SOURCEBOOK IN ABNORMAL PSYCHOLOGY

Leslie Y. Rabkin

University of Rochester

and

John E. Carr

University of Washington

HOUGHTON MIFFLIN COMPANY · BOSTON

New York · Atlanta · Geneva, ILL. · Dallas · Palo Alto

Under the editorship of

LEONARD CARMICHAEL

PREFACE

This book is an attempt to bring together, out of the welter of available materials, a variety of original and important readings in abnormal psychology, with the aim of providing a resource for achieving greater depth and a broader perspective in the classroom study of psychopathology. In our selection process we have tried to maintain a balance between the historically important document, the clinical-dynamic case analysis, the broader empirical investigation, and the more detailed and specific research report.

Our teaching and clinical supervisory experience has constantly brought home to us the importance of working with primary documents based on such criteria. The student's reliance on secondary sources alone, no matter how judicious and well-balanced their viewpoint, involves many pitfalls. Aside from the text's general tendency towards the homogenization of diverse and often disharmonious theories, there are such problems as selective emphasis and erroneous extrapolation. Lost, as well, is the intellectual excitement which develops out of following an enquiring mind on its difficult journey into uncharted territory. Confronted with an original report, the student can begin as well to exercise his own evaluative powers, formulate meaningful questions, and perhaps discover in himself a hitherto unrecognized aptitude for serendipity.

The emphasis in our selection of readings has been on an interactional, dynamic viewpoint. We have sought materials which attempt to answer such basic questions as what is the nature of the interpersonal field of the disturbed person, what is the inner experience of the disordered individual, and out of what kind of family matrix does disturbance arise. Along the way, problems of a more static nature are brought into focus — for example, how can we classify different forms of disturbance and what are the forms of deviation characteristic of the personality structure of disturbed persons.

The format of the book is such that it can be used as an ancilla to any standard text in abnormal psychology. Each of its nine sections is devoted to a particular diagnostic category, a general etiological problem, or a focal issue such as psychotherapy and the definition of normality and abnormality. Prefacing each section is a brief introduction to the subject covered and a resume of the articles which follow.

We wish to express our thanks to the authors and publishers who have allowed us to use their material in this book. Each is credited in a footnote at the beginning of every selection. We wish also to thank our colleagues and students whose critical evaluations have helped us at every stage of the editing process.

LESLIE Y. RABKIN
JOHN E. CARR

iii

CONTENTS

SECTION FOUR: THE PSYCHOSES   190

Contents / **vii**

Normality and Abnormality / 1

There is no more vexing problem in the contemporary study of psychopathology than the delineation of the boundary between the concepts "normal" and "abnormal." The specific meaning of normality, implying a statistical norm, with the abnormal representing any form of behavior deviating from this norm, is hardly a suitable definition. We know, for example, that some phenomena which occur with extreme frequency (e.g., the common cold) are clearly pathological, while others occurring infrequently (e.g., extremes of strength) are indices of heightened "healthiness."

In the search for the meaning of these elusive concepts, two basic paradigms have been used. On the one hand are the positive definitions of normality or mental health; on the other, the negative definitions. The latter suggest that normality can be defined simply as the absence of pathology. The former definition looks to man's positive strivings as the basic criterion for gauging normality or health.

But even within the purview of the positive conception of normality, problems of definition and focus crop up. Is the essence of man's striving a seeking for greater internal cohesiveness, or for a heightened sense of integration in the social world he inhabits? Or both? And are the essential patterns of striving and the criteria of normality culture-bound, relevant only in our own cultural milieu, or are there universal criteria we can employ?

The papers which follow attempt to grapple with these diverse points of view: Heinz Hartmann examines several psychoanalytic concepts of health and normality, concepts which have to do with individual personality functioning and which have found their way into our common jargon — the freedom from anxiety ideal, rationality, and others — and finds them wanting. He attempts to synthesize notions of inner harmony or "being adapted" with the more socially-oriented conception of "achieving adaptation,"

keeping in the forefront the problem of assessing adaptation to what, the nature of man's "typical average environment" and its vicissitudes.

In her seminal contribution to the relationship of anthropology and abnormal psychology, Ruth Benedict takes the extreme cultural relativity position in regard to normality. For her, the basic question is "How far are such categories (of normal-abnormal) culturally determined, or how far can we with assurance regard them as absolute?" Her answer is that, indeed, "Normality is culturally defined." There have been many attempts, of course, to develop pan-cultural standards of normality,[1] but the knotty problem of developing a definition of mental health which has universal application is still unresolved.

Marie Jahoda's social psychological approach to mental health involves a broad perspective and a multi-criterion basis of definition. She suggests that the mental health of an individual can be determined by attention to three criteria:

1. the degree of active mastery manifested,
2. the maintenance of personality cohesiveness, and
3. the person's ability to correctly perceive his environment and himself.

Through her synthesis of social-psychological, psychoanalytic, and anthropological dimensions of the problem, Jahoda develops many possibilities for research into the development and maintenance of mental health, both individual and cultural.

Jules Golden and his associates present a different,

[1] For example, see Wegrocki, H. J., A critique of cultural and statistical concepts of abnormality. J. abn. soc. Psychol., 1939, 34, 166–178. Wegrocki suggests a definition of abnormality as "the tendency to choose a type of reaction which represents an escape from a conflict-producing situation instead of a facing of the problem."

empirical approach to the study of normality. Basing their analysis on a diverse set of psychological tests and interview techniques, they describe the characteristics consistently found in a sample of well-functioning and socially adjusted young men.[2] Although the

validity of their interpretation of the nature of "emotional health" can be questioned, it is interesting to note how close their subjects come to meeting Jahoda's criteria of active adjustment, personality integrity, and accurate perception of self and world. ■

[2] A more recent publication by this research group has examined the wives of these "normal" young men and found them to be a similarly homogeneous and well-adjusted group. See Golden, J. S., Silver, R. J., and Mandel, N. The wives of 50 "normal" American men. Arch. gen. Psychiat., 1963, 9, 614–618.

HEINZ HARTMANN

Psycho-Analysis and the Concept of Health*

Perhaps it would be true to say that we attach less importance in analytical circles to differentiating between healthy and pathological behaviour than is often done outside those circles. But the concepts of 'health' and 'illness' always exert a 'latent' influence, so to say, on our analytical habits of thought and it cannot but serve a useful purpose to clarify the implications of these terms. Moreover, it would be a mistake to suppose that the subject possesses no more than a theoretical interest, that it lacks any practical significance. For, when all is said and done, it often depends upon the analytical concept of health whether we recommend a course of analytical treatment — so that the matter is important as a factor in our judgement of the indications present — or what changes we should like to see effected in a patient, or when we may consider that an analysis is ripe for termination. Differences of outlook in this sphere must ultimately lead to corresponding differences in our therapeutic technique, as was clearly foreseen by Ernest Jones[1] many years ago.

While psycho-analysis was still in its infancy, it seemed a relatively simple matter to define mental health and mental illness. At that period we became acquainted for the first time with the conflicts which give rise to neuroses and believed that we had thereby acquired the right to differentiate between health and illness. Subsequently the discovery was made that conflicts such as those we had come to regard as pathogenic could be shown to exist also in healthy people; it became apparent that the choice between health and illness was determined rather by temporal and quantitative factors. To a greater extent than any theoretical considerations our therapeutic experience has compelled us to recognize this truth. It has been found that our efforts have met with very variable success and we are not always able to accept the familiar explanations of the responsibility for this state of affairs. We are finally forced to the conclusion that the quantitative factor of the strength of

the instincts and a quantitative factor residing in the ego-function have here acquired, side by side with other factors of course, an importance of their own. Moreover, mechanisms are evidently not as such pathogenic but only in virtue of their topographical value in space and their dynamic value in action, if I may so express myself. The process of modifying the original analytical conception of health has been advanced a stage further by the contributions to the psychology of the ego which now have been in the forefront of psycho-analytical interest for nearly twenty years. But the more we begin to understand the ego and its manœuvres and achievements in dealing with the external world, the more do we tend to make these functions of adaptation, achievement, etc. the touchstone of the concept of health.

However, a psycho-analytical definition of health presents certain difficulties which we shall now proceed to examine. As is well known, it is never at any time an easy matter to say what we really mean by 'health' and 'illness' and perhaps the difficulty of differentiating between them is even greater when we are concerned with the so-called 'psychological illnesses' than it is with physical maladies. Health is certainly not a purely statistical average. If it were we should have to look upon the exceptional achievements of single individuals as pathological, which would be contrary to the ordinary usage of speech; and besides this, a majority of people exhibit characteristics which are generally regarded as pathological (the example most frequently given being caries of the teeth). 'Abnormal' then, in the sense of a deviation from the average, is not synonymous with 'pathological.'

In the conceptions of health most widely prevalent, subjective valuations play a considerable part, whether explicitly or implicitly, and that is the chief reason why such conceptions, especially when they relate to mental health and mental illness, may vary considerably at different periods and among different peoples. Here judgement is influenced by a subjective factor depending on cultural and social conditions and even personal values. Within a uniform society these judgements will exhibit a far-reaching similarity, but that does not deprive them in the

* Reprinted by permission from *International Journal of Psycho-Analysis*, Vol. 20, 1939, pp. 308–321.
[1] 'The Attitude of the Psycho-Analytic Physician towards Current Conflicts' (1913), *Papers on Psycho-Analysis*, Third Edition.

least of their subjective character. 'Health' is generally one expression of the idea of vital perfection;
and this in itself implies the subjectivity of the
judgements concerning it. A logical analysis of the
concept of health (I shall barely touch upon the
problem here) would have to devote especial attention to the valuations embodied in the different conceptions of health.

But these are not the only difficulties inherent in a
psycho-analytical definition of health. So long as we
make freedom from symptoms, for instance, the
criterion of mental health, it is comparatively easy
in practice to arrive at a decision. Even by this
standard there exists no absolutely objective basis
for our judgement; for a simple answer is not readily
forthcoming to the question whether a given psychical manifestation is in the nature of a symptom or
whether on the contrary it is to be regarded as an
'achievement.' It is often a difficult matter to decide
whether the pedantry or ambition of an individual
or the nature of his object-choice are symptoms in a
neurotic sense or character-traits possessing a positive
value for health. Nevertheless this standard does
provide us, if not with a basis for objective judgement, at all events with a consensus of opinion which
is usually sufficient for all practical purposes. But
health as it is understood in psycho-analysis is something which means far more than this. In our view,
freedom from symptoms is not enough for health;
and we cherish higher expectations of the therapeutic
effects of psycho-analysis. But over and above this,
psycho-analysis has witnessed the development of a
number of theoretical conceptions of health which
often lay down very severe standards. We have accordingly to ask ourselves what health signifies in a
psycho-analytical sense.

By way of preamble we would remark that man's
relation to health and illness itself often presents
features of a distinctly neurotic order. When these
problems are very much in the foreground one is
sometimes actually tempted to speak of a 'health-
neurosis.' This idea is made the basis of a paper recently published by Melitta Schmideberg.[2] A conspicuous characteristic in certain well-marked types is
their conviction that they themselves enjoy superior
health, accompanied by a compulsive urge to detect
in others deviations, mainly of a neurotic or psychotic kind, from their ideal of health. In certain
circumstances such people are capable of fulfilling a
useful function in society by very reason of their
particular form of neurosis, which may mark them

out for the rôle of eternal sick-nurse to their fellowmen. In the simplest form of this behaviour the
operative mechanism is commonly projection; by
constantly seeing others as patients in need of one's
help one avoids recognition of one's own neurosis.
In the same way Freud once expressed the opinion
that many analysts probably learn to absolve themselves from personal compliance with the obligations
of analysis by exacting it from others. We know too
that a like tendency to overestimate the neurotic and
psychotic reactions of one's fellow-men belongs to
the growing-pains of many analysts. It is a common
feature of 'health-neuroses' that those afflicted by
them cannot allow themselves to suffer or to feel ill
or depressed.[3] But a healthy person must have the
capacity to suffer and to be depressed. Our clinical
experience has taught us the consequences of glossing
over illness and suffering, of being unable to admit
to oneself the possibility of illness and suffering. It
is even probable that a limited amount of suffering
and illness forms an integral part of the scheme of
health, as it were, or rather that health is only
reached by indirect ways. We know that successful
adaptation can lead to maladaptation — the development of the super-ego is a case in point and many
other examples could be cited. But conversely, maladaptation may become successful adaptation. Typical conflicts are a part and parcel of 'normal' development and disturbances in adaptation are included
in its scope. We discover a similar state of affairs in
relation to the therapeutic process of analysis. Here
health clearly includes pathological reactions as a
means towards its attainment.

But we must return to the concept of health and
ask ourselves once more what criteria we possess in
analysis for gauging mental health and illness. I have
already mentioned that we do not identify health
with freedom from symptoms. And we still find ourselves on ground which is comparatively accessible,
from an empirical though not, of course, from a prognostic point of view, if we take into consideration the
extent to which this immunity from symptoms is
durable and capable of withstanding shocks. But
the wider implications which the term health assumes for us and what analysis aims at in this sense
cannot readily be reduced to a scientific formula. At
the same time we find a number of useful theoretical
formulations concerning the attributes of that state
of health to which we are anxious to bring our patients with the help of the methods available to
analysis. Of these the most general is Freud's 'Where
id was, there shall ego be';[4] or there is Nunberg's

[2] ' "After the Analysis . . ." ', *Psychoanalytic Quarterly*,
Vol. VII, 1938. Cf. too the observation made by Glover
in the ensuing discussion, quoted on p. 141.

[3] Cf. Schmideberg, *op. cit.*
[4] *New Introductory Lectures*, 1933, p. 106.

'the energies of the id become more mobile, the super-ego more tolerant, the ego becomes more free from anxiety and its synthetic function is restored.'[5] But the distance between such necessarily schematic formulations and the measurement of actual states of mental health, of the actual degree of mental health enjoyed by a given individual, is far greater than one would like to suppose. It is not at all a simple matter to bring these theoretical conceptions of health into line with what we in actual fact call 'healthy.' Moreover, one gains an impression that individual conceptions of health differ widely among analysts themselves, varying with the aims which each has set for himself on the basis of his views concerning human development, and also of course with his philosophy, political sympathies, etc. Perhaps for the time being it will be advisable to proceed with caution before attempting to arrive at a precise theoretical formulation of the concept of health — otherwise we shall be in danger of allowing our standards of health to become dependent on our moral preoccupations and other subjective aspirations. It is clearly essential to proceed on purely empirical lines, i.e. to examine from the point of view of their structure and development the personalities of those who are actually considered healthy instead of allowing our theoretical speculations to dictate to us what we 'ought' to regard as healthy. This is precisely the attitude that psychoanalysis adopts towards the normative disciplines. It does not ask whether these norms are justified but concentrates on a totally different problem, namely that of the genesis and structure of behaviour which has, in fact, for whatever reason, been assigned a place in a scale of positive and negative values. And besides, theoretical standards of health are usually too narrow in so far as they underestimate the great diversity of types which in practice pass as healthy. Needless to say analysis itself possesses criteria intended to serve as a purely practical guide, such as the tests so frequently applied of a capacity for achievement or enjoyment.

But we propose here to examine in greater detail those theoretical schemes for the classification of mental health and illness which one finds contained, either expressly or by implication, in psycho-analytical literature; and for this purpose we may ask ourselves what conceptions of health have in fact been advanced and not whether certain conceptions 'ought' to be advanced. These descriptions of a healthy or 'biologically adjusted' individual, if we confine ourselves entirely to their broadest general outlines, reveal a pronounced development in two directions. In neither direction, it need scarcely be said, is it merely a question of some subjective factor, some personal predilection achieving expression; they are the results of a rich harvest of clinical experience, and of much valuable experience of the analytical process of cure. These two directions emphasize as the goal of development and health on the one hand rational behaviour and on the other hand instinctual life. This twofold orientation already commands our interest because it reflects the twofold origin of psycho-analysis in the history of thought — the rationalism of the age of enlightenment and the irrationalism of the romantic. The circumstance that these two aspects are emphasized in Freud's work certainly reflects a genuine insight into the dualism which does in fact inform the problem. Now the analytical conceptions of health which have developed on the basis of Freud's suggestions often proceed to assign undue prominence to one of these standpoints at the expense of the other.

When one makes the mistake in analysis of contrasting the id as the biological part of the personality with the ego as its non-biological component, one naturally encourages the tendency to make 'life' and 'mind' into absolutes. When in addition all biological values are acknowledged as supreme, one has approached dangerously near to that malady of the times whose nature it is to worship instinct and pour scorn on reason. To be sure, these tendencies, which lead to a glorification of instinctual man and which at the present time have widely assumed a highly aggressive and political complexion, play a less conspicuous part in the literature pertaining to psychoanalysis or subject to its influence than they do elsewhere.

At the other end of the scale we find the ideal of a rational attitude, and the 'perfectly rational' man is here held up as a model of health and as an ideal figure generally. This conception of mental health deserves closer consideration. That some connection exists between reason and successful adaptation seems clear enough, but it is apparently not such a simple one as is assumed in many psycho-analytical writings. We should not take it for granted that recognition of reality is the equivalent of adaptation to reality. The most rational attitude does not necessarily constitute an optimum for the purposes of adaptation. When we say that an idea or system of ideas is 'in accordance with reality,' this may mean that the theoretical content of the system is true, but it can also signify that the translation of these ideas into action results in conduct appropriate to the occasion. A correct view of reality is not the sole criterion

---

[5] *Allgemeine Neurosenlehre*, 1932, S. 312.

of whether a particular action is in accordance with reality. We must also reflect that a healthy ego should be able to make use of the system of rational control and at the same time take into account the fact of the irrational nature of other mental activities. (This is a part of its co-ordinating function.) The rational must incorporate the irrational as an element in its design. Moreover, we shall have to admit that the advance of the 'rational attitude' is not an even one along a single front, as it were. One often has the impression that a partial progression in this respect may entail a partial regression in other directions. It is evidently very much the same with the process of civilization as a whole. Technical progress may very well be accompanied by mental regression or may actually bring it about by way of mass methods.[6] Here I can only present these ideas in brief outline but I have developed them at greater length elsewhere. They show us the need to revise those analytical conceptions which maintain that the individual who is most rational (in the ordinary sense of the word) is also psychologically the most completely healthy.

Another fundamental criterion of mental health available to psychology has a somewhat less general character, one more firmly rooted in the structural conceptions of analysis: I refer to the criterion of freedom. By freedom is meant not the philosophical problem of free will but rather freedom from anxiety and affects, or freedom to perform a task. The credit for introducing this criterion into analysis belongs to Wälder.[7] I believe that at the root of this conception there lies a well-founded idea; yet I would rather have avoided the term freedom because it is so equivocal in meaning and has been so heavily over-tasked by successive philosophers. In the present context it means no more than control exercised by means of the conscious and preconscious ego and might well be replaced by that description. The mobility or plasticity of the ego is certainly one of the pre-requisites of mental health, whereas a rigid ego may interfere with the process of adaptation. But we would add that a healthy ego is not only and at all times plastic. Important as is this quality, it seems to be subordinated to another of the ego's functions. A clinical example will make this clear. We are all familiar with the obsessional neurotic's fear of losing his self-control — a factor which makes it so very difficult for him to associate freely. The

[6] Karl Mannheim, *Mensch und Gesellschaft im Zeitalter des Umbaus*, Layden, 1935.
[7] 'The Problem of Freedom in Psycho-Analysis and the Problem of Reality-Testing,' this JOURNAL, Vol. XVII, 1936.

phenomenon which I am thinking of is even more clearly marked in those persons who, for fear of losing their ego, are unable to achieve orgasm. These pathological manifestations teach us that a healthy ego must evidently be in a position to allow some of its most essential functions, including its 'freedom,' to be put out of action occasionally, so that it may abandon itself to 'compulsion' (central control). This brings us to the problem, hitherto almost entirely neglected, of a biological hierarchy of the ego's functions and to the notion of the integration of opposites, which we have already met in connection with the problem of rational conduct. I believe that these considerations relative to the mobility of the ego and the automatic disconnecting of vital ego-functions have enabled us to make very considerable progress towards discovering an important condition of mental health. The threads which lead us from this point to the concept of ego-strength are clearly visible. But I do not now wish to discuss this well-worn theme, although one would have to deal with it at considerable length if a systematic exposition of our subject were intended, which is not the case.

I shall now develop this critical exposition of analytical conceptions of health in a direction which will enable us to penetrate more deeply into the realm of ego-theory. For obvious reasons psycho-analysis has hitherto been concerned principally with situations in which the ego finds itself in conflict with the id and the super-ego and, more recently, with the external world. Now one sometimes meets with the idea that the contrast between a conflict-ridden and a peaceful development can automatically be correlated with that afforded by mental health and mental illness. This is a quite mistaken view: conflicts are a part and parcel of human development, for which they provide the necessary stimulus. Nor does the distinction between healthy and pathological reactions correspond to that between behaviour originating or not originating in defence. Nevertheless it is by no means an uncommon thing to discover passages in psycho-analytical literature in which it is maintained that whatever is prompted by the needs of defence, or else results from unsuccessful defence, must somehow be accounted as pathological. Yet it is perfectly clear that a measure which is successful in relation to defensive needs may be a failure from the standpoint of positive achievement, and *vice versâ*. We are really concerned here with two distinct approaches to the classification of the same facts and not with two different sets of facts. This consideration does not invalidate our experience that pathological function offers the most fruitful approach to the problems of mental conflict. Similarly we first became familiar with the mechanisms of defence in their pathogenic aspect and it is only now that we are gradually coming to recognize the part they play in normal development. It would seem that we cannot adequately assess the positive or negative value which such processes possess for mental health so long as we only think of the problems of mental conflict and fail to consider these matters from the standpoint of adaptation as well.

Now if we examine these situations more attentively, we very often make the interesting discovery that the shortest way to reality is not always the most promising from the standpoint of adaptation. It would seem that we often learn to find our bearings in relation to reality by devious ways, and that it is inevitable and not merely 'accidental' that this should be the case. There is evidently a typical sequence here, withdrawal from reality leading to an increased mastery over it. (In its essential features this pattern is already realized in the process of our thinking; the same remark applies to the activity of imagination, the avoidance of unsatisfactory situations, etc.) The theory of the neuroses has always presented the mechanism of turning away from reality solely in terms of pathological processes: but an approach from the standpoint of the problems of adaptation teaches us that such mechanisms have a positive value for health.[8]

In this connection a further problem has a claim upon our interest: I allude to the way in which we use the terms 'regression' and 'regressive' within the analytical system of criteria for measuring mental health. We are generally accustomed to think of regressive behaviour as the antithesis of conduct adapted to reality. We are all familiar with the part which regression plays in pathogenesis and for that very reason I shall not need to consider that aspect of the problem. But in actual fact it would seem that we have to distinguish between progressive and regressive forms of adaptation. We shall have no difficulty in defining a progressive adaptation: it means an adaptation in the direction of development. But we also find instances of successful adaptation achieved by way of regression. These comprise many examples of the activity of the imagination; a further illustration is afforded by artistic activity as well as by those symbolic devices for facilitating thought which are found even in science, where it is most strictly rational.

We do not readily perceive at a first glance why

it is so comparatively often the case that adaptation can only be achieved in these regressive *détours*. Probably the true position is that in his ego, especially as expressed in rational thought and action, in its synthetic and differentiating function,[9] man is equipped with a very highly differentiated organ of adaptation but that this highly differentiated organ is evidently by itself incapable of guaranteeing an optimum of adaptation. A system of regulation operating at the highest level of development is not sufficient to maintain a stable equilibrium; a more primitive system is needed to supplement it.

The objections which we felt obliged to raise against the definitions of mental health and illness last mentioned (in connection with the problems of defence, regression, etc.) may be summarized as follows: these conceptions of health approach the problem too exclusively from the angle of the neuroses or rather they are formulated in terms of contrast with the neuroses. Mechanisms, developmental stages, modes of reaction, with which we have become familiar for the part they play in the development of the neuroses, are automatically relegated to the realm of the pathological — health is characterized as a condition in which these elements are absent. But the contrast thus established with the neuroses can have no meaning so long as we fail to appreciate how much of these mechanisms, developmental stages and modes of reaction is active in healthy individuals or in the development of those who later become so, i.e. so long as an analytical 'normal psychology' is still very largely non-existent. This is one of the reasons why it is precisely the analysis of conduct adapted to reality which is to-day considered of such importance.

I should add that the arbitrary nature of such definitions of mental health and illness is very much less evident in the literature of psycho-analysis itself than in many of its applications to social conditions, artistic activity, scientific production, etc. Where ethical, aesthetic, and political valuations enter very clearly into play and proceed to make use of the concept of health for their special purposes, a considerably wider latitude is allowed to such arbitrary judgement. By skilful conjuring with these kinds of standards it becomes easy enough to prove that those who do not share our political or general outlook on life are neurotic or psychotic or that social conditions to which we are for some reason opposed are to be accounted as pathological. I believe that we are all clear in our own minds that such judgements — whether we personally share them or not — have no

[8] Cf. also Anna Freud, *The Ego and the Mechanisms of Defence*, 1937.

[9] Cf. also Fuchs, 'Zum Stand der heutigen Biologie,' *Imago*, Bd. XXII, 1936.

right to speak in the name of psycho-analytical science.

It will now have become quite obvious to us where many of the conceptions of health and illness discussed in this paper stand most in need of amplification, namely in the direction of the subjects relations with and adaptation to reality. I do not mean to suggest that in these attempts to formulate a definition, to arrive at a theoretical concept of health, the factor of adaptation has been neglected; this is very far from being the case. But in the form in which it is expressed the concept of adaptation itself is in many respects too ill-defined — and, as we have already remarked, 'conduct adapted to reality' has hitherto offered little opportunity for a psycho-analytical approach.

It is obvious that what we designate as health or illness is intimately bound up with the individual's adaptation to reality (or, in the terms of an oft repeated formula, with his sense of self-preservation). I have recently made an attempt to probe more deeply into the problems which confront psycho-analysis at this juncture.[10] Here I shall confine myself to a few suggestions which may seem worth considering in framing a definition of health. The individual's adjustment to reality may be opposed to that of the race. Now it is true that we are accustomed, from the standpoint of our therapeutic aims, to allow a substantial margin of priority to the claims of individual adaptation over those of the race. But if we are to insist that some connection exists between mental health and adaptation, we are bound to admit in the light of our previous remarks that the concept of health may bear inconsistent meanings according to whether we think of it in relation to the individual or to the community. Moreover, we shall deem it expedient to distinguish between the state of being adapted and the process by which it is achieved. And lastly we must point out that adaptation is only capable of definition in relation to something else, with reference to specific environmental settings. The actual state of equilibrium achieved in a given individual tells us nothing of his capacity for adaptation so long as we have not investigated his relations with the external world. Thus an unhampered 'capacity for achievement and enjoyment', simply considered in isolation, has nothing decisive to tell us concerning the capacity for adapting oneself to reality. On the other hand disturbances in one's capacity for achievement and enjoyment (for the sake of simplicity we will keep to these familiar criteria) are not to be evaluated simply as a sign of failure in adaptation. This really goes without saying and I only mention it because it is occasionally overlooked when attempts are made to formulate a definition. As an indispensable factor in assessing an individual's powers of adaptation we would single out his relation to a 'typical average environment'. We must take account of all these aspects of the concept of adaptation if we are to establish criteria of health based on adaptation or the capacity for it. We would insist that the processes of adaptation are always appropriate only to a limited range of environmental conditions; and that successful efforts at adaptation towards specific external situations may in indirect ways lead at the same time to inhibitions in adaptation affecting the organism.

Freud[11] recently characterized this state of affairs by quoting Goethe's 'Reason becomes unreason, beneficence a torment'. Conversely, when viewed from this angle, the proposition that the nature of the environment may be such that a pathological development of the psyche offers a more satisfactory solution than would a normal one loses its paradoxical character.

This necessarily condensed presentation must inevitably make the considerations here adumbrated appear somewhat arid; but I am convinced that no analyst would have any difficulty in illustrating them from his clinical experience. In this connection I should like to insist once more that we shall obviously be in a better position to correlate all these definitions with concrete, clinically manifest conditions and thus to apply the concept of health in an unequivocal and trustworthy manner, when we have been able to advance further in the sphere of analytical 'normal psychology', in the analysis of adapted behaviour. I believe that a more attentive examination of the phenomena of adaptation may also help us to escape from the opposition between 'biological' and 'sociological' conceptions of mental development which plays a certain part in analysis but is fundamentally sterile. It is only when we consider the social phenomena of adaptation in their biological aspect that we can really start 'getting psychology rightfully placed in the hierarchy of science; namely as one of the biological sciences'.[12]

It is important that we should clearly realize both that there exists a close connection between adaptation and synthesis, and the extent of this. An 'organization of the organism', the specific representative

[10] 'Ich-Psychologie und Anpassungproblem', *Internationale Zeitschrift für Psychoanalyse und Imago*, Bd. XXIV, 1939.
[11] 'Analysis Terminable and Interminable', this JOURNAL, Vol. XVIII, 1937.
[12] Ernest Jones, 'Psycho-Analysis and the Instincts' (1935), *Papers on Psycho-Analysis*, Fourth Edition.

of which in the mental sphere we bring into relation with the synthetic function (and also with the differentiating function which has, however, been less fully explored), is a pre-requisite of successful adaptation; on the other hand its efficacy is doubtless dependent on the measure of adaptation achieved. A process when viewed 'from within' may often present itself as a disturbance of mental harmony; when viewed 'from without' we should have to characterize the same process as a disturbance of adaptation. So, too, instinctual conflicts are very frequently bound up with a disturbed relation to the environment. It is also significant in this connection that the same process of defence quite commonly serves the twofold purpose of acquiring mastery over the instincts and of reaching an accommodation with the external world.

By thus seeking to make adaptation, and especially synthesis, the basis of our concept of health, we seem to have arrived at an 'evolutionary' concept of health. And in point of fact this does represent a psychoanalytical contribution to the concept of mental health which should not be underestimated. But on the other hand a conception which relates the degree of mental health to the degree of development actually attained (compare the factor of rational control and, on the instinctual plane, the attainment of the genital stage as a pre-requisite of health) suffers from certain limitations, at least as regards the ego, to which I have briefly alluded.

I shall here conclude this necessarily schematic and fragmentary presentation. I have endeavoured to explain and discuss a number of standpoints which psycho-analysis has in fact adopted towards the concept of health, either expressly or by implication. In a one-sided fashion I proceeded to single out for almost exclusive attention those conditions of mental health which are seen to be related to the ego. I purposely restricted myself in this way. It seemed to me that there were good reasons why the psychology of the id had failed to provide us with a key to the problems of mental health. Moreover, by conducting my survey from the standpoint of the ego I found myself in a position to discuss certain problems of ego-theory which are decidedly no less important than the question of our criteria of health. The contribution that I myself have been able to make towards the further development and criticism of these views certainly does not as yet enable us to formulate a concept of mental health in simple, unequivocal, definitive terms. But I believe that it will have helped us to discern quite clearly in which direction these prolegomena to a future analytical theory of health must be developed.

RUTH BENEDICT

Anthropology and the Abnormal*

Modern social anthropology has become more and more a study of the varieties and common elements of cultural environment and the consequences of these in human behavior. For such a study of diverse social orders primitive peoples fortunately provide a laboratory not yet entirely vitiated by the spread of a standardized world-wide civilization. Dyaks and Hopis, Fijians and Yakuts are significant for psychological and sociological study because only among these simpler peoples has there been sufficient isolation to give opportunity for the development of

* Reprinted by permission from *Journal of General Psychology*, Vol. 10, 1934, pp. 59–82.

localized social forms. In the higher cultures the standardization of custom and belief over a couple of continents has given a false sense of the inevitability of the particular forms that have gained currency, and we need to turn to a wider survey in order to check the conclusions we hastily base upon this near-universality of familiar customs. Most of the simpler cultures did not gain the wide currency of the one which, out of our experience, we identify with human nature, but this was for various historical reasons, and certainly not for any that gives us as its carriers a monopoly of social good or of social sanity. Modern civilization, from this point of view, becomes not a necessary pinnacle of human achievement but one entry in a long series of possible adjustments.

These adjustments, whether they are in mannerisms like the ways of showing anger, or joy, or grief in any society, or in major human drives like those of sex, prove to be far more variable than experience in any one culture would suggest. In certain fields, such as that of religion or of formal marriage arrangements, these wide limits of variability are well known and can be fairly described. In others it is not yet possible to give a generalized account, but that does not absolve us of the task of indicating the significance of the work that has been done and of the problems that have arisen.

One of these problems relates to the customary modern normal-abnormal categories and our conclusions regarding them. In how far are such categories culturally determined, or in how far can we with assurance regard them as absolute? In how far can we regard inability to function socially as diagnostic of abnormality, or in how far is it necessary to regard this as a function of the culture?

As a matter of fact, one of the most striking facts that emerge from a study of widely varying cultures is the ease with which our abnormals function in other cultures. It does not matter what kind of "abnormality" we choose for illustration, those which indicate extreme instability, or those which are more in the nature of character traits like sadism or delusions of grandeur or of persecution, there are well-described cultures in which these abnormals function at ease and with honor, and apparently without danger or difficulty to the society.

The most notorious of these is trance and catalepsy. Even a very mild mystic is aberrant in our culture. But most peoples have regarded even extreme psychic manifestations not only as normal and desirable, but even as characteristic of highly valued and gifted individuals. This was true even in our own cultural background in that period when Catholicism made the ecstatic experience the mark of sainthood. It is hard for us, born and brought up in a culture that makes no use of the experience, to realize how important a rôle it may play and how many individuals are capable of it, once it has been given an honorable place in any society.

Some of the Indian tribes of California accorded prestige principally to those who passed through certain trance experiences. Not all of these tribes believed that it was exclusively women who were so blessed, but among the Shasta (10) this was the convention. Their shamans were women, and they were accorded the greatest prestige in the community. They were chosen because of their constitutional

liability to trance and allied manifestations. One day the woman who was so destined, while she was about her usual work, would fall suddenly to the ground. She had heard a voice speaking to her in tones of the greatest intensity. Turning, she had seen a man with drawn bow and arrow. He commanded her to sing on pain of being shot through the heart by his arrow, but under the stress of the experience she fell senseless. Her family gathered. She was lying rigid, hardly breathing. They knew that for some time she had had dreams of a special character which indicated a shamanistic calling, dreams of escaping grizzly bears, falling off cliffs or trees, or of being surrounded by swarms of yellow jackets. The community knew therefore what to expect. After a few hours the woman began to moan gently and to roll about upon the ground, trembling violently. She was supposed to be repeating the song which she had been told to sing and which during the trance had been taught her by the spirit. As she revived her moaning became more and more clearly the spirit's song until at last she called out the name of the spirit itself, and immediately blood oozed from her mouth.

When the woman had come to herself after the first encounter with her spirit she danced that night her first initiatory shamanistic dance, holding herself by a rope that was swung from the ceiling. For three nights she danced, and on the third night she had to receive in her body her power from her spirit. She was dancing, and as she felt the approach of the moment she called out, "He will shoot me, he will shoot me." Her friends stood close, for when she reeled in a kind of cataleptic seizure, they had to seize her before she fell or she would die. From this time on she had in her body a visible materialization of her spirit's power, an icicle-like object which in her dances thereafter she would exhibit, producing it from one part of her body and returning it to another part. From this time on she continued to validate her supernatural power by further cataleptic demonstrations, and she was called upon in great emergencies of life and death, for curing and for divination and for counsel. She became in other words by this procedure a woman of great power and importance.[1]

It is clear that, so far from regarding cataleptic seizures as blots upon the family escutcheon and

[1] In all cultures behavior which is socially rewarded attracts persons who are attracted by the possibility of leadership, and such individuals may simulate the required behavior. This is as true when society rewards prodigality as when it rewards catalepsy. For the present argument the amount of shamming is not considered though it is of obvious importance. It is a matter which cultures standardize quite as much as they standardize the type of rewarded behavior.

as evidences of dreaded disease, cultural approval had seized upon them and made of them the pathway to authority over one's fellows. They were the outstanding characteristic of the most respected social type, the type which functioned with most honor and reward in the community. It was precisely the cataleptic individuals who in this culture were singled out for authority and leadership.

The availability of "abnormal" types in the social structure, provided they are types that are culturally selected by that group, is illustrated from every part of the world. The shamans of Siberia dominate their communities. According to the ideas of these peoples, they are individuals who by submission to the will of the spirits have been cured of a grievous illness — the onset of the seizures — and have acquired by this means great supernatural power and incomparable vigor and health. Some, during the period of the call, are violently insane for several years, others irresponsible to the point where they have to be watched constantly lest they wander off in the snow and freeze to death, others ill and emaciated to the point of death, sometimes with bloody sweat. It is the shamanistic practice which constitutes their cure, and the extreme physical exertion of a Siberian seance leaves them, they claim, rested and able to enter immediately upon a similar performance. Cataleptic seizures are regarded as an essential part of any shamanistic performance (8).

A good description of the neurotic condition of the shaman and the attention given him by his society is an old one by Canon Callaway (6, pp. 259 ff.) recorded in the words of an old Zulu of South Africa:

"The condition of a man who is about to become a diviner is this; at first he is apparently robust, but in the process of time he begins to be delicate, not having any real disease, but being delicate. He habitually avoids certain kinds of food, choosing what he likes, and he does not eat much of that; he is continually complaining of pains in different parts of his body. And he tells them that he has dreamt that he was carried away by a river. He dreams of many things, and his body is muddied (as a river) and he becomes a house of dreams. He dreams constantly of many things, and on awaking tells his friends, 'My body is muddied today; I dreamt many men were killing me, and I escaped I know not how. On waking one part of my body felt different from other parts; it was no longer alike all over.' At last that man is very ill, and they go to the diviners to enquire.

"The diviners do not at once see that he is about to have a soft head (that is, the sensitivity

associated with shamanism). It is difficult for them to see the truth; they continually talk nonsense and make false statements, until all the man's cattle are devoured at their command, they saying that the spirit of his people demands cattle, that it may eat food. At length all the man's property is expended, he still being ill; and they no longer know what to do, for he has no more cattle, and his friends help him in such things as he needs.

"At length a diviner comes and says that all the others are wrong. He says, 'He is possessed by the spirits. There is nothing else. They move in him, being divided into two parties; some say, "No, we do not wish our child injured. We do not wish it." It is for that reason he does not get well. If you bar the way against the spirits, you will be killing him. For he will not be a diviner; neither will he ever be a man again.'

"So the man may be ill two years without getting better; perhaps even longer than that. He is confined to his house. This continues till his hair falls off. And his body is dry and scurfy; he does not like to anoint himself. He shows that he is about to be a diviner by yawning again and again, and by sneezing continually. It is apparent also from his being very fond of snuff; not allowing any long time to pass without taking some. And people begin to see that he has had what is good given to him.

"After that he is ill; he has convulsions, and when water has been poured on him they then cease for a time. He habitually sheds tears, at first slight, then at last he weeps aloud and when the people are asleep he is heard making a noise and wakes the people by his singing; he has composed a song, and the men and women awake and go to sing in concert with him. All the people of the village are troubled by want of sleep; for a man who is becoming a diviner causes great trouble, for he does not sleep, but works constantly with his brain; his sleep is merely by snatches, and he wakes up singing many songs; and people who are near quit their villages by night when they hear him singing aloud and go to sing in concert. Perhaps he sings till morning, no one having slept. And then he leaps about the house like a frog; and the house becomes too small for him, and he goes out leaping and singing, and shaking like a reed in the water, and dripping with perspiration.

"In this state of things they daily expect his death; he is now but skin and bones, and they think that tomorrow's sun will not leave him alive. At this time many cattle are eaten, for the people encourage his becoming a diviner. At length (in a dream) an ancient ancestral spirit is pointed out to him. This spirit says to him, 'Go to So-and-so and he will churn for you an emetic (the medicine the drinking of which is a part of shamanistic initiation) that you may be a diviner altogether.' Then he is quiet a few days, having gone to the diviner to have the medicine churned for him; and he comes back quite another man, being now cleansed and a diviner indeed."

Thereafter for life when he achieves possession, he foretells events, and finds lost articles.

It is clear that culture may value and make socially available even highly unstable human types. If it chooses to treat their peculiarities as the most valued variants of human behavior, the individuals in question will rise to the occasion and perform their social rôles without reference to our usual ideas of the types who can make social adjustments and those who cannot.

Cataleptic and trance phenomena are, of course, only one illustration of the fact that those whom we regard as abnormals may function adequately in other cultures. Many of our culturally discarded traits are selected for elaboration in different societies. Homosexuality is an excellent example, for in this case our attention is not constantly diverted, as in the consideration of trance, to the interruption of routine activity which it implies. Homosexuality poses the problem very simply. A tendency toward this trait in our culture exposes an individual to all the conflicts to which all aberrants are always exposed, and we tend to identify the consequences of this conflict with homosexuality. But these consequences are obviously local and cultural. Homosexuals in many societies are not incompetent, but they may be such if the culture asks adjustments of them that would strain any man's vitality. Wherever homosexuality has been given an honorable place in any society, those to whom it is congenial have filled adequately the honorable rôles society assigns to them. Plato's *Republic* is, of course, the most convincing statement of such a reading of homosexuality. It is presented as one of the major means to the good life, and it was generally so regarded in Greece at that time.

The cultural attitude toward homosexuals has not always been on such a high ethical plane, but it has been very varied. Among many American Indian tribes there exists the institution of the berdache (12, 15), as the French called them. These men-women were men who at puberty or thereafter took the dress and the occupations of women. Sometimes they married other men and lived with them. Sometimes they were men with no inversion, persons of weak sexual endowment who chose this rôle to avoid the jeers of the woman. The berdaches were never regarded as of first-rate supernatural power, as similar men-women were in Siberia, but rather as leaders in women's occupations, good healers in certain diseases, or, among certain tribes, as the genial organizers of social affairs. In any case, they were socially placed. They were not left exposed to the conflicts that visit the deviant who is excluded from participation in the recognized patterns of his society .

The most spectacular illustrations of the extent to which normality may be culturally defined are those cultures where an abnormality of our culture is the cornerstone of their social structure. It is not possible to do justice to these possibilities in a short discussion. A recent study of an island of northwest Melanesia by Fortune (11) describes a society built upon traits which we regard as beyond the border of paranoia. In this tribe the exogamic groups look upon each other as prime manipulators of black magic, so that one marries always into an enemy group which remains for life one's deadly and unappeasable foes. They look upon a good garden crop as a confession of theft, for everyone is engaged in making magic to induce into his garden the productiveness of his neighbors'; therefore no secrecy in the island is so rigidly insisted upon as the secrecy of a man's harvesting of his yams. Their polite phrase at the acceptance of a gift is, "And if you now poison me, how shall I repay you this present?" Their preoccupation with poisoning is constant; no woman ever leaves her cooking pot for a moment untended. Even the great affinal economic exchanges that are characteristic of this Melanesian culture area are quite altered in Dobu since they are incompatible with this fear and distrust that pervades the culture. They go farther and people the whole world outside their own quarters with such malignant spirits that all-night feasts and ceremonials simply do not occur here. They have even rigorous religiously enforced customs that forbid the sharing of seed even in one family group. Anyone else's food is deadly poison to you, so that communality of stores is out of the question. For some months before harvest the whole society is on the verge of starvation, but if one falls to the temptation and eats up one's seed yams, one is an outcast and a beachcomber for life. There is no coming back. It involves, as a matter of course, divorce and the breaking of all social ties.

Now in this society where no one may work with another and no one may share with another, Fortune describes the individual who was regarded by all his fellows as crazy. He was not one of those who periodically ran amok and, beside himself and frothing at the mouth, fell with a knife upon anyone he could reach. Such behavior they did not regard as putting anyone outside the pale. They did not even put the individuals who were known to be liable to these attacks under any kind of control. They merely fled when they saw the attack coming on and kept out of the way. "He would be all right tomorrow." But there was one man of sunny, kindly disposition who liked work and liked to be helpful. The compulsion was too strong for him to repress it in favor of the opposite tendencies of his culture. Men and women never spoke of him without laughing; he was silly and simple and definitely crazy. Nevertheless, to the ethnologist used to a culture that has, in Christianity, made his type the model of all virtue, he seemed a pleasant fellow.

An even more extreme example, because it is of a culture that has built itself upon a more complex abnormality, is that of the North Pacific Coast of North America. The civilization of the Kwakiutl (1–5), at the time when it was first recorded in the last decades of the nineteenth century, was one of the most vigorous in North America. It was built up on an ample economic supply of goods, the fish which furnished their food staple being practically inexhaustible and obtainable with comparatively small labor, and the wood which furnished the material for their houses, their furnishings, and their arts being, with however much labor, always procurable. They lived in coastal villages that compared favorably in size with those of any other American Indians and they kept up constant communication by means of sea-going dug-out canoes.

It was one of the most vigorous and zestful of the aboriginal cultures of North America, with complex crafts and ceremonials, and elaborate and striking arts. It certainly had none of the earmarks of a sick civilization. The tribes of the Northwest Coast had wealth, and exactly in our terms. That is, they had not only a surplus of economic goods, but they made a game of the manipulation of wealth. It was by no means a mere direct transcription of economic needs and the filling of those needs. It involved the idea of capital, of interest, and of conspicuous waste. It was a game with all the binding rules of a game, and a person entered it as a child. His father distributed wealth for him, according to his ability, at a small feast or potlatch, and each gift the receiver was obliged to accept and to return after a short interval with interest that ran to about 100 per cent a year. By the time the child was grown, therefore, he was well launched, a larger potlatch had been given for him on various occasions of exploit or initiation, and he had wealth either out at usury or in his own possession. Nothing in the civilization could be enjoyed without validating it by the distribution of this wealth. Everything that was valued, names and songs as well as material objects, were passed down in family lines, but they were always publicly assumed with accompanying sufficient distributions of property. It was the game of validating and exercising all the privileges one could accumulate from one's various forbears, or by gift, or by marriage, that made the chief interest of the culture. Everyone in his degree took part in it, but many, of course, mainly as spectators. In its highest form it was played out between rival chiefs representing not only themselves and their family lines but their communities, and the object of the contest was to glorify oneself and to humiliate one's opponent. On this level of greatness the property involved was no longer represented by blankets, so many thousand of them to a potlatch, but by higher units of value. These higher units were like our bank notes. They were incised copper tablets, each of them named, and having a value that depended upon their illustrious history. This was as high as ten thousand blankets, and to possess one of them, still more to enhance its value at a great potlatch, was one of the greatest glories within the compass of the chiefs of the Northwest Coast.

The details of this manipulation of wealth are in many ways a parody on our own economic arrangements, but it is with the motivations that were recognized in this contest that we are concerned in this discussion. The drives were those which in our own culture we should call megalomaniac. There was an uncensored self-glorification and ridicule of the opponent that it is hard to equal in other cultures outside of the monologues of the abnormal. Any of the songs and speeches of their chiefs at a potlatch illustrate the usual tenor:

. . . .
Wa, out of the way. Wa, out of the way. Turn your faces that I may give way to my anger by striking my fellow chiefs.

Wa, great potlatch, greatest potlatch.[2] The little ones[3] only pretend, the little stubborn ones, they only sell one copper again and again and give it away to the little chiefs of the tribe.
Ah, do not ask in vain for mercy. Ah, do not ask in vain for mercy and raise your hands, you with lolling tongues! I shall break,[4] I shall let disappear the great copper that has the name Kentsegum, the property of the great foolish one, the great extravagant one, the great surpassing one, the one

[2] The feast he is now engaged in giving.
[3] His opponents.
[4] To break a copper, showing in this way how far one rose above even the most superlatively valuable things, was the final mark of greatness.

farthest ahead, the great Cannibal dancer among the chiefs.[5]

I am the great chief who makes people ashamed.
I am the great chief who makes people ashamed.
Our chief brings shame to the faces.
Our chief brings jealousy to the faces.
Our chief makes people cover their faces by what he is continually doing in this world, from the beginning to the end of the year,
Giving again and again oil feasts to the tribes.

I am the great chief who vanquishes.
I am the great chief who vanquishes.
Only at those who continue running round and round in this world, working hard, losing their tails,[6] I sneer, at the chiefs below the true chief.[7]
Have mercy on them![8] Put oil on their dry heads with brittle hair, those who do not comb their hair!
I sneer at the chiefs below the true, real chief. I am the great chief who makes people ashamed.

. . . .

I am the only great tree, I the chief.
I am the only great tree, I the chief.
You are my subordinates, tribes.
You sit in the middle of the rear of the house, tribes.
Bring me your counter of property, tribes, that he may in vain try to count what is going to be given away by the great copper-maker, the chief.
Oh, I laugh at them, I sneer at them who empty boxes[9] in their houses, their potlatch houses, their inviting houses that are full only of hunger. They follow along after me like young sawbill ducks. I am the only great tree, I the chief.

. . . .

I have quoted a number of these hymns of self-glorification because by an association which psychiatrists will recognize as fundamental these delusions of grandeur were essential in the paranoid view of life which was so strikingly developed in this culture. All of existence was seen in terms of insult.[9a] Not only derogatory acts performed by a neighbor or an enemy, but all untoward events, like a cut when one's axe slipped, or a ducking when one's canoe overturned, were insults. All alike threatened first and

foremost one's ego security, and the first thought one was allowed was how to get even, how to wipe out the insult. Grief was little institutionalized, but sulking took its place. Until he had resolved upon a course of action by which to save his face after any misfortune, whether it was the slipping of a wedge in felling a tree, or the death of a favorite child, an Indian of the Northwest Coast retired to his pallet with his face to the wall and neither ate nor spoke. He rose from it to follow out some course which according to the traditional rules should reinstate him in his own eyes and those of the community: to distribute property enough to wipe out the stain, or to go head-hunting in order that somebody else should be made to mourn. His activities in neither case were specific responses to the bereavement he had just passed through, but were elaborately directed toward getting even. If he had not the money to distribute and did not succeed in killing someone to humiliate another, he might take his own life. He had staked everything, in his view of life, upon a certain picture of the self, and, when the bubble of his self-esteem was pricked, he had no interest, no occupation to fall back on, and the collapse of his inflated ego left him prostrate.

Every contingency of life was dealt with in these two traditional ways. To them the two were equivalent. Whether one fought with weapons or "fought with property," as they say, the same idea was at the bottom of both. In the olden times, they say, they fought with spears, but now they fight with property. One overcomes one's opponents in equivalent fashion in both, matching forces and seeing that one comes out ahead, and one can thumb one's nose at the vanquished rather more satisfactorily at a potlatch than on a battle field. Every occasion in life was noticed, not in its own terms, as a stage in the sex life of the individual or as a climax of joy or of grief, but as furthering this drama of consolidating one's own prestige and bringing shame to one's guests. Whether it was the occasion of the birth of a child, or a daughter's adolescence, or of the marriage of one's son, they were all equivalent raw material for the culture to use for this one traditionally selected end. They were all to raise one's own personal status and to entrench oneself by the humiliation of one's fellows. A girl's adolescence among the Nootka (16) was an event for which her father gathered property from the time she was first able to run about. When she was adolescent he would demonstrate his greatness by an unheard of distribution of these goods, and put down all his rivals. It was not as a fact of the girl's sex life that it figured in their culture, but as the occasion for a major move in the great game

[5] Himself.
[6] As salmon do.
[7] Himself.
[8] Irony, of course.
[9] Of treasure.
[9a] Insult is used here in reference to the intense susceptibility to shame that is conspicuous in this culture. All possible contingencies were interpreted as rivalry situations, and the gamut of emotions swung between triumph and shame.

of vindicating one's own greatness and humiliating one's associates.

In their behavior at great bereavements this set of the culture comes out most strongly. Among the Kwakiutl it did not matter whether a relative had died in bed of disease, or by the hand of an enemy, in either case death was an affront to be wiped out by the death of another person. The fact that one had been caused to mourn was proof that one had been put upon. A chief's sister and her daughter had gone up to Victoria, and either because they drank bad whiskey or because their boat capsized they never came back. The chief called together his warriors. "Now I ask you, tribes, who shall wail? Shall I do it or shall another?" The spokesman answered, of course, "Not you, Chief. Let some other of the tribes." Immediately they set up the war pole to announce their intention of wiping out the injury, and gathered a war party. They set out, and found seven men and two children asleep and killed them. "Then they felt good when they arrived at Sebaa in the evening."

The point which is of interest to us is that in our society those who on that occasion would feel good when they arrived at Sebaa that evening would be the definitely abnormal. There would be some, even in our society, but it is not a recognized and approved mood under the circumstances. On the Northwest Coast those are favored and fortunate to whom that mood under those circumstances is congenial, and those to whom it is repugnant are unlucky. This latter minority can register in their own culture only by doing violence to their congenial responses and acquiring others that are difficult for them. The person, for instance, who, like a Plains Indian whose wife has been taken from him, is too proud to fight, can deal with the Northwest Coast civilization only by ignoring its strongest bents. If he cannot achieve it, he is the deviant in that culture, their instance of abnormality.

This head-hunting that takes place on the Northwest Coast after a death is no matter of blood revenge or of organized vengeance. There is no effort to tie up the subsequent killing with any responsibility on the part of the victim for the death of the person who is being mourned. A chief whose son has died goes visiting wherever his fancy dictates, and he says to his host, "My prince has died today, and you go with him." Then he kills him. In this, according to their interpretation, he acts nobly because he has not been downed. He has thrust back in return. The whole procedure is meaningless without the fundamental paranoid reading of bereavement. Death, like all the other untoward accidents of existence, confounds man's pride and can only be handled in the category of insults.

Behavior honored upon the Northwest Coast is one which is recognized as abnormal in our civilization, and yet it is sufficiently close to the attitudes of our own culture to be intelligible to us and to have a definite vocabulary with which we may discuss it. The megalomaniac paranoid trend is a definite danger in our society. It is encouraged by some of our major preoccupations, and it confronts us with a choice of two possible attitudes. One is to brand it as abnormal and reprehensible, and is the attitude we have chosen in our civilization. The other is to make it an essential attribute of ideal man, and this is the solution in the culture of the Northwest Coast.

These illustrations, which it has been possible to indicate only in the briefest manner, force upon us the fact that normality is culturally defined. An adult shaped to the drives and standards of either of these cultures, if he were transported into our civilization, would fall into our categories of abnormality. He would be faced with the psychic dilemmas of the socially unavailable. In his own culture, however, he is the pillar of society, the end result of socially inculcated mores, and the problem of personal instability in his case simply does not arise.

No one civilization can possibly utilize in its mores the whole potential range of human behavior. Just as there are great numbers of possible phonetic articulations, and the possibility of language depends on a selection and standardization of a few of these in order that speech communication may be possible at all, so the possibility of organized behavior of every sort, from the fashions of local dress and houses to the dicta of a people's ethics and religion, depends upon a similar selection among the possible behavior traits. In the field of recognized economic obligations or sex tabus this selection is as nonrational and subconscious a process as it is in the field of phonetics. It is a process which goes on in the group for long periods of time and is historically conditioned by innumerable accidents of isolation or of contact of peoples. In any comprehensive study of psychology, the selection that different cultures have made in the course of history within the great circumference of potential behavior is of great significance.

Every society,[10] beginning with some slight inclination in one direction or another, carries its prefer-

[10] This phrasing of the process is deliberately animistic. It is used with no reference to a group mind or a superorganic, but in the same sense in which it is customary to say, "Every art has its own canons."

ence farther and farther, integrating itself more and more completely upon its chosen basis, and discarding those types of behavior that are uncongenial. Most of those organizations of personality that seem to us most incontrovertibly abnormal have been used by different civilizations in the very foundations of their institutional life. Conversely the most valued traits of our normal individuals have been looked on in differently organized cultures as aberrant. Normality, in short, within a very wide range, is culturally defined. It is primarily a term for the socially elaborated segment of human behavior in any culture; and abnormality, a term for the segment that that particular civilization does not use. The very eyes with which we see the problem are conditioned by the long traditional habits of our own society.

It is a point that has been made more often in relation to ethics than in relation to psychiatry. We do not any longer make the mistake of deriving the morality of our own locality and decade directly from the inevitable constitution of human nature. We do not elevate it to the dignity of a first principle. We recognize that morality differs in every society, and is a convenient term for socially approved habits. Mankind has always preferred to say, "It is a morally good," rather than "It is habitual," and the fact of this preference is matter enough for a critical science of ethics. But historically the two phrases are synonymous.

The concept of the normal is properly a variant of the concept of the good. It is that which society has approved. A normal action is one which falls well within the limits of expected behavior for a particular society. Its variability among different peoples is essentially a function of the variability of the behavior patterns that different societies have created for themselves, and can never be wholly divorced from a consideration of culturally institutionalized types of behavior.

Each culture is a more or less elaborate working-out of the potentialities of the segment it has chosen. In so far as a civilization is well integrated and consistent within itself, it will tend to carry farther and farther, according to its nature, its initial impulse toward a particular type of action, and from the point of view of any other culture those elaborations will include more and more extreme and aberrant traits.

Each of these traits, in proportion as it reinforces the chosen behavior patterns of that culture, is for that culture normal. Those individuals to whom it is congenial either congenitally, or as the result of childhood sets, are accorded prestige in that culture, and are not visited with the social contempt or dis-

approval which their traits would call down upon them in a society that was differently organized. On the other hand, those individuals whose characteristics are not congenial to the selected type of human behavior in that community are the deviants, no matter how valued their personality traits may be in a contrasted civilization.

The Dobuan who is not easily susceptible to fear of treachery, who enjoys work and likes to be helpful, is their neurotic and regarded as silly. On the Northwest Coast the person who finds it difficult to read life in terms of an insult contest will be the person upon whom fall all the difficulties of the culturally unprovided for. The person who does not find it easy to humiliate a neighbor, nor to see humiliation in his own experience, who is genial and loving, may, of course, find some unstandardized way of achieving satisfactions in his society, but not in the major patterned responses that his culture requires of him. If he is born to play an important rôle in a family with many hereditary privileges, he can succeed only by doing violence to his whole personality. If he does not succeed, he has betrayed his culture; that is, he is abnormal.

I have spoken of individuals as having sets toward certain types of behavior, and of these sets as running sometimes counter to the types of behavior which are institutionalized in the culture to which they belong. From all that we know of contrasting cultures it seems clear that differences of temperament occur in every society. The matter has never been made the subject of investigation, but from the available material it would appear that these temperament types are very likely of universal recurrence. That is, there is an ascertainable range of human behavior that is found wherever a sufficiently large series of individuals is observed. But the proportion in which behavior types stand to one another in difference societies is not universal. The vast majority of the individuals in any group are shaped to the fashion of that culture. In other words, most individuals are plastic to the moulding force of the society into which they are born. In a society that values trance, as in India, they will have supernormal experience. In a society that institutionalizes homosexuality, they will be homosexual. In a society that sets the gathering of possessions as the chief human objective, they will amass property. The deviants, whatever the type of behavior the culture has institutionalized, will remain few in number, and there seems no more difficulty in moulding the vast malleable majority to the "normality" of what we consider an aberrant trait, such as delusions of reference, than to the normality of such accepted behavior patterns as acquisitiveness. The small proportion of the number of the deviants in any culture is not a function of the sure instinct with which that society has built itself upon the fundamental sanities, but of the universal fact that, happily, the majority of mankind quite readily take any shape that is presented to them.

The relativity of normality is not an academic issue. In the first place, it suggests that the apparent weakness of the aberrant is most often and in great measure illusory. It springs not from the fact that he is lacking in necessary vigor, but that he is an individual upon whom that culture has put more than the usual strain. His inability to adapt himself to society is a reflection of the fact that that adaptation involves a conflict in him that it does not in the so-called normal.

Therapeutically, it suggests that the inculcation of tolerance and appreciation in any society toward its less usual types is fundamentally important in successful mental hygiene. The complement of this tolerance, on the patients' side, is an education in self-reliance and honesty with himself. If he can be brought to realize that what has thrust him into his misery is despair at his lack of social backing he may be able to achieve a more independent and less tortured attitude and lay the foundation for an adequately functioning mode of existence.

There is a further corollary. From the point of view of absolute categories of abnormal psychology, we must expect in any culture to find a large proportion of the most extreme abnormal types among those who from the local point of view are farthest from belonging to this category. The culture, according to its major preoccupations, will increase and intensify hysterical, epileptic, or paranoid symptoms, at the same time relying socially in a greater and greater degree upon these very individuals. Western civilization allows and culturally honors gratifications of the ego which according to any absolute category would be regarded as abnormal. The portrayal of unbridled and arrogant egoists as family men, as officers of the law, and in business has been a favorite topic of novelists, and they are familiar in every community. Such individuals are probably mentally warped to a greater degree than many inmates of our institutions who are nevertheless socially unavailable. They are extreme types of those personality configurations which our civilization fosters.

This consideration throws into great prominence the confusion that follows, on the one hand, the use of social inadequacy as a criterion of abnormality and, on the other, of definite fixed symptoms. The confusion is present in practically all discussions of abnormal psychology, and it can be clarified chiefly by adequate consideration of the character of the culture, not of the constitution of the abnormal individual. Nevertheless, the bearing of social security upon the total situation of the abnormal cannot be exaggerated, and the study of comparative psychiatry will be fundamentally concerned with this aspect of the matter.

It is clear that statistical methods of defining normality, so long as they are based on studies in a selected civilization, only involve us, unless they are checked against the cultural configuration, in deeper and deeper provincialism. The recent tendency in abnormal psychology to take the laboratory mode as normal and to define abnormalities as they depart from this average has value in so far as it indicates that the aberrants in any culture are those individuals who are liable to serious disturbances because their habits are culturally unsupported. On the other hand, it overlooks the fact that every culture besides its abnormals of conflict has presumably its abnormals of extreme fulfillment of the cultural type. From the point of view of a universally valid abnormal psychology the extreme types of abnormality would probably be found in this very group — a group which in every study based upon one culture goes undescribed except in its end institutionalized forms.

The relativity of normality is important in what may some day come to be a true social engineering. Our picture of our own civilization is no longer in this generation in terms of a changeless and divinely derived set of categorical imperatives. We must face the problems our changed perspective has put upon us. In this matter of mental ailments, we must face the fact that even our normality is man-made, and is of our own seeking. Just as we have been handicapped in dealing with ethical problems so long as we held to an absolute definition of morality, so too in dealing with the problems of abnormality we are handicapped so long as we identify our local normalities with the universal sanities. I have taken illustrations from different cultures, because the conclusions are most inescapable from the contrasts as they are presented in unlike social groups. But the major problem is not a consequence of the variability of the normal from culture to culture, but its variability from era to era. This variability in time we cannot escape if we would, and it is not beyond the bounds of possibility that we may be able to face this inevitable change with full understanding and deal with it rationally (9). No society has yet achieved self-conscious and critical analysis of its own normalities and attempted rationally to deal with its own social process of creating new normalities within its next generation. But the fact that it is unachieved is not therefore proof of its impossibility. It is a faint indication of how momentous it could be in human society.

There is another major factor in the cultural conditioning of abnormality. From the material that is available at the present time it seems a lesser factor than the one we have discussed. Nevertheless, disregard of its importance has led to many misconceptions. The particular forms of behavior to which unstable individuals of any group are liable are many of them matters of cultural patterning like any other behavior. It is for this obvious reason that the epidemic disorders of one continent or era are often rare or unreported from other parts of the world or other periods of history.

The baldest evidences of cultural patterning in the behavior of unstable individuals is in trance phenomena. The use to which such proclivities are put, the form their manifestations take, the things that are seen and felt in trance, are all culturally controlled. The tranced individual may come back with communications from the dead describing the minutiae of life in the hereafter, or he may visit the world of the unborn, or get information about lost objects in the camp, or experience cosmic unity, or acquire a life-long guardian spirit, or get information about coming events. Even in trance the individual holds strictly to the rules and expectations of his culture, and his experience is as locally patterned as a marriage rite or an economic exchange.

The conformity of trance experience to the expectations of waking life is well recognized. Now that we are no longer confused by the attempt to ascribe supernormal validity to the one or the other, and realize how trance experience bodies forth the preoccupations of the experiencing individual, the cultural patterning in ecstasy has become an accepted tenet.

But the matter does not end here. It is not only what is seen in trance experience that has clear-cut geographical and temporal distribution. It is equally true of forms of behavior which are affected by certain unstable individuals in any group. It is one of the prime difficulties in the use of such unprecise and casual information as we possess about the behavior of the unstable in different cultures, that the material does not correspond to data from our own society. It has even been thought that such definite types of instability as Arctic hysteria (14) and the Malay running-amok were racial diseases. But we know at least, in spite of the lack of good psychiatric accounts, that these phenomena do not coincide with racial distributions. Moreover, the same problem is quite as striking in cases where there is no possibility of a racial correlation. Running amok has been described as alike in symptoms and alike in the treatment accorded it by the rest of the group from such different parts of the world as Melanesia (11, pp. 54–55) and Tierra del Fuego (7).

The racial explanation is also ruled out of court in those instances of epidemic mania which are characteristic of our own cultural background. The dancing mania (13) that filled the streets of Europe with compulsively dancing men, women, and children in mediaeval times is recognized as an extreme instance of suggestibility in our own racial group.

These behaviors are capable of controlled elaboration that is often carried to great lengths. Unstable individuals in one culture achieve characteristic forms that may be excessively rare or absent in another, and this is very marked where social value has been attached to one form or another. Thus when some form of borderline behavior has been associated in any society with the shaman and he is a person of authority and influence, it is this particular indicated seizure to which he will be liable at every demonstration. Among the Shasta of California, as we have seen, and among many other tribes in various parts of the world, some form of cataleptic seizure is the passport to shamanism and must constantly accompany its practice. In other regions it is automatic vision or audition. In other societies behavior is perhaps closest to what we cover by the term hystero-epilepsy. In Siberia all the familiar characteristics of our spiritualistic seances are required for every performance of the shaman. In all these cases the particular experience that is thus socially chosen receives considerable elaboration and is usually patterned in detail according to local standards. That is, each culture, though it chooses quite narrowly in the great field of borderline experiences, without difficulty imposes its selected type upon certain of its individuals. The particular behavior of an unstable individual in these instances is not the single and inevitable mode in which his abnormality could express itself. He has taken up a traditionally conditioned pattern of behavior in this as in any other field. Conversely, in every society, our own included, there are forms of instability that are out of fashion. They are not at the present time at least being presented for imitation to the enormously suggestible individuals who constitute in any society a considerable group of the abnormals. It seems clear that this is no matter of the nature of sanity, or even of a biological, inherited tendency in a local group, but quite simply an affair of social patterning.

The problem of understanding abnormal human

behavior in any absolute sense independent of cultural factors is still far in the future. The categories of borderline behavior which we derive from the study of the neuroses and psychoses of our civilzation are categories of prevailing local types of instability. They give much information about the stresses and strains of Western civilization, but no final picture of inevitable human behavior. Any conclusions about such behavior must await the collection by trained observers of psychiatric data from other cultures. Since no adequate work of the kind has been done at the present time, it is impossible to say what core of definition of abnormality may be found valid from the comparative material. It is as it is in ethics: all our local conventions of moral behavior and of immoral are without absolute validity, and yet it is quite possible that a modicum of what is considered right and what wrong could be disentangled that is shared by the whole human race. When data are available in psychiatry, this minimum definition of abnormal human tendencies will be probably quite unlike our culturally conditioned, highly elaborated psychoses such as those that are described, for instance, under the terms of schizophrenia and manic-depressive.

REFERENCES

1. BOAS, F. The social organization and the secret societies of the Kwakiutl Indians. *Rep. U. S. Nat. Mus. for 1895*, 1897, 311–738.
2. ———. Ethnology of the Kwakiutl based on data collected by George Hunt. (*Bur. Amer. Ethnol., 35th Ann. Rep. to the Secretary of the Smithsonian Instit.*) (2 vols.) Washington: Govt. Print. Office, 1921. Pp. 1481.
3. ———. Contributions to the ethnology of the Kwakiutl. (*Columbia Univ. Contrib. Anthrop.*, Vol. 3.) New York: Columbia Univ. Press, 1925. Pp. vi+357.
4. ———. Religion of the Kwakiutl. (*Columbia Univ. Contrib. Anthrop.*, Vol. 10.) Vol. II. New York: Columbia Univ. Press, 1930. Pp. vii+288.
5. BOAS, F., & HUNT, G. Kwakiutl texts. (*Mem. Amer. Mus. Natur. Hist.: Jesup North Pacific Expedition*, Vol. 3.) Leiden: Brill; New York: Stechert, 1905. Pp. 532.
6. CALLAWAY, C. H. Religious system of the Amazulu. *Publ. Folklore Soc.*, London, 1884, 15. Pp. viii+448.
7. CORIAT, I. H. Psychoneuroses among primitive tribes. In *Studies in abnormal psychology*, Ser. 6. Boston: Gorham (n.d.). Pp. 201–208.
8. CZAPLICKA, M. A. Aboriginal Siberia: a study in social anthropology. Oxford: Clarendon Press, 1914. Pp. xiv+374. (A convenient summary.)
9. DEWEY, J. Human nature and conduct: an introduction to social psychology. New York: Holt, 1922. Pp. vii+336.
10. DIXON, R. B. The Shasta. *Bull. Amer. Mus. Natur. Hist.*, 1907, 17, 381–498.
11. FORTUNE, R. F. Sorcerers of Dobu. New York: Dutton, 1932. Pp. 346.
12. GRINNELL, G. B. The Cheyenne Indians. New Haven, Conn.: Yale Univ. Press, 1923. Pp. vi+358.
13. HECKER, J. F. C. The black death and the dancing mania. (Trans. from the German by B. G. Babbington.) New York: Humboldt, 1885. Pp. 47.
14. NOVAKOVSKY, S. Arctic or Siberian hysteria as a reflex of the geographic environment. *Ecol.*, 1924, 5, 113–127.
15. PARSONS, E. C. The Zuñi La'mana. *Amer. Anthrop.*, 1916, 18, 521–528.
16. SAPIR, E. A girl's puberty ceremony among the Nootka. *Trans. Roy. Soc. Canada*, 1913, 7 (3rd ser.), 67–80.

MARIE JAHODA

Toward a Social Psychology of Mental Health*†

I. SCOPE AND ORIENTATION

The purpose of this paper‡ is to examine what is known and what should be known about *the impact of community influences on the mental health of the individual.* In one form or another this vast subject, with its virtually unlimited ramifications, has occupied the minds of men for thousands of years. Political philosophers and political scientists in ancient and modern times have often justified the systems they advocate in terms of their impact on the mental well-being of citizens. Hippocrates, for example, in comparing democratic and monarchic forms of government, states that "institutions contribute a great deal to the formation of courageousness." In addition to a vast array of similar insights into the interaction between institutions and mental health which have become available through the observations of men who have followed Hippocrates, anthropologists and psychiatrists of this century have made a host of factual and theoretical contributions to the subject.

The very wealth of these contributions imposes the necessity to choose among them for presentation in this statement. The guiding principle for the selection was largely the wish to furnish information and

* Reprinted by permission from Milton Senn (Ed.), *Symposium on the Healthy Personality.* New York: Josiah Macy, Jr., Foundation, 1950, pp. 211–231.
† Prepared with the financial support and on invitation of the Josiah Macy, Jr. Foundation for use as source material by the Fact Finding Committee of the Midcentury White House Conference on Children and Youth. This statement in preliminary form had the benefit of the critique and judgment of the members and guests of the Josiah Macy, Jr. Foundation Conference on Infancy and Childhood at their special meeting July 3–4, 1950. Grateful acknowledgment is made to that conference group for their support and help in broadening the scope of this paper.
‡ The plan for this paper was developed in conjunction with Dr. Stuart W. Cook; he contributed many of the ideas and formulations it contains. The author is also indebted to Dr. Brewster M. Smith and to Dr. Viola Bernard, who have gone over an earlier draft of this paper and criticized it in considerable detail. Many of their constructive suggestions are incorporated in the present text.

guides for research which would be in accord with the broad purpose of the Midcentury White House Conference on Children and Youth "to consider how we can develop in children the mental, emotional, and spiritual qualities essential to individual happiness and responsible citizenship, and what physical, economic and social conditions are deemed necessary to this development."

To be more specific, we are, then, looking for facts, concepts, and theories on the interaction between community influences and mental health which *can be applied* in the attempt to enhance the mental health of children and young people; this knowledge to be of a nature that it can be applied *widely to groups of individuals* rather than demand application to one person at a time.

In order to be applicable, the knowledge which we are seeking must be related to *situations where there is a genuine choice between alternatives.* If we should arrive at the result that living in the atomic age has unhealthy implications for personality formation, we would be better informed than previously, but since we obviously have no choice about living in the atomic age or at any other period, the application of such knowledge would not be possible. If we are to make constructive discoveries which can be applied, the analysis of the problem must be conducted so as to unearth alternatives possible within the atomic age.

To take another example: any knowledge we might acquire about the differential effect on mental health of, say, life in an urban or a rural setting would not be of the sort we are seeking in view of the fact that the division of labor which results in urban and rural life appears to be inevitable in our society. The community influences on which we wish to concentrate must, then, be of a kind which can be modified and redirected in the interest of the members of the community.

This emphasis on the pragmatic aspects of our task is deliberate and pursued in full recognition of the fact that it is certainly not the only feasible approach to the subject. It must be understood as a limitation of the range and type of community influences with which we are concerned rather than as a lack of concern with theory. We have found, in the past, that the potential usefulness of thought need not detract from, and has on occasion added to, its scientific quality.

A further limitation is contained in this preliminary description of our task: it excludes concern with individual therapy. This, again, is a utilitarian decision. At the present cost of psychiatric treatment and in view of the relative scarcity of psychiatrists and the magnitude of the problem, the knowledge that psychotherapy can restore the mental health of young people contains, unfortunately, no promise that the mental health of a generation can be improved.

II. THE CONCEPT OF MENTAL HEALTH

Perhaps the greatest handicap for a systematic study of the social conditions conducive to mental health is the very elusiveness of this concept. As far as we could discover, there exists no psychologically meaningful and, from the point of view of research, operationally useful description of what is commonly understood to constitute mental health. Yet the establishment of some criteria by which the degree of mental health of an individual can be judged is essential if one wishes to identify social conditions conducive to the attainment of mental health. In an effort to choose such criteria we shall examine below five possibilities chosen either because of their familiarity or their apparent value, or both. The five are: the absence of mental disease, normality of behavior, adjustment to environment, unity of personality, and correct perception of reality.

The Absence of Mental Disease

There is widespread agreement that the absence of mental disease is a necessary, though by no means sufficient, condition of mental health. However, even the definition of mental disease meets with considerable difficulties.

Anthropologists tell us about cultures in which what Western civilization would regard as symptoms of mental disease is generally accepted behavior. According to Ruth Benedict, the Kwakiutl Indians of British Columbia engage in behavior which would be called paranoid and megalomaniac in our culture. Their view of the world has similarities with what we regard as delusions of grandeur (1).

F. Alexander interprets the Buddhistic self-absorption of mystics in India, with its physical manifestation of rigidity and immobility, as an artificial

schizophrenia of the catatonic type (14). Now it is apparently true that the Buddhist can control the onset and end of his "symptoms," a feat which the schizophrenic person in our culture cannot, of course, perform. The example indicates that the similarity in symptoms must not be mistaken for an identical disturbance of functions. It also illustrates — and this is important here — that identical observable symptoms are regarded in one culture as achievement, while in another they are regarded as a severe debility. Examples could be multiplied to indicate that *the evaluation of behavior as sick, or normal, or extraordinary in a positive sense depends largely on accepted social conventions*. This differential evaluation of symptoms is not limited to cross-cultural comparisons. Within our society a farmers' community may well regard as symptoms of mental disorder the behavior of, say, an urban artists' colony. It follows, then, that mental disease is not to be defined in terms of isolated symptoms but rather in conjunction with the social norms and values of the community in which the symptoms are observed.

Even with this qualification, however, the absence of mental disease is not a very satisfactory indication of mental health. For the borderline between what is regarded as normal and as abnormal is dim and ill defined in all but the extreme cases. Neurotic and psychopathic personalities, for example, belong to that large border area to which the application of the label "mental disease" is not much more defensible than that of the label "mental health," unless we can discover more appropriate criteria for one or the other than are implied by the current usage of these terms.

In summary, then, it appears that an effort to arrive at a satisfactory definition of mental disease does not solve our problem but rather adds others. It would seem, consequently, to be more fruitful to tackle the concept of mental health in its more positive connotation.

Normality of Behavior

Here, again, an amount that can hardly be overestimated has been learned from the cultural anthropologists, whose entire work can be regarded as variations on the theme of the plasticity of human nature and, accordingly, on the vast range of what can be regarded as normal. They have convincingly demonstrated the great variety of social norms and institutions invented by different cultures in different parts of the world and the fact that in different cultures different forms of behavior are regarded as normal.

It is generally accepted that normality covers two different concepts which can but need not — and as a rule do not — coincide; namely, normality as a statistical frequency concept and normality as a synonym for the elusive concept of mental health. [The lack of coincidence between the two concepts is most dramatically demonstrated in episodes of mass hysteria, for example, the response to the Invasion from Mars broadcasts, as described by Cantril (3).] In so far as normality is used as a synonym for mental health, the problems of concept definition are, of course, identical. It remains to be seen what can be learned from the frequency concept. Here the practice of anthropologists concerned with the culture of nonindustrialized small tribes and those of social scientists concerned with the culture of this country are often opposed; the former do not, as a rule, apply the statistical normality concept, perhaps because the uniformities are so much more general in the small tribes with which they deal than in our society. However this may be, there are in our culture behavior distributions of very different types. With regard to many forms of behavior, the distribution of the population follows a normal curve; that is, the majority manifests a medium course, with about a quarter of either extreme of behavior. This is true, for instance, for many biological functions (height, weight, and so forth). This type of distribution is so frequently expected that it is actually taken as the basis for the standardization of all tests of psychological functions. However, there are many forms of behavior which do not follow the normal curve. An example is the knowledge of languages, where the overwhelming majority of the population speaks one and only a few two or more. Another is the voting behavior in this country, where only about half the population exercises its privileges to vote, while the other half does not vote. In this case voting would be as "normal" in the statistical sense as not voting. One may assume that these different types of distribution of behavior result, in part, from differential pressures to conformity.

If we are dealing with a distribution of behavior, such as is exemplified in the ability to speak one or more languages, the dividing line between what is normal and abnormal (in the statistical frequency sense) is obviously easier to draw than if we are dealing with a normal distribution curve. It may well be possible to distinguish cultures in terms of the tolerated range of behavior deviant from the statistical norm. In this country, which, according to its explicit creed stands in many respects for a variety of permissible behavior rather than for uniformity, the

criteria for mental health must be such that they do not automatically exclude everything but the average.

Adjustment to Environment

The concept of adjustment implies the establishment of a workable arrangement between personal needs and social conditions. We propose to regard the absence of any such arrangement (observed, for example, in many cases of mental disease) as a definite counterindication of mental health. In such cases individuals lack the ability to adapt themselves to the changing demands of a changing environment; they cannot adjust. While the inability to adjust is a counterindication of mental health, not every form of adjustment is a positive indication of mental health. There are also workable arrangements with the environment which we wish to exclude from a notion of mental health. A case in point is provided by the study of the impact of parental unemployment on children and young people. In a study of an Austrian village in which virtually the entire population was unemployed (12), children and young people had been compelled to adjust to the economic situation by a profound resignation and restriction of personal needs. These children had fewer and more humble wishes, life plans which anticipated failure ("When I grow up I want to be an Indian chief, but I am afraid it will be hard to find a job," a nine-year-old said), and restricted imagination when compared with children of employed families. Their "adjustment" is perhaps better described as *a passive acceptance of social conditions* to the detriment of their mental health. Under conditions of prolonged unemployment or in other situations where the external pressures are extreme, passive acceptance may be the only possible workable arrangement — which is only another way of saying that these conditions are inevitably detrimental to mental health.

Actually, one of the Marienthal youth did find another way: he rebelled against the restrictive features of an unemployed family, committed some minor thefts, and was placed by the juvenile court into a reformatory in which he was trained as an electrician. It is at least a moot question whether his rebellion was mentally not more healthy than the resignation of his contemporaries.

In the case of these young people, their ability to adjust to their environment resulted in a severe curtailment of personal needs. To be sure, they had found a workable arrangement with the conditions of life imposed on them: they had bowed to the dictatorship of circumstances. Such passive acceptance is by no means limited to extreme social conditions. Erich Fromm (6) and David Riesman (26) in their studies of political apathy, among others, have drawn attention to some areas in which passive acceptance threatens to become the rule rather than the exception.

A British study of young factory workers (11) showed the same trend toward passive acceptance. Within a few weeks after these young factory girls had made the transition from school, where the main values were intelligence, industriousness, respect for the teacher and older people in general, to the factory, where intelligence was useless, hard work frowned upon by one's colleagues, and respect for age out of place, they had adopted completely the new set of norms.

To regard such forms of passive acceptance as a counterindication of mental health, notwithstanding the fact that it may be the type of behavior followed by a considerable majority, is ultimately based on social and moral values rather than on objective criteria. If one believes that everything which exists is right by virtue of its existence, then passive acceptance forms a valid criterion for mental health. We do not believe this. Furthermore, it would appear that such a static view of society is untenable in our constantly changing world. Circumstances are better or worse, and are judged and experienced by most people in these terms. Passive acceptance denies or ignores these judgments.

In contrast to passive acceptance there is another form of active adjustment which is indeed linked to our as yet vague notion of mental health. It is perhaps best described as a mastery of environment. An environment which makes it possible to implement Henry V's royal statement, "We are the makers of manners," is by this criterion conducive to mental health.

Active mastery of environment presupposes a deliberate choice of what one does and what one does not conform to and consists of deliberate modifications of environmental conditions. It aims at creating an environment with which one can feel at home. In a society in which regimentation prevails, active adjustment will hardly be possible; in a society where overt regimentation is replaced by the invisible compulsions of conformity pressures, active adjustment will be equally rare. Only where there exists social recognition of alternative forms of behavior is there a chance for the average individual to master his surroundings and attain mental health.

There are, however, periods of life in which active adjustment through a modification of the environment is less feasible than at other periods. Childhood and even adolescence limit the scope of possible modifications of one's surroundings.

Adolescents in our society are inevitably subject to specific discomforts of civilization. At a time when young people are physically mature enough to lead the life of adults, certainly in the economic and the sexual spheres, our civilization interposes a period denying to the adolescent economic and sexual adulthood and providing him, in their stead, with a chance to experiment without having to face the major responsibilities of complete independence.

Adolescence, a period of protected growth, is a time when independence from the parental family is gradually achieved; a time when through rebellion, conflicts, doubts, or through some smoother form of transition, young people acquire a wide range of experiences, undergo the trials and errors of forming personal relationships, develop new group loyalties, change their minds and interests, and commit the creative and destructive errors of youth (24).

If this is a correct description of the function of adolescence, passive acceptance of environmental demands can still stand as a counterindication of mental health. The criterion of active mastery of environment needs some modification in view of the dependence of adolescents which makes it unlikely that they can achieve it in all areas. Here it is the *attempts to modify conditions* in areas where the adolescent is inevitably dependent and the planning for more independent action in the future which should be regarded as symptoms of mental health. For the fully developed adult personality, anticipation and planning without realistic modifications would probably indicate a lesser degree of mental health. However, it should be kept in mind that even in the life of the adolescent there are many areas in which he has freedom of choice and that in these areas he has opportunities for active adjustments of the sort we have discussed.

Unity of Personality

Another possible criterion which has much to recommend itself is the concept of a *unity of personality*, which, though perhaps not formulated in these terms, underlies much of psychoanalytic thought and, it would appear, is the goal of psychoanalytic therapy.

On the basis of evidence derived from psychoanalysis, Heinz Hartmann speaks of "a general trend of human development, the trend towards a growing independence from the immediate impact of present stimuli, the independence from the *hic et nunc;*" and, somewhat later, of the "growing independence from the outside world, in so far as a process of inner regulation replaces the reaction and actions due to fear of the social environment (social anxiety)" (10). Other nonpsychoanalytic authors, in describing similar processes, speak of "self-consistency" or "self-realization."

The proposition being stated here is that the person who acts according to a consistent inner regulation and is relatively free from conflicts among the three constituent parts of personality: id, ego, and superego — in other words an integrated personality — should be regarded as a mentally healthy person. It is perhaps not quite superfluous to add that this does not imply freedom from conflicts with his environment.

Of course it may be true to say that the catatonic patient, for all we know about him, manifests a very high degree of unity of personality; he certainly appears to be entirely self-regulated. The example demonstrates vividly that no single criterion for mental health will ever suffice. If unity of personality is taken as a criterion not alone but in conjunction with active adjustment, the catatonic patient is, of course, immediately ruled out. Indeed, it is the unity of personality, the maintenance of the inner core, which makes active adjustment possible.

Correct Perception of Reality

There is at points in the preceding discussion a hint that the correct perception of reality (including, of course, the self) may serve as another useful criterion of mental health. Unless active adjustment involving the modification of the environment is to rely on hit-or-miss methods, it must be based on correct perception of the environment. If the unity of personality is to persist over a period of time in the face of the inevitable conflicts of life, it must be based on correct self-perception.

The difficulty in the use of this criterion arises over the word "correct." Especially in the perception of more complex phenomena, such as one's own status concern or a country's war-mindedness, it is indeed hard to establish what is correct and what is incorrect perception. A judgment by the majority is not necessarily more correct than one by a single individual. However, there are certain phenomena with respect to which the correctness of perception can be checked objectively. In a biracial housing project (21), one-half Negro and one-half white tenants, many of the white tenants, who were prejudiced against Negroes, consistently overestimated the pro-

portion of Negroes in the project; their perception was, apparently, determined by their fear of being outnumbered. In this sense their prejudices impaired their mental health.

Where the correctness of perception can be ascertained, as in this case, it provides indeed a useful and psychologically meaningful criterion of mental health. Where the objective yardstick is missing, however, the use of the criterion will present difficulties. To establish that the same occurrence can be perceived differently by different people does not yet indicate, of course, whose perception corresponds with reality.

A Multiple Criterion

As will doubtless be clear from the discussions of the individual criteria, we suggest tentatively that a combination of three criteria be used for determining the mental health of an individual: (a) active adjustment or attempts at mastery of his environment as distinct both from his inability to adjust and from his indiscriminate adjustment through passive acceptance of environmental conditions; (b) unity of his personality, the maintenance of a stable, internal integration which remains intact notwithstanding the flexibility of behavior which derives from active adjustment; and (c) ability to perceive correctly the world and himself.

We propose that whether or not a given environment may be considered conducive to mental health depends upon the barriers it erects against the realization of the maximum value for each of these three criteria. It is easy to imagine social conditions which favor one or two but exclude others. Heroic efforts in fighting for a lost cause, for example, obviously exclude correct perception which, in self-defense, is replaced by illusions. Under conditions of unemployment active adjustment may be impossible, as we have seen. Under the conditions of a polysegmented society with many incompatible values and norms, the unity of personality may be abandoned for the sake of opportunistic adjustment in terms of correct perception. In cases such as these, where environmental reality blocks the achievement of full mental health in the sense of maximal realization of all three criteria, we may still ask what is optimum mental health for a given set of circumstances. Granted, for example, that reality makes impossible the achievement of certain personal needs (and is thus detrimental to the realization of full mental health), there will still be some optimum balance of the three criteria of mental health and evaluative comparisons with this optimum may be made.

III. SOME CONCEPTS AND THEORIES RELEVANT TO THE STUDY OF MENTAL HEALTH

With these tentative criteria for mental health in mind, we may now return to the question of the impact of community influences on mental health. It will be helpful here to turn to established psychological theories and concepts which, though not explicitly formulated in relation to the study of community influences on mental health, may, nevertheless, guide it into fruitful channels. We shall briefly examine the psychodynamic theory of personality formation, field theory, modal personality and culture patterns, and the concepts of status and role.

Psychodynamic Theory of Personality Formation

Whether we agree with Ignatius of Loyola that the personality is set by the age of seven, or with early psychoanalytic theory that it is set at an even earlier age, or are in accord with current psychoanalytic thinking which attributes to the latency period up to the age of ten or so a function in personality formation, there appears to be a consensus of opinion as to the decisive influence of early experiences. Granted this, there remains the question of how the social norms to which the individual is exposed *at a later stage* can affect his personality to an extent that it changes the degree of his mental health.

Obviously many events, decisive for personality formation, have occurred before the child is exposed to social conditions other than those inherent in his family. At the Oedipal stage the crucial process of identification with the parents gets under way, and the success or failure of this process is of lasting influence on the development of the superego and the child's capacity to identify in later life with groups and individuals. Even before this stage, in the first year of life, the child has learned to achieve a relation to objects through the gradual constitution of the ego as distinct from the surrounding universe, that is, his mother.

Psychoanalytic theory maintains that serious personality disturbances acquired at any of these crucial stages are irrevocable unless psychoanalytically treated and that environmental change afterward has little remedial value. René Spitz and Catherine Wolf, for example, have presented evidence showing the rapid mental and emotional deterioration of infants separated for some length of time from their mothers or mother substitutes (29).

Psychoanalysts would agree, however, that even if everything went well, relatively speaking, up to the age of the latency period, subsequent social factors may still have a severely disturbing impact. Indeed, the concept of regression exemplifies such a personality change as the result of particular environmental stress and strain in later life.

On the other hand, psychoanalytic theory has been less explicit on other changes which occur in later life under the impact of environmental factors. There can be little doubt that such changes do actually occur under extreme conditions. Bettelheim's analysis of the behavior of inmates of concentration camps (2), for example, provides evidence in this direction. It is quite possible that what happens under extreme conditions can also occur as the result of a prolonged impact of less extreme pressures.

Field Theory

The question can here be legitimately raised as to whether we are talking in the preceding discussion about personality changes or about different behavior of one and the same personality under different external conditions. According to Kurt Lewin's field-theoretical approach (16, 17), behavior is always a function both of personality and of environment, a formulation which encompasses the facts regarding changes in later life and is complementary to, rather than inconsistent with, psychoanalytic theory. It would seem, then, that the answer depends on whether or not the behavioral change persists when the original environmental conditions are restored. All through life environment acts as an agency mobilizing selectively different facets of the personality. There are in every human being, even after the age of ten, many more latent possibilities than meet the eye. It is the pressure of the external world that can alternately favor or reject some personality traits, for shorter or longer periods.

In the light of the psychodynamic and field theories, we may expect that personality and mental health can be modified by community influences in two ways: (a) through the environmental impact on parents which they will transmit to their children from birth onward and (b) through behavior changes demanded by environmental pressures which may establish permanent patterns. It remains to be seen whether some broad aspects of the environment can be specified which tend to influence the mental health of large numbers of people, notwithstanding the fact that the same environment will have a different meaning for different personalities.

Modal Personality and Culture Patterns

One of the most important applications of psychoanalytic theory to the study of environmental impact on personality comes from anthropology through the cooperative effort of Kardiner and Linton. Kardiner has advanced the concept of *basic personality* to describe a phenomenon similar to that referred to by the more widely and vaguely used term "national character;" he has based the concept upon a psychoanalytic interpretation of personality (13). Linton (13) defined basic personality as a configuration of several elements resting upon the following postulates: early experiences have a lasting effect upon personality; similar experiences will tend to produce similar personality configurations; child rearing is culturally patterned and within one society similar in all families although not identical; child rearing differs from one culture to the next. From this he deduces that the members of a given society have many early experiences in common, hence many personality elements in common. It follows that personality norms will differ in different societies.

The crucial aspect of this concept is the emphasis on differences in child rearing practices (differences which may be functionally related to differences in other spheres as, for example, economic organization or sex mores) and their relation to the emergence of different personalities.

Kardiner and Linton's contribution derives its importance from having produced a model of thought and demonstrated the process of concept formation in this difficult area. But the very conception of basic personality, with its emphasis on child rearing, makes its application to contemporary American society difficult. First of all, the question arises whether in the United States we are dealing with one or with many different types of basic personality. In view of the wide range of tolerated deviations in child rearing practices, one is led to assume that more than one basic personality must be formed in this country.

Such evidence as exists on differences in child rearing practices in American society adds to the difficulty of applying Kardiner's concept. Some empirical investigations have, for example, demonstrated considerable and consistent differences in the child rearing practices of the American middle class and the American working class, and also among various ethnic subgroups (23). Kardiner has demonstrated, especially in his interpretation of the Tanala culture, how the entire structure of society — his "rational" and "projective systems" — reinforces and is reinforced by, child rearing practices. While there is not much systematic evidence on the point, it would appear that the American working class and middle class have largely overlapping and identical rational and projective systems (such as the economic organization of the country, or religion). Whether or not the two classes should theoretically be expected to produce different basic personalities is uncertain; whether or not they have different basic personalities has, as far as we know, not been investigated.

To sum up: the concept of basic personality seems to be more applicable to small uniform and self-contained cultures than to American society. If and when its usefulness for describing the impact of American subcultures upon personality formation (and perhaps mental health) can be established, modifications in subcultural characteristics can then be attempted by way of public education about child rearing. Since this is an effort which is rightly proceeding without awaiting the results of further research, it should be stated that in keeping with Kardiner's work and with psychodynamic theory in general, the term "child rearing practices" must not be narrowly interpreted. For it is, after all, not a gesture but the meaning of a gesture in its emotional context which affects the formation of child personality. The most literal obedience to proper weaning procedures will not prevent the development of insecurity and anxiety if the mother's over-all attitude toward the child is rejecting.

Status and Role

The concepts of role and status, and their relation to personality — both acquiring increasing prominence in current socio-psychological thinking (22) — are perhaps more relevant to our problem because their existence has been established beyond doubt in all cultures. According to Linton, even the simplest societies know of at least five different kinds of status: age-sex, occupational, rank and prestige in some hierarchical relation, family or clan, and association group. Status may be either "ascribed," as is the case with the status of the child or minority-group member, or "achieved," as is the case with the status of businessman or president of an organization. A role is, in Linton's words, "the sum total of the culture patterns associated with a particular status. It thus includes the attitudes, values, and behavior ascribed by the society to any and all persons occupying this status. . . . A role is the dynamic aspect of a status" (22).

The notions of status and role lead us one step nearer to the understanding of our task: the impact of the environment on the personality of an individual will be transmitted by way of the status he is ascribed or which he achieves, and the roles that go with such a status. As Newcomb points out in some detail, the various roles one plays in society can be compatible or incompatible with each other. Even where they are compatible, they can be culturally defined in a manner which strains all resources of a personality to an extent that is hardly bearable. One has only to remember the roles assigned to a Jew under the Nazi regime to realize the close link between the definition of roles and the mental well-being of an individual in terms of our criteria of mental health. Where the roles are incompatible, the strain on mental health, especially with respect to the unity of personality criterion, will be considerable.

IV. IN SEARCH FOR ENVIRONMENTAL FACTORS INFLUENCING MENTAL HEALTH

After this sketchy review of our conceptual tools, one fact is established beyond doubt: we do not yet possess a theoretical system, nor even a logically consistent framework, with which to tackle the task of enhancing mental health through the modification of environment. By way of remedy, we would argue that the formulation of theory proceeds best when it is closely linked to empirical research. If we, therefore, now turn to the directions research might take, it is done in the belief that systematic study will, in the end, be the most economic way toward the development of a theory which can safely be applied to guide community change to the benefit of mental health.

Alternative Approaches

One could approach the study of community influences on mental health by selecting individuals manifesting either a high or a low degree of mental health (as defined, for example, in terms of our suggested criteria) and investigating the set of social influences to which they had been exposed throughout their lives. This approach has, undoubtedly, much to recommend it. In a way all forms of psychotherapy present a contribution to the understanding of mental health along these lines. In view of the earlier definition of our task, however, it is not for the present purpose a very economical approach. The chances are that research which sets out to account for the difference between mentally healthy and unhealthy individuals will be led into a study of med-

ical, economic, psychodynamic factors, and the like, as well as of community influences.

A second approach seems to be more directly related to our task. It consists in the study of the mental health of individuals in small, well-defined groups (units, communities). In so far as one is dealing with groups which have distinctive characteristics, these characteristics are kept constant as an influence in the mental health of all members. To the extent that the mental health of individuals in groups with one set of characteristics differs from that of individuals in other groups with different characteristics, we may be in a position to attribute the differences in mental health to the differences between groups. To be sure, one of the basic tenets of the concept of interaction between environment and the individual is that the same situation will be experienced differently by different persons. Nevertheless, if we can describe the common external reality with some objectivity, this may permit the establishment of some regularities in the impact of environmental factors.

The Comparability of Social Units

Having thus identified small communities as the locale on which such studies should most profitably concentrate, one might assume that the considerable number of community studies which have been conducted in this country and abroad could be regarded as a first step in research on community influences on mental health. But this, unfortunately, is not the case. The main difficulties confronting the use of available community studies for our purposes are that these studies are largely descriptive in sociological rather than in sociopsychological dimensions, and that even in the sociological dimensions *they are not comparable to one another*. From published material it is impossible to decide whether living in, say, *Middletown* (18) or living in *Black Metropolis* (4) affects people in any specific way for better or worse because the concepts and dimensions used in these and other community studies are not defined on a comparable basis. Even where the major spheres of human life are treated according to the *Middletown* model (getting a living, making a home, training the young, leisure, play, art, religion, community activities) in different studies, these broad categories do not help much in revealing psychologically meaningful differences or similarities in community influences on the individual.

The establishment of psychologically meaningful attributes of community life is in itself a major research task. Some beginning in this direction has been made in industrial psychology. This has been perhaps most impressively demonstrated in Elton Mayo's wartime studies of absenteeism in three different factories, where the pattern of relations between foremen and workers was regarded as a crucial sociological variable with psychological meaning (19). Other attempts in this direction undoubtedly exist, but much more will have to be done to establish comparable patterns of community life whose psychological relevance can be demonstrated.

There are, however, a set of conditions in community life whose damaging effects need not be demonstrated through research because there is already in our culture an almost unanimous acceptance of the fact that they are detrimental to the individual. The conditions referred to are: hunger, bad housing, lack of medical care, unemployment, low wages, and so forth. There is much evidence on the detrimental effect of these factors on the physical and mental well-being of people (2, 4, 8, 12, 23, 27, 30). While all available social energy is needed to eliminate these conditions, considerations of research strategy suggest that new inquiries should not go out to prove what is already known. On the other hand, however, no community study can neglect to take these basic conditions of human life into account as essential background information.

Some Propositions for Research

The following propositions are only loosely connected with each other, since (as stated earlier) there exists no comprehensive sociopsychological theory of mental health in terms of which they can be interrelated. The only unifying link was provided by the search for community attributes which could be expected to have some bearing on one or more of the tentatively established criteria for mental health, and which occurred in a variety of social units such as villages, factories, colleges, army camps, housing projects, and so forth.

L. S. Cottrell, Jr., has developed a set of propositions about age and sex roles which are of considerable interest in relation to our problem. By way of example, here are two of his propositions: "The degree of adjustment to roles which our society assigns to its age-sex categories varies directly with the clarity with which such roles are defined," and, "The degree of adjustment to a future role varies directly with the degree of clarity with which the future role is defined" (6).

It should be noted that clarity here refers not to a reasoning process in individuals but rather to the institutions and values in society. Some roles in our society are notoriously ill defined, as, for instance, the role of aged parents in the life of their adult children, the role of the unmarried adult, the role of the intellectually trained woman, and so forth. It would be feasible and of considerable importance to apply Cottrell's propositions to these ill defined roles in comparative community studies.

It will be noted that Cottrell does not distinguish in his propositions between passive acceptance and active adjustment. It would appear that either notion could form the basis for a plausible hypothesis, though they are markedly different from one another. In addition, these hypotheses are plausible only when roles are defined so as to be compatible with other roles. No degree of clarity in the definition of the role of a Negro, when this definition implies his inferiority to white citizens, will help him to adjust if he also aspires to the role of a citizen with equal rights.

If, with these qualifications, studies are undertaken which demonstrate the impact on mental health of the clarity with which roles are defined, the implementation of the result through preventive measures will by no means be easy. It will most likely involve a change in role definition, a process about which there is little experience.

Another set of propositions can be developed around the notion of socially recognized individual achievements. If an educational institution like a college, for instance, is organized in such a manner that only the brightest students or only the very good-looking students are rewarded by community recognition, all others will be compelled to strive for the impossible with inevitable frustration and restrictions on personality. If a single type of behavior and achievement is rewarded, the pressure for conformity, that is, passive acceptance, may be dangerously great. This proposition postulates a recognition of the multivalue and multipersonality-type structure of contemporary life. David Riesman, who is continuously concerned with the power of the individual to resist conformity pressures, says in his article, *A Philosophy for "Minority" Living:* "The 'nerve of failure' is the courage to face aloneness and the possibility of defeat in one's personal life or one's work without being morally destroyed. It is, in a larger sense, simply the nerve to be oneself when that self is not approved by the dominant ethics of a society" (25). This admirable ethical principle raises the question as to the factors which contribute to the development of such strength of personality. It may well be that prolonged exposure to a group which recognizes a variety of possible achievements is conducive to such development.

It appears that for Riesman the unity of personality is of much greater importance than active adjustment. While he does not say so explicitly, the resistance against pressures which he advocates presupposes, of course, correct perception of the self and its incompatibility with a given social environment.

The crucial test for the strength of mental health occurs as a person is transposed from one environment to the other when habitual patterns of behavior are challenged and interiorized values of the former environment are contradicted by the socially approved values in the new environment. The intellectual who is drafted into the army, the Sister Carrie who comes from the small isolated village into a metropolitan center, the immigrant from Europe, all are familiar with the strain inherent in such a change of environment. Actually, the experience of the British factory girls mentioned before was of the same nature, though in contrast to the other examples they did not expect to enter a new culture when they went from school to factory. This suggests another set of hypotheses: the correct perception of reality will increase through frequent changes of environment; this will at the same time, however, be conducive to passive acceptance unless the original "home" environment has enhanced the integration of the personality.

At the same time it suggests propositions about the original "home" environment (family, community, school, camp, college, place of work) which bear on the question as to when a protective environment becomes overprotective, that is, detrimental to mental health. The greater the chance to practice active adjustment and to reject passive acceptance at an early stage, the less is the likelihood that environmental changes will prove to be danger points. In the light of this hypothesis, the attempt to spare children and young people the experience and the perception of conflict and irreconcilable value differences is probably an obstacle to the development of mental health.

These arguments are related to another set of propositions concerned with membership in voluntary groups. If a community is organized so as to favor mutually exclusive voluntary group memberships, the dependency of the individual on the one group to which he belongs will be dangerously great. In our multirole society, people need the chance to compensate for frustration and dissatisfaction in one group by more positive experiences in others. One-group membership resembles, in some respects, the overprotective environment discussed above. Examples of the disastrous effect linked with membership in one exclusive all-embracing group are provided by those who, for one reason or another, attempt to leave such a group (Communist party, certain religious groups, juvenile gangs, and so forth). When an individual belongs to other groups which put a less exclusive claim on his loyalty so that his identity as a person will not be threatened when he leaves one group, membership will enhance mental health. Groups which are organized to achieve a specific goal or purpose provide an opportunity for active adjustment.

These are but a few examples of possible research in this area. The scope of study appears to be as great as the need for it. If the research implementation of these propositions appears difficult, their application on a widespread basis will be even more difficult. But there is no other way than to try.

BIBLIOGRAPHY

1. BENEDICT, RUTH. *Patterns of Culture*. Boston and New York: Houghton Mifflin Co. (1934).
2. BETTELHEIM, B. "Individual and Mass Behavior in Extreme Situations," *J. Abnormal and Social Psych.*, 38 (1943).
3. CANTRIL, H. (with the assistance of HAZEL GAUDET and HERTA HERZOG): *The Invasion from Mars*. Princeton: Princeton University Press (1940).
4. CAYTON, H. R., and ST. CLAIRE, DRAKE: *Black Metropolis*. New York: Harcourt Brace (1945).
5. COOK, Stuart W. "The Role of Social Values in Social-Psychological Research," paper presented at the fifty-seventh annual meeting of the American Psychological Association (September, 1949).
6. COTTRELL, JR., L. S.: "The Adjustment of the Individual to His Age and Sex Roles," *Readings in Social Psychology*. New York: Henry Holt and Co. (1947).
7. DEUTSCH, M., and M. COLLINS: *Interracial Housing: A Psychological Evaluaton of a Social Experiment*, University of Minnesota Press (in preparation).
8. FARIS, ROBERT E., and H. W. DUNHAM: *Mental Disorders in Urban Areas: An Ecological Study of Schizophrenia and Other Psychoses*. Chicago: University of Chicago Press (1939).
9. FROMM, E.: *Man for Himself*. New York: Rinehart (1947).
10. HARTMANN, H.: "On Rational and Irrational Action," *Psychoanalysis and the Social Sciences*, 1, (1947).
11. JAHODA, M.: "Some Socio-Psychological Problems of Factory Life," *Brit. J. Psychol.* (January, 1942).
12. JAHODA-LAZARSFELD, M., and H. ZEISL: *Die Arbeitslosen von Marienthal*. Hirzl: Leipzig (1932).
13. KARDINER, A.: *Psychological Frontiers of Society*. New York: Columbia University Press (1945). Preface by R. Linton.
14. KLINEBERG, OTTO: *Social Psychology*. New York: Henry Holt and Co. (1945).
15. KLUCKHOHN, C., and H. MURRAY, eds. *Personality in Nature, Culture and Society*. New York: A. A. Knopf

16. LEWIN, KURT: *The Principles of Topological Psychology*. New York and London: McGraw Hill (1936).

17. LEWIN, KURT: *Resolving Social Conflicts*. New York: Harper & Bros. (1948).

18. LYND, R., and H. LYND: *Middletown*. New York: Harcourt Brace & Co.

19. MAYO, ELTON: *Social Problems of an Industrial Civilization*. Boston: Division of Research, Graduate School of Business Administration, Harvard University (1945).

20. MERTON, ROBERT K.: "The Social Psychology of Housing," *Current Trends in Social Psychology*. Pittsburgh: University of Pittsburgh Press (1948).

21. MERTON, R. K., P. S. WEST, and M. JAHODA: *Explorations in the Social Psychology of Public Housing*. New York: Harper and Brothers (in preparation).

22. NEWCOMB, THEODORE: *Social Psychology*. New York: The Dryden Press (1950).

23. ORLANSKY, H.: "Infant Care and Personality," *Psychol. Bull.*, 46, 1 (January, 1949).

24. RESEARCH CENTER FOR HUMAN RELATIONS: *College Life: A Research Plan*, an unpublished memorandum.

25. RIESMAN, D.: "A Philosophy for 'Minority' Living, New York," *Commentary*, 6, 5 (November, 1948).

26. RIESMAN, D.: *The Lonely Crowd* (in preparation).

27. ROWNTREE, B. S.: *Poverty and Progress*. London: Longmans, Green & Co. (1941).

28. RUMNEY, J., and S. SHUMAN: *The Cost of Slums*. Newark: Housing Authority of the City of Newark (1946).

29. SPITZ, RENÉ: "Hospitalism: An Inquiry into the Genesis of Psychiatric Conditions in Early Childhood," *Study of the Child* (1945).

30. TITMUSS, R.: *Birth, Poverty and Wealth*. London: Hamish Hamilton (1944).

JULES GOLDEN, NATHAN MANDEL, BERNARD C. GLUECK, JR., AND ZETTA FEDER

A Summary Description of Fifty "Normal" White Males[*,1,2]

Personality research in general, and psychiatric research in particular, has been seriously handicapped by the lack of uniformly accepted standards of normality. Until quite recently, the only generally accepted tests were the intelligence tests, where a range of normal intelligence, and ranges of subnormal and supranormal have been established for some years. None of the projective tests, Rorschach, T.A.T., *etc.*, has clearly established and generally accepted normal values or response patterns. Clinical psychiatric description tends to stress the presence or absence of abnormal patterns of behavior, symptoms, and disturbance of normal functioning, without an adequate description or agreement upon what constitutes "normal." Most of the studies reported in the literature deal with segments of personality functioning, as measured by one or more tests, by relatively brief interview; or with a highly selected sample. All of these factors limit the general applicability of the results, especially when one is attempting to set "normal" values.

In the past 15 years several very comprehensive studies have been reported, coming mainly from the highly selected groups represented by college students. In 1945 Heath(7) gave one of the first reports on the Grant Study, describing the general plan of this study of Harvard College sophomores. He states that 60% of the men examined had well integrated basic personalities, while the remaining 40% showed various symptoms such as shyness, mood fluctuations, autonomic instability, asocial behavior, and incomplete integration of basic personality. It is interesting to note that only 6% of the group were felt to be motivated toward creative

* Reprinted by permission from *American Journal of Psychiatry*, Vol. 119, 1962, pp. 48–55.

1 Read at the 117th annual meeting of The American Psychiatric Association, Chicago, Ill., May 8–12, 1961.

2 This research was conducted in the Dept. of Psychiatry, University of Minnesota Medical School.

activity. Heath concludes that normal means a "perpendicular and balanced" personality.

In 1952 Earl Bond(2) reported on 64 of 66 student council members in 3 colleges in the Philadelphia area. In spite of the opinion of one of the college presidents, "It is as normal a group as you will get," only 39 of these students were judged to be well balanced, or to have such strong assets as to outweigh their liabilities. Sixteen of the group showed extraordinary ability and important neurotic traits, "success at the price of unhappiness." Nine of the group were described as gifted, but with serious personality problems: schizoid, depressive, *etc.* Bond concluded that 57% would benefit from psychiatric help, while 14% were in urgent need of help. In discussing the concept of normality Bond stresses a number of negatives, things that normal is not: *e.g.*, "Normal does not mean average — normal does not mean uninteresting — normal is not perfect — a normal person is not one who has no problems." He concludes with several positive statements about normality; it has a wide range and is in a state of flux; normal people are free to focus their energies on main purposes; and in their own culture normal people work and love with ease, happiness and efficiency, somewhat in proportion to their circumstances.

In a paper in 1956, reporting on projective test responses of the same group of students, Cox(3) defines normality as "the ability to maintain an harmonious and productive relationship with the environment and with the self." This is very close to the definition of normal inferred by Ackerman(1) as part of a discussion of goals in therapy. He sees the mentally healthy individual functioning harmoniously in 3 areas: in his internal economy of personality, in his interpersonal adaptation with his significant small group, usually the family, and in his relationships with larger social community.

Epstein(4), in describing some of the problems encountered in a family research study, discusses a number of concepts of normality or emotional health, including the one given by Ackerman, quoted above. On the basis of these various definitions Epstein and his colleagues divided their cases into 4 groups:

A. Absence of structured psychiatric symptoms, adequate social and occupational adaptation, no impairment of dynamic integration.

B. Absence of structured psychiatric symptoms, adequate social and occupational adaptation, mild impairment of dynamic integration with mild anxiety.

C. Absence of structured psychiatric symptoms, presence of social and/or occupational maladapta-

tion, moderate impairment of dynamic integration with moderate anxiety and psychopathology.

D. Structured psychiatric symptoms, social and occupational maladaptation, severe impairment of dynamic integration with severe anxiety and psychopathology.

Groups A and B were considered to be emotionally healthy, although perhaps not normal.

From all of the foregoing material it appears to be obvious that a specific statement of what the normal or emotionally healthy person is like is still in its infancy. The definitions given all imply a large element of subjective evaluation and judgment on the part of the investigator or observer, and suffer inevitably from the various defects inherent in such an appraisal. In an attempt to avoid some of these problems of distortion by the observer, we have utilized the Minnesota Multiphasic Personality Inventory, which is a self-description type of evaluation, as the basic instrument for determining the subjects to be included in this study.

The problem of selection of subjects is never more important than in a study of this type. In all of the groups described above, and in several other reports on "normal" groups, including one on "normal control" volunteers, by Pollin and Perlin(9) in 1958, and a recent report on drug study volunteers by Esecover, Malitz and Wilkens(6), a high incidence of psychopathology is reported. All of these considerations helped to determine the design of the current project, and the method of case selection.

This study of "normal" young males was undertaken primarily to provide a reference group for a study of 100 psychiatric patients, part of a project studying "The Skilled Clinician's Assessment of Personality." We were able to draw upon a large group of young adult males who had first been studied 12 years previously, as part of a project on delinquency being conducted by Monachesi and Hathaway of the University of Minnesota. They had obtained a self-descriptive evaluation, by means of the MMPI, of all ninth grade students in the Minneapolis public schools. These individuals have been followed periodically in the succeeding 12 years, so that those developing known mental illness or delinquency patterns have been identified, and were readily eliminated from our sample. We took as our basic group those individuals who, on self-description at approximately age 14, had indicated an absence of psychopathology in any of the areas measured by the MMPI. This is indicated on the MMPI results by a profile with no score above 55.

Of 1,953 male students tested, 73 gave no indication of significant pathology. Of these 73 potential subjects, 23 were excluded from the study for the following reasons: 13 had moved out of the state, 7 were not locatable, 1 was deceased, 1 could not leave his job in a distant part of the state to come in for interview, and 1 subject refused to cooperate. Of the 50 remaining subjects, all but 5 agreed quite readily to assist in the project. These 5 were primarily concerned about the economic loss occasioned by leaving their jobs, and were persuaded quite readily when they were told they would be recompensed for the time spent in the interviews.

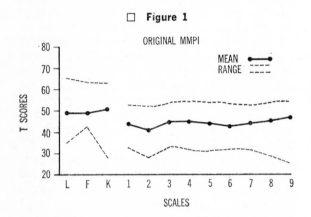

☐ **Figure 1**

Each subject was seen for evaluation at the University. The following procedures were carried out:

1. A 1½-hour unstructured psychiatric interview in which current adjustment, description of home of origin, personal history and aspirations, and mental status were appraised.

2. Examination on additional material to cover an extensive check list type of psychiatric history.

3. A structured mental status examination (check list).

4. A social adjustment rating (MSAS).

5. Psychometrics: (a) Repeat of the Minnesota Multiphasic Personality Inventory (MMPI); and (b) Projective drawings (House-Tree-Person) (HTP).

6. A home visit and unstructured interview with the wife, which included the wife's evaluation of her husband, and the interviewer's evaluation of the wife. (The MMPI, MSAS, and HTP were administered to the wife as well.) The wives of 38 of the 40 married men in the sample were interviewed.[3]

FINDINGS

Our first impression, and one that has continued through subsequent evaluation of the data obtained,

[3] The complete data from this study will be on file with The American Documentation Institute.

was of a remarkable consistency and uniformity in the sample of 50 men. On most of the items in the extensive psychiatric history these men were rated either identically, or within one step, on the variables involved. Some of the similarities were directly influenced by the choice of subjects; for example, 49 of the 50 subjects were born and raised in the Middle West, all were in the 25- to 26-year age range, 48 were currently living in a large metropolitan area.

Some diversity occurs when the current adaptational patterns are examined: 11 men were engaged in professional or semi-professional technical work, 2 were in executive positions, 12 were clerical, sales, or other white collar workers, 13 were craftsmen, skilled workers or foremen, and 12 were operatives and semi-skilled workers. None was in the unskilled, laboring, service, or domestic categories. A narrower spread is observed in their income levels. Only one man was in the $10,000 to $14,000 a year class, 14 were in the $6,000 to $10,000 category, 34 were in the $3,000 to $6,000, and only 1 was earning under $3,000 a year. All of the men had completed high school, 15 had some college education, while 7 had postgraduate education.

The spread becomes somewhat wider when the observers' evaluations of these individuals enter into the picture. On the mental status examination these men were rated as having a spread of from 6 to 40 positive items, with a mean of 22.3 items. This contrasted with a spread of from 1 to 5 negative items, with a mean of .52 negative items per subject.

▨ **TABLE 1 / Mental Status Examination Scores**

Number of Items	Frequency of Positive Items	Frequency of Negative Items
41–60	0	0
36–40	4	0
31–35	1	0
26–30	13	0
21–25	11	0
16–20	10	0
11–15	9	0
6–10	2	0
1–5	0	13
0	0	37
Mean/Subject	22.3	.52

The social adjustment of the subjects was assessed quantitatively by using the Mandel Social Adjustment Scale(8), which gives a quantitative measure of the extent to which an individual meets the overt societal norms of his society. A score of 5 on each of the subcategories of this scale would mean a perfect adjustment. These men had a mean score of 4.43 on the combined 7 scales, with a low of 3.84 on the scale measuring religious adjustment, and a high of 4.80 on the scale measuring health adjust-

ment. This compares favorably with the scores obtained on 3 other groups of subjects as indicated in Table 2.

■ TABLE 2 / Comparison of MSAS Mean Scores

Scale	Study Subjects	U of M Students[1]	R-E-S-T Patients[2]	Hospital Patients[3]
I. Occupational adjustment	4.79	4.40	3.84	3.53
II. Family life adjustment	4.39	4.39	3.62	3.52
III. Economic adjustment	4.36	4.41	3.45	3.06
IV. Health adjustment	4.80	4.53	3.42	2.41
V. Religious adjustment	3.84	3.98	3.81	3.46
VI. Residence adjustment	4.71	4.17	4.35	2.86
VII. Community and social adjustment	4.0	4.11	3.08	2.95
Total scale score	4.43	4.28	3.66	3.11
Total subjects	50	29	58	51

[1] University of Minnesota undergraduate students in Family Life course.
[2] Post-regressive electric shock treatment psychiatric patients from University of Minnesota Hospitals.
[3] University of Minnesota Hospital psychiatric inpatients.

The current MMPI profiles of the subjects were rated by a panel of 5 psychologists, again on a 5-point scale, with a rating of 5 indicating the most healthy end, and a rating of 1 as the most pathological end. Three subjects were rated 5, 23 between 4 and 5, 18 between 3 and 4, 5 between 2 and 3, and 1 between 1 and 2, with a group mean of 3.82.

An appraisal of the overall adjustment of the married subjects, based on the data obtained from the interview with their spouses, was made independently by 3 social workers. Identical ratings were given 19 of the subjects, another 18 subjects were rated identically by 2 of the 3 judges, and only one step off by the third, while in only one case was there lack of agreement between at least 2 of the 3 raters. Two of the men were not rated due to insufficient information, and none of the 10 unmarried subjects was evaluated. The mean rating obtained was 3.16 on a 5-point scale, with a rating of 5 being the ideal, again showing relatively good adjustment. The subjective impression of the 3 raters was that they were confronted with a particularly "normal group of people."

A global evaluation of the subjects based on all of the above information resulted in the distribution by diagnostic categories shown in Table 3.

DISCUSSION

Looking at the last table, showing the distribution of the men by diagnostic categories, one might question the validity of the selection process described above for choosing these men. We would like to raise the question, however, as to whether the "range of normal personality" should not include 47 of the

□ **Figure 2**

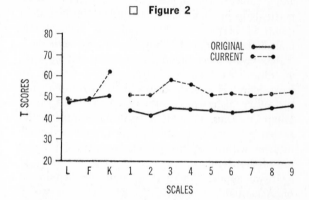

Comparison of original and current mean profiles, N = 50

■ TABLE 3 / Diagnostic Categories

No significant symptomatology	23
Psychoneurotic	9
Minimal (5)	
Mild (4)	
Neurotic character disorder	9
Minimal (5)	
Mild (4)	
Psychosomatic disorders	4
Minimal (3)	
Mild (1)	
Character disorders (acting out)	2
Minimal (1)	
Mild (1)	
Pseudoneurotic schizophrenia	2
Mild (1)	
Moderate (1)	
	49

One subject not included as he had Addison's disease, with psychological symptoms, 3 years before study.

50 men examined. If we evaluate these individuals on the basis of the various definitions of normality described earlier in this paper, we believe that all but 3 of the men would fall within the normal groupings given by the various authors. For example: if we attempted to place our subjects in Epstein's 4 categories we would find that in addition to the 23 men with no evidence whatsoever of symptomatology, 18% listed in the various diagnostic groupings with minimal disturbance would be consistent with category A, since none of these individuals showed structured psychiatric symptoms, disturbance of social or occupational adaptation, or disturbance of their dynamic integration. About 20% of the men would be placed in group B, because of mild impairment of their dynamic integrity with the appearance of some anxiety or its equivalent. One subject with a current history of peptic ulcer, and 2 subjects who showed some antisocial patterns, particularly in traffic violations, might be placed in group C because of the social and occupational maladaptation present. Only 2 men, one with moderately severe pseudoneurotic schizophrenia, one with an obsessive-compulsive pattern, could be said to have definitely structured psychiatric symptoms and the other disturbances of adaptation described in group D. Thus, 45 of the men in our sample would probably be considered by Epstein to be emotionally healthy, within the broad range encompassed by his use of that term.

If we appraise these men from the standpoint of Ackerman's criteria, 70% of the men would appear to have an essentially harmonious relationship in the 3 areas described; 30% showed varying degrees of difficulty, primarily within themselves, although in 2 instances the main disturbances were in the significant small group relationships, and in 3 others in the relationship with the larger social group.

If we assume that any symptomatology is evidence of a need for treatment, we would find that 54% of our sample would be in this category, as compared with 57% reported by Bond. However, we would see only one subject as requiring psychiatric help in order to continue some kind of successful adaptation.

It is also interesting to consider some generalizations about the characteristics of the group, not only as evidence of a current "normal" or "appropriate" adaptation, but also as a prediction for the future involving the impact of these men on their families. The major focus of interest of the subjects appears to be in the home. Those who were married expressed a high order of contentment with their wives and children. There were no separations or broken marriages; with one outstanding exception, the men tended to idealize their wives and the wives were, again with one exception, content with their husbands as stable, responsible, dependable, supportive individuals. If the findings of Epstein and Westley (5) that suggest that the emotional health of children is influenced primarily by the nature of the conjugal relationship are applied to our married men and women, we would predict that the children of the married subjects should develop in a healthy fashion, since the conjugal relationship seems to be so satisfactory in 39 of the 40 married couples.

The marked vocational and residential stability which is characteristic of this group, and the general lack of significant psychopathology, may perhaps be achieved at the price of a more creative, spontaneous type of personality organization. These men were found to have little imagination, and generally limited interests and social activities. They indicate limited educational and vocational aspirations for themselves, and also for their children. This was reflected in the ratings given on various subitems of the psychiatric interviews, with richness of personality and breadth of interests and pleasures being the 2 lowest ratings of the 15 descriptive categories.

■ TABLE 4 / Descriptive Categories

   I.   Contentment with vocational position: Satisfaction with job level and activities.
  II.   Enjoyment of occupation: Extent of pleasure derived from job and associated activities.
 III.   Vocational ambition: Vocational goals and aspirations (in relation to estimated abilities and opportunities).
  IV.   Parents' previous concern with subject's vocational development: Parent's role in influencing subject's vocational choice and progress.
   V.   Contentment with spouse: Satisfaction with choice and relationship with spouse.
  VI.   Compatibility with spouse: Comfort in relationship with spouse.
 VII.   Effectiveness as a husband: Assumption and performance of the role of head of the household.
VIII.   Effectiveness as a parent: Assumption and performance of parental role.
  IX.   Means of handling anger: Mode of expressing assertion and dissatisfaction.
   X.   Symptoms: Manifestations or organized psychopathology.
  XI.   Wishes for 10 years hence: "What would you wish in 10 years if you could write your own ticket?"
 XII.   Use of unlimited finances: "What would you do it you were given $5 million with no strings attached?"
XIII.   Breadth of interests and pleasures: Range of pleasure yielding activities.
 XIV.   Richness of personality: Subject's positive social stimulus value.
  XV.   Overall mental health: Degree of adaptational behavior, considering both personality assets and deficits.

■ TABLE 5 / Mean Ratings of Subjects on Descriptive Categories Derived from Psychiatric Interviews

Descriptive Categories	N	X̄	SD
I. Contentment with vocational position	47	3.53[1]	.66
II. Enjoyment of occupation	47	3.74	.49
III. Vocational ambition	47	3.79	.62
IV. Parents' previous concern with subjects' vocational development	47	2.92	.55
V. Contentment with spouse[2]	38	3.89	.61
VI. Compatibility with spouse[2]	38	3.82	.32
VII. Effectiveness as a husband[2]	38	3.43	.69
VIII. Effectiveness as a father[2]	38	3.48	.77
IX. Expression of anger	47	3.57	.65
X. Symptoms	47	3.77	.92
XI. Wishes (for 10 years hence)	47	3.0	.74
XII. Use of unlimited finances ($5 million)	47	3.39	.62
XIII. Breadth of interests and pleasures	47	2.40	.74
XIV. Richness of personality	47	2.30	.69
XV. Overall mental health	47	3.32	.66

[1] 5-point scale, with 5 indicating the healthiest or the ideal.
[2] Only married subjects rated, 2 subjects not rated as wives not seen.

Contentment with spouse and compatibility with spouse were the two highest ratings, with enjoyment of occupation, and contentment with vocational position also being very high on the list.

CONCLUSION

All of the above raises in our minds a question which has been stated in a number of different ways in the past concerning the balance between the needs and the wants of individuals on the one hand — in this group apparently very much in balance — and the various factors that have been considered to be part of the richer, more creative, spontaneous type of personality. Does "normality," as evidenced by lack of intrapsychic tension, adequate social, economic and familial adaptation, and harmonious integration with other individuals at all levels, necessarily imply a lack of creativity, imagination, and spontaneity? Our data are suggestive of this conclusion. Confirmation would be dependent upon a study of those individuals in the original sample of 1,953 male ninth-graders who have subsequently been more creative, although they showed evidence of some disturbance at that time as measured by their MMPI profiles; at the very least.

It is our opinion that the 23 subjects described in this study as being free of symptomatology and as having made a stable, successful adaptation, represent a very normal, healthy, socially acceptable and desirable group of individuals. We would feel that an additional 12 subjects represent the broader "range of normal," which allows for some degree of intrapsychic tension and some minimal adaptational difficulties, none serious enough to interfere with a basically adequate and successful social and economic adjustment. The remainder of the group, with 2 exceptions, while having somewhat greater difficulty in making an adaptation, are still quite successful in most areas and will probably continue to make a successful adaptation without psychiatric help, although perhaps at the cost of greater tension and psychic stress and strain than might otherwise be the case.

The authors believe that the characteristics of this group of subjects are consistent with a general conception of the well adjusted average American male. Further, that these multi-dimensional data provide a meaningful baseline of personal adaptation within contemporary American society to which other groups may be compared.

BIBLIOGRAPHY

1. ACKERMAN, N. W.: Am. J. Psychoanal., **16**: 9, 1956.

2. BOND, E. D.: Am. J. Psychiat., **109**: 11, 1952.

3. COX R. D.: J. Proj. Tech., **20**: 70, 1956.

4. EPSTEIN, N. B.: Behav. Sci., **3**: 335, 1958.

5. EPSTEIN, N. B., and WESTLEY, W. A.: Grandparents and Parents of Emotionally Healthy Adolescents. *In* Masserman (Ed.), Psychoanalysis and Human Values. New York: Grune & Stratton, 1960, p. 181.

6. ESECOVER, H., MALITZ, S., and WILKENS, B.: Am. J. Psychiat., **117**: 910, 1961.

7. HEATH, C. W.: What People Are, A Study of Normal Young Men. Cambridge: Harvard University Press, 1945.

8. MANDEL, N. G.: Mandel Social Adjustment Scale, University of Minnesota, Minneapolis, Minn., 1959.

9. POLLIN, W., and PERLIN, S.: Am. J. Psychiat., **115**: 129, 1958.

Precursors of Psychopathology / 2

The developing personality moves through a series of crises, each of which must be mastered to create the conditions for emotional health in adulthood. At each stage of this unfolding process, the complex interaction of constitutional and environmental factors determines the individual's reaction pattern and adjustment capacity.

The family represents the chief environmental factor in the socialization of the child and, through the process of family living, roles are learned, attitudes formed, and feelings nurtured. The newborn infant's innate capacities and defects begin immediately to interact with the family patterns of roles and behaviors; he reacts and is reacted to.

The psychogenic view of emotional and mental disorder is concerned with the pernicious effects the earliest home experiences of the child have on his psychological adjustment. The outcome of these basic encounters depends upon an amalgam of factors, discussed in depth in the following articles. These factors involve what the child brings to his postnatal environment in terms of sensory capacities, response readiness, autonomic patterning, and the like, and what sort of family situation he enters, its interpersonal relationships and learning contexts.

Anastasi's paper critically examines the ageless controversy about the relative effects of heredity and environment on behavior. Not content with the extreme and simplistic notions often put forth by the proponents of one or the other of these points of view, she suggests a reorientation of our concern away from questions such as "Which one?" and "How much?" to the more meaningful inquiry into the "How?" of this complex interrelationship. Her approach is interactional, focusing on the relationship between a "continuum of indirectness" of hereditary influences and the "breadth of effect" of environmental factors. Since this article appeared, the exciting discoveries made in the biological substrate of heredity — RNA and DNA — promise new, more sophisticated forms of investigation into the heredity-environment problem.

Thomas and his associates at New York University's College of Medicine have been engaged for a number of years in evaluating what they call the "primary reaction patterns" of children. These patterns — nine have been delineated — are considered "primary" because of their appearance very early in postnatal behavior, their apparent independence of particular environmental influences, and their persistence through at least the first two years of life. Although their study presents methodological problems,[1] they do provide data which is important to understanding early parent-child relationships. As what we have called a "precursor of psychopathology," imagine a mildly anxious but well-meaning mother, whose own personality stresses the importance of high activity, adaptability, and pleasant affect, who gives birth to an infant demonstrating a low activity level, nonadaptability, and a generally negative mood. The resulting interaction of mother and child might well involve expectations and disappointments which could contribute to stressful situations and developmental problems for the child.

Bergman and Escalona examine a specific area of early malfunctioning, that of lack of protection against sensory input. It has repeatedly been shown that severely disturbed children early manifest distinct disabilities in the area of sensory functioning. Sometimes the difficulty involves what appears to be a too-high threshold for sensation in one or another modality; in other cases, a too-low threshold is indicated. In the latter case, as the authors note, the child may develop precocious secondary defenses against stimulation, an ego structure too flimsy to

[1] See, e.g., Escalona, S. B. *Crusade against strawmen?* Contemp. Psychol., 1964, 9, 489–490.

withstand later traumata. A too-high threshold may bring in its wake early sensory deprivation, depriving the child of the cognitive input necessary for learning and emotional development.[2]

The specific problem of early sensory deprivation is taken up by Bruner who presents the view that such deprivation interferes with the organism's formation of cognitive models for coping with his environment. In Bergman and Escalona's children, too much stimulation led to precocious but faulty ego development, a form of self-imposed sensory deprivation situation. For those children who develop in an environment impoverished of stimulation, the result, as Bruner implies, is later disability in the areas of discrimination, coping, exploration, and flexible information-processing. However, this stimulus deficit is not confined to the sensory area, and, as has been amply documented (cf. Clarke and Clarke below), social deprivation is potentially an equally disruptive force.

Following the publication in 1951 of Bowlby's comprehensive summary of the adverse effects of maternal deprivation,[3] much attention was directed to the broad problem of deprivation. At first, the absence of a loving relationship with a mothering figure was emphasized as the key variable. As knowledge accumulated, the focus shifted to the various forms of deprivation, including institutionalization, cultural deprivation, noncontinuous or multiple mothering situations, and adverse family environments per se. Clarke and Clarke briefly review the literature on this problem and comment on some of the variables known to be involved in recovery from its effects. Clearly, the mere absence of a mothering-one is no longer considered a priori an indication of pathology, and such problems as the cognitive impairment resulting from institutionalization are being considered, and more emphasis given to the detailed understanding of the exact parameters of deprivation.

Robert White's contribution on "Motivation reconsidered: the concept of competence" adds an important dimension to the study of personality development and its vicissitudes. Adding to our concepts of motivation his notion of competence, he presents a view of the developmental sequence with many implications for our conceptualizations of psychopathology.[4] Bringing together a wealth of information from the fields of animal psychology, learning theory, and psychoanalysis, White suggests that the modalities of the child's learning to cope effectively with his environment cannot be adequately understood as mere manifestations of primary drives. The forms of behavior which interest White are such things as exploration of the environment, manipulation of objects, and the production of changes in the child's surroundings, all of which, he feels, have at their core a developing sense of competence. The importance of adequate parental models and encouragement at every stage of this process is implicit throughout the article.

Coming a step closer to the interpersonal family aspects of the precursors of psychopathology, Gagnon elaborates on the problems inherent in the child's sexual learning and the family context in which this is carried out. His thesis is that parental behaviors not intended as sexual stimuli do, indeed, "spill over into the sexual area," leading to the child's confusion about these phenomena and expectations concerning them. Since much sexual stimulation is presented unwittingly, and given the nature of the parents' own anxieties in this area, Gagnon questions the efficacy of planning in relation to sex education, and the attempts to titrate the child's learning about this key aspect of his behavior. His analysis of parental techniques of negative labeling, nonlabeling, and rigidity provide insight into family learning contexts.

Perhaps the most important requirement for the child's healthy development is a well-integrated, stable family environment. The maintenance of family equilibrium is a delicate task requiring constant readjustment of the roles, expectations, attitudes, and behavior of all family members. When a state of disequilibrium exists, the entire family suffers. Using aspects of role theory, Spiegel discusses the precipitation of role conflict, or the failure of complementarity in the family, and the methods used to restore a state of equilibrium and dissipate the anxiety and strain which accompanies conflict. How a child, caught in the midst of such parental conflict, can come to be singled out as a "scapegoat" for family troubles is later discussed by Vogel and Bell (see Section 8). ∎

[2] An interesting case in point is reported by Eisen: Eisen, N. H. Some effects of early sensory deprivation on later behavior: the quondam hard-of-hearing child. J. abn. soc. Psychol., 1962, 65, 338–342.

[3] Bowlby, J. Maternal care and mental health. WHO Monogr., 1951, No. 2.

[4] Recently, White has elaborated one aspect of his thinking — the concept of efficacy — in discussing the adaptational deficits involved in schizophrenia. See White, R. W. The experience of efficacy in schizophrenia. Psychiatry, 1965, 28, 199–211.

ANNE ANASTASI

Heredity, Environment, and
The Question "How?"*[1]

Two or three decades ago, the so-called heredity-environment question was the center of lively controversy. Today, on the other hand, many psychologists look upon it as a dead issue. It is now generally conceded that both hereditary and environmental factors enter into all behavior. The reacting organism is a product of its genes and its past environment, while present environment provides the immediate stimulus for current behavior. To be sure it can be argued that, although a given trait may result from the combined influence of hereditary and environmental factors, a specific difference in this trait between individuals or between groups may be traceable to either hereditary or environmental factors alone. The design of most traditional investigations undertaken to identify such factors, however, has been such as to yield inconclusive answers. The same set of data has frequently led to opposite conclusions in the hands of psychologists with different orientations.

Nor have efforts to determine the proportional contribution of hereditary and environmental factors to observed individual differences in given traits met with any greater success. Apart from difficulties in controlling conditions, such investigations have usually been based upon the implicit assumption that hereditary and environmental factors combine in an additive fashion. Both geneticists and psychologists have repeatedly demonstrated, however, that a more tenable hypothesis is that of interaction (15, 22, 28, 40). In other words, the nature and extent of the influence of each type of factor depend upon the contribution of the other. Thus the proportional contribution of heredity to the variance of a given trait, rather than being a constant, will vary under different environmental conditions. Similarly, under different hereditary conditions, the relative contribution of environment will differ. Studies designed to estimate the proportional contribution of heredity

and environment, however, have rarely included measures of such interaction. The only possible conclusion from such research would thus seem to be that both heredity and environment contribute to all behavior traits and that the extent of their respective contributions cannot be specified for any trait. Small wonder that some psychologists regard the heredity-environment question as unworthy of further consideration!

But is this really all we can find out about the operation of heredity and environment in the etiology of behavior? Perhaps we have simply been asking the wrong questions. The traditional questions about heredity and environment may be intrinsically unanswerable. Psychologists began by asking *which* type of factor, hereditary or environmental, is responsible for individual differences in a given trait. Later, they tried to discover *how much* of the variance was attributable to heredity and how much to environment. It is the primary contention of this paper that a more fruitful approach is to be found in the question *"How?"* There is still much to be learned about the specific *modus operandi* of hereditary and environmental factors in the development of behavioral differences. And there are several current lines of research which offer promising techniques for answering the question "How?"

VARIETY OF INTERACTION MECHANISMS
Hereditary Factors

If we examine some of the specific ways in which hereditary factors may influence behavior, we cannot fail but be impressed by their wide diversity. At one extreme, we find such conditions as phenylpyruvic amentia and amaurotic idiocy. In these cases, certain essential physical prerequisites for normal intellectual development are lacking as a result of hereditary metabolic disorders. The individual will be mentally defective, regardless of the type of environmental conditions under which he is reared.

A somewhat different situation is illustrated by

* Reprinted by permission from *Psychological Bulletin*, Vol. 65, 1958, pp. 197–208. Copyright 1958 by the American Psychological Association.
[1] Address of the President, Division of General Psychology, American Psychological Association, September 4, 1957.

hereditary deafness, which may lead to intellectual retardation through interference with normal social interaction, language development, and schooling. In such a case, however, the hereditary handicap can be offset by appropriate adaptations of training procedures. It has been said, in fact, that the degree of intellectual backwardness of the deaf is an index of the state of development of special instructional facilities. As the latter improve, the intellectual retardation associated with deafness is correspondingly reduced.

A third example is provided by inherited susceptibility to certain physical diseases, with consequent protracted ill health. If environmental conditions are such that illness does in fact develop, a number of different behavioral effects may follow. Intellectually, the individual may be handicapped by his inability to attend school regularly. On the other hand, depending upon age of onset, home conditions, parental status, and similar factors, poor health may have the effect of concentrating the individual's energies upon intellectual pursuits. The curtailment of participation in athletics and social functions may serve to strengthen interest in reading and other sedentary activities. Concomitant circumstances would also determine the influence of such illness upon personality development. And it is well known that the latter effects could run the gamut from a deepening of human sympathy to psychiatric breakdown.

Finally, heredity may influence behavior through the mechanism of social stereotypes. A wide variety of inherited physical characteristics have served as the visible cues for identifying such stereotypes. These cues thus lead to behavioral restrictions or opportunities and — at a more subtle level — to social attitudes and expectancies. The individual's own self concept tends gradually to reflect such expectancies. All of these influences eventually leave their mark upon his abilities and inabilities, his emotional reactions, goals, ambitions, and outlook on life.

The geneticist Dobzhansky illustrates this type of mechanism by means of a dramatic hypothetical situation. He points out that, if there were a culture in which the carriers of blood group AB were considered aristocrats and those of blood group O laborers, then the blood-group genes would become important hereditary determiners of behavior (12, p. 147). Obviously the association between blood group and behavior would be specific to that culture. But such specificity is an essential property of the causal mechanism under consideration.

More realistic examples are not hard to find. The most familiar instances occur in connection with constitutional types, sex, and race. Sex and skin pigmentation obviously depend upon heredity. General body build is strongly influenced by hereditary components, although also susceptible to environmental modification. That all these physical characteristics may exert a pronounced effect upon behavior within a given culture is well known. It is equally apparent, of course, that in different cultures the behavioral correlates of such hereditary physical traits may be quite unlike. A specific physical cue may be completely unrelated to individual differences in psychological traits in one culture, while closely correlated with them in another. Or it may be associated with totally dissimilar behavior characteristics in two different cultures.

It might be objected that some of the illustrations which have been cited do not properly exemplify the operation of hereditary mechanisms in behavior development, since hereditary factors enter only indirectly into the behavior in question. Closer examination, however, shows this distinction to be untenable. First it may be noted that the influence of heredity upon behavior is always indirect. No psychological trait is ever inherited as such. All we can ever say directly from behavioral observations is that a given trait shows evidence of being influenced by certain "inheritable unknowns." This merely defines a problem for genetic research; it does not provide a causal explanation. Unlike the blood groups, which are close to the level of primary gene products, psychological traits are related to genes by highly indirect and devious routes. Even the mental deficiency associated with phenylketonuria is several steps removed from the chemically defective genes that represent its hereditary basis. Moreover, hereditary influences cannot be dichotomized into the more direct and the less direct. Rather do they represent a whole "continuum of indirectness," along which are found all degrees of remoteness of causal links. The examples already cited illustrate a few of the points on this continuum.

It should be noted that as we proceed along the continuum of indirectness, the range of variation of possible outcomes of hereditary factors expands rapidly. At each step in the causal chain, there is fresh opportunity for interaction with other hereditary factors as well as with environmental factors. And since each interaction in turn determines the direction of subsequent interactions, there is an ever-widening network of possible outcomes. If we visualize a simple sequential grid with only two alternatives at each point, it is obvious that there are two possible outcomes in the one-stage situation, four outcomes at the second stage, eight at the third, and so on in geometric progression. The actual situation is undoubtedly much more complex, since there will usually be more than two alternatives at any one point.

In the case of the blood groups, the relation to specific genes is so close that no other concomitant hereditary or environmental conditions can alter the outcome. If the organism survives at all, it will have the blood group determined by its genes. Among psychological traits, on the other hand, some variation in outcome is always possible as a result of concurrent circumstances. Even in cases of phenylketonuria, intellectual development will exhibit some relationship with the type of care and training available to the individual. That behavioral outcomes show progressive diversification as we proceed along the continuum of indirectness is brought out by the other examples which were cited. Chronic illness *can* lead to scholarly renown or to intellectual immaturity; a mesomorphic physique *can* be a contributing factor in juvenile delinquency or in the attainment of a college presidency! Published data on Sheldon somatotypes provide some support for both of the latter outcomes.

Parenthetically, it may be noted that geneticists have sometimes used the term "norm of reaction" to designate the range of variation of possible outcomes of gene properties (cf. 13, p. 161). Thus heredity sets the "norm" or limits within which environmental differences determine the eventual outcome. In the case of some traits, such as blood groups or eye color, this norm is much narrower than in the case of other traits. Owing to the rather different psychological connotations of both the words "norm" and "reaction," however, it seems less confusing to speak of the "range of variation" in this context.

A large portion of the continuum of hereditary influences which we have described coincides with the domain of somatopsychological relations, as defined by Barker et al. (6). Under this heading, Barker includes "variations in physiques that affect the psychological situation of a person by influencing the effectiveness of his body as a tool for actions or by serving as a stimulus to himself or others" (6, p. 1). Relatively direct neurological influences on behavior, which have been the traditional concern of physiological psychology, are excluded from this definition, Barker being primarily concerned with what he calls the "social psychology of physique." Of the examples cited in the present paper, deafness, severe illness, and physical characteristics associated with social stereotypes would meet the specifications of somatopsychological factors.

The somatic factors to which Barker refers, however, are not limited to those of hereditary origin. Bodily conditions attributable to environmental causes operate in the same sorts of somatopsychological relations as those traceable to heredity. In fact, heredity-environment distinctions play a minor part in Barker's approach.

Environmental Factors: Organic

Turning now to an analysis of the role of environmental factors in behavior, we find the same etiological mechanisms which were observed in the case of hereditary factors. First, however, we must differentiate between two classes of environmental influences: (*a*) those producing organic effects which may in turn influence behavior and (*b*) those serving as direct stimuli for psychological reactions. The former may be illustrated by food intake or by exposure to bacterial infection; the latter, by tribal initiation ceremonies or by a course in algebra. There are no completely satisfactory names by which to designate these two classes of influences. In an earlier paper by Anastasi and Foley (4), the terms "structural" and "functional" were employed. However, "organic" and "behavioral" have the advantage of greater familiarity in this context and may be less open to misinterpretation. Accordingly, these terms will be used in the present paper.

Like hereditary factors, environmental influences of an organic nature can also be ordered along a continuum of indirectness with regard to their relation to behavior. This continuum closely parallels that of hereditary factors. One end is typified by such conditions as mental deficiency resulting from cerebral birth injury or from prenatal nutritional inadequacies. A more indirect etiological mechanism is illustrated by severe motor disorder — as in certain cases of cerebral palsy — *without* accompanying injury to higher neurological centers. In such instances, intellectual retardation may occur as an indirect result of the motor handicap, through the curtailment of educational and social activities. Obviously this causal mechanism corresponds closely to that of hereditary deafness cited earlier in the paper.

Finally, we may consider an environmental parallel to the previously discussed social stereotypes which were mediated by hereditary physical cues. Let us suppose that a young woman with mousy brown hair becomes transformed into a dazzling golden blonde through environmental techniques currently available in our culture. It is highly probably that this metamorphosis will alter, not only the reactions of her associates toward her, but also her own self concept and subsequent behavior. The effects could range all the way from a rise in social poise to a drop in clerical accuracy!

Among the examples of environmentally determined organic influences which have been described, all but the first two fit Barker's definition of somatopsychological factors. With the exception of birth injuries and nutritional deficiencies, all fall within the social psychology of physique. Nevertheless, the individual factors exhibit wide diversity in their specific *modus operandi* — a diversity which has important practical as well as theoretical implications.

Environmental Factors: Behavioral

The second major class of environmental factors — the behavioral as contrasted to the organic — are by definition direct influences. The immediate effect of such environmental factors is always a behavioral change. To be sure, some of the initial behavioral effects may themselves indirectly affect the individual's later behavior. But this relationship can perhaps be best conceptualized in terms of breadth and permanence of effects. Thus it could be said that we are now dealing, not with a continuum of indirectness, as in the case of hereditary and organic-environmental factors, but rather with a continuum of breadth.

Social class membership may serve as an illustration of a relatively broad, pervasive, and enduring environmental factor. Its influence upon behavior development may operate through many channels. Thus social level may determine the range and nature of intellectual stimulation provided by home and community through books, music, art, play activities, and the like. Even more far-reaching may be the effects upon interests and motivation, as illustrated by the desire to perform abstract intellectual tasks, to surpass others in competitive situations, to succeed in school, or to gain social approval. Emotional and social traits may likewise be influenced by the nature of interpersonal relations characterizing homes at different socio-economic levels. Somewhat more restricted in scope than social class, although still exerting a relatively broad influence, is amount of formal schooling which the individual is able to obtain.

A factor which may be wide or narrow in its effects, depending upon concomitant circumstances, is language handicap. Thus the bilingualism of an adult who moves to a foreign country with inadequate mastery of the new language represents a relatively limited handicap which can be readily overcome in most cases. At most, the difficulty is one of communication. On the other hand, some kinds of bilingualism in childhood may exert a retarding influence upon intellectual development and may under certain conditions affect personality development adversely (2, 5, 10). A common pattern in the homes of immigrants is that the child speaks one language at home and another in school, so that his knowledge of each language is limited to certain types of situations. Inadequate facility with the language of the school interferes with the acquisition of basic concepts, intellectual skills, and information. The frustration engendered by scholastic difficulties may in turn lead to discouragement and general dislike of school. Such reactions can be found, for example, among a number of Puerto Rican children in New York City schools (3). In the case of certain groups, moreover, the child's foreign language background may be perceived by himself and his associates as a symbol of miniority group status and may thereby augment any emotional maladjustment arising from such status (34).

A highly restricted environmental influence is to be found in the opportunity to acquire specific items of information occurring in a particular intelligence test. The fact that such opportunities may vary with culture, social class, or individual experiential background is at the basis of the test user's concern with the problem of coaching and with "culture-free" or "culture-fair" tests (cf. 1, 2). If the advantage or disadvantage which such experiential differences confer upon certain individuals is strictly confined to performance on the given test, it will obviously reduce the validity of the test and should be eliminated.

In this connection, however, it is essential to know the breadth of the environmental influence in question. A fallacy inherent in many attempts to develop culture-fair tests is that the breadth of cultural differentials is not taken into account. Failure to consider breadth of effect likewise characterizes certain discussions of coaching. If, in coaching a student for a college admission test, we can improve his knowledge of verbal concepts and his reading comprehension, he will be better equipped to succeed in college courses. His performance level will thus be raised, not only on the test, but also on the criterion which the test is intended to predict. To try to devise a test which is not susceptible to such coaching would merely reduce the effectiveness of the test. Similarly, efforts to rule out cultural differentials from test items so as to make them equally "fair" to subjects in different social classes or in different cultures may merely limit the usefulness of the test, since the same cultural differentials may operate within the broader area of behavior which the test is designed to sample.

METHODOLOGICAL APPROACHES

The example considered so far should suffice to highlight the wide variety of ways in which hereditary and environmental factors may interact in the course of behavior development. There is clearly a need for identifying explicitly the etiological mechanism whereby any given hereditary or environmental condition ultimately leads to a behavioral characteristic — in other words, the "how" of heredity and environment. Accordingly, we may now take a quick look at some promising methodological approaches to the question "how."

Within the past decade, an increasing number of studies have been designed to trace the connection between specific factors in the hereditary backgrounds or in the reactional biographies of individuals and their observed behavioral characteristics. There has been a definite shift away from the predominantly descriptive and correlational approach of the earlier decades toward more deliberate attempts to verify explanatory hypotheses. Similarly, the cataloguing of group differences in psychological traits has been giving way gradually to research on *changes* in group characteristics following altered conditions.

Among recent methodological developments, we have chosen seven as being particularly relevant to the analysis of etiological mechanisms. The first represents an extension of selective breeding investigations to permit the identification of specific hereditary conditions underlying the observed behavioral differences. When early selective breeding investigations such as those of Tryon (36) on rats indicated that "maze learning ability" was inherited, we were still a long way from knowing what was actually being transmitted by the genes. It was obviously not "maze learning ability" as such. Twenty — or even ten — years ago, some psychologists would have suggested that it was probably general intelligence. And a few might even have drawn a parallel with the inheritance of human intelligence.

But today investigators have been asking: Just what makes one group of rats learn mazes more quickly than the other? Is it differences in motivation, emotionality, speed of running, general activity level? If so, are these behavioral characteristics in turn dependent upon group differences in glandular development, body weight, brain size, bio-chemical factors, or some other organic conditions? A number of recent and ongoing investigations indicate that attempts are being made to trace, at least part of the way, the steps whereby certain chemical properties of the genes may ultimately lead to specific behavioral characteristics.

An example of such a study is provided by Searle's (31) follow-up of Tryon's research. Working with the strains of maze-bright and maze-dull rats developed by Tryon, Searle demonstrated that the two strains differed in a number of emotional and motivational factors, rather than in ability. Thus the strain differences were traced one step further, although many links still remain to be found between maze learning and genes. A promising methodological development within the same general area is to be found in the recent research of Hirsch and Tryon (18). Utilizing a specially devised technique for measuring individual differences in behavior among lower organisms, these investigators launched a series of studies on selective breeding for behavioral characteristics in the fruit fly, *Drosophila*. Such research can capitalize on the mass of available genetic knowledge regarding the morphology of *Drosophila*, as well as on other advantages of using such an organism in genetic studies.

Further evidence of current interest in the specific hereditary factors which influence behavior is to be found in an extensive research program in progress at the Jackson Memorial Laboratory, under the direction of Scott and Fuller (30). In general, the project is concerned with the behavioral characteristics of various breeds and cross-breeds of dogs. Analyses of some of the data gathered to date again suggest that "differences in performance are produced by differences in emotional, motivational, and peripheral processes, and that genetically caused differences in central processes may be either slight or non-existent" (29, p. 225). In other parts of the same project, breed differences in physiological characteristics, which may in turn be related to behavioral differences, have been established.

A second line of attack is the exploration of possible relationship between behavioral characteristics and physiological variables which may in turn be traceable to hereditary factors. Research on EEG, autonomic balance, metabolic processes, and biochemical factors illustrates this approach. A lucid demonstration of the process of tracing a psychological condition to genetic factors is provided by the identification and subsequent investigation of phenylpyruvic amentia. In this case, the causal chain from defective gene, through metabolic disorder and consequent cerebral malfunctioning, to feeblemindedness and other overt symptoms can be described step by step (cf. 32; 33, pp. 389–391). Also relevant are the recent researches on neurological and biochemical correlates of schizophrenia (9). Owing to inadequate methodological controls, however, most of the findings of the latter studies must be regarded as tentative (19).

Prenatal environmental factors provide a third avenue of fruitful investigation. Especially noteworthy is the recent work of Pasamanick and his associates (27), which demonstrated a tie-up between socioeconomic level, complications of pregnancy and parturition, and psychological disorders of the offspring. In a series of studies on large samples of whites and Negroes in Baltimore, these investigators showed that various prenatal and paranatal disorders are significantly related to the occurrence of mental defect and psychiatric disorders in the child. An important source of such irregularities in the process of childbearing and birth is to be found in deficiencies of maternal diet and in other conditions associated with low socioeconomic status. An analysis of the data did in fact reveal a much higher frequency of all such medical complications in lower than in higher socioeconomic levels, and a higher frequency among Negroes than among whites.

Direct evidence of the influence of prenatal nutritional factors upon subsequent intellectual development is to be found in a recent, well controlled experiment by Harrell et al. (16). The subjects were pregnant women in low income groups, whose normal diets were generally quite deficient. A dietary supplement was administered to some of these women during pregnancy and lactation, while an equated control group received placebos. When tested at the ages of three and four years, the offspring of the experimental group obtained a significantly higher mean IQ than did the offspring of the controls.

Mention should also be made of animal experiments on the effects of such factors as prenatal radiation and neonatal asphyxia upon cerebral anomalies as well as upon subsequent behavior development. These experimental studies merge imperceptibly into the fourth approach to be considered, namely, the investigation of the influence of early experience upon the eventual behavioral characteristics of animals. Research in this area has been accumulating at a rapid rate. In 1954, Beach and Jaynes (8) surveyed this literature for the *Psychological Bulletin*, listing over 130 references. Several new studies have appeared since that date (e.g., 14, 21, 24, 25, 35). The variety of factors covered ranges from the type and quantity of available food to the extent of contact with human culture. A large number of experiments have been concerned with various forms of sensory deprivation and with diminished opportunities for motor exercise. Effects have been observed in many kinds of animals and in almost all aspects of behavior, including perceptual responses, motor activity, learning, emotionality, and social reactions.

In their review, Beach and Jaynes pointed out that research in this area has been stimulated by at least four distinct theoretical interests. Some studies were motivated by the traditional concern with the relative contribution of maturation and learning to behavior development. Others were designed in an effort to test certain psychoanalytic theories regarding infantile experiences, as illustrated by studies which limited the feeding responses of young animals. A third relevant influence is to be found in the work of the European biologist Lorenz (23) on early social stimulation of birds, and in particular on the special type of learning for which the term "imprinting" has been coined. A relatively large number of recent studies have centered around Hebb's (17) theory regarding the importance of early perceptual experiences upon subsequent performance in learning situations. All this research represents a rapidly growing and promising attack on the *modus operandi* of specific environmental factors.

The human counterpart of these animal studies may be found in the comparative investigation of child-rearing practices in different cultures and subcultures. This represents the fifth approach in our list. An outsanding example of such a study is that by Whiting and Child (38), published in 1953. Utilizing data on 75 primitive societies from the Cross-Cultural Files of the Yale Institute of Human Relations, these investigators set out to test a number of hypotheses regarding the relationship between child-rearing practices and personality development. This analysis was followed up by field observations in five cultures, the results of which have not yet been reported (cf. 37).

Within our own culture, similar surveys have been concerned with the diverse psychological environments provided by different social classes (11). Of particular interest are the study by Williams and Scott (39) on the association between socioeconomic level, permissiveness, and motor development among Negro children, and the exploratory research by Milner (26) on the relationship between reading readiness in first-grade children and patterns of parent-child interaction. Milner found that upon school entrance the lower-class child seems to lack chiefly two advantages enjoyed by the middle-class child. The first is described as "a warm positive family atmosphere or adult-relationship pattern which is more and more being recognized as a motivational prerequisite of any kind of adult-controlled learning." The lower-class children in Milner's study perceived adults as predominantly hostile. The second advantage is an extensive opportunity to interact verbally with adults in the family. The latter point is illustrated by parental attitudes toward mealtime conversation, lower-class parents tending to inhibit and discourage such conversation, while middle-class parents encourage it.

Most traditional studies on child-rearing practices have been designed in terms of a psychoanalytic orientation. There is need for more data pertaining to other types of hypotheses. Findings such as those of Milner on opportunities for verbalization and the resulting effects upon reading readiness represent a step in this direction. Another possible source of future data is the application of the intensive observational techniques of psychological ecology developed by Barker and Wright (7) to widely diverse socioeconomic groups.

A sixth major approach involves research on the previously cited somatopsychological relationships (6). To date, little direct information is available on the precise operation of this class of factors in psychological development. The multiplicity of ways in which physical traits — whether hereditary or environmental in origin — may influence behavior thus offers a relatively unexplored field for future study.

The seventh and final approach to be considered represents an adaptation of traditional twin studies. From the standpoint of the question "How?" there is need for closer coordination between the usual data on twin resemblance and observations of the family interactions of twins. Available data already suggest, for example, that closeness of contact and extent of environmental similarity are greater in the case of monozygotic than in the case of dizygotic twins (cf. 2). Information on the social reactions of twins toward each other and the specialization of roles is likewise of interest (2). Especially useful would be longitudinal studies of twins, beginning in early infancy and following the subjects through school age. The operation of differential environmental pressures, the development of specialized roles, and other environmental influences could thus be more clearly identified and correlated with in-tellectual and personality changes in the growing twins.

Parenthetically, I should like to add a remark about the traditional applications of the twin method, in which persons in different degrees of hereditary and environmental relationships to each other are simply compared for behavioral similarity. In these studies, attention has been focused principally upon the amount of resemblance of monozygotic as contrasted to dizygotic twins. Yet such a comparison is particularly difficult to interpret because of the many subtle differences in the environmental situations of the two types of twins. A more fruitful comparison would seem to be that between dizygotic twins and siblings, for whom the hereditary similarity is known to be the same. In Kallmann's monumental research on psychiatric disorders among twins (20), for example, one of the most convincing bits of evidence for the operation of hereditary factors in schizophrenia is the fact that the degrees of concordance for dizygotic twins and for siblings were practically identical. In contrast, it will be recalled that in intelligence test scores dizygotic twins resemble each other much more closely than do siblings — a finding which reveals the influence of environmental factors in intellectual development.

SUMMARY

The heredity-environment problem is still very much alive. Its viability is assured by the gradual replacement of the questions, "Which one?" and "How much?" by the more basic and appropriate question, "How?" Hereditary influences — as well as environmental factors of an organic nature — vary along a "continuum of indirectness." The more indirect their connection with behavior, the wider will be the range of variation of possible outcomes. One extreme of the continuum of indirectness may be illustrated by brain damage leading to mental deficiency; the other extreme, by physical characteristics associated with social stereotypes. Examples of factors falling at intermediate points include deafness, physical diseases, and motor disorders. Those environmental factors which act directly upon behavior can be ordered along a continuum of breadth or permanence of effect, as exemplified by social class membership, amount of formal schooling, language handicap, and familiarity with specific test items.

Several current lines of research offer promising techniques for exploring the *modus operandi* of hereditary and environmental factors. Outstanding among them are investigations of: (*a*) hereditary conditions which underlie behavioral differences between selectively bred groups of animals; (*b*) relations between physiological variables and individual differences in behavior, especially in the case of pathological deviations; (*c*) role of prenatal physiological factors in behavior development; (*d*) influence of early experience upon eventual behavioral characteristics; (*e*) cultural differences in child-rearing practices in relation to intellectual and emotional development; (*f*) mechanisms of somatopsychological relationships; and (*g*) psychological development of twins from infancy to maturity, together with observations of their social environment. Such approaches are extremely varied with regard to subjects employed, nature of psychological functions studied, and specific experimental procedures followed. But it is just such heterogeneity of methodology that is demanded by the wide diversity of ways in which hereditary and environmental factors interact in behavior development.

REFERENCES

1. ANASTASI, ANNE. *Psychological testing.* New York: Macmillan, 1954.
2. ANASTASI, ANNE. *Differential psychology.* (3rd ed.) New York: Macmillan, 1958.
3. ANASTASI, ANNE, & CORDOVA, F. A. Some effects of bilingualism upon the intelligence test performance of Puerto Rican children in New York City. *J. educ. Psychol.,* 1953, 44, 1–19.
4. ANASTASI, ANNE, & FOLEY, J. P., JR. A proposed reorientation in the heredity-environment controversy. *Psychol. Rev.,* 1948, 55, 239–249.
5. ARSENIAN, S. Bilingualism in the postwar world. *Psychol. Bull.,* 1945, 42, 65–86.
6. BARKER, R. G., WRIGHT, BEATRICE A., MYERSON, L., & GONICK, MOLLIE R. Adjustment to physical handicap and illness: A survey of the social psychology of physique and disability. *Soc. Sci. Res. Coun. Bull.,* 1953, No. 55 (Rev.).
7. BARKER, R. G., & WRIGHT, H. F. *Midwest and its children: The psychological ecology of an American town.* Evanston, Ill.: Row, Peterson, 1955.
8. BEACH, F. A., & JAYNES, J. Effects of early experience upon the behavior of animals. *Psychol. Bull.,* 1954, 51, 239–263.
9. BRACKBILL, G. A. Studies of brain dysfunction in schizophrenia. *Psychol. Bull.,* 1956, 53, 210–226.
10. DARCY, NATALIE T. A review of the literature on the effects of bilingualism upon the measurement of intelligence. *J. genet. Psychol.,* 1953, 82, 21–57.
11. DAVIS, A., & HAVIGHURST, R. J. Social class and color differences in child rearing. *Amer. sociol. Rev.,* 1946, 11, 698–710.
12. DOBZHANSKY, T. The genetic nature of differences among men. In S. Persons (Ed.), *Evolutionary thought in America.* New Haven: Yale Univer. Press, 1950. Pp. 86–155.
13. DOBZHANSKY, T. Heredity, environment, and evolution. *Science,* 1950, 111, 161–166.
14. FORGUS, R. H. The effect of early perceptual learning on the behavioral organization of adult rats. *J. comp. physiol. Psychol.,* 1954, 47, 331–336.
15. HALDANE, J. B. S. *Heredity and politics.* New York: Norton, 1938.
16. HARRELL, RUTH F., WOODYARD, ELLA, & GATES, A. I. *The effect of mothers' diets on the intelligence of the offspring.* New York: Bur. Publ., Teach. Coll., Columbia Univer., 1955.
17. HEBB, D. O. *The organization of behavior.* New York: Wiley, 1949.
18. HIRSCH, J., & TRYON, R. C. Mass screening and reliable individual measurement in the experimental behavior genetics of lower organisms. *Psychol. Bull.,* 1956, 53, 402–410.
19. HORWITT, M. K. Fact and artifact in the biology of schizophrenia. *Science,* 1956, 124, 429–430.
20. KALLMANN, F. J. *Heredity in health and mental disorder; Principles of psychiatric genetics in the light of comparative twin studies.* New York; Norton, 1953.
21. KING, J. A., & GURNEY, NANCY L. Effect of early social experience on adult aggressive behavior in C57-BL10 mice. *J. comp. physiol. Psychol.,* 1954, 47, 326–330.
22. LOEVINGER, JANE. On the proportional contributions of differences in nature and in nurture to differences in intelligence. *Psychol. Bull.,* 1943, 40, 725–756.
23. LORENZ, K. Der Kumpan in der Umwelt des Vogels. Der Artgenosse als auslösendes Moment sozialer Verhaltungsweisen. *J. Orn., Lpz.,* 1935, 83, 137–213; 289–413.
24. LUCHINS, A. S., & FORGUS, R. H. The effect of differential postweaning environment on the rigidity of an animal's behavior. *J. genet. Psychol.,* 1955, 86, 51–58.
25. MELZACK, R. The genesis of emotional behavior: An experimental study of the dog. *J. comp. physiol. Psychol.,* 1954, 47, 166–168.
26. MILNER, ESTHER A. A study of the relationships between reading readiness in grade one school children and patterns of parent-child interaction. *Child Develpm.,* 1951, 22, 95–112.
27. PASAMANICK, B., KNOBLOCH, HILDA, & LILIENFELD, A. M. Socioeconomic status and some precursors of neuropsychiatric disorder. *Amer. J. Orthopsychiat.,* 1956, 26, 594–601.
28. SCHWESINGER, GLADYS C. *Heredity and environment.* New York: Macmillan, 1933.
29. SCOTT, J. P., & CHARLES, MARGARET S. Some problems of heredity and social behavior. *J. gen. Psychol.,* 1953, 48, 209–230.

30. Scott, J. P., & Fuller, J. L. Research on genetics and social behavior at the Roscoe B. Jackson Memorial Laboratory, 1946–1951 — A progress report. *J. Hered.*, 1951, 42, 191–197.

31. Searle, L. V. The organization of hereditary maze-brightness and maze-dullness. *Genet. Psychol. Monogr.*, 1949, 39, 279–325.

32. Snyder, L. H. The genetic approach to human individuality. *Sci. Mon., N. Y.*, 1949, 68, 165–171.

33. Snyder, L. H., & David, P. R. *The principles of heredity.* (5th ed.) Boston: Heath, 1957.

34. Spoerl, Dorothy T. Bilinguality and emotional adjustment. *J. abnorm. soc. Psychol.*, 1943, 38, 37–57.

35. Thompson, W. R., & Melzack, R. Early environment. *Sci. Amer.*, 1956, 194, (1), 38–42.

36. Tryon, R. C. Genetic differences in maze-learning ability in rats. *Yearb. nat. Soc. Stud. Educ.*, 1940, 39, Part I, 111–119.

37. Whiting, J. W. M., et al. *Field guide for a study of Socialization in five societies.* Cambridge, Mass.: Harvard Univer., 1954 (mimeo.).

38. Whiting, J. W. M., & Child, I. L. *Child training and personality: A cross-cultural study.* New Haven: Yale Univer. Press, 1953.

39. Williams, Judith R., & Scott, R. B. Growth and development of Negro infants: IV. Motor development and its relationship to child rearing practices in two groups of Negro infants. *Child Develpm.*, 1953, 24, 103–121.

40. Woodworth, R. S. Heredity and environment: A critical survey of recently published material on twins and foster children. *Soc. Sci. Res. Coun. Bull.*, 1941, No. 47.

ALEXANDER THOMAS, STELLA CHESS, HERBERT BIRCH, AND MARGARET E. HERTZIG

A Longitudinal Study of Primary Reaction Patterns in Children[*][1]

Growing scientific attention is being accorded to the often expressed view of parents, pediatricians and baby-nurses that even in the neonatal period and in infancy children are behaviorally distinguishable from one another.(2, 7, 13, 19, 21, 26) Implicit in the recent interest is the recognition that careful behavioral study of young children will contribute significantly to our understanding of individual differences in primary reactivity, a basic unresolved problem in child development. Although it has been suggested and presumed that early characteristics of individuality are significant determiners of both normal and pathologic psychological development, (2, 7, 13, 19, 21, 25) a paucity of detailed developmental information makes it difficult to evaluate

the precise relation of initial individuality to psychological growth.(7, 21)

The existence of such primary and possibly constitutional behavioral characteristics is also suggested by the accumulated data which do not support the hypothesis of a one-to-one relationship of parental attitudes and practices and other environmental features to the course of the child's psychological development.(5, 14, 20, 23) While it is clear that these experiential forces profoundly influence the child's functioning, a substantial degree of variance suggests that other factors exert significant influence. Among these factors the organismic characteristics of the infant may very well have an important influence on determining psychological development.

A number of studies have reported observations on individual differences in the infant and young child in specific, discrete areas such as motility,(9) perceptual responses,(3) sleeping and feeding patterns,(8) drive endowment,(1) quality and intensity of emotional tone,(17) social responsiveness,(11)

[*] Reprinted by permission from *Comprehensive Psychiatry*, Vol. I, 1960, pp. 103–112.

[1] Present at New York Divisional Meeting of American Psychiatric Association, November 29, 1959. This study was aided in part by grants from The National Institute of Mental Health (M2805) and the Gralnick Foundation.

autonomic response patterns,(4, 12, 22) biochemical individuality,(18, 28) and electroencephalographic patterns.(27) These various reports emphasized that individual differences appear to be present at birth and are not determined by postnatal experience. Although these studies have provided valuable data and leads for further investigation, there remains the need for a systematic and comprehensive approach to the question of behavioral individuality in childhood. This is neither due to a dearth of behavioral studies, nor to a lack of concern with the development of effective methods for the collection and analysis of developmental data through longitudinal study. However, the general result, as described by a recent exhaustive survey of the literature, has been the accumulation of "incredible amounts of data which defy any degree of organized analysis and have no relation to a specific, experimentally posed hypothesis. Much of this research, therefore, never reaches the manuscript stage, and if it does, it is formulated as impression of the author or as case histories."(24) The problems of such longitudinal studies are seen as small samples, poor testing, and the inability to convert theoretic hypotheses into experimental or operational terms which will identify significant variables.

The present paper reports a longitudinal study of individual behavioral characteristics in children, started in 1956 and comprising a series of 105 children. The paper will report on the existence of primary initial patterns of reactivity in infancy and on the stability of these characteristics through the first two years of life.

METHOD

The difficulties in longitudinal studies of behavioral development have stemmed from three sources: (1) the contamination of the basic data by a confusion of observation with interpretation; (2) the absence of an economical procedure which would permit the gathering of detailed and pertinent behavioral data from a sufficiently large sample; (3) the failure in the analysis of behavioral data to distinguish between the specific content of the behavior observed, which necessarily changes in growth, from the underlying structure or pattern which may be constant.

We have considered elsewhere in some detail the problems which derive from the contamination of first order data by *a priori* interpretation.(25) Most frequently, this error is evidenced by the equivalent treatment of behavioral fact and psychodynamic interpretation, *vide*.(19)

To obtain detailed longitudinal data on a sufficiently large sample of children for the specification of a variety of initial individual patterns of reactivity, it is necessary to define a readily available and investigatively economical source of data. The direct longitudinal observation of the child would require a ratio of one investigator to each child. Consequently, serial cross-sectional study has been substituted in many instances for longitudinal inquiry.(17) It has appeared to us that the parent represents a most valuable source of continual direct observation, and that parental experience, if adequately assessed, constitutes a basic and economical source of longitudinal information. The following problems arise in the use of the parent as a source of data: (1) can the parent supply sufficient explicit behavioral information for analysis? (2) is this information adequate for studying the problem at issue? (3) are the observations valid reflections of the child's actual functioning? If these questions can be answered in the affirmative, then information on a large sample of children can be obtained which could otherwise only be gathered by a large core of investigators who live in the homes of the subjects. To answer these questions, a structured interview of the parents has been utilized. The validity of these data has been checked by comparison with direct observations of the child's behavior.

The distinction between the content and the formal characteristics of behavior is crucial in the longitudinal study of behavioral stability. It is a truism that content is by definition continuously changing and therefore necessarily unstable as an index of the persistence of individual attributes of function. By contrast, formal characteristics of behavior may be constant within a framework of changing content. Thus, distractibility as a formal characteristic may be expressed in terms of the ease with which bottle feeding is interfered with by external stimulation at age six months, and in the ready disturbance of ongoing academic work by extraneous noise in the school years. In each case the formal aspects are the same, though the content of behavior is markedly different. In the present study, attention is directed to the formal and not the content aspect of behavior.

The Interview

The first history is taken when the child is 2 to 3 months old. This is repeated every 3 months for a year, and thereafter at 6 month intervals. Interview data at five points were obtained over the first two years of life. The interviews at each period were scored in accordance with the procedure to be described. The interview has been supplemented by various types of direct observation of the child: in the home, in free play in a standard play room, during the administration of a standard psychological test, and in nursery school.

In gathering longitudinal behavioral data to test the hypothesis of continuity in reaction type, certain principles were strictly observed, to permit objective analysis and independent replication.

1. Behavior is described in objective terms. Strict avoidance of interpretations of behavior by parents, interviewer or observer is maintained throughout. Thus, a statement "the baby hated his cereal" or "he loved his bath" is considered as unsatisfactory for primary data. Instead, the question is always asked "what did he do that made you think he loved or hated it" and a detailed description of the child's actual behavior is recorded. In this way the contamination of the raw data by interpretations based on preconceptions, evident in a number of studies, is avoided. Since interpretations of a specific item of a child's behavior by several simultaneous observers may vary greatly, it is difficult if not impossible to obtain accurate and reduplicable data on an interpretative basis.

2. The basic data are obtained from the details of the child's behavior in the natural daily activities of his life. These include, among others, sleeping, feeding, dressing, bathing, nail-cutting and hair-brushing in the young infant. As the child grows older, other activities such as involvement with individual people, play, toileting, vaccinations, discipline, etc. are added. Detailed information on the child's behavior in his daily life insures that the data will reflect the child's characteristic modes of functioning. This procedure is in contrast to those methods which by relying primarily on observations made in unfamiliar testing situations, raise questions of atypical and unrepresentative behavior in such artificial settings.

3. In comparing the characteristics of responses among infants, obtained differences may be due to two factors. On the one hand the stimulus may vary in intensity or in quality. On the other hand, the stimulus may be constant but differences derive from individual differences in reactivity. This latter factor is the principal focus of interest in this study. However any attempt to define the variations in the individual response of different infants by presenting them with the same constant stimulus would be limited and even undesirable. Such constancy involves artificial test situations, which introduce such new and uncontrolled variables, as strange environment, special manipulations, and testing devices.

Furthermore, a controlled, delineated set of stimuli may elicit responses which represent only a narrow segment of the child's pattern of reactivity.

The present study, therefore, starts with the assumption that no special advantage derives from constancy of stimuli. By acquiring information on the infant's behavioral responses in as many types of situations as possible the data sample becomes representative of the child's functioning. This range of information has been obtained by determining the specific responses which a baby makes to the variegated features of day-by-day living, such as the bath, the taste of different food, periods of food deprivation, loud noises, the crib, bright lights, and so on. The data thus comprise a record of the responses to different stimuli of varying intensity and quality.

In contrast with the artificiality of the limited experiment, this method bases itself on the classic approach used in biological field studies of function in living organisms, namely, the delineation of behavior within the environmental context in which it occurs. The major goal is to obtain detailed and accurate data with regard to a *consistent type of reaction pattern in the individual infant*, whether responding to a hunger stimulus, the taste of new food, the temperature of the bath water, or an attitude of the mother.

4. In data collection special emphasis is placed on the recording of the details of the child's first response to a new stimulus and his subsequent reactions on exposure to the same stimulus until a consistent, long-term response has been established. Such stimuli may be simple, as the first bath, or the introduction of a new food; they may be complex, as the move to a new home or the introduction of a new person into the household. In either case the sequence of responses to new stimuli can give very valuable information as to the individual pattern of reactivity of the child.

Method for Analysis of Behavior Protocols

In order to make interperiod comparisons of behavioral reactivity, nine categories for scoring responses were established by an inductive content analysis of the interview protocols of the first 22 children studied. This procedure avoided the imposition of aprioristic categories derived *a priori* from theoretical schemes. From the inductive content analysis the following nine categories were found to be present and scorable in the interview protocols from early infancy through the second year of life:

1. *Activity Level:* the motor component present in a given child's functioning and the diurnal propor-

tion of active and inactive periods. Protocol data on motility during bathing, eating, playing, dressing and handling, as well as information concerning the sleep-wake cycle, reaching, crawling and walking are used in scoring this category.

2. *Rhythmicity*: the predictability and/or the unpredictability in time of any function. It can be analyzed in relation to the sleep-wake cycle, hunger, feeding pattern and elimination schedule.

3. *Approach or Withdrawal*: the nature of the response to a new stimulus, be it a new food, new toy or new person.

4. *Adaptability*: responses to new or altered situations. One is not concerned with the nature of the initial responses, but with the ease with which they are modified in desired directions.

5. *Intensity of Reaction*: the energy level of response, irrespective of its quality or direction.

6. *Threshold or Responsiveness*: the intensity level of stimulation that is necessary to evoke a discernible response, irrespective of the specific form that the response may take, or the sensory modality affected. The behaviors utilized are those concerning reactions to sensory stimuli, environmental objects, and social contacts.

7. *Quality of Mood*: the amount of pleasant, joyful and friendly behavior, as contrasted with unpleasant, crying and unfriendly behavior.

8. *Distractibility*: the effectiveness of extraneous environmental stimuli in interfering with or in altering the direction of the ongoing behavior.

9. *Attention Span and Persistence*: two categories which are related. Attention span concerns the length of time a particular activity is pursued by the child. Persistence refers to the continuation of an activity in the face of obstacles to the maintenance of the activity direction.

Each category was scored on a three point scale, in terms of two polar extremes, high and low, and one intermediate level. Therefore, every behavioral record was scored for each of the nine categories on a three point scale and resulted in a specific item sum for each category of reactivity.

Each protocol is analyzed for each category independently. No successive interviews of a given child are scored contiguously. This segmented scoring is done to avoid contamination by "halo" effects, whereby the scorer's judgment on one category or interview might be influenced by a judgment already made on another.[2]

[2] A study of the degree to which whole protocol scoring was influenced by content was done by the method of snipanalysis. Individual behavior descriptions of nine (9) protocols were snipped, coded, mounted on cards and scram-

In the gathering of data, as well as in its scoring, use is made of objective, descriptive items, and interpretation is avoided. For example, a statement "he cried because he was hungry" is scored only with regard to the fact of crying. The child may or may not have been hungry, but there is no doubt that he did cry. In training scorers it was found that disagreements derived from attempts to score behavioral descriptions that were not explicit. In such instances the scorer had recorded his interpretation of what the statement meant, since it was impossible to determine the exact meaning because of the ambiguity of the statement. This difficulty was eliminated by strict adherence to the rule that any item where the description was ambiguous or vague was not to be scored.

A few typical behavior items and their scoring will now be given to illustrate the general approach. The item "he lies quietly in the bath and doesn't kick" is scored as low activity level. "He ate cereal well the first time I gave it to him" is scored as an approach response. "At first he spit out his egg but after the third time he took it" is scored as high adaptability. "If he has a bowel movement he is cranky and fusses until I change him" is scored as low threshold of responsiveness. Single behavioral items are frequently scorable in two or more categories. For example, the statement "he kicks wildly, gurgles happily and laughs loudly in his bath and has done so from the very first time" can be scored as (1) high activity level, (2) initial approach, (3) positive mood and (4) intense response. The item "he kicks and whimpers when he has his nails cut, but if we talk to him or show him a toy he is quiet" is scored as (1) high activity level, (2) negative mood, (3) mild intensity and (4) distractibility.

As would be expected, the various parents have shown great variation in the quality of their spontaneous descriptions of their children's behavior. Some are factual and objective, others are subjective and interpretative or concerned with value judgments, some are concise and others ramble. There is also great variation in the wealth of detail given regarding various items of behavior. However, our interview technique which insists on answers in terms of specific factual details of behavior can elicit a great deal of such objective data even from mothers who are subjective, interpretative, preoccupied with

bled. These isolated bits were then scored to criteria. Upon the completion of scoring items were reassembled and the composite scores were compared with the scores made on the continuous whole protocols. No significant differences in scoring were obtained between whole and snipped analysis of the data by 3 independent data analysts.

value judgments, ramble or otherwise tend spontaneously to report insufficient descriptive items. The factual data from any one interview can be broken down into an average of 60 to 70 scorable items of behavior in each.

The reliability of the scoring technic was tested by comparing the results obtained by two independent judges in the scoring of a series of 22 consecutively obtained cases. Ninety per cent agreement was obtained. This high level of interscorer reliability was confirmed by comparing the results obtained by two additional scorers who have been trained recently in this work. Close agreement with the original score was also found in the blind scoring of the same record by the same scorer after an interval of several months.

A final point of method concerns the validity of the parental interviews, namely the degree to which these reports give an accurate description of the essential characteristics of the child's behavior. This was tested by obtaining two to three hour periods of direct observation of the child in the home by two independent observers on separate occasions in 18 unselected cases, and by one observer in five other cases. The protocols of these direct observations were compared with the data reported in the parent interview. It was found that the direct observation agreed with the data reported at the interview closest in time to the observation with a confidence level between 0.05 and 0.01. This quantitative determination of the validity of the parental reports is further sustained by the many observations of the children made by examiners as they interviewed the parents in the home.

SUBJECTS

Thus far 105 children have been followed by the procedures outlined. At present data on 74 of these children are completely gathered through the second year of life, and fully analyzed for consideration in this report.

The families studied represent a fairly homogeneous middle and upper middle-class group. A few of the mothers work full-time, some work part-time, but all accept on a conscious level their major responsibility of having to care for the baby. Child-care practices are highly similar within the group. The parents are permissive, with an emphasis on satisfying the needs of the child. Many of the fathers participate actively in the care of the child.

A fairly homogeneous group of this kind has advantages in an investigation into the occurrence of individual differences in the reactivity of children.

If differences are conspicuous in the young infants of such a group they are unlikely to be due to variations in either general social or cultural factors, or in the general child-care practices of the parents, and therefore more likely to represent differences in the intraorganismic characteristics of the children studied.

RESULTS

When scored for the nine categories it was found that the consistency in interperiod agreement was of such a magnitude that the probability of such agreement occurring by chance sampling factors alone is less than 1 in 100. When each category is analyzed separately the same high level of agreement is sustained. These data leave little doubt that initially determined patterns of reactivity are persistent features of individuality in functioning during the first 24 months of life.

Since each reaction category was scored on a three position scale, lack of predictive relations would be expressed as a random movement from one scale position to another in any category from one age period to another. Such a statement of the problem permits one to determine the degree of confidence with which the hypothesis of no predictive relation can be rejected. Chi-Square analysis permitted the rejection of the null hypothesis at greater than the .01 level of confidence in each of the 74 children for whom data have been analyzed through the first two years of life.

On a qualitative basis, the individual categories may be grouped into clusters. As a consequence, it may be possible to organize the data into a finite number of identifiable types of individuality. At present five cluster types have been identified: (1) Regularity, adaptability, mild intensity, approach, and positive mood; (2) Irregularity, nonadaptability, high intensity, withdrawal, negative mood, and high activity level; (3) Moderate adaptability, mild intensity, withdrawal, negative mood and low or moderate activity level; (4) Low threshold of response, distractibility, short attention span and low persistence; (5) High threshold of response, and nondistractibility. Various other clusters suggest themselves on qualitative inspection of the data, but a detailed quantitative analysis is now being projected and will be required for their precise delineation.

Qualitative examination of the data also permits the delineation of another characteristic of individuality which is of special psychiatric interest. This concerns the character of the child's reactions to a new situation, whether it be the bath or the introduction of solid food in early infancy, vaccinations or the first awareness of strangers, the attempt to enforce the prohibition of dangerous activities or the initiation of toilet training at two years, or the first contact with nursery school at three years. In each instance, there is striking consistency in the pattern of the individual child's reaction to the new situation. This pattern is actually compounded from elements involving certain of the nine categories defined in the quantitative analysis, namely activity level, approach or withdrawal, intensity, mood, adaptability, attention span and persistence. Some children respond quietly and placidly to a new situation, approach it at once and adapt quickly and smoothly. At the other extreme are those children who withdraw sharply and violently from a new situation, persist tenaciously in their old behavior, and adapt irregularly and slowly. Other children show different types of admixture of these two extremes, such as an initial withdrawal reaction of mild intensity, followed by a quick adaptation. Data for the type of reaction to new situations do not appear continuously in the longitudinal study. At some age periods the infant in the usual middle-class family is exposed to a number of new situations, while at other age periods to few or none. We are at present engaged in a special study of this delineation, because of our belief that it may have special functional importance. The character of the initial response to new situations may very well play an important role in the process of mastery and the development of ego functions in general. The initial reaction to social situations may affect the responses of other people involved and influence the whole character of interpersonal interaction.

Other individual characteristics of reactivity can be delineated from the protocols. These include (1) quick conditionability and easy development of anticipatory responses, if, for example the hunger cry of the infant is stopped when the bib is put on preparatory to feeding; (2) variation in the intensity of reaction to different stimuli, manifested in the extreme by the child who has the same all-or-none intense response to all situations, versus the child who has graded, differentiated reactions to different stimuli; (3) very low threshold of responsiveness to one sensory modality, such as auditory or tactile; (4) unusually energetic sucking activity. These characteristics have each been evident in only a few of the children and have not appeared continuously in the longitudinal protocols. Further study is necessary to determine the nature and persistency of these characteristics as independent patterns or derivatives of one or more of the nine general categories. It is also necessary to determine whether they are transient or persist in a stable, consistent form into later childhood.

DISCUSSION

The appearance of definable individual patterns in the first few months of life, before the infant is capable of ideation and conceptualization, strongly suggest their biological rather than psychodynamic basis. We have labeled and defined features of individuality as primary because they are evident early in extra-uterine life without appearing to be the consequence of any other identifiable factor. We have called them reaction patterns, and not behavioral patterns, because the individuality of each child is expressed in a specific consistent type of reactivity to stimuli, and not in any fixed content of behavior. The behavior content changes as the child develops, but the formal pattern of reactivity remains constant.

Our data thus far do not permit a definite answer to the question whether these primary reaction patterns are of an inborn character, formed under the influence of environmental factors in the first few months of life, or the result of the interaction of both. We plan to compare the types of patterns in 6 pairs of twins and 25 other pairs of siblings in our series; and we also intend to determine what correlations, if any, exist between the child's pattern and the parental attitudes and practices.

IMPLICATIONS

Our findings have a number of important implications for the fields of child development and psychiatry.

In the field of child-care practices, it is our strong impression from numerous observations that the effectiveness of the individual parent's approach in caring for the child in feeding, sleeping, discipline and toilet training is very much influenced by the child's primary reaction pattern. What is most effective in one child may be ineffective and even harmful in another. We have recently discussed this question in greater detail elsewhere.(6)

As indicated at the beginning of this paper, various studies have shown the lack of a reciprocal relationship between environmental factors and the healthy or disturbed psychological development of the child. Levy has suggested that the specific direction of psychopathology taken by children subjected to maternal overprotection may be determined by intraorganismic characteristics.(15) In our own material we have already observed differences in the responses of individual children to similar environmental stresses, differences which appear to be related to the character of the primary reaction pattern. We do not desire to minimize the importance of parental attitudes and practice or other environmental factors, as may have been the case in some studies of constitutional typologies in the past. It is our thesis that psychological development is the result of the constant, intimate interplay of environmental and intraorganismic forces. Children with similar primary reaction patterns may emerge with different personality structures and psychologic contents, depending on the environmental forces to which they have been subjected. On the other hand, children with similar environments may also show differing courses of psychological development, if they start with different primary patterns of reactivity.

SUMMARY AND CONCLUSIONS

The present study reports the results of the quantitative and qualitative analysis of behavioral data on 105 children who were studied for two years as part of an ongoing longitudinal study of primary individual characteristics of reactivity during infancy and childhood. The data were obtained by conducting detailed structured parental interviews supplemented and validated by direct observations. The interviews and observational protocols were then subjected to content analysis, and quantitatively scored for 9 defined categories of reactivity. The results of the quantitative analysis of protocols at five periods of development during the first two years of life were analyzed to determine the degree to which individual characteristics of reactivity already identifiable in early infancy persisted or changed during the course of development.

The results obtained provided the following findings:

1. Nine characteristics of reactivity can be identified in early infancy and during the first two years of life: (1) Activity Level, (2) Rhythmicity of Functioning, (3) Adaptability, (4) Approach or Withdrawal, (5) Intensity of Reaction, (6) Threshold or Responsiveness, (7) Quality of Mood, (8) Distractibility, (9) Attention Span and Persistence.

2. The primary reaction characteristics found in the child during the first months of life are persistent and continue to be characteristic of the individual during the first two years with a reliability significant at the 0.01 level of confidence.

3. Clusters of these primary reaction characteristics have been defined by qualitative inspection and yield several patterns of reactivity resulting in a limited number of individual types which appear to have prognostic value for the development of ego functions.

The results are discussed in terms of their implications for the importance of non-psychodynamic factors in the evolution of personality, and in connection with the methodological aspects of longitudinal investigation of psychological development in children.

We can conclude from the evidence presented that our parental interview technique and content analysis procedure has permitted the gathering of meaningful, objective behavioral data in a valid, reduplicable and economical way. It is our belief that these methods can be applied to the study of the longitudinal development of large numbers of children with mental retardation, brain damage and psychopathology.

REFERENCES

1. ALPERT, A., NEUBAUER, P. W., and WEIL, A. P.: Unusual variation in drive endowment. Psychoanalyt. Study of Child 11:125, 1956.
2. AUSUBEL, D. B. Theory and Problems of Child Development. New York, Grune & Stratton, 1957 (pp. 111–113).
3. BERGMAN, P., and ESCALONA, S.: Unusual sensitivities in very young children. Psychoanalyt. Study of Child 3–4:333, 1949.
4. BRIDGER, W. H., and REISER, M. F.: Psychophysiologic studies of the neonate. Psychosomat. Med. 21: 265, 1959.
5. BRUCH, H.: Parent education or the illusion of omnipotence. Am. J. Orthopsychiat. 24:723, 1954.
6. CHESS, S., THOMAS, A., and BIRCH, H.: Characteristics of the individual child's behavioral responses to the environment. Amer. Jour. Orthopsychiat. 29:791–802, 1959.
7. ESCALONA, S., LEITCH, M., et al.: Early phases of personality development. Monograph Soc. Res. Child Develop. 17: No. 1, 1952.
8. —: Emotional development in the first year of life. In: Problems of Infancy and Childhood. New York, Josiah Macy, Jr. Foundation, 1953 (p. 11).
9. FRIES, M., and WOOLF, P.: Some hypotheses on the role of the congenital activity type in personality development. Psychoanalyt. Study of Child 8:48, 1953.
10. FROSCH, J., and WORTIS, S. B.: A contribution to the nosology of the impulsive disorders. Am. J. Psychiat. 111:132, 1954.
11. GESELL, A., and AMES, L. B.: Early evidences of individuality in the human infant. J. Genet. Psychol. 47:339, 1937.

12. GROSSMAN, H. J., and GREENBERG, N. H.: Psychosomatic differentiation in infancy. Psychosomat. Med. 19:293, 1957.

13. JACKSON, E.: Child development patterns in the United States. In: Mental Health and Infant Development, Vol. I, edited by K. Soddy. New York, Basic Books, 1956 (p. 87).

14. KLATSKIN, E. H., JACKSON, E. B., and Wilkin, L. C.: The influence of degree of flexibility in maternal child care practices on early child behavior. Am. J. Orthopsychiat. 26:79, 1956.

15. LEVY, D. Maternal Overprotection. New York, Columbia University Press, 1943.

16. MAHLER, M.: On child psychosis and schizophrenia. Psychoanalyt. Study of Child 7:286, 1952.

17. MEILI, R.: A longitudinal study of personality development. In: Dynamic Psychopathology in Childhood, edited by L. Jessner and E. Pavenstedt. New York, Grune & Stratton, 1959 (pp. 106–123, a summary of a monographic report," Anfänge der Charakterentwicklung," Bern, Hans Huber, 1957).

18. MIRSKY, I. A.: Psychoanalysis and the biological sciences. In: Twenty Years of Psychoanalysis, edited by Alexander and Ross. New York, W. W. Norton, 1953 (pp. 155–176).

19. MURPHY, L. B.: Psychoanalysis and child behavior. Bull. Menninger Clin. 21:177, 1957.

20. ORLANSKY, H.: Infant care and personality. Psychol. Bull. 46:1, 1949.

21. Personality in the Making — Fact-Finding Report of Mid-Century White House Conference on Children and Youth, edited by H. L. Witmer and R. Kotinsky. New York, Harper & Bros., 1952 (pp. 35–36).

22. RICHMOND, J. B., and LUSTMAN, S. L.: Autonomic function in the neonate. Psychosomat. Med. 17:269, 1955.

23. STEVENSON, I.: Is the human personality more plastic in infancy and childhood? Am. J. Psychiat. 114:152, 1957.

24. STONE, A. A., and ONQUE, G. C.: Longitudinal Studies of Child Personality. Cambridge, Harvard University Press, 1959 (p. xiii).

25. THOMAS, A., and CHESS, S.: An approach to the study of sources of individual differences in child behavior. J. Clin. & Exper. Psychopathol. 18:347, 1957.

26. TYLER, L.: Psychology of Human Differences, 2nd ed. New York, Appleton-Century-Crofts, 1956 (pp. 17–18).

27. WALTER, G.: Electroencephalographic development of children. In: Discussion on Child Development, Vol. I, edited by J. M. Tanner and B. Inhelder. New York, International University Press, 1953 (pp. 132–160).

28. WILLIAMS, R. V.: Biochemical Individuality. New York, John Wiley & Sons, 1956.

PAUL BERGMAN AND SIBYLLE K. ESCALONA

Unusual Sensitivities in Very Young Children*

I. INTRODUCTION

It was several years ago that the authors were first struck by the observations to be reported here. Some very young children possessed unusual sensitivities manifesting themselves in several, if not in all, sensory modalities (visual, auditory, tactile, etc.). Colors, bright lights, noises, unusual sounds, qualities of material, experiences of equilibrium, of taste, of smell, of temperature, seemed to have an extraordinarily intensive impact upon these children at a very early age. They were "sensitive" in both meanings

of the word: easily hurt, and easily stimulated to enjoyment. Variations in sensory impression that made no difference to the average child made a great deal of difference to these children. They were also characterized by a certain precocity, though this was very unevenly distributed among the diverse functions of their personality. The first impression which some of their reactions and abilities gave was that of unusual giftedness such as might be observed in the budding of a genius. Further observation, however, suggested comparison with individuals suffering from a traumatic neurosis, or a psychosis, and even with feebleminded children. Closer study and follow-up then made it appear that childhood psychosis was the fate of these children, though we are

* Reprinted by permission from *The Psychoanalytic Study of the Child*, 1949, 3/4, 333–353.

not sure yet that all children of the type to be described eventually develop a clear psychotic picture. The present paper is a report of five cases, followed by a discussion of a way in which the relationship between unusual early sensitivities and psychosis might possibly be conceptualized.

As far as we know, cases of this type have not been described in the literature. Closest to them come the cases of "early infantile autism" described by Kanner (6). These "autistic" children are unable to enter meaningful relationships with other human beings, adults or children. They live emotionally in a solipsistic world, except for their queer interests in some specific intellectual or sensory field. They use language, but not primarily for the purpose of social communication. They may never address themselves to the people with whom they live, while at the same time they may perform amazing feats of memory, e.g., recite by heart scores of poems, or the names of all the presidents. They may show unending fascination with objects and with visual or acoustic stimuli. Only 1 of the more than 30 such children observed by Kanner did not show deep interest in music.[1]

In his paper Kanner does not touch upon the question of general or special sensitivities in the children he describes. The present authors, on the other hand, have been most impressed with the unusual sensitivities in the children under their observation. It is these aspects that will be dealt with in the present discussion. In addition we shall tentatively offer some ideas with the purpose of placing the particular observations into a larger framework of reference. We are not sure that the children described in the present paper belong to the same group as Kanner's autistic children. They might possibly be regarded as a related group of slightly different character. Our children do not quite show the peculiarities of language, the extreme absence of human relationships or the apparent unemotional self-contained intellectuality Kanner describes. Nor is it clear to what extent Kanner's cases possessed unusual early sensitivities.

II. CASE REPORTS[2]

The following case reports are not meant to give complete case histories. We will rather restrict ourselves to a bare outline of biographical data and offer in detail only the material pertinent to the special problem of unusual sensitivities.

[1] Personal communication from the author.
[2] We want to express our appreciation to Dr. Mary E. Leitch for her cooperation in collecting this material.

The cases reported were not all observed in the same manner or under the same conditions.[3] Although we saw all of these children, we did not see the first two until several years after the period with which we are most concerned, namely the first, and to some extent the second, year of life. In these two cases we had to rely on what the parents remembered about the earlier period. We have no reason, however, to cast any special doubts on their statements. The mother who reported Case 2 impressed us as a skilled and reliable observer. Case 3 was brought to us at the age of 25 months and Case 4 at the age of 28 months. Thus we had the opportunity of comparing the parents' reports of a rather recent past with our own actual impressions. Finally, Case 5 was first seen by us at the age of 2.8 months and then followed up at rather frequent intervals to the present age of 14.3 months. In addition to these five cases we have in recent years seen several others that seemed, at least in some respects, to display similar phenomena. We shall not deal with these here, in order to simplify our task.

Case 1. We saw Stanley when he was 6 years old. The father and mother had their problems; the mother particularly could be called nervous; but there was nothing in them that one does not find in parents of many children in the normal or in the neurotic range. Stanley's sister, who was 2 years younger, was reported to be a healthy and active child.

Stanley was born after an uneventful pregnancy (with the exception of a short time in which a miscarriage seemed to threaten). Labor lasted 18 hours. Instruments were used. Birth weight was 8½ lbs. Stanley was believed to be entirely normal, though when about 1 week old, he began to spit up food continuously. An operation for "Pyloric Stenosis" was performed when he was 3 weeks old. Recovery was rapid. Since that time the child has maintained a healthy appetite. He walked and talked at about 1 year, but he was a strange child from the beginning, and became stranger and more bewildering to his parents as he grew older.

Stanley's sleep was always extremely restless. According to the parents, until the age of 18 months, any noise from a thunderstorm to a conversational tone would awaken him. Then he appeared startled and would scream. But sounds seemed to bother him even in the waking state. Later he learned to enjoy certain types of music, in particular, classical music.

[3] However, the Cattell Infant Intelligence Scale, Form A, and the Gesell Developmental Schedules, were administered to all infants seen for psychological examination.

The parents say that he never pounded on the piano as other children do, but always just touched it lightly with his fingers. If the parents' memory can be trusted, Stanley used to like his baths, but always screamed when his penis was washed. He used to smell everything and began to talk about his olfactory perceptions as soon as his vocabulary was ready for it. He is still intensely aware of all odors. He smells his own clothing. He loves perfumes and powders. He is aware of his mother's smell when she comes from the kitchen or other places. When he soiled, his own odor made him sick and he gagged.

Case 2. Berta, whom we saw at the age of 7 years, is the youngest of 5 children. Both parents are psychologically and esthetically unusually sensitive individuals. She was, as far as the mother was concerned, an unwanted child, as the marriage came to a crisis at the time. A very severe cold beset the mother during the last 3 months of the pregnancy.

Berta was during her first months almost too "good" a baby, as she was "always asleep." However, during the first weeks she had several pyloric spasms. From the beginning she was bottle-fed and, except for these occasional spasms, there were no feeding problems. Berta seemed to be quite self-sufficient during the first year of her life, in fact she did not seem to care whether she was picked up or left alone. The mother felt that the baby never looked at her or seemed to expect her. Although Berta spoke a few words when less than 1 year old, she stopped all use of language at 15 months and did not speak again until she was 4 years old. (Her later speech characteristically contained both neologisms and expressions of poetic power and beauty). The child's reactions to sensory stimuli were very much in contrast to her seeming indifference toward people. From early infancy on Berta showed unusually violent reactions to colors and sounds. Often she would wake up and scream when a light was turned on. At the the age of 5 months she seemed fascinated to an unusual degree by a bouquet of flowers containing unusual colors. The mother remembers also that at the age of 10 months Berta almost leaped out of her arms when she saw some red flowers. From the age of 10 months until 24 months she would not eat anything of yellow color, e.g., eggs, corn, pudding, and would become furious when something yellow was offered to her. (On the other hand later, between 2½ and 5 years of age, all her clothes had to be yellow, under no conditions red, and she painted everything in yellow during these years).

From the beginning Berta seemed to get upset by and angry about loud noises. By the age of 5 months certain kinds of modern, dissonant music would disturb her, while she did not mind other music. She too, like Stanley, always played softly on the piano, never banged it. Later, at the age of 4 years, she would hate certain symphonies because they were "too sad", while she would sit entranced listening to others. She would recognize and identify by name many of these symphonies on hearing a small part.

From very early days on Berta seemed to become absorbed in experiences of touch. While she never could tolerate woolly toys — she still does not want them — velvet would put her into paroxysms of laughter. This response was present at 9 months of age. (At a later age Berta discriminated between related tactile experiences to the extent that when sitting cozily with her mother she would ask to have her cheek patted in one direction, but not in another.)

Berta has in recent years shown a very acute sense of smell, and her mother believes that even as a baby she used to smell her food. The mother believes also that Berta used to be unusually discriminating in regard to the taste of food. In addition she never tolerated any of the usual equilibrium stunts which most babies enjoy, like being swung around, lifted up high, etc. One of the fears which she developed in later years was that of being turned upside down.

Case 3. We saw Stella when she was 25 months old. The parents remembered her early reactions quite well. Our own observations were in harmony with the parents' reports.

Pregnancy and birth had been normal. A small umbilical hernia was reduced by repeated applications of adhesive tape. For the first 6 weeks Stella was breast- and bottle-fed. During that time she suffered from colic and cried. At the end of 6 weeks, breast-feeding was discontinued. From then on the child cried very little, but her development did not follow the normal paths. She seemed to live in a world of her own, beyond the reach and influence of her parents. Like Berta, Stella started to talk early, but became mute soon after. When we saw her, she had not yet begun to speak again.

Stella was apparently sensitive to light from an early age on. She used to jerk her head away when sunlight hit her. Her eyes used to squint in bright daylight. Riding in the car at night, she used to blink and duck her head when exposed to lights. (The same was still true at the time of our observation.) It seemed to the parents that Stella "always" had preferred red things.

Stella used to cry when she heard a loud voice or a clap of the hands. She, like the first two children, never banged on the piano, but rather played it very softly. She seemed to enjoy music, to be fascinated by soft musical sounds.

The mother said that Stella "always" used to rock her bed for a time before falling asleep. She enjoyed the rocking provided by the moving automobile so much, that taking her out in the car was a favorite way of quieting her when she was difficult.

Stella used to be very sensitive to cold air. It made her "screw up" her face. Hot weather, on the other hand, seemed also to cause her discomfort. She used to lick cold water and cool things, e.g., metals.

Stella resented being touched at the shoulders, between the legs, and on her face. She never allowed anybody to hold her hand. Until 1 year of age she refused to touch furry or fuzzy toys and since that time has not played with toys at all.

The mother's report stressed also Stella's decided discrimination in regard to taste. She used to gag when certain foods (e.g., spinach, custard, pudding) were given to her. We might mention in this connection again her licking of metals, window glass, the piano and her own hand.

Case 4. Olivia, whom we saw first when she was 28 months old, is the only child of parents both of whom seemed to have many neurotic difficulties. Pregnancy and birth were within normal limits. She had some minor congenital stigmata; two toes grown together and an "odd" facial appearance.

Numerous difficulties occurred very early in Olivia's development. It was hardly possible to establish contact with her and to influence her. She was restless, unhappy, and later fearful and negativistic. This child too showed an interruption of speech development. She had begun to say words when she was 7 months old, then reverted to muteness. At the time of our first observation, she still talked very little, her best being 2-word sentences.

Olivia also showed a number of sensitivities. She used to scream over any noise. At the time of the first examination, however, she had become accustomed to many of the minor noises which previously had disturbed her. She still startled and got frightened at loud noises. Early she discriminated between different kinds of music. If she heard music she did not like, she would cry till it was turned off. She seemed on the other hand deeply pleased with some selections.

Olivia stood alone and walked at the normal time, but gave this up shortly thereafter, and at 28 months had not yet recovered these skills. When the parents attempted to get her to walk by each taking a hand, she "went to pieces" and was more fearful than usual for a week or two. Around the age of 8 months there was a period when Olivia had developed the habit of rocking quite vigorously.

Olivia was at all times rather sensitive to odors. She vomited when smelling certain foods, for example, oranges.

We could not be quite sure whether other sensitivities of Olivia, those to visual and taste stimuli, both reported by the mother as rather unusual, really went beyond what one may expect to see in general.

Case 5. Bruce is an illegitimate child. Delivery and condition at birth were normal. He was breast-fed for 2 weeks. At the age of 2 months he was separated from his mother and sent by an agency to the home of an experienced and trusted boarding mother. At the age of 2.6 months, according to the boarding mother's report, he was sensitive to sudden noises and cried out in his sleep if the door slammed. He sometimes acted frightened when she went to the crib to pick him up or turned him over rather quickly.

We saw Bruce first at the age of 2.8 months. He showed a mild but definite retardation in most areas of development. He characteristically gave delayed responses to stimuli. On the other hand he showed excessive startle reaction to sudden visual stimuli as well as to auditory ones. His responsiveness to the boarding mother was noticeably more mature and more spontaneous than to the examiner who was a stranger to Bruce. Such an observation is rarely made in infants less than 4 months of age and bespeaks a special precocity in this area of development.

At the age of 5.5 months he would be quickly and violently upset by light and other stimuli. For example: He was presented with a cup. He started to approach the cup, bringing his left hand slowly and cautiously over the edge of the table from under it and then stopped. When the cup was moved toward him to encourage his picking it up, he reacted with a violent startle and his face twisted in a peculiarly tense way.

The boarding mother told us at that time that Bruce had a very delicate skin and that pressure marks remained visible for a relatively long time. We were able to verify this observation. His general retardation was again evident at 7.1 months (the I.Q.[4] was 76 at that time), with wide scatter in the level of different achievements, and with inadequate

[4] Cattell Infant Intelligence Scale, Form A.

development in all areas. The observers received the impression that Bruce was a markedly tense baby who failed to relax even when he fell asleep. Being held in someone's arms he quieted somewhat but never lost his tenseness. His response to people and to objects was of the same quality. Both appeared to be disturbing and threatening to him rather than stimulating positive interest or responses. He appeared to be most comfortable when very little attention was paid to him. His posture at such times suggested withdrawal or, more accurately, protection against outside stimuli. Thus, lying on his back, he characteristically shielded his eyes and a portion of his face by drawing one or both arms upwards or he covered his ears with his hands and closed his eyes. When lying on his stomach he buried his face in his arms and drew his legs under his body. When he was held in such a position as to make such withdrawal impossible and toys were presented or social approaches made, he usually reacted with obvious discomfort and anxiety. This manifested itself by anxious, near-crying facial expressions, often accompanied by moaning and whimpering sounds which developed into sobs if stimulation persisted. In addition, an increased rate of breathing, rhythmic rocking motions, a tight interlacing of hands, and bringing his hands before his eyes occurred when stimuli were presented.

At the time of the next observations (at 8.2 months), Bruce was again seen asleep before the test was started. Even in his sleep his forearm was placed over his eyes as though to shield them though he was in a dark room.

At 9.7 months, for the first time since we had known him, Bruce showed some interest in both people and objects. Yet if he was approached too directly, he showed behavior of much the same sort as was seen before.

Shortly before Bruce was 1 year old, he was given a variety of examinations. EEG and neurological examinations did not detect any abnormality at that time, but medical examination detected a general hemorrhagic tendency of unclear etiology.

Later observations and tests, done about once monthly, the last at 14.3 months of age, showed a generalized mental retardation with the I.Q. again in the 70's. He showed little physical activity and was generally lethargic though not truly relaxed. The protective gestures previously so characteristic of him were noted only on few occasions and occurred in mild forms. But he was comfortable only in close physical proximity to the boarding mother and behaved then almost like an infant a few weeks old. The boarding mother confirmed our impression to the effect that Bruce's dependence on her was increased rather than lessened.

III. PROBLEMS OF THE SENSORIUM

How does the presented case material look from the point of view of the sensorium? To answer this question we would have to know, of course, what the sensorium is like in normal infants and very young children. But no normal population, to our knowledge, has ever been systematically investigated in this respect. We have therefore to admit that our impressions of unusual, even extreme, sensitivity in these children are subjective experiences that have arisen against the background of many, but uncontrolled observations made on other children. Nobody will, however, doubt that human beings differ congenitally from each other in their reactions to sensory stimuli. Future observation may give us the normative data necessary for better understanding and safer evaluation of these phenomena.

If we examine more closely those facts that impressed us as bespeaking unusual sensitivity in the described children, we become aware that they differ from each other in several respects, and can be grouped accordingly. We find that we have observed facts pertaining to many parts of the sensorium, i.e., to visual, to auditive, to tactile, to olfactory, to gustatory, to equilibrium, and to temperature experiences. Some of the children reported on reacted very sensitively to light or colors, to noises and music, to materials that came in contact with their skin, to smells and perfumes, to foods, to rocking and swinging, to cold air or cool objects. Thus, one obvious principle of grouping our observations is furnished by the sensory modality.

Then we find that what impressed us in some observations was the reaction to the intensity or quantity of stimulation, while in other cases the observation is more easily understood as a reaction to quality. Thus if any kind of slight sound seems to awaken a sleeping infant, or arouses a reaction from the waking one, we will consider that he reacts to the intensity of the stimulation, in fact here to a very low intensity. But if certain sounds or combinations of sounds attract a child, while other sounds or combinations of sounds of equal loudness repel him, it seems plausible to consider this a reaction to quality. Other reactions to quantity that we find in our material, are e.g., reactions to light of a certain brightness, reactions to normally imperceptible (or at least not usually reacted to) amounts of odor, reactions to slight disturbances of the equilibrium, to slight impressions on the feeling of temperature.

On the other hand, observations pertaining to certain colors, certain materials, specific odors, foods, we can group with reactions to quality. Whether a special fondness of rocking should be grouped with reactions to quality or to quantity may be debatable. With some sensory modalities this distinction does not seem to make much sense. We would not be able to say, e. g., what a reaction to quality would be like in the modality of the sense of temperature.

The reactions to intensity or quantity can be divided into several sub-groups distinguishable without much difficulty. Where a child is found to react to a very slight sound, odor, etc., we might describe the observation with the concept of "lower threshold." The "lower threshold" would be the point on the intensity scale of the minimum stimulus that elicits a sensation or a response. The sensitive child would be expected to have a low "lower threshold", the unsensitive child a high "lower threshold". On the other hand we may group together instances in which the observed children show upset or disturbance because of the too great intensity of the sensory stimulation, for example, too much light, noise, cold air, disturbance of equilibrium, etc. Such observations refer to the "upper threshold", i. e., the maximum stimulus that can be tolerated without eliciting reactions of pain, discomfort, or tendencies of avoidance. While none of the observations in our material pertain to the so-called "difference threshold", that is the smallest difference in intensity between two stimuli that the child perceives or reacts to in a differentiated way, such observations would be very desirable. Future research in this line might, for example, take the form of conditioning experiments with two intensities of the same stimulus that differ only little from each other. If our assumption of unusual sensitivity in the children of the described type is correct, they would — assuming that no other factors interfere — be easier to condition to smaller variations in stimuli than the average child. We would also expect these children to show a low "lower threshold" and a low "upper threshold."

The reactions to quality can also be further grouped. We find in our material several instances of fascination with qualities (colors, sounds, materials, odors, etc.); furthermore, instances of intense dislike of qualities, and finally a few observations that might be interpreted in a manner parallel to the concept of "difference threshold" of intensities, namely small differences in quality that seem sufficient to change the child's emotional reaction from fascination to indifference or dislike, or vice versa.

To convey an impression of these possible groupings we present them in the form of a table using observations from our case material for purposes of illustration. This table should more than anything else remind us of the many data that would be desirable. For not only the blank spaces would need to be filled, in order to achieve a systematic survey of sensitivities, but it has to be remembered also that the illustrations of this table are drawn from several cases and thus conceal how little we actually know, even in these five cases, of sensitivities of the single child. We would need really to know the actual data concerning the various thresholds for each child.

It is also worth mentioning that this table leaves out all possible complications arising from intersensory experience, i. e., the simultaneous involvement of several sensory spheres, which obviously has its own laws. In addition, it is not impossible to conceive, for example, that the sensitivity within a given modality may vary according to the quality of the stimulus. Infant A may prove to be more sensitive to perfume X than infant B, but less sensitive to perfume Y. It is also entirely hypothetical at this time to assume that individual thresholds remain constant over a long period of time. The value of systematic observations in these areas would be considerable. They might for example, throw some light on questions pertaining to constitution and to special gifts. One would like to have answers to questions like these: Can there be unequal sensitivity within one sensory modality, e. g., a low "lower intensity threshold", but a high "upper threshold", or a paradoxical lack of reaction to qualities where sensitivity to intensities seems great? Is it possible for one sensory modality alone to show unusual sensitivity? Do certain sensory modalities tend to have similar characteristics in respect to sensitivity, allowing for the assumption of a closer relationship amongst them as against the rest which do not share these characteristics of sensitivity? Is sensitivity essentially the same in all sensory modalities, i. e., is it a general characteristic of the organism?

We cannot answer any of these questions at present. We should like to return to the observations concerning the particular children we have described. To do this, however, we feel obliged to introduce a concept that will allow us to view the phenomena in a more meaningful framework.

IV. THE "PROTECTIVE BARRIER AGAINST STIMULI" (REIZSCHUTZ)

The concept in reference to which we shall attempt to explain the observed phenomena has been introduced by Freud: the organism's "protective barrier against stimuli" (Reizschutz). It is one of those

TABLE 1 / Data Desired for the Evaluation of Individual Sensitivity with Illustrations from Our Material

Modality	A) Quantity			B) Quality		
	1 Low Threshold	2 Upper Threshold	3 Difference Threshold	1 Fascination	2 Dislike	3 Difference
I Visual		Bruce's upset from light		Berta's excitement with red flowers		
II Auditory	Low voices awakening Stanley	Several children's playing the piano softly		Stanley's enjoyment of certain music	Olivia's dislike of certain music	Berta's distinguishing between music she likes and hates
III Tactile				Berta's paroxysm about velvet	Berta's dislike of wool	
IV Olfactory	Stanley's smelling his own clothing			Stanley's love of perfumes	Olivia's vomiting at the smell of certain foods	
V Gustatory					Stella's gagging certain foods	Berta's discrimination in regard to foods
VI Equilibrium		Berta's intolerance of stunts		Stella's enjoyment of rocking		
VII Temperature		Stella's intolerance of cold air				

concepts which, as marginal by-products of his creativity, Freud has given to us. It is a baffling, ambiguous, yet provocative concept, that Freud apparently applied to a variety of related, but not identical phenomena.

A) He described the "protective barrier" as something common to all living organisms, but most easily discernible in the simplest living substances, the vesicles of protoplasm. Such a living vesicle has an outermost layer,

. . . and this now operates as a special integument or membrane that keeps off the stimuli, i. e., makes it impossible for the energies of the outer world to act with more than a fragment of their intensity on the layers immediately below . . . (1, p. 30).

B) The "protective barrier" functions also in higher organisms, in connection with the sense organs:

In highly developed organisms the receptive external layer of what was once a vesicle has long been withdrawn into the depths of the body, but portions of it have been left on the surface immediately beneath the common protective barrier. These portions form the sense organs, which

essentially comprise arrangements for the reception of specific stimuli, but also possess special arrangements adapted for a fresh protection against an overwhelming amount of stimulus, and for warding off irresistible kinds of stimuli (1, p. 31).

C) Freud uses the concept as an aspect of his psychological construct "perceptive apparatus of the mind". ". . . the perceptive apparatus of our mind consists of two layers, of an external protective barrier against stimuli whose task it is to diminish the strength of excitations coming in, and of a surface behind it which receives the stimuli, namely the system Pcpt. — Cs." (3)

D) A function of the ego, apprehending, is also conceived as part of the "protective barrier against stimuli". This becomes of clinical importance when Freud regards the ordinary traumatic neurosis as the result of an extensive rupture of the "barrier":

What conditions it (i. e., the rupture) is the failure of the mechanism of apprehension to make the proper preparation, including the over-charging of the system first receiving the stimulus . . . We thus find that the apprehensive preparation, together with the over-charging of the receptive systems, represents the last line of defense against stimuli (1, p. 37).

E) In the last years of his life Freud seems to have been inclined to regard "protection from stimuli" as a function of the ego (possibly its primary function) and to consider the organic protective barrier the phylogenetic and ontogenetic precursor of the human ego.

One can hardly go wrong in regarding the ego as that part of the id which has been modified by its proximity to the external world and the influence that the latter has had on it, and which serves a purpose of receiving stimuli and protecting the organism from them, like the cortical layer with which a particle of living substance surrounds itself (4).

Under the influence of the real external world which surrounds us, one portion of the id has undergone a special development. From what was originally a cortical layer, provided with the organs for receiving stimuli and with the apparatus for protection against excessive stimulation, a special organization has arisen which thenceforward acts as an intermediary between the id and the external world. This region of our mental life has been given the name of *ego* (5).

After this review of Freud's thought about "protection from stimuli" we wish to examine whether introduction of this concept may be advisable for the better understanding of our material.

Assuming that the data of our cases would all pertain to the neonatal period rather than to a spread of time between birth and approximately the age of 2 or 2½ years, we would not hesitate to relate them unequivocally to the "protective barrier". We are used to assuming that a functioning ego does not exist at the neonatal period, and we generally see what we regard as its first traces — delay in response to stimuli — only at a much later period. We see in our case material, however (particularly clearly in the case of Bruce, whom we could observe contemporaneously, rather than rely on later reports), indications that these children start life with a high

degree of sensitivity against which they eventually succeed in building some defenses. Furthermore, we see that some of these defenses start early, in fact, as will be discussed later in some detail, that ego functions set in prematurely, apparently in connection with this defensive purpose. It seems therefore justified to us to tentatively regard the unusual sensitivities as not essentially related to qualities of the ego, but rather to something more primitive, constitutional.

The next question to be decided is whether this primitive, constitutional factor necessarily has to be identified as the "protective barrier against stimuli". Does this concept offer any advantages against the idea of over-excitability of the organism we find in the older literature? A word of caution is in place here. We are moving here in realms of abstraction where we might easily fall victims to semantic confusion, unless we are on our guard. We must keep in mind that no different consequences ensue if we call the same phenomena by two different names. In fact, as the following graphic representation shows, degrees of excitability would necessarily be identical with "protective barriers" of different thickness.

Protective barrier and over-excitability are then really not different modes of explanation, but different linguistic forms for the same explanation. There are several advantages, however, to using the concept of the "protective barrier". It simplifies the task of establishing connections with the phenomena that Freud explained with this concept, mainly the traumatic neurosis and phenomena of compulsive repetition against and "beyond" the pleasure principle. It helps, also, as we hope to show later in this paper, to demonstrate in a simple fashion some interrelationships between constitutional and earliest environmental factors and their consequences for ego formation.

The "protective barrier against stimuli" to us is the conceptualization of all (ideally obtainable) data

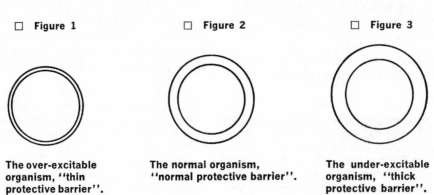

☐ **Figure 1** ☐ **Figure 2** ☐ **Figure 3**

The over-excitable organism, "thin protective barrier".

The normal organism, "normal protective barrier".

The under-excitable organism, "thick protective barrier".

about the sensitivity or excitability of a newborn infant, whether the stimuli come from outside (sensorium) or inside (organic needs). The advantage of our concept lies in that we can point to phenomena which may eventually supply a measure of something that evidently must be assumed to exist in different quantities. In a similar way, in the past, speculation about intelligence eventually led to measurement of intelligence as defined by certain rules of experiment. Obviously "protection against stimuli" is at present more comparable to a map of yet unexplored territory than to a formula that contains in itself all previously obtained knowledge. We cannot, at this time, even make assumptions about possible differences between protection against outer and inner stimuli.[5] It is a matter that has to be decided by observation, or possibly experimentation, whether infants have the same type of reaction (the same "protective barrier") towards outer and inner stimuli.

It may also be premature to make a choice at this time between two possible conceptualizations of the "protection against stimuli" in the person in whom an ego has become established. One choice would be to follow the idea of Freud's later years that the ego grows in the place, as it were, of the original protective barrier, and it alone protects. The other possible way to look at the data would be to assume that the constitutional protective barrier continues to function throughout the individual's life, while the ego adds to the protection. This would mean thinking of two protective layers, one constitutional, organic, either peripheral in the sensory organs or in the adjoining nervous system (Freud's concept B), or within the central nervous system, but without making use of those higher functions of the organism, which we ascribe to the ego and which — through attention, apprehension, symbolization, indirectly also through other functions — would contribute the second protective layer.

What possible observations would make one or the other of these assumptions more advantageous? The decision would have to come from observations of adults or older children. Can we find apparently normal persons, that is to say, persons who can stand a fair amount of frustration, and who show average or better "ego-strength" in relation to id, superego, and the outer world (the three forces with which, according to Freud, the ego has to contend),

but who show in some ways that stimuli reach them with unusual intensity? Would, for instance, indications of physiologic disturbance or introspective testimony about the stimulation received suggest to us that the facts can be easier described in terms of two protective barriers? Could just this be the case in individuals of high sensitivity and great gifts who show adequate or superior ego functioning, to take extreme examples, in persons like Goethe, Rubens, Titian? Or what if only sensory stimulations of a certain kind, e. g., loud noises, bright lights, or a cooling off of the body surface, are unusually disturbing, forcing the person to take special precautions and measures of avoidance? Thus a competent contemporary writer is said to be forced to live in the country and to protect his ears with cottonwool when he has to come near the highways or railroad tracks. Observations of the latter type would, of course, be open to question as to their correct interpretation. One would suspect psychological determination of such sensitivities by experiences in childhood, and by symbolic meaning. But only research can tell eventually what the facts are and what the surviving hypotheses are going to be.

V. EARLY SENSITIVITIES AND PSYCHOSIS

In this last part of our study we will first present some additional material on our cases that we consider weighty enough to exclude almost any other diagnosis but childhood psychosis (except possibly in one of the five cases, that is not quite clear yet). The rest of the discussion will be devoted to an examination of the possible relationships between unusual early sensitivities and childhood psychosis. The hypothesis will be offered that the infant who is not sufficiently protected from stimuli either because of a "thin protective barrier", or because of the failure of maternal protection, may have to resort for such protection to premature formation of an ego. When this premature ego breaks down, possibly as a consequence of a trauma, the psychotic manifestations are thought to set in.

Stanley and Berta, who were older children, showed at the age at which we observed them unmistakable signs of psychosis. Their behavior and their thought processes were found to be deviant and queer far beyond what can be considered neurotic. The thought content also corroborated the presence of psychosis. Stanley was, for instance, almost exclusively preoccupied with fire and destruction, Berta with toilets and "badness". Neither of these children had with anybody around them any relationship that would stand up under the slightest amount of

---

[5] Freud at one point wants the protective barrier directed only against outer stimuli: "Towards the outer world there is a barrier against stimuli, and the mass of excitations coming up against it will take effect only on a reduced scale: towards what is within no protection against stimuli is possible . . ." (1, p. 33).

frustration. They lived almost like strange creatures in the midst of their families.

It was the feeling of all observers (not only of the authors) that Stella and Olivia too could be diagnosed as psychotic children. Our criteria for diagnosing psychosis at the early age of 2 years are, of course, hardly well-established. But here again we had in both cases extremely deviant behavior. Frequently they would not respond in any way when spoken to, called or smiled at.[6] They were beset by many fears, showed extreme negativism, and sometimes outbursts of rage and destructiveness.

All these four children showed spot-like brilliancy and great unevenness in intellectual development, thus differentiating themselves clearly from the feebleminded group. In the case of Bruce, whom we saw last when he was 14.3 months old, we cannot yet offer a diagnosis or prognosis. Our experience and observation of the earliest phases of deviant child development allows us no more than to state our impression that Bruce is a boy significantly deviant from all norms of child development and most likely deviant in a way that will not be compensated for in his later life. We cannot exclude the possibility that he too will turn out to be a psychotic child.

We do not want to give the impression that we regard unusual sensitivities in infants or very young children as a prognostic sign of a developing psychosis. We can definitely state, however, that so far we have seen sensitivities of the described kind and extent only in the most deviant children. Whether children with special gifts without deep personality disturbances would present phenomenologically similar pictures we do not know.[7] The warning may, at any rate, be given not to take such early sensitivities necessarily as signs of an unusually bright future of the child.

It seems possible to us to link in a speculative way the conception of the "thin" protective barrier against stimuli with the development of psychosis in these cases. We may regard an infant as protected

from the onslaught of stimuli in two different ways, on the one hand by the constitutional factor of the protective barrier, on the other hand by the mother who both keeps stimuli from him, and provides them in the right dosage. When such protection from over-dosage and provision of the right dosage of stimuli is given, we have the favorable conditions for ego development. Then the ego becomes gradually organized and in turn is able to control the dosage. If we follow this train of thought we are led to make the assumption that disturbances in ego development may occur when either the organic protective barrier or the mother fail in their function, i. e., provide a protection against stimuli, which is too little, or too much protection for optimal development. It seems logical to assume that in the event of insufficient protection (because of too "thin" protective barrier, or because the mother fails to be protective, or actively overstimulates the infant), a substitute will be developed for the purpose of protection. This substitute might be the ego, precociously organized for the emergency. Too much protection (too "thick" protective barrier, over-protective, or unstimulating mother), on the other hand, may result in delayed and possibly all-too-delayed ego formation.

The idea of an optimal time for the development of each function is not strange to present psychological thinking. Precocious organization of the ego may therefore be considered equally as deleterious a development as its delayed organization, though in a different way. We wish to discuss here only precocious ego formation and its relation to insufficient barrier against stimuli.[8]

Some of our cases showed at an early period a breakdown of functions. Thus loss of language after a normal or even premature start occurred in the cases of Berta, Stella, Olivia. Earlier acquired motoric skills (sitting, standing, walking) were later lost in the case of Olivia. We will not regard the loss of learned habits of cleanliness, which occurred in several of these cases, as a similar ominous sign, for this particular regression occurs rather frequently in young children. We tend to regard as more weighty signs the indications of failure to master traumatic experiences. For example, Stanley, Berta, and Stella reacted very intensely to routine inoculations. In the case of Berta we can definitely state

---

[6] It must at this time remain an open question whether one may attempt to understand the human relationships of our children on the basis of a hypothetical high stimulus value that people would have for them, and against which they would tend to defend themselves.

[7] It is attractive to follow the idea of a "thin" protective barrier against stimuli as a possible constitutional fundament of special gifts. To do so would lead to assumptions of this sort: Only the individual liable to suffer from "bad" stimuli in a certain modality would be likely to be able to develop sufficient interest in procuring or producing "good" stimuli. For example, only he who suffers from noise would be likely to become a good musician.

[8] It may be well to recall here that the concept of the "protective" barrier refers to protection from painful over-excitement. It is not identical with protection of the biological being from damaging influences. A "thick" protective barrier may protect from excitement, but expose to real danger, e. g. when our sense of taste would not warn us against poison.

that in the night after the first diphtheria shot she woke up from sleep with a shriek, and continued to cry for 3 hours in terror: nobody and nothing could calm her, she did not seem to recognize anybody. From that night on this kind of scene repeated itself every night for about a year. In the cases of Stanley and Stella we could not establish when the night terrors had started. However, they were almost as intense as Berta's and lasted also for many months, not unlike those seen in neuroses following a traumatic experience.[9]

It is our impression that there were traces of premature emergence of ego functions to be seen in these cases before their breakdown occurred. For example, we could refer to Bruce's characteristic delay in responding to stimuli, which to the observers had a tentative, inhibited quality. Bruce also distinguished by the age of 2.8 months between his boarding mother — to whom he came only at the age of 2.0 months — and other persons who approached him. Such discriminatory behavior can be regarded as precocious. While it is doubtful to us whether we can distinguish early attention or concentration phenomena in Bruce's defensiveness, we would not hesitate to regard this defensiveness as similar to an ego's attempt to protect the organism from too intensive stimuli through apprehensiveness. We feel that our inability to obtain evidence for precocity of ego functions in the cases we had not been able to observe in early infancy is a real and most regrettable gap in our material and in the structure of this paper, and leaves this part of the paper speculative. The speculation, however, is somewhat supported by observations made on infants who did not have the uninterrupted safety of maternal protection. In such infants, Dr. Escalona and Dr. Leitch observed repeatedly the early occurrence of discriminatory functions, of purposefully directed actions, which resulted temporarily in a relatively high I.Q. on tests. Such early discriminatory behavior may be regarded as evidence of early ego functioning. Thus, while we feel that much further observation will be needed to support the hypothesis of premature ego formation under conditions of insufficiency of the maternal protection or the stimulus barrier, one might nevertheless tentatively regard the material presented as supporting such an assumption. Such a premature ego would be weak, liable to break under stress, and unable to achieve adequate organization later on.

[9] If these connections should be really valid, a noteworthy relationship between early psychosis and the adult's traumatic neurosis would seem to be suggested.

These speculations (if they should prove to be justified) would be in good agreement with Freud's most general formulation of psychosis (2), according to which the essential conflict in psychoses is between the ego and the outer world. Our cases would offer examples for the most primitive type of such conflict, namely, a conflict between an insufficiently protected organism and the stimuli of the outside world.[10] These stimuli set off impulses and excitements within the organism that are overwhelming and destructive through their intensity.

It would be of practical importance to know where the focus of disturbance in these children lies. If our assumption should prove tenable that these children supplement their weak protective barrier against stimuli by a premature ego organization which then breaks and prevents the formation of a mature ego organization, an educational consequence would arise: Parents and others concerned with the welfare of these children would have to protect these children thoroughly from intensive stimulation until such time as the child's ego might be able to take over this function without strain. It would not seem impossible to us that in some cases children with unusual early sensitivities might so be enabled to turn their handicaps to unusual advantages.

After completion of this paper we encountered in the literature the report of an observation similar to our own in a discussion which G. H. J. Pearson gave following a paper of H. M. Little on "The Psychotic Child". Pearson says: "I have noticed, in the two cases with which I have really worked very hard, and a third case with which a friend of mine worked, that these children have a history of having very acute hearing. They are able to hear acutely as babies and are disturbed by noises to a tremendous extent. A little later on they put up a defense against their acuteness of hearing by seeming to be deaf. The two cases of which I spoke later developed an interest in music, which was almost the only interest they had. As a result of these observations, I have wondered whether there is extreme acuteness of hearing in schizo-

[10] Such conflict may even result in the organism's death, if we can trust a news item published in the *Topeka State Journal*, August 13, 1947: *Dies of Fright. Philadelphia, August 13 (AP)* — Two-year-old Nancy Lee Pollock, whose mother said the child was deathly afraid of "anything that sounded like thunder," collapsed and died in her crib as a drum and bugle band practiced nearby, Detective Albert Helvitson reported. Mrs. Elba Pollock, who came from her home in Stockton, California, to visit a sister said Nancy Lee awoke screaming Tuesday night and then fell limp in her bed.

phrenic patients, i. e., whether they are able to hear above and below the normal range." *Pennsylvania Med. Journ.*, Vol. 51, November, 1947, p. 178.

impact of early traumata. The paper indicates a number of questions that might be answered by future research.

SUMMARY

We report in this paper a number of observations in children who very early in life, possibly from birth, showed unusual sensitivities. The general development of these children deviated greatly from normal lines; 4 of 5 described cases could be diagnosed as childhood psychoses. We attempt to understand the observed phenomena with the aid of Freud's concept of the "protective barrier against stimuli" (Reizschutz). An organism insufficiently protected against stimuli by a "thin" barrier may need to precociously develop some ego functions. These ego rudiments appear to break down under the

BIBLIOGRAPHY

1. FREUD, S. *Beyond the Pleasure Principle*, Hogarth, 1922.
2. FREUD, S. "Neurosis and Psychosis," *Coll. Papers*, II, 250–254.
3. FREUD, S. "Notes upon the 'Mystic Writing Pad,'" *Intern. J. Psa.*, XXI, 1940, 472.
4. FREUD, S. *New Introductory Lectures*, Norton, 1933, 106.
5. FREUD, S. "An Outline of Psychoanalysis," *Internat. J. Psa.*, XXI, 1940, 29.
6. KANNER, L. "Early Infantile Autism," *J. Pediat.*, 1944, 211–217.

JEROME S. BRUNER

The Cognitive Consequences of Early Sensory Deprivation[*][1]

Growth in any field of science is almost always uneven. The past decade, for example, has been a period of turbulent growth in the field of perception, a period in which parallel inquiries in neurophysiology, physics and psychology have each in turn thrown light upon the nature of the perceptual process, light of such an order as to dazzle us all a bit with respect to the fundamental nature of perceiving. I should like briefly to review some of these developments before turning to the principal topic of this symposium: the problems of sensory deprivation.

* Reprinted by permission from *Psychosomatic Medicine*, Vol. 21, 1959, pp. 89–95.
[1] The present paper will appear in *Sensory Deprivation and Social Isolation* (Harvard University Press), edited by Dr. Philip Solomon of Boston. I am indebted to Dr. Solomon not only for permission to publish the article in *Psychosomatic Medicine* where it is our hope that it might reach a wider audience, but also for the many arrangements that he made for those of us who participated in the Symposium on Sensory Deprivation in June, 1958, of which he was chairman and which was sponsored jointly by the Office of Naval Research and the Harvard Medical School.

Let me consider first the field of physics. The classical metrics of physics up to the end of the 19th century were the centimeters, grams, and seconds of classical mechanics. Until very recently in psychology, our description of ambient stimuli and of their effect at a sensory surface has been couched in terms of this system. The effort, moreover, to construct a set of experiential attributes for any modality has been guided by this classical system of physical mensuration, and it is not surprising that Titchener (17) and later Boring (2) ended with the ensemble of intensity, protensity, quality, and attensity (the last a never-ending source of embarrassment!). Today, physics has revolutionized its way of looking at the physical world of potential stimulation. In quantum theory, for example, one specifies the state of a system and the set of transitional probabilities leading to next states. Emphasis upon probability of events and transitional probability have become central. These developments in physics have telegraphed themselves into psychology principally via the development of the mathematical theory of communication or information theory, an approach to the analysis of the reduction of uncertainty in physical systems that rests upon Boltzmann's insight that entropy in a system is best described as residual uncertainty. The result of all of this ferment in physics is that attention has been focussed on two related and hitherto neglected features of the physical stimulus: first, the set of *possible* stimulating states that might have occurred at any given moment, and, second, the bias in their likelihood of occurrence. The importance of this probabilistic metric for an understanding of the development of environmentally appropriate sets or attitudes will shortly become apparent.

Developments in neurophysiology have also provided a new challenge to the psychologist interested in perception. As in the case of our contact with physics, we as psychologists have been operating until very recently with a 19th or early 20th century conception of the nervous system, an image of a switching and transmission system made up of an afferent or sensory side, a central segment, and an efferent or motor outflow. The work of Granit, (7) of Galambos, (5) of Magoun and his associates, (e.g., (11), and of Pribram (14) have seriously brought into question whether such a simple input-output model corresponds with the findings of electrophysiology over the past decade and a half. Indeed, we know now that even in so simple a case as the flexion reflex of the spinal mammalian cat, close inspection indicates that a third of the fibres in the efferent nerve trunk going to a muscle has nothing whatever to do with motor activity but with the programming or gating of the sensory stretch receptors in the muscle, setting these receptors to feed back to the spinal cord on the afferent side either a lot or a little sensory information about the state of the muscle. And Granit (7) has shown that centrifugal control fibres operate from the center to the periphery in altering the sensitivity of retinal cells to stimulation. Indeed, Galambos has recently shown that fibres of central origin operate outward to the periphery of the auditory system, serving to "turn off" the sensitivity of hair cells in the organ of Corti when attention is turned elsewhere. Some of these fibres have already been traced back as far as the superior olive, and experiments have been done on the effects of severing them, the result of such section being to prevent centrifugal control from operating. Add to this work the continuing experimentation on the boosting operations of the reticular system in facilitating sensory input to the cortex, discharges which, as Lord Adrian puts it, (1) clear the cortex of alpha activity in order to give sensory

messages a clear field, and still another blow is struck in the interest of freeing psychologists from the rigid model of neural activity that is a heritage from the early Sherrington. What this work indicates, as Robert Oppenheimer put it in his first William James lecture of last year, is that the price of perceiving anything at all is that not everything is perceived that can potentially be perceived. And so, if you will, the problem for an organism which would hope to minimize the suprise of its environment to a level where he might survive, is to match his programming to the likelihood and significance of events in the environment.

Now consider some of the developments in psychology, for we on our part have not been quiet. I want to single out only two of these. The first is the shift in emphasis in the study of perception from a consideration of classical problems of space-time quality organization as so well represented by the work of the Gestalt psychologists to what Prentice (13) has called a functional emphasis. I should take "functional emphasis" to mean that interest has shifted to the manner in which perceiving relates to and is instrumental in the various ongoing enterprises of an organism, whether these enterprises be simply getting around in a familiar environment or as seemingly complex as looking for food or for a mate or for the Holy Grail. What has been healthy about the new emphasis is that, first, it has confused us out of our smug assumption that perception was some sort of fixed relationship between an impinging pattern of physical energy, on the one side, and certain enduring and highly stable properties of the brain on the other, leaving the variability in perception to that favorite American vehicle of variance, the response. The second and more positive effect of the shift in emphasis is that we have been sent scurrying for independent variables that lie outside the comforting stimulus metric of centimeters, grams, and seconds.

A second development in psychology, new work on the effects of early experience, brings us to the heart of the problem to which we are addressing ourselves: the development of perception. It is a problem with a tortured background, tortured by the pains of yesterday's metaphysical dead locks. One such deadlock is the so-called nativist-empiricist controversy which has about it some of the scent of a wrongly formulated dichotomy. I say this unkind thing about the so-called controversy simply because it has had no issue, and because it yields on the very margins where it should stay firm. Nobody in his right mind has ever urged that an organism begins with no built-in equipment for perceiving, nor has anybody been so brashly foolish as to claim that experience has no effect whatever on the nature of what we perceive. If the controversy had any real meaning in the study of space perception, where it originated, it certainly has none in the study of perception generally. Or rather, I should say, it has about the same meaning as a quarrel in physics between those who would proclaim that weight was more important than the force-fulcrum distance in Archimedean Type II levers. It is not a controversy but a question of plotting functions.

For bringing this matter into a proper empirical perspective, we must be grateful for the work of Hebb and his students in investigating the effects of early sensory deprivation in animals. I do not propose to review the work, for it is well known. In general, an impoverished environment, one with diminished heterogeneity and a reduced set of opportunities for manipulation and discrimination produces an adult organism with reduced abilities to discriminate, with stunted strategies for coping with roundabout solutions, with less taste for exploratory behavior, and with a notably reduced tendency to draw inferences that serve to cement the disparate events of its environment such as between the light of a candle flame and the likelihood of its burning when you put your nose into it. Add to these reduced capacities — which may indeed be irreversible, although there has not yet been a full scale attempt to provide adequate therapy toward overcoming these deficits — add to these the fact that there seem to be critical periods operative. Unless certain forms of stimulation-cum-learning take place before a certain point in a puppy's life or a rat's life, there appear to be certain very intractable changes.

Let me speculate a little about the meaning of these challenging findings. But before I do, let me remind you of the parallel findings on prolonged sensory deprivation in adult organisms that have the effect of disorganizing cognitive function, upsetting the constancies, even disrupting the perception of continuous contours that extend beyond the immediate focus of attention at the center of the visual field. I remind you of these matters in advance of setting forth some speculations to underline the likelihood that perception and cognitive activity generally depend upon a dynamically stable though ultimately disruptible equilibrium that depends, even in adult life, upon contact with stimulus heterogeneity and a shifting environment. Indeed, even more dramatic evidence is given by Ditchburn and his associates (4) indicating that if a visual pattern is stabilized on the retina such that it is not even

displaced by the natural tremor of the eye, it will disappear from view within six or so seconds.

Let me see if I can pull the threads of the discussion together now. To operate effectively in an environment, an organism must develop a model of the environment, and this for at least two reasons. In the first place, it is a way of conserving information in the form of concepts or universals, the means whereby, to use the ancient Aristotelian language, we separate essences from accidents, or in modern terms signal from noise. If you will, the recurrent regularities and the higher probability relationships between and among events are conserved in this model. Given such models — call them trace systems or cell assemblies or templates or whatever term seems most appropriate to your imagery — it becomes possible, secondly, for an organism to extrapolate and interpolate on the basis of partial information, to perform the kind of inference that may be called "going beyond the information given." This is a task that is learned gradually at first and then, to use Lashley's (10) phrase, as the grammatical character of learning develops, proceeds at an accelerated pace as we convert masses of connected or associated events into more highly ordered systems, as when the children in the ingenious experiments of Inhelder and Piaget go from trial and error concreteness in bouncing a ball off a wall at a target to the reorganization of the situation as one in which the angle of incidence and the angle of reflexion are recognized as equal. This kind of learning is neither S-S nor S-R in the usual senses of those shopworn terms. It consists of a process of organizing "rules" or "transforms" that conserve and represent the redundant structure of the environment.

Without such prior learning, the centrifugal control functions of the nervous system are without a program — speaking now of a program as one does in computer language. A system without a program, without a basis for predicting that certain events are more likely than others or preclude others, has no basis for selectivity toward stimuli. I would make a small wager at this point. Consider the cats in the experiment of Hernandez-Péon et al. (8) Click stimulation produces large spike discharges in the cochlear nucleus. If now the click stimulation is continued but some white mice are introduced into the field under a bell jar, the electrical discharge produced by continuing click stimulation is markedly reduced. Attention is directed elsewhere with attendant gating of the auditory system. The wager is this: if cats are reared in a highly restricted sensory environment, one with a minimum of stimulus variation in either the visual or auditory fields, the selective gating found will be considerably less marked than in normally reared cats. The prediction is based upon several considerations about the nature of perceptual development as perceptual differentiation, a point of view most intimately associated with the Gibsons. (6) Continued contact with a rich sensory environment, the view would hold, permits the development of differentiation of spheres of activity, of sensory modalities, of events within modalities. Sensory deprivation prevents such differentiation, prevents the development of selective gating.

This leads to another prediction: part of the process of perceptual development consists of the capacity to utilize cues, to extract information from cue-significate encounters. One of the more interesting forms of information utilization is to be found in the weighing of probable in contradistinction to certain cues, for the process requires a sorting out and evaluation of negative and positive instances. A given sign leads not always but sometimes and in excess of chance to a given significate. To master such cues requires either the gradual buildup of excitatory strength as required by such learning theories as Hull's (9) or Spence's, (16) or it requires the use of a strategy like that proposed by such analysts of the decision process as Marschak (12) or Savage. (15) In the first case, the process would be very slow and informationally very inefficient, particularly if one worked with a two-cue discrimination situation where, say, a white signal led to food 70% of the time and to non-food 30% and a black cue to food 30% and to non-food 70%. In the second, more informationally efficient strategy, as soon as the animal discriminated the difference in the probability of payoff, he would opt for the more probable cue and ride with it. Let us take groups of sensorially deprived and normal animals and set them two-choice discrimination tasks where the two cues lead 100:0/0:100 to their respective consequences then 80:20/20:80, and finally 70:30/30:70 as in the well-known experiment of Brunswik. (3) I would predict that the two groups would differ least on the certain cues, and as one moved in the direction of the equiprobable case, the groups would diverge more and more. The reason for the prediction is based on quite a simple premise. Not only does early deprivation rob the organism of the opportunity of constructing models of the environment, it also prevents the development of efficient strategies for evaluating information, for finding out what leads to what and with what likelihood. And robbed of development in this sphere, it becomes the more difficult to utilize probable than certain cues,

the former requiring a more efficient strategy than the latter.

Let me conclude these notes by reference to the problem of transferability in learning. The McGill experiments and those inspired by the work at McGill have given us a striking example of what has been called non-specific transfer of training. Savings effected in learning something new by virtue of having learned something before cannot in such instances be credited to the transfer of specific responses or of priorly established associations. Yet it is precisely this type of so-called non-specific transfer that is perhaps the most typical and the most ubiquitous. It consists of the establishment of models or constructs or concepts that represent the environment in such a way that when one encounters a new task, it is possible to handle it as an exemplar of an old concept in connection with which appropriate responses have already been learned. Such transfer has the function, almost, of saving us from having to do much new learning and it is indeed the case that after a certain age in life, we do indeed get saved from much new learning.

But non-specific or generic transfer also involves the learning of general rules and strategies for coping with highly common features of the environment. And it is here that I think Piaget's vision is the clearest. He remarks upon the fact that cognitive growth consists of learning how to handle the great informational transformations like reversibility, class identity, and the like. In his most recent writing, he speaks of these as strategies for dealing with or, better, for creating usable information. I would propose that exposure to normally rich environments makes the development of such strategies possible by providing intervening opportunity for strategic trial and error. Whether failure to master the elements of such strategies for transforming information before a certain period of growth produces an irreversible loss, I cannot say, nor do I have a clue as to why critical periods are so critical. That there is impairment of strategy under a deprived regimen seems, however, to be fairly evident.

One word of conclusion about the effects of early deprivation. Little is served by fighting over the stale battlegrounds of yesterday's theorizing. I remarked in passing that there has been a strong arousal of interest in the manner in which cognitive functioning and perception are shaped by the instrumental role they play in the enterprises of an organism. In the past there have been pleas of protest that this instrumental bedding of perception played no role in shaping its character or laws, that only responses altered by virtue of instrumental requirements. Such a view comes from the ancient and honorable assumption that all there is to perceiving is the pattern of intensities, durations, and sensory qualities. It is obvious that inference is also a formidable factor in perceiving, else there would not be such a huge difference in recognizing the random word *yrulpzoc* and the fourth-order word *vernalit*, or frequent and infrequent words would be recognized with equal ease. Inference depends upon the establishment of rules and models, and it also depends upon the development of strategies for arriving at rules and models. I have proposed in this paper that early experience with a normally rich perceptual environment is needed for such learning, that deprivation prevents it.

Let me, finally, explore the implication of work on early deprivation for our understanding of the effects of sensory deprivation on the functioning adult organism. It would seem, first of all, that not only are there critical problems in the development of adequate models of the environment and adequate coping strategies, but that there are also maintenance problems of an order of delicacy that were not even imagined before the pioneering experiments of Hebb and his associates at McGill. In listening to the papers of our symposium over the past several days, I have been struck by not only the need for variable sensory stimulation as a condition for maintaining a functioning organism, but also by the need for continuing social contact and stimulation. We have yet to study the relative effects of each of these sources of maintenance, but it would appear as if they may serve a vicarious function for each other: where social contact is maintained, as in the efforts at Mt. Sinai in New York to keep up the family contacts of children in respirators, the cognitively debilitating effects of reduced stimulation are notably reduced. It would not be unreasonable to guess that social contact provides a symbolic analogue or vicar for sensory intake.

What is this maintenance problem? I would like to suggest that it perhaps relates to a kind of continuing feedback-evaluation process by which organisms guide their correction strategies in perceiving, cognizing, and manipulating their environments. Let me suggest that the unhampered operation of this evaluation process is critical in the continuing adaptation of the organism, both in the development of adequate cognitive functioning, as I have suggested, and in moment-to-moment functioning. Consider the massive effects that occur when the evaluation process is interfered with by various means. Disrupt auditory feedback in speech by the conven-

tional technique of delaying the return of the speech pattern to the speaker's ear by a fraction of a second, and the effect is highly disruptive. Stuttering occurs and the speaker reports a lively discomfort, sometimes bordering on panic. So, too, with the discomfort of a visual Ganzfeld, where virtually all orienting cues are removed and only a white unstructured space remains. Distorting spectacles often have the same effect of disrupting and preoccupying the organism, setting him off on a battle for adequate feedback that makes all else seem trivial. One may suggest that one of the prime sources of anxiety is a state in which one's conception or perception of the environment with which one must deal does not "fit" or predict that environment in a manner that makes action possible. If there is anything to this view of anxiety, then it follows that when one prevents an organism from monitoring the fittingness of his percepts and his cognitive structures, one is cutting him off from one of his principal sources of maintaining adjustment.

The work reported by Goldberger and Holt in this symposium on "individual differences in reaction to experimental interference with reality contact" and also by Bennett on the effect of sensory isolation in high altitude flying suggests that people respond differently to the initial stages of isolation, some finding it exciting and even intoxicating, others, terrifying and disrupting. I do not know what bearing this has on our present problem, save that when one is isolated from external stimulation one is thrown on internal resources, and people differ in the degree to which they live comfortably and confidently with their inner impulses and cognitive models. Over and beyond this important distinction, I would make one other in the form of a guess. It is this. To get any pleasure from being cut off temporarily from adequate evaluation of one's coping, whether by sensory deprivation or by "non-problem drinking" of five martinis, say, suggests that one is able to rely more on criteria of congruence and consistency in testing one's notions about the world, that one is less fearful of errors of overdaring and overgeneralization. The "strategies of evaluation" of such a person will tend to be more nominalistic and relativistic in the philosophical meaning of those terms. The person who is more easily thrown off by isolation and sensory deprivation and interference will be more the empiricist and realist, oriented outward for testing ideas. Each will show a different developmental pattern with respect to strategies for dealing with reality. We have seen such differences developing in eleven-year-old children whose cognitive patterns are now being studied intensively by the Cognition Project at Harvard, and as I listened to Drs. Goldberger and Holt reporting their findings, I was tempted to make the guess I am reporting here. Perhaps its only virtue, however, is that it is a testable guess that can be rejected easily!

In conclusion, then, I have suggested that early sensory deprivation prevents the formation of adequate models and strategies for dealing with the environment and that later sensory deprivation in normal adults disrupts the vital evaluation process by which one constantly monitors and corrects the models and strategies one has learned to employ in dealing with the environment.

REFERENCES

1. ADRIAN, E. D. The Physiological basis of perception. In E. D. ADRIAN et al. (Eds.), *Brain mechanisms and consciousness.* Oxford, Blackwell, 1954.
2. BORING, E. G. *The physical dimensions of consciousness.* New York, The Century Company, 1933.
3. BRUNSWIK, E. Organismic achievement and environmental probability. *Psychol. Rev. 50*:255, 1943.
4. DITCHBURN, R. W. Report to the Experimental Psychology Group. Reading, England, January, 1957.
5. GALAMBOS, R. Suppression of auditory nerve activity by stimulation of efferent fibers to cochlea. *J. Neurophysiol. 19*:424, 1956.
6. GIBSON, J. J., and GIBSON, E. J. Perceptual learning: Differentiation or enrichment? *Psychol. Rev. 62*:32, 1955.
7. GRANIT, R. *Receptors and sensory perception.* New Haven, Yale Univer. Press, 1955.
8. HERNANDEZ-PÉON, R., SCHERRER, H., and JOUVET, M. Modification of electric activity in the cochlear nucleus during "attention" in unanesthetized cats. *Science 123*:331, 1956.
9. HULL, C. L. *Principles of behavior.* New York, D. Appleton-Century, 1943.
10. LASHLEY, K. S. Dynamic processes in perception. In E. D. ADRIAN et al. (Eds.), *Brain mechanisms and consciousness.* Oxford, Blackwell, 1954.
11. MAGOUN, H. W. The ascending reticular system and wakefulness. In E. D. ADRIAN et al. (Eds.), *Brain mechanisms and consciousness.* Oxford, Blackwell, 1954.
12. MARSCHAK, J. Rational behavior, uncertain prospects, and measurable utility. *Econometrica 18*:111, 1950.
13. PRENTICE, W. C. H. "Functionalism" in perception. *Psychol. Rev. 63*:29, 1956.
14. PRIBRAM, K. The Brain and Thinking. Paper given at Cambridge Conference on Thinking, Cambridge, England, August, 1955.
15. SAVAGE, L. J. *The foundations of statistics.* New York, Wiley, 1954.
16. SPENCE, K. W. *Behavior theory and conditioning.* New Haven, Yale Univer. Press, 1956.
17. TITCHENER, E. B. *Lectures on the elementary psychology of feeling and attention.* New York, Macmillan Co., 1908.

A. D. B. CLARKE AND ANN M. CLARKE

Some Recent Advances in the Study of Early Deprivation*†‡

INTRODUCTION

During the last 40 years there has been a growing awareness of the importance of early experiences in the development of later personality. The psychoanalysts were the first to stress this, but since then they have been joined by the learning theorists, notably Hebb, who indicated brilliantly that later stages of development depend on the integrity of preceding ones. More recently the ethologists have shown from the animal world that there exist critical periods of development — particularly in early life — during

* Reprinted by permission from *Journal of Child Psychology and Psychiatry*, Vol. 1, 1960, pp. 26–36.
† Based on a paper read to the British Association, York, September 1959.
‡ This study was undertaken in preparation for the production of a book on the effects of deprivation, to be published in the Methuen Manuals of Modern Psychology Series.

which the future of certain behaviour patterns is determined. These diverse trends indicate that from very different approaches a similar stress is laid on the importance of early life experiences.

Much fascinating work on deprivation in animals has been produced by Lorenz, Tinbergen, Beach and others but one must beware of extending the results to man too readily, particularly where infra-primate organisms are concerned. Animals have, unlike man, a relatively short period of immaturity, and the part played during development by learning must be of correspondingly short duration. For survival, particularly in early life, the animal depends on predetermined modes of response, each triggered off by appropriate stimulation. During speedy development the organism tends to be particularly vulnerable, and early deprivation in animals may have very profound effects. For man the situation is different; prolonged development implies prolonged flexibility and hence, although deprivation effects in children may be considerable, there is a greater period for compensatory recovery, sometimes even up to about 30 years of age after which, as William James put it, man's personality tends to be set hard like a plaster cast.

There is theoretical interest in human deprivation because unusual experiences tend to have gross effects, and can therefore tell us something relevant to theories of normal development. The size of the problem is a more practical reason for studying this field. Take physical deprivation as an example: in England, where poverty is no longer a major problem, we tend to forget that well over half the world's children — in whom the foundations for later development are being laid — are at or below the poverty line, suffering from malnutrition. As Morgan (1959) recently put it, vast populations are "struggling with conditions that make sickness and undernourishment the normal state of life." In this country great improvement in physical health has occurred but the same cannot be said for mental health; it is a well-worn statistic that about 44 per cent of our hospital beds are for mental cases. Any studies which throw light on this vast problem — and deprivation studies are one source — must therefore be worthwhile.

One great landmark in this field was Bowlby's (1951) monograph on *Maternal Care and Mental Health*, but its thesis already needs modification, and some advances in understanding have occurred. As will be remembered, Bowlby stated that "what is believed to be essential for mental health is that the infant and young child should experience a warm, intimate and continuous relationship with his mother (or permanent mother substitute) in which both find satisfaction and enjoyment. Given this relationship,

the emotions of anxiety and guilt, which in excess characterize mental ill-health, will develop in a moderate and organized way. . . ." Bowlby's work has of course resulted in many humane changes in hospital practices.

Deprivation and separation from parents, however, tended to become interchangeable and synonymous terms, and much of his evidence implied far more than mere separation. Many studies, for example, concerned children who had suffered unfortunate experiences followed by removal from home and long periods in drab Dickensian institutions, which involved deprivation in a far wider sense than mere separation. Criticisms have been made along these lines by O'Connor (1956), and very recently by Barbara Wootton (1959), who rightly remarks that these findings highlight inadequate public care of children as much as the separation from the mother. Thus perhaps the most obvious feature of deprivation studies is the loose way in which the term is used, and that classification is almost non-existent. We proposed to define deprivation widely as "any external event or constellation of events which significantly interferes with the child's normal developmental processes and which thus affects adversely his mental or physical status." Fig. 1 shows a simple scheme of classification of different types of deprivation.

□ **Figure 1**

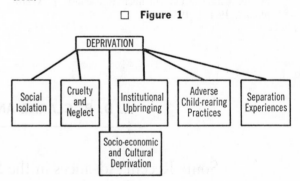

Main types of deprivation.

This scheme is by no means comprehensive; we could add, for example, a large and important category of sensory deprivation. Moreover, each of these main types can and ought to be further subdivided. It will also be noted that from left to right there is a decrease in the severity of deprivation with, however, socio-economic and cultural factors on their own on a rather different plane. Next, in Table 1, other important variables are noted.

Perhaps the only point needing elaboration is the last one. Different aspects of personality may be

■ TABLE 1 / Factors Relevant to Deprivation

1. Duration
2. Intensity
3. Previous experiences
4. Age of occurrence
5. Constitutional vulnerability
   (modifiable by environment)
6. Experiences following deprivation
7. Constitutional resilience
   (modifiable by environment)
8. Aspects of personality affected

damaged by diverse experiences or at different stages of development. For example, a child in a poverty-stricken family *may* be psychologically secure and suffer only physical effects: a child in a tense neurotic family may be intellectually unimpaired yet emotionally disturbed.

SOME RECENT STUDIES

Each type of deprivation shown in Fig. 1 will now be considered briefly in connexion with some recent experiments which have added to our knowledge of this field.

Social Isolation

Studies of social isolation are few and often anecdotal. Accounts of children reared by animals are usually suspect but it is possible that this has in fact happened, and that most, despite care and training, have remained at imbecile or idiot level. The first proper study of such a child was Itard's Wild Boy of Aveyron, itself a major step in the history of psychology, because for the first time a human being was investigated scientifically. The point is often made that such children must have been congenital imbeciles in the first place, but this is untenable. No genuine low-grade defective could survive the hazards of animal life or learn to adapt to animal ways.

There have been a few studies of illegitimate children locked away in attics for 5 or 6 years before discovery. Davis (1940, 1947), for example, reported two cases. When rescued, neither could talk and both functioned at idiot level. In spite of assiduous care one remained an idiot, but the other showed amazing resilience. Within 2 months she could speak in sentences, in 9 months she was reading and writing, and in 16 months had a vocabulary of 2000 words. After 2 years, by the age of 8, she was considered intellectually normal. It so happened that she had not been separated from her deaf mute mother but locked up with her in a darkened attic, while the first had been completely alone, and also had a defective mother.

More recently, Willis (1959, and personal communication) reported very briefly a case of a child kept locked in a hen house between the ages of 2 and 7.

This was the illegitimate son of a widow of 10 years' standing. Half-brothers and sisters on both maternal and paternal sides were normal. After a year of medical and surgical treatment following rescue, Miss Willis saw the child daily for a period of several months. He could not speak, never looked *at* anyone, smelt every new object and was uninterested in movement as such. But after 2 weeks' simple therapy he could be tested with the Seguin Form-board and achieved a mental age of 6½–7 years, his age then being just over 8. The beginnings of the humanization process were observable, but the experiment was abruptly ended when hospital treatment was complete and he was removed to a children's home where at once he regressed — a human and a scientific tragedy.

To summarize, it is clear that extreme isolation can and usually does result in permanent severe intellectual impairment. In one or two cases, however, dramatic recovery has taken place.

Cruelty and Neglect

It is well-known that cruelty and neglect may have very profound effects on young children, but there have been rather few systematic studies. An exception is Hilda Lewis's (1954) research on 500 deprived children in the county of Kent who had been sent to a Reception Centre. She showed the linkage between the child's background and the form of maladjustment exhibited, but Table 2 shows even more interesting data.

■ TABLE 2 / One Hundred Children Included in Special Follow-up Inquiry After Table 50, Lewis (1954)

Condition of Children	At Reception	2 Years Later
Good	15 ⎱ 40	39 ⎱ 75
Fair	25 ⎰	36 ⎰
Poor	39	22
Very poor	21	3

This shows the children's condition as assessed on reception and on follow up. In spite of gross deprivation, 40 per cent were in good or fair psychological condition at reception, and, even more striking, this had increased to 75 per cent 2 years later. Not all children are equally damaged by similar experiences, and in many recovery tends to occur. Lewis points out that removal of children from very adverse homes and separation from bad mothers may be very essential for their mental health. "Some children long exposed to the dislike or indifference of their natural mothers," she writes, "gained rather than lost by separation, provided they passed into kind and sensible hands." This sort of statement tends to redress a common bias in favour of the natural mother, however bad. Similarly, studies at The Manor Hospital have indicated that subnormal deprived persons tend to make great progress after removal from severe deprivation experiences in their own homes.

Institutional Upbringing

An excellent study of the effects of early institutionalization upon speech development in young children has been reported by Kellmer Pringle and Tanner (1958). The subjects were obtained from a day nursery and also from residential nurseries: it was possible to select eighteen reasonably matched pairs of 4–4½ year old children. The home backgrounds of both groups were very poor.

Careful measures of speech showed that in all cases the day nursery group living in their bad homes were in advance of the residential group to the extent, averaging four tests, of 10 months — all this at the early age of 4 years. Such differences in speech foundations are likely to increase with age, and reflect the typical child–other children relationship as against child–adult relationship which is typical for ordinary children. It should, however, be remembered that not all institutions are necessarily bad, and that in fact many are improving.

Adverse Child-rearing Practices

It is proposed to mention here adverse methods *within the limits of social acceptance*, and to report one of several promising approaches. Wittenborn (1956), for example, pointed out the difficulties in accepting at face value correlations between children and their parents where a quality with a possible hereditary basis was concerned; such relationships could be either genetic or environmental or both. However, if foster children were studied (to avoid the effects of selective placement) on non-genetic items of behaviour such as the presence or absence of phobias, then the relationship with the mother's attitude would be likely to be a causal one, and in fact small significant correlations were found between such behaviour and foster-mothers' unsympathetic and rejective attitude.

Several other studies have underlined general parental attitudes such as harshness as well as personal or marital instability as factors related to the child's maladjustment, but obviously nature and nurture intermingle in the natural family. Studies of foster children and their parents are clearly more useful.

Separation Experiences

Much work on separation has been reported recently. Howells and Layng (1955), for example, established that, in a child guidance and a normal control group, about a third of both groups had experienced separation for more than 2 days under the age of 2 years. By the age of 5, about three-quarters of both groups had been separated from their mothers. A little over half the parents believed that harmful effects had resulted, but most thought these were temporary. The authors consider that much mental ill-health arises from the experience of being with unsatisfactory parents and, like Hilda Lewis, believe that some disturbed children may benefit from separation.

Douglas and Blomfield (1958) in their comprehensive study of 5000 randomly selected children, found that half the sample had experienced separation during the first 6 years of life. For 14 per cent this separation lasted for 4 weeks or more. These were carefully matched with a control group of non-separated children. Fairly crude measures of emotional disturbance (such as nightmares, enuresis and solitary play) were used. It was found that, where the child had been separated both from mother and from home, differences between the groups were apparent; 37 per cent of the separated group had nightmares versus 21 per cent of the controls. But where the child remained in his home during the separation period, no differences could be established. This seems a very important finding.

Schaffer (1958) has studied the effects of one or two weeks' hospital experience on seventy-six infants. The main finding at follow-up was the identification of two distinct syndromes (see Table 3), characteristic of the great majority of the children, and each associated with a particular age range — either before or after the age of 7 months.

The main feature of the "global syndrome" was an extreme preoccupation with the environment. Sometimes for hours on end the infant would crane his neck, scanning his surroundings without apparently focusing on any particular feature. It was exceedingly difficult to "break through" this scanning behaviour. The second symptom constellation — the "over-dependent syndrome" — is much more familiar to us, being characterized by unusual and excessive dependence, clinging almost continually, much crying and a fear of strangers.

Schaffer links these very distinct reactions with

■ TABLE 3 / Syndromes Typical of 72 per cent of Infants Following Hospital Experience after Schaffer (1958)

Type	Global	Over-dependent
Features	Extreme preoccupation with environment, "scanning", little vocalization	Excessive crying when mother out of sight, clinging, fear of strangers
Age range	Below 7 months	Above 7 months
Average duration	3 days	14 days
Range	20 min–4 days	1–80 days

the different stages in the child's perceptual and conceptual development and cites Piaget's findings. It is only during the second half of the first year that a new type of cognitive structure emerges which enables the infant to make real relationships. The "global syndrome" is said to emerge as a response to the perceptual monotony of the hospital ward while the "over-dependent syndrome" results both from separation and the trauma of hospital experience.

Prugh et al. (1953) have studied reactions of children to hospitalization. A control and experimental group of 50 children each, the majority aged between 2 and 10 years, were selected. Most of these were admitted to hospital for fairly short periods and for relatively acute illnesses. Matching of the two groups was reasonably successful except that the control group contained before admission a rather larger number of well-adjusted children.

The control group experienced ordinary ward routines and were assessed before, during and after their hospital experience. The experimental group, however, enjoyed special ward routines with visiting by parents at any time, psychological preparation, and support for unpleasant procedures, special play activities and so on. Table 4 shows some of the main results; it should be noted that Prugh's terms "maximal, limited, inadequate" for pre-hospital adjustment and "minimal, moderate, severe," for reactions to hospital, are really synonymous.

It will be seen that the control group showed a shift in the direction of moderate and severe maladjustment under orthodox conditions compared with pre-hospital adjustment. The experimental group under special conditions, however, showed a similar pattern of maladjustment and adjustment before and during their hospital experience.

The younger children were more disturbed than the older, and there was a correlation between previous adjustment and adjustment in hospital.

So far as follow-up is concerned, 92 per cent of the controls and 68 per cent of the experimental group showed significant disturbance of behaviour immediately after discharge. Three months later, the figures had dropped to 58 per cent and 44 per cent respectively. After 6 months 15 per cent of the controls and none of the experimental group showed continued disturbance. The authors have demonstrated without doubt the psychological value of the "humanized" hospital.

A recent paper by Bowlby et al. (1956) has considerably modified some of his earlier views. A group of 60 children admitted for long periods early in life to a T.B. sanatorium was followed up and contrasted with a control group selected as nearest in age to the subjects after their discharge, in their schools. There did appear to be small residual differences between the ex-sanatorium children and their controls but these might reside as much in the sort of home from which a tuberculous child is drawn as in the separation experiences. Bowlby goes on to say courageously that where his expectations proved most wrong was in the sanatorium children's capacity to make friends; unlike those reported on earlier, they appeared relatively normal in this respect. In fact one is able to infer from the data that there appeared to be only a 20 per cent greater incidence

■ TABLE 4 / Pre-Hospital Adjustment and the Reactions of Children to Hospital Data Summarized from Prugh et. al. (1953)

Control group (Orthodox conditions)				Experimental group ("Humanized" conditions)			
Pre-hospital adjustment		Reactions to hospital		Pre-hospital adjustment		Reactions to hospital	
Maximal	56%	Minimal	8%	Maximal	34%	Minimal	32%
Limited	42%	Moderate	56%	Limited	54%	Moderate	54%
Inadequate	2%	Severe	36%	Inadequate	12%	Severe	14%

of maladjustment in the sanatorium as compared with control groups. In particular, Bowlby writes that the statements made earlier by him and by other workers, that children spending long periods in institutions *commonly* develop psychopathic or affectionless characters, are seen to be mistaken. Much will of course depend on the type of institution.

Socio-economic Factors

The study of socio-economic factors in our own culture has provided material relevant to deprivation. For example, in the "Thousand Family Survey," Spence *et al.* (1954) found that half the unsatisfactory mothers came from Social Classes IV and V and that there was a tendency for children in such classes to suffer other handicaps, such as overcrowding and a greater number of illnesses. Douglas and Blomfield (1958) also point to social class differences in growth, health and maternal efficiency with much the same implications. It is clear that particularly the children of unskilled workers tend to start life with a number of handicaps and, in so far as this is true, are deprived.

It has long been known that there are class differences in average intelligence. Nowadays most of us believe that both nature and nurture are relevant, and recent work is giving an indication of some possible environmental mechanisms. Take language as an example: Luria (1959) has shown that language in the first few years of life is not merely a system for intercommunication; it has an additional function as externalized thinking needed for problem solving of all types. Now obviously language does not develop *in vacuo* — it is the result not only of neural maturation but also of language stimulation by parents and others. Hence a very poor language environment (see Kellmer, Pringle and Tanner, 1958) is bound to retard the child's speech and hence certainly in early years, and perhaps later too, to affect the child's intellectual development. Moreover, Bernstein (1958), in an outstanding paper, has described two language systems — the concrete here-and-now "public language" and the "formal language" consisting of abstractions and cause-effect relationships. The public language is the main speech mode of lower socio-economic groups and certainly also occurs in the higher. But the formal language is the main speech mode of the higher groups and, reinforced by the more ambitious attitudes to children of middle-class parents, affects profoundly their language and hence their intellectual development, and this in turn has a bearing on responsiveness to education.

Thus culturally poor language environments must be considered as part of the deprivation problem.

DISCUSSION AND CONCLUSIONS

An attempt will now be made to discuss and to draw together the threads of this exceedingly diverse material, and to state some general conclusions.

The first important point is that, apart from gross deprivation, studies of all other forms show considerable differences in individual vulnerability. Even in poor institutions it seems likely that only a minority develop those very severe disorders of conduct that caused Bowlby so much concern, although maladjustment is certainly a typical outcome. Separation itself is an immensely complex problem — much depends on previous experience and whether it is followed by traumatic situations. And, in spite of the analysts, the mother is not the only figure of importance. The child's conceptual and perceptual rigidity are such that removal from the familiar tends to produce stress, and the familiar includes the actual bricks, mortar and plaster of the particular home. As Woodward (personal communication) puts it, the child has learned expectancies, and depends upon these markedly.

What, then, are the factors determining differences in vulnerability? We know next to nothing about this, but here are some obvious suggestions: inherited predisposition, experiences, preceding and circumstances surrounding the deprivation, and the child's personality *in toto*, in addition to the deprivation itself. In brief, environment does not operate in a mechanically similar way on all children, although there are of course strong "actuarial" tendencies of particular response to various types of severe or prolonged deprivation.

The second important point is that to varying extents there may be recovery from deprivation even of the most severe kind. This again is a highly complex process which among other things seems to involve a basic quality of the organism which we have termed resilience. Earlier there was certainly an error in supposing that deprivation effects were most likely to be permanent. On the contrary one is as much struck by the human being's resilience as by his tendency to break down. Until recently very few studies existed which showed adult outcome of early deprivation, and it is moreover obvious that we tend not to see professionally those who have recovered. Thus we cannot estimate their number completely. The fact that humans remain moderately flexible during the period of development, as mentioned, allows this possibility of compensatory recovery.

To underline this point we will refer briefly to some work carried out at The Manor Hospital. This concerns severely deprived adolescent and young adult defectives drawn either from adverse or exceptionally adverse backgrounds, often involving cruelty, neglect, separation, long periods in many institutions and so forth. This is therefore almost a pure culture (Clarke and Clarke, 1954, 1959; Clarke, Clarke and Reiman, 1958).

During our first year of work with these people we were struck by the frequency of large I.Q. increments particularly in the most deprived. After pilot experiments, all assessments and ratings of social histories were carried out independently, usually by colleagues who did not know the patients at all. Fig. 2 indicates some of the main results.

These graphs cut a very long story short. The vertical axis shows differing percentages of different but comparable groups. The horizontal axis shows test–retest time interval. It will be noted that a larger proportion of those from the most adverse homes had bigger increments, and that the longer the time interval the greater the proportion.

Our data suggest that these results represent recovery from past experiences rather than response to the present. And they seem to be paralleled by change in other aspects of personality. We believe that exceptionally adverse experiences in childhood prolong the immaturity of the organism, and that Hebb's (1949) work is particularly relevant. Many years are needed for learning, in its broadest sense, the experiences missed or disrupted. There is no way of knowing what these persons would have been like if brought up under good conditions — all we do know is that a very different prognostic picture is presented at 25 than at 15 (unless of course the social history is taken into account at the earlier age). This then is further evidence that very severe deprivation effects can fade.

Finally and briefly, some additional points:

□ **Figure 2**

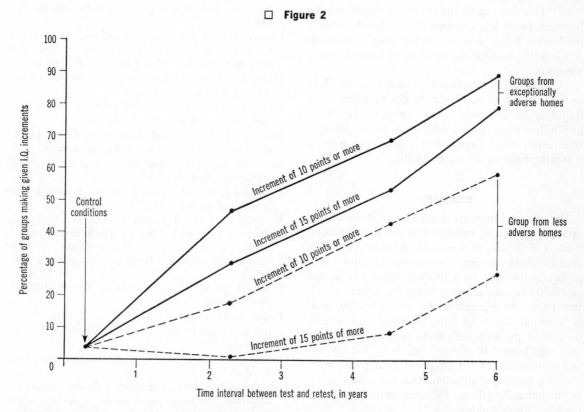

Cognitive recovery from deprivation. This shows the increasing proportion of different but comparable groups of feebleminded patients exhibiting increments in I.Q. of 10 and 15 points with increase in time interval between test and retest. Increments of 20 points or more are not shown, but for the 6 year interval 33 per cent of the group from exceptionally adverse homes and 5 per cent of those from less adverse homes made gains of this order.

(1) Perceptual and conceptual rigidity, a feature of infancy and childhood and very much a function of immature neural mechanisms, is likely to be an important causal factor in early adverse response to hospitalization and other separation experiences. There is also the likelihood, if this rigidity is not broken down by enriching stimulation — whether speech, educational or experiential — that it will continue to varying extents for longer periods than normal. The restricted informational experience of the institution where each drab day is like every other one, and where children's main source of stimulation is other impoverished children rather than adults, serves to retard or fixate perceptual and conceptual development.

(2) Cultures such as ours, which stress a nuclear family structure, are likely to increase the effects of separation in the child. There is some evidence from other societies, such as the Israeli kibbutzim, where the parents play a far less important role, that children grow up more independent and self-sufficient.

(3) One can expect the effects of deprivation to be severe and of long duration *either* when the child's personality before deprivation was poorly adjusted, *or* when the duration and intensity of the experience was great.

(4) Lastly, most deprivation experiences are likely to have an effect on mental health (ranging from transitory to permanent), but obviously mental ill-health has many causes additional to or different from deprivation. Deprivation is important because it is potentially so often preventable.

SUMMARY

Deprivation is important not only in its own right as a vast world-wide problem but also in the general context of theories of personality development. This paper evaluates recent experimental literature with particular reference to individual differences in susceptibility to, and recovery from, the effects of different types of deprivation. Gross deprivation, such as isolation, tends to have profound and usually permanent psychological effects. Earlier work, however, has tended to overestimate both the severity and permanence of the effects of milder and more common types of deprivation. One is as much struck by the human's resilience following suffering as by his tendency to break down.

Acknowledgements — The authors are greatly indebted to Dr J. F. McMahon for his penetrating and helpful criticism; to Dr Hilda Lewis and the Oxford University Press for permission to reproduce part of a Table in her book *Deprived Children*; to Professor Dane G. Prugh for permission to reproduce some of his data; and to Miss B. Willis for her generosity in making available much material concerning a case of social isolation.

REFERENCES

BERNSTEIN, B. (1958) Some sociological determinants of perception. *Brit. J. Sociol.* 9, 159–74.

BOWLBY, J. (1951) *Maternal Care and Mental Health.* World Health Organization, Geneva.

BOWLBY, J., AINSWORTH, M., BOSTON, M. and ROSENBLUTH, D. (1956) The effects of mother-child separation: a follow-up study. *Brit. J. Med. Psychol.* 29, 211–247.

CLARKE, A. D. B. and CLARKE, A. M. (1954) Cognitive changes in the feebleminded. *Brit. J. Psychol.* 45, 173–179.

CLARKE, A. D. B. and CLARKE, A. M. (1959) Recovery from the effects of deprivation. *Acta Psychol.* 16, 137–144.

CLARKE, A. D. B., CLARKE, A. M. and REIMAN, S. (1958) Cognitive and social changes in the feebleminded: three further studies. *Brit. J. Psychol.* 49, 144–157.

DAVIS, K. (1940) Extreme social isolation of a child. *Amer. J. Sociol.* 45, 554–565.

DAVIS, K. (1947) Final note on a case of extreme isolation. *Amer. J. Sociol.* 52, 432–437.

DOUGLAS, J. W. B. and BLOMFIELD, J. M. (1958) *Children under Five.* Allen & Unwin, London.

HEBB, D. O. (1949) *The Organization of Behaviour.* Chapman & Hall, London.

HOWELLS, J. G. and LAYNG, J. (1955) Separation experiences and mental health. *Lancet* ii, 285–288.

KELLMER PRINGLE, M. L. and TANNER, M. (1958) The effects of early deprivation on speech development: a comparative study of 4-year-olds in a nursery school and in residential nurseries. *Language and Speech.* 1, 269–287.

LEWIS, H. (1954) *Deprived Children.* Oxford University Press, London.

LURIA, A. R. (1959) *The Role of Speech in the Formation of Mental Processes.* London: Pergamon Press (in press).

MORGAN, M. (1959) *Doctors to the World.* Robert Hale, London.

O'CONNOR, N. (1956) The evidence for the permanently disturbing effects of mother-child separation. *Acta. Psychol.* 12, 174–191.

PRUGH, D. G., STAUB, E. M., SANDS, H. H., KIRSCHBAUM, R. M. and LENIHAN, E. A. (1953) A study of the emotional reactions of children and families to hospitalization and illness. *Amer. J. Orthopsychiat.* 23, 70–106.

SCHAFFER, H. R. (1958) Objective observations of personality development in early infancy. *Brit. J. med. Psychol.* **31**, 174–183.

SPENCE, J., WALTON, W. S., MILLER, F. J. W. and COURT, S. D. M. (1954) *A Thousand Families in Newcastle upon Tyne.* Oxford University Press, London.

WILLIS, B. E. (1959) A case of extreme isolation in a young child. *Bull. Brit. psychol. Soc.* **38**, 68–69, (Abstract.)

WITTENBORN, J. R. (1956) A study of adoptive children. *Psychol. Monogr.* **40**, 1–115.

WOOTTON, B. (1959) *Social Science and Social Pathology.* Allen & Unwin, London.

ROBERT W. WHITE

Motivation Reconsidered: The Concept of Competence*

When parallel trends can be observed in realms as far apart as animal behavior and psychoanalytic ego psychology, there is reason to suppose that we are witnessing a significant evolution of ideas. In these two realms, as in psychology as a whole, there is evidence of deepening discontent with theories of motivation based upon drives. Despite great differences in the language and concepts used to express this discontent, the theme is everywhere the same: Something important is left out when we make drives the operating forces in animal and human behavior.

The chief theories against which the discontent is directed are those of Hull and of Freud. In their respective realms, drive-reduction theory and psychoanalytic instinct theory, which are basically very much alike, have acquired a considerable air of orthodoxy. Both views have an appealing simplicity, and both have been argued long enough so that their main outlines are generally known. In decided contrast is the position of those who are not satisfied with drives and instincts. They are numerous, and they have developed many pointed criticisms, but what they have to say has not thus far lent itself to a clear and inclusive conceptualization. Apparently there is an enduring difficulty in making these contributions fall into shape.

In this paper I shall attempt a conceptualization which gathers up some of the important things left out by drive theory. To give the concept a name I have chosen the word *competence*, which is intended

in a broad biological sense rather than in its narrow everyday meaning. As used here, competence will refer to an organism's capacity to interact effectively with its environment. In organisms capable of but little learning, this capacity might be considered an innate attribute, but in the mammals and especially man, with their highly plastic nervous systems, fitness to interact with the environment is slowly attained through prolonged feats of learning. In view of the directedness and persistence of the behavior that leads to these feats of learning, I consider it necessary to treat competence as having a motivational aspect, and my central argument will be that the motivation needed to attain competence cannot be wholly derived from sources of energy currently conceptualized as drives or instincts. We need a different kind of motivational idea to account fully for the fact that man and the higher mammals develop a competence in dealing with the environment which they certainly do not have at birth and certainly do not arrive at simply through maturation. Such an idea, I believe, is essential for any biologically sound view of human nature.

As a first step, I shall briefly examine the relevant trends of thought in several areas of psychology. From this it will become clear that the ideas advanced in this paper have already been stated, in one way or another, by workers in animal behavior, child development, cognitive psychology, psychoanalytic ego psychology, and the psychology of personality. If there is novelty in this essay, it lies in putting together pieces which are not in themselves new. They already lie before us on the table, and perhaps

* Reprinted by permission from *Psychological Review*, Vol. 66, 1959, pp. 297–333.

by looking once more we can see how to fit them into a larger conceptual picture.

THE TREND IN ANIMAL PSYCHOLOGY

One of the most obvious features of animal behavior is the tendency to explore the environment. Cats are reputedly killed by curiosity, dogs characteristically make a thorough search of their surroundings, and monkeys and chimpanzees have always impressed observers as being ceaseless investigators. Even Pavlov, whose theory of behavior was one of Spartan simplicity, could not do without an investigatory or orienting reflex. Early workers with the obstruction method, such as Dashiell (1925) and Nissen (1930), reported that rats would cross an electrified grid simply for the privilege of exploring new territory. Some theorists reasoned that activity of this kind was always in the service of hunger, thirst, sex, or some other organic need, but this view was at least shaken by the latent learning experiments, which showed that animals learned about their surroundings even when their major needs had been purposely sated. Shortly before 1950 there was a wave of renewed interest not only in exploratory behavior but also in the possibility that activity and manipulation might have to be assigned the status of independent motives.

Exploratory Behavior

In 1953 Butler reported an experiment in which monkeys learned a discrimination problem when the only reward was the opening of a window which permitted them to look out upon the normal comings and goings of the entrance room to the laboratory. The discriminations thus formed proved to be resistant to extinction. In a later study, Butler and Harlow (1957) showed that monkeys could build up a series of four different discriminations solely for the sake of inspecting the entrance room. Butler concluded that "monkeys — and presumably all primates — have a strong motive toward visual exploration of their environment and that learning may be established on the basis of this motive just as it may be established on the basis of any motive that regularly and reliably elicits responses." Montgomery, in 1954, reported a study with rats in which the animals, their major organic needs satiated, learned to avoid the short arm of a Y maze and to take the path which led them into additional maze territory suitable for exploration. Similar findings have been described by Myers and Miller (1954), whose rats learned to press a bar for the sake of poking their heads into a new compartment and sniffing

around. Zimbardo and Miller (1958) enlarged upon this study by varying the amount of novelty in the two compartments. In their report "the hypothesis advanced is that opportunity to explore a 'novel' environment or to effect a stimulus change in the environment is the reinforcing agent."

These experiments make a strong case for an independent exploratory motive. The nature of this motive can be more fully discerned in situations in which the animals are allowed a varied repertoire of behavior. In 1950 Berlyne published a searching paper on curiosity, a theme which he further developed in subsequent years (1955, 1957, 1958). The rats in his experiments were confronted with an unfamiliar space and later with various novel objects placed in it. Approaching, sniffing, and examining were readily elicited by each novelty, were fairly rapidly extinguished, but were restored nearly to original strength when a fresh novelty was added. Exploration on the part of chimpanzees has been studied by Welker (1956), who put various pairs of objects before the animals and observed the course of their interest. The objects were often first approached in a gingerly manner, with signs of uneasiness, then examined and handled quite fully, then discarded. Introducing a new pair of objects promptly reproduced the whole sequence, just as it did with the rats in Berlyne's experiments. Welker used pairs of objects to find out whether or not the chimpanzees would have common preferences. Bigness and brightness evoked more interest, and greater time was spent upon objects which could be moved, changed, or made to emit sounds and light.

Recent reviews by Butler (1958) and Cofer (1959) show that a great deal of similar work is going on in animal laboratories, generally with similar results.

Exploration as a Drive

The designers of these experiments have favored the idea that exploration should be listed as an independent primary drive. In all cases the experimental plan calls for the elimination of other primary drives by satiation. It is recognized, however, that a confirmed advocate of orthodoxy might bring up two objections to the proposed enlargement of the list of primary drives. He might claim that exploratory behavior could be explained as a consequence of secondary reinforcement, or he might contend that it is reinforced by reduction of anxiety.

The first argument meets an immediate difficulty in Butler's finding that discriminations learned on the basis of visual exploration are resistant to extinction. When reinforcement of primary drive never takes place in the experimental situation, it is to be expected that secondary reinforcement will not prevent extinction (Miller, 1951). But even in those cases where extinction is rapid, as it was with Berlyne's rats and Welker's chimpanzees, serious problems are raised by the quick recovery of exploratory behavior when a novel stimulus is introduced (Berlyne, 1950). In order to sustain the idea that secondary reinforcement accounts for this fact, we should have to suppose that primary rewards have often been connected with the exploration of novelties. It would have to be assumed, for instance, that the securing of food by young animals occurred with considerable frequency in connection with the investigation of novel objects. This image may seem to fit mature animals who search the environment for their food, but it certainly cannot apply to young mammals before they are weaned. Here the learning process can do virtually nothing to reinforce an interest in novelties. Gratification comes from following the same old cues to the same old consummatory responses, and the animal whose attention strays to some novel variation of the breast will only find himself frustrated. One can say that the whole mammalian pattern of infancy works in the opposite direction. The mother is more active than the young in providing gratifications, and the babies must be pursued and retrieved if they stray from the scene of her ministry. However one looks at it, the hypothesis of secondary reinforcement seems to me to demand improbable assumptions about the relationship in the lives of young animals between exploration and primary need gratification.

The hypothesis that exploratory behavior is related to fear and receives its reinforcement from the reduction of anxiety is at first glance considerably more plausible. It seems justified by the observation that Welker's chimpanzees showed uneasiness on first contact with novel objects, and it fits the behavior of rats in a new maze, as reported by Whiting and Mowrer (1943), where initial terror gave place to an exploration so feverish that the food reward was not eaten. Montgomery and Monkman (1955) have undertaken to challenge this hypothesis by a direct experimental attack. They showed that fear induced in rats before entering a novel situation did not increase exploratory behavior, and that fear induced within the novel situation decreased exploration to an extent correlated with the intensity of the fear. They find it more reasonable to suppose that fear and exploration are conflicting forms of behavior, and this view can also be defended on purely logical grounds. Fear shows itself in either freezing or avoidance, whereas exploration is clearly an instance of approach. There is hardly a more perfect example

of conflict between incompatible responses than that of an animal hesitating between investigation and flight. It is clear that exploration can sometimes serve to reduce anxiety, but the proposition that it comes into existence only for this purpose cannot be so easily accepted.

What assumptions have to be made to support the thesis that exploration is motivated by anxiety reduction? It has to be assumed that certain characteristic stimuli arouse anxiety and that exploration of these stimuli is then found to reduce the anxiety. If the characteristics in question are those of novelty and unfamiliarity, we must heed Berlyne's reminder that for the infant all experience is novel and unfamiliar. Berlyne (1950) proposes that the exploratory reaction "may be one that *all* stimuli originally evoke, but which disappears (becomes habituated) as the organism becomes familiar with them." But if all stimuli at first arouse anxious tension, we would have to deduce that all response would consist of avoidance in the interest of reducing that tension. Approaching a stimulus and taking steps to increase its impact could not occur. An exploratory tendency must be there in the first place before it can achieve the function of reducing anxiety. As Woodworth (1958) expresses it, "if there were no exploratory drive to balance and overbalance the fear drive, an animal would be helpless in a novel situation." I find it hard to believe that creatures so liberally endowed with fear could ever achieve a working mastery of the environment if they were impelled toward it only by the pressure of organic needs.

Both hypotheses thus far examined — secondary reinforcement and anxiety reduction — require us to make improbable assumptions. There remains the possibility that exploration should simply be added to the list of primary drives and otherwise treated in orthodox fashion. Myers and Miller (1954) suggest that this is the appropriate course, provided the new drive shows the same functional properties as those already known. "If an exploratory tendency can produce learning like other drives such as hunger, and also show a similar pattern of satiation and recovery, these functional parallels to already known drives would help to justify its classification in the same category." Logically the problem can be dealt with in this way, but we must consider very carefully what happens to the category of drive if we admit this new applicant to membership.

Using hunger as the chief model, the orthodox conception of drive involves the following characteristics: (*a*) there is a tissue need or deficit external to the nervous system which acts upon that system as a strong persisting stimulus; (*b*) this promotes activity which is terminated by a consummatory response with consequent reduction of need; (c) the reduction of need brings about the learning which gradually shapes behavior into an economical pursuit of suitable goal objects. In this scheme the tension of an aroused drive is interpreted as unpleasant, at least in the sense that the animal acts in such a way as to lower the drive and becomes quiescent when it is lowered. There are probably no living champions of so simple an orthodoxy, yet the scheme remains pervasive, and it is therefore worth while to observe that the proposed exploratory drive hardly fits it at all.

In the first place, the exploratory drive appears to bear no relation whatever to a tissue need or deficit external to the nervous system. It is, of course, clearly related to certain characteristics of stimulation from the external environment, a source of motivation which Harlow (1953) would like to see restored to a serious place in contemporary psychology; but it certainly cannot be correlated with a visceral need comparable to hunger, thirst, or sex. Considering the pattern of satiation and recovery shown by Welker's chimpanzees, Woodworth (1958) remarks that "what becomes satiated is not the exploratory tendency in general, but the exploring of a particular place or object." It is possible, as Hebb (1955) has pointed out, that the so-called "reticular activation system" in the brain stem creates a kind of general drive state, and this mechanism might indeed be flexibly responsive to changes in sensory stimulation. This interesting suggestion, however, is still a far cry from viscerogenic drives; it commits us instead to the novel idea of a neurogenic motive, one in which the state of the nervous system and the patterns of external stimulation conspire to produce motivated behavior. There is even a good deal of trouble in supposing that the adequate stimuli for exploration are either strong or persistent. Novelty certainly cannot be equated with strength or persistence, and animals seem readily able to disregard the stimuli to exploration when they are weary.

In the second place, exploratory behavior cannot be regarded as leading to any kind of consummatory response. It is usual for the animal's investigation to subside gradually. If the animal at some point turns away and leaves the once novel object we may say that its curiosity is "satisfied," but we do not mean by this that the equivalent of a consummatory response has just taken place. The sequence suggests rather that curiosity wears out and slowly falls to a level where it no longer guides behavior, at least until a fresh novelty comes into view.

Finally, in the case of exploratory behavior there is real difficulty in identifying reinforcement with need reduction. Montgomery (1954), describing the learning of the Y maze, points out that the short arm, essentially a dead end, would tend to reduce the exploratory drive, whereas the long arm, itself a complex maze, would increase it — but the long arm is chosen. If the long arm functions as a reinforcing agent, "the mechanism underlying this reinforcement is an *increase*, rather than a decrease, in the strength of the exploratory drive." In this experiment, as in their natural habitat, animals do not wait to have novelty thrust upon them, nor do they avoid situations in which novelty may be found. Such behavior can be most readily conceptualized by admitting that under certain circumstances reinforcement can be correlated with an increase in arousal or excitement rather than a decrease. A drive which has no consummatory climax seems almost to require this formulation. It is distinctly implausible to connect reinforcement with the waning of an agreeable interest in the environment or with a general progress from zestful alertness to boredom.

If we admit exploration to the category of drive we are thus committing ourselves to believe that drives need have no extraneural sources in tissue deficits or visceral tensions, that they are not necessarily activated by strong or persistent stimuli, that they do not require consummatory responses, and that drive increase can sometimes be a mechanism of reinforcement.

Activity and Manipulation

Exploration is not the only motive proposed by critics of drive orthodoxy, and novelty is not the only characteristic of the environment which appears to incite motivated behavior. Some workers have suggested a need for activity, which can be strengthened by depriving animals of their normal opportunities for movement. Kagan and Berkun (1954) used running in an activity wheel as the reward for learning and found it "an adequate reinforcement for the instrumental response of bar pressing." Hill (1956) showed that rats will run in an activity wheel to an extent that is correlated with their previous degree of confinement. It is certain that the activity wheel offers no novelty to the animals in these experiments. Nevertheless, they seem to want to run, and they continue to run for such long times that no part of the behavior can readily be singled out as a consummatory response. Perhaps an unpleasant internal state created by inactivity is gradually worked off, but this is certainly accomplished by a tremendous increase of kinaesthetic stimulation and muscular output which would seem to imply increased excitation in the system as a whole.

Harlow and his associates (Harlow, 1953; Harlow, Harlow, & Meyer, 1950) maintain that there is also a manipulative drive. It is aroused by certain patterns of external stimulation and reduced by actively changing the external pattern. The experiments were done with rhesus monkeys, and they involve the solving of a mechanical problem which, however, leads to no further consequences or rewards. The task might be, for instance, to raise a hasp which is kept in place by both a hook and a pin; all that can be accomplished is to raise the hasp, which opens nothing and leads to no fresh discoveries. When the hasp problem is simply installed in the living cages, the monkeys return to it and solve it as many as 7 or 8 times over several days. It seems unlikely that novelty can be postulated as the essential characteristic of the stimulus which evokes this repeated behavior. The simplest interpretation is rather that value lies for the animal in the opportunity, as Zimbardo and Miller (1958) express it, "to effect a stimulus change in the environment." This formulation suggests something like the propensities toward mastery or power that have often been mentioned in discussions of human motivation.

The addition of activity and manipulation to the list of primary drives can only make more serious the difficulties for the orthodox model that resulted from admitting exploration. But recent research with animals has put the orthodox model on the defensive even on its home grounds. It has become increasingly clear that hunger, thirst, and sex cannot be made to fit the simple pattern that seemed so helpful 40 years ago.

Changing Conceptions of Drive

In a brief historical statement, Morgan (1957) has pointed out that the conception of drive as a noxious stimulus began to lose its popularity among research workers shortly after 1940. "On the whole," he says, "the stimulus concept of drive owed more to wishful thinking than to experimental fact." When technical advances in biochemistry and brain physiology made it possible to bring in an array of new facts, there was a rapid shift toward the view that "drives arise largely through the internal environment acting on the central nervous system." One of the most influential discoveries was that animals have as many as a dozen specific hungers for particular kinds of food, instead of the single hunger demanded by Cannon's model of the hunger drive. If an animal's diet becomes deficient in some impor-

tant element such as salt, sugar, or the vitamin-B complex, foods containing the missing element will be eagerly sought while other foods are passed by, a selectivity that obviously cannot be laid to contractions of the stomach. Similarly, a negative food preference can be produced by loading either the stomach or the blood stream with some single element of the normal diet. The early work of Beach (1942) on sexual behavior brought out similar complications in what had for a time been taken as a relatively simple drive. Hormone levels appeared to be considerably more important than peripheral stimulation in the arousal and maintenance of the sex drive. Further work led Beach (1951) to conclude that sexual behavior is "governed by a complex combination of processes." He points out that the patterns of control differ tremendously from one species to another and that within a single species the mechanisms may be quite different for males and females. Like hunger, the sex drive turns out to be no simple thing.

New methods of destroying and of stimulating brain centers in animals have had an equally disastrous effect on the orthodox drive model. The nervous system, and especially the hypothalamus, appears to be deeply implicated in the motivational process. Experimental findings on hypothalamic lesions in animals encourage Stellar (1954) to believe that there are different centers "responsible for the control of different kinds of basic motivation," and that in each case "there is one main excitatory center and one inhibitory center which operates to depress the activity of the excitatory center." As research findings accumulate, this picture may seem to be too cleanly drawn. Concerning sexual behavior, for example, Rosvold (1959) concludes a recent review by rejecting the idea of a single center in the cerebrum; rather, the sex drive "probably has a wide neural representation with a complex interaction between old and new brain structures and between neural and humoral agents." Nevertheless, Miller's (1958) careful work seems to leave little doubt that motivated behavior in every way similar to normal hunger and normal pain-fear can be elicited by electrical stimulation of quite restricted areas of hypothalamus. It is clear that we cannot regress to a model of drives that represents the energy as coming from outside the nervous system. Whatever the effects of peripheral stimulation may be, drives also involve neural centers and neural patterns as well as internal biochemical conditions.

What sort of model becomes necessary to entertain these newly discovered facts? In 1938 Lashley expressed the view that motivation should not be equated with disturbance of organic equilibrium but rather with "a partial excitation of a very specific sensorimotor mechanism irradiating to affect other systems of reaction." Beach (1942) postulated that there must be in the nervous system "a condition analogous to Sherrington's central excitatory state." Morgan, in 1943, undertook to capture the facts in a systematic theory which seems to have been well sustained by subsequent research (Morgan, 1957). He distinguished two types of process which he called *humoral motive factors* and *central motive states*. The humoral factors consist of chemical or hormonal constituents of the blood and lymph, and they are conceived to influence behavior chiefly by a direct sensitizing action on neural centers. The central motive states have several properties: They are partly self-maintaining through neural circuits, they tend to increase the organism's general activity, they evoke specific forms of behavior not strongly controlled by the environment, and they prime or prepare consummatory responses which will occur when adequate stimulation is found. This is a far cry from the orthodox model, but we must nowadays admit that the orthodox model is a far cry from the facts.

In view of this radical evolution of the concept of drive, it is not surprising to find the drive reduction hypothesis in serious difficulties. The earlier identification of reinforcement with drive reduction has been directly attacked in a series of experiments designed to show that learning takes place when drive reduction is ruled out.

In 1950 Sheffield and Roby showed that instrumental learning would take place in hungry rats when the reward consisted not of a nutritive substance but of sweet-tasting saccharine in the drinking water. This finding appeared to be "at variance with the molar principle of reinforcement used by Hull, which identifies primary reinforcement with 'need reduction.'" The authors naturally do not question the vital importance of need reduction, but they point out that need-reducing events may accomplish reinforcement through a mechanism more direct and speedy than the reduction of the need itself. They think that "stimulation and performance of a consummatory response appears to be more important to instrumental learning — in a primary, not acquired, way — than the drive satisfaction which the response normally achieves." Their findings are in line with an earlier experiment with chickens by Wolfe and Kaplon (1941), who used different sizes of food pellets so that the number of pecks and the amount of food received could be thrown out of their usual close connection. The chickens, we might say, would rather peck than

eat; learning was more strongly reinforced when four pecks were necessary than when one peck was enough to take the same amount of food.

The substitution of the consummatory response for need reduction as the immediate reinforcing mechanism is a step in advance, but it soon turns out that another step is required. Can it be shown that an aroused need which does not reach consummation has a reinforcing effect? To test this possibility Sheffield, Wulff, and Backer (1951) provided male rats with the reward of copulating with a female, but not enough times to produce ejaculation. This reward was favorable to instrumental learning even though there was no need reduction and no performance of the final consummatory act. The results were supported by Kagan (1955), whose animals showed substantial learning under the same conditions, though learning was still faster when ejaculation was permitted. Sheffield, Roby, and Campbell (1954) have proposed a *drive-induction* theory according to which the property of reinforcement is assigned to the excitement of an aroused drive. We have already seen that some such assumption is essential if exploration is to be assigned the status of a drive. Here it can be added that the whole theory of pregenital sexuality involves motivation without consummatory acts and without any but the most gradual need reduction. And as a final blow to the orthodox hypothesis comes the finding by Olds and Milner (1954) that positive reinforcement can be brought about by direct electrical stimulation of certain areas of the brain. Once again we learn that neural centers are deeply implicated in the plot of motivation. The simple mechanics of need reduction cannot possibly serve as the basis for a theory of learning.

Twenty years of research have thus pretty much destroyed the orthodox drive model. It is no longer appropriate to consider that drives originate solely in tissue deficits external to the nervous system, that consummatory acts are a universal feature and goal of motivated behavior, or that the alleviation of tissue deficits is the necessary condition for instrumental learning. Instead we have a complex picture in which humoral factors and neural centers occupy a prominent position; in which, moreover, the concept of neurogenic motives without consummatory ends appears to be entirely legitimate. Do these changes remove the obstacles to placing exploration, activity, and manipulation in the category of drives?

Perhaps this is no more than a question of words, but I should prefer at this point to call it a problem in conceptual strategy. I shall propose that these three new "drives" have much in common and that it is useful to bring them under the single heading of competence. Even with the loosening and broadening of the concept of drive, they are still in important respects different from hunger, thirst, and sex. In hunger and thirst, tissue deficits, humoral factors, and consummatory responses retain an important position. The mature sex drive depends heavily on hormonal levels and is sharply oriented toward consummation. Tendencies like exploration do not share these characteristics, whatever else they have in common with the better known drives. It is in order to emphasize their intrinsic peculiarities, to get them considered in their own right without a cloud of surplus meanings, that I prefer in this essay to speak of the urge that makes for competence simply as motivation rather than as drive.

THE TREND IN PSYCHOANALYTIC EGO PSYCHOLOGY

Rather an abrupt change of climate may be experienced as we turn from the animal laboratory to the psychoanalytic treatment room, but the trends of thought in the two realms turn out to be remarkably alike. Here the orthodox view of motivation is to be found in Freud's theory of the instincts — they might be known to us as drives if an early translator had been more literal with the German *Trieb*.

Freud's Theories of Instinct and Ego

In his final work, Freud (1949) described instincts as "somatic demands upon mental life" and as "the ultimate cause of all activity." He wrote further:

It is possible to distinguish an indeterminate number of instincts and in common practice this is in fact done. For us, however, the important question arises whether we may not be able to derive all of these instincts from a few fundamental ones. . . . After long doubts and vacillations we have decided to assume the existence of only two basic instincts, *Eros* and the *destructive instinct* (Freud, 1949, p. 20).

The history of Freud's long doubts and vacillations has been lucidly related by Bibring (1941). Up to 1914 Freud used a two-fold classification of sexual instincts and ego instincts. The ego instincts made their appearance in his case histories in a somewhat moral character, being held responsible for the disastrous represssion of sexual needs, but in systematic usage they were conceived as serving the goal of self-preservation, and hunger was generally taken as an appropriate model. In 1914, when he evolved the concept of narcissism and saw that it threatened to blur the line between sexual and ego tendencies, Freud (1925b) still expressed himself as unwilling to abandon an idea which followed the popular distinction of love and hunger and which reflected man's dual existence "as reproducer and as one who serves his own ends." Various facts, particularly those of sadism and masochism, served to overcome his reluctance, so that he finally united self-preservation and preservation of the species under the heading of Eros or life instincts, establishing destructiveness or the death instinct as the great antagonist in a profound biological sense (Freud, 1948). This highly speculative step proved to be too much for some of his otherwise loyal followers, and the earlier orthodoxy did not become entirely extinct.

It is easier to follow Freud's reasoning when we bear in mind the simultaneous development of his ideas about the mental apparatus. Bibring (1941) points out that even in his early thinking a sharp contrast was always drawn between instinct and mental apparatus. Instinct supplied the energy in the form of powerful, persisting internal stimuli; the apparatus guided it into channels which produced organized behavior and eventually put a stop to the persisting stimulation. In 1915 Freud wrote:

The nervous system is an apparatus having the function of abolishing stimuli which reach it or of reducing excitation to the lowest possible level; an apparatus which would even, if this were feasible, maintain itself in an altogether unstimulated condition. . . . The task of the nervous system is — broadly speaking — *to master stimuli* (Freud, 1925c, p. 63).

During the next decade there was a considerable growth in his ideas about the mental apparatus, culminating in the well known division into id, ego, and superego. The activities of the ego now received much fuller recognition. Freud (1927) assigned to it "the task of self-preservation," which it accomplished through its several capacities of perception, memory, flight, defense, and adaptive action. One can see Freud's thought moving from a mechanical analogy — an engine and its fuel — toward a much more adaptational conception of the mental apparatus. Ego instincts did not wholly disappear, but the decline in their systematic importance was conpensated by the insight that self-preservative tendencies were to some extent built into the whole living system. It is significant that as he took this course he came to question the earlier tension-reduction theory. In the last year of his life he declared it to be probable "that what is felt as pleasure or unpleasure is not the *absolute* degree of the tensions but something in the rhythm of their changes" (Freud, 1949).

Freud's tendency to revise his thinking makes it difficult to pin down an orthodox doctrine, but most workers will probably agree that his main emphasis was upon somatically based drives, a mental apparatus which received its power from the drives, and, of course, the multitude of ways in which the apparatus controlled, disguised, and transformed these energies. His treatment of the ego was far from complete, and it was not long before voices were raised against the conception that so vital and versatile a part of the personality could be developed solely by libidinal and aggressive energies.

An Instinct to Master

In 1942 Hendrick proposed that this difficulty be met by assuming the existence of an additional major instinct. "The development of ability to master a segment of the environment," he wrote, and the need to exercise such functions, can be conceptualized as an "instinct to master," further characterized as "an inborn drive to do and to learn how to do." The aim of this instinct is "pleasure in exercising a function successfully, regardless of its sensual value." The simpler manifestations are learning to suck, to manipulate, to walk, to speak, to comprehend and to reason; these functions and others eventually become integrated as the ego. "The central nervous system is more than a utility," Hendrick declared. The infant shows an immediate desire to use and perfect each function as it ripens, and the adult secures gratification from an executive function efficiently performed regardless of its service to other instincts.

Hendrick's procedure in this and two supporting papers (1943a, 1943b) is quite similar to that of the animal psychologists who propose listing exploration as an additional primary drive. The instinct to master has an aim — to exercise and develop the ego functions — and it follows hedonic principles by yielding "primary pleasure" when efficient action "enables the individual to control and alter his environment." It is to this extent analogous to the instincts assumed by Freud. But just as an exploratory drive seemed radically to alter the whole conception of drive, so the instinct to master implied a drastic change in the psychoanalytic idea of instinct. Critics were quick to point out that Freud had always conceived of instincts as having somatic sources external to the ego apparatus, a condition not met by the proposed instinct to master. There

was nothing comparable to erogenous zones, to orgasm, or to the sequence of painful tension followed by pleasurable release. Mastery, the critics agreed, could not be an instinct, whatever else it might be.

It is of interest that Fenichel (1945), who definitely rejected Hendrick's proposal, gives us another close parallel to the animal work by attributing mastering behavior to anxiety-reduction. He argued that mastery is "a general aim of every organism but not of a specific instinct." He agreed that there is "a pleasure of enjoying one's abilities," but he related this pleasure to cessation of the anxiety connected with not being able to do things. "Functional pleasure," he wrote, "is pleasure in the fact that the exercise of a function is now possible without anxiety," and he contended that when anxiety is no longer present, when there is full confidence that a given situation can be met, then action is no longer accompanied by functional pleasure. We must certainly agree with Fenichel that anxiety *can* play the part he assigns it, but the proposal that all pleasure in ego functions comes from this source raises the same difficulties we have already considered in connection with exploratory behavior. That we exercise our capacities and explore our surroundings only to reduce our fear of the environment is not, as I have already argued, an assumption that enjoys high probability on biological grounds.

Hartmann on the Ego

A less radical change in the orthodox model is proposed by Hartmann, who, in a series of papers since 1939, often in conjunction with Kris and Loewenstein, has been refining and expanding Freud's views on the ego and the instincts. While the ego is conceived as a "substructure" of the personality, this term is somewhat metaphorical because in practice the ego has to be defined by its functions. The list of functions, which includes grasping, crawling, walking, perceiving, remembering, language, thinking, and intention, covers much the same ground that was indicated by Hendrick, but Hartmann does not attribute their growth to an instinct. On the other hand, Hartmann (1950) early came to the conclusion that development could not be explained, as Freud had seemed to conceive it, simply as a consequence of conflict between instinctual needs and frustrating realities. The instincts alone would never guarantee survival; they require mediation by the innate ego apparatus if they are to meet "the average expectable environmental conditions." He therefore proposed that we conceive of an autonomous factor in ego development, an independent maturation of functions taking place in a "conflict-free ego sphere." Functions such as locomotion ripen through maturation and through learning even when they are not caught up in struggles to obtain erotic and aggressive gratification or to avoid anxiety. As Anna Freud (1952) has pointed out, walking becomes independent of instinctual upheavals a few weeks after its beginning; thereafter, it serves the child impartially in situations of conflict and those that are free from conflict.

Hartmann's idea of autonomous ego development has of course been assumed all along by workers in child psychology, but it is an important step to relate it to Freud's disclosures concerning unconscious motivation. In what now looks like an excess of enthusiasm for his own concepts, Freud (1925a) undertook to explain the outgrowing of the pleasure principle and the substituting of the reality principle as a simple and direct consequence of the frustration of instinctual needs. However, the reality principle contained the idea of postponing an immediate gratification in favor of a future one, and Hartmann (1956) properly notes that the capacities for postponement and anticipation cannot be conjured into existence simply by the collision of frustrating reality and ungratified need. Important as frustrations may be, these capacities must already be available, "some preparedness for dealing with reality" must already exist, before the frustration can produce its momentous educative effect. It can be seen from this example that Hartmann's analysis opens the way for profitable commerce between developmental psychologies inside and outside of psychoanalysis.

Hartmann's emphasis on adaptation permits him to perceive much more that is autonomous about the ego than was ever seriously included in Freud's systematic thought. He allows, for instance, that aims and interests which develop in the beginning as defenses against instincts may later become part of conflict-free spheres of activity — become interests in their own right — and thus achieve "secondary autonomy," a concept very close to Allport's (1937) functional autonomy of motives (Hartmann, 1950). He deals with the possibility that adaptive skills developing in the conflict-free sphere may have a decisive influence on the handling of conflicts. These skills have a history of their own, shaped jointly by the child's abilities and by the responses evoked from parents. As Monroe (1955) has expressed it, they have "a very important role in the development of the conscious and semi-conscious psychological self." They may thus have a direct influence upon

the outcome when a child becomes involved in conflict. Rapaport (1958) sees Hartmann's ideas on the autonomy of the ego as vital to the proper understanding not only of healthy development but also of psychopathology itself.

In explaining the autonomous growth of the ego, Hartmann makes generous use of the concept of maturation, but he naturally does not exclude learning. Hartmann (1950) entertains the possibility, mentioned casually from time to time by Freud (1916, 1949), that ego functions are supplied with their own sources of energy independent of instincts, and that there is pleasure connected with their mere exercise. However, he makes little systematic use of this idea, relying instead upon a concept more central in Freud's thinking, that of the neutralization of drive energies. Freud (1927) found that he could "make no headway" in accounting for the varied activities of the ego without assuming "a displaceable energy, which is in itself neutral, but is able to join forces either with an erotic or with a destructive impulse, differing qualitatively as they do, and augment its total cathexis." He speculated that the neutral energy came from Eros and could be conceived as desexualized libido. Hartmann, Kris, and Loewenstein (1949) carried the idea forward a logical step by proposing that the energies of aggressive instincts could similarly be neutralized and placed at the disposal of the ego. Neutralized energy contributes to the development of the ego and makes possible a continuing interest in the objects of the environment regardless of their immediate relation to erotic or aggressive needs. Hartmann (1955) finds this concept particularly helpful in unscrambling the confusions that have arisen over the concept of sublimation.

The doctrine of neutralized instinctual energies is a curious one, and we should bear in mind the complex clinical findings that perhaps suggested it. Freud was an unquestioned genius in detecting the subtle operation of erotic urges and aggressive fantasies, along with elaborate mechanisms of defense, behind the seemingly objective or "neutral" activities of everyday life. Remarkable transformations of interest could sometimes be observed in the course of development. For example, a patient's childhood erotic rivalry and aggressive competition with his father might later disappear beneath a strong objective interest in running the family business; then suddenly, on the brink of success, this interest might come to a total halt, paralyzed by anxiety because the underlying instinctual goals came too close to symbolic fulfilment. The reappearance of instinctual preoccupations in such a case lends a certain color to the idea that they have somehow been driving the behavior all the time, even though the daily pursuit of business goals seems utterly remote from instinctual gratifications.

It is worth noticing that Freud's procedure in making the assumption of neutralized instinctual energy is similar to the one followed by orthodox behaviorists in connection with primary drives. These theorists started from the assumption that all behavior was powered by a limited number of organic drives, and then, in order to protect this assumption, they developed further hypotheses, such as secondary reinforcement, to account for motivated behavior that bore no obvious relation to primary goals. At the point where he could "make no headway" without postulating neutralization, Freud could conceivably have made a good deal of headway if he had been willing to assume that neutral energy, neither sexual nor aggressive, was available as a natural endowment in the first place. But he preferred to protect his assumption of two primary drives and to interpret other energies as transformations of these drives. Even so, the concept seems superfluous if we take Freud at his word about the nature of the life instincts. Freud (1949) made it clear that Eros included more than instincts having a sexual aim; its larger goal was "to establish even greater unities and to preserve them thus — in short, to bind together." Under this formula, it would seem possible to include energies inherently directed toward building up the integrated functions of the ego. But Freud did not exploit the full range of his theory of Eros and proposed only that neutral energies should be conceived as desexualized.

The concept of neutralization has in some respects had a good effect on psychoanalytic ego psychology. In Hartmann's writings, as we have seen, and in Rapaport's (1951, 1954) work on thinking, it has encouraged a strong interest in autonomous ego functions and a fresh analysis of their place in personality. Nevertheless, it seems to me an awkward conceptualization, one which in the end is likely to lead, as Colby (1955) has expressed it, to a "metapsychological snarl." The theory requires that instinctual energies can completely change their aims, which makes one wonder what purpose was served in the first place by defining them as having aims. It preserves an image of mobility of energies that seems much out of line with recent research on animal motivation, where energy is being conceived in a constantly closer relation to specific structures. To my mind it thus compares unfavorably with its quite straight-forward alternative, which is that the alleged neutralized energies are there in the first place as part of the natural make-up of an adaptive organism. I shall later develop this possibility by means of the concept of competence in its motivational aspect, and I believe that this concept gains support from certain other lines of work in the psychoanalytic tradition.

Motility and a Sense of Industry

The trend away from instinct orthodoxy is illustrated by the work of Kardiner (1947) on what he calls "the development of the effective ego." Kardiner's reflections arose from his work on the traumatic neuroses of war. In these disorders the main threat is to self-preservation, and some of the most important symptoms, such as defensive rituals and paralyses, are lodged in the action systems that normally bring about successful adaptive behavior. It thus becomes pertinent to study the growth of action systems, to discover how they become integrated so as to maintain "controlled contact" with the environment and "controlled exploitation of objects in the outer world," and to work out the conditions which either favor or disrupt this acquired integration. Thinking along these lines, Kardiner is led to conclusions just about the opposite of Freud's: It is the successful and gratifying experiences, not the frustrations, that lead to increasingly integrated action and to the discrimination of self from outer world. Frustration produces chiefly disruptions and inhibitions which are unfavorable to the early growth of the ego. Children are gratified when they discover the connection between a movement executed and the accompanying and subsequent sensations. They are still more gratified when they carry out actions successfully; this "gives rise to the triumphant feeling of making an organ obedient to the will of the ego." Such experiences build up "a definite self- or body-consciousness which becomes the center and the point of reference of all purposeful and coördinated activity." Growth of the ego, in short, depends heavily upon action systems and the consequences of action. The course and vicissitudes of this development have to be studied in their own right, and they cannot be understood as side effects of the stages of libidinal development.

A similar theme is pursued to even more radical conclusions by Mittelmann (1954) in his paper on motility. Mittelmann regards motility, which manifests itself most typically in skilled motor actions such as posture, locomotion, and manipulation, as an "urge in its own right" in the same sense that one speaks of oral, excretory, or genital urges. From about 10 months of age it has a distinctly "driven" character, and there is restlessness and anger if it is blocked. During the second and third years the motor urge "dominates all other urges," so that it is proper to "consider this period the motor level of ego and libido development." The child makes tremendous efforts to learn to walk, and to walk well, and he exhibits joyous laughter as he attains these ends. Restrictions of motility may occur because the parents are anxious or because the child's assertiveness troubles them, and a lasting injury to the parent-child relationship may result. Clumsiness in motor or manipulative accomplishments may lead to self-hatred and dependence, for "the evolution of self-assertiveness and self-esteem is intimately connected with motor development." Motility is of central importance in many of the most characteristic functions of the ego. Partly by its means the infant differentiates himself from other objects, and the child's knowledge of objects depends on an extensive activity of manipulation and examination. "Thus motility becomes one of the most important aspects of reality testing." Because it is an element in all cognitive behavior, it can also be considered "the dominant integrative function." Mittelmann bases motor development, in short, on an independent urge, and he sees this urge as the really crucial motive behind the development of the ego.

Like Kardiner, Mittelmann does not attempt to formulate in detail the nature of the motility urge. It is likened not to an instinct but to a "partial instinct," and this seems to place it somewhere between Hendrick's instinct to master and Hartmann's dimly sketched independent energies of the ego. This indefiniteness may irk the systematic theorist, but Mittelmann's account of the part played by motility in ego development easily stands as a significant contribution. Even more influential in this respect is the work of Erikson (1953), who has given a highly detailed timetable of ego development. Erikson stays with the libido theory as far as it will go, but he passes beyond its reach in his account of the latency period and some of the later crises of growth. It is clear that something more than the orthodox instincts is involved in the "enormous value" with which the child in the second year "begins to endow his autonomous will." Something more would seem to be implied in the expanding imagination and initiative of the "phallic" child. Certainly more is involved during the school years, when children address themselves to motor, manual, and intellectual achievements and need "a sense of being able to make things and make them well and even perfectly: this is what I call the *sense of industry*." Erikson's (1952) theory of play is also in-

fluenced by the idea that learning to deal with the animate and inanimate worlds is an important preoccupation of childhood: "the playing child advances forward to new stages of real mastery." Action systems, motility, and a sense of industry all direct our attention to behavior which can scarcely be contained in the old bottle of instinct theory.

Glancing back over these trends in psychoanalytic ego psychology, we cannot fail to be impressed by striking similarities to the trend in animal work. Using Reik's familiar metaphor, we might say that those who listen with their two ears and those who listen with the third ear have apparently been hearing much the same sounds. In both realms there is discontent with drive orthodoxy. In both there is persistent pointing to kinds of behavior neglected or explained away by drive orthodoxy: exploration, activity, manipulation, and mastery. Similar theories have been proposed to account for the energies in such behavior: (*a*) they are derived or transformed in some way from the primary drives or instincts (secondary reinforcement, neutralization of drive energies); (*b*) they are powered by the need to reduce anxiety; (*c*) they can be accounted for only by postulating a new primary drive (exploratory drive, instinct to master). When these explanations are considered to have failed, the one remaining course is to work out a different idea of motivation. In his study of action systems, Kardiner prefers to leave the question of energy sources unanswered, but Erikson's sense of industry and Mittelmann's motility urge point to a motivational base which is only remotely analogous to primary drives or fundamental instincts. I believe that the difficulties in this undertaking can be greatly reduced by the concept of competence, to which we shall shortly turn.

RELATED DEVELOPMENTS IN GENERAL PSYCHOLOGY

If a systematic survey were in order, it would be easy to show a parallel drift of opinion in other parts of the psychological realm. Among theorists of personality, for example, something like drive orthodoxy is to be found in the work of Dollard and Miller (1950), who have translated the main concepts of Freud's psychoanalysis, including processes such as repression and displacement, into the language of reinforcement theory. With them we might put Mowrer (1950), whose searching analysis of fear as an acquired drive has led him to postulate anxiety-reduction as the master motive behind the development of the ego. Discontent with drive orthodoxy has long been expressed by Allport (1937,

1946), who not only argues for a functional autonomy of motives from their infantile roots in primary drives but also seriously questions the law of effect, the very cornerstone of reinforcement theory. Little comfort for the orthodox can be found in Murray's (1938) detailed taxonomy of needs, especially when it comes to needs such as achievement and construction, which can be tied to primary drives only by conceptual acrobatics. Murray and Kluckhohn (1953), moreover, have made a case for pleasure in activity for its own sake, reviving the *Funktionslust* proposed many years ago by Karl Bühler (1924) and recently developed in some detail by French (1952). They also argue for intrinsic mental needs: "the infant's mind is not acting most of the time as the instrument of some urgent animal drive, but is preoccupied with *gratifying itself.*" Murphy (1947) takes the view that all tissues can become seats of tension and thus participants in drive; in addition to visceral drives, he postulates two independent forms, activity drives and sensory drives. Then there are workers such as Goldstein (1939) who approach the whole problem with a holistic philosophy which precludes the dictatorship of any isolated or partial drives. Goldstein (1940) assumes one master tendency, that toward self-actualization, of which the so-called visceral drives are but partial and not really isolated expressions, and which can find expression also in an urge toward perfection — toward completing what is incomplete, whether it be an outside task or the mastery of some function such as walking. It has been shown by the Ansbachers (1956) that Adler, never a friend of instinct orthodoxy, in his later years reached an idea very similar to the urge toward perfection. Maslow (1954, 1955), too, belongs with the heterodox. He insists that we should take account of growth motivation as well as the deficiency motivation implied in the visceral drives, and he offers the valuable idea of a hierarchy of motives, according to which the satisfaction of "lower" needs makes it possible for "higher" needs to emerge and become regnant in behavior.

Mention of these names must suffice here to show that the trends observed in animal psychology and psychoanalytic ego psychology are pervasive in contemporary psychological thought. Doubtless the same controversies and problems could be pointed out in child development, in cognitive psychology, and in other fields. But in order to advance to my main theme, I shall select only certain developments which bear directly on the concept of competence.

Needs for Excitement and Novelty

Human experience provides plentiful evidence of the importance of reducing excessive levels of tension. Men under wartime stress, men under pressure of pain and extreme deprivation, men with excessive work loads or too much exposure to confusing social interactions, all act as if their nervous systems craved that utterly unstimulated condition which Freud once sketched as the epitome of neural bliss. But if these same men be granted their Nirvana they soon become miserable and begin to look around for a little excitement. Human experience testifies that boredom is a bad state of affairs about which something must be done. Hebb (1949) has been particularly insistent in reminding us that many of our activities, such as reading detective stories, skindiving, or driving cars at high speeds, give clear evidence of a need to raise the level of stimulation and excitement. Men and animals alike seem at times bent on increasing the impact of the environment and even on creating mild degrees of frustration and fear. Hebb and Thompson (1954) reflect upon this as follows:

> Such phenomena are, of course, well known in man: in the liking for dangerous sports or roller coasters, where fear is deliberately courted, and in the addiction to bridge or golf or solitaire, vices whose very existence depends upon the level of difficulty of the problems presented and an optimal level of frustration. Once more, when we find such attitudes toward fear and frustration in animals, we have a better basis for supposing that we are dealing with something fundamental if a man prefers skis to the less dangerous snowshoes, or when we observe an unashamed love of work (problem solving and frustration included) in the scientist, or in the business man who cannot retire. Such behavior in man is usually accounted for as a search for prestige, but the animal data make this untenable. It seems much more likely that solving problems and running mild risks are inherently rewarding, or, in more general terms, that the animal will always act so as to produce an optimal level of excitation (Hebb & Thompson, 1954, p. 551).

The concept of optimal stimulation has been developed by Leuba (1955), who sees it as helpful in resolving some of the problems of learning theory. Believing that most theorizing about motivation has been based upon "powerful biological or neurotic drives," Leuba bids us look at the much more common learning situations of nursery, playground, and school, where "actions which increase stimulation and produce excitement are strongly reinforced, sometimes to the dismay of parents and teachers." He proposes that there is an optimal level of stimulation, subject to variation at different times, and that learning is associated with movement toward this optimal level, downward when stimulation is too high and upward when it is too low. A similar idea is expressed by McReynolds (1956) concerning the more restricted concept of "rate of perceptualization." Monotonous conditions provide too low a rate, with boredom; excessive stimulation produces too high a rate, with disruptive excitement; the optimal rate yields the experience of pleasure. These ideas are now amply supported by recent experimental work on sensory deprivation (Lilly, 1956; Hebb, 1958).

In recent papers Young (1949, 1955) has argued for an hedonic theory of motivation, one in which affective processes "constitute a form of primary motivation." According to Young's theory, "an organism behaves so as to maximize positive affective arousal (delight, enjoyment) and to minimize negative arousal (distress)." McClelland (1953) has offered a version of hedonic theory which is of particular value in understanding the significance of novelty. Affective arousal occurs when a stimulus pattern produces a discrepancy from the existing adaptation level. Small discrepancies produce pleasant affect and a tendency to approach; large ones produce unpleasantness and a tendency toward avoidance. The child at play, like the young chimpanzee and the exploring rat, needs frequent novelty in the stimulus field in order to keep up his interest — in order to maintain pleasant discrepancies from whatever adaptation level he has reached. Hebb's (1949) theory of the neurological correlates of learning also deals with novelty, though in a somewhat different way. He equates sustained interest with a state of neural affairs in which "phase sequences" are relatively complex and are growing, in the sense of establishing new internal relations. Such a state follows most readily from a stimulus field characterized by difference-in-sameness; that is, containing much that is familiar along with certain features that are novel. If the field is entirely familiar, phase sequences run off quickly, are short-circuited, and thus fail to produce sustained interest. Hebb's theory, which has the engaging quality of being able to explain why we enjoy reading a detective story once but not right over again, expresses in a neurological hypothesis the familiar fact that well-learned, habituated processes do not in themselves greatly interest us. Interest seems to require elements of unfamiliarity: of something still to be found out and of learning still to be done.

It seems to me that these contributions, though differing as to details, speak with unanimity on their central theme and would force us, if nothing else did, to reconsider seriously the whole problem of motivation. Boredom, the unpleasantness of monotony, the attraction of novelty, the tendency to vary behavior rather than repeating it rigidly, and the seeking of stimulation and mild excitement stand as inescapable facts of human experience and clearly have their parallels in animal behavior. We may seek rest and minimal stimulation at the end of the day, but that is not what we are looking for the next morning. Even when its primary needs are satisfied and its homeostatic chores are done, an organism is alive, active, and up to something.

Dealing with the Environment

If we consider things only from the viewpoint of affect, excitement, and novelty, we are apt to overlook another important aspect of behavior, its effect upon the environment. Moving in this direction, Diamond (1939) invites us to consider the motivational properties of the sensorineural system, the apparatus whereby higher animals "maintain their relations to the environment." He conceives of this system as demanding stimulation and as acting in such a manner as to "force the environment to stimulate it." Even if one thinks only of the infant's exploring eyes and hands, it is clear that the main direction of behavior is by no means always that of reducing the impact of stimulation. When the eyes follow a moving object, or when the hand grasps an object which it has touched, the result is to preserve the stimulus and to increase its effect. In more elaborate explorations the consequence of a series of actions may be to vary the manner in which a stimulus acts upon the sense organs. It is apparent that the exploring, manipulating child produces by his actions precisely what Hebb's theory demands as a basis for continuing interest: he produces differences-in-sameness in the stimulus field.

In a critical analysis of Freud's views on the reality principle, Charlotte Bühler (1954) makes a strong case for positive interests in the environment, citing as evidence the responsiveness and adaptiveness of the new-born baby as well as the exploratory tendencies of later months. The problem is worked out in more detail by Schachtel (1954) in a paper on focal attention. Acts of focal attention are characteristically directed at particular objects, and they consist of several sustained approaches "aimed at active mental grasp" while excluding the rest of the field. These qualities can be observed even in the infant's early attempts to follow a moving object with his eyes, and they show more clearly in his later endeavors to learn how objects are related both to himself and to one another. Such behavior bespeaks "a relatively autonomous capacity for object interest." Schachtel makes the proposal that this interest is pursued precisely at those times when major needs are in abeyance. High pressure of need or anxiety is the enemy of exploratory play and is a condition, as every scientist should know, under which we are unlikely to achieve an objective grasp of the environment. Low need pressure is requisite if we are to perceive objects as they are, in their constant character, apart from hopes and fears we may at other times attach to them. Schachtel doubts that "the wish for need-satisfaction alone would ever lead to object perception and to object-oriented thought." Hence an autonomous capacity to be interested in the environment has great value for the survival of a species.

Being interested in the environment implies having some kind of satisfactory interaction with it. Several workers call attention to the possibility that satisfaction might lie in having an effect upon the environment, in dealing with it, and changing it in various ways. Groos (1901), in his classical analysis of play, attached great importance to the child's "joy in being a cause," as shown in making a clatter, "hustling things about," and playing in puddles where large and dramatic effects can be produced. "We demand a knowledge of effects," he wrote, "and to be ourselves the producers of effects." Piaget (1952) remarks upon the child's special interest in objects that are affected by his own movements. This aspect of behavior occupies a central place in the work of Skinner (1953), who describes it as "operant" and who thus "emphasizes the fact that the behavior *operates* upon the environment to generate consequences." These consequences are fed back through the sense organs and may serve to reinforce behavior even when no organic needs are involved. A rat will show an increased tendency to press a bar when this act produces a click or a buzz. A baby will continue to investigate when his efforts produce rattling or tinkling sounds or sparkling reflections from a shiny object. The young chimpanzees in Welker's experiment spent the longest time over objects which could be lighted or made to emit sounds. Skinner finds it "difficult, if not impossible, to trace these reinforcing effects to a history of conditioning." "We may plausibly argue," he continues, "that a capacity to be reinforced by any feedback from the environment would be biologically advantageous, since it would prepare the organism to manipulate the environment successfully before a given state of deprivation developed."

Woodworth's Behavior-Primacy Theory

The most far-reaching attempt to give these aspects of behavior a systematic place in the theory of motivation is contained in Woodworth's recent book, *Dynamics of Behavior* (1958). Woodworth takes his start from the idea that a great deal of human behavior appears to be directed toward producing effects upon the environment without immediate service to any aroused organic need. "Its incentives and rewards are in the field of behavior and not in the field of homeostasis." This is illustrated by exploratory behavior, which is directed outward toward the environment.

> Its long-range value as the means of making the child acquainted with the world he has to deal with later, and so equipping him through play for the serious business of life, can scarcely lie within the little child's horizon. His goals are more limited and direct: to see this or that object more closely, to find what is behind an obstacle, to hear the noise an object makes when it strikes the floor, to be told the name of a thing or person (Woodworth, 1958, p. 78).

More complex play, such as building with blocks, illustrates the same outgoing tendency and reveals more plainly the element of finding out what one can and cannot do with objects. Even social play falls into the pattern. Playmates do not chiefly supply affection or satisfy organic needs; rather, they "afford the opportunity to do something interesting in the environment."

Woodworth draws a contrast between *need-primacy* theories of motivation and the *behavior-primacy* theory. The latter holds that "all behavior is directed primarily toward dealing with the environment." It is to be noted that "dealing with the environment" means a good deal more than receiving stimuli and making responses. Stimuli must be taken as indicators of objects in space, and responses must be adapted to produce effects upon these objects. Even the so-called "mental" capacities, such as memory and ideational thinking, become in time high-level methods of dealing with the environment. Woodworth leaves no doubt as to what he considers basic in motivation. "We are making the claim that this direction of receptive and motor activity toward the environment is the fundamental tendency of animal and human behavior and that it is the all-pervasive primary motivation of behavior." Organic drives have to break into this constantly flowing stream of activity and turn it in a special direction. But the goals of drives cannot be achieved without effective action upon one's surroundings. The ever-present, ever-primary feature of motivation is the tendency to deal with the environment.

It may appear to some workers that Woodworth has overshot the mark by making primary what has commonly been regarded as secondary, and by reducing the familiar drives to what sounds a little like a subordinate station. Woodworth's theory, however, like Goldstein's concept of self-actualization, probably should be construed not as an attempt to down-grade the drives but rather as an insistence that they be kept in the context of a whole living organism which during its waking hours is more or less constantly active. Woodworth's emphasis on dealing with the environment makes his theory a point of culmination for many of those driftings away from drive orthodoxy which we have found to be persistent in so many different areas of psychology. It will soon appear that the concept of competence, to which I now turn, represents in many respects a similar way of thinking. It emphasizes dealing with the environment, and it belongs in the trend away from drive *orthodoxy*, but it is not intended to supplant, or even to subsume, such dynamic forces as hunger, sex, aggression, and fear, which everyone knows to be of huge importance in animal and human nature.

COMPETENCE AND THE PLAY OF CONTENTED CHILDREN

A backward glance at our survey shows considerable agreement about the kinds of behavior that are left out or handled poorly by theories of motivation based wholly on organic drives. Repeatedly we find reference to the familiar series of learned skills which starts with sucking, grasping, and visual exploration and continues with crawling and walking, acts of focal attention and perception, memory, language and thinking, anticipation, the exploring of novel places and objects, effecting stimulus changes in the environment, manipulating and exploiting the surroundings, and achieving higher levels of motor and mental coordination. These aspects of behavior have long been the province of child psychology, which has attempted to measure the slow course of their development and has shown how heavily their growth depends upon learning. Collectively they are sometimes referred to as adaptive mechanisms or as ego processes, but on the whole we are not accustomed to cast a single name over the diverse feats whereby we learn to deal with the environment.

I now propose that we gather the various kinds of behavior just mentioned, all of which have to do with effective interaction with the environment, under the general heading of competence. According to Webster, competence means fitness or ability, and the suggested synonyms include capability, capacity, efficiency, proficiency, and skill. It is therefore a suitable word to describe such things as grasping and exploring, crawling and walking, attention and perception, language and thinking, manipulating and changing the surroundings, all of which promote an effective — a competent — interaction with the environment. It is true, of course, that maturation plays a part in all these developments, but this part is heavily overshadowed by learning in all the more complex accomplishments like speech or skilled manipulation. I shall argue that it is necessary to make competence a motivational concept; there is a *competence motivation* as well as competence in its more familiar sense of achieved capacity. The behavior that leads to the building up of effective grasping, handling, and letting go of objects, to take one example, is not random behavior produced by a general overflow of energy. It is directed, selective, and persistent, and it is continued not because it serves primary drives, which indeed it cannot serve until it is almost perfected, but because it satisfies an intrinsic need to deal with the environment.

No doubt it will at first seem arbitrary to propose a single motivational conception in connection with so many and such diverse kinds of behavior. What do we gain by attributing motivational unity to such a large array of activities? We could, of course, say that each developmental sequence, such as learning to grasp or to walk, has its own built-in bit of motivation — its "aliment," as Piaget (1952) has expressed it. We could go further and say that each item of behavior has its intrinsic motive — but this makes the concept of motivation redundant. On the other hand, we might follow the lead of the animal psychologists and postulate a limited number of broader motives under such names as curiosity, manipulation, and mastery. I believe that the idea of a competence motivation is more adequate than any of these alternatives and that it points to very vital common properties which have been lost from view amidst the strongly analytical tendencies that go with detailed research.

In order to make this claim more plausible, I shall now introduce some specimens of playful exploration in early childhood. I hope that these images will serve to fix and dramatize the concept of competence in the same way that other images — the hungry animal solving problems, the child putting his finger in the candle flame, the infant at the breast, the child on the toilet, and the youthful Oedipus caught in a hopeless love triangle — have become memorable focal points for other concepts. For this purpose I turn to Piaget's (1952) studies of the growth of intelligence from its earliest manifestations in his own three children. The examples come from the first year of life, before language and verbal concepts begin to be important. They therefore represent a practical kind of intelligence which may be quite similar to what is developed by the higher animals.

As early as the fourth month, the play of the gifted Piaget children began to be "centered on a result produced in the external environment," and their behavior could be described as rediscovering the movement which by chance exercised an advantageous action upon things" (1952, p. 151). Laurent, lying in his bassinet, learns to shake a suspended rattle by pulling a string that hangs from it. He discovers this result fortuitously before vision and prehension are fully coordinated. Let us now observe him a little later when he has reached the age of three months and ten days.

> I place the string, which is attached to the rattle, in his right hand, merely unrolling it a little so that he may grasp it better. For a moment nothing happens. But at the first shake due to chance movement of his hand, the reaction is immediate: Laurent starts when looking at the rattle and then violently strikes his right hand alone, as if he felt the resistance and the effect. The operation lasts fully a quarter of an hour, during which Laurent emits peals of laughter (Piaget, 1952, p. 162).

Three days later the following behavior is observed.

> Laurent, by chance, strikes the chain while sucking his fingers. He grasps it and slowly displaces it while looking at the rattles. He then begins to swing it very gently, which produces a slight movement of the hanging rattles and an as yet faint sound inside them. Laurent then definitely increases by degrees his own movements. He shakes the chain more and more vigorously and laughs uproariously at the result obtained. (Piaget, 1952, p. 185).

Very soon it can be observed that procedures are used "to make interesting spectacles last." For instance, Laurent is shown a rubber monkey which he has not seen before. After a moment of surprise, and perhaps even fright, he calms down and makes movements of pulling the string, a procedure which has no effect in this case, but which previously has caused interesting things to happen. It is to be noticed that "interesting spectacles" consist of such things as new toys, a tin box upon which a drumming noise can be made, an unfolded newspaper, or sounds made by the observer such as snapping the fingers.

Commonplace as they are to the adult mind, these spectacles enter the infant's experience as novel and apparently challenging events.

Moving ahead to the second half of the first year, we can observe behavior in which the child explores the properties of objects and tries out his repertory of actions upon them. This soon leads to active experimentation in which the child attempts to provoke new results. Again we look in upon Laurent, who has now reached the age of nine months. On different occasions he is shown a variety of new objects— for instance a notebook, a beaded purse, and a wooden parrot. His carefully observing father detects four stages of response: (*a*) visual exploration, passing the object from hand to hand, folding the purse, *etc.*; (*b*) tactile exploration, passing the hand all over the object, scratching, *etc.*; (*c*) slow moving of the object in space; (*d*) use of the repertory of action: shaking the object, striking it, swinging it, rubbing it against the side of the bassinet, sucking it, *etc.*, "each in turn with a sort of prudence as though studying the effect produced" (1952, p. 255).

Here the child can be described as applying familiar tactics to new situations, but in a short while he will advance to clear patterns of active experimentation. At 10 months and 10 days Laurent, who is unfamiliar with bread as a nutritive substance, is given a piece for examination. He manipulates it, drops it many times, breaks off fragments and lets them fall. He has often done this kind of thing before, but previously his attention has seemed to be centered on the act of letting go. Now "he watches with great interest the body in motion; in particular, he looks at it for a long time when it has fallen, and picks it up when he can." On the following day he resumes his research.

> He grasps in succession a celluloid swan, a box, and several other small objects, in each case stretching out his arm and letting them fall. Sometimes he stretches out his arm vertically, sometimes he holds it obliquely in front of or behind his eyes. When the object falls in a new position (for example on his pillow) he lets it fall two or three times more on the same place, as though to study the spatial relation; then he modifies the situation. At a certain moment the swan falls near his mouth; now he does not suck it (even though this object habitually serves this purpose), but drops it three times more while merely making the gesture of opening his mouth (Piaget, 1952, p. 269).

These specimens will furnish us with sufficient images of the infant's use of his spare time. Laurent, of course, was provided by his studious father with a decidedly enriched environment, but no observant parent will question the fact that babies often act this way during those periods of their waking life when hunger, erotic needs, distresses, and anxiety seem to be exerting no particular pressure. If we consider this behavior under the historic headings of psychology we shall see that few processes are missing. The child gives evidence of sensing, perceiving, attending, learning, recognizing, probably recalling, and perhaps thinking in a rudimentary way. Strong emotion is lacking, but the infant's smiles, gurgles, and occasional peals of laughter strongly suggest the presence of pleasant affect. Actions appear in an organized form, particularly in the specimens of active exploration and experimentation. Apparently the child is using with a certain coherence nearly the whole repertory of psychological processes except those that accompany stress. It would be arbitrary indeed to say that one was more important than another.

These specimens have a meaningful unity when seen as transactions between the child and his environment, the child having some influence upon the environment and the environment some influence upon the child. Laurent appears to be concerned about what he can do with the chain and rattles, what he can accomplish by his own effort to reproduce and to vary the entertaining sounds. If his father observed correctly, we must add that Laurent seems to have varied his actions systematically, as if testing the effect of different degrees of effort upon the bit of environment represented by the chain and rattles. Kittens make a similar study of parameters when delicately using their paws to push pencils and other objects ever nearer to the edge of one's desk. In all such examples it is clear that the child or animal is by no means at the mercy of transient stimulus fields. He selects for continuous treatment those aspects of his environment which he finds it possible to affect in some way. His behavior is selective, directed, persistent — in short, motivated.

Motivated toward what goal? In these terms, too, the behavior exhibits a little of everything. Laurent can be seen as appeasing a stimulus hunger, providing his sensorium with an agreeable level of stimulation by eliciting from the environment a series of interesting sounds, feels, and sights. On the other hand we might emphasize a need for activity and see him as trying to reach a pleasurable level of neuro-muscular exercise. We can also see another possible goal in the behavior: the child is achieving knowledge, attaining a more differentiated cognitive map of his environment and thus satisfying an exploratory tendency or motive of curiosity. But it is equally possible to discern a theme of mastery, power, or control, perhaps even a bit of primitive self-assertion, in the child's concentration upon those aspects of the environment which respond in some way to his own activity. It looks as if we had found too many goals, and perhaps our first impulse is to search for some key to tell us which one is really important. But this, I think, is a mistake that would be fatal to understanding.

We cannot assign priority to any of these goals without pausing arbitrarily in the cycle of transaction between child and environment and saying, "This is the real point." I propose instead that the real point is the transactions as a whole. If the behavior gives satisfaction, this satisfaction is not associated with a particular moment in the cycle. It does not lie solely in sensory stimulation, in a bettering of the cognitive map, in coordinated action, in motor exercise, in the feeling of effort and of effects produced, or in the appreciation of change brought about in the sensory field. These are all simply aspects of a process which at this stage has to be conceived as a whole. The child appears to be occupied with the agreeable task of developing an effective familiarity with his environment. This involves discovering the effects he can have on the environment and the effects the environment will have on him. To the extent that these results are preserved by learning, they build up an increased competence in dealing with the environment. The child's play can thus be viewed as serious business, though to him it is merely something that is interesting and fun to do.

Bearing in mind these examples, as well as the dealings with environment pointed out by other workers, we must now attempt to describe more fully the possible nature of the motivational aspect of competence. It needs its own name, and in view of the foregoing analysis I propose that this name be *effectance*.

EFFECTANCE

The new freedom produced by two decades of research on animal drives is of great help in this undertaking. We are no longer obliged to look for a source of energy external to the nervous system, for a consummatory climax, or for a fixed connection between reinforcement and tension-reduction. Effectance motivation cannot, of course, be conceived as having a source in tissues external to the nervous system. It is in no sense a deficit motive. We must assume it to be neurogenic, its "energies" being simply those of the living cells that make up the nervous system. External stimuli play an important part, but in terms of "energy" this part is secondary, as one can see most clearly when environmental stimulation is actively sought. Putting it picturesquely, we might say that the effectance urge represents what the neuromuscular system wants to do when it is otherwise unoccupied or is gently stimulated by the environment. Obviously there are no consummatory acts; satisfaction would appear to lie in the arousal and maintaining of activity rather than in its slow decline toward bored passivity. The motive need not be conceived as intense and powerful in the sense that hunger, pain, or fear can be powerful when aroused to high pitch. There are plenty of instances in which children refuse to leave their absorbed play in order to eat or to visit the toilet. Strongly aroused drives, pain, and anxiety, however, can be conceived as overriding the effectance urge and capturing the energies of the neuromuscular system. But effectance motivation is persistent in the sense that it regularly occupies the spare waking time between episodes of homeostatic crisis.

In speculating upon this subject we must bear in mind the continuous nature of behavior. This is easier said than done; habitually we break things down in order to understand them, and such units as the reflex arc, the stimulus-response sequence, and the single transaction with the environment seem like inevitable steps toward clarity. Yet when we apply such an analysis to playful exploration we lose the most essential aspect of the behavior. It is constantly circling from stimulus to perception to action to effect to stimulus to perception, and so on around; or, more properly, these processes are all in continuous action and continuous change. Dealing with the environment means carrying on a continuing transaction which gradually changes one's relation to the environment. Because there is no consummatory climax, satisfaction has to be seen as lying in a considerable series of transactions, in a trend of behavior rather than a goal that is achieved. It is difficult to make the word "satisfaction" have this connotation, and we shall do well to replace it by "feeling of efficacy" when attempting to indicate the subjective and affective side of effectance.

It is useful to recall the findings about novelty: the singular effectiveness of novelty in engaging interest and for a time supporting persistent behavior. We also need to consider the selective continuance of transactions in which the animal or child has a more or less pronounced effect upon the environment — in which something happens as a consequence of his activity. Interest is not aroused and sustained when the stimulus field is so familiar that it gives rise at most to reflex acts or automatized habits. It is not sustained when actions produce no

effects or changes in the stimulus field. Our conception must therefore be that effectance motivation is aroused by stimulus conditions which offer, as Hebb (1949) puts it, difference-in-sameness. This leads to variability and novelty of response, and interest is best sustained when the resulting action affects the stimulus so as to produce further difference-in-sameness. Interest wanes when action begins to have less effect; effectance motivation subsides when a situation has been explored to the point that it no longer presents new possibilities.

We have to conceive further that the arousal of playful and exploratory interest means the appearance of organization involving both the cognitive and active aspects of behavior. Change in the stimulus field is not an end in itself, so to speak; it happens when one is passively moved about, and it may happen as a consequence of random movements without becoming focalized and instigating exploration. Similarly, action which has effects is not an end in itself, for if one unintentionally kicks away a branch while walking, or knocks something off a table, these effects by no means necessarily become involved in playful investigation. Schachtel's (1954) emphasis on focal attention becomes helpful at this point. The playful and exploratory behavior shown by Laurent is not random or casual. It involves focal *attention* to some object — the fixing of some aspect of the stimulus field so that it stays relatively constant — and it also involves the focalizing of *action* upon this object. As Diamond (1939) has expressed it, response under these conditions is "relevant to the stimulus," and it is change in the *focalized* stimulus that so strongly affects the level of interest. Dealing with the environment means directing focal attention to some part of it and organizing actions to have some effect on this part.

In our present state of relative ignorance about the workings of the nervous system it is impossible to form a satisfactory idea of the neural basis of effectance motivation, but it should at least be clear that the concept does not refer to any and every kind of neural action. It refers to a particular kind of activity, as inferred from particular kinds of behavior. We can say that it does not include reflexes and other kinds of automatic response. It does not include well-learned, automatized patterns, even those that are complex and highly organized. It does not include behavior in the service of effectively aroused drives. It does not even include activity that is highly random and discontinuous, though such behavior may be its most direct fore-runner. The urge toward competence is inferred specifically from behavior that shows a lasting focalization and that has the characteristics of exploration and experimentation, a kind of variation within the focus. When this particular sort of activity is aroused in the nervous system, effectance motivation is being aroused, for it is characteristic of this particular sort of activity that it is selective, directed, and persistent, and that instrumental acts will be learned for the sole reward of engaging in it.

Some objection may be felt to my introducing the word *competence* in connection with behavior that is so often playful. Certainly the playing child is doing things for fun, not because of a desire to improve his competence in dealing with the stern hard world. In order to forestall misunderstanding, it should be pointed out that the usage here is parallel to what we do when we connect sex with its biological goal of reproduction. The sex drive aims for pleasure and gratification, and reproduction is a consequence that is presumably unforeseen by animals and by man at primitive levels of understanding. Effectance motivation similarly aims for the feeling of efficacy, not for the vitally important learnings that come as its consequence. If we consider the part played by competence motivation in adult human life we can observe the same parallel. Sex may now be completely and purposefully divorced from reproduction but nevertheless pursued for the pleasure it can yield. Similarly, effectance motivation may lead to continuing exploratory interests or active adventures when in fact there is no longer any gain in actual competence or any need for it in terms of survival. In both cases the motive is capable of yielding surplus satisfaction well beyond what is necessary to get the biological work done.

In infants and young children it seems to me sensible to conceive of effectance motivation as undifferentiated. Later in life it becomes profitable to distinguish various motives such as cognizance, construction, mastery, and achievement. It is my view that all such motives have a root in effectance motivation. They are differentiated from it through life experiences which emphasize one or another aspect of the cycle of transaction with environment. Of course, the motives of later childhood and of adult life are no longer simple and can almost never be referred to a single root. They can acquire loadings of anxiety, defense, and compensation, they can become fused with unconscious fantasies of a sexual, aggressive, or omnipotent character, and they can gain force because of their service in producing realistic results in the way of income and career. It is not my intention to cast effectance in the star part in adult motivation. The acquisition of motives is a complicated affair in which simple and sovereign theories grow daily more obsolete. Yet it may be that the satisfaction of effectance contributes significantly to those feelings of interest which often sustain us so well in day-to-day actions, particularly when the things we are doing have continuing elements of novelty.

THE BIOLOGICAL SIGNIFICANCE OF COMPETENCE

The conviction was expressed at the beginning of this paper that some such concept as competence, interpreted motivationally, was essential for any biologically sound view of human nature. This necessity emerges when we consider the nature of living systems, particularly when we take a longitudinal view. What an organism does at a given moment does not always give the right clue as to what it does over a period of time. Discussing this problem, Angyal (1941) has proposed that we should look for the general pattern followed by the total organismic process over the course of time. Obviously this makes it necessary to take account of growth. Angyal defines life as "a process of self-expansion;" the living system "expands at the expense of its surroundings," assimilating parts of the environment and transforming them into functioning parts of itself. Organisms differ from other things in nature in that they are "self-governing entities" which are to some extent "autonomous." Internal processes govern them as well as external "heteronomous" forces. In the course of life there is a relative increase in the preponderance of internal over external forces. The living system expands, assimilates more of the environment, transforms its surroundings so as to bring them under greater control. "We may say," Angyal writes, "that the general dynamic trend of the organism is toward an increase of autonomy. . . . The human being has a characteristic tendency toward self-determination, that is, a tendency to resist external influences and to subordinate the heteronomous forces of the physical and social environment to its own sphere of influence." The trend toward increased autonomy is characteristic so long as growth of any kind is going on, though in the end the living system is bound to succumb to the pressure of heteronomous forces.

Of all living creatures, it is man who takes the longest strides toward autonomy. This is not because of any unusual tendency toward bodily expansion at the expense of the environment. It is rather that man, with his mobile hands and abundantly developed brain, attains an extremely high level of competence in his transactions with his surroundings.

The building of houses, roads and bridges, the making of tools and instruments, the domestication of plants and animals, all qualify as planful changes made in the environment so that it comes more or less under control and serves our purposes rather than intruding upon them. We meet the fluctuations of outdoor temperature, for example, not only with our bodily homeostatic mechanisms, which alone would be painfully unequal to the task, but also with clothing, buildings, controlled fires, and such complicated devices as self-regulating central heating and air conditioning. Man as a species has developed a tremendous power of bringing the environment into his service, and each individual member of the species must attain what is really quite an impressive level of competence if he is to take part in the life around him.

We are so accustomed to these human accomplishments that it is hard to realize how long an apprenticeship they require. At the outset the human infant is a slow learner in comparison with other animal forms. Hebb (1949) speaks of "the astonishing inefficiency of man's first learning, as far as immediate results are concerned," an inefficiency which he attributes to the large size of the association areas in the brain and the long time needed to bring them under sensory control. The human lack of precocity in learning shows itself even in comparison with one of the next of kin: as Hebb points out, "the human baby takes six months, the chimpanzee four months, before making a clear distinction between friend and enemy." Later in life the slow start will pay dividends. Once the fundamental perceptual elements, simple associations, and conceptual sequences have been established, later learning can proceed with ever increasing swiftness and complexity. In Hebb's words, "learning at maturity concerns patterns and events whose parts at least are familiar and which already have a number of other associations."

This general principle of cumulative learning, starting from slowly acquired rudiments and proceeding thence with increasing efficiency, can be illustrated by such processes as manipulation and locomotion, which may culminate in the acrobat devising new stunts or the dancer working out a new ballet. It is especially vivid in the case of language, where the early mastery of words and pronunciation seems such a far cry from spontaneous adult speech. A strong argument has been made by Hebb (1949) that the learning of visual forms proceeds over a similar course from slowly learned elements to rapidly combined patterns. Circles and squares, for example, cannot be discriminated at a glance without a slow apprenticeship involving eye movements, successive fixations, and recognition of angles. Hebb proposes that the recognition of visual patterns without eye movement "is possible only as the result of an intensive and prolonged visual training that goes on from the moment of birth, during every moment that the eyes are open, with an increase in skill evident over a period of 12 to 16 years at least."

On the motor side there is likewise a lot to be cumulatively learned. The playing, investigating child slowly finds out the relationships between what he does and what he experiences. He finds out, for instance, how hard he must push what in order to produce what effect. Here the S-R formula is particularly misleading. It would come nearer the truth to say that the child is busy learning R-S connections — the effects that are likely to follow upon his own behavior. But even in this reversed form the notion of bonds or connections would still misrepresent the situation, for it is only a rare specimen of behavior that can properly be conceived as determined by fixed neural channels and a fixed motor response. As Hebb has pointed out, discussing the phenomenon of "motor equivalence" named by Lashley (1942), a rat which has been trained to press a lever will press it with the left forepaw, the right forepaw, by climbing upon it, or by biting it; a monkey will open the lid of a food box with either hand, with a foot, or even with a stick; and we might add that a good baseball player can catch a fly ball while running in almost any direction and while in almost any posture, including leaping in the air and plunging forward to the ground. All of these feats are possible because of a history of learnings in which the main lesson has been the effects of actions upon the stimulus fields that represent the environment. What has been learned is not a fixed connection but a flexible relationship between stimulus fields and the effects that can be produced in them by various kinds of action.

One additional example, drawn this time from Piaget (1952), is particularly worth mentioning because of its importance in theories of development. Piaget points out that a great deal of mental development depends upon the idea that the world is made up of objects having substance and permanence. Without such an "object concept" it would be impossible to build up the ideas of space and causality and to arrive at the fundamental distinction between self and external world. Observation shows that the object concept, "far from being innate or ready-made in experience, is constructed little by little." Up to 7 and 8 months the Piaget children searched for vanished objects only in the sense of trying to continue the actions, such as sucking or grasping, in which the objects had played a part. When an object was really out of sight or touch, even if only because it was covered by a cloth, the infants undertook no further exploration. Only gradually, after some study of the displacement of objects by moving, swinging, and dropping them, does the child begin to make an active search for a vanished object, and only still more gradually does he learn, at 12 months or more, to make allowance for the object's sequential displacements and thus to seek it where it has gone rather than where it was last in sight. Thus it is only through cumulative learning that the child arrives at the idea of permanent substantial objects.

The infant's play is indeed serious business. If he did not while away his time pulling strings, shaking rattles, examining wooden parrots, dropping pieces of bread and celluloid swans, when would he learn to discriminate visual patterns, to catch and throw, and to build up his concept of the object? When would he acquire the many other foundation stones necessary for cumulative learning? The more closely we analyze the behavior of the human infant, the more clearly do we realize that infancy is not simply a time when the nervous system matures and the muscles grow stronger. It is a time of active and continuous learning, during which the basis is laid for all those processes, cognitive and motor, whereby the child becomes able to establish effective transactions with his environment and move toward a greater degree of autonomy. Helpless as he may seem until he begins to toddle, he has by that time already made substantial gains in the achievement of competence.

Under primitive conditions survival must depend quite heavily upon achieved competence. We should expect to find things so arranged as to favor and maximize this achievement. Particularly in the case of man, where so little is provided innately and so much has to be learned through experience, we should expect to find highly advantageous arrangements for securing a steady cumulative learning about the properties of the environment and the extent of possible transactions. Under these circumstances we might expect to find a very powerful drive operating to insure progress toward competence, just as the vital goals of nutrition and reproduction are secured by powerful drives, and it might therefore seem paradoxical that the interests of competence should be so much entrusted to times of play and leisurely exploration. There is good reason to suppose, however, that a strong drive would be precisely the wrong arrangement to secure a flexible, knowledgeable power of transaction with the environment. Strong drives cause us to learn certain lessons well, but they do not create maximum familiarity with our surroundings.

This point was demonstrated half a century ago in some experiments by Yerkes and Dodson (1908). They showed that maximum motivation did not lead to the most rapid solving of problems, especially if the problems were complex. For each problem there was an optimum level of motivation, neither the highest nor the lowest, and the optimum was lower for more complex tasks. The same problem has been discussed more recently by Tolman (1948) in his paper on cognitive maps. A cognitive map can be narrow or broad, depending upon the range of cues picked up in the course of learning. Tolman suggests that one of the conditions which tend to narrow the range of cues is a high level of motivation. In everyday terms, a man hurrying to an important business conference is likely to perceive only the cues that help him to get there faster, whereas a man taking a stroll after lunch is likely to pick up a substantial amount of casual information about his environment. The latent learning experiments with animals, and experiments such as those of Johnson (1953) in which drive level has been systematically varied in a situation permitting incidental learning, give strong support to this general idea. In a recent contribution, Bruner, Matter, and Papanek (1955) make a strong case for the concept of breadth of learning and provide additional evidence that it is favored by moderate and hampered by strong motivation. The latter "has the effect of speeding up learning at the cost of narrowing it." Attention is concentrated upon the task at hand and little that is extraneous to this task is learned for future use.

These facts enable us to see the biological appropriateness of an arrangement which uses periods of less intense motivation for the development of competence. This is not to say that the narrower but efficient learnings that go with the reduction of strong drives make no contribution to general effectiveness. They are certainly an important element in capacity to deal with the environment, but a much greater effectiveness results from having this capacity fed also from learnings that take place in quieter times. It is then that the infant can attend to matters of lesser urgency, exploring the properties of things he does not fear and does not need to eat, learning to gauge the force of his string-pulling when the only penalty for failure is silence on the part of the attached rattles, and generally accumulating for himself a broad knowledge and a broad skill in dealing with his surroundings.

The concept of competence can be most easily discussed by choosing, as we have done, examples of interaction with the inanimate environment. It applies equally well, however, to transactions with animals and with other human beings, where the child has the same problem of finding out what effects he can have upon the environment and what effects it can have upon him. The earliest interactions with members of the family may involve needs so strong that they obscure the part played by effectance motivation, but perhaps the example of the well fed baby diligently exploring the several features of his mother's face will serve as a reminder that here, too, there are less urgent moments when learning for its own sake can be given free rein.

In this closing section I have brought together several ideas which bear on the evolutionary significance of competence and of its motivation. I have sought in this way to deepen the biological roots of the concept and thus help it to attain the stature in the theory of behavior which has not been reached by similar concepts in the past. To me it seems that the most important proving ground for this concept is the effect it may have on our understanding of the development of personality. Does it assist our grasp of early object relations, the reality principle, and the first steps in the development of the ego? Can it be of service in distinguishing the kinds of defense available at different ages and in providing clues to the replacement of primitive defenses by successful adaptive maneuvers? Can it help fill the yawning gap known as the latency period, a time when the mastery of school subjects and other accomplishments claim so large a share of time and energy? Does it bear upon the self and the vicissitudes of self-esteem, and can it enlighten the origins of psychological disorder? Can it make adult motives and interests more intelligible and enable us to rescue the concept of sublimation from the difficulties which even its best friends have recognized? I believe it can be shown that existing explanations of development are not satisfactory and that the addition of the concept of competence cuts certain knots in personality theory. But this is not the subject of the present communication, where the concept is offered much more on the strength of its logical and biological probability.

SUMMARY

The main theme of this paper is introduced by showing that there is widespread discontent with theories of motivation built upon primary drives. Signs of this discontent are found in realms as far apart as animal psychology and psychoanalytic ego psychology. In the former, the commonly recognized primary drives have proved to be inadequate in explaining exploratory behavior, manipulation, and general activity. In the latter, the theory of basic instincts has shown serious shortcomings when it is stretched to account for the development of the effective ego. Workers with animals have attempted to meet their problem by invoking secondary reinforcement and anxiety reduction, or by adding exploration and manipulation to the roster of primary drives. In parallel fashion, psychoanalytic workers have relied upon the concept of neutralization of instinctual energies, have seen anxiety reduction as the central motive in ego development, or have hypothesized new instincts such as mastery. It is argued here that these several explanations are not satisfactory and that a better conceptualization is possible, indeed that it has already been all but made.

In trying to form this conceptualization, it is first pointed out that many of the earlier tenets of primary drive theory have been discredited by recent experimental work. There is no longer any compelling reason to identify either pleasure or reinforcement with drive reduction, or to think of motivation as requiring a source of energy external to the nervous system. This opens the way for considering in their own right those aspects of animal and human behavior in which stimulation and contact with the environment seem to be sought and welcomed, in which raised tension and even mild excitement seem to be cherished, and in which novelty and variety seem to be enjoyed for their own sake. Several reports are cited which bear upon interest in the environment and the rewarding effects of environmental feedback. The latest contribution is that of Woodworth (1958), who makes dealing with the environment the most fundamental element in motivation.

The survey indicates a certain unanimity as to the kinds of behavior that cannot be successfully conceptualized in terms of primary drives. This behavior includes visual exploration, grasping, crawling and walking, attention and perception, language and thinking, exploring novel objects and places, manipulating the surroundings, and producing effective changes in the environment. The thesis is then proposed that all of these behaviors have a common biological significance: they all form part of the process whereby the animal or child learns to interact effectively with his environment. The word *competence* is chosen as suitable to indicate this common property. Further, it is maintained that competence cannot be fully acquired simply through behavior instigated by drives. It receives substantial contributions from activities which, though playful and exploratory in character, at the same time show direction, selectivity, and persistence in interacting with the environment. Such activities in the ultimate service of competence must therefore be conceived to be motivated in their own right. It is proposed to designate this motivation by the term effectance, and to characterize the experience produced as a *feeling of efficacy*.

In spite of its sober biological purpose, effectance motivation shows itself most unambiguously in the playful and investigatory behavior of young animals and children. Specimens of such behavior, drawn from Piaget (1952), are analyzed in order to demonstrate their constantly transactional nature. Typically they involve continuous chains of events which include stimulation, cognition, action, effect on the environment, new stimulation, *etc.* They are carried on with considerable persistence and with selective emphasis on parts of the environment which provide changing and interesting feedback in connection with effort expended. Their significance is destroyed if we try to break into the circle arbitrarily and declare that one part of it, such as cognition alone or active effort alone, is the real point, the goal, or the special seat of satisfaction. Effectance motivation must be conceived to involve satisfaction — a feeling of efficacy — in transactions in which behavior has an exploratory, varying, experimental character and produces changes in the stimulus field. Having this character, the behavior leads the organism to find out how the environment can be changed and what consequences flow from these changes.

In higher animals and especially in man, where so little is innately provided and so much has to be learned about dealing with the environment, effectance motivation independent of primary drives can be seen as an arrangement having high adaptive value. Considering the slow rate of learning in infancy and the vast amount that has to be learned before there can be an effective level of interaction with surroundings, young animals and children would simply not learn enough unless they worked pretty steadily at the task between episodes of homeostatic crisis. The association of interest with this "work," making it play and fun, is thus somewhat comparable to the association of sexual pleasure with the biological goal of reproduction. Effectance motivation need not be conceived as strong in the sense that sex, hunger, and fear are strong when violently aroused. It is moderate but persistent, and in this, too, we can discern a feature that is favorable for adaptation. Strong motivation reinforces learning in a narrow sphere, whereas moderate motivation is more conducive to an exploratory and experimental attitude which leads to competent interactions in general, without reference to an immediate pressing need. Man's huge cortical association areas might have been a suicidal piece of specialization if they had come without a steady, persistent inclination toward interacting with the environment.

REFERENCES

ALLPORT, G. W. *Personality: A Psychological interpretation.* New York: Holt, 1937.

ALLPORT, G. W. Effect: A secondary principle of learning. *Psychol. Rev.*, 1946, **53**, 335–347.

ANGYAL, A. *Foundations for a science of personality.* New York: Commonwealth Fund, 1941.

ANSBACHER, H. L., & ANSBACHER, R. R. (Eds.) *The individual psychology of Alfred Adler.* New York: Basic Books, 1956.

BEACH, F. A. Analysis of factors involved in the arousal, maintenance and manifestation of sexual excitement in male animals. *Psychosom. Med.*, 1942, **4**, 173–198.

BEACH, F. A. Instinctive behavior: Reproductive activities. In S. S. Stevens (Ed.), *Handbook of experimental psychology.* New York: Wiley, 1951. Pp. 387–434.

BERLYNE, D. E. Novelty and curiosity as determinants of exploratory behavior. *Brit. J. Psychol.*, 1950, **41**, 68–80.

BERLYNE, D. E. The arousal and satiation of perceptual curiosity in the rat. *J. comp. physiol. Psychol.*, 1955, **48**, 238–246.

BERLYNE, D. E. Attention to change, conditioned inhibition ($S^{I}R$) and stimulus satiation. *Brit. J. Psychol.*, 1957, **48**, 138–140.

BERLYNE, D. E. The present status of research on exploratory and related behavior. *J. indiv. Psychol.*, 1958, **14**, 121–126.

BIBRING, E. The development and problems of the theories of the instincts. *Int. J. Psychoanal.*, 1941, **22**, 102–131.

BRUNER, J. S., MATTER, J., & PAPANEK, M. L. Breadth of learning as a function of drive level and mechanization. *Psychol. Rev.*, 1955, **62**, 1–10.

BÜHLER, C. The reality principle. *Amer. J. Psychotherap.*, 1954, **8**, 626–647.

BÜHLER, K. *Die geistige Entwicklung des Kindes.* (4th ed.) Jena: Gustav Fischer, 1924.

BUTLER, R. A. Discrimination learning by rhesus monkeys to visual-exploration motivation. *J. comp. physiol. Psychol.*, 1953, **46**, 95–98.

BUTLER, R. A. Exploratory and related behavior: A new trend in animal research. *J. indiv. Psychol.*, 1958, **14**, 111–120.

BUTLER, R. A., & HARLOW, H. F. Discrimination learning and learning sets to visual exploration incentives. *J. gen. Psychol.*, 1957, **57**, 257–264.

COFER, C. N. Motivation. *Ann. Rev. Psychol.*, 1959, **10**, 173–202.

COLBY, K. M. *Energy and structure in psychoanalysis.* New York: Ronald, 1955.

DASHIELL, J. F. A quantitative demonstration of animal drive. *J. comp. Psychol.*, 1925, **5**, 205–208.

DIAMOND, S. A neglected aspect of motivation. *Sociometry*, 1939, **2**, 77–85.

DOLLARD, J., & MILLER, N. E. *Personality and psychotherapy.* New York: McGraw-Hill, 1950.

ERIKSON, E. H. *Childhood and society.* New York: Norton, 1952.

ERIKSON, E. H. Growth and crises of the healthy personality. In C. Kluckhohn, H. A. Murray, & D. Schneider (Eds.), *Personality in nature, society, and culture.* (2nd ed.) New York: Knopf, 1953. Pp. 185–225.

FENICHEL, O. *The psychoanalytic theory of neurosis.* New York: Norton, 1945.

FRENCH, T. M. *The integration of behavior.* Vol. I. *Basic postulates.* Chicago: Univer. Chicago Press, 1952.

FREUD, A. The mutual influences in the development of ego and id: Introduction to the discussion. *Psychoanal. Stud. Child,* 1952, 7, 42–50.

FREUD, S. *Wit and its relation to the unconscious.* New York: Moffat, Yard, 1916.

FREUD, S. Formulations regarding the two principles in mental functioning. *Collected papers.* Vol. 4. London: Hogarth Press and Institute of Psycho-analysis, 1925. Pp. 13–21. (a)

FREUD, S. On narcissism: An introduction. *Collected papers.* Vol. 4. London. Hogarth Press and Institute of Psycho-analysis, 1925. Pp. 30–59. (b)

FREUD, S. Instincts and their vicissitudes. *Collected papers.* Vol. 4. London: Hogarth Press and Institute of Psycho-analysis, 1925. Pp. 60–83. (c)

FREUD, S. *The ego and the id.* (Trans. by J. Riviere) London: Hogarth Press, 1927.

FREUD, S. *Beyond the pleasure principle.* London: Hogarth Press, 1948.

FREUD, S. *An outline of psycho-analysis.* (Trans. by J. Strachey) New York: Norton, 1949.

GOLDSTEIN, K. *The organism.* New York: American Book, 1939.

GOLDSTEIN, K. *Human nature in the light of psychopathology.* Cambridge, Mass.: Harvard Univer. Press, 1940.

GROSS, K. *The play of man.* (Trans. by E. L. Baldwin) New York: D. Appleton, 1901.

HARLOW, H. F. Mice, monkeys, men and motives. *Psychol. Rev.,* 1953, 60, 23–32.

HARLOW, H. F., HARLOW, M. K., & MEYER, D. R. Learning motivated by a manipulation drive. *J. exp. Psychol.,* 1950, 40, 228–234.

HARTMANN, H. Comments on the psycho-analytic theory of the ego. *Psychoanal. Stud. Child,* 1950, 5, 74–95.

HARTMANN, H. Notes on the theory of sublimation. *Psychoanal. Stud. Child,* 1955, 10, 9–29.

HARTMANN, H. Notes on the reality principle. *Psychoanal. Stud. Child,* 1956, 11, 31–53.

HARTMANN, H. *Ego psychology and the problem of adaptation.* (Trans. by D. Rapaport) New York: International Univer. Press, 1958.

HARTMANN, H., KRIS, E., & LOEWENSTEIN, R. Notes on the theory of aggression. *Psychoanal. Stud. Child,* 1949, 3/4, 9–36.

HEBB, D. O. *The organization of behavior.* New York: Wiley, 1949.

HEBB, D. O. Drives and the c.n.s. (conceptual nervous system). *Psychol. Rev.,* 1955, 62, 243–254.

HEBB, D. O. The motivating effects of exteroceptive stimulation. *Amer. Psychologist,* 1958, 13, 109–113.

HEBB, D. O., & THOMPSON, W. R. The social significance of animal studies. In G. Lindzey (Ed.), *Handbook of social psychology.* Vol. I. Cambridge, Mass.: Addison-Wesley, 1954. Pp. 532–561.

HENDRICK, I. Instinct and the ego during infancy. *Psychoanal. Quart.,* 1942, 11, 33–58.

HENDRICK, I. Work and the pleasure principle. *Psychoanal. Quart.,* 1943, 12, 311–329. (a)

HENDRICK, I. The discussion of the 'instinct to master.' *Psychoanal. Quart.,* 1943, 12, 561–565. (b)

HILL, W. F. Activity as an autonomous drive. *J. comp. physiol. Psychol.,* 1956, 49, 15–19.

JOHNSON, E. E. The role of motivational strength in latent learning. *J. comp. physiol. Psychol.,* 1953, 45, 526–530.

KAGAN, J. Differential reward value of incomplete and complete sexual behavior. *J. comp. physiol. Psychol.,* 1955, 48, 59–64.

KAGAN, J., & BERKUN, M. The reward value of running activity. *J. comp. physiol. Psychol.,* 1954, 47, 108.

KARDINER, A., & SPIEGEL, H. War stress and neurotic illness. New York: Hoeber, 1947.

LASHLEY, K. S. Experimental analysis of instinctive behavior. *Psychol. Rev.,* 1938, 45, 445–471.

LASHLEY, K. S. The problem of cerebral organization in vision. In H. Klüver, *Visual mechanisms.* Lancaster, Pa.: Jaques Cattell, 1942. Pp. 301–322.

LEUBA, C. Toward some integration of learning theories: The concept of optimal stimulation. *Psychol. Rep.,* 1955, 1, 27–33.

LILLY, J. C. Mental effects of reduction of ordinary levels of physical stimuli on intact, healthy persons. *Psychiat. res. Rep.,* 1956, No. 5.

MASLOW, A. H. *Motivation and personality.* New York: Harper, 1954.

MASLOW, A. H. Deficiency motivation and growth motivation. In M. R. Jones (Ed.), *Nebraska symposium on motivation 1955.* Lincoln, Neb.: Univer. Nebraska Press, 1955. Pp. 1–30.

McCLELLAND, D. C., ATKINSON, J. W., CLARK, R. A. & LOWELL, E. I. *The achievement motive.* New York: Appleton-Century, 1953.

McDOUGALL, W. *Introduction to social psychology.* (16th ed.) Boston: John Luce, 1923.

McREYNOLDS, P. A restricted conceptualization of human anxiety and motivation. *Psychol. Rep.,* 1956, 2, 293–312. Monogr. Suppl. 6.

MILLER, N. E. Learnable drives and rewards. In S. S. Stevens (Ed.), *Handbook of experimental psychology.* New York: Wiley, 1951. Pp. 435–472.

MILLER, N. E. Central stimulation and other new approaches to motivation and reward. *Amer. Psychologist,* 1958, 13, 100–108.

MITTELMANN, B. Motility in infants, children, and adults. *Psychoanal. Stud. Child,* 1954, 9, 142–177.

MONTGOMERY, K. C. The role of the exploratory drive

in learning. *J. comp. physiol. Psychol.*, 1954, **47**, 60–64.

MONTGOMERY, K. C., & MONKMAN, J. A. The relation between fear and exploratory behavior. *J. comp. physiol. Psychol.*, 1955, **48**, 132–136.

MORGAN, C. T. *Physiological psychology*. New York: McGraw-Hill, 1943.

MORGAN, C. T. Physiological mechanisms of motivation. In M. R. Jones (Ed.), *Nebraska symposium on motivation 1957*. Lincoln, Neb.: Univer. Nebraska Press, 1957. Pp. 1–35.

MOWRER, O. H. *Learning theory and personality dynamics*. New York: Ronald, 1950.

MUNROE, R. *Schools of psychoanalytical thought*. New York: Dryden, 1955.

MURPHY, G. *Personality: A biosocial approach to origins and structure*. New York: Harper, 1947.

MURRAY, H. A. *Explorations in personality*. New York & London: Oxford Univer. Press, 1938.

MURRAY, H. A. & KLUCKHOHN, C. Outline of a conception of personality. In C. Kluckhohn, H. A. Murray, & D. M. Schneider (Eds.), *Personality in nature, society, and culture*. (2nd ed.) New York: Knopf, 1953.

MYERS, A. K., & MILLER, N. E. Failure to find a learned drive based on hunger; evidence for learning motivated by "exploration." *J. comp. physiol. Psychol.*, 1954, **47**, 428–436.

NISSEN, H. W. A study of exploratory behavior in the white rat by means of the obstruction method. *J. genet. Psychol.*, 1930, **37**, 361–376.

OLDS, J., & MILNER, P. Positive reinforcement produced by electrical stimulation of septal area and other regions of rat brain. *J. comp. physiol. Psychol.*, 1954, **47**, 419–427.

PIAGET, J. *The origins of intelligence in children*. (Trans. by M. Cook) New York: International Univer. Press, 1952.

RAPAPORT, D. *Organization and pathology of thought*. New York: Columbia Univer. Press, 1951.

RAPAPORT, D. On the psychoanalytic theory of thinking. In R. P. Knight & C. R. Friedman (Eds.), *Psychoanalytic psychiatry and psychology*. New York: International Univer. Press, 1954. Pp. 259–273.

RAPAPORT, D. The theory of ego autonomy: A generalization. *Bull. Menninger Clin.*, 1958, **22**, 13–35.

ROSVOLD, H. E. Physiological psychology. *Ann. Rev. Psychol.*, 1959, **10**, 415–454.

SCHACHTEL, E. G. The development of focal attention and the emergence of reality. *Psychiatry*, 1954, **17**, 309–324.

SHEFFIELD, F. D., & ROBY, T. B. Reward value of a non-nutritive sweet taste. *J. comp. physiol. Psychol.*, 1950, **43**, 471–481.

SHEFFIELD, F. D., ROBY, T. B., & CAMPBELL, B. A. Drive reduction vs. consummatory behavior as determinants of reinforcement. *J. comp. physiol. Psychol.*, 1954, **47**, 349–354.

SHEFFIELD, F. D., WULFF, J. J., & BACKER, R. Reward value of copulation without sex drive reduction. *J. comp. physiol. Psychol.*, 1951, **44**, 3–8.

SKINNER, B. F. *Science and human behavior*. New York: Macmillan, 1953.

STELLER, E. The physiology of motivation. *Psychol. Rev.*, 1954, **61**, 5–22.

TOLMAN, E. C. Cognitive maps in rats and men. *Psychol. Rev.*, 1948, **55**, 189–208.

WELKER, W. L. Some determinants of play and exploration in chimpanzees. *J. comp. physiol. Psychol.*, 1956, **49**, 84–89.

WHITING, J. W. M., & MOWRER, O. H. Habit progression and regression — a laboratory study of some factors relevant to human socialization. *J. comp. Psychol.*, 1943, **36**, 229–253.

WOLFE, J. B., & KAPLON, M. D. Effect of amount of reward and consummative activity on learning in chickens. *J. comp. Psychol.*, 1941, **31**, 353–361.

WOODWORTH, R. S. *Dynamics of behavior*. New York: Holt, 1958.

YERKES, R. M. & DODSON, J. D. The relation of strength of stimulus to rapidity of habit-formation. *J. comp. Neurol. Psychol.*, 1908, **18**, 459–482.

YOUNG, P. T. Food-seeking drive, affective process, and learning. *Psychol. Rev.*, 1949, **56**, 98–121.

YOUNG, P. T. The role of hedonic processes of motivation. In M. R. Jones (Ed.), *Nebraska symposium on motivation 1955*. Lincoln, Neb.: Univer. Nebraska Press, 1955. Pp. 193–238.

ZIMBARDO, P. G., & MILLER, N. E. Facilitation of exploration by hunger in rats. *J. comp. physiol. Psychol.*, 1958, **51**, 43–46.

Sexuality and Sexual Learning in the Child*†

One of the most impressive aspects of this century is its exceptional concern with children. This is not to say that our children are loved more intensely or that their loss is mourned more deeply than in previous times, but that there is a special awareness of them as *children*. Only occasionally in preineteenth-century literature is a child depicted in present-day terms; rather children are represented as smaller and weaker versions of the adults surrounding them. A reading of Chaucer and Shakespeare fails to reveal a special world of the child, and it is not until the nineteenth century that such writers as Wordsworth in poetry and Dickens in the novel attest a new and prepossessing concern for the life of the child,[1] and childhood becomes a unique stage during which perceptions and learning are related to age as well as to station. In contrast, the execution of the Princes in Shakespeare's *Richard the Third*, and even the labor of children in the mines and factories in the nineteenth century, were consequences of children sharing with adults the assets and dangers of their common social positions of nobility or proletariat. There was no universal dispensation for age independent of social status even in the nineteenth century, though a change of consciousness was beginning to appear in the genius of the era.

This newfound concern, not only in England, with the child as an entity unlike an adult presaged the fundamental assessment of the impact of a child's experience on his character as an adult, which was the basic contribution of Freud. While much of the discussion of childhood in the late nineteenth century was idyllic and asexual, this tendency would seem to be partially a result of the honorable desire to protect the child from the vicissitudes of adulthood. At the same time, however, the quality of protection given to any individual child often depended upon his presumed innocence. Concurrent with this increasingly prevalent image of children, which is often conceived to have been universal and wrong-headed by modern scholars reacting to "Victorian prudery," there was writing about the sexual capacity of children in British medical literature, focusing upon its dangers, but certainly not denying its existence.[2] Thus the shock for adults of Freud's discoveries was not that children might be involved in sexual activity, but that this activity was not confined to a few evil children and was, in fact, an essential precursor and component of the development of the character structure of the adult. What superficially appeared to be an aspersion on the innocence of childhood was an assault upon the antisexuality and asexuality of adults. Freud pointed out the many permutations of the sexual impulse, the most important of which was that it never failed to be manifest.

In this process of realization that there was a special character to childhood, and indeed that it might require a special psychology, a new consciousness of children developed. While this change has not been universal, it is a characteristic of the United States and other countries of the Western European tradition, and more than likely it will be the dominant orientation of the future.

One of the consequences of this recognition is that adults now have a greater conscious concern with the processes by which children learn about sexuality. During the nineteenth century the popular method of dealing with childhood sexuality when it intruded upon adults was either to suppress the behavior or to deny its existence, and to avoid thinking about it at all as long as it was not a public issue. These methods are to this day the most

* Reprinted by special permission of The William Alanson White Psychiatric Foundation, Inc., from *Psychiatry*, Vol. 28, 1965, pp. 212–228. Copyright by The William Alanson White Psychiatric Foundation, Inc.

† This is a revised version of a paper originally published in Italian as "Sessualita ed apprendimento sessuale de bambino," *Scuola e Citta* (1964) 15:249–258. This research was supported by the National Institute of Mental Health Grant No. MH-07742.

[1] An analysis of this historical change, particularly in France, is the work by Phillipe Arles, *Centuries of Childhood*; New York, Knopf, 1962. For changes in attitudes toward sexuality see especially pp. 100–127. A remarkably original work tracing from an existentialist point of view the general implications of this change in consciousness is Jan. H. van den Berg, *The Changing Nature of Man*; New York, Dell, 1964.

[2] Steven Marcus, "Mr. Acton of Queen Anne Street, or, The Wisdom of Our Ancestors," *Partisan Review* (1964) 31:201–230.

popular ways of dealing not only with the sexuality of children, but also with that of adults.

However, as sexuality has become more and more of a public concern in the United States, a growing desire has been expressed to instruct children appropriately in sexual matters. Appropriate instruction is usually considered to be that which teaches without provoking either discussion or overt behavior. In this way, it is hoped, the alleged traumas that result either from incomplete information or mislearning may be avoided, and the essential nonsexual character of the child is preserved. In addition, the development of textbooks of sexual knowledge relieves parents of the anxieties and embarrassments of talking about sexuality to their children.[3] Part of this reluctance to talk about sexuality to one's offspring arises from the fact that such discussion may suggest to the child the sexual character of the adult. If the parent describes coitus to the child, then there is the risk that the child will make the correct supposition about parental participation. As will be discussed later in this paper, only a minority of sexual information is in fact learned by children in a legitimate, formal manner either through the school or the parents. However, when discussions are held about the methods of such instruction, it is usually these formal informational channels that are emphasized. Thus such questions as, "What, how much, by what means, and when should I tell my child about sex?", are always cognitively framed as if a rational pedagogy were the solution to the proper ordering of the sexual life, not only of the child, but of the adult. Out of these questions a small but growing literature on how to tell children about sex is appearing, ori-

ented not only to parents but to formal youth groups; in addition, there is some interest in programs of sex education, to be carried on usually in the high schools for children of 15 to 18 years of age. It is in this mode that the majority of effort is directed, even though there is some evidence that it is misdirected and that, even if directed properly, it occurs at considerably later ages than it should.

The rest of this paper is concerned with what seem to be some of the central elements in the development of sexuality and sexual knowledge in children and the role that the formal processes of information-giving may have in this development.

THE SEXUAL VALUE SYSTEM OF ADULTS

A prerequisite in any discussion of the sexuality of children is some description of the sexual value system of the adult members of the community. The discussion here, as elsewhere in the paper, is restricted to the United States, less specifically to Western Europe, and probably not at all to non-Western cultures.

The most apparent element in the sexual culture of adults is the degree to which there is no real community of values.[4] There is a cluster of negative values that represents the total body of public sexual norms, but as Lionel Trilling says in evaluating the larger cultural significance of the book, *Sexual Behavior in the Human Male*,[5] "Nothing shows more clearly the extent to which modern society has atomized itself than the isolation in sexual ignorance which exists among us. . . . Many cultures, the most primitive and the most complex, have entertained sexual fears of an irrational sort, but probably our culture is unique in strictly isolating the individual in the fears that society has devised."[6]

What consensus there is usually is worked out by indirection or through the behavior of sexual pairs. The public system of values in reference to sexuality is clearly supportive of only marital coitus as a legitimate expression of either virtuous or mature sexuality. However, there is a substantial body of evidence

[3] An example of the confused thought that results from this dilemma — that children should know about sex but not act out their knowledge — is provided by the following paragraph in a relatively sensible popular work on the sexual development of children. "Shielding children from the awareness of adult sex conduct goes without saying. Much more injurious than any play among themselves would be the observation of adult behavior and loose significant talk. As in the case of vulgarities — the greater the prudery the greater the pornography — so the greater the freedom among adults the greater the freedom among children. Also, the greater the denial of legitimate understanding among them, the greater the exploration. Far from being an abnormal or perverted or precocious entrance into heterosexuality, sex play in children is a normal, if socially unacceptable instance of sex interest, an expression of a normal developmental need. If they are not to provide an answer to that need themselves, we must provide it for them, not only in knowledge of the life processes, but in legitimate though vicarious participation in those processes. Words alone do not satisfy." Francis Bruce Strain, *The Normal Sex Interests of Children*; New York, Appleton-Century-Crofts, 1948; p. 139.

[4] It may, in fact, be a myth of the intellectualizing classes that value consensus as an outcome of rational deliberation exists to any extent in lower-class populations. There is a strong tendency among those to whom ideas and language are important to impute the same significance to others for whom words are inadequate or unimportant.
[5] Alfred C. Kinsey, Wardell B. Pomeroy, and Clyde E. Martin, *Sexual Behavior in the Human Male*; Philadelphia, Saunders, 1948.
[6] Lionel Trilling, "The Kinsey Report," in *The Liberal Imagination*; New York, Doubleday Anchor Books, 1953; p. 216.

that marital coitus has not been the only source of sexuality for the majority of adults, especially males. This capacity of the system of values and the system of behavior to exist side by side not only within groups, but within the same person, is indeed remarkable, so that it is possible for the same individual to report the majority values as well as behavior contradictory to them.

An examination of the specific sexual adjustment of pairs of persons reveals that it is quite possible for extensive and long-term sexual relationships — even, and possibly especially, in marriage — to work out to the apparent satisfaction of the two persons involved without a word being spoken about sexual behavior and its consequent pleasure or pain. This seems to be primarily a function of the character of the male and female roles brought to the marriage. The exchange of information between males in American culture is not sexually informative except in an indirect sense. The information comes as part of tales of sexual prowess or of humor in which emphasis is placed on heterosexual expertise or exploits. What evolves from this male-to-male interaction is an image of the sexual self rather than knowledge about sexuality. Among females, on the other hand, while a certain amount of sexual information is exchanged, by far the majority of discussion is related to affection and love. Thus the male is cast in the role of the technical expert, and this expertise is related to his masculine role. Even if he is not expert, there is a substantial constraint on the female not to point this out and not to help in the sexual adjustment, because there is always the problem of revealing to the male how she acquired her knowledge and arousing his anxiety about her ability to make invidious comparisons. Consequently the sexual relation is learned by and large through the exchange of cues and gestures rather than through discussion or direct experimentation.

This development of adult sexual consensus about acceptable overt behavior through the interaction of pairs of individuals rather than among larger social groups in the community has serious consequences for the nature of public discussion of sexuality, especially in times of controversy. The privatization of sexual consensus means that no one can be sure of the behavior of others, and this insecurity is accompanied by a belief that statements that differ from the conventional norms will be taken as evidence of sexual deviation. The only system of values that can be invoked in a time of sexual controversy is the most conservative, and this often results in the most puritan of the community defining the content

of public sex education for children.[7] This lack of consensus makes it very difficult for a body of disinterested opinion about sexuality to exist. Any statement by an individual about sexuality is commonly presumed to be related to the sexual preferences and desires of that individual. In this sense all sexual statements are assumed to be ideological in character. Another consequence of this lack of knowledge and consensus is the degree to which fantasy may be projected into and then shape the sexual situation. In most areas of social activity, a reality check upon individual fantasies is provided either by interaction with other persons or by contact with the mass media; but the sexual area lacks such checks, and the proportion of fantasy probably outweighs the proportion of reality. With these conditions prevalent in the adult sexual community, it is not difficult to see some of the difficulties inherent in parent-child interaction, out of which come the primary experiences that shape character structure and sexual behavior.

PARENT-CHILD INTERACTION

It was Freud who developed the first fully articulated theory of psychosexualality,[8] and the stages of psychosexual development, which he called the oral, anal, and genital, have now passed into what might be called the "conventional wisdom." Freud conceived of the sexual character of the child and the processual changes by which the undifferentiated drive becomes the infrastructure of adult sexual life. To a striking extent, Freud's hypotheses were put to use as part of therapeutic programs without conventional empirical testing — except as they were tested in relation to individual patients. The result of this historical accident was that instead of the ideas being adequately judged, two warring camps developed, one believing in Freud as revealed wisdom, and the other rejecting his insights as absolutely unscientific. It is only in recent years that these ideas have received serious treatment from a scientific point of view — that is, one that treats the ideas as subject to confirmation or disproof. This is, in fact, the most important honor that could be done to Freud's work.

[7] This is not always true, since in some communities sex education in schools has successfully weathered rather extreme conflicts. However, it is the fear of this situation that keeps most adults silent.
[8] Sigmund Freud, "Three Essays on Sexuality," *Standard Edition of the Complete Psychological Works* 7:135–245; London, Hogarth, 1953.

There are two primary difficulties in the Freudian scheme that are relevant to the problem of childhood sexuality. The first is the location of the instinctual energy within the child; the child is invested with initiatory capacities that would seem to be better allocated to the parent. The second is the rather over-general presumption that all contacts with or stimulation of the end organs of the infant have either a protosexual or completely sexual meaning.[9]

The first of these difficulties has been the emphasis on the instinctual character of the sexual energy source in the child. The child is seen as possessing certain sexual characteristics which express themselves regardless of parental action systems. These actions of the child are viewed, in an older sense of the concept of instinct, as rooted in the constitutional nature of the organism. It is possible to reconceptualize this notion to include that of a transactional information system which exists between the child and the mother, and while maintaining many of the clinical insights of Freud to abandon the psychic instinctual model.[10] To suggest this does not require that such central insights as the unconscious and the irrational bases of action be abandoned, but rather that they be reorganized into another noninstinctual theoretical system. It is interesting that Freud should have allocated certain initiatory elements in the interaction between parent and the child to the child's own "nature." This theory projects upon the child — who is less differentiated sexually and therefore less initiatory — the sexual desires of the parents, who are the primal agents in developing, promoting or repressing the sexual behavior and attitudes of the child. In some sense this may have made it easier for the parent to accept a sexual element in the child by placing it in the realm of constitutional forces. However, it seems more likely that parents may unknowingly be sexually initiatory to their children, and may interpret nonspecific behavior as sexual and respond to it, giving it such a definition to the child.

The second difficulty is the primitive Freudian view that all actions of parents that impinge upon the child or that all of the child's actions of a specific class — for example, thumbsucking — have direct control over or stand in place of certain sexual actions or functions. It is clear that this is too general a formulation, but it does lead to fruitful considerations of the relationships between "nonsexual" parent-child interaction and the resultant sexual behavior of the child. The specific mechanisms by which the parents' behavior in reference to, say, bowel control is related to the sexual functioning of the child, and the hierarchy of significance of the various activities involved in the teaching of this earliest form of control, are currently unknown.

However, there is substantial evidence that the experiences of the child early in life have certain lasting and defining influences on the way in which he conducts his sexual life.

The convergence of the early work of Spitz[11] on mother-deprived infants and that of Harlow and others[12] on the Rhesus monkey are two of the most important examples of research pointing out the significance of early learning for sexual development.[13] Spitz found that infants observed in normal homes with excellent mother-child relations had a significantly greater incidence of genital play in the first year of life than did children reared either in an institution with mother-child relations of varying emotional quality, or in a foundlings' home without mother-child relations. Spitz concluded that genital play was part of the normal pattern of development of the healthy child in contact with an accepting mother. This remains rather global terminology since the acts and attitudes of the mother are not so

---

[9] It is clear that not all psychoanalysts hold these positions in whole or in part. Unfortunately little effort has been devoted to redefinition. A reconstruction of the Oedipus complex by Rado bears upon the first point very directly. Sandor Rado, *Psychoanalysis of Behavior: Collected Papers*; New York, Grune & Stratton, 1956; p. 197.

[10] The functions of the sex hormones as an alternative energy source in preparing the organism to receive sexual information is discussed in the following work by John Money: "Components of Eroticism in Man: I. The Hormones in Relation to Sexual Morphology and Sexual Desire," *J. Nervous and Mental Disease* (1961) 132:239–248. "Sex Hormones and Other Variables in Human Eroticism," in *Sex and Internal Secretions*, edited by William C. Young; Baltimore, Williams and Wilkins, 1961; pp. 1383–1400.

[11] René A. Spitz, with the collaboration of Katherine M. Wolf, "Autoeroticism; Some Empirical Findings and Hypotheses on Three of its Manifestations in the First Year of Life," in *The Psychoanalytic Study of the Child*, 3/4:85–120; New York, Internat. Univ. Press, 1949.

[12] See the following works by Harry F. Harlow: "The Nature of Love," *Amer. Psychol.* (1958) 13:673–685. "Love in Infant Monkeys," *Scientific Amer.* (1959) 200:68–74. "Sexual Behavior in the Rhesus Monkey," paper presented to the Conference on Sex and Behavior, Berkeley, Calif., 1961 (mimeographed). Harry F. Harlow and M. K. Harlow, "Social Deprivation in Monkeys," *Scientific Amer.* (1962) 207:137–146.

[13] This convergence has been noted by Spitz himself in René A. Spitz, "Autoeroticism Re-examined: The Role of Early Sexual Behavior Patterns in Personality Formation," in *The Psychoanalytic Study of the Child* 17:283–315; New York, Internat. Univ. Press, 1962.

much specified as hidden in the description; however, it still points to the importance of the early experience. The work of Harlow in rearing Rhesus monkeys in a variety of experimental situations is of equal significance, and, since the adult activities of the monkeys were observed, of even more convincing character. Some of the monkeys were reared with surrogate mothers made alternatively of wire or cloth; others were reared in various combinations of play groups and present or absent mothers. A series of powerful findings was generated by these researches. One was that adult monkeys who had been reared in isolation from both mothers and peers were completely incapable of adult heterosexual contacts, and exhibited symptoms which looked very much like human mental disease. In addition, an important element in the development of the sexual capacity of these animals was the presence of peers; when the infant monkeys were reared with peers but without mothers the sexual capacity did not seem to be disturbed. Deprivation of peers from the age of three to six months, Harlow contends, "irreversibly blights the animal's capacity for social adjustment."[14] He further suggests, "It is apparent also that sexual activity is stimulated by the mother's grooming of the infant.[15] In this research there is specific evidence that particular patterns of activity of a mother with an infant animal have lasting and permanent impact on the sexual life of that infant when he is an adult.

Thus there exists the beginning of a body of empirical evidence that is supportive of the general Freudian presumptions about early childhood experience. Further, there is some value in viewing the original Freudian conceptions which specified basic developmental sequences as a prototype of the critical-period hypothesis. This hypothesis, which originated in ethological research, has, as pointed out by Caldwell, two possible meanings. One is that beyond a certain point in time the organism becomes immune or resistant to certain types of stimulation, and the second is that during a particular period of time the organism is especially susceptible or sensitive to certain types of modifiers.[16] This is, of course, what is involved in the Harlow findings about deprivation of peer interaction during the period of from three to six months of age in the Rhesus monkey.

14 See footnote 12, Harlow and Harlow; p. 138.
15 See footnote 14; p. 144.
16 Bettye M. Caldwell, "The Usefulness of the Critical Period Hypothesis in the Study of Filiative Behavior," *Merrill Palmer Quart.* (1962) 8:229–242. It is implicit that prior to a certain point in time the organism may well be resistant to learning.

It would appear reasonable to suggest that the developmental sequences suggested by Freud might well be of the critical-period type.[17] However, at this point, while there is evidence that the early period of life is extremely significant, the systems of transactions which are causal are not as yet clearly delineated.

Much of the behavior described above may have sexual consequences for the child; however, except for a few adults who are conscious of Freud, there is little recognition of the significance of differences in parental behavior that have different outcomes for the child. Indeed, even among those who have some recognition of the current fads in child-rearing, there is little evidence to suggest that conscious planning of child-parent interaction has done any more than confuse the child about what to expect next. The parent often seems to be working out fundamentally unconscious needs in a pattern of habitual response rather than planning his interaction with the child.[18]

One of the obvious areas in which the behavior of parents toward children has clear-cut sexual consequences is the separate behavioral syndromes that are related to the rearing of male and female children. The work of Money and the Hampsons[19] indicates clearly the early development of gender role, which they describe as ". . . all those things that a person says or does to disclose himself or herself as having the status of boy or man, girl or woman, respectively. . . . A gender role is not established at birth, but is built up cumulatively through experiences encountered and transacted — through casual and unplanned learning, through explicit instruction and inculcation, and through spontaneously putting two and two together to make sometimes four and sometimes, erroneously, five."[20] These

17 An alternative formulation of the findings on infant behavior from a learning theory point of view may be found in Jacob L. Gewirtz, "A Learning Analysis of the Effects of Normal Stimulation, Privation and Deprivation in the Acquisition of Social Motivation and Attachment," in *Determinants of Infant Behavior*, edited by Brian M. Foss; New York, Wiley, 1961; pp. 213–290.
18 The most thoroughgoing of the planners have been those who have used the Skinner Box with infants, but the outcomes of these experiments are still unclear.
19 See the following papers by John Money, Joan G. Hampson, and John L. Hampson: "Hermaphroditism: Recommendations Concerning Assignment of Sex, Change of Sex, and Psychologic Management," *Bull. Johns Hopkins Hosp.* (1955) 97:284–300. "Sexual Incongruities and Psychopathology: The Evidence of Human Hermaphroditism," *Bull. Johns Hopkins Hosp.* (1956) 98:43–57. Joan G. Hampson, "Hermaphroditic Genital Appearance, Rearing and Eroticism in Hyperadrenocorticism," *Bull. Johns Hopkins Hosp.* (1955) 96:265–273.
20 See footnote 19, 1955; p. 285.

scientists demonstrated that in their cases gender role was usually set by a little after two years of age, and attempts after this time to change the orientation in children who had been placed in the incorrect sex category because of external genital ambiguity had various negative psychic consequences for the child. Other criteria — gonadal or chromosomal — for sex assignment were of minor importance even though they have been assumed to have biological priority .

It is possible to argue, as indeed Money and the Hampsons do, that their research is antithetical and in basic contradiction to theories of innate bisexuality such as those of Freud. However, a more modest middle ground which will admit directionality based on prenatal potentiation of the organism through hormonal effects on the nervous system seems to be the one to take at present.[21] It is possible, as has been pointed out by Diamond, that the abnormal cases studied by Money and the Hampsons may have been less directed toward maleness or femaleness because of lowered hormonal levels and therefore more liable to misprinting in the sense that the latter authors use the term.[22] The biological substrate produced by prenatal hormonal effects may differentially ready the organism to receive the definitions and inputs of masculinity and femininity from the parents. The gender role and its components will then be built on the bisexual biological character, and the gender role will be a resultant of these two kinds of forces rather than the unique product of either. Further, data have been gathered that suggest that persons with anomalous genitalia who have been reared in a gender role opposite that of their biological internal structure have made successful shifts in gender role late in life, and these shifts were often made because the patients felt "something was wrong."[23] This finding suggests that the management of the sexually misidentified child should also take into account his own self-conception and desires rather than simply adhering to one or another rigid therapeutic orientation derived from a specific theory.

Since many of these inputs of information to the child occur without thought upon the part of the parent, it is clear that the actions that are involved even in the development of gender role are quite obscure; however, the fact that the parents are clear

in their belief that the infant is either male or female has permanent consequences for the child.[24] Thus the vigor of play, the frequency of father-child as opposed to mother-child interaction, and the tolerance for aggression in the male as opposed to the female infant and child all contribute to the development of the self defined as masculine or feminine. Indeed, one of the purely physical elements that may be connected with the greater intensity of the Oedipus conflict when compared with the Electra conflict is the sheer frequency with which the mother handles the genitalia of the male child in contrast to the frequency with which the father handles the female, and the period in development when the contacts take place. In addition, the mother may have a more sexual definition of the phallus than she does of the vagina. The period of contact, the frequency of contact, and the psychological set of the parents can be expected to have differential consequences for gender role development.

This is an example of sets of actions which spill over indirectly into the sexual area. The phenomenon of indirect learning is probably more important in sexuality than in any other zone of development. These early experiences are primarily important in setting the capacity of the organism to respond to information that comes later on. Therefore the child in the first years of life does not develop a fully articulated sexual structure, but rather there are limits and parameters set, within and around which the growing child will operate. Thus the experiences of the child with nurturance and the character of his toilet training define to a greater or lesser degree his capacities to deal in the future with situations which are homologous or analogous to the early experience.

NEGATIVE LABELING, NONLABELING, AND RIGIDITY

Upon examining the interaction of parents and children, one is struck by the frequency of both negative injunctions and what appear to be — at least to adults — unambiguous instructions given to children in their early years. A simple household item like the stove is an example; the toddler is taught that the stove is hot, and whether it is hot or cold at any given moment he is told not to touch it, for a single failure in learning might well be disastrous. As the child grows older, more flexible

[21] William C. Young, Robert W. Goy, and Charles H. Phoenix, "Hormones and Sexual Behavior," *Science* (1964) 143:212–218.
[22] Milton Diamond, "A Critical Evaluation on the Ontogeny of Human Sexual Behavior," *Quart. Review Biology* (in press).
[23] From studies cited in footnote 22.

[24] John L. Hampson and Joan G. Hampson, "The Ontogenesis of Sexual Behavior in Man," in *Sex and Internal Secretions*, edited by William C. Young; Baltimore, Williams and Wilkins, 1961; pp. 1401–1432.

information and attitudes about fire, temperature, and the stove are learned. The stove may be touched when there is no fire, cooking may be experimented with, and finally a series of rather fine discriminations are learned in order to deal with a common household object. This new information comes in both positive and negative forms and overlays the original information about the hot stove. This form of training is necessary for the child who is operating in a complex environment where the dangers of injury are high. However, as the child grows older, explanations of negative injunctions tend to be based more and more frequently upon rational calculations. Thus the infant who has been warned only about "hot" when he approaches the stove, is informed as he grows older about the dangers of burning himself, and is given a complicated set of responses to use in dealing with the stove.

This early instruction of the child comes from adults in whom the child invests considerable affect. However, in most areas of behavior the influence of the parents, while setting limits upon the capacity of the child to respond, is made less pervasive by the impact of other and later experiences. It is in the area of sexual behavior that this body of apparently unambiguous and negative instructions is least modified by later experience. If the child exhibits behavior which the adult perceives as sexual — and, as I have noted before, the majority of adults often do not understand the relevance of most of these behaviors to sexuality since in the adult state sexuality and genitality are usually assumed to be congruent — the adult's response is one of two types. The first is to tell the child that it is wrong to behave in that way — that is, to label the behavior as unequivocally wrong. This type of information often will not come as a shock to the child, since parents who respond in this way have already communicated some elements of this attitude to the child in nonverbal learning situations. The second type of response is to nonlabel or mislabel the behavior.[25] When the behavior is observed, the parent attempts to distract the child from what he is doing by interposing tasks which are suggested to be more enjoyable, or by pointing out negative consequences which are not related to the sexual aspect of the behavior — for example, giving hygienic reasons against kissing. As part of the process of mislabeling, the infantile words for the genitals and for the acts of excretion

are only replaced fragmentarily by another vocabulary. The negative control of sexual information extends to single words, and the child is left to nonparental agencies for learning the specific informational content of sexuality.

The nonlabeling phenomenon has two major consequences. The first is that the primary negative and dichotomous informational inputs to the child are never revised. The primitive form of conditioning, which constructs only black and white consequences for behavior, maintains itself independently, since the parental figures, who create the sexual capacity of the child through both direct action and indirection, are not reassessed or newly judged. This may be partially related to Freud's discovery of the requirement of transference for successful treatment of neurosis. One of the commonplaces of our time is the ease with which people adjust to a changing technological environment; however, an even greater commonplace is the difficulty in the treatment of mental disease. Freud says in reference to this:

> In the absence of such a transference (bearing a 'plus' sign) . . . the patient would never even give a hearing to the doctor and his arguments. In this his belief is repeating the story of its own development; it is a derivative of love and, to start with, needed no arguments. Only later did he allow them enough room to submit them to examination, provided they were brought forward by someone he loved.[26]

Thus it is possible for the child to reevaluate his parents' attitudes toward politics, vocations, and religion, for in these areas the parents have interacted with the child not only in the primitive negative manner, but also in a more complex and rational way. The child, as he matures, construes the parent as a religious, political, vocational being, and therefore the original inputs to the child are modified by consequent experience. This is not to say that even such reevaluations, especially if negative, are not accompanied by pain and grief and that in many cases they never take place; however, there is little doubt that most children and most adults are unable to consciously conceive of their parents as sexual creatures. Even those persons who remember having observed the primal scene — as well as the larger numbers who have repressed all such memories — should be included in this class. This observation of parental coitus, even if it occurs more than once

25 Robert R. Sears, Eleanor E. Maccoby, and Harry Levin, *Patterns of Child Rearing*; Evanston, Ill., Row, Peterson, 1957; pp. 176–217. See pp. 215–216 for the origin of the term *nonlabeling*.

26 Sigmund Freud, "Transference," *Standard Edition of the Complete Psychological Works*, 16:431–447; London, Hogarth, 1963; p. 445.

in poor and crowded circumstances — is not sufficient to create an articulated sexual image of the mother or the father, whatever else it might do.[27] — which is more likely to happen to those living It is very difficult for children to believe that their parents even existed prior to their birth, and this primacy of mother as only mother and father as only father continues long into adolescence. Even after the experience of coitus, it is extremely difficult for a young man or woman to conceive of his parents in the same roles. It is of great significance that the original organization of sexual learning and attitude is never challenged in any major way, and it is not easily possible for the growing child to revise these early conceptions. Of course, in addition to the parents, other agencies of socialization serve to modify early nonsexual learning, but once again the absence of such processes in the area of sexuality should be noted.

The second consequence of nonlabeling is that of spillover from one training experience to another. As pointed out above, there is an influence on sexual behavior arising from early contact between parents and children which is not recognized as sexual by the parents, and the character of which is not clearly understood at the present time. However, there is one element which seems of greater significance than many others — the problem of the control of aggression and the manner in which training for aggression spills over into sexuality. If the sexual domain is left relatively empty and undefined by processes of nonlabeling, there seems to be a flow of aggression into this area. This has very basic consequences for both males and females, for if the sexual area is left empty, or if only the primitive forms of learning are in the child's repertoire, the differential training and control of aggression in the boy or the girl can come to characterize their sexuality as well. The fact that male children are usually more aggressive than females, and that this aggression is aided and abetted by parents, suggests that it is through the aggressive component of the personality that the male child frees himself from the repression of the

sexual drive. In the case of females the sexual component is both nonlabeled and repressed, and the aggressive component is repressed as well; and so the typical adult female has a more responsive and less initiatory personality structure.[28]

This phenomenon of nonlabeling or ignoring sexuality may not always have deleterious results for children. Since many parents have intense anxiety about their own sexuality, the manner and content of their direct instruction about sexual matters might be more damaging to the child than the nonfamilial and informal structures that actually supply the information. In addition to protecting the child from parental anxieties about giving sexual information, it is possible that lack of recognition by adults of the sexual consequences of certain kinds of contacts with children — such as cleaning the genitals or body contact — may free the adults to perform such tasks with lowered anxiety. If they did recognize the fundamentally sexual character of certain of these experiences which are necessary for the development of the child, they might be inhibited from performing them or at least be unable to do so without displaying considerable guilt and upset.

Even after infancy parents create, unawares, situations of sexual learning. Mother-daughter look-alike costumes are an example of this. The mother wears the costume because it makes her attractive, which is an ultimately sexual consideration, while the child ostensibly dresses the same way because it is "cute." The child is modeling elements of adult female sexual attributes without the conscious awareness of the parent. In this example the linkage is relatively direct. In other situations, such as those involving cleanliness and aggression after the child is verbal, and types of handling and contact with the preverbal child and infant, the adult is even less likely to see these relationships — possibly properly so.

Adult provocation of childhood sexual experiences as actual occurrences, rather than as part of a universal childhood fantasy as posited by Freud after the first crisis in psychoanalytic thought, has been of

---

[27] The chronic use of the term "motherfucker" by American Negro slum dwellers is a case in point. Rather than being directed toward anyone's "real" mother or calling to mind coitus with her, it has an extremely abstract referent. In its use in verbal games which function as outlets for aggression and therefore social ranking among males it is clear that the reference is to womankind. See Roger D. Abrahams, *Deep Down in the Jungle*; Hatboro, Pa., Folklore Associates, 1964, for examples and discussion of urban Negro folklore, and especially pp. 259–262 for the meaning of this and other obscenities.

[28] The work of Maslow supports this hypothesis. He shows that women who had higher dominance scores on a dominance-submission scale were more similar to men in other characteristics than similar to low-dominance women. It is quite likely that this shift in characteristics may have resulted from differences in the training for aggression rather than in training for sexuality. Abraham H. Maslow, "Dominance, Personality and Social Behavior in Women," *J. Social Psychology* (1939) 10:3–39; and "Self-Esteem (Dominance-Feeling) and Sexuality in Women," *J. Social Psychology* (1942) 16:259–294.

concern not only to present-day analysts, but to the contemporaries of Freud.[29] The position of Johnson and Szurek, as well as others, is that certain sexual acting-out may be a function of unconscious provocation by the parents, serving to gratify their repressed desires which they project onto their children.[30]

Since the acting-out of the children is often restricted to a single area of behavior — often nonsexual — Johnson and Szurek have labeled this phenomenon as superego lacunae.[31] Since it is the function of parents to provide and indeed call forth certain sexual functions in the child, the acting-out of the child who needs therapy must be distinguished from the patterns of development of "normal" children who at least do not make the kinds of signs of distress that provoke the interest of treatment agencies. What is distinctive of the parents of the acting-out child is the openly sexual content of interactions between parent and child; and even though the parents may not be conscious of the consequences of the interaction, they remember (without analytic uncovering of repressed material) specifically sexual discussions and characterizations of the child's behavior.[32] It would seem that the distinction between these parents and those who do not have acting-out children is the fact that the latter are less likely to freely and aggressively define the children sexually. Indeed, it may be really impossible for any adult to consciously intervene in the sexual life of the child without a burden of guilt that will perhaps overwhelm both him and the child. Ferenczi suggests that in this situation the child will come to identify with the adult and will introject the adult's guilt and anxiety so that the child feels both innocent and culpable at the same time.[33] In the case of certain pathological adults, the calling forth of sexuality on the part of the child by the adult — a customary

characteristic of the learning of sexual patterns — becomes a disorganizing and disruptive sexual experience.

THE CHILDREN'S WORLD

The capacity for specifically sexual pleasure (as defined by orgasm) has been observed in both male and female children as early as four months.[34] This is clearly not present in all children; however, the capacity seems to develop steadily over time, with more and more children at each age level being able to respond to specifically sexual stimuli. Shortly after puberty most males in the United States (90 percent by age 16) have had orgasmic experience, and this same figure is attained by age 29 among females.[35]

However, the development of the physical capacity to respond in a specifically sexual manner probably only complicates the already difficult situation in which children learn to deal with sexual information. As noted above, the phenomenon of nonlabeling or mislabeling leaves the young child without a vocabulary with which to describe his physical or psychic experiences.[36] This specific absence of terminology has two major consequences. The first is the tendency for fantasy to overrun the sexual life of the child. The mysterious penis that must exist behind the female pubic hair, the feeling that females have been castrated, and other childhood fantasies are common because there has been no system of naming which will adequately control the child's nascent interest in his own or others' bodies.[37] The second consequence of the lack of a controlling set of symbols is probably related to the tendency for children to identify their sexual organs with excretory functions, and many psychoanalysts have noted that the emphasis on the dirtiness of the excretory function utilized to enforce sphincter control surely has consequences for the child's perception of the cleanliness

[29] Bernard C. Glueck, Jr., "Early Sexual Experiences in Schizophrenia," in *Advances in Sex Research*, edited by Hugo G. Beigel; New York, Harper and Row, 1963; pp. 248–255. Karl Abraham, "The Experiencing of Sexual Traumas as a Form of Sexual Activity," *Selected Papers of Karl Abraham*, M.D.; London, Hogarth, 1927; pp. 47–63. Sandor Ferenczi, "Confusion of Tongues Between the Adult and the Child," *Internat. J. Psycho-Anal.* (1949) 30:225–230.
[30] Adelaide M. Johnson and S. A. Szurek, "The Genesis of Antisocial Acting Out in Children and Adults," *Psychoanal. Quart.* (1952) 21:323–343. Edward M. Litin, Mary E. Griffin, and Adelaide M. Johnson, "Parental Influence in Unusual Sexual Behavior in Children," *Psychoanal. Quart.* (1956) 25:37–55.
[31] See Johnson and Szurek, in footnote 30; p. 323.
[32] See the case reports in Litin, Griffin, and Johnson, in footnote 30.
[33] See Ferenczi, in footnote 29; p. 228.

[34] Alfred C. Kinsey, Wardell B. Pomeroy, Clyde E. Martin, and Paul H. Gebhard, *Sexual Behavior in the Human Female*; Philadelphia, Saunders, 1953; p. 103.
[35] See footnote 34; p. 717.
[36] This has also been discussed by Albert Bandura and Richard H. Walters in *Adolescent Aggression: A Study of the Influence of Child-Training Practices and Family Interrelationships*; New York, Ronald, 1959; pp. 184–187.
[37] I have already noted the lack of consensus about sexuality among adults who have at least had some sexual experience; how much more mysterious must sexual functions appear to the inexperienced child. The role of language as imposing order on the external world may be found explicitly in the works of Kenneth Burke and George Herbert Mead and implicitly in those of Erving Goffman.

of his own genitalia and of their sexual function. This may also be related to some of the sexual differences between girls and boys; since boys may get dirty — therefore dirt is not so bad — and girls may not, the association may be more firmly entrenched among the latter.

In addition to the fantasy-proneness of childhood, there is the tendency for the unsatisfied curiosity of children to lead them directly into sexual play. This is probably true of many aspects of childhood behavior where the child does not possess a meaningful vocabulary with which to communicate or to elicit information. From the data on adults in the United States gathered in the samples of the Institute for Sex Research, about 57 percent of the males and 48 percent of the females who were interviewed as adults remembered sociosexual play prior to puberty, with most of it occurring between ages 8 and 13.[38] Of a small sample of males interviewed before puberty, about 70 percent reported such sex play, suggesting that it is an even more widespread phenomenon, and that the memory of it is apparently often repressed by adult respondents.[39] Most of the play was sporadic and primarily motivated by curiosity about the body of either the same or the opposite sex.[40] Similar to children's other patterns of behavior, the learning situation was usually initiated by a child slightly older either in age or experience, and most commonly the behavior did not continue. The lack of labeling may make experimental play more likely in that it creates a zone of the body about which there is some fundamental mystery and concern.[41]

Given this framework of repression and avoidance by parents, it is not surprising that the child gets the bulk of his sexual information, though not his attitudes, through peer relationships. Though the parents are not providing cognitive information about sexuality for the child, they are creating attitudes and orientations through which information from other children will be filtered. In the peer relationships, since no children — or, at most, few — have accurate information about even reproductive functions, they will systematically misinform each other just as they are systematically misinformed by their parents about being brought by the stork, being brought in the doctor's bag, or having been found in a cabbage patch. Unfortunately these belief systems and their origins among children have not been systematically studied, and the most likely reason for this is that the research itself must be a form of sex education.[42] In the exchanges between child and interlocutor the child will not remain unchanged, and even if he is asked only the meaning of certain terms, he will be in that moment informed or made curious. In this case there can be nothing but action research.

In all of the American studies it is clear that the primary source of sex information is peers. This has been a stable characteristic of most populations studied beginning with the Exner study of 1915 (85 percent of 948 college men),[43] and continuing

---

[38] See footnote 34; p. 107. Also see footnote 5; pp. 165–167.

[39] See footnote 38; p. 167.

[40] See footnote 38; p. 182.

[41] There is a body of evidence that among young children there is a large amount of game and folklore material that is rapidly forgotten after puberty. A certain amount of this material is sexual; however, the folklorists who work with children usually fail to keep records of this, or if they do so, do not publish it. An interesting aspect of this material is its eternal character — that is, it is passed on from generation to generation; for example, children in England are currently singing a recognizable variant of a song about Bonaparte popular in the early nineteenth century. See Iona Opie and Peter Opie, *The Lore and Language of School Children*; London, Oxford, 1959; pp. 98–99. This evidence for the historical continuity of children's culture makes the contention in the earlier part of the paper concerning the change in the modern consciousness about children somewhat more complex; however, what seems to have happened is that the culture of children existed despite parental ignorance, and it had traditions of some viability independent of the adult community. It is unclear to what extent an adequate vocabulary for children would influence their overt behavior, but most likely it would not stimulate additional activity. This fear that is often expressed by parents is a function of their own anxiety and not necessarily related to the motives and drives of their children. Thus the parent placing himself in the role of the child presumes that exposure to certain types of stimulation or knowledge of certain types of behavior would cause the child to react in the same way as an adult would.

[42] A series of reports has appeared about a study of this sort conducted through the use of doll play and interviews with 200 children. The general good sense of these researchers is attested to in the following: ". . . no series of scientific terms can 'immunize' a child against the inevitable language of the street. The child may need both in order to become an effective member of his group." See the following papers by Jacob Conn: "Sexual Curiosity of Children," *Amer. J. Diseases Children* (1940) 60:1110–1119. "Children's Reactions to the Discovery of Genital Differences," *Amer. J. Orthopsychiatry* (1940) 10:747–754. "Children's Awareness of the Origins of Babies," *J. Child Psychiatry* (1948) 1:140–176. See also Jacob Conn and Leo Kanner, "Children's Awareness of Sex Differences," *J. Child Psychiatry* (1947) 1:3–57.

[43] Cited in Glenn Ramsey, "The Sex Information of Younger Boys," *Amer. J. Orthopsychiatry* (1943) 13:347–352.

through Hughes in 1926 (78 percent of 1,029 schoolboys),[44] Ramsey in 1943 (90 percent of 291 high school students, either from peers or by self-discovery),[45] Gebhard and co-workers in 1965 (91 percent of 477 lower-class men, 89 percent of 888 incarcerated criminals, and 89 percent of 1,356 convicted sex offenders).[46]

In approximately one-half of the cases in all of the studies, neither parent contributed any information. In the Ramsey study of 1943, 60 percent of the mothers and 82 percent of the fathers had given no sexual information.[47] In the study by Gebhard and co-workers, approximately three-quarters of the parents of both sexes had failed to give any direct sexual information.[48]

The information that mothers give is usually related to menstruation and pregnancy; however, less than one boy in four in the Ramsey study received even this information from his mother. Learning about contraceptives, prostitution, and coitus was practically restricted to peers (over 90 percent in each instance). The role of the father is most ambiguous in this whole area; the myth of the good heart-to-heart talk between father and son seems to be exactly that. The father even less than the mother serves as a source of sexual information, and this seems to be a surprising finding. Apparently the father either assumes the boy will learn in his own good time, or that he has no real role to play in this area.[49] Unfortunately the questions asked have not ascertained whether the father ever made an attempt to teach his children anything about sex and then found out he was too late.

The Ramsey study also focused upon the age at which learning took place, and it is clear that pregnancy was learned of first (69 percent by age 10), intercourse usually next (57 percent by age 10), and masturbation next (43 percent by age 10). By age 14, the point at which it is suggested that most sex education programs should start, nearly all (92 to 100 percent) of the boys had learned about the previous three categories, and as many had learned of female prostitution. They remained most ignorant of menstruation (38 percent) and venereal disease (57

percent).[50] However, there is nothing in this learning process which suggests that the children have any integrated body of sexual knowledge. The young boy with experience in sex play may not associate his firsthand knowledge of the anatomical differences between boys and girls with the fact that babies grow inside of his mother and the biological facts of fertilization may never dawn on him at all. Even though the large body of data on females in the files of the Institute for Sex Research has not been analyzed for these variables, it would seem safe to speculate that except for menstruation females are unlikely to have learned the facts in any more logical or coherent order. In the case of females it is clear that the mother may often play a more decisive role because it is more appropriate that she inform her daughter of the dangers of sexuality and the possibility of menstruation. This is certainly not always the case, since a fair number of females in our sample report that they first learned of menstruation when it occurred for them the first time.

What is learned is important; however, it is the context in which it is learned that is more important. The exchange of sexual information among children is clandestine and subversive, and the manner in which parents attempt to teach their children reinforces this learning structure. The admonitions of parents, since they are general and diffuse, do not result so much in cessation of either interest or behavior, but in their concealment and the provoking of guilt. It is clear that few males have been deterred by the horror stories attached to masturbation. Madness, degeneration, and physical stigmata have all at various times been attributed to this behavior in the face of the evidence that the majority of males, especially in adolescence, have masturbated and that they have suffered none of these consequences. Those they have suffered have been related to the anxiety produced by worrying about the nonexistent consequences.

Thus children interact and exchange information on a sporadic and unconnected basis, usually but not always with some guilt.[51] The novelist Richard Wright recalled in his autobiography that in his early childhood he repeated an obscenity to his grandmother and received a ferocious beating for it, but did not know why he had been beaten.[52] This seems to happen fairly often — that the child behaves in a manner an adult perceives as sexual, and the child is punished without being able to

[44] See footnote 43; p. 349.
[45] See footnote 43; pp. 349–350.
[46] Paul H. Gebhard, John H. Gagnon, Wardell B. Pomeroy, and Cornelia V. Christenson, *Sex Offenders: An Analysis of Types*; New York, Harper and Row, 1965.
[47] See footnote 43; pp. 350–351.
[48] See footnote 46. Also, the data for 5,000 college males is currently being analyzed at the Institute for Sex Research; this should provide some evidence about the experience of this social level.
[49] See footnote 36; pp. 150–154.

[50] All figures from Ramsey, footnote 43.
[51] See footnote 41; pp. 93–97.
[52] Richard Wright, *Black Boy*; New York, Signet, 1963; pp. 49–53.

make a connection between stimulus and response. The punitive action of the parent may have little inhibitory power since it is nonspecific to the child's behavior, but it may provoke intense anxiety.

The development of guilty knowledge occurs extremely quickly, and the children's world resembles a secret society keeping information from parents.[53] This secret society is under enormous strain from two sources, both of them pointed out by Simmel. One is the tendency of children to express spontaneously what they know or feel, and the second is the difficulty of keeping a secret in a "small and narrow circle."[54] There is a positive value set on the ability of adults to talk to children about their problems, and the quality of child-rearing is often judged by whether the child will go to the parents with his difficulties. Even with all of these tensions organized to force the communication of sexual attitudes and information between the parents and the child, the barriers of mutual distrust and anxiety are too high. Thus the sexual learning process contributes another element to the child's future character structure — the capacity and need to keep sexuality secret, especially from those one loves.

After adolescence a different set of sexual problems appears, many of which are more or less restricted to the United States and relate less to the areas of Western Europe. Free dating and open inter-sexual social contact result from very special American conditions. Even with these special conditions many of the preparatory attitudes and belief systems that originated in childhood and infancy continue to play a powerful role.

Despite a rapidly changing society, especially in the technological realm, the power of these early experiences may be attested to by the stability (for the last fifty years at least) in patterns of overt sexual behavior. For the male the only basic overt behavioral change in his sexual repertoire has been a substantial decline in the frequency of coitus with prostitutes, although the proportion of men who have had at least one such experience seems not to have changed.[55] The use of prostitutes as a stable and substantial source of coitus seems to be a phenom-

enon of the past. Two attitudinal changes have occurred that are of some importance. First, the intensity and duration of anxiety about masturbation have declined (although the incidence and frequency of the behavior have remained remarkably constant) and, second, the proportion of males who seriously adhere to the "double standard" has declined, with a shift to a position described by Reiss as "permissiveness with affection."[56] The most radical change in sexual patterns has been the substantial increase in the incidence of premarital coitus among females born after 1900, who grew up during the 1920's when contrasted with females born before 1900, who grew up before the first World War.[57] There has been no recent change similar to this, as surveys of college students have shown.[58] The bulk of this coitus is restricted to one male and to the year before marriage, indicating that premarital coitus in the female seems linked more directly to age at marriage and falling in love than it is to the attributes that are most important in determining male sexual behavior.[59] Attitudinal shifts have taken place among females, but often they are situation-specific, changing from a more permissive stance when the girl is in the process of courtship and is about to get married to a less permissive one when she has teen-age daughters.[60] The connection between these changes in attitudes and how they are translated into overt behavior is still obscure.

The long predicted change in American sexual patterns has not, in fact, occurred, despite the advent of the automobile and other artifacts of a changing technology. Since most of the sexual orientations of the adult personality are results of events that are not reversible through conventional means, there are no grounds for predicting that the sexual life can be easily changed. Given our difficulties in changing the behavior of schizophrenics, drug addicts, or juvenile delinquents, or even of changing the political party affiliation of others, there seems to be a curious contradiction in the belief that sexual behavior is immediately amenable to change from the slightest external impulse. This anxious belief may arise from

[53] This also has been pointed out by Freud. "We are shown . . . above all, how the secret of sexual life begins to dawn on her indistinctly and then takes complete possession of the child's mind; how, in the consciousness of her secret knowledge, she at first suffers hurt, but little by little overcomes it." Sigmund Freud, *Standard Edition of the Complete Psychological Works* 14:341; London, Hogarth, 1963.
[54] Kurt H. Wolff, editor, *The Sociology of George Simmel*; Glencoe, Ill., Free Press, 1950; pp. 330–335.
[55] See footnote 5; pp. 394–417.

[56] See footnote 5. Ira Reiss, *Premarital Sexual Standards in America*; Glencoe, Ill., Free Press, 1960; pp. 126–145.
[57] See footnote 34; pp. 298–302. Winston Ehrmann, *Premarital Dating Behavior*; New York, Holt, 1959; pp. 32–36.
[58] Mervin B. Freedman, "The Sexual Behavior of American College Women: An Empirical Study and an Historical Survey," *Merrill Palmer Quart.* (1965) 11:33–48.
[59] See footnote 34; pp. 282–345.
[60] Robert R. Bell and Jack V. Buerkle, "Mother and Daughter Attitudes to Premarital Sexual Behavior," *Marriage and Family Living* (1961) 23:390–392.

the facts that practically all sexual behavior is taboo, that violations of the norms are widespread, and that the transgressions are systematically ignored. These violations, which are as constant as the norms, are assumed, when discovered, to be the product of changes in behavior rather than to represent the persistence of previous patterns.

PLANNING AND THE UNPLANNABLE

The forces that mold childhood and thereby provide the structure around which the personality of the adult is formed are still only vaguely understood. Even such an insightful work as Erikson's *Childhood and Society* primarily provides a set of labels, albeit useful, and only intimations of possible explanations of process and change.[61] Even if these processes were understood at some high level of scientific sophistication, it does not follow that many parents would be able to utilize the available knowledge. A large portion of the actions of parents toward children is based upon irrational grounds, often repetitive of the experiences that the parents had as children. I am not suggesting a simplistic cyclical theory, but attempting to point out a differential amenability to change in various areas of both the personality and social life.

It is experiences in infancy and childhood that ready the child for integration of sexual knowledge and sexual behavior. This readiness is the consequence of systems of parental behavior that have no direct sexual bearing but spill over into the sexual area. The actions of the parents are not planned or rational, and when there is an attempt to make them so, the child often becomes confused — he must respond at one level to the habitual character of the parents and then at another to the parents' rational plans. In the midst of these plans the irrational components of the parents' character tend to erupt, and the child is unclear as to the actual nature of the parents' expectations.

These confusions on the part of parents and the consequent disorderliness of the child's life are now commonly placed at the door of permissive child-rearing. It is now suggested by psychiatrists as well as Dr. Spock that discipline — when not carried too far — is a good thing and that good discipline is needed for the child's own sense of security.[62] The

sentiment of psychiatrists that parents should return to punishment — administered "wisely" is the usual codicil — is based on two disparate but mutually supporting experiences. The first is related to the stresses of the therapeutic life for the therapist, for whom treatment failure and changes in the presenting syndromes of new patients have endlessly complicated the problems of traditional psychoanalysis. (In contrast to Freud, it is possible to argue that the success or failure of psychoanalytic therapy is unconnected to the explanatory value of the theory in reference to human behavior; however, since psychoanalysis has been primarily used as part of a treatment program, this distinction is usually not made.) As Freudian analytic techniques are rejected, so are the pronouncements about the processes of normal childhood development and the role of permissiveness. This reaction is especially notable among those therapists who deal with criminal or other deviant populations or mass groups such as school children.[63] The intractability of the case or the dimensions of the problem (often simply in terms of size) are enough to make people suggest a return to techniques which are applicable in the mass and by the number.

The second experience is the difficulty which parents have in applying the suggested methodology and the responsibility that it implies. The popular literature is replete with anxious parents unhinged by the dangerousness and difficulty of the child-rearing task, and much talk to parents is bent upon reducing parental anxiety. The opening line of Dr. Spock is the summation of all such reassurance: "You know more than you think you do."[64] The current mode is to tell parents to rely upon their common sense, whatever that might be. The import of these admonitions is to remove the onus from the parent of the terrifying (and rightly so) responsibility of rearing children,

---

[61] Erik H. Erikson, *Childhood and Society*; New York, Norton, 1950.

[62] The revision of Spock's classic in 1957 to include a greater concern with discipline is noted in Martha Weinman, "Now 'Dr. Spock' Goes to the White House," *The New York Times Magazine* (December 4, 1960) pp. 26,

120–121. The cause of the revision was "permissiveness running away with itself." The child-rearing column of the Magazine section of *The New York Times* is increasingly running to titles such as, "Relearning What Permissiveness Means," or "When Discipline is Called For." The column often translates psychiatric positions into layman's information.

[63] Many of these impressions come from personal interaction with psychiatrists, but the *J. Offender Therapy*, which is directed toward dealing with criminal populations explicitly, says what many therapists feel when confronted with these kinds of problems. See Ernst Schmidhofer, "Acting Up or Acting Out," *J. Offender Therapy* (1964) 8:1–4, or Mark D. Altschule, "The Alleged Value of Anti-Social Self Expression," *J. Offender Therapy* (1963) 7:73–74.

[64] Benjamin S. Spock, *The Pocket Book of Baby and Child Care*; New York, Pocket Books, 1946; p. 3.

for this is often too much for the consciousness of the parent; he cannot reconcile the seriousness of his task, the lack of accurate guide rules (as opposed to clichés) for his behavior, and his emotional involvement in the child who is demanding his attention. The new literature even deflects from parental responsibility by pointing out elements such as inherent differences between children, as if this provided an exclusionary clause. It is not that the techniques of permissive child-rearing are necessarily indicted by the failures of parents in using them, but rather that parental incapacities have made adherence to the principles so sporadic and of such uneven intensity that they resulted only in confusion for the child.

In addition to the parents' incapacity to deal with the indirect elements which affect sexuality, they are also unable to deal with the problem of the supply of specifically sexual information. Since the parents persist in patterns of information control that are mostly composed of negative sanctions and nonlabeling and mislabeling of behavior, the child must search for information in the meager resources of his equally misinformed friends. As has been suggested earlier, given the troubled quality of adults when they deal with sexuality, it may be better for the children to learn through the informal channels of other children, since material from parents that might be over-loaded with anxiety is reduced in significance and impact.

The overwhelmingly unplanned and unplannable elements in the development of the sexual life of children make it extremely difficult to discuss the role that planning in sex education might play. It is, however, possible to suggest that information imparted to children in schools or in other educational contexts should be communicated in each grade as part of the general curriculum. While it may be too rapid for some children and too slow for others, in general, if there is a source of accurate information that the children may tap anonymously and which is presented in a nonpejorative manner, at least the methods of communicating the information to the children will not in themselves be particularly destructive.[65] The specific age at which a child receives this information, as well as the specific items of information to be imparted, are of less significance than the preparation of the child for receiving this knowledge. The child who is traumatized by the sight of a nude body, or by learning that intercourse occurs, or by learning that babies grow inside of the

[65] *Symposium on Sex Education*, edited by E. C. Cumings; New York, Amer. Social Hygiene Assn., November, 1957.

mother, has previously developed a background of experience such that sooner or later, in one context or another, he would have been unable to cope with similar sexual stimuli. The specific triggering event is less important than the accumulation of readying experiences that prepared the child for such responses.

Planning of sex education should then be viewed as a rather secondary force in the development of the sexual life of the child, and while humanitarian values suggest that such planning should be done, the bulk of the evidence suggests that it will play a minor role in setting patterns of sexual life. There may be some long-run value in the teaching of sex education in schools, since it reduces the role of the parent who may only reproduce his own anxieties in the child. Whatever patterns of sexual life are considered desirable to maintain in a society, or whatever changes men may seek to make in these patterns, it is certain that it will be more difficult to resist or accomplish these goals because of the roots of sexuality in childhood. Even the accumulation of scientific knowledge about human sexual behavior may not accelerate much the pace or direction of change, for in this area of behavior — as is probably true in others — the statement that "Ye shall know the truth, and the truth shall make you free," may not apply. In a society that is addicted to the ideology of limitless possibilities in human engineering it is perhaps important to focus on some of the refractory elements in human development. While it is possible to be more hopeful about the human capacity for change than was Freud in his later years, his statement about the limited potentials of sex education should be kept in mind. It occurs during his discussion of the limited consequences for mental health that either the purely intellectual discussion of instinctual conflicts or the reading of psychoanalytic writings have. Freud says of these activities:

We have increased his knowledge, but altered nothing else in him. . . . We can have analogous experiences, I think, when we give children sexual enlightenment. I am far from maintaining that this is a harmful or unnecessary thing to do, but it is clear that the prophylactic effect of this liberal measure has been greatly over-estimated. After such enlightenment, children know something they did not know before, but they make no use of the new knowledge that has been presented to them. We come to see that they are not even in so great a hurry to sacrifice for this new knowledge the sexual theories which might be described as a natural growth and which they have constructed in harmony with, and dependence on, their imperfect libidinal organization — theories about the part played by the stork, about the nature of sexual intercourse and about the way in which babies are made. For a long time after they have been given sexual enlightenment they behave like primitive races who have had Christianity thrust upon them and who continue to worship their old idols in secret.[66]

[66] Sigmund Freud, "Analysis Terminable and Interminable." *Standard Edition of the Complete Psychological Works* 23:216–253; London, Hogarth, 1964; pp. 233–234.

JOHN P. SPIEGEL

The Resolution of Role Conflict within the Family*†

In an investigation of the relations among cultural value conflict, family conflict, and the emotional adjustment of the individual, in which I am participating with Florence R. Kluckhohn and a number of co-workers, the concept of social role is being used to observe and analyze the details of behavior which is functional or dysfunctional for the family as a whole. The social role concept is useful for this purpose because it facilitates observation of the way the individual members of the family become involved in the family as a superordinate system of behavior. (See, for example, Ackerman, 1951; Ackerman and Sobel, 1950; Parsons and Bales, 1955; Pollak, 1952; Spiegel, 1954.) It helps to describe not only the interaction of two members as they adjust to each other, but also the transactions of a plurality of members as they interweave in the special type of compulsiveness or control which a going system always imposes on its members. (See: Bentley, 1950; Dewey and Bentley, 1949; Kluckhohn and Spiegel, 1954; Spiegel, 1956.) Since the uniquely compulsive elements of the family system leave a characteristic stamp upon the personality development of the child, it is important to have a way of tearing apart the rather subtle elements of which it is composed.

In studying a group of families of emotionally disturbed children and comparing them with families in which the children are free of clinically manifest disturbance, we have found evidence of what promises to be a consistent difference between the two groups. In the first group, the children inevitably become involved in a conflict or disequilibrium situation which exists between the parents. Most frequently neither the child nor the parents are aware of this fact, nor are they aware of the ways in which it comes about. In the second group of families, although there may be sources of tension between the parents, the children are minimally involved in it. In order to avoid excessive variability in our two sets of families, we have kept them similar with respect to size, ethnic, regional, and class variables. Nevertheless, the sources of tension can be related in every case to differences and incompatibilities in cultural value orientations and, as a corollary, in definitions of social role expectations. These incompatibilities have a pronounced bearing upon the object relations and unconscious psychodynamics of the transacting members of the family. However, this is not the place to deal with the origin of the cultural value conflict or its direct relation to the intrapsychic process. These connections will be reported in subsequent communications. In this paper they will be assumed to underlie the role conflict in the family, and our attention will be centered rather on the ways in which the role conflict[1] is handled.

[1] The expression, "role conflict," has been used in two different ways. In the first, and perhaps more common, usage it refers to a situation in which ego is involved in a difficult or impossible choice between two different roles toward two different alters. No matter what decision he makes, he is in trouble with one or the other of his role partners in the situation. In the second usage, ego and alter have conflicting or incompatible notions of how to play their reciprocal role. The conflict is not over which

* Reprinted with permission of The Free Press from *The Patient and the Mental Hospital*, M. Greenblatt, D. J. Levinson, and R. H. Williams, Eds., pp. 545–565. Copyright © 1957, The Free Press, A Corporation.
† This study is supported by research grants from the National Institute of Mental Health, and the Pauline and Louis G. Cowan Foundation.

While we were studying the ways in which parents unwittingly involve one or more children in their own conflicts, it became clear that this process, so ably reported by Adelaide Johnson and her coworkers (1952; 1953), could be described in the usual psychodynamic terms. Through identification with the unconscious wishes of the parent the child acts out the parent's unconscious emotional conflict. The acting-out serves as a "defense" for the parent, making it unnecessary for him to face his own conflicts. This vocabulary is adequate for most purposes, and besides, confers a kind of credibility upon the description because of long usage and ready acceptance in the mind of the user. Nevertheless, it left us unsatisfied. Even with the qualifications of the term "unconscious," the description sounds too planned, too much under the control of one or more individuals. A constant observer of the family — or of any other persistent group process — has a somewhat contrary impression that much of what occurs in the way of behavior is not under the control of any individual or even set of individuals, but is rather the upshot of complicated processes beyond the ken of anyone involved. Something in the group process itself takes over as a steering mechanism, and brings about results which no one anticipates or wants, consciously or unconsciously. Or the steering mechanism may bring about a completely unexpected pleasant effect. On the basis of numerous observations, we were struck with the fact that so often what is functional for one member of the family group may be dysfunctional for the family as a whole. The opposite also holds: What is functional for the family as a whole, may have very harmful effects on an individual. Then phenomena take place unwittingly not only because of the unconscious dynamics within the individual but also because of the operations of the system of relations in which the members of the family are involved.

To describe the characteristics of a system of relations within a group accurately over a considerable span of time is no small task. The most successful attempt to do this known to us is the method of interaction process analysis devised by Parsons and Bales (Chap. V, 1953). However, the categories of interaction used by these workers is at too high a level of abstraction for our purposes. We decided, therefore, to use their basic concepts of behavior occurring within role systems of ego and alter, or any

number of alters, but to devise our own set of categories for observing the roles involved. Thus the basic concept used in analyzing the family as a system consists of describing the behavior of an individual in terms of his role in transaction with a role partner or partners. A role is defined as a goal-directed pattern or sequence of acts tailored by the cultural process for the transactions a person may carry out in a social group or situation. It is conceived that no role exists in isolation but is always patterned to gear in with the complementary or reciprocal role of a role partner (alter). Thus all roles have to be learned by the individuals who wish to occupy them in accordance with the cultural (or subcultural) values of the society in which they exist. If that society is fairly homogeneous and well integrated, then the roles will be patterned in such a way that their complementary structure is obvious and stable.

The roles pertinent to the family as a system consist of husband and wife, mother and father, son and daughter, brother and sister. This is not an exhaustive list, and refers to the nuclear rather than the extended family. But if one compares these roles on any axis of variation, such as ethnic or class affiliation, it is apparent that they are defined differently, and their complementary structure varies according to the particular mode of family organization characteristic of that class or ethnic group. It is true that even within a class or ethnic group there is considerable variation of pattern. Nevertheless, one mode of organization tends to be typical or dominant compared to the others. For example, an American middle-class wife tends to expect her husband to treat her as an equal. She expects of her husband a good deal of independence, initiative, and planning for future success in his occupation, but in his relations with her and with the children, she expects coöperation, sharing of responsibility, and individual consideration. Reciprocally, the husband expects his wife to help in his plans for future economic and social success, notably, by putting his success goals above any personal career or occupational goals of her own, and by developing the social and domestic skills suitable to his particular occupational status. There is evidence that these complementary role expectations may not be precisely reciprocal — that is, there may be some built-in strain — but on the whole they fit with each other fairly well.

By way of comparison, it is illuminating to select some of the complementary role patterns in the lower-class Italian family. Here the wife has no wish that her husband spend a great deal of time thinking or planning about occupational success. She expects her husband to work steadily and do his best to bring

---

of several possible roles to take, but rather how to enact the role they have both decided to take. It is the second definition which is used in this paper. Settlement of the terminology problem should not prove too difficult, but will have to be postponed for the present.

in enough money to satisfy the needs of the family, but she doesn't expect his economic or social status to change. She expects rather to have a large number of children who will soon join the husband in trying to increase the economic intake of the family, but in the meantime there is always help to be expected from relatives and friends if there is real need. On the other hand, she does expect him to spend a lot of time keeping up contacts with the extended and complicated networks of relatives and friends in order to keep their own position secure. At home she doesn't expect to be treated as an equal. Rather she expects to be relieved of responsibility through his making the chief decisions so that she can tend to the needs of the large brood of children. For his part, the husband expects submission but also a good deal of nurturant care from his wife. He wants her to be chiefly concerned with his children. Everything else is secondary. For both of them there is an accent on enjoyment and a sense of festivity in family life which is of greater importance than hard work and planning for the sake of social ambition. Again, although definite strains can be noted here and there, the roles of the family members *vis-à-vis* each other are characterized by a complementarity of expectations which fit each other in fairly smooth and systematic ways.

THE EQUILIBRIUM-DISEQUILIBRIUM BALANCE

I hope these all too brief examples of contrasting husband-wife role patterns illustrate how complementarity can be maintained in spite of variation in goals, values, and concrete sequences of acts within the role systems. The principle of complementarity is of the greatest significance because it is chiefly responsible for that degree of harmony and stability which occurs in interpersonal relations. Because so many of the roles in which any of us are involved are triggered off by cultural cues in a completely complementary fashion, we tend not to be aware of them. We enact them automatically, and all goes well. This automatic function of role systems has significance for psychological economy of effort. We are spared the necessity of coming to decisions about most of the acts we perform because we know our parts so well. This saves our efforts for those acts which occur in less stabilized role systems. In this way role reciprocity confers spontaneity upon human behavior. Self-consciousness and self-guarding enter the scene along with role conflict which sharply raises the number of decisions which have to be made with respect to any sequence of acts. As long as comple-

mentarity is maintained at high levels of equilibrium,[2] decisions are decentralized, so to speak. They are taken care of by the system of role relations rather than by the individual acting in a self-conscious manner.

However, it is a part of the human condition that high levels of equilibrium figured by precise complementarity of roles are seldom maintained for long. Sooner or later disharmony enters the picture. Complementarity fails; the role systems characterizing the interpersonal relations move toward disequilibrium. The role partners disappoint each others' expectations. The failure of complementarity feeds back into the awareness of the participants in the form of tension, anxiety or hostility, and self-consciousness. If the process continues without change, it will end in the disruption of the system. This process is so familiar and inevitable that it seems to merit no further comment. Yet, it has appeared to us that it may contain some general elements which can throw light on family behavior, if it were to be subjected to critical scrutiny. The key to its analysis would consist of a study of the conditions leading to the breakdown of complementarity and to its subsequent restoration. Although this study has not been carried as far as I would like, our current experience indicates that there are at least five causes for failure of complementarity in role systems within the family. Because of limitations of time and space, I will review them here very briefly, without the extended discussion and illustration which they deserve.

Cognitive Discrepancy

One or both individuals involved in the role system may not know or have sufficient familiarity with the required roles. This is especially likely to occur with respect to age roles, and therefore frequently characterizes sources of disequilibrium between parents and children. When the pattern of acts constituting the role is not clearly mastered or not cognitively mapped or internalized, complementarity can be maintained only with difficulty. Cues are misinterpreted, and misunderstanding reduces complementarity of expectations. Both participants must have a relatively high tolerance of frustration and failure, and both must alternatively assume informally the roles of teacher and learner alternately. This alternation and reversal of roles will be discussed later in connection with the mechanisms of restoration of complementarity. In our culture cognitive discrepancy is a character-

[2] In this context "equilibrium" does not denote a rigid, static state, but rather a balancing of process in a moving or changing state. The phrase "moving equilibrium" might, perhaps, be a better name.

istic problem between adolescents and the adult world. It also occurs between husband and wife at various developmental crises, or with respect to any sudden, new situation. For example, the wedding and immediate post-nuptial situation requires much new learning of roles. So does the birth of the first child, the first severe illness, and so forth.

Discrepancy of Goals

Roles are patterns of acts directed toward immediate or ultimate goals. The goal of ego, interlocking with the goal of alter, determines the motivational principle behind the individual's taking of the role. Some goals serve the purpose of gratification, while others are chosen for the sake of defense. The same goal may serve either purpose, but if there is a shift in motivation, there is usually a shift in the definition of the role. For example, in one of our "sick" Italian families an eleven-year-old daughter, the middle one of three girls, repeatedly made demands upon her father for gifts of all sorts. Her motive was originally desire for gratification, but it was mixed with a defensive need to test whether she were being rejected or not. At first the father gratified her demands intermittently and inconsistently. He gave when he felt like and at other times refused. Both giving and refusing represented satisfactions for him, and he included rewarding and withholding as legitimate goals in his conception of the father's role. However, the daughter gradually defined his withholding as confirmation of her fear of rejection and tested more intensively by increasing her demands. The father defined this as "pestering" and responded with increased withholding and disapproval while claiming that he was trying his best to satisfy her. This claim was not true since he consistently rewarded the older sister more than this middle girl. But now the goal of withholding had become defensive against the implied meaning of her demands — that he actually preferred the older sister. In this complicated transaction, the defense was accomplished on the father's side through defining the daughter's motivation as coercive and pinning this down in the informal role, "pest," while giving himself the informal role of "victim." Although a tenuous complementarity was maintained by the defensive establishment of the informal "pest-victim" relation, actually their goals became more and more discrepant. This discrepancy of goals was one of the chief reasons why the family brought the girl into the psychiatric clinic for treatment. The parents verbalized the failure of complementarity by characterizing the girl to our interviewers as a bad and disobedient daughter. They had tried their best to teach her "right" from "wrong" but she was unable to "learn." It is significant of the defensive problem in this family that her behavior was ascribed to a cognitive and value discrepancy — that she couldn't "learn" the correct behavior — when actually it was due to a motivational problem concerning unavowed goals.

Another source of discrepancy in goals is biologically determined, rather than of motivational origin. Fatigue, illness, and lack of maturation are accompanied by a *restricted capacity for goal attainment*. Other biological limitations such as deficiency of intelligence have the same effect. Such limitations produce disequilibrium when one of the role partners is unable to accommodate through a change in level of expectancy of goals as rewards, for example, the parent who can't accept the limited intelligence of his child.

Allocative Discrepancy

In any particular social situation there is a question of the individual's right to the role he wishes to occupy. There are four principal ways in which roles are sorted out among those who contend for them.

(1) Some roles, such as age and sex roles, are *ascribed*, (Linton, 1936). This means that they are universally expected and the individual has practically no leeway: He is not free to decide to change his sex or age role. If a man tries to change his sex role, as in transvestism, he is likely to invoke intense criticism. The same is true, though to a lesser extent, of age roles. The child who tries to act like an adult usually produces a critical response, and the same thing holds for the reverse situation.

(2) Some roles, such as occupational and some domestic roles, have to be *achieved*, (Linton, 1936). As an allocative principle, achievement involves effort, the satisfaction of prerequisites, and some form of ceremonial recognition such as licensure, contract, conferring of a diploma, appointment, and so forth. There is more leeway than in the case of ascribed roles, but strong sanctions will be invoked if an achieved role is simply taken without observing the required formalities.

(3) Some roles, in the main of an informal character, can be taken simply through *adoption*. No one has to ask permission to take an adopted role, although there may not always be approval for it. For example, the father in the Italian family just discussed adopted the role of "victim." He could have responded to his daughter's demands with some other role activity. He could have treated them as childish antics and laughed them off in the role of

amused "spectator." This was actually a tack he frequently took when his feelings were not so intensely involved. By adopting the role of "victim," however, he *assigned* her the complementary role of "pest." The assignment was implicit rather than explicit. This is to say that it was concealed or masked, and that on the whole he treated her as if she had spontaneously adopted the role of pest toward him. Thus adoption-assignment describes for role transactions what is denoted for the individual by the concepts of introjection-projection. If he had been able to laugh off her demands, he would have treated her behavior as essentially playful.

(4) Playfulness is the sign of the last allocative principle, which is based on *assumption*. Assumed roles are not serious. They are taken in games or play, and are held to be at some distance from "reality." The child who plays "mother" is not really confusing herself with her mother. Thus there are no sanctions invoked for assumed roles, provided the individual has emitted the culturally appropriate cue indicating the assumption of a role. The facial configuration referred to in the expression — "smile when you say that" — is such a cue. It is obvious that assumed roles are of the greatest importance to the development and socialization of the child. But they are of equal importance to adults, not only for the sake of recreation and informality, but also to escape from a disequilibrium situation. The formula — "I was only kidding" — changes an adopted or achieved role into an assumed one, and thus establishes a new type of complementarity when the old one was threatened with failure. In this connection, withholding a cue indicating whether a role is adopted or assumed is frequently used to conceal or mask motivation. Alter is left in the dark or misinterprets whether ego was serious or not.

The most common sources of allocative discrepancy leading to a failure of complementarity are: (a) use of a culturally invalid or inappropriate allocative principle; (b) withholding of a clue indicating the allocative principle being used; and (c) emission of a misleading cue which gives alter the impression that one allocative principle is in use when in fact another one is actually present. For example, in the Italian family that I have been discussing, the mother was angry about the favoritism and excessive attention which the father showed toward their oldest daughter. In her eyes his behavior was largely seductive. At the same time she was ambivalent about his behavior, and unable to express the full range of her feelings. She preferred to attack him on the grounds that he was not a typical American Daddy.

She reproached him for showing favoritism, for being unfair to the other children, saying nothing about the competitive feelings toward her daughter which his behavior stimulated in her. His response was to deny anything inappropriate in his behavior toward his daughter, and to accuse his wife of being irritable and unduly apprehensive in this situation. Actually neither of them wanted to push the situation to the full extent of their feelings. There was an implicit agreement to avoid it and to substitute in its place their coöperative concern with the excessive demands and "disobedience" of the middle daughter.

An analysis of the allocative principles involved in this source of disequilibrium between the parents reveals that (a) the mother defines the father's role as invalid. In her eyes he acts like a lover to his daughter and this is doubly inappropriate. It is not a part of his ascribed role as a father, nor of his achieved role as a husband. He has no right to this role. (b) The father agrees with the mother's view of the allocative principles but denies that he has taken a lover's role. But since both accusation and the denial are implicit — that is, they are only hinted at, not directly verbalized — we have to look for the operations through which the potentially explosive aspects of this situation are avoided. This occurs by a mutually unconscious shift of the dispute to the ground of a cultural value discrepancy — the father's failure to be a typical American rather than a misguided Italian Daddy. At the same time, according to the observations of the interviewers who are studying the family, there is an ill-defined but quite intense intimacy between the father and daughter. It is hard to decide whether it is merely a playful aspect of filial attention and devotion, or whether it is something more than this. At times the daughter seems actually to take the mother's role toward the father. The cue distinguishing this as an assumed, adopted, achieved, or ascribed role is missing. But the father's direct description of his activity (how he perceives his behavior) on being questioned is that it is merely a part of his generally ascribed role as father. He even goes so far as to deny to the interviewer that he shows any favoritism, claiming that he treats all his children alike.

Withholding allocative cues or emitting misleading cues are in part attempts to avert the full denouement of failure of complementarity with its accompanying intense disequilibrium. Insofar as they have this function they will be discussed below in connection with that step in the restoration of equilibrium for which I will propose the term *masking*. It is probably obvious that these are general processes occurring in transactions at all levels of the social system. Withholding allocative cues universally produces a masked or ambiguous situation favorable for the "reading in" or projection of intentions. Emitting misleading cues is also a familiar device, whether in the hands of spies, at the international level, or confidence men on home territory. Be that as it may, their connection with failure of complementarity is this: That at the point at which the situation becomes unmasked, the allocative discrepancy is revealed in all its starkness. The disequilibrium is characterized by disillusionment ("You deceived me!"), protest ("You have no right to do what you did!"), alarm ("I've been robbed!"), and various similar phrasings in the vocabulary of victimization.

Instrumental Discrepancy

A review of the origins of failure to maintain complementarity in role relations can not neglect the fact that nonhuman events and objects form part of the context of all behavior. Insofar as role activities require technical instruments, equipment, furniture, props, costumes, climate and other appropriate physical facilities (including money!), a deprivation or insufficiency of these instrumental prerequisites interferes with role transactions. The point is so obvious that it is represented in various traditional and contemporary maxims, of somewhat dubious accuracy. When equestrian skills were at a premium, instrumental discrepancy was pictured as "For want of a nail, the shoe was lost. For want of a shoe, the horse was lost. For want of a horse, the battle was lost. . . ." Today, in a less heroic cultural climate, one frequently hears, "There's nothing wrong with him that money won't cure!"

Despite the therapeutic oversimplification, such sentiments underscore the potential for severe frustration inherent in instrumental discrepancy. In addition to legitimate and actual deprivation, instrumental discrepancy easily assumes displaced or symbolic functions. For example, in our Italian family, the father complained that he did not have the money to buy the things that his family demanded. Actually he tried desperately to earn more money by taking extra jobs in addition to his main employment. These frenzied efforts defined him as a failure in the dominant American cultural pattern of occupational and economic success because he was unable to plan, budget, or save any money. On the other hand, this strenuous activity relieved him of the potential accusation of neglect — of not caring for his family's welfare. Yet the need to neglect underlay much of his over-compensatory striving. Unconsciously he resented having to take the role of the

father, the provider, and would have preferred to compete with his children as the recipient of parental care and concern. This source of role discrepancy, however, had to be hidden from his conscious awareness and its energy had to be partly displaced into other types of activity or passive avoidance of activity.

Unconsciously contrived instrumental deficiency admirably served this purpose. The family suffers from protean forms of equipment failure. The screens had holes, the cellar frequently flooded, the car broke down, the ice box was constantly in need of repair, fuses blew, pipes broke, paint peeled. In the midst of this chaos, the father gave the impression of much activity, rushing about to attend to the latest crisis, accompanied by strident advice from his wife. Actually, he neglected repairing obvious defects until it was too late. The result of the neglect was painful to the wife who had high standards of housekeeping. He met all criticism from her with the attitude, "What can I do? I'm doing my best!"

From this description, it is apparent that instrumental discrepancy can be consciously or unconsciously motivated. To the extent that this is true, it is closely related to goal discrepancy. It must be kept in mind, however, that it can occur quite fortuitously, as in the case of accidental loss or deprivation by fire, robbery, or some other external agent.

Discrepancy in Cultural Value Orientations

As was said before, roles are patterned in accordance with the value orientations of a culture or subculture. In mixed marriages, in families that have moved suddenly from one culture to another as in emigration, and in families that are moving up or down the social class ladder, the possibilities of confusion or outright conflict in cultural values are very great. However, even in families not involved in such dramatic transitions, there is a possibility of discrepancy of cultural value orientations. This is especially true in the United States, because of the extreme mixture of values beneath the surface layers of apparent uniformity of the social system. In this country, cultural traditions are so various and so frequently at odds with each other that almost any individual will have internalized some degree of cultural conflict.

In our project we are using the scheme of variation in cultural value orientations proposed by Florence Kluckhohn (1953; 1957) to keep track of the cultural attitudes which can give rise to conflict. This has proved very useful, but it is too detailed and involved to set forth here. However, the way in which cultural value discrepancies can give rise to disequilibrium can be illustrated again in the case of the Italian family discussed above. The mother was born in this country of native Italian parents. The father was born in Italy and did not come to the United States until he was eight years old. Consequently, the mother considers herself, correctly, to be more Americanized than the father. In both of them there is a great deal of conflict and confusion over the transition to the American patterns, but on any specific issue between them, she is always closer to the American middle-class cultural orientation. She would like to cook only American food, but he insists on Italian dishes. She would like to get away from the home, visit with friends and ultimately obtain a job, but he insists that she stay home and care for the children constantly. She would like her husband to show more initiative and independence though she has the capacity for making decisions and solving problems. He backs away from responsibility and is unable to discipline the children. She would like to plan for their future and the future of the children, but he is occupied with present concerns and he can't get his eyes on the future as a good American would.

These discrepancies in cultural values are associated with incompatible definitions of their roles as husband and wife, mother and father. Thus the complementarity of their role relations is always somewhat strained. The strain would be reduced if the father were moving, culturally, in the direction the mother wants to go. But her activity toward him makes it impossible for him to utilize what potentials for movement he possesses, since he is continuously defined as a failure in terms of the American patterns. He defends himself by pleading incapacity, by claiming that he is "trying" as hard as he can, and by asking that she accept as culturally adequate substitutes other informal roles. One of these is the role of comedian which he plays with great skill, offering entertainment in the place cf successful performance. However, his position *vis-à-vis* the value of discrepancy is essentially destructive to his self-esteem. He takes his revenge on his wife through his seductive relations with his oldest daughter. In this way a value discrepancy, in which he is the loser, is compensated by an allocative and goal discrepancy in which he is the victor. Since these complicated transactions represent attempts to stabilize or restore equilibrium through *masking* and *compromise*, their further discussion will be postponed until we take up the discussion of these processes.

It is apparent that in discussing the varieties of failure of complementarity in any concrete empirical focus it is virtually impossible to avoid discussing simultaneously the efforts occurring in the system of transactions to compensate or re-establish equilibrium. Failure of complementarity is so disruptive that it is almost always accompanied by processes of restoration for which I would like to use the term, *re-equilibration*. In any ongoing system of relations such as a family, then, one can observe re-equilibration occurring whenever the balance of equilibrium to disequilibrium in the state of the system moves too close to the disequilibrium pole. It seems to me that it is the empirical admixture of these three processes — that is, of equilibrium (high complementarity), disequilibrium (low complementarity), and re-equilibration — that has made the processes involved in the stabilization or healthy internal adjustment of the system so difficult to recognize.

RE-EQUILIBRIUM

The restoration of equilibrium, once complementarity is threatened with failure, is itself an extremely complicated process. I have distinguished eleven steps in the process which I will here describe briefly. I believe these steps have a temporal order and that this order has a kind of internal logic. Unfortunately, I am unable to discern the basis of the order and must therefore leave the presentation in an excessively descriptive and "*ad hoc*" condition. The description has heuristic value, though it will not leave the reader free of the suspicion that it is arbitrary and incomplete. I am myself dissatisfied with it, but at least it is a method of systematically noting processes in the family which are subtle and difficult to observe.

With respect to the problem of internal logic or the underlying process connecting the various categories, one thing can be said. The eleven categories fall into two groups which are basically different. The first five categories belong together as do the last five. The sixth forms a connecting link between the two groups. The difference between the two groups is concerned with the method by means of which the role conflict is handled and the equilibrium restored. In the first group the resolution is affected by means of a unilateral decision. Ego resolves the discrepancy by giving in to alter, or *vice versa*. One or the other parties to the conflict agrees, submits, goes along with, becomes convinced, or is persuaded in some way. For this group, therefore, I would propose the term, *role induction*.[3] The net

[3] H. S. Sullivan used the term "induction" for the process through which anxiety in the parent elicits anxiety in the child. However, Sullivan applied the word only to the transmission of anxiety; in this paper it refers to a variety

effect, whatever the particular step may be, is that alter is induced to take the complementary role which will restore the equilibrium with ego. Ego's role, on the other hand, does not essentially change. The techniques of induction are dealt with in the classical tradition of Rhetoric and have been given a contemporary analysis by Kenneth Burke (1950). They have also been considered in contemporary studies of propaganda devices. I am very much indebted to Burke for his detailed and illuminating studies of the relation between persuasion and discrepancy.

In the second group of categories, re-equilibration is accomplished through a change in roles of both ego and alter. Complementarity is re-established on a mutually new basis. Because of the novel solution of the conflict, I suggest for this group the term, *role modification*. The change in role expectations is bilateral and the modification techniques are based on interchanges and mutual identifications of ego with alter. Although the distinction may be somewhat vague, induction techniques are founded on manipulative and instrumental procedures, while modification techniques are based on insight and communicative procedures.

ROLE INDUCTION

(1) *Coercing* holds first place as the most universally available induction technique. It may hold its primacy either on biological or cultural grounds or both. It can be defined as the manipulation of present and future punishments. Thus it ranges from overt attack to threats of attack in the future, and from verbal commands to physical force. It varies in intensity from mildly aversive manipulations to cruel and unusual torture. It owes its universality to its connection with the hostile-aggressive patterns of behavior in the individual. The reverse is, of course, also true. This is to say that the hostile-aggressive behavior would have no biologically useful function if coercion did not exist as a culturally patterned mode of settling role conflicts. It exists in every family we have studied, and it is probably safe to say that it is present in every enduring social system, no matter how much it may be veiled. If it is successful, the role conflict is settled through submission in which ego accepts the complementary role enforced by alter. However, none of the in-

duction techniques can guarantee success. They may all be met in one of two ways: Either by a specific neutralizing technique or by a counter-induction. The specific neutralizing technique for coercing is *defying*. The counter-inductions may vary from retaliatory coercion to any of the other re-equilibration categories.

(2) *Coaxing* is in second place not because it is less universal than coercion but because it seems somewhat less readily available as an induction technique. It is probably not the best term for this category, though it specifies the basic principle involved in it. Coaxing can be defined as the manipulation of present and future rewards. Thus it includes asking, promising, pleading, begging, and tempting. Ego accedes to alter's request in order to gain alter's reward, just as in coercing ego submits in order to escape alter's punishment. The child who says, "Please!", by word or gesture, rewards his mother with love or compliance when she gratifies his request. In tempting, bribing, or seducing, alter's rewards are likely to be more concrete! However, in seduction, the behavior is invaded by masking — insofar as the seducer conceals his actual motives — and consequently this is probably not a pure case.

Coaxing owes its universality (and its irresistability) to the fact that it expresses ego's wish for gratification and stimulates a wish to gratify in alter. It epitomizes desire. In spite of its power, it is no guarantee of success in resolving role conflict. As with the other induction techniques, it can misfire if ego responds with a specific neutralizing technique or a counter-induction. The specific neutralization for coaxing is *refusing* or *withholding*. All specific neutralizing techniques are essentially without affect. The affective neutrality occurs because the response is simply a technical way of meeting a persuasion. However, the neutrality may be hard to maintain, and some degree of affective response may creep into it. To the extent that this happens, the response becomes transformed into a counter-induction. For example, defying is simply a holding out against threat and is not in itself affectively toned. But, if ego feels anxiety over the success of defying as a way of warding off threat, then he is likely either to submit, or to become hostile and respond with counter-coercion. Similarly, refusing is merely a way of warding off the pressure of coaxing, but if ego is anxious about its effect — for example, if he feels guilty — he may respond by coercing or postponing, or some other induction.

(3) *Evaluating* operates upon the role conflict in a somewhat more derived way than coercing and

---

of interpersonal influences. A further distinction is that Sullivan regarded the process as somewhat mysterious — a unitary phenomenon, incapable of analytic penetration. For further details, see Sullivan (1953).

coaxing. In the usual case it follows upon them, and therefore is likely to be a counter-induction, though this is not necessary or inevitable. In evaluating, alter responds to ego's behavior by identifying or categorizing it in a value context. Thus it includes such activities as praising, blaming, shaming, approving, and disapproving. For example, if alter tries to resolve the role conflict through coercion, ego may evaluate his behavior by saying, "Stop behaving like a fool!", or, "Quit trying to act like a little Hitler!". The "Stop" and "Quit" signal defiance, but ego clearly is responding as if defiance were not enough either to express the degree of affect mobilized in him or to neutralize the degree of coercion emitted by alter.

The effect of this kind of induction is based upon the manipulation of reward and punishment. It differs from coercing and coaxing in that the reward or punishment is generalized, categorized, and thus placed in a class of value judgments — either positive or negative — linked by verbal and visual imagery to the category. When ego says, "acting like a fool," he is linking alter's behavior to a class of punished or devalued activities symbolized by the figure of the fool. He establishes an identity between alter and all other fools. If alter accepts the identity, then he will define his having coerced as punishable or noneffective and will terminate or extinguish his coercive activity. He may then substitute some other induction, such as coaxing, to resolve the role conflict. However, he may not accept the identity employed in the evaluation, and if so, he may use the specific neutralizing technique to be employed against evaluation. This is *denying*. For example, alter may respond to ego's evaluating by saying, "I am *not* behaving like a fool, and if you don't do what I've asked you to do, you'll have to suffer the consequences!" After denying, ego returns to coercing, showing the circular pattern characteristic of any protracted quarrel.

The same mechanisms hold true for positive evaluating such as praising. Of course, positive evaluating is more likely to be accepted, since it is a reward, though it may not be so interpreted as in the case of what is held to be unwarranted flattery. The case of flattery, however, is another example of a compound induction because it is likely to be mixed with various degrees of masking. Alter is apt to perceive ego's flattering as concealing a hidden motive. Apart from masking, there are still good reasons for denying positive evaluating. Since the motive behind ego's positive evaluation is to induce alter to take the complementary role which will restore equilibrium, alter may deny in order to ward off this outcome. This is

certainly what happens in the case of praise, encouragement or support, if alter is resisting the induction process. A mother, attempting to encourage her reluctant son to go to school for the first time, may say, "Johnny, I'm sure you'll enjoy school. You'll have a good time, and Mommy will be proud of you, just like she is of Freddy (older brother)." First the mother coaxes, by holding out the promise of future reward (enjoyment) and then she reinforces with a positive evaluation, putting Johnny with Freddy in a class of rewarded objects (pride). Such an inducement can easily backfire. Johnny bursts into tears and says, "No! I don't wanna go. I won't have a good time." (Refusal of coaxing.) "And I don't care about Freddy. I'm not *like* him!". (Denial of identity and of evaluation.) This leaves the discrepancy of goals about where it started, at high disequilibrium, and the mother may now try coercing, or she may postpone the settlement of the conflict until Daddy comes home, or until tomorrow when Johnny's resistance may be lowered.

(4) *Masking* is another universal induction technique, more indirect than the three discussed so far. It may be defined as the withholding of correct information or the substitution of incorrect information pertinent to the settlement of the conflict. It includes such behavior as pretending, evading, censoring, distorting, lying, hoaxing, deceiving, etc. These words are taken from ordinary usage and are apt to have a negative connotation. However, it is not my intention to give masking (nor any other induction technique) either a positive or negative value. It occurs universally in the course of organism-environment transactions, and has its biological and cultural aspects. The tiger stalking its prey is masking as is the camouflaged bird sitting on its nest. Every culture has its patterned ways of concealing information and its criteria for determining what information may or may not be revealed, with or without distortion. In studying masking my intention is merely to determine its *function* for the way the system is working. I believe it is as significant to the function of the social system, large or small, as is *repression* to the function of the personality as a system. Repression is universal as an intrapsychic process, and it means that information available to certain components of the personality is either completely unavailable to another component or reaches it only in disguised form. Repression has a biological basis in the function of the organism, but the content of what is repressed is related to the content of what is masked in the social system. This is a point which Sullivan (1953) repeatedly stressed in calling attention to the significance of interpersonal relations

to the function of the personality. However, Sullivan tended to see only the negative side of masking. He noted how it produces obstacles to successful communication which the individual internalized, but he was not interested in its function for the social system itself.

Masking is so complex and so intrinsic to re-equilibrating processes in the family that it is impossible to discuss it adequately in this small compass. "Little white lies" and minor disguises of motives take place so automatically that they are scarcely noticeable. For example, displacement and substitution of roles between parent and child are ubiquitous. A child bumps itself on a chair, and the mother says, "Naughty chair!", assigning the chair a human activity and then evaluating that activity as if it were part of a coercive induction. Why does she do this? Pain produces anger and in order to avoid the potential role conflict which may be precipitated between herself and her child, she involves the child in a make-believe conflict with the chair, with herself in the role of referee. Furthermore, she denies thereby the potential negative evaluation of herself as insufficiently protective of the child, by displacing the carelessness to the chair. This preserves equilibrium between herself and the child and thus is functional for that role system. But one can ask whether what is functional for their role system may not be dysfunctional for the child's ability to test reality. She conceals the important information that pain and accidents can occur without motive and need to be endured in the inevitable process of maturation and acquisition of autonomy by the child. Thus her masking ties the child to her in a dependent relation in which she plays the role of protector. She conceals both from herself and her child information about her resentment at the growing independence of the child, which, if it were available as a message, would read, "If you're going to act so independent, you ought to be punished. But I don't want you to know that I think this, so I'll pretend that it's not your behavior I resent but the chair's. You will understand that the world is full of hostile chairs, and you need me to protect you from them." If the child does not see through this masking, he will take the complementary dependent role which his mother desires for him.

In studying the family it is often difficult to disentangle the significance of minor masking, such as the example just discussed, from major transactions in which the masking is very dramatic. For example, in the Italian family discussed above both the cultural value discrepancy and the sexual goal discrepancy between the parents were masked and the role conflict displaced to the middle daughter who was explicitly defined by both parents as the major source of all their difficulties. The test of significance is to discover what happens when the induction technique is unmasked. *Unmasking* is the specific neutralizing technique for masking. The role partners confront each other with what has been concealed or disguised. Where the masking has averted a major disequilibrium, unmasking can be extremely explosive. As a result of therapy with the mother, father, and middle child in this Italian family, the mother began to displace less of her role conflict to the middle child and to pay more attention to the father's relation to the oldest daughter. The change was registered in a violent scene in which the mother openly voiced her resentment to the father who then lost his temper and threw a lighted cigarette at his wife, denying all the while the truth of her accusation. This unmasked the sexual situation, but left the cultural discrepancy still concealed, that is, not directly stated as a source of role conflict between the parents. It is our hunch that when this conflict opens up, the violence in their feelings will be even greater.

(5) *Postponing* may seem to fit uneasily as an induction technique since it appears to be merely a negative or passive way of dealing with role conflict. Nevertheless, it is undertaken with the expectation in both ego and alter that "in the interval he will change his mind." The process by which the conflict is to be settled is deferred in the hope of change of attitude. Indeed, this is very likely to be successful since the intrapsychic process always tends to work toward a resolution of conflict. The implied instruction, "think it over," or "I'll sleep on it," often achieves the desired effect. Most role conflicts in the family are not settled at the moment, but are deferred and taken up afresh, time and time again. From the point of view of persuasion, the question between ego and alter is: Who has the most to gain from postponing? If ego considers that he has very little to gain, he may attempt the specific neutralizing technique when alter attempts to postpone. This is *provoking*. If ego is afraid of postponement, he may provoke or incite the conflict to appear in full force.

(6) *Role reversal*[4] is a transitional re-equilibration midway between role induction and role modifica-

---

[4] Like "role conflict," the expression "role reversal" has also been used in two different ways. In one usage it refers to a situation in which ego and alter permanently exchange roles. For example, a husband and wife settle on an arrangement in which the husband stays home and looks after the house and children while the wife takes a

tion. It can be defined in G. H. Mead's (1936) sense as the process of taking the role of alter. Ego proposes that alter put himself in ego's shoes, try to see it through his eyes. Or ego initiates the reversal in the hope that alter will do the same. Ego may say, "Well, I think I'm beginning to see your point, but. . . ." Or, "It doesn't make too much sense to me, but I think I see what you mean." Insofar as this is a nonmanipulative approach, it can't be classified as an induction, and it therefore requires no specific neutralizing technique. On the one hand, if alter responds to role reversal with an induction, then ego may give up the attempt to reverse roles, and the whole process will revert to inductive and counter-inductive maneuvers. On the other hand, the role reversal may well kick the process of re-equilibration toward role modification and a novel resolution. It is this ambivalent position that makes it impossible to classify role reversal as belonging to either group; it is really transitional between both of them.

Whether role reversal is effective or not depends in large part on the intensity of masking procedures in the family relations. The more energy in disequilibrium being defended by masking, the less likely is role reversal to take effect. In our Italian family, the interviewers, seeing the parents, tried repeatedly to test their ability to reverse roles with Joanne, the middle daughter. For example, the mother's interviewer would say, "Do you think Joanne is sort of feeling left out in the family; maybe she feels she isn't getting enough attention." To this sort of approach, the mother, for a long time, would respond with the statement, "But how could she?" We try so hard to treat them all the same!" The same sort of thing tended to happen with respect to Joanne's stealing. Joanne was not given an allowance nor permitted to baby-sit in order to earn some money. This was always defended on the basis of the evaluative induction: Joanne steals. She's not reliable. We can't trust her, etc. The interviewer asked how Joanne could ever learn to take responsibility if she were not given some. After a while this role reversal "took" with the mother who started to treat Joanne as if she were not an irretrievably deviant daughter. This coincided with an intensive role reversal program between the interviewer and the mother in which the interviewer tried con-

tinuously to understand how the mother was feeling. The double-barreled procedure moved Joanne out of the masking process in which she had been held as if in a vise. In turn this led to the unmasking of the sexual conflict between the mother and father with respect to Rosemarie, the oldest daughter.

ROLE MODIFICATION

(7) *Joking* is an outgrowth of role reversal. It is the first sign that role modification is in progress. The role partners having successfully exchanged places with each other and thus having obtained some insight into each other's feelings and perceptions are now able to achieve some distance from their previous intense involvement in the conflict. They are able to laugh at themselves and each other. The laughing proceeds in part, as Freud pointed out, from the saving of psychic energy coincident with the partial solution of the conflict. The jokes also permit the expression in sublimated form of some of the induction techniques which are about to be relinquished — such as coercing and evaluating. The joking process moves the allocative base of the transaction to a whole set of assumed roles, and thus introduces playfulness into what was previously a tense set of achieved or adopted roles. In play the role partners try on for size a series of weird or impossible solutions, out of which is gradually fabricated the substance of the possible solution.

(8) *Referral to a third party*. Role reversal and joking may not of themselves create a role modification. They are helpful but not necessarily sufficient for this type of re-equilibration. Therefore, ego or alter may suggest that the conflict be referred to a third person (or organization) for help in its solution. The assumption is that the third party is less intensely involved in the conflict and has information or skills not available to ego or alter. Thus he can visualize a solution with greater ease. There are two difficulties which may arise from this re-equilibrating procedure. First, the third party chosen may steer the process back to a manipulative procedure and thereby restimulate the induction process. Secondly, and coincidental with this, the third person may form a coalition with ego against alter, or *vice versa*. In families, the attempted solution through referral frequently gets grounded on the rocks of a coalition. The third person, who was to have taken the role of impartial judge or referee, actually teams up with either ego or alter. This triadic situation has been studied by Simmel, (1950) and more recently by Mills, (1953; 1954) in artificially composed groups. However, the process involved in it needs much more extensive investigation. In our Italian family, third

---

job and earns the income for the family. In the second usage, the phrase refers to a process in which ego and alter temporarily exchange roles, in action or in imagination, for the sake of gaining insight into each other's feelings and behavior. This definition has been extensively used by J. L. Moreno and his associates, to whom I am much indebted. For examples, see Moreno (1955).

party referral always seemed to end in a coalition. At the outset, the parents were allied against Joanne. As unmasking proceeded, the father and Rosemarie were revealed in a coalition against the mother. There was evidence that the youngest child and the mother were in alliance against the father. These shifting triadic relations are among the most difficult transactions to unearth and keep track of in the family. Yet they are of the greatest importance to the dynamics of role conflict and thus to the way in which the family system is organized and functions.

Referral is invoked whenever a family comes to a community agency for help and is inevitably associated with the role of the psychiatrist or other mental health worker. Implicitly or explicitly, the helper is asked to judge, referee, or take sides. The interviewers seeing our families are inevitably pitted against each other in a semi-coalition with the particular member of the family they are seeing. This process is neutralized by our team approach in which the interviewers exchange information continuously with each other. If there is delay in the collaborative interchange between interviewers, then the coalitions are apt to get out of hand. The high level of communication between the interviewers permits all of them to obtain a balanced view of the over-all family process. In this way excessive identification with the member they are seeing is avoided. It seems a good working rule that the more information available to the person taking the role of the third party, the easier it is to avoid getting entangled in a coalition. As a corollary to this proposition, the more information available to the third person, the easier it is for him to help the role partners to a novel solution and to avoid a manipulated solution of the conflict.

(9) *Exploring* is the next step in role modification. Ego and alter probe and test each other's capacity to establish a novel solution. This process was already initiated in the joking phase but now it is undertaken more seriously. If a third party has been able to avoid becoming entangled in a coalition, he can be of great help in promoting exploration. To a considerable extent this describes the activity of the psychiatrist, case worker, nurse, or whoever is involved in the solution of a family problem. It is almost always accompanied by temporary relapses to an induction procedure, but once initiated, it tends to be self-steering. Ego and alter propose and reject possible solutions. This is accomplished not so much through verbal formulations as through actual behavior, though both paths toward the solution are probably necessary.

(10) *Compromising*. After a sufficient amount of exploration, ego and alter come to see that restora-

tion of equilibrium involves some change in the goals each desired or in the values by which they were guided. Thus they must settle for somewhat different complementary roles than those with which they started. If the process of re-equilibration has involved a successful referral, the third person takes very little part in the actual compromise solution. His role has accomplished its function when exploration moves re-equilibration to the threshold of compromise.

(11) *Consolidating* is the last step and it is required because the compromise solution, which is characterized by novelty and cognitive strain, is still present. Even though ego and alter establish a compromise, they must still learn how to make it work. To put the matter somewhat differently, compromise can be defined as the adjustment and redistribution of goals. Then consolidating is associated with the adjustment and redistribution of rewards. The roles are modified through the redistribution of goals. The new roles still have to be worked through and internalized by ego and alter as they discover how to reward each other in playing the new roles.

CONCLUSION

The study of how the family functions and maintains itself as a going system is greatly facilitated by the observation of role transactions concerned with equilibrium (high complementarity of roles), disequilibrium (low complementarity of roles), and re-equilibration (restoration of complementarity). I suspect that these same processes occur in other small-scale social systems such as a factory or a mental hospital. To what extent they can be detected in large-scale social systems, such as a total society, I do not know. In a small-scale system like the family, most of the process which can be seen by the observer is concerned with equilibrium. Complementarity of roles is high, decision-making is low, and most events take place automatically, leaving a considerable degree of spontaneity to the individuals in transaction with each other. This is the "routine," the way the system usually works. However, there are inevitable strains in any such system, and these give rise to disequilibrium. The strains can be analyzed in terms of the cognitive, goal, allocative, instrumental, and value structures of the roles. A strain represents a discrepancy in the expectations of any ego and alter with respect to these role structures. Thus it can be described in terms of role conflict. Strain gives rise to anxiety because, if left unchecked, it will lead to a rupture of the role relations, and thus to a disruption of the system. Without discussing the origin of this anxiety in the basic structure and function of the intrapsychic process in the individual, it can be said that the role conflict gives rise to defensive processes both in the individual and in the family system. For the family system this reactive process can be described as an attempt to restore the threatened complementarity of roles. The process itself can be called re-equilibration since its effect is to restore the equilibrium which has been shattered.

Re-equilibration can be analyzed as an eleven-step process. The first five of these steps are manipulative. Ego attempts to persuade or get alter to comply with his expectations. If compliance is achieved and alter takes the necessary complementary role, then equilibrium is restored. For this reason, these steps are grouped together as a process called role induction. The last five steps are based on mutual insight rather than manipulation. They lead to a novel solution of the role conflict underlying the disequilibrium. These steps are grouped together in a process called role modification. The sixth step is intermediate between the two groups since it can lead either to induction or modification.

If modification is successful, then the new solution of the role conflict sinks into the normal "routine" of the family. The "problem" has disappeared. In this way modification differs from induction. Induction is primarily defensive. It wards off the disequilibrium but it is always likely to crop up again. It is an unsettled problem to the system and the resolution of the strain is more apparent than real. In this way it becomes internalized by the members of the family where it is likely to be productive either of a neurotic symptom or of difficulties in interpersonal relations. In dealing with emotionally disturbed individuals, whether in office practice or in a mental institution, one observes new versions of the old, unsettled, family role conflict appear. Therefore, it is fruitful to examine the role systems which the patient recreates in these settings to see in what way they reproduce the defensive, inductive procedures which were experienced in the family. Also, it is necessary to discover in what way the new institutional settings may have elaborated role conflicts and inductive re-equilibrations — because of their own internal organization — which resemble the original strain in the family.

REFERENCES

ACKERMAN, N. W. and SOBEL, R. Family diagnosis: an approach to the pre-school child. *American Journal of Orthopsychiatry*, 1950, 20, 744–753.

ACKERMAN, N. W. 'Social role' and total personality. *American Journal of Orthopsychiatry*, 1951, 21, 1–17.

BENTLEY, A. F. Kennetic inquiry. *Science*, 1950, 112, 775–783.

BURKE, K. A *rhetoric of motives*. New York: Prentice-Hall, 1950.

DEWEY, J. and BENTLEY, A. F. *Knowing and the known*. Boston: Beacon Press, 1949.

JOHNSON, ADELAIDE M. and SZUREK, S. A. The genesis of antisocial acting out in children and adults. *Psychoanalytic Quarterly*, 1952, 22, 323–343.

JOHNSON, ADELAIDE M. Factors in the etiology of fixations and symptom choice. *Psychoanalytic Quarterly*, 1953, 22, 475–496.

KLUCKHOHN, FLORENCE R. Dominant and variant value orientations. In: Kluckhohn, C., Murray, H. A. and Schneider, D. M. (Eds.), *Personality in nature, society, and culture*. New York: Knopf, 1953.

KLUCKHOHN, FLORENCE R. *Variants in value orientations*. Evanston, Ill.: Row-Peterson, to be published 1957.

KLUCKHOHN, FLORENCE R. and SPIEGEL, J. P. *Integration and Conflict in family behavior* (Report N. 27). Topeka, Kansas: Group for the Advancement of Psychiatry, 1954.

LINTON, R. *The study of man*. New York: Appleton-Century, 1936.

MEADE, G. H. *Mind, self, and society*. Chicago: Univer. Chicago Press, 1936.

MILLS, T. M. Power relations in three-person groups. In: Cartwright, D. and Zander, A. (Eds.), *Group Dynamics*. Evanston, Ill.: Row-Peterson, 1953.

MILLS, T. M. The coalition pattern in three person groups. *American Sociological Review*, 1954, 19, 657–667.

MORENO, J. L. The discovery of the spontaneous man — with special emphasis on the technique of role reversal. *Group Psychotherapy*, 1955, 8, 103–129.

PARSONS, T., BALES, R. F., and SHILS, E. A. *Working papers in the theory of action*. Glencoe, Ill.: The Free Press, 1953.

PARSONS, T. and BALES, R. F. *Family, socialization, and interaction process*. Glencoe, Ill.: The Free Press, 1955.

POLLAK, O. *Social science and psychotherapy for children*. New York: Russell Sage Foundation, 1952.

SIMMEL, G. Quantitative aspects of groups. In: Wolff, K. J. (Trans. & Ed.), *The sociology of Georg Simmel*. Glencoe, Ill.: The Free Press, 1950.

SPIEGEL, J. P. The social roles of doctor and patient in psychoanalysis and psychotherapy. *Psychiatry*, 1954, 17, 369–376.

SPIEGEL, J. P. A model for relationships among systems. In: Grinker, R. R. (Ed.), *Toward a unified theory of human behavior*. New York: Basic Books, 1956.

SULLIVAN, H. S. *The interpersonal theory of psychiatry*. New York: Norton, 1953.

The Neuroses / 3

The neuroses are by far the most common single group of behavior disorders. Estimates of their incidence in the general population tend to vary depending upon how one defines the term, but they are clearly ubiquitous. For example, in the most recent comprehensive epidemiological survey, the Midtown Manhattan Study[1] fully 23.4 per cent of the population sampled revealed symptomatology severe enough to be considered as psychologically impaired, and 67.8 per cent of this group were classified as suffering from neuroses or forms of personality disorder. Despite the problems involved in assessing the validity of such data,[2] it is clear that the neuroses represent a major health problem. It is clear, as well, that the concept of neurosis does not describe a homogeneous syndrome, but rather refers to a disparate assortment of disorders varying in their symptomatic manifestations, although having several functional characteristics in common.

Every major theory of personality has been put to the test of accounting for neurotic malfunctioning and the factors which determine its various forms (the "choice of neurosis"). Some of these conceptualizations are quite divergent in their assessment of predisposing and precipitating variables, but to varying degrees each is probably correct, for the "causes" of neurotic behavior are extraordinarily complex, involving genetic, social, intrapsychic, and cultural factors, to mention but a few.

Freud described anxiety as "the fundamental phenomenon and the central problem of neurosis," a characterization which is as relevant for the behavior-

ist approach to neurotic behavior as it is for the psychoanalytic. Indeed, anxiety has been portrayed as one of the most common and potentially painful human experiences. Fromm-Reichmann's paper reviews the basic theories of anxiety and concludes that its origins lie in the individual's inability to escape the distortions of his earliest interpersonal relationships, resulting in constriction of freedom to grow and realize his full potential.

Kubie's view of the neuroses is based on psychoanalytic theory, taking as its starting point man's inherent capacity for symbolic behavior. He suggests that in the course of development various guilt-laden and psychologically painful experiences, feelings, and thoughts are repressed and buried in the child's unconscious where they undergo a process of symbolization, and thus remain ever present but unamenable to modification through the normal processes of learning. Later, given a series of events symbolically representing the earlier painful situation, the neurotic state, in its various symptomatic forms, crystallizes and emerges. Kubie's distinction between normality and neurosis, based on the role of the unconscious in determining behavior, calls our attention to the important difference between phenotype and genotype, between behavior as it is manifested and the root causes of the behavior.

Mowrer presents a contrasting view of the genesis of neurosis, finding its core not in what he calls a "learning excess," the result of a too-harsh socialization process, but in a "learning deficit," a disorder of problem-solving. He questions the Freudian conception of neurosis which is based, he feels, on the assumption that the individual's suffering is due to the repression of instinctual feelings by an oppressive conscience or superego. The theory Mowrer proposes is rooted in what Sartre calls "bad faith," the individual's refusal to accept responsibility for his acts

[1] Srole, L., Langner, T. S., Michael, S. T., Opler, M. K., & Rennie, T. A. C. Mental Health in the metropolis. New York: McGraw-Hill, 1962.
[2] For a critique of the Midtown Manhattan Study, see Gruenberg, E. M. A review of "Mental health in the metropolis: Midtown Manhattan Study." Milbank Memorial Fund Quarterly, 1963, 42, 77–94.

resulting in a process of self-deception and "conscience killing," culminating in a personality lacking in integrity and based on false premises.

As Fromm-Reichmann's paper makes clear, neurotic symptoms can be understood as the result of the breakthrough of anxiety in a relatively pure and unmodulated form, or of an attempt to defend against its intrusion. These defense mechanisms are many and varied,[3] and each major form of neurosis has its characteristic defensive pattern. For example, the psychoanalytic position with regard to obsessional and phobic behavior emphasizes the role of "substitution" or displacement, the shifting of one's anxiety from an unconscious impulse or object to an external, symbolically-linked object. Displacement's central role in the development of phobic fear was dramatically defined by Freud in his case of "Little Hans."[4]

Rachman and Costello's article contrasts the psychoanalytic and the more contemporary behavior-therapy position with regard to the etiology of phobias. As associates of Hans Eysenck at the University of London, it is natural that their presentation takes a firmly behaviorist stand. They present a brief synopsis of the analytic and behaviorist theories on phobias, and critically review the evidence supporting each view. Noteworthy is their learning theory approach to the well-known phenomenon of the "spreading" of phobic fears along associative lines, as in Albert's fear of a white rat which generalized to similar white, furry objects. Important, too, is their succinct enumeration of behavior-therapy approaches which can be applied in the treatment of behavior disorders, one of which (Wolpe's "systematic desensitization") is discussed in greater detail in Section 9.

The clinical syndrome of hysteria (now more commonly called "conversion reactions") occupies an especially important place in the history of the study of psychopathology since it was in the course of the examination and treatment of this condition that Freud developed the method of psychoanalysis and many of its basic theories. Hysteria has been described as the "great imitator," for its manifestations frequently include patterns of somatic complaint which can be easily confused with symptoms of

organic illness. In addition to these psychogenic somatic symptoms, there may also be a puzzling complacency on the part of the patient, what Janet called "la belle indifférence," as well as periodic disturbances in consciousness during which potentially disturbing thoughts or emotions are repressed and blocked from awareness. Hysterical functioning has been more frequently observed in females, a phenomenon originally interpreted to mean that this is primarily a feminine disorder, but more recently viewed as a cultural artifact. Similarly, the apparent seductiveness of such women, once seen as reflecting a hypersexuality, has been explained in terms of the emotional immaturity and dependency so characteristic of the hysterical personality.

The paper by Ziegler and Imboden represents an empirical approach to the study of conversion reactions and their relation to hysterical character functioning. In their review of the psychiatric usage of the term "conversion," they critically discuss the mechanical "transmutation of energy" theory, and conclude that such a conception can only be used metaphorically, not in an explanatory sense. Interestingly, they find no evidence of a clear link between the conversion reactions and the hysterical personality. Their own analysis ties these reactions to role-playing, with the patient's symptoms developing in an interpersonal context out of an amalgam of vague expectations, iatrogenic (physician-caused) factors, and symbolic suitability of the body's various organs.

The term "depression" refers not only to an affective symptom, but to a clinical syndrome as well. The depressed or "melancholic" individual has been the focus of study at least since Hippocrates, and his symptoms seem eternally the same. For example, compare Ostow's portrayal with this analysis by a seventeenth-century clergyman, Richard Baxter:

> Melancholy Persons are commonly exceeding fearful. . . . Their Fantasie most erreth in aggravating their Sin, or Dangers or Unhappiness. . . . They are still addicted to Excess of Sadness, some weeping they know not why, and some thinking it ought to be so; and if they should Smile or speak merrily, their Hearts smite them for it, as if they had done amiss. . . . They are continual Self-Accusers, turning all into matter of Accusation against themselves, which they hear or read, or see, or think of; quarreling with themselves for every thing they do, as a contentious Person doth with others.[5]

Ostow focuses his attention less on a descriptive approach than on the psychodynamics of depression,

---

[3] In their study of maternal adjustment to pregnancy, Bibring and her associates enumerated 39 such defense mechanisms, some of which they called first-order defenses while others were viewed as more complex, second-order defenses. See Bibring, G. L., Swyer, T. F., Huntington, D. S., & Valenstein, A. F. A study of the psychological processes in pregnancy and of the earliest mother-child relationship. Psychoanalytic study of the child, 1961, 16, 9–72.

[4] Freud, S. Analysis of a phobia in a five-year-old boy. Collected papers. New York: Basic Books, 1959, Vol. III, pp. 149–289.

[5] Quoted in Hunter, R. and Macalpine, I. Three hundred years of psychiatry 1535–1860. London: Oxford Univ. Press, 1963, pg. 241.

emphasizing its relationship to the loss of a love object or the anticipation of such loss. The differentiation between various forms of this disorder, ranging from mild grief reactions through full-blown neurotic and psychotic depressive states, is a problem Ostow approaches from a clinical point of view.[6]

[6] For further elaboration on the normal grief reactions, see Lindemann, E. Symptomatology and management of acute grief. Amer. J. Psychiat., 1944, 101, 141–148. The etiologic and prognostic importance of differentiating between neurotic depression and that caused by situational factors is discussed in a recent paper: Kiloh, L. G. and Garside, R. F. The independence of neurotic depression and endogenous depression. Brit. J. Psychiat., 1963, 109, 451–463.

Whatever the form neurotic disturbance may take, it clearly arises and is maintained within an interpersonal, family context. The process of "contagion," the transmission of disturbed functioning across generational lines, is the subject of Ehrenwald's paper. As he notes, emotional attitudes and patterns of fantasy, because of their diffuse and primitive quality, wind their insidious way through several generations of a family.[7] ■

[7] A similar investigation, involving the use of psychological tests, is Fisher, S. and Mendell, D. The communication of neurotic patterns over two and three generations. Psychiatry, 1957, 19, 41–46.

FRIEDA FROMM-REICHMANN

Psychiatric Aspects of Anxiety*

The most unpleasant and at the same time the most universal experience, except loneliness, is anxiety. We observe both healthy and mentally disturbed people doing everything possible to ward off anxiety or to keep it from awareness.

Mentally disturbed people try to dispel anxiety by developing mental symptoms. In fact as first stated by Freud, mental symptoms are at the same time both the expression of unbearable anxiety and the means of warding it off. (9) In other words mental symptoms and mental illness can be understood simultaneously as the outcome of anxiety and as a defense against it. Mental illness can be understood as a person's response to unbearable anxiety. Therefore, anxiety constitutes an essential problem in psychotherapy.

This holds true even though we consider anxiety to be an experience by no means limited to the mentally disturbed. As initially stated, we realize that anxiety in its milder forms is a universal human phenomenon. Philosophers and psychologists have known and advanced this knowledge for a long time. In their eagerness to be great helpers and healers, psychiatrists have been and are still partly inclined

* Reprinted from C. Thompson, M. Mayer, and E. Witenberg, Eds., An Outline of Psychoanalysis. New York: Random House, 1955, pp. 113–133.

to overlook the difference between what may be called the normal anxieties of the emotionally healthy and the neurotic or psychotic excess anxiety which should be subject to psychotherapy. For a long time, psychiatrists and psychotherapists have also overlooked the fact that anxiety not only has negative, disintegrative facets but also some positive, constructive ones. As we set out to clarify the philosophy of psychotherapy regarding neurotic and psychotic anxieties, we must keep these two aspects of anxiety clearly in mind.

Anxiety, as we know, shows in a great variety of ways. Subjectively it may be experienced as a most unpleasant interference with thinking processes and concentration, as a diffuse, vague and frequently objectless feeling of apprehension or as a discomforting feeling of uncertainty and helplessness. As it arises in its milder forms, it may show objectively by a shift in tone of voice, and/or tempo of speech, by a change of posture, gesture and motion, also by the anxious person's intellectual or emotional preoccupation or blocking of communication. In people who are even more anxious, anxiety manifests itself psychologically in more or less marked degrees of paralysis of thought and action. The well known physical manifestations that may be caused by anxiety are symptoms of a hyperactive sympathetic system such as change of turgor, perspiration, tremor, sensation of a lump in the throat, sinking abdominal sensations, diarrhea, vomiting, changes in pupillar reactions, in heart beat, pulse rate and respiration. If anxiety-states become so severe that the anxiety-stricken person cannot handle them, mental symptoms and mental illness are the final outcome.

In the rare cases when anxiety is so severe that all these expressions of it and all defenses against it fail to bring relief, panic or terror may be the outcome. Panic, as defined by H. S. Sullivan, is an extreme concentration of attention and the direction of all available energy toward only one goal — escape, swift flight from internal dangers which are poorly envisaged, and in the case of failure to escape, by a temporary disintegration of personality with random destructive tendencies against oneself and others. Also according to Sullivan, terror is anxiety of a cosmic quality in the face of a primitively conceived threat of danger. The terror-stricken person feels himself to be alone among deadly menaces, more or less blindly fighting for his survival against dreadful odds. (29, 30) Fortunately, terror and panic are short lived. The organism produces quick defenses against the devastating influence which panic or terror of prolonged duration would exert. John Vassos' empathic pictorial work on Phobia (which, incidentally, is dedicated to H. S. Sullivan) should be mentioned here as an impressive contribution to the understanding of terror and panic. (34)

In contrast to these various forms of anxiety, fear is a useful, rational kind of fright elicited by realistic external dangers. To be described presently, and in contrast to fear, are the dangers from within, which elicit anxiety.

What is anxiety in terms of its conceptions in dynamic psychiatry? Freud says in "The Problems of Anxiety," that anxiety is felt by a person at the realization of formerly repressed inacceptable drives and wishes; his anxiety is with regard to loss of love and punishment, i.e. along the lines of Freud's libidinal concepts, castration-fear. (9)

We need not go into the discussion of Freud's older explanation of anxiety as the result of repressed sexual desires, (5) because he rejected it himself in "The Problems of Anxiety."

Sullivan shares with Freud the concept of the anxiety-arousing power of inacceptable thoughts, feelings, drives, wishes and actions. But in the framework of his interpersonal conceptions he sees these forbidden inner experiences as interpersonal ones, not as instinctual drives per se; also the expected punishment is not seen as castration-fear. Rather, it is experienced by the anxious person as the antici-

pated disapproval, i.e. loss of love, from the significant people of his early life, from whom he has originally learned to discriminate between acceptable and inacceptable drives, attitudes, and actions. Later on this fear of disapproval may be transferred from the original significant people who trained and educated the anxious person to their emotional successors. Guilt feelings, separately described by other authors, are obviously inherent in Sullivan's conception of anxiety. (29, 30, 31, 32)

This disapproval by the significant people of one's early life, to which both Freud and Sullivan refer, is vital enough to account for severe anxieties because the infant and the young child are dependent upon the early important people for fulfillment of their basic needs. The infant's survival depends upon the loving care he is given by the mothering ones of his infancy.

Nearly all psychological concepts of anxiety have, in common with Freud and Sullivan, this one basic conception: that anxiety is tied up with the inner danger of inacceptable thoughts, feelings, wishes or drives which elicit the expectation of loss of love and approval or of punishment. No matter how much these conceptions may differ in their explanatory details and regardless of whether or not this aspect of anxiety is explicitly mentioned in these conceptions, it is a viewpoint now commonly shared.

Let me quote a few outstanding representatives of various psychiatric schools of thinking. Rank speaks of separation anxiety which people first experience at birth and subsequently throughout their lives, present at all phases of personality-development and individuation, from weaning, i.e. separation from mother's breast, to separation from one's fellowmen, by death. (26)

Adler uses his concept of inferiority feelings where other authors speak of anxiety. He asserts that these inferiority feelings can be overcome by people only in affirmation and strengthening of their social bonds with society, by enforcing the sense of belonging to a social group. (1)

Horney emphasizes the central significance of the interrelatedness between anxiety and hostility — anticipated in others and sensed in the anxious person himself; here again anxiety is seen as being tied up with the fear of disruption of one's interpersonal relationships. (19)

Fromm, Berdyaev, Halmos, Kardiner, Riesman and other social psychologists find the source of man's anxiety in his psychological isolation, his alienation from his own self and from his fellowmen. They consider this the common fate of man in modern society, irrespective of his state of emotional health. (3, 10, 18, 22, 27) A poetic version of this viewpoint may be found in Auden's "Age of Anxiety." (2)

Goldstein's conception of anxiety as being the subjective experience of a danger to existence in the face of failure may also imply anxiety regarding loss of love and recognition by those who recognize the anxious person's failure. (15, 16)

The same holds true for Rollo May's definition of anxiety as "the apprehension set off by a threat to some value which the individual holds essential to his existence as a personality."[1] (23) Again this concept implies the fear of losing interpersonal recognition or acceptance since this could be tied up with the loss of essential values in the life of the individual. I will return later to the discussion of some other aspects of the conceptions of these authors. At this point I am primarily interested in demonstrating the ubiquitously implied acceptance of the concept that anxiety is connected with anticipated fear of punishment and disapproval, withdrawal of love, disruption of interpersonal relationships, isolation or separation.

This conception of anxiety as the expression of the anticipated loss of love and approval, or separation, social isolation, or disruption of one's interpersonal relationships implies its close psychological affinity to loneliness. In fact, I believe that many of the emotional states to which psychiatrists refer as anxiety actually are states of loneliness or fear of loneliness.[2]

Now I wish to return to the discussion of the psychodynamics of anxiety. According to Sullivan, the infant and child's need for love and approval and the anxiety connected with rejection and disapproval are utilized by the significant adults in handling the necessary early processes which are designed to train the infant and child for his interpersonal adjustment, his socialization and acculturalization. Out of this educative process evolves the part of human personality which Sullivan has called "self system." This self-system operates in the service of people to obtain satisfaction without incurring too much anxiety. In the process of establishing the self-system certain infantile trends must be barred

[1] Rollo May's book is most stimulating as a monograph in its own right, but also as an excellent survey of the theories of anxiety. The proceedings of the 39th Annual Meeting of the American Psychopathological Association, 1949; Grune & Stratton, 1950; edited by Hoch & Zubin ought to be quoted as another useful compendium on the subject.
[2] I will elaborate on this topic in my forthcoming publication "Philosophy of Psychotherapy." (See footnote on page 113.)

from awareness, dissociated. If they break into awareness anxiety will reappear because the structure of the self-system, the nature of which tends toward rigid maintenance of its protective status quo, is threatened with change. This defensiveness against change makes for the danger of personal rigidity, which in turn increases the potentialities for further anxiety. (29, 30) This anxiety connected with change is eternally in conflict with man's general innate tendencies toward growth, toward the change which is implied and particularly with the innate motivation of mental patients toward health. One of the great responsibilities of the psychotherapist is to help patients face and overcome this conflict constructively. (12)

I would like to offer an additional explanatory concept about the factors which make people expect punishment, disapproval and loss of love and which has helped me to understand better than I did previously the psychological significance of the anxieties of people in general and of mental patients in particular. Let us ask again: what do people disapprove of most gravely in themselves, i.e. which trends in themselves do they expect will bring the most severe disapproval on the part of the significant people in their lives? Are there other significant causes for the anxiety-arousing anticipation of disapproval and isolation in addition to those we have quoted? Let me offer the following hypothetical answer.

It is a well-known psychological fact that a person will misvalue the significant people of his childhood to the extent to which his early interpersonal tie-ups remain unresolved. If these early interpersonal patterns stand uncorrected, people will distort the image of various people whom they meet in the course of their lives. They may or may not dimly sense that they do so, but they will not recognize the interpersonal misconceptions of their early childhood as the root of the distortions of their interpersonal relationships.

An adult person who finds himself compulsively appraising other people inadequately, incorrectly evaluating their reactions, acting upon and responding to them in line with these misconceptions in terms of early patterns of living, may many times become semi-aware of his erroneous judgment and behavior. However, he may feel inadequate and helpless in his dim wish or attempt to change and correct his judgment and his emotional reactions because he is unaware of their unconscious roots, the unmodified fixations to the patterns of interpersonal relationships which he acquired in his early years. This helplessness in the face of the need to change anachronistic, distorted patterns of interpersonal relationships meets with self-disapproval and discontent; it interferes with the innate tendency to self-realization; it produces deep insecurity in people and meets with the anticipated disapproval of others; thus, it is the expression of anxiety and it produces further anxiety. Goldstein could demonstrate this type of anxiety in his brain-injured patients. When they were faced with a simple task which they could not accomplish for reasons unknown to them, stemming from their neurological brain injury, they became the prey of an abject feeling of helplessness, of nothingness, or a "catastrophic reaction," as Goldstein has called it. (15, 16)

The hypothesis is offered that mentally disturbed people frequently develop a "catastrophic reaction," anxiety, in response to their compulsively determined inability to change their distorted, immature patterns of interpersonal relationships. This task may be set by the demands of their own conscience or by the actual or assumed demands of their elders or friends. This helplessness in the presence of the need to envision and to relate oneself adequately to other people, i.e. in accordance with one's chronological age and with one's psychological reality without full awareness of its causes, is most frightening, for more than one reason. It elicits a general feeling of helplessness and paralysis. It means that the person concerned is living in an unreal psychological world and that he feels he is in danger of pulling the people of his environment actually or in fantasy into the same threatening abyss of unreality. Being unable to successfully avail himself of the possibility of using new means of evaluating people and of relating himself meaningfully to them amounts to being blocked in the utilization of learning processes which serve growth and change. This absence of growth and change is tantamount to psychological stagnation and emotional sterility, i.e. psychological death. (14) In other words, the repetition-compulsion to follow early patterns of interpersonal evaluation and relatedness and the inability to learn to replace them by new patterns, deprives a person of the freedom to live and move about in the world of psychological reality which should be his, deprives him of the freedom for self-realization and conveys feelings of stagnation and sterility, hence the fear of psychological death, of Tillich's "not being," or Goldstein's "nothingness." (15, 16, 33)

By "self-realization" I mean (to repeat a definition I have previously given (12) a person's use of his talents, skills and powers to his satisfaction within the realm of his own freely established realistic set of values. Furthermore, I mean the uninhibited ability of patients to reach out for and to find fulfillment of their needs for satisfaction and security, as far as it can be obtained, without interfering with the laws and customs which protect the needs of their fellowmen. Goldstein's "self-actualization," Fromm's "productive character," Whitehorn's "mature personality" and the "self-affirmation" of the existentialists are formulations of the same concept. (10, 15, 35) In the classical psychoanalytic literature insufficient attention has been given so far to the concept of self-realization as a great source, if not the greatest source, of human fulfillment. Freud has referred to it in his teachings on secondary narcissism and ego-ideal formation, but he has dealt more with the investigation of the origin of the phenomenon than with the elaboration on the psychological significance of the end-product, mature self-realization. (7, 8)

The lack of freedom for self-realization and the feeling of stagnation and "nothingness" that goes with it, this sense of psychological death, seems to me to be at the root of many people's anxiety. To repeat, they cling to infantile interpersonal patterns, and as a result feel helpless without really knowing why. They are unable to grow emotionally, to develop or change. They are not able to think, feel, and act according to their chronological age. They live anachronously in a deadening emotional rut where they compulsively continue to distort their interpersonal images of new people whom they meet, and to misvalue the interpersonal reactions and behavior of these people along the line of the conceptions gained in their unresolved interpersonal childhood contacts.

Example: A young woman, Anna, went to see her older friend and confidant, Mr. N., whom she trusted unequivocally. Anna asked him to contact certain significant people in her family and explain to them some facts about her life which she felt would be of immeasurable value for them and for her in the general family picture. Mr. N. assured Anna of his complete willingness to do this and when Anna left him she was confident that Mr. N. would take care of the situation with understanding and skill. For valid rational reasons, which are beside the point of our discussion, Mr. N. decided later not to meet the members of the family and have a talk with them along the lines suggested by Anna. He did not have an opportunity to discuss this with her. When Anna found out about it a few days later, she felt deep resentment against Mr. N. and developed a spell of severe anxiety. Why? She felt that her friend had not accepted her appraisal of the total situation nor given it serious consideration. She also felt he had treated her the same way her parents had always done; to judge everything the little girl suggested or offered for consideration as not being worthy of serious thought on their part, "little girls are too emotional." Anna realized though, that her resentment against Mr. N., whom she felt had betrayed her and had not taken her suggestion seriously was, somehow, unfounded and sensed dimly that he might well have fallen down on their agreement for valid, rational reasons. However, she felt completely incapable of overcoming her resentment and her severe spell of anxiety lasted for hours. The semi-awareness she had about the irrationality of her anxiety and resentment did not help any until, by psychoanalytic investigation, she finally discovered the reasons, of which she had been unaware. Then she recognized that her resentment was due to a distortion of the present situation between her and Mr. N., in the light of the unresolved interpersonal pattern of living with the parents of her childhood. ("little girl" — "too emotional" — judgment and suggestions deserve no consideration.)

Jurgen Ruesch's interesting new concept of anxiety which he gained from observation and investigation of people under stress, fits into this context. He says that anxiety arises as a result of overstimulation which cannot be discharged by action. (28) The anxious people who have been described are barred from discharging tension by action, from converting anxiety into euphoria because they live in a state of "not-being," or "nothingness."

The anxiety producing aspects of people's unresolved early tie-ups and involvements, of which they are only partially aware, receive additional reinforcement because so many of these anxiety producing aspects are experienced as forbidden and elicit anxiety connected guilt feelings. Love for the parent of the opposite sex and competitive hatred of the parent of the same sex should be mentioned here as the most outstanding example of such anxiety and guilt evoking psychological constellations.

The resolution of such early tie-ups with the parents of one's childhood, which I have implicitly recommended as a preventive against anxiety, should not be confused with manifestations of a child's outwardly breaking away from his parents. Children who succeed in breaking away from their parents early may experience increased anxiety, since this emerging independence of a child meets with a sense of loss on the part of the parents, hence frequently with their disapproval of the child.

The psychology of masturbation is illustrative of our last statement. There has been much discussion about the following question: Why are there so many children who never have been exposed to any warning against masturbation and many adults who intellectually do not consider masturbation forbidden or dangerous and yet there are practically no people who masturbate without feeling guilty and anxious about it? How can we explain this fact? I believe that guilt eliciting masturbatory fantasies are only partly, if at all, responsible. Many cases of masturbatory feelings of guilt and anxiety seem to be connected with the fact that masturbation represents a child's first act of independence from his parents or others who have raised and mothered him. He needs his elders for the fulfillment of all his basic needs; getting food and fresh air and for being kept clean and getting fresh clothes and bedding. Masturbation is the only pleasure he can obtain without their help. As such, it constitutes an act of breaking away from one's parents, for which the child feels guilty and anxious regardless of the permissive or non-permissive attitude of the elders towards the act of masturbation per se.

It has been stated that practically no one in this culture gets ideally rid of his early interpersonal tie-ups and the resulting interpersonal problems. In other words, almost no one is entirely prepared to face the anxiety provoking dangers of his present life, fully undistorted by interpersonal entanglements with the "ghosts of his past" and with full command of his adult emotional equipment. As Grinker puts it, in his research on "Anxiety and Psychosomatic Transactions:" "The stimulus" (which arouses anxiety) "must be perceived in the light of inner expectation originating at an early and particularly helpless time in the organism's history, to be dangerous to its protective attachments and hence to his existence," i.e. to have the power to produce anxiety. (17)

People's fear of nothingness, of helplessness in the face of "psychological death," as it has been postulated here as being a central cause of human anxiety, has a factual correlate in the practically universal experience of anxiety with regard to actual death as a general phenomenon. The fact that life ends with death remains to most people an inconceivable experience of ultimate psychobiological separation. To others, the fact that time and cause of death are unpredictable conveys a painful sense of ultimate powerlessness. This fear and anxiety of death gains reinforcement from the fact that it does not stand only for itself but is also an expression and a symbol of other unknown and unpredictable forces which govern human existence. "It is this fact of our being in a finite and limited time, the awareness of (our) mortality and uncertainty of the future," which renders us helpless and anxious, as Podolsky puts it. (25) That is, people seem to feel the same helplessness and anxiety in the face of the phenomenon of actual death as they do in the face of the above defined personal experience of "psychological death."

There are various ways in which people may try to counteract the anxiety and the narcissistic hurt inflicted on them when they are faced with the necessity of accepting the reality of death. The powerfulness of these defenses is a measuring rod for the intenseness of the anxiety which people try to fight off with them.

The religious concept of the Hereafter is the greatest attempt to counteract the inconceivable separation experience which is death.

The well known phenomenon of people's guilt feelings after the death of a close person is, in my judgment, caused not only by the ambivalence toward the deceased, but also and more so by people's anxiety about the uncertainty and unpredictability which go with the very nature of life and death. Feeling guilty about someone's death means assuming part of the responsibility. If we are partly responsible, the inconceivable, unpredictable character of death is mitigated; it is put into some more acceptable context with that which man can influence — or fails to influence — by virtue of his own skills and powers.

A more pathological way of counteracting the anxiety connected with death is used by certain emotionally disturbed people to whom its uncertainty is so anxiety provoking and unbearable that they evade its acceptance, or at least find satisfaction in fantasying that they can evade it, by committing suicide. To these people, suicide means doing away with the unpredictability of the end of their lives. As if, by their own determination, they take the power of decision out of the hands of the Lord, of fate or of nature, as their conceptions may be. (36, 37)

These examples show that the defenses people feel the need to erect against the anxieties connected with actual death are just as powerful as the symptoms with which mental patients try to protect themselves against the anxiety connected with "psychological death."

Some psychoanalysts may ask at this point, how this concept of anxiety in the face of psychological and factual death ties up with the classical psychoanalytic concept of the death instinct? Freud postulated, in his metapsychological treatise, "Beyond the Pleasure Principle," that man is born with aggressive and destructive impulses against himself and others. (6) Man's death instinct, according to Freud, operates throughout his life as the expression of these self-destructive tendencies against himself.

Other psychoanalysts in writing about this topic have tried to prove the existence of the death instinct in terms of what, in their judgment, are self-destructive operations which we can observe in most people, such as their neglect in seeking medical help for obviously harmful pathological processes. (24) I believe this seemingly self-destructive behavior can be better understood as the outcome of man's fear of death than as the response to his death-instinct. He does not consult the doctor lest he be faced with a fatal prognosis of his ailment which might increase his fear of death.

I find myself in agreement with Sullivan, Fromm and several other dynamic psychiatrists and psychoanalysts who do not find any evidence of primary in-born hostile and destructive tendencies in the human mind, but who deduct from their psychiatric experience that the rise of hostile and destructive tendencies is the outcome of and the response to the adversities of people's interpersonal experiences throughout their lives. Consequently, these authors do not see any evidence of the original existence of self-destructive tendencies, of a death instinct, as a given ubiquitous phenomenon. (11, 29)

Irrespective of the controversial issue of Freud's concept of the death instinct, we agree with his conceptions that man must have some kind of an inner awareness, or sense some kind of reflection of the changes of the organism which take place daily and hourly in the direction of its final dissolution and death. I believe that man's inner awareness of these changes of the organism on its gradual way from birth to death contribute to his fear of death and to his anxiety of the unknown which is connected with the facts of death, rather than their being an expression of his death instinct.

So much about the anxiety connected with what I have called "psychological death" and about the anxiety connected with the psychological facts of actual death as a general human phenomenon. Our data corroborates our introductory statement about there being almost no one permanently free from anxiety. Yet, healthy people learn to handle their anxieties without converting them into symptoms. They may even be able to turn them into assets, a topic on which I have elaborated elsewhere. (13)

In the same context, let me also quote Horney who states that both types of anxiety, that of the mentally healthy and of mentally disturbed people, render them helpless and this helplessness in turn produces more anxiety, "secondary" anxiety. However, Horney says that anxiety in the face of actual death and of the other powers of nature must be accepted and does not call for the development of the defense mechanism and of the hostility and destructiveness which people develop in response to other — neurotic or psychotic — forms of helplessness and anxiety. The contrary may even be true. (19) Grinker corroborates this viewpoint when he states: "If anxiety is mild, it is stimulating and facilitates increased and efficient action or thought." (16)

As Fromm pointed out, anxiety in the face of the overwhelming and unpredictable powers of nature, which is the common fate of all of us, may be used as a motivation for increasing the common bonds between human beings.

Freud, and also Adler, have emphasized the viewpoint that human efforts to allay anxiety have led to the development of civilization. Jung and Adler also emphasize the positive powers of constructive defense which may be aroused in people for the sake of counteracting their anxiety. (1, 6, 21)

The existentialists, including one of the outstanding psychiatrists among them, Binswanger, stress the constructive aspects of anxiety even more. They consider it the equivalent of the tension aroused in a person who is able to face the universe and the task which is set to men, to conquer the emanations of the universe by action. (4, 35)

States of anxiety which are severe enough to call for expression and defense by mental symptoms, i.e. the states of excess anxiety of which neurotic and psychotic patients suffer, are, of course, not constructive except for the times when they are reduced to milder degrees.

It should not be overlooked though, that the anxiety of mental patients under treatment can be psychotherapeutically utilized as a signpost indicating underlying conflicts and as a challenge to solve them. This holds true for neurotic patients as well as for psychotics. In fact, it may be generally stated that mild degrees of anxiety, discomforting as they may be, can be useful danger signals to mentally healthy and to mentally disturbed people. (9, 35)

Some readers may be surprised that I suggest psychotherapeutic intervention not only with excess anxiety in neurotic patients but also in psychotics. Clinical experience during the last 25 or 30 years has taught dynamic psychiatrists that both neurotic and psychotic excess anxieties can be successfully treated with psychoanalysis or psychoanalytically oriented dynamic psychotherapy. Time and space permitting, I could corroborate this statement with many examples from my own experience and that of many other psychiatrists who work with both types of patients. We cannot enter into a discussion of the psychotherapeutic techniques which dynamic psychiatrists use in the treatment of anxiety. If our initial statement is correct, that anxiety is at the root of every mental disturbance, then it is also true that

any discussion of psychotherapeutic methods in the treatment of neurotic and psychotic anxieties would amount to writing a paper on psychotherapy at large.

I will restrict myself, therefore, to the following brief comments: We have seen that people who suffer from anxiety are at best only semi-aware of its causes. Therefore, the focal point of all psychotherapeutic guidance or treatment of anxiety states is to help the anxious person uncover and understand the unconscious reasons for his helplessness and anxiety. Beyond that it follows from our distinction between mild degrees of anxiety and their predominantly constructive aspects and severe degrees of anxiety with their predominantly disjunctive aspects, that the specific psychotherapeutic usefulness of dynamic psychiatrists in helping anxious patients, encompasses three central therapeutic tasks. One therapeutic goal should be to guide people in understanding and then accepting and learning to live with and to utilize mild degrees of anxiety. In the case of more intensive states of anxiety, the psychotherapeutic goal should be to help people (patients), for preventive reasons, uncover, resolve and integrate the causes of these anxieties, lest they lead up to an expression by mental symptoms which simultaneously are used as defenses against the awareness of these anxiety states. In cases where a person's anxiety is severe enough to express itself in mental symptomatology and mental illness, the psychotherapeutic goal should be to help the mental patient with the methods of intensive psychoanalytically oriented dynamic psychotherapy to gain insight into the emotional roots of his anxiety and of his symptomatology, to understand the psychodynamic linkage between anxiety and symptomatology and to face, work through and eventually vanquish his excess anxiety. Caution is indicated regarding the timing and the dosage of therapeutic intervention and enlightenment, lest a patient be made to face more dynamic insight into his anxiety and greater amounts of open anxiety than he can accept at a given time.

The discussion of the psychotherapeutic aspects of anxiety would be more than incomplete if its focus were not extended to the problem of anxiety in psychotherapists. If it is true that there is practically no one who is permanently free from anxiety, and/or none in whom anxiety cannot be temporarily aroused by all kinds of adverse experiences, then this fact, of course, holds true for psychotherapists as well. In their case, we are especially interested in the feelings of anxiety which may, sometimes, be brought forth in them by their patients.

A psychotherapist who does not know and integrate this fact, who dreams about his non-vulnerability to anxiety, be it aroused in his exchange with patients or other persons, a psychotherapist who dreams about "complete emotional security" as an unreal goal for his own inner life, cannot guide his mental patients to wholesome, constructive testing and evaluation of their anxieties and to a constructive adjustment to the facts and data of their internal and external reality. Awareness of his anxiety, not freedom from or denial of it and sufficient emotional security to accept and handle it is the philosophical attitude toward anxiety to be expected of a competent, mature psychiatrist. Incidentally, there was a time when it was my belief that a well-analyzed psychotherapist should be altogether free from anxiety and emotional insecurity. As a matter of fact, my printed elaborations on such utopianism can still be read in my book "Principles of Intensive Psychotherapy." (12) To repeat, I now believe, or better still, I know that a state of mind permanently free of anxiety is utopianism for the psychotherapist by the same token that it is for anyone else.

There are many pitfalls in the psychiatrist's interaction with patients and for that matter, in the interaction of other people engaged in responsible interpersonal guidance of their fellowmen, if they are not willing and able to accept the awareness of a certain amount of anxiety and emotional insecurity within themselves. Conversely, there is a great and constructive source of help for psychotherapeutic effectiveness in the psychiatrist's awareness and creative acceptance of his own anxieties whenever they are elicited. The therapist's anxiety is frequently indicative of emotional experiences in patients which arouse anxiety in him. Thus the psychiatrist's anxiety becomes an important divining rod for the discovery of many emotional experiences of patients, which might otherwise remain undiscovered and hidden for a long time, as in the case of a psychiatrist who would not feel free to use his own anxiety as a guide to anxiety provoking emotional experiences in patients.

A therapist's denial of his own anxieties may cause him to overlook the possibility of his contaminating patients with them, a danger which in extreme cases may only be eliminated or corrected by its free discussion between patient and doctor, or for that matter between any other two participants in such an experience. Furthermore, in a therapist, denial of anxiety may arouse all kinds of defenses in him which will interfere with his therapeutic usefulness. That is, he may feel he must reassure himself against the onslaught of anxiety aroused in him by a patient by giving the patient uncalled for reassurance. Or, he may try to propitiate his patient by assuming, for his own defense, all types of roles in the therapeutic process (e.g. the "better" parent, the "great" doctor), instead of operating for the benefit of the patient. A psychotherapist (like any other person participating in an interpersonal exchange) is only able to listen with unimpaired alertness, perceptiveness and creative responsiveness, i.e. he is only able to operate effectively, to the extent to which there is no interference from defense against his own recognized anxiety.

At present, I am engaged along with several colleagues at Chestnut Lodge, in a research project on the intuitive elements in the doctor's therapeutic approach to schizophrenics. There, we have ample opportunity to observe clearly the marked interference with free utilization of intuitive abilities stemming from our anxiety, with regard to our patients, as well as with regard to our colleagues in the research group, as long as this anxiety operates unrecognized.

There is one more important psychotherapeutic issue which is in danger of being obscured in cases of psychiatrists' unrecognized anxiety. A therapist who fails to recognize and to accept his own anxieties will also fail to differentiate correctly between the type and the degree of pathological excess anxiety in mental patients, which is subject to treatment, and the general human experience of non-pathological anxieties which everyone may suffer and utilize as part of the business of living. To put the same thought differently: psychotherapists are not Gods who can change man's fate, which includes everyone, at times, being submitted to states of anxiety. In their role as individual psychiatrists, they cannot alter, except very slowly and imperceptively, the structure of a culture and a society which may elicit anxiety in its members. However, psychiatrists can and should be useful in man's fight against his individual, irrational excess anxieties, and in encouraging people to accept and integrate constructively and without psychotherapeutic help the milder degrees of anxiety which we may loosely call "normal" anxiety.

SUMMARY

Anxiety is seen as a universal emotional experience. The reader's attention is directed toward the realization that milder degrees of anxiety have both disintegrative and constructive aspects.

Severe degrees of anxiety are described as leading up to the development of mental illness, mental symptoms being simultaneously an expression of severe anxiety and a defense against it.

The existing genetic theories on anxiety are briefly reviewed and the fear of anticipated disapproval, withdrawal of love, and separation from significant environmental figures is discussed as a factor, about the genetic significance of which most authors agree.

The hypothesis is offered that the genesis of anxiety may also be understood as a result of unresolved early emotional tie-ups with significant persons of one's early environment. People are stuck with these early interpersonal patterns and with their early interpersonal evaluation which remain uncorrected. These fixations, of which people are only partially aware, if at all, render them psychologically helpless, interfere with their ability to change, with their growth, maturation and self-realization, and with their correct evaluation of their own and other peoples' interpersonal interactions. The result is "psychological death," which elicits anxiety. This anxiety is compared to the anxiety which is called forth in most people by factual death and similar phenomena which are beyond human control and, therefore, arouse helplessness and anxiety.

A distinction is proposed between psychotherapeutic guidance in cases of milder forms of anxiety and psychotherapeutic intervention in cases of severe forms of anxiety, which lead to neurotic or psychotic symptom-formation and mental illness.

Finally, the anxieties which may be elicited in psychotherapists during the treatment situation are discussed in their constructive and in their disintegrative aspects.

REFERENCES

(1) ADLER, ALFRED: *The Neurotic Constitution*. Translated by Bernard Glueck. New York: Moffat, Yard & Co., 1917.

(2) AUDEN, W. H.: *The Age of Anxiety*. New York: Random House, 1946.

(3) BERDYAEV, NICHOLAS: *Solitude and Society*. London: 1938.

(4) BINSWANGER, LUDWIG: *Grundformen und Erkenntnis Menschlichen Daseins*. Zurich: Max Niehans Verlag, 1942.

(5) FREUD, SIGMUND: *A General Introduction to Psychoanalysis*. New York: Liveright, 1935; Garden City Publ. Co., 1943. (Chapter on Anxiety)

(6) ———: *Beyond the Pleasure Principle*. London: Hogarth Press, 1942.

(7) ———: "On Narcissism: An Introduction." In: *Collected Papers* 4:30–59. London: Hogarth Press, 1946.

(8) ———: *The Ego and the Id*. London: Hogarth Press, 1935.

(9) ———: *Problems of Anxiety*. New York: Norton, 1936.

(10) FROMM, ERICH: *Man for Himself*. New York: Rinehart, 1947.

(11) ———: "Selfishness and Self-love." *Psychiatry*, 2:507–23 (1939).

(12) FROMM-REICHMANN, FRIEDA: *Principles of Intensive Psychotherapy*. Chicago: Univ. of Chicago Press, 1950.

(13) ———: "Remarks on the Philosophy of Mental Disorders." *Psychiatry*, 9:293–308 (1946).

(14) ———: "Psychoanalysis and Dynamic Psychotherapy. Similarities and Differences." *Journal Am. Ps. An. Assn.*, 2:711–721 (1954).

(15) GOLDSTEIN, KURT: *Human Nature in the Light of Psychopathology*. Cambridge: Harvard Univ. Press, 1940.

(16) ———: *The Organism*. New York: American Book Co., 1939.

(17) GRINKER, ROY R.: *Psychosomatic Research*. New York: Norton, 1953.

(18) HALMOS, PAUL: *Solitude and Privacy*. New York: Philosophical Library, 1953.

(19) HORNEY, KAREN: *New Ways in Psychoanalysis*. New York: Norton, 1939.

(20) ———: *The Neurotic Personality of Our Time*. New York: Norton, 1937.

(21) JUNG, C. G.: *Collected Papers on Analytical Psychology*. Translated by C. E. Long; London: Baillere, Tindall & Cox, 1920.

(22) KARDINER, ABRAM: *The Psychological Frontiers of Society*. New York: Columbia Univ. Press, 1945.

(23) MAY, ROLLO: *The Meaning of Anxiety*. New York: Ronald Press, 1951.

(24) MENNINGER, KARL: *Man Against Himself*. New York: Harcourt, Brace, 1938.

(25) PODOLSKY: "The Meaning of Anxiety"; *Diseases of the Nervous System*. 14:4 (1953).

(26) RANK, OTTO: *Will Therapy and Truth and Reality*. New York: Knopf, 1945.

(27) RIESMAN, DAVID: *The Lonely Crowd*. New Haven, Yale Univ. Press, 1950.

(28) RUESCH, JURGEN: "The Interpersonal Communication of Anxiety." *Symposium of Stress*; Walter Reed Army Medical Center, Wash., D.C.: 154–164 (1953).

(29) SULLIVAN, H. S.: *Conceptions of Modern Psychiatry*. Wash., D.C.: The Wm. Alanson White Found., 1947. New Edition, New York: Norton, 1953.

(30) ———: *The Interpersonal Theory of Psychiatry*. New York: Norton, 1953.

(31) ———: "The Meaning of Anxiety in Psychiatry and in Life." *Psychiatry*, 11:1–13 (1948).

(32) ———: "The Theory of Anxiety and the Nature of Psychotherapy." *Psychiatry*, 12:3–12 (1949).

(33) TILLICH, PAUL: *The Courage To Be*. New Haven: Yale Univ. Press, 1952.

(34) VASSOS, JOHN: *Phobia*. New York: Covici-Friede, 1931.

(35) WEIGERT, EDITH: "Existentialism and Its Relation to Psychotherapy." *Psychiatry*, 12, 399–412 (1949).

(36) ZILBOORG, GREGORY: "Considerations on Suicide with Particular Reference to that of the Young." *Am. J. Orthopsychiat.* (1937).

(37) ———: "Suicide Among Civilized and Primitive Races." *Am. J. Psychiat.*, 92:1347–69 (1936).

LAWRENCE S. KUBIE

Social Forces and the Neurotic Process*

INTRODUCTION

There is a widespread conviction that a close interdependence exists between individual psychopathology and the pathology of social structure and of cultural forces. If this is true, it is of utmost importance for the future of the human race as a whole, for human society, and for each individual human being. For this very reason, however, it is essential not to oversimplify the nature of their interdependence nor to delude ourselves with the many easy clichés and deceptive fallacies with which this subject is infested.

Let me give point to this by citing some frequent simplifications. Each statement will be an exaggeration, yet in the literature each recurs in many disguises, often hedged around with qualifications which seem to bring it closer to the truth but do not eliminate the essential error.

1. "Neuroses are due to poverty." A more careful statement is that without poverty you would have no, or fewer, or less severe, or different kinds of, neuroses. A still more careful formulation is the one by Leavy and Freedman (9).

2. "Neuroses are due to wealth and leisure." Again stated more carefully, it is the surfeit of wealth, the inability to use leisure, the lack of anything to do, the lack of occupation, the lack of work, idleness which produces neuroses or intensifies them. It is not irrelevant that in quick succession the same individual will defend both of these opposing positions without realizing their irreconcilability.

3. Neuroses are due either to overwork or to underwork, to excessive fatigue or to excessive indolence.

4. Again, we find neuroses attributed to ignorance and/or to excessive education, to being an "egghead," to superstition, or to supersophistication.

5. Neuroses are attributed to lack of love or to an excess of loving.

6. Neuroses are due to neglect or, obversely, to overprotection.

* From *Explorations in Social Psychiatry*, edited by Alexander H. Leighton, John A. Clausen and Robert N. Wilson, © Basic Books, Inc., Publishers, 1957, New York, pp. 78–99 and 409–410.

7. Still others blame neuroses on the simplicity, the barrenness, and the isolation of country life or, conversely, on the pace, the congestion, and the complexities of urban existence.

8. Primitivism in all its forms is blamed; but against this is balanced the attribution of the neurotic process to the highly rarefied and precious air of the most cultivated and "civilized" modern existence.

9. Neurosis is blamed by some on superstition and credulity and also on an overcompliant, passive acceptance of religious faith. Conversely, neurosis is blamed on irreligion and skepticism.

10. Neurosis is blamed on puritanism and moralistic taboos or, conversely, on license, instinctual self-indulgence, and vice.

11. There was a period, not long past, when neuroses were blamed on inbred family life. For instance, the novels of Louis Couperus described the fetid air of neurosis in the intricate network of family life in Amsterdam. Swiss writers were painting similar pictures of Basel. Others were doing the same for Jewish families, for the red damask era of established American Jewry and for the Jewish immigrant, for the Anglicized Jew in Britain (Louis Golding, G. B. Stern, and others), and for the continental Jew (Wassermann, Feuchtwanger, etc.).

These stressed the secret accumulation of inexpressible patricidal, matricidal, and fratricidal tensions in close-knit families, and the parallel pressures of equally inexpressible incestuous needs, as the soil out of which neurosis is born. Today, however, because of the current emphasis on domestic turbulence, superficial observers seem to forget these recent arguments and place the blame almost exclusively on the breakdown and attenuation of family life as a major source of the neurotic process, rather than viewing this as one of its important current manifestations.

Another evidence of this easy misinterpretation of the influence of family disruption is the fact that it overlooks the statistics of the situation. In a recent article (5) I pointed out that the statistics gathered by Paul H. Jacobson of the Metropolitan Life Insurance Company and others indicate that although the disruption rate due to divorce had risen in the years between 1890 and 1940, the disruption rate due to early deaths had dropped even more. The net result is that more families were holding together in 1940 than in 1980. Family disruption is not a new phenomenon. The reshuffling of marriages because of early deaths does not necessarily have the same impact upon youngsters as does a reshuffling through divorce; but there has been no objective comparative study of the effects of the two types of family disruption on the development of children.

It does not clarify the basic issue to acknowledge that every extreme position contains a measure of truth. Nor does it reconcile their inconsistencies to point out that in each instance there are "feedback" relations, in that the conditions which may be an outcome of the neurotic process (e.g., family disruption) can also influence it in turn. In the interplay of psychosocial forces, cause and effect relationships are always circular. Yet the basic question remains unanswered — to wit, what initiates the neurotic process in infancy and what role, if any, do social forces exercise in its inception? These questions must be clearly differentiated from questions concerning the role of social forces in the secondary molding and shaping of the neurotic process and in determining the price paid by an individual, his family, and the community for his neurosis. All of these issues will be explored more fully after a description of the nature of the neurotic process itself.

THE NATURE OF THE NEUROTIC PROCESS

Probably nothing has been less conclusively defined than the nature of the neurotic process; and about nothing is there more confusion between laymen and behavioral scientists, among the several varieties of behavioral scientists, and even within the close fraternity of psychiatrists and the even closer fraternity of analysts. Therefore no definition can be looked upon as one to which all will agree. All that I have any right to hope is that if I express my own convictions clearly about the nature of the neurotic process, then for the purposes of my argument the reader may understand what I personally mean. If at the same time I also convince even a few readers that my definition goes to the heart of the matter, then my argument will in addition have a wider usefulness.

In the explication that follows, it will be clarifying to rule out the current popular and quasi-scientific misuses of the concept of neurosis which contribute to the universal confusion.

In the first place, I will not use the words *neurotic process* to characterize any fully developed illness,

although the neurotic *state* as an illness evolves out of a preexisting neurotic *process* which may have been well hidden (7). Nor will I apply the words to any behavior merely because that behavior is strange, unusual or infrequent, asocial, unconventional, and non-conformist in contrast to that which is statistically frequent, socially acceptable and approved, and conforms to the mores of any particular culture. The term will not be used as a synonym for behavior which is socially destructive as contrasted with socially creative and valuable. Statistical frequency has nothing to do with health. Common colds are illnesses no matter how many people suffer from them. Conformity and rebelliousness may equally be sick or well, normal or neurotic, depending upon whether they are voluntary or automatic; which, in turn, depends upon their determining circumstances, as will be explained below. Furthermore, there are many more neurotic do-gooders than do-badders, or the world would be in an even more parlous state than already exists. Nor will the words have to do with the strangeness or eccentricity or peculiar unfamiliarity or flamboyance of any pattern of behavior, since many manifestations of the neurotic process are masked behind a meticulously obscure, mediocre, and self-effacing façade.

Perhaps most important of all is the fact that I will not be talking about neurotic personalities or neurotic constitutions or neurotic cultures. A great deal is written and claimed about this in the technical literature of psychoanalyses and psychiatry — in the literature of cultural anthropology and social psychology, in the law, and in the lay press. Yet our data are not sufficiently clear to make it possible to apply these terms with accuracy either to whole personalities or to whole cultures. Furthermore, without a broad area of meaning which is common to all, we cannot even be sure that we are communicating about the same phenomena. My conviction therefore is that for the present we must limit ourselves to trying to understand what determines whether any given moment of behavior is "normal" or "neurotic" or, as is the rule, an admixture of both.

To clarify this, I will venture to repeat an already published hypothesis which utilizes the dynamics of behavior as the basis for a crude pragmatic test: "Thus the essence of normality is flexibility, in contrast to the freezing of behavior into patterns of unalterability which characterize every manifestation of the neurotic process, whether in impulses, acts, thoughts, or feelings. Whether or not a behavioral event is free to change depends not upon the quality of the act itself but upon the nature of the constellation of forces that has produced it. No moment of behavior can be looked upon as neurotic unless the processes that have set it in motion also predetermine its automatic repetition, irrespective of the situation, the utility, or the consequences of the act" (4).

Naturally, the question that will arise immediately is what is the nature of that peculiar constellation of forces which can predetermine a tendency to the automatic repetition of any act? The answer to this requires a few additional words of technical explanation. We view every moment of behavior as being the product of three groups of concurrent psychological forces: a group that operates on the *conscious* level, another group that operates on what is called the *preconscious* level, a third group that influences behavior from behind an iron curtain which can be penetrated only by special exploratory devices — to wit, the *unconscious* level. Wherever unconscious forces play the preponderant role in this constellation, dominating over the other two, then for a variety of reasons the behavior which results from the interplay among these three groups of forces is subject to a tendency to automatic and obligatory repetition. This is, in part, because the unconscious conflicts and purposes are represented by symbolic patterns of activity through which their objectives can never be reached. Futhermore, because their dominant determinants are unconscious, these action patterns are not modifiable by conscious experiences of pleasure or pain, success or failure rewards or punishment, argument or exhortation. Consequently, they are automatic, rigid, incapable of attaining satiation for their unconscious purposes, and incapable of being modified by learning from experience of any kind. Moreover, this is true whether the forces are expressed through frank neurotic symptoms, through art forms, through creative acts in science, or through those subtle deformations of general patterns of behavior which together constitute deformations of general patterns of behavior which together constitute what we call the personality.

In contrast to all of this, wherever conscious and preconscious forces are in the saddle, the resulting patterns of activity are alterable by experience. Since desired goals can be achieved through such patterns of activity, a state of comfortable satiety can be reached. Or, when goals prove unattainable, the corrective experience of defeat will result in the modification of the patterns — either toward change or cessation. Therefore, behavior which is determined by a constellation of processes in which conscious and preconscious forces predominate is alterable by the impact of success and failure, rewards and punishments, pleasure and pain, argument, logic and exhortation. It is a further consequence that such behavior is anchored in reality and remains freely flexible. It

is adaptive. It can be modified by learning. This is the essential difference between a normal and a neurotic act; between the normal and the neurotic process. It is the difference between eating to satisfy hunger and the compulsive eating of the neurotic child who eats until he vomits and then must eat again. I must repeat that the difference lies *not* in the act but in the constellation of forces which determines the act and which predetermines at the same time its automatic repetition.

If we generalize from this to a concept of mental health in a broader sense, it is fair to say that greater health is achieved whenever important areas of life can be brought under the domination of conscious and preconscious processes (never exclusively, but to a major degree). Therefore, the goal of therapy is to shrink those areas of life which are dominated preponderantly by the inaccessible unconscious processes. This is a wholly reasonable concept of normality, which leaves ample room for all of the vital and creative economies of preconscious functioning and also for those unconscious processes which are not in irreconcilable conflict with conscious and preconscious goals.

At this point I should reemphasize the fact that this concept of the neurotic process is far removed from the usual derogatory connotations of the term. In the first place, it starts from the fact that there is a neurotic potential in human nature which is universal (4, 7) because it is inherent in our psychological development, depending as it does upon the special role which symbolic functions play in human development. It is the power of symbolic thinking and feeling which endows Man with his unique creative potential, and it is also the vulnerability of these symbolic functions to distortions which gives rise to that aspect of the neurotic process which is peculiar to the human being. It is the symbolic process plus its vulnerability which gives rise to the neurotic potential.

Furthermore, out of this universal neurotic potential a neurotic process evolves in some degree in everyone. It varies in form and direction and intensity; but in some measure it plays a basic role in every life and in every personality, including those lives which we think of as being approximately normal. Finally, the point of view presented here implies that this variable but ubiquitous neurotic process in appropriate circumstances precipitates something called "the neurotic state." Actually, this neurotic state (or "neurosis") occurs universally as transient episodes in childhood. In some children these transient neurotic episodes gradually merge to become the more enduring neuroses of adolescence and of adult life. In others, the transient neurotic states of childhood disappear below the surface. Rarely, if ever, are they basically resolved. Usually they leave the individual scarred. For years he may remain free from crystallized neurotic illness; but in time the cumulative effects of these scars catch up with him and the neurotic process then "decompensates" with the eruption of the full-blown neurosis or psychosis of later life. The influence of those neurotic episodes, which seem to disappear spontaneously, actually persists as a process which may warp and color an entire life. Consequently, in the adult population the so-called normal is usually an individual who does not have a symptomatic neurosis but in whom the neurotic process plays a more subtly concealed role, influencing the make-up of his personality, his life adjustment, his work and play, his loves and hates, and his health in general. The so-called "neurotic" among adults is merely one in whom there are, in addition, those crystallized neurotic states which we call the psychoneuroses. These are self-diagnosing. Their recognition requires no skill or subtlety. Indeed, such patients come to us without urging, telling us that they have fears, depressions, compulsions, obsessions, etc. With few exceptions they seek help on their own initiative for the relief of their painful symptoms. Yet the more subtly concealed neurotic process, which may be devoid of overt neurotic symptoms, is often far more destructive of human health and happiness. The concealed neurotic mechanisms are so interwoven into the fabric of the personality that most human beings defend to the death their right to retain their prized neurotic quirks.

Here is where culture exercises a profound influence (Hollingshead and others [2, 3]). The cultural tolerance for overt neurotic symptoms may vary widely in different settings, as will the cultural tolerance for those personality quirks which manifest in concealed ways the subtle influence of the neurotic process. Therefore, culture is one of the forces which determine if and when a patient will look upon himself as ill or at least as needing help and whether he will seek help. Ultimately, however, what determines a patient's attitude toward his own neurotic process and neurotic symptoms is the amount of pain these cause him. Everyone, if he lives long enough, in the end pays a high price for his own neurotic process; but, as will be evident in some of the illustrations to be given below, the pain of a neurotic symptom may be urgent, insistent, and immediate in its demand for help, whereas for many years the neurotic process may cause pain to others and not to the patient himself. Consequently he may not turn to treatment until late in life. Many a successful man comes to

grief in the later decades of life because the neurotic process, with which he has sparred successfully for years and which he has even used successfully, finally catches up with him. Many a campus hero comes for treatment in his thirties or forties only to reveal the fact that underneath the surface of a seemingly smooth adjustment in school and college, neurotic mechanisms had been at work which, until that moment, he had been able to utilize and exploit. Indeed, the universal but masked neurotic ingredient in all human nature is the ultimate basis of that human discontent which occurs in even the most successful and the most privileged among us.

There is one other point that I should clarify here, because it concerns the nature of the neurotic process and its relationship to the psychosis. This again is an issue about which there is both uncertainty and disagreement. Nor is it possible to go into it in detail without overextending this chapter. I can say only that, apart from those psychoses which are caused by organic disruption of nervous structure and function, the psychosis arises when an acute failure occurs in the defenses against a neurotic process. Sometimes this occurs in early years (8); sometimes only after the defenses have worked satisfactorily for years. Either way, when the break occurs it results in chaotic disorganization of all psychological processes. The resulting state of psychosis has many special psychological characteristics and symptomatic manifestations; but I do not believe that it is necessary or relevant to detail these in this connection.

With this triad in mind (*i.e.*, a universal neurotic potential which is inherent in human nature, a highly variable but ubiquitous neurotic process which evolves out of this universal potential, and a neurotic state which in appropriate circumstances precipitates out of the neurotic process) our next problem becomes the question of what forces determine the evolution of this neurotic process.

Many variables determine this — *e.g.*, physiological, cultural, and social forces, individual idiosyncratic events, catastrophic early experiences, and early but continuous stresses. All of these influence the development of our psychological processes and their symbolic representations on all three levels or systems — to wit, conscious, preconscious, and unconscious. At this point we can anticipate what is to follow by saying that cultural influences play an obvious role in those imitative steps which determine the acquisition of conscious psychological processes. They play a subtler role in all preconscious imitative and repetitive processes, which are inherent in the learning process and in which, at the same time, individual emotional experiences also play an important role.

When, however, we ask what role cultural influences play in the splitting off of unconscious processes from the main stream of conscious and preconscious function (which is the quintessence of the neurotic process) we face an issue which is not yet understood even vaguely.

It is easy to characterize this splitting off of the representatives of inner events so as to render them unconscious as the operation of a mechanism called "repression." But the mere naming of it does not explain it. Nor has the role of cultural forces in repressive processes been explored, although it is precisely here that the impact of highly charged individual experiences plays a major role. It would be hazardous to claim that cultural forces, operating in subtle forms, exercised no influence on the repressive process. But one can say with certainty only that the precise interaction remains obscure and that it is related to many unresolved issues, as for instance the role of heredity both in cultural patterning in general and in repression in particular — i.e., whether or not the experience of the race becomes incorporated in our nervous system in such a way as to determine whether certain impulses and conflicts will be experienced consciously or unconsciously and whether in turn these impulses are transmitted by hereditary forces and not by imitation. If racial history exercises such an effect, then we must also conclude that there are unconscious processes which have never been either preconscious or conscious and which consequently have never been subjected to the processes of repression. It is experimentally proven that some experiences can be preconsciously perceived and buried in the unconscious without ever having been consciously experienced. The precise relation of this process to neurotogenic repression is still unclear. About these critical issues there is heated disagreement but no conclusive evidence; and until these basic alternatives have been subjected to critical experimental investigation, all formulations about the impact of culture must be made quite tentatively.

THE ROOTS, TRUNK, AND BRANCHES OF THE NEUROTIC PROCESS

It will be helpful and clarifying to bear in mind the many banal experiences which should make us ask ourselves whether we are dealing with the roots of the neurotic process or with those many later forces which shape and alter its subsequent evolution, secondary forces which make an enormous difference in the price which the individual pays for his neurosis but not in its genesis. It is conceivable that environmental forces may alter both the matured forms of the neurotic process and its individual and social consequences without necessarily playing a significant role in its genesis.

All of us can think of examples which demonstrate that the relationship between the roots of the neurotic process and cultural forces is subtle and elusive and not to be dismissed by the easy generalizations of which I gave a few examples in the introductory section.

During the war, whenever a group of soldiers from a common origin chanced to be placed in the same unit (whether in training camp or in combat) for a considerable period, they would develop neurotic symptoms or somatic disturbances the forms of which were influenced by their national or cultural backgrounds. Here the influence of culture was not on the incidence or primary origins of neurosis but on its form. Similarly, the price one will pay for an agoraphobia or a claustrophobia will be quite different if one lives in a New York City tenement or on an Australian sheep ranch; and the price one pays for a height phobia will be different in the Rockies or on the Great Plains. In one situation one may be symptom-free and in another haunted by terror.

Again, we should not overlook the fact that society rewards some neuroses even as it punishes others. Thus the consequences to society, to the family of the patient, and to the patient himself are quite different for compulsive benevolence or compulsive greed. I cite these only to underscore the fact that the interaction between social forces and the neurosis is easily traced in terms of the secondary and tertiary consequences of the neurotic process. The difficult issue concerns the relationship of culture to the origins of the neurotic process.

I have frequently cited a group of Scotch-Canadian woodsmen, who enjoyed economic and physical security and lived a physically challenging and toughening existence, in comfortable seclusion and yet with ready access to others. During a period of seven weeks in which I lived in the midst of two such families, I was consulted professionally by every member of both families. Not only was it evident that the neurotic process was universal in the group but even more impressive was the fact that the quality of their neuroses was indistinguishable from that which challenged me daily in my private office and in the psychiatric out-patient clinic of a general hospital in New York, the origins of whose patients were predominantly Italian, Jewish, and Latin-American.

I could cite the example of a family in which a simple event occurred to a series of four children whose ages were nine, seven, five and two-and-one-half years. This event made a significant impact on the psychopathological development of each child, the difference depending on the age of the child, its sex, and the ordinal position of each child in the group. The culture was constant. The neurotic process was as varied as four lives could be.

I recall the children in a family of sturdy, loving, "healthy" people. The father of this apparently well-adjusted family was somewhat compulsively disorderly, happy-go-lucky, and irresponsible in the details of existence, whereas the mother was compulsively orderly, meticulously clean, and overcompensating for the father's heedlessness by her responsibility in all daily and financial routines. The "neurosis" of each parent was expressed in a form which was easily acceptable, falling well within the social norm. In the eyes of the world each made a happy social and familial adjustment. Only the fact that professional training brought each parent into analysis brought to light these well-masked, well-compensated neuroses. In no statistical table would this have been called a family dominated by neurotic parents. Yet it was not the culture but the subtle interplay between these two "normally" neurotic yet conflicting personalities, plus the ordinal positions, age intervals, and sexual sequence among the children, that were the critical forces which determined the evolution of each of the children and the shape of the neuroses that developed in each.

I can compare a number of sets of identical twins who were brought up with the closest possible mutual identification, treated almost as two halves of a single human being, yet showed remarkable divergences in the patterns of the neuroses which evolved. In one instance two little girls were the last in a family of fourteen. One grew up with an unconscious identification with the father's aggressive, eloquent, and boisterous temperament, an identification which colored every detail of her life until her death at the age of seventy-eight. The other evolved an equally strong but purely consolatory identification with a gloomy, defensive, conscience-ridden, sourly benevolent mother. This colored her behavior until her death at seventy-five.

Again, early in life a set of monozygotic male twins diverged to such a degree that one developed an obsessional-compulsive work drive and the other an obsessional block in both work and play. The initiating steps which had preceded this bifurcation in the two neurotic processes had been identical; yet under the later influence of deep unconscious rivalry they split to follow divergent paths. The subsequent evolutions of the two neuroses were as different as day and night. One went on to a career of external achievement and success, which for many

decades won him, as the rewards for his neurosis, social prestige, economic advantages, and considerable academic distinction; until finally in the fifties his neurosis decompensated into an involutional depression. The other twin led a life of incessant pain, frustration, and humiliation which by his late teens had driven him into a chronic hypochondriacal depression. This gradually acquired secondary paranoid features which colored all his years as he moved slowly to his death.

In another family group the father and mother married for unconscious reasons which expressed another set of well-masked and evenly balanced neurotic forces. Unwittingly, the father had married the mother as a heterosexual mask for his unconscious homosexual attachment to her brothers. Equally unwittingly, the mother had married the father as a mask for her incestuous attachment to the same brothers and also as an effort to salve the deep hurts which their rejection of her had always caused. Out of this painful struggle came children, every detail of whose orientation in life bore the imprint of the interplay between these two "sick" parents, both of whom were making exemplary social adjustments — the husband as a lawyer, the wife as a research scientist.

These are types of stresses which play an obvious role in the secondary evolution and shaping of the neurotic process. What role they play in its initial origins is by no means so clear. The answer to this question demands such microscopic examination as is accessible almost exclusively in analysis only. Yet even in analysis such basic data are obtainable only in the most favorable and controlled and cross-checked circumstances. For such studies we need special research institutes. For many reasons, private practice alone does not yield dependable data of this type and depth. Rarely if ever are such data accessible to cultural anthropological scrutiny. Yet, without it, one is unable to evaluate accurately the relative influence of the more easily accessible external social forces. Without such data in depth it is all too easy either to overemphasize the role played by the surface forces of society or to dismiss them as inconsequential.

UNIVERSALS IN THE EVOLUTION OF THE HUMAN NEUROTIC PROCESS

Such considerations as these reinforce my conviction that we must begin our efforts to understand the role of social forces in the neurotic process by seeking to characterize the neurotogenic universals — *i.e.*, those forceful processes which, as far as we now know, exist in every human life in every culture known to man and which are repeated in every existence. These universals are the baseline. Once they are determined, we will be in a position to evaluate the influence of variables introduced by different cultural, economic, social, educational, and religious patterns. But until we understand the universals and their role in neurotogenesis, it will remain impossible to evaluate accurately the influence of these other variables.

If we allow ourselves to assume that we have solved the many technical problems of adequate representative sampling, of communication, of long-term observations, of cross-checking, recording, and evaluating, and if we assume that we are at last competent to evaluate both the universal and the variable social and cultural forces, what then will be the critical questions which we would have to ask ourselves about their impact? Our answers to this will depend upon what we consider to be the essential ingredients in the neurotic process. I will not presume here to try to give an exhaustive catalogue of these. I will mention only those which at the moment seem to me to be of primary importance.

1. In the preverbal and largely presymbolic phase of infancy, I would place primary emphasis on a type of experience the importance of which Spitz (10) has demonstrated irrefutably; namely, the preverbal security, warmth, stillness, comfort, monotony, peace, closeness, ease, and familiarity which is engendered by being surrounded by familiar inanimate and animate objects. The first epitome of this is the mother's face and the interwoven visual, oral, and olfactory experiences of the mother's body (the constellation of breast, bottle, and supporting arms), plus the incessant slow play of familiar sensory stimulation from handling, cleansing, feeding, cooing, rocking, carrying, and playing. Into this infantile nirvana of constancy comes the primary disruptive impact of separation, pain, startle, neglect, starvation. The duration of that nirvana, its quality, constancy, and consistency, when and how it is disrupted (*i.e,* whether gradually, intermittently, or suddenly), what constant substitutes are provided if any; all of these make the first profound and lasting imprint on the emotional organization of that infant.

I would link closely to these a type of experience which follows soon after; namely, the long years, which to every human child seem endless, in which he lives as one helpless Lilliputian among hordes of brutal rival Lilliputians in a Brobdingnagian world of giants who are always giving either too much protection or too little. (How different cultures handle these stressful, banal realities of every life has many consequences.)

2. It seems probable that these basic early experiences accumulate to establish in each individual a central emotional position to which the personality returns automatically from any excursion to other emotional states. This central position can be pleasant and comforting, in which case the individual spends his life seeking it, protecting it, preserving it, and attempting to recreate and recapture it by every conscious, preconscious, and unconscious device at his disposal. Alternatively, the central emotional position may be one of pain (*i.e.,* fear, depression, rage), against which the individual spends his life defending himself by conscious, preconscious, and unconscious devices whose aim it is to avoid this pain-filled central emotional position. I must repeat that these defensive maneuvers, like those that seek to regain happy central emotional positions which have been lost, are carried out unconsciously, preconsciously, and consciously in varying proportions. Among these it is the unconscious maneuvers, whether designed to regain and protect a happy state or to avoid a painful state, which play a vital role in neurotogenesis. (Parenthetically, I would point out that we do not know today to what extent these patterns are alterable merely by gaining analytic insight into them.) The important point is that, whether we are protecting and seeking a pleasant central position or defending against a painful one, whenever such maneuvers are preponderantly unconscious they enter into the structure of the universal masked neurotic component which is to be found in all personalities. This is not true where the same maneuvers are carried on consciously and/or preconsciously.

These considerations pinpoint for us two ways in which cultural forces may influence the origins of the neurotic process. In the first place, economic and social forces play a significant role in the parent-child environment in general and in encouraging or limiting sudden changes and disruptive separations in the infant world. The young widow who is forced to go out to work, the ambitious young woman who wishes to be both a mother and a career woman, and the frivolous young mother who leaves her infant for long hours out of every day to shop and play golf or cards are equally the instruments of separations which will help to create the central emotional position which will shape a human life throughout its existence. Nor does it matter to the infant or child whether the mother is absent playing cards or scrubbing floors. Indeed, the pitiful paradox is that the frivolous card-playing absentee who comes home relaxed and gay may inflict less damage on her child than does the dour self-sacrificing worker-mother who returns to her home tense and tired and who extends her daytime of physical absence by an evening of psychological absence behind a wall of glum self-absorption and resentment.

But what role do social forces play in determining *the level of awareness* on which the subsequent searching and defending maneuvers will operate? Where and how does repression enter and establish the dichotomy between the conscious-preconscious levels on the one hand and the unconscious processes on the other? And what role do social forces play in determining this primal step in the ontogeny of the neurotic process? As I have said, the search and defense may be painful on any level, but unless they are carried on under the dominant influence of unconscious forces they are not neurotogenic. Therefore the role of culture in neurotogenesis focuses sharply and precisely on the issue of how culture influences the psychological level on which conflicts are lived out. This would seem to be one of the basic questions which no one has hitherto either asked or answered.

3. Closely related to the central emotional positions and their unconscious maneuvers of search and/or defense are the many *trigger mechanisms* which precipitate human beings out of one emotional set and into another.

The relation of endogenous and social forces to the various phenomena of trigger mechanisms is another unexplored issue. Trigger stimuli can explode almost any ingredient of human behavior; *e.g.*, the familiar phenomena of laughter, tears, and rage as well as fear; an explosive return to a central emotional position; the release of obsessional and compulsive furors either of erotic or of destructive impulses or alternatively of symptomatic defenses against them; the precipitation of sudden states of acute blocking and dissociation; the induction of various degrees of hypnotic dissociation; the precipitation into sleep or out of it. Indeed, we are bombarded by trigger stimuli through all of our waking hours and during sleep as well. The role of sociocultural influences in establishing and shaping such mechanisms has not been studied.

In view of the fact that trigger mechanisms are so widespread in behavior, it is surprising that their general importance has been overlooked both in normal psychology and in psychopathology. Even clinical consideration of them has been limited chiefly to their most familiar manifestation, the classical phobia.

By trigger mechanisms we mean reactions which can be touched off by stimuli which are inherently neutral, but which have become highly charged not merely by conditioning but also through their preconscious and especially their unconscious overtones.

About these there are many questions to ask: Are trigger mechanisms inherent in the structural organization and biochemistry of the nervous system? Do they vary from one individual to another, because of variations in structure and biochemistry? If such differences exist, are they determined by inherited genetic factors? Can experience in turn modify such hypothetical innate factors or the trigger mechanisms which they establish? In other words, do social and cultural forces influence a tendency which may be inherent in every human nervous system to establish trigger reactions, their thresholds, and/or the intensity of what is released by them? One would also have to consider the impact of social and cultural forces, apart from the cumulative effects of individual experience, in: (1) establishing trigger mechanisms in the first place; (2) determining what trigger stimuli are effective; (3) determining thresholds of perception of trigger stimuli and of responses to them; (4) influencing the form of the behavior which is released; (5) maintaining these reactions.

If it should turn out that social and cultural forces play little or no role in these phenomena, then we would be forced to conclude that here is one important aspect of the neurotic process in which such forces are of little consequence. Certainly, for our understanding of the role of cultural and social forces in the genesis and the shaping of the neurosis, it is as important to know what areas are relatively uninfluenced by them as to know what areas are patterned by them.

There are many forms of trigger stimuli in which it is reasonable to expect that social and cultural forces play a role in determining which trigger stimuli are effective: animals, facial expressions, Love and Hate signals, Yes or No signs, Stop and Go indicators, Hurry or Wait signals, wordless gestures or speech, silence or a loud noise, the seasons, changes in the weather, the daily cycle of light and dark, the rustling of the wind through grass. Inevitably these would have different connotations to city-bred and country-bred children: but differing connotations do not correlate in any necessary fashion with trigger phenomenology; and it may be that the same is true of differing cultural implications. For instance, certain foods are forbidden in certain religions; but not all adherents to that faith develop phobic taboos about such foods.

Similarly, there are many forms of triggered reactions about which it is reasonable to expect that cultural and social variants will play a role in determining what is released: whether free exhibition of affect or its inhibition and internalization, tears or exultant laughter, etc. Will social and cultural forces determine whether a certain trigger mechanism releases alertness or sleep, the paralysis and freezing of action or freedom to act? Or will social and cultural forces play a role in determining whether the discharge takes place largely through the autonomic nervous system?

Merely to compile a systematic and exhaustive list of the questions to be explored would require a separate chapter. At this point all I can do is to emphasize both the basic importance of the issue and its neglect.

4. Dependent in part on the early establishment of central emotional positions is the acquisition of perceptual processes and of motor organization and integration. This is a learning process which occurs during the ontogeny of the subverbal animal as well as in that of man. Every animal breeder can testify that the acquisition of these skills occurs in a field of emotional forces which influence it at every step. As this evolves in the human animal, however, one critical complication is added: to wit, the acquisition of the symbolic process, to which reference has already been made and to which further consideration will now be given.

In the acquisition of perceptual, motor, and symbolic skills, inherited or acquired differences in the organic structure of the central nervous system and of the perceptual and motor apparatus exercise an obvious influence. At the same time, the environment of every developing infant will also vary with respect to the amount of activity, handling, and play, the amount of light and noise, the amount and quality of song, speech, and gesture, of companionship and loneliness, of talkativeness or silence. His exposure to all of these will vary through his parents (and especially through his mother or her substitutes), and through older siblings. Later the toddler's rivalry with older and/or younger siblings, his association with playmates who are more or less advanced, his conscious and unconscious fears of exposure and retaliation and therefore of victory, all influence his step-by-step acquisition of bodily and intellectual skills. At a later age the youngster who compensates in athletics for his limitations in the classroom, or his opposite number who does the reverse, is familiar to all of us. But always in the background lurk the figures of the parents, living out through their children their own fears, ambitions, and vengeful retaliations for the unresolved aches and pains of their own childhoods.

All of these social and familial forces, and many others as well, influence the equipment which the child acquires and with which he meets the demands of life. These are of great importance, because the freedom with which this learning process evolves will determine the richness and freedom with which the child will be able to utilize the vitally creative and essential economies of preconscious symbolic functions throughout the rest of his days.

5. This brings us to the next critical question; namely, at what stage in the evolution of the symbolic process are social influences recognizable as playing a role in determining on the one hand the distribution between conscious and preconscious function and on the other those distortions of the symbolic process which occur when any part of the symbolic process is split off from the rest and rendered unconscious by repression. (Whether comparable neurotic distortions occur through the influence of those ingredients in the unconscious system which have never been conscious and which consequently need never to have been subjected to the same kind of repression is an issue which is relevant but not yet solved. Nor is it essential for our consideration of the central issue.)

With respect to our knowledge of every aspect of human development, it is fair to say that we are in a transitional period. We have learned enough to ask better questions. We have learned enough to know what we do not know. We have learned enough even to know a great many things that are wrong in human development. But we do not yet know how to improve, or even to alter, them. For instance, we know that the human child develops with an enormous burden of masked and dissimulated hatred, rivalry, and destructiveness. We know that to be sufficiently permissive toward the child to give him the right to know what he feels makes a profound difference in the evolution of his processes of hate. Yet the child's destructive impulses remain intolerable to himself, causing him so much guilt and terror that he has to repress some measure of realization of them even in a tolerant environment. Thus cultural and familial tolerance makes a difference in the *point* at which repression occurs. But it does not eliminate repression. An eleven-year-old who was being helped to understand and to accept his blinding hatred of a younger sister suddenly turned suspicious eyes on his father and said with anger and with fear: "You mean I have to carry this hate around with me for the rest of my life?" Certainly it made a difference that the boy was able to ask the question. But it would be naïve to assume that he did not still have to repress major aspects of his violent hatred.

Similarly, we may try to help children to accept the body, body products, and body apertures without the destroying and corroding fear and loathing of the body and all its works which a blindly and crudely repressive educational system will engender. But in spite of efforts in this direction, we have not yet found out how to teach a child cleanliness and sphincter control and a reasonable degree of modesty without infecting him with body shame. We have not found out how to make that shift from the potty as a social event in the middle of the nursery floor to the toilet in the bathroom behind a closed door without doing deep violence to the small child's self-acceptance. And in that act of violence, "modesty" is transmuted into shame and repression arises.

Again we can make a difference in the social attitude toward sexual play and bodily curiosity. We can shift the point at which a barrier is interposed. It makes a difference whether a child has never seen an adult who is not fully clothed, has seen an adult in underclothes, or has seen an adult naked. But the child who has seen the naked adult is not satisfied. He still wants to look inside. One child crouches in front of his mother and tries to look up through the screen of pubic hair "to look up her little hole." Another says: "I wish you had a window in your belly so I could see what is inside." Curiosity is not satisfied with words or with inspection from a distance. The gratification of a child's curiosity requires touching and examining and smelling and tasting and exploring and looking inside. What a child sees he wants to get his hands on, and what he gets in his hands he wants to put in his mouth. Therefore tolerance does not rid us of barriers but only changes their positioning.

This does indeed make a difference in the influence of repression. But it does not eliminate it. As a little boy was being bathed, he held on to his penis with one hand. Very gently his mother took the sponge, washed his face and his back and his chest and the free hand, and then, with careful, casual nonchalance, moved the hand that was engaged with his genital and sponged it too. Later the boy was restless and tense, and he told the story in these words: "And then a great big hand like a giant's hand came and tore my hand away." Subsequently, this evolved into a series of dreams of buzzard-like birds coming to pluck off his penis; because, as he said, the urine was their milk. Then he added reassuringly that his penis would grow back. Surely the careful attempt of the parent not to distort the child's attitudes toward his own genitals had made a difference. But the forces which distorted his perceptual processes of the mother's hand and produced their later symbolic representation were by no means controlled by the parent's careful attitude. In the end, repression took over, to produce a dream which masked and altered the original experience, condensing with it the masked representation of recent experiences centering around watching his mother nursing his baby sister.

A woman of sixty looks back over the years to the age of three. She recalls the tin wash-tub in front of a pot-bellied stove on the sandy floor of a cabin on the western range where she grew up. She recalls the loving figure of her grandmother pouring hot water into the tub and then sponging her down. Then comes the dark moment when in an altered voice the old woman thrusts the sponge into the little girl's hand and says, "And now you finish yourself off down there. . . ." The words "down" and "down there" ring in her ears throughout the years like bells tolling a doom of fear and shame. "There is a dreadful nameless 'down-there' place on me to which even my loving grandmother will not apply a sponge or a name." Here was the birth of repression and of a "down-there" phobia that nearly blasted a brilliant life.

This is why I say that the forces of culture, whether deliberate and individual or represented in the mores of a group, may battle against these deep repressive tendencies but do not eliminate them. Nor do we know the full story of their interaction. Therefore we do not yet know the role of culture in this most critical moment in the evolution of the neurotic process.

6. Early in life, under influences which are so obscure that they have never been satisfactorily described, the phenomena of fixation enter the story of the development of the neurotic process. In the history of analytic theory, this problem has been oversimplified by a general acceptance of the hypothesis that inherent and congenital characteristics of erogenous zones determine the roles to be played by successive recognizable stages of instinctual development, which in turn determine the intensity of the "demands" made by the various zones and organs for specific forms of gratification. These hypotheses beg vital questions: namely, what is fixation and what determines its advent on the scene — *i.e.*, what constellation of constitutional, physiological, individual, and social forces produces it? Later in life the manifestations of this same process constitute the familiar phenomenology of symptomatic compulsions, obsessions, and phobias. It is at least possible that in early life similar compulsive mechanisms produce an obligatory and repetitive accentuation of some phase of instinctual activity or focus on certain objects of instinctual need and on the defenses which are set up against instinctual needs whenever they become compulsively overdriven. If so, then fixations themselves are merely the early symptoms of a neu-

rotic process which is already organized, and which is focused on instinctual functions. Later consequences of the original fixation should then be viewed as secondary derivatives of primary steps in neurotogenesis, with all of the neurotic distortions to which instinctual derivatives are vulnerable. This leaves the same plaguing questions still unanswered: (a) What role do social forces play in the formation of these primary fixations — *i.e.*, the early compulsive and phobic involvements of instinctual processes? (b) What role do social forces play in the secondary and tertiary consequences of such primary fixations? (cf. Kubie [6]).

7. Interwoven throughout each phase of this is the influence of those processes of identification which depend only indirectly on society or social structure or economic forces or cultural organization, but which are directly dependent upon the nature of the family organization, the size of the family unit, the number and variety of adults in whose aura the child develops, the presence or absence of aunts, uncles, and grandparents, the size, age, and sex distribution in the sibling group, the patriarchal or matriarchal domination of each family group, the monogamous-polygamous or uniandrous or polyandrous base of family formation, etc. Whether the family is happy or unhappy, whether it is a center of love or of hostility and rivalry, these determine the identifications with adults which the child makes automatically and which influence the evolution of the symbolic process, of the central emotional position, of compulsive distortions of instinctual processes, of compulsive and phobic defenses, and of the trigger mechanisms which can set any or all of these in motion.

These, then, are seven of the ingredients in the neurotic process. These ingredients are always at work. But we do not as yet have any precise methods by which to evaluate the influence of varying social, economic, cultural, and educational influences on them. That there is an interplay is obvious. My argument is that in our effort to understand this interplay it is of great importance that we do not oversimplify it and that we recognize the fact that as a first step in this direction we must become clearer about the impact of those universal individual experiences which occur in every culture of which we have any knowledge and which initiate that most unique of all developmental phenomena in the human — namely, the distortion of symbolic function which we call the neurotic process.

This distortion of symbolic functions, which is an essential ingredient in the neurotic process in the human being, is in itself a complex process composed of several ingredients. It involves the severing of the relationship between the symbol and its root by repression. It involves the short-cutting of preconscious perceptual experiences into unconscious and autonomic functions without conscious representation and their subsequent representation by disguising symbolic images. It involves the introduction of time gaps between symbol and what it represents. It involves the automatic regression to infantile phases in the development of language, with fluctuations in levels of consciousness, with the consequence that symbolic relationships become multiple and overlapping as in infancy, instead of unique and specific as in maturity. And all of this interacts in a continuous feedback relation to dissociations between affects and their original stimuli, between affects and symbolic processes at all levels, with central emotional positions and their defenses and triggers.

A penetrating and economical summary of the contribution of the allied disciplines to our understanding of psychopathology is to be found in Sidney Axelrad's paper in the 1955 "Symposium on Progress in Orthopsychiatry" (1), together with a carefully selected bibliography. His concluding paragraph is in many ways the essence of what I have been trying to say here.

"It seems to me that part of the confusion in the relation of the social sciences and orthopsychiatry is caused by an assumption that the social sciences stand to psychology as biochemistry and anatomy and physiology stand to medicine, or to the normal functioning of the individual. I am afraid that the situation is reversed. It is psychology, the study of what goes on inside the individual, and very largely of what goes on at a level not accessible to consciousness, that is the basis science for the social sciences. The clearer we are about this, the richer will be the cooperation between the social sciences and orthopsychiatry."

SUMMARY

We must in short consider the interaction of developmental universals and of cultural variables on those ingredients of the neurotic process which are unique for humankind — to wit, the establishing of central emotional positions, the unconscious efforts to preserve certain of these and to defend against others, the acquisition of perceptual and motor patterns, the dichotomy or trichotomy of the evolving symbolic process, the subordination of instinctual development and of the defenses against its various ingredients to unconscious symbolic functions, the fixation of instinctual development by superimposed obsessional, compulsive, and phobic processes and also by dreamlike infantile delusions, the development of manifold disruptive trigger mechanisms, and the integrative and dispersive influences which arise through distortions of the normal processes of identification.

The error which has been made in most considerations of the interaction between developmental and cultural forces in the neurotic process is identical with the fallacy which crops up repeatedly in work on the so-called experimental neurosis. This has been to confuse the seed or the soil with the plant, the part with the whole. Significant external stresses and the emotional disturbances which arise in certain phases of the neurotic process (but which are not the essential distinguishing mark of the human neurosis) have been confused with the unique neurotic process itself. It is this double fallacy which I have tried to avoid in this chapter.

BIBLIOGRAPHY

1. AXELRAD, S.: Symposium on progress in orthopsychiatry. *Am. J. Orthopsychiat.*, 25, No. 3:524–537, 1955.

2. HOLLINGSHEAD, AUGUST B., and REDLICH, F. C.: Social stratification and psychiatric disorders. *Am. Social Rev.*, 18, No. 2:163–169, 1953.

3. ———, and FREEDMAN, LAWRENCE Z.: Social class and the treatment of neurotics. *Social Welfare Forum*, 194–205, 1955.

4. KUBIE, L. S.: The fundamental nature of the distinction between normality and neurosis. *Psychoanalyt. Quart.*, 23:167–204, 1954.

5. ———: "Husband and Wife," in Margaret M. Hughes, ed., *The People in Your Life.* Knopf, 1951, pp. 28–63.

6. ———: The influence of symbolic processes on the role of instincts in human behavior. *Psychom. Med.*, 18:189–208, 1956.

7. ———: The neurotic potential, the neurotic process, and the neurotic state. *U.S. Armed Forces Med. J.*, 2:1–12, 1951.

8. KUBIE, L. S., and ISRAEL, H. A.: "Say You're Sorry," in *The Psychoanalytic Study of the Child.* Internat. Univ. Press, Vol. X, 1955, pp. 289–299.

9. LEAVY, STANLEY A., and FREEDMAN, LAWRENCE Z.: *Psychoneurosis and Economic Life.* Unpublished ms.

10. SPITZ, R. A.: "Hospitalism," in *The Psychoanalytic Study of the Child.* Internat. Univ. Press., Vol. I, 1945, pp. 53–75; Vol. II, 1946, pp. 113–119.

O. H. MOWRER

Symposium, 1952

The Therapeutic Process

*III. Learning Theory and the Neurotic Fallacy**

On an earlier occasion, I have presented a paper before this Association entitled "Learning Theory and the Neurotic Paradox" (3). Here I propose to take up again the thesis of that paper and, so to say, bring it up to date.

* Reprinted from *American Journal of Orthopsychiatry*, Vol. 22, 1952, pp. 679–689. Copyright, the American Orthopsychiatric Association, Inc. Reproduced by permission.

I. THE NEUROTIC PARADOX

In the earlier paper, attention has been called to the fact that neurosis or at least the modern conception of neurosis, involves a paradox. It is today very generally believed that neurosis presents a *learning excess* and that, more specifically, this excess consists of fears which are no longer warranted by the individual's life situation but which persist in spite of their unrealistic nature.[1] Where physical traumata, such as those of war or natural catastrophe, cannot be demonstrated, it is common to assume that the individual who later becomes neurotic must, in childhood, have been treated with unusual harshness by his parents or parent substitutes and must in this way have developed, as Freud was wont to say, "an excessively severe superego." Such a superego, or conscience, reflecting the overseverity and strictness of parents, has been assumed by Freud and his followers to impede the free and healthy expression of the "instincts" and thus to generate anxiety and the varied attempts to deal therewith which we call neurotic "symptoms." Now in "Learning Theory and the Neurotic Paradox," it was pointed out that laboratory learning studies have repeatedly demonstrated that fears, however powerful, always disappear eventually if there is a change in circumstances which makes such fears genuinely unrealistic, genuinely non-functional. It may take several repetitions of the stimulus, or situation, which was previously associated with danger to bring about full extinction of the fear reaction; but sooner or later the subject becomes convinced of the safety of the situation and reacts accordingly (8). In light of these facts, one is moved to ask: Why is it, then, that in neurosis we have fears which appear to have long outlived any real justification but which stubbornly persist or which may even augment to the point of seriously incapacitating the individual?

It can, of course, be pointed out, quite properly, that the learning laboratory is not the same as life and that principles demonstrated in the former may or may not hold in the wider experience of the individual. Yet the dilemma just described seemed sufficiently real and important to prompt Freud to make numerous attempts to resolve it. These took the form of speculations regarding "erotic fixation," the "timelessness of the repressed," the "repetition compulsion," the "death instinct," constitutional variables, and the "racial unconscious." But Freud himself was never fully content with any of his attempted resolutions of this paradox, and on more than one occasion expressed his uncertainties and misgivings on this score. Perhaps his most extended comment in this connection — and surely an eloquent one — is the following:

> Why are not all neuroses merely episodes in the individual's development which become a closed chapter when the next stage of development is reached? Whence comes the element of perma-

nency in these reactions to danger? Whence springs the preference over all other affects which the affect of anxiety seems to enjoy in alone evoking reactions which we distinguish from others as abnormal and which in this inexpediency obstruct the stream of life? In other words, we find ourselves abruptly confronted once again by the oft-repeated riddle: What is the source of neurosis, what is its ultimate, its specific, underlying principle? After decades of analytic effort this problem rises up before us, as untouched as at the beginning (2, p. 120).

II. PROPOSED RESOLUTION OF THE NEUROTIC PARADOX

In the earlier paper, an extended review of the writings of Freud and numerous other investigators in this field led to the conclusion that the neurotic paradox arises because of a false premise: namely, the premise that the neurotic is suffering from excessive and unrealistic fears. This conclusion, that the neurotic paradox is a spurious one because based upon a false premise, was stated and interpreted as follows:

> As defined at the outset of this paper, the neurotic paradox lies in the fact that human behavior is sometimes indefinitely perpetuated despite the fact that it is seriously self-defeating. Freud's major attempt to resolve this paradox involves the assumption that in neurosis there are acts and feelings which have been appropriate at one stage of the individual's life history but are no longer so. More specifically, Freud believed that it was the superego which, as a result of too zealous childhood training, retained its over-severity into adult life despite altered circumstances and in this way produced the distressing, hampering effects seen in neurosis. But this approach to the problem goes counter to one of the best-established principles in the psychology of learning, which is that all learning tends to undergo extinction unless it is at least periodically reinforced.

Recognizing this difficulty in Freud's formulations, Horney and others have sought to rectify it by positing that the wasteful, self-defeating habits and attitudes which constitute neurosis do indeed become periodically reinforced through the operation of so-called vicious circles. But here again neurosis is conceived as a *learning excess*, and it is assumed that if one can but stop the cyclic sequence of events which keeps this learning reinforced, neurosis will be self-correcting.

Against these and similar attempts to resolve the neurotic paradox, we have posited the view that

---

[1] For a detailed review of the evidence for this statement see Mowrer (5).

neurosis is not a learning excess but a *learning deficit*. Because of resistances which the infantile ego sets up against the socializing forces and because of the opposition which it later exerts against the internalized agent of these forces, namely, the superego, the ego remains immature, asocial, id-dominated.

That such an ego continues to experience anxiety is in no way surprising since it is still at war with the superego, which is constantly being kept alive and vigorous by the very nature of the social realities which it represents. We do not ask why the criminal continues to be a fearful individual. There is the ever-present danger that he will be apprehended and punished for his rebellious, antisocial behavior. And much the same is true of the neurotic. It is not that he is suffering from unreal or "childish" fears. He, too, faces a real danger, the danger of having his immaturities and "delinquencies" discovered — the danger, as one patient expressed it, of being "unmasked" — and of having to resume the painful task of renouncing the pleasure principle of infancy and accepting the reality principle of adulthood.

The problem, then, is not to explain why the neurotic does not *unlearn*; it is rather to account for the fact that he does not *learn*. We have already touched upon some of the reasons why small children resist primary socialization and why in later life the ego of the neurotic continues to fight with the superego. And we have also seen the way in which this intrapsychic struggle again becomes externalized in therapy and to what extent the transference behavior is essentially defensive, defensive in the sense of trying to avert the learning involved in further "growing up."

Having thus established the thesis that the neurotic is an "underdone" human being, in some respects not unlike the criminal, rather than an overdone, superhuman sort of creature, we must now turn and make an important modification of an earlier statement. We have repeatedly characterized the neurotic as a victim of underlearning, immaturity, ignorance; but this underlearning is of a special kind and is vouchsafed by what is, in one respect, "overlearning." Preston [9] has remarked that mental health is a matter of attitudes, and it is with respect to *attitudinal learning* that the neurotic is most deficient. To say that an individual is neurotic is not to say that there is anything deficient about his problem-solving learning ability. Indeed, it is the very fact that he has been so skillful in parrying the early attempts of his elders, and later of his conscience, to socialize him that has kept him neurotic. The essence of the difficulty is precisely that, through problem-solving learning, or the primitive pleasure

principle, he has learned how to keep from learning in the sense of being conditioned, i.e., changed emotionally and attitudinally. To put this matter somewhat paradoxically but succinctly, the neurotic is an individual *who has learned how not to learn*. . . .

When we see the development of human personality in this light, not only is the neurotic paradox formally resolved; we are also enabled to conceive the task of therapy, not as that of attempting to stay or actually reverse the process whereby the human animal is converted into a full-fledged member of his society; rather do we see therapy as the more promising venture of reinstituting and, if possible, in some measure completing the education of the laggard learner.

At the time it was written, some four years ago, the above excerpt represented the best statement I could then make of my view of neurosis and its origin. This view still stands, but further experience as a therapist and certain related developments in behavior theory now make it possible to be more concrete and, it is hoped, more cogent and convincing with respect to this argument. In what follows an attempt will therefore be made to give the stated position greater precision and to develop its logical implications along some previously unexplored lines.

III. THE NEUROTIC FALLACY AND ITS PROFESSIONAL ACCEPTANCE

In the preceding section it is pointed out that the neurotic paradox, as I have called it, rises because of a debatable assumption: the assumption that the neurotic is excessively and unrealistically fearful. We have seen that although Freud was well aware of the paradoxical implications to which this assumption leads, he nevertheless continued to hold to it; and a recent review of current theorizing in respect to neurosis and its treatment (5) shows that acceptance of this assumption is still very widespread in the professions most concerned with these matters.

Now it is surely arresting and perhaps also instructive to discover that the same assumption is very widely held by neurotics themselves. This assumption takes myriad forms. One of the commonest of these is the tendency on the part of neurotics to see others — especially parents and "society" — as responsible for their difficulties. Having persuaded themselves of the baleful influence which these "significant others," to borrow Sullivan's phrase, have had upon them, patients are full of self-vindication and resentment. Certainly their view of the situation is that they have been grievously wronged and mistreated.

If a therapist uses the approach that neurosis results from inhibition of sexual and aggressive instincts by an unreasonable, overly severe superego (which reflects the irrationality and malevolence of parents and "society"), he is sure to get a strong "positive transference" from patients. Here at last, they feel, is a person who understands them and who is willing and, they hope, able to help them on their own terms (6, Chap. 18). Then, when this "honeymoon" ends and disillusionment begins to develop in the patient, his reactions are said to represent "negative transference," and one settles down comfortably to "analyze" it for two or three years.

If one wishes to see the same forces at work in a different setting, then let him proceed on the assumption that what is repressed in the neurotic is not so much the forces of the id as those of conscience. Promptly and emphatically the patient will point out that his problems arise precisely because he is *too conscientious*, and in support of this thesis he will again tell you of symptoms which might appear to make of him a veritable monster of morality, a victim of such scruples as one can hardly imagine.

Surely these are suspicious circumstances! It is one thing to say that a therapist must take the patient's "point of view" if by this we mean being willing to listen long and carefully to what he says. But a therapist whose conception and philosophy of neurosis does not differ perceptibly from that of persons who have themselves fallen victim of this disorder can hardly be expected to provide either the conceptual leadership or the curative efficiency of which we are in such need in this field.

In fairness let us grant that a therapist with the orientation which is here under scrutiny will not *wholly* agree with his patients. He will, for example, be the first to tell you that whereas the patient believes or, at some crucial point in the past, has believed in the strategy of resolving psychic conflicts by denial and repression, he, the therapist, stands for a policy of facing conflicts and resolving them without repression; and to this end the therapist will try, by interpretation of dreams, symptoms, slips, etc., to bring back into consciousness those impulses which, in the interests of psychological peace, have been pushed into "the unconscious."

But even here such a therapist is playing into the patient's hands and sharing with him the neurotic fallacy. He is basing his interpretations, his campaign for reality-facing, upon an assumption which the patient would like to believe is true but which, it seems, rarely is. The patient is only too ready

to believe that he suffers because of inhibited lust and hostility and is willing to spend much time, effort and money trying to root out these fear-induced barriers to a better life. But if, in point of fact, the patient's dissociative strategies have worked in another way, i.e., if he has repressed not sex and aggression but instead the forces of his own conscience, all the allegiance in the world to the "reality principle" and the utmost belief in the importance of making the unconscious conscious will not achieve the desired end.

Is it, then, too cynical a view to suggest that a therapist who follows the traditional Freudian line or some currently popular variation of it agrees with the patient in areas where the patient is almost certainly wrong and that in those areas where the therapist *disagrees* with the patient, he is, in effect, accusing the patient of something which the patient actually has not done? We are often charged with basing our theories of personality too much upon our experience with "the abnormal." Certainly the insights of those who make a speciality of studying "only normal people" have not been very helpful or profound. But we cannot easily escape the suspicion that those clinicians who have taken the neurotic patient as their standard have been more victimized in this respect than is commonly recognized.

IV. A CASE ILLUSTRATION

During the course of her college career, Margaret L. became increasingly tense, developed rashes, and entered into a full-blown anxiety state. At this point she went to a clinic and was referred to a woman therapist. However, Margaret obtained no relief from this contact and soon entered into a suicide pact with the young man with whom she was currently involved. Following the suicide attempt, both of these young people had to be hospitalized for a few days, but their physical recovery was rapid and they were soon discharged. Margaret was now assigned to a male therapist who took the following view of her problems. He told her that her basic difficulty was that she "hated men" and supported this pronouncement as follows. Margaret, he said, obviously had exorbitant guilt in connection with sex, and since she perceived her father as the stricter of her two parents, it was he that Margaret blamed and hated most for the irrational and unfair way in which she had been trained. Her hatred of her father generalized, said this therapist, to all men and thus prompted Margaret's need to kill her lover, as well as herself.

Upon entering therapy a third time, Margaret was still chanting, "I hate men," which she said Dr.

K had told her was her trouble; and she was trying to believe this was true but that it had not seemed to help very much. She said that she had been so terrorized by her experiences of the past year and was so afraid of the future that no sacrifice would be too great if she could only be relieved of her suffering.

During the course of the first seven interviews with this patient, it became apparent that it was not so much "men" as herself that she hated and that the basis of her self-reproaches was likewise not so much the illicit sexual activities in which she had been engaged as the fact that she was borrowing money from her parents to complete her education and while presenting a picture of great industry and ambition to them was actually spending most of her time and energy seeking solace from her anxiety in one love affair after another.

At the eighth interview Margaret announced that she had an opportunity to drive to her home in a nearby city over the week end and that she had about decided to do so and have a "talk" with her father. She said that it seemed that she was not going to have any peace until she told her parents, particularly her father, what the real state of affairs was; but she said she felt she could not do this unless she said her therapist had *told* her to. Margaret was advised not to undertake this enterprise until she was herself convinced of its soundness and was able to take full responsibility for it. She made the trip, with results which are given in the following excerpts from the ninth interview. After some preliminary comments, Margaret said:

"Uh — Up until the time that I started talking to my folks I was feeling pretty good. I — just the usual uh — amount of tension; but I wasn't feeling any particular anxiety. And uh — pretty soon after I got up I told my folks that uh — I was still nervous and uh — uh — I was — My father said, 'Why don't you take some shots?' I said, 'No, Dad, they're — the nervousness I'm talking about is neurotic nervousness. You notice I'm talking as loud as — I'm racked with nervousness, I'm feeling anxiety.' And he said, 'About what? About the money we owe you?' [This was a slip; she should have said, ". . . the money you owe us?"] And I said, no, I didn't think it was that. And I felt that — uh — it was more a question of the way I acted; it was more a question of the fact that I wanted to be more honest; I wanted to talk to them. And throughout the conversation with my father he would go off on another vein and try to get me off the subject, but I kept with it. Ah-h-h [big sigh]. It ended up that I seemed to make it more impersonal. At first, when I was losing my nerve about talking I started to talk about neurotic behavior and the value of psychology and what is nervousness and all that sort of thing. On the other hand, my father just — it was just as well that I did that because he was all set to tell once again that I needed vitamin pills and so forth. Uh — we started talking about honesty, as I said, and I asked him if — if he thought sex was evil. And he said, no, he didn't think so, not in the right time and place; and — and then my mother broke in and said — and — and said, 'Oh, well, don't bother talking like this.' And I said, no, I was going to, and then I said uh — well, I had always gotten the impression, I think, from him that he felt it was. And he said, no, he didn't; he thought that I had a lot of impressions about things that he thought [which] he didn't have. And I asked him if he — 'Do you want me to go out on dates? Do you want me to get married?' and he said, 'Yes, of course I want you to do all those things.' And uh — then I said, 'Well, Dad, do you object to the fact that I've had love affairs with men?' He said, 'Well, one thing at a time. You're in school now and don't bother with love affairs.' And I realized then that he thought that I meant by that just going together and being serious about getting married. And he said, 'Never mind about being uh — being serious about someone.' And I said to him, 'Well, I am serious and I have been.' And he said, 'Well, never mind about that. One thing at a time. If those fellows want to get married, let 'em — have him come and talk to me.'

"At which time my mother said, 'That isn't done any more.' And then I completely lost my nerve. I uh — I felt as if someone was tightening a band around my head and I was feeling a *great* deal of anxiety. And I wanted very much to tell them what I meant by 'love affairs,' but I started to open my mouth and it just — nothing came out; I couldn't do it. So I sat around a long time and I thought about it and thought about it and thought about it and tried to get up some nerve, and then I called up Jerry, who drove me to my home this week end. I was whining on the phone to him, 'This is all so foolish. I don't want to do this. I'm just hurting my father. You come over and tell him.' He said — I said, 'I don't know what to say to him.' And I said, uh — 'This is just some silly experiment and I don't — I don't want to do it.' He said to me, 'Well, you're either going to do it now or in the future — take your choice.' And then I tried to — I — I tried to make him say — make me say to hi- — make him say to me that I didn't have to do it. I used every trick I knew. I said, 'This is going to make a big difference in our friendship. I'm liable to feel guilty about a whole lot of things and — and so forth.' But he stuck to his guns and he said, 'You have to tell it; it's better for you.' And he said, 'You want to feel anxiety or do you want to tell them?' And I said, 'I want to feel the anxiety!' And he said, 'Just go in there and tell them!'

"So I went back and — and uh — I said — by that time my father was listening to the radio, and I said uh — 'Look, Dad, I don't — I don't think we understand each other by what we mean by love affairs.' And then my nerve was gone again and I started to hem and haw. And I said — and then he said to me, 'Are you talking about intercourse?' And I said, 'Yes, I am.' And he said uh — 'Well —' He just sat there for a minute. And I said, 'Yes, Dad, that's exactly what I'm talking about.' But I never said it myself; I couldn't bring myself to do it. I couldn't say, 'Yes, I have had love affairs, including intercourse, with men.' It was he that said it, and I just sat there and agreed with him on the fact that that's what I was talking about. I was very relieved when he said it. And uh — I said, 'You see, Dad, I've gotta make a decision here whether I'm going to feel extreme nervousness or whether I'm going to tell you about these things and — and it's uh — I've made a decision that I'm going to tell you this that I have — that uh —' I don't remember how I worded that — oh, I just went that far and he said, 'Well, that's all right.' He said uh — 'Everything in its place though. You're in school now.' And he said, 'If those — don't let anyone give you a line.' And I said, no, no one had given me a line. My mother said something to the effect of Tom, who is the fellow I used to go with. My dad said, 'Oh, Tom's a liar.' What he meant by that I don't know. Probably he thought that Tom had talked me into this situation and then didn't want to marry me. And I said, no, that wasn't true.

"And I said, 'Well, then, you don't reject me on this score.' He said, 'No, I don't.' And then he said, 'I want you to go to school and when you get out of school, make your decisions about anything. Don't do thinking about other things now.' I said, 'Don't you uh — you just told me you didn't care if I went out on dates.' And he said, 'Well, better just go to school now.' By that time I was really feeling physically ill. So I could — I wanted to say more at that point, but I managed to say that I want to make some decisions of my own. And he said, 'Decisions about what?' And then I just regressed into my childlike behavior. I — I started talking to my mother and kidding with her and then later on I told her. I said, 'Well, I do want to make my own decisions; I want to be captain of my own ship or get to the point where I can be.' He said, 'Well, that's all right; that's fine; that's what you

should do.' And when I left I felt better than I ever have in a year — a year and a half.

"And yesterday I felt a great deal different. . . . It was just like a miracle how much better I felt. But I didn't, I really didn't think I'd ever make it through towards the — and I — it just kept going through my head what you said about — I kept wanting to leave it at the word love affairs. Maybe he understood and maybe he didn't. And I wa- — I was trying to talk myself into the fact that oh, he probably did. And I realized that he really didn't. And it — it took a great deal for me to go on with it after that. I didn't think I'd make it. That's the first time that I've *ever* said anything to my father, in any sense of the word, about sex. And then to come out with *all* of this and I — I know he felt very strangely.

"I kept thinking about that, after how much better I felt, that maybe lots of things that Dr. K said were wrong. I just don't feel those things at all. [Pause.] I still feel I have a long way to go; I — but I've — I've certainly developed different — [long pause]. . . .

"But again, I must say, I certainly felt different after Sunday. I felt a great deal relieved. [Long pause.] Oh, I certainly don't feel entirely at ease or entirely confused or unconfused rather, or entirely sure of what I want to do in the future. But I know — this is for sure — that it was a very wise thing for me to do, and I'm certainly very happy that I did it."

As this girl herself realizes, there is still work to be done before she achieves a fully integrated personality; but she has taken a significant step toward recovery and, barring unforeseen events, her progress should now be swift and sure. One case does not, to be sure, prove a theory; but growing experience indicates that by following precepts delineated in the foregoing pages it is possible to achieve in 30 to 70 interviews results which seem to be more satisfactory than those obtained after hundreds of hours of orthodox Freudian analysis (5).

V. SOME CONCLUDING COMMENTS AND REJOINDERS

1. If the conception of neurosis which has been presented in this paper is sound, then the contemporary scene would seem to reflect more of an attempt to devise a theory and a therapy which will be popular with neurotics than to devise a theory and a therapy which will fit facts and produce results. This inference — that the "neurotic fallacy" has been widely accepted in those professions which are most concerned with these matters — may in some measure account for the generally backward nature of

both treatment and prevention of personality disorder in our time.

2. Confusion with respect to masculinity and femininity (i.e., the tendency toward "homosexuality," unmanliness, unwomanliness) is a common feature of neurosis. How can this fact be related to the assumption that neurosis is more a matter of faulty and perverted problem-solving by the patient than of mistraining and malconditioning by others? Freudian theory makes character development contingent upon libidinal development. The present approach puts matters differently. Psychosexual development and orientation are features — one can almost say, by-products — of general character development (4, Chap. 21); and if one sees the neurotic with "homosexual" trends as a person who is trying to avoid full adulthood in the manner appropriate to one's particular sex, as a person who, like Achilles of old, hides from manly duty and danger among the women, active therapeutic movement replaces the slow and questionable results produced by Freudian "analysis" of such problems.

3. It is sometimes inferred that personal consistency demands absolute social conformity, and conformity is assumed to mean an end to "creativity" and "progress." The resolution of this seeming dilemma consists merely of *taking consequences*. One can be as much of a nonconformist or innovator as one wishes and remain mentally healthy, *provided* one does not "cheat," i.e., does not try to have the advantages of conformity and nonconformity simultaneously.

4. How can one hold to a scientific conception of human motivation and behavior and yet see the neurotic as in any way "responsible" for his difficulties? Here we encounter another aspect of the "neurotic fallacy." Neurotics commonly complain of the meaningless and mechanistic nature of human life; they speak of fate and predestination; and they report being haunted by the feeling of helplessness in the face of causal determinism. This is a large issue which will not be settled philosophically or logically in a few words. Clinically, however, the matter is often resolved for all practical purposes by the discovery that the patient has, in the manner of Faust, bartered his sense of freedom to the devil for the dubious comfort of feeling no responsibility, no guilt. As many writers, especially older writers such as Kierkegaard, have pointed out, to be free is to be responsible, capable of guilt. To the extent that our professional efforts are directed toward banishing guilt, not in the sense of helping the patient become guiltless but in the sense of diminishing his capacity for guilt, may we not be leading him further into the kind of helplessness, isolation and enslavement of which the neurotic so often complains?

5. We are beginning to hear a good deal about the implications of "information" or "communication" theory for mental disorder and health. Mind, we are told, is a system, an organization which is built and depends upon communication, particularly communication of the feedback or "servo" variety. In both deception and dissociation there is a distortion, an impairment of "communication." As Professor Deutsch (1) has observed, there is a loss of "openness." If mind is so composed, small wonder, then, that in neurosis the patient feels he is "losing his mind." More literally, he is destroying it, destroying it, paradoxically enough, in an attempt to preserve it; i.e., he is trying to eliminate contradiction and strain within himself; but he does so, not integratively, communicatively, constructively, but by "cutting connections." The neurotic, in the interest of easy solutions and avoiding consequences, first cuts "connections" between himself and other persons (evasion, duplicity); and when there is self-reproach on this account, he then begins to deny, dissociate, cut off from the main body of the self-system those segments which are producing undesirable internal consequences. "Thou shalt not bear false witness" and "Know thyself," *know*, acknowledge, communicate with yourself, may yet guide us to surer ground in our quest for psychological healing and wholeness (7).

REFERENCES

1. DEUTSCH, K. M. *Communication Theory and Social Science.* Am. J. Orthopsychiatry, 22:469–483, 1952.

2. FREUD, S. *The Problem of Anxiety.* Norton, New York, 1936.

3. MOWRER, O. H. *Learning Theory and the Neurotic Paradox.* Am. J. Orthopsychiatry, 18:571–610, 1948.

4. ———. *Learning Theory and Personality Dynamics.* Ronald Press, New York, 1950.

5. ———. "Neurosis: A Disorder of Conditioning or Problem Solving?" in *Comparative Conditioned Neuroses in Human and Other Animals* (E. J. Kempf, Ed., in press).

6. MOWRER, O. H. (Ed.). *Theory and Research in Psychotherapy.* Ronald Press, New York (in press).

7. MOWRER, O. H. "Neurosis and Its Treatment as Learning Phenomena," In *Progress in Clinical Psychology* (Brower and Abt, Eds.). Grune & Stratton, New York, 1952.

8. ———. *A Note on Methodology and Interpretation in Certain Types of Animal Experimentation* (in preparation).

9. PRESTON, G. H. *Psychiatry for the Curious.* Rinehart, New York, 1940.

The Aetiology and Treatment of Children's
Phobias: A Review*

The past few years have seen the establishment of two conflicting views regarding phobias in children. Most workers in this field, psychiatrists and psychologists, are influenced to a greater or lesser extent by either the psychoanalytic theory or the behavior theory in their approach to the subject of phobias. For this reason we have restricted our review primarily to these two theories.

PSYCHOANALYTIC THEORY

The psychoanalytic theory of phobias derives very largely from Freud's case history of Little Hans(14) which was published in 1909. The essentials of the phobic theory were presented in this paper and appear to have undergone little change in the past 50 years.

The theory states that the basis for phobic disturbances is the Oedipus Complex. The child desires to possess the mother sexually and is jealous and hostile towards the father. The child fears his father because of these hostile wishes and, in particular, dreads castration. The fear of the avenging father is then projected onto some external and formerly innocuous object. The outbreak of the phobia is generally preceded by a period of privation and/or intensified sexual excitement.

This development of phobias may be analysed into the following components.

1. The child "is fixated at the oedipal or pre-oedipal level"(22).

Freud(11) states that psychoanalysis has "often showed that animal (phobic object) was a substitute for the father, a substitute on to which the fear of the father derived from the Oedipus complex has been displaced."

(1a) The child has a sexual desire for the mother.

This aspect of the theory is stressed in the case of Little Hans(14). In a discussion on the psychogenesis of agoraphobia in childhood, Abraham(17) illustrates Freud's theory by referring to case material: The phobic child had "an incestuous wish for sexual possession of her (the mother)."

(1b) The child is jealous of, and hostile to, the father.

In the discussions by Abraham mentioned above, he also makes explicit the child's hostility to the father — he had "a death wish against his father."

2. The child fears the father.

Freud(12) states that "the animals which play a part in the animal-phobias of children are generally father-substitutes."

He also says that "the instinctual impulse subjected to repression here (in animal phobias) is a libidinal attitude to the father, coupled with a dread of him. After repression this impulse vanishes out of consciousness"(15).

(2a) The child has castration fears.

The anxiety experienced by the child when he is confronted by the object of his phobia is a danger signal set off by his ego and the danger which is being signalled in this way is invariably the danger of castration(13).

And again, "the fear in zoophobia is castration anxiety on the part of the ego"(13).

3. The fears of the father and of castration are projected onto a neutral external object.

Castration anxiety, states Sarason, et al. (26) results in

the displacement or projection of the dangerous connotations upon an external (previously innocuous) object or situation. After this occurs the original castration anxiety is elicited by a different object and therefore is expressed only in a distorted form.

In Freud's words(9) ". . . castration anxiety is given another object and a distorted expression — namely that of being bitten by a horse . . . instead of being castrated by the father."

4. The onset of the phobia is often preceded by a period of privation and/or sexual excitement.

"An increase in sexual longing, fear or guilt, reactivates the oedipal or pre-oedipal fear of sexual injury to the mother . . ."(22).

Freud(14) attaches importance to this precipitant

* Reprinted by permission from *American Journal of Psychiatry*, Vol. 118, 1961, pp. 97–105.

in the Little Hans case as does Bornstein(2) in the case of Lisa.

5. The onset of the phobia is generally preceded by an anxiety attack which is associated with the phobic object.

Freud(13) states that "a phobia generally sets in after a first anxiety attack has been experienced in specific circumstances such as in the street or in a train or in solitude." Similarly, Abraham is quoted as stating that "in general, the phobic reaction to a specific object or situation becomes established only after the child has experienced an anxiety attack while interacting in some way with the particular object or situation"(26). The initial anxiety attack itself however is produced by castration fears. "The phobic process begins when the ego recognizes the danger of castration and consequently gives a signal of anxiety"(26).

6. Phobias only develop in people with disturbed sexual adjustments.

Freud(10) states that, "the main point in the problem of phobias seems to me that *phobias do not occur at all when the vita sexualis is normal*," (original italics).

He says further, "My theory is only to be gainsaid by evidence of phobias occurring together with a normal vita sexualis."

Watson and Rayner's(31) laboratory demonstration of the development of a phobia in little Albert (see below) must bring into question 5 of the 6 elements of the psychoanalytic theory as does the evidence discussed in the works of Wolpe(32), Eysenck (7, 8) and Jones(19). Point 5, however, approaches close to the learning theory account of phobias described below. The learning theory position is that the onset of the phobia is not merely preceded by an anxiety attack which is associated with the phobic object but that the anxiety attack is generally the major cause of the phobia.

More generally, Ellis(6) argues that

the vague, suppositional and multi-interpretive terms in which the theoretical framework of orthodox analysis is usually stated make it almost impossible to test its concepts by normal psychological methods of investigation.

And we may add, it also makes it almost impossible to appraise the internal consistency and logic of psychoanalytic theory — as a theory.

Ellis(6) has criticised the unscientific nature of psychoanalysis and emphasizes the inadequacies and confusion of the theory, the unreliability of the supportive evidence, the failure to submit any part of the theory or practice of psychoanalysis to acceptable scientific test. One of Ellis's most insistent complaints is against the rampant speculation so common in psychoanalysis. As we hope to demonstrate below, one of Ellis's comments on a passage of Freud's writings seems in fact to be applicable to a large body of psychoanalytic literature. He remarks that, "the ratio of speculative statements to empirically adduced facts . . . is slightly overpowering."

PSYCHOANALYTIC EVIDENCE

Clinical evidence serves a double purpose in psychoanalysis. It is used in order to construct the theory and also to support the theory. Some serious deficiencies present in psychoanalytic case material have been discussed in a critical examination of Freud's treatment of the famous Little Hans case (33). Although the criticisms which we offer here may all be applied equally well to the Little Hans case, we have restricted our comments to other well-known case histories in order to emphasise that these flaws are the rule rather than the exception.

ELABORATION

Bornstein(2) presents an account of a girl of 2 yrs. 4 mths. who developed a phobia of lying down. At one point, Bornstein writes, "She was asked directly what she really had to fear in bed. She replied with a recital of misdeeds having the character of severe self-reproach." The following is an example of what the child said, "See cup ow." Bornstein states that this means ("translated into the language of the adult") "See the cup is broken, has pain (ow) and it is my fault." We suggest that this is an elaboration, particularly the claim that the child felt at fault.

Later we read that the child used to masturbate by rubbing her legs together. Then, the mother reported, she stuck diapers or table napkins between her legs. Bornstein comments "As if wishing to demonstrate that her genitalia were not 'Ow,' not damaged, that in other words she possessed a male genitalia."

A more extensive elaboration is given in an account of one of the child's dreams. The child reported the dream thus, "Opa dudu." Bornstein gives as a direct literal translation "Grandpa naughty naughty," but writes also that it "meant that her grandfather had appeared to her in a dream and had either threatened or spanked her." Later the dream was apparently better understood and Bornstein writes, "The little girl's favourite game before she was sick had been the 'Kuckuck game.' This consisted in hiding and then calling "Kuckuck" which the child who still spoke very imperfectly often used to pronounce 'Duduck' or really almost 'Dudu.' The dream therefore said 'Grandfather is hiding, has gone away.' "

Further elaborations are given in connection with two incidents. (a) The grandfather on one occasion when out with the child had gone behind a tree and urinated. (b) The grandfather had taken the child's mother away for a short period in order to look after the sick grandmother. "Opa Dudu" finally means "If I am not good mother will be taken away by grandfather." But over and above this, it also expressed the wish that "her grandfather would play Dudu again — that is disappear and expose his penis." We suggest that this also reveals a tendency towards over-elaboration.

SUGGESTION

Schnurmann(27) gives an account of a girl, Sandy, who developed a dog phobia at the age of 2 yrs. 5 mths. At that time (1944) she was in the Hamstead Nursery. One night she had a nightmare: "She told the nurse a dog was in her bed." Schnurmann comments later that,

As Sandy had up to then not shown any special interest in dogs it seems strange that in the dream the dog was invested with great significance. An explanation may be found in the following facts: "When the nursery children were taken out in a group an encounter with a dog was usually met by some kind of emotion on the part of the other children. The fear of dogs at night continued for the next three nights. Statements like "Out, out, out, doggie coming" were made. On the fourth night, "Sandy undertook a thorough inspection of her genitals. She was deeply absorbed in this activity and did not take any notice of our presence (two therapists). The worker told her that everything was all right there and that all girls looked like that.

The next day, "On the way to the nursery some of our children started to play with a strange dog. I explained to them that he might bite if they frightened him." It is noteworthy that it was only from this time that the child showed signs of fear of dogs in the street. The main point, however, is that it was only after the worker had drawn the child's special attention to her genitals and after the worker had suggested that the dog might bite, that Sandy herself began to talk about biting. Two nights later Sandy said to the worker, "Bite Annie Bite."

"I asked 'Where bite?' She lifted her nightie pointed to her genitals and said, 'There bite.' "

There was a considerable amount of talk about biting for the remainder of the therapy which enabled the therapist to conclude that, "In the nightmare — as it became clear in Sandy's subsequent behaviour and remarks — a dog was assaulting Sandy in her bed, injuring her genitals, *i.e.*, biting off her penis."

It is also noteworthy that after Sandy's attention had been drawn to the 'rightness' of her genitals she became quite concerned about the rest of her body and clothes — fingers, legs, coat, hat. They all became penis symbols by displacement apparently.

It is felt that, after having given the child the idea that genitals are all right (or all wrong) and also warning her that dogs bite, to regard her subsequent concern with these ideas as confirming the analysis is unsatisfactory and not convincing.

INVERSIONS AND NON-ACCEPTANCE

A common feature of psychoanalytic case reports is the refusal to accept the patient's accounts and to attach instead a reversed meaning to his testimony. The tendency is clearly illustrated in the case of Frankie, aged 4½, reported by Bornstein(3). For example, the boy reported a dream in which he, the room and two other persons were falling down. Bornstein comments, "Actually, the emphasis on 'going down' was a representation of its opposite being lifted up."

We feel then the psychoanalytic theory of phobias is inadequate for the following reasons: 1. The theory is complex and loosely formulated. 2. The evidence is not related clearly to the theory by means of predictions from the theory. 3. The evidence is manipulated through over-elaboration and inversion to fit into the theory and sometimes the patient himself is manipulated by suggestion so that his behavior may fit into the theory.

We will now proceed to an account of an alternative theory — Behavior Theory — which has been presented to account for the development and treatment of phobias.

A BEHAVIOR THEORY OF PHOBIA

The past decade has seen the growth of a new theory of neurotic behavior which has been developed from learning theory. Expositions of the general theory are provided by Wolpe(32) Eysenck(7, 8), Jones(19).

The position adopted by this theory is that neurotic behavior is acquired. The process of acquisition implied in the theory is derived from Hull's system.

Wolpe(32) defines neurotic behavior as "any persistent habit of unadaptive behavior acquired by learning in a physiologically normal organism." Anxiety is "usually the central constituent of this behavior, being invariably present in the causal situations."

In similar vein, Eysenck(7) postulates that "neurotic symptoms are *learned patterns of behavior* which for some reason or another are *unadaptive*," (original italics). Neurotic behavior patterns persist paradoxically, because they are unpleasant. Having acquired an unpleasant association and reaction to a particular stimulus or situation, the person will tend to avoid exposure to these noxious circumstances. As learned patterns of behavior can only be extinguished by repeated unreinforced evocations, the tendency to avoid the noxious situation often precludes the possibility of a spontaneous disappearance of the neurotic behavior. Furthermore, if the person does come into contact with the noxious stimulus he generally responds by withdrawing. This withdrawal is followed by a reduction in anxiety and will reinforce the avoidance behavior mentioned above. This then is what Eysenck(7) refers to as "the vicious circle which protects the conditioned fear response from extinction."

As is the case in all learned responses, neurotic reactions are subject to stimulus generalization. That is, a range of stimuli similar to the original noxious stimulus may also evoke the neurotic reaction.

It should be noted also that neurotic symptoms may under certain circumstances result "not from the learning of an unadaptive response, but from the failure to learn an adaptive response"(19). An instance of this type is enuresis nocturna.

The experimental evidence which supports the behavior theory of neurosis is discussed in Wolpe (32), Eysenck(7, 8), Jones(19).

In terms of the behavior theory, *phobias* may be regarded as conditioned anxiety (fear) reactions.

Any neutral stimulus, simple or complex, that happens to make an impact on an individual at about the time that a fear reaction is evoked acquires the ability to evoke fear subsequently. If the fear at the original conditioning situation is of high intensity or if the conditioning is repeated a good many times the conditioned fear will show the persistence that is characteristic of *neurotic* fear; and there will be generalization of fear reactions to stimuli resembling the conditioned stimulus(33).

The experimental evidence supporting this view of phobias is discussed in Wolpe(32) and Wolpe

and Rachman(33) and is derived from studies of the behavior of children and of animals. The classical demonstration of the development of a phobia in a child was provided by Watson and Rayner(31) in 1920. Having first ascertained that it was a neutral object, the authors presented an 11-month-old boy, Albert, with a white rat to play with. Whenever he reached for the animal the experimenters made a loud noise behind him. After only 5 trials Albert began showing signs of fear in the presence of the white rat. This fear then generalized to similar stimuli such as furry objects, cotton wool, white rabbits. The phobic reactions were still present when Albert was tested 4 months later.

The process involved in this demonstration provides a striking illustration of the manner in which phobias develop and may be represented in this way:

1. Neutral Stimulus (rat) $\rightarrow$ Approach R
2. Painful noise stimulus (UCS) $\rightarrow$ Fear (UCR)
3. Rat (CS) + noise (UCS) $\rightarrow$ Fear
4. Rat (CS) $\rightarrow$ Fear (CR)
5. Rabbit (GS^1) $\rightarrow$ Fear (GCR)
6. Cotton Wool (GS^2) $\rightarrow$ Fear (GCR)

The essentials of the theory may be summarized in 6 statements.

1. Phobias are learned responses.
2. Phobic stimuli, simple or complex, develop when they are associated temporally and spatially with a fear-producing state of affairs.
3. Neutral stimuli which are of relevance in the fear-producing situation and/or make an impact on the person in the situation, are more likely to develop phobic qualities than weak or irrelevant stimuli.
4. Repetition of the association between the fear situation and the new phobic stimuli will strengthen the phobia.
5. Associations between high intensity fear situations and neutral stimuli are more likely to produce phobic reactions.
6. Generalization from the original phobic stimulus to stimuli of a similar nature will occur.

Each of these 6 statements is based on experimental evidence and would also appear to be consistent with clinical experience(32, 8). All are supported by Wolpe's experiments(32) and evidence for specific statements is provided by Liddell(25), Jones(19), Watson and Rayner(31), Eysenck(8) and Gantt(16) among others. It can be legitimately argued in fact that these propositions are supported by the full weight of almost all the evidence accumulated in research on the learning process.

BEHAVIOR THERAPY

The essence of Behavior Therapy is clearly deducible from the theory. If neurotic behavior is acquired (learned) it should be amenable to 'unlearning' in a manner similar to that whereby nonneurotic acquired behavior is extinguished. The two major decremental processes in learning are inhibition and extinction. Numerous therapeutic procedures based on these processes have already been developed(32, 8) and additional techniques are now under investigation. The indications are that these methods are successful in a variety of neurotic disturbances(7, 8, 32), but a definitive conclusion must be postponed until a properly designed and controlled experimental test has been conducted. Such an investigation admittedly poses serious and difficult practical problems but on theoretical grounds, behavior therapy is eminently suited for such an investigation. The hypotheses and procedures are clearly defined and manipulable and a satisfactory study can be expected to provide a relatively unambiguous answer.

Most of the case-reports available to date which deal with the treatment of children's phobias involve the use of Wolpe's 'inhibitory therapy.' He defines the principle of reciprocal inhibition psychotherapy:

If a response antagonistic to anxiety can be made to occur in the presence of anxiety-evoking stimuli so that it is accompanied by a complete or partial suppression of the anxiety responses, the bond between these stimuli and the anxiety responses will be weakened(32).

The method may be illustrated by referring to some actual case reports which we summarize briefly here.

A 3-year-old boy, Peter, evinced fear of white rats, rabbits, fur, cotton wool and other stimuli along this continuum. He was treated by Jones(21) using deconditioning methods. It was decided to work on the rabbit phobia as this seemed to be a focus of Peter's fears. Peter was gradually introduced to contacts with a rabbit during his daily play period. He was placed in a play group with 3 fearless children and the rabbit was brought into the room for short periods each day. Peter's toleration of the rabbit was gradually improved. The progressive steps observed in the process included: "rabbit in cage 12 feet away tolerated . . . in cage 4 feet away tolerated . . . close by in cage tolerated . . . free in room tolerated . . . eventually, fondling rabbit affectionately." Another measure employed by Jones involved the use of feeding responses. "Through the presence of the pleasant stimulus (food) whenever the rabbit was shown, the fear was eliminated gradually in favor of a positive response."

Using these techniques Jones overcame not only Peter's fear of rabbits but all the associated fears. The follow-up of this case showed no resurgence of the phobia.

Lazarus and Rachman(24) describe the treatment of a 14-year-old boy who had suffered from a fear of hospitals and ambulances for 4 years. The phobia had developed after the prolonged illness and suffering experienced by his mother. She had been taken from the house several times by ambulance and spent over a year in hospitals.

The boy was first trained to relax. Hierarchies of disturbing situations concerning ambulances and hospitals were then constructed, ranging from mildly upsetting to extremely upsetting items. The lowest item in the ambulance hierarchy for example, was a mental image of a derelict ambulance in a scrapyard and the highest item an image of sitting beside the driver in a moving ambulance. The therapist then slowly worked up the hierarchies desensitizing each item by relaxation responses. After 10 interviews, the boy was much improved and was able to visit a hospital. Four months later he was still quite well.

The third case, reported by Lazarus(23), deals with an 8-year-old boy who developed a fear of moving vehicles 2 years after having been involved in a motor accident. Initially the therapist rewarded the boy whenever he made a positive comment concerning vehicles, by giving him a piece of his favorite chocolate. By the third interview the boy was able to talk freely about all types of moving vehicles. Next a series of "accidents" with toy motor cars was demonstrated. The boy, John, was given chocolate after each accident. Later John was seated in a stationary vehicle and slow progress (with chocolate feeding reinforcements used at each point) was made until John was able to enjoy motor travel without any anxiety.

Lazarus also describes the successful treatment of a case of separation anxiety and a case of dog-phobia. Case reports describing the treatment of phobias in adults are provided in Eysenck(8).

REINTERPRETATION OF PSYCHOANALYTIC CASES

A further advantage of behavior theory is that it can account for and incorporate a good deal of evidence presented by psychoanalysts. We will illustrate this with several examples from the literature.

A number of psychoanalysts when discussing school phobia have stressed the importance of getting the child back to school early. Eisenberg(5) writes, "In general, the longer the period of absence from school before therapeutic intervention is attempted the more difficult treatment becomes." In explanation he writes, "Left at home the patient . . . is reinforced to persist in infantile manoeuvering by the 'success' of his efforts." This point has also been stressed by the workers at the Judge Baker Guidance Center(4, 18, 29, 30). No attempt is made, however, to incorporate this important aspect of therapy in the psychoanalytic theory. This therapeutic procedure is in a sense even contradictory to the theory insofar as it is symptom-oriented. This failure to account for important data by means of the theory can be added to the list of deficiencies above.

The importance of the early return to school can be accounted for by the behavior theory of phobias in the following manner:

As learned responses (including fear) can only be abolished by extinction or inhibition, no reduction of the school phobia can be expected to occur if the person is entirely isolated from the noxious situation. Furthermore, continued absence from school will certainly reinforce the phobic pattern. It will have this effect because of the reduction in school-anxiety which is produced when the person refrains from attending school. Like all learned behavior, phobic responses are strengthened by drive reduction, in this case, reduction of the anxiety drive.

Another aspect of therapy for school phobias has been stressed by some psychoanalytic writers. Klein (22) writes:

The child is told he must go to school every day, but does not have to stay there and does not have to attend the classroom. The child can stay in an office, assist the office staff, read or draw and can leave at any time.

This graded approach is another aspect of therapy not in keeping with the general psychoanalytic approach and not accounted for by the theory. It is on the other hand a procedure which directly follows from the behavior theory of phobias.

Though the psychoanalytic case histories referred to in this paper are long and complex, most of the data presented are taken from the analytic sessions and the phobic situation itself is seldom described adequately. For this reason it is not possible to give precise accounts in terms of behavior theory of the development and treatment of the phobias reported. But one or two general observations can be made.

We referred earlier in this paper to Bornstein's case of the girl who developed a phobia of lying down(2). From the point of view of behavior theory the following points are of importance. "Training in cleanliness was begun in the sixth month. The child was held over the pot at regular hours." Towards the end of the first year, the child's grandmother took over the toilet training and apparently imposed severe measures. After the age of one year the child wet herself on very few occasions. One of these occasions was the day before her mother's return from an illness, when she wet herself several times. "The members of the household thought it probable that when this happened they said to her 'Wait until your mother hears you have wet yourself again! She won't love you any more. She will go away again and won't want to come back.'"

Bornstein comments,

We believe that she could not allow herself to lie down because she was afraid that when lying down or sleeping she would be unable to control the wish to defecate in bed . . . Moreover we know of an historical factor which had connected the motif 'incontinence' with the motif 'not sitting': *After her illness with diarrhoea the child could no longer sit up.*

(original italics). Bornstein is referring here to the fact that when the child was 7-months-old she had an attack of diarrhoea which left her so weak that she could no longer sit alone.

From the point of view of behavior theory the development of the phobia can be accounted for in the following way: Because of her severe toilet training the stimulus to urinate or defecate had become associated with anxiety. The association of defecation with lying down (at the time of her illness) resulted in the act of lying down also producing the anxiety response. The child then attempted to avoid anxiety by sitting up all the time.

Concerning the child's recovery from the phobia, the following observation is noteworthy:

The child on one occasion refused to resume even a sitting position in bed. As was usual she was left. She soiled herself, the bed was changed and the girl asked her mother to give her a hug which she was given. Then to the mother's astonishment the girl happily lay down in bed for the first time in five weeks.

It would seem unlikely that this one association of soiling with an accepting and affectionate response was sufficient to produce a recovery. Although we are not informed whether, after this "astonishing" result, the mother altered her attitude and behavior to her child we will assume that she used this experience in her future handling of the girl. If she continued to use affection and re-assurance to dampen the child's anxiety, such a procedure would almost certainly have brought about a reduction of the phobia.

In the case of Sandy's dog phobia(27) and Frankie's elevator phobia(3) we do not have sufficient information to give a convincing account of the development of the phobia. But we have already seen that in both cases the phobic objects were associated with fear producing stimuli. In the case of Sandy, we have the nightmare involving a dog and the therapist's warning that dogs bite. But one may be justified in asking why the child had a nightmare involving a dog in the first place. In the case of Frankie we have the nurse's threats that she would call the elevator man to teach him not to disturb people.

Regarding Sandy's and Frankie's recovery from their phobias we again do not have sufficient information. But it is of interest that Sandy frequently encountered dogs when out walking with the therapist which would at least present an opportunity for the extinction of the fear response. Secondly Schnurmann writes that on one occasion Sandy played quite happily with a doll's pram, "I asked her whom she had covered with the blankets. She produced a dog. I said 'A doggie.' Sandy replied, 'No pussy cat.' " It is possible that further play with the toy dog would have produced some desensitization. Finally Sandy had played dogs with other children and the therapist and it is of interest that the phobia ended in the following way: "When on the way to the nursery school we met a dog who was on a lead. Sandy at first made a withdrawing movement, then she approached the dog hesitatingly. When another dog came into sight, Sandy walked directly towards him and barked." Sandy responded in other words in a manner learned while playing at being dogs.

CONCLUSIONS

Mention has been made of Mary Cover Jones's (20, 21) classic studies in which she describes her attempt to develop techniques for eliminating chil-

dren's fears. The significance of this early work is only now becoming recognized. She gives an account of several methods of treatment. Four of these appear to be promising, practical and in accord with present-day learning theory. They are the methods of:

1. Direct conditioning.
2. Social imitation.
3. Systematic distraction and
4. Feeding responses.

The fruitfulness of the behavior theory approach to phobias is well demonstrated if we add to Jones' list the additional new methods which have been, or could be used in overcoming children's phobias.[2]

5. Systematic desensitization (Wolpe)
6. Assertive responses (Wolpe)
7. Relaxation responses (Wolpe)
8. "Pleasant" responses in the life situation — with drug enhancement (Wolpe)

In a suggestive article by Jersild and Holmes(17) further possible methods for treatment of children's fears are discussed. From their survey of parent's experiences in dealing with children's fears, Jersild and Holmes suggest these techniques (among others): Prompting the child to acquire skills which will enable him to cope with the feared situation; progressive contact with, and participation in, the feared situation; verbal explanation and reassurance; practical demonstration of fearlessness.

Some of these techniques are already employed by prevailing therapies without receiving explicit acknowledgement.

All these methods certainly provide therapists with a formidable armamentarium to begin with. What is now required is careful, thorough investigation of these methods and above all a major project to establish the degree and permanence of improvements which may be obtained by these techniques.

In the meantime, active therapists may consider conducting their own investigations of these methods when faced with children suffering from phobic conditions. Obviously the choice of the method will depend to a considerable extent on the nature of the phobia. It is worth remembering also that these methods are not mutually exclusive and it is probable that in many cases a combination of these techniques may offer the most promising approach.

[2] Naturally, many of these methods are equally applicable to the treatment of adults' phobias.

BIBLIOGRAPHY

1. ABRAHAM, K.: Clinical Papers and Essays in Psychoanalysis. New York: Basic Books, 1955.
2. BORNSTEIN, B.: Psychoanal. Quart., 4:93, 1935.
3. BORNSTEIN, B.: In: The Psychoanalytic Study of the Child. Vol. III/IV, pp. 181–226. New York: International Univ. Press, 1949.
4. COOLIDGE, J. C., HAHN, P. B., and PECK, A. L.: Am. J. Orthopsychiat., 27:296, 1957.
5. EISENBERG, L.: Am. J. Psychiat., 114:712, 1958.
6. ELLIS, A.: Genetic Psychol. Monog., 41:147, 1950.
7. EYSENCK, H. J.: Proc. Roy. Soc. Med., 53:504, 1960a.
8. EYSENCK, H. J. (Ed.): Behaviour Therapy and the Neuroses. London: Pergamon Press, 1960b.
9. FREUD, S.: The Problem of Anxiety. New York: Norton, 1936.
10. FREUD, S.: Collected Papers, Volume I. London: Internat. Psychoanalytic Library, 1946.
11. FREUD, S.: An Autobiographical Study. London: Hogarth Press, 1948.
12. FREUD, S.: Collected Papers, Volume IV. London: Internat. Psychoanalytic Library, 1949a.
13. FREUD, S.: Inhibitions, Symptoms and Anxiety. London: Hogarth Press, 1949b.
14. FREUD, S.: Collected Papers, Volume III. London: Hogarth Press, 1950.
15. FREUD, S.: A General Selection from the Works of Freud. (Ed. J. Rickman) London: Hogarth Press, 1953.
16. GANTT, W. H.: Experimental Basis for Neurotic Behavior. New York: Hoeber, 1944.
17. JERSILD, A., and HOLMES, F. B.: J. Psychol., 1:75, 1935.
18. JOHNSON, A. M., FALSTEIN, E. I., SZUREK, S. A., and SVENDSEN, M.: Am. J. Orthopsychiat., 11:702, 1941.
19. JONES, H. G.: In: Handbook of Abnormal Psychology. (Ed. Eysenck, H. J.) London: Pitman, 1960.
20. JONES, M. C.: J. Exp. Psychol., 7:383, 1924a.
21. JONES, M. C.: Pedagogical Sem., 31:308, 1924b.
22. KLEIN, E.: In: The Psychoanalytic Study of The Child. Vol. I. New York: Int. Univ. Press, 1945.
23. LAZARUS, A. A.: In: Behaviour Therapy and the Neuroses. (Ed. Eysenck, H. J.) London: Pergamon Press, 1960.
24. LAZARUS, A., and RACHMAN, S.: S. African Med. J., 31:934, 1957.
25. LIDDELL, H. S.: In: Personality and the Behavior Disorders. (Ed. J. McV. Hunt) New York: Ronald Press, 1944.
26. SARASON, S. B., DAVIDSON, K. S., Lighthall, F. F., WAITE, R. R., and RUEBUSH, B. K.: Anxiety in Elementary School Children. New York: John Wiley & Sons, 1960.
27. SCHNURMANN, A.: In: The Psychoanalytic Study of the Child. Volume III/IV, 253. New York: Int. Univ. Press, 1949.
28. TALBOT, M.: Am. J. Orthopsychiat., 27:286, 1957.
29. WALDFOGEL, S.: Am. J. Orthopsychiat., 27:754, 1957.
30. WALDFOGEL, S., TESSMAN, E., and HAHN, P. B.: Am. J. Orthopsychiat., 29:324, 1959.
31. WATSON, B. J., and RAYNER, R.: J. Exp. Psychol., 3:1, 1920.
32. WOLPE, J.: Psychotherapy by Reciprocal Inhibition. Stanford: Stanford Univ. Press, 1958.
33. WOLPE, J., and RACHMAN, S.: J. Nerv. Ment. Dis., 131:135, 1960.

FREDERICK J. ZIEGLER AND JOHN B. IMBODEN

Contemporary Conversion Reactions
II. A Conceptual Model*†

It is apparent that recent contributions to the literature dealing with conversion reactions are derived from a variety of premises. For our continuing study of conversion phenomena, we decided to examine critically some of the implicit and explicit assumptions of current writers, in order to evolve a conceptual model which would be useful to us as a working theory. The present paper is a statement of our

* Reprinted from the *Archives of General Psychiatry*, April, 1962, Volume 6, pp. 279–287. Copyright 1962 by American Medical Association. Reprinted by permission.

† Read in summary form at the 117th Annual Meeting of the American Psychiatric Association, Chicago, May 12, 1961.

current viewpoint, with comments on positions of other contributors.

HISTORIC AND SEMANTIC CONSIDERATIONS

The now partially discarded term "hysteria" long outlived the Hippocratic concept denoting a clinical condition caused by the wandering uterus or by some variation of this (i.e., the engorged uterus, uterine "suffocation," or "furor"). Charcot's(11) conception of hysteria (apparently still with some vestigial influence in continental psychiatry) implicitly accepted Morel's theory of nervous degeneration and led him to stress the presence of "stigmata" as more or less enduring earmarks of an hysterical diathesis. Much earlier, the clinically astute Sydenham regarded a variety of somatic symptoms as having no organic basis and as being "hysterical" but, as usual, he avoided speculation about mechanisms.(2) Brodie should be credited with the first psychodynamic model of what we now classify as conversion reactions for his statement in 1837 that "fear, suggestion, and unconscious simulation are the primary factors" in the development of certain hysterical symptoms.(9) Later, the concepts of Möbius(39) (that "hysterical" symptoms are shaped by unconscious ideas about disease) and of Babinski(4) (that suggestibility has a role in symptom shaping and in the treatment of this disorder) were contributions that today still retain substantial validity.

Freud first used the term "conversion" in 1894 (22) defining it as a process by which the "unbearable idea is rendered innocuous by the quantity of excitation attached to it being transmuted into some bodily form of expression;" this was a modification of his earlier position(26) that hysteria results from "psychic trauma." Unlike other nosological psychiatric terms which describe or connote some essential symptomatic or behavioral feature of the disorders they designate, the term "conversion" refers to a theoretical conception of a clinical disorder. The term is in this respect similar to the nosology of the ancients, who often named disorders according to their theory of etiology (e.g., hysteria); and we might speculate that "conversion reaction" was able to displace "hysteria" as a nosological term in part because of the fact that the theory connoted by the latter had long been an absurdity, while that connoted by the newer term seemed to make considerable sense. It is also apparent that the extreme variability of clinical manifestations of conversion reactions made the task of descriptively naming the condition difficult.

The clinical designation of a disorder by an explanatory theory has, we feel, important and some-

times undesirable theoretical and practical consequences. The verbal fusion of phenomenon with theory tends automatically to promote a conceptual fusion as well, so that the unwary student finds himself unwittingly defining and describing the disorder according to his notion of the theory of conversion; that is, the range of observable clinical syndromes included under the term "conversion reaction" will be enormously broadened or narrowed depending upon the particular investigator's assumed theory of conversion. If 2 investigators do not mean the same thing when they speak of the *theory* of conversion, they probably do not mean the same thing when they speak of the *phenomenon* designated "conversion," and communicative difficulties loom.

In a recent study of genetic aspects of "hysteria," Slater(52) concluded that "the hypothesis of a genetical basis of a specific or indeed important kind has had to be discarded," and questioned that there was any basis for regarding "hysteria" as a syndrome. The authors concur with other investigators(1, 12, 36, 44, 56, 59) that manifest conversion reactions and "hysterical" or histrionic personality traits are by no means invariably associated and, in this paper, only the problem of conversion reactions per se is considered. Because of this point of departure, our model is therefore not comparable with many of those of "hysteria," such as Wisdom's nuclear-introject, phallocentric model.(58) Current "explanatory" psychodynamic models of the conversion reaction contain at least 2 of the following 3 distinct, but interrelated, major elements: (*a*) conversion reactions serve as defenses against anxiety, (*b*) in the conversion process, there is a "transmutation" of "psychic energy" into a somatic symptom or syndrome, and (*c*) the particular somatic symptom or syndrome is symbolically expressive of underlying conflict. In the following sections we will critically review these elements in this order, and present a conceptual model of conversion reaction which we have found useful.

CONVERSION REACTIONS AS DEFENSES AGAINST ANXIETY

The general proposition that neurotic symptoms serve to attenuate anxiety became jelled in 1926, following the publication of Freud's work *The Problem of Anxiety*.(23) This work, that of Anna Freud in 1936,(20) and the "psychobiologic reaction" concept of Adolf Meyer, are reflected in our present system of nomenclature. *The Diagnostic and Statistical Manual: Mental Disorders*(16) states: "The chief characteristic of these (psychoneurotic) disorders is anxiety, which may be directly felt and expressed or which may be unconsciously and automatically controlled by the utilization of various psychological defense mechanisms (depression, conversion, displacement, etc.)." Conversion reactions, then, are described as follows: "Instead of being experienced consciously . . . the impulse causing the anxiety is converted into functional symptoms in organs or parts of the body, usually those that are mainly under voluntary control. The symptoms serve to lessen conscious (felt) anxiety and ordinarily are symbolic of the underlying mental conflict." Our officially sanctioned American model is, then, clearly stated, and the proposition that the conversion symptom is a defense against anxiety is widely accepted. Recent evidence and critical thinking now require examination of the adequacy of the term "anxiety" to designate that which is defended against by the conversion reaction.

In examining the existing evidence to support or to require modification of the "anxiety model," it first should be noted that the small number of well studied or "analyzed" cases in reports which tend to confirm this model requires scientific caution. Scientific conceptual models in general, if they derive from a small number of studied prototypes or observations, are properly thought of as "mechanical models," in which the elements of the model are of the same scale as those studied.(35) However, when models are designed to be *generally* applicable to a large number of experimental or observed phenomena, they must often be modified to include a range of interchangeable factors, and to exclude those features from individual observations that are neither essential nor generally valid. These more generally applicable models have been termed "statistical models." The methodologic error of using mechanical models as if they were generally valid (i.e., generalizing from an "n" of 1) has been, and is, easy to fall into in our discipline.[1] In the light of accumulating clinical experience with conversion reactions, it seems as if the assumption that anxiety is always the specific affect defended against should be revised.

In examining a recent series of 134 conversion reaction patients seen at The Johns Hopkins Hospital over a 4-year period, it became apparent that this group was not homogeneous but was composed of various subgroups.(59) There were 40 patients with clinical features of depression, 19 with evidence of incipient schizophrenia, some adolescents and adults with ego identity problems, and still others with features of "neurotic anxiety" in the clinical sense of that term. This investigation suggested that conversion reactions may serve to reduce or avoid a variety of painful affects. To apply the term "anxiety" to a variety of painful affects presents real semantic difficulty, especially since even Freud made only a quantitative distinction between "signal anxiety" and clinically overt anxiety.[2] The "defense mechanism" theory of conversion symptoms might actually be challenged on logical grounds since, except for abundant inferential clinical data, no experimental evidence or "proof" has heretofore been produced. We wish to cite 2 additional studies that also seem to provide some of this (to us) desirable evidence. In the first, of delayed convalescence following acute brucellosis,(30) individuals who had recovered quickly from the disease were compared with patients who had developed "chronic brucellosis." Both groups were given the TDMA "Self-Concept Scale" (which provides some indication of the degree to which the subject perceives himself "positively"). As expected, the control ("acute, recovered") group scored significantly higher on this scale than did the chronic group. However, those patients who had had "chronic brucellosis," but had symptomatically recovered by the time of the investigation, scored *lower* on the Self-Concept Scale than did those patients who still had symptoms at the time of this study. This finding, which was confirmed by data derived from the psychiatric interviews, strongly supported the view that the somatic symptoms had a significant function in the maintenance of self-esteem. In another study, of delayed convalescence after the Asian influenza epidemic,(29) it was demonstrated that those patients who showed objective test evidence of depression before the epidemic retained symptoms significantly longer (tending toward chronicity) than did undepressed controls.

On the one hand, these studies all support the concept that the conversion symptom or syndrome is a personality defense. On the other hand, they strongly suggest that there are any number of dysphoric affects which may be defended against with conversion symptoms. (The relationship between depression and conversion symptoms has also been noted by

---

[1] Perhaps the most obvious example of this sort of error has been the problem of paranoia which, since Freud's(25) study of Schreber's autobiography (i.e., one case), has often been considered erroneously to be invariably due to projection specifically of homosexual impulses.(43, 50) The elucidation of the psychological mechanism of projection was a brilliant and invaluable contribution, but the now clinically evident fact that a *variety* of unacceptable impulses and ideation might be projected has been too often overlooked.

[2] "The development of anxiety induces symptom formation — nay more, it is a *sine qua non* thereof . . . there is an obvious tendency on the part of the ego to restrict the development of anxiety to a minimum, to employ anxiety only as a signal."(23)

Abse[1]). Moreover, we are not now in a position from which the range of various dyphoric affects, which are defended against with conversion symptoms, can be delineated satisfactorily. Although there are important recent contributions to affect theory, (7, 17, 40, 41) there seems to be no generally accepted classification. Therefore we merely consider, schematically, that there are a number of dysphoric affects, any of which (singly or in combination) might evoke utilization of psychological defense mechanisms, including conversion symptoms. In support of a broad defense mechanism view of conversion, Szasz(55) quotes Fairbairn(19): "Hysterical conversion is, of course, a defensive technique — one designed to prevent the conscious emergence of emotional conflicts involving object relationships. Its essential and distinctive feature is the substitution of a bodily state for a personal problem; and this substitution enables the personal problem as such to be ignored." Szasz further develops concepts of object relationships making it explicit that, essentially, he is talking about affects.

To recapitulate this element of our model, we consider that current evidence confirms the proposition that conversion reactions and syndromes serve as personality or "ego" defenses, but that it requires replacement of the specific term "anxiety" by the generic term "dysphoric affect," to designate that which is defended against.

CONVERSION AS TRANSMUTATION OF ENERGY

As originally defined by Freud, the term "conversion" referred to a process in which a "quantity of excitation" is "transmuted into some bodily form of expression."(22) Later, this "quantity of excitation" came to be further elaborated as "psychic energy" deriving from instinctual drives or libido; so, in effect, the freudian view hypothesizes the conversion of postulated energy. To illustrate how this postulated energy may be transmuted, Freud(24) used a hydrodynamic analogy: "When the bed of a stream is divided into two channels, then, if the current in one of them is brought up against an obstacle, the other will at once be overfilled." Since the energy transformation theory per se does not impose any limitations on the type of somatic process into which the energy may be transformed, the *literal* acceptance of this theory leads to an enormous expansion of the range of clinical disorders that may be categorized as conversion reactions. This is epitomized by Deutsch, who describes the process of conversion as "transformation of great amounts of libido into organic manifestations at the cellular level." In a recent monograph(14) he asserts that "fundamentally, organic symptoms due to the conversion process may occur in all organs according to their erogenicity." In the same monograph, Ludwig illustrates this point of view in reporting the case of a patient with laryngeal malignancy and commenting that: "In view of the large quantities of energy and the intensity of the conflict cathected in the larynx, one might have predicted that this man's vocal cords would become the seat of the disease. Quite possibly the interference with his drinking . . . dangerously shifted the cathexis to his larynx and may have precipitated the outbreak of malignancy localized there."(15) Thus carried to its logical extreme, libido, pent-up and convertible, becomes an all-encompassing *élan maladif*.

Current scientific evidence, coming from several quarters, seems decidedly against the energy transmutation hypothesis. Oken and others(42) consider that their studies of physiologic, emotional, and behavioral parameters of stress interviews provide ". . . no indication that stimulus effects are shunted away from the psychological system into alternate somatic channels, as has been postulated for certain psychosomatic disorders. Rather, it would seem that when the defensive system is operating, stimuli do not significantly impinge on the organism." Such a formulation implies selective inattention rather than diversion of repressed instinctual energy. Biologists have long tended to disdain the notion of a unique type of psychological energy and have preferred to restrict the term "instinctual" to certain readily observed, apparently inborn (as opposed to learned) potential behavior patterns; and Beach(5) predicts eventual replacement of the term "instinct" when various aspects of so-called instinctual patterns are identified. Stanley Cobb has commented on the mischief resulting from translating Freud's *Triebe* into "instincts."(13) As more has been learned of biological energy, in terms of adenosine-phosphate systems and the Krebs citric acid cycle, the notion of unique psychic energy has become even more untenable. Biochemical energy systems in nervous tissue are considered to be identical with those in other tissues.(28) Among psychoanalysts, Alexander(3) has objected to the term "conversion" because of its transmutation of energy connotation. Bieber(6) has suggested that libido theory has estranged psychoanalysis from science. Szasz(54) has remarked; "It would appear as if the point had now been reached at which, in the interests of progress, the classic libido theory would have to be transformed into a theory of development based essentially upon object relationships." Kubie(32) has commented that his "own conviction is that the libido theory violates much basic knowledge both of energetics in general and of the physiology of the nervous system in particular, and that it is possible, through a proper expansion of our understanding of the functions of the symbolic process . . . to get along well without it." Kardiner(31) and his associates have, in recent series of penetrating articles, concluded that "energetic (and instinctive) explanations . . . are forms of circular reasoning that add nothing to our understanding of ego functions." Assumed instances of "libidinal" conversion to somatic processes have been of a *post facto* anecdotal sort which, in conjunction with lack of operationally precise terms,(34) have been subject to the influence of the investigators' preconceptions.

The authors know of no scientific evidence that would warrant further delay of the long overdue abandonment of libidinal, energetic, and "instinctual" implications connoted by the term "conversion." We do, however, retain the term "conversion," used in a *metaphorical* sense, because no better term immediately suggests itself to denote the observable alteration of function.

SYMBOLIC AND COMMUNICATIVE ASPECTS

The symbolic functions of conversion symptoms have been stressed since the Breuer-Freud(8) monograph appeared. It is commonly inferred, with supporting anecdotal evidence, that symbolic requirements of an incipiently symptomatic patient partially determine the nature of the conversion symptoms. According to this view, then, the patient's need to express unconscious affect and fantasy symbolically plays an important *etiological* role in the conversion reaction (i.e., in the selection and molding of specific symptoms). Quite in contrast to the global view of conversion possible, if one assumes energy transmutation, symbolization requirements fairly sharply *restrict* conversion reactions to those organ systems which are capable of conveying "bits of information." The somatic motor and sensory systems are capable of differentiated responses to cortical influence and, therefore, presumably are capable of expressing unconscious ideas or feelings. On the other hand, the autonomic nervous system is extremely limited in its capacity for making differential responses to cortical influence, so it seems most unlikely that sympathetic or parasympathetic responses to cortical activity could differentiate one complex of ideas from another. Similarly, those metabolic processes under predominantly humoral influence are viewed by us as incapable of serving as communication systems. In short, if primary symbolization is viewed as a *sine qua non* of the conversion process, the latter is perforce restricted to somatic sensory and motor functions. Autonomic dysfunction, hematopoietic disease, neoplasms, etc., would all be excluded from the category of conversion reaction. Alexander(3) and Grinker(27, 42) have recently favored this clinical restriction, as do the present authors. "Psychophysiologic" disorders apparently become symbolically invested only secondarily; as Schur(51) has stated, "once a lesion has been established, it can add to confusion of identity by its localization, its character, or its secondary symbolic elaboration." The distinction between "meaning" and "cause" as elaborated by Whitehorn(57) is most important when symbolic aspects of symptomatology are considered. Szasz, in a lucid discussion of symbolization, considered conversion symptoms to be iconic signs.(65)

THE CONVERSION REACTION AS SOCIAL ROLE ENACTMENT

We have found it useful to consider the patient with a conversion symptom as someone enacting the role of a person with "organic" illness, symbolically communicating his distress — dysphoric affect and/or unacceptable fantasy — by means of somatic symptoms. In our conceptual model, this somatic mode of communication does not serve to "discharge" pent-up emotion but, rather like any other language, it is useful as an instrument in negotiating interpersonal transactions. Through the conversion reaction, the fact that the patient is in distress is formulated to himself and communicated to others in the ego-syntonic terms of "physical illness," and the patient thereby distracts himself (with varying degrees of success) from the more immediate perception of his dysphoric affect. Human beings may communicate their feelings and ideas to themselves[3] and others in a variety of modes such as ordinary consensual language, sign language, dreams, autistic verbal symbols of schizophrenia, or autistic somatic symbols of conversion reaction. Conversion may be viewed as operating, in this way, like other psychological processes.

The language of information handling and communication theory, as it has been applied by Ruesch, (45, 46, 48, 49) seems appropriate to this aspect of conversion reactions. In many conversions reactions seem clinically the message of emotional distress is

---

[3] Intrapsychic communication mechanisms have been discussed by Meyer and Mendelson.(38)

communicated primarily in nonverbal ways (to the patient himself as well as to the others in his transactional field) in terms of somatic symptoms which are, in effect, an "analogic code."[4] Szasz(55) has recently proposed a very similar view, elaborating many of these points.[5]

Within the framework of the symbolically communicative function of conversion reactions, we now need to consider the question of determinants which *restrict* the choice of specific symptoms among the myriad available. Several dynamic factors operate together or in sequence to narrow the range of available symptoms. First, the patient unconsciously chooses particular symptoms according to his conception of illness, as derived from his own past experiences with illness[6] or from his observation of others. The patient's need to adopt the role of an

acceptably ill person, as viewed in the light of his own unique preconception,(53, 59) results in a substantial narrowing of the range of available somatic symptoms. His particular symptoms will then simulate physical illness in a relatively expert or a relatively crude manner, depending upon the degree of congruity between his imagery of illness and that of the observer. Medically sophisticated patients are often relatively expert unconscious simulators, while patients with "classical" symptoms are more often found in "backwoods" cultures. (1, 59)

Another factor often operating in the selection of specific symptoms is that of the patient's psychologic identification with another person who has or has had an illness. A common example of this is seen in unresolved grief reactions in which the patient portrays with conversion symptoms some or all of the clinical characteristics of the deceased's terminal illness. In such a situation, identification with the lost "object" facilitates the patient's choice of a particular set of symptoms from his mental repertory of syndromes. Abse has reviewed this identification aspect.(1)

Within this context of unconsciously simulated illness, specific symptoms may develop or receive prominence because they are especially suited to the symbolic representation of specific fantasies, affects, and motivational conflicts. For example, an ex-secretary of a neurologist, who had intermittently simulated multiple sclerosis for some months, expressed unconscious rejection of her pregnancy with her complaint of progressive weakness of her arms, which she fantasied would prevent her from holding the unwanted baby. In this connection we cautiously speculate upon the relative contributions of ideational as opposed to affective expression of the conversion symptom. Our clinical experience suggests that unconscious affect contributes heavily to the subjective sensation of the symptom, i.e., that the affect is reflected in how the symptom feels. For example, our experience would lead us to believe that unconscious or denied[7] feelings of depression are apt to be associated with pain. An unconscious denial of anxiety related to aggressive impulses is apt to be associated with feelings of weakness or numbness. On the other hand, revealing clues of unconscious fantasy are often reflected in the patient's

---

[4] These theoretical considerations seem to have significant implications for therapy, which some(10, 33, 50) have found presents difficulties because the patient remains convinced that his problem is somatic rather than emotional. The physician, then, must realize that at first the patient is only able to communicate his distress in the language of somatic complaints; and abrupt attempts to shift the focus of treatment to the successfully fended-off emotional problems are not tolerated by the patient because they do not seem appropriate. Any transactions that seem pertinent to the patient must, therefore, begin at this analogically codified level. As Ruesch has said: "The understanding of nonverbal denotation is based upon the participant's empathic assessment of biological similarity."(47) The tactical goal of enabling the patient to communicate eventually in ordinary consensual word language about his emotional reactions would seem most desirable.

[5] Szasz, of course, may not concur that his and our models are similar. Of the old term "conversion hysteria," he preferred to drop "conversion" and we prefer to drop "hysteria." We assume that "conversion reaction" as we use it accounts for most of the variance covered by "hysteria" as he uses it, but are not sure. (For example, Eysenck(18) uses "hysteria" to refer to a rather specific degree of extroversion and neuroticism and apparently does not accept the defense mechanism model at all.) We infer underlying "dysphoric affects," while Szasz covers this in a discussion of object relations. We both stress ego-defensive, learned and patterned social role enacting, information handling, symbolic and communicative aspects, which Szasz further elaborates into a game-playing model. We regard his analysis of conversion phenomena as a significant contribution, but consider that the logic of using this model as a basis for other arguments in his book is more apparent than real (if, indeed, it is apparent). We are not ourselves prepared to abandon the physician's role, as it is institutionalized in our culture, since we find it a most useful vantage point for the collaborative (with other physicians and other behavioral scientists) investigation and attempted modification of these and allied disorders.

[6] Freud put it this way: "It appears to be far more difficult to create fresh conversion than to form paths of association between a new thought which is in need of discharge and an old one, which is no longer in need of it."(22)

[7] E. Meyer(37) points out that the concepts of repression and denial are often implicitly related to libido theory. However, they "may instead be viewed as ego functions directed to the regulation of more specific and recognizable affects and affect states. The latter view suggests an uninterrupted continuum between the normal process of inattention and the repression involved in the formation of a conversion symptom."

verbalized interpretations of symptoms. Such correlations are methodologically difficult to validate at present but are tentatively useful in the attempt to understand the meanings of symptoms.

SUMMARY

A brief review of psychiatric usage of the term "conversion" has been presented. The semantic problems inherent in using a term which connotes an explanatory theory for the purpose of designating a clinical phenomenon are discussed. The authors found no scientific evidence in support of the "transmutation of energy" (or of "libido") theory of the mechanism of conversion, and consider that the term "conversion reaction" should be used only in a metaphorical sense, not a literal sense.

Currently reported studies, including ours, have cited evidence that clinical conversion reactions and histrionic (or "hysterical") personality traits are not always correlated. We cite our own and other data in support of the currently accepted propositions that conversion symptoms are employed as psychological or personality defenses against conscious awareness of emotional distress. However, we consider that the conventional formulation of conversion as a defense against "anxiety" is too restrictive, and evidence is cited that there are in all probability a number of dysphoric affects, imminent perception of which may evoke conversion symptoms.

In our conceptual model, the patient with a conversion reaction is enacting the role of a person with "organic" illness, communicating his emotional distress in the symbols of somatic symptoms while at the same time distracting himself from the perception of dysphoric affects. Physiologic requirements for symbolic communication would seem to limit conversion phenomena chiefly to motor and sensory systems. Within this conceptual framework, other factors which operate to narrow or to predetermine symptom choice include: (1) the patient's conceptions of physical illness, usually determined by previously experienced or observed illness; (2) identification with persons with whom an ambivalent relationship has been disrupted; (3) the suitability of specific symptoms for the symbolic representation of particular fantasies and affects.

REFERENCES

1. ABSE, D. W.: Hysteria, in American Handbook of Psychiatry, Vol. 1, edited by S. Arieti, New York, Basic Books, Inc., 1959, chap. 14.
2. ACKERNECHT, E. H.: A Short History of Psychiatry, New York, Hafner Publishing Company, 1959, p. 28.
3. ALEXANDER, F.: Fundamentals of Psychoanalysis, New York, W. W. Norton & Company, Inc., 1948, pp. 245–251.
4. BABINSKI, J., and FROMENT, J.: Hysteria or Pithiatism, translated by J. D. Rolleston, London, University of London Press, Ltd., 1918.
5. BEACH, F. A.: The Descent of Instinct, Psychol. Rev. 62:401–410, 1955.
6. BIEBER, I.: A Critique of the Libido Theory, Amer. J. Psychoanal. 18:52–68, 1958.
7. BOWLBY, J.: Separation Anxiety, Int. J. Psychoanal. 41:89–113, 1960.
8. BREUER, J., and FREUD, S.: Studies in Hysteria, Nervous and Mental Disease Monograph Series, New York and Washington, Nervous and Mental Disease Publishing Company, 1936.
9. BRODIE, B. C.: Lectures Illustrative of Certain Nervous Affectations, No. 11, London, 1837; cited by Zilboorg, G., and Henry, G.: A History of Medical Psychology, New York, W. W. Norton & Company, Inc., 1941, p. 374.
10. BROWN, W., and PISETSKY, J.: Sociopsychologic Factors in Hysterical Paraplegia, J. Nerv. Ment. Dis. 119:283–298, 1954.
11. CHARCOT, J. W.: Maladies du système nerveux, Oeuvres complètes, tome premier, Paris, Bureaux du Progrès Medical, 1892.
12. CHODOFF, P., and LYONS, H.: Hysteria, the Hysterical Personality and "Hysterical" Conversion, Amer. J. Psychiatr. 114:734–740, 1958.
13. COBB, S.: Instincts, Amer. J. Psychiat. 112:149–151, 1955.
14. DEUTSCH, F., Editor: On the Mysterious Leap from the Mind to the Body: A Workshop Study on the Theory of Conversion, New York, International Universities Press, Inc., 1959, p. 41.
15. DEUTSCH,(14) pp. 106–107.
16. Diagnostic and Statistical Manual, Mental Disorders, Washington, D.C., American Psychiatric Association, 1952, pp. 31–32.
17. ENGEL, G. L.: Towards a Classification of Affects, read before the American Association for the Advancement of Science, New York, Dec. 30, 1960, to be published.
18. EYSENCK, H. J., Editor: Handbook of Abnormal Psychology, New York, Basic Books, Inc., 1961, v. chap. 1.
19. FAIRBAIRN, W. R. D.: Observations on the Nature of Hysterical States, Brit. J. Med. Psychol. 27:105, 1954.
20. FREUD, A.: The Ego and the Mechanisms of Defense, translated by C. Baines, New York, International Universities Press, Inc., 1946.
21. FREUD, S.: Analysis of a Case of Hysteria, Collected Papers, Vol. 3, London, Hogarth Press, Ltd., 1956, p. 66.
22. FREUD, S.: The Defense Neuro-Psychoses, Collected Papers, Vol. 1, London, Hogarth Press, Ltd., 1956, p. 63.

23. FREUD, S.: The Problem of Anxiety, translated by H. A. Bunker, New York, The Psychoanalytic Quarterly Press and W. W. Norton & Company, Inc., 1936, pp. 85–86.

24. FREUD, S.: Five Lectures on Psycho-Analysis, Standard Edition [His] Complete Psychological Works, Vol. 11, London, Hogarth Press, Ltd., 1955, pp. 3–55.

25. FREUD, S.: Psycho-Analytic Notes Upon an Auto-Biographical Account of a Case of Paranoia (Dementia Paranoides) (1911), Collected Papers, Vol. 3, London, Hogarth Press, Ltd., 1956, p. 444.

26. FREUD, S., and BREUER, J.: On the Psychical Mechanism of Hysterical Phenomenon, Collected Papers, Vol. 1, London, Hogarth Press, Ltd., 1956, p. 32.

27. GRINKER, R. R., and ROBBINS, F. P.: Psychosomatic Case Book, New York, Blakiston Division, McGraw-Hill Book Company, Inc., 1954, p. 74.

28. HASTINGS, A. B.: Personal communication to the authors.

29. IMBODEN, J. B.; CANTER, A., and CLUFF, L. E.: Asian Influenza — Influence of Psychological Factors in Convalescence, Arch. Intern. Mod. 108:393–399, 1961.

30. IMBODEN, J. B.; CANTER, A.; CLUFF, L. E., and TREVER, R. W.: Brucellosis: III. Psychologic Aspects of Delayed Convalescence, A.M.A. Arch. Intern. Med. 103:406–414, 1959.

31. KARDINER, A.; KARUSH, A.: and OVESEY, L.: A Methodological Study of Freudian Theory: IV. The Structural Hypothesis, the Problem of Anxiety, and Post-Freudian Ego Psychology, J. Nerv. Ment. Dis. 129:341–356 (v. 354) 1959.

32. KUBIE, L., in discussion of Szasz, T.: An Attempt at the Systematic Restatement of the Libido Theory: I. A Critical Analysis of Some Aspects of the Libido Theory: The Concepts of Libidinal Zones, Aims, and Modes of Gratification, Ann. N.Y. Acad. Sci. 76: 994, 1959.

33. LAUGHLIN, H.: The Neuroses in Clinical Practice, Philadelphia, W. B. Saunders Company, 1956, p. 278.

34. LEHRMAN, N. S.: Precision in Psychoanalysis, Amer. J. Psychiat. 116:1097–1103, 1960.

35. LEVI-STRAUSS, C., in Anthropology Today, edited by A. L. Kroeber, Chicago, University of Chicago Press, 1953, p. 528.

36. MEYER, E., Review of Deutsch,(14) J. Nerv. Ment. Dis. 132:350, 1961.

37. MEYER, E.: Personal communication to the authors.

38. MEYER, E., and MENDELSON, M.: Psychiatric Consultations with Patients on Medical and Surgical Wards: Patterns and Processes, Psychiatry, 24:197–220, 1961.

39. MÖBIUS, P. J.: Über den Begriff der Hysterie, Neurologisch Beitrage, I. Heft, Leipzig, Ambr. Abel, 1894.

40. NOVEY, S.: A Clinical View of Affect Theory in Psychoanalysis, Int. J. Psychoanal. 40:94–104, 1959.

41. NOVEY, S.: Further Considerations of Affect Theory in Psycho-Analysis, Int. J. Psychoanal. 42:21–31, 1961.

42. OKEN, D.; GRINKER, R. R.; HEATH, H. A.; SABSHIN, M., and SCHWARTZ, N.: Stress Response in a Group of Chronic Psychiatric Patients, Arch. Gen. Psychiat. 3:451–466 (v. 463) 1960.

43. OVESEY, L.: Pseudohomosexuality, the Paranoid Mechanism and Paranoia: An Adaptational Revision of the Classical Freudian Theory, Psychiatry 18:163–173, 1955.

44. RANGELL, L.: The Nature of Conversion, J. Amer. Psychoanal. A. 7:632–662, 1959.

45. RUESCH, J.: Disturbed Communication, New York, W. W. Norton & Company, Inc., 1957.

46. RUESCH, J.: General Theory of Communication in Psychiatry, in American Handbook of Psychiatry, Vol. 1, edited by S. Arieti, New York, Basic Books, Inc., 1959, chap. 45, pp. 895–908.

47. RUESCH, J.: Nonverbal Language and Therapy, Psychiatry 18:323–330, 1955.

48. RUESCH, J.: Synopsis of the Theory of Human Communication, Psychiatry 16:215–243, 1953.

49. RUESCH, J., and BATESON, G.: Communication — The Social Matrix of Psychiatry, New York, W. W. Norton & Company, Inc., 1951.

50. SALZMAN, L.: Paranoid State — Theory and Therapy, A.M.A. Arch. Gen. Psychiat. 2:679–693, 1960.

51. SCHUR, M.: Comments on the Metapsychology of Somatization, Psychoanal. Study Child 10:146, 1955.

52. SLATER, E.: The Thirty-Fifth Maudsley Lecture: "Hysteria 311," J. Ment. Sci. 107:359–381, 1961.

53. STAINBROOK, E.: The Community of the Psychiatric Patient, in The American Handbook of Psychiatry, Vol. 1, edited by S. Arieti, New York, Basic Books, Inc., 1959, p. 150.

54. SZASZ, T. S.: An Attempt at the Systematic Restatement of the Libido Theory: I. A Critical Analysis of Some Aspects of the Libido Theory: The Concepts of Libidinal Zones, Aims, and Modes of Gratification, Ann. N.Y. Acad. Sci. 76:975–1009 (v. 985) 1959.

55. SZASZ, T. S.: The Myth of Mental Illness, New York, Paul B. Hoeber, Inc. (Medical Book Department of Harper & Brothers), 1961.

56. WALTERS, A.: Psychogenic Regional Pain Alias Hysterical Pain, Brain 84:1, 1961.

57. WHITEHORN, J. C.: The Concepts of "Meaning" and "Cause" in Psychodynamics, Amer. J. Psychiat. 104:289–292, 1947.

58. WISDOM, J. O.: A Methodological Approach to the Problem of Hysteria, Int. J. Psychoanal. 42:224–237, 1961.

59. ZIEGLER, F. J.; IMBODEN, J. B., and MEYER, E.: Contemporary Conversion Reactions: A Clinical Study, Amer. J. Psychiat. 116:901–909, 1960.

The Psychology of Depression and Its Management[*][1]

Depression is one of the common affective phenomena of daily living and it is also one of the most common symptoms of serious psychic illness. When a symptom consists of the pathologic exaggeration of a normal function, studies of physiology and pathology are mutually illuminating. The phenomenon of depression is therefore presented here in the contexts of both normal function and disease. The formulations offered are derived from observations made during psychoanalytic and psychiatric practice and correspond fairly closely, I believe, to classic psychoanalytic theory. The approach, however, is primarily clinical.

DEFINITION AND DESCRIPTION

Depression is an affect. The word affect refers to the pure subjective feeling component of the somewhat more general concept of emotion which is often considered to include elements of thoughts, fantasies, wishes and prejudices. Affects in general may be divided into those that are pleasurable and those that are painful. Depression is clearly one of the latter group which includes also, for example, anxiety, guilt, shame, embarrassment, resentment and anger. The distinction between depression and other painful affects cannot be made without resort to the use of some question begging term as sadness to characterize depression. Since the essence of every affect is a subjective and intangible sensation, the definition of an affect can distinguish one from the others only by appeal to ancillary data such as physical concomitants, circumstances of evocation and behavioral consequences. In a sense then, the definition of depression will have to be completed by the remainder of this paper.

Nevertheless there are certain visible signs by which an affect may declare itself to an observer. These signs become more pronounced and their number increased the more pronounced the affect. Depression is usually betrayed by a fairly characteristic facial expression. It is usually accompanied by weeping especially when the subject is alone. A psychic and physical inertia usually accompanies depression. The depressed individual is inclined neither to think, nor to imagine, nor to plan, nor to work, nor even to move. Such psychic and physical activity as does appear, is performed slowly and with a sense of great effort. Anorexia is fairly constant and in severe cases may be replaced by a positive aversion to food, or nausea. Unusual and unpleasant sensations may be referred to the gastrointestinal tract in instances of pronounced depression, a frequent complaint being a sense of "gnawing." The depressed individual will sometimes compare his "stomach" sensations to those which might be produced by some living organism restlessly churning about and clawing. Sexual desire is diminished in mild depression and completely abolished in severe depression. Sexual performance is often impaired as well. In some seriously depressed individuals the usual inertia is replaced by a visible restlessness which often precludes sleep, and it betrays a pronounced psychic agitation. Confessions of unwarranted or exaggerated guilt especially toward loved ones are common. In instances of serious depression there may be feelings of worthlessness and wickedness. Of course the greatest threat in cases of pathologic depression is suicide. There are no signs by which a physician can be assured in any given case that a suicidal outcome is not possible. In general it seems that suicidal outcomes are more likely in cases in which there is a family history of suicide or a previous personal attempt at suicide. However, the absence of such a history cannot be depended upon to exclude the possibility of suicide.

The occasions upon which depression characteristically appears may also serve to distinguish depression from other painful affects. During the course of normal day to day living, depression is most frequently encountered following some serious loss or disappointment. The depression following the death of a loved person is typical. Mild depression persisting a few days or weeks often follows childbirth especially among women who have enjoyed their pregnancy. Depression falls into the category of disease when it occurs in the absence of any overt loss or when its persistence or severity is immoderate

* Reprinted by permission from the *Bulletin of the New York Academy of Medicine*, Vol. 31, 1955, pp. 757–773.
[1] Presented at a meeting of the Section on Neurology and Psychiatry of The New York Academy of Medicine, November 9, 1954.

even though the precipitating loss be significant. The sixth decade of life is the period in which pathologic depression is most likely to appear or is likely to be most severe if episodes of depression have occurred earlier.

FUNCTIONS AND NATURE

Since depression is so obviously a component of normal daily life one may assume that it has a function. This problem may be approached by first considering the function of affects in general. I have suggested elsewhere that affects might be considered labels by which individuals might anticipate the results of any proposed course of action. Thus, given any set of environmental circumstances, the individual attempts experimentally to ascertain what opportunity these circumstances offer for the gratification of instinctual wishes. For example, a sexually active male, introduced to a woman he has not known before will automatically want to know what she would be like as a sex partner. He proceeds to imagine the liaison accomplished and as he does so becomes aware of an effect. The experiment is performed swiftly, almost instantaneously and none of it may arise to the level of awareness save for the affect. If the affect is a pleasant one, the individual may proceed to live out his fantasy. If on the other hand considerations of morality, propriety, or personal safety, or the difficulty of accomplishment veto the project, one of the negative affects appears in consciousness and the project is not only abandoned but often its consideration is not acknowledged. In this way the affect is used as a guide for ascertaining the suitability of environmental circumstances for the gratification of instinctual wishes. However, affects appear not only during experimental contemplation of proposed behavior, but also in the course of actual living. Just as the affect which appears during experimental contemplation determines whether that or a similar fantasy is to be pursued or elaborated on the one hand or whether an entirely different mode of procedure is to be used on the other, so the affect which appears during an actual experience determines whether the individual shall strive to continue or intensify that experience or to change or replace it.

In light of this discussion we may ask what kind of activity is anticipated with the feeling of depression, and further, in what type of experience depression is likely to appear. Merely by referring to the conditions under which depression appears in normal life we are able to offer prompt replies. Obviously, when the consequence of any act is the loss of something or someone which one loves, the individual is warned by anticipation depression. Also following the actual experience of loss, the affect of depression conspires to undo the loss or at least the impact of the loss.

We may now ask, what is the nature of the loss against which anticipatory depression warns us and which post hoc depression attempts to undo. Addressing ourselves once more to the occasions on which normal depression appears, the most obvious instance, we realize is the loss of a loved person, in psychoanalytic terminology, the love object. The love may be based on family ties as in the parent-child or in the sibling relation, or it may be a romantic love. The loss may be occasioned by death, departure, separation or by rejection. Depression is equally likely to be concerned with a loss of the physical integrity of the person himself. Such losses include for example the amputation of a limb or the surgical removal of some organ which formed part of the individual's mental image of himself, such as an eye or a breast. Even the realization of the gradual loss of youth as for example on the occasion of some biologic or chronologic landmark may be associated with depression. A loss of physical attractiveness whether gradually by aging or abruptly by a disfiguring injury may be a cogent cause of depression. Capacity for sexual performance is thought of in the same way. Moreover since the individual usually considers his social and economic status and his personal property to be in a sense a part of himself, their loss too may be associated with depression. It is interesting that even a loss of physical integrity or social prestige can be understood in terms of a loss of love object. In the first place the individual always reserves a sizable proportion of his capacity to love for himself, that is, for his body, his social position and his intellectual creations. Therefore a loss in any of these spheres may be considered a loss of love object. Secondly, since these features make for the individual's attractiveness to others as a love object, a loss of any of them makes him less desirable to others and therefore less able to attract and hold a love object.

However the situation is less simple in cases of neurotic or psychotic depression. Here we are often able to see no obvious loss, or a loss which is trivial. When individuals with pathologic depression come under the scrutiny of psychoanalysis, a fantasied loss of love object in any of the forms mentioned above is invariably seen. The fantasy of loss is usually the consequence of wishes for the destruction or desertion of the love object. An especially common though incredible fantasy of this type resembles the idea of killing the goose that laid the golden eggs.

The individual becomes so desirous, and greedy with respect to the virtues and potential gifts of the love object, that he finds himself destroying the loved person to acquire his virtues. The fantasy that the loss has actually occurred, while really a consequence of the unconscious wish, is often precipitated by some minor loss which the individual interprets as symbolic of the major deprivation for which he has wished. In such an instance the depression is disproportionately severe with respect to the magnitude of the loss which the individual considers responsible.

Briefly, then, we may conclude that where there is depression, there has been a loss. Where the degree of depression is commensurate with the magnitude of the loss, we consider the depressive reaction to be a normal response. Where no loss at all is visible or where the degree of depression is disproportionately great, in the light of the actual loss, the depression is considered pathologic.

If I have succeeded in establishing that the affect of depression is related to a loss, either anticipatory or post hoc, then I might with justice be asked how the elements of the depressive reaction can be understood to be specifically concerned with the loss of the love object. Since the affect itself is a painful one, it has the effect of urging the individual either to avoid or to attempt to undo the state of deprivation which it signals. The depressed individual has the conviction that relief is to be obtained only by a restitution of the loss and in no other way. While a state of depression may be succeeded by a state of determination, resolution or ambition, the depression itself contains none of these other feelings. The depressed individual is in no mood to attempt to restore his loss by his own efforts but believes that the loss can be restored by the efforts of a loving person, who will protect, redeem and rescue. It is this attitude which is responsible for the discrepancy between the strength of the individual's desires and the state of inertia which accompanies depression. One is reminded of course, of the small child's relation to its mother who alone can undo the child's deprivations and can provide for the child's wants. Since in the first and second years of life, the child will accept no substitute for the mother, or at least for the adult who customarily takes care of it, we are led to suspect that the pattern of depression in response to the loss of a loved person, is first established in early childhood when the child has to learn that it is expected, naturally but inevitably to wean itself from dependence upon its mother. It is a fact that when depressed patients are psychoanalyzed, circumstances of the early childhood depression are reconstructed. Although these early depressions are often unnoticed, ignored or resented by parents, occasionally parents are aware of a tendency to brood, sulk and be moody or mean. The characteristic facial expression of depression, as well as the loss of erectness of posture, signify to every observer the individual's need for external help and affection. When confronted with this signal, every individual feels the need to comply by offering gifts, consolation and affection. This need is so compelling that it is exploited both by legitimate social agencies and by unscrupulous swindlers and mendicants to obtain gifts. The compelling nature of this phenomenon is occasionally resented by the individual who is so obligated. There is the familiar story of a wealthy man, who upon being confronted by a beggar with a particularly sad story, instructs his butler, "Get that man out of here! He's breaking my heart." Such resentment is more regular and more pronounced among the families of patients who are pathologically depressed and who respond not at all to the sympathetic efforts of those who love them to cheer them up. The fact that the patient doesn't respond in the face of the stubborn demand implicit in his appearance and deportment, evokes resentment and anger in the family.

The combination of miserable appearance and inertia together with a sense of helplessness, appears also in an entirely different syndrome of purely physical origin, namely, surgical shock. It is probably true that every element of this syndrome can be accounted for as part of a set of integrated neural and hormonal reaction patterns. It has occurred to many that the syndrome could be imagined to be purposefully devised. In the presence of physical injury so serious that the individual's only chance for survival lies in complete rest and assistance from another individual, the injured individual develops insuperable inertia and a miserable, sympathy-evoking appearance. It seems reasonable to imagine that the resemblance between the syndrome of surgical shock and depression betrays a common origin in a phylogenetically inherited response pattern devised for the purpose of enforcing a dependent relation of the subject individual to another person.

THE ROLE OF AGGRESSION AND GUILT

A frequent component of normal depression and a constant component of pathologic depression is an aggressive tendency. Considering the formulation offered above, that depression is the response to deprivation of a love object and includes a wish for its restoration by the agency of some loving individual, one may be surprised to find that hostility is a significant element in the syndrome. However if we note that it occurs constantly in pathologic depression and if we assume that the extent to which it appears in a so-called normal depression is related to the degree of psychopathology included in such a depression, we will obtain a clue about the meaning of the aggression and also about the nature of pathologic depression. It will be recalled that the essential difference between a pathologic depression and a normal depression is that a normal depression is a response to a real loss, while in pathologic depression, either no loss is evident to the observer, or any loss which is evident is trivial in contrast to the profundity of the response evoked. We may infer, and this inference is confirmed by clinical observation, that in cases of pathologic depression, the loss is either wholly or largely a fantasied loss — any loss preceding the depression being merely a symbol for a more serious loss in fantasy. Now why should an individual be troubled by the fantasy of a serious deprivation? Clinical psychoanalytic observation discloses that pathologic depression is regularly preceded by fantasies, and often not very well disguised acts of aggression directed against the love object. At a given point, either because of the achievement of certain quantitative thresholds within the psyche, or as a result of some actual loss which is taken as a symbolic demonstration that the wished for destruction has actually taken place, the depressive reaction sets in. In a sense a certain amount of aggression exists in all erotic ties and to a certain extent, at least, every loss of a love object, no matter how real and actual, is symbolic of the attainment of a wish.

If the suggestion I made above, to the effect that the purpose of depression is to obtain restitution of the love object, then it should follow that depression automatically cancels any aggression against the love object. The sense of helplessness and the inertia almost seem to guarantee that that effect will be achieved. To explain the persistence of aggression within depression, we may turn to one of Freud's most brilliant observations which he called "the return of the repressed." This is a fairly universal phenomenon but it is especially striking in outspoken cases of neurosis. Freud observed that when he had succeeded in recognizing the instinctual drive, that was struggling against repression, and against the measures adopted by the individual to defend himself against the appearance in consciousness and the execution of this drive, he was then astonished to discover that the defensive measure itself often served as the vehicle for the very drive which was repressed.

The classic example of this appears in the case of the fanatic moralist who insists that the public be protected against obscenity by censorship of the press, and then has himself appointed to a committee to examine all printed material which is suspected of obscene content for the purpose of censorship. It is clear that his intense concern for the morality of society, is a reflection of his difficulty in controlling his own wish to derive pleasure from pornography. By sitting on a committee of censors, he not only satisfies his conscience and acquires a feeling of righteousness but simultaneously gratifies the wish for enjoyment of pornography against which he struggles so hard and which he denies everyone else. One may observe a similar situation among anti-vivisectionists. Here are individuals with such difficulty in controlling their wish to kill fellow humans that they become fanatic protectors of the lives of lower animals. They project their own sadistic wishes upon the physiologists who use experimental animals and attempt to prevent experimentation upon living animals. Of course, if they were successful, the ultimate sufferers would be their fellow humans against whom their unconscious aggressive wishes are directed in the first place.

To return to the subject of pathologic depression, we may explain the persistence of aggression after the depressive reaction has set in, as an instance of the return of the repressed. True, physical assault does not occur and almost all rebukes are directed against the individual himself, the loved ones who are concerned about him being spoken of most respectfully. Nevertheless passive resistance is recognized as a powerful tool of aggression. As noted above, the pathologically depressed individual, by his unresponsiveness to the most extravagant efforts of his loved ones, tortures these very loved ones before whom he pretends to be so humble. In such cases, it is usually apparent to the consulting psychiatrist that the family is much more eager to obtain medical assistance than the patient. This torturing of the family is a part of every pathologic depression and those normal depressions which were preceded by significant amounts of hostility to the person lost. Thus the aggression towards loved ones in pathologically depressed individuals represents the same aggressive tendency which existed towards them before the onset of the depression and can appear during depression only because it has circumvented the inhibitory effect of the depressive syndrome. Such aggression as may become apparent even to the patient may be utilized by him. He may scold his family for failing to provide him with the gratification he wishes. The sense of shame and the humiliation which necessarily accompany depression may become associated with the aggressive tendency and give rise to a bitterness and meanness in the patient.

The most dangerous and most striking aspect of aggression in the depressed individual is the self-directed aggression. The patient scolds himself, starves himself, will not permit himself any enjoyment, rejects any erotic approaches and finally may commit suicide. Such behavior is considered to be aggression directed against the self because it is clear that the patient does to himself what psychoanalytic investigation discloses he wants to do to others. It is interesting to note that the same aggression against the self which becomes so obvious during depression, can be observed even when the patient is not depressed and especially when he is hypomanic. Thus we may infer, that aggressive tendencies towards others and towards the self exist together in the individual prone to depression. When he is depressed the aggression against others seems to be more inhibited and the aggression against the self reinforced, while during a hypomanic state, the aggression against the self is attenuated and the aggression against others is facilitated. The agitation which appears in many cases of pronounced depression and in mania is derived from this aggression and may be considered an attempt to dissipate it harmlessly.

Another prominent component of the depressive syndrome is the affect of guilt. The pathologically depressed individual reproaches himself for failure to be adequately just and loving, for being a drain on the family resources and for all sorts of wickedness of which he seems to be innocent. It is only when one becomes aware of the aggressive unconscious fantasy that one understands the justice behind the self reproaches. We must remember that depression has the purpose of discouraging acts which would result in significant loss to the individual. However, any given act need not be restrained by only one controlling mechanism. There is another device which has the function of controlling destructive acts directed by one individual against other members of his group or against humans in general, even where no significant personal loss is involved — that is the guilt mechanism. Therefore any hostile wish against a love object necessarily activates both the depressive and the guilt mechanisms. The association of guilt with depression arises not from any necessary dynamic relation between the two, but from the circumstance that both are activated by the same pathologic wish fantasy, namely, the wish to destroy the love object. The principle effect of the guilt is to facilitate the suicidal tendency by turning the outward-directed aggression back upon the subject, thus gratifying the hostile wishes and the need for punishment, in the same act.

Most Christian and Jewish funeral services include the repetition of the following verse from Job: "The Lord has given and the Lord has taken, blessed be the name of the Lord." While the repetition of this verse is generally understood to be a gesture of resignation which it obviously was in its original context, it seems to me that it has an additional meaning. It is as though the bereaved individual were assuring himself and others that it was not he who was responsible for his loss, but the Lord. It is as if he were saying, "The Lord created him and it's his job to sustain him, and if he didn't, I cannot be held responsible."

MODE OF RESOLUTION

The foregoing constitutes a fairly hopeless picture of depression and the number of vicious circles implied suggests that there is a spontaneous tendency for depressions to become more severe. And yet it is well known that depressed individuals recover, often spontaneously. Moreover since depression is an effect which appears normally, there must be some normal mechanism for dissipating the depression and arranging for succession by another state of mind. Freud discovered several such mechanisms and I shall present some of the most important. Freud noticed that mourning was not simply a mental state which the individual experienced passively. The most important aspect of mourning is the psychic task of dissolving all emotional ties with the lost love object. This task is accomplished laboriously and painfully by reviewing mentally all gratifying experiences which were recorded in memory. As each experience is recalled, the affect associated with it appears in consciousness and is followed by sadness at the thought that the experience will never be repeated. When this task has been completed the work of mourning is over and the depression accompanying it is lifted. When however a significant amount of aggression is incorporated in the memories so that their recollection gives rise to guilt, the guilt may halt or slow the mental reviewing process so that the depression persists for an unusually long time. Since in cases of pathologic depression, the onset of depression follows aggressive fantasies directed against the love object and since the depression itself occurs in response to the phantasy of separation from the love object, this process of dissolution of ties cannot proceed because of large amounts of guilt liberated whenever this psychic reviewing process is initiated. While this is an active psychic task and while the affective experience appears in consciousness, it is driven by unconscious sources so that it neither requires nor waits upon voluntary resolution.

The second device for overcoming depression is the substitution of a new object for the one lost. This is seldom successful until a certain amount of dissolution of ties has already been accomplished. Thus the death of one parent will often be followed by increased affection for the other; the death of either parent may be followed by increased affection for a child and the death of a mate followed by a second marriage. Various customs of naming children after parents or grandparents are derived from the tendency to substitute one object for another.

One particular instance of this substitution of a new object for one that was lost is the use of the self as the new object. One can frequently observe that following the death of the husband, the widow adopts his mannerisms, character traits, activities and values and sometimes even his appearance as well. She may take over his business and some of his social activities in an attempt to recapture within herself the person whom she has lost. In a similar fashion a child will identify with a dead parent especially if the parent is of the same sex. In this manner the bereaved individual becomes in a sense independent of the love object and can continue to obtain erotic gratification by loving those traits in himself which he has taken over from the lost object. This gives rise to self love and is one of the bases of what Freud called narcissism.

It was mentioned above that often the work of dissolution of ties during mourning is slowed down or halted by the recollection of aggressive fantasies which induce guilt which, in turn, inhibits the work of mourning. On such occasions there may be an effort to expiate the guilt so as to permit the work of mourning to continue. This guilt expiation is accomplished by any of a number of well known procedures such as ritualized religious penitence and prayer, by charity and by self castigation and sacrifices. Although not directly concerned with undoing the deprivation, these measures can facilitate that process.

I have just described the device for facilitating recovery from depression which is called identification, that is, the mechanism by which the depressed individual acts as though he were the lost love object. The psychodynamic mechanisms by which identification is accomplished are complex and not well understood. Suffice to say that under psychoanalytic

scrutiny, it often appears that identification is accomplished by the fantasy of incorporating the lost object into one of the body cavities and among depressed subjects particularly by the fantasy of eating and swallowing the lost object. During analysis, the anorexia and other gastrointestinal subjective symptomatology which are characteristic of depression, are readily seen to be correlated with such fantasies of identification by oral incorporation. While this sounds like a rather bizarre idea to those who are unfamiliar with unconscious processes and fantasies, the reader can be assured that it is a particularly commonplace fantasy, especially among the depressed patients. One can imagine that the aggressive tendencies mentioned above may come to serve the interests of these incorporation fantasies. This is, however, not an unmixed blessing because as soon as the aggressive tendencies are utilized they give rise to guilt which in turn inhibits the utilization of the identification technique for recovery.

It was noted above that in the depressed patient the aggressive tendency is often directed against the self. An all too frequent outcome of this self-directed aggression is suicide. While the erotic wishes which are responsible for the feeling of deprivation, strongly oppose the suicidal drive, the latter occasionally becomes associated with the fantasy of reunion with the lost object by death. This fantasy whether unconscious or conscious makes the suicide drive practically irresistible. Suicide wishes also promise to satisfy the guilt arising from aggressive wishes towards others. For these reasons, suicide offers itself to the depressed individual as a particularly satisfactory method of resolving his depression.

I shall mention only one more device used to facilitate recovery from depression. This is the fantasy of rebirth. The idea that one can be born anew, and make a fresh start in life, is a fantasy which is common among children and can be detected in unconscious form among most adults. Attempts to start afresh are not uncommon as conscious resolutions, and analysis discloses that the unconscious fantasy motivating the wish to start afresh, is usually a fantasy of rebirth. Sometimes the rebirth fantasy becomes associated with a suicide drive so that the depressed individual comes to believe that he will be born anew by killing himself. More often appearance of a rebirth fantasy in depression has a therapeutic effect and it may sometimes presage recovery.

It should be understood that none of these processes aiming at the resolution of the feeling of deprivation is the sole occupant of the psychic scene. In most cases, many or all of these mechanisms and others are utilized simultaneously or in an overlapping consecutive fashion. When they are mutually facilitating, recovery may be especially prompt but it may be delayed when these various components of the recovery process work at cross purposes. Probably the only process which is indispensable is that of dissolution of ties. The other processes perhaps cannot begin until a certain amount of dissolution of ties has been effected. While they may facilitate that process they cannot be substituted for it. From the foregoing it may be anticipated that the course and prognosis of depression are not easily predicted. Similarly its management must depend in each case upon the specific clinical picture.

MANAGEMENT

Cases of normal depression require no specific treatment since they usually resolve spontaneously in a period of a few weeks or months. The methods by which recovery is accomplished include those listed above, namely, dissolution of ties, substitution of objects, identification with the object, undoing guilt and fantasies of rebirth. When a certain amount of the work of mourning has been accomplished, consolation and assistance from others are usually welcome and the process of recovery facilitated. It should be emphasized, however, that a definite amount of time is required for the accomplishment of this mourning work and that the speed at which the work is performed and therefore its duration, are highly variable from individual to individual for reasons that we do not understand and which obviously have to do with the constitutional endowment of the individual. Nevertheless formalized mourning rituals, such as are offered by religion are often useful in keeping the psychic recovery process on the right track.

With pathologic depression, however, the problem is considerably more difficult. Realizing that most pathologic depressions terminate sooner or later spontaneously, one may be inclined to temporize, waiting for a spontaneous recovery. There are a number of objections to such an approach. In the first place the patient may commit suicide while the doctor is waiting for his recovery. When a patient is really determined to do so, even hospitalization with close supervision may not prevent him from accomplishing his purpose. Second, a depression may last a number of years and during this time the patient is not only unproductive but is actually a great financial burden to his family. If treatment can shorten the period of depression, then obviously it should be used. Finally, there are some depressions which continue for many years, in fact for the rest

of the patient's life. Since one cannot predict at the onset the probable duration of a depression, the pathologic depression should be treated as soon as the diagnosis is made.

Fortunately, most pathologic depressions respond promptly and well to electric shock treatment. I shall not discuss the indication for, the hazards and the technique of treatment; however, its effect is often dramatic and it is especially valuable when the depression is not precipitated by a real loss which must be faced again after the termination of treatment. When there has been a significant real loss, the depression returns almost as soon as the amnesia, which is regularly produced by electric shock treatment, disappears. How electric shock treatment achieves its effect has been the subject of much speculation but no real knowledge. I may mention in passing, that it is my opinion, that the entire structure of psychic fantasies including aggressive wishes against a love object followed by the unconscious conviction of destruction of that object or desertion by it, dissipated by the treatment. If the fantasy life is reorganized around a new nucleus, then the patient stays well for a while. If on the other hand, the depression has been precipitated by a real loss or if the patient has a tendency to fall into the psychic pattern leading to depression as though into an inescapable psychic rut, the electric shock treatment has less chance of being effective. Aside from the hazards of fracture or other physical accident, electric shock treatment has only one other serious shortcoming; that is, its failure to prevent subsequent depressions or even to lengthen the interval between periodic depressions. Accepting this limitation, one should try electric shock therapy in every serious case of pathologic depression when there is no physical contraindication.

Does psychotherapy have any place in the management of depression? If we confine ourselves to the question of management during depression rather than during intervals, then it would seem to me that the indications for psychotherapy are: (1) Those cases who have had adequate trial of electric shock treatment and who have either not responded or who have relapsed within a few weeks; (2) those cases in whom a physical contraindication to electric shock treatment exists; (3) those cases in whom depression is only slight or moderate, particularly when it is not too disabling, and when frequent recurrences and chronicity make the depressive tendency rather than any single episode the target of treatment. The chief hazard in psychotherapy is that of suicide. Hospitalization is not an answer to the problem for several reasons. One is that good authentic psychoanalysis is available within relatively few institutions. The second is that in the case of a particularly persistent patient, even hospitalization will not prevent suicide. Third, let us consider an individual who is seriously depressed and occupied with suicidal fantasies, but is nevertheless able to carry along in his vocation and to a certain extent even socially at an acceptable level. When such a patient does not respond to shock treatment, if he is hospitalized for psychotherapy, the very fact of removing him from his home and job to be hospitalized may make him sufficiently desperate to pass from suicidal fantasy to suicide itself. Finally, hospitalization may be economically ruinous to the patient and to his family. Under such circumstances the psychiatrist has first to weigh the possibility of suicide against the disadvantage of prolonged mental hospitalization. The decision is often a difficult one to make and different psychiatrists may reach different conclusions in the same case. If one is risking suicide by extra-mural treatment, the family should be notified and their approval obtained, if that is possible within the strictures of the therapeutic relation.

There are several forms of psychotherapy. In depression the simplest form of psychotherapy consists of the therapist's offering himself to the patient as a substitute for the lost love object. In a few cases of depression which are not too severe and which are about to remit, this procedure alone may suffice. However, most cases of pathologic depression do not wait for a love object to appear; when they are ready for one they manage to find it. Then there are the various interpretative types of therapy of which the most elegant and indeed the only definitive type is psychoanalysis. If interpretive psychotherapy is to be offered at all in pathologic depression, intensive authentic analysis is the treatment of choice. Analysis facilitates the spontaneous recovery process by bringing to consciousness and thereby loosening the inhibitions stemming from aggressive fantasies and feelings of guilt. This procedure requires the active cooperation of the patient; it requires patience on the part of the patient and his family. Since several months, or even years, may elapse before the patient emerges from depression, if competent psychoanalysis is to be obtained there must be ample financial resources. If spontaneous recovery requires a period of months to years, then how can one know that the treatment is responsible for the recovery rather than spontaneous forces? To my knowledge there are no adequately controlled statistical studies of the effects of authentic psychoanalysis on depression. However, one should not completely ignore the subjective impressions of the psychoanalyst who follows psychic progress in his patient, becomes aware of the harbingers of recovery before there is an overt sign of improvement and is able to see that each step in the recovery process follows the interpretation of the immediately preceding fantasy material in the same way that improvement occurs in cases of psychoneurosis. One may be more convinced of the efficacy of analysis if the therapeutic procedure prevents recurrences in a patient previously subject to attacks of depression. To accomplish this the analysis must usually be carried past the point of recovery from depression well into the period of normality. Certainly if a hypomania follows the depression the hypomania must be completely analyzed. I believe that there is enough cumulative experience to warrant the belief that authentic psychoanalysis can facilitate the termination of pathologic depression and prevent its recurrence.

Given a patient subject to recurrent depressions, can anything be done during the interval when he is free from depression? Prophylactic single electric shocks at intervals of about a month have been advocated by some and statistical proof of the efficacy of this procedure has been adduced. When one contemplates the number of shocks that would be given over the course of a few decades at this rate, one might be less sanguine about the innocuousness of this procedure. Moreover, one should not underestimate the value of the normal flow of instinctual drives and their derivative fantasies for the richness and meaningfulness of living. Periodic electric shock means periodic disruption of this normal flow so that although a major breakdown may be prevented, the cost in terms of inner satisfactions of living may be excessive.

A more constructive approach to the prevention of relapses is therapeutic psychoanalysis. Of course, there are drawbacks to this procedure. The cost in terms of both time and money is great, though certainly it is not excessive when measured against the results obtained. Secondly, psychoanalysis can be accomplished only when driven by motivation. Though the patient may be desperate when depressed, the same individual is often irrationally confident of the permanence of his recovery once he has emerged from the depression. Therefore he will have no motivation for initiating treatment when well and will discontinue treatment which was begun in a depression. Finally, one or more full cycles of depression and recovery may have to be traversed before the analysis can be successfully completed. However, if these obstacles can be surmounted and a good analysis completed, the results in terms of both immunity to relapse and undoing the neurotic aspects of the interval personality, cannot be surpassed.

SUMMARY

Depression is an affect which appears either in response to the loss of a love object or in anticipation of some act which would result in the loss of a love object. The characteristic psychic and physical components of the depression syndrome can be understood as devices to compel protective acts on the part of those who love the patient. When depression follows an externally imposed significant loss, it may be considered normal. When it follows no loss or a trivial loss it is pathologic. In such a case, the depression is provoked by the unconscious fantasy that a wish to destroy or injure the love object has been realized. However, the ensuing depression is usually not successful in terminating the hostile tendency which continues to express itself against love objects in passive and indirect ways, and because of the guilt which the aggression evokes, reflexively in self-destruction.

Depression drives the process of dissolution of ties in such a way that something of the lost object remains by means of a process of identification. Normal depression requires no treatment and neither can, nor should be circumvented. The management of abnormal depression depends upon such factors as danger of suicide, accessibility of the patient to psychotherapy, the presence of contraindications to electric shock therapy and the chronicity of the depression. In general, abnormal depression is most rapidly dissipated by electric shock therapy, while the propensity to recurrent depressions and the interval neurotic personality will be most effectively treated by psychoanalysis.

JAN EHRENWALD

Neurosis in the Family
A *Study of Psychiatric Epidemiology**

For obvious reasons the epidemiological analysis of mental disorders takes the various recognized nosological entities as its point of departure. It studies the incidence of manic-depressive psychosis, schizophrenic reactions, neurosis, senile or epileptic disorders, alcoholism, and suicide or psychological infertility in a given society.(1–5) It has accumulated an enormous amount of data concerning their relationships to culture, class, family environment, and changing socioeconomic and political conditions.(6, 7) All this does not, however, amount to a conceptually systematized body of knowledge regarding the epidemiology of mental illness.

It is suggested here that the reason for this state of affairs lies in several tacitly implied but unwarranted

* Reprinted by permission from the *Archives of General Psychiatry*, Vol. 3, September 1960, pp. 232–242. Copyright 1960, by American Medical Association.

presuppositions. First, it is implied that mental illness can be compared with the various more or less distinct nosological entities studied in general medicine. Second, their presumed transmission from person to person is discussed in largely metaphorical terms, taking their communicable or contagious nature for granted. Third, insufficient allowance is made for the still existing diagnostic and conceptual difficulties of distinguishing hereditary transmission of abnormal behavior patterns from the effects of imitation, primitive learning, imprinting, and other factors emanating from the familial and sociocultural environment. Fourth, prevailing attention is focused on the horizontal, geographical study of populations while contagion spreading along vertical, genealogical pathways is left outside the frame of reference of psychiatric epidemiology.

The present study proposes to shift the focus of

interest from the traditional Kraepelinian nosological entities to a limited number of elementary units of behavior which are characteristic of human interaction in health and disease. The rationale of such an essentially sociometric approach has been presented in a previous article.(8) It is based on the study of 10 triads or clusters of traits and attitudes which may be used by the clinical observer to describe the habitual behavior of one member of a family pair towards the other member, e.g., of a mother to son, of son to mother, of husband to wife, of wife to husband, etc. With certain qualifications, these behavioral configurations can be considered just as "real" as the diverse colors of the rainbow or the eight tones of an octave. It should be noted that Gordon Allport(11) has gone so far as to assign to them the status of "ultimate realities" in our psychological organization. Our Inventory of Traits and Attitudes ranges from such positive, socially desirable clusters as "giving-supportive-affectionate," to "destructive-sadistic-castrating," or "erratic-eccentric-defective," on the negative side of the scale. The clinical observer is asked to tell which of the 30 traits or attitudes listed in the Inventory are, in his order of preference, the most characteristic of the relationships of one family member to the other. This preferential rating or ranking can be further refined by the use of two independent observers functioning as judges. Yet even in the absence of a second judge, the scores of a single observer, guided by the consistent use of well-defined criteria, can serve as efficient tools for the study of patterns of interaction within a given family. If, in a concrete example, a mother's attitude towards her son can be characterized as "domineering-controlling," while her son's corresponding attitude is chiefly "submissive-masochistic," their mutual relationship can be described in terms of a "domineering-submissive" configuration. This configuration is in turn an example of a wide variety of patterns of interaction which emerge from such an inquiry. The patterns can be grouped under four major headings: (1) patterns of sharing, (2) patterns of contagion, (3) complementary patterns, and (4) patterns of resistance and rebellion.

It is readily understood that in the present context the patterns of sharing and contagion are of principal interest. Their diagnosis is based on the clinical impression that the prevailing attitude of one member of a family pair tends to call forth a similar attitude in his opposite member. If so, it is apt to reinforce the existing pattern of interaction characteristic of the pair. This may be further strengthened by identical patterns characteristic of the mutual relationships of other family pairs. Thus, both patterns of sharing (i.e., the mutual reinforcement of socially desirable traits and attitudes) and patterns of contagion (i.e., the sharing of socially undesirable or "sick" traits and attitudes) may spread over and envelop all aspects of family interaction. Again, since families do not live in a social vacuum, a prevailing pattern of contagion may spread from one family to another and thus form the focus of a veritable epidemic of socially undesirable, i.e., sick behavioral patterns in the community at large. It should, however, be emphasized once again that it is not a particular type of neurosis or psychosis which is subject to transmission in the manner just described. What is transmitted are such elementary units of behavior as are included in our Inventory of Traits and Attitudes, much in the same way as in the epidemiology of bacterial infection it is not the red skin rash or hacking cough which is communicated from one person to another but the streptococcus responsible for scarlet fever, the virus responsible for measles, the Koch-bacillus responsible for pulmonary tuberculosis, or the Bacillus pestis responsible for pulmonary plague.

ILLUSTRATIVE CASE MATERIAL: THE OBSCOMP PEDIGREE AND FOUR SHORT FAMILY HISTORIES*

The following family history contains the description of a minor psychiatric epidemic which has extended over four successive generations of the Obscomp family and its collaterals. It is based on information concerning 14 family members obtained in the course of prolonged psychoanalytic psychotherapy and in a number of diagnostic interviews over a period of 13 years involving all but the two deceased members of the clan. The aggregate number of hours spent with all persons covered by the present report is 859. This made a fairly exhaustive clinical and analytic study of each individual possible. At the same time, each member of a family pair was in a position to supply corroborative information concerning the attitudes of his or her opposite number as well as concerning the mutual interrelationships of other members.

The Obs' are an upper middle class family of business and professional people, most of them college educated. They have an impressive record of social and economic achievement bought at the price of driving ambition and a marked obsessive-compulsive trend. They are Protestants of German extraction. In the third generation there have been two instances of intermarriage with Jewish spouses.

_____
* "Obscomp" stands for obsessive compulsive.

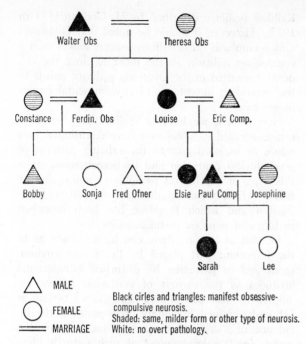

Bobby | Sonja | Fred Ofner | Elsie Paul Comp | Josephine

Sarah | Lee

△ MALE
○ FEMALE
═══ MARRIAGE

Black cirles and triangles: manifest obsessive-
compulsive neurosis.
Shaded: same, milder form or other type of neurosis.
White: no overt pathology.

The Obscomp Pedigree illustrating transmission of homonymic contagion along genealogical pathways.

The story begins with Walter Obs, the patriarch of the family, now deceased. He is described as a typical compulsion neurotic who had suffered two or three "nervous breakdowns" in the course of his life. His wife, Theresa Obs, at present in her eighties, has been domineering-controlling with her two children, Louise and Ferdinand. Mrs. Obs too shows evidence of an obsessive compulsive trend. She has an excessive preoccupation with order and cleanliness, keeps a tight hold on her money, and tends to exercise a despotic rule over her children, her in-laws, and a ladies' companion in her employ. Her daughter, Louise, at present in her early fifties, also exhibits all the symptoms of an obsessive-compulsive neurosis. She has undergone psychoanalysis of three years' duration. Louise's husband, Eric Comp, now deceased, and likewise of German descent, is described as a strict authoritarian, a rigid, compulsive personality. He was a hardworking, successful business executive who had little time to spend with his family. Louise was clinging and dependent with her husband and overprotective, controlling-domineering with her two children, Elsie and Paul, now in their late twenties. At the same time they were both exposed to their mother's latent — or thinly disguised — sadistic impulses. Elsie and Paul responded to this situation in terms of passive-submissive, masochistic pat-

terns which in turn served as reaction formations against their own underlying defiant-rebellious attitudes towards their mother. In effect, throughout their childhood and adolescence Elsie and Paul used the pattern of violent sibling rivalry as the principal outlet for their hostilities. They both developed full-fledged compulsion neuroses showing striking family resemblance to the clinical pictures presented by their mother Louise and their grandmother, Theresa Obs, the tight-fisted matriarch of the family. Both Elsie and Paul have undergone intensive psychoanalytic therapy.

Thus the pattern running through both the Obs and the Comp families can be described in terms of psychological contagion barely mitigated by coexisting complementary and subdued rebellious patterns. In fact, the same pattern is very much in evidence in the third generation, as well as in the collateral families and their descendants. It is characteristic of Elsie's and Paul's marital relationship. Elsie is married to Fred Ofner, a cultured man of Jewish background, but otherwise in many respects resembling her "kid brother" Paul. Elsie married Fred fully aware of the fact that he had been suffering from serious sexual difficulties. She is controlling, demanding, and at times destructive or frankly sadistic with her spouse. Fred, in turn, tends to be passive-compliant with his wife and puts up very little resistance to her tendency to involve him in the sadomasochistic pattern characteristic of marital relationships in her family of orientation.

Esie's brother, Paul Comp, a man of many outstanding qualities, also married a spouse of wealthy Jewish background. His wife Josephine is a passive-dependent woman, four years his senior which, incidentally, is also the age difference between Paul and Elsie, his sister-rival. Josephine too shows a variety of compulsive features. Her clinical picture is, however, one of latent or pseudoneurotic schizophrenia for which she is receiving psychoanalytic treatment by a colleague. Despite her clinging-dependent attitude towards her husband, Josephine too tends to become increasingly demanding and at times destructive-sadistic with him, thus repeating the pattern characteristic of the Comp family.

Elsie's and Paul's mother, Louise, has a younger brother, Ferdinand Obs, who can likewise be described as a textbook case of obsessive-compulsive neurosis. True to the family tradition, his wife Constance is a clinging dependent woman some 15 years his junior. Significantly, the age difference between Louise and her husband, Eric, is of the same order. Put in clinical-diagnostic terms, Constance, now in her thirties, is an hysteric, acting-out type of personality and her submissive-masochistic attitudes are a perfect match to her husband's demanding-controlling and at times frankly sadistic behavior towards her. It should also be noted at this point that Constance is herself the daughter of an erratic, at times punitive, at times overindulgent father and of a weak, overprotective, oversolicitous mother of the anxiety-hysteric type.

Ferdinand and Constance's son, Bobby is at present 8 years of age. He is described by the school authorities as emotionally immature, overanxious, and inhibited. He suffers from a reading disability for which he is receiving outpatient treatment in a child guidance clinic. Ferdinand's attitude towards his son is much the same as towards his wife Constance, while Constance is overtly oversolicitous but covertly hostile and rejecting towards Bobby. Bobby's younger sister, Sonja, now aged 3, seems to be a well-adjusted child. She has not, however, reached as yet what epidemiologists call the "period of risk."

Paul and Josephine Comp have two daughters, Sarah, aged 6, and Lee, aged 2. Sarah is a shy and withdrawn child, docile and compliant with her parents and competitive with Lee. She is suffering from bronchial asthma which tends to become worse in fall and winter. Her shyness and withdrawal has come to the notice of the school authorities who requested her psychological evaluation. The psychologist describes Sarah as a pretty but unsmiling little girl of superior intelligence. Her Rorschach and TAT tests show evidence of a mixed neurosis in a passive-aggressive character structure. The child seems to be dominated by harsh superego demands. Sarah's little sister, Lee, is described as an active, well-adjusted child. She too has not as yet reached the "period of risk." The marriage of Fred and Elsie Ofner has remained childless so far.

Space does not permit to pursue the far-flung network of disturbed interaction in the Obscomp pedigree and its collaterals in greater detail. Nor would the description of two or three more, prevailingly schizophrenic, family groups, studied at present at the Out-Patients' Department of Roosevelt Hospital, supply much added information relevant to our issue. It is, however, instructive to compare the Obscomp pedigree with the systematic investigations devoted to such families by T. Lidz and his associates,(12, 13) by M. Bowen,(14) W. M. Broadey,(15) and others in recent years, or with the studies of F. J. Kallmann,(3) E. Slater,(16) and others concerning the genetics of manic-depressive psychosis, neurosis, epilepsy, or various organic brain syndromes. Again, it would be interesting to compare — or to contrast — the Obscomp family with the Kallikak pedigree described by H. Goddard(17) in 1912. However, it should be noted that Goddard's undue emphasis on hereditary aspects makes such a comparison difficult, all the more so since the evidence presented in the Obscomp pedigree points to the overriding importance of environmental factors in our case.

Nevertheless, we have to realize that even here gene-controlled variables may have contributed to a minor or major degree to the existing patterns of psychological contagion and its perpetuation. It is this type of psychiatric pathology running in the family which seems to duplicate hereditary transmission and which therefore has been described in terms of neurotic pseudoheredity.

Be that as it may, there can be no doubt as to the important part played by the family environment and in particular by disturbed interpersonal attitudes as the carriers of contagion in our example. It must be assumed that given a certain as yet undetermined hereditary predisposition, the incidence of "sick" traits and attitudes forms the matrix for the development of such virtually identical clinical manifestations affecting three or four successive generations as our example illustrates. This is what can be described as *homonymic contagion*. It can be contrasted with the pattern of *heteronymic contagion* in which a similar cluster of disturbed interpersonal attitudes may be conducive to the development of different types of neurosis, mental disorder, or even psychosomatic pathology. Such a change in clinical symptomatology is in fact a well-known feature of a great many family histories. A child may respond to a compulsive mother, exhibiting a cluster of controlling, demanding, and rejecting attitudes by becoming a compulsion neurotic himself. But we also know that, as another alternative, he may develop bronchial asthma, paranoid schizophrenia, or turn into an overt homosexual.(10) Here, again, space does not permit to document this type of heteronymic contagion by reference to specific case histories or to the wealth of literature dealing with this problem.

The following brief family history is, however, an informative example of heteronymic contagion manifesting itself in an apparently paradoxical shift of the clinical picture from neurosis to psychosomatic symptoms in marriage partners, while the only daughter of the family emerged psychologically unscathed. The father, Mr. Ross, now in his early fifties, is a compulsion neurotic suffering from hypertension and cardiac involvement. He is the son of an equally obsessive-compulsive father and of a weak, doting, overindulgent mother. His wife,

Mrs. Ross, now in her middle forties, had been a well-adjusted girl throughout her childhood and adolescence. She had been compliant, passive-submissive in relation to her husband and giving, supportive and affectionate with her daughter, Henrietta, now aged 23. Mrs. Ross, in the course of the past 24 years, seems to have withstood without overt neurotic manifestations the relentless pressures, demands, and controlling-authoritative attitudes of her husband. However, with the gradual deterioration of his health and following her daughter's marriage at 21, Mrs. Ross seemed to have reached the limits of her endurance. Under growing stress emanating from Mr. Ross and deprived of her daughter's support, she developed a series of urticarial rashes of the giant type, alternating with massive angioneurotic edema in the face, tongue, and other parts of the body. Antihistaminics administered over a year's period brought these symptoms under control. But they were soon replaced by clinical signs of thyroid hyperactivity culminating in the picture of Graves' disease.

Henrietta had in turn responded to her father's controlling, demanding, authoritarian ways with growing defiance and rebellion and ultimately escaped into marriage to a placid, easygoing young man of her own age.

No attempt at a deeper analytic evaluation of this situation can be made in the present context. Nor is it possible to go into a detailed discussion of the presumable psychodynamics responsible for Mrs. Ross' specific psychosomatic dysfunctions. It is, however, safe to assume that her personality make-up and early childhood conditioning protected her from responding to continued stress in terms of a homonymic neurotic reaction, dovetailing with or duplicating her husband's compulsive trend. Nor does it appear that the route towards hysteric or hostile acting out, depression, or alcoholism was open to her. Instead, it was the autonomic nervous system which gave way and responded with the development of her psychosomatic dysfunction. It is interesting to note that as a child Mrs. Ross had been subject to occasional mild attacks of hives or angioneurotic edema.

In this family, the heteronymic pattern of contagion is unmistakable. Indeed, the shift from neurotic to psychosomatic pathology is so radical that doubts may be raised as to the contagious nature of or to the dynamic correlation existing between the two conditions. There are, however, a number of clinical observations pointing in the same direction. (9) They indicate that heteronymic contagion tends to occur not only among married partners (that is, among individuals unrelated by genetic bonds), but also among blood relatives.

Whether and how far the existence of such bonds tends to reinforce the tendency to homonymic contagion must at present remain an open question. The following observation would seem to underscore the part played by a genetic factor in the contagious transmission of compulsive symptomatology from parent to child.

The Dale family consists of four members. Mr. Dale is a highly cultured man of superior intelligence and achievements. He is an obsessive-compulsive personality, greatly concerned with order and cleanliness in his household. He married late in life and tends to be controlling, driving and in a subtle way sadistic with his wife, Lottie, 15 years his junior. Mrs. Dale is an hysterical, acting-out type of personality, passive-submissive in relation to her husband. Their two children are twins, Danny and Judy, aged 2. Danny is a self-willed, obstinate, aggressive boy — the "spitting image" of his father. Judy is a placid, compliant girl, easy to handle, with a ready smile for both parents and for strangers.

At 18 months, before he was able to speak, Danny would motion to the maid cleaning the nursery floor to wipe off a spot she had overlooked. On going to bed he would notice that one of the Venetian blinds was unevenly drawn and insist that it be straightened out. When being dressed in the morning he would point to the various articles of clothing he wanted to put on in the first, second, or third place. "He is all the time one step ahead of me," as his mother put it. His twin sister, Judy, brought up under identical environmental conditions, shows no evidence of compulsive behavior in *statu nascendi*, as it were.

Observations like these are familiar to the child psychiatrist. They are usually attributed to imitation and learning. But the striking fact is that both Danny and Judy have very little contact with their father, a busy business executive working late hours and leaving the upbringing of his children entirely to his wife and a full-time maid. The different reaction of the two fraternal twins to seemingly identical environmental situations may thus have to be attributed to one of two things. It may be due to differences in their innate hereditary equipment. But it may also be attributed to the effect of Mrs. Dale's different attitude to her two babies. The fact is that Danny represented to her a carbon copy of her controlling, demanding husband, while she saw in Judy a reflection of her own compliant, submissive, feminine self. This may have influenced her behavior toward Danny in such a way that he reacted to her — and to other mother figures — in a precociously controlling-demanding and, in effect, compulsive fashion. In a similar vein, it could be argued that in the absence of such cues emanating from Judy there was nothing in Mrs. Dale's behavior towards her daughter which would have elicited similar compulsive patterns in the little girl. If this is true, Danny's early infantile neurosis could be well explained in psychoanalytic, that is, essentially environmental terms.

The following brief family history throws light on the dynamics of psychological contagion in the absence of a genetic factor which could conceivably have facilitated the occurrence of contagion. Mrs. Nelson is an obsessive-compulsive woman of 37, married to a weak, ineffectual, passive-submissive husband. The couple was childless. However, by circumventing legal authorities they succeeded in adopting an apparently healthy baby girl of 2 months. Soon thereafter the child became colicky and more and more difficult to manage. She cried for hours, resisted early attempts at toilet training, became destructive with toys and other articles within reach. When the baby was 6 months old, Mrs. Nelson suffered a "mental breakdown" and was hospitalized. During her absence her husband's sister, a placid, sensible woman, moved into the household to take care of the baby. Within four weeks the child's behavior was markedly improved; the colic subsided and all evidence of neurotic contagion or rebellious behavior disappeared.

COMMENT

The elaborate pedigree of the Obscomp family and the three clinical thumbnail sketches described in the preceding section are apt to raise more questions than can be answered. Yet, it is precisely the raising of the proper questions aiming at a methodical approach to psychiatric epidemiology which is the main purpose of the present inquiry. The principal questions raised can be conveniently discussed under four headings.

1. *Homonymic Versus Heteronymic Contagion.* — *Homonymic* contagion is the environmental transmission of clinically similar disturbed attitudes within the family and in the community at large. It may lead to the communication of obsessive-compulsive, phobic, hysteric, or other psychiatric disorders from parent to child and from one generation to another. It may extend to collateral families in ever-widening circles and reach the proportions of a veritable family epidemic. The Obscomp family illustrates the tendency of contagion to

spread in the parameter of time, that is, along genealogical pathways. Although the epidemic has already enveloped three or four generations, it is too early to say whether or not it has already reached the descending limb of its course.

For obvious reasons, *heteronymic* contagion is more difficult to trace. This is illustrated by the Ross family in which the husband's severe obsessive-compulsive pattern was conducive not to overtly neurotic but to psychosomatic manifestations. But for the rather transparent psychodynamic situation in this family the shift from one to another type of clinical symptomatology might have indeed obscured the reactive — that is, the essentially contagious — nature of Mrs. Ross' illness. Contagious patterns involving psychosomatic dysfunctions may the more readily escape attention since the latter seem to transgress the boundaries of strictly psychiatric disorders. It will be readily understood, however, that making proper allowance for this pattern of contagion is an essential prerequisite for the study of psychiatric epidemiology. Confining attention to such homonymic types of contagion as traumatic, obsessive-compulsive, or anxiety neuroses, etc., running in the family, would be just as self-defeating as to pay exclusive attention to the occurrence of an erythematous rash as the only diagnostic clue in an epidemic of syphilis or scarlet fever, while the presence or absence of tonsillitis or of a primary lesion is assiduously overlooked. In effect, it could be stated that at the present state of our knowledge the study of psychiatric epidemiology is beset by the same difficulties as was the proper understanding of infectious diseases before the discovery of pathogenic microorganisms.

2. *The Time Factor in Mental Contagion.* — Attitudes are by definition specific behavioral configurations manifesting themselves in time. In effect, it is only owing to their relatively enduring character that they qualify as attitudes or, if sustained over a lifetime, as "character traits" or "character defenses." Patterns of contagion presuppose the slow, grinding interpersonal effect of such sustained attitudes or traits. The example of the Obscomp family suggests that the cumulative effect of such attitudes may reinforce their contagious potential over successive generations. Eventually, they may develop into basic features or subcultural traits characteristic of a given family group. Put in a capsule, it can be stated that a demanding, controlling and, clinically speaking, compulsive mother is more likely to have a contagious effect on her child than a compulsive gradeschool teacher, and that such a teacher is in turn more likely to elicit a contagious response

in his pupil than an occasional baby sitter to whom the child happens to be exposed for a few hours only. If this is true, it would be indicative of a simple linear correlation between the time of exposure and the contagious potential of a cluster of disturbed attitudes.

However, the example of little Danny, aged 2, one of the twins in the Dale family, shows that contagion involving the apparent transmission of compulsive attitudes may occur within a comparatively short period of time. The same is true for some of the youngest descendants of the Obscomp family. Again, the case of Mrs. Nelson's adopted baby likewise tends to show that susceptibility to contagion may be greatly increased in early childhood. This is, of course, in good keeping with the available evidence concerning the quicker pace of learning in infancy and childhood, with basic psychoanalytic observations, and particularly with the spectacular effects of imprinting studied by the ethologists. R. W. Gerard (18) has summed up this state of affairs, stating "The earlier the material trace, the more profound is its effect; inherited influences are likely to be more far reaching than are congenital ones, those of early infancy more than those of maturity."

There undoubtedly are other critical periods in an individual's life history during which susceptibility to contagion may be increased. Such periods are puberty and involution, as well as certain dynamically determined fluctuations of ego strength. Panic and other manifestations of the "herd instinct" belong in the same category. So do states of psychological regression produced in transference neuroses, by suggestion, hypnosis, and mediumistic trance.

Disregarding, at least for the moment, these psychological and biological variables — including the part played by maturational and developmental factors discovered by the ethologists — it could be stated that psychological contagion is directly proportional to the duration of exposure and inversely proportional to the age at the time exposure occurs.

3. *Susceptibility Versus Resistance.* — It goes without saying that susceptibility to contagion is determined by several more factors besides those mentioned above. Reference has already been made to such subcultural influences as the prevalence of certain traits running through the family. Similar trends prevailing in the cultural environment at large may have the identical effect. Variables of this order can be compared to the influence of geographic, climatic, or seasonal factors upon the spread of infectious diseases. The part played by regres-

sion or fluctuations of ego strength, as it can be gauged by psychoanalytic inquiry, has already been mentioned. To this we have to add what can be described as hereditary or constitutional factors. Although the present trend in psychiatric research tends to emphasize the part played by environmental influences, many authorities are still inclined to attribute susceptibility to neurosis to a "neurotic personality factor" (H. J. Eysenck and D. B. Prell, (4) F. J. Kallmann,(3) and others) that is, to essentially gene-determined variables. Such factors, it is assumed, predispose to neurotic illness and, by implication, to psychological contagion.

Gardner Murphy,(19) in a recent lecture, has pointed out that genetic influences have a potentiating effect upon "favoring circumstances in the patient's environment" and vice versa. Such a potentiation of existing "homonymic" environmental influences may well be suspected in the Obscomp family and its dependents. It may conceivably account for the early appearance of compulsive features in little Danny, who was described as the "spitting image" of his compulsion neurotic father. Continued interaction and potentiation of genetic and environmental factors would then explain the tendency for psychological contagion to be carried along genealogical pathways and to be handed down the family tree from one generation to the other — whether it be called the Kallikaks, the Obscomps, or the Houses of Laius, or Atreus whose tragic family histories have been recorded by the bards of ancient Greece.

In the face of this tendency to potentiation, the question of resistance — or immunity — to contagion is of paramount importance to the psychiatrist concerned with matters of prevention. It should be noted that resistance in the present context has to be taken in the literal sense. It was pointed out in a previous article(8) that patterns of resistance, defiance, and rebellion may be effective antidotes against the spread and perpetuation of disturbed patterns in the family and in the community at large. They bring the element of change into a given culture and can be compared to mutations in the biological sphere. It is true that such attitudes, if carried too far, may be conducive to strife and dissension, to political radicalism, to delinquent, or otherwise antisocial behavior. It should be noted that, by contrast, in the third and fourth successive generations of the Obscomp family there was not one black sheep to mar its record of exemplary civic virtue. Their family crest could be fittingly emblazoned with the insignia of scrupulous righteousness and compulsive morality.

Observations like these seem to lend support to Freud's thesis concerning Civilization and Its Discontents.(20) They suggest once more that our contemporary western culture is precariously poised between neurosis on one side and delinquency or other forms of antisocial acting out on the other side of the scale. There are, however, two redeeming features in this picture. One is that the same cluster of attitudes which has given rise to compulsive patterns in the Obscomp family can also call forth vastly different types of clinical responses. They may provoke psychosomatic symptoms, hysteric, or phobic reactions. Or else they may be conducive to complementary patterns with little or no overt clinical pathology. They may thus lead to a shift in the direction of heteronymic contagion. Another redeeming feature derives from the fact that the spread of psychological contagion may be counteracted and cancelled out by patterns of sharing and cooperation which, by definition, are instrumental in the transmission of socially desirable attitudes. It is apparently due to this trend that there are a great many families and societies which, after all, have succeeded in walking the "straight and narrow path" without tripping and coming to grief.

4. *Contagious Potential, Penetrance, or Virulence of Attitudes.* — Some brief comment is called for concerning the nature of the potentially contagious modes of interaction between person and person. It is a well-known fact of social psychology and communication theory that the various modes of verbal, preverbal, and nonverbal communication are possessed of widely divergent contagious potential. This is least marked on the level of verbal communication based on signs and symbols of the type used by the mathematician in its purest form. The contagious potential increases as we move from here to what J. Ruesch(21) has described as action language of the person in the throes of affect, or of the organ or somatic language characteristic of the infant or the regressed patient. J. Meerloo(22) has called attention to the highly contagious quality of such archaic communications as blushing, yawning, scratching, rhythmic body movements, etc. Their contagious quality, he states, is the greater the more archaic is the communication which they convey. Paracelsus' description of epidemics of Chorea lasciva is a classical example of this kind. The medieval dance epidemics and the modern Rock and Roll craze belong in the same category. So do the small-scale epidemics of various hysteric conversion symptoms that tend to occur in boarding schools, military barracks, or prison camps. Tics,

panic reactions, manifestations of neurotic anxiety are variations on the same theme. Again, it may well be that the marked emotional charge underlying the cluster of attitudes characteristic of obsessive-compulsive, phobic, or paranoid behavior is responsible for the high contagious potential or penetrance of such attitudes. It may well be compared to the penetrance of dominant genes studied by the geneticists, or to the virulence of certain strains of microorganisms responsible for epidemics of infectious diseases. In summary, it could be stated that the contagious potential of disturbed interpersonal attitudes is directly proportional to their archaic nature, coupled with their emotional charge, and that it is inversely proportional to their discursive quality and to the quantity of semantic information which they convey.

SUMMARY

The present study of psychiatric epidemiology focuses on the potentially contagious or communicable nature of disturbed interpersonal attitudes as they were described in a previous article. It proceeds on the assumption that it is maladjusted attitudes, not specific nosological entities, which are subject to psychological contagion. They may thus account for the spread of mental disorder in the family and the community at large. This principle was applied to the pedigree of the Obscomp family covering four generations and to three smaller family groups presenting obsessive-compulsive, psychosomatic, and hysteric features. Their study suggests four major propositions: (1) Psychological contagion may be conducive to the development of similar or dissimilar clinical symptomatology. This is described as homonymic *versus* heteronymic contagion. (2) Other things being equal, psychological contagion is directly proportional to the duration of exposure and, within certain limitations, inversely proportional to the age at which exposure takes place. (3) Psychological contagion is further determined by an individual's susceptibility and resistance to it. Though due to environmental influences, contagion is facilitated by existing hereditary predispositions. This may aid in its communication along genealogical pathways from one generation to the other. Patterns of psychological resistance and rebellion and, to a lesser extent, complementary patterns, may mitigate this tendency or may shift it in the direction of heteronymic contagion. The presence of socially desirable patterns and their sharing also tends to counterbalance the spread of contagious patterns in both the horizontal and vertical co-ordinates. (4)

The fourth proposition is concerned with the contagious potential, virulence, or penetrance of the disturbed attitudes and messages which they convey. It is suggested that this is in direct proportion to their archaic nature, coupled with their emotional charge, while it is inversely proportional to their semantic value and to the quantity of information which they convey. The primitive nature and the affective charge underlying hysteric, phobic, compulsive, or frankly psychotic manifestations may thus tend to facilitate their transmission. This may in turn be aided by an existing tendency to conformity and compliance prevailing in the family or in the community at large.

REFERENCES

1. LEMKAU, P. V.: The Epidemiological Study of Mental Illness and Mental Health, Am. J. Psychiat. 111: 801, 1955.
2. MALZBERG, B.: Important Statistical Data About Mental Illness, in American Handbook of Psychiatry, edited by S. Arieti, Vol. 1, 1959, p. 161.
3. KALLMANN, F. J.: Heredity, Health and Mental Disorder, New York, W. W. Norton, 1953.
4. EYSENCK, H. J., and PRELL, D. B.: The Inheritance of Neuroticism: An Experimental Study, J. Ment. Sc. 97:441, 1951.
5. HALLIDAY, J. L.: Psychosocial Medicine, New York, W. W. Norton, 1948.
6. HOLLINGSHEAD, A. B., and REDLICH, F. C.: Social Class and Mental Illness, New York, John Wiley & Sons, Inc., 1958.
7. Opler, M.: Culture, Psychiatry and Human Values, Springfield, Ill., Charles C Thomas, Publisher, 1956.
8. EHRENWALD, J.: Neurotic Interaction and Patterns of Pseudoheredity in the Family, Am. J. Psychiat. 115:2, 1958.
9. EHRENWALD, J.: Patterns of Neurotic Interaction: A Study of Empathy and Enkinesis, Am. J. Psychotherapy 7:24, 1953.
10. EHRENWALD, J.: The Symbiotic Matrix of Paranoid Delusions and the Homosexual Alternative, Am. J. Psychoanalysis 20:49–65, 1960.
11. ALLPORT, G.: Personality: A Psychological Interpretation, New York, Henry Holt & Company, 1937.
12. LIDZ, R. W., and LIDZ, T.: The Family Environment of Schizophrenic Patient, Am. J. Psychiat. 106: 332, 1949.
13. FLECK, S.; FREEDMAN, D. X.; CORNELISON, A.; JERRY, D., and LIDZ, T.: Intrafamilial Environment of the Schizophrenic Patient, read before the Annual Meeting of the American Psychiatric Association, Los Angeles, May, 1957.
14. BOWEN, M.: A Family Concept of Schizophrenia, in The Etiology of Schizophrenia, edited by Don Jackson, New York, Basic Books, Inc., 1960.
15. BROADEY, W. M.: Some Family Operations and Schizophrenia, A.M.A. Arch. Gen. Psychiat. 1:379, 1959.
16. SLATER, E.: Psychiatric Genetics, Vol. 2, Recent Progress in Psychiatry, edited by G. W. Fleming, London, J. & A. Churchill, Ltd., 1950.
17. GODDARD, H. H.: The Kallikak Family, New York, The Macmillan Company, 1912.
18. GERARD, R. W.: Neurophysiology: Brain and Behavior, in American Handbook of Psychiatry, edited by S. Arieti, Vol. 2, 1959.
19. MURPHY, G.: Potentiation: A Clue to Integration in the Living System, Flowerman Memorial Lecture, New York, December, 1959.
20. FREUD, S.: Civilization and Its Discontents, New York, W. W. Norton, 1930.
21. RUESCH, J.: Disturbed Communication, New York, W. W. Norton, 1957.
22. MEERLOO, J. A. M.: Mental Contagion, Am. J. Psychother. 12:66, 1959.

The Psychoses / 4

Any attempt to summarize briefly the essential meaning of the psychotic experience founders on the rocks of ambiguity and the inexpressible. Delineating the major clinical aspects of these maladjustments of personality is not hard to do: the psychotic, we are told, loses contact with reality and retreats into a world of fantasy, demonstrates disturbances of thought and perception, called delusions and hallucinations, and suffers a marked inability to cope with interpersonal relations. For the clinician involved in work with psychotic people, their strange, disturbed, and disturbing language and behavior is taken as an elliptical and symbolic, but nonetheless meaningful, statement about their condition. But the "translation" difficulties are severe, and in desperation one often feels a need to retreat once again to a flat description of behavior or obsessive ruminations about classification and syndrome "types."

We suggest that in the psychological study of the psychoses there appear to be two distinct schools of investigation. One group is concerned with the descriptive aspects of psychotic states, the other with the inner experience of the sufferers themselves. We have tried below to present material pertinent to both forms of study, which also provides an historical perspective on the problem. The bulk of the papers are concerned more specifically with the schizophrenic disorders, the most common of these maladjustments. These have been studied more intensively than any other form of psychopathology, and out of these studies have come many of our most insightful hypotheses concerning processes of development and maldevelopment in such areas as speech, perception, motor abilities, emotional control, and general systems of adaptation.

Freud's brief paper of 1924 expresses his view of the essential difference between neurosis and psychosis: "neurosis does not disavow the reality, it only ignores it; psychosis disavows it and tries to replace it." This paper is as clear and concise an exposition of the psychoanalytic viewpoint on the intrapsychic mechanisms of these forms of maladaptive behavior as one is likely to find. Particularly interesting are Freud's comments on the linkage of normal, neurotic, and psychotic behavior in terms of the individual's relationship to reality.

The term "schizophrenia" has its origin in the work of the Swiss psychiatrist, Eugen Bleuler. Before Bleuler's introduction of this term, the common designation for these disorders was Kraepelin's "dementia praecox," meaning early mental deterioration, and implying just that — a disease developing in young people, characterized by a process of intellectual and psychological deterioration. Bleuler, as this brief excerpt makes clear, attempted to define these disorders in terms not of their course but of their primary and secondary symptomatology. The primary defects in schizophrenia, as he presents it, are disorders of thinking, feeling, and the relationship to external reality. The secondary results of these defects are the oft-noted symptoms of schizophrenia — delusions, hallucinations, bizarre association and so on. Bleuler also delineates four types of schizophrenia, a typology which has persisted to the present time. Even the most cursory examination of the immense literature on schizophrenia will show the indebtedness of all workers in this field to Bleuler's reconceptualization of the problem.

Knight's paper brings into relief some important aspects of the "borderline state," a common clinical condition. He describes an individual who displays many levels of psychological functioning, sometimes concomitantly, ranging from the healthy and adaptive to the disorganized and disruptive. His stress on the need for assessing the situational variables involved, that is, how the individual functions in various milieux, is a key concept in diagnostic evaluation. Work by Rudolf Ekstein and his associates at the

Menninger Clinic and the Reiss-Davis Clinic in Los Angeles has extended the "borderline" concept to disorders of childhood as well.[1]

With Goldman's analysis of the comparative-developmental approach to schizophrenia, we turn to a consideration of the characteristic functioning of these profoundly disturbed individuals. The developmental viewpoint, as promulgated by the late Heinz Werner, is concerned with the formal structure of behavior as distinguished from its content. For example, whereas the psychoanalytic theorist may deal with the content of a psychotic delusion, in terms of its symbolic referents, the developmental approach focuses on the structural similarity between delusional behavior and similar "not-me" phenomena which emerge in the course of normal development (for example, the infant's inability to recognize the consequences of his own behavior, the result of an action being considered an effect of some external force). By thus placing schizophrenia in the context of a general theory of behavior, the apparently bizarre and disruptive behavior so characteristic of this disorder becomes more explicable and amenable to research.

The fascinating paper by Bateson and his colleagues takes us into the realm of concern with the etiology of schizophrenia, the development and maintenance of schizophrenic behavior. Basing his theory on important formal aspects of communication theory, Bateson discusses the key concept of the "double bind," a basic form of pathological communication. This concept, which has since been incorporated into common psychiatric parlance, refers to a communication situation involving an intense relationship (such as mother-child), the expression by an important person of two orders of messages which are incongruent with each other, and a stricture on the "receiver" of this message making it impossible for him either to comment on its essentially confusing nature or leave the field.

Haley takes up and expands the problem of family interaction in relation to schizophrenia. In his closely reasoned paper, emphasis is placed on the nature of family communication patterns, the way in which each member "manifests an incongruence between what they say and how they qualify what they say." As he carefully notes, these qualifications can take place at several levels, making the ongoing family interaction a kaleidoscopic array of messages in collision with each other.[2]

Lidz and his co-workers at Yale have been involved in a long-term study of schizophrenia, investigating a variety of etiological variables in the family interaction patterns. Here they attempt to answer a question basic to the study of family pathology: "If the family milieu is critical to the production of schizophrenia in a particular offspring, if it exerts a serious pathogenic influence upon the child, what about the siblings? Why are they not affected?" What emerges from their analysis is that the pathological communication patterns and interpersonal transactions described by Bateson and Haley have a pernicious effect on all family members. Thus, as the authors note, the question is not why do other children in the family of the schizophrenic remain "normal" (for it is clear that a large percentage are psychotic as well), but what are the factors in the family environment which lead to the choice of a certain child as the "lightning rod" for the family disturbance. In their discussion of "divergent influences upon the offspring within the family," they touch on points relevant to Spiegel's role-conflict theory (see Section 2) and to Sarvis and Garcia's discussion of autism (see Section 8).

In the papers noted so far, the emphasis has been on formal, structural problems in the investigation of schizophrenia. Little concern has been evinced with the content of schizophrenic thought or the descriptions of his psychotic behavior patterns, what could be described as the experience of schizophrenia. Much, of course, has been written on this subject, some of it extremely moving as well as frightening, the element of fear creeping in when one is confronted with descriptions of experiences so uncanny and devastating that they touch a deeply buried source of anxiety concerning one's own humanness.[3] However, instead of presenting a professional paper on this aspect of the problem, we felt that a sensitive first-person account of the experience of psychosis would come even closer to illuminating the heart of the matter. With such an object in mind, we have included "The onset of psychosis — a diary account."

---

[1] See Ekstein, R. and Wallerstein, J. Observations on the psychology of borderline and psychotic children. Psychoanalytic Study of the Child, 1954, 9, 344–369.

[2] For a more elaborate presentation of these concepts as they relate to family communication patterns, as well as to psychotherapy, see Haley, J. Strategies of psychotherapy. New York: Grune & Stratton, 1963.

[3] A handful of therapists have devoted their careers to working with chronic, deeply regressed schizophrenics, and their writings beautifully communicate these feelings. See Bullard, D. M. (Ed.) Psychoanalysis and psychotherapy, selected papers of Frieda Fromm-Reichmann, Chicago: Univ. of Chicago Press, 1959; Searles, H. F. Collected papers on schizophrenia and related subjects. New York: Internat. Univ. Press, 1964; and Hill, L. B., Psychotherapeutic intervention in schizophrenia. Chicago: Univ. of Chicago Press, 1955. A collection of first-person accounts of mental illness has recently been published: Kaplan, B. The inner world of mental illness. New York: Harper & Row, 1964.

The article by Gibson and his associates on manic-depressive psychosis turns our attention to the consideration of other forms of psychotic maladjustment. Their evaluation of the developmental aspects of manic-depressive disturbance stresses the child's early home environment, with its excessive concern for social approval and prestige strivings, and an atmosphere of competitiveness and envy. The child is considered as the family flag-bearer who will, through his achievements, raise the family's prestige; but conformity demands linked to achievement demands create an intensely stressful psychological dilemma for the manic-depressive.

The paranoid individual, with his intricate delusional ideas, has been a fertile source of hypotheses for theorists of various persuasions. The challenge of this form of disorder lies in the paranoid's development of a system of thought which is refractory to influence and unmodifiable by experience. For psychoanalytic theory the core of the paranoid's persecutory delusions is a conflict over homosexual impulses. This model begins with the experience of a sexual impulse ("I love him") followed by the denial of this impulse ("No I don't love him"), leading to the counterclaim "I hate him — he is a homosexual," ending with the reemergence of the loved person as a dangerous enemy, a persecutory villain. In the Sullivanian model, the basis of the problem is the paranoid's deep feeling of inferiority and worthlessness which leads to dramatic but unfortunate distortions of reality in an attempt to provide himself with some semblance of self-esteem and interpersonal viability. Cameron sees the thought processes of the paranoid as a distortion of certain aspects of normal self-referent thinking and feeling. Because of his lack of interpersonal security and social isolation, the paranoid must face emotional crises alone. Driven by anxiety, he attempts to piece together fragments of his hostile world into some coherent system. Ultimately the paranoid pseudo-community is formed, a reconstruction of reality which organizes the actual and projected behavior of the people around him into a "comprehensible" conspiracy against the paranoid. This crystallization often takes place with a sudden flash of insight, the "ah-ha" experience as described by Sullivan and brilliantly portrayed in fiction by Chekhov in his story Ward No. 6. ■

SIGMUND FREUD

The Loss of Reality in Neurosis and Psychosis*

I have recently[1] indicated as one of the features which differentiate a neurosis from a psychosis the fact that in a neurosis the ego, in its dependence on reality, suppresses a piece of the id (of instinctual life), whereas in a psychosis, this same ego, in the service of the id, withdraws from a piece of reality. Thus for a neurosis the decisive factor would be the predominance of the influence of reality, whereas for a psychosis it would be the predominance of the id. In a psychosis, a loss of reality would necessarily be present, whereas in a neurosis, it would seem, this loss would be avoided.

But this does not at all agree with the observation which all of us can make that every neurosis disturbs the patient's relation to reality in some way, that it serves him as a means of withdrawing from reality, and that, in its severe forms, it actually signifies a flight from real life. This contradiction seems a serious one; but it is easily resolved, and the explanation of it will in fact help us to understand neuroses.

For the contradiction exists only as long as we keep our eyes fixed on the situation at the *beginning* of the neurosis, in which the ego, in the service of reality, sets about the repression of an instinctual

* Acknowledgment due to Sigmund Freud Copyrights Ltd., Mr. James Strachey and The Hogarth Press Ltd. to quote The Loss of Reality in Neurosis and Psychosis, 1924, Volume XIX of the Standard Edition of The Complete Psychological Works of Sigmund Freud. (Permission granted by Basic Books, Inc. This chapter is also available in Volume II, Collected Papers of Sigmund Freud, edited by Ernest Jones, translated by Joan Riviere, Basic Books, Inc., Publishers, New York, 1959.)
[1] 'Neurosis and Psychosis' (1924b) [this volume, p. 149].

impulse. This, however, is not yet the neurosis itself. The neurosis consists rather in the processes which provide a compensation for the portion of the id that has been damaged — that is to say, in the reaction against the repression and in the failure of the repression. The loosening of the relation to reality is a consequence of this second step in the formation of a neurosis, and it ought not to surprise us if a detailed examination shows that the loss of reality affects precisely that piece of reality as a result of whose demands the instinctual repression ensued.

There is nothing new in our characterization of neurosis as the result of a repression that has failed. We have said this all along,[2] and it is only because of the new context in which we are viewing the subject that it has been necessary to repeat it.

Incidentally, the same objection arises in a specially marked manner when we are dealing with a neurosis in which the exciting cause (the 'traumatic scene') is known, and in which one can see how the person concerned turns away from the experience and consigns it to amnesia. Let me go back by way of example to a case analysed a great many years ago,[3] in which the patient, a young woman, was in love with her brother-in-law. Standing beside her sister's death-bed, she was horrified at having the thought: 'Now he is free and can marry me.' This scene was instantly forgotten, and thus the process of regression,[4] which led to her hysterical pains, was set in motion. It is instructive precisely in this case, moreover, to learn along what path the neurosis attempted to solve the conflict. It took away from the value of the change that had occurred in reality, by repressing the instinctual demand which had emerged — that is, her love for her brother-in-law. The *psychotic* reaction would have been a disavowal[5] of the fact of her sister's death.

We might expect that when a psychosis comes into being, something analogous to the process in a neurosis occurs, though, of course, between different agencies of the mind; thus we might expect that in a psychosis, too, two steps could be discerned, of which the first would drag the ego away, this time from reality, while the second would try to make good the damage done and re-establish the subject's relations to reality at the expense of the id. And, in fact, some analogy of the sort can be observed in a psychosis. Here, too, there are two steps, the second of which has the character of a reparation. But beyond that the analogy gives way to a far more extensive similarity between the two processes. The second step of the psychosis is indeed intended to make good the loss of reality, not, however, at the expense of a restriction of the id — as happens in neurosis at the expense of the relation to reality — but in another, more autocratic manner, by the creation of a new reality which no longer raises the same objections as the old one that has been given up. The second step, therefore, both in neurosis and psychosis, is supported by the same trends. In both cases it serves the desire for power of the id, which will not allow itself to be dictated to by reality. Both neurosis and psychosis are thus the expression of a rebellion on the part of the id against the external world, of its unwillingness — or, if one prefers, its incapacity — to adapt itself to the exigencies of reality, to Ἀνάγκη [Necessity].[6] Neurosis and psychosis differ from each other far more in their first, introductory, reaction than in the attempt at reparation which follows it.

Accordingly, the initial difference is expressed thus in the final outcome: in neurosis a piece of reality is avoided by a sort of flight, whereas in psychosis it is remodelled. Or we might say: in psychosis, the initial flight is succeeded by an active phase of remodelling; in neurosis, the initial obedience is succeeded by a deferred attempt at flight. Or again, expressed in yet another way: neurosis does not disavow the reality, it only ignores it; psychosis disavows it and tries to replace it. We call behaviour 'normal' or 'healthy', if it combines certain features of both reactions — if it disavows the reality as little as does a neurosis, but if it then exerts itself, as does a psychosis, to effect an alteration of that reality. Of course, this expedient, normal, behaviour leads to work being carried out on the external world; it does not stop, as in psychosis, at effecting internal changes. It is no longer *autoplastic* but *alloplastic*.[7]

---

[2] [The notion that the 'return of the repressed' constitutes 'the illness proper' is already stated in Draft K of the Fliess correspondence, of January 1, 1896 (Freud 1950a). A little later Freud restated this, using the actual words 'failure of defence' as equivalent to 'return of the repressed,' in Section II of the second paper on 'The Neuro-Psychoses of Defence' (1896b).]

[3] In *Studies on Hysteria* (1895d). *Standard Ed.*, 2, 156 and 167. The words of the patient, Frau Elisabeth von R., are not here quoted verbatim.]

[4] [The German word is '*Regression*,' not '*Verdrängung*' ('repression'), in all editions.]

[5] [See Editor's footnote to 'The Infantile Genital Organization' (1932e), p. 143 above.]

[6] [See 'The Economic Problem of Masochism' (1924c), p. 168 above.]

[7] [These terms are possibly due to Ferenczi, who used them in a paper on 'The Phenomena of Hysterical Materialization' (1919a, 24; English trans., 1926, 97). But he there appears to attribute them to Freud, who, however, does not seem to have used them elsewhere than in this passage.]

In a psychosis, the transforming of reality is carried out upon the psychical precipitates of former relations to it — that is, upon the memory-traces, ideas and judgements which have been previously derived from reality and by which reality was represented in the mind. But this relation was never a closed one; it was continually being enriched and altered by fresh perceptions. Thus the psychosis is also faced with the task of procuring for itself perceptions of a kind which shall correspond to the new reality; and this is most radically effected by means of hallucination. The fact that, in so many forms and cases of psychosis, the paramnesias, the delusions and the hallucinations that occur are of a most distressing character and are bound up with a generation of anxiety — this fact is without doubt a sign that the whole process of remodelling is carried through against forces which oppose it violently. We may construct the process on the model of a neurosis, with which we are more familiar. There we see that a reaction of anxiety sets in whenever the repressed instinct makes a thrust forward, and that the outcome of the conflict is only a compromise and does not provide complete satisfaction. Probably in a psychosis the rejected piece of reality constantly forces itself upon the mind, just as the repressed instinct does in a neurosis, and that is why in both cases the consequences too are the same. The elucidation of the various mechanisms which are designed, in the psychoses, to turn the subject away from reality and to reconstruct reality — this is a task for specialized psychiatric study which has not yet been taken in hand.[8]

There is, therefore, a further analogy between a neurosis and a psychosis, in that in both of them the task which is undertaken in the second step is partly unsuccessful. For the repressed instinct is unable to procure a full substitute (in neurosis); and the representation of reality cannot be remoulded into satisfying forms (not, at least, in every species of mental illness). But the emphasis is different in the two cases. In a psychosis it falls entirely on the first step, which is pathological in itself and cannot but lead to illness. In a neurosis, on the other hand, it falls on the second step, on the failure of the repression, whereas the first step may succeed, and does succeed in innumerable instances without overstepping the bounds of health — even though it does so at a certain price and not without leaving behind traces of the psychical expenditure it has called for. These distinctions, and perhaps many others as well, are a result of the topographical difference in the initial situation of the pathogenic conflict — namely whether in it the ego yielded to its allegiance to the real world or to its dependence on the id.

A neurosis usually contents itself with avoiding the piece of reality in question and protecting itself against coming into contact with it. The sharp distinction between neurosis and psychosis, however, is weakened by the circumstance that in neurosis, too, there is no lack of attempts to replace a disagreeable reality by one which is more in keeping with the subject's wishes. This is made possible by the existence of a *world of phantasy*, of a domain which became separated from the real external world at the time of the introduction of the reality principle. This domain has since been kept free from the demands of the exigencies of life, like a kind of 'reservation';[9] it is not inaccessible to the ego, but it is only loosely attached to it. It is from this world of phantasy that the neurosis draws the material for its new wishful constructions, and it usually finds that material along the path of regression to a more satisfying real past.

It can hardly be doubted that the world of phantasy plays the same part in psychosis and that there, too, it is the storehouse from which the materials or the pattern for building the new reality are derived. But whereas the new, imaginary external world of a psychosis attempts to put itself in the place of external reality, that of a neurosis, on the contrary, is apt, like the play of children, to attach itself to a piece of reality — a different piece from the one against which it has to defend itself — and to lend that piece a special importance and a secret meaning which we (not always quite appropriately) call a *symbolic* one. Thus we see that both in neurosis and psychosis there comes into consideration the question not only of a *loss of reality* but also of a *substitute for reality*.

[8] [Cf., however, some beginnings made by Freud himself in the case of paranoia (*Standard Ed.*, **12**, 69–71) and of 'paraphrenia, (ibid., **14**, 86–7, 203–4 and 230).]

[9] [Cf. the paper on the 'Two Principles of Mental Functioning' (1911*b*), *Standard Ed.*, **12**, 222 and footnote.]

E. BLEULER

The Definition of the Disease*

By the term "dementia praecox" or "schizophrenia" we designate a group of psychoses whose course is at times chronic, at times marked by intermittent attacks, and which can stop or retrograde at any stage, but does not permit a full *restitutio ad integrum.* The disease is characterized by a specific type of alteration of thinking, feeling, and relation to the external world which appears nowhere else in this particular fashion.

In every case we are confronted with a more or less clear-cut splitting of the psychic functions. If the disease is marked, the personality loses its unity; at different times different psychic complexes seem to represent the personality. Integration of different complexes and strivings appears insufficient or even lacking. The psychic complexes do not combine in a conglomeration of strivings with a unified resultant as they do in a healthy person; rather, one set of complexes dominates the personality for a time, while other groups of ideas or drives are "split off" and seem either partly or completely impotent. Often ideas are only partially worked out, and fragments of ideas are connected in an illogical way to constitute a new idea. Concepts lose their completeness, seem to dispense with one or more of their essential components; indeed, in many cases they are only represented by a few truncated notions.

Thus, the process of association often works with mere fragments of ideas and concepts. This results in associations which normal individuals will regard as incorrect, bizarre, and utterly unpredictable. Often thinking stops in the middle of a thought; or in the attempt to pass to another idea, it may suddenly cease altogether, at least as far as it is a conscious process (blocking). Instead of continuing the thought, new ideas crop up which neither the patient nor the observer can bring into any connection with the previous stream of thought.

Primary disturbances of perception, orientation, or memory are not demonstrable. In the severest cases emotional and affective expressions seem to be completely lacking. In milder cases we may note only that the degree of intensity of the emotional reactions is not commensurate with the various events that caused those reactions. Indeed, the intensity of the affective reactions may range from a complete lack of emotional expression to extremely exaggerated affective responses in relation to different thought-complexes. The affectivity can also appear to be qualitatively abnormal; that is, inadequate to the intellectual processes involved.

In addition to the often discussed signs of "deterioration," many other symptoms are present in a majority of the hospital cases. We find hallucinations, delusions, confusion, stupor, mania and melancholic affective fluctuations, and catatonic symptoms. Many of these accessory symptoms and symptom-complexes betray a specific schizophrenic character so that their presence may be utilized in diagnosing the disease. Outside the hospital, there are schizophrenics in whom accessory symptoms are less apparent, or absent altogether.

At the present time, we divide dementia praecox tentatively into four subdivisions:

1. *Paranoid.* Hallucinations or delusions continuously hold the forefront of the clinical picture.
2. *Catatonia.* Catatonic symptoms dominate continuously, or for rather long periods of time.
3. *Hebephrenia.* Accessory symptoms appear but do not dominate the picture continually.
4. *Simple Schizophrenia.* Throughout its whole course only the specific, basic symptoms can be found.[1]

* Reprinted by permission from *Dementia Praecox or the Group of Schizophrenias.* New York: International Universities Press, 1950, pp. 9–10.

[1] For more details see Section II.

Borderline States*†

The term "borderline state" has achieved almost no official status in psychiatric nomenclature, and conveys no diagnostic illumination of a case other than the implication that the patient is quite sick but not frankly psychotic. In the few psychiatric textbooks where the term is to be found at all in the index, it is used in the text to apply to those cases in which the decision is difficult as to whether the patients in question are neurotic or psychotic, since both neurotic and psychotic phenomena are observed to be present. The reluctance to make a diagnosis of psychosis on the one hand, in such cases, is usually based on the clinical estimate that these patients have not yet "broken with reality"; on the other hand the psychiatrist feels that the severity of the maladjustment and the presence of ominous clinical signs preclude the diagnosis of a psychoneurosis. Thus the label "borderline state," when used as a diagnosis, conveys more information about the uncertainty and indecision of the psychiatrist than it does about the condition of the patient.

Indeed, the term and its equivalents have been frequently attacked in psychiatric and psychoanalytic literature. Rickman(13) wrote in 1928: "It is not uncommon in the lax phraseology of a Mental O. P. Department to hear of a case in which a psychoneurosis 'masks' a psychosis; I have used the term myself, but with inward misgiving. There should be no talk of masks if a case is fully understood and certainly not if the case has not received a tireless examination — except, of course, as a brief descriptive term comparable to 'shut-in' or 'apprehensive' which carry our understanding of the case no further." Similarly, Edward Glover(8) wrote in 1932: "I find the terms 'borderline' or 'pre'-psychotic, as generally used, unsatisfactory. If a psychotic mechanism is present at all, it should be given a definite label. If we merely suspect the possibility of a breakdown of repression, this can be indicated in the term 'potential' psychotic (more

accurately a 'potentially clinical' psychosis). As for larval psychoses, we are all larval psychotics and have been such since the age of two." Again, Zilboorg(18) wrote in 1941: "The less advanced cases (of schizophrenia) have been noted, but not seriously considered. When of recent years such cases engaged the attention of the clinician, they were usually approached with the euphemistic labels of borderline cases, incipient schizophrenias, schizoid personalities, mixed manic-depressive psychoses, schizoid manics, or psychopathic personalities. Such an attitude is untenable either logically or clinically. . . ." Zilboorg goes on to declare that schizophrenia should be recognized and diagnosed when its characteristic psychopathology is present, and suggests the term "ambulatory schizophrenia" for that type of schizophrenia in which the individual is able for the most part, to conceal his pathology from the general public.

I have no wish to defend the term "borderline state" as a diagnosis. I do wish, however, to discuss the clinical conditions usually connoted by this term, and especially to call attention to the diagnostic, psychopathological, and therapeutic problems involved in these conditions. I shall limit my discussion to the functional psychiatric conditions where the term is usually applied, and more particularly to those conditions which involve schizophrenic tendencies of some degree.

I believe it is the common experience of psychiatrists and psychoanalysts currently to see and treat, in open sanitaria or even in office practice, a rather high percentage of patients whom they regard, in a general sense, as borderline cases. Often these patients have been referred as cases of psychoneuroses of severe degree who have not responded to treatment according to the usual expectations associated with the supposed diagnosis. Most often, perhaps, they have been called severe obsessive-compulsive cases; sometimes an intractable phobia has been the outstanding symptom; occasionally an apparent major hysterical symptom or an anorexia nervosa dominates the clinical picture; and at times it is a question of the degree of depression, or of the extent and ominousness of paranoid trends, or of the severity of a character disorder.

* Reprinted by permission from *Bulletin of the Menninger Clinic*, Vol. 17, 1953, pp. 1–12.
† Read at the joint session of the American Psychoanalytic Association and the Section on Psychoanalysis of the American Psychiatric Association, Atlantic City, May 12, 1952.

The unsatisfactory state of our nosology contributes to our difficulties in classifying these patients diagnostically, and we legitimately wonder if a "touch of schizophrenia" is of the same order as a "touch of syphilis" or a "touch of pregnancy." So we fall back on such qualifying terms as latent or incipient (or ambulatory) schizophrenia, or emphasize that it is a *severe* obsessive-compulsive neurosis or depression, adding, for full coverage, "with paranoid trends" or "with schizoid manifestations." Certainly, for the most part, we are quite familiar with the necessity of recognizing the primary symptoms of schizophrenia and not waiting for the secondary ones of hallucinations, delusions, stupor, and the like.

Freud(4) made us alert to the possibility of psychosis underlying a psychoneurotic picture in his warning: "Often enough, when one sees a case of neurosis with hysterical or obsessional symptoms, mild in character and of short duration (just the type of case, that is, which one would regard as suitable for the treatment) a doubt which must not be overlooked arises whether the case may not be one of incipient dementia praecox, so-called (schizophrenia, according to Bleuler; paraphrenia, as I prefer to call it), and may not sooner or later develop well marked signs of this disease." Many authors in recent years, among them Hoch and Polatin,(9) Stern,(17) Miller,(10) Pious,(11) Melitta Schmideberg,(15) Fenichel,(3) H. Deutsch,(2) Stengel,(16) and others, have called attention to types of cases which belong in the borderline band of the psychopathological spectrum, and have commented on the diagnostic and psychotherapeutic problems associated with these cases.

SOME DIAGNOSTIC CONSIDERATIONS

In attempting to make the precise diagnosis in a borderline case there are three often used criteria, or frames of reference, which are apt to lead to errors if they are used exclusively or uncritically. One of these, which stems from traditional psychiatry, is the question of whether or not there has been a "break with reality"; the second is the assumption that neurosis is neurosis, psychosis is psychosis, and never the twain shall meet; a third, contributed by psychoanalysis, is the series of stages of development of the libido, with the conceptions of fixation, regression, and typical defense mechanisms for each stage.

No psychiatrist has any difficulty in diagnosing a psychosis when he finds definite evidence of falsification of reality in the form of hallucinations and delusions, or evidence of implicit loss of reality sense in the form of self-mutilation, mutism, stupor, stereotypies, flight of ideas, incoherence, homicidal mania, and the like. But these are all signs of advanced psychosis, and no present day psychiatrist of standing would be unaware of the fact that each patient with one or more of these psychotic manifestations had carried on for some previous years as a supposedly normal individual, albeit with concealed potentialities for a psychotic outbreak, and that there must have been warning signs, various stages of development, and a gradually increasing degree of overtness of these gross expressions of psychotic illness. All science aims at the capacity to *predict*, and psychiatry will become a science the more it can detect the evidences of strain, the small premonitory signs of a psychotic process, so that it can then introduce the kinds of therapeutic measures which have the best chance of aborting the psychotic development. The break with reality, which is an ego alteration, must be thought of not as a sudden and unexpected snapping, as of a twig, but as the gradual bending as well, which preceded the snapping; and sound prognosis must inevitably take into account those ego factors which correspond to the tensile strength of the twig, as well as the kinds and degree of disruptive forces which are being applied.

A second conception which leads to misdiagnosis is that neurosis and psychosis are mutually exclusive, that neurosis never develops into psychosis, and that neurotics are "loyal to reality" while psychotics are "disloyal to reality." It is, to be sure, one of the contributions of psychoanalysis that neurotic mechanisms are different from psychotic mechanisms, and that psychosis is not simply a more severe degree of neurosis. However, it is quite possible for both psychotic and neurotic mechanisms to have developed in the same individual, and this is the crux of the problem in many borderline cases. Furthermore, there is a sense in which there is a loss of reality even in neurosis. As Freud(4) pointed out: "The difference at the beginning comes to expression at the end in this way: in neurosis a part of reality is avoided by a sort of flight, but in psychosis it is remodelled. Or one may say that in psychosis, flight at the beginning is succeeded by an active phase of reconstruction, while in neurosis obedience at the beginning is followed by a subsequent attempt at flight. Or, to express it in yet another way, neurosis does not deny the existence of reality, it merely tries to ignore it; psychosis denies it and tries to substitute something else for it. A reaction which combines features of both these is the one we call normal or 'healthy'; it denies reality as little as neurosis, but then, like a psychosis, is concerned with effecting a change in it. This expedient normal attitude leads naturally to some active achievement in the outer world and is not content, like a psychosis, with establishing the alteration within itself; it is no longer *autoplastic* but *alloplastic*." Again, on the point of gradations in loss of reality, Freud(6) discussed normal jealousy, projected jealousy, and delusional jealousy, pointing out their transitions from one to the other, and describing how an individual may for a time maintain his critical judgment over paranoid ideas which are already present but do not yet have the strength of conviction of delusions.

Anna Freud(7) describes how children can use the defense of denial — denial in fantasy and denial in word and act — in ways which represent temporary breaking with reality while retaining an unimpaired faculty of reality testing. However, if adolescents and adults persist in, or resume, this kind of denial after the normal development of ego synthesis has taken place "the relation to reality has been gravely disturbed and the function of reality-testing suspended." The varieties of channelling psychotic (usually paranoid) tendencies in eccentric or fanatical ways — even to the point of developing a following of many people — and the various degrees of inappropriate emotions seen in many individuals further highlight the vagueness of the criterion of reality testing, and of the distinction between neurotic and psychotic. Also, we are well aware that in these and other borderline conditions the *movement* in the case may be toward or away from further psychotic development.

The third frame of reference, that of the levels of psychosexual development — oral sucking, oral biting, anal expulsive, anal retentive, phallic, and genital — and of the attempts to build a classification of mental disorders by linking a certain clinical condition to each level of libidinal fixation, has presented a one-sided, libidinal theory of human functioning. This psychoanalytic contribution has been of major value, but it needs to be supplemented extensively with the findings of ego psychology which have not, as yet, been sufficiently integrated with the libido theory. Reliance on the "ladder" of psychosexual development, with the line of reality testing drawn between the two anal sub-stages, has resulted in many blunders in diagnosis — especially in the failure to perceive the psychosis underlying an hysterical, phobic, or obsessive-compulsive clinical picture.

I believe it was Freud who used the metaphor of a retreating army to illuminate the mixed clinical picture in libidinal regression. I should like to borrow the metaphor and elaborate it for the purpose of illuminating ego-defensive operations. Various segments or detachments of the retreating army may make a stand and conduct holding or delaying operations at various points where the terrain lends itself to such operations, while the main retreating forces may have retired much farther to the rear. The defensive operations of the more forward detachments would, thus, actually protect the bulk of the army from disaster; but these forward detachments may not be able to hold their positions, and may have to retreat at any time in the face of superior might. On the other hand, the main army may be able to re-group itself, receive reinforcements or gain new leadership, and recapture its morale. In that event, the forward positions may hold long enough for the main forces to move forward to, or even well beyond, the stubbornly defended outposts.

I believe this metaphor conceptualizes in an important way the psycho-economy and the indicated therapy in the borderline cases. The superficial clinical picture — hysteria, phobia, obsessions, compulsive rituals — may represent a holding operation in a forward position, while the major portion of the ego has regressed far behind this in varying degrees of disorder. For the sake of accurate diagnosis, realistic prognosis, and appropriate therapy, therefore, the clinician must be able to locate the position, movement, and possibilities of re-synthesis of the main ego forces and functions, and not be misled by all the shooting in the forward holding point. An important corollary of this conception is that the therapy should not attempt to attack and demolish the forward defensive operations when to do so would mean disaster for the main ego operations. Some forward defensive operations are a matter of life and death.

Without defending the term "borderline state" as a diagnostic label, I have thus far developed the argument to show that there is a borderline strip in psychopathology where accurate diagnosis is difficult. I have tried to show the general characteristics of such borderline conditions, and to point out why the often used diagnostic criteria of break with reality, mutual exclusiveness of neurosis and psychosis, and the libido theory are insufficient and misleading in reaching accurate diagnosis, prognosis, and appropriate therapeutic recommendations for such cases. What, then, are the more reliable methods of evaluating these cases so that one will not have to be content with using as a diagnosis the unspecific term "borderline state"? The attempt to answer this question will involve a discussion of certain dynamic considerations as they relate to the diagnostic techniques available to us — the psychiatric interview, the free-association interview, and the use of psychological diagnostic tests.

SOME DYNAMIC CONSIDERATIONS

We conceptualize the borderline case as one in which normal ego functions of secondary process thinking, integration, realistic planning, adaptation to the environment, maintenance of object relationships, and defenses against primitive unconscious impulses are severely weakened. As a result of various combinations of the factors of constitutional tendencies, predisposition based on traumatic events and disturbed human relationships, and more recent precipitating stress, the ego of the borderline patient is laboring badly. Some ego functions have been severely impaired — especially, in most cases, integration, concept formation, judgment, realistic planning, and defending against eruption into conscious thinking of id impulses and their fantasy elaborations. Other ego functions, such as conventional (but superficial) adaptation to the environment and superficial maintenance of object relationships may exhibit varying degrees of intactness. And still others, such as memory, calculation, and certain habitual performances, may seem unimpaired. Also, the clinical picture may be dominated by hysterical, phobic, obsessive-compulsive, or psychosomatic symptoms, to which neurotic disabilities and distress the patient attributes his inability to carry on the usual ego functions.

During the psychiatric interview the neurotic defenses and the relatively intact adaptive ego functions may enable the borderline patient to present a deceptive, superficially conventional, although neurotic, front, depending on how thoroughgoing and comprehensive the psychiatric investigation is with respect to the patient's *total* ego functioning. The face to face psychiatric interview provides a relatively structured situation in which the conventional protective devices of avoidance, evasion, denial, minimization, changing the subject, and other cover-up methods can be used — even by patients who are genuinely seeking help but who dare not yet communicate their awareness of lost affect, reality misinterpretations, autistic preoccupations, and the like.

Several interviews may be necessary to provide the psychiatrist with a sufficiently comprehensive appraisal of the total ego functioning, and to provide the patient with enough sense of security to permit him to verbalize his more disturbing self-observations. In spite of the patient's automatic attempts at concealment, the presence of pathology of psychotic degree will usually manifest itself to the experienced clinician. Occasional blocking, peculiarities of word usage, obliviousness to obvious implications, contaminations of idioms, arbitrary inferences, inappropriate affect, and suspicion-laden behavior and questions are a few possible examples of such unwitting betrayals of ego impairment of psychotic degree.

In regard to such manifestations the appraisal of total ego functioning can be more precise if the psychiatrist takes careful note of the degree of ego-syntonicity associated with them. Momentary halting, signs of embarrassment, and attempts at correction of the peculiarity of expression are evidences of a sufficient degree of ego intactness for such psychotic intrusions to be recognized and repudiated as ego-alien; whereas unnoticed and repeated peculiarities and contaminations provide evidence that the ego has been overwhelmed or pervaded by them and has lost its power to regard them as bizarre. Likewise the expression of suspicions accompanied by embarrassed apologies or joking indicates preservation of the ego's critical function with respect to paranoid mistrust; whereas unqualified suspiciousness indicates the loss of that important ego function. Sometimes this capacity for taking distance from these psychotic productions has to be tested by questions from the psychiatrist which call attention to the production and request comments from the patient about them. Obviously such confrontations should be made sparingly and supportively.

In addition to these microscopic evidences of ego weakness in respect to id eruptions in borderline cases, there are more macroscopic manifestations which may be either frankly stated by the patient or may be implicit in his attitudes and productions. Lack of concern about the realities of his life predicament, usually associated with low voltage wishes for help or grossly inappropriate treatment proposals of his own, is one such macroscopic sign. Others are the fact that the illness developed in the absence of observable precipitating stress, or under the relatively minor stress which was inevitable for the point where this patient was in his life course; the presence of multiple symptoms and disabilities, especially if these are regarded with an acceptance that seems ego-syntonic, or are viewed as being due to malevolent external influence; lack of achievement over a relatively long period, indicating a chronic and severe failure of the ego to channelize energies constructively, especially if this lack of achievement has been accompanied by some degree of disintegration of the ordinary routines of looking after one's self; vagueness or unrealism in planning for the future with respect to education, vocation, marriage, parenthood, and the like; and the relating of bizarre dreams, or evidence of insufficient contrast between dream content and attitudes on the one hand and waking activities and attitudes on the other. All of these macroscopic manifestations will be observable, if they are present, only if the psychiatrist keeps as his frame of reference the patient's total ego functioning, with appropriate allowances for the patient's age, endowment, cultural background, previous level of achievement, and the degree of severity of the recent or current life stresses.

The question of using the free association interview, with the patient on the couch, frequently comes up with borderline cases. The associative anamnesis has been advocated by Felix Deutsch,(1) and many analysts use free association interviews either as a limited diagnostic tool or as a more extended trial period of analytic therapy. This technique changes the fairly well structured situation of the face to face psychiatric interview into a relatively unstructured one, so that the patient cannot rely on his usual defensive and conventionally adaptive devices to maintain his front. Borderline patients are then likely to show in bolder relief the various microscopic and macroscopic signs of schizophrenic illness. They may be unable to talk at all and may block completely, with evidence of mounting anxiety; or their verbalizations may show a high degree of autistic content, with many peculiarities of expression; or their inappropriate affect may become more obvious. The diagnosis is aided by the couch-free association technique, but the experience may be definitely anti-therapeutic for the patient. Definitive evidence of psychotic thinking may be produced at the expense of humiliating and disintegrating exposure of the patient's naked pathology. Clinical judgment must be used as to how far the psychiatrist should go in breaking through the defenses in his purpose of reaching an accurate diagnosis.

In the face to face psychiatric diagnostic interview the patient is in a fairly well structured situation and is reacting to the interested listening and active questioning of a visible and supportive physician; in the couch-free association interview the patient is in a relatively unstructured situation, more or less abandoned to his own fantasies, and relatively unsupported by the shadowy and largely silent listener. Diagnostic psychological tests combine the advantages of support from a visible and interested professional listener, as in the face to face psychiatric interview, and the diagnostically significant unstructured situation of the couch-free association interview.

The various test stimuli are unusual and unconventional, and there are no "correct" answers, so that the patient does not know what he is revealing or concealing. The psychological tests also have one significant advantage over either of the two kinds of diagnostic interview. The tests have been standardized by trials on thousands of cases, so that objective scoring can be done and comparisons can be made of this patient's responses to typical responses of many other patients with all kinds of psychiatric illness, whereas even the experienced psychiatric interviewer must depend on impressions and comparisons of the patient's productions with those of other remembered patients in his particular experience. The psychologist can also determine the patient's capacity to take critical distance from his more pathological responses, and thus assess the degree of ego-alienness or ego-syntonicity of the pathological material, by asking questions which elicit comments from the patient about certain of the unusual responses.

As Rapaport, (12) Schafer, (14) and others have pointed out, the interpretation of diagnostic psychological test results is far from being a mere matter of mathematical scoring followed by comparisons with standard tables. There is also required a high degree of clinical acumen, and it is just in the field of the borderline cases that expert interpretation of the test results is essential. The Rorschach is probably the most sensitive test for autistic thinking, and the word association and sorting tests are most valuable for detecting the loosening of associations and disruption of concept formation. The Thematic Apperception Test is less sensitive to schizophrenic pathology but can give a sharply etched picture of the patient's projected image of himself and of the significant people in his life, while describing what the patient feels he and these significant people are doing to each other. The Bellevue-Wechsler intelligence test may, on the other hand, especially in borderline cases, show excellent preservation of intellectual functioning. The relatively clean and orderly responses of the Bellevue-Wechsler do not cancel out the contaminated and disorderly responses of the other tests and thus make the diagnosis doubtful. Instead, the former highlight the preservation of certain ego functions in the face of the impairment of other ego functions revealed by the latter, and thus provide a basis for critical appraisal of ego strengths in relation to threatening eruptions from the id. The Rorschach alone is often given as a test to check on possible schizophrenia, but only a balanced battery of tests can provide the range of responses which will permit accurate appraisal of total ego functioning.

In all of these diagnostic methods, then, the aim should be to take a complete inventory of ego functioning in order to discover the kind of equilibrium which exists between ego controls on the one hand and threatening impulses on the other, and to learn whether the *movement* in this patient is toward less ego control and poorer adaptation. The qualitative appraisal of ego functions is, if anything, even more important than the quantitative estimation of impulse-control balance. Even quite severely neurotic defenses may be capitalized, through therapy, and become reintegrating forces leading to a dynamic shift away, for example, from dereistic thinking to fairly well organized compulsive striving, with marked improvement in both the defensive and adaptive aspects of ego functioning.

Some final comments are in order regarding the clinical picture in the borderline group of cases before turning to the therapeutic considerations. A useful distinction can be made between internalized or autoplastic illnesses, such as the schizophrenias, depressions, and clinical psychoneuroses, and the externalized or alloplastic illnesses, such as the neurotic and psychotic characters. In the autoplastic conditions, the ego, in various stages of enfeeblement, is attempting to hold out against a barrage of ego-alien impulses and their autistic elaborations; in the alloplastic conditions, or character disorders, the ego itself has been moulded and distorted by the gradual infiltration of pathogenic impulses and defenses, and the invasion of id impulses appears much more ego-syntonic. In some respects the alloplastic conditions thus represent greater integration of the ego, but just because of this integrated infiltration of pathogenic impulses into the ego these cases are more difficult to influence therapeutically. On the other hand, the autoplastic conditions may appear more severely ill than the alloplastic ones but the prognosis for therapy may be more favorable. Both the psychiatric interview and the psychological test results can aid in establishing whether the structure of the illness is primarily autoplastic or alloplastic.

SOME THERAPEUTIC CONSIDERATIONS

The ego of the borderline patient is a feeble and unreliable ally in therapy. In the incipient schizo-phrenias the ego is in danger of being overwhelmed by the ego-alien pathogenic forces, and in the psychotic character disorders the ego is already warped by more or less ego-syntonic pervasion by the same pathogenic forces. Yet a few adaptive functions remain, and certain psychoneurotic defense measures may still be in operation, even though the impulse-defense balance is precarious. In an environment which maintains its over-taxing demands on such patients, further regression is likely. If these patients are left to their own devices, in relative isolation, whether at home or in closed hospital, they tend toward further intensification of autistic thinking. Similarly, if they are encouraged to free associate in the relative isolation of recumbency on the analytic couch, the autistic development is encouraged, and the necessary supportive factor of positive transference to an active, visible, responding therapist is unavailable. Thus even though a trial analysis may bring forth misleading "rich" material, and the analyst can make correspondingly rich formulations and interpretations, the patient's ego often cannot make use of them, and they may only serve the purpose of stimulating further autistic elaborations. Psychoanalysis is, thus, contraindicated for the great majority of borderline cases, at least until after some months of successful analytic psychotherapy.

Psychotherapists can take their cue from the much better front these patients are able to present and maintain in face to face psychiatric interviews, where the structured situation and the visible, personal, active therapist per se provides an integrating force to stimulate the patient's surviving adaptive, integrative, and reality-testing capacities. Our therapeutic objective then, would be the strengthening of the patient's ego controls over instinctual impulses and educating him in the employment of new controls and new adaptive methods, through a kind of psychotherapeutic lend-lease. With our analytic knowledge we can see how he defends himself, and what he defends himself against, but we do not attack those defenses except as we may modify them or educatively introduce better substitutes for them. Our formulations will be in terms of his ego operations rather than of his id content, and will be calculated to improve and strengthen the ego operations.

The psychoneurotic defenses and symptoms especially are not attacked, for just these ego operations protect the patient from further psychotic disorganization. Particularly the obsessive-compulsive defense line is left untouched, except as it can be modified educatively. To return for the moment to the metaphor of the retreating army, our therapy should by-pass the outposts of neurotic defenses and symptom formation, and should act as a *rescue force* for the main army of ego functions to the rear, helping to regroup them, restore their morale, and provide leadership for them. Then we might hope to bring them forward to or beyond the neurotic outpost which we by-passed. We may even take our cues for morale building and leadership from the kind of neurotic outpost we observed. If it was primarily obsessive-compulsive we might strive therapeutically for a reintegration based on strengthened compulsive trends. If it was phobic we could attempt to build counter-phobic defenses.

Not only do we try to consolidate the more neurotic defenses available, but we also attempt to convert autoplastic (self-crippling) defenses into alloplastic (externally adaptive) ones. This attempt will often require considerably more therapeutic impact than can be provided in an hour a day of modified analytic psychotherapy. Both the motivation and the specific opportunities for alloplastic adaptation can be provided through group dynamics measures — group discussions, group projects, and initiative-stimulating group and individual activities. In a comprehensive attempt at providing such a setting in which to conduct the individual psychotherapy of these borderline cases, we have discovered that many such patients can be carried on a voluntary basis and in an open hospital facility, thus avoiding the encouragement toward isolation, regression, and inertia which closed hospital care sometimes introduces.

SUMMARY

Borderline cases have been discussed in their diagnostic, dynamic, and therapeutic aspects. The term borderline case is not recommended as a diagnostic term, for a much more precise diagnosis should be made which identifies the type and degree of psychotic pathology. Far more important, however, than arriving at a diagnostic label is the achievement of a comprehensive psychodynamic and psycho-economic appraisal of the balance in each patient between the ego's defensive and adaptive measures on the one hand, and the pathogenic instinctual and ego-disintegrating forces on the other, so that therapy can be planned and conducted for the purpose of conserving, strengthening, and improving the defensive and adaptive functions of the ego.

BIBLIOGRAPHY

1. DEUTSCH, FELIX: *Applied Psychoanalysis; Selected Objectives of Psychotherapy.* New York, Grune & Stratton, 1949.
2. DEUTSCH, HELENE: Some Forms of Emotional Disturbance and Their Relationship to Schizophrenia. *Psychoanalyt. Quart.* 11:301–321, 1942.
3. FENICHEL, OTTO: *The Psychoanalytic Theory of Neurosis.* New York, Norton, 1945.
4. FREUD, SIGMUND: Further Recommendations in the Technique of Psycho-Analysis. On Beginning the Treatment. The Question of the First Communication. The Dynamics of the Cure. *Collected Papers,* Vol. II. London, Hogarth, 1924. Pp. 342–365.
5. ———: The Loss of Reality in Neurosis and Psychosis. *Collected Papers,* Vol. II. London, Hogarth, 1924. Pp. 277–282.
6. ———: Certain Neurotic Mechanisms in Jealousy, Paranoia and Homosexuality. *Collected Papers,* Vol. II. London, Hogarth, 1924. Pp. 232–243.
7. FREUD, ANNA: *The Ego and the Mechanisms of Defence.* New York, International Universities Press, 1946.
8. GLOVER, EDWARD: A Psycho-Analytical Approach to the Classification of Mental Disorders. *J. Ment. Sc.* 78:819–842, 1932.
9. HOCH, PAUL AND POLATIN, PHILLIP: Pseudoneurotic Forms of Schizophrenia. *Psychiat. Quart.* 23:248–276, 1949.
10. MILLER, WILBUR R.: The Relationship Between Early Schizophrenia and the Neuroses. *Am. J. Psychiat.* 96:889–896, 1940.
11. PIOUS, WILLIAM L.: Obsessive-Compulsive Symptoms in an Incipient Schizophrenic. *Psychoanalyt. Quart.* 19:327–351, 1950.
12. RAPAPORT, DAVID, GILL, MERTON AND SCHAFER, ROY: *Diagnostic Psychological Testing.* Chicago, Yearbook Publishers, 1946.
13. RICKMAN, JOHN: *The Development of the Psycho-Analytical Theory of the Psychoses, 1893–1926.* London, Bailliere, Tindall & Cox for the Institute of Psycho-Analysis, 1928.
14. SCHAFER, ROY: *The Clinical Application of Psychological Tests.* New York, International Universities Press, 1948.
15. SCHMIDEBERG, MELITTA: The Treatment of Psychopaths and Borderline Patients. *Amer. J. Psychotherapy* 1:45–70, 1947.
16. STENGEL, ERWIN: A Study on Some Clinical Aspects of the Relationship Between Obsessional Neurosis and Psychotic Reaction Types. *J. Ment. Sci.* 91:166–187, 1945.
17. STERN, ADOLPH: Psychoanalytic Therapy in the Borderline Neuroses. *Psychoanalyt. Quart.* 14:190–198, 1945.
18. ZILBOORG, GREGORY: Ambulatory Schizophrenics. *Psychiatry* 4:149–155, 1941.

ALFRED E. GOLDMAN

A Comparative-Developmental Approach to Schizophrenia*

There is a growing number of social and biological scientists who feel the need for a comprehensive theory of behavior — a theory of which schizophrenia in particular, or psychopathology in general, is only one facet. The theory should be broad enough to encompass data from such apparently diverse fields as anthropology, phylogenesis, human development, and states of lowered consciousness. Data from all of these areas contribute to our understanding of human behavior, and it would seem that the law of parsimony would be better served if these data could be subsumed under the same concepts and interpreted in terms of a common set of principles.

This paper attempts to outline a comparative-developmental approach to schizophrenia. It is comparative in that it relates data from the study of schizophrenia to many different fields of inquiry. It is developmental insofar as it is suggested by, and draws its basic facts from developmental studies — the development from conception to birth, the development from childhood to adulthood, the development from the single-celled organisms to man, and from developmental studies of human cultures.

For the particular organization of the approach to schizophrenia presented here, the author accepts responsibility; the original formulation of the comprehensive comparative-developmental theory is that by Heinz Werner (1940) and his co-workers at Clark University.

Werner's comparative-developmental approach aims at viewing the total behavior of all organisms in terms of a common set of developmental principles. It is his belief that such an approach is fruitful in coordinating, within a single descriptive framework, psychological phenomena observed in phylogenesis, ontogenesis, ethnopsychology, and psychopathology. This paper confines itself to what this theoretical position has had to contribute to an understanding of schizophrenia. It attempts to indicate the comprehensiveness and heuristic value of the approach without, however, attempting to present an exhaustive review of the large body of relevant research.

Behavior proceeds through given stages in its development. A formal similarity obtains between the organization and structure of processes in young children, in organisms low on the phylogenetic scale, in human adults of technologically backward societies, and in certain states of lowered consciousness in educated normal adults of technologically advanced societies. In order for developmental theory to encompass schizophrenic processes it requires the introduction of constructs which suggest a parallelism of various aspects of schizophrenia with developmental patterns in all of these spheres of inquiry, but especially with development in childhood. To this end developmental theorists have introduced the concept of "regression." The progression seen in the normal course of development is reversed in pathology; thus, in schizophrenia we may expect to find a regression in the direction of greater primitivization of process.

A frequently raised objection to developmental theory is that it seeks only generic similarities between various groups and tends to ignore their differences.

Exploration of developmental theory does require seeking for systematic patterns of generic similarities in cognitive performance among certain groups. Thus focused on similarities, developmental theorists have not always taken explicit account of specific differences that have appeared between groups.

The heuristic value of such an approach has already been demonstrated by the considerable number of investigations that have been provoked by or conducted under the purview of development theory. Its clinical value is suggested by its contributions to psychodiagnostic testing, in particular to the scoring and interpretation of the Rorschach technique. Genetic theory does not question that differences exist between the child and adult schizophrenic. It does hold that similarities in cognitive structure exist between young children and adult schizophrenics both of which are exemplifications of an ideal construct, namely, developmental primitivity.

* Reprinted by permission from *Psychological Bulletin*, Vol. 59, 1962, pp. 57–69. Copyright 1959 by the American Psychological Association.

A word now about the use of the term "primitive" (Werner & Kaplan, 1956). Much of the criticism leveled at the use of this term is based on the assertion that it is moralistic in character and thus has little place in scientific endeavor. No such evaluative connotation is intended. While "primitivity" is not evaluative in this moralistic sense, it is evaluative in that it may either impede or facilitate attainment of certain goals or states. Primitivity pertains to the psychologically prior stages of development. In essence the concept of primitivity is a theoretical construct referring to a kind of cognition characterized by developmentally early processes. Processes that appear early in the development sequence — that is, early in childhood, or early in the temporal development of an idea — are more primitive than those which appear later in the sequence.

The term "regression" as used by Werner (1940) refers to the structural re-emergence of developmentally lower levels of functioning as the more advanced and more recently developed levels are disorganized. Regression in this sense differs in emphasis from the meaning given this term by psychoanalytic orthodoxy[1] which focuses on impulses and the methods by which these are gratified and controlled. While psychoanalysis has emphasized the *function* and *content* of psychopathology, the developmental approach considers only the *formal structure* of psychopathological processes.

By similarity in *process* between childhood and pathological primitivization reference is made to structural similarity, not to similarity in content. The regressed adult is, of course not a child; rather, similar organizations or forms of process are identifiable in both. Our interest here is not primarily in *what* children or schizophrenics think or perceive, but rather, *how* they think or perceive. Schizophrenia thus is seen as a regression in cognitive processes; that is, it is conceived as a reversal of those patterns of thinking, perceiving, and so on which are encountered in the normal course of development. Further, developmental theorists are not concerned with the nature of the conditions that have caused the regressed behavior or the historical antecedents of such conditions. Rather they focus on the structural or formal consequences of these predisposing experiences.

It should be made clear that the psychoanalytic

and the comparative-developmental approaches are not mutually exclusive; rather, they focus on different aspects of schizophrenia (Arieti, 1955). Each may be clinically useful and theoretically productive. Devoting attention in this paper to the structural point of view does not attribute less value or validity to the psychodynamic viewpoint. Where the psychodynamic approach is particularly helpful in therapy, the structural approach is useful in developing hypotheses, describing developmental phenomena within a consistent framework, and — most important to the clinician — it provides a gauge by which psychopathological states and modifications in those states may be assessed and understood in terms of developmental criteria (Siegel, 1953). The concept of schizophrenia which is proposed here proceeds from a basic developmental principle; wherever development takes place it initiates in a globality or lack of differentiation and becomes increasingly more differentiated, terminating in a state of integration. The development of motor coordination may serve to illustrate this developmental principle.

When stimulated, the newborn typically reacts with mass nondirected motor activity. In the normal course of maturation, this mass action becomes more focalized and better directed with respect to the stimulating agent. That is, from the total involvement of the whole body emerges a differentiated activity of certain parts of the body — arms, legs, head, etc. These now differentiated movements become integrated into a single smooth-flowing response in which all parts of the body may participate appropriately in achieving a goal or solving a task.

Now let us turn to the separate functions that this approach encompasses.[2] In each case the comparison will be made between human ontogenesis and schizophrenia.

EMOTIONAL BEHAVIOR

Ontogenetic changes in emotional behavior proceed along, at least, three continua: (*a*) From overt motor expression of emotion to increasingly more internalized experience of emotion. Crying (Bayley, 1932), and other motor activity decreases with age. (*b*) From globality of emotional experience to greater differentiation (Bridges, 1932). At first there are only undifferentiated affective states of relative excitement or quiescence. With development there

---

[1] Although Freud considered ego regression as well as impulse regression, many psychoanalytic practitioners are inclined to overemphasize the latter at the expense of the former.

[2] A comprehensive survey of developmentally oriented research in childhood may be found in Werner (1946).

is greater specificity of emotion. For example, global negative affect becomes more differentiated into increasingly more subtle nuances, such as hate, despise, contempt, dislike, etc. (c) From lability of emotional experience to increased stability. In the young child there is characteristically momentary change in the nature of his emotional experiences and its expression (Jersild, 1939). What starts out as a laugh may end up in bitter tears or vice versa. Crying can be quickly changed to giggling by a well placed tickle.

In accordance with the regression hypothesis, in schizophrenia there is the expectation of a reversal in each of these three progressions:

1. In the acute stage of the illness, before chronicity becomes manifest in affective blunting, emotion is uncontrolled; impulse is expressed overtly without adequate intellectual intervention. Not only is the expression of affect likely to be more public, but there is an increase in the degree of motor involvement. Thus, the motoric hyperactivity of the excited schizophrenic and the motoric hypoactivity of the chronic "burnt-out" schizophrenic both exhibit the degree to which the emotional state is syncretically (Werner, 1940) fused in its expression with the motoric system. Although the affective and motoric are never wholly independent (Wolff, 1943) of each other, the immediacy, directness, and overtness of this relationship tends to increase in schizophrenia.

2. The increasing differentiation and subtlety of feelings seen in ontogenesis is reversed in schizophrenia. Clinical practice, in particular experience with the projective techniques, reflects the dedifferentiation of feelings. Aggressive and sexual components are not infrequently fused into an indistinguishable whole. Even more striking is the blatant admixture of positive and negative impulses.

3. Though perhaps not to the same degree, the emotional experience of the acute schizophrenic is similar to that of the young child's in that it, too, is highly labile and unpredictable.

PERCEPTION

The progression from globality to differentiation to integration is perhaps best seen in perception. For the neonate and very young child the visual field is not well organized or structured. Figure and ground, contours, patterns of light and shadow, movement, all merge into an undifferentiated perceptual mass, or in William James' classic terminology, "a blooming, buzzing confusion." From this globality emer-

ges stages of increasingly differentiated perception. Here visual patterns acquire object-properties, with definitive contours and localized in three-dimensional space. This development then terminates in a stage in which these differentiated aspects of the perceptual field are integrated, or synthesized, into a single meaningful percept (Werner, 1940).

This developmental sequence has been corroborated by a number of experiments, the most convincing of which have used the Rorschach blots as stimulus material (Hemmendinger, 1953). Use of this technique reveals the following changes to take place with increasing age.

Three-year-olds are whole-perceivers; they see few details and their perception is best described qualitatively in terms of their undifferentiated character. Four- and 5-year-olds react less in terms of wholes and more often notice and comment on the parts. At 6 years another, and distinct, change occurs: an abrupt and marked increase in perceptual responses to the small and rarely noticed areas in the blots. This attraction to tiny details is interpreted as an intensification of the development of differentiation. At 9 years begins the final phase of perceptual development — that of synthesis and integration. This final phase terminates in the appearance of predominantly synthesizing activity. In the integrated whole response, the blot is perceptually articulated and then reintegrated into a well differentiated unified whole.

Having considered perceptual development in children we would expect, according to the regression hypothesis, a reversal of this pattern in schizophrenia. Further, we would expect that the greater the pathology the more immature the perception.

Experiments, particularly those by Friedman (1953) and Siegel (1953), reveal the following relationships in perceptual function between schizophrenics and children:

With respect to the developmentally immature response, there exists no significant difference between children and schizophrenics, and both groups differ significantly from normal adults. The same is true of the most advanced percepts. The integrated whole response discriminates each of the three groups from each other. Thus, these findings justify the conclusion that schizophrenics, in some respects, respond perceptually in a manner similar to that of children, and in other aspects, they occupy an intermediate position between normal adults and children. This may be understood in terms of the hypothetical construct of regression. In this regard regression seems evident, but it is not of such a total nature as to completely eradicate the history of the individual who has once operated on a higher developmental level.

Now, what may be said regarding the schizophrenic subtypes? There is little or no evidence on which to discriminate the perceptual functioning of the hebrephrenics and catatonics from each other, and no work has been done with simple schizophrenics. However, developmentally comparing paranoid schizophrenics with the combined hebrephrenic and catatonic group (Siegel, 1953) we find the following: while the perception of paranoid schizophrenics is typically fractionated and fragmented with emphasis on perceptual analysis, resembling the performance of children from 6 to 10, that of the hebrephrenic and catatonic schizophrenics is characteristic of the global, amorphous perceptual activity of 3–5 year old children.

Comparative-developmental theory thus permits the location of catatonics, hebrephrenics, and paranoids on a developmental scale. In all aspects of cognitive functioning, in addition to perception, paranoid schizophrenics are expected to perform more like the normal adult than the catatonic or hebrephrenic schizophrenic. It does not, however, attempt to state the conditions which facilitate or inhibit the depth of regression in these diagnostic categories. At this stage in its development the theory has paid relatively little attention to motivational aspects of schizophrenia. Among clinical practitioners this conceptual vacuum has been filled by psychodynamic theories.

There are other aspects of perceptual development and regression that are instructive here:

The extreme lability that we see in primitive emotional behavior is also seen in the perceptual sphere. Those who have worked intensively with schizophrenics or with young children cannot avoid being impressed by the extreme lability of their attention. This, in both the child and in the schizophrenic, may be attributable to a kind of perceptual passivity in which competing stimuli have equal potential for evoking a perceptual response. This notion of stimuli equipotentiality may be useful in understanding the severe stimulus boundedness of the child and schizophrenic.

The child is stimulus bound in that the stimulus *must* be attended to. An infant's eyes *must* follow the hand that goes before it. His hand must grasp the object that is placed in it.

The schizophrenic is similarly stimulus bound. Stimuli that compete for a perceptual response cannot be adequately discriminated in terms of their relevance to a task. Thus, the schizophrenic com-

plains of a rapidly shifting, kaleidoscopic world. A patient seen by the author complained continually that he could not attend to anything for very long because everything and anything disrupted his thoughts. Apparently irrelevant details demanded his attention: a noise outside, lights passing by at night, an apparently random thought, or a bodily sensation had equal demand on his attention as the topic being discussed or the task at hand. This extreme interpenetration of the schizophrenic's attention and thought by apparently random stimuli is a well known phenomenon and has been well described by Cameron (1939), Kasanin (1944), and others.

LEARNING

The developmental approach to learning derives from the notion that development is characterized by qualitatively different processes and modes of organization, rather than by simply quantitative variations in process. This approach is therefore in opposition to those theoretical orientations which view learning as reduceable to a single process. Developmental theory does not conceive of any one process as being paradigmatic of the whole range of human learning. A view which reduces all learning to a single process conceives of the adult as having available *more* response alternatives than the child. A genetic point of view conceives of the adult and child as utilizing *different* processes which may not be distinguishable in terms of efficiency or achievement.

Developmental theorists thus seek to understand the nature of human learning through the exploration of qualitatively distinct organizational stages. Such an exploration was undertaken in a recent study by Goldman and Denny (in press). They presented two kinds of learning tasks to children 5–14 years old. Performance in the first learning task depended on apprehending the regular pattern of the pre-established program (response to two switches in a right-right-left-left sequence). Performance in this task increased steadily with age and IQ. In the second task rewards were received according to a predetermined, random "probability" program in which one response was rewarded 25% of the time and the other response was rewarded 75%. Performance in this task was essentially invariant with age and IQ with the trend somewhat favoring the younger children. Insofar as these developmental curves were strikingly different they were interpreted as indicating that the performances on the two learning tasks reflected different processes. Insofar as the sequential, or "recursive," task required an active seeking for a general rule for its solution, it was interpreted as requiring a more advanced mode of functioning than that on the probability or "stochastic" task which permitted a more passive orientation to the task in that it did not provide for such an easily generalizable solution.

A third learning process that may represent the most primitive level for humans is classical conditioning, in which the stimulus is presented wholly at the discretion of the experimenter and the response is usually of a physiological or reflexive nature. Developmental studies of classical conditioning suggest that conditioned responses can be established very early in life and indeed that young children can be more easily conditioned than older children and adults (Jones, 1928, 1930a, 1930b; Kasatkin & Levikova, 1935; Mateer, 1918; Razran, 1933, 1935). The developmental primitivity of classical conditioning is further suggested by studies which indicate that susceptibility to conditioning is enhanced in states of lowered consciousness (Leuba, 1940, 1941; Scott, 1930).

Thus, at least three modes of learning are suggested which, in the order from most primitive to most advanced, are: learning by classical conditioning, stochastic learning (instrumental conditioning), and recursive learning (problem solving). The first level appears to be characteristic of the learning of very young children and of infrahuman animals. Here the learner is a kind of passive "victim" of his environment in that he does little of an active nature to learn; learning, the pairing of stimuli and response, is imposed upon him.[3] The second learning mode is distinguished from the first in that the learner is active or "instrumental" in the learning process, yet the learning process is essentially by rote. In this learning mode young children and adults do equally well, as do subjects of varying intelligence. The third learning mode is not only the most active in that there is a deliberate seeking for order and regularity, but there is a vigorous development and testing of solution hypotheses. This learning mode favors older and more intelligent subjects.

With growth — phylogenetic and ontogenetic — classical conditioning is less adaptive and recedes to the background until called upon when the task situation calls for no more profound level of intellection. The other modes of learning emerge later to better serve the individual's needs.

In schizophrenia it is proposed that this development is reversed, with sequential learning and other forms of complex learning situations being effected

[3] A similar viewpoint was expressed by Gesell (1938).

most and classical conditioning ascending in relative importance.

Schizophrenics have been found to be more readily conditioned than normals in relatively simple situations in which the response alternatives are limited and the response reflexive. This has been demonstrated for the knee jerk (Pfaffman & Schlossberg, 1936), the psychogalvanic response (Mays, 1934; Shipley, 1934), and eyeblink (Spence & Taylor, 1953). Schizophrenics have also been shown to exceed neurotics in eyeblink conditioning (Taylor & Spence, 1954). However, since some studies have failed to demonstrate the greater conditionability of schizophrenics over normals (Howe, 1958; Paintal, 1951), the question is raised as to what stimulus conditions enhance the establishment of the conditioned response in schizophrenics as compared to normals.

In accordance with the regression hypothesis, the increase in susceptibility to conditioning in schizophrenia should be accompanied by a decrement in performance of complex tasks. By "complex" task is meant tasks which permit wide response alternatives, among which are many irrelevant ones, and in which an active role of the learner is required. Schizophrenics have been found to perform poorly relative to the performance of control normals in these complex tasks (Cameron, 1939; Hanfmann, 1939; Hanfmann & Kasanin, 1942; Rapaport, 1945).

The increased conditioning performance and the decreased performance in complex tasks, in schizophrenia as compared to normals, has been interpreted by Mednick (1958) and other learning oriented theorists (e.g., Taylor & Spence, 1954) in terms of the effect of drive intensification (anxiety) on the response strength of the conditioned response. A difficulty with this type of Hullian interpretation is that it fails to take into account developmental data. The superior performance of children and infrahuman animals relative to normal adults in conditioning experiments can hardly be incorporated within such a theoretical framework unless one postulates the existence of a heightened drive state in these more primitive organisms. Genetic theory offers the parsimonious incorporation of data from all of these areas within a single theoretical structure.

When a stable stimulus-response relationship has been established the response may be elicited by other stimuli similar in some manner to the initial stimulus. This is stimulus generalization.

The genetic principle that differentiation proceeds from an initial stage of globality would suggest that in development stimulus generalization would decrease. Reiss (1946) found that young children tend to generalize readily to homophones but this tendency disappears at about 11 years of age. Mednick and Lehtinen (1957) found that amount of stimulus generalization reactivity, measured along a visual-spatial dimension of similarity, was significantly greater for young children (7–9 years) than for older children (10–12 years).

The expectation then would be that in schizophrenia stimulus generalization would be higher than in normals of comparable intelligence. A number of studies testify that this is so (Cameron, 1938; Garmezy, 1952; Mednick, 1955).

THINKING AND LANGUAGE

Thinking and language may be investigated from the vantage of many dimensions. Three which appear to the author to be most central and inclusive are the development from idiosyncrasy to consensuality of concepts, from lability to stability of concepts, and from contextualization to autonomy of concepts.

The development from idiosyncrasy to consensuality refers to the increasingly more public and predictable thinking of which the child becomes capable as he grows older (Pollack, 1953; Werner & Kaplan, 1952). Thus, the agreement in the meaning of words among members of a given speech community increases with age. Children, in contrast to adults, use words in a private, highly individualistic manner (Hayakawa, 1954).

In psychopathological regression the development toward greater consensuality in thinking is reversed. Idiosyncratic thought then reduces the schizophrenic to virtual social isolation (Cameron, 1938; Goldman, 1960).

The second dimension is the development from lability to stability of concepts. In the young child concepts are typically labile (Pollack, 1953). The nature of the concept changes rapidly and in a seemingly capricious manner (Eng, 1931).

An example from performance on the Object Sorting Test (Rapaport, 1945) may serve to illustrate concept lability. The test consists of a number of everyday, common objects that are placed on a desk before the subject. The typical adult, when asked to place these objects into meaningful groups so that the objects within any one group belong together, will form objects into groups according to their color, or material, or perhaps their use. A subject may pick out all red objects and put them together, or all wooden objects, or all tools. Young children will frequently switch the

relationship in a very labile manner (Reichard, Schneider, & Rapaport, 1944). Thus, a young child will select first a red ball and then this is placed with a red plate, the two objects having redness in common. Then a toy knife is selected because it goes on the table, too, like the red plate, and then pliers are chosen because it is metal like the knife, and then a pipe because "the workman uses the pliers and smokes a pipe."

Similar chain concepts are developed by schizophrenics in the same task situations. The response of a young schizophrenic girl in a task involving a linear schematization technique may serve as an illustration of the extreme equivocality, or lability, of the relationship between the symbol and the meaning it symbolizes (Goldman, 1960). Linear schematization requires the subject to represent a word, in this case a mood term, by drawing a line. The subject is asked to draw an "angry" line, or a line that expresses the word "misery," and so on. This subject was asked to draw a line that represented the word "healthy." She drew a series of different lines. When asked what there was in the lines she drew that suggested health she responded: "A seven upside down, lightning going up, the medusa, and this is the medical sign of health." While the patient could not clarify the way in which all of these concepts are related to health, the response invites speculation about the way each thought was related to the one that preceded it. While the experiment was in progress she was drinking 7-Up and remarked that it was "good for you." Lightning going up may represent a denial of the destructive (i.e., unhealthy) effects of lightning. The medusa may be related to "the medical sign of health" (the caduceus) by clang association, or by the snakes which are common to both.

In the extreme case concept lability may be reflected in one word or symbol subsuming not only different concepts but opposite ones. This has been established in dreams (Jones, 1913), in archaic language (Freud, 1950), and also in schizophrenia (Goldman, 1960).

The equivocal nature of symbol meaning in childhood and in schizophrenia appears to be determined by the close bond between the symbol and some particular situation, event, or person with which it is associated. This is the third dimension —the development from contextualization to autonomy of a concept. Concepts in childhood are determined by personally relevant experience (Binet, 1916; Chodorkoff, 1952; Feifel, 1949; Hayakawa, 1954; Kasanin, 1944; Terman, 1916). A newspaper, for example, may be defined as "what the paper boy brings and you wrap the garbage with it" (Hayakawa, 1954, p. 80). With growth these concepts become increasingly independent or autonomous of these personally meaningful contexts (Werner, 1940; Werner & Kaplan, 1950, 1952).

In schizophrenia we expect the reverse of this development; concepts should become increasingly less autonomous and more contextualized. There is extensive evidence — clinical and experimental (Arieti, 1948; Baker, 1953; Cameron, 1938; Goldman, 1960; Kasanin, 1944) that this is so. The vocabulary test performances lend further credence to the statement that in comparison to normals, schizophrenics tend to use words in terms of their concrete functions rather than in terms of abstract autonomous properties (Chodorkoff, 1952; Feifel, 1949; Harrington, 1954; Yacorzyncki, 1941).

This regression may be illustrated by referring again to linear schematization. A group of schizophrenics were asked to represent the meaning of a word in a line. Then inquiry was made into the relationship between the line and the word it expressed. Typically, the line was justified in terms of some personally relevant experience. For example, the word "gentle" was represented by a patient as a hay stack when she replied to the inquiry with "lying in the hay is gentle." Another patient drew two lines which she said represented the path taken by the hand of a mother "gently" caressing a child. Still a third patient represented the word "gentle" with a leaf, which "is 'gently' blowing in the breeze." Gentleness in all of these cases is represented by unique personal experiences and associations. Similarly, in the Object Sorting Test, schizophrenics are more inclined than normals, to relate objects in a highly personal manner — "All of these things were in my mother's house" or "I think they are all pretty."

Thus, three dimensions of concepts are suggested. Underlying the first, idiosyncrasy-consensuality, is the increasing stability of concepts. A concept must be stable in reference before it can be public, or consensual. Underlying, in turn, the second dimension, is the contextuality-autonomy dimension. If a concept has meaning only in terms of personal contexts, its reference will be as labile as one's personal experiences, and therefore not available for use as a vehicle for social interaction.

The second and third dimensions both reflect the developmental progress from globality to differentiation, and its dedifferentiation in psychopathological regression. To the extent that a concept is labile, or in the extreme, in that it encompasses opposite meanings, it is undifferentiated. In schizophrenia the vehicles of thinking and communication become progressively dedifferentiated in that they, the symbol and referent, are not related in a stable manner. With regard to contextualization it may be said that the more autonomous a meaning, the more it is differentiated from a particular context. Thus, in development there is progressive meaning-context differentiation, while in schizophrenia meaning and context are dedifferentiated.

Normal subjects more frequently reflect less situational meanings and attempt to represent some essential quality of gentleness. The word "gentle" is typically symbolized by normals by a light curved line, expressing the "soft," "light" aspects of "gentle." The autonomous meaning of a word is essential in that it abstracts from each of the many situations with which it is associated (lying in hay, mother caressing child, etc.), a commonity that each shares. The essential meaning of a concept is abstracted from but is relatively autonomous of concrete contexts.

SOCIALIZATION

In the development of social behavior we again see the increasing differentiation out of the state of globality which terminates in integration. We have little reason to believe that in the neonate the self is distinguished from others. According to psychoanalytic theorists the mother, her breast, her voice, the warmth of her body, the sensations from within the infant's own body, are an indistinguishable whole. With development, there is an increasing awareness of the self as an entity.

The development in social integration is seen in patterns of play (Buehler, 1935; Loomis, 1931). At first, young children play in isolation with their hands, feet, or other objects. Later, children prefer to play in the presence of other children — not *with* other children, but in "parallel" play. Differentiation has taken place, with this first step toward integration and will eventually lead to genuine interpersonal interaction.

This development toward social integration is also seen in the increasing complexity of the social groups, and in their increasing stability (Zaluzhni, 1930).

In schizophrenia we find similar processes, except in reverse. On the ward we can see interaction representing all of these phases. The suspicious, hostile paranoid that still seeks social interaction; the hallucinating, babbling chronic schizophrenic that somehow still prefers to hallucinate and babble in the presence of others, although not with or in concert with others; and finally, the totally regressed isolate who withdraws into the social vacuum of a corner of the ward and devotes himself to his own bodily sensations.

MOTOR FUNCTIONS

One of the most striking developments to take place in the motor sphere is the increase in the implicitness of motor activity. Vicarious movements replace overt activity in reasoning, problem solving is less vocal and more silent, motion in general is less gross.

Relative to the massive debilitation in other spheres there is relatively little motor involvement in schizophrenia. It is only in the most severe regression that motor impairment is found, such as in catatonic *cerea flexibilitas,* and in the hyperactivity and restlessness that sometimes characterizes the acute stage of schizophrenia. In chronic schizophrenia, too, there is frequently evidence of incessant repetitive movements of head, trunk, or limbs.

The fact that there is little motor involvement in schizophrenia, except in severe cases, is consistent with Hughlings Jackson's principle that those functions which are the latest to develop are the first to be impaired in pathology. Since motor functions are amongst the first to develop in infancy, we would therefore expect impairment in this sphere to develop last.

There are other dimensions that have not been considered. In each of those that have been discussed focus has been on structural similarities between young children and schizophrenic functioning. Such similarities in process are also distinguishable in primitive cultures and in states of lowered consciousness, such as dreams, drug states, and hypnogogic conditions.

A comparative-genetic approach is fruitful in our effort to understand the essential nature of schizophrenia because it seeks to expose process rather than assess achievement and it is an approach in which structure is no less important than content and function.

Although a structural point of view has been central in the systems of some theorists for some time (Arieti, 1957; Munroe, 1955; Rapaport, 1951a, 1951b), psychoanalytic orthodoxy has not given sufficient attention to structural elements until recently. Having concerned itself in its early development predominantly with primary process, psychoanalysis is now turning increasingly more to a consideration of secondary process. Merton Gill (1959) has formalized this emphasis of the structural point of view in psychoanalysis.

This more energetic phychoanalytic consideration of ego functions, and the theoretical approach that has been offered in this paper have a similar goal — the formulation of a comprehensive theory of human behavior. Such genetic approaches remind us that in our consideration of the schizophrenic, oral deprivation is a no more significant datum than is the inability to conceive of square things in terms of their squareness.

REFERENCES

ARIETI, S. Special logic of schizophrenia and other types of autistic thought. *Psychiatry,* 1948, **11**, 325–338.

ARIETI, S. *Interpretation of schizophrenia.* New York: Robert Brunner, 1955.

ARIETI, S. The two aspects of schizophrenia. *Psychiat. Quart.,* 1957, **31**, 403–416.

BAKER, R. W. The acquisition of verbal concepts in schizophrenia: A developmental approach to the study of disturbed language behavior. Unpublished doctoral dissertation, Clark University, 1953.

BAYLEY, NANCY. A study of the crying of infants during mental and physical tests. *J. genet. Psychol.,* 1932, **40**, 306–329.

BINET, A., & SIMON, T. *The development of intelligence in children.* Vineland, New Jersey: Training School, 1916.

BRIDGES, K. Emotional development in early childhood. *Child Develpm.,* 1932, **3**, 324–334.

BUEHLER, CHARLOTTE. *From birth to maturity.* London: Kegan Paul, 1935.

CAMERON, N. S. Reasoning, regression and communication in schizophrenics. *Psychol. Monogr.,* 1938, **50**(1, Whole No. 221).

CAMERON, N. S. Schizophrenic thinking in a problem-solving situation. *J. ment. Sci.,* 1939, **85**, 1–24.

CHODORKOFF, B., & MUSSEN, P. Qualitative aspects of the vocabulary responses of normals and schizophrenics. *J. consult. Psychol.,* 1952, **16**, 43–48.

ENG, H. *The psychology of children's drawings.* London: Kegan Paul, 1931.

FEIFEL, H. Qualitative differences in the vocabulary responses of normals and abnormals. *Genet. psychol. Monogr.,* 1949, **39**, 151–204.

FREUD, S. The antithetical sense of primal words. In E. Jones (Ed.), *Collected papers.* Vol. 4. London: Hogarth, 1950.

FRIEDMAN, H. Perceptual regression in schizophrenia: An hypothesis suggested by the use of the Rorschach test. *J. proj. Tech.,* 1953, **17**, 171–185.

GARMEZY, N. Stimulus differentiation by schizophrenic and normal subjects under conditions of reward and punishment. *J. Pers.,* 1952, **20**, 253–267.

GESELL, A. The conditioned reflex and the psychiatry of infancy. *Amer. J. Orthopsychiat.*, 1938, 8, 19–30.

GILL, M. The present state of psychoanalytic theory. *J. abnorm. soc. Psychol.*, 1959, **58**, 1–9.

GOLDMAN, A. Symbolic representation in schizophrenia. *J. Pers.*, 1960, **28**, 293–316.

GOLDMAN, A. Classification of sign phenomena. *Psychiatry*, in press.

GOLDMAN, A., & DENNY, J. Ontogenesis of choice behavior in stochastic and recursive programs. *J. genet. Psychol.*, in press.

GOLDSTEIN, K. *The organism.* New York: American Book, 1939.

HANFMANN, E. Thought disturbance in schizophrenia as revealed by performance in a picture completion test. *J. abnorm. soc. Psychol.*, 1939, **34**, 249–264.

HANFMANN, E., & KASANIN, J. Conceptual thinking in schizophrenia. *Nerv. ment. Dis. Mongr.*, 1942, No. 67.

HARRINGTON, R., & EHRMANN, J. Complexity of response as a factor in the vocabulary performance of schizophrenics. *J. abnorm. soc. Psychol.*, 1954, **49**, 362.

HAYAKAWA, S. I. *Language in action.* New York: Harcourt, Brace, 1954.

HEMMENDINGER, L. Perceptual organization and development as reflected in the structure of the Rorschach test response. *J. proj. Tech.*, 1953, **17**, 162–170.

HOWE, E. S. GSR conditioning in anxiety states, normals, and chronic functional schizophrenic subjects. *J. abnorm. soc. Psychol.*, 1958, **56,**, 183–189.

JERSILD, A. T. *Child psychology.* New York: Prentice-Hall, 1939.

JONES, E. *Papers on psychoanalysis.* London: Bailliere, 1913.

JONES, H. E. Conditioned psychogalvanic responses in infants. *Psychol. Bull.*, 1928, **25**, 183–184.

JONES, H. E. The galvanic skin reflex in infancy. *Child Develpm.*, 1930, **1**, 106–110.

JONES, H. E. The retention of conditioned emotional responses in infancy. *J. genet. Psychol.*, 1930, **37**, 485–498.

KASANIN, J. S. *The disturbance of conceptual thinking in schizophrenia.* Berkeley: Univer. California Press, 1944.

KASATKIN, N. I., & LEVIKOVA, A. M. On the development of early conditioned reflexes and differentiation of auditory stimuli in infants. *J. exp. Psychol.*, 1935, **18**, 1–19.

LEUBA, C. Images as conditioned sensations. *J. exp. Psychol.*, 1940, **26**, 345–351.

LEUBA, C. The use of hypnosis for controlling variables in psychological experiments. *J. abnorm. soc. Psychol.*, 1941, **36**, 271–274.

LOOMIS, A. M. A technique of observing the social behavior of nursery school children. *Child develpm. Monogr.*, 1931, No. 5.

MATEER, F. *Child behavior.* Boston: Badger, 1918.

MAYS, L. L. Studies of catatonia: V. Investigation of the perseverational tendency. *Psychiat. Quart.*, 1934, 8, 728.

MEDNICK, S. A. Distortions in the gradient of stimulus generalization related to cortical brain damage and schizophrenia. *J. abnorm. soc. Psychol.*, 1955, **51**, 536–542.

MEDNICK, S. A. A learning theory approach to research in schizophrenia. *Psychol. Bull.*, 1958, **55**, 316–327.

MEDNICK, S. A., & LEHTINEN, L. F. Stimulus generalization as a function of age in children. *J. exp. Psychol.*, 1957, **53**, 180–183.

MUNROE, RUTH. *Schools of psychoanalytic thought.* New York: Dryden, 1955.

PAINTAL, A. S. A comparison of the GSR in normals and psychotics. *J. exp. Psychol.*, 1951, **41**, 425–428.

PFAFFMAN, C., & SCHLOSBERG, H. The conditioned knee jerk in psychotic and normal individuals. *J. Psychol.*, 1936, **1**, 201–206.

POLLACK, R. H. A genetic study of intuitive word meanings. Unpublished doctoral dissertation, Clark University, 1953.

RAPAPORT, D. The conceptual model of psychoanalyses. *J. Pers.*, 1951, **20**, 56–81. (a)

RAPAPORT, D. *Organization and pathology of thought.* New York: Columbia Univer. Press, 1951. (b)

RAPAPORT, D., GILL, M., & SHAFER, R. *Diagnostic psychological testing.* Vol. 1. Chicago: Year Book, 1945.

RAZRAN, G. Conditioned responses in children. *Arch. Psychol.*, NY, 1933, No. 148.

RAZRAN, G. Conditioned responses: An experimental study and a theoretical analysis. *Arch. Psychol.*, NY, 1935, No. 191.

REICHARD, SUZANNE, SCHNEIDER, MARION, & RAPAPORT, D. The development of concept formation in children. *Amer. J. Orthopsychiat.*, 1944, **14**, 156–161.

REISS, B. F. Genetic changes in semantic conditioning. *J. exp. Psychol.*, 1946, **36**, 143–152.

SCOTT, H. D. Hypnosis and the conditioned reflex. *J. gen. Psychol.*, 1930, **4**, 113–130.

SHIPLEY, W. C. Studies of catatonia: VI. Further investigation of the perseverative tendency. *Psychiat. Quart.*, 1934, 8, 736–744.

SIEGEL, E. L. Genetic parallels of perceptual structuralization in paranoid schizophrenia: An analysis by means of the Rorschach test. *J. proj. Tech.*, 1953, **17**, 151–161.

SPENCE, K. W., & TAYLOR, J. A. The relation of conditional response strength to anxiety in normal, neurotic, and psychotic subjects. *J. exp. Psychol.*, 1953, **45**, 265–277.

TAYLOR, J. A., & SPENCE, K. W. Conditioning level in the behavior disorders. *J. abnorm. soc. Psychol.*, 1954, **49**, 497–503.

TERMAN, L. M. *The measurement of intelligence.* Boston: Houghton Mifflin, 1916.

WERNER, H. *Comparative psychology of mental development.* New York: Harper, 1940.

WERNER, H. Genetic experimental psychology. In P. L. Harriman (Ed.), *Encyclopedia of psychology.* New York: Philosophical Library, 1946.

WERNER, H., & KAPLAN, B. The developmental approach to cognition: Its relevance to the psychological interpretation of anthropological and ethnolinguistic data. *Amer. Anthropologist,* 1956, **58**, 866–880.

WERNER, H., & KAPLAN, EDITH. Development of word meaning through verbal context: An experimental study. *J. Psychol.,* 1950, **29**, 251–257.

WERNER, H., & KAPLAN, EDITH. *The acquisition of word meanings: A developmental study.* Evanston, Ill.: Child Development, 1952.

WOLFF, W. *The expression of personality.* New York: Harper, 1943.

YACORZYNSKI, G. K. An evaluation of the postulates underlying the Babcock Deterioration Test. *Psychol. Rev.,* 1941, **48**, 261–267.

ZALUZHNI, A. S. Collective behavior of children at preschool age. *J. soc. Psychol.,* 1930, **1**, 367–378.

GREGORY BATESON, DON D. JACKSON, JAY HALEY, AND JOHN WEAKLAND

Toward a Theory of Schizophrenia*

Schizophrenia — its nature, etiology, and the kind of therapy to use for it — remains one of the most puzzling of the mental illnesses. The theory of schizophrenia presented here is based on communications analysis, and specifically on the Theory of Logical Types. From this theory and from observations of schizophrenic patients is derived a description, and the necessary conditions for, a situation called the "double bind" — a situation in which no matter what a person does, he "can't win." It is hypothesized that a person caught in the double bind may develop schizophrenic symptoms. How and why the double bind may arise in a family situation is discussed, together with illustrations from clinical and experimental data.

This is a report[1] on a research project which has been formulating and testing a broad, systematic view of the nature, etiology, and therapy of schizophrenia. Our research in this field has proceeded by discussion of a varied body of data and ideas, with all of us contributing according to our varied experience in anthropology, communications analysis, psychotherapy, psychiatry, and psychoanalysis. We have now reached common agreement on the broad outlines of a communicational theory of the origin and nature of schizophrenia; this paper is a preliminary report on our continuing research.

THE BASE IN COMMUNICATIONS THEORY

Our approach is based on that part of communications theory which Russell has called the Theory of Logical Types (17). The central thesis of this

* Reprinted by permission from *Behavioral Science,* Vol. 1, 1956, pp. 251–264.

[1] This paper derives from hypotheses first developed in a research project financed by the Rockefeller Foundation from 1952–54, administered by the Department of Sociology and Anthropology at Stanford University and directed by Gregory Bateson. Since 1954 the project has continued, financed by the Josiah Macy, Jr. Foundation. To Jay Haley is due credit for recognizing that the symptoms of schizophrenia are suggestive of an inability to discriminate the Logical Types, and this was amplified by Bateson who added the notion that the symptoms and etiology could be formally described in terms of a double bind hypothesis. The hypothesis was communicated to D. D. Jackson and found to fit closely with his ideas of family homeostasis. Since then Dr. Jackson has worked closely with the project. The study of the formal analogies between hypnosis and schizophrenia has been the work of John H. Weakland and Jay Haley.

theory is that there is a discontinuity between a class and its members. The class cannot be a member of itself nor can one of the members *be* the class, since the term used for the class is of a *different level of abstraction* — a different Logical Type — from terms used for members. Although in formal logic there is an attempt to maintain this discontinuity between a class and its members, we argue that in the psychology of real communications this discontinuity is continually and inevitably breached (2), and that a priori we must expect a pathology to occur in the human organism when certain formal patterns of the breaching occur in the communication between mother and child. We shall argue that this pathology at its extreme will have symptoms whose formal characteristics would lead the pathology to be classified as a schizophrenia.

Illustrations of how human beings handle communication involving multiple Logical Types can be derived from the following fields:

1. *The use of various communicational modes in human communication.* Examples are play, nonplay, fantasy, sacrament, metaphor, etc. Even among the lower mammals there appears to be an exchange of signals which identify certain meaningful behavior as "play," etc.[2] These signals are evidently of higher Logical Type than the messages they classify. Among human beings this framing and labeling of messages and meaningful actions reaches considerable complexity, with the peculiarity that our vocabulary for such discrimination is still very poorly developed, and we rely preponderantly upon nonverbal media of posture, gesture, facial expression, intonation, and the context for the communication of these highly abstract, but vitally important, labels.

2. *Humor.* This seems to be a method of exploring the implicit themes in thought or in a relationship. The method of exploration involves the use of messages which are characterized by a condensation of Logical Types or communicational modes. A discovery, for example, occurs when it suddenly becomes plain that a message was not only metaphoric but also more literal, or vice versa. That is to say, the explosive moment in humor is the moment when the labeling of the mode undergoes a dissolution and resynthesis. Commonly, the punch line compels a re-evaluation of earlier signals which ascribed to certain messages a particular mode (e.g.,

literalness or fantasy). This has the peculiar effect of attributing *mode* to those signals which had previously the status of that higher Logical Type which classifies the modes.

3. *The falsification of mode-identifying signals.* Among human beings mode identifiers can be falsified, and we have the artificial laugh, the manipulative simulation of friendliness, the confidence trick, kidding, and the like. Similar falsifications have been recorded among mammals (3, 13). Among human beings we meet with a strange phenomenon — the unconscious falsification of these signals. This may occur within the self — the subject may conceal from himself his own real hostility under the guise of metaphoric play — or it may occur as an unconscious falsification of the subject's understanding of the other person's mode-identifying signals. He may mistake shyness for contempt, etc. Indeed most of the errors of self-reference fall under this head.

4. *Learning.* The simplest level of this phenomenon is exemplified by a situation in which a subject receives a message and acts appropriately on it: "I heard the clock strike and knew it was time for lunch. So I went to the table." In learning experiments the analogue of this sequence of events is observed by the experimenter and commonly treated as a single message of a higher type. When the dog salivates between buzzer and meat powder, this sequence is accepted by the experimenter as a message indicating that "the dog has *learned* that buzzer means meat powder." But this is not the end of the hierarchy of types involved. The experimental subject may become more skilled in learning. He may *learn to learn* (1, 7, 9), and it is not inconceivable that still higher orders of learning may occur in human beings.

5. *Multiple levels of learning and the Logical Typing of signals.* These are two inseparable sets of phenomena — inseparable because the ability to handle the multiple types of signals is itself a *learned* skill and therefore a function of the multiple levels of learning.

According to our hypothesis, the term "ego function" (as this term is used when a schizophrenic is described as having "weak ego function") is precisely *the process of discriminating communicational modes either within the self or between the self and others.* The schizophrenic exhibits weakness in three areas of such function: (*a*) He has difficulty in assigning the correct communicational mode to the messages he receives from other persons. (*b*) He has difficulty in assigning the correct communi-

---

[2] A film prepared by this project, "The Nature of Play; Part I, River Otters," is available.

cational mode to those messages which he himself utters or emits nonverbally. (*c*) He has difficulty in assigning the correct communicational mode to his own thoughts, sensations and percepts.

At this point it is appropriate to compare what was said in the previous paragraph with von Domarus' (16) approach to the systematic description of schizophrenic utterance. He suggests that the messages (and thought) of the schizophrenic are deviant in syllogistic structure. In place of structures which derive from the syllogism, Barbara, the schizophrenic, according to this theory, uses structures which identify predicates. An example of such a distorted syllogism is:

> Men die.
> Grass dies.
> Men are grass.

But as we see it, Von Domarus' formulation is only a more precise — and therefore valuable — way of saying that schizophrenic utterance is rich in metaphor. With that generalization we agree. But metaphor is an indispensable tool of thought and expression — a characteristic of all human communication, even of that of the scientist. The conceptual models of cybernetics and the energy theories of psychoanalysis are, after all, only labeled metaphors. The peculiarity of the schizophrenic is not that he uses metaphors, but that he uses *unlabeled* metaphors. He has special difficulty in handling signals of that class whose members assign Logical Types to other signals.

If our formal summary of the symptomatology is correct and if the schizophrenia of our hypothesis is essentially a result of family interaction, it should be possible to arrive a priori at a formal description of these sequences of experience which would induce such a symptomatology. What is known of learning theory combines with the evident fact that human beings use *context* as a guide for mode discrimination. Therefore, we must look not for some specific traumatic experience in the infantile etiology but rather for characteristic sequential patterns. The specificity for which we search is to be at an abstract or formal level. The sequences must have this characteristic: that from them the patient will acquire the mental habits which are exemplified in schizophrenic communication. That is to say, *he must live in a universe where the sequences of events are such that his unconventional communicational habits will be in some sense appropriate.* The hypothesis which we offer is that sequences of this kind in the external experience of the patient are re-

sponsible for the inner conflicts of Logical Typing. For such unresolvable sequences of experiences, we use the term "double bind."

The Double Bind

The necessary ingredients for a double bind situation, as we see it, are:

1. *Two or more persons.* Of these, we designate one, for purposes of our definition, as the "victim." We do not assume that the double bind is inflicted by the mother alone, but that it may be done either by mother alone or by some combination of mother, father, and/or siblings.

2. *Repeated experience.* We assume that the double bind is a recurrent theme in the experience of the victim. Our hypothesis does not invoke a single traumatic experience, but such repeated experience that the double bind structure comes to be an habitual expectation.

3. A *primary negative injunction.* This may have either of two forms: (*a*) "Do not do so and so, or I will punish you," or (*b*) "If you do not do so and so, I will punish you." Here we select a context of learning based on avoidance of punishment rather than a context of reward seeking. There is perhaps no formal reason for this selection. We assume that the punishment may be either the withdrawal of love or the expression of hate or anger — or most devastating — the kind of abandonment that results from the parent's expression of extreme helplessness.[3]

4. A *secondary injunction conflicting with the first at a more abstract level, and like the first enforced by punishments or signals which threaten survival.* This secondary injunction is more difficult to describe than the primary for two reasons. First, the secondary injunction is commonly communicated to the child by nonverbal means. Posture, gesture, tone of voice, meaningful action, and the implications concealed in verbal comment may all be used to convey this more abstract message. Second, the secondary injunction may impinge upon any element of the primary prohibition. Verbalization of the secondary injunction, may, therefore, include a wide variety of forms; for example, "Do not see this as punishment"; "Do not see me as the punishing agent"; Do not submit to my prohibitions"; "Do not think of what you must not do"; "Do not question my love of which the primary prohibition is (or is not) an example"; and

---

[3] Our concept of punishment is being refined at present. It appears to us to involve perceptual experience in a way that cannot be encompassed by the notion of "trauma."

so on. Other examples become possible when the double bind is inflicted not by one individual but by two. For example, one parent may negate at a more abstract level the injunctions of the other.

5. *A tertiary negative injunction prohibiting the victim from escaping from the field.* In a formal sense it is perhaps unnecessary to list this injunction as a separate item since the reinforcement at the other two levels involves a threat to survival, and if the double binds are imposed during infancy, escape is naturally impossible. However, it seems that in some cases the escape from the field is made impossible by certain devices which are not purely negative, e.g., capricious promises of love, and the like.

6. Finally, the complete set of ingredients is no longer necessary when the victim has learned to perceive his universe in double bind patterns. Almost any part of a double bind sequence may then be sufficient to precipitate panic or rage. The pattern of conflicting injunctions may even be taken over by hallucinatory voices (14).

The Effect of the Double Bind

In the Eastern religion, Zen Buddhism, the goal is to achieve Enlightenment. The Zen Master attempts to bring about enlightenment in his pupil in various ways. One of the things he does is to hold a stick over the pupil's head and say fiercely, "If you say this stick is real, I will strike you with it. If you say this stick is not real, I will strike you with it. If you don't say anything, I will strike you with it." We feel that the schizophrenic finds himself continually in the same situation as the pupil, but he achieves something like disorientation rather than enlightenment. The Zen pupil might reach up and take the stick away from the Master — who might accept this response, but the schizophrenic has no such choice since with him there is no not caring about the relationship, and his mother's aims and awareness are not like the Master's.

We hypothesize that there will be a breakdown in any individual's ability to discriminate between Logical Types whenever a double bind situation occurs. The general characteristics of this situation are the following:

1. When the individual is involved in an intense relationship; that is, a relationship in which he feels it is vitally important that he discriminate accurately what sort of message is being communicated so that he may respond appropriately.

2. And, the individual is caught in a situation in which the other person in the relationship is expressing two orders of message and one of these denies the other.

3. And, the individual is unable to comment on the messages being expressed to correct his discrimination of what order of message to respond to, i.e., he cannot make a metacommunicative statement.

We have suggested that this is the sort of situation which occurs between the pre-schizophrenic and his mother, but it also occurs in normal relationships. When a person is caught in a double bind situation, he will respond defensively in a manner similar to the schizophrenic. An individual will take a metaphorical statement literally when he is in a situation where he must respond, where he is faced with contradictory messages, and when he is unable to comment on the contradictions. For example, one day an employee went home during office hours. A fellow employee called him at his home, and said lightly, "Well, how did you get *there*?" The employee replied, "By automobile." He responded literally because he was faced with a message which asked him what he was doing at home when he should have been at the office, but which denied that this question was being asked by the way it was phrased. (Since the speaker felt it wasn't really his business, he spoke metaphorically.) The relationship was intense enough so that the victim was in doubt how the information would be used, and he therefore responded literally. This is characteristic of anyone who feels "on the spot," as demonstrated by the careful literal replies of a witness on the stand in a court trial. The schizophrenic feels so terribly on the spot at all times that he habitually responds with a defensive insistence on the literal level when it is quite inappropriate, e.g., when someone is joking.

Schizophrenics also confuse the literal and metaphoric in their own utterance when they feel themselves caught in a double bind. For example, a patient may wish to criticize his therapist for being late for an appointment, but he may be unsure what sort of a message that act of being late was — particularly if the therapist has anticipated the patient's reaction and apologized for the event. The patient cannot say, "Why were you late? Is it because you don't want to see me today?" This would be an accusation, and so he shifts to a metaphorical statement. He may then say, "I knew a fellow once who missed a boat, his name was Sam and the boat almost sunk, . . . etc.," Thus he develops a metaphorical story and the therapist may or may not discover in it a comment on his being late. The convenient thing about a metaphor is that it leaves it up to the therapist (or mother) to see an accusation in the statement if he chooses, or to ignore it if he chooses. Should the therapist accept the accusation in the metaphor, then the patient can accept the statement he has made about Sam as metaphorical. If the therapist points out that this doesn't sound like a true statement about Sam, as a way of avoiding the accusation in the story, the patient can argue that there really was a man named Sam. As an answer to the double bind situation, a shift to a metaphorical statement brings safety. However, it also prevents the patient from making the accusation he wants to make. But instead of getting over his accusation by indicating that this is a metaphor, the schizophrenic patient seems to try to get over the fact that it is a metaphor by making it more fantastic. If the therapist should ignore the accusation in the story about Sam, the schizophrenic may then tell a story about going to Mars in a rocket ship as a way of putting over his accusation. The indication that it is a metaphorical statement lies in the fantastic aspect of the metaphor, not in the signals which usually accompany metaphors to tell the listener that a metaphor is being used.

It is not only safer for the victim of a double bind to shift to a metaphorical order of message, but in an impossible situation it is better to shift and become somebody else, or shift and insist that he is somewhere else. Then the double bind cannot work on the victim, because it isn't he and besides he is in a different place. In other words, the statements which show that a patient is disoriented can be interpreted as ways of defending himself against the situation he is in. The pathology enters when the victim himself either does not know that his responses are metaphorical or cannot say so. To recognize that he was speaking metaphorically he would need to be aware that he was defending himself and therefore was afraid of the other person. To him such an awareness would be an indictment of the other person and therefore provoke disaster.

If an individual has spent his life in the kind of double bind relationship described here, his way of relating to people after a psychotic break would have a systematic pattern. First, he would not share with normal people those signals which accompany messages to indicate what a person means. His metacommunicative system — the communications about communication — would have broken down, and he would not know what kind of message a message was. If a person said to him, "what would you like to do today?" he would be unable to judge accurately by the context or by the tone of voice or gesture whether he was being condemned for what he did yesterday, or being offered a sexual invitation, or just what was meant. Given this inability to judge accurately what a person really means and an excessive concern with what is really meant, an individual might defend himself by choosing one or more of several alternatives. He might, for example, assume that behind every statement there is a concealed meaning which is detrimental to his welfare. He would then be excessively concerned with hidden meanings and determined to demonstrate that he could not be deceived — as he had been all his life. If he chooses this alternative, he will be continually searching for meanings behind what people say and behind chance occurrences in the environment, and he will be characteristically suspicious and defiant.

He might choose another alternative, and tend to accept literally everything people say to him; when their tone or gesture or context contradicted what they said, he might establish a pattern of laughing off these metacommunicative signals. He would give up trying to discriminate between levels of message and treat all messages as unimportant or to be laughed at.

If he didn't become suspicious of metacommunicative messages or attempt to laugh them off, he might choose to try to ignore them. Then he would find it necessary to see and hear less and less of what went on around him, and do his utmost to avoid provoking a response in his environment. He would try to detach his interest from the external world and concentrate on his own internal processes and, therefore, give the appearance of being a withdrawn, perhaps mute, individual.

This is another way of saying that if an individual doesn't know what sort of message a message is, he may defend himself in ways which have been described as paranoid, hebephrenic, or catatonic. These three alternatives are not the only ones. The point is that he cannot choose the one alternative which would help him to discover what people mean; he cannot, without considerable help, discuss the messages of others. Without being able to do that, the human being is like any self-correcting system which has lost its governor; it spirals into never-ending, but always systematic, distortions.

A DESCRIPTION OF THE FAMILY SITUATION

The theoretical possibility of double bind situations stimulated us to look for such communication sequences in the schizophrenic patient and in his family situation. Toward this end we have studied the written and verbal reports of psychotherapists who have treated such patients intensively; we have studied tape recordings of psychotherapeutic interviews, both of our own patients and others; we have interviewed and taped parents of schizophrenics; we have had two mothers and one father participate in intensive psychotherapy; and we have interviewed and taped parents and patients seen conjointly.

On the basis of these data we have developed a hypothesis about the family situation which ultimately leads to an individual suffering from schizophrenia. This hypothesis has not been statistically tested; it selects and emphasizes a rather simple set of interactional phenomena and does not attempt to describe comprehensively the extraordinary complexity of a family relationship.

We hypothesize that the family situation of the schizophrenic has the following general characteristics:

1. A child whose mother becomes anxious and withdraws if the child responds to her as a loving mother. That is, the child's very existence has a special meaning to the mother which arouses her anxiety and hostility when she is in danger of intimate contact with the child.

2. A mother to whom feelings of anxiety and hostility toward the child are not acceptable, and whose way of denying them is to express overt loving behavior to persuade the child to respond to her as a loving mother and to withdraw from him if he does not. "Loving behavior" does not necessarily imply "affection"; it can, for example, be set in a framework of doing the proper thing, instilling "goodness," and the like.

3. The absence of anyone in the family, such as a strong and insightful father, who can intervene in the relationship between the mother and child and support the child in the face of the contradictions involved.

Since this is a formal description we are not specifically concerned with why the mother feels this way about the child, but we suggest that she could feel this way for various reasons. It may be that merely having a child arouses anxiety about herself and her relationships to her own family; or it may be important to her that the child is a boy or a girl, or that the child was born on the anniversary of one of her own siblings (8), or the child may be in the same sibling position in the family that she was, or the child may be special to her for other reasons related to her own emotional problems.

Given a situation with these characteristics, we hypothesize that the mother of a schizophrenic will be simultaneously expressing at least two orders of message. (For simplicity in this presentation we shall confine ourselves to two orders.) These orders of message can be roughly characterized as (*a*) hostile or withdrawing behavior which is aroused whenever the child approaches her, and (*b*) simulated loving or approaching behavior which is aroused when the child responds to her hostile and withdrawing behavior, as a way of denying that she is withdrawing. Her problem is to control her anxiety by controlling the closeness and distance between herself and her child. To put this another way, if the mother begins to feel affectionate and close to her child, she begins to feel endangered and must withdraw from him; but she cannot accept this hostile act and to deny it must simulate affection and closeness with her child. The important point is that her loving behavior is then a comment on (since it is compensatory for) her hostile behavior and consequently it is of a different *order* of message than the hostile behavior — it is a message about a sequence of messages. Yet by its nature it denies the existence of those messages which it is about, i.e., the hostile withdrawal.

The mother uses the child's responses to affirm that her behavior is loving, and since the loving behavior is simulated, the child is placed in a position where he must not accurately interpret her communication if he is to maintain his relationship with her. In other words, he must not discriminate accurately between orders of message, in this case the difference between the expression of simulated feelings (one Logical Type) and real feelings (another Logical Type). As a result the child must systematically distort his perception of metacommunicative signals. For example, if mother begins to feel hostile (or affectionate) toward her child and also feels compelled to withdraw from him, she might say, "Go to bed, you're very tired and I want you to get your sleep." This overtly loving statement is intended to deny a feeling which could be verbalized as "Get out of my sight because I'm sick of you." If the child correctly discriminates her metacommunicative signals, he would have to face the fact that she both doesn't want him and is deceiving him by her loving behavior. He would be "punished" for learning to discriminate orders of messages accurately. He therefore would tend to accept the idea that he is tired rather than recognize his mother's deception. This means that he must deceive himself about his own internal state in order to support mother in her deception. To survive with her he must falsely discriminate his own internal messages as well as falsely discriminate the messages of others.

The problem is compounded for the child because the mother is "benevolently" defining for him how he feels; she is expressing overt maternal concern over the fact that he is tired. To put it another way, the mother is controlling the child's definitions of his own messages, as well as the definition of his responses to her (e.g., by saying, "You don't really mean to say that," if he should criticize her) by insisting that she is not concerned about herself but only about him. Consequently, the easiest path for the child is to accept mother's simulated loving behavior as real, and his desires to interpret what is going on are undermined. Yet the result is that the mother is withdrawing from him and defining this withdrawal as the way a loving relationship should be.

However, accepting mother's simulated loving behavior as real also is no solution for the child. Should he make this false discrimination, he would approach her; this move toward closeness would provoke in her feelings of fear and helplessness, and she would be compelled to withdraw. But if he then withdrew from her, she would take his withdrawal as a statement that she was not a loving mother and would either punish him for withdrawing or approach him to bring him closer. If he then approached, she would respond by putting him at a distance. *The child is punished for discriminating accurately what she is expressing, and he is punished for discriminating inaccurately — he is caught in a double bind.*

The child might try various means of escaping from this situation. He might, for example, try to lean on his father or some other member of the family. However, from our preliminary observations we think it is likely that the fathers of schizophrenics are not substantial enough to lean on. They are also in the awkward position where if they agreed with the child about the nature of mother's deceptions, they would need to recognize the nature of their own relationships to the mother, which they could not do and remain attached to her in the *modus operandi* they have worked out.

The need of the mother to be wanted and loved also prevents the child from gaining support from some other person in the environment, a teacher, for example. A mother with these characteristics would feel threatened by any other attachment of the child and would break it up and bring the child back closer to her with consequent anxiety when the child became dependent on her.

The only way the child can really escape from the situation is to comment on the contradictory position his mother has put him in. However, if he did so, the mother would take this as an accusation that she is unloving and both punish him and insist that his perception of the situation is distorted. By preventing the child from talking about the situation, the mother forbids him using the metacommunicative level — the level we use to correct our perception of communicative behavior. The ability to communicate about communication, to comment upon the meaningful actions of oneself and others, is essential for successful social intercourse. In any normal relationship there is a constant interchange of metacommunicative messages such as "What do you mean?" or "Why did you do that?" or "Are you kidding me?" and so on. To discriminate accurately what people are really expressing we must be able to comment directly or indirectly on that expression. This metacommunicative level the schizophrenic seems unable to use successfully (2). Given these characteristics of the mother, it is apparent why. If she is denying one order of message, then any statement about her statements endangers her and she must forbid it. Therefore, the child grows up unskilled in his ability to communicate about communication and, as a result, unskilled in determining what people really mean and unskilled in expressing what he really means, which is essential for normal relationships.

In summary, then, we suggest that the double bind nature of the family situation of a schizophrenic results in placing the child in a position where if he responds to his mother's simulated affection her anxiety will be aroused and she will punish him (or insist, to protect herself, that *his* overtures are simulated, thus confusing him about the nature of his own messages) to defend herself from closeness with him. Thus the child is blocked off from intimate and secure associations with his mother. However, if he does not make overtures of affection, she will feel that this means she is not a loving mother and her anxiety will be aroused. Therefore, she will either punish him for withdrawing or make overtures toward the child to insist that he demonstrate that he loves her. If he then responds and shows her affection, she will not only feel endangered again, but she may resent the fact that she had to force him to respond. In either case in a relationship, the most important in his life and the model for all others, he is punished if he indicates love and affection and punished if he does not; and his escape routes from the situation, such as gaining support from others, are cut off. This is the basic nature of the double bind relationship between mother and child. This description has not depicted, of course, the more complicated interlocking gestalt that is the "family" of which the "mother" is one important part (11, 12).

ILLUSTRATIONS FROM CLINICAL DATA

An analysis of an incident occurring between a schizophrenic patient and his mother illustrates the "double bind" situation. A young man who had fairly well recovered from an acute schizophrenic episode was visited in the hospital by his mother. He was glad to see her and impulsively put his arm around her shoulders, whereupon she stiffened. He withdrew his arm and she asked, "Don't you love me any more?" He then blushed, and she said, "Dear, you must not be so easily embarrassed and afraid of your feelings." The patient was able to stay with her only a few minutes more and following her departure he assaulted an aide and was put in the tubs.

Obviously, this result could have been avoided if the young man had been able to say, "Mother, it is obvious that you become uncomfortable when I put my arm around you, and that you have difficulty accepting a gesture of affection from me." However, the schizophrenic patient doesn't have this possibility open to him. His intense dependency and training prevents him from commenting upon his mother's communicative behavior, though she comments on his and forces him to accept and to attempt to deal with the complicated sequence. The complications for the patient include the following:

1. The mother's reaction of not accepting her son's affectionate gesture is masterfully covered up by her condemnation of him for withdrawing, and the patient denies his perception of the situation by accepting her condemnation.

2. The statement "don't you love me any more" in this context seems to imply:

(a) "I am lovable."

(b) "You should love me and if you don't you are bad or at fault."

(c) "Whereas you did love me previously you don't any longer," and thus focus is shifted from his expressing affection to his inability to be affectionate. Since the patient has also hated her, she is on good ground here, and he responds appropriately with guilt, which she then attacks.

(d) "What you just expressed *was not* affection," and in order to accept this statement the patient must deny what she and the culture have taught him about how one expresses affection. He must also question the times with her, and with others, when he thought he was experiencing affection and

when they *seemed* to treat the situation as if he had. He experiences here loss-of-support phenomena and is put in doubt about the reliability of past experience.

3. The statement, "You must not be so easily embarrassed and afraid of your feelings," seems to imply;

(a) "You are not like me and are different from other nice or normal people because we express our feelings."

(b) "The feelings you express are all right, it's only that *you* can't accept them." However, if the stiffening on her part had indicated "these are unacceptable feelings," then the boy is told that he should not be embarrassed by unacceptable feelings. Since he has had a long training in what is and is not acceptable to both her and society, he again comes into conflict with the past. If he is unafraid of his own feelings (which mother implies is good), he should be unafraid of his affection and would then notice it was she who was afraid, but he must not notice that because her whole approach is aimed at covering up this shortcoming in herself.

The impossible dilemma thus becomes: "If I am to keep my tie to mother I must not show her that I love her, but if I do not show her that I love her, then I will lose her."

The importance to the mother of her special method of control is strikingly illustrated by the interfamily situation of a young woman schizophrenic who greeted the therapist on their first meeting with the remark, "Mother had to get married and now I'm here." This statement meant to the therapist that:

1. The patient was the result of an illegitimate pregnancy.

2. This fact was related to her present psychosis (in her opinion).

3. "Here" referred to the psychiatrist's office and to the patient's presence on earth for which she had to be eternally indebted to her mother, especially since her mother had sinned and suffered in order to bring her into the world.

4. "Had to get married" referred to the shot-gun nature of mother's wedding and to the mother's response to pressure that she must marry, and the reciprocal, that she resented the forced nature of the situation and blamed the patient for it.

Actually, all these suppositions subsequently proved to be factually correct and were corroborated by the mother during an abortive attempt at psychotherapy. The flavor of the mother's communications to the patient seemed essentially this: "I am lovable, loving, and satisfied with myself. You are lovable when you are like me and when you do what I say." At the same time the mother indicated to the daughter both by words and behavior: "You are physically delicate, unintelligent, and different from me ('not normal'). You need me and me alone because of these handicaps, and I will take care of you and love you." Thus the patient's life was a series of beginnings, of attempts at experience, which would result in failure and withdrawal back to the maternal hearth and bosom because of the collusion between her and her mother.

It was noted in collaborative therapy that certain areas important to the mother's self-esteem were especially conflictual situations for the patient. For example, the mother needed the fiction that she was close to her family and that a deep love existed between her and her own mother. By analogy the relationship to the grandmother served as the prototype for the mother's relationship to her own daughter. On one occasion when the daughter was seven or eight years old the grandmother in a rage threw a knife which barely missed the little girl. The mother said nothing to the grandmother but hurried the little girl from the room with the words, "Grandmommy really loves you." It is significant that the grandmother took the attitude toward the patient that she was not well enough controlled, and she used to chide her daughter for being too easy on the child. The grandmother was living in the house during one of the patient's psychotic episodes, and the girl took great delight in throwing various objects at the mother and grandmother while they cowered in fear.

Mother felt herself very attractive as a girl, and she felt that her daughter resembled her rather closely, although by damning with faint praise it was obvious that she felt the daughter definitely ran second. One of the daughter's first acts during a psychotic period was to announce to her mother that she was going to cut off all her hair. She proceeded to do this while the mother pleaded with her to stop. Subsequently the mother would show a picture of *herself* as a girl and explain to people how the patient would look if she only had her beautiful hair.

The mother, apparently without awareness of the significance of what she was doing, would equate the daughter's illness with not being very bright and with some sort of organic brain difficulty. She would invariably contrast this with her own intelligence as demonstrated by her *own* scholastic record. She

treated her daughter with a completely patronizing and placating manner which was insincere. For example, in the psychiatrist's presence she promised her daughter that she would not allow her to have further shock treatments, and as soon as the girl was out of the room she asked the doctor if he didn't feel she should be hospitalized and given electric shock treatments. One clue to this deceptive behavior arose during the mother's therapy. Although the daughter had had three previous hospitalizations the mother had never mentioned to the doctors that she herself had had a psychotic episode when she discovered that she was pregnant. The family whisked her away to a small sanitarium in a nearby town, and she was, according to her own statement, strapped to a bed for six weeks. Her family did not visit her during this time, and no one except her parents and her sister knew that she was hospitalized.

There were two times during therapy when the mother showed intense emotion. One was in relating her own psychotic experience; the other was on the occasion of her last visit when she accused the therapist of trying to drive her crazy by forcing her to choose between her daughter and her husband. Against medical advice, she took her daughter out of therapy.

The father was as involved in the homeostatic aspects of the intrafamily situation as the mother. For example, he stated that he had to quit his position as an important attorney in order to bring his daughter to an area where competent psychiatric help was available. Subsequently, acting on cues from the patient (e.g., she frequently referred to a character named "Nervous Ned") the therapist was able to elicit from him that he had hated his job and for years had been trying to "get out from under." However, the daughter was made to feel that the move was initiated for her.

On the basis of our examination of the clinical data, we have been impressed by a number of observations including:

1. The helplessness, fear, exasperation and rage which a double bind situation provokes in the patient, but which the mother may serenely and ununderstandingly pass over. We have noted reactions in the father that both create double bind situations, or extend and amplify those created by the mother, and we have seen the father passive and outraged, but helpless, become ensnared in a similar manner to the patient.

2. The psychosis seems, in part, a way of dealing with double bind situations to overcome their in-

hibiting and controlling effect. The psychotic patient may make astute, pithy, often metaphorical remarks that reveal an insight into the forces binding him. Contrariwise, he may become rather expert in setting double bind situations himself.

3. According to our theory, the communication situation described is essential to the mother's security, and by inference to the family homeostasis. If this be so, then when psychotherapy of the patient helps him become less vulnerable to mother's attempts at control, anxiety will be produced in the mother. Similarly, if the therapist interprets to the mother the dynamics of the situation she is setting up with the patient, this should produce an anxiety response in her. Our impression is that when there is a perduring contact between patient and family (especially when the patient lives at home during psychotherapy), this leads to a disturbance (often severe) in the mother and sometimes in both mother and father and other siblings (10, 11).

CURRENT POSITION AND FUTURE PROSPECTS

Many writers have treated schizophrenia in terms of the most extreme contrast with any other form of human thinking and behavior. While it is an isolable phenomenon, so much emphasis on the differences from the normal — rather like the fearful physical segregation of psychotics — does not help in understanding the problems. In our approach we assume that schizophrenia involves general principles which are important in all communication and therefore many informative similarities can be found in "normal" communication situations.

We have been particularly interested in various sorts of communication which involve both emotional significance and the necessity of discriminating between orders of message. Such situations include play, humor, ritual, poetry, and fiction. Play, especially among animals, we have studied at some length (3). It is a situation which strikingly illustrates the occurrence of metamessages whose correct discrimination is vital to the cooperation of the individuals involved; for example, false discrimination could easily lead to combat. Rather closely related to play is humor, a continuing subject of our research. It involves sudden shifts in Logical Types as well as discrimination of those shifts. Ritual is a field in which unusually real or literal ascriptions of Logical Type are made and defended as vigorously as the schizophrenic defends the "reality" of his delusions. Poetry exemplifies the communicative power of metaphor — even very unusual metaphor — when labeled as such by various signs, as contrasted to the obscurity of unlabeled schizophrenic metaphor. The entire field of fictional communication, defined as the narration or depiction of a series of events with more or less of a label of actuality, is most relevant to the investigation of schizophrenia. We are not so much concerned with the content interpretation of fiction — although analysis of oral and destructive themes is illuminating to the student of schizophrenia — as with the formal problems involved in simultaneous existence of multiple levels of message in the fictional presentation of "reality." The drama is especially interesting in this respect, with both performers and spectators responding to messages about both the actual and the theatrical reality.

We are giving extensive attention to hypnosis. A great array of phenomena that occur as schizophrenic symptoms — hallucinations, delusions, alterations of personality, amnesias, and so on — can be produced temporarily in normal subjects with hypnosis. These need not be directly suggested as specific phenomena, but can be the "spontaneous" result of an arranged communication sequence. For example, Erickson (4) will produce a hallucination by first inducing catalepsy in a subject's hand and then saying, "There is no conceivable way in which your hand can move, yet when I give the signal, it must move." That is, he tells the subject his hand will remain in place, yet it will move, and in no way the subject can consciously conceive. When Erickson gives the signal, the subject hallucinates the hand moved, or hallucinates himself in a different place and therefore the hand was moved. This use of hallucination to resolve a problem posed by contradictory commands which cannot be discussed seems to us to illustrate the solution of a double bind situation via a shift in Logical Types. Hypnotic responses to direct suggestions or statements also commonly involve shifts in type, as in accepting the words "Here's a glass of water" or "You feel tired" as external or internal reality, or in literal response to metaphorical statements, much like schizophrenics. We hope that further study of hypnotic induction, phenomena, and waking will, in this controllable situation, help sharpen our view of the essential communicational sequences which produce phenomena like those of schizophrenia.

Another Erickson experiment (12) seems to isolate a double bind communicational sequence without the specific use of hypnosis. Erickson arranged a seminar so as to have a young chain smoker sit next to him and to be without cigarettes; other participants were briefed on what to do. All was ordered so that Erickson repeatedly turned to offer the young man a cigarette, but was always interrupted by a question from someone so that he turned away, "inadvertently" withdrawing the cigarettes from the young man's reach. Later another participant asked this young man if he had received the cigarette from Dr. Erikson. He replied, "What cigarette?", showed clearly that he had forgotten the whole sequence, and even refused a cigarette offered by another member, saying that he was too interested in the seminar discussion to smoke. This young man seems to us to be in an experimental situation paralleling the schizophrenic's double bind situation with mother: An important relationship, contradictory messages (here of giving and taking away), and comment blocked — because there was a seminar going on, and anyway it was all "inadvertent." And note the similar outcome: Amnesia for the double bind sequence and reversal from "He doesn't give" to "I don't want."

Although we have been led into these collateral areas, our main field of observation has been schizophrenia itself. All of us have worked directly with schizophrenic patients and much of this case material has been recorded on tape for detailed study. In addition, we are recording interviews held jointly with patients and their families, and we are taking sound motion pictures of mothers and disturbed, presumably preschizophrenic, children. Our hope is that these operations will provide a clearly evident record of the continuing repetitive double binding which we hypothesize goes on steadily from infantile beginnings in the family situation of individuals who become schizophrenic. This basic family situation, and the overtly communicational characteristics of schizophrenia, have been the major focus of this paper. However, we expect our concepts and some of these data will also be useful in future work on other problems of schizophrenia, such as the variety of other symptoms, the character of the "adjusted state" before schizophrenia becomes manifest, and the nature and circumstances of the psychotic break.

THERAPEUTIC IMPLICATIONS OF THIS HYPOTHESIS

Psychotherapy itself is a context of multilevel communication, with exploration of the ambiguous lines between the literal and metaphoric, or reality and fantasy, and indeed, various forms of play, drama, and hypnosis have been used extensively in therapy. We have been interested in therapy, and

in addition to our own data we have been collecting and examining recordings, verbatim transcripts, and personal accounts of therapy from other therapists. In this we prefer exact records since we believe that how a schizophrenic talks depends greatly, though often subtly, on how another person talks to him; it is most difficult to estimate what was really occurring in a therapeutic interview if one has only a description of it, especially if the description is already in theoretical terms.

Except for a few general remarks and some speculation, however, we are not yet prepared to comment on the relation of the double bind to psychotherapy. At present we can only note:

1. Double bind situations are created by and within the psychotherapeutic setting and the hospital milieu. From the point of view of this hypothesis we wonder about the effect of medical "benevolence" on the schizophrenic patient. Since hospitals exist for the benefit of personnel as well as — as much as — more than — for the patient's benefit, there will be contradictions at times in sequences where actions are taken "benevolently" for the patient when actually they are intended to keep the staff more comfortable. We would assume that whenever the system is organized for hospital purposes and it is announced to the patient that the actions are for *his* benefit, then the schizophrenogenic situation is being perpetuated. This kind of deception will provoke the patient to respond to it as a double bind situation, and his response will be "schizophrenic" in the sense that it will be indirect and the patient will be unable to comment on the fact that he feels that he is being deceived. One vignette, fortunately amusing, illustrates such a response. On a ward with a dedicated and "benevolent" physician in charge there was a sign on the physician's door which said "Doctor's Office. Please Knock." The doctor was driven to distraction and finally capitulation by the obedient patient who carefully knocked every time he passed the door.

2. The understanding of the double bind and its communicative aspects may lead to innovations in therapeutic technique. Just what these innovations may be is difficult to say, but on the basis of our investigation we are assuming that double bind situations occur consistently in psychotherapy. At times these are inadvertent in the sense that the therapist is imposing a double bind situation similar to that in the patient's history, or the patient is imposing a double bind situation on the therapist. At other times therapists seem to impose double

binds, either deliberately or intuitively, which force the patient to respond differently than he has in the past.

An incident from the experience of a gifted psychotherapist illustrates the intuitive understanding of a double bind communicational sequence. Dr. Frieda Fromm-Reichmann (5) was treating a young woman who from the age of seven had built a highly complex religion of her own replete with powerful Gods. She was very schizophrenic and quite hesitant about entering into a therapeutic situation. At the beginning of the treatment she said, "God R says I shouldn't talk with you." Dr. Fromm-Reichmann replied, "Look, let's get something into the record. To me God R doesn't exist, and that whole world of yours doesn't exist. To you it does, and far be it from me to think that I can take that away from you, I have no idea what it means. So I'm willing to talk with you in terms of that world, if only you know I do it so that we have an understanding that it doesn't exist for me. Now go to God R and tell him that we have to talk and he should give you permission. Also you must tell him that I am a doctor and that you have lived with him in his kingdom now from seven to sixteen — that's nine years — and he hasn't helped you. So now he must permit me to try and see whether you and I can do that job. Tell him that I am a doctor and this is what I want to try."

The therapist has her patient in a "therapeutic double bind." If the patient is rendered doubtful about her belief in her god then she is agreeing with Dr. Fromm-Reichmann, and is admitting her attachment to therapy. If she insists that God R is real, then she must tell him that Dr. Fromm-Reichmann is "more powerful" than he — again admitting her involvement with the therapist.

The difference between the therapeutic bind and the original double bind situation is in part the fact that the therapist is not involved in a life and death struggle himself. He can therefore set up relatively benevolent binds and gradually aid the patient in his emancipation from them. Many of the uniquely appropriate therapeutic gambits arranged by therapists seem to be intuitive. We share the goal of most psychotherapists who strive toward the day when such strokes of genius will be well enough understood to be systematic and commonplace.

REFERENCES

1. BATESON, G. Social planning and the concept of "deutero-learning." *Conference on Science, Philosophy, and Religion, Second Symposium.* New York: Harper, 1942.
2. BATESON, G. A. A theory of play and fantasy. *Psychiatric Research Reports,* 1955, 2, 39–51.
3. CARPENTER, C. R. A field study of the behavior and social relations of howling monkeys. *Comp. Psychol. Monogr.,* 1934, 10, 1–168.
4. ERICKSON, M. H. Personal communication, 1955.
5. FROMM-REICHMANN, F. Personal communication, 1956.
6. HALEY, J. Paradoxes in play, fantasy, and psychotherapy. *Psychiatric Research Reports,* 1955, 2, 52–58.
7. HARLOW, H. F. The formation of learning sets. *Psychol. Rev.,* 1949, 56, 51–65.
8. HILGARD, J. R. Anniversary reactions in parents precipitated by children. *Psychiatry,* 1953, 16, 73–80.
9. HULL, C. L., *et al. Mathematico-deductive theory of rote learning.* New Haven: Yale Univ. Press, 1940.
10. JACKSON, D. D. An episode of sleepwalking. *J. Amer. Psychoanal. Assn.,* 1954, 2, 503–508.
11. JACKSON, D. D. Some factors influencing the Oedipus complex. *Psychoanal. Quart.,* 1954, 23, 566–581.
12. JACKSON, D. D. The question of family homeostasis. Presented at the Amer. Psychiatric Assn. Meeting, St. Louis, May 7, 1954.
13. LORENZ, K. Z. *King Solomon's ring.* New York: Crowell, 1952.
14. PERCEVAL, J. A narrative of the treatment experienced by a gentleman during a state of mental derangement, designed to explain the causes and nature of insanity, etc. London: Effingham Wilson, 1836 and 1840.
15. RUESCH, J., & BATESON, G. *Communication: the social matrix of psychiatry.* New York: Norton, 1951.
16. VON DOMARUS, E. The specific laws of logic in schizophrenia. In J. S. Kasanin (Ed.), *Language and thought in schizophrenia.* Berkeley: Univ. of California Press, 1944.
17. WHITEHEAD, A. N., & RUSSELL, B. *Principia mathematica.* Cambridge: Cambridge Univ. Press, 1910.

JAY HALEY[1]

The Family of the Schizophrenic:
A Model System*

This paper will attempt to show that schizophrenic behavior serves a function within a particular kind of family organization. The emphasis in this description will be on the interactive behavior of the schizophrenic and his parents rather than on their ideas, beliefs, attitudes, or psychodynamic conflicts. This work is largely based on an examination of a small sample of families participating in therapeutic sessions where parents and schizophrenic child, as well as siblings, are seen together and recorded. An excerpt from a recording of a family session will be presented and analyzed in terms of the observable behavior of family members, to illustrate the hypothesis that the family of the schizophrenic is a special kind of system which can be differentiated from other family systems.

The hypothesis that schizophrenia is of family origin has led to a number of investigations of schizophrenic patients and their parents. These studies include both impressions of family members and attempts at statistical measurement of individual traits of parents or the conflict between them. Typically the mother of the schizophrenic is described as dominating, overprotective, manipulative of the child and father, and also overtly rejecting (18). The father is usually described as weak and passive, holding aloof from the patient (15, 17), and occasionally overtly rejecting and cruel (8). Many investigators mention a certain percentage of fathers or mothers who appear "normal."

Besides reporting descriptions of the individuals in the family, investigators report on the relationship between the parents on the assumption that conflict between father and mother could be related to disturbance in the child. Lidz and Lidz (13) reported in 1949 that 20 of 35 schizophrenic patients had parents who were clearly incompatible. Tietze (20) reported in the same year that 13 of 25 mothers of schizophrenic patients reported unhappy marriages and nine marriages which were described as "perfect" were found by the investigator to be otherwise. In 1950 Gerard and Siegal (7) found strife between 87 per cent of the parents of 71 male schizophrenic patients in contrast to 13 per cent found in the controls. In the same year Reichard and Tillman (17) noted the unhappy marriages of parents of schizophrenics. Frazee (8) in 1953 reported that 14 of 23 parents were in severe conflict with each other and none had only moderate conflict in contrast to 13 control parents who had only moderate conflict. Lidz (16) reported in 1957 that all of 14 families of schizophrenic patients contained marital relationships which were seriously disturbed. Bowen (6) describes the parents in this type of family as experiencing "emotional divorce." Wynne uses the term "pseudo mutuality" to describe the difficulties family members have with each other (23).

These studies provide strong evidence for conflict between the parents of schizophrenics, but do not clarify what strife between parents has to do with schizophrenia in a child. After all, there is conflict between parents who do not have schizophrenic children. Similarly to show that the mothers of schizophrenic patients are dominating and overprotective and the fathers weak and passive does not clarify how schizophrenia is appropriate in families with such parents. Psychiatric terminology seems particularly unsuited to this problem. The language of psychiatry either describes the processes within an individual, such as his needs, fantasies, anxieties, and so on, or provides static descriptions of two individuals in dominant-submissive or rejecting or dependent relationships. When schizophrenia is described in the traditional psychiatric way, and when other family members are seen with the biased emphasis upon the processes in the in-

[1] Project for the Study of Schizophrenic Communication, directed by Gregory Bateson. Staff consists of Jay Haley and John H. Weakland, Research associates, Dr. Don D. Jackson, consultant, Dr. William F. Fry, consultant. The research project is located at the Veterans Administration Hospital, Palo Alto, California, and is financed by grants from the Macy Foundation and the Foundations' Fund for Research in Psychiatry.

* Reprinted by permission from *The Journal of Nervous and Mental Diseases*, Vol. 129, 1955, pages 357–374. Copyright ©, 1955. The Williams & Wilkins Co., Baltimore, Md. 21202, U.S.A.

dividual, it is difficult to relate schizophrenia to a family.

Currently most groups investigating schizophrenia and the family are recognizing that the total family unit is pathogenic, and there are attempts to develop a language which will describe the interaction of three or more people. A transition would seem to have taken place in the study of schizophrenia; from the early idea that the difficulty in these families was caused by the schizophrenic member, to the idea that they contained a pathogenic mother, to the discovery that the father was inadequate, to the current emphasis upon all three family members involved in a pathological system of interaction. Although it would seem impossible at this time to provide a satisfactory language for describing the complex interaction of three or more people, this paper will suggest a rudimentary approach to such a descriptive system. An essential requirement of any such description is that it show the adaptive function of schizophrenic behavior within the family system.

The present paper is a product of the current research conducted by the Bateson project. Historically this project began as a general investigation of the nature of communication and began to focus on the communication of the schizophrenics in 1953. The observation that the schizophrenic consistently mislabels his communication led Bateson to deduce that he must have been raised in a learning situation where he was faced with conflicting levels of message. From this came the "double bind" hypothesis (5) which was put together with Jackson's emphasis on schizophrenia serving a homeostatic function in the family (12). The research project then brought together the families of schizophrenics to observe the actual behavior in the family. Basically the double bind hypothesis was a statement about two-person interaction and it has been extended to areas outside of schizophrenia (9, 11). When the family was seen as an interactive unit, there was an attempt to extend the double bind concept to a three person system (21). Currently the project is attempting to devise a theoretical system for describing the family as a unit and this attempt had led to several papers (2, 3, 4) including this one.

The importance of describing a total system rather than elements within it may explain some of the inconsistencies in the description of individuals in the family and conflict between them. For example, it is possible that a mother could show rejecting traits when her child is ill and dependent upon her, and overprotective traits when he begins

to recover and attempt to achieve independence from her. Similarly, parents may not show discord when their child is psychotic and they are drawn together by this burden, but conflict could appear should the child behave more assertively and so threaten to leave them. Alanen (1) studied mothers of schizophrenic patients and found many of them within the limits of the "normal" on the basis of Rorschach tests and individual interview. He mentions, almost in passing, "Some of the cases in which the mother of a schizophrenic patient had been relatively healthy belong to those in which the father was seriously disturbed. The wives of all fathers who had developed chronic psychosis belong, for example, to this category." If the 'normality' or the pathology of a family member depends upon the influence of the behavior of other family members at that time, only a study of the total family system will show consistent findings.

The focus of a family study should be on the total family and on the interaction of parents and children *with each other* rather than on the interaction of family members with interviewers or testers. What a family member reports to an investigator about his relationship with another family member is only hearsay evidence of what actually takes place. To study the system of interaction in the family of the schizophrenic it is necessary to bring family members together over a period of time and directly observe them relating to one another. Inevitably the fact of observing the family introduces a bias into the data for they may behave differently when observed than when not observed. It would seem to be impossible to leave the observer out of this sort of study, and the problem is to include him in the situation in such a way as to maximize the information he can gain. The most appropriate type of observation would seem to be in a therapeutic context. There is serious doubt as to whether this type of family can be brought together without therapeutic support. If the parents are merely asked to be observed interacting with their schizophrenic child, the question is automatically raised whether they have something to do with the illness of the child; accordingly guilts and defenses are aroused and must be dealt with in the situation. Long-term observation of the family is also necessary since they may give one impression in a single interview and quite another when they have talked together many times and pretenses are dropping. The presence of a therapist is necessary as sensitive areas in the relationships are touched upon when family members get more intensively involved with one another. Long-term observation also provides an opportunity to verify hypotheses and make predictions as family patterns are observed occurring again and again. Finally, the introduction of a therapist makes possible the observation of a family responding to planned intervention. As ideas are presented to the family, or as therapeutic change is threatened, the family can be observed maintaining their system under stress.

Although the expense of regular filming of therapy sessions is prohibitive, the occasional use of film and the constant use of tape recordings provides data which may be studied at leisure.

AN ILLUSTRATION OF FAMILY BEHAVIOR

Since few investigators have the opportunity to observe a schizophrenic and his parents interacting with one another, an illustration is offered here. The following excerpt is transcribed verbatim from a recording of an interview where a patient and his parents were seen weekly as an adjunct to his individual therapy, because of his previous inability to see his parents for even a few minutes without an anxiety attack. The patient, a thirty nine year old man, suffered a breakdown in the army and was diagnosed as a schizophrenic. After discharge he returned home and remained with his parents for the following ten years. There were several abortive attempts to leave home and go to work. He was employed for little more than a year during those ten years and was supported by his parents during his temporary absences from home. When he entered the hospital, at the insistence of his parents, he was hallucinating, behaving in a compulsive way, exhibiting bizarre mannerisms, and complaining of anxiety and helplessness.

Earlier in the interview the patient had been saying he felt he was afraid of his mother, and finally she brought out a Mother's Day Card she had just received from him. It was a commercial card with the printed inscription, "For someone who has been like a mother to me." The patient said he could see nothing wrong with the card nor understand why his mother was disturbed about receiving it.

Patient: Uh, read the outside again.

Mother: All right, the outside says, "On Mother's Day, with best wishes" — everything is very fine, it's wonderful, but it's for someone else, not for your mother, you see? "For someone who's *been* like a mother to me."

Father: In other words, this card made mother think. So mother asked me . . .

Mother: (interrupting) When you . . .

Father: (continuing) what I think about it. So I said, "Well, I don't think Simon — meant that way, maybe he . . .

Patient: (interrupting) Well, I mean you can interpret it, uh — uh, you've been like a mother is uh supposed to be.

Father: No, no.

Patient: (continuing) a good — a real good mother.

Therapist: Why don't you like the idea that he might have deliberately sent that?

Father: Deliberately? Well . . .

Mother: (overlapping and interrupting) Well, that's what I . . .

Father: (continuing) well, he says he didn't, he agrees . . .

Mother: (continuing) Well, I mean I believe our son would have . . .

Father: (overlapping and continuing) that he couldn't get another card.

Patient: (interrupting) Well, I meant to sting you just a tiny bit by that outside phrase.

Mother: (overlapping) You see I'm a little bit of a psychiatrist too, Simon, I happen to be — (laughing) So I felt so — when you talked to (the therapist) I brought along that card — I wanted to know what's behind your head. And I wanted to know — or you made it on purposely to hurt me — Well, if you did, I — I . . .

Patient: (interrupting) Not entirely, not entire . . .

Mother: (interrupting and overlapping) I'll take all — Simon, believe me, I'll take all the hurt in the world if it will help you — you see what I mean?

Therapist: How can you . . .

Mother: (continuing) Because I never meant to hurt you — Huh?

Therapist: How can you hurt anybody who is perfectly willing to be hurt? (short pause)

Father: What's that?

Mother: I uh — a mother sacrifices — if you be — maybe a mother you would know too. Because a mother is just a martyr, she's sacrificing — like even with Jesus with his mother — she sacrificed too. So that's the way it goes on, a mother takes over anything what she can help . . .

Therapist: (interrupting) What mother?

Mother: (continuing) her children.

Patient: (interrupting and overlapping) Well, uh, I'll tell you Ma — listen, Ma, I didn't mean to sting you exactly that outside part there.

Therapist: Well, you said so.

Patient: Oh, all right, but it — it wasn't that exactly. No, I'm not giving ground — uh — it's hard to explain this thing. Uh — uh — What was I going to say. Now I forgot what I was going to say. (short pause) I mean I felt that this — this is what I mean, uh — that I felt that you could have been a better mother to me than you were. See there were things.

Mother: Uh . . .

Father: Well you said . . .

Patient: (interrupting) You could have been better than you were. So that's why — that's that — I felt — it was, uh — uh, was all right to send it that way.

Mother: Well, if you meant it that way that's perf — that's what I wanted to know — and that's all I care — you see. But I still say, Simon, that if you would take your father and mother just like they're plain people — you just came here and you went through life like anybody else went through — and — and don't keep on picking on them and picking them to pieces — but just leave them alone — and go along with them the way they are — and don't change them — you'll be able to get along with everybody, I assure you.

Patient: (interrupting) I mean after all a card is a card — why I d — it seems to me kind of silly (anguish in his voice and near weeping) to bring that thing in here — they have sold them at the canteen, Ma . . .

Therapist: Are you anxious now . . .

Patient: Why . . .

Therapist: Are you anxious now because she said . . .

Patient: I shouldn't be blamed for a thing like that, it's so small . . .

Mother: (overlapping) I'm not blaming you.

Patient: (continuing) I don't even remember exactly what the thing was.

Mother: (overlapping) Well, that's all I wanted to know (laughs)

Patient: (continuing) I didn't want to — to — to — to blame you or nothing.

Therapist: Will you slow down a minute. Are you anxious now because she said she didn't like to be picked on? And you've sort of been picking on her today. Is that what's making you so — upset?

Patient: No, it's now what's making me upset. That they s — after all, mother's got to realize that those people — the people that sell the cards — they sell them and people buy them — the wording isn't exactly right — I've stood for half an hour in a store sometimes picking — picking out a card to send mother or to send to one of the family where I wanted to get the wordings just so — and the picture on the thing just so. I was just too particular, that was before I took sick . . .

Therapist: I think you did that this time too —

Patient: (continuing) And came back to the hospital. No I wasn't — I bought that thing in five minutes. There was only a choice of four cards — but of course that helped. But I — I — I — uh, I — I do have — I've changed now with those cards, I'm not as particular as I used to be. I mean uh — peop — they sell those cards and, uh — I don't think that they — they got — they don't mean anything by the words. Uh, — they're sold for people to buy, they're sold for people to buy.

Therapist: (overlapping) The person who sends them ought to mean something by the words.

Patient: No, but I . . .

Therapist: And you seem to be denying that you sent . . .

Patient: No, I think that can be interpreted in different ways.

Therapist: Sure, it's pretty safe, but not quite safe enough apparently.

Patient: Is that the way you feel too?

Therapist: I feel you tried to say something indirectly so you'd be protected.

Patient: (interrupting) No, I wasn't, I just felt that — that — that thing.

Therapist: Now you're . . .

Patient: (continuing) was — was — all right I'm changing a little bit. Uh, — that the mother was a good enough mother. It says "For someone that's been like a mother to me."

Father: A *real* mother.

Patient: Yeah, a *real* mother — so that's all.[2]

---

[2] This excerpt is not offered as an example of family therapy but rather as an example of family behavior. The parents in this case were not considered to be patients and the family as a unit was not officially undergoing treatment.

Despite its brevity, this excerpt illustrates a typical kind of interaction in this type of family. From the point of view of psychiatric diagnosis, the patient manifests such symptoms as: 1) blocking and forgetting what he was going to say, 2) showing concretistic thinking when he says "a card is a card," 3) implying that someone else caused the difficulty ("They sell them in the canteen" and later in the interview implying in a rather paranoid way that it was the fault of a post office clerk for mailing it) and 4) claiming amnesia ("I don't even remember what the thing was"). Although less dramatic than symptoms manifested by the full-blown psychotic patient, his behavior could be said to be schizophrenic.

Another family could have responded in this situation rather differently. Should a child in another family send his mother such a card, she might respond to it in any of a variety of ways. And whatever way chosen, her husband and child would also have a range of possible ways to respond to her. This particular family selects these ways, and a description of this family must 1) describe the formal patterns in this type of interaction in such a way as to 2) differentiate the patterns from other possible ones, or those in other families.

POSSIBILITIES OF A THREE-PERSON SYSTEM

One way to describe a particular family is to present its type of interaction against the background of the potential ways a mother, father, and child might interact with one another. If any set of parents and child are brought together in a room, what sort of communicative behavior is potentially possible between them?

1. Whatever they do together can be seen as communication between them; each will do something and each will respond. Although it seems obvious, it is particularly important to emphasize that family members cannot avoid communicating, or responding, to one another when they are in the same room. If one speaks to another and he does not answer, his not-answering is a response in a real and meaningful sense.

2. Not only must parents and child communicate with each other, but each must communicate on at least two levels. Whatever one says and does will inevitably be qualified by the other things he says and does, and when any piece of communication is *about*, or qualifies, another piece of communication they can be said to be of different levels. Whenever anyone speaks to another person he must qualify what he says because he must speak in a tone of voice, with a body movement, with other verbal statements, and in a particular context. What he says will be qualified with an indication of what sort of statement it is, *i.e.* a joking statement, a sincere one, an unimportant one, a command, a suggestion, and so on. A man can smile and murder as he smiles, and if his behavior is to be described both levels of communication must be included.

If a man says, "I won't stand for that any more!" in a tone of voice which indicates anger and with a gesture of putting a stop to it in a situation where what he says is appropriate, then his statement and qualifications can be said to be congruent, or to "affirm," each other. Messages and their qualifiers can also be incongruent. If a mother makes a punishing statement while labeling what she does as benevolent, she is disqualifying what she says, or manifesting an incongruence between her levels of message. It is important to note that she is not contradicting herself. Contradictory statements are of the same level, such as, "I will do it," and "I won't do it." Incongruent statements are of different levels: "I will do it," said in a tone of voice which indicates, "Don't take what I say seriously." Whether family members qualify their own statements incongruently or congruently, and under what circumstances they do so, can be described as they interact with one another.

3. The three people in the room must also qualify each other's statements. As they respond to one another, they are inevitably commenting upon, or classifying, each other's statements. They may affirm what each other says, or they may disqualify the other's statements by indicating that isn't the sort of thing that should be said. If mother says, "I brought you some candy," and her son says, "You treat me like a child," the son is disqualifying his mother's communication. If he accepts it with a statement of thanks, he is affirming her statement. A description of parents and child must include whether, and under what circumstances, they affirm or disqualify each other's behavior.

4. When three people are in a room, some sort of leadership will take form, even if only in terms of who will speak before the others do. Any one of the three may initiate something, and the other two may go along with him or attempt to take leadership themselves. In some families, father and child may consistently turn to mother for a decision, other families may label father as the final arbiter, while other parents may lean on their child for the initiation of what is to happen.

5. The three people may also form any or all of various possible alliances. It is possible for the three

of them to ally against the outside world, or for one to ally with someone in the outside world against the other two, or two may ally against the third. In some families father and mother may form a coalition against the child, in others the child may ally with one of his parents against the other, and so on.

6. Finally, when something goes "wrong," there are a variety of possible arrangements for the three people to handle blame. All three may each acknowledge blame, one may never accept blame for anything, two may consistently blame the third, and so on.

This list of some of the possibilities in a three person system is made more complex by the fact that a family member may form an alliance but indicate he isn't forming one, or may take blame but qualify his statement with an indication that he really isn't to blame. The possible range of maneuvers is considerably increased when people are seen to communicate at multiple levels.

THE RULES IN THE FAMILY OF THE SCHIZOPHRENIC

Given a potential range of behavior between three people in a family system, it becomes possible to look at any one type of family as restricted to a certain range of that potential. No one family will interact in all possible ways: limited patterns of interaction will develop. The patterns described here are those in a particular sample and are those which occur when parents and schizophrenic child interact *with each other*. They may behave differently with other people, including psychiatric investigators or siblings of the schizophrenic child. Although siblings are included in our observation of this type of family, the description offered here is of the three person system, partly for simplification in this presentation and partly because parents and schizophrenic child form a special triadic system in the larger family unit.

The Ways Family Members Qualify Their Own Statements

Consistently in this type of family the individual members manifest an incongruence between what they say and how they qualify what they say. Many people do this under certain circumstances, but when these family members interact they confine themselves almost entirely to disqualifying their own statements.

In this excerpt, the mother confronts her son with the Mother's Day Card because she didn't like it, but she emphasizes what a wonderful card it

is. Then she says she wants to know what was behind his head and if he sent it to hurt her, and she laughs. In a context of accusing him of hurting her, she says she wants to be hurt and is willing to take all the hurt in the world to help him. Her description of herself as a special person who will sacrifice all is qualified a few moments later by the statement that she and her husband are just plain people and her son should treat them like anybody else. This "benevolent advice" is offered in a punishing tone of voice and context. When her son says she shouldn't blame him, she qualifies her statements as not being blaming. Consistently what she communicates she qualifies in an incongruent way.

The father is only briefly in this excerpt, but while there he indicates that the son didn't mean to say what the card said, and, besides, the card said she was a real mother.

The son also manifests incongruent behavior. He sends a card to his mother on Mother's Day which indicates she is not really his mother. He further qualifies this message by indicating there was nothing wrong with it and then suggests that it says she is like a mother is supposed to be. Following this, he indicates that it means she could have been a better mother than she was. He then protests that it was silly of her to bring the card in, and qualifies this with the statement that they sell them in the canteen. Besides he doesn't remember what the thing was. After indicating that he bought the card hurriedly, he qualifies this by saying it took him five minutes to choose among four cards. He adds that one should be careful in choosing cards with exact wording, but people sell those cards and they don't mean anything by the words. Finally, he qualifies his greetings by saying that it meant she was not only a good enough mother but a real mother.

The more extreme incongruence between the son's levels of message differs from that of his mother, and this difference will be discussed later. Yet basically a similar pattern of communication is apparent. The mother does not say, "You shouldn't have said me this card — what do you mean by it?" which is implied by her bringing the card to the session. The son doesn't say, "I sent it to you to sting you, but I'm sorry I did now." The mother is condemning him for sending her the card, but she qualifies her messages in such a way that she indicates she isn't condemning him. The son apologizes for sending the card, but he qualifies his apology in such a way that he isn't apologizing. Father indicates the son didn't mean what he said, and the card didn't say what he didn't mean anyhow. Although these incongruencies between what is said and how it is qualified are apparent in the verbal transcript, they are even more apparent when the vocal inflections on the recording are heard. Mother's tone of voice and laughter are inappropriate and thereby disqualify what she is saying, and father and son similarly do not make a flat statement which is affirmed by the ways they say it.

One can listen to many hours of recordings of conversations between parents and schizophrenic child without hearing one of them make a statement which is affirmed. Usually if one finds an exception, it proves on closer examination to fit the rules. For example, during a filmed session a family was asked to plan to do something together and the father said in a positive way that they were going to do this and do that. He fully affirmed his statements by the ways he said them. However, a few minutes later he said he was only saying these things because they should say something in front of the camera, thus disqualifying his previous statements.

How Family Members Qualify Each Other's Statements

Although it is possible for family members to affirm or disqualify each other's statements, in this type of family the members consistently disqualify what each other says. In this excerpt it is difficult to find any statement by one person affirmed by another. The son has actually disqualified his mother's whole past maternal behavior at one stroke by sending her such a card. When she protests, he indicates her protests are not valid. Similarly, the mother disqualifies the greeting she received from her son and also his defenses of it. When he indicates there is nothing wrong with it, she labels this as in error. When he indicates he knew what he was doing and meant to "sting" her a bit, she indicates this was in error. Father joins them to disqualify both the son's message, since he didn't meant it, and his defense of the message. No one affirms what anyone says except 1) when the son says he doesn't remember what the card was, and his mother says that is all she wanted to know; 2) when the father says the card means she is a real mother, and the son agrees. Both of these affirmations involve symptomatic behavior by the son: amnesia and distortion of reality. From this excerpt one might hypothesize that the family members will disqualify what each other says except when the child is behaving in a symptomatic way. Such a hypothesis requires more careful investigation. Apparently even symptomatic

behavior by the child is usually disqualified except in certain contexts. When the mother is under attack, the parents may affirm psychotic behavior but not necessarily at other times.

It might be argued that the behavior in this excerpt is exceptional since it deals with a moment of crisis. However, analysis of other interviews suggests that the pattern is typical. In a previous paper (5) the relationship between mother and schizophrenic child was described as a "double bind" situation in that the mother imposed incongruent levels of message upon the child in a situation where the child must respond to conflicting requests, could not comment on the contradictions, and could not leave the field. Further investigation indicates that this kind of communication sequence is a repetitive pattern between all three family members. Not only is each constantly faced with conflicting levels of message, but each finds his response labeled as a wrong one. (Family therapy with this type of family has its unrewarding aspects since almost any comment by the therapist is similarly disqualified.)

Typically if one family member says something, another indicates it shouldn't have been said or wasn't said properly. If one criticizes the other, he is told that he misunderstands and should behave differently. If one compliments the other, he is told he doesn't do this often enough, or he has some ulterior purpose. Should a family member try to avoid communicating, the others will indicate this "passivity" is demanding and indicate he should initiate more. All family members may report they always feel they are in the wrong. However, they do not necessarily directly oppose each other or openly reject one another's statements. If one suggests going to a particular place, the other may not say "No," but rather he is likely to indicate, "Why must we always go where you suggest?" Or the response may be the sigh of a brave martyr who must put up with this sort of thing. Typically the family members may not object to what one another says, but to their right to say it. Often open disagreements are prevented by an atmosphere of benevolent concern and distress that the other person misunderstands. Family members may also respond in an affirmative way when their response would be appropriate only if the person had made some other statement.

It is important to emphasize that a formal pattern is being described here which may manifest itself in various ways. A mother may be overprotective and thereby disqualify what the child does as insufficient or inadequate. She may also be rejecting and similarly disqualify what he does as unacceptable. She may also withdraw when the child initiates something as a way of disqualifying his offer. Similarly, father may viciously condemn mother or child or merely be passive when they seek a positive response from him and in both cases he is disqualifying their communication.

Although it is not uncommon for people to disqualify each other's statements, ordinarily one would expect affirmation also to occur. However, when observing these families one does not hear even affectionate or giving behavior appreciated or affirmed. If one person indicates a desire for closeness, another indicates this is done in the wrong way or at the wrong time. (However, if one suggests separation the other will also indicate this is the wrong thing to do. Typically in these families the mother regularly threatens separation but does not leave, and the father does not often threaten separation but spends a good deal of his time away from home or "leaves" by drinking heavily while staying home.) Typically family members behave as if they are involved in what might be called a *compulsory relationship*. For example, a mother in one family indicated with some contempt that her husband was afraid to leave her because he could not stand being alone. She suggested he was cruel to her because he was angry at being tied to her. She also rejected his affectionate overtures because she considered them only a kind of bribery to insure staying with her. She herself was unable to leave him even for a night, though he was drunk several nights a week and beat her regularly. Both felt the association was not voluntary, and so neither could accept as valid any indication from the other about wanting to be together. A compulsory relationship is also typical of the parent and schizophrenic child. Since the child is considered incapable of leaving home and associating with others, his staying at home is taken as involuntary. Therefore should he indicate a desire to be with his parents, they tend to disqualify his overtures as merely a request that they not turn him out, and he finds his affectionate gestures disqualified.

Leadership in the Family

Since family members tend to negate their own and each other's communication, any clear leadership in the family is impossible. Typically in these families the mother tends to initiate what happens, while indicating either that she isn't, or that someone else should. The father will invite her to initiate what happens while condemning her when she does. Often they suggest the child take the lead, and then disqualify his attempts. These families tend to become incapacitated by necessary decisions because each member will avoid affirming what he does and therefore is unable to acknowledge responsibility for his actions, and each will disqualify the attempts of any other to announce a decision. Both the act of taking leadership and the refusal to take leadership by any one family member is condemned by the others. The family "just happens" to take actions in particular directions with no individual accepting the label as the one responsible for any action.

Alliances

Similarly, no labeled alliances are permitted in the family. A family coalition against the outside world (represented, say, by an observer), breaks down rather rapidly. Such individuals are also unable to form an alliance of two against one. Often they may appear to have such an alliance, as they tend to speak "through" one another. For example, the mother may ask for something for her child as a way of indicating that her husband deprives her, and so appear in alliance with the child. Or when the parents begin to express anger at each other, they may turn on the child for causing their difficulties and so appear in a coalition against him. Yet should the coalition be labeled, it will break down. If the child says, "You're both against me," one or the other parent will disqualify this remark and so deny the coalition. If father should say to mother, "Let's stick together on this," she is likely to say, "I'm afraid you'll back down at the last minute," or "It isn't my fault when we don't stick together." The mother and child may appear to form a coalition against the father, but should the child say, "Father treats us badly," mother is likely to say, "He has his troubles too," even though a moment before she may have been complaining to the child about how badly they were both treated by the father. Family members behave as if an alliance between two of them is inevitably a betrayal of the third person. They seem to have difficulty functioning in a two-person relationship, and as a result the separation of any one of the three from the others is a particular threat.

What confines the members so rigidly within their system is the prohibition on intimate alliances of one member with someone outside the family. As a result, the family members are inhibited from learning to relate to people with different behavior

and so are confined to their own system of interaction.

Defense Against Blame

Characteristically the mothers in these families
defend themselves by "transfer of blame." Such a
defense follows from the mother's consistent manifestation of incongruent levels: what she does, she
qualifies as not having been done or not done in
that way. If the child becomes disturbed, it happens "out of the blue." If anything goes wrong,
mother indicates it is the fault of someone else. In
those rare instances where she does admit she did
something wrong, she indicates she did it only because she was told to, or out of duty, so that it
wasn't her fault. She may also indicate that something must be wrong with the other person, since
he ought not to have been affected by what she did,
particularly when she didn't really do it. Even when
her behavior affects someone pleasantly, she must
deny that it was her fault. Typically she presents
herself as helplessly pushed by forces outside her
control.

The fathers also follow the family rule of incongruently qualifying their messages, yet they cannot
use the same denial of blame and remain with their
wives. They tend to use types of defense which
complement her defense, and these are of three
kinds. 1) Fathers who are withdrawn and passive,
accept the blame their wives put upon them, but
indicate by their unresponsiveness that they are
blamed falsely and do not agree with her. 2)
Fathers who have temper tantrums and blame their
wives, put the blame on false or exaggerated grounds
so the wife can easily point out her innocence. This
type of father is easily blamed since he is dominating and tyrannical, yet by going too far he indicates
he is an innocent victim driven by forces outside
his control. 3) Some fathers do not blame their
wives but also do not blame themselves or anyone
else. Such fathers make an issue of semantic difference. If asked if they or their wives are at fault, a
typical reply is, "Just what do you mean by 'fault'?"
By accepting no implicit definition and not defining
anything themselves, they obscure everything. Any
particular father may manifest these three types of
defense, all of which involve both disqualification
of one's own statements and a disqualification of the
other person's statements.

The child tends to use two types of defense.
When "sane" he may blame himself and indicate
that everything wrong with the family centers in
him, an attitude the parents encourage, while at
the same time he gives an impression of being

blamed unjustly. When "insane" he negates his
own statements and those of others by denying that
anything happened. Or, if it did, he wasn't there —
besides it wasn't him and it happened in another
place at a time when he had no control over himself. The "withdrawal from reality" maneuvers of
the schizophrenic make it impossible for him to
blame himself or his parents since he defines himself as not of this world.

THE "DIFFERENT" BEHAVIOR OF THE SCHIZOPHRENIC

The inability of the schizophrenic to relate to
people and his general withdrawal behavior seems
understandable if he was raised in a learning situation where whatever he did was disqualified and if
he was not allowed to relate to other people where
he could learn to behave differently. Should he be
reared in a situation where each attempt he made
to gain a response from someone was met with an
indication that he should behave in some other way,
it would be possible for an individual to learn to
avoid trying to relate to people by indicating that
whatever he does is not done in relationship to
anyone. He would then appear "autistic." However, the peculiar distortions of communication by
the schizophrenic are not sufficiently explained by
this description of his learning situation. If schizophrenic behavior is adaptive to a particular type of
family, it is necessary to suggest the adaptive function involved when a person behaves in a clearly
psychotic way.

The recovering schizophrenic patient, and perhaps the pre-psychotic schizophrenic, will qualify
what he says in a way similar to that used by his
parents. His behavior could be said to be "normal"
for that family. However, during a psychotic episode the schizophrenic behaves in a rather unique
manner. To suggest how such behavior might serve
a function in the family, it is necessary both to
describe schizophrenia in terms of behavior and to
suggest the conditions under which such behavior
might occur. To describe schizophrenic behavior,
it is necessary to translate into behavioral terms such
diagnostic concepts as delusions, hallucinations, concretistic thinking, and so on.

What appears unique about schizophrenic behavior is the incongruence of all levels of communication.
The patient's parents may say something and disqualify it, but they will affirm that disqualification.
The schizophrenic will say something, deny saying
it, but qualify his denial in an incongruent way.
Schizophrenic behavior described in this way has

been presented elsewhere (10), but it may be summarized briefly here.

Not only can a person manifest an incongruence between levels of total message, but also between elements of his messages. A message from one person to another can be formalized into the following statement: *I (source) am communicating (message) to you (receiver) in this context.*

By his body movement, vocal inflections, and verbal statements a person must affirm or disqualify each of the elements of this message. The symptoms of a schizophrenic can be summarized in terms of this schema.

1) *Source.* A person may indicate that *he* isn't really the source of a message by indicating that he is only transmitting the idea of someone else. Therefore he says something but qualifies it with a denial that *he* is saying it. The schizophrenic may also qualify the source of the message in this way, but he will qualify his qualifications in an incongruent way. For example, a male schizophrenic patient reported that his name was Margaret Stalin. Thus he indicated that *he* wasn't really speaking, but by making his denial clearly fantastic he disqualified his denial that he was speaking. Similarly a patient may say that "voices" are making the statement. In the excerpt presented, the patient denies that *he* is responsible for the greeting card message by saying "they sell them in the canteen," and yet this denial is by its nature self-disqualifying and so his messages become incongruent at all levels.

2) *Message.* A person may indicate in various ways that his words or action are not really a message. He may indicate, for example, that what he did was accidental if he blurts something out or if he steps on someone's foot. The schizophrenic may indicate that his statement isn't a message but merely a group of words, or he may speak in a random, or word salad, way, thus indicating that he isn't really communicating. Yet at the same time he manages to indicate some pertinent points in his word salad, thus disqualifying his denial that his message is a message. In the excerpt given above, the patient says, "a card is a card," as a way of denying the message communicated. He also says that he doesn't remember what the thing was, thus denying the message existed for him. However, both these qualifications of the message are also disqualified: the card obviously isn't merely a card, and he can hardly not remember what the thing was when he is looking at it.

3) *Receiver.* A person may deny this element in a message in various ways, for example by indicating he isn't really talking to the particular person he is addressing, but rather to that person's status. The schizophrenic patient is likely to indicate that the doctor he is talking to isn't really a doctor, but, say, an FBI agent. Thereby he not only denies talking to the physician, but by labeling the receiver in a clearly fantastic way he disqualifies his denial. Paranoid delusionary statements of this sort become "obvious" by their self-negating quality.

4) *Context.* A person may disqualify his statement by indicating that it applies to some other context than the one in which it is made. *Context* is defined broadly here as the situation in which people are communicating, including both the physical situation and the stated premises about what sort of situation it is. For example, a woman may be aggressively sexual in a public place where the context disqualifies her overtures. The typical statement that the schizophrenic is "withdrawn from reality" seems to be based to a great extent on the ways he qualifies what he says by mislabeling the context. He may say his hospital conversation is taking place in a palace, or in prison, and thereby disqualify his statements. Since his labels are clearly impossible, his disqualification is disqualified.

These multiple incongruent levels of communication differentiate the schizophrenic from his parents and from other people. If a person says something and then negates his statement we judge him by his other levels of message. When these too are incongruent so that he says something, indicates he didn't, then affirms one or the other, and then disqualifies his affirmation; there is a tendency to call such a person insane.

From the point of view offered here, schizophrenia is an intermittent type of behavior. The patient may be behaving in a schizophrenic way at one moment and in a way that is "normal" for this type of family at another moment. The important question is this: Under what circumstances does he behave in a psychotic way, defined here as qualifying incongruently all his levels of message?

In this excerpt of a family interaction, the patient shows psychotic behavior when he is caught between a therapist pressuring him to affirm his statements and his parents pressuring him to disqualify them. From this point of view, the patient is faced with a situation where he must infringe the rules of his relationship with the therapist or infringe his family rules. His psychotic behavior can be seen as an attempt to adapt to both.[3] By behaving in a psy-

---

[3] An attempt to synthesize two incompatible situations by a perceptual change is suggested in Weakland and Jackson (22). Describing an incident during a psychotic

chotic way he could 1) affirm his statement about his mother, thus following the rule in the therapeutic relationship for affirmative statements, 2) disqualify his critical statement of the mother, thus following the family rules that mother is not to be blamed in a way so that she can accept blame and all statements are to be disqualified, and 3) synthesize these two incompatible theses by indicating that the message wasn't his (it wasn't really a message, he couldn't remember it, and he didn't really send it). It can be argued that psychotic behavior is a sequence of messages which infringe a set of prohibitions but which are qualified as not infringing them. The only way an individual can achieve this is by qualifying incongruently all levels of his communication.

The need to behave in a psychotic way would seem to occur when the patient infringes a family prohibition and thereby activates himself and his parents to behave in such a way that he either returns within the previous system of rules or indicates somehow that he is not infringing them. Should he successfully infringe the system of family rules and thereby set new rules, his parents may become "disturbed." This seems to occur rather often when the patient living at home "improves" with therapy. When improving in therapy he is not only infringing the family prohibitions against outside alliances but he may blame the mother in a reasonable way and affirm his statements or those of others. Such behavior on his part would shatter the family system unless the parents are also undergoing therapy. The omnipotent feelings of the schizophrenic patient may have some basis, since his family system is so rigid that he can create considerable repercussions by behaving differently.

A patient is faced with infringing family prohibitions when 1) two family prohibitions conflict with each other and he must respond to both, 2) when forces outside the family, or maturational forces within himself, require him to infringe them, or 3) when prohibitions special to him conflict with prohibitions applying to all family members. If he must infringe such prohibitions and at the same time not infringe them, he can only do so through psychotic behavior.

Conflicting sets of prohibitions may occur when the individual is involved with both mother and therapist, involved with a therapist and administrator in a hospital setting (19), or when some shift

within his own family brings prohibitions into conflict. This latter would seem the most likely bind the patient would find himself in when living at home, and an incident is offered here to describe psychotic behavior serving a function in the family.

A twenty one year old schizophrenic daughter arrived home from the hospital for a trial visit and her parents promptly separated. The mother asked the girl to go with her, and when she arrived at their destination, the grandmother's home, the patient telephoned her father. Her mother asked her why she turned against her by calling the father, and the daughter said she called him to say goodbye and because she had looked at him with an "odd" look when they left. A typical symptom of this patient when overtly psychotic is her perception of "odd" looks, and the problem is how such a message is adaptive to the family pattern of interaction.

The incident could be described in this way. The mother separated from father but qualified her leaving incongruently by saying it was only temporary and telling him where she was going. The father objected to the mother's leaving, but made no attempt to restrain her or to persuade her to stay. The daughter had to respond to this situation in accord with the prohibitions set by this family system: she had to disqualify whatever she did, she had to disqualify what her mother and father did, she could not ally with either mother or father and acknowledge it, and she could not blame the mother in such a way that the mother would accept the blame.

The girl could not merely do nothing because this would mean remaining with father. However, by going with the mother she in effect formed an alliance and so infringed one of the prohibitions in the family system. The girl solved the problem by going with mother but telephoning her father, thus disqualifying her alliance with mother. However, her mother objected to the call, and the daughter said she only called him to say goodbye, thus disqualifying her alliance with father. Yet to leave it this way would mean allying with mother. She qualified her statement further by saying she called father because she gave him an "odd look" when she left him. By having an odd look, she could succeed in not siding with either parent or blaming mother. She also manifested schizophrenic behavior by qualifying incongruently all levels of message and thereby adapting to incongruent family prohibitions. Previously the girl could withdraw to her room to avoid the alliance problem, but when mother stopped staying home while saying she was

breakdown, they say, "Psychotic delusions allowed him to free himself of decision making. For example, the cab driver is a hospital attendant in disguise. There is no problem in Home vs. Hospital; it has been resolved."

going to leave, and left while saying she was not really leaving, the girl was threatened by a possible alliance whether she went with her mother or stayed at home. Her incongruent, schizophrenic behavior would seem necessary to remain within the prohibitions of the family at those times. If one is required to behave in a certain way and simultaneously required not to, he can only solve the problem by indicating that *he* is not behaving at all, or not with this particular person in this situation. The girl might also have solved the problem by disqualifying her identity, indicating the context was really a secret plot, indicating that what she did was what voices told her to do, or speaking in a random or word salad way. In other words, she could both meet the prohibitions in the family and infringe them only by disqualifying the source of her messages, the nature of them, the recipient, or the context, and so behave in a psychotic fashion.

It is important to emphasize that schizophrenic behavior in the family is adaptive to an intricate and complicated family organization which is presented here in crude simplicity. The network of family prohibitions confronts the individual members with almost insoluble problems. This particular incident was later discussed with the parents of this girl, and the mother said her daughter could have solved the problem easily. She could have stayed with father and told him he was wrong in the quarrel which provoked the separation. This would seem to be the mother's usual way of dealing with this kind of situation — she stays with father while telling him he is wrong. However, the mother leaves herself out of this solution by ignoring the fact that she asked her daughter to go with her. This request was even more complicated — the mother asked the daughter to go with her during a period when the mother was saying the daughter must return to the hospital because she could not tolerate associating with her. When the parents reunited later that week, the girl was returned to the hospital because mother said she could not stand daughter in the room watching her, and she could not stand daughter out of the room thinking about her.

The approach offered here differs from the usual psychodynamic explanations. It would be possible to say that the mother's concern about leaving the daughter with the father, even when she could not tolerate the girl's company, might center in the family's concern about incestuous desires between father and daughter. Such a psychodynamic hypothesis could be supported. Later in therapy the father and daughter planned a picnic alone together

when they decided they should see more of each other without the mother being present. The evening of the day this was arranged, the therapist received a telephone call from the disturbed mother. She reported that she and her husband had been drinking and arguing all evening and she reported that her husband had told her it was natural for a father to have sexual relations with his daughter. The husband's report was that he had not said this. (He had said it was natural for a father to have sexual *feelings* for his daughter, but this did not mean he would do anything about it.) This crisis over suggested possible incest could be explained by saying that the threat of closeness between father and daughter aroused forbidden incestuous desires in them. However, it was the mother who made an issue over the possible incest. From the psychodynamic point of view, hints and discussions of incest would represent unconscious conflicts. From the point of view offered here, this type of discussion is an aspect of family strategy. To label a relationship as possibly incestuous would be one further way of enforcing a prohibition on alliances between father and daughter. Such a maneuver is similar to one where the mother inhibits a relationship between father and daughter by insisting that the father should associate more with the daughter, thus arousing his negative behavior as well as the issue of whether he neglected the daughter. The approach offered here does not deal with supposed motivating forces within the individuals concerned, but with the formal characteristics of their behavior with each other.[4]

THE FUNCTION OF FAMILY BEHAVIOR

The difficulty for this type of family would seem to lie in the inflexibility of their family system. They often maintain the system despite the sturdy attempts of a family therapist to help them deal with each other more amicably. Apparently family members gain only discord, dissension, and a constant struggle with one another, or periods of withdrawal in a kind of truce, yet they continue so to behave. It would be possible to postulate psycho-

[4] Although statements in the form of family rules deal with observable behavior and are therefore verifiable, the verification depends to some extent upon the skill of the observer. Such statements are more reliably documented by placing the family in a structured experimental situation where the results depend upon whether or not the family functions under certain prohibitions. The Bateson project is now beginning a program of experiments with families similar to the small group experiments of Alex Bavelas.

dynamic causes for this type of behavior, or self-destructive drives could be sought, but an attempt is made here to develop an alternative descriptive language centering on the peculiar sensitivity of people to the fact that their behavior is governed by others.

When people respond to one another they inevitably influence how the other person is to respond to them. Whatever one says, or doesn't say, in response to another person is a determinant of the other person's behavior. For example, if one criticizes another, he is indicating that critical statements from him are permissible in the relationship. The other person cannot not respond, and whatever response he makes will govern the critical person's behavior. Whether the criticized one gets angry, or weeps helplessly, or passively accepts the criticism, he must either be accepting the rules or countering with other rules. These rules for relationships which people establish with each other are never permanently set but are in a constant process of reinforcement as the two people interact and govern each other's behavior.

Every human being depends upon other people not only for his survival but for his pleasure and pain. It is of primary importance that he learn to govern the responses of other people so they will provide him satisfaction. Yet a person can only gain satisfaction in a relationship if he permits others to cooperate in setting the rules for the relationship and so influence and govern him. The person who dare not risk such control over him would seem to provoke his own misery by attempting to avoid it. If someone has suffered a series of hurts and frustrations with people he trusted, he tends to try to become independent of people — by not getting involved with them in such a way that they can gain control over his feelings or his behavior. He may literally avoid people; he may interact with them only on his own terms, constantly making an issue of who is going to circumscribe whose behavior; or he may choose the schizophrenic way and indicate that nothing he does is done in relationship to other people. In this fashion he is not governing anyone and no one is governing him.

The family of the schizophrenic would seem to be not only establishing and following a system of rules, as other families do, but also following a prohibition on any acknowledgement that a family member is setting rules. Each refuses to concede that he is circumscribing the behavior of others, and each refuses to concede that any other family member is governing him. Since communication in-evitably occurs if people live together, and since whatever one communicates inevitably governs the behavior of others, the family members must each constantly disqualify the communications of one another. Should one affirm what he does or what another does, he risks conceding that he is governed by the other with all the consequences that follow being disappointed again by an untrustworthy person. Schizophrenic behavior can be seen as both a product and a parody of this kind of family system. By labeling everything he communicates as not communicated by him to this person in this place, the schizophrenic indicates that he is not governing anyone's behavior because he is not in a relationship with anyone. This would seem to be a necessary style of behavior at times in this type of family system, and it may become habitual behavior. Yet even psychotic behavior does not free the individual from being governed or from governing others. The person who insists that he does not need anyone at all and is completely independent of them requires people to put him in a hospital and to force feed him. To live at all one must be involved with other people and so deal with the universal problem of who is going to circumscribe whose behavior. The more a person tries to avoid being governed or governing others, the more helpless he becomes and so governs others by forcing them to take care of him.

A MODEL FOR DIFFERENTIATING TYPES OF FAMILIES

What is lacking in the study of interpersonal relations is a method of describing, by way of some analogy, the process which takes place when two or more people interact with one another. Although there are models for inner activity, e.g., the id-ego-superego metaphor, there is not yet a model for human interaction. Implicit in the approach to the schizophrenic family offered here there is such a model. The essential elements of it are:1) the proposition that human communication can be classified into levels of message, 2) the cybernetic idea of the self-corrective, governed system. If a family confines itself to repetitive patterns within a certain range of possible behavior, then they are confined to that range by some sort of governing process. No outside governor requires the family members to behave in their habitual patterns, so this governing process must exist within the family. A third essential point is that when people respond to one another they govern, or establish rules, for each other's behavior.

To describe families, the most appropriate analogy would seem to be the self-corrective system governed by family members influencing each other's behavior and thereby establishing rules and prohibitions for that particular family system. Such a system tends to be error-activated. Should one family member break a family rule, the others become activated until he either conforms to the rule again or successfully establishes a new one.

A system of three organisms each governing the range of behavior of the other two, and each communicating at multiple levels, is both a simple idea and a complex model. Yet such an approach offers a general theoretical framework within which the specific rules of any one type of family system can be classified. The rudiments of such a system are suggested here at the most general level. The family of the schizophrenic is a particularly good model for this approach because of the narrow limits of their system. Our few preliminary observations of families containing children without symptoms, children who are delinquent, and children with asthma, lead us to believe that the interaction in the family of the schizophrenic is unique. Members of other types of family sometimes disqualify each other's statements but only under certain circumstances. Mutual affirmation will also occur. We have observed, for example, parents of an asthmatic child finishing each other's sentences and having this approved. Should the father of a schizophrenic finish the mother's sentence, it seems inevitable that she would indicate he provided the wrong ending. In other families leadership will stabilize into a pattern accepted by family members. Certain alliances will be allowed in some types of families, notably the delinquent where the child is capable of forming labeled alliances in gangs outside the family. In the family of the schizophrenic the range of behavior is as limited and inflexible as is the behavior of the schizophrenic in contrast to other people.

The observation of this type of family system inevitably takes place after the child has manifested a schizophrenic episode. Whether the family behaved in a similar way prior to his diagnosis is unknowable. In this sense it is difficult to assert that the interaction in his family "caused" schizophrenia. There are two possibilities. 1) If the family is a self-corrective system and the child behaves intermittently in a schizophrenic way, then schizophrenic behavior is a necessary part of this family system. 2) Alternatively, schizophrenic behavior as a result of a particular family system which has been disrupted by forces outside the system, such as maturation of the child or environmental influence. The family then reorganizes a new system which includes the schizophrenic behavior as an element, and this is what we are presently examining. The evidence leads us to believe that schizophrenic behavior in the child is reinforced by the present family system.

Although psychotic behavior may serve a function in a family system, a risk is also involved. The patient may need to be separated from the family by hospitalization and so break up the system, or he may enter therapy and change and so leave the system. Typically the parents seem to welcome hospitalization only if the patient is still accessible to them, and they welcome therapy for the patient up to the point when he begins to change and infringe the rules of the family system while acknowledging that he is doing so.

REFERENCES

1. ALANEN, Y. The mothers of schizophrenic patients. Acta psychiat. et neurol. scandinav., **33**: Suppl. 124, 1958.

2. BATESON, G. Cultural problems posed by a study of schizophrenic process. Presented at the American Psychiatric Association, Conference on Schizophrenia, Honolulu, 1958. In press.

3. BATESON, G. The group dynamics of schizophrenia. Presented at the Institute on Chronic Schizophrenia and Hospital Treatment Programs, Osawatomie State Hospital, Osawatomie, 1958. In press.

4. Bateson, G. The new conceptual frames for behavioral research. Presented at the Sixth Annual Psychiatric Institute Conference at the New Jersey Neuro-Psychiatric Institute, Princeton, New Jersey, 1958. In press.

5. BATESON, G., JACKSON, D. D., HALEY, J. AND WEAKLAND, J. Toward a theory of schizophrenia. Behavioral Sc., **1**: 251–264, 1956.

6. BOWEN, M., DYSINGER, R. H. AND BASAMINIA, B. The role of the father in families with a schizophrenia patient. Paper presented at the annual meeting of the American Psychiatric Association, May, 1958.

7. GERARD, D. L. AND SIEGEL, J. The family background of schizophrenia. Psychiat. Quart., **24**: 47–73, 1950.

8. FRAZEE, H. E. Children who later became schizophrenic. Smith. Coll. Stud. Social Work, **123**: 125–149, 1953.

9. HALEY, J. Control in psychoanalytic psychotherapy. Progr. Psychotherapy, **4**: 48–65, 1959.

10. HALEY, J. An interactional description of schizophrenia. Psychiatry, to be published.

11. HALEY, J. An interactional explanation of hypnosis. Am. J. Clin. Hypnosis, **1**: 41–57, 1958.

12. Jackson, D. D. The question of family homeostasis. Psychoanalyt. Quart., 31: Suppl.; 79–90, 1957.

13. Lidz, R. W. and Lidz, T. The family environment of schizophrenic patients. Am. J. Psychiat., 106: 332–345, 1949.

14. Lidz, T., Parker, B. and Cornelison, A. R. The role of father in the family environment of the schizophrenic patient. Am. J. Phychiat., 113: 126–132, 1956.

15. Lidz, T., Cornelison, A. R., Fleck, S. and Terry, D. The intrafamilial environment of schizophrenic patients. I. The Father. Psychiatry, 20: 329–342, 1957.

16. Lidz, T., Cornelison, A. R., Fleck, S. and Terry, D. The intrafamilial environment of schizophrenic patients. II. Marital schism and marital skew. Am. J. Psychiat., 114: 241–248, 1957.

17. Reichard, S. and Tillman, G. Patterns of parent-child relationships in schizophrenia. Psychiatry, 13: 247–257, 1950.

18. Rosen, J. N. Direct Analysis. Grune & Stratton, New York, 1951.

19. Stanton, A. H. and Schwartz, M. S. The Mental Hospital. Basic Books, New York, 1954.

20. Tietze, T. A study of the mothers of schizophrenic patients. Psychiatry, 12: 55–65, 1949.

21. Weakland, J. The double bind hypothesis of schizophrenia and three-party interaction. In The Study of Schizophrenia. Basic Books, New York. In press.

22. Weakland, J. H. and Jackson, D. D. Patient and therapist observations on the circumstances of a schizophrenic episode. A. M. A. Arch. Neurol. & Psychiat., 79: 554–574, 1958.

23. Wynne, I. D., Ryckoff, I. M., Day, J. and Hirsch, S. E. Pseudo-mutuality in the family relations of schizophrenics. Psychiatry, 21: 205–220, 1958.

THEODORE LIDZ, STEPHEN FLECK,
YRJÖ O. ALANEN, AND ALICE CORNELISON

Schizophrenic Patients and Their Siblings*†

A number of studies carried out by ourselves and others have demonstrated that schizophrenic patients virtually always grow up in seriously disturbed homes.[1] Since the finding provides one of the most consistent leads concerning the etiology of schizophrenia, we have been seeking to describe the characteristics of these families and to isolate factors that may be specific to the genesis of schizophrenia. The question has been raised repeatedly: If the family milieu is critical to the production of schizophrenia in a particular offspring, if it exerts a serious pathogenic influence upon this child, what about the siblings? Why are they not affected?

We designed our entire intensive study of the families of patients around this question, selecting only families in which the schizophrenic child had at least one sibling who could be studied. This permitted a comparison of the patients with persons who were not schizophrenic but who had been raised by the same parents and exposed to many similar intrafamilial influences. The siblings rather than some other arbitrarily selected person form a comparative group — and we are pointedly avoiding the term controls, since we do not believe that a

* Reprinted by special permission of The William Alanson White Psychiatric Foundation, Inc., from Psychiatry, Vol. 26, 1963, pp. 1–18. Copyright by The William Alanson White Psychiatric Foundation, Inc.

† The research upon which this paper is based is supported by grants from the National Institute of Mental Health and from the Social Research Foundation.

[1] Yrjö O. Alanen, "The Mothers of Schizophrenic Patients," Acta Psychiat. et Neurol. Scandinav. (1958) 33: Supplement 124. Murray Bowen, "The Family as the Unit of Study and Treatment: I. Family Psychotherapy," Amer. J. Orthopsychiatry (1961) 31:40–60. Warren M. Brodey, "The Family as the Unit of Study and Treatment: 3. Image, Object and Narcissistic Relationships," Amer. J. Orthopsychiatry (1961) 31:69–73. Stephen Fleck, "Family Dynamics and Origin of Schizophrenia." Psychosomatic Med. (1960) 22:333–344. Ruth W. Lidz and Theodore Lidz, "The Family Environment of Schizophrenic Patients," Amer. J. Psychiatry (1949) 106:332–345. Theodore Lidz, "Schizophrenia and the Family," Psychiatry (1958) 21:21–27. Lyman C. Wynne, Irving M. Ryckoff, Juliana Day, and Stanley I. Hirsch, "Pseudo-Mutuality in the Family Relations of Schizophrenics," Psychiatry (1958) 21:205–220.

true control series can be established in this type of study.

Of course, we do not aspire to a definitive answer, for if the question of why one child in a family rather than another becomes schizophrenic could be answered, the cause of schizophrenia would be virtually found. Genetic investigations, despite the impressive findings of twin studies, have thus far failed to produce evidence for either a dominant or a recessive trait.[2] Their failure may be due to primary reliance upon hospital records and the incidence of overt and flagrant schizophrenia. The contribution of the various genetic studies has recently been reviewed by Jackson, and currently Rosenthal is carefully examining their methodologies and findings.[3] The evidence indicates that extragenetic influences play a very significant role. The scrutiny of our data can help clarify the problem, particularly along two lines: First, by noting the incidence of serious psychopathological conditions among the siblings. Second, by examining the differences in the intrafamilial influences impinging upon the siblings within a family with particular reference to (a) the changes in family circumstances and intrafamilial role relationships that alter the conditions under which siblings are raised; (b) the mother's capacities to provide affectionate nurturant care to the various siblings during infancy; (c) the different role allocations and role assumptions of the children in the family dynamics; (d) how the parental personalities and the configuration of their relationship lead children of one sex to be confronted by greater developmental problems than children of the opposite sex; (e) idiosyncratic problems; and (f) the influence of the siblings upon one another.

The findings to be presented are based upon the intensive study of sixteen families who had an adolescent or young adult offspring hospitalized in the Yale Psychiatric Institute. Inclusion in the series was based upon the availability of the mother and at least one sibling for repeated interviews, projective testing, and observation. In all except two families, the father was living and was included in the study, creating a bias toward unbroken families. With the exception of two upwardly mobile lower-middle-class families, all were upper-middle-class and upper-class families capable of supporting an off-spring in a private hospital for prolonged periods. The distinct bias toward families with some degree of prestige in their communities was welcomed to minimize the potential effects of poor extrafamilial socioeconomic environments. The basic means of gaining information were repeated interviewing of all family members by the same social worker and by psychiatrists — the latter interviewing in some instances becoming synonymous with fairly intensive psychotherapy;[4] observing the interaction of family members with each other and hospital staff;[5] and projective testing of all family members.[6] Diaries, family friends, former teachers, and nurse-maids were drawn into the study whenever feasible, and home visits were made in most cases. Families were studied for periods ranging from six months to six years, and, except for the first three cases, all were actively studied for more than a year. Any attempt to reconstruct a family environment as it existed over a period of fifteen to thirty years will have grave deficiencies, but, with a few exceptions, these families are probably known more intimately than any series of families that have been studied for any purpose.

All of the families were seriously disturbed. The difficulties pervaded the entire family interaction and could not be encompassed by focusing upon isolated segments of the data alone, even though in a series of papers we have sought to focus on differing aspects of the family milieu and to analyze the family transactions from various perspectives. We have noted the severe psychopathology of the fathers as well as of the mothers,[7] and we have found that these families were either schismatic —

[2] Franz J. Kallmann, *Heredity in Health and Mental Disorder*; New York, Norton, 1953. David Rosenthal, "Confusion of Identity and the Frequency of Schizophrenia in Twins," *Arch. General Psychiatry* (1960) 3:297–304. Dorothy T. Sohler, Jules D. Holzberg, Stephen Fleck, Alice R. Cornelison, Eleanor Kay, and Theodore Lidz, "The Prediction of Family Interaction from a Battery of Projective Tests," *J. Projective Techniques* (1957) 21: 199–208.
[3] Don J. Jackson, Editor, *The Etiology of Schizophrenia*; New York, Basic Books, 1960. David Rosenthal, "Some Factors Associated with Concordance and Discordance with Respect to Schizophrenia in Monozygotic Twins," *J. Nervous and Mental Disease* (1959) 129:1–10. See also Rosenthal (1960) in footnote 2, and Rosenthal, unpublished data.

[4] Alice R. Cornelison, "Casework Interviewing as a Research Technique in a Study of Families of Schizophrenic Patients," *Mental Hygiene* (1960) 44:551–559.
[5] Stephen Fleck, Alice R. Cornelison, Nea Norton, and Theodore Lidz, "The Intrafamilial Environment of the Schizophrenic Patient: II. Interaction Between Hospital Staff and Families," PSYCHIATRY (1957) 20:343–350.
[6] See Sohler and others, in footnote 2.
[7] Theodore Lidz, Alice R. Cornelison, Stephen Fleck, and Dorothy Terry, "The Intrafamilial Environment of the Schizophrenic Patient: I. The Father," PSYCHIATRY (1957) 20:329–342. Theodore Lidz, Stephen Fleck, Alice R. Cornelison, and Dorothy Terry, "The Intrafamilial Environment of the Schizophrenic Patient: IV. Parental Personalities and Family Interaction," *Amer. J. Orthopsychiatry* (1958) 28:764–776.

that is, divided into two antagonistic and competing factions — or were "skewed" in that the serious personality disturbance of one parent set the pattern of family interaction.[8] We have described the irrational and paralogical modes of thinking and communicating that prevailed in these families, suggesting that the children received a very faulty training in reality testing.[9] We have also discovered that the parents commonly struggled with incestuous and homosexual tendencies themselves, and that the ensuing difficulties, together with the faulty family dynamics, left the schizophrenic offspring unable to resolve his Oedipal problems and gain a secure identity as a member of his or her sex.[10] Our findings, though at times expressed in different terms, are very much in accord with those of Bateson and Jackson, Weakland, Wynne, Bowen, Brodey, Alanen, and others who have studied families of schizophrenic patients.[11] To summarize, we do not consider it likely that any single factor such as a faulty mother-infant relationship will prove to be responsible in itself for causing schizophrenia, but we have found that the structure and interaction of these families are highly detrimental to the ego development of children raised in them.

[8] Theodore Lidz, Alice R. Cornelison, Stephen Fleck, and Dorothy Terry, "The Intrafamilial Environment of the Schizophrenic Patient: II. Marital Schism and Marital Skew," *Amer. J. Psychiatry* (1957) 114:241–248.
[9] Theodore Lidz, Alice R. Cornelison, Dorothy Terry, and Stephen Fleck, "The Intrafamilial Environment of the Schizophrenic Patient: VI. The Transmission of Irrationality," *Arch. Neurology and Psychiatry* (1958) 79:305–316. Theodore Lidz, Alice R. Cornelison, Sarah Schafer, Dorothy Terry, and Stephen Fleck, "Ego Differentiation and Schizophrenic Symptom Formation in Identical Twins," *J. Amer. Psychoanalytic Assn.* (1962) 10:74–90. Theodore Lidz, C. Wild, Sarah Schafer, and Stephen Fleck, "The Thought Disorders of Parents of Schizophrenic Patients," paper presented at the Third World Congress of Psychiatry, Montreal, 1961.
[10] Stephen Fleck, Alice R. Cornelison, Sarah Schafer, Dorothy Terry, and Theodore Lidz, "The Intrafamilial Environment of the Schizophrenic Patient: Incestuous and Homosexual Problems," pp. 142–159, in *Science and Psychoanalysis, Vol. II: Individual and Familial Dynamics,* edited by Jules H. Masserman; New York, Grune & Stratton, 1959. See also Lidz and others, "Ego Differentiation and Schizophrenic Symptom Formation in Identical Twins," in footnote 9.
[11] Gregory Bateson, Don D. Jackson, Jay Haley, and John H. Weakland, "Toward a Theory of Schizophrenia," *Behavioral Science* (1956) 1:251–264. John H. Weakland, "The 'Double Bind' Hypothesis of Schizophrenia and Three-Party Interaction," Chapter 13, in *The Etiology of Schizophrenia,* edited by Don D. Jackson; New York, Basic Books, 1960. See, in footnote 1, Wynne and others; Bowen; Brodey; and Alanen. See also Jay Haley, "The Family of the Schizophrenic: A Model System," *J. Nervous and Mental Disease* (1959) 129:357–374.

Studying these families has led to a search for the fundamentals in the organization of the family that are requisite for reasonably stable development of its off-spring. We find that these parents fail to provide a satisfactory family milieu because they cannot form a coalition as members of the parental generation, maintaining their appropriate sex-linked roles, or transmit instrumentally valid ways of thinking, feeling, and communicating suited to the society into which the child must emerge. The child who grows up in a family lacking in these fundamentals has confused and confusing models for identification, has difficulty in achieving a sex-linked identity, in overcoming his incestuous attachments, and in finding meaningful and consistent guides for relating to others because of the deviant perception and cognition of himself and the world which he has acquired in his family.

Comparing the intrafamilial factors influencing the schizophrenic patient with those affecting his siblings obviously presents difficulties. The investigators are aware of the bias that can arise from the knowledge that one sibling is schizophrenic and another is not. As the difficulty is inherent in the study, nothing could be done except to take it into account. Another problem is that an intensive study including all family members could not encompass a large sample, and unless the study was intensive, it could not expect to gain meaningful answers. In the sixteen families the various combinations and sequences of brothers and sisters were limited, and some factors of potential pertinence require study of various permutations of gender and sequential placement within the family. Another limitation arises in presenting the material: It is difficult to compare the developmental situations of the siblings briefly, for the material is inordinately complex and properly would require a thorough exposition of each family.

THE 'NORMAL' SIBLING

Any intent to compare the development of the schizophrenic patient with that of 'normal' siblings had to be modified greatly for the simple but incontrovertible reason that only a small minority of the siblings could be considered reasonably well adjusted. While normality cannot be readily defined, everyone who has examined the material has been struck by the serious personality problems of the siblings as a group. The sixteen patients have a total of twenty-four siblings. Only five or six of the siblings are making reasonably adequate adjustments, and of these only three are considered well adjusted, even if the assessments are slanted favorably.[12] Examining the siblings for the presence of serious psychopathology, we find that three are clinically schizophrenic and another six or seven, including one who is a severe psychopathic personality, are making borderline and very tenuous adjustments. The remaining eight or nine siblings suffer from a variety of clinical neuroses, acting-out tendencies, and psychosomatic ailments, alone or in combination, for which four had required psychiatric treatment prior to the time of study (see Figure 1).

tending to be highly suspicious of the motives of others. The youngest sister had withdrawn from the family and had married. She refused to use her inherited wealth, tying herself down to her housework and children in a bizarre, obsessive manner, maintaining a very precarious balance. She is a borderline or ambulatory schizophrenic.

While the nonschizophrenic personality disorders of the siblings may be of little interest to those who consider schizophrenia to be a clearly circumscribed

□ **Figure 1**

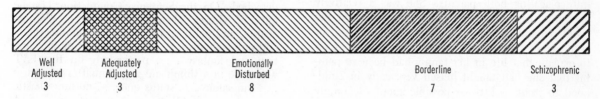

Well Adjusted	Adequately Adjusted	Emotionally Disturbed	Borderline	Schizophrenic
3	3	8	7	3

Range of adjustment of 24 siblings of schizophrenic patients.

The listing of psychiatric diagnoses for the siblings would serve little. The range and severity of their problems can be illustrated by citing the problems of the children in the two families with the largest number of siblings. By chance, one contained four sons and the other four daughters. In the Schwartz family,[13] the youngest son was the patient, a paranoid schizophrenic with delusions that people were against him, accusing him of homosexuality. His oldest brother was a severe sociopath, an embezzler, forger, and gambler. The second son had been disturbed in adolescence and may have been transiently delusional in early adult life, but had become a successful mathematician and had moved far away from the family and its problems. The third son was seriously phobic, suffered from anxiety, and was unable to practice his profession, although he managed to hold a routine job and to marry, living with his wife in the parental home.

The second daughter in the Thomas family had been schizophrenic for many years, the most chronic and withdrawn patient in the series. Her older sister had been in analysis for several years because of serious and diffuse emotional and marital difficulties. The third daughter, who also was in psychiatric treatment, had severe marital problems, had a violent temper, and felt chronically frustrated,

disease entity, or to those seeking a predominantly genetic etiology, these disorders have pertinence to psychiatrists who entertain the hypothesis that schizophrenia is related to deviant personality development. If the intrafamilial transactions play a major role in shaping the personality of the offspring raised within the family, each child in these seriously disturbed families may well be affected in different ways and to differing degrees, and not all need reach the extreme of a schizophrenic reaction.

The personality problems of the siblings will receive further scrutiny during the discussion of the influences affecting their development within their families. However, two defensive maneuvers, marked constriction and flight from the family, require special comment because they were strikingly characteristic, particularly of the siblings who had made reasonably good adaptations.

Of the four best adjusted siblings, only one, a girl who had two psychotic brothers, seemed reasonably free and imaginative. The other three, as well as many of the more distrubed siblings, suffered from marked constriction of their personalities with notable limitations in their range of emotional maturity, their perceptiveness, and the use of their intellectual resources.[14] A sibling may, for example, successfully pursue a scientific career that requires minimal interpersonal awareness and remain relatively impoverished in other areas. The constricted person-

[12] Margaret Thaler Singer, in an unpublished investigation, estimated the stability of fourteen siblings of eleven schizophrenic patients through a study of their projective tests. She considered four to be constricted normals, five as moderately or severely neurotic, and five as clearly schizoid or latently schizophrenic.

[13] All names are fictitious.

[14] Margaret Thaler Singer has also emphasized personality constriction as a major defense of siblings of schizophrenic patients from her unpublished study of the projective tests of a series investigated at the National Institute of Mental Health by Lyman Wynne and his co-workers.

ality usually utilizes the defense of isolation to prevent recognition of the extent of the intrafamilial difficulties, for facing the total situation would be shattering. In some, whole periods of the past have been completely repressed and particularly traumatic experiences have produced amnesias. In the investigation, where intensive therapy could not be offered the siblings, such defenses had to be respected as essential to the sibling's ego integrity.

A sister of a young schizophrenic woman had managed to avoid involvement in the parental conflict in which her sister had been enmeshed, carefully placating both parents. She was a relatively poor informant about the family, insisting that she could remember very little about her childhood, or even about many recent occurrences. She went on to explain that life in her family had been so painful that she had taught herself very early in childhood to think as little as possible about the family quarrels, never letting herself review a day's happenings. She tried to concentrate upon avoiding trouble, pleasing her parents, and doing well at school until she could leave college and lead her own life. She did not consciously know how she felt about her strange and difficult parents. While we have counted this young woman among the more stable siblings — indeed the most stable sibling of the same sex as the patient — Margaret Thaler Singer, who interpreted the projective tests of the members of this family without any knowledge about them, wrote the following excerpt:[15]

> To coin a phrase, this girl is "her parents' child." One can see the impact of their communication styles upon her. She uses fragmented remarks, tells a story [on the TAT], then takes it back saying that she didn't find a meaning! Nothing gets validated and confirmed. She often describes interactions as rather pointless, fragmented affairs which she then denies. . . . people are not responsible for their own wrongdoings . . . children might need their attention brought back to concrete realities — they are seen as inattentive and drifting — people in general are not good, and interactions hardly ever lead to anything pleasant. She is more than willing to leave crazily incompatible acts hanging together as if they made sense or were sequitors. . . . Men are seen in very poor light. . . . Mother is not seen in a positive way at all. On one card she told no story at all where a mother is usually seen. On another two stories the wife poisons the husband. . . .

Thus the projective tests bore out the clinical impression that this woman had managed to deal with potentially serious disturbance by constriction, isolation, and denial.

One of the most successful siblings, the brother of a schizophrenic girl, had knowingly or unknowingly gratified his parents' ambitions for him by choosing a wealthy spouse and becoming a capable physician. He was pleasant and affable, but communicated little of pertinence. Singer, again without knowledge of the subject, stated, on the basis of the projective tests:

> He is obsessive. He has learned from his father to take an intellectual position and try to seem detached. On the Sentence Completion Test he talks of viruses, chemistry, Beethoven, pharmaceutics, and politics. He senses he is nonrevealing and unimaginative. . . . He is repudiating imagination and fantasy . . . particularly on the TAT where he says things are a . . . matter of course . . . innocuous . . . status quo . . . nothing drastic . . . just a passing thing . . . no outcome . . . just simply another thing, etc. He has learned the Pollyanna-like style both his parents have. . . .

Although personality constriction was prominent in the siblings in this study, we know that some siblings of schizophrenic patients are reasonably stable and also highly sensitive and productive. A number of outstanding authors have had schizophrenic siblings, and some have apparently abreacted their traumatic lives in their artistic productions. Psychiatrists with schizophrenic siblings have sensitively used the insights gained within their own families to understand and treat schizophrenic patients.

Some siblings realize that they must flee from the disturbing family environment as soon as possible in order not to be overwhelmed. Several of them recounted how they had maintained an emotional aloofness for several years until they could get away; in others, the predicament of the schizophrenic sibling became so intolerable and frightening that they impulsively left home, as did a character in *The Glass Menagerie*.[16] In leaving the home, they are apt to try to block out the past and disengage themselves from their families. Of course, these siblings are often more able to leave the parental attachments and survive on their own than are the patients, in whom such attempts at disengagement may precipitate an acute psychotic break. The sister whose constriction has just been noted had no intention of returning home after finishing college and married promptly upon being graduated. In another instance, a college girl became bedridden soon after her brother was hospitalized, and then with the support of her

---

[15] The excerpts which follow are from Singer's unpublished data. See also Sohler and others, in footnote 2; and Jules D. Holzberg, unpublished notes.

[16] Tennessee Williams, *The Glass Menagerie*; New York, Hawthorne, 1955.

psychiatrist moved away from the home and severed contact with her mother; even many years later she continued to avoid her parents, and she visited her brother, who was hospitalized very close to her home, only two or three times in four years. The brother of a male patient kept away from his mother — who was schizophrenic, divorced, and pathetically lonely — because, in his frenzy at her engulfing ways, he found himself planning ways of murdering her. The most stable of the four Schwartz brothers was the only one who had left the family; he lived at a great distance and kept himself absorbed in his mathematics. One sister in the Thomas family, but not the best adjusted, had made a complete break with her family, not only avoiding contact with them but also consciously seeking to lead a totally different type of life.

DIVERGENT INFLUENCES UPON THE OFFSPRING WITHIN A FAMILY

The Effects of Changing Family Circumstances

The family is not static but is an organization with a dynamic configuration in which role relationships change constantly. Time is a factor in these changes, as children enter new developmental phases and parents grow older. Sometimes marked shifts in the family occur, leading to a loss of equilibrium or to deleterious defensive measures to maintain a semblance of role reciprocity between members. In some instances the family situation and the parental attitudes altered so markedly that the patient was raised altogether differently from his siblings, and a similar outcome of the developmental process could not be expected. The Forel family offers a clear example.

The Forel marriage had never been compatible. The father, a weak man, had struggled ineffectually against the domination of the family by his wife, who was abetted by her two older sisters. All three sisters were contemptuous of men, and the oldest was a virago who despised and sought to control men. Mrs. Forel was cold, highly narcissistic, and a teasing flirt. She refused to move away from the neighborhood where her mother and sisters lived, and each summer abandoned her husband to vacation with them for two months. The marriage became increasingly schismatic, with Mr. Forel feeling himself an outcast in his own home, his opinions devalued, and his wishes ignored. His frequent tantrums increased his wife's contempt for him.

There were three children; the patient, a boy, was the youngest child, with a sister thirteen years older and a brother eleven years older. All of the children suffered from the family atmosphere. The older brother considered his childhood to have been abysmal, but far better than the patient's. For the two older children the parental influences had been modified by close contact with the extended families of both parents. The older son had been a favorite of his grandparents and aunts, gaining their admiration and praise by ingratiating himself in an obsequious fashion that enraged his father. He became highly neurotic, terrified of male authorities. He believed that he had escaped very serious disorganization by, first, his attachment to a male teacher, identifying himself with him and trying to follow in his footsteps, and then by developing a psychogenic dermatitis that led him into intensive psychotherapy. The sister became a seriously constricted and anxious woman.

Shortly before the conception of the patient, the parents had verged upon the separation they had often considered. Mr. Forel had been offered an opportunity to establish a business in another state, but his wife refused to move away from her sisters. When Mr. Forel issued an ultimatum and threatened divorce, his wife capitulated and agreed to move, and also agreed to resume the sexual relationship she had terminated eleven years before. The patient was a product of the brief reconciliation. Finding herself pregnant, Mrs. Forel became enraged at her husband and sought unsuccessfully to terminate the pregnancy. After the child was born, she paid little attention to him, and, feeling lost without her sisters, upon whom she had always been dependent, she began to drink heavily and to entertain male friends. During the patient's childhood, both parents were frequently intoxicated, and the older children reported that the father often carried his wife home dead drunk. The older siblings and the father tried to fill a mothering role toward the patient. Then, when the patient was six, Mrs. Forel was seriously disfigured in an auto accident which occurred when her husband fell asleep while driving. She became depressed and refused to leave her room until her appearance could be restored surgically, more than a year later. Feeling guilty, the father sought to make amends by becoming subservient to her, and was treated more contemptuously than ever. Then in rapid succession, the brother left for college, the sister married, and the father failed in his business. The family moved again, and shortly thereafter the father developed a malignancy. As he went downhill, his wife totally neglected him, fearing that she might catch cancer from him. The father died when the patient was eleven, and from then on the boy never had a real home. They lived with his married sister for a time; and then his mother moved in with her oldest sister. This aunt hated the patient,

who was defiant toward her, and refused to permit
him to live in her house. He boarded in the neighborhood, visiting his mother when his aunt was not
at home.

In at least half of the families, the sequential
position of the offspring formed a significant differentiating influence because of changing family circumstances, although the changes were less dramatic
in the other case than in the one described above.
The children's position in a family can, however,
make considerable difference in the parents' attitudes
toward them even when they are of the same sex
and closely proximate in age because of the places
they fill in the dynamic equilibrium of the family.
We have considered two of the most difficult problems of differentiation in our series in previous
papers: The differing role and identity assignments
of a set of identical twins,[17] and the very different
situations confronting two sisters born less than two
years apart, the older of whom is schizophrenic and
the younger reasonably well adjusted.[18] The mother
of the twins had selected the older twin to live out
her masculine fantasies of the life denied her because
she was a woman and was herself a less favored
younger twin, while she identified the younger of
the twins with her feminine, passive, and masochistic
self. In the other case, the older of the sisters had
become the focal point and scapegoat in a conflict
between her parents that had antedated her birth
and had been brought to a crisis by her conception,
whereas the younger sister had remained relatively
peripheral to the continuing parental quarrel.

The Mother's Capacity to Provide Nurturant
Care During the Patient's Infancy

In half of the cases studied, a clear disturbance
was found to have existed in the relationship of the
mother with the patient as an infant — a disturbance that was not present, or at least not to the
same degree, in her relationship with her other
children. This is in keeping with theories of the
importance of infantile deprivation and maternal
rejection in the genesis of schizophrenia. Three
mothers had been physically incapacitated for many
months following the patient's birth, disabilities that
had been aggravated by their emotional problems at
the time. One mother had been fearful of handling
her oldest child, particularly of bathing him, a task
which the father had to carry out. The mother of
the two schizophrenic Robb sisters had been too
insecure to take care of her oldest daughter and had

[17] Lidz and others, "Ego Differentiation and Schizophrenic
Symptom Formation in Identical Twins," in footnote 9.
[18] Lidz and others (1958), in footnote 7.

turned her care, as an infant and small child, over to
a nurse; when her son was born, three year later, she
had cared for him herself; but when the younger
daughter was born, she paid little attention to her,
for she was preoccupied with hostility toward her
unfaithful husband, had started an affair, and was
considering divorce. Another mother of two daughters had suffered "gloomy thoughts" following the
birth of the younger girl, who became the patient,
whereas the birth of the older child had been a
joyous occasion — and a clear preference for the
older child continued during the ensuing years.
Mrs. Forel, already referred to, had sought to abort
her youngest child, who became the patient, and had
been emotionally withdrawn from him during his
infancy, as well as during his later years. At least
one other mother's efforts at mothering were seriously impeded by her husband's extreme jealously
of any attention she sought to give her son, a situation that did not recur after the birth of a daughter. In several other instances, the mother had
difficulty in providing proper nurturant care for her
children as infants, but notable differences in the
care provided the patient and the siblings were not
apparent.

It is difficult properly to assess such influences in
the first year of the patient's life. The problem is
partly one of retrospective assessment, but even
more one of sorting out what is pertinent and decisive in families where serious difficulties had existed
prior to the patient's birth and then continued
throughout his developmental years. Two things
are apparent: That these difficulties in nurturing the
infant did not occur in all cases, and that this problem was but one among many parent-child difficulties.
However, such deprivation may be important in predisposing the child to schizophrenia. It may also
indicate the start of a chronically faulty mother-
child relationship, and such unsatisfactory parent-
infant interaction may set a pattern aggravated by
constant feedback from child to mother, mother to
child, and one parent to the other, involving the
sibling relationships as well.

The Child's Role in the Family Dynamics

The Child and Parental Conflicts — In those
families that we have designated as "schismatic,"
the parents were in open conflict, trying to coerce
each other, each encountering from the other either
defiance or, at best, a temporary hostile and resentful submission. Each undercut the worth and self-
esteem of the other and divided the family, the
mother wooing the children to side with her, and
the father wooing them to side with him in the

conflict, each parent fostering distrust and devaluation of the other. In many cases a constant threat of family dissolution hung over the children. The parents were preoccupied with their marital problems, and, in the absence of affection and support from each other, turned to a child to fill their emotional needs. In our experience, the child who becomes schizophrenic is caught in the schism to a greater degree than are the others in a variety of ways: First, he may fill the role of the "scapegoat" whose difficulties preoccupy the parents and mask their basic unhappiness with one another. Second, he may insert himself into the split, seeking to widen the gap between them to gain one parent for himself. Third, he may devote his energies and attention to bridging the gap between the parents. He straddles issues, divides his loyalties, and seeks to become a different person for each parent in order to fill the emotional needs of both, consuming his energies in preserving the parents' marriage and in salvaging their lives, rather than in the interests of his own independent ego development. Fourth, he may be caught in a bind in which loyalty to one parent means rejection by the other; because of their opposing standards and needs, he cannot satisfy and feel accepted by one without arousing dissatisfaction or hostility in the other. The widely discrepant attitudes and directives of the parents cannot be integrated within the single child — the irreconcilable parents become irreconcilable introjects.[19]

The reasons why one offspring rather than another becomes most intensively involved are diverse: The sequential position, the child's sex, changes in the family situation, childhood illnesses, and others not so readily categorized. However, the patient's involvement commonly relieves the other children of much of the burden. The following case excerpts illustrate how one child became more caught up in the family schism than the siblings.

In the Nussbaum family, the parents, preoccupied with their own problems, could invest little in their daughter from the time she was born, resenting her because her birth had prevented the divorce which they had considered. The baby became irritable and difficult and filled the role of scapegoat, diverting attention from the parents' dissension, and eventually she widened the gulf between the parents by displacing the mother in the father's affections to the extent of near incestuous involvement.

[19] Fleck and others, in footnote 10. Stephen Fleck, Theodore Lidz, and Alice R. Cornelison, "Comparison of Parent-Child Relationships of Male and Female Schizophrenic Patients," *Arch. General Psychiatry* (1963) 8:1–7. See also Weakland, in footnote 11.

Mrs. Nussbaum had been delighted with her first-born son and very proud of him. When the daughter was born three years later, the mother was unable to care for the infant, supposedly because of a back injury that she blamed on her husband's neglect during the pregnancy. During the year before the daughter's birth, the couple had had a severe disagreement as a consequence of a feud between their parental families. The couple never became reconciled and lived together in an atmosphere of resentment, at times not speaking to one another for weeks. Mrs. Nussbaum felt trapped in an intolerable marriage, grew increasingly sullen and caustic, and eventually became severely disturbed. Although she could not act warmly toward her daughter, she continued to find solace and pleasure in her son.

Mr. Nussbaum remained away from home as much as possible, and turned to his daughter for affection and admiration he could not gain from his wife. At times, he seemed to be spiting his wife by the alliance with the girl. He became very seductive toward his daughter, sleeping with her when she became anxious at night and cuddling her to sleep until she began, during adolescence, to express fears of becoming pregnant. The child's problems became a major concern to both parents, but also a source of mutual recrimination. The mother sought to devote herself to her daughter's care when she became increasingly difficult during adolescence, but would lose patience and go into rages in which she would tell the girl that she wished she were dead. The mother, fairly typically, lacked empathy for her daughter, and because of her inconsistent behavior and the father's devaluation of her formed an unacceptable model, while the father seductively substituted the daughter for his wife. Thus the patient was at times a scapegoat and at other times a divisive influence. In contrast, the son received affection from both parents, for his father was very much interested in him, and although he was affected by the parental conflict, he was never in the center of it and was two years old before it arose. Further, his father as a professional man provided an excellent career model for him, even in his mother's eyes.

The older of the two daughters in the Grau family was caught in a particularly difficult bind because of the parents' dissensions that antedated her birth and their irreconcilable ideas about religion, which focused upon how the child should be raised. Her Protestant father refused to permit her to be baptized into Catholicism despite his written promise, he constantly condemned Catholicism and all Catholics, and he later refused to permit her to go with Catholic boys. Her Catholic mother fought back, sought to woo the girl to Catholicism, and secretly circumvented her husband. She was constantly anxious about her unbaptized child, and eventually had her baptized without her husband's knowledge. The parents' religious quarrels were but symptomatic of many areas of discord.

The patient struggled with these irreconcilable introjects until she finally defiantly sided with her paranoid father and sought to win him away from her mother. The younger daughter, while also subjected to the conflict, never became the focus of it. To some extent, the father relinquished her to his wife; since the older sister preempted the father's attention and affection, the younger could form an alliance with her mother. As we shall note later in the paper, the sister learned at an early age to sidestep the difficulties in which the patient became involved.

In the Benjamin family the son who became schizophrenic sought to satisfy the disparate ambitions his parents held for him, to fill their unmet needs, and to keep them from separating. When they were at odds, he would become frightened by their seductiveness toward him; yet he would become jealous and more disturbed whenever they became more compatible. Both parents used the son's indications of affection and his criticisms of the other parent as a vindication of themselves, wooing him as an ally. At the same time, the father could not permit his son to gain a better education than he himself had obtained, and he unconsciously sabotaged his wife's hopes and the boy's ambitions. The confusions in the sexual sphere were even greater, with both parents behaving seductively toward their son. The patient's older sister could simply side with her father and did not seek to hold the parents together. She was not threatened by seduction from the mother, and her father was less physically seductive toward her than toward his son. Less involved in the parents' difficulties and hence less burdened by guilt, she could also exploit the parents' disagreements to gain goals of her own, which her brother could not do.

The Child's Role in "Skewed" Families — Not all of the parents were in overt conflict. In the families that we have termed "skewed" — predominantly families with male schizophrenic offspring[20] — the serious personality problems and deviant ways of the dominant parent were not count-ered by the spouse. The patient, in contrast to his siblings, is the object of a particular intrusiveness by the dominant parent, usually the mother, which blurs the ego boundaries between parent and child and ties the patient to satisfying the parent's needs and to continuing a primary relatedness with her. The boy's differentiation from the initial symbiotic bond to his mother and the development of identification with his passive father are impeded. The symbiotic attachment leads to confusion of sexual identity, incestuous concerns, and a greater assimilation of the disturbed parent's deviant and paralogical ways. The siblings may resent the patient's special relationship with the mother, but they are freer to develop into independent persons. The oldest child may be selected as the object of this intrusive relationship, but in some instances the mother holds on to the youngest child as the older children grow away from her.

In the family with the identical twins, the mother never established ego boundaries between herself and her twins. From the time of their birth, her entire life was wrapped up in these phallic extensions of herself. The older brother of the twins, together with the father, became outcasts. The mother banished the father from her room and bed, and she considered the older son to be uncouth and unimportant. The older brother hated the twins, envied them, and suffered; and he became accident-prone, seriously unstable, and given to acting-out tendencies. Yet he could identify with his father, who, despite his wife's contempt and ridicule, was a far more stable person than she. The older brother did not need to struggle to differentiate himself from his mother or to escape her bizarre demands; and eventually he felt very free to leave home and seek fulfillment elsewhere.

The Siblings' Gender

While most of the siblings were emotionally unstable, our data indicate that the most generalized and consistent factor related to the severity of the disturbance was the sex of the sibling. This factor is complex; since it is a function of the parental personalities and their interrelationships, its origins can antedate the birth of any of the children.[21] The significant finding is that siblings of the same sex as the schizophrenic patients were, as a group, clearly more disturbed than siblings of the opposite sex. The developmental tasks confronting children of opposite sexes in a particular family were very dif-

[20] Fleck and others, "Comparison of Parent-Child Relationships of Male and Female Schizophrenic Patients," in footnote 19.

[21] Fleck and others, "Comparison of Parent-Child Relationships of Male and Female Schizophrenic Patients," in footnote 19.

ferent. While the sample in this series is small and unsuited for statistical analysis, the finding is in accord with the studies of concordance rates for schizophrenia in dizygotic twins, with studies of *folie à deux*, and with the findings of Penrose and others concerning concordance rates for schizophrenia in siblings of schizophrenic patients.[22] Such findings have led to the consideration of a sex-linked genetic factor, but Rosenthal's recent analysis of the collective data from the various studies shows that the gender-linkage within the more extended family does not appear to follow genetic lines.[23]

As shown in Figure 2, the nine male patients in our series had fourteen siblings — eight brothers and six sisters. Three had only brothers, two had a brother and sister, and four only a sister.

may attain reasonable stability despite some acting-out tendencies. Two other sisters of male schizophrenics are living reasonably satisfying lives despite fairly serious personality problems; one is seriously constricted and insecure in her marital relationship, and the other has psychopathic traits that have thus far not led to serious difficulties. The remaining two women, the sisters of the most chronic male patients, were both seriously disturbed at one time, and both sought psychotherapeutic help; one is now pursuing a profession effectively, and the other has married and is raising a family, but is seriously constricted and insecure and is making a tenuous adjustment.

The Brothers of Male Schizophrenics — In contrast to the sisters, none of the eight brothers can be considered to have remained reasonably stable.

□ **Figure 2**

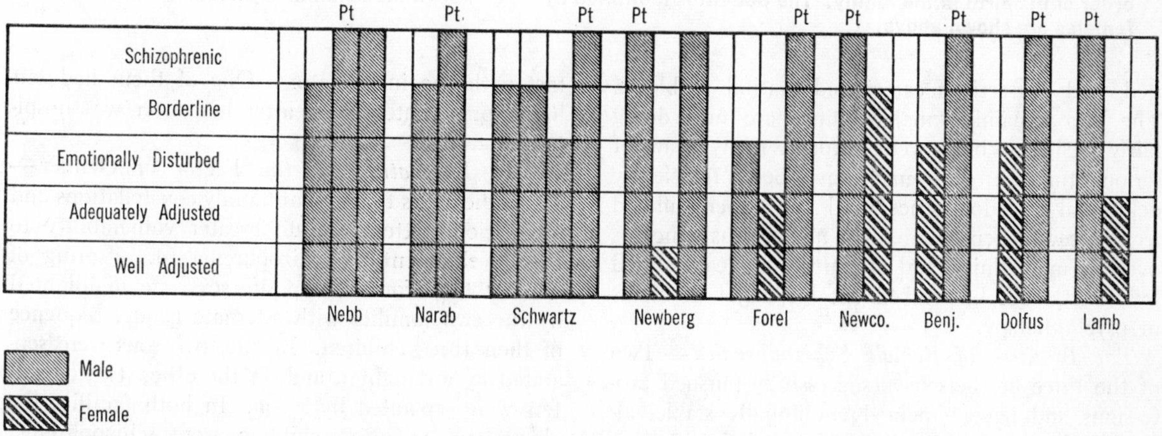

Estimated adjustments of male patients and their siblings. Each vertical column represents a child in the order of his birth in the family. The patient is identified by ''Pt'' above the column. Symbols for males and females are shown above.

Figure 3 shows the female patients and their siblings. The seven female patients had a total of ten siblings — seven sisters and three brothers. The paucity of brothers is unfortunate and limits the usefulness of the data. Four of the female patients had only sisters; one had a brother and a sister; and two had only a brother.

The Sisters of Male Schizophrenics — The only sibling of a male schizophrenic who could be considered emotionally healthy and well adjusted is a sister. One other sister, now a young adolescent,

Two have been psychotic; one became paranoid in childhood, and the other, an identical twin of a patient, has been a transvestite with bizarre fantasies and thought processes.[24] Another brother is a criminal sociopath; a fourth is making a tenuous borderline adjustment and shows many schizophrenic features on his projective tests. The fifth, the older brother of the identical twins, is accident-prone and severely obsessive, and has many other disrupting personality problems. The sixth is phobic and lim-

[22] David Rosenthal, unpublished data on studies of concordance rates for schizophrenia in dizygotic twins. For concordance rates in siblings, see: Phillip H. Greenberg, "Folie à Deux: An Historical and Clinical Study," unpublished thesis written as Registrar at Guy's Hospital, Lon-

don. Kallman, in footnote 2. L. S. Penrose, "Survey of Cases of Familial Mental Illness," *Digest Neurology and Psychiatry* (1945) Series 13: 644. See also studies by Rosenthal, in footnotes 2 and 3.

[23] See Rosenthal, in footnote 2, and unpublished data.

[24] Lidz and others (1962), in footnote 9.

□ **Figure 3**

	Pt	Pt	Pt	Pt	Pt	Pt	Pt
Schizophrenic							
Borderline							
Emotionally Disturbed							
Adequately Adjusted							
Well Adjusted							
	Reading	Grau	Ubanque	Thomas	Robb	Nussb.	Lerner

MALE

FEMALE

Estimated adjustments of female patients and their siblings. Each vertical column represents a child in the order of his birth in the family. The patient is identified by "Pt" above the column. Symbols for males and females are shown above.

ited, and has serious career and marital problems. The two remaining male siblings are now doing fairly well, but both went through many years of serious turmoil: One may have been transiently delusional in adolescence, and the other suffered from a severe neurodermatitis, had serious concerns over his masculinity, and at times was incapacitated by anxiety, but he worked out his major problems in psychotherapy.

The Brothers of Female Schizophrenics — Two of the three brothers have successfully pursued professions and have remained emotionally stable, although they are both limited by constriction of their personalities. The third brother, a man with two chronically schizophrenic sisters, has had considerable difficulty in both work and marriage and is rather schizoid.

The Sisters of Female Schizophrenics — Only one of the seven sisters of the female patients has made a reasonably stable adjustment, and her limitations have already been mentioned. Her skillful avoidance of crippling involvement in a very bad family situation has been discussed in detail in another paper.[25] One sister is chronically schizophrenic, and another, who completely withdrew from her family, is making a borderline schizophrenic adjustment. The remaining four sisters are rather seriously unstable, but the extent of the disabilities of two could not be clearly determined because of their fear of involvement and avoidance of frequent con-

tact with the investigators. One of them had left home precipitately soon after her sister was hospitalized.

Two Illustrations of the Factor of Gender — The indications that certain family constellations and interaction patterns create greater vulnerability to the development of schizophrenia for offspring of one sex than for the opposite sex[26] are highlighted by the two families with alternate gender sequence of their three children. In one, two sons were separated by a daughter, and, in the other, two daughters were separated by a son. In both families the oldest and youngest children were schizophrenic, while the middle child of the opposite sex was not. While this finding probably is partly a matter of chance, the family situations will be presented briefly to illustrate how the family configurations created very different developmental tasks for the boys and girls within these families.

In the Newberg family the oldest son became acutely schizophrenic at the age of fifteen. The daughter, who was thirteen at the time, has remained well and is probably the most stable and adaptable of any of the siblings in our series. The third child, a boy who was then nine years old, suffered from night terrors and paralyzing separation problems, and soon after his brother's hospitalization developed delusional beliefs about his teachers and schoolmates.

[25] Lidz and others (1958), in footnote 7.

[26] Fleck and others, "Comparison of Parent-Child Relationships of Male and Female Schizophrenic Patients," in footnote 19.

The Newberg marriage had been filled with mutual recrimination and frequent threats of separation almost from its inception, with most of the quarrels focusing on the intense attachment of both spouses to their natal families. Mr. Newberg was the most poorly organized father of any of the male patients. Raised in a disorganized family abandoned by the father, he had at an early age assumed responsibility for the support of his mother. He remained intensely attached to her, was jealous of his brothers, and spent much of his spare time in his mother's home. He was equally rivalrous with his sons, behaving in many ways like another child in the family. He talked incessantly, in a driven way that the interviewers found difficult to endure for even an hour at a time. He was scattered, pursuing one fixed idea after another. Although a steady provider, he was caught between his ambitions and his needs for security, and he constantly threatened to leave his job to pursue some hairbrained scheme. In his free time he worked upon a sequence of inventions that never materialized or a succession of hobbies each of which he was going to turn into a business. He talked constantly of his great abilities but accomplished little, and he created great confusion when at home.

Mrs. Newberg, in contrast, was one of the most stable mothers in our series. She depended greatly upon her older son, and sought compensation for her unhappy marriage in her children. Although she was oversolicitous, she maintained a reserve that probably impeded her relationships with them. She was firmly attached to her three sisters and refused to move away from the street on which they all lived, which caused her husband great inconvenience. While she justifies this, in part correctly, by her husband's unreliability and her need for companionship and help in raising the children, her husband resented her lack of confidence in him. Mrs. Newberg's sisters intruded themselves into the affairs of the Newberg household, and one in particular was openly hostile and contemptuous of Mr. Newberg, constantly belittling him even in the presence of his children.

In this family, the sons had a very faulty paternal model in a man who boasted much and achieved little, who was highly inconsistent and given to suspiciousness, and who was more of a rival to them than a father. The mother and her sisters constantly denigrated him and placed little trust in him, conveying to the boys that they must not resemble him. They lived in an atmosphere where women dominated the extended family and were highly critical of men. For a son to become like the father meant becoming virtually psychotic, subject to constant hostile criticism and contempt, and almost intolerable to the mother whose love they sought.

The daughter's situation was very different. Surrounded by women who were mutually supportive, she had a number of positive feminine models. Although her father was frequently angry with her mother, he also expressed considerable admiration for her. The daughter was clearly her father's favorite, and her mother was not jealous or rivalrous. Further, the daughter did not need to fill the place in her mother's life that her father had left unsatisfied; she did not have to achieve as a man in a world in which her grandiose father could accomplish little; nor did she have to face the issue, which confronted her brothers, of how a man could satisfy and be lovable to a woman when the father was so unsatisfactory to their mother and aunts.

The Robb family, in which two chronically schizophrenic daughters were separated by a son who, despite serious difficulties and several bad starts, has managed to achieve a career and marry, presents an analogous situation. Mr. Robb, a professor of education, married a troubled heiress who was seriously lacking in self-esteem. The couple had very different ideas of family life, child rearing, and the types of people with whom they wished to associate. Mrs. Robb accepted her dominating husband's decisions and choice of friends and quietly suffered in associating with people whom she despised. When, however, her husband started a series of sexual liaisons, she followed suit to vent her anger and gain quiet vengeance. Then Mr. Robb invited female exchange students from abroad to live with the family, ignoring his wife's protests. Soon he was spending evenings talking with them and ignoring his wife, and he turned to one of these, who was a teacher doing advanced study, for guidance in raising the children. For many years Mrs. Robb had had little authority in her own home, but now her inadequate self-esteem and confidence fell markedly as her opinions were pointedly ignored and belittled. Deeply resentful and preoccupied with her unhappiness, she could invest little in her children.

The oldest daughter was cared for by a nursemaid during her infancy, but when the son was born the nurse was discharged, and the mother gained considerable satisfaction from caring for him. However, it was soon after the second daughter was born that the mother discovered that her husband was having an affair and in revenge also started an affair. From then on she gave little thought or attention to her children. Even though the situation has been presented only in barest outline, one can note that the daughters were uncherished by their mother and that they gained a strange view of the worth and role of a woman, since she was unempathic as a mother, and consistently devalued and held in contempt as a wife. The girls could readily feel that they could not satisfy or gain the affection of their oversolicitous and seductive father by growing up to resemble their mother. The son, who also developed rather serious problems, had at least received maternal affection and attention during his infancy and early childhood; and he had a successful and renowned father who provided a model — and whose example he eventually followed by marrying a wealthy woman from an unstable family.

When the families with schizophrenic sons and those with schizophrenic daughters were examined as separate series, notable differences in their configurations became apparent. Because of the parental personalities and the nature of their interactions, the families with schizophrenic sons presented more serious impediments to the integrated ego development of boys than of girls, and the opposite was true for the families with schizophrenic daughters, although a few families were probably equally noxious to children of both sexes.

The parent of the same sex as the patient — the fathers of sons and the mothers of daughters — formed a very poor model for the patient to internalize in order to gain identity as a man or woman because of the parent's serious psychopathology, because of the parent's attitudes toward the child, or because of the spouse's derogatory and undermining behavior toward this parent, and commonly for all three reasons. To maintain the approval and affection of the parent of the opposite sex, the child sought to differentiate himself from, rather than identify himself with, the parent of the same sex, and thus lacked a positive sex-linked model to follow in order to gain maturity as a man or a woman. The situation was aggravated because the parent of the opposite sex from the child seductively used the child as a replacement for the unsatisfactory spouse in filling his own emotional needs and thus interfered with the child's development into an independent person. Although the case illustrations have emphasized the child's difficulty in achieving identity as a member of his own sex, the problems created for his development go far beyond this. The resolution of the Oedipal ties is impeded, and incestuous wishes remain conscious into adolescence;

fears of vindictiveness by the parent of the same sex are heightened by the realistic rivalries existing in the family; and narcissistic and homosexual proclivities are fostered by the confused and confusing sexual identities of the parents.[27]

The case material reveals that with but rare exception the mother of the male patient is engulfing of the son, seeking to maintain a symbiotic closeness with him, while the father is distant and rivalrous toward the son or is himself but a weak, emasculated appendage of his wife. In contrast, the mother of the female patient is aloof and distant from her, either because she is unable to accept in a daughter the femininity she rejects in herself or because she seeks to ward off homosexual impulses, while the father tends to be derogatory of women in general but seductive of the daughter, whose admiration he needs to bolster his insecure masculinity and narcissism. A more detailed examination of these differences in another paper suggests that satisfactory ego development and integration in boys and girls depends upon different requisites in the family structure and interaction.[28] A boy's ego development will be injured more seriously than a girl's by a mother who cannot establish clear ego boundaries between herself and the child, since to achieve a firm masculine identity he must break away from the initial mother-child symbiosis more completely than a daughter needs to. In addition, a father who fails to fill a masculine instrumental role in the family will be more detrimental to a boy, who needs to learn this role, than to a girl. Conversely, a girl will be harmed more seriously by a cold and aloof mother, for the attainment of maternal affectional characteristics through empathic absorption of maternal feelings is more critical to a girl's development than to a boy's; and a father who dominates and derogates the mother and tends to be antagonistic and belittling toward all women will affect a girl's development more deleteriously than a boy's. The exposition of the different developmental tasks confronting boys and girls and how they are furthered or impeded by the family configuration goes beyond the purposes of this paper; here we are seeking only to indicate why a child of one sex may be more vulnerable to personality disorganization within a given family than a child of the opposite sex.

[27] Fleck and others, in footnote 10.
[28] Fleck and others, "Comparison of Parent-Child Relationships of Male and Female Schizophrenic Patients," in footnote 19.

Idiosyncratic Problems in the Parents' Relationship to the Schizophrenic Offspring

The comparison of some of the patients with their siblings must take into account certain special problems related to unique circumstances. Expectations before birth as well as many circumstances at and following confinement can set the stage for certain interaction patterns in the family or certain attitudes toward a particular infant. For example, differences in temperament present at birth may influence the ensuing child-parent relationship and interaction, although this, like many other such influences, is difficult to assess retrospectively.

The Nebb twins, one of whom was overtly schizophrenic and the other a transvestite who might also be considered schizophrenic, were, in contrast to their older brother, placed at birth in a special and unusual situation because their mother had been competing with her own twin sister to see which of them could produce twins. The birth of the twin sons was a major triumph for Mrs. Nebb, who had been the deformed and neglected member of her family, and they were to be her means of achieving prestige and dominance.[29]

In another family, the daughter who became the patient had manifested artistic talent to an unusual degree by the age of three. Two relatives in the maternal line who had been similarly gifted from earliest childhood had become psychotic. The patient's mother had been directed away from developing a similar talent lest it lead to insanity, but the patient's unusual ability could not be suppressed. The mother was naturally ambivalent about the patient's dominant activity and vacillated between encouraging and seeking to guide the girl into more conventional channels. The bright but untalented older brother had not been subjected to such ambivalent guidance, nor to an a priori expectation of great vulnerability to psychosis.

It must be noted, however, that there were other problems in both families that were just as serious as in the other families in the series.

The Interaction Between the Siblings

In our scrutiny of the divergent influences upon the siblings within a family, we must also note the effects of the interaction between the siblings themselves, although this topic extends beyond the limits and purposes of this paper. In the Narab family, the overtly schizophrenic mother considered both of her sons to be geniuses — even, at times, Messiahs

[29] See Lidz and others (1962), in footnote 9.

— and her extreme intrusiveness into the lives of both was not countered by the father. The younger son became schizophrenic while the older traversed a narrow path, skirting overt psychosis. He was filled with venom toward his mother and feared that he might act out his homicidal fantasies about her if he remained near her; and, at times, he was almost equally hostile toward his younger brother. While ex post facto analysis is particularly hazardous in this instance, several factors seem important. Mrs. Narab had been smotheringly dominant of her first-born, but with the birth of the second son she turned her major energies toward him; and as the older son began to move away from her, she clung all the more tenaciously to the younger. The first-born could express his jealousy and anger toward his brother, dominating him and forcing him into a passive and masochistic position — one might say into developing a more Messiah-like personality and possibly emulating his father, whom both sons considered homosexual. The absorption of the mother's needs by the younger son appears to have provided greater freedom for the older.

Illness in one offspring — whether the schizophrenic patient or the nonschizophrenic sibling — affects the siblings differentially. At least three of our patients experienced comparative neglect when the prolonged illness of older siblings — rheumatic fever in one instance — required a great deal of the mother's attention. In the Schwartz family, the severe psychopathy of the oldest brother preempted the economic and emotional resources, as has already been noted. It was the youngest son who became psychotic. Not only had his father become ineffectual as a husband and father shortly after his birth, but his mother's attention had become absorbed by the oldest son's markedly antisocial and delinquent behavior. The family lived in a "tough" neighborhood, and the next older brother had protected the patient, as the baby of the family, and fought his battles for him — abetting his development as a passive, dependent child who was very insecure of his masculinity.

In the Grau family, the patient's difficulties throughout her childhood had had a very different impact on the younger sister. She explained that her older sister had borne the brunt of her mother's insecurity in raising children; the mother had relied on books with her first child but raised the second daughter according to less rigid directions. Moreover, the second daughter had avoided involvement in the parental conflicts by noting how her sister became embroiled with one or the other parent at each phase of development, and her major guide in life had been sidestepping situations that had caused difficulties for her sister. It also became clear that her antagonism to her older sister who created so much difficulty had led her to side with her mother rather than to seek the affection of the paranoid father.

The influences of the siblings upon one another may be diverse, but the child who becomes schizophrenic often lessens the impact of the parental pathology upon the siblings by serving as a target of the parents' intrusiveness, as a scapegoat, or as an example for the siblings of what not to do.

This comparison of sixteen schizophrenic patients with their twenty-four siblings, in an effort to clarify why the patient rather than his siblings became schizophrenic, has presented only a general survey of the problems, for any careful scrutiny from a genetic-dynamic orientation would require a separate article, if not a monograph, for each family. Several general findings that warrant attention have emerged from the study. One of these is that the question of why one child within a family becomes schizophrenic while the others remain 'well' or 'normal' requires restatement. As many siblings were psychotic as reasonably well integrated, and all except five or six of the twenty-four siblings suffered from serious personality disorders.

A definite gender-linkage was found in the occurrence and severity of the psychiatric disturbances in the siblings. The brothers of the male schizophrenic patients were clearly more disturbed than the sisters; and the sisters of schizophrenic females were sicker than the brothers, although the value of his finding is limited by the paucity of brothers of female patients in our series. Only one sibling of the same sex as the patient was considered to be reasonably stable; and no sibling of the opposite sex from the patient was overtly psychotic.

The influence of the parents and of their interaction with one another upon sons and daughters differed. In general, different configurations of parental personalities existed in the families with male and female schizophrenic offspring.

Other differentiating influences upon the development of the children occurred with varying fre-- quencies and in various combinations. In half of the cases, the mother had been either physically incapacitated, too intensely preoccupied with her marital problems, or too anxious and insecure to provide nurturant mothering care during the patient's infancy, while such conditions did not apply during the infancy of the siblings. In half of the families the patient was raised under conditions that were different from those under which the siblings were brought up; in a few families the difference was very marked.

When the siblings were close in age — and even when they were identical twins — they were also subjected to very different intrafamilial influences. The child who becomes schizophrenic may become a pawn or scapegoat in the parental conflict; he may be caught in a bind between the conflicting needs and wishes of the parents, who become irreconcilable introjects; he may invest his energies in seeking to salvage the parents' marriage and to satisfy the needs of both; he may insert himself into the split between the parents, and become a needed complement to one parent. The patients' energies during their developmental years were deflected from developing an integrated independent ego, and failure of closure of their Oedipal attachments left them prone to incestuous conflicts during adolescence. The influence of the siblings upon one another may create more or less precarious circumstances and greater or lesser vulnerability.

We have not, of course, included all of the factors that may have been conducive to the production of schizophrenia. Little attention has been given to family characteristics that were reasonably similar for all of the siblings, particularly the paralogic modes of thinking and communicating of one or both parents that were present in all the families.

Although any reconstruction of the intrafamilial circumstances that influenced the development of these patients and their siblings cannot be fully satisfactory, the material offers clear and reasonable grounds for the understanding of why one child rather than another in a family becomes schizophrenic. The data support rather than refute the hypothesis that the intrafamilial environment plays a critical role in the etiology of schizophrenia.

MALCOLM BOWERS

The Onset of Psychosis — A Diary Account*

The main portion of this paper consists of a diary kept by a young man during the two weeks prior to his hospitalization for an acute psychotic reaction. It is presented as a unique source of information for the study of the experiential aspects of the acute psychosis. Most theoretical approaches in this area emphasize inferentially the motivational determinants in a patient's speech or behavior with a view toward clarifying unconscious processes. However, recently there have been several attempts in the literature to examine the elements of the psychotic reaction in a way more designed to elucidate the psychosocial significance of the experience. Erickson, for instance, has presented the view that the psychotic reaction should be considered in the light of the life tasks of a given age group.[1] Jackson and Watzlawick have suggested that in some instances the acute psychosis can be viewed as a manifestation of a growth experience.[2] Such an approach takes seriously the conscious experiential aspects of psychosis, the psychiatric clinician having access to such information within the framework of the psychotherapeutic interview. Thus, how the patient feels inwardly and what growth tasks he has been struggling to master become topics of direct mutual investigation for patient and therapist.

In the present account there is an opportunity for observing firsthand the inner struggle of a person in the throes of what might be called a telescoped growth experience — a period in which a number of maturational skills are put rigorously to test. The author treated the patient during four months of his hospitalization, during which time there was also extensive family contact. The names of the principals have been changed in the anamnestic material and in the body of the diary.

HISTORICAL DATA

David F was a 21-year-old senior at an Eastern university at the time of his hospitalization. He was approaching the end of his college career with a great deal of concern about his future. Though already accepted by a prominent law school, David was not certain about this choice of vocation and had also given some consideration to medicine and writing. David knew that his father, a lawyer, had also encountered difficulty in choosing a vocation and had taken a kind of moratorium after college by going abroad to participate in the Spanish Civil War. This had been a disillusioning experience, however, and Mr. F had given up his idealism completely, directing his attention to making money. In many ways, Mr. F considered himself a failure, and though he made a good living for his family, he was unhappy with his accomplishments. He had managed to purchase a very expensive home, though there always seemed to be outstanding debts.

Mrs. F, long intimidated by her husband, sought psychiatric assistance for intractable colitis two years before David's hospitalization. As a result she became more assertive toward her husband in ways that frequently took the form of undercutting his authority in the home and belittling his sexual ability. Mr. F was usually very passive toward his wife, dealing with her aggression with a kind of sarcastic banter. However, following bouts of drinking he would engage in violent outbursts, and on such occasions David, his 18-year-old sister, and his 13-year-old brother were often witnesses to the abusive arguments of their parents. Mrs. F held the threat of divorce constantly over the heads of the other family members.

David had a special girl friend, Laura, who had been in psychotherapy for two years. Their relationship was characterized by a great deal of sexual experimentation, with David frequently doubting his own sexual ability. Separations and reconciliations were violent, highly-charged experiences, much

* Reprinted by special permission of The William Alanson White Psychiatric Foundation, Inc., from *Psychiatry*, Vol. 28, 1965, pp. 346–358. Copyright by The William Alanson White Psychiatric Foundation, Inc.

[1] Erik H. Erikson, "Introduction," in *Emotional Problems of the Student*, edited by Graham B. Blaine and Charles C. McArthur; New York, Appleton-Century-Crofts, 1961; p. xiii.
[2] Don D. Jackson and Paul Watzlawick, "The Acute Psychosis as Manifestation of a Growth Experience," in *Acute Psychotic Reaction*, Psychiatric Research Report No. 16, 1963; pp. 89–94.

in the fashion of the relationship between David's parents. In mid-February Laura had dated a boy in another city and refused to tell David the details. He immediately fantasied that Laura had engaged in intercourse with her date and wrote a very vindictive poem to her, calling her a whore. Having mailed the poem, he felt angry and guilty. A trip to Buffalo, where he visited friends, served only to assure David that they had their own troubles. Following his return he wrote a short story entitled "Test To Be a Man" in which the storyteller finds that his best friend has stolen his sweetheart. He became even more overwrought when he learned that a lifelong friend, Nathan, sided with Laura in her quarrel with David. This discovery prompted him to write Nathan a "hate letter," accusing him of betraying their friendship. At this point David essentially confined himself to his room at college, attended a few classes, but spent most of his time — day and night — at the typewriter attempting to get his thoughts on paper. At one point he seemed to view this process as a self-analysis. He recorded the progress of events in calendar form as follows.

Sunday, Feb. 22 — wrote letter to Laura, severing.

Weekend, Feb. 28 — fled to Buffalo, no good.

Monday, March 2 — wrote story "Test To Be a Man."

Friday, March 6 — found Nathan sympathetic to Laura, story comes true.

Sunday & Monday, March 8 & 9 — two hate letters to Nathan.

Monday & Tuesday, March 9 & 10 — intense anxiety.

Wednesday, March 11 — partial solution (intuitive) in letter to Nathan.

Friday, March 13 — ended diary.

Saturday, March 14 — began self-analysis.

March 17 — case closed.

The following day he found his way to the hospital emergency room where he presented a picture of intense fright, pressure of speech, ideas of influence and reference, and autistic thinking. Diagnosis based on clinical data and psychological tests was acute undifferentiated schizophrenic reaction. Later, when his parents visited his room at school, they found the following typed account. There has been some deletion and condensation where certain sections were repetitive but otherwise the account has not been altered in any way. The stream-of-consciousness style has been left as written by the patient, who has given his consent for the publication of this material. Brief explanatory footnotes have been included where they seem indicated.

SLIGHT DEPRESSION
OR
WATCHING YOURSELF LIVE
OR
JUST A WEEK LIKE ANY OTHER

Monday, March 9, 1964

She had said she loved me (bopping off to Providence in between protests I suppose I could swallow that though) but I don't think if it were ever true, that she still does. (N told me that, told me just like that and the reason he hadn't called was cause he was playing pickup sticks with her date he's so charmingly forthright I puke).

His logic is so good he can laugh at his own [girl] having her insides torn out he's so positive and rational and knows just how everything works including one divorce, one abortion that he's undoubtedly reassured her everything's all right such a good friend midwife to disasters a cool guy that's what so even if she does still love me (she was so cold on the phone) anyway so cold her voice on the phone she wanted to chat I fantasied suicide for twenty four hours . . . twenty four hours you begin to scare yourself like that wanted to chat bragged she'd burned 'everything' (I wanted to ask if that everything included thirty dollar cashmeres doubt it) chat about her date etc. If he had been alone I would have killed I promise if I believe anything is left in myself I promise I would have killed but he was only there as a friend so that solution would have been disproportionate honor among friends (I had asked him not to meddle asked him as a friend ha ha) being outdated anyhow no one not even me would have understood not being able to kill him and less able to kill myself I just got drunk alone in Harlem. If she still loves me if if then still I can't see her talk to her until I am worthy if I can ever be of her of anything until at least say (stinkin symbolism runs my life) even then if I see her at all it must be to propose to say here I am me at last me I respect myself can respect love marry you can bolt myself onto life and ride ride ride we'll ride together some say its a good thing I'd like to give it a try when I trust myself and what I am when the times comes I shall say I love you.

I have a right I do have a right to hold that bastard responsible . . . my game wasn't pretty perhaps; I wanted her to relent first, that's all, just relent first that much of the double standard I hold by if that means double standard but she bore the burden she ran off on me I had a right . . . she made no attempt at apology that night none none so we're both prideful but all I wanted was an I'm sorry even to the letter I wrote, horrible letter designed to humble and that's all just asking an emotional sacrifice an ego sacrifice on her part something she had been as little willing to make as I was . . . but she couldn't do it with that snake whispering in her ear someone for her anyone for her to talk to excuse herself to but me.[3]

Tuesday, March 10, 5 A.M.

Story will be turned down today for the simple reason that it's lousy. I don't realize things like that before I've shown them all over town . . . at least then I'd avoid having my vanity take as bad a beating as my pride . . . and there's old Hawthorne's bosom serpent for you eating away hissing all night I lie there and I lie there and think and think and think all the time trying not to think I think anyway or reminisce rather (delightful pastime) until pow I feel like the top of my head blows off and I smash my fist into something and begin all over again like a one cycle engine. As far as the stories go its a good thing I'm going to make money as a lawyer. Quite ingenuously it is hard for me to believe I write so poorly. Hemingway says it should be two against the world the religion the New Faith and all nothing like that just her there exclaiming how she made it or worried about her mother or trying to beat me in ping pong and when I got off the boat last fall I announced I was going to rescue and protect her! I'm getting warts on my neck, I deserve them. Tonight I composed three different suicide notes in my head and I think I broke the pinkie on my left hand when the pow came. What a joy if insanity were still the romantic mysterious brain fever type thing it was in the 19th century then I could try going mad instead of writing, I'd probably be better at it.

Hemingway lost a whole suitcase full of his earliest stories and was thus forced by the world (conveniently that world which kills the bravest, gentlest, best etc.) to start again. Maybe if I can find a suitcase and put all my writing in it, maybe the suitcase will get lost. The one real advantage of suicide is that at least there wouldn't be a reception at the Master's house afterwards. I want a war like Hemingway had . . . it isn't fair . . . I never learned to shoot squirrels either.

What a sad thing! There is nobody any good around anymore . . . I was going to be the last one and then mucked it. Will spring never come?? Or maybe they could make insomnia less painful by changing the time system: IST . . . insomniac savings time.

[3] The foregoing passage deals with his presumed betrayal by Laura and Nathan's willingness to be Laura's confidant in the argument.

March 10, 5 P.M.

I'm becoming a monomaniac its incredible it just doesn't stop there are moments when I can do no more than tear up matchbooks futile futile things and others of greater lucidity when I can see so clearly what went wrong why we were unable to commit ourselves each coming to the brink at different moments I came to her that evening at her house felt my insides dissolve with wanting, expecting to burst free she put me off good put me off and put me off and then 12 hours later when the thing lay sticky like bile inside me then only then we went to bed together and she had her orgasm and I did crossword puzzles. Did she ever come at me yes I suppose, at the beginning, too fast to desperately when she knew there was no chance and was doing it on her doctor's advice and I kept telling her I was no therapist that wasn't my job not my job. But that letter should have been a test it was a test I wanted her to make it on her own without help confronting everything but she dragged in a surrogate she dragged in my lilly-livered friend and he came galloping to the rescue in all the accoutrements of maiden rescue and good will. There are moments of lucidity when I see how close hate and love can lie, back to back, moment to moment I could kill I could love I lie here tearing up matchbooks. My story was rejected and I think I mucked an english test this morning. Will do the same for a French test tomorrow. The big test is still ahead or behind I tear up matchbooks. First a tragedy then a comedy I keep trying to laugh. Someone said you can refuse a man a loan you can refuse him your sympathy but you can't refuse him a fight if he wants to fight. I'll beat him on the streets I'll beat him in front of Susan or before his parents. He'll fight. Anyhow at last that second self is returning the one that wants to turn his life into a work of art its returning a little in writing momentary sweet breaths of sanity in the end perhaps its the only way I must write even poorly.[4]

Tuesday, March 10, 10 P.M.

I can't cope, I can't come to grips . . . it's Hawthorne's disease blazing away, red guilt or little stringy black warts (they're growing with a virulence I swear I never noticed before) . . . music helps a bit and I've conducted the Eroica all over the room three times already today, waving my arms and occasionally hitting things . . . all very dramatic . . . to think I worried myself about sleeping too much

[4] In these entries he seems preoccupied with his lack of success as a writer, which was a progressive and painful realization for him.

last fall! I've given the jargon a once over; it stems from incest drives, castration fears, masturbation complexes, homosexual doubts, oedipal fixations bullshit bullshit it was around before the jargon and its got me . . . already at table I've been making curious unconscious slips as if the synapses suddenly rot away and I come disconnected its all right its all right I'm going to be a lawyer and make lots of money and grow up to be as weak as my father as torn as my mother look ahead!! Be a good little benjy franklin and don't despair; simply write down your virtues on one side of the page like this and then your vices on the other (that's a good boy) now add them up, divide by the fraction of a normal life already lived (that's right, one third) nice going benjy you're doing fine, now multiply by your abilities as scored by the IBM machine and factor by your various ambitions (what's the matter bengy?? haven't got any? Come on now boy, you always did want to invent a lightening rod, didn't you? Or build a fire house? Sure you did. . . . well skip it and just multiply by the height of the statue you want built after your death) now . . . what have you got? (now don't be corny benjy, Hemingway has already been through that for you . . . try something else) (be a good boy benjy and don't seek escapes in vulgarity, try again) (look here, benjy, we'll have none of your morbidity, be positive boy, reach down way deep inside you and tell the world what you find) HATE HATE HATEHATEHATE (what a cornball! A lousy sensationalist . . . what kind of founding father would you make?) Founding father? Are you kidding? I'm well on my way to becoming a blithering schizoid its too bad really too bad I have too much of a sense of humor to believe that adam eve and apple stuff . . . I rather think that Beckett's got the right idea and original sin was trying to climb out of the mud we must have had a good time back then never overeaching, no such thing as hubris or stargazing or breasts the size and texture of (dear diary! How can I begin, you mean I really never tried before? Who was I kidding did I never chance to look in the mirror and see the warts) of Christ the more fool you.

Tuesday, March 10, 11 P.M.

It's silly to stop now, I've got a good rhythm going. I type for twenty minutes and then read back over the past two months for forty. That makes an hour. Then I begin again. Pretty soon I'll get sleepy from all this banging down on the keys and then I'll go to sleep and start fresh in the morning. I ought to entitle this to my future headshrinker cause Mr. White says this is about the age

when the snap occurs . . . he says anything can set it off if it's there to begin with (what that means, of course, he's not sure . . . I am) any drop in (get this) "esteem income" occasioned by test situations or symbolic maturity crises like graduation, or tests or even, even a love affair (what a bland term!) So I'm waiting. Where and when does it begin? Do you at some point decide to go crouch in a corner talking to yourself unable to shit? Except maybe I'm pulling myself out of it, kind of reeling out the intestines of it diseased inch by inch . . . sublimating in otherwords. My concerns are once again pretentiously self-conscious, I notice in my rereadings an increasing number of quotes and witticisms . . . I'm showing off again, what a good thing: Like the eighty year old women in the asylum to whom the scientists gave estrogen just to see what would happen . . . sure enough, they began combing their hair and fixing their dresses and primping, in short preparing like mad to go out and have their hymens busted again. Everybody, doctors, and relatives and other patients thought Oh what a good thing that they're taking a renewed interest in life! I thought it was a rather touching thing myself. So I'm taking a renewed interest in life . . . I even began criticising certain turns of construction in the pages just written . . . hot diggity, pretty soon I'll be sitting around in a pile of writing up to my ears and simply tickled pink! Like feces I'll play with the paper make gliders and little sailor hats and be innocent again.[5]

Rereading this time, I just noticed a terrible thing . . . I'm such a short sighted misanthrope that I will never be able (in a particularly severe paroxysm of self pity of course) to give this to any of my friends . . . There isn't a single one I've spared much less said a good word of! I'm sorry really. The obvious solution is to send it to Laura and then blow my brains in (I'd prefer to fall on a sword but I'd probably take it through the forearm) that way she'd feel bad about burning it. Egotism the bosom serpent, I need a good priest.

Midnight, Tuesday-Wednesday

Every last bit of it, right to the bottom of the stable get out all the crusted horse dung leave it spic and span so there will be place for more. Cause like they say there is knowing and then there is knowing and I know a lot of things but I don't know anything at all. . . . I know how to type ten

[5] Here, as in other places, he seems to flirt with the idea of going insane even to the point of addressing, in a sense, his future psychiatrist.

hours running and drink beer (thank god the beer was around I'm broke and down to my last two cigars and not a bit sleepy yet) but I don't know what to DO and that's what counts most of all. Or does it? It appears I'm out to prove the cliche about the intellectual . . . except I'm no intellectual so that is solved, or maybe it proves the cliche about the tortured jew, but then I'm no jew either. I sure know all about what I'm not. This little dispatch from hell is really turning in on itself like a seashell winding smaller and smaller; I see now where I picked up the theme of insanity mentioned flippantly and in passing, and succeeded in running it into the ground . . . I ought to skip the verbiage and go find a good crown of thorns, or do like Bruce did in Buffalo drink somebody's blood and lie back blissfully in their vomit . . . but then he was drunk and that doesn't count and shouldn't discourage the happy people. Boy, that Nathan and Laura business really pulled the cork I'm bad or mad or just dull? Down on my knees before the crescent moon I got my pants dirty. This is undoubtedly one of the most prolix records of a scarringover process (I'm sealing like one of those puncture proof tires, but in slow motion) I should be back to my habitual state of callousness in a couple of days with no apparent damage, maybe I can even go on staving off like this ("a poem is a momentary stay against confusion" Frost . . . this is quite a poem) till I die. I guess you shouldn't be alone in a moment like this, what you need is a good friend . . . ha . . . today he gets the letter, the second letter, the one in which I spoke his own language . . . nothing assuages nothing (oh don't do that again you've already done that twice before, try something new, quote some more big names).

One ray of hope (the first branch, Mt. Arrarat is in sight, get all the animals ready to debark the hell out of here particularly the snakes and spiders) that is my regrets and nostalgias seem to be coming closer on the heels of my debacles last time it took me two years to realize that I'd made a mistake with Laura, this time it took me two weeks, but maybe next time (three strikes you know the pitch?) well maybe next time I will have killed Nathan first . . . a little foresight should do the trick . . . what drives that bastard anyway? I think I've taken him to represent my own rational sickness and not seen what he is at all, its myself I hate in him . . . but then the old empirical hard core fact remains that this is the second time he snivelled around in the wake of my romance with Laura . . of course, she begged him to . . . they can both go to hell (redundancies boy, esthetic considerations are replacing

moral ones for the sweet sake of sanity and the coming spring) skip it

How can I hate myself like this?

Thursday, March 12, 11 A.M.

I'm out! I'm through . . . boomed out of the tunnel sometime last night and it's raining stars . . whooey . . . its nice out there's time for everything . . . I can do it I did it and if it happens again I'll do it again twice as hard I got a dexamyl high going and I'm not on dexamyl and I've been up for forty eight or more hours and giddygiddygiddy and I took a test this morning and it was on Voltaire and I kicked him a couple of good ones for being down on Pascal that poor bastard with his shrivelled body and bottomless abysess they're not bottomless!! You get down far enough and it gets thick enough and black enough and then you claw claw claw your way out and pretty soon you're on top again. And I licked it by myself, all alone. No pandering psychiatrists or priests or friends by myself. Now, I must admit I'm a little leery; I dashed back to the typewriter to give it form to write it down and sew it in my vest like Pascal so if the Thing hits me again I'll have this in my vest and I'll kick it in the teeth again but Pascal saw God and yet still it hit him again . . . will it hit me again? Who cares . . . I just sat in on one of those weddings of the soul and I tooted tooted . . . I don't care I can use it I can run on it it will be my psychic gasoline now I don't have to sleep sleep all the time to get away with it . . . but if I lose my typewriter? So my hand will get tired too bad. The tail ain't going to wag this dog no more . . . at least not as ferociously. The passions, the humors, the libido, the original sin, the blood curse I'm going to put them all in a suitcase and then I'm going to lose that damn suitcase or maybe I'll just keep throwing it away. But I can do it. I licked this school and I licked my blue bear. Maybe I can even lick Laura . . . she can't do it for herself. Maybe I've got enough left over for two. I took that test without having read three quarters of the material with my head still going whooey and I licked that. Maybe I can lick Laura.[6]

I got a few confessions to make. Still, I think I did overflow a bit on other people and that is just a trifle bit humiliating since I knew they couldn't help anymore than a psycho and then, yesterday afternoon I trotted over to the third floor of Univ. Health and the woman said Well, we have two openings next

[6] This passage exemplifies one of several passages in which some relief and a sense of resolution and clarification break through his mounting anxiety.

week maybe we can fit you in and I thought about that guy who got put off like that and launched himself from the roof and will never fly again and thought for a while how bad I was going to make them feel having history repeat itself and came near to slamming my fist on the receptionists desk (having made that great sacrifice in the first place . . . ah pride) and nearly shouted That's nonsense I just want a little offhand advice this business should be more convenient and stormed out noting on the way a slightly terrified look in the poor receptionist's eye that was fun . . . I can always do that again too if the Blue Bear ever comes growling back. Poor Voltaire, the son of a bitch never understood never did spent a frenetic life throwing well turned witticisms into Pascal's yawning pit and eternal silences ah the Sound and the fury I'd better get some sleep now. Or maybe I'm a manic-depressive. Maybe the pills did it to me. It's coming back step on it step on it shave that Blue Bear. No. I've got it now. Just don't reread anything but the good parts. That's it. Underline them.

Oh jesus christ I *still* don't really believe in anything I just got myself too worn out to care. I'm pretty sure Kierkegaard had something to say about this but if I get any more names and quotes and things in my head my ability to make fun of them is just going to go pachunk and I'll give out altogether. No dice. Me I'm still flying.

The coincidence of my break up with Laura with imminent graduation and the inevitability of law school combined with pressures from home have kicked off these bouts of self-doubt and account for the virulence of the blue bear (subconscious, warts, dreams etc.) White is wrong or Freud or whoever insisted that dreams are pure wish fulfillment . . . or rather, the wish may be very subtle . . . a wish to punish oneself . . . because certainly my greatest wish at the moment is to beat this thing and I certainly haven't dreamed any victories yet. How many years did it take Freud? I'll bet he didn't have any french paper to write for tomorrow. No that's for sure.

But the biggest step has been made . . . I have objectified my disturbances in the person of Blue Bear (we'll deal with that one later) torn them apart from myself in the moment of tooting and prevented them from wrecking me. Now I must destroy the blue bear once and for all.

ANNOUNCEMENT: A new campaign is on against the word "maybe." When I stamp out maybe maybe I'll stop smoking. I tremble seeing how close I came to the brink. How do you like that? I repressed the whole reason for writing this time . . . I knew I had missed something (ha ha won't get away from me blue bear I'm hot on your tail) my story was truer than I wished to believe (changing hair color location and all etc.) I had taken Nathan as symbolic of some male principle and was tormenting myself with him . . . he's just as stuck as most of us, he just has great and clever specialized intellectual faculties . . . so that the irony of my story coming semi-true was also too much to take and aggravated my sense of betrayal. That letter to him then was not completely sincere . . . I don't want him to do my courting (that was the doubt about the manliness of the favor) I just wanted to apologise to both of us and maybe duck the decision to go after Laura myself because after all, I'm not sure that I need her if she represents no more than a test. Well, we'll see . . . maybe the test wasn't such a bad idea because if she's got the guts to take me back she's a big enough girl for me and we'll see what comes of it. I was half exposing myself, half proving myself, half boasting to her and hurting her, half admitting my problem and half challenging her to save me. . . . no one saves you Christ was a fool you save yourself. Let me qualify that, you don't save yourself all at once up on a cross that's what Nathan would like to do and Pascal and all the absolute hunters craving to die in orgasm before the starry heavens shaking their fists or down on their knees life doesn't work that way . . . novels and poems do and should . . . to live "enbonne foi" in good faith with yourself you have to save yourself each day . . . not in some corny way helping old ladies across the street . . . but in a little soul plunging before breakfast . . . a picker-upper. You can do it with the setting up exercises.

March 12, Midnight

I mustn't test it yet . . . I've got to keep quiet . . . I've got momentum habits of exhibitionism and I've come to grips with my own doubts but the resolution hasn't been strong enough to sustain the doubts of others . . . I can't be a proselytizer because the essence of my discovery is that there ARE NO doctrines that living is a day by day affair I do much better talking about monopoly I LIKE to talk about monopoly I LIKE to touch things and listen to things I CAN'T support Greg's problems I start proving myself to him QUIET QUIET SHUT-UP AND SILENCE I can see too well what happens I go on a grand flight and halfway up it sounds hollow and then to save face I begin to force and push and I can carry him along for a minute but he always comes down before I do and then my stomach just caves in . . . the thing is too fragile to test yet . . . if it were only based on a permanent thing on an absolute on God capital g on Love capital L but it isn't and I don't want it to be even Fromm became a doctrinaire and then he was no good any-more I wish I could pray god give me just a couple of years of this that is all that will be enough I am so big now my body has such stretching potential it gallops like Thomas Wolfe's character it bounds along and it doesn't touch ground until someone like Greg casts a shadow.[7]

I must pursue the analysis and not talk about it. I know what I must do. Right now, with eight hours to go I must stay awake (I feel like I've been up for two weeks) and do the french paper . . . Laura once said it is going to be fun falling in love with you I was flattered but I didn't understand now I do . . . what do they say? Take it as it comes? Right that's it . . . just take it as it comes too bad we didn't . . . too bad? What am I saying . . . a damn tragedy . . . .

HUMILITY let's go right back to the text books right back to the puritan primers cause after all they know what they were talking about and if I've done it then what I've done is to secularize and person-alize their solution and I must keep my trap shut.

But jesus I feel that I've changed I really do I've never felt this way before I'm even beginning to trust it a little bit . . . so if you are introspective then BE introspective . . . all the way . . . you come through the bottom and out the other side and there's a world out there just waiting to be eaten played on lived with worked for jumped up and down upon made love to sung about man I'm six years old.

I could be simply overawed but in rereading this I see an incredible, an astonishing structure . . . automatic writing but there is development, there is almost an internal plot . . . the hand of god? Or of the subconscious? or of both at the same time? Grace and peace and inner peace. Or have I gone mad? Am I talking rationally . . . skip the french paper I've got to get out of this room this typewriter and find out no . . . I'm okay

I think I just passed the acid test. I passed through an absolute web of complexities involving the person who had posed the greatest threat and did so with what came close to serenity . . . I wasn't dead (as John later tried to suggest in a veiled form of attack) . . . I liked the music and the coffee and the people and the perfume and the women but I wasn't upset! I wasn't driven back against that wall

of incriminations self-accusations self doubts etc. that used to clutter up my people encounters. It went like this:

John[8] and I were talking on the usual subjects of identity and function in life (he talks so beauti-fully one would never guess!) I was attacking him as the symbolic beatnik the person who has given free reign to his unconscious who refuses to live a structured existence and identifying him with his brother-in-law Richard who did so badly by his sister etc. I can't do John I haven't even begun to do myself . . . suffice it to say he got back to his high school experience which represents for him a dangerous but exciting search for identity in others, in various attempts to graft himself onto more stable environments (that's where he picked up the business about the Jewish home . . . boy did that bug me when he first came out with it!)

My resistences must have been immense because now I remember that night he got drunk he said straight out that he was trying to seduce me (intel-lectually of course). Lastly, he keeps wanting to tell me what REALLY is the story between me and Laura and I keep stopping him short . . . I'm still not ready to take it . . . I'm still shaky, but less so. When I left him he looked sad. I can't help him and he certainly can't help me . . . I wonder if I can get away from him without feeling like I'm running scared. I must never feel scared again. I must never again feel as if I'm swimming uphill against life. I'm going to sit at this machine until morning if need be . . . until next year . . . (no, until next morning because I've got to see Laura tomorrow) taking things topic by topic, systematizing, ordering, making as little or as much headway as I can. There must be an end and in any case, I have reassured myself that I won't go mad trying. Besides, I didn't dream at all (or probably, the repressant mechanism is healthy again . . . all this is symbolic language who knows what really happens who cares . . . I'm getting better . . . I was close to being sick. Very close.) when I finally got to sleep this afternoon.

I have been leafing through Jones on Freud again (I shouldn't . . . I can and should do this on my own maybe I should? What am I afraid of finding out?) I will and it was a positively thrilling dis-covery that Freud's feelings of greatest worthless-ness, as evidenced in his letters came just prior to his greatest discoveries. But that went on all his life . . . will mine? who cares . . . Freud lived on,

---

[7] Greg is an acquaintance who occasionally drops in to visit as David types out his thoughts.

[8] John is another friend whom David spends some time with during the period of the diary. He becomes con-cerned about the possibility of homosexual attraction to John.

riddled with cancer thru a world falling apart with his religion being exterminated exiled from his own country and he kept working . . . he still knew what he had to do . . . that's what counts . . . that much optimism and you don't need much else . . . or do you? Have religions and books and castles been built as mere excuses? No . . . they mean something but you don't have to flagallate yourself to know what they mean as, precisely, the beatnik tenet would say . . . you can do them and dig them and do and dig yourself all at the same time like a great big ninety ring circus . . . that's what it means the act of living . . . the act not the significance of life is real . . . more real anyway. holy cow it's a jigsaw puzzle and it all falls together and lord human beings are big big animals! My hands are literally shaking with excitement . . . this is all so new so new . . . just like they say why why why does nobody believe them? It's like a dam that builds and builds and builds and fills up behind with dark things that putrefy and finally something or someone (I must see Laura if only to thank her) pulls the cork and out it comes gushing and making a terrible mess and leaving you shaking and cleaner I want to be still cleaner. I want to stay up all night and shine with cleanliness when I see her tomorrow . . . can I take it? Is it too soon? . . . no I have to go on living this isn't a monomania its just a rebirth, that's all . . . a mere rebirth.

You go in and out deeper and shallower and you come back you always come back its like a drug but without the excuse of being drugged drugs do that they make you think you're going to know yourself and then make you forget yourself so they promise and then they take away promise and take away someone promised and took her the bitch Laura my mother my mother promised to love me and then took it away and gave it back to him and kept doing that taking it away and giving it back to him you can't trust them they're not to be trusted they give and then take back and they make you cry and leave you frightened and crying and watching from your crib as they walk away walk away back to their room bedroom her room they don't rock you anymore they always stop rocking you and leave you there in the dark to cry and cry and cry boy I must have cried like hell as a baby . . . my mother said I cried a lot . . . post nasal drip or something she said, the bitch she was lying I knew what they were doing she was covering up hiding it from me she was scared and guilty about it and I knew and cried coming out . . . I'm trembling also smoking a lot cause it hurts it hurts to know this but I MUST MUST MUST know this I don't want any more

secrets I've had enough secrets secrets kept me from my beautiful lovely Laura in the purple velvet dress no more secrets cause of that bitch my mother whip out the happiness kit its your key your safety valve your proof it can be done you did it you saw that morning sometime that morning when it rained stars it will rain stars again no question about it so I figured I'd do it to my sister to get him back cause he liked my sister too come to think of it I kind of did it with my mother with her her her (oh go on say it we'll burn the thing) with her panties a fetish that's all it was no it wasn't. Like my grandfather said my penis would fall off if I played with it so I played with it and played with it and am still playing with it and I suppose I'm still waiting for it to fall off . . . suppose who are you kidding buster . . . you want it to fall off want it to wish it would you hate it because because because it did all those things what things things with mother and father and freddie and sister and brother that's enough.

Saturday, March 14, 11 A.M.

Everything now conspires to my cure, my whole body aches to be better (slips of the typewriter . . . is that possible?) I hadn't realized how sick I was . . . the bloody stools or at least my queer satisfaction with them was in my head . . . or libido or whatever one calls that amazing thing! I awoke after four hours sleep so as to continue . . . went to take a shower, brought along vitamin pills (after all I don't want to die physically in the process of living emotionally) joked into the mirror saying automatically "Swallowing a bitter pill eh?" And then, instead of leaving the pills on the tray over the sink I went right into the shower with them clutched in my hand . . . I can't stop now . . . and didn't realize until I was standing there staring at them in amazement (absent mindedness and what I do under it is another subject for analysis . . . absent mindedness was on a terrifying increase just prior to the Day) . . . . Falling asleep last night a thousand million thoughts bubbled then the number the age 18 what happened when I was 18? (my stomach hurts . . . it really physically does . . . that blue bear has all kinds of tricks . . . I'm going out for coffee) Well I DO have to go out to get some money but I MUST be merciless with the blue bear. He has no quarter for me . . . he keeps asking too much demanding too much (my father kept asking too much love of me more than I could show him because my mother would have beaten me what a funny reversal of roles come to think of it that is about what I was going to do) in any case it threw up tests too hard to meet I've recently said that if I can't commit myself both to marry Laura and to apply immediately to med school then I'm no good . . . I know I can't meet tests like that just yet and that creates anxiety, self punishment. . . . I had a bad moment when the money Nathan promised to send didn't come (I knew rationally that I could get a blank check had money in the bank could charge at the Co-op). I felt the old surge of hatred as I had against my father this last summer in Spain when money didn't come . . . when love didn't come. . . . Everybody knows or accepts by now that such things "the jargon" homosexual conflicts etc. are within them. . . . everyone knows that what they do every day has something to do with that jargon, but very few are willing to find out EXACTLY what the connecting links are, what the psychic energy has to do with its product . . . most don't have to until they are shown by some disaster that what they do is foolish, or harmful or too painful for themselves to bear and only then do they ask themselves what those connecting links are, HOW EXACTLY they have been exteriorizing . . . John is driving me crazy (scaring me, still threatening) I called to get that lift down to New York I stumbled on some word (inside myself, still inside myself) and he jumped on it said "Do you feel guilty about something, daddy?" for himself he meant guilty about trying to escape him last night, refusing to let him bother me . . . whatever he meant by Daddy is his problem I suppose the guy you want to make love to has to ressemble your father. It's just too uncanny having him take me down to try and come to terms with Laura I had a fear a while back that something inside him would make us crash and although objectively that may yet be my own fear comes from a desire that that should be so, that I should go no further with this analysis but instead give myself up to him as he desires (desires . . . desires . . . there's another word I used in that letter to Nathan.) . . . Acquiesce to my desires I want to beat (love) you that damn letter was in part a love letter. . . . (No no it can't be that just stated them in their undeniable form so that I had to face it both the wish to beat and love my father and the wish to love healthily, heterosexually) I mustn't shake John's grip if I'm going to ride in the same car with him that's silly you have to go pretty far crazy to kill yourself even subconsciously directed because you are threatened he probably believes there are plenty of others besides me the fact is I MUST shake John's grip on myself and not scare myself with eery consequences . . . the newspaper odds are AGAINST automobile

deaths, that was the resistance mechanisms trying to stop me again I'm hot on your tail blue bear that doesn't mean anything what does that mean it means that I'm feeling the denied homosexual instinct, feeling the woman in me and getting over her that's it that's what Faulkner's bear was a woman I have the quotes up on my wall I wrote them down a week ago. . . . woman is a bear you must kill the bear to be a man no that isn't what I've got on my wall the quotes go "Anyone could be upset by his first lion."

DISCUSSION

There are many ways of viewing the material contained in this diary account. The characteristics of the thought processes lend a note of diffuse symbolism, and the record could profitably be examined as raw data from which to construct motivational hypotheses. On the other hand, one can see in it the patient's-eye view of what the experience was all about. In this frame of reference one accepts as a useful observation the patient's evaluation of the adaptional pressures he faces and of the way he experiences himself and the world in this crisis. One agrees to meet the patient on his level, to appreciate what his subjectivity is like, and thereby to see what sense the psychotic reaction makes in terms of his life tasks.[9]

In the present case, one can see this patient wrestling with those life tasks he has been called upon to master but has not. Faced with graduation and a career choice which would identify him with his unhappy father, overwhelmed by failure and guilt in a sexual relationship, and plagued by a conflict-laden family environment he must learn to leave, this man sits down to set in order in a few days a young lifetime of difficult relationships. He seems curiously drawn to the task as if he felt that adequate resolution of it would result in significant inner growth. It is as if something were forcing a number of issues at this stage of his life, and he seems to have well in mind — even if they are hopelessly entangled — the principal people involved in these issues.

If from the diary one obtains an appreciation of this man's struggles, one also comes to a sense of how he felt inwardly during them. Many items could be pointed out in this regard: His pervasive sense of mission, his inner drivenness, his bed-rock depression, and his fear. Of particular note are the affective swings. Periodically he seems to experience

9 See footnotes 1 and 2.

a kind of illumination which temporarily sets his mounting anxiety aside, as when he writes, "I'm out! I'm through . . . boomed out of the tunnel sometime last night and it's raining stars," or "I could be simply overawed but in rereading this I see an incredible, an astonishing structure . . . automatic writing but there is development, there is almost an internal plot. . . ." At other times he is floundering at the nadir of despair: "I can't cope, I can't come to grips . . . it's Hawthorne's disease blazing away, red guilt or little stringy black warts. . . ."

From such an account one gains a new appreciation of what Federn called *Erlebnis*, the concept of the ego as subjective experience or self-awareness.[10] This diary, written on the threshold of psychosis, provides an inner chronicle of the vicissitudes of self-awareness, even as the "self" is swallowed up. We psychiatrists need more information about this very process — the inner experience of becoming psychotic. In many ways our "objective" ways of characterizing ego disruption — either by formal testing or clinical observation and inference — have failed to take into account the patient's actual experience. Most of the literature on this subject is contained in the collection of self-reports edited by Kaplan.[11] These accounts make fascinating reading and source material, but the term "psychosis" is applied so broadly that considerable weeding out would need to be done if one were to learn from them something about the subjective process of becoming psychotic. Laing has recently written an appeal for more concentration on the subjective experience of the psychotic reaction.[12] He contrasts this approach with that of behavioristic description on the one hand, and that of psychoanalytically-oriented investigation on the other. A study in preparation suggests that the ego state at the onset of some psychoses gives rise to self-experiences which are rather limited in number and that these experiences have a great deal in common with other climactic ego states such as religious conversion, mystical states, and certain drug experiences.[13]

There are two main purposes of emphasizing the need for a careful delineation of the subjective experience of becoming psychotic. First, from a practical viewpoint, this is where the therapist needs to be working with his patient. He needs to have a sense of what his patient has been feeling, what the subjective history of the transition from relative sanity to psychosis has been. Second, if serious work is to be done on comparative psychopathological states, ways of characterizing these states *from the point of view of the person who experiences them* need to be worked out.

This patient was hospitalized for approximately six months and has been in psychotherapy elsewhere since his discharge. I have seen him on several occasions since discharge to discuss the publication of his diary. He seems to have gained some insight into the difficulties his parents have in living together and is trying to keep his own future separate from their conflicts. He has gained a good deal of distance from his relationship with Laura; he seems to recognize some of the more destructive aspects which he previously tended to gloss over. Presently he plans to attend college an additional year in order to complete requirements for medical school. He sees this as a "practical" decision, having resulted from a realistic view of his abilities and interests as a writer. He hopes to be a "body doctor, not a mind doctor." He has also gained distance from the diary account presented here, which he now regards as "so bitter, I really can't see how I ever wrote it. It doesn't bother me to read it because it just doesn't seem like me."

[10] Paul Federn, *Ego Psychology and the Psychoses;* New York, Basic Books, 1953.

[11] *The Inner World of Mental Illness*, edited by Bert Kaplan; New York, Harper and Row, 1964.

[12] R. D. Laing, "Is Schizophrenia a Disease?," *Internat. J. Social Psychiatry* (1964) 10:184–193.

[13] Malcolm B. Bowers and D. X. Freedman, "Psychedelic Experiences in Acute Psychoses" (in preparation).

**ROBERT W. GIBSON, MABEL B. COHEN,
AND ROBERT A. COHEN**

On the Dynamics of the Manic-Depressive Personality[*][1]

The primary goal of psychoanalytic therapy is the relief of the patient's symptoms and the promotion of further growth of his personality. However, data elicited in these intensive relationships have served a most important additional function; they have formed the basis for a theory of personality development and of human relations which may aid man in the greater realization of his potentialities. The problem of generalizing from these data is complex. To what extent are the patterns of thought and behavior described in our patients characteristic of all other patients with the same clinical symptoms? To what extent are they similar to those of normal individuals in our own and other cultures? How do they compare to patients with other severe emotional disorders? An important criticism leveled at psychoanalytic data is that the sample is skewed. For example, a recent study (1) of the patients treated by psychoanalysts in the United States indicates that 60% are college graduates, as compared to 6% in the general population. They tend to be predominantly middle class and upwardly mobile. Adequate studies with lower class patients have not yet been reported. There are a host of other problems which remain to be resolved before our theories can be validated.

In this report we have attempted to make a contribution to some of these issues at several levels. Treatment of the schizophrenic patient, studies of his interactions with others, and of his family relationships have been the objects of considerable psychoanalytic attention. This has led not only to the formulation of important principles in therapeutic technique, but also to an increased understanding of personality structure and dynamics — particularly of the vicissitudes of ego development. By reexamining the course of intensive psychotherapy of a group of manic-depressive patients, we hoped to delineate the special problems of therapeutic technique posed by these individuals. Coincident with this we tried to define some characteristic personality qualities, especially those which seem to be quite different from those of schizophrenic patients with whom we had worked similarly. By studying the development of the transference-countertransference relationships and by considering such events of their early life experiences as they seemed to have in common, we postulated some tentative ideas as to the possible relationships between intrapersonal forces and early familial and other environmental experiences which might account for the type of personality development we had observed. Finally, having defined those qualities which our group of intensively treated patients appeared to have in common, one of us who had not participated in the original study examined a series of case histories of manic-depressive patients from a large state mental hospital to determine which of the original observations seemed to apply also to this different population.

In this paper we shall briefly summarize the findings of the two studies and then discuss some of their therapeutic and theoretical implications. And finally, we raise some of the questions which must be answered through further research.

The first study (2) was done on a group of 12 cases of manic-depressive psychosis who were, or had been in intensive psychoanalytic psychotherapy for periods ranging from 1 to 5 years. Nine of these cases were reviewed in a research seminar which met twice monthly for a period of 3 years. Subsequently, these reports were restudied for 2 more years, together with material from 3 other patients currently in treatment.

THE MANIC-DEPRESSIVE PERSONALITY

In brief summary, the personality patterns of the manic-depressive patient which impressed the seminar group as being most conspicuously related to difficulties in adjustment and ultimately to the development of the psychosis were:

1. The patients' dependency drives; 2. The extreme difficulty in dealing with feelings of envy and competition; 3. The common use of denial as a

* Reprinted by permission from the *American Journal of Psychiatry*, Vol. 115, 1959, pp. 1101–1107.
[1] Read at the 114th annual meeting of The American Psychiatric Association, San Francisco, Calif., May 12–16, 1958.

defense, there being a notable lack of subtlety, and of awareness of their own or of the feelings of others in their interpersonal relations; and 4. The almost total orientation of values in terms of social convention and of what others think.

Our findings supported those of Freud (3, 4), Abraham (5), and others that a frequent precipitating event in the psychosis is the loss of a love object. On studying the nature of the patient's relationship with the object, it was found to be an intensely dependent one. The patient had sacrificed his own maturity and self-sufficiency; his gratification and security seemed to rest on his success in gaining the approval of the object by gratifying the other's needs and desires. Coupled with this dependency was an extreme degree of envy and competitiveness not only toward potential rivals but also toward the highly-valued object. The experience of envy directed toward others was associated with a fear of being envied or of being in an enviable position, with the result that achievement of dependent strivings was invariably associated with feelings of vulnerability and danger.

This complex of dependency drives and envious fear of others was almost totally out of awareness. In many patients it was covered by a superficial, apparently affable relationship with a large circle of acquaintances; in others it was expressed in an over-conscientious, martyr-like integration with the important person. In the service of the successful maintenance of this dependency, the patient's value system was oriented toward gaining the approval of others, and toward fitting in with the conventional standards of his group. There appeared to be an absence of, or a lack of conscious appreciation for, empathy and psychological feeling. The patient seemed to avoid awareness of the meaning and significance of his experiences with others, both in terms of his own feelings and the manifest expressions of the attitudes of his associates. Nevertheless, although they were not consciously aware of their envy, competitiveness, and dependent strivings, on a behavioral level they seemed to take such factors into account, and so manipulated the important figures in the environment that they were often temporarily successful in achieving gratification.

For example, such a patient might attempt to mobilize another into helpful action by means of an indirect request. The problem is laid before the other in such a manner that not offering to step up and perform the desired action seems at the least ungracious and at the most downright harmful to the patient. Thus one patient while on an out-of-town assignment desired to change jobs and believed

that his analyst could use influence to bring about the hoped-for change. He wrote a letter outlining the prospects but without making any request for assistance. A non-committal reply by the analyst was promptly followed by a renewal of depressive symptoms. Subsequent discussion of the sequence brought recognition to the patient of his covert expectation that the analyst would make the new job possible, his feelings of anxiety and rejection when this was not done, and the subsequent depression. Supporting the impression of the causal relationships in this sequence was the lifting of the depression after it was reviewed.

EARLY PARENT-CHILD RELATIONSHIPS

A comparison of the inner experiences, as reported in psychotherapy, of the manic-depressive patient with those of the schizophrenic during periods of intense anxiety led us to hypothesize that the manic-depressive's early anxiety experiences with the mother interfered with his succeeding in very young childhood in integrating his concepts of the good mother and bad mother into a single person. This kept him dependent and suppliant to an ambivalently-viewed object who would be good and rewarding to the extent that the child conformed, but tyrannical and condemning whenever he acted independently. This was in contrast to the schizophrenic who failed to develop a self clearly differentiated from the other. While both relationships can be considered dependent, the quality of the dependency is different. The schizophrenic ego is relatively weaker, his concept of self more tenuous. In moments of panic his ego boundaries appear to dissolve; he has the greatest difficulty in distinguishing between himself and objects, and desperately struggles to maintain his own identity by such mechanisms as withdrawal or projection. The manic-depressive, on the other hand, has a sturdier ego, and distinguishes more clearly between himself and his objects. However, he is equally dependent, and attempts to manipulate the object in order to find acceptance by it and to acquire, if possible, exclusive possession of it.

THE PSYCHOTIC ATTACK

The prepsychotic person with a manic-depressive personality can be thought of as living in an equilibrium in which there is enough gratification of his dependency needs to minimize his anxiety, his fear of abandonment, and his competitive envy of others. This equilibrium can be threatened by a variety of life situations: the object may be factually lost by death; there may be a change in relationship merely by change in circumstance; the object may rebel at the dependency relationship and refuse to continue his role; some circumstance of success on the part of the patient may alter his relationship with the object and arouse his fears of being envied; or some outstanding success of the other's may also threaten the dependency and arouse the patient's envy.

When the depression comes on, it seems to be an exaggeration and intensification of the habitual personality patterns. When the dependent equilibrium is disrupted, the patient uses depressive techniques — suffering, self-reproaches, and complaints — in an effort to elicit the desired response. These become offensive to the other, who as a consequence responds even less; the patient redoubles his efforts and receives still less. Finally he loses hope and enters into the psychotic state where the pattern of emptiness and need is repeated over and over in the absence of any gratifying relationship. During the depressed phase, the patient carries on a chronic, largely fantastic acting-out of the pattern of dependency. He addresses his complaints and appeals for help to his previous object, though now chiefly in fantasy, and in addition rather indiscriminately makes his appeal to hospital personnel or others in his immediate environment. The appeal is highly stereotyped, however, and the efforts of relatives, doctors, nurses, *etc.*, bring no comfort. The patient is unable to establish a constructive working relationship with his therapist for 2 main reasons: first, he does not see a realistic goal to strive for, since he is immersed in his repetitious efforts to attain the much-valued dependent relationships; and second, the therapist is not recognized by him as a real person with whom a reliable working relationship can be established. Much time is spent in fruitlessly going over the stereotyped list of fears, self-reproaches, and complaints.

Our experience has been primarily with the depressive attack. Our limited experience with the manic attack leads us to agree with Freud, Lewin (6) and others that manaic behavior can be understood as a defense against the basic depressive pattern. It represents the patient's efforts to escape from the unbearable feelings of isolation and emptiness of the depressive state.

THERAPEUTIC TECHNIQUE

In the light of this picture of the dynamics of the manic-depressive and also as the result of their experience in therapy, the research group developed some concepts of techniques of treatment. It was noted that most of the group found psychotherapy with these patients quite difficult. This was partly on the basis of frustration and helplessness in establishing a communicative relationship, and partly due to the irritation and counter-aggression which the patient's demands and denials aroused. Despite these difficulties, however, the group found that therapy showed some promise, and particularly that as they gained experience, the therapists' feelings of helplessness and defeat grew less. The concensus was that the chief therapeutic problem was that of breaking through the barriers to a communicative relationship set up by the patient's conventional stereotypes and denial of emotional meanings in his interactions. Various methods were advocated for achieving this break-through, many of which were related to the personality of the therapist. Regardless of the specific manner of approach, a general attitude of active involvement with the patient was thought desirable, in contrast to the more passive attitudes appropriate in treating neurotics. However, it was agreed by all that the active involvement must also carry with it an equally active refusal to be manipulated into the position of meeting the patient's dependency needs. Should this occur, the patient will merely be repeating his pre-psychotic pattern with a new object. There is also the danger that the therapist, having drifted into the position of being the source of the patient's dependent gratifications, will eventually free himself from this entanglement by withdrawing from or rejecting the patient. In our experience, the dangers of suicide were greatest when the patient felt unrelated; even a hostile integration with another seemed to lessen this risk. The patient's sense of his own importance or of his meaningfulness as a person may be promoted by the therapist's attempt to convey to him some of the therapist's own feeling attitudes. Even negative responses to his destructive attitudes or his manipulative attempts may be usefully expressed to him if they are genuinely and warmly felt.

EARLY LIFE HISTORY AND FAMILY BACKGROUND

Having developed this working model of the manic-depressive personality, the patients' early life histories were scrutinized for the kinds of experience and types of relationship which might have contributed to the establishment of such patterns. The family histories, as reconstructed during treatment, were examined for elements common to all or most of them. An effort was also made to establish that such elements were unique; that is, that the particular patterns of interaction did not occur in the family history of the schizophrenic or neurotic patient. As will be discussed later, it is highly speculative whether such a characterization can be made. In any event, the most consistent observation made in all 12 histories was that each family was set apart in its social environment by some factor which singled it out as different. This varied from racial to economic difference or to difference resulting from mental illness in a parent. All the families felt this social difference keenly and reacted to it with attempts to maintain or raise the family's prestige by excessive and literal adherence to conventional standards of proper behavior. The patients, as children, were used as instruments for attaining prestige. The child conceived of his worth as being proportional to the degree of his success in being conventionally good. He came to fear that family catastrophe would result from lack of conformity, and that he would be completely rejected and abandoned in such a circumstance. This emphasis on material and conventional success was associated with strong competitive feelings toward others who were seen only as rivals or as objects whose favor was to be sought. The competitive feelings were accompanied by equally strong feelings of envy.

A less consistent observation in the majority of our cases was the finding that the mother was the more driving and ambitious parent, while the father was relatively ineffectual and — even more important — was blamed by the mother for the family's difficulties. In such a situation the child came to depend upon and fear the mother, while finding the father warmer but also less reliable. This led to identity problems as well as to those which arise from inconsistencies in the authority figures.

It was felt that these findings from the group of patients studied by intensive psychotherapy should be checked by the investigation of a larger number of patients and of a control group where the data had been collected in the course of less intensive psychiatric evaluation. We are greatly indebted to Dr. Winfred Overholser and members of his staff for their assistance and cooperation in allowing one of the authors to carry out the second part (7) of the study at St. Elizabeths Hospital in Washington, D. C. The patients in this group differed from the original group in that they were from other social classes, although the social status was not precisely defined for any of them.

A careful study was made of the family relationship patterns and early life experience of 27 manic-depressive and 17 schizophrenic patients. Only those patients were included in whom an unequivocal diagnosis could be made; an additional requirement was the availability of relatives to supplement the information contained in the hospital records. Social workers obtained detailed histories from all informants, special emphasis being given to those aspects of the history related to the hypotheses derived from the first part of the study.

In order to evaluate the information uniformly, a questionnaire was designed in which all the findings of the research group pertaining to family background were stated in the form of 16 questions. By rating the historical data according to this questionnaire, it was possible to determine how closely a patient's history corresponded to the pattern described by the research group. The reliability of the questionnaire was checked by comparing ratings made by several people independently, and by comparing re-ratings made several months later. The reliability studies indicated that the ratings represented adequate, stable judgments, and that the technique of rating could be communicated to uninvolved research assistants.

After all the data had been collected, comparisons were made between the two groups of patients from St. Elizabeths Hospital and the original group of 12 manic-depressive patients. Statistical evaluation indicated that there were only minor differences between the two groups of manic-depressive patients, but there were some highly significant differences between the manic-depressive and schizophrenic patients. In their relations to the community, the families of the manic-depressives had made much greater efforts than the families of the schizophrenics to rise in social status and prestige. They showed greater concern for social approval. The patient was involved in this effort and concerned in a major way. He was often dealt with by his family as if he were an instrument for achieving social prestige rather than a person in his own right. The incidence of envy and competitiveness was particularly high. Most often the patient had been the principal object of this envy and had engaged in self-defeating behavior. The research group had noted this self-defeating behavior and had interpreted it as a defense against the patient's own competitive strivings.

The research group had hypothesized that the parents of manic-depressive patients would show a split, with the mother being relatively cold, unloving but reliable, the father warm, affectionate, and unreliable. No differences in this regard could be found among the families of the 3 groups studied. They had also hypothesized that the manic-depressive would have grown up in a family where there was excessive dissension and great inconsistency with harsh discipline alternating with over-indulgence. In this respect, also, no significant differences were found among the 3 groups of patients.

Thus, the study of the St. Elizabeths' patients supported certain of the concepts of the research group. The manic-depressive can be distinguished from the schizophrenic in that he commonly fits this pattern: he comes from a family where there has been special concern about social approval. The patient has usually borne the brunt of the family's striving for social prestige. There is a background of intense envy and competitiveness. The patient has commonly been the object of this envy within the family, and in later life — presumably to counteract this envy — has developed a pattern of underselling himself and of not utilizing his capacities at anywhere near their potential level.

DISCUSSION AND SUMMARY

We have suggested that two sets of factors are important in the development of the manic-depressive personality: 1. The state of ego development when major anxiety-provoking experiences occur; 2. The dynamics of interpersonal relationships between the family members. How much confidence can we place in the findings which led to these hypotheses? In the first place, it should be emphasized that we worked only with patients who actually had a manic-depressive illness, and our descriptions of the "manic-depressive personality" apply to this group at times when they were free from phychosis. For the most part we worked on the depressive phase of the psychosis, and gave only secondary attention to the manic attack. We do not present any data on the much broader group of cyclothymic personalities.

Is it legitimate to emphasize the social and psychodynamic factors in the development and maintenance of these disorders over and above the biological and hereditary? We do not deny, of course, that the behavioral manifestations of the illness are mediated by physiological alterations. However, it is doubtful that genetic and biological factors could so influence the development of interpersonal relations as to account for the remarkably consistent dynamic descriptions of the personalities of these patients. Further, the fairly consistent family relationship patterns lend support to a primarily psychogenic theory. This view is further strengthened by the fact that with successful psychotherapy the patient abandons his stereotyped pattern of envious, competitive, manipulative dependency and moves into a more mature, independent relationship.

Nevertheless, it is clear that the family pattern as described could not be a sufficient cause for the patient's specific personality development. Not all children in these families developed similar personalities; many of the patterns were also seen in families

of schizophrenic patients. Further, it is characteristic of the American middle class generally, especially of upper middle class families, that they have the status consciousness and concern and the upward mobility which we have described for the families of our manic-depressive patients. Obviously, much more research into family patterns is needed, in normals as well as in the various forms of mental disorder, in other cultures as well as in our own, and in the epidemiology of mental illness in the various social classes.

Despite these reservations concerning the reliability of our ideas about them, we believe these family patterns may be influential in the genesis of the manic-depressive personality. Our work to date does not permit us to make a precise statement regarding the mode of action and intermediate steps between the early environmental family influences and the manic-depressive illness. However, inferences drawn from reports of patients in psychotherapy have led us to formulate some tentative hypotheses.

As the child moves from the helplessness of early infancy to the more self-assertive and active phases of late infancy and childhood, he will be increasingly exposed to the anxiety engendered by the family's needs for prestige and social conformity as well as to the conflictful situation arising out of envy and competitiveness. At this time the primary closeness based upon the identifications of early infancy will have diminished but the more mature closeness based on the ability to relate to others as individuals distinct from oneself will be in the most rudimentary stage. Thus the child could be expected to feel peculiarly alone and consequently vulnerable to any threat of abandonment. This particular sensitivity and vulnerability persists into adult life leading to a central conflict in the manic-depressive. It may also be that the repression of feelings and discharge of tensions *via* the manipulative exploitative activity on the part of a parent may provide the child with a model which is later modified in his personality to a hypomanic way of life. In any given case there may be a wide variation dependent upon individual attributes of the infant that serve as stimuli to arouse anxieties in the parents. For example, age, sex, or physical appearance of a child may cause the parent to see the child as a hated sibling, leading to specific kinds of overexpectation and demands. Further, the quality of parent-child interaction may be of specific importance. Thus, the mother-child relationship in schizophrenia has been described as symbiotic; while in the manic-depressive we have visualized it as being less close, with the child serving a somewhat mechanistic role as his mother's instrument. Longitudinal studies of child development will make it possible to check the validity of such hypotheses as these. All that we can offer in their support at present is that such reconstructions in the course of psychotherapy appeared to have been instrumental in the development of a favorable change in the patient.

Although we have stressed the importance of environmental influences as mediated through the significant interpersonal relationships, we do not deny that differences in drive intensity or innate ego strength may be thought of as determining what makes one person a successful extrovert and another a manic-depressive. Predictive description would have to go far beyond what is presently possible, in the direction primarily of the identification and quantitative appraisal of the resources of the personality. Possibly the character and degree of reaction to psychotomimetic drugs such as LSD-25 and the current studies of the responses to sensory deprivation might contribute to the problem of the assessment of ego strength — both in its defensive and integrative aspects.

Finally, we believe that the methods used in this study have some merit. The seminar made it possible to review the data from a larger number of cases than can usually be reported in psychoanalytic therapy. By virtue of this review we found ourselves steadily narrowing the number of "positive" findings until at last we proposed those which we thought were most consistently present in the 12 patients. These were subjected to further screening by the survey of the larger sample and the schizophrenic controls. This led to a revision of the description of the family relationship patterns and served to highlight those areas requiring more precise definition and investigation. It is to be hoped that further and more sophisticated elaboration of such cross-checking efforts will help organize the great mass of valuable data which lies imbedded in every psychotherapeutic effort.

BIBLIOGRAPHY

1. WEINSTOCK, HARRY I.: Summary and Final Report of the Central Fact-Gathering Committee of the Am. Psychoanalytic Assoc.
2. COHEN, M. B., BAKER, GRACE, COHEN, R. A., FROMM-REICHMANN, FRIEDA, AND WEIGERT, E. V.: Psychiatry, 17: 103, May 1954.
3. FREUD, S.: Mourning and Melancholia. *In:* Collected Papers, 4: 152.
4. FREUD, S.: Group Psychology in the Analysis of the Ego. London: Hogarth Press, 1922.
5. ABRAHAM, K.: Selected Papers on Psychoanalysis. New York: Basic Books, 1953.
6. LEWIN, B.: The Psychoanalysis of Elation. New York: W. W. Norton, 1950.
7. GIBSON, ROBERT W.: Psychiatry, 21: 71, Feb. 1958.

NORMAN CAMERON

The Paranoid Pseudo-Community Revisited*

ABSTRACT

The pseudo-community is reformulated as a cognitive structure which attempts to solve the problem of reconciling social reality with the products of paranoid projection. Delusional development follows regression and the loss of social reality. It begins with the estrangement experienced by a partially regressed person when he attempts to regain object relations and proceeds through successive provisional reconstructions of reality until a cognitive solution is reached which seems to justify paranoid action. Aggressive action is likely to make social reality confirm the expectations of the pseudo-community.

* Reprinted by permission from *American Journal of Sociology*, Vol. 65, 1959, pp. 52–58. Copyright 1959 by The University of Chicago Press.

A decade of experience with intensive clinical studies of paranoid thinking, in the course of psychoanalyzing psychoneurotics and in the long-term therapy of ambulatory psychotics, has led me to a reworking of the concept of the pseudo-community as formulated in this *Journal*[1] and further developed elsewhere.[2] The social aspects of the concept require little change. It is in its individual aspects — in a greater concern with the evidence of internal changes and with the signs that forces are operative which are not open to direct observation — that the pseudo-community acquires deeper roots and greater usefulness.

Original Presentation — In the normal evolution and preservation of socially organized behavior the most important factor is the developing and maintaining of genuine communication. In each individual, language behavior grows out of preverbal interchange between infant and older person. It evolves in accordance with whatever traditional patterns prevail in the immediate environment, since communication is always, at first, between a child who operates at preverbal levels and older individuals whose language is already a highly organized interactive system. Through sharing continuously in such language and prelanguage interchange, each child develops shared social perspectives and skill in shifting from one perspective to another in time of need.

A highly significant result of this gradual process is that, as time goes on, the child normally acquires an increasingly realistic grasp of how other people feel, what their attitudes, plans, hopes, fears, and intentions are, and in what ways these all relate to his own. Eventually, he is able to take the roles of other people around him in imagination and to view things more or less realistically from their perspectives as well as from his own. In this way he also develops a workable degree of objectivity toward himself, learning to respond to his body, his personality, and his behavior more or less as others do. In the final product, there is considerable difference

[1] Norman Cameron, "The Paranoid Pseudo-Community," *American Journal of Sociology*, XLIX (1943), 32–38. Reprinted in A. M. Rose (ed.), *Mental Health and Mental Disorder: A Sociological Approach* (New York: W. W. Norton & Co., 1955).

[2] Norman Cameron, *The Psychology of Behavior Disorders: A Biosocial Interpretation* (Boston: Houghton Mifflin Co., 1947), and "Perceptual Organization and Behavior Pathology," in R. Blake and G. Ramsey (eds.), *Perception: An Approach to Personality* (New York: Ronald Press Co., 1951); and Norman Cameron and A. Magaret, *Behavior Pathology* (Boston: Houghton Mifflin Co., 1951), chap. xiii, "Pseudo-Community and Delusion."

between the socialization achieved in behavior publicly shared and genuinely communicated and behavior that has remained private and little formulated or expressed in language.

The adult who is especially vulnerable to paranoid developments is one in whom this process of socialization has been seriously defective. His deficient social learning and poorly developed social skills leave him unable to understand adequately the motivations, attitudes, and intention of others. When he becomes disturbed or confused under stress, he must operate under several grave handicaps imposed by a lifelong inability to communicate freely and effectively, to suspend judgment long enough to share his tentative interpretations with someone else, to imagine realistically the attitudes that others might have toward his situation and himself, and to imagine their roles and thus share their perspectives.

Left to his own unaided devices in a crisis, the paranoid person is able only to seek and find "evidence" that carries him farther in the direction he is already going — toward a more and more delusional interpretation of what seems to be going on around him.[3] This process may culminate in a conviction that he himself is the focus of a community of persons who are united in a conspiracy of some kind against him. It is this supposed functional community of real persons whom the patient can see and hear, and of other persons whom he imagines, that we call the *paranoid pseudo-community*. It has no existence as a social organization and as soon as he attempts to combat it, or to flee, he is likely to come into conflict with his actual social community.

Incompleteness of the Descriptive Pseudo-community — This, in brief, is the background and structure of the paranoid pseudo-community, as originally described. As it stands, it still seems valid; but it is unnecessarily restricted. In the first place, the account of the delusional development pays scant attention to internal dynamics because of the limits imposed by a behavioristic orientation. Patients, of course, recognize no such limitations. In the course of long-term intensive therapy they can sometimes furnish important information about what is going on within them to a therapist who is ready to receive it. Some of this they describe as it happens, in their own terms, and often in their own idiom. Some of it one can infer from what is said and done, with the help of material commu-

[3] For a detailed discussion of this process of *desocialization* see "Desocialization and Disorganization," in Cameron and Magaret, *op. cit.*, pp. 448–517.

nicated in parallel cases. Some of it one must postulate in an effort to make one's observations and direct inferences more intelligible, just as is done in other empirical sciences.

In the original account not enough emphasis was given to the positive achievements of delusion formation. As we shall see, the pseudo-community is the best means a paranoid patient has at the time for bridging the chasm between his inner reality and social reality. Its use for this purpose may lead to a progressive reduction in desocialization and the reappearance of more normal communicative channels.

And, finally, the concept of the pseudo-community needs a background of structural postulates. In order to make sense out of the experiences which people actually have in fantasies, daydreams, dreams, and psychoses, one is obliged to go beyond such impermanent concepts as perception, response, and behavior — upon which the writer earlier relied — and to assume probable forces and mechanisms operating within personality systems and interacting subsystems. Here, again, the patient often comes to the rescue with empirical data. And, every now and then, one comes across a patient who describes with naïve simplicity and directness — but consistently over a long period of time — phenomena which seem purely theoretical and highly abstruse, as reported in the literature. Exposed to such material the therapist may still be left with a sense of strangeness; but his previous feeling of their abstruseness and incredulity sooner or later vanishes.[4]

Paranoid Loss of Social Reality — Paranoid delusional development begins with an impairment of social communication. It is preceded by experiences of frustration to which, like many normal persons, the paranoid individual reacts by turning away from his surroundings, and taking refuge in fantasy and daydream. This is the phase of withdrawal and preoccupation which is sometimes obvious even to an untrained observer.

When a paranoid person withdraws like this, he is far more likely than a normal person to lose effective contact with his social environment (i.e., with social reality) and to undergo regression. If this happens, he may abandon social reality for a time completely and become absorbed in primitive regressive thinking and feeling. Occasionally, a patient openly expresses some of his regressive experiences at the time; more often they can be inferred only from what emerges later on.

[4] See, e.g., the clinical material in Norman Cameron, "Reprojection and Introjection in the Interaction between Schizophrenic Patient and Therapist" (submitted for publication).

Precursors of the Pseudo-community. I. Beginning Restitution — It is a fact, of both clinical observation and subjective report, that paranoid patients, while still withdrawn, preoccupied, and regressed, begin to make attempts to regain their lost relationships with social reality. We may conceptualize these as marking the tapering-off of regression and the beginning of the reintegration of personality. The attempts fail to recover the lost social reality, however, because the patient's internal situation is not what is was before his regression. It is no longer possible for him to regain social reality as, for example, a normal person does when he wakes up in the morning. Instead, as we shall see, paranoid reintegration involves a restitutive process, the construction of a pseudo-reality which culminates in the paranoid pseudo-community.

Paranoid personalities suffer all their lives from defective repressive defenses and a heavy reliance upon the more primitive defenses of denial and projection. If they undergo a pyschotic regression, which involves partial ego disintegration, their repressive defenses become still more defective. Primitive fantasies and conflicts now begin to emerge and to threaten ego disruption. The patient is forced to deal with them somehow, if he is to preserve what personality integration he still has and avoid further regression. Since he cannot successfully repress them, he vigorously denies them and projects them. An immediate result of the intense projective defense is that the products of the patient's emerging fantasies and conflicts now appear to him to be coming from outside him. Thus he seems to escape disintegration from within only to be threatened with destruction from without.

Precursors of the Pseudo-community. II. Estrangement and Diffuse Vigilance — In the process of denying and projecting, the paranoid patient makes a start toward regaining contact with his surroundings. But this process neither simplifies nor clarifies the situation for him; and it does not bring about a return to social reality. On the contrary, the surroundings now seem somehow strange and different. Something has unquestionably happened. The patient misidentifies this "something" as basically a change in the makeup of his environment instead of what it actually is, a fundamental change within himself. If he expresses his feelings at this point, he is likely to say that things are going on which he does not understand; and this, of course, is literally true.

It is hardly surprising that the patient, finding himself in a world grown suddenly strange, should become diffusely vigilant. He watches everything uneasily; he listens alertly for clues; he looks everywhere for hidden meanings. Here his lifelong social incompetence makes matters still worse. He lacks even ordinary skill in the common techniques for testing social reality. He is unable to view his threatening situation even temporarily from the perspective of a neutral person. The more anxious and vigilant he grows, the less he can trust anybody, the less he dares to share with anyone his uneasiness and suspicion. He is condemned to pursue a solitary path, beset by primal fears, hates, and temptations which he cannot cope with nor escape.

Precursors of the Pseudo-community. III. Increased Self-reference — Strong tendencies toward self-reference are characteristic of paranoid personalities. When a paranoid adult becomes deeply and regressively preoccupied, his habitually egocentric orientation is greatly increased. And when he next resorts to wholesale projection, he in effect converts his environment into an arena for his projected fantasies and conflicts. This destroys whatever neutrality and objectivity the environment may have previously possessed for him. He is now engrossed in scrutinizing his surroundings for signs of the return of what he is denying and projecting. To these he has become selectively sensitive. He is watching out for something that will explain away the strangeness and enable him to escape his frightening sense of isolation.

It is an unfortunate fact that a badly frightened person — even a normal one — is likely to notice things and make interpretations that increase rather than diminish his fear. And this is especially the case if he feels alone, in strange surroundings, and threatened by an unknown danger. Many non-paranoid adults, for example, walking alone through a large cemetery at night, or lost at night in a forest, become extremely alert and feel personally threatened by harmless things wholly unrelated to them. The paranoid adult, who is peopling his surroundings with projected phantoms from his own past, likewise creates a situation in which everything seems somehow dangerously related to him. Since he cannot escape, he tries to understand the situation he has unconsciously created, in the vain hope that he may then be able to cope with it.

Precursors of the Pseudo-community. IV. Preliminary Hypotheses — Being human, the paranoid patient is driven irresistibly to make hypotheses; but, having partially regressed, and being paranoid as well, he cannot test them. He tends, therefore, to pass from one guess or one suspicion to another like it. Using the materials provided by his environment and by his projected fantasies and conflicts, he constructs a succession of provisional hypotheses, discarding each as it fails to meet the contradictory

demands of his internal needs and the environment. This is characteristic also of complex normal problem-solving. It is an expression of what is called the synthetic function of the ego.

Everyone who works with paranoid patients discovers that some kind of delusional reconstruction of reality is essential to their continued existence as persons. Even a temporary and unsatisfactory delusional hypothesis may be at the time a patient's sole means of bridging the gap between himself and his social environment. It gives a distorted picture of the world; but a distorted world is better than no world at all. And this is often a regressed person's only choice. To abandon his projected fears, hates, and temptations might mean to abandon all that he has gained in the reconstruction of reality, to have his world fall apart and fall apart himself. Patients sense this danger, even expressing it in these words, and they rightly refuse to give up their delusional reality. Their fear is not unrealistic, for clinically such catastrophes actually occur, ending in personality disintegration.

A great many paranoid persons never go beyond the phase of making and giving up a succession of preliminary delusional hypotheses. Some of them regain a good working relationship with social reality, something approaching or equaling their premorbid status. Some are less successful and remain chronically suspicious, averse, and partially withdrawn but manage even so to go on living otherwise much as they had lived before. They may appear morose, irascible, and bitter; but they do not fix upon definite enemies or take definite hostile action. At most they suffer brief outbursts of protest and complaint without losing their ability to retreat from an angry delusional position. In this paper, however, we are concerned primarily with paranoid patients — by no means incurable — who go on to crystallize a more stable delusional organization.

Final Crystallization: The Pseudo-community — A great many paranoid persons succeed in crystallizing a stable conceptual organization, the pseudo-community, which gives them a satisfactory cognitive explanation of their strange altered world and a basis for doing something about the situation as they now see it. Their problem is exceedingly complex. It is impossible for them to get rid of the unconscious elements which they have denied and projected, but which now return apparently from the outside. They cannot abandon or even ignore their environment without facing a frightening regression into an objectless world. Their task is somehow to integrate these internal and external phenomena which appear before them on a single plane into a unified world picture.

The human environment which others share (*social reality*) provides the patient with real persons having social roles and characteristics which he can utilize in making his delusional reconstruction. It also provides real interaction among them, including interaction with the patient himself. Many things actually happen in it, some of them in direct relation to the patient, most of them actually not.

Internal reality provides two sets of functions. One is made up of the previously unconscious impulses, conflicts, and fantasies — now erupted, denied and projected. This, as noted, introduces imagined motivation, interaction, and intentions into the observed activities of other persons. It gives apparent meaning to happenings which do not have such meaning for the consensus. The other set of functions is included in the concept of ego adaptation. It is the ego synthesis mentioned above, by means of which the demands of internal reality and the structure of social reality are integrated into a meaningful, though delusional, unity.

What the paranoid patient does is as follows: Into the organization of social reality, as he perceives it, he unconsciously projects his own previously unconscious motivation, which he has denied but cannot escape. This process now requires a perceptual and conceptual reorganization of object relations in his surroundings into an apparent community, which he represents to himself as organized wholly with respect to him (delusion of self-reference). And since the patient's erupted, denied, and projected elements are overwhelmingly hostile and destructive, the motivation he ascribes to the real persons he has now organized into his conceptual pseudo-community is bound to be extremely hostile and destructive.

To complete his conceptual organization of a paranoid conspiracy, the patient also introduces imaginary persons. He ascribes to them, as to real persons, imagined functions, roles, and motivations in keeping with his need to unify his restitutional conception and make it stable. He pictures helpers, dupes, stooges, go-betweens, and master-minds, of whose actual existence he becomes certain.

It is characteristic of the pseudo-community that it is made up of both real and imaginary persons, all of whom may have both real and imaginary functions and interrelations.[5] In form it usually corresponds to one or another of the common dangerous, hostile groups in contemporary society, real or fictional —

[5] This is in contrast to the autistic community, which is composed of wholly imaginary persons (see "Autistic Community and Hallucination," in Cameron and Magaret, *op. cit.*, pp. 414–447.

gangs, dope and spy rings, secret police, and groups of political, racial, and religious fanatics. Many paranoid patients succeed in creating a restitutional organization which has well-formulated plans. The chief persecutor is sometimes a relative or acquaintance, or a well-known public figure, while the rest of the imaginary personnel forms a vague, sinister background. Sometimes one finds the reverse — the chief persecutor is unknown, a malevolent "brain" behind everything, while the known dangerous persons play supporting roles in the delusional cast.

The final delusional reconstruction of reality may fall into an integrated conceptual pattern that brings an experience of closure: "I suddenly realized what it was all about!" the patient may exclaim with obvious relief at sudden clarification. The intolerable suspense has ended: the strangeness of what has been "going on" seems to disappear, and confusion is replaced by "understanding," and wavering doubt by certainty. A known danger may be frightening; but at least it is tangible, and one can do something about it. In short, the pseudo-community reduces the hopeless complexity and confusion to a clear formula. This formula — "the plot" — the patient can now apply to future events as he experiences them and fit them into the general framework of his reconstruction.

The organization of a conceptual pseudo-community is a final cognitive step in paranoid problem-solving. It re-establishes stable object relations, though on a delusional basis, and thus makes integrated action possible. To summarize what this reconstruction of reality has achieved for its creator:

a) *Reduction in estrangement.* — As a direct result of paranoid problem-solving, experienced external reality is distorted so as to bring it into line with the inescapable projected elements. This lessens confusion and detachment and allows the patient to recover some of his lost sense of ego integrity. The world seems dangerous but familiar.

b) *Internal absorption of aggression.* — Construction and maintenance of a conceptual pseudo-community absorb aggression internally, in the same sense that organizing a baseball team, a political ward, or a scientific society absorbs aggression. This reduces the threat of ego disintegration which the id eruptions pose.

c) *Basis for action.* — Any new cognitive construct can serve as a basis for new action; in this respect the paranoid pseudo-community is no exception. It organizes the drive-directed cognitive processes, leads to meaningful interpretations in a well-defined pseudo-reality structure, and paves the way for overt action with a definite focus. The patient is enabled to go ahead as anyone else might who had powerful urges and felt sure that he was right.

d) *Justification of aggressive action.* — Finally, a persecutory pseudo-community justifies attack or flight, either of which involves a direct aggressive discharge in overt action. Fighting or running away is less disintegrative psychologically than prolonged frightened inaction. And under the circumstances, as the patient now conceptualizes them, he need feel neither guilt for attacking nor shame for fleeing.

Paranoid Cognition and Paranoid Action — When a patient succeeds in conceptualizing a pseudo-community, he has taken the final cognitive step in paranoid problem-solving. He now "knows" what his situation is. But he is still faced with his need to do something about it. As a matter of fact, the crystallization of a hostile delusional structure usually increases the urge to take action. A circular process may quickly develop. The imagined threats of the now structured imaginary conspiracy seem to the patient concrete and imminent. They stimulate more and more his anxiety and defensive hostility — and the latter, being as usual projected, further increases the apparent external threat. Often this kind of self-stimulation spirals upward, while more and more "incidents" and people may be drawn into the gathering psychotic storm.

Paranoid action, however inappropriate it may be, still represents the completion of restitutional relationships and the fullest contact with his human environment of which the patient is capable at the time. He switches from his previous passive role of observer and interpreter, with all its indecision and anxiety, to that of an aggressive participant in what he conceives as social reality. For him this is genuine interaction, and he experiences the gratification that comes with certainty and with a massive discharge of pent-up aggressiveness. He may give a preliminary warning to the supposed culprits or make an appeal for intervention to someone in authority before taking direct action himself, which, when it comes, may be in the form of an attack or sudden flight, either of which may be planned and executed with considerable skill.

Making Social Reality Conform to the Pseudo-community — Paranoid patients who take aggressive action often achieve a pyrrhic victory. They succeed finally in making social reality act in conformity with the delusional reality which they have created. As long as a patient confines himself to watching, listening, and interpreting, he need not come into open conflict with the social community. But, when he takes overt action appropriate only in his private pseudo-community, a serious social conflict will arise.

Social reality is the living product of genuine sharing, communication, and interaction. Valid social attitudes, interpretations, and action derive continuously from these operations. The restitutional reality in which the patient believes himself to be participating has no counterpart outside of himself: it is illusory. Other persons cannot possibly share his attitudes and interpretations because they do not share his paranoid projections and distortions. Therefore they do not understand action taken in terms of his delusional reconstruction. The patient, for his part, cannot share their attitudes and interpretations because he is driven by regressive needs which find no place in adult social reality.

When an intelligent adult expresses beliefs and makes accusations which seem unintelligible to others, as well as threatening, he may make the people around him exceedingly anxious. This is particularly the case when his words tend to activate their unconscious fantasies and conflicts. And when such a person begins to take aggressive action, which seems unprovoked as well as unintelligible, he inevitably arouses defensive and retaliatory hostility in others. The moment the social community takes action against him, it provides him with the confirmation he has been expecting — that there is a plot against him.

Thus, in the end, the patient manages to provoke action in the social community that conforms to the expectation expressed in his pseudo-community organization. His own internal need to experience hostility from without — as a defense against being overwhelmed by internal aggression — is satisfied when actual persons behave in accordance with his projections. His need for a target against which to discharge hostility is also met. This is his victory and his defeat.

The defeat need not be final. Much will depend, of course, upon the patient's basic personality organization, particularly his emotional flexibility, his potentiality for internal change, and his residual capacity for establishing new ego and superego identifications. The depth and extent of his regression are also important, as are the fixity and the inclusiveness of his delusional structure. Much will also depend upon his potential freedom to communicate, to develop reciprocal role-taking skills with another person, and to include another's alternative perspectives in his own therapeutic orientation.

Therapy — The primary therapeutic consideration, of course, is not the character of the delusional structure but what makes it necessary. A reduction in anxiety is among the first objectives. The source of anxiety lies in the regressive changes and in the threat these have brought of an unconscious breakthrough. But it is also aggravated by anything in the environment which tends to increase the patient's hostility and fear. Once the setting has been made less anxiety-provoking, the most pressing need is for someone in whom the patient can ultimately put his trust — someone not made anxious by the patient's fear and hostility or driven to give reassurances and make demands.

For the paranoid patient who is ready to attempt social communication, an interested but neutral therapist can function as a living bridge between psychotic reality and social reality. Through interacting with such a person, who neither attacks the delusional structure nor beats the drums of logic, a patient may succeed in gaining new points of reference from which to build a new orientation. The therapeutic process now involves another reconstruction of reality, one which undoes the restitutional pseudo-community without destroying the patient's defenses and forcing him to regress further.

As anxiety and the threat of disintegration subside, paranoid certainty becomes less necessary to personality survival. The patient can begin to entertain doubts and consider alternative interpretations. Such changes, of course, must come from within if they are to come at all. If he is able to work through some of the origins and derivatives of his basic problems, the patient may succeed eventually in representing to himself more realistically than ever before how other people feel and think. In this way the conceptual structure of his pseudo-community may be gradually replaced by something approaching the conceptual structure of social reality.

Character and Personality Disorders / 5

A great deal of confusion and controversy surrounds the group of disturbances known as the personality disorders. Under this heading have been grouped a hodgepodge of individuals, including those who repeatedly rebel against authority, who commit murder, who manipulate and cheat others, and who make an inadequate response to the ordinary demands of life or have difficulty in self-control. Ranging even further, this diagnostic category covers those persons who maintain socially unsanctioned sexual relations, or overindulge in alcohol, or engage in the use of drugs. In popular psychiatric jargon, any and all of these individuals may be designated a "psychopath." Broadly defined (and the moral implications of this label should be clear from the use of such terms), the psychopath is the kind of person who seems insensitive to social demands, who is irresponsible and shows poor judgment, who appears to lack the ability to take the role of the other, who is impulsive and shallow, incapable of maintaining a love relationship, and who doesn't learn by experience, inexorably invoking a cycle of behavior culminating in self-defeat. It should come as no surprise that these warped personalities are remarkably resistant to therapeutic change.

Thorne, in the opening paper, offers an explanation of the dynamics of these sociopathic or psychopathic states centering around Alfred Adler's concept of the "style of life." He proposes that the sociopath learns his particular life style because, to some degree, it provides immediate gratification of short-term needs and impulses. There is an echo of Mowrer's conception of the development of neurosis in Thorne's portrait of the psychopath as an attractive and intelligent child, who learns at an early age how to capitalize on his assets in order to manipulate the adults around him. In this paper, Thorne counters several common assertions about the sociopath, including the theory of a constitutional, hereditary factor, and the supposed lack of guilt and anxiety concerning their interpersonal, anti-social behavior.

Satten and his colleagues at the Menninger Clinic attempt a description of the characteristics of a personality disorder type rarely encountered in the literature on the subject, the individual who commits impulsive, senseless murder. Emerging from a background of parental violence and emotional deprivation, such individuals develop such weak egos that periodic explosions of aggression may result in homicidal acts. A brilliant account of such an individual can be found in Truman Capote's recent book, In Cold Blood (New York: Random House, 1966).

Glueck's paper presents a report of an intensive study of over two hundred men convicted and imprisoned for sex offenses. While admittedly a biased sample, all the men having been convicted of felonies, the implications for the psychodynamic patterns of sex offenders in general are appropriate. Glueck discusses the legal and emotional aspects of the sex offense which complicate any attempt to delineate the psychodynamics of the offender.

Brown examines a more familiar form of sexual disorder, male homosexuality, presenting evidence for the importance of family interaction patterns and child-rearing practices in sexual development and behavior. The combination of a dominant, overly intimate ("close-binding") mother, and a detached, hostile, or weak father appears to have direct bearing upon the development of male homosexuality.

In his paper on narcotic addiction, Ausubel argues that the addict's dependence upon the continued use of narcotics to avoid withdrawal symptoms is not a significant factor in causing drug addiction, but is instead a function of the addict's reliance upon the drug for its adjustive value and euphoric properties. Ausubel distinguishes between two types of drug addicts: a chronic type of disorder with a very poor prognosis, and a more transitory disturbance, similar to juvenile delinquency, and he enumerates a series of factors which bear on the development and maintenance of these patterns of behavior. These include long-standing motivational immaturity, external social pressures, an internal predisposing factor, the particular adjustive value of the drug, its availability and the community's tolerance for drug addiction.

But beyond its social aspects, drug use is an extremely personal experience, involving deep-rooted emotional and attitudinal components. Becker's paper is an intriguing analysis of the "natural history" of the marihuana smoker's contact with the drug. He portrays the marihuana user as engaged in a learning process involving instrumental behaviors, perceptual and cognitive reorganization, and alterations in motivational and emotional factors, culminating in a new conception of the drug and his use

of it. As Becker comments, "On completion of this process he (the marihuana user) is willing and able to use marihuana for pleasure."

One of the most common forms of personality disorder is the alcoholic. Whether confined in definition only to alcohol "addicts" or used more broadly to designate any form of excessive drinking, alcoholism is a disorder symptomatic of underlying psychological and social pathology. Joan Jackson's paper draws attention to the impact of alcoholism on the family. As she describes it, alcoholism precipitates a cumulative crisis in the family which passes through seven critical stages, from the initial denial of the problem to a final family reorganization. Jackson argues, contrary to the popular conception that the wife's personality plays a "causal" role in the onset of alcoholism, that the wife's personality picture may well be a reflection of the family crisis at any one of its stages. ■

FREDERICK C. THORNE

The Etiology of Sociopathic Reactions*

To date, the literature contains few convincing formulations of the etiology and personality dynamics of the large group of character disorders variously known as sociopathic reactions, character neuroses or psychopathic personality. On the contrary, a large number of misconceptions or partial truths concerning the symptomatology of the syndrome have gained widespread acceptance and resulted in further confusion concerning the essential nature of these perplexing cases. The purpose of this paper is to offer an hypothetical model of the dynamics of sociopathic reactions, in general, based on a survey of the literature and on our clinical experience with a group of intensively treated cases.

THE OBSERVATIONS TO BE EXPLAINED

Sociopathic behavior occurs in all degrees of severity, ranging from single sociopathic actions occurring once in a life-time to the most complex char-

* Reprinted by permission from the *American Journal of Psychotherapy*, Vol. 13, 1959, pp. 319–330.

acter disorders involving the whole personality and manifested almost continuously. We propose to define sociopathic reactions *operationally* in this paper by outlining the characteristic symptomatology of the syndrome under discussion. The distinction should be made between sociopathic behaviors occurring as symptoms of other clinical groups such as defectives, psychoneurotics or psychotics, and the sociopathic reactions occurring as primary personality disorders with their own specific etiology and dynamics. A difficult problem in differential diagnosis often exists in attempting to discriminate the asocial behaviors observed in alcoholism, sexual offenders and other psychiatric classifications where the symptomatology is secondary to more primary disorders.

Cleckley (3) has presented descriptively a museum collection of severe sociopathies, providing a typical sampling of the symptomatology which characterizes this group, but he offers no convincing etiologic hypotheses. Karpman (5) also has collected a large series of cases presenting sexual psychopathies which he interpreted psychoanalytically. In our opinion, while analytic formulations may apply validly to the dynamics of specific aspects of the symptomatology in individual cases, no unified theory has developed from psychoanalysis capable of clarifying the dynamics of the syndrome in general. This author (7) has stressed defective conditioning and unhealthy ego development, wherein the sociopath attempts to satisfy his inflated and unrealistic ego needs by socially unacceptable mechanisms. From the literature and our own clinical observations, we have collected a list of symptoms considered typical of this syndrome, and which are outlined below:

Normal Intelligence — Except for a small group of cases with organic involvement demonstrable by electroencephalography or neurologic findings, there is little convincing psychometric evidence of marked intellectual deficits in this group. This confutes the older hypothesis that these were "moral imbeciles" unable to distinguish right from wrong.

Social Intelligence — To the contrary, sociopaths show high social intelligence, as manifested by their ability to influence and manipulate people, to know what to say to appear convincing, to understand and manipulate motives, and to successfully operate confidence games and frauds based on knowledge of the psychology of people and situations.

Attractive Physical Appearance and Personality — As a group, many sociopaths are above average in physical and personality attractiveness. This characteristic gains them early entree into adult groups, resulting in a precocious initiation to sexuality, alcohol, gambling and high life in general.

Not Hereditary — No convincing evidence of hereditary transmission is available. Sociopaths usually occur one to a family as in the classical description of the "black sheep." Although underprivileged environments, presumably populated by less adequate persons, appear to contribute an higher incidence, the relationship is far from universal, in that many sociopaths occur in the best of families, and the primary factors appear to be environmental rather than hereditary.

Inability to Learn from Experience — This characteristic is cited in the literature as evidence of a defect of intelligence or learning ability, as evidenced by the facts that reward or punishment (typically) does not modify sociopathic behavior. If anything, many sociopaths actually become more efficient in their asocial ways, seem to learn from experience *what not to do*, to avoid being caught. Perhaps the constancy of the undesirable behavior is due to a relative constancy of conditions of inner motivation and style of life rather than to inability to learn from experience. Sociopaths learn very well what they *need* to learn.

Level of Anxiety — The literature stresses a relative lack of anxiety in sociopaths in the consequences of their actions both on others and for themselves, citing as evidence the common observation that most sociopaths seem callous and oblivious to guilt, regret, penitence, or the need to assume responsibility for one's own conduct. For this reason, it is often postulated that sociopathy is the result of defective super-ego development wherein normal anxiety over misbehavior is not experienced by the sociopath. Here again, our experience questions this conclusion since many of the sociopaths in our series manifested extreme anxiety in all its classic symptomatology. Its strength as a motive, however, was not great enough to displace other motives.

Impulsivity — Most sociopaths show high impulsivity, lack of inhibition and low frustration tolerance. These characteristics are particularly conspicuous in early life but may show some improvement with training, especially toward middle age, if they are treated patiently, and gradually taught to delay impulses. Some authorities believe that this impulsivity, or tendency to "act out" impetuously, is a constitutional characteristic because of its early appearance.

Attitudinal Traits — In many cases we find distinctive patterns of attitudinal structure reflecting both a deviant *Weltanschauung* and defensive rationalizations of their conduct. Many of them act as though usual laws and limitations did not apply to them, saying, "I have a right to something in life," "the world owes it to me," "I know my dad wouldn't punish me if I took it," etc. Conveniently disregarding the usual rules about having to work for what you get, the sociopath typically regards it as "smart" to "take what you can get" by "using your wits." Cleverness in defrauding other people becomes a mark of distinction.

Multi-formed Symptomatology — In the developmental course of the disorder, many sociopaths show a changing pattern of symptoms reflecting maturational factors, conditioned behavior disorders, psychoneurotic reactions and even transient psychotic disorders. This is evidenced by the fact that many sociopaths have received a variety of clinical diagnoses at various stages of the disorder. It may be interpreted after Menninger (6) as reflecting the manifold symptomatology of an unitary mental disease, or alternatively, in terms of a variety of personality reactions occurring during the vicissitudes of a distinct clinical entity.

Societal Factors — Insufficient attention has been

given in the literature to social conditions which stimulate and perpetuate the development of socio-pathies. Of primary importance are "centers" where sociopaths tend to congregate and regale each other with tales of their methods and exploits. Such centers include bars and grills (the poor man's clubs), sporting establishments, corrective institutions and social resorts where a coterie of parasites and hangers-on tend to gather. Of secondary importance are persons and business establishments who have learned to recognize and capitalize on the weaknesses of the sociopaths. Thus we have the people who will cash their checks knowing they can always collect from the family, the bartenders who allow them to drink though knowing of the consequences, the dishonest business men who connive to permit them to benefit from fraudulent accounts, etc.

Developmental History — In our opinion, socio-pathic reactions develop in a definite developmental sequence which fulminates in direct relation to the degree to which sociopathic patterns are effective in gratifying personal needs. Isolated sociopathic behaviors may be observed in normal persons, their incidence seems to vary in different life periods, their severity and social consequences occurring in all degrees, and with considerable fluctuations being observable in different life situations according to the need for their utilization and the amount of gratification derived therefrom. It is probable that many sociopathic reactions may be nipped in the bud if they are not reinforced or can be displaced by more adaptive behavior. If it is hypothesized that most sociopathic patterns are conditioned, then it is theoretically possible for them to be unlearned and relearned.

Reversibility — Until recently, few convincing claims of positive therapeutic results were advanced and it was concluded generally that sociopathic reactions were irreversible permanent character disorders unsusceptible to any known treatment. In the last decade, however, isolated cases of successful therapeutic intervention have been reported, usually involving the most intensive therapy on a total push basis.

Ego-inflation — The typical sociopath manifests a large discrepancy between ego-ideals and actual status. There is an almost insatiable need to "be somebody," to have the best, to "keep up with the Joneses," etc. The sociopath tends to "act out" these inflated ego-ideals, repeatedly, even though their inefficiency is demonstrated.

Conditioned Utilization of Mechanisms — The sociopath typically learns to use his wits to secure objectives ordinarily gained by normal persons by hard work. The sociopath learns to "take" what the normal person has to "earn." Various mechanisms of projection, rationalization, defense and escape are progressively utilized by the sociopath to maintain this way of life. An increasing weight of evidence supports this interpretation of sociopathic reactions as learned patterns, producible under certain standard conditions, reversible in early stages, subject to fluctuations to some degree controllable under optimum conditions, but if left too long uncorrected becoming unmodifiably built-in to the personality structure.

Any valid theory of the nature and etiology of sociopathic behavior must be able to explain all the symptoms described above. In our opinion, the most valid approach is an organismic approach which can demonstrate how sociopathic behavior becomes a "style of life" and is effective enough in satisfying personal needs to be incorporated into a systematized offensive-defensive strategy for living. We assume that the sociopath learns his particular style of life because it to some degree provides immediate gratification of short-term needs and impulses. What the sociopath perceives, what he learns, what motivates him, and his distinctive utilization of mechanisms, can be understood in terms of the particular style of life around which his personality integration is organized. Many sociopathic reactions appear to be true style of life disorders.

The sociopath has a private map of the world which is inadequate to reality because his perceptions are so selectively and defensively oriented (to protect his life style) as to result in a functional isolation from reality. Again, the sociopath does not lack environmental opportunities to relate socially in healthy modes toward meaningful and contributive relations with the world, but is unable to take advantage of normal training and rehabilitation facilities because what he can learn is determined by his maladaptive life style. The defect of the sociopath is not inability to learn but, rather, the tendency to learn the wrong things, as a consequence of his specific motivational status in defense of a maladaptive life style.

The defective superego development of the sociopath may be viewed as being continuously blocked, weakened and conflicted by the struggle to maintain an untenable life schema. The self-centeredness of the sociopath may be interpreted in terms of the need to consolidate personal security and worth before much attention and energy is left over for social ends. Many of the impulses of the sociopath are basically good; but the strategy for working them out is unacceptable. Sociopaths can be very generous with funds obtained by fraud, making lavish gifts or supporting worthy social causes. They often perceive what is right (at least for others) but their life style does not permit them to act it out in their own lives. Identifying themselves with the roles of achievement and material success, their attempts to act them out without having developed suitable resources only results in a vicious circle of fraud, self-deception, detection and punishment, defensive retaliation, escape into alcohol or drugs, and a sequence of progressively outrageous behaviors.

AN HYPOTHETICAL MODEL

Adler's concept of *life style* (1) may be considered as a key to the understanding of sociopathic reactions. Recognizing that there may be constitutional differences in drive strength and impulsivity, and viewing life style as the person's conscious-unconscious strategy for satisfying his needs in an environment which may subtly stimulate and reinforce sociopathic reactions, it becomes important to analyze the *specific* offensive-defensive mechanisms, whereby personality needs are expressed or gratified. We propose to interpret sociopathic reactions as disorders of the *style of life* in which an initially normal person is conditioned to depend upon unhealthy mechanisms to gratify his needs. The resulting sociopathic behavior is viewed as the outcome of a vicious circle of interpersonal reactions tending to exacerbate rather than alleviate the condition. Sociopathic reactions may be regarded as interactional disorders in which the organism "acts out" the distorted perceptions, conditionings and motivations of his unrealistic life style. Adler (2) described the sociopath tentatively as the "receptive type" variety of the "pampered life style," thus recognizing the determinants of getting something for nothing in a situation of being pampered.

An hypothetical formulation of etiologic factors contributing to the development of the full-blown sociopathic reaction is postulated as follows:

A physically attractive child of intelligence within normal limits, early learns to capitalize on behavioral attractiveness in social relations, particularly with the opposite sex. He early learns to use his wits in influencing and manipulating other people.

In a typical developmental sequence, the attractive child learns to charm people, to behave so attractively that others will excuse shortcomings and withhold punishment which another child could not escape. The child early learns to get around his female relatives, susceptible teachers and less attractive age peers.

Or if he is not so behaviorally attractive, he may learn that if he takes aggressively enough, he may get away with it because he knows that his relatives will not prosecute him.

A typical sequence is that the developing sociopath is prematurely introduced to adult pleasures, accepted by older persons in recreation and vices, early seduced and seducing sexually, and precociously acquiring tastes for money, expensive things, liquor, drugs, and high life in general.

The young sociopath quickly learns to use his wits to avoid hard work (too slow to satisfy short term gratifications) and typically fails to acquire the solid educational background which serves as a positive resource for the normal child. Instead he learns a large variety of dishonesties, frauds, confidence games and shady tricks for taking what others are earning. As he progressively falls behind his peers in developing healthy habits and skills, his deceits become progressively more maladaptive and outrageous as he attempts to compensate for his deficits.

The young sociopath succeeds more or less in getting away with his depredations until ages 16–21, or as long as he remains in school. Tolerant parents and authorities excuse increasingly serious misconduct, hope that it will be outgrown, or even unconsciously reinforce it by making it work. The child is bailed out of difficulties repeatedly, being allowed to escape normal punitive consequences of misbehavior. Some environments even encourage sociopathic behavior as when parents or authorities defy law and order themselves.

Repressive social checks usually become operative at the critical point where the young sociopath is forced to go out on his own. Here, when he is required to succeed in a job, expend and save money wisely, the defects of his training become painfully obvious. He is unable to deliver on the job, is fired repeatedly with a typical pattern of poor work history with frequent job changes, lack of skills, interpersonal difficulties, etc. Because of inability to earn a living commensurate with the extravagant tastes, dishonesty and deceits become progressively accumulated as the increasing burden of insolvency makes necessary greater depredations. Here again, overprotective relatives and sympathetic authorities excuse misbehaviors. The sociopath oscillates between prison and mental hospital, being considered too sick to punish and too well to hospitalize. Few states provide special resources for their care.

The sociopath leaves a swath of disillusioned, hurt and seriously damaged people in his wake. Because of behavioral attractiveness, there are many too-easy sex adventures, leaving broken engagements, illegitimate pregnancies, divorce, infidelity, broken homes and child neglect. Other persons are at first bewildered and then enraged by the growing life record of irresponsibility and misbehavior. Soon the entire community learns what to expect and the sociopath has to move on to new fields. Multiple marriages with or without divorce, sex irregularities, business failures, frauds and swindles, bouts of alcoholism, and progressive financial and personal bankruptcy ensue.

But contrary to the literature, the sociopath does not emerge unscathed from his irregularities. At heart, he knows what he is, and this causes an increasing burden of self-hate, however well disguised or repressed. In the beginning, the sociopath can escape from anxiety by simply leaving the site of failure, and securing ego-inflation from the spurious security of new sexual conquests. But gradually it becomes necessary to consume increasing amounts of alcohol or drugs to anesthetize anxiety. Also, the sociopath is getting older, less physically attractive, and outwardly ravaged by the wages of sin. Conquests of the opposite sex become more difficult and with less attractive partners. Gradually the sociopath gravitates socially downward until finally ending in the slums, broken financially, in and out of delirium tremens, shunted from prison to hospital, and finally expiring in the poor house or mental hospital.

A few sociopaths show a reversal of the pattern, becoming less impulsive and irresponsible in middle age, apparently learning to gratify their needs in more socially acceptable ways, and even occasionally becoming harnessed to work and positions of social responsibility. But apparently, this desirable outcome requires the investment of great patience and material resources in loving them in spite of their misbehaviors "until they come to their senses."

This pattern, with endless variants, reflects the essential inadequacy and progressive breakdown of the sociopath's style of life. Whereas the normal person develops sufficient security from the successful results of his work so as to have enough energies to develop motivations "to go beyond the self" in the direction of altruism, the motivational system of the sociopath must necessarily be concerned with "private profit" because it is endlessly involved in efforts to gain security. Their distorted perceptions, faulty learnings and private map of the world are simply not adequate to reality.[1]

[1] I am indebted to Dr. Heinz Ansbacher for suggestions concerning the formulation of the material presented here.

IDENTIFICATION OF UNHEALTHY MECHANISMS

Perhaps the outstanding mechanism of the sociopath is *to take* what ordinarily would be earned. The development of this pattern is not difficult to understand since the operation of the *expansion tendency* (4) in children causes them to take everything they can. Unless controlled by social limits, this tendency to gratify pleasures immediately, to live for the moment, becomes habitual. It starts when the child is not punished when he steps out of bounds, when the parents are too divided, inconsistent or weak to establish discipline. With a very attractive child, the environment may purchase their indulgence at any cost. Gradually, the sociopath may take so ruthlessly that curtailment is impossible even to the point of self-destruction.

Secondary to the taking mechanism is the development of blame-avoidance mechanisms such as rationalization, projection and escape. Most sociopaths show well developed paranoid trends which may be relatively effective in tension reduction even though more or less anxiety and guilt eventually break through. Alcoholism and drug addiction are the typical escape mechanisms which not only anesthetize anxiety and tension but also permit him to undertake progressively more outrageous escapades.

Most sociopaths are unqualified hedonists, compulsively seeking immediate impulse gratification to the total disregard of the Reality Principle and long-term goals. The patient may succeed in "acting-out" a fairly convincing role of the successful man-about-town, deriving feelings of power and fulfillment through the temporary success of his frauds, and succeeding in juggling his deceits with sufficient dexterity to fool some of the public part of the time. Such behavior is reinforced by the false values of our culture as depicted in advertising, portraying the man of distinction wearing the surface trappings of success and with a glass of whiskey in his hands. *Upward social mobility* is the theme of American life, with everyone offered the prospects of gracious living and personal distinction, but few actually achieving genuine success so that most must either renounce it or assume an artificial veneer of what passes for culture. Most sociopaths are early infected with class consciousness and the virus of upward striving but lack the skills to achieve success. So the sociopath "acts-out" in imitation of the genuine articles which he perceives about him.

Partial evidence that this "acting-out" behavior is to some degree deliberate and subject to conscious control lies in the fact that most sociopaths seem able to discriminate the limits of what society will tolerate and rarely commit the more serious felonies. Although they may be very ruthless in taking the property of others in situations where they are relatively certain of not being prosecuted or punished, such actions usually are perpetrated within the framework of fraud rather than robbery. The sociopath typically depends upon his knowledge of the psychology of persons and situations to "gull" them out of their possessions voluntarily, and thereby making coercion unnecessary as in the case of the "criminal." With many sociopaths, a moderate degree of intoxication is necessary to inhibit anxiety and guilt, but after enough successful deceits even such fears are allayed and dishonesty becomes habitual and callous.

Further evidence of the conditioned nature of sociopathic behaviors results from observations of the manner in which sociopaths "learn" their deceitful tricks either from other sociopaths or from unscrupulous normals who exploit them. Such tricks as having unscrupulous business men issue false bills to parents for goods or money advanced to the sociopath, the ways of passing bum checks, dodges for getting gifts or handouts, methods of seducing or victimizing unsophisticated women, and for working more complicated confidence games, are an interesting source of group conversations among sociopaths who avidly experiment with each new technique they hear of.

No discussion of the etiology of sociopathic reactions is complete without consideration of group attitudes which tacitly encourage or reward such behavior. Such attitudes as "beating the game", "getting something for nothing", "soldiering" or "bugging out", admiring the "wise guy" or the "smart money", "taking the suckers", etc., are widely accepted in segments of our society and may constitute a way of life for the budding sociopath. The style of living "on one's wits" is reinforced by the existence of a large group of unadjusted youth, "lonely hearts", frustrated persons of the opposite sex, or sado-masochists who tolerate the depredations of the sociopath to have his company.

REQUIREMENTS FOR SUCCESSFUL PSYCHOTHERAPY WITH SOCIOPATHS

Since 1947, we have undertaken intensive psychotherapy with a series of seven sociopaths with successful results in cases where all the conditions enumerated below could be satisfied. Our treated cases represent a very selected group in that all came from well-to-do families able to assume the financial costs of expensive case handling over a

period of years. Without large financial resources, we consider these cases untreatable since neither the therapist nor society can afford to make large investments in a single case unless the family is able to assume all costs. Such cases represent an almost intolerable drain on the patience and resources of all concerned. In several cases of our series, it required an investment of over $15,000 per year over periods as long as ten years to effect a satisfactory outcome. The method of case handling which we have worked out over a period of ten years is outlined below.

1. *Financial supervision.* Apart from the threat of legal prosecution or institutionalization, complete control over finances is the most effective motive or incentive for influencing the behavior of the sociopath. In each case, we have insisted on taking over control of all funds advanced to the sociopath by his family, acting as trustee over his accounts. We have insisted that no funds should be made available from any other source, thus effectively requiring the psychopath to report for therapy if he expects to receive any funds. This type of coercion is not an ideal condition for therapy but it at least insures regular contacts of the sociopath with the therapist.

2. *No further "bail-outs."* Relatives or other interested parties must agree not to "bail-out" the sociopath from any further escapades, but must refer each subsequent incident to the therapist. The principle here is that from the beginning of therapy, the sociopath must progressively face and assume the consequences of his own behaviors.

3. *Limits and controls.* Great patience must be utilized in gradually requiring the sociopath to accept some limits and controls. It cannot be expected that the sociopath will immediately discontinue his asocial behaviors at the onset of therapy. On the contrary, the therapist may have to be very patient in excusing numerous sociopathic actions at the start of therapy but which may be expected to dwindle off as gradually the sociopath begins to accept some limitations of his conduct.

4. *Punishments.* While the therapist should never administer punishments himself, on the other hand he should not protect the sociopath from the consequences of his actions. The principle is that the sociopath must experience and come to expect the same corrective actions on the part of the environment as normal persons have to face. Thus, we routinely require sociopaths to go back and settle bad checks, frauds, etc., out of their own allowance. If the sociopath commits any misdemeanor, he must face the court and work out the terms of the sen-

tence. Or if he becomes acutely psychotic or out of control from alcoholism, he must submit to hospitalization until he is ready and able to assume responsibility for his own conduct.

5. *Interpretive structuring.* We consider it desirable routinely to acquaint the sociopath with the fact that the therapist understands him thoroughly. This is accomplished by outlining in a friendly but serious manner exactly what the therapist expects to go through with the sociopath, discussing how the sociopath has operated in the past, and how the therapist expects to handle recurrences in the future. Or, perhaps, the therapist may outline the typical behavior of the sociopath. In any case, the therapist should convey to the sociopath that he understands him thoroughly, knows what to expect, and will be convinced of good intentions only through actions and not words.

6. *Modes of communication.* Usually, it is effective for the therapist to communicate with the sociopath in his own jargon, thus establishing further evidence in the mind of the sociopath that he is understood. Such handling often earns a grudging admiration from the sociopath who accepts that he is confronted by someone who is "on to him."

7. *Insight into self-defeating mechanisms.* We are convinced that the only motive strong enough to "convert" the sociopath from his errant ways is the final insight into the fact that sociopathic behavior is eventually too painful and self-defeating to be continued. The sociopath must learn that short-term pleasures usually exert too great a toll when long term retribution will inevitably be exacted. Translated into the vernacular, the sociopath must be shown repeatedly that he is "screwing himself."

8. *The search for a leverage point.* Although the usual appeals to decency and higher motives are usually lost on the sociopath, most of them have some ego ideal which can be used as a powerful motive leverage to stimulate more socially acceptable behaviors. In any case, the incentive of money is the hidden resource of the therapist who controls it.

9. *Tenable ego ideals.* We usually exert an unceasing pressure on the sociopath to be more realistic about himself and to test reality more effectively. This involves the clear recognition by the sociopath of his ego-involved activities, renouncing them, and trying to act out what he really is. This means giving up expensive cars, unrealistic affectations, luxurious tastes, etc.

10. *Self-consistency.* The core of health must be complete self-consistency. The sociopath must accept that he has two personalities, one potentially normal, and the other completely pathological. He must learn to be self-consistent with his more normal personality.

11. *Undercutting secondary gains.* The sociopath must be taught to renounce the secondary gains of his "acting-out" behaviors. This is accomplished mainly by not allowing him to get away with anything.

12. *Patience.* It may require hundreds or thousands of conditioning experiences carried out over periods of months or years to gain the desired results. The sociopath will continue to act-out his old patterns as long as they are to any degree rewarding. It must not be expected that therapy will be effective quickly when dealing with such deep personality disorders.

This therapeutic plan is most effective when the sociopath gains insight into the inconsistency and painfulness of his old life style and begins to discover that "honesty is the best policy" actually works to satisfy needs formerly satisfied in sociopathic ways.

SUMMARY

This paper presents an hypothetical model of the etiology of sociopathic reactions as *style of life disorders.* A survey of the literature on sociopathic or psychopathic behavior results in the collection of a list of symptoms which must be explained by any valid theory. The typical pattern of development of the sociopathic life style is outlined in an hypothetical case summarizing the salient features of the syndrome. A plan of requirements for effective therapy with sociopaths is presented on the basis of our experience with the successful therapy of a limited series of cases.

BIBLIOGRAPHY

1. ADLER, A.: *The Pattern of Life.* London: Kegan Paul, 1931.
2. ADLER, A.: The fundamental views of Individual Psychology. *Int. J. Indiv. Psychol.,* 1935, **1**, 5–8.
3. CLECKLEY, H.: *The Mask of Sanity.* St. Louis: Mosby, 1941.
4. FOREST, HERMAN: Biological expansion and psychology. *J. Indiv. Psychol.,* 1958, **14**, 105–110.
5. KARPMAN, B.: *Case Studies of the Psychopathology of Crime.* Washington, D.C.: Medical Science Press, 1948. Vols. 1–4.
6. MENNINGER, K.: The Unitary Concept of Mental Illness. *Bull. Menninger Clinic,* 1958, **22**, 4–12.
7. THORNE, F. C.: Etiological Studies of Psychopathic Personality: The Ego-Inflated, Defectively Conditioned Type. *J. Consult. Psychol.,* 1947, **11**, 299–309.

JOSEPH SATTEN, KARL MENNINGER, IRWIN ROSEN, AND MARTIN MAYMAN

Murder Without Apparent Motive:
A *Study in Personality Disorganization*[*][1]

In attempting to assess the criminal responsibility of murderers, the law tries to divide them (as it does all offenders) into two groups, the "sane" and the "insane." The "sane" murderer is thought of as acting upon rational motives that can be understood, though condemned, and the "insane" one, as being driven by irrational senseless motives. When rational motives are conspicuous (for example, when a man kills for personal gain) or when the irrational motives are accompanied by delusions or hallucinations (for example, a paranoid patient who kills his fantasied persecutor), the situation presents little problem to the psychiatrist. But murderers who seem rational, coherent, and controlled, and yet whose homicidal acts have a bizarre, apparently senseless quality, pose a difficult problem, if courtroom disagreements and contradictory reports about the same offender are an index(1).

It is our thesis that the psychopathology of such murderers forms at least one specific syndrome which we shall describe. In general, these individuals are predisposed to severe lapses in ego control which makes possible the open expression of primitive violence, born out of previous, and now unconscious, traumatic experiences. The syndrome of periodic breakdown in control and its place in a homeostatic concept of mental illness has previously been described by two of the authors(6). It is the purpose of this paper to illustrate that concept in a clinical study of one type of murder.

The authors examined 4 men convicted of bizarre, apparently senseless murders, as part of an appeal process. All had been examined by psychiatrists prior to their trials, and found to be "without psychosis" and "sane." Three of the 4 were under death sentence, and one of them was serving a long prison term. Further psychiatric investigation was requested because someone in each of these cases, either the lawyer, a relative, or friend, was dissatis-

fied with the psychiatric explanations previously given, and asked: "How can a person, as sane as this man seems to be, commit an act as crazy as the one he was convicted of?"

DESCRIPTION OF CASES

A. — Thomas: A 31-year-old chief petty officer in charge of a hospital, while talking casually to the 9-year-old daughter of one of his superior officers, suddenly grabbed the child, choked her, and held her head under water long after she was dead. A discontinuity existed in Thomas' mind as to what happened; he could not remember the beginning of the assault, but "suddenly discovered" himself strangling his young victim.

B. — Adams: A 24-year-old corporal looking for a prostitute near a French town, was approached by a 13-year-old boy who persistently asked him to change Army scrip into French currency; when refused, the boy seemed to mock or make fun of him, whereupon he struck the boy. Adams insisted he had no intention of killing the victim and did not recall the actual killing. When Adams "found out" what he was doing, the victim's body had been severely mutilated.

C. — Mason: A 20-year-old laborer and truck driver, frightened and angry following an argument with a friend, picked up a 14-year-old boy to whom he suggested homosexual relations. The boy refused, and kept "nagging" Mason to take him back home. Mason struck the boy, and began choking him. He said he didn't intend to kill the boy, but "found" the victim was dead.

D. — Elliot: A 43-year-old married Negro soldier lapsed into a dreamlike dissociative state under the taunting and mocking of a prostitute attempting to seduce him and get his money. He struck her with a tire jack, killed her, and then mutilated and dismembered her body.

For the most part, the murderers themselves were puzzled as to why they killed their victims. Attempts to reconstruct a rational motive were unsuc-

* Reprinted by permission from *American Journal of Psychiatry*, Vol. 117, 1960, pp. 48–53.
[1] Read at the 115th annual meeting of the American Psychiatric Association, Philadelphia, Pa., Apr. 27–May 1, 1959.

cessful. In each case, there was no gain to the murderer by killing the victim, nor was there any accompanying crime. The victims were relatively unknown to the murderers, and the method of the murder was haphazard and impromptu. In no case did the murderer use a conventional weapon, but killed either with his bare hands or whatever could immediately be pressed into use. In all instances, however, the murder was unnecessarily violent, and sometimes bizarre, and there was evidence that the assaults on the bodies continued until long after the death of the victims.

Our study was primarily "cross sectional." It consisted of a careful exploration of the patient's mental functioning in 10 to 12 hours of clinical interviews and 5 to 6 hours of psychological testing. A history of the patient, as given by himself and others, was used in an attempt to understand the early roots of the behavior disturbance, and its course throughout his life. Physical and neurological examinations, including EEG's, were also done.

HISTORICAL FINDINGS

The most uniform, and perhaps the most significant, historical finding was a longstanding, sometimes lifelong, history of erratic control over aggressive impulses. For example, 3 of the men, throughout their lives, had been frequently involved in fights which were not ordinarily altercations, and which would have become homicidal assaults if not stopped by others. Officers who observed one of these men during several such attacks reported that it required 7 to 10 strong men to restrain him until sedatives took effect, for he was able to break through strap restraints and restraining jackets. This same man had been involved in sadistic attacks on children over a period of many years; on one occasion he nearly drowned a girl in a swimming pool; on another occasion he was thought to have killed a patient while working in a hospital; and he himself gave a history of unnecessarily killing children and civilians while on duty in wartime Europe.

Despite the violence in their lives, all of the men had ego-images of themselves as physically inferior, weak, and inadequate; and the histories revealed in each a severe degree of sexual inhibition. To all of them, adult women were threatening creatures, and in two cases, there was overt sexual perversion. All of them, too, had been concerned throughout their early years about being considered "sissies," physically undersized, or sickly.

In all 4 cases there was historical evidence of periods of altered states of consciousness, frequently in connection with the outbursts of violence. Two of the men reported severe dissociative trance-like states during which violent and bizarre behavior was seen, while the other two reported less severe, and perhaps less well-organized, amnesic episodes. During moments of actual violence, they often felt separated or isolated from themselves, as if they were watching someone else. One of them, Thomas, in relating the details of the murder said, "I knew that I was doing it, but somehow it didn't seem like me. It was as if I was watching myself do it." This feeling that it was not he who committed the murder enabled him to successfully pass a "lie detector" test, at the conclusion of which, however, he impulsively confessed.

Also seen in the historical background of all the cases was the occurrence of extreme parental violence during childhood, a finding which has also been reported in studies of murderers by Duncan, et al. (2). One man said he was "whipped every time I turned around." The theme of open violence dominated his early experiences. His earliest memory of himself was of almost being killed in a cotton gin; his earliest memories of his father were of him coming home beaten up, bloody, and with broken ribs. Severe corporal punishment was something he took for granted as one of the natural phenomena of life. Another of the men had many violent beatings in order to "break" him of his stammering and "fits," as well as to correct him for his allegedly "bad" behavior.

In some of these cases, the violence was associated with the sexual behavior of grown-ups. One man, Elliot, from his early life onward was an observer of much drunkenness, fighting, and promiscuity among his parental figures, and he was frequently drawn into their physical violence. Another reported that, as a child, he was frequently kept awake by the drunken fighting accompanying the sexual activity of a couple next door, whom he could observe or hear through the common wall separating their bedroom from his. Although our examination stopped considerably short of the intensive exploration of the unconscious necessary to fully confirm psychoanalytic hypotheses, our data permit the inference that the murderers probably fantasied or actually observed the primal scene as something overwhelmingly violent and sadistic.

The history relating to *extreme* violence, whether fantasied, observed in reality, or actually experienced by the child, fits in with the psychoanalytic hypothesis that the child's exposure to overwhelming stimuli, before he can master them, is closely linked to early defects in ego formation and later severe disturbances in impulse control.

In all of these cases, there was evidence of

severe emotional deprivation in early life. This deprivation may have involved prolonged or recurrent absence of one or both parents; a chaotic family life in which the parents were unknown; or an outright rejection of the child by one or both parents with the child being raised by others. Although the depth of the examinational data varied, in some cases it was possible to demonstrate links to early and severe oral deprivation. For example, Mason had been a colicky, crying baby who was suddenly weaned in two days at the age of one year but remained a feeding problem for several years thereafter, during which time he ate dirt, gravel, and sand and acted as if he was constantly craving food.

Three of the men had a definite history of stuttering in childhood, and under stress, traces of this could be seen in their adult functioning. The fourth one, though without a history of speech disturbances, frequently found himself inarticulate and groping helplessly for verbal expression. This finding confirms that of Greenacre(4), who correlates early speech difficulties with the ego's failure to develop adequate mechanisms for delaying impulse discharge, or for diverting impulses into ideational and verbal, rather than motor outlets.

EXAMINATIONAL DATA

In addition to the similarity in historical findings described above, a number of common characteristics emerged in the clinical examinations. The data cited below illustrate the total functioning of these men and no single item in itself should be taken as a diagnostic sign of the personality disorder we are describing.

The most striking similarity in the examinational findings was in disturbances of impulse control. During the examination, a pattern of erratic impulsivity was observed: their speech could quickly shift from a blocked, groping, at times almost aphasic inarticulateness to an explosive gushing of words; their bodies would grow stiff with tension as they sought to contain the rising charge of affect and anxiety that would sporadically well up within them. They tended to show either extreme over-control and inhibition, or marked restlessness and hyperkinesis (pacing the room during the testing and clinical interviews was not an uncommon occurrence).

Evidence of this brittle quality of impulse control was seen clearly in the psychological tests. In general, the test picture for all of the men added up to an "all or none" pattern of functioning. Inhibition of action required great amounts of psychic energy and lacked flexibility; once controls began to weaken, the men were almost completely overwhelmed by affect,

morbid fantasy, and a proneness to immediate unreflective action. The test pictures were uniformly consistent with indications of a severe ego deficiency which permits impulse to flow too directly into action and not be easily shunted into thinking or verbalization. Details of test responses are described in another paper(11).

Manifestations of a bizarre, violent, and primitive fantasy life were seen in each of the men we examined. Repetitive dreams of violently killing, mutilating, burning, or destroying others were seen; the brief TAT stories of these men were filled with a quality of primitive, murderous hostility, in some cases glibly rationalized on the basis of the victims having "provoked" their murderers, and in others precipitated by rejection or rebuff, usually implying oral deprivation. Although the hostility and destruction pervading their fantasy lives were easily observed, conscious fantasy or ideational activity was minimal. Brief constricted Rorschach records and meager, frequently autobiographical, TAT stories were the rule. Certainly the usual role of thinking (as a delay of, and attenuated substitute for, action) was conspicuously absent in these cases.

There was a blurring of the boundaries between fantasy and reality, and there were transient feelings of depersonalization. In one extreme example, Elliot, what really occurred, or what the man thought, or dreamed, were all blurred in a hazy, nebulous series of memories, and it was extremely difficult to construct a verifiable sequence of what actually happened. In response to a Rorschach card, for example, he began to describe not only the blot in front of him but a confused mixture of dreams, memories, and waking fantasies. Two of the men described episodes in which they thought they might have killed people, sometimes later returning to the scene of the "killing" to find a dead body, but they remained still unsure as to whether the episode was real, a dream, or a fantasy.

Evidence of disturbances in affect organization was seen. Most typically the men displayed a tendency not to experience anger or rage in association with violent aggressive action. None reported feelings of rage in connection with the murders, nor did they experience anger in any strong or pronounced way, although each of them was capable of acts of enormous and brutal aggression. The tolerance for affect and anxiety in these individuals was also extremely limited. All showed marked disturbance in dealing with color on the Rorschach test and their TAT stories showed a preponderance of violence, most typically without accompanying affect. As formulated by Rapaport, affect is conceived of as an impulse derivative, generated through the ego mechanisms of delay and control(10). For the murderers, these mechanisms were too brittle to produce the methods for "damming up" and appropriately discharging impulses that are necessary for a graduated and variegated affective experience.

Their relationships with others were of a shallow, cold nature, lending a quality of loneliness and isolation to these men. People were scarcely real to them, in the sense of being warmly or positively (or even angrily) felt about. In their early memories and psychological test material appears the re-institution of an idealized, all-giving mother figure, but always in the context of loss or rejection, leaving the world, for these men, bleak and empty.

The 3 men under sentence of death had shallow emotions regarding their own fate and that of their victims. Guilt, depression, and remorse were strikingly absent.

The most questionable examinational finding involved the evidence relating to organic brain damage. Two of the men showed neither historical evidence, neurological nor EEG findings, that would in any way be consistent with organic brain pathology — nor were there any such indications on the psychological tests. The other two men in our sample revealed ambiguous findings. One reported a history of childhood convulsions, and his associational blocking, severe constriction, and aphasic-like speech difficulty raised the question of the possibility of organic brain pathology. The psychogenic meaning of these symptoms was clearly demonstrated in some hypnotherapeutic sessions(3), and in the face of negative neurological studies, organic damage seemed ruled out. The organic findings on the other man were the most definite of our sample (previous EEG studies were "suggestive" of organic brain damage), and his history revealed a severe head injury at age 10 followed by personality disturbances of even greater severity than those noted prior to the accident.

The negative evidence, however, was not absolute, for we used only regular and sleep EEG's in search for evidence of a convulsive disorder. We did not use EEG activation techniques, such as metrazol, photic stimulation, *etc.* It would not be surprising, however, in view of the equivocal evidence with routine methods, to find evidence of some organic or physiological factors with more refined methods of neurophysiologic investigation(5, 7, 12).

THE ROLE OF UNCONSCIOUS MOTIVATION

The individuals described above can be considered to be murder-prone in the sense of either carrying a surcharge of aggressive energy or having an unstable ego defense system that periodically allows the naked and archaic expression of such energy. The murderous potential can become activated, especially if some disequilibrium is already present, when the victim-to-be is unconsciously perceived as a key figure in some past traumatic configuration. The behavior, or even the mere presence, of this figure adds a stress to the unstable balance of forces that results in a sudden extreme discharge of violence, similar to the explosion that takes place when a percussion cap ignites a charge of dynamite.

One man, Mason, had such varying targets of aggression that it was impossible to delineate precisely their meaning in his unconscious conflicts from the data obtained. For Elliot, whose case included a series of hypnotherapeutic interviews, his victim seemed to have multiple unconscious meanings, although the predominant one related to his deceased girl friend, toward whom his feelings were intense but ambivalent. In Thomas, sodium amytal interviews yielded material suggesting that the victim mainly represented a dead sister, with whom he had a conflictual, incestuous relationship. For Adams, the murder appeared to have been a deflected suicide, as impulsive murders have occasionally been interpreted(8, 9, 13). The victim represented by the murderer's own hated self-image; the young boy he killed was a camp pet who ran errands for the soldiers, just as he himself had been a mascot for the men in his father's lumber camp.

The hypothesis of unconscious motivation explains why the murderers perceived innocuous and relatively unknown victims as provocative and thereby suitable targets for aggression. But, why murder? Most people, fortunately, do not respond with murderous outbursts even under extreme provocation. The cases described, on the other hand, were predisposed to gross lapses in reality contact and extreme weakness in impulse control during periods of heightened tension and disorganization. At such times, a chance acquaintance or even a stranger was easily able to lose his "real" meaning and assume an identity in the unconscious traumatic configuration. The "old" conflict was re-activated and aggression swiftly mounted to murderous proportions.

Such outwardly senseless attacks on relatively unknown persons are different from those arising out of protracted but conflict dominated relationships, such as with a wife, child, or parent, *e.g.* catathymic crises(13). The question of the factors involved in the "choice" of the "unknown" victim in these cases goes beyond the scope of this paper. Research now in process suggests a range of selection factors whereby, for some impulsive murderers, almost any other human being can activate the tremendous destructive potential, while for others, only a highly specific person or action is required.

A finding significant for social administration is the fact that 3 of these 4 murderers had conveyed their fears of losing control to legal officials or psychiatrists *before the murders took place.* The warnings were disregarded.

SUMMARY

In this paper we have described a number of common characteristics found in individuals who have committed impulsive senseless murders. These characteristics were: severe weakness of impulse control; blurring of the boundaries between fantasy and reality, with periods of altered states of consciousness; blunted and shallow emotional reactions; and a violent and primitive fantasy life.

This constellation seems to have grown out of a history characterized by extreme parental violence and early severe emotional deprivation. In these cases, there appeared an ego weakness which allowed the periodic breakthrough of intense aggressive impulses, sometimes of homicidal proportion.

When such apparently senseless murders occur, they are seen to be an end result of a period of increasing tension and disorganization in the murderer starting before the contact wth the victim who, by fitting into the unconscious conflicts of the murderer, unwittingly serves to set into motion his homicidal potential.

It remains a task of future research to: 1. Differentiate these individuals from other murderers as well as from others with similar disturbances but who do not kill; 2. Weigh the significance of the individual factors described; 3. Devise measures for identifying and effectively controlling these individuals before they commit murder.

BIBLIOGRAPHY

1. COHEN, L. H., and COFFIN, T. E.: J. Criminal Law and Criminoloy of Northwestern University, **37:** 4, 262, 1946.
2. DUNCAN, G. M., FRAZIER, S. H., LITIN, E. M., JOHNSON, A. M., and BARRON, A. J.: J.A.M.A., **168:** 1755, 1958.
3. EHRENREICH, GERALD A.: Headache, Necrophilia, and Murder: A Brief Hypnotherapeutic Investigation of a Single Case. Read at the Joint Conventions of the Southwestern Psychological Association and the Kansas Psychological Association, Topeka, Kan. 1959.
4. GREENACRE, PHYLLIS: Psa. Quart., **19:** 4, Oct. 1950.
5. LEFFMAN, HENRY, and PERLO, V. P.: Electroencephalog. & Clin. Neurophysiol., 7: 61, 1955.
6. MENNINGER, KARL, and MAYMAN, MARTIN: Bull. of Menninger Clinic, **20:** 153, 1956.
7. MERLIS, SYDNEY, and DENBER, H. C. B.: Electroencephalog. & Clin. Neurophysiol. Suppl. No. 3, 1953, p. 92.
8. PODOLSKY, E.: Int. J. Social Psychiatry, 1: 4, Spring, 1956.
9. PODOLSKY, E.: Samiksa, **10:** 65, 1957.
10. RAPAPORT, DAVID: Emotions and Memory. Baltimore: Williams and Wilkins, 1942.
11. ROSEN, IRWIN C., SATTEN, JOSEPH, MAYMAN, MARTIN, and MENNINGER, KARL: A Study of Episodic Dyscontrol Eventuating in Homicide. Read at the Joint Conventions of the Southwestern Psychological Association and the Kansas Psychological Association, Topeka, Kan., 1959.
12. SCHWADE, E. D., and GEIGER, SARA: Electroencephalog. & Clin. Neurophysiol. Suppl. No. 3, 1953, p. 60.
13. WERTHAM, FREDERIC: Arch. Neurol. and Psychiat., **37:** 974, 1937.

BERNARD C. GLUECK, JR.

Psychodynamic Patterns in the Sex Offender[*][1]
Fifth Annual Hutchings Memorial Lecture

Of the many problems that plague our society, that of the sex offender is one of the most disturbing. Society reacts with greater fear, disgust, hysteria and anger to only one other crime, murder. Many explanations can be advanced for this intense emotional reaction, depending upon the particular frame of reference of the individual giving the interpretation. Thus we may have religious, moralistic, philosophical, sociological and psychological explanations, among others. In the course of the last 60 years, largely as a result of the pioneer efforts of Sigmund Freud, and those who followed the trail he blazed, a new approach to the age-old problem of understanding human behavior has been developed, the science of psychodynamics. This is the particular frame of reference for the present remarks.

In the years immediately following World War II, an increasing concern by society about the activities of "sex offenders," spot-lighted by a furor in the press over "the depraved machinations of sex fiends," culminated in the establishment in New York State, among others, of a research project under the joint auspices of the commissioners of Correction and Mental Hygiene. Its purpose was to be "the development of information as to the underlying causes of sex crimes and the development of treatment for persons committing such crimes."

The raw material for this research was the group of men incarcerated at Sing Sing Prison, who had been convicted of sex felonies. Included in this group of felonies are: first and second degree rape, first and second degree sodomy, carnal abuse of a child under 10 years, carnal abuse of a minor be-

tween 10 and 16 — if a second offense, and assault in the second degree with intent to rape, sodomize or carnally abuse. The lesser sexual offenses such as exhibitionism, voyeurism and statutory rape, are not considered felonies, so that men convicted of these offenses are not sentenced to Sing Sing Prison. This selective process has a very important bearing on the statistics gathered by the research group, since only the more serious sex offenses are represented in the men studied. This may account, at least in part, for the marked psychopathology found in the group.

In March 1950, a preliminary report[2] was issued on 102 men who had been studied up to that time. The general conclusions reached included a statement that every man studied suffered from some type of mental or emotional disorder, though not usually so pronounced as to meet the legal definition of mental illness. They were not, in other words, sufficiently psychotic to be certifiable. Additional information on the same men — coming from further psychiatric observation, psychological studies, and the changes in their adjustment to prison, or in a few cases, to parole — as well as information on new cases, confirm the psychopathology present in this group. The major question, at the present writing, is not: Does pathology exist? Instead, we are primarily concerned with an attempt at quantification of the pathology and the development of some kind of adequate diagnostic system which will reflect the psychodynamic aspects of each case, and give a more accurate description of the phenomena observed than the present diagnoses permit. It is unnecessary to stress the benefits from more accurate diagnosis. To mention only two points: There would be improved statistical reporting; and there are possible therapeutic and prognostic implications stemming from a given diagnosis. The last point has an added importance in dealing with psychiatric problems because of the rather divergent attitudes

* Reprinted by permission from *Psychiatric Quarterly*, Vol. 28, 1954, pp. 1–21.
1 The Fifth Annual Richard H. Hutchings Memorial Lecture was delivered at Syracuse, N. Y., October 5, 1953 by Dr. Glueck as director of the New York State Sex Delinquency Research Project. Dr. Hutchings was professor emeritus of clinical psychiatry of the College of Medicine of Syracuse University, had been superintendent of St. Lawrence and Utica (N. Y.) State Hospitals, and was editor of this QUARTERLY at the time of his death in October 1947.

2 Report on Study of 102 Sex Offenders at Sing Sing Prison. Albany. March 1950.

of the extremists who favor either psychotherapy or organic therapy as mutually exclusive techniques, and because of the rather nihilistic attitude of many psychiatrists where the diagnosis of schizophrenia is concerned.

Unquestionably, in the light of present therapeutic results, one tends to be somewhat pessimistic regarding the outcome when a diagnosis of schizophrenia or psychopathic personality is made. There is, however, sufficient evidence available, in the form of well-documented statistics collected over long periods, indicating a basic 30 to 35 per cent remission rate in schizophrenia, regardless of the type of psychosis or kind of treatment. We can, therefore, expect one out of every three schizophrenics to have a remission, even though nothing is done in terms of specific therapy. Furthermore the remission rate can be improved, if only for relatively short periods, by the various therapeutic approaches currently available. The writer is, therefore, of the opinion that the argument against making a diagnosis of schizophrenia, on the grounds of the "death sentence" implications of such a diagnosis, no longer applies, and should not influence decision about diagnosis. Of even greater importance in forensic psychiatry, is the effect of the diagnosis, when made before trial or sentencing, on the disposition of the particular case.

The present legal interpretations of the terms "sane" and "insane" have been repeatedly challenged by both lawyers and psychiatrists, as being totally inadequate in the light of modern concepts of psychopathology and psychodynamics. The concern of the courts still centers, for the most part, around the need to punish the offender, and the fear that a plea of insanity will protect the "guilty" individual from the just retribution that society demands.

The discovery of extensive pathology in every individual studied by the research group has already been mentioned. All of the men in this first group of 102, covered in the research project's first report were, in spite of clear-cut clinical evidence of psychosis in several cases, and very suspicious symptoms in over half of the group, diagnosed as being without psychosis when examined psychiatrically before trial or sentencing. The same failure to detect overt psychotic symptoms and behavior has been apparent in many of the additional cases studied in the past three years. This has been true in both groups, those entering the prison under the usual short-term definite sentence, and those entering under provisions of the new, indeterminate-sentence

law. Failure to establish an accurate diagnosis is especially disturbing in the second group of cases, since one of the provisions of the law is that, "No person convicted of a crime punishable in the discretion of the court with imprisonment for an indeterminate term, having a minimum of one day and a maximum of his natural life, shall be sentenced until a psychiatric examination shall have been made of him and a complete written report thereof shall have been submitted to the court." This examination is made according to certain paragraphs of the code of criminal procedure and involves observation and examination by two qualified psychiatrists.

In spite of these provisions, four men out of 46 who were received at Sing Sing Prison under the new law have been committed to Dannemora State Hospital with overt psychoses. Two of the four were committed within 60 days of reception at Sing Sing, and were held for that interval only to obtain a psychiatric appraisal for the research studies. A fifth individual was suspected of being feebleminded because of his general behavior in the prison community. On psychological testing he was found to have an IQ in the 60's and was committed to the state institution for defective delinquents. A brief description of the symptoms of two of these men will illustrate the type of gross pathology that was apparent shortly after reception at Sing Sing, and was undoubtedly present for some time previous to the Sing Sing observations.

CASE A.

The first case, A., is that of a 39-year-old white man who was sentenced to Sing Sing for a term of "one day to life" after pleading guilty to carnal abuse of a nine-year-old girl. The offense, as described in the probation reports, consisted of his placing his hand on the girl's genitals in an amusement park. When first arrested he denied any guilt, stating that he was sitting in his car with the girl and his six-year-old son. The girl complained that she was cold, and got him to touch her panties to prove that she had two pairs on. During the course of his trial, he changed his plea to guilty, but has since denied any intent to molest the girl.

Six weeks after the offense, A. was examined by two psychiatrists, at the request of the court, in accordance with the provisions of the new sex offender law. The findings at that time were: negative physical and neurological; psychometric, an IQ of 97; mental, a "quiet, co-operative, smiling, talkative and active individual. He shows no remorse for his present difficulty and he denies the charge against him definitely stating that he did nothing wrong. No delusions or hallucinations. He does admit being nervous and being in X State Hospital and the Y State Hospital for the Criminal Insane. He also admits many other anti-social acts during the past twenty years." The second report stated, "Extreme emotional lability is associated with defective judgment in this patient to a degree that, in my opinion, renders him a potential menace to society at all times." The conclusions reached were, "He is not psychotic or mentally defective and not suitable for commitment to a state hospital or a state school," and "Diagnosis: Constitutional Psychopathic Personality."

This inmate was received at Sing Sing Prison five days after these examinations, having been declared legally sane. His behavior shortly after entering the prison was so bizarre, that an immediate psychiatric consultation was requested by the principal keeper. At this time, the man showed a very bizarre affect, with much inappropriate smiling and laughing. He would burst into fits of wild sobbing and crying, without apparent cause. These episodes would last a few minutes, and were often followed by more smiling, laughing and grimacing, again quite inappropriate. His ideas were poorly correlated, with much circumstantiality and paralogical thinking. He also showed a persistent paranoid trend toward his wife, giving a very involved story of her relationships with other men — at the same time admitting that these ideas had been proved false in the past. He also admitted hallucinations in the past, but denied them at present.

A. was kept under observation at Sing Sing for six weeks, during which time he began to hallucinate, hearing voices, usually male, talking about him and about his wife. He attached the "voice" to an inmate in a nearby cell, and finally attempted to attack him. His general contact with reality became less and less adequate, and he was finally transferred to Dannemora State Hospital, with a diagnosis of paranoid schizophrenia, six weeks after entering Sing Sing. He has remained at Dannemora for the past three years.

This inmate's history reveals an early life in poor economic circumstances, in slum neighborhoods, where there was considerable violence, inter-racial conflict, and delinquency. He apparently developed normally, although he was always very small, being five feet, two inches tall and weighing 90 pounds at the age of 14. There was considerable friction between the parents, both father and mother being described as "nervous, high strung, and difficult to get along with." Four siblings have extensive anti-social and criminal histories.

The first evidence of A.'s behavior disturbance appears from the ages of eight to 10, when he failed in the third grade on four occasions. He finally left school at 16, having completed the sixth grade. Since repeated psychometric tests have indicated an IQ in the 90's, one may suggest an emotional disturbance rather than intellectual deficit as the cause of his school difficulties. Upon leaving school A. became a bootlegger, specializing in "bathtub gin." After the repeal of prohibition he became a welterweight boxer, having 112 fights in nine years, winning 96. He denies ever being knocked unconscious, losing on decisions or technical knockouts. His criminal history begins in 1930, and runs through 10 arrests with seven convictions, including the present sentence. In addition, he was committed to a state hospital in 1943, being discharged after two months with a diagnosis of psychosis with psychopathic personality. At that time, he showed marked emotional lability, with weeping, euphoria and silly grimacing. He denied hallucinations or delusions, but was assaultive on one occasion.

He was committed to a state hospital for the criminal insane three years later, from Bellevue, following his arrest for the attempted rape of a nine-and-one-half-year-old girl. His explanation of this offense was that his wife had refused to submit to sexual intercourse that day, and as a result of feeling overpassionate he took this girl into a lot in daylight, got on top of her, but did not open his trousers. At Bellevue, "he showed marked emotional lability, at times weeping loudly in an almost hysterical fashion, with much histrionic display. He was overproductive with excessive detail. On one or two occasions he was suspicious, claiming that he saw his wife sign a paper for one of the doctors on the ward, and he became quite argumentative about this even when it was found out and conveyed to him that she had merely signed a receipt for his bank book which he had authorized her to take from his property. . . . He relates persecutory ideas, for example, that the Parole Commission influenced foremen on the jobs where he worked to get him into trouble. He felt that everybody in Bellevue was against him and wanted to make trouble for him. The diagnosis of Psychosis with Psychopathic Personality was made."

The record from the first state hospital shows the following: "On examination he was overproductive, at times rambling. He showed emotional variability, crying and then laughing. He showed brief irritability on one occasion. Gave an account of his past life in conformity with the above recorded details. In speaking of his boxing career, he said his managers were a bunch of crooks who robbed him and did not treat him properly. He denied the use of alcohol and drugs. He referred to his ideas about his wife before he married as 'illusions.' He thought at that time, 1943, that she was a prostitute and was taking drugs and was having intercourse with negroes. He recalled his disturbed state while in the state hospital. He gave the same account of the crime as he gave at Bellevue. He denied that he exposd his privates and claimed that the detective in the police station forced the girl to say that he did. He said that he was excited and cried when he was admitted to Bellevue and claimed that he told the doctors there several lies because the lawyer put ideas into his head. No delusions or hallucinations otherwise could be elicited. He was correctly oriented, showed no memory impairment, good retention and immediate recall, poor counting and calculation. There was nothing unusual about his reading or writing, school and general knowledge were limited, intelligence rating was considered possibly borderline, insight partial."

"DIAGNOSIS: The basic problem in diagnosis is to decide whether the emotional instability is due to a constitutional disorder, psychopathic personality or an organic condition, hemorrhagic encephalitis associated with the trauma of boxing. There is also an hysterical quality to the easily aroused and variable emotional display. The emotional lability has some organic characteristics. However, his instability is described as temperamental and preceded his boxing career, as did also his delinquency. We lack any corroborative neurological or encephalographic evidence of organic involvement. The high incidence of psychopathic traits in the family also suggests a constitutional disorder. The diagnosis of Psychopathic Personality, Episode of Emotional Instability is suggested, although head trauma might be an aggravating factor."

After 18 months a certificate of recovery was issued, the final diagnosis being psychosis with psychopathic personality. Two and one-half years later, A. was again arrested and charged with disorderly conduct, especially with annoying a 10-year-old girl. He was again examined at Bellevue and found to be "well oriented and his memory appeared intact. No definite delusional trends or hallucinations could

be elicited at this time. During the interview however, he at times displayed considerable emotional instability, becoming tearful and obviously attempted to gain the sympathy of the examiners. No definite psychotic symptoms could be demonstrated." He was given a six-month sentence. Three days after his release, he committed the new offense.

CASE B.

The second case, B., is that of a 30-year-old white male who was indicted and sentenced for first degree sodomy, having performed anal intercourse on a 10-year-old boy. As in the previous case, he was studied by two psychiatrists, in a psychiatric hospital. Their very complete report on this man contained the following, "The defendant's father, who is said to have been alcoholic, died when the defendant was four years old. Shortly thereafter his mother lost her eyesight in an accident and was therefore unable to care for her three children, of whom the defendant was the middle. The children were subsequently reared by the grandmother and uncle. As a child, the defendant was healthy but suffered from a speech impediment which handicapped him socially and in his school work.

"He was always bashful and of somewhat limited intelligence. These factors combined with his speech impediment made school difficult for him, and he quit after the second year of high school at the age of 18. During the next two years he had various odd jobs; the longest period of employment was five months as a handyman at a sanatorium.

"The defendant has described his early years as unhappy because his relatives were 'cranky' and 'picked' on him. On one occasion, at the age of 14, he ran away and stayed overnight with a friend.

"His service record was good during three years in the army. In the army, he began to drink heavily, continuing to 1950, when he reduced his intake at the behest of a girlfriend. Also while in the army, he began to be more active sexually. He had intercourse with at least one 12-years-old 'native girl,' and had frequent anal intercourse, usually with 'native boys.' In these homosexual relations the defendant took the active role, with the passive cooperation of his partner.

"About seven months after his discharge from the army, the defendant married. He states that his marriage was happy and that sexual relations with his wife were satisfactory. In spite of this he continued to masturbate periodically. In October 1946, he was arrested for writing letters to two young girls, inviting them to the firehouse, where he was working as a janitor. The police believed his intent was immoral, but he denied this. He received a suspended sentence. In August 1947, while his wife was in her seventh month of pregnancy, he was arrested for carnal knowledge of a six-year-old girl. It is said that he took this girl in his car, parked in an isolated spot, played with her genitals and attempted intercourse with her. He was unable to penetrate but was able to satisfy himself. As a result of his action, the child was severely bruised in the genital area and received medical treatment for vaginitis. Prior to his trial for this offense, he was examined in a state hospital to determine his sanity. He was released as "non-commitable," tried, convicted and served two and one-half years of a three-year term in state prison. His psychiatric examination prior to trial showed that he had an IQ of 96 on the Wechsler-Bellevue Test.

"When he was released from prison in July 1950, he went 'out west' where he found work. In the spring of 1951, he became involved with a young boy, whom he grabbed and pressed close to his own body. The police released him on condition that he leave the community and return home.

"After his return in April 1951, he got along well until June 20, 1951, at which time he had anal intercourse with a 10-year-old boy. This led to his arrest and subsequent indictment. Since his arrest he has continued to experience frequent sexual tension which he has relieved by masturbation.

"During the defendant's stay in this hospital he has been pleasant, co-operative and sociable. During interviews, we have found him to be alert, co-operative and friendly. He still shows a mild speech impediment. There is no formal disorder of talk. He is not abnormally depressed or elated. He has no abnormal preoccupations and is experiencing no delusions or hallucinations. He is correctly oriented. His memory is excellent and he shows no formal disturbance of intellectual functions. He states he believes he is not insane, but feels he is sexually abnormal. He expresses a sincere desire to receive treatment. He does not feel that he could be sure of controlling his perverse sexual impulses if he were at liberty now. Psychological studies confirmed a normal intelligence, with an IQ of 96. Summary of the Rorschach examination is as follows, 'The patient appears to be much duller than he actually is, with the test results placing him in the lower limits of the average group. He displays a lack of personality integration, however, in that the ego is weak. His thinking is inclined to be autistic, and though he

is self-absorbed, he lacks insight or real self-awareness. Since he lacks mechanisms which would help him inhibit his behavior, he would be inclined to act out his sexual fantasies and impulses to satisfy his instinctual needs or promptings. While treatment should be attempted, long term prognosis seems very guarded.' "

On the basis of these findings he was diagnosed as "psychopathic personality with pathologic sexuality," and was discharged to the county jail. From there he entered Sing Sing on a "day to life" sentence.

In 1947, B. had been admitted to a state hospital in another state, the emergency certificate stating, "marked affective blunting, paranoid tendencies, disorganized vague thinking, perversion, suicidal tendencies. Impression: schizophrenia." Description of his mental state at that time included, "Patient appeared dull, facies was flattened. He was rather hesitant and slowed in his responses, appeared to be preoccupied; there was some blocking of thought and he was apathetic. He tended to be seclusive and somewhat surly. . . . Content — stated he had heard voices 'before' but no longer did — had communications from the Lord while he was praying which were 'like a feeling.' There was severe patchy defect of mentation especially apparent when attention and concentration play a part in arriving at correct answers. He was, however, oriented for time, place, person, and situation. Insight was entirely lacking. In summary, the mental status indicated that this man had been depressed and was still moderately depressed and that in all likelihood he was suffering from some form of schizophrenic psychosis."

In spite of this, he was discharged in three weeks since he was judged non-committable. At a later staff conference he was again diagnosed as dementia præcox, simple type.

This inmate was received at Sing Sing eight days after his discharge from the observation hospital. Psychiatric consultation was again requested, during his first week in prison, by the administration, because of his bazarre behavior. He was very co-operative on examination, but showed serious disturbance in performance, due to a combination of depression and markedly shallow, flattened affect. He could not give subjective feeling responses, was circumstantial and dwelt on irrelevant details. He had repeated quarrels with the other inmates, particularly in the movies, saying he was "picked on," and made to change his seat. He had also been observed by the officers to be masturbating frequently at times in public, such as in the mess hall, in a corner of the exercise yard, or in the shop where he worked.

A sample of his productions at this time shows his difficulty in verbalizing and the paralogical thinking present. This was written down and given to the psychiatrist studying his case.

"FUNDAMENTAL reason Why on Sodomy"

"The reason a lot of boys does it to boys is this simple reason. Lots of them getting discourage with women on the important part. The girls say they can cook. Then after you marry them and find out more things on them you get discourage and you do it to boys which you can get the same satisfaction as you can from a girl. It also make you feel just as good as it was a girl. Another thing you can't trust a girl anymore. In the olden days you could trust them but can't no more. Here some reason why a boy like to do it to a boy.

"1. He will not tell as easy as a girl

"2. On an average a boy will like to do it to each other

"3. He doesn't have to worry about having a child.

"4. He doesn't have to spend money on him providing he can do it also.

"5. If you do spend money you can get away by treating him to something an the lowest price is a $.10

"6. He pal around with you much better then a girl that you would be really in love with."

This communication was one of many written by B. during the seven months that he was in Sing Sing. In spite of two years of high school and an IQ of 107 to 112 on tests done at Sing Sing, he has marked difficulty in expressing his ideas. The writer explains this discrepancy as a measure of the emotional blocking of intellectual functioning, and uses it as one of the criteria in diagnosis of a schizophrenic illness.

B. was held at Sing Sing for a period of seven months, primarily for adequate investigation by the research team. During this time his behavior became progressively more disturbed, with increasing paranoid preoccupations, and a growing sense of depersonalization and disintegration. He began to ruminate on suicide, and talked constantly of ways to commit it. One of his last notes contained the following, "I can't write or say what I really want to write down for you. But it have to be written before the ends come for me. . . . Another thing,

I can read a book and I my mind forget what I read after I read it. . . . I also still got the feeling I want to kill myself and getting around more sure of myself and if there isn't something done I probably will take a stab at it." He was transferred to Dannemora State Hospital nine months after entering Sing Sing, and is still there, 13 months later.

These two cases have been used as illustrations because the psychopathology was overt and obvious from the moment these men entered Sing Sing. It was so obvious, in fact, that laymen, the guards on duty at the prison entrance and in the reception cells, knew these men were "nuts" or "bugs," to use their vernacular. Yet these very same men, one week before, had been declared legally sane after psychiatric examination by qualified psychiatrists. Small wonder, then, that the men with borderline, masked, or sub-clinical schizophrenic disturbances escape detection and proper diagnosis. Why does this happen? Can a man develop such marked symptoms, and show such extensive psychopathology in the short space of a week? The possibility that such an acute, fulminating illness can develop does exist, but it is not apt to happen with the frequency seen in the sex offender research project cases.

How then can one explain the discrepancies between the pre-trial examination of these men, and the research findings, frequently within one or two weeks? One explanation can be considered and discarded in the same breath; that is the competence of the psychiatrists doing the examinations on these men. They are, for the most part, men of considerable clinical experience, especially in the rapid evaluation of patients hospitalized for psychiatric observation as potential psychotics. In many of the cases studied one finds, in the record, a rather extensive description of symptoms indicative of psychopathological processes, incuding statements about ideas of reference, persecutory ideas, extreme emotional lability and defective judgment; and yet the diagnosis of a psychotic illness, specifically schizophrenia, is avoided, and the individual is diagnosed as a psychopathic personality, a sexual psychopath, a psychopath with sexual perversions, and so forth. The writer believes that the critical factors influencing the judgment of these psychiatrists are three-fold: first, the patient's antisocial behavior, the fact that he has been indicted for a felony; second, stemming directly from the first, the concern that society, as represented by the prosecution and the court, will complain that the offender is being "protected medically" from receiving proper punishment if a diagnosis of psychosis is made; third, and here one treads on dangerous ground, the psychiatrist's own unconscious reaction to the sexual character of the felony, which may motivate him toward punishment rather than treatment in such a case.

In the writer's opening remarks, he indicated the horror, resentment, anger, fear and demand for retribution that make up society's response to a sexual offense. The reasons for this reaction cannot be gone into in this paper. But the writer does raise the question, on the basis of the psychiatric and psychological appraisals of the sex offenders studied at Sing Sing, of whether punishment is the optimum answer to this problem, or of whether a therapeutically-oriented program would not be preferable. Before arguing the pros and cons of this question, let us consider further the diagnostic problem in these cases.

If these men are psychopathic personalities, sexual or otherwise, they should show specific psychopathological characteristics that are the criteria for diagnosing this condition. In one of the widely-quoted books on the psychopath, Cleckley's *The Mask of Sanity*,[3] the characteristics of this type of individual are given as follows, "Superficial charm and good intelligence, absence of delusions and other signs of emotional 'thinking,' absence of 'nervousness' or psychoneurotic manifestations, unreliability, untruthfulness and insincerity, lack of remorse or shame, inadequately motivated anti-social behavior, poor judgment and failure to learn by experience, pathologic egocentricity and incapacity for love, general poverty in major affective reactions, specific loss of insight, unresponsiveness in general interpersonal relations, fantastic and uninviting behavior, with drink and sometimes without, suicide rarely carried out, sex life impersonal, trivial, and poorly integrated, and lastly, failure to follow any life plan." Let us consider these 16 points, one by one, and see whether they fit the data collected from over 200 sex offenders during the course of the project's investigations.

Superficial Charm and Good Intelligence — The test scores of intelligence in the research project cases range from the middle 60's — four men were transferred to the institution for defective delinquents — to a high of 140, with the mean being slightly over 100. This would indicate that the sex offenders have the same intelligence spread as the general population, and do not fall into a high

[3] Cleckley, H.: The Mask of Sanity. Mosby. St. Louis. 1950.

or low group. They are, however, anything but a charming group, even superficially. Many have definite physical deformities, and they all show marked social awkwardness, stemming from their withdrawn, isolated personality patterns.

Absence of Delusions and Other Signs of Irrational Thinking — The men studied do have the ability to cover up ideas and experiences that they have learned are not acceptable when related to their families, friends or others. The distortions in their perception of reality may be very subtle, requiring close contact with the inmate, over a considerable time, to detect. These perceptive disturbances can also be elicited, and this is particularly useful if the subject is trying to cover up, by the use of projective techniques, such as the TAT and the Rorschach examinations. It is the initial perceptive distortions, magnified and further altered by the disturbances of mood and affect, that in many instances lead to the antisocial sexual act; e. g., in the second case, B. relates his discouragement with women, their unreliability, and his lack of satisfaction from contact with them. In the light of his reality situation these would appear to be definite perceptual and reasoning distortions. Cleckley also speaks of the absence of valid depression. About 70 per cent of the cases in this study show mild to severe depression, with some expressing suicidal ideas.

Absence of "Nervousness" or Psychoneurotic Manifestations — The absence of anxiety and tension in the psychopath has been stressed repeatedly. In contrast, the writer has found moderate to severe anxiety in 90 per cent of the project cases, with little or no anxiety appearing only in those individuals with overt psychoses or marked organic cerebral impairment.

Unreliability — While this is the hallmark of the psychopath, particularly when subjected to the slightest pressure in the form of frustrations or obligations to perform, the opposite is true for the Sing Sing cases. The majority of these men are considered steady, reliable, even compulsive workers, especially in the older age groups, with the exception of their sexual behavior; and, in many of the cases studied, their difficulties with alcohol.

Untruthfulness and Insincerity — These qualities are extremely difficult to evaluate in individuals being studied in a prison setting, especially when they feel that their chances for parole may be influenced or determined by the information given to the investigator, a conviction that persists in spite of all reassurances to the contrary. Unquestionably, many of the men studied "put the best foot forward," in that they withhold information rather than concoct deliberate falsehoods. There is, however, a sizable group who persistently deny their guilt, in the face of overwhelming evidence in probation records and admissions of guilt at the times of arrest. These are, however, the more seriously-disturbed individuals, largely those with paranoid personality patterns, rather than the typical glib and very plausible psychopath.

Lack of Remorse or Shame — The amount of depression and guilt, already referred to, in the Sing Sing cases would indicate considerable shame and remorse as a consequence of the anti-social acts. While direct expressions of shame are obtained in less than half the cases studied, indirect evidence, such as the attempt to hide or deny the sex offense from the rest of the prison population, is rather common. This is true even in the group who deny their guilt, since the clinching argument for their innocence is often, "Why I couldn't do such a terrible thing, I'd feel too ashamed."

Inadequately Motivated Anti-Social Behavior — While many of the individuals in the Sing Sing group could give no immediate reason for committing their anti-social act or acts, in fact frequently asked for assistance in understanding their aberrant sexual behavior, immediate precipitating factors, such as sexual frustration by their wives, economic reverses, and other threats to status or security were found in about one-third of these men. The absence of such specific events does not, however, imply inadequate motivation. Overwhelmingly influential unconscious motivations can be discovered in these individuals, given an adequate — which does not of necessity mean lengthy — examination. The more bizarre and chaotic the sexual expression becomes, the more severe the degree of schizophrenic involvement, in the writer's experience.

Poor Judgment and Failure to Learn by Experience — This is another of the commonly-accepted characteristics of the psychopath, and is one of the factors that makes punishment for his activities so futile. While there are many recidivists in the sex offender group, and while many of them show remarkably poor judgment in the commission of their sexual acts, frequently choosing times and places that appear to invite detection and apprehension, this behavior, as already indicated, does not have the apparent purposelessness of the psychopath, as it is compulsively motivated in most instances. It is likely, however, that the apparent failure to learn by past experience, shown in the repetition of their sexual acts, is the critical factor in determining the diagnosis of "sexual psychopath" made on 95 per cent of the men who have had psychiatric examinations before sentencing to Sing Sing.

Pathologic Egocentricity and Incapacity for Love — Superficial appraisal of the behavior of the "sexual psychopath," with its apparent concentration on the satisfaction of the individual's own sexual needs, to the exclusion of any and all other considerations, would seem to fit the Sing Sing offender into this category very neatly. When one looks beneath this superficial manifestation, however, the anti-social behavior is found to be the resultant of forces, largely unconscious, that have been in conflict for long periods, and that reach external expression — in the majority of the cases — only when the repressive factors are weakened by alcohol, organic brain damage, or the disorganization that accompanies an overt schizophrenic illness. The capacity for object relationships is certainly disturbed in these individuals, largely, one feels, as the result of incapacitating inhibitions and fears over establishing emotional contact and interpersonal give-and-take with others. It is the impression, however, that these disturbances result in a weakened, childish kind of behavior toward libidinal objects, rather than in the absence of capacity for object relationships that is described in the psychopath. Since therapeutic contact is dependent upon the ability to make some kind of object relationship, accurate estimation of this capacity in these individuals has an important bearing on the therapeutic possibilities and therefore on the ultimate prognosis.

General Poverty in Major Affective Reactions — In this area, as in the factor just considered, the importance of distinguishing between the "feebleness of affect" of the psychopath, and the affective blunting of the schizophrenic is emphasized by the superficial similarity of behavior in the two groups. This distinction has been attempted in the Sing Sing study by rating each case on "ability for emotional rapport and reactivity." None of the Sing Sing cases has been rated as having a "mature and adequate" ability. Approximately 50 per cent are rated as having ability "present but suppressed," 25 per cent as having "limited" ability, and 25 per cent as having "none or slight." This would indicate a disturbance of affect in all of these cases, the disturbance being both qualitative and quantitative, in contrast to the simple quantitative deficiency in the psychopath. These affective disturbances are interpreted as an indication of the fear experienced by these men when they attempt affective ties with others. As a defense against these fearful situations, they remain emotionally encapsulated, isolated and detached.

Specific Loss of Insight — Under this heading, Cleckley discusses the psychopath's inability "to see himself as others see him." This is in marked contrast to his perfect orientation, his ability to reason, and his freedom from delusions. The information on this point obtained by the estimate of insight in the Sing Sing prisoners studied, shows normal insight to be lacking. It is found, however, that one-third of the men have partial insight, another 50 per cent have some awareness of their difficulties, while less than 20 per cent are essentially without insight. This last group is comprised of the more overtly psychotic individuals in the series. The majority of the sexual offenders are keenly aware of the attitude of society in general, and prison society in particular, toward their sexual aberrations: and they show, as has already been stated varying degrees of shame and remorse.

Unresponsiveness in General Interpersonal Relations — The contrast is drawn here between the superficial ease and affability of the psychopath, and his basic lack of response to the usual emotional interplay existing in close interpersonal relationships. The difficulties in interpersonal relations seen in the Sing Sing cases stem, it is felt, from these offenders' marked anxiety and fear of close emotional contact with others, particularly with adults. This is a pervasive difficulty, so that these men show little social ability, and are a significantly isolated and withdrawn group. This isolation continues, even in the prison setting.

Fantastic and Uninviting Behavior with Drink and Sometimes Without It — The bizarre behavior in all areas of personality-functioning described under this heading in Cleckley's book has rarely been encountered in the Sing Sing cases. Again excluding overtly psychotic individuals, who may exhibit as bizarre behavior as can be imagined, the acting out seen in the majority of the men who were alcoholics tends to be confined to the specific area of their sexual difficulties. In addition, when sober, they are over-controlled, rigid conformists, for the most part.

Suicide Rarely Carried Out — In respect to suicide, the psychopath seems to resemble the Sing Sing sex offenders. One encounters mention of suicidal ideas or attempts infrequently, even though depression and guilt are relatively common. Again it is the more disturbed psychotics in the group who have shown the suicidal tendencies found. For example, B. speaks of suicide as an escape from the torment of his immediate situation.

Sex Life Impersonal, Trivial, and Poorly Integrated — This is the third, and perhaps most im-portant area of agreement between the description of the psychopath and the Sing Sing group of sex offenders. In contrast to the generally accepted belief that the sexual offender is a "sex fiend," motivated by an uncontrollable need for sexual gratification, one finds that close to 90 per cent of the men studied show markedly impaired erotic drives. They are satisfying some need other than sexual while performing the aberrant sexual act — such as retaliation or revenge, for the trauma experienced with a hostile, rejecting or castrating mother or wife. There is also a marked lack of integration, extending to chaotic confusion, based primarily on the intense sexual fears generated by their traumatic childhood sexual experiences. A high percentage of such traumatic episodes is found in these men. Analysis of their sexual disturbances reveals a schizophrenic type of disorganization and shallowness, consistent with, and part of, the marked disturbances in interpersonal relationships already described.

Failure to Follow Any Life Plan — The inconsistency of the psychopath in working toward a definite goal or goals is seldom encountered in this group of offenders. A high percentage are compulsive workers, showing enormous energy and drive in their attempts to gain social and economic status and security. While there may be temporary interruptions because of alcoholism and anti-social sexual activities, they stick closely to patterns of achievement, and have very specific goals and objectives in all areas, including in some instances, fairly realistic sexual goals. Again those in the Sing Sing group who come closest to Cleckley's foregoing description are the more seriously disturbed, disintegrating schizophrenics, who may show very pointless, nomadic and irresponsible lives.

It is found, then, after careful scrutiny of the various characteristics of the psychopath, that the individuals in the present research group, most of them diagnosed as psychopathic personalities, show relatively few of the traits listed by Cleckley as typical of the true psychopath. In fact, in only five of the 16 characteristics given by Cleckley is there even superficial agreement. In four of the five — pathological egocentricity and incapacity for love; general poverty in major affective reactions; unresponsiveness in general interpersonal relations; and sex life impersonal, trivial and poorly integrated — the common psychodynamic denominator is the disturbance of affective capacity which manifests itself in impoverished emotional relationships, and a sharp dampening in external attachments and interests. This autistic withdrawal from interpersonal contacts is one of the earliest, and most significant symptoms of psychological decompensation, an indication of the dangerously narrow margin of competence remaining to the weakened and brittle ego structure of the individual. The fifth factor, poor judgment and failure to learn by experience, is an additional indication of the failure of the ego to perform satisfactorily in all three major areas of its function: the perceptive, integrative, and executive.

That the disintegration or collapse of ego function is not complete, thereby enabling the individual to maintain a façade of normal behavior, does not, in the writer's opinion, vitiate the diagnosis of a schizophrenic illness. The individual is not, to be sure, grossly decompensated, that is, overtly psychotic. But it is precisely because he maintains some semblance of normal behavior that he presents such a problem and threat to the community. The behavior disturbances of the overt psychotic cause him, as a general rule, to be detected rapidly and disposed of properly, in our highly-organized and complex modern society. It is the borderline individual, who can still maintain some semblance of control, but who loses this control episodically, or is about to lose control chronically, who winds up in prison, having had the opportunity to commit one or more anti-social acts, and who is diagnosed as "without psychosis, not mentally defective, psychopathic personality." It is the writer's contention that such a diagnosis does not indicate the true state of affairs, in fact effectively hides the psychodynamic status of the inmate, and causes confusion and apathy regarding treatment and eventual disposition of the inmate.

On the basis of clinical investigations on the Sing Sing sex offenders, corroborated by the findings on psychological examination, the writer would propose that these individuals be diagnosed, for the most part, somewhere along the continuum ranging from schizo-adaptive personality structure[4] through pseudoneurotic schizophrenia,[5] pseudopsychopathic schizophrenia,[6] and ambulatory schizophrenia to overt, clinically demonstrable schizophrenic psychosis. Without becoming involved in the controversy that is ever present regarding the genetic basis of schizophrenia, the usefulness of the concept of a schizotype — or to use Sandor Rado's term, a schizo-adaptive personality — in dealing with the problems of therapy and prognosis in this group of cases, has become increasingly evident over the past three years. In the field of therapy, for example, while the prognosis in schizophrenia is still not a rosy one, as has been mentioned, therapeutic techniques are available, and do modify the pattern of illness in many patients. On the other hand, there is a universal pessimism, and rightly so, about therapeutic efforts with the psychopath, and this may have an adverse effect upon the treatment of individuals so diagnosed.

In the field of prognosis, which in prison psychiatry includes not only a prediction about the medical future of the inmate patient, but also involves or implies a prediction about his future social behavior, the use of the diagnostic continuum just described, with its implication of movement in either direction, gives a flexibility to statements about therapeutic response that cannot be achieved using terms like "cured" or "improved." Every psychiatrist who has had to decide, or help decide on the ability of a hospitalized patient to adjust to life outside the institution is keenly aware of the difficulties and problems surrounding such decisions. When the "patient" has committed an anti-social act, and may have a history of recidivism, the decision, from the psychiatric standpoint, on his suitability for release, is an even weightier one. The device of attaching a diagnostic label never suffices. The administrative officials in the probation offices, parole boards and courts are increasingly interested in a statement of the psychodynamics of the particular case, reduced of course to understandable lay terminology, and are willing, even eager, to be guided in their decisions by the implications about the future behavior of the individual that are contained in such a statement. In order, therefore, to meet most adequately the dual responsibility which medicine has always accepted — to society on the one hand, and to the individual patient on the other — and which has been intensified in recent years by the willingness of the courts and correctional authorities to accept medical, especially psychiatric, opinion about problems of human misbehavior, we must attempt as accurate a description as possible of the behavior pattern in question. This must be dynamically oriented, if a proper understanding of the motivational context, as well as the actual behavior, is to be achieved. Prediction of future behavior is dependent to a greater extent on a clear understanding of the motivations and goals, both conscious and unconscious, of the individual, than on any other factor.

[4] Rado, Sandor: Academic Lecture. Am. J. Psychiat., 110:6, 406, December 1953.
[5] Hoch, P., and Polatin, P.: Pseudoneurotic forms of schizophrenia. PSYCHIAT. QUART., 23, April 1949.
[6] Dunaif, S., and Hoch, P.: Pseudopsychopathic schizophrenia. Presentation at 1953 meeting of American Psychopathological Association.

DANIEL G. BROWN

Homosexuality and Family Dynamics*†

In considering the subject of sexual development and behavior, it is necessary to differentiate three different, independently varying components. These are: (1) the *biological-constitutional* component, which refers to hereditary, congenital, and maturational factors; (2) the *sex role* component, which pertains to the individual's identification with one sex or the other, and (3) the *genital* component which refers to the source, aim, and direction of sexual stimulation, desire, activity, and satisfaction.

Disturbances in any one of these areas have occasioned confusion in the mind of the public, at least. Physical disturbances, such as hermaphroditism, are not evidence of abnormality in other components. Disturbance in the sex role is particularly variable in degree, ranging from very mild forms to such practices as transvestitism. It does not necessarily involve inverted sex relations. On the other hand, individuals who seek sexual activity with persons of the same sex as themselves may or may not display evidence of abnormality in the other two realms. The situation is further confused by the fact that these individuals are sometimes active sexually with both sexes.

The term homosexuality is properly applied only to the specific deviation from the norm in the third component, in which sexual desire and activity is directed toward the same sex.

There is a need for clarification in the area of disturbances in sexual development, but this study is concerned only with the relationship of male homosexuality (as defined above) to certain parent-child experiences and particular family dynamics.

Research studies(7, 8) indicate there are several million individuals in the United States who are predominately or exclusively homosexual and that among these millions, there are two or three times more males than females. The widespread occurrence of homosexuality has prompted the reference to homosexuals as those individuals within our society who do not biologically reproduce themselves, yet whose number seems to be steadily increasing. Why is this so? And, parenthetically, the question might be raised, why has so little been done by society (and the social, psychological, and medical sciences) to understand, to correct, to prevent, to cope with this behavioral abnormality? While millions have been spent on research for the control and prevention of various ailments of mankind, very little has been spent on psychological disturbances such as homosexuality, although certainly the unhappiness and misery that are often found in such individuals and their families may be as real and painful as other human afflictions.

There are a number of factors that occur in childhood which appear to be related to the development of homosexuality in adults. Such conditions as prolonged segregation of the sexes; specific, intensely exciting, and gratifying homosexual experiences in childhood; seduction by adult homosexuals; threatening and painful experiences in connection with sex play or relationships with the opposite sex; these and related factors in childhood and adolescence are correlated with the occurrence of homosexuality in adulthood. The focus of the present discussion, however, is on the child's early experiences and relationships with parental figures, specifically with the opposite-sex parent compared to the same-sex parent in the etiology of male homosexuality.

There is now sufficient evidence to warrant the following general conclusion: male children who become predominantly or exclusively homosexual in adulthood often have childhoods in which there was an excessively close and abnormally strong mother-son relationship. Typically, this relationship involved exaggerated amounts of fondling, caressing, and petting by the mother who, at the same time, was dominating and overcontrolling of her son. Such activities as dressing and undressing, bathing, and sleeping with the boy along with frequent and overintense "love" attachments long after infancy appear to provide the kind of psychological climate that results in a developmental predisposition for the boy later becoming homosexually rather than

* Reprinted with permission from the *Bulletin of the Menninger Clinic*, Vol. 27, pp. 227–232. Copyright 1963 by The Menninger Foundation.
† Paper presented at the Annual Air Force Clinical Psychology Meeting, USAF School of Aerospace Medicine, Brooks AFB, Texas, January 10, 1963.

heterosexually adjusted. In simple learning terms, such a relationship early becomes and remains a source of fear arousal and avoidance conditioning. With the incest barrier in human society, the boy is conditioned against the female figure as a sexual love object because of the prolonged attachment and *excessive* emotional-physical contacts with the mother.[1] This psychologically unhealthy attachment seems to be instigated by the mother who, consciously or unconsciously, handles the boy in an an erotic and often seductive manner. In addition, the family constellation usually involves a father who is, in one way or another, a predominantly negative figure as far as the son is concerned. Such a father is passive, weak, and ineffective as a member of the family and in relation to the son, or else is abusive, hostile, rejecting, or indifferent to the son. There is consequently an absence of emotional closeness and attachment between the male child and the father. It is this family pattern that sets the stage for the development of homosexuality in males.

How valid and well substantiated is the above formulation? What evidence is there for it? Before briefly reviewing the major clinical and research investigations, mention might be made of observations of the author during the past eight years of active duty in the Air Force. During this period there was the opportunity to interview and test approximately 40 male airmen in whom predominant or exclusive homosexuality was the major problem. In more than 30 of these cases, the mother-son and father-son relationship conformed to the family pattern described above. Not one of these airmen had a close, warm, affectionate attachment to his father or a father-substitute in childhood. There may be such cases but they were not among this group.

Some 30 years ago, Terman and Miles,(11) on the basis of a careful study of 77 male homosexuals, 17 to 44 years of age, concluded as follows: "If the case history data supplied by these individuals can be accepted as anywhere near the truth, the psycho-social formula for developing homosexuality in boys would seem to run somewhat as follows: 'Too demonstrative affection from an excessively emotional mother — a father who is unsympathetic, autocratic, brutal, much away from home, or de-

ceased; treatment of the child as a girl, coupled with lack of encouragement to associate with boys — overemphasis of neatness, niceness, and spirituality; lack of vigilance against the danger of seduction by older homosexual males.' "

Psychoanalytic theory also has emphasized the mother-son factor in the development of male homosexuality. Freud,(5) Schilder,(9) Fenichel(4) and other psychoanalytic writers refer to a *very intense* mother fixation in childhood in practically all cases of adult, male homosexuality. In Hamilton's report(6) of his study and evaluation of a number of male homosexuals, invariably one factor stood out in childhood: the presence of an intense mother-son relationship that made it difficult for the boy to accept his own sexual feelings as natural and acceptable. Hamilton refers to the "unmistakable eroticism" and "incestuous aggressiveness" that mothers expressed toward their sons who became homosexual adults; he considers the fear of incest to be the most important factor involved. Bender and Paster(1) in a study of 19 actively homosexual children, found either a grossly deficient or very negative relationship with the same-sex parent, coupled with an overly intimate attachment to the opposite-sex parent. And, in a recent publication by West,(12) a number of contemporary investigators are cited who independently have reached the same conclusion concerning the mother-son factor in male homosexuality. In this same publication, West presents his own study in England of 50 homosexual males and 50 matched control (nonhomosexual) males. His findings clearly show that male homosexuals are much more likely to come from a family constellation involving an overintense mother *and* unsatisfactory father relationship. West emphasizes that it is this *combination* of parental relationship that characterized the homosexual group. This suggests clearly that it is not simply the psychologically "smothering mother" but also the psychologically "starving father" that provides the basis for predisposing the male child to homosexuality. Thus, even with a smothering mother, homosexuality probably will not develop provided the father maintains a close, positive relationship with the son.

Finally, the most recent research study of family dynamics and homosexuality is the book by Bieber and collaborators.(2) This reference reports in detail the findings of a study of 106 homosexual males and a comparison group of 100 heterosexual males, all of whom had received psychoanalytic therapy. This study represents a comprehensive analysis of the problem and is one of the most significant contributions that has yet appeared. The basic over-all

[1] This underlying dynamic factor probably explains in part why the typical adult male homosexual finds the heterosexual relationship revolting and even frightening. To him there is nothing sexually attractive or exciting about the female figure; he is impotent as far as women are concerned.

finding is summarized as follows: "The 'classical' homosexual triangular pattern is one where the mother is close-binding-intimate with the son and is dominant and minimizing toward a husband who is a detached father, particularly a hostile-detached one. From our statistical analysis, the chances appear to be high that any son exposed to this parental combination will become homosexual or develop severe homosexual problems." In the clear majority of these cases *the mother* was described as "close-binding-intimate" and seductive; she suppressed normal heterosexual interests and discouraged masculine patterns; she interfered with the father-son relationship by preferring the son to the father, fostering father-son rivalry, and using the son as a romantic substitute for the father; she interfered with the peer relations of the son and discouraged friendships with "regular" boys; and she interfered with the development of the son's independence by overprotection, "babying," etc. Concerning the role of the father, the authors write: "The father played an essential and determining role in the homosexual outcome of his son." "Profound interpersonal disturbance is unremitting in the homosexual father-son relationships. Not one of the fathers (of homosexual sons) . . . could be regarded as reasonably 'normal' parents. . . ." These fathers typically were emotionally detached and hostile, spent little time with their sons, failed to serve as a masculine model, and failed to protect the son from destructive maternal influences.

It is recognized that individuals with this family constellation do not necessarily or invariably become homosexual, i.e., this pattern may be found in the childhood of individuals who do not become adult homosexuals. It might be predicted that many such nonhomosexuals would show other kinds of psychiatric disturbance, immaturity reactions, or character problems. The question then arises: given the psychopathological family dynamics described in this paper, what psychosocial factors differentiate those males who become or do not become adult homosexuals?

More research is necessary, of course, before this question can be answered. One important over-all variable would be the *timing* and *continuity or discontinuity* of the family pattern, *i.e.*, did this pattern exist from the birth of the son, continue through childhood, and into adolescence? For example, it would make a difference if the child were exposed to this configuration before rather than after the second or third or fourth year of life. What would be the effect on a child's psychosexual development of a change in the family structure by the death of

a parent or the prolonged or permanent separation of the parents? Also, what would be the effect of the subsequent replacement of one parent by a stepparent? It would seem safe to assume that the particular effect would depend to a significant degree on the *age* of the child at the time he experiences the loss, and the availability of a parental substitute. In other words, the concept of a "critical period" in the child's development and learning is relevant here.(10) It is quite conceivable that there is a crucial period in the early years of a child for establishing the basic capacity for heterosexual adjustment. In this connection, evidence indicates that sex role differentiation and identity occur in most children between the ages of one and one-half and three, and that heterosexual stimulation and responsiveness develop between the third and sixth year of life.(2, 3)

In summary, then, it would seem that the family pattern involving a combination of a dominating, overly intimate mother *plus* a detached, hostile or weak father is beyond doubt related to the development of male homosexuality. Beginning with the penetrating clinical insights of Freud 50 years ago, the systematic investigation by Terman and Miles some 30 years ago, the independent findings of a number of clinical and research workers, and the recent noteworthy contributions of West and Bieber, there is now strong evidence and considerable agreement as to family dynamics in the development of male homosexuality. It is surprising there has not been greater recognition of this relationship among the various disciplines that are concerned with children. A problem that arises in this connection is how to inform and educate teachers and parents relative to the decisive influence of the family in determining the course and outcome of the child's psychosexual development. There would seem to be no justification for waiting another 25 or 50 years to bring this information to the attention of those who deal with children. And there is no excuse for professional workers in the behavioral sciences to continue avoiding their responsibility to disseminate this knowledge and understanding as widely as possible.

REFERENCES

1. BENDER, LAURETTA and PASTER, SAMUEL: Homosexual Trends in Children. *Amer. J. Orthopsychiat.* 11:730–743, 1941.
2. BIEBER, IRVING and others: *Homosexuality.* New York, Basic Books, 1962.
3. BROWN, D. G.: Sex-Role Development in a Changing Culture. *Psychol. Bull.* 54:232–242, 1958.
4. FENICHEL, OTTO: *The Psychoanalytic Theory of Neurosis.* New York, Norton, 1945.

5. FREUD, SIGMUND: Three Contributions to the Theory of Sex. In *The Basic Writings of Sigmund Freud*, A. A. Brill, ed. New York, Modern Library, 1938.
6. HAMILTON, G. V.: Incest and Homosexuality. In *Encyclopaedia Sexualis*, Victor Robinson, ed. New York, Crown, 1936.
7. KINSEY, A. C. and others: *Sexual Behavior in the Human Male*. Philadelphia, Saunders, 1948.
8. ———: *Sexual Behavior in the Human Female*. Philadelphia, Saunders, 1953.
9. SCHILDER, PAUL: On Homosexuality. *Psa. Rev.* 16:377–389, 1929.
10. Scott, J. P.: Critical Periods in Behavioral Development. *Science* 138:949–958, Nov. 30, 1962.
11. TERMAN, L. M. and MILES, C. C.: *Sex and Personality*. New York, McGraw-Hill, 1936.
12. WEST, D. J.: Parental Figures in the Genesis of Male Homosexuality. *Int. J. Soc. Psychiat.* 5:85–97, 1959.

DAVID P. AUSUBEL

Causes and Types of Narcotic Addiction: A *Psychosocial View*[*]

Addiction to narcotic drugs is one of the most serious but least understood medico-social problems of our time. The grievous lack of public enlightenment about this problem reflects in part its inherent complexity as well as the paucity of definitive research findings dealing with physiological, psychological, and social aspects of addiction. But an even more important cause, perhaps, of both lay and professional misunderstanding of the drug addiction problem is the continuous stream of lurid and sensational misinformation about this topic which appears in the various mass media.

THE ADDICT'S VIEW

Let us examine first the addict's own view of the cause of drug addiction. According to him, all human beings are equally susceptible to addiction. The unlucky victim need only have the misfortune to be introduced to the drug as a result of abnormal curiosity, chance encounters with addicts and narcotic peddlers, or prolonged illness. Then, once he is caught in the "iron grip" of physical dependence on the drug he is allegedly powerless to help himself. He is obliged to continue using more narcotics "just to stay normal," that is, to avoid the "un-bearable" symptoms that ensue when the drug is discontinued.

This dangerously distorted account of the causes of drug addiction is a great comfort to the addict. It puts his illness in the most favorable possible light and also absolves him of all responsibility. Unfortunately, however, he has not only successfully deluded himself, but has also managed, with the unwitting co-operation of the mass media, to foist his understandably biased view on a credulous American public. Physical dependence and withdrawal symptoms are genuine physiological phenomena, and association with confirmed addicts or drug peddlers *is* the typical way in which candidate addicts are introduced to narcotics. But neither factor explains *why* an individual becomes a drug addict.

Physical Dependence

How credible is the physical dependence explanation? In the first place, although the symptoms of withdrawal are distressing, they are generally no worse than a bad case of gastro-intestinal influenza, and, in any event, largely disappear within 10 days. Thus, unless other potent satisfactions were derived from the narcotic habit, it is difficult to believe that any individual would be willing to pay the fantastic price of the drug and risk imprisonment and social ostracism merely to avoid a moderately severe 10-day illness. Second, every year thousands of persons

[*] Reprinted by permission from *Psychiatric Quarterly*, Vol. 35, 1961, pp. 523–531.

with serious fractures, burns and surgical conditions receive opiates long enough to develop physiological dependence, but are nevertheless able to break this dependence quite easily. Third, the dosage of morphine (or equivalent) required to prevent withdrawal symptoms is never more than one to two grains daily. Hence, why will drug addicts take up to 20 grains a day if they take the drug, as they claim to, "just to feel normal"? Fourth, withdrawal symptoms can be adequately prevented and relieved if morphine is taken hypodermically. Therefore, why will addicts run the risk of thrombophlebitis and septicemia by injecting the drug "main-line" — or directly into their veins — with crude, homemade syringes? The answer to both third and fourth questions is that the large dose and the "main-line" route increase the "kick" or euphoric effect. Fifth, new, synthetic opiate-like drugs have been developed which have all of the analgesic and euphoric properties of opiates, but for which withdrawal symptoms are minimal. Nevertheless, the evidence is conclusive that addiction develops just as rapidly for these drugs as for other opiates.(1)

Last, if physical dependence were a significant causal factor in drug addiction, how could we explain the fact that a least 75 per cent of all addicts discharged from federal hospitals start using the drug almost immediately after release?(2) By the time of release, it is at least a year since physical dependence was broken. If addicts are really so terrified by withdrawal symptoms, why should they start developing the habit all over again after suffering the symptoms once and then escaping their clutches?

MULTIPLE CAUSALITY IN DISEASE

Generally speaking, research on drug addiction has been hampered by the same type of faulty thinking that has plagued the investigation of the causes of such other complex disorders as cancer, tuberculosis and juvenile delinquency. This is the error of assuming that since the disorder in question *appears* to be identical in all individuals, it must necessarily have the same *single* cause in all instances. Actually, there are many different kinds of drug addicts, and the causes of drug addiction are multiple and additive in their impact rather than mutually exclusive.

As in most other diseases, the causes of drug addiction include both *internal* factors originating within the affected individual (e.g., hereditary susceptibility) and *external* factors originating within the environment. Each type of factor may be fur-

ther categorized with respect to whether its impact occurs immediately prior to, and is essential for, the appearance of the disease (*precipitating*), or is operative over a longer period of time and merely contributory (*predisposing*). In tuberculosis, for example, hereditary susceptibility to the inroads of tubercle bacilli is the predisposing internal cause, and temporary lowering of general resistance (as in overexertion or exposure to extremes of temperature) is the precipitating internal cause. Comparable external causes would include overcrowded living conditions, on the one hand, and actual exposure to an adequately large dose of tubercle bacilli, on the other.

It makes little sense, therefore, to talk about *the* cause of tuberculosis. Exposure to a reasonably large dose of virulent organisms is a necessary causal factor but is rarely a sufficient cause in the absence of particular hereditary susceptibility to tuberculosis, depressed standards of living, and transitory lapses in general resistance to disease. In any given case, one particular factor may overshadow all others and thus provide a spurious appearance of single causality; but this neither guarantees that this same factor will be equally prominent in other cases nor excludes the operation of other factors in the same case. All we can say in this regard, is that if any one of the relevant causes is especially salient, the other contributory factors are less necessary to bring about the disease. If one individual, for example, by virtue of his heredity, happened to be highly susceptible to tuberculosis, whereas his neighbor happened to be highly resistant to this disease, the former would obviously succumb to a much smaller dose of tubercle bacilli than would be necessary to strike down the latter. It also follows that both the severity of the disease and the outlook for recovery would vary in accordance with the relative prominence of the various causal factors.

MULTIPLE CAUSALITY IN DRUG ADDICTION

The causal picture in drug addiction is quite analogous to that just described for tuberculosis. Availability of narcotics (that is, exposure to addicts and drug peddlers, or, in the case of physicians and others, even more direct access to the drug) is the *external precipitating* factor. No matter how great an individual's susceptibility, he obviously cannot become a drug addict unless he has regular access to narcotics. The factor of relative availability explains why the rate of addiction is so much higher in slum areas and among members of the medical and allied professions than in middle-class neighborhoods and among other occupational groups. To account for the higher Puerto Rican addiction rate in comparably exposed Negro and Puerto Rican sections of New York City's Harlem slum area,(3) and for the much higher addiction rate in China than in Japan,(4) one must invoke a major predisposing factor, also of environmental origin, namely, degree of community or cultural tolerance for the practice.

But *external* factors alone cannot explain all of the known facts about the incidence and distribution of drug addiction. In a given slum area of uniformly high exposure to and tolerance for the drug addiction habit, why is the practice limited to a relatively small minority of the residents, and why do male adolescents constitute such a disproportionately large percentage of the affected group? Why do some addicts originate in middle-class neighborhoods despite little exposure to narcotics and strong community disapproval of the habit? To explain these facts, we must turn to the important internal factor of differential susceptibility. In the same sense that individuals are not equally susceptible to tuberculosis, they are not equally susceptible to drug addiction.

TYPES OF ADDICTION

Maturational Deficiency

The most serious, and prognostically least hopeful, variety of drug addiction occurs among individuals who fail to undergo adult personality maturation, that is who fail to develop the long-term drives and corresponding motivational traits characteristic of normally mature adults in our society. Such motivationally immature persons are typically passive, dependent, irresponsible, lacking in perseverance and self-discipline, and preoccupied with achieving immediate, pleasurable self-gratification. They are unconcerned about marriage, raising a family, socially useful employment, vocational achievement, financial independence, and constructive service to the community.(5) The euphoria (objectively unwarranted feelings of ecstasy, well-being and self-confidence) induced by narcotics has uniquely efficient adjustive value for them. It provides immediate and effortless pleasure and dulls their self-critical faculties, thereby enabling them to feel supremely contented with their immature and inadequate adjustment to life's problems. Hence, since few other adjustive mechanisms are able to compete with drugs in attractiveness to persons possessing this type of personality structure, the disorder tends to be chronic, and the outlook for recovery is poor.

What are the sources of the motivational immaturity that constitutes the internal predisposing factor in drug addiction? Apart from hereditary proclivities toward such personality traits as passivity, self-indulgence, and excessive need for pleasurable self-gratification, the principal causes of motivational immaturity are particular kinds of unsatisfactory parent-child relationships. Considerations of space do not permit a full discussion of this topic. But examination of the kinds of relationships that drug addicts as children and adolescents have had with their parents reveals several typical patterns: (1) the extremely *overprotecting* parent, who shields the child from all independent experience and all possibility of failure so that he never gets the opportunity to set mature goals for himself or to act independently; (2) the extremely *underdominating* parent, who makes no demands on the child for mature behavior and leads him to believe that he is a specially privileged person whose needs will always be satisfied by others; and (3) the extremely *overdominating* parent, who imposes excessively high goals on the child, thereby inviting complete sabotage of the goals of adult maturation as soon as the child can escape from parental control.(6)

Reactive Addiction

Reactive addiction is the most common type of addiction found in the United States today, having increased spectacularly since the end of World War II. It is a transitory, developmental phenomenon, occurring principally among slum-dwelling adolescents with essentially normal personalities. The adjustive value of drugs for these individuals is simply that they provide an outlet both for the exaggerated rebelliousness and defiance of conventional norms (which is not uncommon among American adolescents generally), and for the particular aggressive attitudes associated with membership in an underprivileged and often ethnically stigmatized segment of the urban population. These precipitating internal factors are further compounded by such external factors as the ready availability of drugs, high community tolerance for addiction, and coercive pressures from addict associates in the closely-knit predatory gangs of the urban slum. Dabbling or experimenting with drugs has no unique adjustive value for the tensions and attitudes operative in this context. It is just one of many possible nonspecific ways of expressing aggression, hostility, nonconformity, and identification with deviant agemates. Like juvenile delinquency, therefore, this type of addiction gradually diminishes and is eventually discarded by most of the reactive drug users, with the approach of adult life, as normally mature family and vocational interests assert themselves and as adolescent identification with deviant norms correspondingly declines.

A difficult problem in differential diagnosis is posed by the fact that the motivationally immature type of addict is found most commonly (although by no means as exclusively as is the reactive type of addict) among adolescent and young adult males in urban slum areas. This is hardly surprising, when one considers that motivational immaturity is no more rare in such areas than elsewhere, and that the actual development of addiction in highly susceptible individuals is further abetted by adolescent stresses, gang influences, racial and social class tensions, social demoralization, high availability of narcotics, and high community tolerance for the drug habit. How then does one distinguish between these two basically different types of addicts, both of whom are often represented in the same gang?

Data collected by the Research Center for Human Relations of New York University(7) suggest several feasible criteria for differential diagnosis. Motivationally immature addicts tend to use narcotics more regularly, in larger quantities, and more for their adjustive values than "for kicks." They also tend to manifest more serious and deep-seated personality problems, to be peripheral rather than active members of delinquent gangs, and to participate more in the remunerative, criminal ventures of the gangs than in their athletic, heterosexual and gang warfare activities. Reactive users, on the other hand, are typically week-end "joy-poppers" who much more rarely take the drug regularly enough or in sufficient quantity to develop physical dependence. They are more likely to be delinquent before addiction, to come from the economically more depressed homes in the neighborhood, and to use drugs either to conform to age-mate standards or as just another nonspecific means of expressing antisocial attitudes. After the age of 18, the reactive drug user tends to abandon both his active, predatory gang interests and his casual use of drugs in favor of more mature, conventional concerns with vocation and family; but the motivationally immature habitual user retreats further from normal adult adjustment into drug-induced euphoria.

Miscellaneous Varieties of Drug Addiction

A relatively rare form of narcotic addiction is found sometimes among individuals suffering from neurotic anxiety and depression. These addicts, usually professional persons who have easy access to the drug, tend to use small, stabilized doses of opiates for the *sedative* rather than euphoric effects. Possessing strong achievement drives and normally mature motivational traits, they value the drug solely for its anxiety-reducing properties and for its ability to soften the unreasonably harsh and critical view that anxious and depressed individuals take of themselves. But since many other adjustive mechanisms (e.g., rationalization, compensation, delusion, fantasy, phobia, compulsion) are available, and since the barbiturates and tranquilizers are, in any case, both more efficient and legally accessible for the desired purposes, this type of addiction is becoming increasingly more rare. Drug addiction also occurs occasionally among certain vicious, remorseless criminals, the aggressive antisocial psychopaths, who use the addiction habit merely as a nonspecific means of expressing hostile and destructive personality trends.

SUMMARY

The addict's dependence on continued use of narcotics to avoid withdrawal symptoms is not a significant factor in causing drug addiction, even though the drug addict has been amazingly successful in deluding both himself and the American public into believing that it is the primary causal consideration. Physical dependence cannot account convincingly for the surplus dosage and intravenous route habitually taken by the confirmed addict, or for the latter's willingness to risk social ostracism and incarceration just to avoid a moderately severe 10-day illness. Neither does it adequately explain the recurrence of addiction long after physical dependence is lost, nor the strong addicting-potential of new opiate-like drugs which give rise to only minimal degrees of physical dependence, nor the ease with which normal persons are able to overcome the physical dependence on narcotics which they may inadvertently acquire during the course of prolonged illness. All of these facts suggest that susceptibility to drug addiction is variable rather than uniform, and that addicts use opiates primarily for their euphoric properties.

The causes of drug addiction are both multiple and additive in their impact. As in most other diseases, they include factors originating both within the person (internal) and within his environment (external), and each category in turn may be further divided into predisposing and precipitating causes. The major external and necessary precipitating factor is the ready availability of the drug, a factor which is reinforced by the predisposing environmental factor of high community or cultural tolerance for the practice. These external factors are sufficient to induce the disorder in individuals who are highly susceptible to addiction.

Susceptibility to drug addiction (the internal factor) is largely a reflection of the relatively great adjustive value which narcotic drugs possess for potential addicts. This adjustive value is most specific and efficient in the case of those individuals for whom the euphoric properties of opiates are most attractive. These are persons who manifest the internal predisposing factor (failure to develop the drives and motivational traits characteristic of normally mature persons in our society). This internal predisposing factor (motivational immaturity) is itself largely an outcome of particular kinds of unsatisfactory parent-child relationships, as well as partly a reflection of various temperamental traits of hereditary origin.

Susceptibility to drug addiction is less marked when the euphoric effects of opiates have less specific and efficient adjustive potential. This occurs when the susceptibility reflects internal precipitating factors of a more transitory nature, such as adolescent revolt against conventional norms, gang pressures, and attitudes associated with residence in a socially demoralized urban slum or membership in a racial minority group.

On the basis of the relative prominence of these various causal factors, it is both possible and diagnostically important to distinguish between two major and essentially different types of drug addicts. In instances where increased susceptibility to addiction is indicative of long-standing motivational immaturity (the internal predisposing factor), the highly specific and efficient adjustive value of the drug makes for a chronic type of disorder with a very poor prognosis. Where external causal factors are more prominent and internal factors are of a more temporary (precipitating) nature, the adjustive value of the drug is less specific and efficient, and the resulting (reactive) type of addiction accordingly tends to be a transitory aberration similar to juvenile delinquency. Both types of addiction, however, the motivationally immature as well as the reactive, are found most commonly among adolescent males in the urban slums. This is because motivational immaturity occurs just as frequently there as elsewhere, and because all of the other internal and external causal factors (the various developmental and social stresses, the high availability of the drug, the high community tolerance) tend to converge on teen-age boys who reside in such areas.

REFERENCES

1. WIKLER, A.: Opiate Addiction. P. 50. Thomas. Springfield, Ill. 1953.
2. PESCOR, M. J.: Follow-up study of treated narcotic drug addicts. Public Health Report, Supplement No. 170, 1943.
3. COMMITTEE ON PUBLIC HEALTH RELATIONS, New York Academy of Medicine: Conference on Drug Addiction among Adolescents. P. 64. Blakiston. New York. 1953.
4. MERRILL, F. T.: Japan and the Opium Menace. Institute of Pacific Relations, and the Foreign Policy Association. New York. 1942.
5. PESCOR, M. J.: A statistical analysis of the clinical records of hospitalized drug addicts. Public Health Report, Supplement No. 143, 1938.
6. AUSUBEL, D. P.: Drug Addiction: Physiological, Psychological and Sociological Aspects. Pp. 43–44. Random House. New York. 1958.
7. RESEARCH CENTER FOR HUMAN RELATIONS OF NEW YORK UNIVERSITY: Report No. II, Personal Background of Drug Users, Delinquents, and Controls. New York. 1957.

Becoming a Marihuana User*†

The use of marihuana is and has been the focus of a good deal of attention on the part of both scientists and laymen. One of the major problems students of the practice have addressed themselves to has been the identification of those individual psychological traits which differentiate marihuana users from nonusers and which are assumed to account for the use of the drug. That approach, common in the study of behavior categorized as deviant, is based on the premise that the presence of a given kind of behavior in an individual can best be explained as the result of some trait which predisposes or motivates him to engage in the behavior.[1]

This study is likewise concerned with accounting for the presence or absence of marihuana use in an individual's behavior. It starts, however, from a different premise: that the presence of a given kind of behavior is the result of a sequence of social experiences during which the person acquires a conception of the meaning of the behavior, and perceptions and judgments of objects and situations, all of which make the activity possible and desirable. Thus, the motivation or disposition to engage in the activity is built up in the course of learning to engage in it and does not antedate this learning process. For such a view it is not necessary to identify those "traits" which "cause" the behavior.

Instead, the problem becomes one of describing the set of changes in the person's conception of the activity and of the experience it provides for him.[2]

This paper seeks to describe the sequence of changes in attitude and experience which lead to the use of marihuana for pleasure. Marihuana does not produce addiction, as do alcohol and the opiate drugs; there is no withdrawal sickness and no ineradicable craving for the drug.[3] The most frequent pattern of use might be termed "recreational." The drug is used occasionally for the pleasure the user finds in it, a relatively casual kind of behavior in comparison with that connected with the use of addicting drugs. The term "use for pleasure" is meant to emphasize the noncompulsive and casual character of the behavior. It is also meant to eliminate from consideration here those few cases in which marihuana is used for its prestige value only, as a symbol that one is a certain kind of person, with no pleasure at all being derived from its use.

The analysis presented here is conceived of as demonstrating the greater explanatory usefulness of the kind of theory outlined above as opposed to the predispositional theories now current. This may be seen in two ways: (1) predispositional theories cannot account for that group of users (whose existence is admitted)[4] who do not exhibit the trait or traits considered to cause the behavior and (2) such theories cannot account for the great variability over time of a given individual's behavior with reference to the drug. The same person will at one stage be unable to use the drug for pleasure, at a later stage be able and willing to do so, and, still later, again be unable to use it in this way. These changes, difficult to explain from a predispositional or motivational theory, are readily understandable in terms

* Reprinted from American Journal of Sociology, Vol. 54, 1953, pp. 235–242, by permission of The University of Chicago Press. Copyright 1953 by The University of Chicago Press.
† Paper read at the meetings of the Midwest Sociological Society in Omaha, Nebraska, April 25, 1953. The research on which this paper is based was done while I was a member of the staff of the Chicago Narcotics Survey, a study done by the Chicago Area Project, Inc., under a grant from the National Mental Health Institute. My thanks to Solomon Kobrin, Harold Finestone, Henry McKay, and Anselm Strauss, who read and discussed with me earlier versions of this paper.
1 See, as examples of this approach, the following: Eli Marcovitz and Henry J. Meyers, "The Marihuana Addict in the Army," War Medicine, VI (December, 1944), 382–91; Herbert S. Gaskill, "Marihuana, an Intoxicant," American Journal of Psychiatry, CII (September, 1945), 202–4; Sol Charen and Luis Perelman, "Personality Studies of Marihuana Addicts," American Journal of Psychiatry, CII (March, 1946), 674–82.

2 This approach stems from George Herbert Mead's discussion of objects in Mind, Self, and Society (Chicago: University of Chicago Press, 1934), pp. 277–80.
3 Cf. Roger Adams, "Marihuana," Bulletin of the New York Academy of Medicine, XVIII (November, 1942), 705–30.
4 Cf. Lawrence Kolb, "Marihuana," Federal Probation, II (July, 1938), 22–25; and Walter Bromberg, "Marihuana: A Psychiatric Study," Journal of the American Medical Association, CXIII (July 1, 1939), 11.

of changes in the individual's conception of the drug as is the existence of "normal" users.

The study attempts to arrive at a general statement of the sequence of changes in individual attitude and experience which have always occurred when the individual has become willing and able to use marihuana for pleasure and which have not occurred or not been permanently maintained when this is not the case. This generalization is stated in universal terms in order that negative cases may be discovered and used to revise the explanatory hypothesis.[5]

Fifty interviews with marihuana users from a variety of social backgrounds and present positions in society constitute the data from which the generalization was constructed and against which it was tested.[6] The interviews focused on the history of the person's experience with the drug, seeking major changes in his attitude toward it and in his actual use of it and the reasons for these changes. The final generalization is a statement of that sequence of changes in attitude which occurred in every case known to me in which the person came to use marihuana for pleasure. Until a negative case is found, it may be considered as an explanation of all cases of marihuana use for pleasure. In addition, changes from use to nonuse are shown to be related to similar changes in conception, and in each case it is possible to explain variations in the individual's behavior in these terms.

This paper covers only a portion of the natural history of an individual's use of marihuana,[7] starting with the person having arrived at the point of willingness to try marihuana. He knows that others use it to "get high," but he does not know what this means in concrete terms. He is curious about the experience, ignorant of what it may turn out to be, and afraid that it may be more than he has bargained for. The steps outlined below, if he undergoes them all and maintains the attitudes developed in them, leave him willing and able to use the drug for pleasure when the opportunity presents itself.

[5] The method used is that described by Alfred R. Lindesmith in his *Opiate Addiction* (Bloomington: Principia Press, 1947), chap. i. I would like also to acknowledge the important role Lindesmith's work played in shaping my thinking about the genesis of marihuana use.

[6] Most of the interviews were done by the author. I am grateful to Solomon Kobrin and Harold Finestone for allowing me to make use of interviews done by them.

[7] I hope to discuss elsewhere other stages in this natural history.

I

The novice does not ordinarily get high the first time he smokes marihuana, and several attempts are usually necessary to induce this state. One explanation of this may be that the drug is not smoked "properly," that is, in a way that insures sufficient dosage to produce real symptoms of intoxication. Most users agree that it cannot be smoked like tobacco if one is to get high:

Take in a lot of air, you know, and . . . I don't know how to describe it, you don't smoke it like a cigarette, you draw in a lot of air and get it deep down in your system and then keep it there. Keep it there as long as you can.

Without the use of some such technique[8] the drug will produce no effects, and the user will be unable to get high:

The trouble with people like that [who are not able to get high] is that they're just not smoking it right, that's all there is to it. Either they're not holding it down long enough, or they're getting too much air and not enough smoke, or the other way around or something like that. A lot of people just don't smoke it right, so naturally nothing's gonna happen.

If nothing happens, it is manifestly impossible for the user to develop a conception of the drug as an object which can be used for pleasure, and use will therefore not continue. The first step in the sequence of events that must occur if the person is to become a user is that he must learn to use the proper smoking technique in order that his use of the drug will produce some effects in terms of which his conception of it can change.

Such a change is, as might be expected, a result of the individual's participation in groups in which marihuana is used. In them the individual learns the proper way to smoke the drug. This may occur through direct teaching:

I was smoking like I did an ordinary cigarette. He said, "No, don't do it like that." He said, "Suck it, you know, draw in and hold it in your lungs till you . . . for a period of time."
I said, "Is there any limit of time to hold it?"
He said, "No, just till you feel that you want to let it out, let it out." So I did that three or four times.

[8] A pharmacologist notes that this ritual is in fact an extremely efficient way of getting the drug into the blood stream (R. P. Walton, *Marihuana: America's New Drug Problem* [Philadelphia: J. B. Lippincott, 1938], p. 48).

Many new users are ashamed to admit ignorance and, pretending to know already, must learn through the more indirect means of observation and imitation:

> I came on like I had turned on [smoked marihuana] many times before, you know. I didn't want to seem like a punk to this cat. See, like I didn't know the first thing about it — how to smoke it, or what was going to happen, or what. I just watched him like a hawk — I didn't take my eyes off him for a second, because I wanted to do everything just as he did it. I watched how he held it, how he smoked it, and everything. Then when he gave it to me I just came on cool, as though I knew exactly what the score was. I held it like he did and took a poke just the way he did.

No person continued marihuana use for pleasure without learning a technique that supplied sufficient dosage for the effects of the drug to appear. Only when this was learned was it possible for a conception of the drug as an object which could be used for pleasure to emerge. Without such a conception marihuana use was considered meaningless and did not continue.

II

Even after he learns the proper smoking technique, the new user may not get high and thus not form a conception of the drug as something which can be used for pleasure. A remark made by a user suggested the reason for this difficulty in getting high and pointed to the next necessary step on the road to being a user:

> I was told during an interview, "As a matter of fact, I've seen a guy who was high out of his mind and didn't know it."
> I expressed disbelief: "How can that be, man?"
> The interviewee said, "Well, it's pretty strange, I'll grant you that, but I've seen it. This guy got on with me, claiming that he'd never got high, one of those guys, and he got completely stoned. And he kept insisting that he wasn't high. So I had to prove to him that he was."

What does this mean? It suggests that being high consists of two elements: the presence of symptoms caused by marihuana use and the recognition of these symptoms and their connection by the user with his use of the drug. It is not enough, that is, that the effects be present; they alone do not automatically provide the experience of being high. The user must be able to point them out to himself and consciously connect them with his hav-

ing smoked marihuana before he can have this experience. Otherwise, regardless of the actual effects produced, he considers that the drug has had no effect on him: "I figured it either had no effect on me or other people were exaggerating its effect on them, you know. I thought it was probably psychological, see." Such persons believe that the whole thing is an illusion and that the wish to be high leads the user to deceive himself into believing that something is happening when, in fact, nothing is. They do not continue marihuana use, feeling that "it does nothing" for them.

Typically, however, the novice has faith (developed from his observation of users who do get high) that the drug actually will produce some new experience and continues to experiment with it until it does. His failure to get high worries him, and he is likely to ask more experienced users or provoke comments from them about it. In such conversations he is made aware of specific details of his experience which he may not have noticed or may have noticed but failed to identify as symptoms of being high:

> I didn't get high the first time. . . . I don't think I held it in long enough. I probably let it out, you know, you're a little afraid. The second time I wasn't sure, and he [smoking companion] told me, like I asked him for some of the symptoms or something, how would I know, you know. . . . So he told me to sit on a stool. I sat on — I think I sat on a bar stool — and he said, "Let your feet hang," and then when I got down my feet were real cold, you know.
> And I started feeling it, you know. That was the first time. And then about a week after that, something pretty close to it, I really got on. That was the first time I got on a big laughing kick, you know. Then I really knew I was on.

One symptom of being high is an intense hunger. In the next case the novice becomes aware of this and gets high for the first time:

> They were just laughing the hell out of me because like I was eating so much. I just scoffed [ate] so much food, and they were just laughing at me, you know. Sometimes I'd be looking at them, you know, wondering why they're laughing, you know, not knowing what I was doing. [Well, did they tell you why they were laughing eventually?] Yeah, yeah, I come back, "Hey, man, what's happening?" Like, you know, like I'd ask, "What's happening?" and all of a sudden I feel weird, you know. "Man, you're on, you know. You're on pot [high on marihuana]." I said, "No, am I?" Like I don't know what's happening.

The learning may occur in more indirect ways:

> I heard little remarks that were made by other people. Somebody said, "My legs are rubbery," and I can't remember all the remarks that were made because I was very attentively listening for all these cues for what I was supposed to feel like.

The novice, then, eager to have this feeling, picks up from other users some concrete referents of the term "high" and applies these notions to his own experience. The new concepts make it possible for him to locate these symptoms among his own sensations and to point out to himself a "something different" in his experience that he connects with drug use. It is only when he can do this that he is high. In the next case, the contrast between two successive experiences of a user makes clear the crucial importance of the awareness of the symptoms in being high and re-emphasizes the important role of interaction with other users in acquiring the concepts that make this awareness possible:

> [Did you get high the first time you turned on?] Yeah, sure. Although, come to think of it, I guess I really didn't. I mean, like that first time it was more or less of a mild drunk. I was happy, I guess, you know what I mean. But I didn't really know I was high, you know what I mean. It was only after the second time I got high that I realized I was high the first time. Then I knew that something different was happening.
> [How did you know that?] How did I know? If what happened to me that night would of happened to you, you would've known, believe me. We played the first tune for almost two hours — one tune! Imagine, man! We got on the stand and played this one tune, we started at nine o'clock. When we got finished I looked at my watch, it's a quarter to eleven. Almost two hours on one tune. And it didn't seem like anything.
> I mean, you know, it does that to you. It's like you have much more time or something. Anyway, when I saw that, man, it was too much. I knew I must really be high or something if anything like that could happen. See, and then they explained to me that that's what it did to you, you had a different sense of time and everything. So I realized that that's what it was. I knew then. Like the first time, I probably felt that way, you know, but I didn't know what's happening.

It is only when the novice becomes able to get high in this sense that he will continue to use marihuana for pleasure. In every case in which use continued, the user had acquired the necessary concepts with which to express to himself the fact that he was experiencing new sensations caused by the drug.

That is, for use to continue, it is necessary not only to use the drug so as to produce effects but also to learn to perceive these effects when they occur. In this way marihuana acquires meaning for the user as an object which can be used for pleasure.

With increasing experience the user develops a greater appreciation of the drug's effects; he continues to learn to get high. He examines succeeding experiences closely, looking for new effects, making sure the old ones are still there. Out of this there grows a stable set of categories for experiencing the drug's effects whose presence enables the user to get high with ease.

The ability to perceive the drug's effects must be maintained if use is to continue; if it is lost, marihuana use ceases. Two kinds of evidence support this statement. First, people who become heavy users of alcohol, barbiturates, or opiates do not continue to smoke marihuana, largely because they lose the ability to distinguish between its effects and those of the other drugs.[9] They no longer know whether the marihuana gets them high. Second, in those few cases in which an individual uses marihuana in such quantities that he is always high, he is apt to get this same feeling that the drug has no effect on him, since the essential element of a noticeable difference between feeling high and feeling normal is missing. In such a situation, use is likely to be given up completely, but temporarily, in order that the user may once again be able to perceive the difference.

III

One more step is necessary if the user who has now learned to get high is to continue use. He must learn to enjoy the effects he has just learned to experience. Marihuana-produced sensations are not automatically or necessarily pleasurable. The taste for such experience is a socially acquired one, not different in kind from acquired tastes for oysters or dry martinis. The user feels dizzy, thirsty; his scalp tingles; he misjudges time and distances; and so on. Are these things pleasure? He isn't sure. If he is to continue marihuana use, he must decide that they are. Otherwise, getting high, while a real enough experience, will be an unpleasant one he would rather avoid.

9 "Smokers have repeatedly stated that the consumption of whiskey while smoking negates the potency of the drug. They find it very difficult to get 'high' while drinking whiskey and because of that smokers will not drink while using the 'weed'" (cf. New York City Mayor's Committee on Marihuana, *The Marihuana Problem in the City of New York* [Lancaster, Pa.: Jacques Cattell Press, 1944], p. 13).

The effects of the drug, when first perceived, may be physically unpleasant or at least ambiguous:

> It started taking effect, and I didn't know what was happening, you know, what it was, and I was very sick. I walked around the room, walking around the room trying to get off, you know; it just scared me at first, you know. I wasn't used to that kind of feeling.

In addition, the novice's naïve interpretation of what is happening to him may further confuse and frighten him, particularly if he decides, as many do, that he is going insane:

> I felt I was insane, you know. Everything people done to me just wigged me. I couldn't hold a conversation, and my mind would be wandering, and I was always thinking, oh, I don't know, weird things, like hearing music different. . . . I get the feeling that I can't talk to anyone. I'll goof completely.

Given these typically frightening and unpleasant first experiences, the beginner will not continue use unless he learns to redefine the sensations as pleasurable:

> It was offered to me, and I tried it. I'll tell you one thing. I never did enjoy it at all. I mean it was just nothing that I could enjoy. [Well, did you get high when you turned on?] Oh, yeah, I got definite feelings from it. But I didn't enjoy them. I mean I got plenty of reactions, but they were mostly reactions of fear. [You were frightened?] Yes. I didn't enjoy it. I couldn't seem to relax with it, you know. If you can't relax with a thing, you can't enjoy it, I don't think.

In other cases the first experiences were also definitely unpleasant, but the person did become a marihuana user. This occurred, however, only after a later experience enabled him to redefine the sensations as pleasurable:

> [This man's first experience was extremely unpleasant, involving distortion of spatial relationships and sounds, violent thirst, and panic produced by these symptoms.] After the first time I didn't turn on for about, I'd say, ten months to a year. . . . It wasn't a moral thing; it was because I'd gotten so frightened, bein' so high. An' I didn't want to go through that again, I mean, my reaction was, "Well, if this is what they call bein' high, I don't dig [like] it." . . . So I didn't turn on for a year almost, accounta that. . . .
> Well, my friends started, an' consequently I started again. But I didn't have any more, I didn't have that same initial reaction, after I started turning on again.

> [In interaction with his friends he became able to find pleasure in the effects of the drug and eventually became a regular user.]

In no case will use continue without such a redefinition of the effects as enjoyable.

This redefinition occurs, typically, in interaction with more experienced users who, in a number of ways, teach the novice to find pleasure in this experience which is at first so frightening.[10] They may reassure him as to the temporary character of the unpleasant sensations and minimize their seriousness, at the same time calling attention to the more enjoyable aspects. An experienced user describes how he handles newcomers to marihuana use:

> Well, they get pretty high sometimes. The average person isn't ready for that, and it is a little frightening to them sometimes. I mean, they've been high on lush [alcohol], and they get higher that way than they've ever been before, and they don't know what's happening to them. Because they think they're going to keep going up, up, up till they lose their minds or begin doing weird things or something. You have to like reassure them, explain to them that they're not really flipping or anything, that they're gonna be all right. You have to just talk them out of being afraid. Keep talking to them, reassuring, telling them it's all right. And come on with your own story, you know: "The same thing happened to me. You'll get to like that after awhile." Keep coming on like that; pretty soon you talk them out of being scared. And besides they see you doing it and nothing horrible is happening to you, so that gives them more confidence.

The more experienced user may also teach the novice to regulate the amount he smokes more carefully, so as to avoid any severely uncomfortable symptoms while retaining the pleasant ones. Finally, he teaches the new user that he can "get to like it after awhile." He teaches him to regard those ambiguous experiences formerly defined as unpleasant as enjoyable. The older user in the following incident is a person whose tastes have shifted in this way, and his remarks have the effect of helping others to make a similar redefinition:

> A new user had her first experience of the effects of marihuana and became frightened and hysterical. She "felt like she was half in and half out of the room" and experienced a number of alarming physical symptoms. One of the more experienced users present said, "She's dragged because she's high like that. I'd give anything to

---

[10] Charen and Perelman, *ob. cit.*, p. 679.

get that high myself. I haven't been that high in years."

In short, what was once frightening and distasteful becomes, after a taste for it is built up, pleasant, desired, and sought after. Enjoyment is introduced by the favorable definition of the experience that one acquires from others. Without this, use will not continue, for marihuana will not be for the user an object he can use for pleasure.

In addition to being a necessary step in becoming a user, this represents an important condition for continued use. It is quite common for experienced users suddenly to have an unpleasant or frightening experience, which they cannot define as pleasurable, either because they have used a larger amount of marihuana than usual or because it turns out to be a higher-quality marihuana than they expected. The user has sensations which go beyond any conception he has of what being high is and is in much the same situation as the novice, uncomfortable and frightened. He may blame it on an overdose and simply be more careful in the future. But he may make this the occasion for a rethinking of his attitude toward the drug and decide that it no longer can give him pleasure. When this occurs and is not followed by a redefinition of the drug as capable of producing pleasure, use will cease.

The likelihood of such a redefinition occurring depends on the degree of the individual's participation with other users. Where this participation is intensive, the individual is quickly talked out of his feeling against marihuana use. In the next case, on the other hand, the experience was very disturbing, and the aftermath of the incident cut the person's participation with other users to almost zero. Use stopped for three years and began again only when a combination of circumstances, important among which was a resumption of ties with users, made possible a redefinition of the nature of the drug:

It was too much, like I only made about four pokes, and I couldn't even get it out of my mouth, I was so high, and I got real flipped. In the basement, you know, I just couldn't stay in there anymore. My heart was pounding real hard, you know, and I was going out of my mind; I thought I was losing my mind completely. So I cut out of this basement, and this other guy, he's out of his mind, told me, "Don't, don't leave me, man. Stay here." And I couldn't.

I walked outside, and it was five below zero, and I thought I was dying, and I had my coat open; I was sweating, I was perspiring. My whole insides were all . . . , and I walked about two

blocks away, and I fainted behind a bush. I don't know how long I laid there. I woke up, and I was feeling the worst, I can't describe it at all, so I made it to a bowling alley, man, and I was trying to act normal, I was trying to shoot pool, you know, trying to act real normal, and I couldn't lay and I couldn't stand up and I couldn't sit down, and I went up and laid down where some guys that spot pins lay down, and that didn't help me, and I went down to a doctor's office. I was going to go in there and tell the doctor to put me out of my misery . . . because my heart was pounding so hard, you know. . . . So then all week end I started flipping, seeing things there and going through hell, you know, all kinds of abnormal things. . . . I just quit for a long time then.

[He went to a doctor who defined the symptoms for him as those of a nervous breakdown caused by "nerves" and "worries." Although he was no longer using marihuana, he had some recurrences of the symptoms which led him to suspect that "it was all his nerves."] So I just stopped worrying, you know; so it was about thirty-six months later I started making it again. I'd just take a few pokes, you know. [He first resumed use in the company of the same user-friend with whom he had been involved in the original incident.]

A person, then, cannot begin to use marihuana for pleasure, or continue its use for pleasure, unless he learns to define its effects as enjoyable, unless it becomes and remains an object which he conceives of as capable of producing pleasure.

IV

In summary, an individual will be able to use marihuana for pleasure only when he goes through a process of learning to conceive of it as an object which can be used in this way. No one becomes a user without (1) learning to smoke the drug in a way which will produce real effects; (2) learning to recognize the effects and connect them with drug use (learning, in other words, to get high); and (3) learning to enjoy the sensations he perceives. In the course of this process he develops a disposition or motivation to use marihuana which was not and could not have been present when he began use, for it involves and depends on conceptions of the drug which could only grow out of the kind of actual experience detailed above. On completion of this process he is willing and able to use marihuana for pleasure.

He has learned, in short, to answer "Yes" to the question: "Is it fun?" The direction his further use of the drug takes depends on his being able to continue to answer "Yes" to this question and, in addition, on his being able to answer "Yes" to other questions which arise as he becomes aware of the implications of the fact that the society as a whole disapproves of the practice: "Is it expedient?" "Is it moral?"[11] Once he has acquired the ability to get enjoyment out of the drug, use will continue to be possible for him. Considerations of morality and expediency, occasioned by the reactions of society, may interfere and inhibit use, but use continues to be a possibility in terms of his conception of the drug. The act becomes impossible only when the ability to enjoy the experience of being high is lost, through a change in the user's conception of the drug occasioned by certain kinds of experience with it.

In comparing this theory with those which ascribe marihuana use to motives or predispositions rooted deep in individual behavior, the evidence makes it clear that marihuana use for pleasure can occur only when the process described above is undergone and cannot occur without it. This is apparently so without reference to the nature of the individual's personal makeup or psychic problems. Such theories

[11] Another paper will discuss the series of developments in attitude that occurs as the individual begins to take account of these matters and adjust his use to them.

assume that people have stable modes of response which predetermine the way they will act in relation to any particular situation or object and that, when they come in contact with the given object or situation, they act in the way in which their makeup predisposes them.

This analysis of the genesis of marihuana use shows that the individuals who come in contact with a given object may respond to it at first in a great variety of ways. If a stable form of new behavior toward the object is to emerge, a transformation of meanings must occur, in which the person develops a new conception of the nature of the object. This happens in a series of communicative acts in which others point out new aspects of his experience to him, present him with new interpretations of events, and help him achieve a new conceptual organization of his world, without which the new behavior is not possible. Persons who do not achieve the proper kind of conceptualization are unable to engage in the given behavior and turn off in the direction of some other relationship to the object or activity.

This suggests that behavior of any kind might fruitfully be studied developmentally in terms of changes in meanings and concepts, their organization and reorganization and the way they channel behavior, making some acts possible while excluding others.

JOAN K. JACKSON

The Adjustment of the Family to the Crisis of Alcoholism*[1]

I. INTRODUCTION

Although the subjects *families under stress and alcoholism* have both received increased attention from sociologists in recent years, very little has appeared on the families of alcoholics. Standard

* Reproduced by permission from the *Quarterly Journal of Studies on Alcohol*, Vol. 15, pp. 562–586, 1954. Copyright 1954 by Journal of Studies on Alcohol, Inc., New Brunswick, N.J.
[1] From the Department of Psychiatry, University of Washington School of Medicine, Seattle, Washington.

textbooks on the family devote a few pages or a chapter to "the disgraced family" and, in passing, comment that one type of disgraced family is that of the alcoholic. In a few books dealing with alcoholism, the family's problems are recognized and advice is offered to its members on how to treat the alcoholic. But there is little information on

This report is part of an alcoholism project at the University of Washington which has been supported by the State of Washington Research Fund under Initiative 171.

the effect of alcoholism on the division of labor within the family, on the interaction patterns, on the family's integration, on the roles of family members, or on the ongoing functions of the family.

Mowrer (1), based on case studies of alcoholics and their wives, and of controls, stated that the status of the male alcoholic in marriage becomes inferior to that of his wife. Sexual relationships are unsatisfactory due to the inadequacies of both partners. In the conclusion, there is a suggestion that family attitudes towards alcoholics are direct resultants of the alcoholism.

Bacon (2) suggested that although on the whole "excessive drinking and factors in personality leading to excessive drinking tend to preclude or debar marriage," some of those alcoholics who do marry become excessively dependent on their wives. Baker (3) noted that treatment of the wife is often as important as treatment of the inebriate. She also mentioned the personality disturbances frequently found in children of alcoholics.

A few articles have dealt with the wives of alcoholics from a psychological viewpoint. Futterman (4) concluded that there is much clinical evidence to suggest that the wife "unconsciously, because of her own needs, seems to encourage her husband's alcoholism." He suggested that when the husband becomes sober the wife often decompensates and begins to show symptoms of neurotic disturbance. Whalen (5) and Price (6) substantially agree that the wife contributes to the alcoholism of the husband and shows personality difficulties. Whalen delineates four types of personalities common to wives of alcoholics. She goes further than Futterman, suggesting that certain types of women marry alcoholics in order to satisfy deep, unconscious needs. Price found wives of alcoholics to be nervous, hostile, basically dependent people, although on the surface they appeared to be adequate. They were unable to cope with the drinking by their husbands and accepted no responsibility for it. The wife at the time of her marriage was depicted as an insecure person who expected her husband to be a strong, dependable, responsible person.[2]

None of the studies deals with the way in which the family as a unit attempts to adjust to an alcoholic parent. None views these adjustments on a time continuum.

[2] It may be noted that this is the culturally prevalent expectation of a husband by women in American society. This may be evidence that most American women are dependent but, if so, dependency loses its relevance to the problem of selecting or adjusting to an alcoholic spouse.

The studies of the wives of alcoholics impute psychological traits to the wife, as judged from her behavior after her husband has reached an advanced stage of alcoholism, and posit that these psychological traits would have been found prior to the onset of drinking. None of the articles conceptualizes the behavior of the wife, or the personality traits inferred from this behavior, as a reaction to a cumulative crisis in which the wife experiences progressively more stress.

These articles imply or state directly that the wife is responsible for some of her husband's drinking and, because of her own unconscious personality needs, encourages his excessive drinking. The reasoning seems to be somewhat as follows: The wife takes some kind of action; the husband soon thereafter resumes drinking. A causal connection is assumed to exist between the two events, and this assumption may receive further reinforcement when the husband states that this action was the reason why he drank. As the wife's behavior (from the viewpoint of an observer) was dysfunctional in achieving her consciously stated ends, and as she may persist in this behavior over a period of time, it is assumed that she is driven to act in this manner by an unconscious need to have her husband drink. These conceptions raise several problems. (1) There is no evidence that the husband drank because of this or any other form of action on the part of his wife. Nor is there any evidence that if the wife had not taken this action he would not have resumed his drinking. To make a causal connection between the behavior of the wife and the drinking of her husband requires that we know why alcoholics drink excessively, and can specify the type of behavior or other personal relationships, which will precipitate or minimize drinking episodes. Our present verified knowledge of alcoholism does not include this information. (2) Before a conclusion can be reached that the wife has an unconscious need to have her husband continue to drink, we must be able to demonstrate that if she were given information on how to terminate the drinking, she would not or could not make use of this information. Again, knowledge of the appropriate behavior which would lead to the end of drinking is lacking, both to the wife who consciously wishes to have a sober husband, and to those who attempt to advise her. The question of unconscious needs will thus remain in the realm of theory until knowledge of alcoholism expands sufficiently to permit a test of this hypothesis. Alternate hypotheses might be: (a) that some of the wife's behavior has a more immediate motivation, that is, that it serves to release situationally induced tension, and that such behavior is followed only incidentally by more drinking by the husband; (*b*) that some of the wife's behavior is intended to stabilize the family and that, in so doing, it precipitates a situation which leads to further drinking by the husband. When viewed in the context of what is best for the husband, such behavior might be judged as dysfunctional; viewed in the context of the rest of the family, it might appear to be functional.

Sources of Data

Over a 3-year period, the present investigator has been an active participant in the Alcoholics Anonymous Auxiliary in Seattle. This group is composed partly of women whose husbands are or were members of Alcoholics Anonymous, and partly of women whose husbands are excessive drinkers but have never contacted Alcoholics Anonymous. At a typical meeting one fifth would be the wives of Alcoholics Anonymous members who have been sober for some time; the husbands of another fifth would have recently joined the fellowship; the remainder would be equally divided between those whose husbands were "on and off" the Alcoholics Anonymous program and those whose husbands had as yet not had any contact with Alcoholics Anonymous.

At least an hour and a half of each formal meeting of this group is taken up with a frank discussion of the current family problems of the members. As in other meetings of Alcoholics Anonymous the questions are posed by describing the situation which gives rise to the problem and the answers are a narration of the personal experiences of other wives who have had a similar problem, rather than direct advice. Verbatim shorthand notes have been taken of all discussions, at the request of the group, who also make use of the notes for the group's purposes. Informal contact has been maintained with past and present members. In the past 3 years 50 women have been members of this group.

The families represented by these women are at present in many different stages of adjustment and have passed through several stages during the past few years. The continuous contact over a prolonged period permits generalizations about processes and changes in family adjustments.

In addition, in connection with research on hospitalized alcoholics, many of their wives have been interviewed. The interviews with the hospitalized alcoholics, as well as with male members of Alcoholics Anonymous, have also provided information on family interactions. Further information has been derived from another group of wives, not connected with Alcoholics Anonymous, and from probation officers, social workers and court officials.

The following presentation is limited insofar as it deals only with families seeking help for the alcoholism of the husband. Other families are known to have solved the problem through divorce, often without having attempted to help the alcoholic member first. Others never seek help and never separate. There were no marked differences between the two groups seeking help, one through the hospital and one through the A.A. Auxiliary. The wives of hospitalized alcoholics gave a history of the family crisis similar to that given by women in the Auxiliary.

A second limitation is that only the families of male alcoholics are dealt with. It is recognized that the findings cannot be generalized to the families of alcoholic women without further research. Due to differences between men and women in their roles in the family as well as in the pattern of drinking, it would be expected that male and female alcoholics would in some ways have a different effect on family structure and function.

A third limitation is imposed for the sake of clarity and brevity: only the accounts of the wives of their attempts to stabilize their family adjustments will be dealt with. For any complete picture, the view of the alcoholic husband would also have to be included.

It must be emphasized that this paper deals with the definitions of the family situations by the wives, rather than with the actual situation. It has been noted that frequently wife and husband do not agree on what has occurred. The degree to which the definition of the situation by the wife or husband correlates with actual behavior is a question which must be left for further research.

The families represented in this study are from the middle and lower classes. The occupations of the husbands prior to excessive drinking include small business owners, salesmen, business executives, skilled and semiskilled workers. Prior to marriage the wives have been nurses, secretaries, teachers, saleswomen, cooks or waitresses. The economic status of the childhood families of these husbands and wives ranged from very wealthy to very poor.

Method

From the records of discussions of the Alcoholics Anonymous Auxiliary, the statements of each wife were extracted and arranged in a time sequence. Notes on informal contacts were added at the point in the sequence where they occurred. The interviews with the wives of hospitalized alcoholics were similarly treated. These working records on individual families were then examined for uniformities of behavior and for regularities in changes over time.

The similarities in the process of adjustment to an alcoholic family member are presented here as stages of variable duration. It should be stressed that only the similarities are dealt with. Although the wives have shared the patterns dealt with here, there have been marked differences in the length of time between stages, in the number of stages passed through up to the present time, and in the relative importance to the family constellation of any one type of behavior. For example, all admitted nagging but the amount of nagging was variable.

When the report of this analysis was completed it was read before a meeting of the Auxiliary with a request for correction of any errors in fact or interpretation. Corrections could be presented either anonymously or publicly from the floor. Only one correction was suggested and has been incorporated. The investigator is convinced that her relationship wih the group is such that there would be no reticence about offering corrections. Throughout her contact with this group her role has been that of one who is being taught, very similar to the role of the new member. The over-all response of the group to the presentation indicated that the members individually felt that they had been portrayed accurately.

The sense of having similar problems and similar experiences is indicated also in the reactions of new members to the Auxiliary's summarization of the notes of their discussions. Copies of these summaries are given to new members, who commonly state that they find it a relief to see that their problems are far from unique and that there are methods which successfully overcome them.

Statement of the Problem

For purposes of this presentation, the family is seen as involved in a cumulative crisis. All family members behave in a manner which they hope will resolve the crisis and permit a return to stability. Each member's action is influenced by his previous personality structure, by his previous role and status in the family group, and by the history of the crisis and its effects on his personality, roles and status up to that point. Action is also influenced by the past effectiveness of that particular action as a means of social control before and during the crisis. The behavior of family members in each phase of the crisis contributes to the form which the crisis takes in the following stages and sets limits on possible behavior in subsequent stages.

Family members are influenced, in addition, by the cultural definitions of alcoholism as evidence of weakness, inadequacy or sinfulness; by the cultural prescriptions for the roles of family members; and by the cultural values of family solidarity, sanctity and self-sufficiency. Alcoholism in the family poses a situation defined by the culture as shameful but for the handling of which there are no prescriptions which are effective or which permit direct action not in conflict with other cultural prescriptions. While in crises such as illness or death the family members can draw on cultural definitions of appropriate behavior for procedures which will terminate the crisis, this is not the case with alcoholism in the family. The cultural view has been that alcoholism is shameful and should not occur. Only recently has any information been offered to guide families in their behavior toward their alcoholic member and, as yet, this information resides more in technical journals than in the media of mass communication. Thus, in facing alcoholism, the family is in an unstructured situation and must find the techniques for handling it through trial and error.

II. STAGES IN FAMILY ADJUSTMENT TO AN ALCOHOLIC MEMBER

The Beginning of the Marriage

At the time marriage was considered, the drinking of most of the men was within socially acceptable limits. In a few cases the men were already alcoholics but managed to hide this from their fiancées. They drank only moderately or not at all when on dates and often avoided friends and relatives who might expose their excessive drinking. The relatives and friends who were introduced to the fiancée were those who had hopes that "marriage would straighten him out" and thus said nothing about the drinking. In a small number of cases the men spoke with their fiancées of their alcoholism. The women had no conception of what alcoholism meant, other than that it involved more than the usual frequency of drinking, and they entered the marriage with little more preparation than if they had known nothing about it.

Stage 1 — Incidents of excessive drinking begin and, although they are sporadic, place strains on the husband–wife interaction. In attempts to minimize drinking, problems in marital adjustment not related to the drinking are avoided.

Stage 2 — Social isolation of the family begins as incidents of excessive drinking multiply. The increasing isolation magnifies the importance of family interactions and events. Behavior and thought become drinking-centered. Husband–wife adjustment deteriorates and tension rises. The wife begins to feel self-pity and to lose her self-confidence as her behavior fails to stabilize her husband's drinking. There is an attempt still to maintain the original family structure, which is disrupted anew with each episode of drinking, and as a result the children begin to show emotional disturbance.

Stage 3 — The family gives up attempts to control the drinking and begins to behave in a manner geared to relieve tension rather than achieve long-term ends. The disturbance of the children becomes more marked. There is no longer an attempt to support the alcoholic in his roles as husband and father. The wife begins to worry about her own sanity and about her inability to make decisions or act to change the situation.

Stage 4 — The wife takes over control of the family and the husband is seen as a recalcitrant child. Pity and strong protective feelings largely replace the earlier resentment and hostility. The family becomes more stable and organized in a manner to minimize the disruptive behavior of the husband. The self-confidence of the wife begins to be rebuilt.

Stage 5 — The wife separates from her husband if she can resolve the problems and conflicts surrounding this action.

Stage 6 — The wife and children reorganize as a family without the husband.

Stage 7 — The husband achieves sobriety and the family, which had become organized around an alcoholic husband, reorganizes to include a sober father and experiences problems in reinstating him in his former roles.

Stage 1. Attempts to Deny the Problem

Usually the first experience with drinking as a problem arises in a social situation. The husband drinks in a manner which is inappropriate to the social setting and the expectations of others present. The wife feels embarrassed on the first occasion and humiliated as it occurs more frequently. After several such incidents she and her husband talk over his behavior. The husband either formulates an explanation for the episode and assures her that such behavior will not occur again, or he refuses to discuss it at all. For a time afterward he drinks appropriately and drinking seems to be a problem no longer. The wife looks back on the incidents and feels that she has exaggerated them, feels ashamed of herself for her disloyalty and for her behavior. The husband, in evaluating the incident, feels shame also and vows such episodes will not recur. As a result, both husband and wife attempt to make it up to the other and, for a time, try to play their conceptions of the ideal husband and wife roles, minimizing or avoiding other difficulties which arise

in the marriage. They thus create the illusion of a "perfect" marriage.

Eventually another inappropriate drinking episode occurs and the pattern is repeated. The wife worries but takes action only in the situations in which inappropriate drinking occurs, as each long intervening period of acceptable drinking behavior convinces her that a recurrence is unlikely. As time goes on, in attempting to cope with individual episodes, she runs the gamut of possible trial and error behaviors, learning that none is permanently effective.

If she speaks to other people about her husband's drinking, she is usually assured that there is no need for concern, that her husband can control his drinking and that her fears are exaggerated. Some friends possibly admit that his drinking is too heavy and give advice on how they handled similar situations with their husbands. These friends convince her that her problem will be solved as soon as she hits upon the right formula for dealing with her husband's drinking.

During this stage the husband–wife interaction is in no way "abnormal." In a society in which a large proportion of the men drink, most wives have at some time had occasion to be concerned, even though only briefly, with an episode of drinking which they considered inappropriate (7). In a society in which the status of the family depends on that of the husband, the wife feels threatened by any behavior on his part which might lower it. Inappropriate drinking is regarded by her as a threat to the family's reputation and standing in the community. The wife attempts to exert control and often finds herself blocked by the sacredness of drinking behavior to men in America. Drinking is a private matter and not any business of the wife's. On the whole, a man reacts to his wife's suggestion that he has not adequately controlled his drinking with resentment, rebelliousness and a display of emotion which makes rational discussion difficult. The type of husband–wife interaction outlined in this stage has occurred in many American families in which the husband never became an excessive drinker.

Stage 2. Attempts to Eliminate the Problems

Stage 2 begins when the family experiences social isolation because of the husband's drinking. Invitations to the homes of friends become less frequent. When the couple does visit friends, drinks are not served or are limited, thus emphasizing the reason for exclusion from other social activities of the friendship group. Discussions of drinking begin to be sidestepped awkwardly by friends, the wife and the husband.

By this time the periods of socially acceptable drinking are becoming shorter. The wife, fearing that the full extent of her husband's drinking will become known, begins to withdraw from social participation, hoping to reduce the visibility of his behavior, and thus the threat to family status.

Isolation is further intensified because the family usually acts in accordance with the cultural dictate that it should be self-sufficient and manage to resolve its own problems without recourse to outside aid. Any experiences which they have had with well-meaning outsiders, usually relatives, have tended to strengthen this conviction. The husband has defined such relatives as interfering and the situation has deteriorated rather than improved.

With increasing isolation, the family members begin to lose perspective on their interaction and on their problems. Thrown into closer contact with one another as outside contacts diminish, the behavior of each member assumes exaggerated importance. The drinking behavior becomes the focus of anxiety. Gradually all family difficulties become attributed to it. (For example, the mother who is cross with her children will feel that, if her husband had not been drinking, she would not have been so tense and would not have been angry.) The fear that the full extent of drinking may be discovered mounts steadily; the conceptualization of the consequences of such a discovery becomes increasingly vague and, as a result, more anxiety-provoking. The family feels different from others and alone with its shameful secret.

Attempts to cover up increase. The employer who calls to inquire about the huband's absence from work is given excuses. The wife is afraid to face the consequences of loss of the husband's pay check in addition to her other concerns. Questions from the children are evaded or they are told that their father is ill. The wife lives in terror of the day when the children will be told by others of the nature of the "illness." She is also afraid that the children may describe their father's symptoms to teachers or neighbors. Still feeling that the family must solve its own problems, she keeps her troubles to herself and hesitates to seek outside help. If her husband beats her, she will bear it rather than call in the police. (Indeed, often she has no idea that this is even a possibility.) Her increased isolation has left her without the advice of others as to sources of help in the community. If she knows of them, an agency contact means to her an admission of the complete failure of her family as an inde-

pendent unit. For the middle-class woman particularly, recourse to social agencies and law-enforcement agencies means a terrifying admission of loss of status.

During this stage, husband and wife are drawing further apart. Each feels resentful of the behavior of the other. When this resentment is expressed, further drinking occurs. When it is not, tension mounts and the next drinking episode is that much more destructive of family relationships. The reasons for drinking are explored frantically. Both husband and wife feel that if only they could discover the reason, all members of the family could gear their behavior to making drinking unnecessary. The discussions become increasingly unproductive, as it is the husband's growing conviction that his wife does not and cannot understand him.

On her part, the wife begins to feel that she is a failure, that she has been unable to fulfill the major cultural obligations of a wife to meet her husband's needs. With her increasing isolation, her sense of worth derives almost entirely from her roles as wife and mother. Each failure to help her husband gnaws away at her sense of adequacy as a person.

Periods of sobriety or socially acceptable drinking still occur. These periods keep the wife from making a permanent or stable adjustment. During them her husband, in his guilt, treats her like a queen. His behavior renews her hope and rekindles positive feelings toward him. Her sense of worth is bolstered temporarily and she grasps desperately at her husband's reassurance that she is really a fine person and not a failure and an unlovable shrew. The periods of sobriety also keep her family from facing the inability of the husband to control his drinking. The inaccuracies of the cultural stereotype of the alcoholic — particularly that he is in a constant state of inebriation — also contribute to the family's rejection of the idea of alcoholism, as the husband seems to demonstrate from time to time that he can control his drinking.

Family efforts to control the husband become desperate. There are no culturally prescribed behavior patterns for handling such a situation and the family is forced to evolve its own techniques. Many different types of behavior are tried but none brings consistent results; there seems to be no way of predicting the consequences of any action that may be taken. All attempts to stabilize or structure the situation to permit consistent behavior fail. Threats of leaving, hiding his liquor away, emptying the bottles down the drain, curtailing his money, are tried in rapid succession, but none is effective. Less punitive methods, as discussing the situation when he is sober, babying him during hangovers, and trying to drink with him to keep him in the home, are attempted and fail. All behavior becomes oriented around the drinking, and the thought of family members becomes obsessive on this subject. As no action seems to be successful in achieving its goal, the wife persists in trial-and-error behavior with mounting frustration. Long-term goals recede into the background and become secondary to just keeping the husband from drinking today.

There is still an attempt to maintain the illusion of husband–wife–children roles. When father is sober, the children are expected to give him respect and obedience. The wife also defers to him in his role as head of the household. Each drinking event thus disrupts family functioning anew. The children begin to show emotional disturbances as a result of the inconsistencies of parental behavior. During periods when the husband is drinking the wife tries to shield them from the knowledge and effects of his behavior, at the same time drawing them closer to herself and deriving emotional support from them. In sober periods, the father tries to regain their favor. Due to experiencing directly only pleasant interactions with their father, considerable affection is often felt for him by the children. This affection becomes increasingly difficult for the isolated wife to tolerate, and an additional source of conflict. She feels that she needs and deserves the love and support of her children and, at the same time, she feels it important to maintain the children's picture of their father. She counts on the husband's affection for the children to motivate a cessation of drinking as he comes to realize the effects of his behavior on them.

In this stage, self-pity begins to be felt by the wife, if it has not entered previously. It continues in various degrees throughout the succeeding stages. In an attempt to handle her deepening sense of inadequacy, the wife often tries to convince herself that she is right and her husband wrong, and this also continues through the following stages. At this point the wife often resembles what Whalen (5) describes as "The Sufferer."

Stage 3. Disorganization

The wife begins to adopt a "What's the use?" attitude and to accept her husband's drinking as a problem likely to be permanent. Attempts to understand one another become less frequent. Sober periods still engender hope, but hope qualified by

skepticism; they bring about a lessening of anxiety and this is defined as happiness.

By this time some customary patterns of husband–wife–children interaction have evolved. Techniques which have had some effectiveness in controlling the husband in the past or in relieving pent-up frustration are used by the wife. She nags, berates or retreats into silence. Husband and wife are both on the alert, the wife watching for increasing irritability and restlessness which mean a recurrence of drinking, and the husband for veiled aspersions on his behavior or character.

The children are increasingly torn in their loyalties as they become tools in the struggle between mother and father. If the children are at an age of comprehension, they have usually learned the true nature of their family situation, either from outsiders or from their mother, who has given up attempts to bolster her husband's position as father. The children are often bewildered but questioning their parents brings no satisfactory answers as the parents themselves do not understand what is happening. Some children become terrified; some have increasing behavior problems within and outside the home; others seem on the surface to accept the situation calmly.[3]

During periods of the husband's drinking, the hostility, resentment and frustrations felt by the couple is allowed expression. Both may resort to violence — the wife in self-defense or because she can find no other outlet for her feelings. In those cases in which the wife retaliates to violence in kind, she feels a mixture of relief and intense shame at having deviated so far from what she conceives to be "the behavior of a normal woman."

When the wife looks at her present behavior, she worries about her "normality." In comparing the person she was in the early years of her marriage with the person she has become, she is frightened. She finds herself nagging and unable to control herself. She resolves to stand up to her husband when he is belligerent but instead finds herself cringing in terror and then despises herself for her lack of courage. If she retaliates with violence, she is filled with self-loathing at behaving in an "unwomanly" manner. She finds herself compulsively searching for bottles, knowing full well that finding them will change nothing, and is worried because she engages in such senseless behavior. She worries about her inability to take con-

---

[3] Some effects of alcoholism of the father on children have been discussed by Newell (8).

structive action of any kind. She is confused about where her loyalty lies, whether with her husband or her children. She feels she is a failure as a wife, mother and person. She believes she should be strong in the face of adversity and instead feels herself weak.

The wife begins to find herself avoiding sexual contact with her husband when he has been drinking. Sex under these circumstances, she feels, is sex for its own sake rather than an indication of affection for her. Her husband's lack of consideration of her needs to be satisfied leaves her feeling frustrated. The lack of sexual responsiveness reflects her emotional withdrawal from him in other areas of family life. Her husband, on his part, feels frustrated and rejected; he accuses her of frigidity and this adds to her concern about her adequacy as a woman.[4]

By this time the opening wedge has been inserted into the self-sufficiency of the family. The husband has often been in difficulty with the police and the wife has learned that police protection is available. An emergency has occurred in which the seeking of outside help was the only possible action to take; subsequent calls for aid from outsiders do not require the same degree of urgency before they can be undertaken. However, guilt and a lessening of self-respect and self-confidence accompany this method of resolving emergencies. The husband intensifies these feelings by speaking of the interference of outsiders, or of his night in jail.

In Stage 3 all is chaos. Few problems are met constructively. The husband and wife both feel trapped in an intolerable, unstructured situation which offers no way out. The wife's self-assurance is almost completely gone. She is afraid to take action and afraid to let things remain as they are. Fear is one of the major characteristics of this stage: fear of violence, fear of personality damage to the children, fear for her own sanity, fear that relatives will interfere, and fear that they will not help in an emergency. Added to this, the family feels alone in the world and helpless. The problems, and the

---

[4] It is of interest here that marriage counselors and students of marital adjustment are of the opinion that unhappy marriage results in poor sexual adjustment more often than poor sexual adjustment leads to unhappy marriage. If this proves to be true, it would be expected that most wives of alcoholics would find sex distasteful while their husbands are drinking. The wives of the inactive alcoholics report that their sexual adjustments with their husbands are currently satisfactory; many of those whose husbands are still drinking state that they enjoyed sexual relationships before the alcoholism was established.

behavior of family members in attempting to cope with them, seem so shameful that help from others is unthinkable. They feel that attempts to get help would meet only with rebuff, and that communication of the situation will engender disgust.

At this point the clinical picture which the wife presents is very similar to what Whalen (5) has described as "The Waverer."

Stage 4. Attempts to Reorganize in Spite of the Problems

Stage 4 begins when a crisis occurs which necessitates that action be taken. There may be no money or food in the house; the husband may have been violent to the children; or life on the level of Stage 3 may have become intolerable. At this point some wives leave, thus entering directly into Stage 5.

The wife who passes through Stage 4 usually begins to ease her husband out of his family roles. She assumes husband and father roles. This involves strengthening her role as mother and putting aside her role as wife. She becomes the manager of the home, the discipliner of the children, the decision-maker; she becomes somewhat like Whalen's (5) "Controller." She either ignores her husband as much as possible or treats him as her most recalcitrant child. Techniques are worked out for getting control of his pay check, if there still is one, and money is doled out to her husband on the condition of his good behavior. When he drinks, she threatens to leave him, locks him out of the house, refuses to pay his taxi bills, leaves him in jail overnight rather than pay his bail. Where her obligations to her husband conflict with those to her children, she decides in favor of the latter. As she views her husband increasingly as a child, pity and a sense of being desperately needed by him enter. Her inconsistent behavior toward him, deriving from the lack of predictability inherent in the situation up to now, becomes reinforced by her mixed feelings toward him.

In this stage the husband often tries to set his will against hers in decisions about the children. If the children have been permitted to stay with a friend overnight, he may threaten to create a scene unless they return immediately. He may make almost desperate efforts to gain their affection and respect, his behavior ranging from getting them up in the middle of the night to fondle them, to giving them stiff lectures on children's obligations to fathers. Sometimes he will attempt to align the males of the family with him against the females.

He may openly express resentment of the children and become belligerent toward them physically or verbally.

Much of the husband's behavior can be conceptualized as resulting from an increasing awareness of his isolation from the other members of the family and their steady withdrawal of respect and affection. It seems to be a desperate effort to regain what he has lost, but without any clear idea of how this can be accomplished — an effort to change a situation in which everyone is seen as against him; and, in reality, this is becoming more and more true. As the wife has taken over control of the family with some degree of success, he feels, and becomes, less and less necessary to the ongoing activity of the family. There are fewer and fewer roles left for him to play. He becomes aware that members of the family enjoy each other's company without him. When he is home he tries to enter this circle of warmth or to smash it. Either way he isolates himself further. He finds that the children discuss with the mother how to manage him and he sees the children acting on the basis of their mother's idea of him. The children refuse to pay attention to his demands: they talk back to him in the same way that they talk back to one another, adding pressure on him to assume the role of just another child. All this leaves him frustrated and, as a result, often aggressive or increasingly absent from home.

The children, on the whole, become more settled in their behavior as the wife takes over the family responsibilities. Decisions are made by her and upheld in the face of their father's attempts to interfere. Participation in activities outside the home is encouraged. Their patterns of interaction with their father are supported by the mother. Whereas in earlier stages the children often felt that there were causal connections between their actions and their father's drinking, they now accept his unpredictability. "Well," says a 6-year old, "I'll just have to get used to it. I have a drunken father."

The family is more stabilized in one way but in other ways insecurities are multiplied. Pay checks are received less and less regularly. The violence or withdrawal of the father increases. When he is away the wife worries about automobile accidents or injury in fights, which become more and more probable as time passes. The husband may begin to be seriously ill from time to time; his behavior may become quite bizarre. Both of these signs of increasing illness arouse anxiety in the family.

During this stage hopes may rise high for father's "reform" when he begins to verbalize wishes to stop drinking, admits off and on his inability to stop, and sounds desperate for doing something about his drinking. Now may begin the trek to sanitariums for the middle-class alcoholic, to doctors, or to Alcoholics Anonymous. Where just the promise to stop drinking has failed to revive hope, sobriety through outside agencies has the ability to rekindle it brightly. There is the feeling that at last he is "taking really constructive action." In failure the discouragement is deeper. Here another wedge has been inserted into the self-sufficiency of the family.

By this time the wedges are many. The wife, finding she has managed to bring some semblance of order and stability to her family, while not exactly becoming a self-assured person, has regained some sense of worth which grows a little with each crisis she meets successfully. In addition, the very fact of taking action to stabilize the situation brings relief. On some occasion she may be able to approach social agencies for financial help, often during a period when the husband has temporarily deserted or is incarcerated. She may have gone to the family court; she may have consulted a lawyer about getting a restraining order when the husband was in a particularly belligerent state. She has begun to learn her way around among the many agencies which offer help.

Often she has had a talk with an Alcoholics Anonymous member and has begun to look into what is known about alcoholism. If she has attended a few Alcoholics Anonymous meetings, her sense of shame has been greatly alleviated as she finds so many others in the same boat. Her hopes rise as she meets alcoholics who have stopped drinking, and she feels relieved at being able to discuss her problems openly for the first time with an audience which understands fully. She begins to gain perspective on her problem and learns that she herself is involved in what happens to her husband, and that she must change. She exchanges techniques of management with other wives and receives their support in her decisions.

She learns that her husband is ill rather than merely "ornery," and this often serves to quell for the time being thoughts about leaving him which have begun to germinate as she has gained more self-confidence. She learns that help is available but also that her efforts to push him into help are unavailing. She is not only supported in her recently evolved behavior of thinking first of her family, but now this course also emerges from the realm of the unconceptualized and is set in an accepted rationale. She feels more secure in having a reason and a certainty that the group accepts her as "doing the right thing." When she reports deviations from what the group thinks is the "right way," her reasons are understood; she receives solid support but there is also pressure on her to alter her behavior again toward the acceptable. Blaming and self-pity are actively discouraged. In group discussions she still admits to such feelings but learns to recognize them as they arise and to go beyond them to more productive thinking.

How much her altered behavior changes the family situation is uncertain, but it helps her and gives her security from which to venture forth to further actions of a consistent and constructive type, constructive at least from the point of view of keeping her family on as even a keel as possible in the face of the disruptive influence of the husband. With new friends whom she can use as a sounding board for plans, and with her growing acquaintance with the alternatives and possible patterns of behavior, her thinking ceases to be circular and unproductive. Her anxiety about her own sanity is alleviated as she is reassured by others that they have experienced the same concern and that the remedy is to get her own life and her family under better control. As she accomplishes this, the difference in her feelings about herself convinces her that this is so.

Whether or not she has had a contact with wives of Alcoholics Anonymous members or other wives who have been through a similar experience and have emerged successfully, the very fact of taking hold of her situation and gradually making it more manageable adds to her self-confidence. As her husband is less and less able to care for himself or his family, she begins to feel that he needs her and that without her he would be destroyed. Such a feeling makes it difficult for her to think of leaving him. His almost complete social isolation at this point and his cries for help reinforce this conviction of being needed.

The drinking behavior is no longer hidden. Others obviously know about it, and this becomes accepted by the wife and children. Already isolated and insulated against possible rejection, the wife is often surprised to find that she has exaggerated her fears of what would happen were the situation known. However, the unpredictability of her husband's behavior makes her reluctant to form social relationships which could be violently disrupted or to involve others in the possible consequences of his behavior.

Stage 5. Efforts to Escape the Problems

Stage 5 may be the terminal one for the marriage. In this stage the wife separates from her husband. Sometimes the marriage is reestablished after a period of sobriety, when it appears certain that the husband will not drink again. If he does revert to drinking, the marriage is sometimes finally terminated but with less emotional stress than the first time. If the husband deserts, being no longer able to tolerate his lack of status in his family, Stage 6 may be entered abruptly.

The events precipitating the decision to terminate the marriage may be near-catastrophic, as when there is an attempt by the husband to kill the wife or children, or they may appear trivial to outsiders, being only the last straw to an accumulation of years.

The problems in coming to the decision to terminate the marriage cannot be underestimated. Some of these problems derive from emotional conflicts; some are related to very practical circumstances in the situation; some are precipitated by the conflicting advice of outsiders. With several children dependent on her, the wife must decide whether the present situation is more detrimental to them than future situations she can see arising if she should leave her husband. The question of where the money to live on will come from must be thought out. If she can get a job, will there be enough to provide for child care also while she is away from home? Should the children, who have already experienced such an unsettled life, be separated from her to be cared for by others? If the family still owns its own home, how can she retain control of it? If she leaves, where can she go? What can be done to tide the family over until her first earnings come in? How can she ensure her husband's continued absence from the home and thus be certain of the safety of individuals and property in her absence? These are only a small sample of the practical issues that must be dealt with in trying to think her way through to a decision to terminate the marriage.

Other pressures act on her to impede the decision-making process. "If he would only stay drunk till I carry out what I intend to do," is a frequent statement. When the husband realizes that his wife really means to leave, he frequently sobers up, watches his behavior in the home, plays on her latent and sometimes conscious feelings of her responsibility for the situation, stresses his need for her and that without her he is lost, tears away at any confidence she has that she will be able to manage by herself, and threatens her and the children with injury or with his own suicide if she carries out her intention.

The children, in the meantime, are pulling and pushing on her emotions. They think she is "spineless" to stay but unfair to father's chances for ultimate recovery if she leaves. Relatives, who were earlier alienated in her attempts to shield her family but now know of the situation, do not believe in its full ramifications. They often feel she is exaggerating and persuade her to stay with him. Especially is this true in the case of a "solitary drinker." His drinking has been so well concealed that the relatives have no way of knowing the true nature of the situation. Other relatives, afraid that they will be called on for support, exert pressure to keep the marriage intact and the husband thereby responsible for debts. Relatives who feel she should leave him overplay their hands by berating the husband in such a manner as to evoke her defense of him. This makes conscious the positive aspects of her relationship with him, causing her to waver in her decision. If she consults organized agencies, she often gets conflicting advice. The agencies concerned with the well-being of the family may counsel leaving; those concerned with rehabilitating the husband may press her to stay. In addition, help from public organizations almost always involves delay and is frequently not forthcoming at the point where she needs it most.

The wife must come to terms with her own mixed feelings about her husband, her marriage and herself before she can decide on such a step as breaking up the marriage. She must give up hope that she can be of any help to her husband. She must command enough self-confidence, after years of having it eroded, to be able to face an unknown future and leave the security of an unpalatable but familiar past and present. She must accept that she has failed in her marriage, not an easy thing to do after having devoted years to stopping up the cracks in the family structure as they appeared. Breaking up the marriage involves a complete alteration in the life goals toward which all her behavior has been oriented. It is hard for her to rid herself of the feeling that she married him and he is her responsibility. Having thought and planned for so long on a day-to-day basis, it is difficult to plan for a long-term future.

Her taking over of the family raises her self-confidence but failure to carry through on decisions undermines the new gains that she has made. Vacil-

lation in her decisions tends to exasperate the agencies trying to help her, and she begins to feel that help from them may not be forthcoming if she finally decides to leave.

Some events, however, help her to arrive at a decision. During the absences of her husband she has seen how manageable life can be and how smoothly her family can run. She finds that life goes on without him. The wife who is working comes to feel that "my husband is a luxury I can no longer afford." After a few short-term separations in which she tries out her wings successfully, leaving comes to look more possible. Another step on the path to leaving is the acceptance of the idea that, although she cannot help her husband, she can help her family. She often reaches a state of such emotional isolation from her husband that his behavior no longer disturbs her emotionally but is only something annoying which upsets daily routines and plans.

Stage 6. Reorganization of Part of the Family

The wife is without her husband and must reorganize her family on this basis. Substantially the process is similar to that in other divorced families, but with some additions. The divorce rarely cuts her relationships to her husband. Unless she and her family disappear, her husband may make attempts to come back. When drunk, he may endanger her job by calls at her place of work. He may attempt violence against members of the family, or he may contact the children and work to gain their loyalty so that pressure is put on the mother to accept him again. Looking back on her marriage, she forgets the full impact of the problem situation on her and on the children and feels more warmly toward her husband, and these feelings can still be manipulated by him. The wide circulation of information on alcoholism as an illness engenders guilt about having deserted a sick man. Gradually, however, the family becomes reorganized.

Stage 7. Recovery and Reorganization of the Whole Family

Stage 7 is entered if the husband achieves sobriety, whether or not separation has preceded. It was pointed out that in earlier stages most of the problems in the marriage were attributed to the alcoholism of the husband, and thus problems in adjustment not related directly to the drinking were unrecognized and unmet. Also, the "sober personality" of the husband was thought of as the "real" personality, with a resulting lack of recognition of other factors involved in his sober behavior, such as remorse and guilt over his actions, leading him to act to the best of his ability like "the ideal husband" when sober. Irritation or other signs of growing tension were viewed as indicators of further drinking, and hence the problems giving rise to them were walked around gingerly rather than faced and resolved. Lack of conflict and lack of drinking were defined as indicating a perfect adjustment. For the wife and husband facing a sober marriage after many years of an alcoholic marriage, the expectations of what marriage without alcoholism will be are unrealistically idealistic, and the reality of marriage almost inevitably brings disillusionments. The expectation that all would go well and that all problems be resolved with the cessation of the husband's drinking cannot be met and this threatens the marriage from time to time.

The beginning of sobriety for the husband does not bring too great hope to the family at first. They have been through this before but are willing to help him along and stand by him in the new attempt. As the length of sobriety increases, so do the hopes for its permanence and efforts to be of help. The wife at first finds it difficult to think more than in terms of today, waking each morning with fear of what the day will bring and sighing with relief at the end of each sober day.

With the continuation of sobriety, many problems begin to crop up. Mother has for years managed the family, and now father again wishes to be reinstated in his former roles. Usually the first role reestablished is that of breadwinner, and the economic problems of the family begin to be alleviated as debts are gradually paid and there is enough left over for current needs. With the resumption of this role, the husband feels that the family should also accept him at least as a partner in the management of the family. Even if the wife is willing to hand over some of the control of the children, for example, the children often are not able to accept this change easily. Their mother has been both parents for so long that it takes time to get used to the idea of consulting their father on problems and asking for his decisions. Often the father tries too hard to manage this change overnight, and the very pressure put on the children toward this end defeats him. In addition, he is unable to meet many of the demands the children make on him because he has never really become acquainted with them or learned to understand them and is lacking in much necessary background knowledge of their lives.

The wife, who finds it difficult to conceive of her husband as permanently sober, feels an unwillingness to let control slip from her hands. At the same time she realizes that reinstatement of her husband in his family roles is necessary to his sobriety. She also realizes that the closer his involvement in the family the greater the probability of his remaining sober. Yet she remembers events in the past in which his failure to handle his responsibilities was catastrophic to the family. Used to avoiding anything which might upset him, the wife often hesitates to discuss problems openly. At times, if she is successful in helping him to regain his roles as father, she feels resentful of his intrusion into territory she has come to regard as hers. If he makes errors in judgment which affect the family adversely, her former feelings of being his superior may come to the fore and affect her interaction with him. If the children begin to turn to him, she may feel a resurgence of self-pity at being left out and find herself attempting to swing the children back toward herself. Above all, however, she finds herself feeling resentful that some other agency achieved what she and the children could not.

Often the husband makes demands for obedience, for consideration and for pampering which members of the family feel unable to meet. He may become rather euphoric as his sobriety continues and feel superior for a time.

Gradually, however, the drinking problem sinks into the past and marital adjustment at some level is achieved. Even when this has occurred, the drinking problem crops up occasionally, as when the time comes for a decision about whether the children should be permitted to drink. The mother at such times becomes anxious, sees in the child traits which remind her of her husband, worries whether these are the traits which mean future alcoholism. At parties, at first, she is watchful and concerned about whether her husband will take a drink or not. Relatives and friends may, in a party mood, make the husband the center of attention by emphasizing his nondrinking. They may unwittingly cast aspersions on his character by trying to convince him that he can now "drink like a man." Some relatives and friends have gone so far as secretly to "spike" a nonalcoholic drink and then cry "bottoms up!" without realizing the risk of reactivating patterns from the past.

If sobriety has come through Alcoholics Anonymous, the husband frequently throws himself so wholeheartedly into A.A. activities that his wife sees little of him and feels neglected. As she worries less about his drinking, she may press him to cut down on these activities. That this is dangerous, since A.A. activity is correlated with success in Alcoholics Anonymous, has been shown by Lahey (9). Also, the wife discovers that, though she has a sober husband, she is by no means free of alcoholics. In his Twelfth Step work, he may keep the house filled with men he is helping. In the past her husband has avoided self-searching; and now he may become excessively introspective, and it may be difficult for her to deal with this.

If the husband becomes sober through Alcoholics Anonymous and the wife participates actively in groups open to her, the thoughts of what is happening to her, to her husband and to her family will be verbalized and interpreted within the framework of the Alcoholics Anonymous philosophy and the situation will probably be more tolerable and more easily worked out.

III. SUGGESTIONS FOR FURTHER RESEARCH

The above presentation has roughly delineated sequences and characteristics of family adjustment to an alcoholic husband. A more detailed delineation of the stages is required. The extent to which these findings, based on families seeking help, can be generalized to other families of alcoholics needs to be determined, and differences between these families and others specified. Consideration should be given to the question of correspondence between the wife's definition of the situation and that which actually occurs.

Further research is needed on the factors which determine the rate of transition through the stages, and on the factors which retard such a transition, sometimes to the extent that the family seems to remain in the same stage almost permanently. In the group studied, the majority passed from one stage to the next but took different lengths of time to make the transition. Those wives whose husbands have been sober a long time had all passed through all the stages. None of the long-term members remained in the same stage throughout the time that the group was under study.

Other problems which require clarification are: (a) What are the factors within families which facilitate a return to sobriety or hamper it? (b) What variations in family behavior are determined by social class? (c) What problems are specific to the different types of drinking patterns of the husband — for example, the periodic drinker, the steady drinker, the solitary drinker, the sociable drinker, the drinker who becomes belligerent, and the drinker who remains calm? There are indications in the data gathered in the present study that such specific problems arise.

IV. SUMMARY

The onset of alcoholism in a family member has been viewed as precipitating a cumulative crisis for the family. Seven critical stages have been delineated. Each stage affects the form which the following one will take. The family finds itself in an unstructured situation which is undefined by the culture. Thus it is forced to evolve techniques of adjustment by trial and error. The unpredictability of the situation, added to its lack of structure, engenders anxiety in family members which gives rise to personality difficulties. Factors in the culture, in the environment and within the family situation prolong the crisis and deter the working out of permanent adjustment patterns. With the arrest of the alcoholism, the crisis enters its final stage. The family attempts to reorganize to include the ex-alcoholic and makes adjustments to the changes which have occurred in him.

It has been suggested that the clinical picture presented by the wife to helping agencies is not only indicative of a type of basic personality structure but also of the stage in family adjustment to an alcoholic. That the wives of alcoholics represent a rather limited number of personality types can be interpreted in two ways, which are not mutually exclusive.

(a) That women with certain personality attributes tend to select alcoholics or potential alcoholics as husbands in order to satisfy unconscious personality needs;

(b) That women undergoing similar experiences of stress, within similarly unstructured situations, defined by the culture and reacted to by members of the society in such a manner as to place limits on the range of possible behavior, will emerge from this experience showing many similar neurotic personality traits. As the situation evolves some of these personality traits will also change. Changes have been observed in the women studied which correlate with altered family interaction patterns. This hypothesis is supported also by observations on the behavior of individuals in other unstructured situations, in situations involving conflicting goals and loyalties, and in situations in which they were isolated from supporting group interaction. It is congruent also with the theory of reactions to increased and decreased stress.

REFERENCES

1. Mowrer, H. R. A psychocultural analysis of the alcoholic. Amer. sociol. Rev. **5**: 546–557, 1940.

2. Bacon, S. D. Excessive drinking and the institution of the family. In: Alcohol, Science and Society; Lecture 16. New Haven; Quarterly Journal of Studies on Alcohol; 1945.

3. Baker, S. M. Social case work with inebriates. In: Alcohol, Science and Society; Lecture 27. New Haven; Quarterly Journal of Studies on Alcohol; 1945.

4. Futterman, S. Personality trends in wives of alcoholics. J. psychiat. soc. Work **23**: 37–41, 1953.

5. Whalen, T. Wives of alcoholics: four types observed in a family service agency. Quart. J. Stud. Alc. **14**: 632–641, 1953.

6. Price, G. M. A study of the wives of 20 alcoholics. Quart. J. Stud. Alc. **5**: 620–627, 1945.

7. Club and Educational Bureaus of Newsweek. Is alcoholism everyone's problem? Platform, N. Y., p. 3, Jan. 1950.

8. Newell, N. Alcoholism and the father-image. Quart. J. Stud. Alc. **11**: 92–96, 1950.

9. Lahey, W. W. A Comparison of Social and Personal Factors Identified with Selected Members of Alcoholics Anonymous. Master's Thesis; University of Southern California; 1950.

Psychosomatic Disorders | 6

No psychiatric term is handled with such misguided casualness as is "psychosomatic." As Phyllis McGinley's poem reminds us, psychosomatic has come, in everyday parlance (and in some scientific writing), to refer to all forms of organic-physiologic disorders in which the faintest trace of a psychological component can be found to exist concurrently. While it is true that any disease or disability will have associated with it such psychological phenomena as anxiety, frustration, depressive feelings, and passivity, their mere presence does not make the disorder a psychosomatic one. To use this term in a more meaningful way we must confine its application to those somatic disorders for which psychological factors have been more or less clearly found to be of etiological significance. For examples in this sphere fall ulcerative colitis, migraine, bronchial asthma, and peptic and duodenal ulcers.

Emotional and physiological factors are both implicated in many illnesses. Both ancient and primitive medicine, in devising their empirical curative processes, have clearly recognized this connection. We know, too, that for any form of disorder we must treat "the whole patient," focusing on both psychological and somatic factors in his hospital regimen. But, beyond these generalities, many specific problems have been examined and theories set forth. Present theoretical trends tend to regard these disorders as complex-determined, multi-etiological in nature, with roots in the earliest parent-child relationships and in the development of stress-coping patterns. Stress refers to the sum total of disruptive agents, whatever their origin, which lead to organismic decompensation. Hans Selye, the endocrinologist, has postulated a three-stage reaction to stress, the result of which may be psychosomatic symptomatology. These three stages are the alarm reaction, during which the body's adaptive mechanisms are called into play, the stage of resistance, in which a maximum state of adaptation has been achieved, and the stage of exhaustion, resulting from prolonged stress, in which adaptation fails and organismic damage takes place. In one form or another, concepts of stress, stress tolerance, and excessive stress are discussed in this Section as important links in the sequence leading to psychosomatic disturbance.

The Kaplans present a succinct outline of the various important theories in psychosomatic medicine, generally identified as the specificity theories, based on psychoanalytic concepts, and the nonspecific theories, rooted more in experimental laboratory approaches. As they note, it is likely that the necessary and sufficient conditions for the development of psychosomatic disorder involve processes important to both schools of thought, as well as a vulnerable organ, its symbolic meaning to the patient, and a more general psychological susceptibility to the inroads of stress.[1]

The excellent paper by Weiner and his associates on the development of duodenal ulcers highlights the interactive, multi-causal theme. Instead of using a post hoc procedure of investigating patients after the development of their symptoms, Weiner obtained data on psychological and physiological

[1] For a more detailed discussion of these two theoretical viewpoints, see Alexander, F., and Szasz, T. S. The psychosomatic approach in medicine. In Franz Alexander and Helen Ross (Eds.), Dynamic psychiatry. Chicago: Univ. of Chicago Press, 1952, pp. 369–400, and Wolff, H. G. Life stress and bodily disease — a formulation. Res. Nerv. Ment. Dis. Monogr. Baltimore: Williams and Williams, 1950, pp. 1059–1094. For a more complete and up-to-date expression of the Kaplans' viewpoint see Freeman, A. M. and Kaplan, H. I. (Eds.), Comprehensive textbook of psychiatry. Baltimore: Williams and Williams, 1966.

measures of his subjects before they demonstrated ulcerous lesions. A picture of a complex interrelationship of physiological, psychological, and contextual variables emerges from this investigation.

The study by Hinkle and his associates is an attempt to correlate life experiences with the development of physical and psychological disturbance in groups of men and women of diverse backgrounds. The premise of this investigation is drawn from the work of Harold Wolff, that the perception of a situation as stressful leads to adaptive maneuvers which, should they prove difficult to achieve successfully, will culminate in the onset of various forms of illness. As Hinkle demonstrates, the individual's problems in adjustment to his perceived environment, rather than the vicissitudes of the physical setting or the presence of pathogenic agents, most profoundly effect his health status.

Titchener, Riskin, and Emerson present a family-oriented view on the origin of psychosomatic illness. Their study attempts to move away from the usual concern with the etiological role of maternal attitudes and behavior to the process of family relationships as it effects the shifting balance of individual and group needs, emotions, and beliefs. It is interesting to note how key themes in the etiology of ulcerative colitis, such as helplessness, repressed hostility, and dependency needs, are reflected in all family members and all family transactions. A real advance in our understanding of psychosomatic illness, as with all other problems of living, would be a longitudinal study of the interaction of constitutional and family-process events throughout the individual's life cycle, particularly during the crisis periods of greatest change. ■

PHYLLIS MCGINLEY

Don't Shake the Bottle, Shake Your Mother-in-law*

When I was young and full of rhymes
  And all my days were salady,
Almost I could enjoy the times
  I caught some current malady.
Then, cheerful, knocked upon my door
  The jocular physician,
With tonics and with comfort for
  My innocent condition.
Then friends would fetch me flowers
  And nurses rub my back,
And I could talk for hours
  Concerning my attack.
But now, when vapors dog me,
  What solace do I find?
My cronies can't endure me.
The doctors scorn to cure me,
And, though I ail, assure me
  It's all a state of mind.

It's psychosomatic, now, psychosomatic.
Whatever you suffer is psychosomatic.
Your liver's a-quiver? You're feeling infirm?
Dispose of the notion you harbor a germ.
Angina,
  Arthritis,
    Abdominal pain —
They're nothing but symptoms of marital strain.
They're nothing but proof that your love life is minus.
The ego is aching
Instead of the sinus.
So face up and brace up and stifle that sneeze.
It's psychosomatic. And ten dollars, please.
There was a time that I recall,
  If one grew pale or thinnish,
The pundits loved to lay it all
  On foods unvitaminish,
Or else, dogmatic, would maintain
  Infection somewhere acted.
And when they'd shorn the tonsils twain,
  They pulled the tooth impacted.
But now that orgies dental

Have made a modish halt,
Your ills today are mental
    And likely all your fault.
Now specialists inform you,
    While knitting of their brows,
Your pain, though sharp and shooting,
Is caused, beyond disputing,
Because you hate commuting
    Or can't abide your spouse.

It's psychosomatic, now, psychosomatic.
You fell down the stairway? It's psychosomatic.

That sprain of the ankle while waxing the floors —
You did it on purpose to get out of chores.
Nephritis,
    Neuritis,
        A case of the ague?
You're just giving in to frustrations that plague you.
You long to be coddled, beloved, acclaimed,
So you caught the sniffles.
And aren't you ashamed!
And maybe they're right. But I sob through my
    wheezes,
"They've taken the fun out of having diseases."

HAROLD I. KAPLAN AND HELEN S. KAPLAN [2/3]

Current Theoretical Concepts in Psychosomatic Medicine[*][1]

Before discussing current theoretical approaches in psychosomatic medicine, we think it would be salutary to play devil's advocate for just one moment. We should like to point out that a definite and significant causal relationship between psychological factors and true organic ailments is as yet merely an assumption. Psychogenesis in physical illness has never, to our knowledge, been rigorously proved. However, the assumption of a significant psychosomatic relationship rests on a great deal of what appears to be solid circumstantial evidence, and, furthermore, such a relationship is very attractive from a theoretical standpoint. Psychosomatic theoreti-

* Reprinted by permission from the *American Journal of Psychiatry*, Vol. 115, 1959, pp. 1091–1096.
[1] Read before the 5th annual meeting of the Academy of Psychosomatic Medicine, N.Y.C., Oct. 11, 1958.
[2] Harold I. Kaplan, M.D., Professor of Psychiatry & Director of Psychiatric Education and Training, New York Medical College; Helen S. Kaplan, M.D., Ph.D., Associate Professor of Psychiatry and Chief of Psychosomatic Training, New York Medical College.
[3] For a more complete and up-to-date expression of the authors' views in psychosomatic medicine, the reader is referred to *Comprehensive Textbook of Psychiatry*, edited by Alfred M. Freedman, M.D., and Harold I. Kaplan, M.D., Baltimore, Williams and Wilkins Co., 1966.

cians therefore agree in assuming that psychic factors play a noteworthy etiological role in many common ailments. There is, however, little agreement about the basic mechanisms by which psychological and physical factors interact to produce disease. *There is, in fact, currently no one theory, construct, or set of variables adequate to explain the observed and assumed relationship between psychological difficulty and physical malady.* Indeed, even the definition and limitation of what constitutes a "psychosomatic disease" is controversial. For example, some workers consider every disease *psychosomatic* in that psychic and somatic phenomena are two aspects of the same process, and, since all disease is multicausal, psychic factors must play some role in every pathological process(1). Others feel that the definition should be limited to those disease processes in which psychic factors are assumed to play a *major* etiological role. In this paper we shall restrict the term *psychosomatic* to diseases in which psychological events appear to contribute heavily to etiology and to such diseases as peptic ulcer and ulcerative colitis, in which manipulation of psychological factors seems markedly to influence the course of the illness.

There are several reasons for the lack of agreement in psychosomatic theory. 1. One of these is conceptual confusion. Such confusion may understandably follow when an attempt is made to describe in one theory, phenomena which have previously been studied by entirely separate and distinct sciences, namely psychopathology and medical pathology as well as psychology and physiology. The psychological and the physiological disciplines operate at different levels of description, use different systems of semantics and symbols, and are at different stages of theoretical development. They use essentially different methods of inquiry. Many of the early as well as some of the current difficulties in theoretical formulations in the field of psychosomatic medicine may be attributed to the inappropriate and uncritical equating of concepts derived from different levels of description(2). Compounding these difficulties is the uncritical application of unproved psychiatric and, in particular, psychoanalytic concepts to psychosomatic theory. Among such controversial concepts are "libido" and a fixed pattern of psychosexual development(3). Although such psychoanalytic concepts have been of immense theoretical and practical value in working therapeutically with psychiatric patients, their undiscriminating transfer to psychosomatic medicine, is, we feel, questionable.

2. Another reason for lack of agreement is the underdeveloped state of psychology, psychiatry, and psychoanalysis. These sciences suffer from deficiencies in language and methods of description, frequent conceptual confusion, and a lack of experimental and clinical validation of many of their theoretical and therapeutic principles. We believe that at this point the greatest single obstacle to the development of a satisfactory psychosomatic theory and the definitive demonstration of a significant relationship between psyche and soma is the relatively backward state of the psychological sciences. We feel that there must be progress in psychological theory and technique to bring these disciplines to a level of development *comparable* to that of the physical and biological sciences in order that psychosomatic phenomena may be described in comparable terms.

3. Finally, the idea must be entertained that one "unified theory" of psychosomatic disease, which has been sought by almost all investigators in this field, may never be possible, *i.e.*, that different psychosomatic diseases may prove to be psychosomatic by virtue of entirely different mechanisms, so that different workers studying different diseases may

very correctly emerge with distinctly different and yet valid psychosomatic theories.

THE MAJOR THEORETICAL APPROACHES

We will now try to describe the salient features of the current theoretical psychosomatic approaches. For the sake of brevity, we arbitrarily divide the theories into 3 groups. The first group may be termed "specificity" theories, according to which, specific psychological events cause specific psychosomatic diseases. Another group, the so-called "nonspecific" group, attributes psychosomatic disease to general psychogenic stress reactions, which may be triggered off by a variety of psychological stimuli. The third group has developed out of the recognition of the limitations of the other two.

The *specificity* theories vary in their explanation of the mechanisms by which psychosomatic diseases are produced. Included in this group are the historically important but no longer accepted "personality profiles" of Flanders Dunbar(4), in which she suggested that various personality constellations are etiologically associated with specific diseases — for example, that coronary occlusion is associated with the driving, ambitious male.

Another "specific" approach derives from Freud's libido theory(5) as applied to the etiology of conversion hysteria. Freud suggested that various hysterical somatic affections, such as paralysis, might be caused by specific unconscious psychological conflicts that were defensively transformed into *symbolically significant* functional somatic symptoms involving organs innervated by the voluntary nervous system. Freud, incidentally, never applied his hysteria formulation clearly to visceral diseases, although other workers have. For example, Garma (6) has now suggested a libido theory formulation with some Kleinian modifications in his hypothesis about the causation of peptic ulcer, in which ulcer is explained as the result of the symbolic bite of the patient's gastric mucosa by his introjected hostile mother.

Most of these aforementioned "specific" approaches, which clearly suffer from the uncritical application of inappropriate psychological concepts, have been displaced in acceptance and popularity by Alexander's much more sophisticated but still controversial specificity theory(1), which has its conceptual roots in the amalgamation of the best of Freud's, Cushing's and Cannon's work(7, 8). Alexander suggests that specific typical unconscious conflict situations result in specific diseases by virtue of the following mechanism, presented in a very simplified form. He believes that a specific conflict situation will arouse anxiety in a particular patient. The anxiety, which in psychoanalytic theory is regarded as a signal of danger to the patient's ego, then sets in motion a series of specific unconscious psychological reactions which involve characteristic psychological defenses and regressive phenomena. Alexander believes that specific emotional reactions have specific parasympathetic and/or sympathetic concomitants, which affect specific visceral organs. The excessive autonomic-organ innervation caused by the chronic tension of *repressed* conflicts may lead to disturbance in function, which may eventually lead to organic pathological changes in susceptible individuals.

Thus, for example, blocking of dependency needs in adult life in a patient with a passive-dependent character structure causes anxiety, with a resultant specific defensive regression to an infantile oral state. The discharge of "psychic energy" through the parasympathetic nervous system is associated with increased gastric acid secretion. If chronically aroused, this concomitant vegetative pattern may lead to peptic ulcer in susceptible individuals.

Alexander's studies have been criticized on theoretical as well as experimental grounds. First, theoretically Alexander discounts the role of the voluntary nervous system in the genesis of psychosomatic disease; second, he has assumed as fact certain hypothetical and questionable psychoanalytic concepts and has proposed a series of fixed unconscious conflictual constellations as causative factors in various diseases; third, he assumes that certain psychological conflicts or stresses have specific physiological concomitants. This latter point has been experimentally challenged and represents an example of the conceptual confusion resulting from mixing concepts from two levels of description.

Although there is some validation of Alexander's studies, there has been considerable disagreement on whether it is possible to demonstrate the same specific conflicts in all cases of the same disease. It is also questionable whether the conflicts postulated for one disease differ from those associated with others. In other words, it has not been possible up to this time to predict disease from conflict, or vice-versa. In addition, it is highly doubtful whether specific psychological conflicts can be correlated clinically or experimentally with specific physiological vegetative changes.

Alexander's views have received significant support from several hundred case histories reported in the literature as well as from the fine and continuing experimental studies of Mirsky(9). The latter investigator has demonstrated that gastric secretory activity is paralleled by the excretion of uropepsin in the urine and has therefore been able to correlate stomach activity with a variety of psychological stimuli which have been interpreted psychoanalytically. He concluded from his studies that there was a positive relationship between augmentation of uropepsin excretion, and hence gastric activity, and the mobilization of oral dependency wishes in various subjects. If true, this finding would support Alexander's theoretical views particularly in reference to peptic ulcer pathogenesis. However, it is important to note that there are many dissenting opinions about the interpretation of the psychological data presented by many of the aforementioned supporting investigators.

Thus, even though Alexander's theory of the typical unconscious conflict remains a major theoretical force in the psychosomatic field, it is at this time a basically unvalidated hypothesis resting on unvalidated underlying assumptions.

The *nonspecific* theoretical approaches to psychosomatic medicine include the theories of Wolff, Mahl, Selye and various animal experimentalists such as Liddell and Gantt. Their approach rests on the assumption that there is no correlation between the type of psychological stress and the nature of the organ selected for the disease.

In general, the work of this group is not rooted in psychoanalytic theory. Therefore, although the resultant formulations may suffer from a limited insight into some psychological complexities, they gain the advantage of being unhampered by unvalidated and often misleading assumptions.

Among the outstanding experimentalists of the so-called nonspecific group are Harold Wolff(10) and his associates at the Cornell Medical College. Wolff's main contribution to the field of psychosomatic medicine is the application of the experimental method to the study of the physiological and pathological functioning of various bodily organs and the correlation of these functions with various types of psychological stimuli. Using laboratory and clinical experimental techniques, he has amply demonstrated physiological and pathological changes in various organs and systems — notably the stomach (11), the colon(12), and the nasal musoca(13) under emotional stress as well as during ordinary life situations. The changes he describes generally involve variations in the swelling, vascularity, and motility of various viscera, and it is assumed that these changes are the logical precursors of potentially permanent pathological changes which constitute psychosomatic disease. He describes, for example, two variations of physiological change in the gastrointestinal and respiratory mucosa, namely, hyperfunction and hypofunction in the vascular and secretory activity. In general, emotions such as hostility are associated with physiological overactivity, while fear and sadness involving a feeling of withdrawal are accompanied by diminished physiological function. The character of the conflict evoking these emotions, although not specific for any particular illness, is specific for the individual patient and has its roots in the events of his sociopsychological development.

More recently, Wolff has concluded that psychosomatic disease is a result of attempts of the total organism to protect itself against psychogenic stress in the form of threatening symbols or situations. In interpreting his data, Wolff suggests that many of the physiological changes described above, although originally unconditioned protective reaction patterns and responses to noxious physical stimuli, may later become conditioned to noxious psychological stimuli. He further suggests that the resultant physiological reactions ultimately also acquire symbolic psychological meanings; for example nasal hyperemia associated with nasal obstruction represents a "shutting out — shutting in pattern" of non-participation in stressful life situations.

Wolff has been criticized as naive in his selection and interpretation of psychological data. Margolin (14), typifying the psychoanalytic approach, feels that Wolff has failed to take account of important "unconscious" psychological data and has dealt with the behavioral aspect of his correlations on too superficial a level. We, on the other hand, tend to agree with most of Wolff's work, which we believe includes some very important basic contributions to the field, but we differ with his recent conclusion that psychosomatic disease is protective, defensive, and symbolic in nature. We shall clarify this point when we present our own theoretical approach.

Other workers in this nonspecific group have demonstrated various possible mechanisms by which psychologically induced stress may cause organic disease in man and animals. Selye(15) feels that the hypophyseal-adrenocortical axis responds to various types of physical and psychic stress with hormonal changes which can ultimately cause a variety of organic diseases, such as rheumatoid arthritis and peptic ulcer. Selye views such diseases as a side product of the body's attempt to adapt to stress from any source.

Mahl(16), an experimental psychologist with a learning theory conception of behavior, has studied the effects of chronic unrelieved anxiety in men and animals and has found that gastric hydrochloric acid production increases under such circumstances. Since such acidity is a precursor of peptic ulcer, he had concluded that chronic anxiety, derived from any source whatsoever, is the variable intervening between the behavioral and physical events involved in psychosomatic illness.

Other animal experimentalists, such as Gantt(17) and Liddell(18), have successfully produced a variety of psychosomatic symptoms, *e.g.*, certain respiratory conditions, in animals, by experimentally creating stressful situations and inducing conflicts. Since it can be assumed that animals do not have man's capacity for symbolic thought, and since they nevertheless demonstrate psychosomatic phenomena in response to psychogenic stress, one wonders whether it is necessary or practicable to postulate the operation of specific psychological conflicts, which can hardly be meaningful to an animal, in the etiology of such disease.

Our own theoretical predilection lies along nonspecific lines(2). We believe that as long as a patient can deal with unpleasant emotions and with the anxiety engendered by his conflicts by means of various psychological defenses and mechanisms, there will be no abnormal psychogenic physical functioning nor resultant psychosomatic illness. If, however, a patient's psychological defenses are inadequate to reduce his excited or anxious state, so that he is left in a chronic state of emotional tension, then a variety of psychosomatic diseases may be produced in constitutionally susceptible individuals as a result of the physiological concomitants of chronic tension. According to this view, many psychosomatic diseases are a consequence of the *breakdown* of psychological defenses. It should be added that we do not consider the aforementioned mechanism to account for all instances of psychosomatic illness; other mechanisms, such as conditioning, may play a role in certain diseases. Nor do we believe that there is sufficient evidence to indicate that the nature of the psychological stimulus setting off the emotional tension determines the type of disease that develops. The problem of "organ selection," *i.e.*, what accounts for the type of disease suffered by a particular patient, is unsolved as yet. Interesting work by Malmo(19) suggests that constitutional factors may be the prime determinants of organ selection in psychosomatic disease.

A criticism that has been justly leveled against the nonspecific theorists is that their approach is too general: they say, in effect, that a person is nervous and that this makes him sick. The object, however, is to use modern psychodynamic and psychopatho-logical concepts in order to define more precisely what the etiological factors in psychosomatic disease are. Alexander, in criticizing Mahl's use of the concept of chronic anxiety as a causative agent in psychosomatic disease, notes that he too recognizes the importance of anxiety, but, whereas Mahl believes that the physiological concomitants of anxiety cause psychosomatic disease, Alexander believes that it is anxiety which triggers off a series of psychodynamic processes which terminate in psychosomatic illness. The controversy seemingly is a semantic one, hinging on the meaning of anxiety. It goes deeper, however. The psychoanalysts generally feel secure in their complex conceptualization of the psyche and try to correlate physical events with specific but highly theoretical psychological events. The other group of theorists, on the other hand, believe that psychological knowledge has developed to a point where only the most general correlations are possible.

Many workers recognize the limitations in the current state of knowledge and theory of psychosomatic medicine and have suggested that a multi-disciplinary approach might facilitate progress in this field. Among these are Galdston(20) who believes that psychoanalysts tend to concentrate excessively on the psychological aspects of the problem. Grinker(21) and his co-workers have suggested a "field theory" in which they advocate that in psychosomatic medicine one must appraise all factors, external and internal, past and present, that bring their influence to bear upon the patient and represent a disturbance of his homeostatic equilibrium. Grinker would have investigators of different disciplines, e.g., sociology, physiology, psychology, etc., study the same disease at the same time using their own frame of reference. Grinker contends that "most psychiatrists, psychologists or social scientists are too deeply specialized and immersed in their own disciplines to be able to observe accurately the relationships or bridges to other disciplines involved in studying co-variables. Each should indicate when and where his observations lose their sharpness and when other specialists at different positions in the total field are necessary" (21).

SUMMARY

We have outlined, for the sake of simplicity, 3 groups of psychosomatic theorists. One assumes that the psychological make-up of the individual and the character of the psychological trauma determine the nature of organic illness. Another group believes that the structure of the patient's personality and the nature of his conflicts and psychological trauma have no direct bearing on the type of organic pathology he will develop. They assume that any kind of psychological stress may be associated with a pathogenic physiological concomitant leading to organic disease, the nature of which depends probably more on the physical than on the psychological make-up of the individual. The third group is not really worthy as yet of being characterized as a theoretical group. It consists of those who object to the lack of validation of the intellectually attractive specificity theories and yet are dissatisfied with the over-generalized nonspecific theories. These theorists are using the "shotgun," or multidisciplinary, approach in an attempt to clarify the complex problems of psychosomatic medicine.

You may well ask, where does this leave me? That, we suggest, depends on your aims and the level of your interest. For example, it is important for the nonpsychiatric medical practitioner to be aware of the existence of the psychosomatic relationship and of the fact that different opinions about etiology exist. Each patient should be treated as an individual, and no formula or set treatment regimen can as yet be applied to any particular problem. When treating an ulcer patient, it would in our opinion, be unwise to assume that he is therefore dependent and has problems in this area; what is important is to attempt to diminish his anxiety level in any way that will work uniquely for him.

The same general attitude ought to be taken by the psychiatrist. He will probably have a tendency to espouse a psychosomatic theory consistent with his particular psychiatric orientation: this is constructive so long as it gives him a useful frame of reference in working with patients. He should, however, be sufficiently flexible to be aware that he is dealing with theoretical constructs, not with proved facts. He should also be aware that his interpretations and psychotherapeutic manipulations may have profound physical effects on his psychosomatic patients and may seriously affect the course of the organic phase of the disease process.

And lastly we come to the "egghead," the "theoretical psychosomaticist." He should not be at all discouraged by the disagreements and the contradictions; to the contrary, he should thrive on them. There is a great joy in working on untrodden soil, especially when that soil is of as much intrinsic interest and importance as psychosomatic medicine. We are faced with a myriad of unknown phenomena and imperfectly understood relationships. As each theory is proposed, it should be scrutinized under the harsh and impartial light of the scientific method, which demands rigorous proof and validation.

We find it stimulating to work amidst such mystery, and rather than finding the lack of conclusiveness distressing, consider it one of the personal attractions offered by the field of psychosomatic medicine.

BIBLIOGRAPHY

1. ALEXANDER, F.: Psychosomatic Medicine. New York: W. W. Norton and Co., 1950.
2. KAPLAN, H. I. and KAPLAN, H. S.: Am. J. Psychother., 9: 16, 1957.
3. MENDELSON, M., HIRSCH, S., and WEBBER, C. S.: Psychosom. Med., 18: 363, 1956.
4. DUNBAR, F.: Emotions and Bodily Changes. New York: Columbia University Press, 1954.
5. FREUD, S.: Fragment of an analysis of a case of hysteria. In Collected Papers, Vol. III. London: Hogarth Press and the Institute of Psychoanalysis, 1948.
6. GARMA, A.: Internat. J. Psychoanal., 31: 53, 1950.
7. CUSHING, H.: Surgery, Gynecology and Obstet., 55: 39, 1932.
8. CANNON, W. B.: The Wisdom of the Body. New York: W. W. Norton and Co., 1932.
9. MIRSKY, I. A.: Psychoanalysis and the biological sciences. In Twenty Years of Psychoanalysis. Ed. by F. Alexander and H. Ross. New York: W. W. Norton and Company, 1953.
10. WOLFF, H. G.: Assn. Res. Ner. Ment. Dis., 29: 1059, 1950.
11. WOLF, S. and WOLFF, H. G.: Human Gastric Function. New York: Oxford University Press, 1943.
12. GRACE, W., WOLF, S. and WOLFF, H. G.: The Human Colon. An Experimental Study Based on Direct Observation of Four Fistulous Subjects. New York: Harper and Bros., 1951.
13. HOLMES, T. H., GOODELL, H., WOLF, S. and WOLFF, H. G.: The Nose: An Experimental Study of Reactions Within the Nose in Human Subjects During Varying Life Experiences. Springfield, Illinois, C. C. Thomas, Publisher, 1950.
14. MARGOLIN, S. G.: Psychoanal. Quart., 20: 349, 1951.
15. SELYE, H.: The Physiology and Pathology of Exposure to Stress, Montreal: Acta, 1950.
16. MAHL, G. F.: Psychosom. Med., 12: 158, 1950.
17. GANTT, W. H.: Experimental Basis for Neurotic Behavior: Origin and Development of Artificially Produced Disturbances of Behavior in Dogs. New York: Paul Hoeber, 1944.
18. LIDDELL, H.: The role of vigilance in the development of animal neuroses. In Anxiety. Edited by P. Hoch and J. Zubin. New York: Grune and Stratton, 1950.
19. MALMO, R., SHAGASS, C. and DAVIS, F. H.: Res. Pub. Ass. Nerv. Ment. Dis., 29: 231, 1950.
20. GALDSTON, I.: Arch. Neurol. and Psychiat., 74: 441, 1955.
21. GRINKER, R.: Psychosomatic Research. New York: W. W. Norton and Co., 1953.

**HERBERT WEINER, MARGARET THALER,
MORTON F. REISER, AND I. ARTHUR MIRSKY**

Etiology of Duodenal Ulcer*
I. Relation of Specific Psychological Characteristics to Rate of Gastric Secretion (Serum Pepsinogen)

The life history of a clinical syndrome and the various factors that contribute to the predisposition and precipitation of the syndrome in any particular person are usually inferred from data obtained after the clinical disorder has developed. Such inferences are frequently biased by the investigator's particular orientation. Thus, there are those who claim that the development of duodenal ulcer is determined solely by "organic" factors,(11) whereas others claim that "psychic" factors are the sole determinants.(8) Such polar attitudes are inevitable when the data being considered is *post hoc* in nature. The ideal approach for evaluating the determinants responsible for precipitating any clinical disorder is to study the subject who is going to develop the disorder before he does so. This *propter hoc* approach requires criteria that will permit the selection of individuals who are susceptible to the development of the particular syndrome.

Previous studies have established that the concentration of pepsinogen in the blood is dependent upon the rate of pepsinogen production by the stomach.(15) In 87 per cent of patients with duo-

denal ulcer, the pepsinogen concentration is greater than the mean of values found in subjects without duodenal or other gastrointestinal disturbances.(16) This observation is consistent with the general consensus that patients with duodenal ulcer tend to secrete more gastric juice, hydrochloric acid, and pepsin than do healthy subjects.(10) The fact that the high concentration of pepsinogen in the sera of such patients was found to persist even after the duodenal lesion was healed,(16) as does also the increased rate of gastric secretion,(13) suggested that gastric hypersecretion is an essential but not the sole determinant in the development of the lesion.

The concentration of pepsinogen in the blood of 14 per cent of subjects without any gastrointestinal disturbance is greater than the mean of values found in patients with duodenal ulcer.(16) Presumably, the stomachs of such "healthy" subjects are hypersecreting pepsinogen. If gastric hypersecretion is an essential determinant in the development of duodenal ulcer, it may be postulated that the high pepsinogen secretors represent that segment of the population with a maximal secretory capacity(9) that is most likely to develop duodenal ulcer when exposed to those circumstances responsible for precipitating the sequence of physiological events that result in the characteristic lesion. In accord with this hypothesis is the observation that apparently healthy subjects, without any previous history of gastrointestinal derangement, but with serum pepsinogen values in the range of those of patients with duodenal ulcer may go on to develop the lesion without any further significant increase in the concentration of pepsinogen in the blood.(16, 17, 18)

The precise circumstances responsible for the precipitation of duodenal ulcer remain unknown. The consensus, however, is that psychic tension initiated by exposure to some environmental event is a prepotent factor. Although numerous studies have established that various manifestations of psychic

* Reprinted by permission from *Psychosomatic Medicine*, Vol. 19, 1957, pp. 1–10.

Presented at the Thirteenth Annual Meeting of the American Psychosomatic Society, Boston, Mass., March 25, 1956.

The authors wish to acknowledge their indebtedness to Dr. David McK. Rioch, Director, and Col. Albert J. Glass, M. C., Deputy Director, Neuropsychiatry Division, Walter Reed Army Institute of Research, Walter Reed Army Medical Center, Washington, D.C., Col. Robert Skinner, M. C., Commanding Officer, and Lt. Col. R. Gonzales, M. C., Chief of Radiology, Fort Dix Army Hospital, New Jersey, Capt. John Finn, M. S. C., Walter Reed Army Institute of Research, Washington 12, D.C., Cpl. Robert Freeman, Sgt. Jules Van Praag, and Pfc. William H. Swayze for their invaluable assistance in administering and helping score the psychological material; and M/Sgt. H. A. Becker, Sgts. M. J. Colton and R. Nixon, formerly of Walter Reed Army Hospital, Washington, D.C.

tension can be related to a variety of gastrointestinal changes, no clue to the source of the tension became apparent until Alexander and his colleagues applied psychoanalytical principles to the study of patients with peptic ulcer.(1, 2) Such studies by Alexander and others(2, 12, 19) led to the generalization that patients with duodenal ulcer have in common a conflict related to the persistence of strong infantile wishes to be loved and cared for, on the one hand, and the repudiation of these wishes by the adult ego or by external circumstances, on the other hand. This psychic conflict is postulated to be responsible for initiating a sequence of physiological changes that result in the development of the duodenal lesion. Yet, as Alexander(1) and others(12) have stressed, similar psychodynamic patterns can be demonstrated in subjects without any gastrointestinal disturbance or in subjects with some other derangement. Consequently, as Alexander indicated, psychic conflict, specific or otherwise, cannot be the sole determinant in the precipitation of duodenal ulcer.

It is generally acknowledged that the response to some environmental event is a major factor in initiating the process responsible for the precipitation of peptic ulcer. Yet, there is nothing specific about the social situation that so frequently precedes the precipitation of duodenal ulcer.(20) The only inference that can be made is that the specific meaning of the environmental event to the particular individual determines whether or not the event is responded to as a noxious one.

From the preceding it would appear that there are three parameters which may contribute to the precipitation of duodenal ulcer: a physiological parameter, which determines the susceptibility of the duodenum to ulceration; a psychological parameter, which determines the relatively specific psychic conflict that induces psychic tension; and a social parameter, which determines the environmental event that will prove noxious to the particular individual. Accordingly, a duodenal ulcer should develop when an individual with a sustained rate of gastric hypersecretion and the aforementioned psychic conflict is exposed to an environmental situation that mobilizes conflict and induces psychic tension.

This report deals with part of a study designed to evaluate the role of the three parameters in the precipitation of duodenal ulcer. The degree of gastric secretion gauged by the concentration of pepsinogen in the serum comprised the physiological parameter; subjects with serum pepsinogen values beyond one standard deviation of the mean were regarded as hypersecretors, and subjects with pepsinogen values below one standard deviation of the mean were regarded as hyposecretors. The selection of subjects representative of those with the highest and lowest concentrations of pepsinogen in the blood permitted one group to serve as a control for the other. The style of interpersonal interactions that could be inferred from projective and other psychological techniques comprised the psychological parameter. The exposure to 16 weeks of basic training comprised the environmental situation that might prove noxious to some and not to other subjects.

METHOD

A total of 2073 draftees between the ages of 17.5 years and 29.2 years were chosen at random while being processed at induction at an army camp. Before entering service all had resided in the northeastern United States. Ten ml. of blood was drawn from each man. The sample was identified by code number, refrigerated, and sent to one of us (IAM) for analysis. The concentration of pepsinogen in the serum was determined by a method described in an earlier paper.(15) The Cornell Medical Index,(5) the Saslow Screening Inventory,(2) and a sociological rating scale[1] were administered to each man. Approximately 300 men were processed per week.

At the end of each week, the code numbers of 20 men were returned to the research group at the Induction Center without their levels of serum pepsinogen being revealed. These numbers identified men who were chosen for more detailed study because they were in the range of the highest and lowest values obtained in the group of men tested during the previous week. At the end of seven weeks, a total of 120 men had been selected for special study.

During the second week the 20 men who had been selected at the end of the first week were given a battery of psychological tests (Rorschach Test, Blacky Pictures, and Draw-A-Person Test). Each man was interviewed briefly by a psychiatrist and social worker, and each man was given a complete gastrointestinal roentgenological examination. The psychological tests were administered by a technician, and the test material was then sent to three of us (MT, HW, and MR) for evaluation.

After these studies were completed the men were sent to the basic training area. Subsequently, all but 13 men were again given the psychological tests

[1] Devised and evaluated by 1st Lt. Sidney Croog, WRAIR, Walter Reed Army Medical Center, Washington 12, D.C.

and roentgenological examinations some time between the eighth and sixteenth week of the basic training period.

The Rorschach results were submitted both to a formal scoring(3) and to that devised by DeVos, which divides content into various categories and subcategories "concerned with the symbolic expressions of affect."(6) Each drawing from the Draw-A-Person Test was classified as primitive, distorted, boyish, masculine, or adult. The Cornell Medical Index,(5) Saslow(21) and Blacky(4) tests were scored as recommended by their originators. In addition, Card II of the Blacky Test was scored as to whether Blacky was seen as openly expressing anger or whether the expression of such affect was denied, rationalized, or ignored.

RESULTS

Figure 1 illustrates the normal distribution of the values for the concentration of pepsinogen in the sera of the population of 2073 men who were screened. The hypersecretor group selected for special study consisted of 63 of the 300 men who comprised those with the upper 15 per cent of the serum pepsinogen values. The hyposecretor group selected for special study consisted of 57 of the 179 men who comprised those with the lowest 9 per cent of the serum pepsinogen values.

The first roentgenological examination revealed evidences of a healed duodenal ulcer in three, and of an active ulcer in one of the 63 men with gastric hypersecretion. Of these four men with evidence

Figure 1

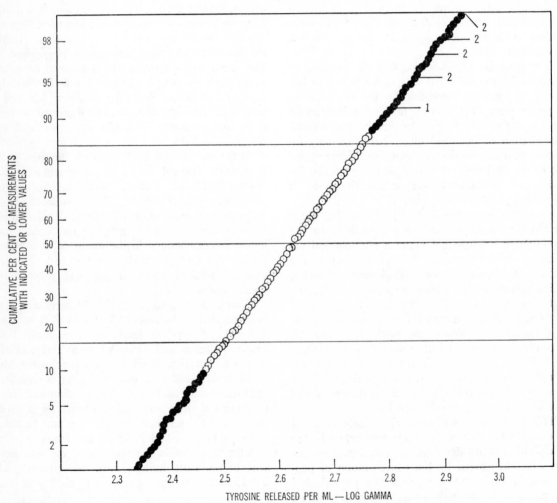

Distribution of blood serum pepsinogen concentrations: the frequency distribution of the logarithm of the concentration of the pepsinogen in the serum plotted on a probit scale. The subjects selected for special study were among those designated with closed circles. The numerals refer to individuals with duodenal ulcer.

of duodenal lesions at the outset, one became a disciplinary problem and was confined to the stockade, one went "absent without leave," one went through his basic training without incident, and the fourth man, who had the active duodenal lesion, was discharged from the service.

The second roentgenological examination at the eighth to sixteenth week revealed evidences of active duodenal ulcer in an additional five men who had no evidences of a gastrointestinal derangement at the outset of the study. All the subjects who had or developed evidences of duodenal ulcer were found among the 63 individuals with high blood pepsinogen values (Fig. 1).

With no knowledge of the pepsinogen levels or roentgenological findings, we evaluated the psychological test material to test the hypothesis that the hypersecretor could be differentiated from the hyposecretor and that men with or prone to duodenal ulcer could be identified. These hypotheses were based on clinical observations that suggested that the hypersecretor, like the patient with duodenal ulcer, would exhibit evidences of intense infantile oral dependent wishes, marked "immaturity," tendencies to please and placate, and difficulties revolving particularly about the management of oral impulses and hostility.(17, 18) Similar clinical observations suggested that the hyposecretor, like the patient with pernicious anemia, would exhibit evidences of pseudomasculine defenses and paranoid trends.(17) Accordingly, in order to categorize those who might belong among the hypersecretor group, the psychological test material was examined specifically for the presence of strong direct references to the acts of feeding, of being fed, and of incorporation. Indirect or inferred oral symbolism such as talking, smoking, kissing, blowing, etc., and responses referable to heat and cold (e.g., snow, people warming themselves, flowers growing in the snow) were also sought. It was anticipated that the hypersecretors would reveal diffuse anxiety in their answers, that many records might be characterized by depressive associations, and that the drawings would be those of boys, or primitive and gross, or asexual.

To categorize those who might belong to the hyposecretor group, special attention was paid to indications of problems referable to activity and passivity, submissiveness and assertiveness, femininity and masculinity, as evidenced by responses suggesting conflict over sexual identification, passive sexual longing, and anal symbolism. It was postulated that the test material of the hyposecretors, in contrast to the hypersecretors, would show little or no oral, depressive, or anxiety content and a paucity of indications of a need to please and placate.

Using the above criteria, one psychologist and two psychiatrists independently rated the test records to determine whether the subject belonged to the hypersecretor or hyposecretor group. On the basis of a majority opinion, 61 per cent of the 120 men — 71 per cent of the hypersecretors and 51 per cent of the hyposecretors — were correctly designated on the basis of the postulated traits.

It had been anticipated that the psychological test material and social histories would permit the prediction of the way in which each individual would react to the social situation represented by the period of basic training. This anticipation, however, proved incorrect since no technique could be devised *post hoc* to permit the selection of individuals who would react to the situation as if it were a noxious one. Consequently, based on previous experience with test patterns from patients with duodenal ulcer(23) and on inferences derived from psychoanalytical and other clinical observations of such patients,(1, 2, 7, 12, 14, 17, 19, 20, 22, 24) an attempt was made to predict which individual would develop a duodenal ulcer during the 16 weeks of basic training. It was postulated that the subject most likely to develop an ulcer during the period of basic training would show all the characteristics of the hypersecretor but with a much greater intensity than the individual who was not likely to develop the lesion. Accordingly, the psychological test material of the inductees was evaluated *before* the biochemical and roentgenological data became available.

Ten men were selected as those most likely to develop an ulcer because their test material not only suggested that they belong to the group of hypersecretors but also showed evidences of intense needs to maintain relationships with others. Their anxieties centered around a fear of expressing hostility lest there be a loss of supplies for their needs; they went out of their way to rationalize, deny, and displace such feelings. The need to please and placate authority figures as potential sources of affection was particularly striking. The predictions were accurate in seven out of the ten. Of the three who did not have or did not develop an ulcer, two were hypersecretors.

Post hoc studies revealed that all of the nine men who had or developed a duodenal ulcer during the period of basic training had been classified correctly as belonging to the group with high serum pepsinogen values on the basis of the psychological criteria given above. Other than the intensity of their attempt to maintain relationships, no criterion was found to distinguish the hypersecretor who developed an ulcer from the hypersecretor who did not.

The attempt to differentiate the hypersecretors from the hyposecretors on the basis of clinical impressions of the available psychological test material indicated that the criteria used for such differentiation were inadequate. To develop a more accurate diagnostic tool, a variety of criteria from the test material of the hypersecretors and hyposecretors were analyzed statistically. Only those criteria that were significant at less than the 5 per cent level of confidence were used for a final classification. By means of a cluster of 20 such criteria it was possible to distinguish the two groups to the extent that 85 per

cent of the 120 men could be assigned accurately to their group at a 0.001 level of confidence. Thus, of the 120 men, only 6 hypersecretors and 12 hyposecretors could not be correctly classified on the basis of the cluster of psychological test criteria.

The twenty criteria that permitted the relatively correct differentiation of the hypersecretor from the hyposecretor are listed in Table 1. No single criterion permitted the separation of the two groups with an accuracy exceeding 64.2 per cent, but all were significant at the 5 per cent level of confidence or better. The combinations of items, however, permitted the more accurate designation.

The overall impression of the psychological make-up of hypersecretors gained from the use of these

■ TABLE 1 / Criteria Distinguishing Subjects with High and Low Concentration of Pepsinogen in the Blood

Criterion	Responses: Cut-off Score	Serum Pepsinogen Concentration		No. Correctly Classified	% of Total Corr. Classified	X^2	P Level
		High	Low				
1. Rorschach: Color-form	Present	31	17	71	59.2	4.684	< .05
	Absent	32	40				
2. Rorschach: Childish and authority-dependency	Present	37	21	73	60.8	5.741	< .02
	Absent	26	36				
3. Rorschach: Texture	Present	33	18	72	60.0	5.299	< .05
	Absent	30	39				
4. Rorschach: Oral symbolism	31% or more	35	19	73	60.8	5.971	< .02
	30% or less	28	38				
5. Draw-A-Person: Boyish drawings	Present	24	8	73	60.8	7.67	< .01
	Absent	39	49				
6. Rorschach: Openly symbolized hostility	3 or more	27	14	70	58.3	5.010	< .05
	2 or less	36	43				
7. Rorschach: Per cent hostile responses	24% or less	50	30	77	64.2	9.624	< .01
	25% or more	13	27				
8. Blacky Test: Anger on Card II	Absent	32	18	71	59.2	4.546	< .05
	Present	31	39				
9. Blacky Test: Denial of aggression, Card IIIb	Present	29	16	70	48.3	4.119	< .05
	Absent	34	41				
10. Saslow Test: Anger expressed (N = 110)	No	36	22	66	60.0	4.296	< .05
	Yes	22	30				
11. Rorschach: Per cent small details	8% or more	36	20	73	60.8	5.849	< .02
	7% or less	27	37				
12. Rorschach: Poorly perceived responses	20% or less	31	14	74	61.7	7.755	< .01
	21% or more	32	43				
13. Cornel Medical Index: No. of items	15 or less	46	26	75	62.5	9.153	< .01
	16 or more	16	29				
14. Saslow Text: Anxiety expressed (N = 109)	No	30	14	67	61.5	6.64	= .01
	Yes	28	37				
15. Rorschach: Hostile-sado-masochistic content	Absent	52	37	72	60.0	4.853	< .05
	Present	11	20				
16. Rorschach: Feminine identification	Absent	52	37	72	60.0	4.853	< .05
	Present	11	20				
17. Rorschach: Anxious face details	Absent	62	49	70	58.3	5.010	< .05
	Present	1	8				
18. Rorschach: Hybrid combinations	1 or less	62	47	72	60.0	7.335	< .01
	2 or more	1	10				
19. Rorschach: Per cent unpleasant content	39% or less	33	18	72	60.0	5.299	< .05
	40% or more	30	39				
20. Rorschach: Per cent neutral content	35% or more	33	18	72	60.0	5.299	< .05
	34% or less	30	39				
Total Classification (20 Criteria)	10 or more	57	45	102	85.0	....	< .001

scoring criteria was one of marked dependency in their relationships to others, of compliance, and of passiveness. Thus the affect of a greater number was childishly toned (criteria 1 and 2); they gave more texture responses (criterion 3), suggesting a greater awareness of, or need for tactile contact with others. A greater incidence of responses symbolizing oral needs (criterion 4) and dependency on authority figures (criterion 2) were given by the hypersecretors. This group also displayed a greater incidence of immature body images on human drawings (criterion 5).

The majority of the hypersecretors gave responses symbolizing the expression, explicit or implicit, of anxiety (criterion 6), the source of which appeared to be hostile impulses (criterion 7) that they felt must not be revealed or directly expressed (criteria 8, 9, and 10). This was inferred from the resulting formal evidences of depression that were evident in the Rorschach scores (criteria 11 and 12). The hypersecretors had relatively few complaints about bodily symptoms, be they of discomfort, physical illness (criterion 13), or of the anxiety reaction (criterion 14). It is noteworthy, however, that the Rorschach associations of some individuals indicated both the presence of anxiety (criterion 6) in freely associated material, and a tendency not to complain of its physical concomitant and not to be aware of and/or acknowledge its presence on direct questioning (criteria 13 and 14). Thus, of the 27 individuals with high serum pepsinogen levels who gave anxiety associations (criterion 6), 12 denied that they felt anxious on the Saslow questionnaire. Yet anxiety associations (criterion 6) were given by 14 hyposecretors, 11 of whom admitted their anxiety openly (criterion 14).

Although the above features, so common to many of the hypersecretors, were also present in 12 of the hyposecretors, the incidence of such features was insignificant among the latter (criteria 1, 2, 4, and 5). The greater "immaturity" of the hypersecretors, when compared with the hyposecretors, is also revealed in the fact that they consistently showed two of the three categories which best reveal juvenile traits (criteria 1, 2, and 5) when these criteria were combined to evaluate this feature.

Another distinction between the two groups was that the hyposecretors showed high hostility scores (criterion 7) in which sadomasochistic associations figured prominently (criterion 15), or they openly expressed their anger (criteria 8 and 10).

To test the consistency with which the hypersecretor group appeared to avoid or evade the evidences of the expression of hostility, responses to criteria 7, 8, 9, 10, and 15 were combined. Using a simple majority tally as a cut-off score, the direct expression of hostility was found to be rarer among the hypersecretors than among the hyposecretors ($P < 0.001$).

Bodily preoccupation (criterion 13) and more complaints about bodily symptoms generally characterized individuals in the group with low serum pepsinogen concentrations. The hyposecretors gave a mean of 19 complaints, whereas the hypersecretors gave a mean of 12 complaints. Furthermore, using Brodman's criterion of 30 or more complaints as an indicator of potentially inadequate military performance,(5) there were 4 hypersecretors and 15

TABLE 2 / Checklist of "Disturbed" Records

Sign	Responses: Cut-off Score	Serum Pepsinogen Concentration		No. Correctly Classified	% of Total (120) Corr. Classified	X^2	P Level
		High	Low				
1. *Formal Rorschach. N-33*							
a) P %	12% or less	8	7	20	60.0	....	N.S.
	13% or more	6	12				
b) F minus % and i % combined	49% or more	9	9	19	57.0	....	N.S.
	48% or less	5	10				
c) W %	20% or less	9	8	20	60.0	....	N.S.
	21% or more	5	11				
d) Feminine on Card 3	Absent	14	12	21	63.0	4.417	< .05
	Present	0	7				
e) Elaboration	Absent	14	10	23	69.0	6 76	< .01
	Present	0	9				
2. *DeVos Scoring*:							
f) Ahyb	1 or less	13	13	19	57.0	....	N.S.
	2 or more	1	6				
g) AA and Aa combined	2 or more	13	6	26	78.0	9.874	< .01
	1 or less	1	13				
h) Oral	2 or more	10	6	23	69.0	4.515	< .05
	1 or less	4	13				

hyposecretors who gave 30 or more of these answers; the difference is statistically significant (P < 0.01).

Twenty of the 57 hyposecretors drew very masculine and adult figures on the Draw-A-Person Test, but 20 of these had an apparent difficulty in sexual identity, revealed by their identifying the figures on the third Rorschach card as women or by giving only female human content on the entire test.

That a small number of hyposecretors handle their anxiety by focusing on profile details on the Rorschach test is indicated by criterion 17. Other subjects gave two or more autistic and hybrid combinations of humans and animals (criterion 18).

■ TABLE 3 / Overall Clinical Judgment of Rorschach Record

DeVos Index No. of Responses	Hypersecretors		Hyposecretors	
	Not Disturbed (49)	Disturbed (14)	Not Disturbed (38)	Disturbed (19)
0	32	4	22	5
1	12	1	9	3
2 and more	5	9	7	11
	$X^2 = 8.75$ p < .01		$X^2 = 7.399$ p < .01	

In the overall group of 120 soldiers, there were 33 (14 hypersecretors and 19 hyposecretors) whose test records on inspection indicated sufficient psychological difficulties to rate the protocols as "disturbed."(6) The contrast between "disturbed" hyper- and hyposecretors was consistent with the inference drawn above for the entire group. In fact, the "disturbed" records of hypersecretors revealed that their anxieties were the product of variants of primitive oral impulses in dependent relationships. The hyposecretors, in contrast, evidenced marked somatic preoccupation, predominantly projective defenses, and an elaborate form of thought disorder.

DISCUSSION

In the present study, the criterion chosen as an index of the susceptibility to the development of duodenal ulcer was the concentration of pepsinogen in the serum. This criterion was selected because long-term studies still in progress have indicated that duodenal ulcer develops only in those with high serum pepsinogen concentrations.(17, 18)

The data reported herein reveal a remarkable correlation between the concentration of pepsinogen in the serum and specific personality characteristics of a group of young men inducted into the army.

The group of subjects with high serum pepsinogen concentrations show intense needs that are principally "oral" in nature and which are exhibited in terms of wishing to be fed, to lean on others, and to seek close bodily contact with others. Satisfaction of these needs for external support and external sources for satiation is attempted by many means. When such attempts fail, the resultant frustration arouses anger that cannot be expressed lest there ensue a loss of supply for their needs. Consequently these subjects usually do not make complaints or express any feelings of anger.

In contrast to the above, the subjects with low concentrations of pepsinogen in the serum exhibit fewer problems about and less dependency on external sources of supply and support. They are more narcissistic and exhibit more problems relative to internal, bodily discomfort, and react to the sources of the discomfort with intense hostility which they express relatively freely. They show evidences of a disturbance in language style that is characterized by elaboration and pretentiousness. Some of the subjects show a hostile feminine identification which they defend themselves against by a masculine overcompensation. Projective defenses against anxiety are common.

In accord with the hypothesis stated at the outset, the men who had or developed a duodenal lesion were among those with high concentrations of pepsinogen in the circulation; that is, among the hypersecretors. Further, the personality characteristics of those who did develop a duodenal ulcer are essentially the same as most of the subjects comprising the hypersecretor group. Although the predictions were accurate in seven of nine subjects who had or developed duodenal ulcer, it proved impossible in the present study to use the available data to determine why only some of the hypersecretors reacted as they did to the social situation or developed the duodenal lesion. In another study in which psychoanalytically oriented anamnestic interviews were conducted, however, it has been possible to predict the character of the social situation that would prove noxious to the specific individual, and subsequently to observe that when such exposure occurred, a duodenal ulcer ensued. These observations, as well as the mechanism whereby exposure to a social event that is noxious to the individual induces the development of a duodenal lesion, will be described in another communication.

The present study does not provide an explanation for the high correlation between the serum pepsinogen concentration and the relatively specific personality characteristics. Studies on siblings and twins reveal that the secretory capacity of the gastric mucosa as gauged by the serum pepsinogen concentrations is genetically determined.(18) Even at birth, the concentration of serum pepsinogen is distributed normally with some newborn infants having values that are beyond the mean of patients with duodenal ulcer. Consequently, it is improbable that the psychological characteristics described above are responsible for the physiological state of the stomach. Although the psychological development of the infant is largely dependent upon his human environment, the secretory capacity of the stomach with which the child is born may play a significant role in his relationship with that environment. (17) Studies on the manner in which the quantitative aspects of a physiological system influences the child-mother unit and thereby the child's psychological development are in progress and should provide data that may clarify the mechanisms involved.

Although it is possible to postulate that the inherited secretory capacity of the stomach plays a role in determining not only the psychological development of the infant but also his physiological predisposition, it does not account for the marked individual differences that characterize the manner in which the needs described above are handled. Study of these individual differences suggest that the vagaries of each person's life experiences determine the manner in which impulses and wishes are mastered, whereas the hypersecretor's persistent wishes for support and succor from the external environment are determined by early childhood factors. The manner in which he handles these wishes is determined by all his life experiences, that is, by the factors that determine his integrative capacity.

SUMMARY

1. Serum pepsinogen was determined for each of 2073 army inductees. Sixty-three with values in the upper 15 per cent and 57 with values in the lower 9 per cent of the blood pepsinogen distribution were selected for special study. Each of these was given the Rorschach, Blacky, Draw-A-Person, Cornell Medical Index, and Saslow tests, and a complete upper gastrointestinal roentgenological examination before being sent to basic training.

2. One hundred and seven subjects were reexamined between the eighth and sixteenth week of basic training. The first roentgenological examination revealed healed duodenal ulcers in three subjects and an active ulcer in one. The second roentgenological examination revealed active duodenal ulcers in five additional men. All nine subjects with peptic ulcer were in the upper 15 per cent of the blood pepsinogen distribution, eight of them being in the upper 5 per cent. Thus, 15 per cent of men in the top 5 per cent developed peptic ulcer.

3. Independent evaluation of the psychological data revealed that subjects with peptic ulcer displayed evidence of major unresolved and persistent conflicts about dependency and oral gratification, the characteristics of which are described.

4. Classification of the selected test population into two groups on the basis of criteria derived from the psychological tests was found to correlate (85 per cent) with the two groups (hyper- and hypo-pepsinogen secretors) derived from the physiological tests.

5. The study indicates that neither a high rate of gastric secretion nor a specific psychodynamic constellation is independently responsible for development of peptic ulcer. Together, however, these two parameters constitute the essential determinants in the precipitation of peptic ulcer on exposure to social situations noxious to the specific individual.

REFERENCES

1. ALEXANDER, F. The influence of psychologic factors upon gastrointestinal disturbances: General principles, objectives and preliminary results. *Psychoanalyt. Quart.* 3:501, 1934.
2. ALEXANDER, F. *Psychosomatic Medicine.* New York, Norton, 1950.
3. BECK, S. J. *Rorschach's Test.* New York, Grune and Stratton, 1947.
4. BLUM, G. S. Revised scoring system for research use of the Blacky pictures. (Male form — 1951). Ann Arbor, Mich., Univ. of Mich., 1951.
5. BRODMAN, K., ERDMANN, A. J., JR., LORGE, I., DEUTSCHBERGER, J., and WOLFF, H. G. The Cornell Medical Index — Health Questionnaire VII: The prediction of psychosomatic and psychiatric disabilities in army training. *Am. J. Psychiat.* 111:37, 1954.
6. DeVos, G. A quantitative approach to affective symbolism in Rorschach responses. *J. of Proj. Tech.* 16:133, 1952.
7. GILDEA, E. G. Special features of the personality which are common to certain psychosomatic disorders. *Psychosom. Med.* 11:273, 1949.
8. GARMA, A. Internalized mother as harmful food in peptic ulcer patients. *Internat. J. Psycho-analysis* 34:102, 1953.
9. HUNT, J. N., and KAY, A. W. The nature of gastric hypersecretion of acid in patients with duodenal ulcer. *Brit. M. J.* 2:1444, 1954.
10. IVY, A. C., GROSSMAN, M. I., and BACHRACH, W. H. *Peptic Ulcer.* Philadelphia, Blakiston, 1950.
11. JONES, F. A. The problem of peptic ulcer. *Ann. Int. Med.* 44:63, 1956.

12. KAPP, F. T., ROSENBAUM, M., and ROMANO, J. Psychological factors in men with peptic ulcer. *Am. J. Psychiat.* 103:700, 1947.

13. LEVIN, E., KIRSNER, J. B., and PALMER, W. L. Twelve-hour nocturnal gastric secretion in uncomplicated duodenal ulcer patients: Before and after healing. *Proc. Soc. Exper. Biol. Med.* 69:153, 1948.

14. MINSKI, L., and DESAI, M. M. Aspects of personality in peptic ulcer patients. *Brit. J. M. Psychol.* 28:113, 1955.

15. MIRSKY, I. A., FUTTERMAN, P., KAPLAN, S., and BROH-KAHN, R. H. Blood plasma pepsinogen: I. The source, properties, and assay of the proteolytic activity of plasma at acid reactions. *J. Lab. and Clin. Med.* 40:17, 1952.

16. MIRSKY, I. A., FUTTERMAN, P., and KAPLAN, S. Blood plasma pepsinogen: II. The activity of the plasma from "normal" subjects, patients with duodenal ulcer, and patients with pernicious anemia. *J. Lab. and Clin. Med.* 40:188, 1952.

17. MIRSKY, I. A. Psychoanalysis and the biological sciences. In Alexander and Ross, *Twenty Years of Psychoanalysis.* New York, Norton and Co., 1953.

18. MIRSKY, I. A. In preparation.

19. RUESCH, J. The infantile personality. *Psychosom. Med.* 10:134, 1948.

20. RUESCH, J., CHRISTIANSEN, C., DEWEES, S., HARRIS, R. E., JACOBSON, A., and LOEB, M. B. Duodenal ulcer, a sociopsychological study of naval enlisted personnel and civilians. Berkeley, Cal., University of California Press, 1948.

21. SASLOW, G., COUNTS, R. M., and DUBOIS, P. H. Evaluation of a new psychiatric screening test. *Psychosom. Med.* 13:242, 1951.

22. STREITFELD, H. S. Specificity of peptic ulcer to intense oral conflicts. *Psychosom. Med.* 16:315, 1954.

23. THALER, M. B., WEINER, H., and REISER, M. F. An exploration of the doctor-patient relationship through projective techniques. Presented at 111th Annual Meeting, American Psychiatric Association, Atlantic City, N. J., May 12, 1955.

24. ZANE, M. Psychosomatic considerations in peptic ulcer. *Psychosom. Med.* 2:372, 1947.

Lawrence E. Hinkle, Jr. / Norman Plummer / Rhoda Metraux
Peter Richter / John W. Gittinger / William N. Thetford
Adrian M. Ostfeld / Francis D. Kane / Leo Goldberger
William E. Mitchell / Hope Leichter / Ruth Pinsky
David Goebel / Irwin D. J. Bross / Harold G. Wolff

Studies in Human Ecology

Factors Relevant to the Occurrence of Bodily Illness and Disturbances in Mood, Thought and Behavior in Three Homogeneous Population Groups[*][1]

This is an initial summary of the findings from 3 studies which have been carried out during the past 5 years. Two have been completed; the third is still in progress. Twenty-four investigators from the fields of internal medicine, psychiatry, psychology, sociology, cultural anthropology, and medical statistics have taken part in these investigations with the technical assistance of 8 others. The 3 population groups which have been studied provided a total of 2924 individuals upon which the general conclusions are based.

These studies were designed to investigate the influence which man's relation to his social environment has upon his health. They are based upon the premise that in a group of people unselected

* Reprinted by permission from the *American Journal of Psychiatry*, Vol. 114, 1957, pp. 212–220.
[1] Read at the 112th annual meeting of The American Psychiatric Association, Chicago, Ill., April 30–May 4, 1956.

with regard to health, and essentially equal with regard to the various factors known to affect health, each individual's relation to his own life situation is an outstanding variable. In such a group, a study of the relationship between this variable and the state of health of the individual members is facilitated. It is not possible, of course, to obtain any group of human beings which is literally homogeneous with regard to all of the various factors which may affect the health of its members. One can, however, find groups which closely approach homogeneity with regard to the major factors, and in which the minor and unrecognized factors are presumably scattered at random, thus minimizing the influence of these variables as compared to the variable under study.

Among the major factors that are known to have an effect upon the health of humans are age, sex, genetic inheritance, constitution, the effects of previous disease processes, cultural background, socioeconomic status (with all that this implies in terms of diet, housing, etc.), occupation, the general physical environment, and the opportunities for encountering the external causative agents relevant to disease. We have studied 3 groups, each quite different from the other 2, and each remarkably homogeneous with regard to most of these factors. The genetic inheritance and constitution of individual members, of course, cannot be controlled; but the effect of this and other variables can be assessed to some extent by a consideration of the individual case material, as will be described later.

The characteristics of these 3 groups are outlined in Table 1. There were independent and complete records of all the periods of disability, and of the nature of all illnesses, which had occurred in the adult lives of the members of the two American groups, both of which were employed by a corporation that kept meticulous records of its employees' health and attendance. In the Chinese group we were forced to rely upon the medical histories given by the informants, their descriptions of the symptomatic manifestation of their illnesses, and the results of physical examinations and diagnostic tests, in order to obtain our information about their health. Information obtained in this manner from the American informants, when compared with that obtained independently from their records, was found to be reliable, and it is our belief that we have a reliable estimate of the health of our Chinese informants.

In the 2 American groups the following investigative procedure was used: the initial group was made up of all people employed in the same type of work in a division of a corporation in a large city — approximately 1,800 men in one case and approximately 1,700 women in the other. From these initial groups there were excluded all those for whom complete records were not available, leaving 1,527 men and 1,297 women. These larger groups were used for statistical studies of the distribution sickness disability and the occurrence of various illnesses among their members, over a number of years.

There were many women and men who had been observed continuously for 20 years or more. All of these women (336) and one-third of the men (279) were studied intensively, using statistical methods.

■ TABLE 1 / Characteristics of the Three Groups

	Group I	Group II	Group III
1. Total number studied	1297	1527	100
2. Number studied intensively	336	279	100
3. Age	17–50	17–55	19–72
4. Sex	Women	Men	Men and women
5. Cultural background	2nd Generation Irish and Italian American	Mixed indigenous American	Chinese
6. Socio-economic background	Upper-lower class	Lower-middle class	Upper class
7. Education	Grammar school	High school	College
8. Occupation	Unskilled white-collar	Skilled workmen	Graduate students professional men
9. Lifetime environment	Metropolitan New York	Metropolitan New York	Various parts of China (Later United States)
10. Sanitation of general surroundings	Generally high	Generally high	Generally very low
11. Exposure to pathogens and trauma	Low	Moderate	High
12. Physical deprivations, pressures and dislocations	Few	Few	Many
13. Social dislocations and situations of uncertainty	Few	Few	Many

When the distribution of illness over a 20-year period in these 2 smaller groups had been obtained, the 20 in each group who had been disabled for the greatest number of days, and the 20 disabled for the smallest number of days, were identified. The records of these 40, and those of many others selected at random from the middle range of each group, were examined carefully to ascertain the nature of the illness episodes which had been experienced. The informants, themselves, were interviewed by an investigator who obtained from them a complete medical history, and carried out a physical and psychiatric examination, as well as additional diagnostic procedures if any were necessary in order to complete his understanding of the case. At the same time, a life history was obtained covering the pertinent aspects of the early development and later life experiences of the informant.

A somewhat different procedure was used with the Chinese. All members of this group of 100, selected at random from a larger group of approximately 5,000 Chinese graduate students and professional men, were studied intensively for a total of 16 hours. Four hours of this were spent with an internist, 4 hours with a psychiatrist, 4 hours with a cultural anthropologist and sociologist, and 4 hours with a clinical psychologist, who administered a battery of tests including the Wechsler-Bellevue Intelligence Scale, Form I, the Rorschach Test, the Lowenfeld Mosaic, a Projective Questionnaire, the Sacks Sentence Completions, the Thurstone Temperament Scale, and Human Figure Drawings. The TAT was given to about 30 of the informants also.

Sickness disability was not distributed at random among the members of any of these groups. In each group there were many members who had more illness, and many who had less illness, than would be expected if chance alone were the determining factor. In the group of American men, upon whom the statistical studies are most complete, the distribution of sickness episodes closely approximates the negative binomial distribution — a distribution which is based upon the assumption that some factor in addition to chance determines the occurrence of such episodes. In this group, approximately 10 percent of the men show a statistical "risk" of becoming ill which is at least twice as great as the average "risk" for the group, and another 10 percent show a correspondingly smaller "risk" (Fig. 1). The general effect of this skewed distribution of illness is that approximately one-fourth of the individuals experienced more than half of all the illnesses and upwards of 75 percent of the total days disability.

□ **Figure 1**

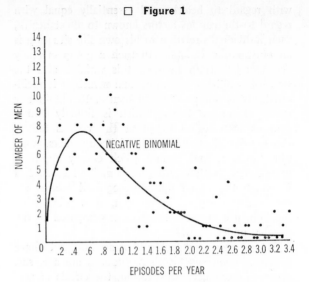

AMERICAN MEN / Distribution of informants by episodes of illness. (twenty years of observation.)

Our general inference from this finding is that, in all of these groups, some factor other than chance determines the occurrence of sickness in the individual members. Since this appears to be a consistent finding, we suspect that the same phenomenon occurs in the population at large.

An investigation of the nature of the illnesses experienced by the various members of each group revealed that in all 3 groups, those who had the greatest amount of sickness disability had experienced a wide variety of illnesses of various types, and various etiologies, involving a number of body systems. While one or two recurrent or chronic illnesses might predominate in the sickness pattern of an individual, it was a universal finding that those who had a great many episodes of illness, and a great many days of total disability, experienced illnesses involving a number of body systems. This is illustrated in Fig. 2, from the study of the American men, in which the number of illnesses experienced by each informant is plotted against the number of body systems involved. As the amount of illness experienced by each informant increases, the number of involved body systems increases.

There appears to be a similar relationship between bodily illnesses and disturbances of mood, thought, and behavior. Figure 3, taken from the study of the Chinese, illustrates this. Those having the greater number of bodily illnesses, regardless of their nature or etiology, in general, experience a

□ **Figure 2**

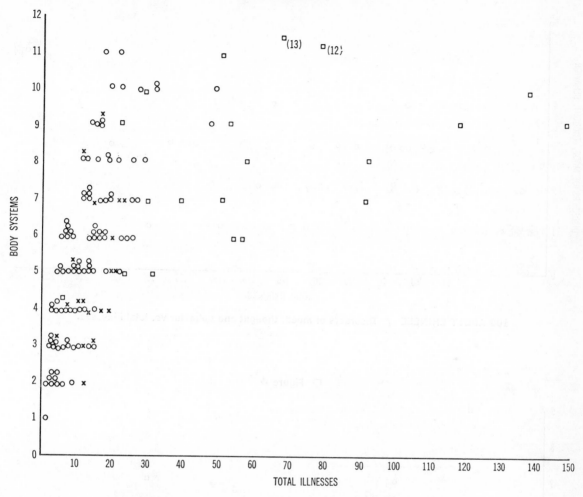

AMERICAN MEN / Number of body systems involved vs. total illnesses.

greater number of disturbances of mood, thought, and behavior.

Between major and minor illnesses, the same type of relationship appears to hold. In each group, those experiencing the greater number of minor illnesses in general experience the greater number of major illnesses. Usually it was found that major illnesses involved the same body systems most frequently involved in minor illnesses. For example, individuals having a great many colds appear to be more likely to have an episode of pneumonia, and those having many minor disturbances of mood, thought, or behavior appear to be more likely to have major disabling illnesses in this category. But major illnesses may appear in other body systems also; the general relationship is shown in Fig. 4 which is taken from the study of the American men.

An example of the illnesses experienced by a frequently ill informant is shown in Table 2. This American working woman was selected for intensive study because she had had 1,041 days of sickness disability over a period of 35 years.

Our general inferences from the foregoing findings are that humans, when they move from a state of "health" into a state of "sickness" are likely to manifest disturbances of function and pathological processes involving a number of body systems. If illness persists long enough, it is likely to be manifested by disturbances in a majority of body systems, as well as by disturbances of mood, thought, and behavior. We infer that whatever factors are responsible for this operate upon man as a whole and influence illnesses regardless of their nature or etiology. They evidently influence irreversible path-

☐ **Figure 3**

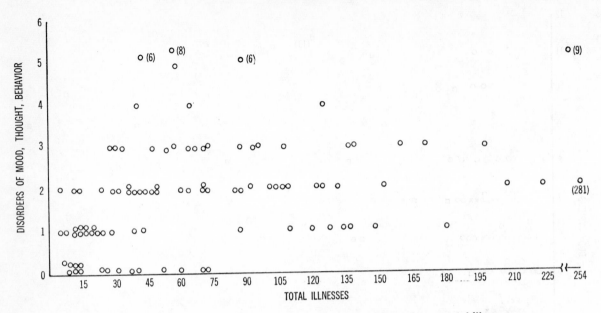

100 ADULT CHINESE / Disorders of mood, thought and behavior vs. total illnesses.

☐ **Figure 4**

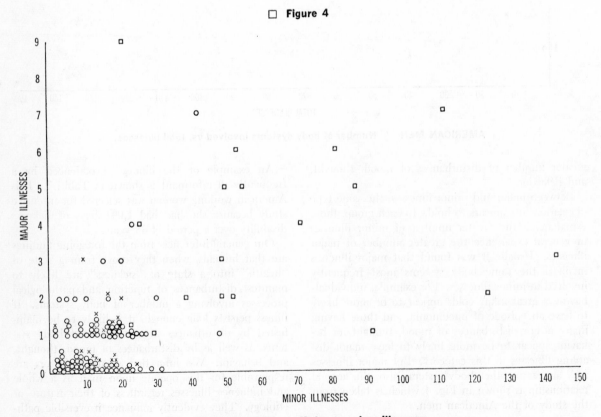

AMERICAN MEN / Major vs. minor illnesses.

■ TABLE 2 / An "Ill" American Working Woman: Illnesses Experienced From Age 16 to Age 51

"Body System"	Syndrome	Episodes of Disability
1. Respiratory system	Influenza	1
	Pertussis	1
	Minor upper respiratory infections (Approx.)	44
	Severe tonsillitis	2
2. Gastrointestinal system	Cholecystitis and cholelithiasis	2
	Diaphragmatic hernia	5
	Duodenal diverticulum	0
	Postoperative biliary symptoms	4
	Mucous colitis	4
	Infectious gastroenteritis	3
	(Chronic, nondisabling constipation, low abdominal pain, "gas," and nausea, present for many years)	
3. Cardiovascular system	Essential hypertension	0
4. Genital system	Myomata of uterus	1
	Dysmenorrhea (chronic)	
	Postmenopausal flushes, severe	
5. Urinary system	Pyelonephritis	1
	Cystitis	1
6. Blood	Hypochromic anemia	
7. Musculoskeletal system	"Low back pain"	4
	Osteoarthritis	1
8. Head	Vascular headaches	2
	(Nondisabling headaches occurred about once a month)	
9. Ears	Otitis Media	2
	Menière's syndrome	1
10. Eyes	Conjunctivitis	1
11. Teeth	Dental caries	3
	(Total extractions)	
12. Skin	Urticaria	2
	Cellulitis	1
13. Breast	Fibroma	1
14. Metabolic	Obesity	
15. Mood, thought, behavior	Moderately severe depressions	3
	Anxiety-tension states	5
	(Symptoms of anxiety, tension, depression chronically present)	
Accidents	Contusions	8
	Lacerations	3
	Sprains	1
Operations	1. Cholecystectomy	
	2. Hysterectomy and oophorectomy	
	3. Excision of fibroma of breast	
	4. Total dental extractions	

Summary

Total days disabled	1041
Disabling episodes of illness	95
"Major" illnesses	9
Disabling disturbances of mood, thought, and behavior	8
"Body systems" involved	15
Accidents	12
Operations	4

ological processes as well as reversible disturbances of function, and diseases which are potentially fatal as well as those which are usually transient and relatively harmless. They influence the occurrence of disturbances of mood, thought, and behavior and the occurrence of bodily illnesses in a roughly parallel manner. The relation between these two categories of illness thus appears to be one of general parallelism. As a group, those who have

more of one are likely to have more of the other.

When the distribution of illness in the lives of our informants was studied, it was found that sickness episodes frequently appeared in clusters; usually they were not distributed at random throughout a lifetime. Typically, an informant would have periods of relatively good health, alternating with several years during which he would have a number of illnesses of a variety of etiologies and involving several body systems, running consecutively or concurrently. This is a common phenomenon in all 3 groups, and it appears to be uniformly distributed in each. It occurs among those who have small and intermediate amounts of illness as well as among those who have many illnesses. Some illnesses and accidents do, of course, appear as isolated phenomena; but most illnesses seem to occur in clusters. An example of this is shown in Fig. 5 taken from the study of the Chinese.

□ **Figure 5**

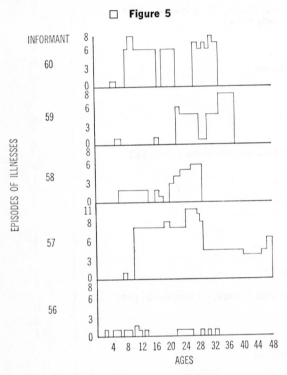

CHINESE GROUP / Distribution of illnesses by age at time of occurrence in five informants.

From this phenomenon of "clustering," we infer that whatever factors are operating to affect the general susceptibility of our informants to illness do not exert a constant influence at all times. Their effect is greater at some times, and less at others. There is no predictable period of life when such clusters appear, and they have no consistent duration or magnitude. From this we infer that these factors probably arise out of some changing and unpredictable relationship between each individual and his environment.

By correlating events and situations in the life histories of our informants with the occurrence of clusters of illness, we have attempted to ascertain what consistent features of the individual's relationship to his environment might be associated with fluctuations in his general health. So far as we have been able to determine, physical hardship, geographic and climatic change, and changing exposures to toxic or infectious agents, are not the significant variables. Only occasionally does it appear that the development of an isolated illness, or a cluster of illnesses, is simply the result of some fortuitous encounter with bacteria, trauma, or other influences arising from the physical environment. Genetic inheritance and constitutional endowment undoubtedly play a role in general susceptibility to illness, and probably have an important influence upon the total sickness experienced by an individual throughout his life. But the data in general suggest that, as compared to the effects of the life situation, these factors are relatively unimportant in determining the distribution of illness in any of the groups. In any case, it is difficult to invoke them as an explanation of the clustering of illness at special times in the lives of individual informants.

We find that clusters of illness usually are associated with periods when an individual is attempting to adapt to a difficult life situation (Figs. 6 and 7). That is to say, such clusters commonly occur during periods of demonstrable conflict with parents, siblings, or spouse, threat to social position, loss of significant supports, or excessive demands created by the sickness or aggressive behavior of other members of the family, employers, associates, and so on. Such observable difficulties in the relationship to the social environment are usually directly stated by the informants to be difficult or unpleasant, with a detailed description of why they are difficult and with appropriate feelings. From such data alone it is possible to say that, in each of these informant groups, the relationship of the informants to their social environment has an important influence upon the occurrence of clusters of illness, and that it is much more consistently related to this than any other factors which have been considered. But the correlation between clusters of illness and such "objective" evidences of difficult life situations is by no means complete. There are a great many instances of informants existing in what are objectively "difficult life situations," with no observable evidence of illness; and, conversely, there are many other instances in which clusters of illness appeared in the lives of informants at times when they were existing in what objectively appear to be benign life situations.

It is axiomatic that man does not react to his environment as it is "objectively" perceived by other

□ **Figure 6**

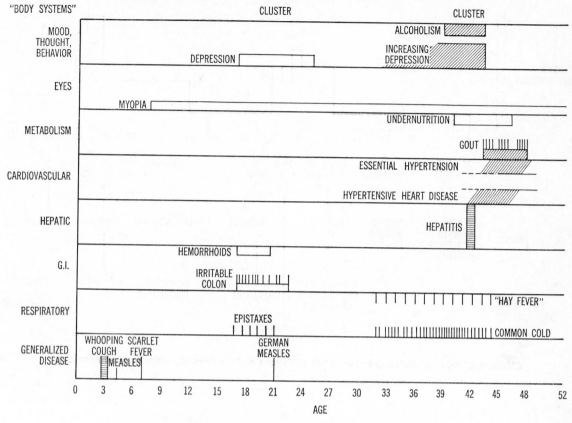

CHINESE STUDY / **Illnesses experienced by one informant.**

people; rather he reacts to it, as he, himself, perceives it in terms of his own needs and aspirations (using "perceive" to include both conscious and unconscious processes). There is no way to ascertain how a man perceives his life situation without using his own subjective impressions, or the inferences of an observer, or both. Information obtained in this manner is always biased by the attitudes of the informant, and is very likely to be biased by those of the observer. Such information, therefore, does not lend itself to being counted or quantified in a mathematical fashion. On the other hand, the observer can validly state his inferences and present the original case material upon which these inferences are based. It has been the general inference of all of the observers who have participated in these studies that the great majority of the clusters of illness which have occurred in the lives of our informants have occurred during life situations which the informant, himself, perceived as stressful, even though this situation might appear benign to an "objective" observer; conversely, when "objectively"

difficult life situations are not associated with illness the informants usually did not perceive these life situations as difficult, even though the observer might expect them to do so. This was a consistent observation among the informants in all of the groups, regardless of their general state of health.

CONCLUSION

Our inferences from our studies are these: man's relation to his social environment as perceived by him has a profound effect upon his general health. It influences the development and progression of all forms of illness, regardless of their nature, and regardless of the influence of other etiological factors. Its effect often far outweighs the influence of changes in the physical environment and the effects of random exposure to pathogenic or noxious agents. As a group, those who are experiencing difficulty in adapting to their social environment have a disproportionate amount of all of the illness which occurs among the adult population.

☐ **Figure 7**

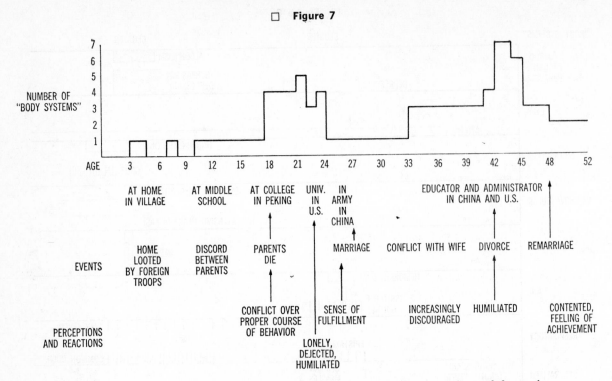

CHINESE STUDY / Relation between life situations and clusters of illness in one informant.

JAMES L. TITCHENER, JULES RISKIN, AND RICHARD EMERSON

The Family in Psychosomatic Process
A Case Report Illustrating a Method of Psychosomatic Research*†

This paper is the report of a study of an entire family in which one son developed ulcerative colitis. It has been written to point out a method by which one of the conditions specific to the etiology of psychosomatic processes may be further understood.

* Reprinted by permission from *Psychosomatic Medicine,* Vol. 22, 1960, pp. 127–142.
† Research reported in this paper was supported by research grants M999 and M2534 from the National Institute for Mental Health, U.S. Public Health Service, Bethesda, Md.

In setting forth this method we propose an expansion of current hypotheses regarding the object relations factors in the causes of and predisposition to psychosomatic illness.

In his thorough review of the ulcerative colitis syndrome Dr. George Engel writes: "Elucidation of the specific aspects of the object relations constitutes a most important problem for further research."(1). This comment seems appropriate for the whole field of psychosomatic investigation. From his own research and from his extensive review of the work of others, Engel has formulated the recurrent patterns of significant relationships in ulcerative colitis patients and he has pointed out how these rigid and confining patterns predispose these individuals to psychosomatic illness. This formulation is part of a theory of the etiology of ulcerative colitis.

Dr. Engel views ulcerative colitis as a response of the whole organism with a particular locus in the lining of the large bowel. The effective and healthy bowel lining serves as a selective barrier against penetration of organisms and other substances from the "outside," i.e., the lumen of the colon. In ulcerative colitis the physiologic function of the bowel lining quite probably becomes affected in such a way that organisms in the lumen can penetrate and are, thereafter, no longer innocuous, but pathogenic. It is considered likely that a constitutional predisposition is necessary for this situation. Among the other possible factors, some still unknown, is the psychophysiologic factor; there is imposing clinical evidence to support the significance of a psychosomatic relationship.

The reports of Engel and others reviewed by him are persuasive that the essential psychological condition operating with somatic factors towards the onset of ulcerative colitis is an affective state characterized by helplessness and despair arising from a deep disturbance in a key object relation which is lost or threatened, or whose loss is imagined. The ulcerative colitis patient is unable to accomplish the grief work nor any other adjustment to object loss and so suffers a deep disruption of previous adaptation, with consequent development of a state of helplessness. It is probable that this drastic change in psychological systems breaks through to affect the operation of somatic systems, particularly if they are predisposed to dysfunction.

This unfortunate lack of adaptive capacity, combined with incessant need, develops, in Engel's view, from the early, very much prolonged symbiosis between mother and child. In very brief summary, the mother-infant and mother-child relationship are conditional ones in which mother will give love if she can control. The necessary submission of the child lays the groundwork for uninterrupted need for similar relationships throughout life. Such relationships in adolescence and adulthood, when society rules against the maintenance of a symbiosis with mother, are very difficult to find and to maintain with potential substitutes. Usually the patient-to-be manages to find someone who will fill the bill at least partially. But almost always this chosen person, who perhaps unwittingly finds himself or herself a "key" person, cannot stand the strain and the interpersonal needs of the potential patient are frustrated or threatened. Such individuals are so sensitive to the vicissitudes of the mutually controlling relationship that almost any occurrence may upset the tenuous equilibrium.

THE FAMILY IN A PSYCHOSOMATIC PROCESS

In launching our study we have assumed the conditions for the onset of ulcerative colitis as Engel has hypothesized them. Our contribution toward a new look at this hypothesis is confined to the object relation aspects of the formulation.

Our investigative approach may be likened to the one used by cultural anthropologists who, if interested in the psychodynamics of a relationship in a culture would study not one but both persons involved and, further, would seek any others who could offer intimate observations upon the relationship in question.

Our methods of study of whole families provide us with corroborating and contrasting observations by each family member, including comments upon individual feelings, upon the feelings and behavior of others, and upon their own and other relationships. We are enabled to derive a stereoscopic view of the family as a field and of the individuals' functions in this field. In addition, we can develop concepts of the family's working as a whole system — a social unit with a structure and a dynamic pattern.

We assume that, as with personality, there are patterns of adaptation for a family too. A particular person or a particular relationship — for example, mother and child — are involved continually in mutually influencing transactions with the whole family, as a social system. Let us now return to Engel's hypotheses about the prolonged mother-child symbiosis which becomes a mutually controlling relationship, pathogenic, in some cases, of ulcerative colitis. We would add that this relationship is, from the beginning and during its later vicissitudes, conditioned by the milieu in which it exists — the family. The mother-child axis turns in a social field of which the family constitutes a large and important segment.

To put our case more strongly, our approach would seem to obviate a concept of a colitigenic mother, as it would also the schizophrenogenic mother, for the relationship is not one in which the mother *per se* forces herself in a pathogenic way upon a child, but one made by the mother and conditioned by the dynamics of the family in which she and her child live. The significant element is not simply the mother's personality, but the way she acts in the particular relationship with the particular child in a particular period — all in the context of the *whole* family's psychodynamic patterns.

Let us imagine a study in which personality assessments of 20,000 mothers of ulcerative colitis patients were compared with those of 20,000 mothers of children without colitis. We would surmise that, though there would be a contrast in the groups, the correlation of colitis patients with mothers having certain traits of personality at the time of assessment would *not* be especially high. We are of the opinion that colitigenic mothers are not born nor even made in their own childhood. Their ways of relating to their children come into being *in a family situation* and their special relationships with future ulcerative colitis patients are largely determined by the dynamics of the family environment. The figure of the mother obtained in the anamnestic data from the patient is not reality, nor totally a mythical figment of the patient's psychopathology. Truly, the mother figure, like other figures in the family, is largely *a family legend* created by the relationships of *all* the individuals in the family with a central figure. The patient, then, presents us this image compounded of reality, of his own distortions, and of the family's idea of mother. One thing is probably true, however: Whatever the mother "really" is beneath the figure and the role and the image represented in the family, she is this way most of all with the patient. We can speculate that the deeper, intrapsychic conflicts, emerge most strongly in the relationship with the patient-to-be. This selection of the patient for the focus of family conflict is determined by a number of factors — environmental, individual, and constitutional. For a real understanding of the forces which motivate object choice and which bring about sensitivity to object loss we need to examine early and late object relations from this multidimensional point of view, rather than being concerned only with the binary relationship in a vacuum.

A study correlating mothers' personalities with a psychosomatic illness is in our theory, likely to produce unimpressive results because of the existence of so many other factors crucial in the moulding of the object relations which are the really essential aspects of pathogenesis. More important, studies of this kind fail to provide us with much information about *how* the mother's relations with a patient have influenced him.

In the following case study we wish to demonstrate how object relations can be seen in depth. We shall attempt to illustrate our opinion that the mother's attitudes and behavior alone are not etiologically responsible for the predisposition and onset of the illness. If her characteristics were so responsible, might she not have started a small epidemic of ulcerative colitis in this family? Instead, the theoretically pathogenic object relations are moulded by the whole interlocking set of relations, although the mother is a central figure. We shall further try to demonstrate how the affected member of the family becomes a focus of conflict for the parents and his siblings.

The case report was assembled as part of a larger and more general research on family dynamics, (2) which is related to the expanding interest in the dynamics of the individual and his family. Ackerman, (3) Chance, (4) and Kluckhohn and Spiegel (5) have provided extensive review and bibliography in this area.

The methods of our research included an observed interaction session including all family members, a number of interviews with each member individually, and a family relations inventory designed by our research team. For the purposes of this report we shall include only the individual interviews, although we learned about some aspects of the family inadvertently in some informal sessions with several of the family members. The individual interviews have a sequence which lends them some extra value. One member (J. T.) of the research team does all of the interviewing with a family, seeing its members in sequence. Then, when a series has been completed, it is repeated. In the family studied, the series was repeated four times with the exception of the patient's brother who could be interviewed only once for somewhat more than an hour. In this case we also have notes from a course of psychotherapy undergone by the patient. The interlocking or revolving sequence of interviewing tends to bring out some aspects of a family's characteristic transactions. The interviewer's ear soon becomes very sensitively tuned to the communication of the family group he is seeing, and the material covered in the associative anamnesis interviewing is directed somewhat by what the interviewer hears from all the family members. For example, in this family there was a surprising tendency for all to comment upon some early memories first reported by the patient. This tendency was encouraged by the interviewer. The fact that several people involved in a fairly intimate situation comment upon the same current issues is also extremely helpful in seeing, almost *in vivo*, what characteristically transpires in a family.

CASE HISTORY

Our acquaintance with the Neal family (pseudonym) began in early 1957 when Bob, Jr. was admitted to our psychosomatic study service upon the urgent recommendation of an internist and a psychiatric consultant. By that time Bob had lived through more than 12 months of discouraging battle with his ulcerative colitis. The anniversary of onset had passed just before Christmas without signs of improvement and, in fact, it had seemed to be marked by a moderate relapse. His self-respect had suffered with the suggestion of psychiatric treatment and his reluctant agreement to the hospital admission had carried some degree of last-resort submission on his part.

As far as we know, the illness began about the middle of December 1955 with twelve watery and bloody stools per day, diffuse abdominal pain, and nausea. Through December and January 1955–6 the diagnosis of ulcerative colitis was confirmed by proctosigmoidoscope and x-ray. He improved slowly with antibiotics and supportive care although there was a gradual decline in weight from his original 170 lb., and an anemia that stabilized at medium-low levels. A psychiatrist had one brief contact in February 1956, but his interview and the suggestion of hospitalization in a Veterans Administration psychiatric service resulted only in a petulant change of physicians. After Bob left the hospital, his condition improved a little, then relapsed a little, each setback shaking further his hope of final relief. By the fall of 1956 the relapses were more severe and enduring than the remissions, while home medical care became less effective and less resourceful.

When we first met him, Bob was a long, thin young man of 24, usually huddled and curled in his bed with a stool-chair close by. He weighed about 115 lb. Any conversation of more than 10 minutes had to be interrupted by a rush from the bed and a burst of diarrhea. He had long, dark-blond hair falling over a pale, strained, and thin face. Talking with others was painful for him, not so much because it was fatiguing and he was ill, but more because it was emotionally difficult. Medically he was toxic and psychiatrically he was helpless and hopeless. The alternate sides of Bob's character can, even at this point, be illustrated by the contrasting picture of him 12 months later, after treatment, surgery, and steroids. Then we see him standing, emerged from the cocoon of bedclothes and psychic withdrawal, with a full, heavy face and an air of complacent, assured stiffness.

Mrs. Neal was seen the day of admission. She is a moderately obese woman of slightly more than average height. She seemed relaxed, accessible, and poised. She talked easily, gave quick assurance of understanding our methods, and promised cooperation. She appeared to be empathic towards her son's recent ordeal, although first impressions could have been mistaken. She never showed much tension in response to the course of Bob's illness. Nevertheless, even a researcher oriented to the subtleties of family dynamics was surprised by the occurrence that took place immediately after this first interview, when the mother went from the office to her son's room and burst in saying, "Your father is in an agony of stomach pain from worrying about you." This drastic double-bind (6) and conflictful expression of common family problems, which will be explained more completely below, expresses the divided pity of the mother and forces Bob, in a loving way, to accept the responsibility for the father's illness. It would be impossible to say whether the occurrence had a physiological effect, since the bowel was already operating at near maximum speed of contraction, secretion, and hemorrhage. Soon thereafter, Bob was seen in his room. He was tightly huddled, sometimes trembling and almost unable to talk except to emit short bursts of anger at his father for not taking care of himself and his stomach. The conversation was strategically directed towards introductory small-talk. A little anxious himself, the interviewer strayed to the window and there spoke aimlessly of promises to bring magazines and of the hospital's need for new buildings to replace the old, dreary ones. While the interviewer was looking away, the patient hurried from his bed and had a torrential bowel movement. With the decision, then, that the patient needed a nurse more than a doctor, the interviewer ended the first contact.

Mr. Neal (Bob, Sr.) is a stout, full-faced man of about 50, with silver hair and moustache. He leaned back in his chair in a posture of confidence, but sometimes would tilt forward on his elbows to make a point. With a few exceptions his manner was that of a man of straightforward half sincerity. He exuded a confidential and friendly air which is useful in business and was usual in his interviews, although he spoke meaningfully of personal feelings and of his observations of others in the family. Several brief times in each interview the impact of events would change his voice a little to an imploring tone.

There were three other children: Doris, 29, and Dottie, 22, were not available, although we know something of them. Ken, 27, is a trim air force officer with a quiet, friendly, but noncommittal manner.

Precipitation of the Illness

The precipitating events of a serious illness seem to gather in one period linking and joining forces to upset a psychosomatic equilibrium. Bob Neal's difficulties were preceded by a set of associated occurrences, some of which were probably not truly separate precipitating factors, but rather representations or subordinates of the more significant ones.

By the fall of 1955 Bob was out of the Navy 2 years and in a business college, where his work was deteriorating. He seemed distracted, while his parents were urging him on and demanding to know why he could not do better. He partially supported himself, feeling a little angry that he had to but, at the same time, ashamed and guilty that he was being helped by his parents. It was impossible for him to know whether it was proper to be dependent upon his father while attending college, since it was never decided whether he appreciated the financial strain on his parents. His younger sister was being sent to the same college at the same time; was this reason to pay his own way or justification for expecting more?

These circumstances further affected object relations. The mother, by her own report and from those of others, had entered menopause in early 1955. She seemed less attracted by previous interests, was more likely to be irritated, and withdrew from her previous maternal attitudes. She was subject to crying spells, manifesting less energy, more complaints, and increased expectations of others.

About the same time (and also related to the uncertainties regarding college) Bob became puritanically angry at his younger sister, although they had previously had a close and sympathetic relationship. He felt she was "running with the wrong crowd," that she had involved herself with the "wrong" man and, worst of all, was behaving in a disrespectful, irresponsible, and impudent manner. He knew, and said, that he could not have escaped censure had he acted that way. But, most important, his criticism and bitterness, openly expressed, brought about resentful quarrels and a subsequent break with his sister. Coincident with Bob's near failure in college and the financial complications arising from his attendance, his father began to show, in the form of gastrointestinal symptoms, the effects of strain. However, these symptoms did not deter him from his exhausting work, but rather forced an even more frenzied and hard-driving application to business interests. The father's response to the mother's emotional change was that of strenuous work over long hours while, as an executive, he took on complex tasks that promised one crisis after another. Mother and son shared the worry over the father's alleged foolhardiness; in Bob's case it turned to exasperation. Perhaps realistically, he wondered how necessary it was for his father to exert and punish himself so much when the return of a peptic ulcer threatened. The father's ways of dealing with his illness affected Bob's relations with both parents, adding to his problems of self-respect and feelings of inadequacy. While the father strove mightily and while he obviously had pain, he urged his son as he always had, to fear not and to perform better — At what price? the son might ask. Bob must have known the frustrations his father suffered in his self-incurred struggles. Perhaps as a parable of his attitudes to his father, Bob reported an incident that occurred in the fall of 1955 and involved his relations with a part-time employer. As assistant to a bartender, he was caused anguish by the demands of the latter that he have the courage to throw out unruly customers. Bob knew that at the same time this same man was stealing from the cash drawer.

For several years Bob had been courting a girl, with whom there was an informal understanding about marriage. This girl, named Dottie, as was his younger sister, we know little about, except that the state of his relationship with her heavily affected our patient's equilibrium. In very gross summary it seems to be true that by the fall of 1955 the courtship had gotten to the point where he felt pressed to commit himself, yet he did not feel secure enough to set a date for marriage. In early 1955, he thought he was involved in a pregnancy case as a result of a presumed interval of dalliance with another girl. The latter had married by that time out of malice toward Bob, but claimed to be pregnant by him. This episode threatened scandal, but proved a false alarm and taught him a stern lesson in fidelity. Bob thought he wanted to marry late in 1955, while his father, particularly, thought it a good idea that Bob become a "family man" and show his independence. The couple tacitly agreed upon the spring of 1956. In the midst of this excitement and during some celebrating at college, where he had very recently acquired the habit of taking some alcohol every night, he found himself on edge about the coming holidays and the trip home. He vaguely remembers having some diarrhea before the vacation, but this symptom dims in importance relative to the acute onset of his illness soon after coming home for Christmas.

From this account three main currents stand out, yet even these cannot be clearly disentangled.

First, there is evidence concerning the change in Bob's mother in the direction of withdrawal, depression, irritability, and less maternal dependability.

Secondly, perhaps as consequence of the change in Mrs. Neal, the father began to manifest a recurrence of his gastrointestinal illness and, at the same time, an increase in the over-compensating drive expressed through the search for business crises. He doubted more the advantages of supporting his son in college, urging better performance and more independence upon him, and advising incessantly that fear of the future should be shunned. Meanwhile, Bob did poorly in school and became dreadfully uncertain that he would have the funds to finish.

Thirdly, there was the commitment to marry, which seemed something thrust upon him rather than being sought and desired. He wondered whether he had dealt with another girl cruelly, and was partially relieved to find that he had not. In spite of insecurity about marriage, he felt that he was obliged to marry and hoped that he would find someone dependable. His troubles with his sister seem to represent the conflicts involving his fiancee and his mother, as well as the malice of an old rivalry that added to his guilt and shame. He felt an ambivalence involving anger and a wish to break from all three of these women, but this wish was opposed by his continuing needs. We know from both Bob and his mother that very shortly after the onset of the disease the older brother and sister petitioned the mother by letter (since Bob was then home and ill) that she not "baby" him as she always had.

The force of these trends in the year that preceded the onset of the illness is made more evident from what we learned about the patient's life history and from his reactions during the months of psychotherapy that followed admission.

FAMILY HISTORY

The Neal family had two children by 1932. The father tells us that he left home early in his life and fought hard to protect his family during the depression. Though the Neals always had an income, the father's early experience warned him that he must be industrious if poverty were not to overtake him. The arrival of Bob, Jr., in the depth of the depression in 1932 undoubtedly posed some threat to the family security, although we have no way to really knowing how much. The Neals tell a story about Bob's birth that may reflect upon the significance to them of his arrival in the family. Mr. Neal tells it most dramatically: "But Bob was a little bit different than the rest of them. Did she tell you the way he was born? Well the children had the mumps when she was carrying Bob — or the whooping cough, that's what it was. So I took them up to my folks and left them and I went up to see them one night a week. When I got back, my gosh, the police was swarming all over the place. I went in there thinking, 'What in the world is wrong!' Well, her and this woman were sitting out on the front porch and my wife got up to go in the house to do something and a nigger came running out of the bedroom around the bed and jumped out the window. It liked to scare her to death. So she run out — we didn't have a telephone — she ran out the front door and started over to the neighbors and the neighbor's dog jumped off the porch and scared her. She was a nervous wreck! Well, the next morning Bob was born. That was on Friday night 'cause Saturday I had to get the payroll out. I don't know whether that could affect a child or whether it would have made her feel any different towards him, but he was a good child, he slept good, and had very little sickness or anything else."

We have little doubt of the truth of this story with respect to the essentials of its plot. We have interpreted the story for its current significance as a kind of family legend to explain to the rest of the family why Bob is "different." The way that the parents tell the tale and the portentous meaning they attach to it make this episode a family legend with symbolic significance. They seem to speak of the anxiety Bob's birth signified. Each parent attributes the main fright to the other. Most evident is the indication of an intruder entering the home. Several times we have been asked for our opinion on the effect of this incident upon Bob's later development. In other words, they ask what effect their feelings had upon the intruder.

We know from the comments of everyone in the family that this child, with his father's name, was given extra care and protection by the mother. The mother admits to some of it, but denies that the term baby is descriptive of her attitudes. She claims to have sensed that this boy needed more, particularly in rivalrous situations with his siblings.

Some of Bob's memories constitute comments upon the effects of early childhood. He recalls the financial strain of buying a new house shortly after the birth of his younger sister, and that this house was endangered by the flooding river. The mother comments that actually the new house had been a step forward for the family, and that this same house was one of those most safe from the floods threatening their community. This memory at once depreciates the father and adopts his feeling of threat and insecurity. Bob relates another memory of childhood as though it were an episode of childish rebellion. He recalls collecting Christmas trees from the neighborhood and piling them in the driveway to the extent that they blocked the father's entrance to the garage. Mother tells of the incident as though it was a bit of sportive behavior on the part of her son. Bob also tells — with some of the original terror — of being cornered in the back yard by rats and of being rescued by his mother. No one else remembers this incident, but there is little wonder that his mother felt he needed help in relations with his siblings. We know little of his later childhood, except that after the age of five or six, Bob was an appealing and outgoing boy according to the reports of both parents. By the time he entered high school he had acquired a severe form of examination anxiety, although he did his best to conceal his fear. This hiding was reinforced by his father's incessant and particular advice to stifle all recognition and expression of anxiety. "When it came to butting his head against a wall, when he *had* to do something, he had a psychological fear of it," his father said.

Nevertheless, Bob became a reasonably successful athlete as a high school varsity football and basketball player. This activity had his mother's enthusiastic sponsorship, an attitude she had acquired from her brothers. She was a spectator at all of his games, although the father never could find the time to attend even one of them. Although he had been more successful in these activities than in anything else in his life, Bob never talked of his athletic experience with any pride or pleasure.

He finished high school at the start of the Korean conflict and, managing to overcome his mother's stout resistance, entered the Navy, as had his brother before him. His recollection of the service career is characterized by a feeling of isolation and loneliness in relation to his fellow sailors. He recoiled from the language commonly used by the others, but he felt ashamed when he found himself speaking it. His ship was hit off the Korean coast by shore batteries. When his mother read the news, she became distraught, expecting to receive the announcement of his death. Bob was disgusted when he heard of his mother's reaction. This event had none of the terror for him that he felt when caught with a soiled uniform during an admiral's inspection.

THERAPY

It can be appreciated that the doctor (J. R.) responsible for the psychotherapeutic part of the total treatment faced some difficult tasks. However, anyone experienced in such matters will know that the coordination and balance of the three methods of treatment (psychiatric, medical, and surgical) in a complicated case is difficult to maintain. Try as the psychotherapist may to coordinate the efforts of the internist and the surgeon with his own work, at times the collaboration becomes imperfect. Occasionally the psychiatrist will find himself making surgical and medical decisions certain to influence his relationship with the patient; at other times he will find that a decision has been made without his consultation and with which he would not have agreed. His treatment goals, his comprehension, his therapeutic anxieties, and his countertransference are all complicated by the delicate imbalances inevitably occurring in a three-way collaborative treatment. Although these were factors influencing the treatment of Bob Neal, they never completely upset his progress. Over the approximately 16 months of Bob's treatment on our service, his principal therapies consisted of steroids, two operations (an ileostomy and a colectomy, 10 and 13 months after hospital admission), and his work with the psychotherapist. To describe the nuances of the interactions between these approaches would require another study. In fact, it will be necessary to be cautious in interpreting the occurrences of relapse and remission as responses to psychotherapy. In this study we can hope only to learn more about the patient's conflicts and defenses, leaving aside the question of the absolute value of psychotherapy for ulcerative colitis.

Analysis of the purely verbal interaction of the first month of psychotherapy is of little use. In the interviews there was a halting and stereotyped expression of thought and feeling. He really doubted the value of this work, but tried to conform. Certainly, the acute phase of his physical illness affected his participation, and he slowly made some adjustment to the ward, the nurses, and other patients. Rorschach tests done shortly after admission and then repeated a month later show some change. In the beginning he was seen as an outwardly adjusted and conforming person with underlying detached and depreciative attitudes toward others. At a still deeper level there was evidence of angry frustration — of an individual who wanted much but expected only husks of things or token gratifications. He seemed regressed to an infantile level, but even there he was depressed. A month later, after improvement on steroids, Rorschach tests found him much the same, although there were increased indications of hostility and other signs of an enhanced willingness for emotional expression.

After this very halting, difficult beginning, Bob began to express some material relevant to his suspicion of the frightening power of his needs and feelings. He noted that he was worse when home on pass or when the psychotherapist was away. A struggle for power and control began to emerge as a feature of his relationship with his fiancee: "She is the one who can relax me." However, it was necessary that she be there at the right time and do the right things or she would disturb him more than anyone else. Meanwhile, he worried about the drain of the hospital expenses upon his father. Following one interview in which these problems with father and fiancee became associated, he suddenly acquired a sensitivity to one of his medicines and developed a distressing and massive urticaria. "Amazingly," the observer's notes state, the diarrhea and cramps disappeared for the duration of his skin disorder. Prior to this anxiety occurrence the therapist had decided to facilitate the relationship through a bit of role playing in which he became the "good doctor," on the patient's side, against the "bad doctors" who unfeelingly prescribed things to make him uncomfortable. We cannot say whether this maneuver was necessary, but it appeared to raise the question of the trust the patient could have in the relationship. He first doubted the therapist's reliability, then relaxed with him and hinted, shamefully, that he found himself at the apex of a triangle involving his doctor and the head nurse. However, at the same time, the therapist's role of siding with the patient led to expressions indicating that the doctor would bend to the patient's will, which produced tension in both Bob and the therapist. Bob could not find the relationship really gratifying and the doctor found Bob "demanding" and "oral-aggressive" — both irritating qualities. But then, for reasons no longer manifest, the psychotherapist began to take control enough to balance some of the patient's drives and, at that point, Bob seemed more a master of his own feelings and less fearful of abandonment. The therapy could by no means settle on this plateau, for there were other forces to contend with: problems with the family and fiancee, and difficult issues concerning the ulcerative colitis. However, Bob tried to hold the relationship at this mutually controlled level. He feared the anger that might break it and he resented the therapist when a decrease in his defensiveness was urged. He wondered how much was demanded of him in terms of psychiatric performance in therapy. The latter has a realistic basis, since it appeared that with physiological improvement the expectations of everyone — therapist, family, fiancee, and nurses — increased.

These trends in therapy brought from him memories of submission to his mother's urging during the year of illness before admission to our hospital. She would cheerfully suggest that he "go out" and enjoy himself to prove his strength, and that he widen his shrinking perspective. Although he had no enthusiasm at all for such activity, he would be afraid not to humor her. He also submitted, despite his own opinions, to her repeated suggestion that he ignore the doctor's advice and eat foods not on his prescribed diet. In fact, he was not tempted by these foods, but his mother thought he should be. Her urging seemed to say: "I am offering you signs of love, but you won't accept them." He felt guilty about resisting the foods that he thought it wrong to eat. These memories were associated with a description of the tenseness that had been present in the relationship with the mother since his return from the service. The "change of life" previously noted required more energy and more appeasement from the patient in order to maintain the old equilibrium. His father had warned that the mother had changed while Bob was away. He recalled ruefully in the same interview the closeness with his mother when he had been a successful athlete. It is possible that he longed for the days when the mother-son relationship had been mutually most gratifying.

Meanwhile, there seemed to be little chance for relaxation in the psychotherapy. This was never a relationship which permitted some quiet and rewarding reflection upon thoughts and feelings. There was a tautness, difficult to analyze at the time, which represented a push and pull in the interaction between doctor and patient. There could be no sharing, no peaceful discussion. Remarks had to be expressed or shamefully withheld while the patient expected to be pushed and pulled in the same manner. He tested repeatedly to see what would be required from him and what he could safely resist without the danger of severing the relationship. It was difficult as a therapist to see beyond the patient's stubbornness and his tendency to deal with every event in strictly literal terms. Although we see now that he wanted a dependent relation with the therapist, he wanted it to be without intrusion into emotions on the verbal level and without danger of anything unexpected. He said once, "You're just like my mother: you asked me if I wanted another appointment; I said, 'No,' and you came anyway." He went on to say that he could not understand why the therapy had to concern itself with such irritating matters as his worry over finances (father), dreams, and the idea "that I'm trying to hang on to some feelings." He could talk somewhat about his irritation towards his mother, since he felt at fault for that.

Thereafter, the more open hostility towards the therapist increased until headaches replaced bowel symptoms. This phase, in which the therapist was becoming pessimistic and shifting to the viewpoint that the patient needed surgery, seemed to be preparation for the next phase in the treatment. A more frankly dependent move occurred in which, in Bob's mind, the therapist became a clearly reliable person who made decisions, commiserated with the patient over his need for surgery and, in general, had taken or had been given the control of the relationship. Most likely this mutually controlled relationship repeated in an assuring way the early mother-child relationship. With very little trouble Bob provoked his fiancee to defy him and thus to give him reason for breaking the engagement. His reaction to this break was not intense. It seemed to have meaning only in the context of his new and more reliable symbiosis. He could afford to give up the fiancee at this point.

However, by this time surgery did seem indicated. The patient had had steroids so long and in such doses that it did not seem that he could soon relinquish them. Hence, rather than serving as a start for a long process of psychiatric treatment, the relationship was instead an aid in helping the patient through surgery.

For the purposes of this study the events in psychotherapy demonstrate for us the type of object relations our patient tends to form. We can see the push and pull, arduous for both Bob and his therapist, and how the interaction finally settled to some form of equilibrium in which the stronger member of the symbiosis has control but is also controlled.

In the following section, the causes of Bob's need for this kind of situation are sought in the milieu in which such habits were made necessary, the network of relationships within which Bob's personality developed — his family.

THE NEAL FAMILY

Throughout the worst of Bob's illness, Mrs. Neal had been his faithful, though often insistent nurse. During some of the most difficult times at home Bob was close to morphine addiction, and the prevention of this was arduous for mother and son.

His sleep pattern reversed, and his mother sat with Bob through the hours from midnight to day talking endlessly of his childhood days. She commented: "I think it's been rough on me, since on top of it I'm going through the change of life. I said to a friend that maybe it's been a blessing in disguise, since maybe I would have given up to my own feelings had I not had him to worry about this year." In discussing this remark she explains at length that she "swallowed my own feelings." Anger, her disappointment regarding the lack of financial and social success, and depression were diverted into maternal care, pity, and worry over the adversities of another. Bob's illness revived, in many of its essentials, the guilt-appeasing, controlling, emotionally expensive symbiotic relationship of earlier days — but not quite!

In talking of herself Mrs. Neal was the most guarded of all. Although immensely voluble and indirect in telling of her life, she dealt with her own feelings and her personal history on a chatty and bland level. She was an only girl with three brothers, one of whom — the youngest — died when she was about seven. She had no memory of feelings about his death. She recalls a tiny and sickly mother, some kindly brothers, and a strong, authoritarian, and distant father. Family solidarity and respectability, without sign of emotional disturbance, was her ideal and a treasured memory of her childhood experience. She revealed slightly the feelings of insecurity imparted by her husband and reinforced by the realities of the economic depression, but these emotions were not nearly as intense as her perception of other's needs, particularly those of her husband and her third child, Bob. As mentioned above, she has no doubt that Bob required her special attention during childhood; she also knows that her husband has always disagreed and even resented this tendency. She said that the rest of the family thought she "favored" the third child, but she knows that it was simply that he needed her more.

Mr. Neal (Bob, Sr.) was far more open in talking of himself, at least in so far as he reveals his character. We see more clearly in him the nature of the equilibrium between needs and reactions to them, and between conflicts and adaptive techniques to quiet the anxiety arising from them.

In addition, Mr. Neal's personality stands out in his relations with Bob, Jr. He spoke first, and with affect, of his perception of an inability to speak effectively and comfortably to his children and particularly to the one who bore his name. He could see that his lifelong absorption in his work, and his consistently long hours had deprived him of the feelings of closeness and other gratifications his family might have afforded him. But, more selfrighteously, he repeatedly told of how he had tried to convey a belief in fearlessness and independent strength. He felt he had demonstrated to his son what hard work could do for a man, and he emphasized hard work because he had known poverty in a large family as a boy, because it had been necessary that he support himself when he was 16, and because his mother had died shortly before he left home. The evidence is clear that the hard driving suited his angry fight against material insecurity, that it helped withdraw him from his need for love, that it reassured him that he could overcome his difficulties — in a word, overcompensation. In later years when economic adversity was not so threatening, Mr. Neal sought out and obtained executive positions which were not so financially rewarding as they were filled with unending crises and laced with complicated troubles. He is known in his business circles as one whom employers have given the thankless, troublesome tasks that require much worry and a 70-hour week. Mr. Neal enjoyed voicing his unconvincing complaints and he was genuinely proud that he had almost never had a vacation except for sick leaves.

The woman he left at home through all this — Mrs. Neal — was allowed to respond to his wishes for loving care only when he was troubled by his ulcer. He knew that he was usually too tired, too headachy, and too preoccupied to ask from her or give to her. When he wanted to yield a bit to his needs he had to "shove off" his wife's sympathy and affection. Currently he sometimes feels that even when he is ill his wife has lost her ways of approaching him, presumably because she had been held off so often.

There are indications that Mr. Neal permitted some warmth between himself and his older son and two daughters; but he was alienated from Bob somehow. He thinks that perhaps it was because of the protectiveness Mrs. Neal lavished on the boy, making it necessary for him to strengthen the child by the opposite treatment; it also seems that the special attitude of the mother towards Bob may further have shut out the father. The latter idea neatly rationalizes the father's own participation in frustration of his own needs.

He explains his conviction that his son needed to cultivate independence and fearlessness with an incident from Bob's boyhood: One evening, Bob was out when supper was served. His father went to fetch him and, finding him, called his name. The boy retreated further into the shadows. The father called again and walked towards him, but Bob ran again. Ignominiously he called and called into the silence, but had to go back without his son. He was deeply hurt and the question he never could face was, had he, the father, caused fear in his son? From that time he sought often to extinguish signs of anxiety in Bob and, in doing so, warned him repeatedly of the things feared by himself. His rivalry with his namesake could not help but emerge. When the mother was overprotective, father was "rough." It was this offspring who had to do the most to get his college education. It was Bob who, by implication, was the greatest drain on finances even before his illness. When young Bob was home long his father forcefully suggested marriage and a job elsewhere. When the mother worried about the son's illness, the father reassured her that death too could be tolerated; for after all, he had known the death of both parents and two siblings.

Mr. Neal had a recurrence of his ulcer just before Bob's admission to our hospital. Then, when the events in the hospital were most acute, Mr. Neal decided that, for the first time in more than 10 years, a vacation and rest were in order. Mrs. Neal agreed that her husband needed this trip with her; for once he seemed to be submitting to her wish to care for him. Near the end of Bob's hospitalization, when plans were being made, Mr. Neal again put forth his idea that his son would be better alone in a distant city. As we reflect on the problem the father, of course, seems to be wrong — but he was also right.

Ken Neal, 27, and Bob's older brother is, in many respects, a model of his father. He has the self-assurance and complacent ease, but his exterior is not quite so brittle. He has rather successfully adopted the themes of independence and strength and he does not find it necessary to struggle quite so much to compensate for his need for some emotional attachment. He is a successful career officer in the Air Force, risen from the ranks. He moved from post to post, always seeking another technical school and cheerfully taking the distant assignment, claiming he needed no place to "light." In his relationships he was outwardly noncommittal and nonchalant. He was matter-of-fact about his mother's forceful attitudes. He recognized her needs and put distance between himself and her. He was sympathetic, but not especially worried or stirred emotionally by his brother's illness. In fact, he seemed not at all surprised that an illness would bind his mother and brother. He agreed with the father's idea that Bob should depart from his parents' home. In our contacts with Ken he revealed the conflictful side of himself in only two ways; one of these was characteristic, the other a surprise. First, he told us with little affect that he had been twice engaged. He had drifted rather easily from the first relationship and the second was near a break at the time of our interviews. About a week before, he had planned a marriage after his fiancee had proposed it; a law suit involving the girl had then intervened. He rather dispassionately accepted the interruption and seemed little concerned whether the marriage would ever take place.

Near the end of our last talk, Ken was asked if he had any questions. Without change in facial expression he said, "Well, I get lonely sometimes." Then he halted and floundered a little before adding, "I have one thing that bothers me. I can't express any emotion. I have a terrible time with it. I want to stay just as far away from emotion as I can. I hate to get emotionally involved, even with my family. It hurts me . . . it hurts them sometimes, I know." This sudden expression is surprising from a taciturn young man who joins the rest of his family in the unity of dampening feeling, and in upholding the family ideal that emotional quiet and a respectable calm must be maintained in family life.

We are not at all certain of our data concerning the two sisters, since we have not seen them. However, from the corroborating comments of the others we have strong hints that Doris, 29, the oldest, is a slightly more rigid and imperious version of her mother. Dottie, 22, must have been — in the view of this family — "spoiled," since she is more truly independent and boisterous than the rest. She was obviously a rugged competitor with her brother.

AN ATTEMPT AT FAMILY ANALYSIS

Remaining is the goal of demonstrating from the above account that, in Bob's case, the rigid and confining patterns of object relations were not only formed in the binary mother-child symbiosis, but were conditioned by the multidimensional matrix of object relations constituting the field in which his personality developed. When we attempt, in studies of human behavior, to analyze events occurring in multidimensional fields rather than in simple binary systems, we compound our difficulties. However it is the argument of this paper that the ways of forming and selecting object relations are shaped in a complex system such as the family.

We have chosen to simplify this task for ourselves and the reader in the following paragraphs by describing a number of interpersonal cycles which, in time, fixed the type of interpersonal relations Bob would have to make in adolescence and maturity. These cycles are conceptually designed to depict the flow of feelings and conflicts among family members. It is possible to construct an almost endless number of these cycles. Their schematic nature allows only a summary of the complexity of incessantly interacting systems. We hypothesize that most of these cycles operate simultaneously, and that the one on which we concentrate at any moment is determined by our point of view at the time. However, one or more may predominate in particular aspects of the family transactions and also at one time in the family's history. It is our thesis that the whole field — that is, all the individuals — is involved and influenced by each of the cycles. For the sake of convenience and simplicity in this paper the field will be limited to the mother, father, and patient — a system complex enough for a first attempt. The others, nevertheless, influence this three-person system in many ways.[1]

The basic cycle operating in the relationship of these three began before Bob was born. It had its overt impact briefly and then was deeply buried, although it made the succeeding family adaptations necessary. The following is a graphic representation of the cycle (Fig. 1).

In this and subsequent representations, M, F, and S signify mother, father, and son, respectively.

The mutual frustration of dependency needs in a mother who needed more than she seemed and a father who, for a long time greatly feared poverty, led to the unconscious wish that they could exclude an additional burden from their family and home. Maintenance of equilibrium in a system functioning like this cycle is impossible. It is potentially explosive, and each of the three family members must be driven off.

Hence, two more cycles come into almost immediate operation (Fig. 2).

In the first of these two cycles the mother compensates partially for her dependency needs and counteracts her guilt by maternalizing the new son. In a sense, the mother obtains an opportunity for expression of her own needs, but the father gets only a rival. Later, the son adopts the style of his mother's angry feelings toward the husband and father. In the second cycle the mother's "babying" of her son intensified the father's competitive feelings.

The father's defensiveness is the main impetus for another set of cycles in which we can use the almost identical terms given us by father and son for their feelings towards the mother: shoving her off when they perceive any need for her (Fig. 3).

---

[1] Lindemann(7) has used a similar conceptual scheme in the explanation of his hypotheses concerning the key object relation in the pathogenesis of ulcerative colitis.

☐ **Figure 1**

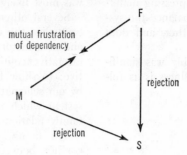

☐ **Figure 2**

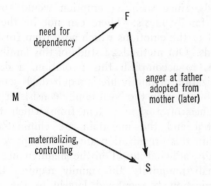

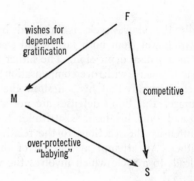

☐ **Figure 3**

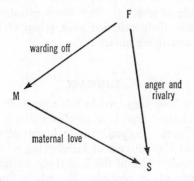

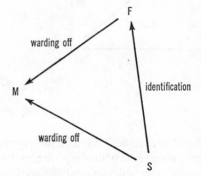

Father has to ward off mother as part of his over-compensation, but still feels the rivalry towards his son as the mother is pushed into expressing maternal love to him. However, to help balance the system, the son identifies with the father, and does his own warding off.

The situations which most probably was significant in the precipitation of Bob's illness is as follows (Fig. 4).

□ **Figure 4**

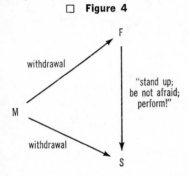

Essentially the above cycle is initiated by the mother's withdrawal from both father and son as a result of a menopausal depression. The father reacts in his usual manner (with overcompensation) and competitively demands that his son show the same alleged courage. But Bob's defenses are not so well developed, and thus his father's attitudes towards him only intensify the reactions to the relative loss of the mother. An attempt at renewal of the old symbiosis leads to a cycle which involves the whole family (Fig. 5).

□ **Figure 5**

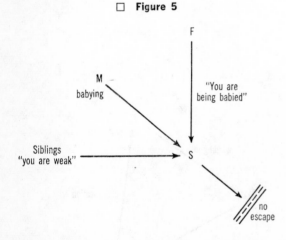

The siblings' and father's feelings in response to the mother's withdrawal stimulates rivalry toward the one who has supposedly enjoyed the most maternalizing in this family. There are not many possibilities for achieving an equilibrium in this cycle unless the illness causes a major shift in the total family adaptation. An escape was needed, and it was most likely that this would involve sickness.

Several other reconstructions are possible to conceptualize the dynamics of this family as a history and as a factor in the precipitation of our patient's ulcerative colitis. Our motive is primarily illustrative: to show that reconstructions can be made — by our schematic cycles or by some other evaluative system which attempts to span the entire field of family relations.

The family's adaptation involved resolution of a conflict between frustrated needs for dependency and the family ideal of independence, respectability, and avoidance of allegedly selfish desires. To do this, the members of the family must remain, for as long as possible, deeply committed to each other. In the process of this devotion to common needs there must be no overt demonstration of individual needs, since such an eruption would compromise the family ideals. There can not be the slightest hint of the emotions which arise from frustration of needs. Our methods of study of this family revealed that, to accomplish this resolution, a definite organization of family life is required. Essentially, the organization in the Neal family consists of the maintenance of a rigid system from which the unexpected and the uncertain are eliminated. Roles within this organization are carefully prescribed and rigidly adhered to. For the maintenance of emotional tranquillity this family requires that communication be confined largely to the matter-of-fact; vagueness, excitement, or disturbance are shunned. Nevertheless, there must be some breakthrough and when this occurs it can be extreme. The stereotyped form of communication can not permit much perception of another's inner feelings. In our summarizing phrase — anxious cohesion — for a family of this kind, we refer to a quality of family life in which the individuals maintain almost desperately their cohesion as a group at the high cost of *underlying* anxiety.

SUMMARY

1. We have suggested in this case study that the object relations aspects of psychosomatic hypotheses may be more comprehensively investigated by inquiry into the patterns of interlocking relationships in the family. Use of the field study method of the anthropologist in observing the whole family provides a view in depth of important relationships, instead of reports from the individual patient.

2. We have proposed an expansion of current

hypotheses concerning the object relations aspects of predisposition and etiology in psychosomatic research. In the case discussed we have attempted to show that the patient's adaptation was conditioned by an interlocking set of relationships within the family. The crucial mother-child relationship was itself conditioned by the family setting as a transacting field object relations between its members. In our opinion it is not the *mother* who affects the child, but the *family's mother*, whose relationship with the child is a product of the dynamics operating within the family as a social system.

REFERENCES

1. ENGEL, G. L. Studies of ulcerative colitis III. The nature of the psychological processes. *Am. J. Med.* 19:231, 1955.

2. TITCHENER, J., and EMERSON, R. Some methods for the study of family interaction in personality development. *Psychiat. Res. Rep.* 10:72, 1958.

3. ACKERMAN, N. W. *The Psychodynamics of Family Life.* New York, Basic Books, 1958.

4. CHANCE, E. *Families in Treatment.* New York, Basic Books, 1959.

5. KLUCKHOHN, F., and SPIEGEL, J. (Eds.) Integration and conflict in family behavior; a report of the Committee of the Group for the Advancement of Psychiatry. Report #27, 1954.

6. BATESON, G., JACKSON, D., HALEY, D., and WEAKLAND, J. Toward a theory of schizophrenia. *Behavioral Science* 1:4, 1956.

7. LINDEMANN, E. Modifications in the course of ulcerative colitis in relationship to changes in life situations and reaction patterns. Life stress and bodily disease. *Proc. A. Res. Nerv. & Ment. Dis.* 29:706, 1950.

Brain Disorders and Mental Retardation / 7

Organic dysfunction is an area of interest to the student of psychopathology not only because of the direct effects brain damage has upon intellectual and motor functioning, but because of its profound impact upon personality organization and emotional adjustment. Recent advances in neurophysiology have increased our knowledge of the complex functioning of the central nervous system and brought about a revival of interest in the study of the interrelationship between brain and behavior. Growing social concern with the problems of aging, with its resulting decline in cerebral competence and adaptive capacities, have also spurred research efforts in the area of brain functioning.[1]

Current neurophysiologic conceptions of brain functioning stress the interdependence of functional areas and their subordination to total integrative processes, calling into question simplistic localization notions. Greater emphasis is now placed on psychosocial factors, the need for evaluating the setting in which brain damage occurs, and the meaning of the setting for the individual.

The late Kurt Goldstein was one of the earliest investigators to note the difficulty in distinguishing between organic and functional disorders as far as symptomatology and therapy are concerned. In both conditions one deals with pathological functioning of the total organism and with the attempts of that organism to come to terms with the environment. It is this concept of self-actualization, the striving of the brain-damaged individual to adjust to his world, which typifies Goldstein's viewpoint.

This problem of environmental adjustment after brain injury is taken up by Gertrud Lewin, using the theoretical notions of her late husband, the social

psychologist Kurt Lewin. She describes the feeling of social isolation of the epileptic and his unclear self-boundaries, with the resulting confusion and passivity so often seen in these individuals. These conceptions lead her to propose a therapeutic approach based on a reintegration of the epileptic into his social world through group discussion and a clarification of expectations and goals.[2]

Since the Kennedy administration's President's Panel on Mental Retardation, which culminated in a 1962 report, "A Proposed Program for National Action to Combat Mental Retardation," a great deal of attention has been focused on the problems of the defective child. As Mandlebaum and Wheeler point out, the emphasis has been placed upon the intellectual and social limitations of the child, with little consideration given to the emotional burdens of the parents. In their sensitive analysis of the complex feelings and conflicts of parents of defective children they remind us of the necessity to help parents to gain understanding and plan realistically for the care of their child.

The diagnosis of mental retardation quite frequently depends upon intelligence quotients derived from standard psychological tests. Psychologists familiar with these instruments have known that the I.Q. is susceptible to socio-cultural influences and that estimates of intellectual functioning may be of questionable validity among the more socially or educationally deprived members of the population. While more severe grades of mental retardation therefore are likely to be attributable to biological defects, mild and borderline retardation may often be due to "social-psychological lacks." In his timely and chal-

---

[1] These problems are summarized and examined in Cumming, E., and Henry, W. E., Growing Old, New York: Basic Books, 1961.

[2] The inner experience of the epileptic has been brilliantly described by Dostoevski in The Idiot, and more contemporaneously by Margiad Evans in her book A Ray of Darkness, London: Arthur Barker, Ltd., 1952.

lenging paper Wortes concludes that prevention of mental retardation must include social reforms in terms of better education and the relief of poverty, as well as improved comprehensive medical services, especially in the areas of maternal and child care.

The increased concern for the potential etiological importance of social and cultural factors in mental retardation represents a significant trend in professional thinking, of which Wortes' paper is a cogent and convincing example. ∎

KURT GOLDSTEIN

The Effect of Brain Damage on the Personality*†

When I was asked to speak before the Psychoanalytic Association about the changes of the personality in brain damage, I was somewhat hesitant because I was not quite sure that I would be able to make myself understood by an audience which thinks mainly in such different categories and speaks in such a different terminology from my own. I finally accepted the invitation, because I thought that members of the Association apparently wanted to hear what I think and because it brought me the opportunity to express an old idea of mine — the idea that it is faulty in principle to try to make a distinction between so-called organic and functional diseases, as far as symptomatology and therapy are concerned.[1] In both conditions, one is dealing with abnormal functioning of the same psychophysical apparatus and with the attempts of the organism to come to terms with that. If the disturbances — whether they are due to damage to the brain or to psychological conflicts — do not disappear spontaneously or cannot be eliminated by therapy, the organism has to make a new adjustment to life in spite of them. Our task is to help the patients in this adjustment by physical and psychological means; the procedure and goal of the therapy in both conditions is, in principle, the same.

This was the basic idea which induced a group of neurologists, psychiatrists, and psychotherapists — including myself — many years ago, in 1927, to organize the Internationale Gesellschaft für Psychotherapie in Germany and to invite all physicians interested in psychotherapy to meet at the First Congress of the Society. Psychotherapists of all different schools responded to our invitation, and the result of the discussions was surprisingly fruitful. At the second meeting in 1927, I spoke about the relation between psychoanalysis and biology.[2] During the last twenty years, in which I have occupied myself intensively with psychotherapy, I have become more and more aware of the similarity of the phenomena of organic and psychogenic conditions.

It is not my intention to consider the similarities in this paper. I want to restrict myself to the description of the symptomatology and the interpretation of the behavior changes in patients with damage to the brain cortex, particularly in respect to their personality, and would like to leave it to you to make comparisons.

The symptomatology which these patients present is very complex.[3] It is the effect of various factors of which the change of personality is only one. Therefore, when we want to characterize the change of personality, we have to separate it from the symptoms due to other factors: (1) from those which are the effect of *disturbance of inborn or learned patterns* of performances in special performance fields — such as motor and sensory patterns;

* Reprinted by special permission of The William Alanson White Psychiatric Foundation, Inc., from *Psychiatry*, Vol. 15, 1952, pp. 245–260. Copyright by The William Alanson White Foundation, Inc.
† This paper was presented, by invitation, at the Annual Meeting of the American Psychoanalytic Association, Atlantic City, May 1952.
[1] See K. Goldstein, "Ueber die gleichartige functionelle Bedingtheit der Symptome in organischen und psychischen Krankheiten," *Monatschr. f. Psychiat. u. Neurol.* (1924) 57:191.

[2] K. Goldstein, "Die Beziehungen der Psychoanalyse zur Biologie"; in *Verhandlungen d. Congresses für Psychotherapie in Nauheim; Leipzig, Hirzel,* 1927.
[3] See K. Goldstein, *Aftereffects of Brain Injuries in War*; New York, Grune & Stratton, 1942.

(2) from those which are the *expression of the so-called catastrophic conditions*; and (3) from those which are the *expression of the protective mechanisms* which originate from the attempt of the organism to avoid catastrophies.

In order to avoid terminological misunderstandings, I want to state what I mean by personality: Personality shows itself in behavior. Personality is the mode of behavior of a person in terms of the capacities of human beings in general and in the specific appearance of these capacities in a particular person. Behavior is always an entity and concerns the whole personality. Only abstractively can we separate behavior into parts — as for instance, bodily processes, conscious phenomena, states of feelings, attitudes, and so on.[4]

According to my observation, all the phenomena of behavior become understandable if one assumes that all the behavior of the organism is determined by one trend,[5] the *trend to actualize itself* — that is, its nature and all its capacities. This takes place normally in such harmony that the realization of all capacities in the best way possible in the particular environment is permitted. The capacities are experienced by a person as various *needs* which he is driven to fulfill with the cooperation of some parts of the environment and in spite of the hindrance by other parts of it.

Each stimulation brings about some disorder in the organism. But after a certain time — which is determined by the particular performance — the organism comes back, by a process of *equalization,* to its normal condition. This process guarantees the constancy of the organism. A person's specific personality corresponds to this constancy. Because realization has to take place in terms of different needs and different tasks, the behavior of the organism is soon directed more by one than by another need. This does not mean that organismic behavior is determined by separate needs or drives. All such concepts need the assumption of a controlling agency. I have tried to show in my book, *The Organism,* that the different agencies which have been assumed for this purpose have only made for new difficulties in the attempts to understand organismic behavior; they are not necessary if one gives up the concept of separate drives, as my theory of the organism does. All of a person's capacities are always in action in each of his activities. The

capacity that is particularly important for the task is in the foreground; the others are in the background. All of these capacities are organized in a way which facilitates the self-realization of the total organism in the particular situation. For each performance there is a definite figure-ground organization of capacities; the change in the behavior of a patient corresponds to the change in the total organism in the form of an alteration of the normal pattern of figure-ground organization.[6]

Among patients with brain damage we can distinguish between alterations which occur when an area belonging to a special performance field — such as a motor or sensory area — is damaged somewhat isolatedly, and alterations which occur when the personality organization itself is altered. In lesions of these areas — according to a dedifferentiation of the function of the brain cortex[7] — qualities and patterns of behavior (both those developing as a result of maturation and those acquired by learning) are disturbed. Indeed, these patterns never occur isolatedly. They are always embedded in that kind of behavior which we call personality. The personality structure is disturbed particularly by lesions of the frontal lobes, the parietal lobes, and the insula Reili; but it is also disturbed by diffuse damage to the cortex — for instance, in paralysis, alcoholism, and trauma, and in metabolic disturbances such as hypoglycemia. The effect of diffuse damage is understandable when we consider that what we call personality structure apparently is not related to a definite locality of the cortex[8] but to a particular complex function of the brain which is the same for all its parts. This function can be damaged especially by lesions in any of the areas I have mentioned. The damage of the patterns certainly modifies the personality too. Although for full understanding of the personality changes, we should discuss the organization of the patterns and their destruction in damaged patients, that would carry us too far and is not absolutely necessary for our discussion. I shall therefore restrict my presentation to consideration of the symptoms due to damage of the personality structure itself.[9]

There would be no better way of getting to the heart of the problem than by demonstrating a patient. Unfortunately I have to substitute for this a description of the behavior of patients with severe

[4] See K. Goldstein, *The Organism: A Holistic Approach to Biology*; New York, Amer. Book Co., 1939; pp. 310 ff.
[5] See K. Goldstein, *Human Nature in the Light of Psychopathology*; Cambridge, Harvard Univ. Press, 1940; p. 194.

[6] Reference footnote 4; p. 109.
[7] Reference footnote 4; p. 131.
[8] Reference footnote 4; pp. 249 ff.
[9] See K. Goldstein, *Handbuch der normalen und pathologischen Physiologie*; Berlin, J. S. Springer, 1927; vol. 10, pp. 600 ff. and 813.

damage of the brain cortex. Let us consider a man with an extensive lesion of the frontal lobes.[10] His customary way of living does not seem to be very much disturbed. He is a little slow; his face is rather immobile, rather rigid; his attention is directed very strictly to what he is doing at the moment — say, writing a letter, or speaking to someone. Confronted with tasks in various fields, he gives seemingly normal responses under certain conditions; but under other conditions he fails completely in tasks that seem to be very similar to those he has performed quite well.

This change of behavior becomes apparent particularly in the following simple test: We place before him a small wooden stick in a definite position, pointing, for example, diagonally from left to right. He is asked to note the position of the stick carefully. After a half minute's exposure, the stick is removed; then it is handed to the patient, and he is asked to put it back in the position in which it was before. He grasps the stick and tries to replace it, but he fumbles; he is all confusion; he looks at the examiner, shakes his head, tries this way and that, plainly uncertain. The upshot is that he cannot place the stick in the required position. He is likewise unable to imitate other simple figures built of sticks. Next we show the patient a little house made of many sticks — a house with a roof, a door, a window, and a chimney. After we remove it, we ask the patient to reproduce the model. He succeeds very well.

IMPAIRMENT OF ABSTRACT CAPACITY

If we ask ourselves what is the cause of the difference in his behavior in the two tasks, we can at once exclude defects in the field of perception, action, and memory. For there is no doubt that copying the house with many details demands a much greater capacity in all these faculties, especially in memory, than putting a single stick into a position which the patient has been shown shortly before. A further experiment clarifies the situation. We put before the patient two sticks placed together so as to form an angle with the opening pointing upward ($\vee$). The patient is unable to reproduce this model. Then we confront him with the same angle, the opening downward this time ($\wedge$), and now he reproduces the figure very

well on the first trial. When we ask the patient how it is that he can reproduce the second figure but not the first one, he says, "This one has nothing to do with the other one." Pointing to the second one, he says, "That is a roof"; pointing to the first, "That is nothing."

These two replies lead us to an understanding of the patient's behavior. His first reply makes it clear that, to him, the two objects with which he has to deal are totally different from one another. The second answer shows that he apprehends the angle with the opening downward as a concrete object out of his own experience, and he constructs a concrete thing with the two sticks. The two sticks that formed an angle with the opening upward apparently did not arouse an impression of a concrete thing. He had to regard the sticks as representations indicating directions in abstract space. Furthermore, he had to keep these directions in mind and rearrange the sticks from memory as representatives of these abstract directions. To solve the problem he must give an account to himself of relations in space and must act on the basis of abstract ideas. Thus we may conclude that the failure of the patient in the first test lies in the fact that he is unable to perform a task which can be executed only by means of a grasp of the abstract. The test in which the opening of the angle is downwards does not demand this, since the patient is able to grasp it as a concrete object and therefore to execute it perfectly. It is for the same reason that he is able to copy the little house, which seems to us to be so much more complicated. From the result of his behavior in this and similar tasks we come to the assumption that these *patients are impaired in their abstract capacity.*

The term "abstract attitude," which I shall use in describing this capacity, will be more comprehensible in the light of the following explanation.[11] We can distinguish two different kinds of attitudes, the concrete and the abstract. In the concrete attitude we are given over passively and bound to the immediate experience of unique objects or situations. Our thinking and acting are determined by the immediate claims made by the particular aspect of the object or situation. For instance, we act concretely when we enter a room in darkness and push the button for light. If, however, we reflect that by pushing the button we might awaken someone asleep in the room, and desist from pushing the button, then we are acting abstractively. We transcend the immediately given specific aspect of sense

[10] K. Goldstein, "The Significance of the Frontal Lobes for Mental Performances," *J. Neurol. and Psychopathol.* (1936) 17:27–40; and "The Modifications of Behavior Consequent to Cerebral Lesions," *Psychiatric Quart.* (1936) 10:586.

[11] See K. Goldstein and M. Scheerer, *Abstract and Concrete Behavior; Psychol. Monogr. No. 239, 1941.*

impressions; we detach ourselves from these impressions, consider the situation from a conceptual point of view, and react accordingly. Our actions are determined not so much by the objects before us as by the way we think about them: the individual thing becomes a mere accidental representative of a category to which it belongs.

The impairment of the attitude toward the abstract shows in every performance of the brain-damaged patient who is impaired in this capacity. He always fails when the solution of a task presupposes this attitude; he performs well when the appropriate activity is determined directly by the stimuli and when the task can be fulfilled by concrete behavior. He may have no difficulty in using known objects in a situation that requires them; but he is totally at a loss if he is asked to demonstrate the use of such an object outside the concrete situation, and still more so if he is asked to do it without the real object. A few examples will illustrate this:

The patient is asked to blow away a slip of paper. He does this very well. If the paper is taken away and he is asked to think that there is a slip of paper and to blow it away, he is unable to do so. Here the situation is not realistically complete. In order to perform the task the patient would have to imagine the piece of paper there. He is not capable of this.

The patient is asked to throw a ball into open boxes situated respectively at distances of three, nine, and fifteen feet. He does that correctly. When he is asked how far the several boxes are from him, he is not only unable to answer this question but unable even to say which box is nearest to him and which is farthest.

In the first action, the patient has only to deal with objects in a behavioral fashion. It is unnecessary for him to be conscious of this behavior and of objects in a world separated from himself. In the second, however, he must separate himself from objects in the outer world and give himself an account of his actions and of the space relations in the world facing him. Since he is unable to do this, he fails. We could describe this failure also by saying that the patient is unable to deal with a situation which is only possible.

A simple story is read to a patient. He may repeat some single words, but he does not understand their meaning and is unable to grasp the essential point. Now we read him another story, which would seem to a normal person to be more difficult to understand. This time he understands the meaning very well and recounts the chief points. The first story deals with a simple situation, but a situation which has no connection with the actual situation of the patient. The second story recounts a situation he is familiar with. Hence one could say the patient is able to grasp and handle only something which is related to himself.

Such a patient almost always recognizes pictures of single objects, even if the picture contains many details. In pictures which represent a composition of a number of things and persons, he may pick out some details; but he is unable to understand the picture as a whole and is unable to respond to the whole. The patient's real understanding does not depend on the greater or smaller number of components in a picture but on whether the components, whatever their number, hang together concretely and are familiar to him, or whether an understanding of their connection requires a more abstract synthesis on his part. He may lack understanding of a picture even if there are only a few details. If the picture does not reveal its essence directly, by bringing the patient into the situation which it represents, he is not able to understand it. Thus one may characterize the deficiency as an inability to discover the essence of a situation which is not related to his own personality.

Memory and Attention

This change in behavior finds its expression in characteristic changes in memory and attention. Under certain circumstances the faculty for reproduction of facts acquired previously may be about normal. For example, things learned in school may be recalled very well, but only in some situations. The situation must be suited to reawakening old impressions. If the required answer demands an abstract attitude on the part of a patient or if it demands that he give an account of the matter in question, the patient is unable to remember. Therefore he fails in many intelligence tests which may seem very simple for a normal person, and he is amazingly successful in others which appear complicated to us. He is able to learn new facts and to keep them in mind; but he can learn them only in a concrete situation and can reproduce them only in the same situation in which he has learned them. Because the intentional recollection of experiences acquired in infancy requires an abstract attitude toward the situation at that time, the patient is unable to recall infancy experiences in a voluntary way; but we can observe that the aftereffect of such experiences sometimes appears passively in his behavior. Such a patient has the greatest difficulty in associating freely; he cannot assume the attitude of mind to make that possible. He is incapable of recollection when he is asked to recall things which have nothing to do with the given situation. The patient must be able to regard the present situation in such a way that facts from the past belong to it. If this is not the case, he is completely unable to recall facts which he has recalled very well in another situation. Repeated observation in many different situations demonstrates clearly that such memory failures are not caused by an impairment of memory content. The patient has the material in his memory, but he is unable to use it freely; he can use it only in connection with a definite concrete situation.

We arrive at the same result in testing attention. At one time the patient appears inattentive and distracted; at another time, he is attentive, even abnormally so. The patient's attention is usually weak in special examinations, particularly at the beginning before he has become aware of the real approach to the whole situation. In such a situation he ordinarily seems much distracted. If he is able to enter into the situation, however, his attention may be satisfactory; sometimes his reactions are even abnormally keen. Under these circumstances he may be totally untouched by other stimuli from the environment to which normal persons will unfailingly react. In some tests he will always seem distracted; for example, in those situations which demand a change of approach (a choice), he always seems distracted because he is incapable of making a choice. Consequently, it is not correct to speak of a change of attention in these patients in terms of plus or minus. The state of the patient's attention is but part of his total behavior and is to be understood only in connection with it.

Emotional Responses

The same holds true if we observe the emotions of the patients. Usually they are considered emotionally dull and often they appear so, but it would not be correct to say simply that they are suffering from a diminution of emotions. The same patients can be dull under some conditions and very excited under others. This can be explained when we consider the patient's emotional behavior in relation to his entire behavior in a given situation. When he does not react emotionally in an adequate way, investigation reveals that he has not grasped the situation in such a way that emotion could arise. In fact, we might experience a similar lack of emotion through failing to grasp a situation. The patient may have grasped only one part of the situation — the part which can be grasped concretely — and

this part may not give any reason for an emotional reaction. The lack of emotion appears to us inappropriate because we grasp with the abstract attitude the whole situation to which the emotional character is attached. This connection between the emotions and the total behavior becomes understandable when we consider that emotions are not simply related to particular experiences but are, as I have shown on another occasion,[12] inherent aspects of behavior — part and parcel of behavior. No behavior is without emotion and what we call lack of emotion is a deviation from normal emotions corresponding to the deviation of behavior in general. From this point of view, one modification of reactions that is of particular interest in respect to the problem of emotions in general, becomes understandable. Often we see that a patient reacts either not at all or in an *abnormally quick manner*. The latter occurs particularly when the patient believes he has the correct answer to a problem. Although this behavior might seem to be the effect of a change in the time factor of his reactivity, it is rather the *effect of an emotional factor* — that is, it is the modification of his emotional feelings because of the impairment of his ability for abstraction — which in turn modifies the time reaction.

Pleasure and Joy

These patients are always somewhat in danger of being in a catastrophic condition — which I shall discuss later — as a result of not being able to find the right solution to a problem put before them. They are often afraid that they may not be able to react correctly, and that they will be in a catastrophic condition. Therefore, when they believe they have the right answer, they answer as quickly as possible. Because of impairment of abstraction, they are not able to deliberate; they try to do what they can do as quickly as possible because every retardation increases the tension which they experience when they are not able to answer. The quick response is an effect of their *strong necessity to release tension;* they are forced to release tension because they cannot handle it any other way. They cannot bear anything that presupposes deliberation, considering the future, and so on, all of which are related to abstraction.

This difference in behavior between these patients and more normal people throws light on the nature of the *trend to release tension.* These patients must, so to speak, follow the "pleasure principle." This

12 See K. Goldstein, "On Emotions: Considerations from the Organismic Point of View," *J. Psychol.* (1951) 31: 37–49.

phenomenon is one *expression of the abnormal concreteness* which is a counterpart to the impairment of abstraction. The *trend to release tension appears to be an expression of pathology* — the effect of a protective mechanism to prevent catastrophic condition. To normal behavior belong deliberation and retardation; but in addition there is the ability to speed up an activity or a part of it to correspond to the requirements of the task, or at least part of the requirements, so that its performance guarantees self-realization. Sometimes the ability to bear tension and even to enjoy it are also a part of this normal behavior. In contrast, the patients that I am talking about are only able to experience the pleasure of release of tension; they never appear to enjoy anything — a fact which is often clearly revealed by the expression on their faces. This becomes understandable if we consider that immediate reality is transcended in any kind of joy and that joy is a capacity we owe to the abstract attitude, especially that part of it concerned with possibility. Thus brain-injured patients who are impaired in this attitude cannot experience joy. Experience with brain-injured patients teaches us that we have to distinguish between *pleasure by release of tension,* and the active *feeling of enjoyment* and freedom so characteristic of joy. Pleasure through release of tension is the agreeable feeling which we experience on returning to a state of equilibrium after it has been disturbed — the passive feeling of being freed from distress. Pleasure lasts only a short time till a new situation stimulates new activity; we then try to get rid of the tension of the new situation which acts to shorten the span of pleasure. In contrast, we try to extend joy. This explains the different speeds of joy and pleasure. Because of the capacity for joy, we can experience the possibility of the indefinite continuation of a situation. The two emotions of joy and pleasure play essentially different roles in regard to self-realization; they belong to different performances or different parts of a performance; they belong to different moods. Pleasure may be a necessary state of respite. But it is a phenomenon of standstill; it is akin to death. It separates us from the world and the other individuals in it; it is equilibrium, quietness. In joy there is disequilibrium. But it is a productive disequilibrium, leading toward fruitful activity and a particular kind of self-realization. This difference in approach between the normal person and the brain-injured patient is mirrored in the essentially different behavior of the latter and the different world in which he lives. The different significance of the two emotional states in his total behavior is related to their time difference.

Edith Jacobson,[13] in the outline of her paper presented to the Psychoanalytic Association, speaks about the speed factor in psychic discharge processes and comes to the conclusion that discharge is not the only process which produces pleasure — that we have to distinguish between different qualities of pleasure in terms of the slow rising and the quick falling of tension. That is very much in accordance with my conclusions derived from experience with brain-injured patients. If one distinguishes two forms of pleasure, one should, for clarity's sake, use different names for them; I think that my use of pleasure and joy fits the two experiences. But I would not like to call them both discharge processes: the one is a discharge process; the other one a very active phenomenon related to the highest form of mental activity — abstraction. From this it becomes clear why they have such an essentially different significance in the totality of performance: the one is an equalization process which prepares the organism for new activity; the other one is an activity of highest value for self-realization. They belong together just as in general equalization process and activity belong together. Therefore they cannot be understood as isolated phenomena.

The Phenomenon of Witticism

From this viewpoint of the emotions of brain-injured patients, the phenomenon of witticism appears in a new aspect. We can see that even though a patient makes witty remarks, he is not able to grasp the character of situations which produce humor in an average normal individual. Whether or not some situation appears humorous depends upon whether it can be grasped in a concrete way which is suited to producing the emotion of humor. In accordance with the impairment of his ability for abstraction, such a patient perceives many humorous pictures in a realistic way, which does not evoke the expected humor. But of course any of us who might at a given time perceive a humorous picture in a realistic way would respond similarly. On the other hand a patient may make a witty remark in relation to a situation which is not considered humorous by us, because he has experienced the situation in another way. Thus we should not speak of witticism as a special characteristic of these pa-

[13] Edith Jacobson, "The Speed Pace in Psychic Discharge Processes and Its Influence on the Pleasure-Unpleasure Qualities of Affects," paper read before the Amer. Psychoanal. Assn., Atlantic City, May, 1952.

tients. It is but one expression of the change in their personality structure in the same way that their inability to understand jokes under other conditions expresses this change. Indeed, these patients are in general dull because of their limited experience, and their witticisms are superficial and shallow in comparison with those of normal people.

Friendship and Love

The drive towards the release of tension, which I have already mentioned, is one of the causes of the strange behavior of these patients in friendship and love situations. They need close relationships to other people and they try to maintain such relationships at all cost; at the same time such relationships are easily terminated suddenly if the bearing of tension is necessary for the maintenance of the relationship.

The following example is illustrative: A patient of mine, Mr. A, was for years a close friend of another patient, Mr. X. One day Mr. X went to a movie with a third man. Mr. X did not take Mr. A along because Mr. A had seen the picture before and did not want to see it a second time. When Mr. X came back, my patient was in a state of great excitement and refused to speak to him. Mr. A could not be quieted by any explanations; he was told that his friend had not meant to offend him, and that the friendship had not changed, but these explanations made no impression. From that time on, Mr. A was the enemy of his old friend, Mr. X. He was only aware that his friend was the companion of another man, and he felt himself slighted. This experience produced a great tension in him. He regarded his friend as the cause of this bad condition and reacted to him in a way that is readily understandable in terms of his inability to bear tension and to put himself in the place of somebody else.

Another patient never seemed to be concerned about his family. He never spoke of his wife or children and was unresponsive when we questioned him about them. When we suggested to him that he should write to his family, he was utterly indifferent. He appeared to lack all feeling in this respect. At times he visited his home in another town, according to an established practice, and stayed there several days. We learned that while he was at home, he conducted himself in the same way that any man would in the bosom of his family. He was kind and affectionate to his wife and children and interested in their affairs insofar as his abilities would permit. Upon his return to the hospital from such a visit he would smile in an embarrassed way and give evasive answers when he was asked about his family; he seemed utterly estranged from his home situation. Unquestionably the peculiar behavior of this man was not really the effect of deterioration of his character on the emotional and moral side; rather, his behavior was the result of the fact that he could not summon up the home situation when he was not actually there.

Lack of imagination, which is so apparent in this example, makes such patients incapable of experiencing any expectation of the future. This lack is apparent, for instance, in the behavior of a male patient toward a woman whom he later married.[14] When he was with the girl, he seemed to behave in a friendly, affectionate way and to be very fond of the girl. But when he was separated from her, he did not care about her at all; he would not seek her out and certainly did not desire to have a love relationship with her. When he was questioned, his answers indicated that he did not even understand what sexual desire meant. But in addition he had forgotten about the girl. When he met her again and she spoke to him, he was able immediately to enter into the previous relation. He was as affectionate as before. When she induced him to go to bed with her and embraced him, he performed an apparently normal act of sexual intercourse with satisfaction for both. She had the feeling that he loved her. She became pregnant, and they were married.

Change in Language

Of particular significance in these patients is the change in their language because of their lack of abstract attitude.[15] Their words lose the character of meaning. Words are not usable in those situations in which they must represent a concept. Therefore the patients are not able to find the proper words in such situations. Thus, for instance, patients are not able to name concrete objects, since as shown by investigation, naming presupposes an abstract attitude and the abstract use of words. These patients have not lost the sound complex; but they cannot use it as a sign for a concept. On other occasions, the sound complex may be uttered; but it is only used at those times as a simple association to a given object, as a property

[14] K. Goldstein and J. I. Steinfeld, "The Conditioning of Sexual Behavior by Visual Agnosia," *Bull. Forest Sanit.* (1942) vol. 1, no. 2, pp. 37–45.
[15] See K. Goldstein, *Language and Language Disturbances*; New York, Grune & Stratton, 1948; p. 56.

of the object, such as color and form, and not as representative of a concept. If a patient has been particularly gifted in language before his brain is damaged and has retained many such associations or can acquire associations as a substitute for naming something, then he may utter the right word through association, so that an observer is not able to distinguish between his uttering the sound complex and giving a name to something; only through analysis can one make this distinction.[16] Thus we can easily overlook the patient's defect by arriving at a conclusion only on the basis of this capacity for a positive effect. In the same way we can be deceived by a negative effect which may only be an expression, for instance, of the patient's fear that he will use the wrong word. I have used the term *fallacy of effect* to describe the uncertain and ambiguous character of a conclusion which is based only upon a patient's effective performance. This term applies not only to language but to all performances of the patients. It is the source of one of the most fatal mistakes which can be made in interpretation of phenomena observed in organic patients; incidentally, it is a mistake which can be made also in functional cases.

Frontal Lobotomy

In reference to the fallacy of effect, I want to stress how easily one can be deceived about the mental condition of patients who have undergone frontal lobotomy. The results of the usual intelligence test, evaluated statistically, may not reveal any definite deviation from the norm; yet the patient can have an impairment of abstraction that will become obvious through tests which take into consideration the fallacy of effect.[17] My experience with frontal lobotomy patients and my evaluation of the literature on frontal lobotomy leave no doubt in my mind that at least many of these patients show impairment of abstract capacity, although perhaps not to such a degree as do patients with gross damage of the brain. Because of the fallacy of effect, which tends to overlook the defect in abstraction, the reports of the relatives that the lobotomized patient behaves well in everyday life

are often evaluated incorrectly by the doctor.[18] In the sheltered, simple life that these patients have with their families, the patients are not often confronted with tasks which require abstract reasoning; thus the family is likely to overlook their more subtle deviations from the norm. Sometimes peculiarities of the patient are reported which definitely point to a defect in abstraction, which is more serious than it is often evaluated: for instance, a patient who in general seems to live in a normal way does not have any relationship with even the closest members of his family and manifests no interest in his children; another patient exists in a vacuum so that no friendship is possible with him.

A woman patient after lobotomy still knows how to set a table for guests, and how to act as a perfect hostess. Before lobotomy, she was always a careful housewife, deciding everything down to the last detail; but now she does not care how the house is run, she never enters the kitchen, and the housekeeper does all the managing, even the shopping. She still reads a great number of books, but she does not understand the contents as well as before.

A skilled mechanic, who is still considered an excellent craftsman, is able to work in a routine way; but he has lost the ability to undertake complicated jobs, has stopped studying, and seems to have resigned himself to being a routine worker; apparently all this is an effect of the loss of his capacity for abstraction, which is so necessary for all initiative and for creative endeavor. Thus we see that even when the behavior of the patients appears not to be overtly disturbed, it differs essentially from normal behavior — in the particular way which is characteristic of impairment in abstract attitude. Freeman,[19] who was originally so enthusiastically in favor of the operation, has become more cautious about its damage to the higher mental functions. He writes:

> The patients with frontal lobotomy show always some lack of personality depth; impulse, intelligence, temperament are disturbed; the creative capacity undergoes reduction — the spiritual life in general was affected. They are largely indifferent to the opinions and feeling of others.

He apparently discovered the same personality changes in his patients as those which we have described as characteristic of the behavior of patients

16 Reference footnote 15; p. 61.
17 Thirty years ago we constructed special tests when we were faced with the problem of re-educating brain-injured soldiers. (See K. Goldstein and A. Gelb, "Ueber Farbennamenamnesie," *Psychol. Forsch.* [1924] 6:127.) These tests, which were introduced in America by Scheerer and myself (reference footnote 11), proved to be particularly useful not only for studying the problem of abstraction in patients, but also for the correct organization of treatment.

18 See K. Goldstein, "Frontal Lobotomy and Impairment of Abstract Attitude," *J. N. and M. Disease* (1949) 110: 93–111.
19 W. Freeman and J. Watts, *Psychosurgery*, second edition; Springfield, Ill., Thomas, 1950.

with impaired capacity for abstraction. Thus we should be very careful in judging personality change following frontal lobotomy. Although I would not deny the usefulness of the operation in some cases, I would like to say, as I have before, that the possibility of an impairment of abstraction should always be taken into consideration before the operation is undertaken.

I would now like to present a survey of the various situations in which the patient is unable to perform. He fails when he has: (1) to assume a mental set voluntarily or to take initiative (for instance, he may even be able to perform well in giving a series of numbers, once someone else has presented the first number, but he cannot begin the activity); (2) to shift voluntarily from one aspect of a situation to another, making a choice; (3) to account to himself for his actions or to verbalize the account; (4) to keep in mind simultaneously various aspects of a situation or to react to two stimuli which do not belong intrinsically together; (5) to grasp the essence of a given whole, or to break up a given whole into parts, isolating the parts voluntarily and combining them into wholes; (6) to abstract common properties, to plan ahead ideationally, to assume an attitude toward a situation which is only possible, and to think or perform symbolically; (7) to do something which necessitates detaching the ego from the outer word or from inner experiences.

All these and other terms which one may use to describe the behavior of the patients basically mean the same. We speak usually, in brief, of an *impairment of abstract attitude.* I hope that it has become clear that the use of this term does not refer to a theoretical interpretation but to the real behavior of the human being and that it is suitable for describing both normal and pathological personality.

In brief, the patients are changed with respect to the most characteristic properties of the human being. They have lost initiative and the capacity to look forward to something and to make plans and decisions; they lack phantasy and inspiration; their perceptions, thoughts, and ideas are reduced; they have lost the capacity for real contact with others, and they are therefore incapable of real friendship, love, and social relations. One could say they have no real ego and no real world. That they behave in an abnormally concrete way and that they are driven to get rid of tensions are only expressions of the same defect. When such patients are able to complete a task in a concrete way, they may — with regard to the effect of their activity — not

appear very abnormal. But closer examination shows that they are abnormally rigid, stereotyped, and compulsive, and abnormally bound to stimuli from without and within.

To avoid any misunderstanding, I would like to stress that the defect in patients with brain damage does not always have to manifest itself in the same way — not even in all frontal lobe lesions. To what degree impairment of abstraction appears depends upon the extensiveness, the intensity, and the nature of the lesion. To evaluate the relationship between a patient's behavior and his defect, we have to consider further that personal experience plays a role in determining whether a patient can solve a problem or not. One patient reacts well — at least at face value — when he is given a task, although another patient has failed the same task; to the first patient the task represents a concrete situation; for the second patient it is an abstract situation. But in both cases, the defect will always be revealed by further examination.

CATASTROPHIC CONDITIONS

Impairment of abstraction is not the only factor which produces deviations in the behavior of patients, as I have stated before. Another very important factor is the occurrence of a catastrophic condition.[20] When a patient is not able to fulfill a task set before him, this condition is a frequent occurrence. A patient may look animated, calm, in a good mood, well-poised, collected, and cooperative when he is confronted with tasks he can fulfill; the same patient may appear dazed, become agitated, change color, start to fumble, become unfriendly, evasive, and even aggressive when he is not able to fulfill the task. His overt behavior appears very much the same as a person in a state of anxiety. I have called the state of the patient in the situation of success, *ordered condition;* the state in the situation of failure, *disordered or catastrophic condition.*

In the catastrophic condition the patient not only is incapable of performing a task which exceeds his impaired capacity, but he also fails, for a longer or shorter period, in performances which he is able to carry out in the ordered state. For a varying period of time, the organism's reactions are in great disorder or are impeded altogether. We are able to study this condition particularly well in these patients, since we can produce it experimentally by demanding from the patient something which we know he will not be able to do, because of his

[20] Reference footnote 4; pp. 35 ff.

defect. Now, as we have said, impairment of abstraction makes it impossible for a patient to account to himself for his acts. He is quite unable to realize his failure and why he fails. Thus we can assume that catastrophic condition is not a reaction of the patient to failure, but rather belongs intrinsically to the situation of the organism in failing. For the normal person, failure in the performance of a nonimportant task would be merely something disagreeable; for the brain-injured person, however, as observation shows, any failure means the impossibility of self-realization and of existence. The occurrence of catastrophic condition is not limited therefore to special tasks; any task can place the patient in this situation, since the patient's self-realization is endangered so easily. Thus the same task produces anxiety at one time, and not at another.

Anxiety

The conditions under which anxiety occurs in brain-injured patients correspond to the conditions for its occurrence in normal people in that what produces anxiety is not the failure itself, but the resultant danger to the person's existence. I would like to add that the danger need not always be real; it is sufficient if the person imagines that the condition is such that he will not be able to realize himself. For instance, a person may be in distress because he is not able to answer questions in an examination. If the outcome of the examination is not particularly important, then the normal person will take it calmly even though he may feel somewhat upset; because it is not a dangerous situation for him, he will face the situation and try to come to terms with it as well as he can by using his wits, and in this way he will bring it to a more or less successful solution. The situation becomes totally different, however, if passing the examination is of great consequence in the person's life; not passing the examination may, for instance, endanger his professional career or the possibility of marrying the person he loves. When self-realization is seriously in danger, catastrophe may occur together with severe anxiety; when this occurs, it is impossible for the person to answer even those questions which, under other circumstances, he could solve without difficulty.

I would like to clarify one point here — namely, that anxiety represents an emotional state which does not refer to any object. Certainly the occurrence of anxiety is connected with an outer or inner event. The organism, shaken by a catastrophic shock, exists in relation to a definitive reality; and

the basic phenomenon of anxiety, which is the occurrence of disordered behavior, is understandable only in terms of this relationship to reality. But anxiety does not originate from the experiencing of this relationship. The brain-injured patient could not experience anxiety, if it were necessary for him to experience this relationship to reality. He is certainly not aware of this objective reality; he experiences only the shock, only anxiety. And this, of course holds true for anxiety in general. Observations of many patients confirm the interpretation of anxiety by philosophers, such as Pascal and Kierkegaard and by psychologists who have dealt with anxiety — namely, that the source of anxiety is the inner experience of not being confronted with anything or of being confronted with nothingness.

In making such a statement one must distinguish sharply between *anxiety* and *fear* — another emotional state which is very often confused with anxiety.[21] Superficially, fear may have many of the characteristics of anxiety, but intrinsically it is different. In the state of fear we have an object before us, we can meet that object, we can attempt to remove it, or we can flee from it. We are conscious of ourselves, as well as of the object; we can deliberate as to how we shall behave toward it, and we can look at the cause of the fear, which actually lies before us. Anxiety, on the other hand, gets at us from the back, so to speak. The only thing we can do is to attempt to flee from it, but without knowing what direction to take, since we experience it as coming from no particular place. We are dealing, as I have shown explicitly elsewhere, with qualitative differences, with different attitudes toward the world. Fear is related, in our experience, to an object; anxiety is not — it is only an inner state.

What is characteristic of the object of fear? Is it something inherent in the object itself, at all times? Of course not. At one time an object may arouse only interest, or be met with indifference; but at another time it may evoke the greatest fear. In other words, fear must be the result of a specific relationship between organism and object. What leads to fear is nothing but the experience of the possibility of the onset of anxiety. What we fear is the impending anxiety, which we experience in relation to some objects. Since a person in a state of fear is not yet in a state of anxiety but only envisions it — that is, he only fears that anxiety may befall him — he is not so disturbed in his

[21] See K. Goldstein, "Zum Problem der Angst.," *Allg. ärztl. Ztschr. f. Psychotherap. u. psych. Hygiene* (1929) 2:409–437. Also, reference footnote 4; p. 293.

judgment of the outer world as the person in a state of anxiety. Rather, driven as he is by the tendency to avoid the onset of anxiety, he attempts to establish special contact with the outer world. He tries to recognize the situation as clearly as possible and to react to it in an appropriate manner. Fear is conditioned by, and directed against, very definite aspects of the environment. These have to be recognized and, if possible, removed. Fear sharpens the senses, whereas anxiety renders them unusable. Fear drives to action; anxiety paralyzes.

From these explanations it is obvious that in order to feel anxiety it is not necessary to be able to give oneself an account of one's acts; to feel fear, however, presupposes that capacity. From this it becomes clear that our patients do not behave like people in a state of fear — that is, they do not intentionally try to avoid situations from which anxiety may arise. They cannot do that because of the defect of abstraction. Also from our observation of the patients we can assume that they do not experience fear and that they only have the experience of anxiety.

Anxiety, a catastrophic condition in which self-realization is not possible, may be produced by a variety of events, all of which have in common the following: There is a discrepancy between the individual's capacities and the demands made on him, and this discrepancy makes self-realization impossible. This may be due to external or internal conditions, physical or psychological. It is this discrepancy to which we are referring when we speak of "conflicts." Thus we can observe anxiety in infants, in whom such a discrepancy must occur frequently, particularly since their abstract attitude is not yet developed or not fully. We also see anxiety in brain-injured people, in whom impairment of abstraction produces the same discrepancy. In normal people, anxiety appears when the demands of the world are too much above the capacity of the individual, when social and economic situations are too stressful, or when religious conflicts arise. Finally we see anxiety in people with neuroses and psychoses which are based on unsolvable and unbearable inner conflicts.

THE PROTECTIVE MECHANISMS

The last group of symptoms to be observed in brain-injured patients are the behavior changes which make it possible for the patient to get rid of the catastrophic condition — of anxiety.[22] The ob-

[22] Reference footnote 4; p. 40 ff.

servation of this phenomenon in these patients is of special interest since it can teach us how an organism can get rid of anxiety without being aware of its origin and without being able to avoid the anxiety voluntarily. After a certain time these patients show a diminution of disorder and of catastrophic reactions (anxiety) even though the defect caused by the damage to the brain still exists. This, of course, can occur only if the patient is no longer exposed to tasks he cannot cope with. This diminution is achieved by definite changes in the behavior of the patients: They are withdrawn, so that a number of stimuli, including dangerous ones, do not reach them. They usually stay alone; either they do not like company or they want to be only with people whom they know well. They like to be in a familiar room in which everything is organized in a definite way. They show extreme orderliness in every respect; everything has to be done exactly at an appointed time — whether it is breakfast, dinner, or a walk. They show excessive and fanatical orderliness in arranging their belongings; each item of their wardrobe must be in a definite place — that is, in a place where it can be gotten hold of quickly, without the necessity of a choice, which they are unable to make. Although it is a very primitive order indeed, they stick fanatically to it; it is the only way to exist. Any change results in a state of very great excitement. They themselves cannot voluntarily arrange things in a definite way. The orderliness is maintained simply because the patients try to stick to those arrangements which they can handle. This sticking to that which they can cope with is characteristic for their behavior; thus any behavior change can be understood only in terms of this characteristic behavior.

An illustration of this characteristic behavior is the fact that they always try to keep themselves busy with things that they are able to do as a protection against things that they cannot cope with. The activities which engross them need not be of great value in themselves. Their usefulness consists apparently in the fact that they protect the patient. Thus a patient does not like to be interrupted in an activity. For instance, although a patient may behave well in a conversation with someone he knows and likes, he does not like to be suddenly addressed by someone else.

We very often observe that a patient is totally unaware of his defect — such as hemiplegia or hemianopsia — and of the difference between his state prior to the development of the symptoms and his present state. This is strikingly illustrated by the fact that the disturbances of these patients play a very small part in their complaints. We are not dealing simply with a subjective lack of awareness, for the defects are effectively excluded from awareness, one might say. This is shown by the fact that they produce very little disturbance — apparently as the result of compensation. This exclusion from awareness seems to occur particularly when the degree of functional defect in performance is extreme. We can say that defects are shut out from the life of the organism when they would seriously impair any of its essential functions and when a defect can be compensated for by other activities at least to the extent that self-realization is not essentially disturbed.

One can easily get the impression that a patient tries to deny the experience of the functional disturbance because he is afraid that he will get into a catastrophic condition if he becomes aware of his defect. As a matter of fact, a patient may get into a catastrophic condition when we make him aware of his defect or when the particular situation does not make possible an adequate compensation. Sometimes this happens — and this is especially interesting — when the underlying pathological condition improves and with that the function.

A patient of mine who became totally blind by a suicidal gunshot through the chiasma opticum behaved as if he were not aware of his blindness; the defect was compensated for very well by his use of his other senses, his motor skill, and his knowledge and intelligence. He was usually in a good mood; he never spoke of his defect, and he resisted all attempts to draw his attention to it. After a certain time, the condition improved; but at the same time he realized that he could not recognize objects through his vision. He was shocked and became deeply depressed. When he was asked why he was depressed, he said, "I cannot see." We might assume that in the beginning the patient denied the defect intentionally because he could not bear it. But why then did he not deny it when he began to see? Or we might assume that in the beginning he did not deny his blindness but that in total blindness an adjustment occurred in terms of a change of behavior for which vision was not necessary; and because of this it was not necessary for him to realize his blindness. The moment he was able to see, he became aware of his defect and was no longer able to eliminate it. The exclusion of the blindness defect from awareness could thus be considered a secondary effect of the adjustment. But in this patient who was mentally undisturbed a more voluntary denial cannot be overlooked. A voluntary denial is not possible in patients with

impairment of abstraction as in brain-injured patients. Here the unawareness of the defect can only be a secondary effect — an effect of the same behavior, which we have described before, by which the brain-injured person is protected against catastrophes which may occur because of his defect. As we have said, the patient, driven by the trend to realize himself as well as possible, sticks to what he is able to do; this shows in his whole behavior. From this point of view, the patient's lack of awareness of his defect, as well as his peculiarities in general, becomes understandable. For instance, in these terms, it is understandable why an aphasic patient utters a word which is only on the normal fringe of the word that he needs; for the word that he needs to use is a word that he cannot say at all or can say only in such a way that he could not be understood and would as a result be in distress.[23] Thus a patient may repeat "church" instead of "God," "father" instead of "mother," and so on; he considers his reaction correct, at least as long as no one makes him aware of the fact that his reaction is wrong. The same kind of reaction occurs in disturbance of recognition, of feeling, and so on.

One is inclined to consider the use of wrong words or disturbances of recognition, actions, and feelings as due to a special pathology; but that is not their origin. Since these disturbances are reactions which represent all that the individual is able to execute, he recognizes them as fulfillment of the task; in this way, these reactions fulfill this need to such a degree that no catastrophe occurs. Thus the protection appears as a passive effect of an active 'correct' procedure and could not be correctly termed denial, which refers to a more intentional activity, 'conscious' or 'unconscious.'

This theory on the origin of the protective behavior in organic patients deserves consideration, particularly because the phenomena observed in organic patients shows such a similarity to that observed in neurotics. One could even use psychoanalytic terms for the different forms of behavior in organic patients. For instance, one might use the same terms that Anna Freud[24] uses to characterize various defense mechanisms against anxiety. Both neurotic and organic patients show a definite similarity in behavior structure and in the purpose served by that structure. In organic patients, however, I prefer to speak of protective mechanisms instead of defense mechanisms; the latter refers to

[23] Reference footnote 15; p. 226.
[24] A. Freud, *The Ego and the Mechanisms of Defense*; New York, Internat. Univ. Press, 1946.

a more voluntary act, which organic patients certainly cannot perform, as we have discussed earlier. In neurotics, the development of defense mechanisms generally does not occur so passively through organismic adjustment, as does the development of protective mechanisms in the organic patients; this is in general the distinction between the two. It seems to me that this distinction is not true in the case of neurotic children, however; some of these children seem to develop protective mechanisms in a passive way, similar to organic patients. Such mechanisms can perhaps be found in other neurotics. Thus, in interpreting these mechanisms, one should take into account the possibility of confusing the neurotic patient with the organic patient.

I would like to add a last word with regard to the restrictions of the personality and of the world of these patients which is brought about by this protective behavior. The restrictions are not as disturbing in the brain-injured patients as is the effect of defense mechanisms in neuroses. In a neurotic, defense mechanisms represent a characteristic part of the disturbances he is suffering from; but the organic patient does not become aware of the restriction since his protective mechanisms allow for some ordered form of behavior and for the experience of some kind of self-realization — which is true, of course, only as long as the environment is so organized by the people around him that no tasks arise that he cannot fulfill and as long as the protecting behavior changes are not hindered. This is the only way the brain-damaged person can exist. The patient cannot bear conflict — that is, anxiety, restriction, or suffering. In this respect he

differs essentially from the neurotic who is more or less able to bear conflict. This is the main difference which demands a different procedure in treatment; in many respects, however, treatment can be set up in much the same way for both.[25] In treating these patients, it is more important to deal with the possible occurrence of catastrophe rather than with the impairment of abstraction, for my observations of a great many patients for over ten years indicate that the impairment of abstraction cannot be alleviated unless the brain damage from which it originated is eliminated. There is no functional restitution of this capacity by compensation through other parts of the brain. Improvement of performances can be achieved only by the building up of substitute performances by the use of the part of concrete behavior which is preserved; but this is only possible by a definite arrangement of the environment.

I am well aware that my description of the personality change in brain damage is somewhat sketchy. The immense material and the problems involved, so manifold and complex, make a more satisfactory presentation in such a brief time impossible. I hope that I have been successful in outlining, to the best of my ability, the essential phenomena and problems of these patients. In addition, trust that I have shown how much we can learn from these observations for our concept of the structure of the personality, both normal and pathological, and for the treatment of brain-damaged patients and also, I hope, of patients with so-called psychogenic disorders.

[25] See K. Goldstein, "The Idea of Disease and Therapy," Rev. Religion (1949) 14:229–240.

GERTRUD W. LEWIN

Some Characteristics of the Socio-Psychological Life Space of the Epileptic Patient[*][1]

Research on how a particular illness or disability tends to affect the person's perception of himself and of his social situation is only in its beginning (3). Recent studies (1, 10) point out that difficulties in the social area may be caused by conditions inherent in the physical disability itself, or may arise from limitations imposed on the disabled person by society. Finally the feelings of the handicapped person about himself and his response to the first two factors affect his social situation. It is obvious that these three factors function interdependently constituting a system of interaction between the person and his environment that is of great complexity. Such a system, comprising the total situation of a person as experienced by him, has been called the 'life space' of the person (7, 9). The life space represents the person in his environment, at a given unit of time, including his action, thinking, wishing, striving, valuing, etc. The present study will employ the term 'life space' and related concepts in an attempt to gain increased insight into some of the interrelations of the sociopsychological forces induced by epilepsy.

Epilepsy is understood today not as a disease entity *per se*, but as a symptom of various kinds of brain pathology amenable to treatment by medication or surgery. Better diagnostic procedures and the development of anti-convulsive drugs have meant a sizeable reduction or elimination of seizures for many patients. From a strictly medical point of view alone, many epileptics could lead a normal or near normal life (4, 5).

However, the socio-psychological situation within our culture has not kept pace with medical progress. Old superstitions and the discouraging experiences of centuries combine to create a 'stereotype' of 'the epileptic', a picture that may vary from that of a person possessed by evil spirits to the more scientific conception of the 'epileptic personality.'[2]

In the practice of casework with epileptics it becomes evident that many professional people, including social workers, tend to share such stereotyped views, and that referrals of patients may be rejected for such reasons as 'epileptics are practically unemployable' or 'are not good prospects for casework'. Such broad generalizations indicate that the patient is not accepted as an individual in a specific situation.

The subjects of this study were patients of the National Veterans Epilepsy Center at Cushing Veterans Administration Hospital (now Boston Veterans Administration Hospital). They were hospitalized for diagnostic work-up and treatment. Many patients were followed in the out-patient clinic and some were readmitted for further diagnostic exploration and treatment. The social worker had contact with the out-patients as well as with those on the ward. In many cases relatives also were interviewed.

A discussion group with hospitalized patients seemed to offer particularly significant material and provided a rich, fairly well-rounded picture in the patient's own words of how they saw their total situation.

These varied contacts sharpened our perception of the patients' anxieties and difficulties related to epilepsy, extending over a wide range of problems and situations. From these combined data, individual casework interviews with ward and out-patients and their relatives as well as our observations in the group discussion, we attempted to outline a conceptual representation of the life space of the epileptic patient.

A theoretical derivation of this kind involves the use of such concepts as the position and potency (weight, importance) of regions in the life space,

* Reprinted by permission from *Human Relations*, Vol. 10, 1957, pp. 249–256.
1 This study was developed while the writer was connected with the Social Service Department and the National Veterans Epilepsy Center, Boston Veterans Administration Hospital, Boston, Massachusetts.

2 That cultures develop stereotypes related to certain physical disabilities has, among others, been stressed by Hines (2).

boundaries and barriers of regions, positive and negative vectors, tensions and forces inherent in the situation.[3]

A region representing concern and activities in the area of 'health and disease' may be assumed to exist in the life space of every person in our culture at a certain stage of maturity. For a healthy, normally functioning person it would be rather peripherally located, and of small potency (representing such matters as getting enough sleep, eating a balanced diet, securing dental care, etc.). With the onset of serious illness it would move from a peripheral to a more central position in the life space of the person and would gain greatly in potency. Since the life space is an interdependent field, other regions and their properties will be affected. The person finds himself in a *new situation*.

Psychological field theory assumes inner personal regions and corresponding regions in the life space (environment). The following considerations however will not differentiate between regions within the person and in the life space.

'From both the theoretical and practical point of view the most important characteristics of a situation are what is possible and what is not possible for the person in this situation' (7, p. 14).

The person with a recent onset of epilepsy, i.e. the person in whose life space 'region E' (E= Epilepsy) developed, is faced with a new situation with an unclear cognitive structure. He does not know what it will be possible for him to do and what will be impossible from now on.

Such new situations arising from changes in physique (such as growth in adolescence) or from physical handicap or illness with concomitant unclear cognitive structure have been analysed by Barker *et al.* (1, pp. 30 ff.). Their general properties are:

1. The directions towards a desired goal are unknown.
2. Valences are simultaneously positive and negative (each act may place one closer to the goal (positive) or move one further from it (negative)).
3. The perceptual structure is unstable, indefinite, and ambiguous.

This situation is comparable to that of a man on thin ice, or of a person on a new job, where

[3] For definition and discussion of these concepts see Lewin (7).

the requirements, the personalities of significant people and their power relations are unknown. Finding oneself in such a situation leads to trial-and-error behavior, to false steps at the very time one wants to be most cautious, resulting in frustration and emotionality. It may cause a prolonged state of conflict, over-alertness to every small cue that might clarify perception. It may produce vacillating unstable behavior.

Such tendencies could clearly be observed in our epileptic patients, who appeared to be overwhelmingly concerned with trying to understand their mysterious condition, seeking clarification of its medical, social, and psychological aspects. Their cognitively ill-structured situation — due to the newly arisen and very potent region E — produces all the frustrations, tensions, and anxieties that occur normally in the wake of such radically restructured life space in which one is not yet oriented.

There are other reasons why the situation of epileptics tends to lack adequate cognitive structure over a long period of time:

1. If a diagnosis of epilepsy has been established the most important information given to the patient is that, while he cannot be cured, an attempt will be made to 'control' the condition. To the layman-patient who is accustomed to think in dichotomies (either healthy or ill) this is an ambiguous statement which helps him little towards orientation in the new situation. We find extreme responses:

A patient who, after only two seizures, was well controlled on medication gave up his job at the post office (a civil service job considered to be especially suited for an epileptic) because 'if he goes to work he might fall into the subway pit'. Other patients deny or minimize the implications and try to avoid making any changes in their way of life.

2. If a diagnosis has been made and if, over the necessary period of time, medication has been satisfactorily adjusted, the cognitive structure of a life space with region E is still very unclear and ambiguous. In epilepsy more than in some other physical disabilities we have to deal frequently with a constellation of overlapping regions. The person finds himself in region E in so far as he is an epileptic. But at the time he has no seizures he may experience himself to be in region H (health). Actually he is never conscious when fully in region E. (This does not hold for patients with Jacksonian seizures.) The relative potency of the two regions, E and H, is dynamically important for the behavior of the patient. If he feels uncertain whether to behave at any time as an epileptic or as a healthy

person, he will be in conflict and under tension. Similar tensions have been described for the adolescent who does not know whether to behave as an adult or as a child in a specific situation. Members of racial or religious minority groups may feel uncertain in a situation whether to act within the frame of reference of their minority group belongingness or whether this is irrelevant or inappropriate at the moment. Similarly a woman may feel torn between her role as a wife and her role as a mother, if the overlapping regions 'marriage' and 'mother of children' are felt to be in conflict. Compared to the situation of a cripple with a permanent, visible handicap (such as an amputated leg) the epileptic is more apt to find himself within two overlapping regions with vacillating potency.

But overlapping regions are not necessarily conflicting or antagonistic; e.g. being a wife and mother is a situation that not only occurs frequently, but may be felt to be compatible.[4] Therefore, one requirement for an adjustment to epilepsy is: to learn to experience the overlapping regions H and E as compatible regions.

To give concrete instances of conflicts due to the overlapping of regions: a patient with an amputated leg may have to give up skiing or mountain climbing; he may be frustrated, but cannot vacillate. An epileptic may know that he should give up driving a car or working on moving machinery. However while he has no seizure he feels himself to be in the region H and may decide to act according to the possibilities open to him in region H.

Adjustment would mean here neither to give up completely like the post office clerk nor to take irresponsible chances, but to lead 'a normal life' in region H within the limits set by region E (not to go on scaffolds at a construction job, but to work as draftsman in the office).

3. The epileptic is often in overlapping subregions even within region E, in so far as there is uncertainty whether E is a physical or mental condition. Our material shows how strongly the patients want to be perceived as patients with a physical condition and how persistently they suffer from the nagging doubt that they might be mentally sick. In view of the frequency of borderline cases, and the occurrence of both 'true' and psycho-genic seizures in the same patient, this vacillating perception (experiencing oneself alternately in region EP (physically sick) and region EM (mentally sick)) is not unrealistic. The patient who has

[4] For properties of overlapping regions see Barker, *et al.* (1, pp. 39 ff.).

been told that the electro-encephalogram or pneumo-encephalogram established an epileptogenic lesion and who is later referred for psychotherapy because of the strong psychological overlay is naturally confused, frightened, and defensive. Helping such a patient to accept psychotherapy is a difficult and not infrequent casework task.

4. Topologically the area of two overlapping regions is equivalent to the boundary zone between the two regions. It is evident in politico-geographical life that such boundary zones are apt to be areas of conflict and tension which spread over the wider field. (The Saarbasin and the zone of Trieste are such boundary zones in the political system of Europe which may be considered part of one of two contesting regions, according to different frames of reference.)

In the life space of a person, clear boundaries between regions facilitate purposeful action and mental stability. Educators and parents know that it is often less important to give a child a wider space of free movement than it is to be consistent, to make the boundaries of a situation very clear. In psychotherapy one speaks of the therapist 'setting limits' and of the patient 'testing the limits'. Unclear or inconsistent limits are said to produce increased tension and guilt feelings. The life space of the epileptic seems to be characterized by lack of normally sharp boundaries. Just as in relation to employment, he is uncertain about his position in relation to courtship and marriage, about his fitness to have children, or about his desirability as a friend in a social group. Even if he had made sufficient adjustment to accept his condition, he is up against the fact that the unsharpness of boundaries also exists in the way he is perceived by others; and he is aware of being perceived in this doubtful way.

5. Boundaries and barriers (boundaries that offer resistance to locomotion) are often experienced by the epileptic as not 'factual' or 'objective' such as physical barriers are.

For example, the amputee who gives up skiing, experiences skiing as physically impossible, and may ascribe his frustration to 'fate' or to 'forces of nature'. The epileptic veteran who was forbidden by his doctor in line with state laws to use 'that beautiful new DeSoto' he bought with his mustering-out pay, experienced the barrier as arbitrary, set up by social forces. Limitations set by society seem to create more resentment and more tension (in this case leading to a depression) than the inexorable forces of nature.

6. Patients speak of living within an 'iron curtain' or in a 'blockade'. Thus they see themselves use something like topological terms to describe their feelings of social isolation and of being excluded from desirable activities. Isolation is felt most keenly and is most detrimental when it involves not a group but a single individual. The isolation imposed on the physically handicapped is therefore especially pathogenic: the adolescent has the friendship group of his age mates; the minority group member may return from discrimination of the majority group to his family, church, or club where he is among his kind. Handicapped individuals such as the epileptic feel the 'blockade' possibly most strongly in relation to the closest group, the family, another tension-producing factor in the situation.[5]

7. Identification with other epileptics requires a high degree of acceptance of the condition and is often associated with ambivalent feelings (valences are both positive and negative); if a certain degree of identification can be achieved, it is, as our material shows, a source of great comfort to the patient. In this respect the situation on the epilepsy ward has dynamic properties similar to that of the ghetto; the situation in the community after discharge functions like the dispersion (8, pp. 153 ff.). Hence patients whose seizures seem well controlled at the hospital may suffer again from frequent seizures after discharge.

8. If we include in the force field a projection in time (a perception of past and future as part of a person's present experience) we find again that the epileptic meets unsharp boundaries, indistinct goals, much cause for fear, vague hopes. Only comparative research can decide in what respect the time perspective for the epileptic is similar or different from that of other patients with severe illness (cancer, tuberculosis, manic-depressive psychosis with its changing ways of looking at the world). All these diseases may alternate between improvement, remission, and exacerbation; however, the sudden and unpredictable occurrence of the single seizure superimposes a peculiar rhythm upon the curve that would represent the vicissitudes of a disease over a period of weeks, months, and years. Possibly the situation of the cardiac patient may be similar to that of the epileptic in certain aspects of time perspective. Barker states that tuberculosis is one of the chronic diseases where 'definite plans can be

---

[5] It has been reported by O'Connor and Simon (11) that deaf children tend to be better adjusted if they have deaf relatives.

made and gradually achieved . . . In the chronic stages change is usually slow, either for better or for worse, and the patient can look forward to months or years of a stable situation' (1, p. 172). This is in definite contrast to the situation of the epileptic, both in its medical and in its social aspects.

In summarizing — with the onset of epilepsy, as with the onset of any severe, chronic illness, a new region (E) of considerable centrality and potency is formed that affects profoundly all other regions in the patient's life space. The patient is forced to go through a period of adjusting to a new situation by means of a difficult and painful process. Even if from a medical point of view control of seizures may be said to be successful, such process of psycho-social adjustment can be achieved only over a considerable period of time. The new situation is characterized topologically by the fact that region E has unsharp boundaries. The resulting unclear cognitive structure leads to doubt, fear, vacillating, seemingly unpurposeful behavior. Few goals can be clearly perceived and consistently pursued. Dynamically such a situation produces a system of tension, permeating every region of the life space, those representing family and wider social relationships, economic and social status, leisure-time activities, etc. Valences (goals) become ambivalent. Wherever the patient turns he is confronted with these uncertain boundaries or outright barriers that induce forces both towards and away from any region. Such limitation of the space of free movement may finally lead to a 'giving up', to a high degree of passivity (6, pp. 95 ff.). Casework contacts indeed reveal passivity as an outstanding behavioral characteristic of many epileptic patients.

II

From this representation of the life space of the epileptic, certain recommendations for the practice of casework in a hospital or clinic setting may be derived. During the initial period of diagnostic work-up that involves much waiting and suspense for the anxious patient, casework will have to be basically supportive; but clarification of diagnostic and treatment procedures is often indicated. As the medical diagnosis becomes known, a primary casework goal consists in helping to clarify the new situation. The patient must be helped to express his hopes and fears; misconceptions must be clarified both with the patient and with members of his family. While understanding and accepting that the condition is not a rational process alone, intellectual clarification has its place in the casework process, because so much ignorance and misknowledge is in the way of realistic perception. At the same time the caseworker has to be sensitive to the emotional meaning of the new situation for the patient and his family.

Our findings demonstrate to what extent a group setting is able to support and complement these casework goals. The patient who, for emotional reasons, can hardly pronounce the word 'epilepsy' in individual contacts, experiences in the group how his co-sufferers are able to speak frankly and to raise the very questions that he himself has on his mind, however vaguely formulated. Thus tendencies towards denial and suppression are reduced. The group offers intellectual clarification, emotional catharsis releasing tensions caused by the hospital situation and by the threatening diagnosis. It seems to fuse the co-sufferers into some kind of a unit to a higher degree than just living on the ward together usually does (but living on the ward together is a strong factor in the development of this more structured unit). The group may show the patients possible outlets for action to improve their social situation as a group.

In all these respects the situation of the newly diagnosed patient is, of course, different from that of the readmitted one. In the group the former gets the benefit of the latter's experience.

At the time the newly treated patient is being discharged from the hospital, it is often difficult to arrive at some kind of 'social diagnosis' and 'social prognosis' and to assess the ego strength of the patient. The stresses in the community and his response to them are unknown.

The patient who at first thinks that his life has come to an abyss may go back to family and job and may live as before, for all practical purposes. The patient who before discharge stated that he will certainly be able to return to his former job, may report at follow-up clinic that he was fired and has been refused several other jobs. Only after discharge did he feel the full impact of the new social situation. The patient who quite sensibly planned to return to the firm where he is known and appreciated, but to ask for transfer to a job involving no driving, reported at the time of the first clinic visit that he found himself unable to accept this transfer and the cut in salary and status involved. He preferred to find a similar position in a different, new place of employment.

For such reasons the first clinic visit after discharge is often the critical contact, in which the pattern of the patient's adjustment becomes apparent, not only in terms of seizure control by medication, but also in terms of the social situation that is beginning to develop. It is at this point that the caseworker may be of much help, again by acceptance and support, by clarification and reinterpretation, by suitable referrals, sometimes by working with other members of the family, sometimes by direct contact with the employer. Anything that will make the boundaries of a region sharper and can help structure the time perspective in a realistic way should help towards adjustment.

How much explanation and clarification should be given by the doctor and how much by the caseworker will depend on the policy and philosophy of the setting and on the personalities involved. There seems no cause to fear overlapping or duplication of function, because the patient's need for clarification is insatiable and these new and frightening matters are not assimilated when they are explained just once. The only thing to fear is contradictory information, lack of teamwork, anything else that increases the patient's confusion instead of resolving it. Where teamwork is really functioning at its best, the social worker will have avenues to know the medical procedures planned for the patient, the results of psychological testing, the medical diagnosis once it is made. The doctor will be interested in the social and psychological implications of his diagnosis. Channels of communications will exist by which he can plan with the psychologist, with the social worker, and with the vocational guidance worker for the best possible way to help the patient structure his future.

REFERENCES

1. BARKER, R. G., WRIGHT, BEATRICE A., MEYERSON, L., and GONICK, MOLLIE R. *Adjustment to Physical Handicap and Illness: a Survey of the Social Psychology of Physique and Disability.* New York: Social Science Research Council, 1953.

2. HINES, J. S., Jr. 'Social Concepts of Blindness in American Culture.' *Social Casework,* Vol. 31, No. 10, 1950.

3. LEDERER, H. D. 'How the Sick view their World.' *J. Soc. Issues,* Vol. 8, No. 4, 1952.

4. LENNOX, W. G. 'Seizure States.' In Hunt, J. McV. (Ed.), *Personality and the Behavior Disorders.* New York: Ronald Press, 1944.

5. LENNOX, W. G. *Science and Seizures.* New York: Harper, 1946.

6. LEWIN, K. A *Dynamic Theory of Personality.* New York: McGraw-Hill, 1935.

7. LEWIN, K. *Principles of Topological Psychology.* New York: McGraw-Hill, 1936.

8. LEWIN, K. *Resolving Social Conflicts.* New York: Harper, 1948.

9. LEWIN, K. *Field Theory in Social Science.* New York: Harper, 1941.

10. MEYERSON, L. 'The Social Psychology of Physical Disability,' *J. soc. Issues,* Vol. 4, No. 4, 1948.

11. O'CONNOR, C. D., and SIMON, EDNA. A *Preliminary Survey into Problems of Adjustment among Pupils of the Lexington School for the Deaf.* Philadelphia: F. A. Davis, 1926.

ARTHUR MANDELBAUM AND MARY ELLA WHEELER

The Meaning of a Defective Child to Parents*

During the past decade the defective child has been the object of considerable professional concern. The focus of concern however, has largely been on the defective child himself, with attention given not only to his intellectual handicaps and social limitations but to his potentialities. Increasingly, emphasis has been placed on the value of the child's remaining in his own home and being cared for by his parents. This trend has given impetus to parents to organize themselves into groups for mutual support. Little professional consideration, however, has been given to the problems of parents who must carry the emotional burden of this tragic problem.

The purpose of this paper is to analyze the troubled and complex feelings of parents of defective children as revealed during the diagnostic study at our clinic. Attention will also be given to ways by which parents may be helped, through gaining some understanding of their feelings, to make realistic decisions for the care of their child and to plan constructively for themselves and other members of the family.

Our report is based on cases studied at the Children's Service of the Menninger Clinic. Many of the children were defective to such a degree that they were disturbed in most areas of functioning. Because they had had so many difficulties in their growth and development, the parents often questioned whether they could adjust to any social situation. Frequently the responses of the children were so scattered that their behavior caused be-

wilderment and confusion in the family, the school, and the community. The parents, in addition to feeling bewildered and confused, had an acute sensitivity to the rejecting attitudes of others. Although present attitudes toward defective children are more enlightened than they were in earlier days, when explanations were rooted in myth and superstition, considerable rejection still prevails.

SOCIAL ATTITUDES TOWARD DEFECTIVE CHILDREN

From ancient times societies have had some method of dealing with defective children. In some cultures, such children were destroyed when it became evident that they could not be incorporated into society in a useful capacity. Even when defective children escaped this fate, the attitudes of society toward them were still hostile and fearful. In medieval times, the mentally defective person sometimes became the court fool or jester, where he was both mocked and ridiculed and protected and shown favor. The defective person was sometimes regarded with awe and was given superstitious reverence as if he possessed magical power. Defective children were often called "les enfants du bon Dieu" while Luther and Calvin described them as "filled with Satan."[1] Within our own recent historical past, mental defectiveness has often been confused with insanity, and the defective person has been considered a potentially dangerous criminal.

Although the extremely negative attitudes of ear-

* Reprinted by permission from *Social Casework*, 1960, Vol. 41, No. 7, pp. 360–367.

[1] Alfred Stuart Queen, *Social Work in the Light of History,* J. B. Lippincott Co., Philadelphia, 1922, p. 155.

lier times no longer prevail in our society, certain residual feelings of anger and fear about the defective child remain in most of us — parents and professional people alike. Such feelings, rooted in our past culture, militate against acceptance of the present-day humane philosophy and produce inner conflict, guilt, and bitterness. These feelings must be recognized and understood if help is to be given to the child and his parents.

CHARACTERISTIC ATTITUDES OF PARENTS

The attitudes manifested by parents when they initiate their request for help with the child may be viewed as a preface to the themes that unfold during the total diagnostic process. For example, parents may protest about the time required for the study, as if they feared the pain caused by too long an exposure of their feelings. They may also protest about the cost of the study, doing so in a manner that leaves no doubt that they feel further investment of effort is futile. Frequently parents who bring their defective child to the Menninger Clinic for a diagnostic evaluation already have been seen in one or more other clinics. Although they have previously been given a clinic's findings, they complain about confused diagnoses or unjust treatment. They are frantic in their questioning about the etiology of the disorder and they constantly seek for reassurance. Sometimes parents are clear about previous findings but complain about being left with the burden of reaching a solution. When we ask that they send reports of previous studies, they sometimes protest, fearing that we then will be prejudiced or less objective. Parents often express concern during the evaluation process because they think we may see the child at his "worst" and that our findings, therefore, will be distorted and false. Some parents, in contrast, think we may see the child at his "best" and will not recognize the seriousness of his difficulties.

Because most people regard organic causes of dysfunctioning as final and irreversible, many parents hope that a psychiatric examination will reveal functional causes for the child's behavior which can be corrected through treatment. Furthermore, by coming to Topeka, which is often far from their home communities, parents may hope that a fresh and objective viewpoint will be given by people who do not know about their problems. Underlying these hopes and fears is the very real wish that we will understand them; that we will perceive their readiness for realistic solutions; and that we will assist them in facing the truth which they sense but cannot admit.

We believe that it is essential for both parents to accompany the child when he is brought for diagnostic study. Each parent then has an opportunity to present his individual concerns and the depth of his personal reactions and emotional investment. If only one parent comes, there is risk that the presentation of the problem will be distorted, since it is rare for both parents to have identical reactions and concerns. The parent who remains at home may be the one who has chief resistance to securing help; he may also fear exploration of his acutely felt pain. The parent who brings the child for study may so dominate and control the home situation that, either directly, or subtly, he excludes the other person from the study process. Of particular importance is the fact that it is not possible for the participating parent to convey to the absent partner the full extent of the emotional and therapeutic force of the evaluation process.

Since few couples view the child's problems in the same way, it is not surprising that they seldom are united in their struggle to find a solution. An important function of the diagnostic study, therefore, is to help the parents resolve their conflicting views. When they continue to be competitive and inconsistent, they tend to reject both the child and the clinical findings. For example, if one parent wishes to place the child, the other parent, who opposes placement, may feel that he is the child's staunchest defender. This attitude may call forth resentment in the parent who seeks placement. Thus, the conflict may serve to bind the opposing parent to the child, making the other parent feel guilty and disloyal. It is in this way that a destructive cycle of feelings may be set in motion.

Mrs. A often insisted that her husband take Ben with him when he went out, although she knew Ben's behavior was often unpredictable and likely to be embarrassing. If Mr. A protested, Mrs. A would accuse him of not loving the boy. Mr. A admitted that frequently this was true, but it no longer caused him to feel guilty. There was a time when he shared his wife's belief that a miracle might happen and Ben would suddenly become a normal boy. "But," he explained, "I no longer have that faith — only a little hope." Feeling his marriage jeopardized and lacking a shared belief in "love, faith, and hope," Mr. A proposed that his wife either place Ben or agree to a divorce. He said, in effect, "Choose between us — either my son or me."

In the above example, the mother tried to use her own troubled feelings about the child to punish her husband and make him feel guilty. Quite often disagreements about a child and his potentialities spread throughout the marriage and threaten total disintegration of the family. In such cases, it is difficult to determine whether the child is the major cause of marital tension and if so, whether the parents have enough stability and find sufficient gratification in other areas of their relationships to indicate possibilities for saving the marriage. A profound disagreement between the partners about a child — if it cannot be resolved — acts as a dangerous infection in the entire family, often culminating in a severe emotional crippling of all members.

DEFENSE PATTERNS

A mother whose guilt makes her feel she alone is responsible for the problem may carry the full burden for the physical and emotional care of the defective child. Ostensibly, she does this to shield and protect her husband, but she may actually view him as too weak and too passive to share the burden. As the responsibilities become heavier with time, she tends to become resentful of her husband's apparent indifference and he, in turn, feels excluded. Acutely sensitive to the unexpressed attitudes of his wife, the father attributes his exclusion to his weakness. He assumes that his wife is more able than he to assume the responsibility for their child.

Mrs. H assumed the major physical and emotional burden of caring for their daughter, Inge. On the basis that the husband was busy with his work, the mother rarely shared with him the daily problems created by the girl. In reality, however, she felt she was the stronger of the two and better able to deal with Inge. Although she gave care uncomplainingly, she deeply resented her husband's acceptance that she carry the burden. She interpreted his behavior as rejection of Inge and his silence as a lack of concern about the child and an inability to make decisions for the family. Although Mr. H was relieved not to have to be bothered about the care of Inge, he felt guilty about his lack of involvement and resentful of his wife's implication that he was inadequate.

In such a situation, the father's withdrawal into work may be viewed as his method for handling his grief and depression. His withdrawal, although partially desired by the mother, creates in her a fear that she has been left alone to deal with the child. She feels that her husband has deserted her and their handicapped child as well. It is hard for either spouse fully to understand this kind of withdrawal as a defense against grief. A mother has fewer environmental methods of withdrawal. She cannot easily leave the child and family to seek solace in work. Therefore, we frequently find mothers using such defenses as emotional isolation, retreat into depression, and outbursts of anger.

Some mothers try to deal with their distress by not having other children. Others want another child, hoping that they can prove their adequacy and their capacity to bear healthy children. In some instances, having another child serves as a justification for the mother's withdrawal from the defective child, since a new infant demands her central attention and activity. This solution, however, creates a conflict of loyalties and therefore adds to her guilt. During pregnancy, the mother's thoughts and energies are psychologically turned toward the unborn infant but, after his birth, the problem of the defective child returns with increased vigor; it is felt again as an inescapable reality. The mother may then view the new infant as a symbol of her rejection and abandonment of the defective child. One mother expressed fear that her defective child, who had been placed, would accuse her of having "thrown him away" and would therefore never forgive her. Her intense wish to have him visit the home was understandable only in terms of her wish that he would find pleasure in seeing his new sibling. She felt that his pleasure would relieve her guilt at having displaced him with a normal child.

Some mothers who cannot give birth to another child turn to adoption of a child as a defense against their troubled inner thoughts. Frequently the adopted child becomes the "target" for the parents' unresolved anger. Because he has talents and skills their defective child can never have, the adopted child comes to be jealously resented. The resentment directed against the adopted child, however, is often a displacement — he becomes the object of the anger the parents feel, but can never express, toward their own defective child. To be angry with their own child, who "did not choose to be born," is often seen by such parents as a cowardly, immoral act.

Another common defense utilized by parents is their frantic search for the "cause" of their child's defectiveness, with the hope that it can be attributed to heredity or family background.

Mr. F often referred to his own siblings, each of whom in some aspect resembled his defective son George. For example, one brother in a fit of rage accidentally shot and killed another brother. One brother was always considered "stupid," although he had made a fair adjustment to farm work. Still another was "so dumb that he let himself be kicked by a mule" and later died of tetanus. Mr. F insisted he had no choice but to believe George's condition was inherited.

Frequently, one of the parents attributes the child's condition to the family background of the spouse. He may refer to the "poor stock" of the family. In other instances, a parent may point out that the child's defectiveness is attributable to too much brilliance in either his or his spouse's family, calling attention to a member who was a "genius." The implication is that genius has erratic, fragile, esoteric qualities that are akin to those found in the mentally defective person.

Some parents, in speaking of their child, may suggest that he has certain grotesque qualities that are frightening to them. They may say he treats "life as a joke" and point to his clown-like appearance. They may also refer to the attitudes expressed by neighborhood children who view him as silly and funny. Parents who describe their child in this way are subtly conveying the idea that life has played a cruel joke on them about which they are both dismayed and angry. They may also feel that somehow the child has wilfully produced his defectiveness and is attacking them with it. They do not realize that the desperate efforts such a child makes to confabulate in order to conceal his inadequacies may give him an appearance of joking or teasing. The parents are unable to see that behind this facade the child is making desperate attempts to please them.

In another context, Schilder has pointed out that "the neurotic tendency gets a great influence from the inferior organ."[2] In the same way, the impact of a defective child on his family influences neurotic tendencies and may call forth latent conflicts. When the child fails to achieve normal development, the parents' latent conflict may emerge at varying levels of intensity and complexity. On the simplest level, the parents will recall unconscious aggressive thoughts, frustrated dependency needs, and ambivalent wishes. These may appear singly or in combination. When they come to the surface during an evaluative study, the parents sense them as intrusive thoughts or guilt reactions, and tend to think of them as the secret cause of the child's defectiveness. In relatively mature parents, such thoughts and concerns dissolve quickly when their reality is evaluated.

When Mrs. J was pregnant with Karl, she had an "uneasy" feeling that something was wrong either with her or with the unborn infant. When Karl was born, she was miserably disappointed because she had so much wanted a girl. As he grew and developed, Mrs. J was unable to take any delight in him; she "just knew" something was wrong. When the diagnostic findings confirmed her fear that Karl was brain damaged, Mrs. J thought that his condition was God's punishment for her acute disappointment because her child was not a girl.

On a more complicated level, parents may view their feelings of rejection as the cause of the child's damage. This reaction is common with parents who have marked feelings of inadequacy and low self-esteem. Their self-blame, hitherto latent, is likely to come to the surface during the evaluative process and become a powerful dynamic against making realistic plans. Such parents find it easier to focus on the past than on the current problem that is the cause of their immediate pain.

It has been postulated that "the more intense the defensive reaction toward the child and the longer its duration, the more probable it is that the retarded child has become an integral part of the parents, total psychological functioning."[3] We have found, as Mahoney has observed, that parents who have achieved a relatively satisfying adjustment are likely to be able to bear the pain of having a defective child without prolonged personality disturbance. On the other hand, parents who have not been able to achieve a satisfying adjustment in their previous years tend to react with severe personality difficulties. It is these parents with pathological reactions — who involve their child in their own psychological dysfunction in a pervasive manner — who have difficulty in separating reality from unreality.

Mrs. L stated with a smile that on this day she was coming in to see me as a "patient." Her eyes were bright and her body tense as she leaned forward to say that, even though she is a college graduate, her problems are the same as those of her defective child. She made a vague gesture as she explained that she had been a premature infant too, and that this was the reason she had never learned to think, to reason things out for herself, or to make decisions. The major difference between herself and her son was that he could think and reason better than she; he can make decisions, she cannot. She said she felt like a puppet on a string and she wept as she described her hatred for her mother and the maltreatment and emotional neglect she had suffered as a child. Her mother still seemed to exert control over her, even though many miles separated

[2] Paul Schilder, M.D., Ph.D., *Brain and Personality*, Nervous and Mental Disease Publishing Company, Washington, D.C., 1931, p. 22.

[3] Stanley C. Mahoney, "Observations Concerning Counselling with Parents of Mentally Retarded Children," *American Journal of Mental Deficiency*, Vol. LXIII, No. 81 (1958), p. 83.

them. She confused the child with herself, although she knew she was trying to give him things her mother had not given to her.

As some parents become aware of their own un-expressed anger toward a child who is a disappointment to them, they begin to express fear of the child's aggressiveness. Such parents are keenly aware of the difficulty they had as children in controlling their destructive impulses. Some may even speak of their own sense of confused sexual identity, re-lating their confusion to their child's struggles with problems of growth. They may recall memories of feeling rejected by their parents and of their fears about their bodies when they were children. Some mothers have stated that their bodies were unsuited to produce children; that they had "immature" reproductive organs or that their pelvic bones were "funnel shaped."

It is not unusual for these mothers to recall that during pregnancy they experienced an obsessive fear of giving birth to a damaged infant. Some think that their child was damaged as a result of their destructive wishes and fantasies, which the mothers still regard as omnipotent. A few mothers reported that during pregnancy they felt unusual activity in the womb — the fetus kicked and squirmed in an unusual manner. One mother stated that her un-born child had an "epileptic fit in utero." When a mother feels that her child has been magically dam-aged because of her forbidden wishes, angry feel-ings, or fantasied acts of cruelty, she may be too immobilized to assume appropriate responsibility. Such feelings may also serve as rationalizations for feelings of dependency, helplessness, and bewilder-ment. Sometimes a mother may insist on viewing the child as a symbol of her martyrdom and sacrifice.

On an even deeper level, a mother may be so psychologically fused with the child that she makes no differentiation between herself and the child, seeing the child as a reflection of herself. She may remember that her own parents regarded her as inadequate and damaged; thus, her child is really herself. Such closeness serves as a potent force pre-venting the mother from expressing angry feelings toward the child. It also serves to keep alive their intense mutual dependency on each other.

THE HELPING PROCEDURES

It is presumptuous to think that within the rela-tively short period of the diagnostic study the total-ity of the parent-child interaction can be uncovered, unraveled, or resolved. It is possible, however, to identify some of the complex feelings that exist between the parents and their child and to help them understand some of their interrelationships.

Parents come to the diagnostic study with an accumulation of months, and frequently years, of pain and distress. The patterns of the interrelation-ship are set, as if in concrete. At the time of the study it may seem that all three — the two parents and the child — have reached an impasse.

One of the purposes of the study is to assist the parents to take action once again, but this time with a clearer view of their individual and mutual needs. The parents' feeling of hope must be founded on reality and plans must be based on a true estimate of whatever strengths they may pos-sess. It should be emphasized that we consider the diagnostic study only a beginning step in the help-ing process, although an important one. The help-ing process is set in motion by the caseworker who helps both parents, individually and together, to express their bitterness, their confusions, their shat-tered hopes. It gains direction when the parents are encouraged to observe and reflect on their thoughts and feelings, to make connections between pertinent fragments of experience, to begin to ex-press their frustrations and bewilderment, as well as their hopes and joys, and to consider together their own needs as they examine alternative solutions for themselves and their child.

Too often, the caseworker underrates the im-portance of this beginning phase of help and thinks of it as a total process, to be completed within a week or ten days. He may throw aside patience, calmness, and consistency, and thereby give the parents the impression that he is more concerned, for reasons of prestige, to have them accept the recommendations than he is to have them use their own strengths to arrive at a satisfactory solution to their problem.

It is important, therefore, to examine some of the reasons why caseworkers feel such a desperate need to have parents accept the clinical findings of mental deficiency. Such feelings of desperation are often found to be linked with frustration as well as guilt if the caseworker must tell the parents that their child's condition is irreversible; he seems to be saying "There is no help." The caseworker may resist accepting the clinical findings and be angry at having to tell the parents about the child's limita-tions and handicaps. Caseworkers, as well as par-ents, may have magical wishes and deep resentment against the "senselessness of nature." Resistance may also stem from the fact that deep within all of us are feelings about the worthlessness of persons who deviate markedly from normal standards and about the futility of endeavoring to help them. We may feel deep guilt about the fact that such misfortune has happened to others and that we have "escaped" this fate. Many parents do not hesitate to mention this fact. Our frustration from being unhelpful heightens our self-doubts, and we may question our ability to be of help to parents who must come to grips with such a problem.

The caseworker, therefore, if he is to be of help, must be aware of the possibility that he may have many of the same feelings that trouble the parents. He should recognize the similarities in feelings, but he must also be aware of his different position and outlook. If he trusts his technical skills, he will feel less inner pressure to persuade parents to accept the clinic's diagnosis and the recommendations.

The primary aim of a diagnostic study is to assist the parents toward arriving at some resolution of their painful, conflicted feelings, of the anger and guilt that torment them, of the self-doubts that assail them, and of the distortions of reality that lead to irrational planning. If this aim is even partially achieved, the parents will experience a resurgence of whatever strengths they have and will then be able to deal with the problem as best they can. Too strenuous attempts on the part of the caseworker to have the parents accept the diagnosis or recommendations can only result in making the parents more guarded and cautious, since such an approach is viewed as an attack, both on them and on their child. If the worker has no emotional investment in a particular course of action, the parents feel free to do whatever they are able to do.

The parents of a defective child will always have difficulty with the concept of acceptance of one's problems. There are some burdens that can never be truly accepted. These parents may not accept the fact that a major portion of the child's limitations can never be reversed — that he will always have certain serious defects. Also, they may not fully accept the fact that any help provided for the child will not accomplish all that they wish.

The future, as well as the present, contains many frightening questions for such parents. Will the child be able to live as an adult without their parental care? If not, who will care for him? Will he be exploited and maltreated? Will he be able to marry? The parents deeply fear the child's physical maturation, not only because of the accompanying increase in aggression and expressions of sexuality, but also because the growing-up process exposes the child to more experiences in which he will meet defeat. Nearly all parents can tolerate the dependency needs of a child during his early

years because there is promise that his dependence will diminish as the child matures. But for parents of the defective child, there is no such promise.

As we have worked with parents toward a resolution of their conflicts, and tried to consider with them healthy solutions to the problem the defective child poses for them and the family, our least successful effort has been in discussing the effect of the child on other family members. Efforts to call attention to the neglected needs of other siblings usually arouse anger and deep resentment.

Bewildered and confused by the complexity of their feelings, parents often cling to many unrealities. One parent insisted that, if he had the time, patience, and the ability to be firm with his child, he was sure the child could be taught to do many things for himself and would eventually become an independent adult. To confront the parent with the unreality of his ideas would not alter his attitude. In this instance the worker commented on the importance of the father's beliefs, his hopes, and his refusal to accept defeat, assuring him that no one would try to change his convictions. The worker then helped the father to examine the source of these feelings, to identify the pressures behind them, and to explore what they meant in his relationship to his child. Such an intellectual approach often leads into emotional channels; the worker may then, with a light touch, explore these guarded feelings.

Despite the intense resistance parents show in accepting the fact of their child's retardation, their rigid and hostile defenses often give way under the consistent warmth and empathy of the worker. Through warmth and understanding, the parents come to feel that not only they, but they and their child, are loved. Their need, therefore, to defend both him and themselves is no longer so intensively felt. They can then apply themselves in a more constructive manner to the task of securing necessary help for the child, themselves, and the total family.

As parents present a picture of their child and their relationship to him, the worker must be keenly sensitive to overt and subtle affects. He must allow sufficient time to secure details, to clarify obscure points, and to explore ambiguities and contradictions. The parents are thus led into a comfortable, supportive, and relatively deep relationship that can sustain them in dealing with the truths about the child's condition as these slowly emerge during the diagnostic study process. For example, one mother in describing her child referred to him several times as a "throwback." When the worker suggested that she seemed to see her son as a "primitive" being, the mother thoughtfully agreed. With surprise in her voice, she told with feeling that she thought her son was some kind of atavistic organism, potentially dangerous and representing an accumulation of all that was bad in the "blood lines" of her own and her husband's family. The caseworker's exploration served to turn the client's rigid defense into a flow of feeling, in which she expressed both her suffering and her confused ideas.

Sometimes parents use the casework interviews as a form of self-punishment. They may make passive complaints about their helplessness, or they may protest their fate with quiet anger. Such parents look upon the casework contact during the diagnostic study as a means of gaining help for themselves; they hope the worker will view them as the patient and provide psychotherapy. Such parents prefer talking about their own dependency needs, their infantile conflicts, and their sexual thoughts rather than about their feelings as parents and as marital partners. It is much easier for a parent to talk about himself as weak and helpless, although his life situation and performance contradict this self-portrait, than to talk about the helplessness of his defective child. But, beneath this defense, the parent is often filled with self-doubt about the adequacy of his past care of the child. Should he accept the reality of his child's handicaps, he must then face the question as to whether he is adequate to meet this chal-

lenge and whether he can fulfil his parental role. Although the worker may offer understanding and empathy, the parent may strenuously resist a relationship with the worker because, to him, such a relationship is dangerous. To succumb to it, even slightly, may mean assuming the overwhelming responsibility of dealing with the truth of his child's limitations.

Skilled casework may remove the parent's temptation to regress. The caseworker, by assuming that parents come to the diagnostic study with strengths, may provide a creative experience that will affirm the integrity of the parents and set in motion new energy to cope with the many family problems.

A final question should be raised. Is the "shopping" for a diagnosis, which many parents do, a healthy or unhealthy adaptive mechanism? Their efforts to "leave no stone unturned" may be a reflection of their strength and not, as is often assumed, an indication of their inability to face their misfortune. Their refusal to yield, their rebellion, and their conscious effort to make sense out of senselessness, are not always efforts to deny their problems. Perhaps if we had better understanding of the parents' need to leave no stone unturned, we would be more successful in curtailing futile efforts. It is important for those working with these parents to recognize that sometimes their resistance and rebellion may be healthy adaptive mechanisms.

JOSEPH WORTIS

Prevention of Mental Retardation*†

Mental retardation is a relative term. It generally is defined as a degree of arrested intellectual development that disqualifies a child for ordinary education or an adult for ordinary employment. For present

* Reprinted from the *American Journal of Orthopsychiatry*, October 1965, Vol. 35, No. 5, pp. 886–895. Copyright, the American Orthopsychiatric Association, Inc. Reproduced by permission.
† Presented at the 1965 annual meeting of the American Orthopsychiatric Association, New York, New York, in the panel, "Research Approaches to Mental Retardation."

purposes we quickly can acknowledge that both biological handicaps and social-psychological vicissitudes may render a child or adult intellectually unfit or unprepared for the ordinary demands of life. For effective prevention we have to influence an extraordinarily wide range of factors (social, psychological, medical, genetic, etc.) that contribute to the problem. Moreover, since the concept of retardation is relative, we must realize that broader opportunities and fewer demands reduce the problem, while higher standards and demands will magnify it. That is why the diagnosis of retardation is made most often during the school years, when academic demands are greatest, and least often in infancy and in adult life, when the demands are less intense. Conversely, the lack of education in the broadest sense can retard an individual's mental development even if he were born with normal potential, while inborn defects can hinder development even in the best of circumstances. The more severe the retardation the greater is the likelihood that we are dealing with a biological handicap. The milder and more common degrees of retardation are more likely to be caused altogether or in part by lack of educational opportunity.

There is unfortunately still a good deal of ambiguity about the term, mental retardation, even among some of the professional people who work in the field. Some think it always implies a kind of innate or biological deficiency that limits the individual's capacity for mental development. Others think the term also is meant to encompass individuals of normal capacity who have fallen behind for social-psychological reasons. This confusion can be resolved very simply: I shall use the term mental retardation to denote all those whose IQs are below two standard deviations from the mean on one of the commonly used tests, such as the Stanford-Binet, WISC or Arthur Scale. This will generally be an IQ just below 70. Our definition thus certainly will implicate some individuals with normal and some with defective biological equipment. Binet and Simon, who can be fairly credited with the first systematic development of intelligence tests, never believed that retardation merely reflected biological endowment. Quite the contrary. Half a century ago they wrote:

> As a general rule, the children classed as retarded are the victims of disease, constitutional debility or malnutrition. We find included in our lists some who are the children of migratory parents; some who have been kept from school; some who have attended a religious school, where they learned little but sewing and writing; some who have changed their school too often; some also who are foreigners and understand little French, and lastly, some who have been kept back in their studies by unrecognized myopia . . .

That is why they proposed very cautious methods of diagnosis, including not only an intelligence test but also a careful consideration of history and circumstances, as well as a medical examination, before they would place a child in a special class for defectives.

On the basis of these considerations there should therefore be at least three elements in a program for the prevention of retardation.

First, we have to do as good a job in *education* as we possibly can, not only to allow the handicapped to develop to their fullest capacities, but also to prevent developmental failures.

Second, we already know that the health of the mother, particularly in pregnancy, the conduct of the birth act, and the health care of the child can greatly affect the child's mental equipment. We therefore have to provide the best possible *health care* for mother and child.

Third, we have to know much more about the causes of mental retardation. In at most half of the cases of retardation we can diagnose the disease, define the condition or make plausible guesses about what might be involved. In the rest we frankly admit ignorance or can make only the vague and general surmise that there is something wrong with the brain ("encephalopathy") without knowing the cause; and even at autopsy we usually cannot do much more than describe the lesion or defect. We therefore require *research* to increase our knowledge of such cases before we can set about preventing them.

I shall say very little about research, but I want to emphasize the need to apply the knowledge we already have in the two areas of education and health services.

What has education to do with mental retardation and its prevention? A great deal. It is commonly said that 3 percent of the population is retarded. Where does that figure come from? The distribution curve for the Stanford-Binet Form L is so plotted, or to put it differently, the test is so constructed that in a random population IQs below 70 should be found in close to 3 percent of the population. On this particular distribution curve IQs in the range of 50 to 69 should occur 10 times more frequently than IQs below 50. This means that if our schools depend on IQ tests to classify their pupils (as they do) about 90 percent of the retarded population is mildly retarded, educable or in the older terminology can be described as morons. The interesting thing, however, is that it is precisely in this range of the mildly retarded that we find the closest relation between social status and retardation. By almost every available measure: correlation with family income, with social class, with parent's vocation, by comparison of white with Negro, white with Puerto Rican, white with Mexican-American, white with native Indian, we find this same marked tendency to higher concentration of the retarded in the more disadvantaged sections of our population.

In the last war Negro registrants rejected for so-called mental deficiency outnumbered white rejected registrants by six to one. The rejection rates throughout the country, however, paralleled the per capita expenditures for education, so that the whites from the South did worse than the Negroes from the West.

About 10 years ago in Syracuse, N.Y., a census was taken of all children under the age of 18 who had been found or were suspected to be retarded by any responsible child-care agency in the city. It was found that about 3 percent of the children were so regarded with a peak of cases in the age range 10 to 14, where they amounted to about 7 percent. It we focus our attention on children in this age group in four districts of low economic level we find that the percentage of ascertained cases in these districts was more than twice as high (15.2 percent) for the white children, compared with the rest of the city, and more than four times as high (31.8 percent) for the Negro children in these districts in this age group compared with the rest of the city. Thus nearly one-third of the Negro children in these poor districts between the ages of 10 to 14 had been regarded by some responsible city agency as a diagnosed or suspected case of retardation. Gruenberg, who directed this study, concluded "that both the physical and cultural environments create a higher risk of impaired intellectual development for the children of these areas — more so for the nonwhite than for the white child." In New York City Saenger also found that though only 7 percent of the city population lives in the two areas with lowest median income (under $2,500 per annum) these two areas contributed 33 percent of the high-grade retarded who remained in the community. These two areas are inhabited mostly by Negroes and Puerto Ricans. This relation to ethnic and economic status relates only to the population with IQs above 50. Below that no relation was found to ethnic or economic groups. However, with regard to institutionalization, we find the disadvantaged sections of our population again contributing disproportionately high numbers to our institutions in all IQ ranges with this poor 7 percent of the population accounting for 39 percent of the institutionalized cases. Thus, while 1 out of every 21 known low-grade, retarded Jewish children was committed to a state institution, and 1 out of every 11 white, low-grade, retarded Protestant or

Catholic children, we find that 1 out of every 5 low-grade, retarded Negro children, and 1 out of every 2 low-grade, Puerto Rican retardates was sent to an institution.

But it might be argued that the defectives are found in larger numbers in our depressed social classes because that is where they drift. But suppose we could raise some of these children predestined to retardation, in better circumstances? How would they turn out? This is precisely what was done recently with adopted children whose mothers were retarded, as Skeels recently reported. Findings to date indicate that these children are quite normal and that their children in turn are average or better though the original mothers all had IQs from 32 to 75. Moreover, if known retarded children are taken from ordinary institutions and given enriched programs, their IQs go up quite significantly, while their companions who are left behind deteriorate and decline. Obviously, retardation and intelligence depend on other things besides biological equipment.

A serious scientific obstacle to progress in the mental retardation field has been Galton's old concept of a normal distribution curve for intelligence with all its implications. The assumption was that intelligence was one of those natural or God-given attributes you were born with; if you had it you were part of an intellectual elite; the less fortunate members of our society were then treated with more or less kindly solicitude by their superiors while the very defective idiots were put away for safe-keeping. Even if we all had equally good educations, the concept might at best be valid for the middle ranges, but in the lower ranges we are dealing not with normal variation but with products of both social and medical pathology: there is every reason to believe on clinical and empirical grounds that the true intelligence distribution for the population is not Gaussian but negatively skewed to the left, or lower, ranges. Moreover, it should be kept in mind that the Stanford-Binet Form L was standardized in 1937 on a white population and that the most recent revision, Form L-M (1960), was standardized on a population "somewhat biased in the direction of superior social and economic status."

It is true that the poor tend to be intellectually undernourished (we see them every day in our clinic in Brooklyn, especially the Negro poor). For them the conventional family unit is usually not known; the father is often nonexistent or absent; the mother is out working or the child lives with a grandmother, aunt or neighbor; books are rarely seen at home, or indeed any reading matter; toys are seldom used, and there is the constant intellectual stultification produced by the long hours before the television screen. It is not surprising that in this atmosphere the reading skills of New York City public school pupils have declined to the point where more than a third of the junior high school children (aged 12 to 14) are two or more years behind in their reading ability.

Better and earlier and more comprehensive school education could help a great deal, but with the serious social dislocation now developing in these slums, the children come to school with few intellectual or cultural interests or aspirations, little preparation or capacity for organized group work and with rebellious and combative attitudes that overtax the teacher's ability to maintain order and leave her little time, energy and opportunity to teach. It is obvious that even here it will take more than the schools to promote optimal educational opportunities. What is needed is a change in the total life situation of these children, starting with (but not limited to) the alleviation of their poverty. Let us have no illusions: there is much more to the educational process than the activities in the classroom.

Further down toward the lower end of the intelligence distribution curve, three or more standard deviations away from the mean (IQ below 50) we find a miscellany of backward individuals; some of them may have been biologically normal but they never had much of a developmental chance. However most of these backward individuals are biologically handicapped. Nobody knows exactly what the proportions are of these two groups respectively, but even after we have faced up to the fact that a distressingly large proportion of our population is uneducated, we are still left with a substantial number, perhaps 1 to 2 percent of our general population, who are biologically handicapped in a way that significantly affects their intellectual capacities. If we leave the major responsibility for the first group to the educators and social reformers, what can we say about prevention of mental defect involving the biologically unfit?

But here too we must first ask: what are the main biological causes of mental defect? We know something about this, but not enough. Yet we can make some reasonable surmises.

If three percent of our population is retarded, and we make the plausible assumption that half of these are mostly educationally deprived, we are left with a possible one and a half percent whose mental retardation is presumably of non-psychological origin. Of these about one-seventh, or 15 percent, are mongoloid. The diagnosable chromosomal anomalies other than mongolism do not now comprise more than one or two percent of the retarded population, while other genetic metabolic defects (phenylketonuria, galactosuria, sucrosuria, histidinuria, homocystinuria and other aminoacidurias) are quite rare and altogether probably do not comprise more than another 1 or 2 percent of this retarded population. A miscellany of other specific causes (brain infections, brain trauma, certain rare dysplastic syndromes, heavy metal poisoning and the like) also do not comprise in their totality more than a few percent. A somewhat larger group is made up of those children whose development has been hampered by general weakness, chronic debilitation, malnutrition and neglect.

The big remaining category thus comprises the so-called encephalopathies. These are the biologically abnormal cases that present us with a compromising history of impaired pregnancy or gestation, prematurity, complicated or traumatic births, or who on direct clinical examination show signs of faulty neural integration either in terms of very early developmental lags or demonstrable impairments of neurologic function.

Seventy percent of the retarded cases in our clinic were designated as some form of encephalopathy, and in the majority of these cases we had no idea what the cause might be. The two diagnostic categories, encephalopathy of unknown cause and mental retardation of unknown cause, together comprise more than half of our retarded clinic cases. In time no doubt we shall discover new metabolic and genetic entities among them (and the large preponderance of males in this group suggests important genetic mechanisms), but for the present it is safe to assume that these two large miscellaneous categories will be found to consist mainly of four kinds of cases: (1) directly inherited conditions, (2) induced genetic mutations, (3) products of disturbed or abnormal gestation and (4) products of perinatal complications or injuries.

To define these groups is almost automatically to define the preventive measures they require. I shall comment on each.

With several conditions known to us we can tell parents quite accurately what the probabilities are of having another affected child. It is now also possible to detect the heterozygotes for both galactosuria and phenylketonuria, and methods for detecting heterozygotes for other genetic metabolic disorders no doubt will be found. But in other known congenital syndromes and for genetic conditions still unknown we will need more knowledge of genetic mechanisms and modes of transmission; we need more and better diagnostic facilities, more and better genetic counselling, more knowledge of the relationship between genetics and chemistry and better nongenetic methods for treatment and correction of genetic faults.

Such enlarged facilities would provide some more or less specific measures that could reduce the incidence of certain genetic diseases. But what can we say about general eugenic measures designed to limit the productivity of the unintelligent by compulsory (or voluntary) sterilization? The Nazis tried it, but there is no indication that it helped. Thousands of defectives have been sterilized in recent decades in the U.S.A., but the social usefulness of such a step is highly questionable to say the least. Penrose says:

It is difficult to justify compulsory sterilization of defectives on genetic grounds. . . . Owing to the fact that the great majority of defectives of all grades are born to parents who cannot be classed as defective themselves, the reduction of defect in the community by preventing all known cases from having children would not be spectacular. . . . There is no precise genetics of social inefficiency, so that the idea that it can be prevented on the basis of genetic theory is essentially invalid.

But if eugenics, in Galton's original sense, no longer can be regarded as an important tactic in prevention, genetics is opening up new possibilities for social improvement by affording us opportunities for correcting the genetic fault by chemical means. I again quote Penrose:

Many people consider that identification of abnormal karyotypes in mental disability makes alleviation seem out of the question. I do not find this so myself. The effects of aneuploidy in plants are not necessarily unfavorable. The distortions of growth which can follow may be simply a question of water balance in the cells, not of the production of abnormal enzymes. The existence of a new aspect of human pathology has now suddenly been demonstrated and at present almost nothing is known about it. The fact that cytologically anomalous individuals can exist in the population and be perfectly healthy indicates that there are compensatory factors. These must be investigated.

The basic error in the eugenics of the past was the assumption that mental retardation like intelligence was a genetic entity that was transmitted along classical genetic lines. The assumption was false: mental retardation is a complex entity, only

partially genetic, where specific genetic diseases transmitted along classic lines play only a partial role in the total problem. Most chromosomal anomalies so far discovered are associated with mental defect, but except for mongolism they are rare. Compulsory sterilization involves serious dangers to civil rights; but voluntary sterilization and contraceptive birth control, if supported by sound genetic counselling, can reduce the incidence of such cases as translocation mongolism, tuberous sclerosis, galactosemia, phenylketonuria, gargoylism, Tay-Sachs disease, etc.

In addition to direct inheritance there is the problem of induced mutation. Hiroshima and Nagasaki revealed in an appalling but impressive way what ionizing radiation can do to produce fetal death, deformity and mental retardation. We need to minimize all exposure to radiation, including X-Ray and background radiation. The nuclear test ban was a step in this direction, but much more must be done. Aside from radiation there are many other agents that can induce gene mutations and teratogenic deformities: drugs, dietary deficiencies, mechanical insults, anoxia. The thalidomide scandal has raised the index of suspicion for all drugs, and no doubt new sources of trouble now will be discovered.

Our obstetrical practices are being reviewed and corrected in the light of developmental studies of children delivered in different ways. The crude method of judging the safety of an obstetrical procedure by relating it to survival rates or gross injury is now inadequate. The greatest risk in obstetrical practice is that of diffuse and minimal brain damage, and only developmental studies will disclose which obstetrical practices thus impair the child. There is good reason to suspect that some widely used obstetrical methods (anesthesia, induced labor and other practices) may prove to be more harmful than is now realized.

Now that we know that not only German measles but at least several other virus diseases can adversely affect the developing fetus, we have begun to think of protective immunizations of prospective mothers. In one recent survey nearly one-fifth (17.5 percent) of the women had no demonstrable antibody against the rubella virus. This is the virus which will damage one-fifth of all offspring if the mother is infected in the first trimester of pregnancy. A promising protective vaccine is now being developed which could be given to young women prior to pregnancy. Low placental estrogen production rates are now known to endanger the fetus, and remedial measures can be undertaken here.

Attempted abortions probably play a significant role in some fetal defects, since the mechanism of induced abortion is invariably to kill the fetus. Three percent of our own clinic patients admit attempted abortion; the true percentage is undoubtedly higher.

Other specific examples could be given of ways in which prenatal care could prevent fetal damage, but they all would lead to the same conclusion: pregnant mothers need prenatal care. It is well known that there is a direct relationship between pregnancy risks and prenatal care. That is why the President's Panel on Mental Retardation strongly urged the creation of maternity clinics for the high-risk mothers.

The present state of health services for pregnant women is deplorable. Dr. Arthur L. Lesser, for example, has recently cited a report by Dr. John D. Thompson, professor of obstetrics and gynecology at Emory University School of Medicine, Atlanta, Georgia, who says:

> On the obstetrical services of these large charity hospitals. . . . It is simply impossible to give adequate prenatal care. . . . 23 percent of all patients delivered came to the hospital first when they were in labor, having had no prenatal care. Only 11 percent . . . came . . . in the first trimester of their pregnancy.

In Dallas one-third of the low-income patients received no prenatal care; at the Los Angeles County Hospital in 1958, 20 percent; at the D.C. General Hospital in Washington, D.C., 45 percent, etc.

It is for such reasons that the President's Panel strongly emphasized the great importance of maternal care (including genetic counselling) and recommended increased expenditure for this purpose on all government levels with an emphasis on the needs of the low-income, high-risk mothers. The Panel called for more laboratory facilities for the diagnosis of genetic anomalies, Rh and other blood anomalies, the detection of metabolic types of retardation, detection of maternal infection, etc. It called for renewed emphasis upon and expansion of the educational opportunities of the underprivileged, and quite correctly stated that poverty hurts both body and mind. The corrective process must start early, and school should start at three years.

The Panel also made a number of specific recommendations to reduce the danger of teratogenic drugs, ionizing radiation, head injuries in children, etc., but it must be said to their credit that the two major areas of emphasis were prenatal care and education, and both of them in turn were especially

related to poverty. The management and care of pregnant women, they said, are "too often based on economics rather than on medicine."

The Panel was not asked to propose changes in our system of medical care, and its recommendations are strictly within the framework of existing arrangements: more money to the Children's Bureau for its state aid program for maternal and child welfare, more money to various USPHS departments for demonstration, training and research purposes, enlarged public health laboratory and diagnostic facilities, more public education and the like. It has, however, become clear to many that our existing arrangements for medical care are both disorganized and inadequate.

By almost every measurable standard, American medical services for the general public are extremely poor: we are *eighth* in the world in perinatal mortality, *seventh* in congenital malformations, and *ninth* in the world in infant mortality rate (just a little better than Singapore). Of all the 13 countries listed in the most recent Vital Statistics report of the World Health Organization (No. 1–2, 1964) the United States had the worst record for infant deaths due to birth injury, postnatal asphyxia and atelectasis (1961), a rate nearly twice as high as Norway's. But even these figures do not tell the whole story because the fair level of services to our middle classes obscures the picture of the extremely inadequate services to the poor. In New York City, for example, the prematurity rate in one white, middle-class district is 6.2 percent and in another poor Negro district, 16.5 percent. Last month (February) the American Journal of Public Health declared editorially:

> An effort to break the vicious cycle linking poverty and ill health has to take account of various elements, but one of the most important must be a system of health services.

But the paying patients do not always fare better. In that same issue Dr. Ray E. Trussell, commissioner of hospitals in New York City, gives an appalling picture of the medical inefficiency of the proprietary hospitals in New York City: 45 percent of their laboratories could not diagnose a bacteriological specimen correctly; 25 percent could not do adequate chemistries and in blood typing errors ran as high as 5 to 7 percent. When we consider our enormously rich productive capacities, our high technological development, high per-capita income and high level of medical training and competence, this is especially striking and points up the need for vastly improved methods for the distribution of medical services, including maternal and child care.

In summary, the prevention of mental retardation in the years just ahead will depend on two things: (1) the alleviation of poverty together with a vastly expanded and improved educational, cultural and social welfare program for the underprivileged and (2) a much expanded, better coordinated and greatly improved program of medical services.

It should be emphasized that any piecemeal program of improved maternal care, mental health centers, well baby clinics, etc., however useful each may be, will not prove to be a satisfactory substitute for rationalized, comprehensive and universally available health services.

If both these things come to pass, we can accept the conservative statement of the President's Panel that with present knowledge at least half of the mental retardation now known to us is preventable.

REFERENCES

1. BINET, A. and T. SIMON. 1914. Mentally Defective Children. W. B. Drummond. Trans. Longmans, Green Co., New York.
2. EDITORIAL. 1965. Quality of medical care: public health problem. Amer. J. Public Health. 55: 169–170.
3. GINZBERG, E., and D. W. BRAY. 1953. The Uneducated. Columbia Univ. Press, New York.
4. GRUENBERG, E. M. 1964. Epidemiology, pp. 259–306. In Mental Retardation. H. A. Stevens and R. Heber, eds. Univ. of Chicago Press, Chicago.
5. LESSER, A. J. 1963. Current problems of maternity care. Lecture delivered at the School of Public Health, University of California, Berkeley.
6. LESSER, A. J. 1964. Accent on prevention through improved service. Children. 11: 13–18.
7. PENROSE, L. S. 1962. The Biology of Mental Defect. 2nd Ed. Grune & Stratton, New York.
8. PENROSE, L. S. 1962. Biological Aspects. Proc. London Conf. Scient. Study Ment. Deficiency. 1: 11–18.
9. A Proposed Program for National Action to Combat Mental Retardation. 1962. President's Panel on Mental Retardation. U.S. Government Printing Office, Washington, D.C.
10. SAENGER, G. 1960. Factors influencing the Institutionalization of Mentally Retarded Individuals in New York City. N.Y. State Interdepartmental Health Resources Board, Albany.
11. SKEELS, H. M. 1965. Effects of adoption on children from institutions. Children. 12: 33–34.
12. TERMAN, L. M., and M. A. MERRILL. 1960. Stanford-Binet Intelligence Scale Manual for the Third Revision, Form L-M. Houghton-Mifflin Co., Boston.
13. TRUSSELL, R. E. 1965. The quality of medical care as a challenge to health. Amer. J. Public Health. 55: 173–182.
14. WORLD HEALTH Organization Epidemiological and Vital Statistics Report 1963 and 1964. Vols. 16 and 17.
15. WORTIS, H. 1964. Social class and premature birth. Social Casework. 45: 541.

Childhood Disturbances / 8

We have tried to maintain throughout this volume an orientation towards the appreciation of family processes in the development (and maldevelopment) of personality. In every area of psychopathology research, investigation into family transactional patterns has begun to take the place of the examination of static, intraindividual symptom complexes.

This trend is most dramatically seen in current work with children. The disruptions and distortions in a child's growth process, which we call emotional disturbance, are seen as the result of a breakdown in family homeostasis, in the adaptive coping patterns developed by the family over time. As one authority has commented:

> A disturbed child referred for professional help is only one link in the chain of family disturbance. He may be the most sick or the least sick member of the family. The warp of the family interaction invades the child's emotional life; the child's behavior in turn penetrates and modifies the processes of family interaction. The child absorbs and reprojects the pathogenic contagion of the family group. He must be viewed not only as a distressed individual, but also as a symptom of a psychopathically twisted family group. His behavior offers a specific clue to the distortion of homeostatic control of family functions.[1]

As Ackerman's comments make clear, the disturbed child is not the mere recipient of pathological parental attitudes, but a participant in ongoing family interaction patterns. The nature of his "twisted family group," as well as some of the forms of disturbance he manifests, are analyzed in the following selections.

[1] Ackerman, N. *Preventive implications of family research. In G. Caplan (Ed.) Prevention of mental disorders in children. New York: Basic Books, 1961, p. 154.*

The basic premises of the diagnostic evaluation of the disturbed child are schematically set forth in the selection from the Group for the Advancement of Psychiatry's report on The Diagnostic Process in Child Psychiatry. Emphasis is placed here on the vicissitudes of the child's response to anxiety, whether this arises out of self-perception or environmental stress. As an outline for understanding children's difficulties, the GAP suggestions are quite comprehensive, involving problems of family interaction, self-concept, and biological factors, concepts examined in greater detail above in Section 2.

Vogel and Bell once again take us directly into the sphere of family interaction processes. Their work, carried out within the same framework of role theory as that of Spiegel (see above, "The Resolution of Role Conflict within the Family"), attempts to delineate the reasons why a child is assigned a certain unfortunate role in the family and how he is locked into this role. The scapegoated child suffers, and there are many dysfunctional aspects of this role assignment for the family, but such a channeling of conflict allows for the continued maintenance of some degree of family-group integration.

Spitz reviews the earliest manifestations of psychological disturbance, appearing during the infant's first year of life. He suggests two basic etiological factors, based on the acknowledged importance of the mother-child relationship during this period. These are the wrong kind of mother-child interaction, which leads to the psychotoxic diseases, in which the mother becomes a toxic substance to the infant, and the insufficient mother-child relationship or maternal deprivation, resulting in the deficiency diseases. Spitz's classification scheme, while clearly only a beginning step, does provide a convenient framework for investigating the primary forms of infant maladjustment.

Eisenberg, in a paper originally written for pediatricians, discusses the symptomatology, development, and management of a common and disruptive childhood disturbance known as school phobia. He stresses the etiological importance of the mother-child relationship, with its extreme manifestations of dependency, muted hostility, and guilt, terms reminiscent of Green's discussion of the middle-class child's family environment. As most of these phobic children stem from middle-class homes, school phobia may be seen, in this light, as one form of response to the nonspecific pathogenic influences Green outlines.

If such factors as parental ambivalence concerning love and aggression and "smothering" of the child are seen as etiological agents in the development of neurotic problems, what form of parent-child interaction appears to lie behind the eruption of antisocial behavior, in any of its myriad forms? Giffin and her associates put forth the concept of the "superego lacunae," a defect of conscience which develops in the child through incorporation of ambivalent parental attitudes with respect to the antisocial behavior. Thus, the child grows up in a family environment which fosters the very behavior it condemns; the parents obtaining vicarious gratification for their own hidden impulses through the behavior of their child. Giffin makes it clear that unlike the neurotic, overinhibited child, who needs help in developing self-expression and freedom of action, the antisocial child is desperately in need of external controls, a sense of limits which he can eventually internalize.

One of the most distressing of childhood disturbances, and one of its most enigmatic forms, is the syndrome known as infantile autism. First delineated and labeled by the psychiatrist Leo Kanner at Johns Hopkins,[2] early infantile autism is characterized by extreme isolation and withdrawal from human contact and an intense preoccupation with the maintenance of sameness. The syndrome manifests itself within the first two years of life, and the disturbance in interpersonal relations is usually evident from the earliest postnatal period. Sarvis and Garcia examine the wider range of autistic disturbances, both primary and secondary types, and present an outline of various etiological factors which alone or in concert lead to the development of autistic behavior. As can be noted, they see this development in a transactional framework involving child and parents, each reacting and counteracting to the other's behavior on the basis of their own predispositions and needs. What it is like for a family to cope with the behavior of an autistic child, whatever the cause of his disturbance, is beautifully portrayed in the reprinted selection from Life magazine's report on a University of California research team's use of reinforcement techniques in the treatment of autism. Billy, the subject of the article, is a seven-year-old whose bizarre and frightening behavior had all but driven his family crazy before he was brought to UCLA for treatment. Whether the techniques used with Billy — based on the reinforcement of adaptive behaviors and the punishment of maladaptive ones — will signal a breakthrough in our treatment of such disturbed children is still an open question, but results so far show great promise. ■

_____

[2] For Kanner's views on this disturbance see: Kanner, L. Autistic disturbances of affective contact. Nerv. Child, 1943, 2, 217–250 and Kanner, L. Early infantile autism, 1943–55. Amer. J. Orthopsychiat., 1956, 26, 556–566. For a most extensive coverage of the literature on autism and the proposal of an interesting theoretical position on its etiology, see Rimland, B. Infantile autism. New York: Appleton-Century-Crofts, 1963. Finally, for a poignant fictional account of the world of an autistic child, see Rubin, T. Jordi. New York: Macmillan, 1960.

The Diagnostic Process in Child Psychiatry
II. Basic Assumptions*

In preparing this report the Committee agreed that certain basic assumptions are essential to the consideration of the diagnostic process in child psychiatry. These basic assumptions relate to current knowledge concerning the development of human personality.

The concept that a child's behavior reflects his attempts to adapt to a series of tension-producing situations is fundamental to the diagnostic study of children. The well-adjusted child's methods of adaptation are personally gratifying and socially appropriate. The emotionally disabled child's adaptive attempts are ineffectual and only partially satisfying, and they may be experienced internally as distressing symptoms. As outer signs of the disability they may be manifested in behavior which is socially unacceptable and often disturbing to others.

Diagnosis involves primarily an investigation of the child's relative successes and failures in mastering in orderly sequence certain universal anxieties which confront all children as they move through the several stages of personality development. In general, the major tasks in this growth are directed toward the achievement of a biologically satisfying utilization of life energies (the libidinal or psychosexual and the aggressive drives) through constructive patterns which are socially and ethically satisfactory.

The delineation of those specific areas which have been seriously impeded at a particular chronological age must be based on the body of knowledge concerning normal personality growth. It is a distinctive feature of child psychiatry that all findings are weighed against the developmental norms for the successive, changing stages of growth. Basic to this concept is the belief that normal personality patterns evolve out of interpersonal relationships. As a unique and distinct biological organism, the child is always interacting in varying degrees with external

* Reprinted by permission of the copyright owner, Group for the Advancement of Psychiatry, from Report #38 "The Diagnostic Process in Child Psychiatry," formulated by the Committee on Child Psychiatry, Group for the Advancement of Psychiatry, New York, 1957.

social forces, especially within the family in early years. In infancy he depends totally on his parents for the primary satisfaction of loving care and for the protection necessary to sustain life. These lay the foundation for his further biological and psychological maturation which in turn progressively stimulates the inherent and newly emerging energies that increasingly strive for satisfying expression. To meet these successive changing needs the child again depends on adults, first on his parents and later on others in his broadening society. As the unique aspect of childhood, the dependency relationships provide the framework through which the child is helped to develop an awareness of himself as an organized separate individual whose behavior patterns are consistent with both individual and group living.

The growth of the child's sense of his own identity as a unique and distinct individual is accomplished within the successive developmental phases through certain observable processes of differentiation. In the earliest months the infant is in a relatively undifferentiated state of oneness with his mother. But gradually as the child experiences minimal and hence tolerable frustrations of his basic needs and is satisfied repetitively by his mother, he more actively turns toward her with increasing confidence and patience. He learns that he is separate and different from his mother yet dependent on her and his environment. In the normal, mutually gratifying, symbiotic relationship with his mother the infant's and mother's needs are complementary, for in anticipating and meeting her child's needs the mothering-person is also fulfilling her own mothering function.

Intimately associated and concurrent with this process, the child's neuro-muscular, intellectual and emotional growth leads to an awareness of his bodily parts and their functional differentiation. He also becomes aware of his increasing needs and greater energies for pleasurable and rewarding muscular activities such as reaching, walking, talking and controlling elimination. He strives to master some of his bodily functions so that voluntarily and purposefully he can direct his own actions to satisfy some of his needs. This self-sufficiency is attained through certain appropriate prohibitions and prescriptions. From the parents the child needs some actual protective limitations along with their support and guidance in becoming aware of socially approved standards and in learning the skills and techniques required for gratifying and acceptable behavior. In a sense the outcome of infant development is the increasing ability to bear tension.

Continued physiological maturation and expanding social experiences within the family contribute additional qualities to the child's sense of his own identity. When he begins to recognize the relationships between his parents and siblings, his egocentricity and possessiveness yield to a more precise ego differentiation. He also modifies his previous self-image of narcissistic omnipotence when he is confronted by the unique and exclusive relationship between his mother and father, as he naturally at this stage directs toward them his first diffuse and early genital tensions and his curiosity about the differences between the sexes and between children and adults. To resolve the resultant conflicting feelings of love, anger, rivalry, guilt and fear inevitably created by these universal triangular life experiences, he again needs the guidance of others. He needs adult understanding; a kindly, firm, appropriate balance of limits and permissiveness; and sound parental standards for identification in order to attain a valid acceptance of himself, — of his own biological sex, of his actual native aptitudes, and of his realistic position with his parents, siblings, peers and teachers. The adaptive capacities of the parents help the child achieve this type of identity enabling him to take some initiative and responsibility for his own behavior. The child needs parents who, first individually and somewhat differently as man and woman, and then together as husband and wife, and later as father and mother, having attained the maturity of enjoying and sharing their mutual creative responsibilities in fostering his continued growth.

The diagnostic process, therefore, must include two essential areas of investigation, each with its special characteristics but each understood more fully in its reciprocal relationship with the other. These are (1) the child himself, his basic physical and intellectual endowment and the inner biological and psychological forces and behavior patterns or ego mechanisms which emerge in the development of his own individual identity, and (2) the environment and its social forces which influence the child as he matures. In the exploration of dynamic and genetic factors, any unilateral approach precludes accurate diagnosis. Both the child and his society must be understood separately and in their interactions. The recognition of this necessity for including the family in the diagnostic process has differentiated child psychiatry from *traditional* adult psychiatry. In contrast to the adult with a more structured ego, the child is still developing as an individual and is not only more flexible but also more vulnerable to the environmental forces around him.

The diagnosis of child pathology requires first of all the accurate delineation of those aspects of development which are primarily disturbed together with some reasonable hypotheses concerning the multiple factors that might have operated to cause the deviation. To construct a psychodynamic formulation requires a frame of reference which is based on the assumptions derived from accumulated clinical data. One basic assumption is that behavioral disabilities arise in an interpersonal milieu in connection with experiences that evoke or reactivate within the child a feeling of helplessness or vulnerability felt as an anxiety. This anxiety may be provoked by either realistic or fantasied threatening situations or by the child's actual or contemplated counter-measures directed against those situations. Its intensity, which reflects the child's valid or distorted estimate of the potential destructiveness of the threatening experience, will depend partly on the nature and intensity of the external challenge or precipitating factor and partly on the child's adaptive capacity as determined by his particular personality structure. Certain common challenges are inevitably experienced during the course of the child's growth. The degree to which they become severe threats varies with the age of the child and with the level of psycho-socio-sexual maturity that he has reached at any given chronological age. The usual challenges of life may be experienced as severe threats by the immature child with limited ability to tolerate stress, while exposure to extraordinary environmental stress may threaten even the relatively stable child.

The universal primary anxiety connected with loss of love and protection is intensified initially or reactivated later by actual or expected abandonment or deprivation. This might occur with any separation from the parents, such as hospitalization, or with punitive threats of desertion. The common anxiety associated with mutilation and disability may become overwhelmingly great if the child is physically assaulted or threatened with any bodily harm, such as accident, disease, or even the physical injury inherent in a simple tonsillectomy or other surgical procedures. He may also be more vulnerable to this anxiety if, burdened with illogical guilt, he anticipates retaliation for his own destructive impulses. The anxiety associated with his sense of defeat about his performance and his feeling of inferiority and disgrace about his adequacy as a person compared to his own and others' standards may also disrupt the child's adjustment. This is often true for the child who actually has some disability but it occurs also when a child imagines he is defective.

When the child fails to deal adequately with these external conflicts or environmentally-stimulated anxieties, the process of symptom formation is set in motion. He may resort to earlier behavior patterns which had once been successful in coping with previous developmental tasks. But at best this attempt is only temporarily effective. This process of symptom formation might be illustrated by excerpts from the case history of Jimmy, a greatly over-indulged child of 8, whose basic insecurity was intensified by the arrival of a new sibling. He reverted to the earlier pleasure of persistent thumb-sucking which had previously been relinquished at age 3. This method of coping with his reactivated infantile needs was incompatible with society's expectations of the older child as well as with his own internalized standards and wishes as a growing boy. Moreover, he developed anxiety and guilt over the forbidden hostility he felt in response to the environment which frustrated his infantile impulses. Jimmy first attempted to solve his various internal and external conflicts by compulsively and aggressively repeating the former self-satisfying activity, namely the thumb-sucking. But this method failed as an adequate compromise; it afforded only partial satisfaction for which his guilt, nevertheless, demanded the penalty of personal suffering, energy diffusion and social disharmony. His various tensions were reflected in marked irritability, distractibility, feelings of shame and inferiority, and social withdrawal. In Jimmy's case his continued internal conflicts as well as further parental disapproval led to another equally unsuccessful solution when, along with a diminution of the thumb-sucking, he developed a new combination of patterns manifested as a severe animal phobia. In the face of similar conflicts some children might develop anorexia or vomiting, or over-eating and biting, or demanding, possessive attitudes. In each case, the child has resorted to some compulsive repetitive pattern or to a composite unitary action derived from earlier mechanisms. Although these methods result in

some dependency satisfaction through the parental interest and care elicited by the disabilities, the child is distressed and maladjusted. The degree to which his energies are bound and depleted by these conflicts determines the extent to which he is blocked in his further growth.

The type of emotional or behavioral disability which results is determined by the specific configuration of ego mechanisms utilized by the particular child. It is manifested in physiological, psychological or conduct disturbances which are the clinical signs and symptoms of anxiety itself or of the child's attempts to allay the anxiety. In any case the symptom consciously or unconsciously selected is often related to specific areas of parental emotional disturbance. Although the behavioral pattern may be dissatisfying to the child and unsatisfactory to society, it does serve the child in reducing or avoiding some of his anxieties.

The child's pathological response to anxiety may represent varying degrees of ego-disintegration. He experiences the threats as a destruction of his internalized body images — either of the existence of the body as a whole, or of its internal or external organs, or of its continued functioning in an effective and acceptable manner. This breakdown of ego integration is a psychological regression and may be called a "de-differentiation", analogous to the more primitive physiological dysfunctioning in organic pathology. On both the physical and psychological levels, the organism reacts to stress with a defensive attack against the dangerous stimuli by reverting to some previously effective pattern as a starting-point for re-establishing its structure and healthy functioning. In physical healing the cellular response is helpful in attacking noxious agents and restoring the physical integrity. An analogy might be found in the response to psychological stress; earlier successful behavior patterns are reactivated as defense mechanisms for mastering anxiety and for re-integrating the appropriate functional capacity of the ego.

Diagnosis in child psychiatry must be seen as a dynamic process through which are evaluated all the growth-promoting and growth-retarding forces in the child's life as they interact to produce various conflicts and the particular modes of solving them. It is more than the classification of a child in a nosological system based on the clinical observation and description of the presenting signs and symptoms of deviant behavior. In a sense then, it consists of an evaluation of the functioning of the child's ego, of his integrative capacity, strength and flexibility. It involves an assessment of the nature and intensity of specific anxieties including the time and setting of their onset. Child psychiatric diagnosis delineates the areas and degree of regression as well as those pathological defense mechanisms used in the regression. It identifies also the healthy ego mechanisms utilized in the past and present in adapting to the normal developmental tasks of ordinary experiences and to any unusual or critical life situations. It takes into account any unevenness in the different spheres of personality development. It encompasses the concept that the disability itself represents a strategic withdrawal to a partially regressed level for re-grouping or rallying the child's strengths and that this constructive aspect of the child's disability can be supported for his recovery. In this appraisal it is also important to weigh the ego functions against the nature and strength of the internal drives arising in the biological processes and to recognize that the effectiveness of the ego's defenses against anxiety and the efficiency of its executive mechanisms are largely determined by the intactness and healthy functioning of the total organism, especially the neuro-muscular system.

The comprehensive evaluation of the child's ego functioning takes into account the two-way nature of his relationship with society. The child himself plays an active part in the interaction with his parents and others. Certain constitutional factors may lower his inherent capacity for the effective utilization of positive life experiences. Even in infancy certain characteristics of the child, such as his motility pattern and degree of sensitivity may influence the maternal attitude. A young child's repetitive unrewarding responses to mothering efforts may foster tensions and lead to the vicious cycle of an uncomforted child and a frustrated mother trying desperately to be a good mother. On the other hand, this process may be set in motion by the mother who, in a distorted identification with her child, responds to him as a symbol of an unsettled past. Unhealthy parental attitudes arising from previous or current significant relationships or from social or cultural factors may be displaced to the child so that the parent does not realistically perceive him or his needs. The child thus threatened and deprived may react aggressively in his frustration; he may be forced to turn back to earlier self-satisfying activities. His behavioral responses then reinforce the distorted identifications of the mother so that tensions increase, and neither mother nor child gains from their relationship the gratifications necessary for each. As an example, severe emotional disturbance in the mother may so distort her percep-

tion of early infantile needs that adequate normal symbiosis is never attained. Such children, when they do not die of intercurrent disease, are likely to show primary atypical development or mental retardation. Their behavior may represent fragmented aspects of developmental stages which have never been fully mastered or integrated into the personality.

Basic to the understanding of parent-child interactions is the recognition that the parental capacity to meet a child's needs may vary greatly in his different phases of growth. The child's normal behavior at one stage may elicit healthy parental responses whereas at another it may reactivate the parents' immaturities around old conflicts pertinent to that level of development. In defining parental attitudes such terms as "rejecting mother" or "competitive father" are as stultifying as is the diagnostic label of "conduct disorder." Dynamic diagnosis is dependent on an accurate determination of those specific developmental areas in which a parent may be "rejecting" or "competitive." For example, a mother may satisfy completely her child's needs for oral dependency only to fail seriously, because of her own anxieties, to meet his increasing need for greater self-expression. Similarly significant is the evaluation of whether a "competitive father" is rivalrous with the dependency of his young son or with the masculine strivings of his growing son. Inadequate parental responses to the child at any level may vary from over-indulgence and the excessive permissiveness of prolonged earlier satisfactions to the overly ambitious and premature stimulation of more grown-up behavior in anticipation of a later stage in development. For normal growth the child needs to exact the appropriate satisfactions to be derived from each stage of development in order to proceed to the next. At the same time the mature gratification of the parents in helping the child at each step serves as a foundation for a continuing mutually beneficial relationship. A major aim of the diagnostic process is the understanding of the breakdown or lack of development of this healthy interaction as it gives rise to behavioral disabilities.

The diagnostic study is a dynamic process which offers new relationships and potentially meaningful experiences to the child and his parents as they are helped to face their problems together and to reveal the various biological, psychological and social factors involved. It is based on a sound knowledge of both normal and pathological development and function and on an awareness of the continuous interaction of all the psychobiological and psychosocial forces. This understanding demands a multi-faceted approach; no unilateral study can effectively reveal the cross currents and significant forces in a total family situation. Sufficient historical data about physical, psychological and social factors; an adequate evaluation of the child's current levels of physical and psychological functionings; and valid appraisals of his native physical equipment and intellectual endowment are all necessary. Therefore, the psychiatric clinics for children are staffed and structured on the basic assumption that the diagnostic process is a collaborative process utilizing the specialized methods of several professional disciplines

to investigate the various diagnostic areas. In addition, the psychiatric clinics and other child diagnostic facilities take into account that a special sensitivity to the meaning of the different diagnostic areas is essential in planning comprehensive studies and in insuring their final integration. The diagnostic process for children is therefore developed through the leadership and direction of the child psychiatrist whose specialized training provides the skill and experience for carrying the ultimate responsibility of synthesizing the various diagnostic data into a comprehensive diagnosis of the child in his environment.

EZRA F. VOGEL AND NORMAN W. BELL

The Emotionally Disturbed Child as the Family Scapegoat*

The phenomenon of scapegoating is as old as human society. Sir James Frazer records, in *The Golden Bough*,[1] numerous instances, reaching back to antiquity, of public scapegoats, human and other. He views the process of scapegoating as one in which ". . . the evil influences are embodied in a visible form or are at least supposed to be loaded upon a material medium, which acts as a vehicle to draw them off from the people, village, or town."[2] The scapegoat's function ". . . is simply to effect a total clearance of all the ills that have been infesting a people."[3] Frazer was dealing with the phenomenon at the level of a society, tribe, village, or town. It

is the purpose of this paper to examine the same phenomenon within families, by viewing an emotionally disturbed child as an embodiment of certain types of conflicts between parents. This pattern is a special case of a common phenomenon, the achievement of group unity through the scapegoating of a particular member. It is, perhaps, more widely known that a group may achieve unity through projection of hostilities to the outside,[4] but there are also a large number of cases where members of a particular group are able to achieve unity through scapegoating a particular member of that group. Thus, the deviant within the group may per-

* Reprinted with permission of The Macmillan Co. from *A Modern Introduction to the Family*, by Norman W. Bell and Ezra F. Vogel, pp. 382–397, 667–668. Copyright © 1960, The Free Press, a Corporation. The material was specially prepared for that volume on the basis of work done by the authors in connection with a broader research project, "Cultural Values, Family Roles, and the Mental Health or Illness of the Individual." The research was directed by Drs. John P. Spiegel and Florence R. Kluckhohn and supported by the National Institute of Mental Health and the Pauline and Louis G. Cowan Foundation.

[1] Sir James Frazer, *The Golden Bough* (abridged ed.; New York: Macmillan, 1927).

[2] *Ibid.*, p. 562.

[3] *Ibid.*, p. 575.

[4] In addition to Frazer, *op. cit.*, see also Emile Durkheim, "Deux lois de l'évolution pénale," *L'Année Sociologique*, IV (1899), 55–95; Henri Hubert and Marcel Mauss, "Essai sur la nature et la fonction du sacrifice," *L'Année Sociologique*, II (1897), 29–138; William Robertson Smith, *The Religion of the Semites* (London: A. and C. Black, Ltd., 1927); Roger Money-Kyrle, *The Meaning of Sacrifice* (London: Hogarth Press, 1930); George Herbert Mead, "The Psychology of Punitive Justice," *American Journal of Sociology*, XXIII (1918), 577–620; Ruth S. Eissler, "Scapegoats of Society," in Kurt R. Eissler (ed.), *Searchlights on Delinquency* (New York: International Universities Press, 1949), 288–305; and Clyde Kluckhohn, "Navaho Witchcraft," *Papers of the Peabody Museum of American Archaeology and Ethnology*, Harvard University, Vol. XXII (1944).

form a valuable function for the group, by channeling group tensions and providing a basis for solidarity.

The notion that the family is in large part responsible for the emotional health of the child is a compelling one in contemporary behavioral science. By and large, however, the research has focused largely on the mother-child relationship, and the independent variable by which the mother-child relationship and the child-rearing practices are usually explained is the personality and developmental history of the mother. Recently, an attempt has also been made to treat the father-child relationship, again largely in terms of the personality and developmental history of the father. While in clinical practice there is some awareness of family dynamics, in the literature, the family has largely been treated simply as a collection of personalities, and the child's personality development has been seen almost exclusively as a direct result of the separate personalities of his parents.[5] Rarely is the interaction of parents treated as a significant independent variable influencing childhood development. Even when broader cultural patterns have been considered, childhood development has been related to child-rearing practices and socialization into the culture, with little consideration of the family as the mediating unit.

Data for this paper are derived from the intensive study[6] of a small group of "disturbed" families, each with an emotionally disturbed child, and a matched group of "well" families without clinically manifest disturbance in any child. Of the nine families in each group, three were Irish-American, three Italian-American, and three old-American. The families were seen by a team including psychiatrists, social workers, psychologists, and social scientists. The disturbed families, on which this paper is based, were seen weekly in the offices of a psychiatric clinic and in their homes over periods ranging from one to four years. Detailed information was gathered about the members' developmental histories and character structure, but even more specific data were obtained about current processes.

The present paper is concerned with how a child in the family, the emotionally disturbed child, was used as a scapegoat for the conflicts between parents and what the functions and dysfunctions of this scapegoating are for the family.

In all the disturbed families it was found that a particular child had become involved in tensions existing between the parents.[7] In the "well" families used for control purposes, either the tensions between the parents were not so severe or else the tensions were handled in such a way that the children did not become pathologically involved. In general, both parents of the emotionally disturbed child had many of the same underlying conflicts, but in relationship to each other, they felt themselves to be at opposite poles, so that one spouse would act out one side of the conflict and the other would act out the other side of the conflict. They had developed an equilibrium in which they minimized contact with each other and minimized expressions of affect, particularly hostility, which they strongly felt for each other, and this made it possible for them to live with each other.[8] But this equilibrium had many difficulties, the most serious of which was the scapegoating of a child.

1. SOURCES OF TENSION THAT LEAD TO SCAPEGOATING

It is our contention that scapegoating is produced by the existence of tensions between parents which have not been satisfactorily resolved in other ways. The spouses in the disturbed families had deep fears about their marital relationship and about the partner's behavior. They did not feel they could predict accurately how the other would respond to their own behavior. Yet, the other's response was of very great importance and was thought to be potentially very damaging. The partners did not feel they

[5] This is not to deny relevance of psychological aspects. The same facts can be related to a number of different theoretical systems, but here focus is on the group dynamics.

[6] For other reports of this research, see John P. Spiegel, "The Resolution of Role Conflict Within the Family," *Psychiatry*, XX (1957), 1–16; Florence Rockwood Kluckhohn, "Family Diagnosis: Variations in the Basic Values of Family Systems," *Social Casework*, XXXIX (1958), 1–11; and John P. Spiegel, "Some Cultural Aspects of Transference and Countertransference," in Jules H. Massermann (ed.), *Individual and Family Dynamics* (New York: Grune and Stratton, Inc., 1959). A more inclusive statement of the conceptual framework will be published in the near future as, John P. Spiegel, "The Structure and Function of Social Roles in the Doctor-Patient Relationship." Lectures delivered at Tulane University, 1958.

[7] It should be noted that only families which had never been separated or divorced were included in the present sample. Of course, there are also cases of emotionally disturbed children where only one parent is living with other relatives. Hence, tensions between parents cannot be the universal cause of emotional disturbance. A more general hypothesis would be that the emotionally disturbed child is always the focus of primary-group tension.

[8] This is spelled out in more detail in Ezra F. Vogel, "The Marital Relationship of Parents and the Emotionally Disturbed Child" (Unpublished Ph.D. thesis, Harvard University, 1958).

could deal with the situation by direct communication, because this might be too dangerous, and they resorted to manipulations of masking, evading, and the like. This atmosphere of tension has several sources. One of the sources was the personality problems of each spouse, but in the present analysis the focus will be on the group sources of the tension. These tensions usually have several sources. At a very general level, one of the main sources of tension was conflict in cultural value orientations.[9] Value orientations are abstract, general conceptions of the nature of human nature and man's relationship to it, of man's relation to man, of the most significant time dimension, and of the most valued type of activity. All societies have preferences and alternative preferences to these basic dimensions; these preferences are expressed within a wide range of phenomena. In complex ways, they are related to personality and social structure and to more specific values. When people are in the process of acculturation, as was the case with the families of Irish and Italian backgrounds, many possibilities for value-orientation conflict arise. Any one individual may have been socialized into conflicting or confused patterns, and be unsuccessful in bridging the gap. Marriage partners may have been socialized into different patterns and be working on different assumptions. All our disturbed families had problems of these sorts. Some were trying to shift quickly to a set of orientations they had not thoroughly internalized, and without having neutralized previous orientations. Others were trying to live by conflicting orientations.[10]

A common example of the cultural value conflicts was the conflict centered around the problems of individual performance. There were considerable pulls toward the American middle-class achievement patterns. In families which had partially internalized both sets of value orientations, it was impossible to live up to both sets of values, and whichever the family chose, this meant that certain conflicts would result.

Another source of tension was the relations of the family and the larger community. Disturbed families usually had problems in this area, rejecting and/or being rejected by the community. In some cases, a family had very severe disapproval of a very close-knit ethnic neighborhood directed at them. In other cases, families had moved from ethnic neighborhoods to more fashionable suburbs and suffered in their own eyes by comparison to their new neighbors. Consequently, their social relationships with these neighbors were often minimal; when they did exist, they were usually strained or else one spouse had fairly good relationships with some friends and the partner had poor relationships with these friends. All families, to a greater or lesser extent, had problems in their relationships with families of orientation. Typically, the wife was strongly attached to her parents and antagonistic towards her husband's family, while the husband was attached to his parents and antagonistic to his wife's family. If either spouse was critical of his in-laws, the partner typically defended his own parents and became more critical of his in-laws. If one spouse was critical of his own parents, the partner was often friendly to them. The unbalanced attachments to parents and parents-in-law was not resolved. Changes usually produced more tension, but the basic sources of strain remained unchanged.[11]

2. THE SELECTION OF THE SCAPEGOAT

The tensions produced by unresolved conflicts were so severe that they could not be contained without some discharge. It is not surprising that some appropriate object was chosen to symbolize the conflicts and draw off the tension. Conceivably, some person or group outside the family could serve in this capacity. However, in these disturbed families, the parents had by and large internalized the standards of the surrounding community sufficiently so that they had great difficulty in finding a legitimate basis for scapegoating outsiders. In addition, most of these families had very tenuous ties with the community, and since they were very concerned about being accepted, they could not afford to antagonize their associates. While some of the families did, at times, have strong feelings of antagonism toward various members of the community in which they lived, they could rarely express this antagonism directly. Even if at times they were able to manifest their antagonism, this usually led to many additional complications, and the family preferred to scapegoat its own child.[12]

[9] See Florence R. Kluckhohn, *loc. cit.*; and F. Kluckhohn, Fred L. Strodtbeck and others, *Variations in Value Orientations* (Evanston, Ill.: Row, Peterson & Co., forthcoming).

[10] Well families, by contrast, had bridged the gap between the orientations of different ethnic or class groups. They had succeeded in neutralizing old orientations before taking on new ones. Usually such families were changing in a slower and more orderly fashion.

[11] Discussed at length in Norman W. Bell, "The Impact of Psychotherapy Upon Family Relationships" (Unpublished Ph.D. thesis, Harvard University, 1959).

[12] The one family which did occasionally express antagonism directly to outsiders was the most disturbed family

Channeling the tensions within the family did not lead to difficulties with the outside, but usually the latent hostilities between the husband and wife made it very difficult to deal with problems openly between them. There was always danger the partner might become too angry, which would lead to severe and immediate difficulties. A number of factors made a child the most appropriate object through which to deal with family tensions. First of all, the child was in a relatively powerless position compared to the parents. While he was dependent on the parents and could not leave the family, he was not able effectively to counter the parents' superior power. Although the parents' defenses were fairly brittle in comparison with those of well parents, still their defenses were much stronger than those of their children. Because the child's personality is still very flexible, he can be molded to adopt the particular role which the family assigns to him. When the child does take on many of the characteristics which the parents dislike in themselves and each other, he becomes a symbolically appropriate object on which to focus their own anxieties. Since the person scapegoated often develops such severe tensions that he is unable to perform his usual task roles, it is important that those family members performing essential, irreplaceable functions for the family not be scapegoated. The child has relatively few tasks to perform in the family, compared to the parents or other elders, and his disturbance does not ordinarily interfere with the successful performance of the necessary family tasks. The "cost" in dysfunction of the child is low relative to the functional gains for the whole family.

In all cases, with partial exception of one family, a particular child was chosen as the scapegoat, while other children were relatively free of pathology. The selecting of a particular child is not a random matter; one child is the best symbol. Just as a dream condenses a variety of past and present experiences and a variety of emotional feelings, the scapegoat condenses a variety of social and psychological problems impinging on the family.

_____

in the sample. The expression of hostility to neighbors was filled with such conflicts and added complications that it inevitably proved inadequate and the family returned to the scapegoating of their child.

While many members of these families did express prejudice towards minority groups, this prejudice did little to drain the severe tensions within the family. Perhaps the minority group was not symbolically appropriate for the handling of any of the family conflicts, or perhaps they were not sufficiently available to serve as a continual focus of family tensions.

Who is selected as the scapegoat is intimately related to the sources of tension. Where value-orientation conflicts existed, the child chosen was the one who best symbolized these conflicts. For example, if the conflicts revolved about achievement, a child who failed to achieve according to expectations could become the symbol of failure. Alternatively, a child might be an appropriate object because he was achieveing independently and thus violating norms of loyalty to the group.

The position of the child in the sibling group frequently became a focus for the unresolved childhood problems of the parents. If the parents' most serious unresolved problems were with male figures, the child chosen to represent the family conflict was usually a male child. Similarly, sibling order could be a strong factor. If one or both parents had difficulties with older brothers, an older boy in the family might become the scapegoat.

In two cases, the sex or sibling position of the child seemed to be particularly important in the selection of a particular child as the family scapegoat. In one of these cases, the mother was the oldest of three siblings and had considerable feelings of rivalry with her next younger sister which had never been effectively resolved. Although the father had two older siblings, they were so much older that to him they were a separate family. In his effective family environment, he was the older of two children and had considerable feelings of rivalry toward a younger brother who displaced him and for whom he subsequently had to care. This couple has three children, and there was an unusual amount of rivalry between the oldest and the second sibling. Both the parents sided very strongly with the oldest child. They were continuously conscious of the middle child bothering the older, for which they severely criticized this middle child. There are many striking parallels, even to small details, in the relationship between the parents and their next younger siblings and the relationship between their oldest child and the next younger sibling.

Another pattern revolved about the identification of a child with a parent whom he resembled. This was found in all families, sick and well, in one form or another; but in the disturbed families, the child was seen as possessing very undesirable traits, and although the parent actually possessed the same traits, the focus of attention was the child and not the parent. In one family, in particular, this pattern was striking. The father and the eldest son had very similar physical characteristics; not only did they have the same first name but both were called by the same diminutive name by the mother. At times, the social worker seeing the mother was not certain whether the mother was talking about her husband or her son. The wife's concerns about the husband's occupational adequacy were not dealt with directly, but the focus for her affect was the child and his school performance. In fact, the son was criticized by his mother for all the characteristics which she disliked in her husband, but she was unable to criticize her husband directly for these characteristics. She channeled all her feelings, especially anxiety and hostility, to the child, although her husband had similar problems. Furthermore, in order to control her feelings toward her husband, she remained very aloof and distant and was not able to express to him her positive or negative feelings. While she channeled many criticisms and anxieties through the child, she also expressed many of her positive feelings to the child, thereby leading to severe Oedipal conflicts. The husband was not happy about his wife being so aloof from him, but on the other hand he found that by co-operating with his wife in criticizing the child, he was able to keep the burden of problems away from himself. He thus joined with the wife in projecting his own difficulties and problems onto the child and in dealing with them as the child's problems rather than as his own.

In three of the families, the scapegoat had considerably lower intelligence than did the other children in the family. In all these families, there were serious conflicts about the value of achievement, and the parents had great difficulty themselves in living up to their own achievement aspirations. In all these three cases, the parents were unable to accept the fact that their children had limited abilities, and they continually held up impossible standards for these children. Although all three children had I.Q.'s in the 80's or below and had failed one grade or more, all three mothers stated that they intended that their children should go to college. At the beginning of therapy, one of the mothers hoped her son would attend medical school and become a doctor; another had begun to put away a small amount of money from a very tight budget for her daughter's college education, even though the daughter's intelligence was that of a moron. At the beginning of therapy, none of the parents was able to deal directly with his own difficulties in achievement. In contrast, in one of the families, there were two children in the family who had very low intelligence, one of whom had failed a grade in school, but the family scapegoat was a boy who had normal intelligence. In this case, the

parents, who had average intelligence, had resolved their conflicts about achievement by denying that they were interested in achievement and accepting their social position. This child of slightly higher intelligence and greater physical activity was seen by them as a very aggressive child who was always doing too much, and the parents were continually worried that he was "too smart."[13]

In a number of cases, the disturbed child either had a serious physical disease when he was young or a striking physical abnormality such as a hare lip, bald spots in the hair, or unusually unattractive facial features. The mere existence of some such abnormality seemed to draw attention to one particular child, so that if there were some sorts of anxieties or problems in the family at all, the child with the physical peculiarities seemed to become the focus of the family problems. Here again, however, it was not the mere existence of a physical defect but its meaning[14] in the life of the family which gave it its significance. For example, in some families there was a feeling that they had committed certain sins by not living up to their ideals, for instance by using contraceptives. This was a very common problem, since many families could not possibly live up to the two opposing sets of ideals which they had at least partially internalized. The child's physical abnormality became a symbol of the family's sin for not having lived up to some partially-internalized values, and the malformed child was seen as a sinful child who was not living up to the standards of the group. Since the family's relationship with the community was often tenuous, the fact that one of their children had physical abnormalities that made the child the focus of neighborhood ridicule, served to make the parents increasingly ashamed of the child's physical characteristics and to focus increasingly more attention on this child. For example, one of the main concerns of the family with the unusually ugly child was that other children were continually teasing her about

---

[13] While in virtually all these families, there were considerable problems about achievement, another family seen by one of the authors as part of another investigation was very closely tied to the traditional ethnic patterns and had not yet seriously begun to incorporate American achievement values. In this family, there was one child, seriously substandard in intelligence, with very ugly physical features, who had epileptic seizures. There were also some children who were above average in intelligence. This family had no serious conflicts about achievement, and none of the children were scapegoated.

[14] Alfred Adler, *Understanding Human Nature* (New York: Greenberg, 1927), and Alfred Adler, "The Cause

her appearance. However, the concern was less for the child herself, and more for the whole family. Her problems symbolized the parents' past and present problems with the neighborhood; rather than sympathize with the child, they abused her all the more. In another case in which a female child's physical illness became a focus of the family's problems, the parents were extremely concerned about her safety, which was again related in part to the potential dangers in social relationships with the outside world. As a result of the girl's illness, the family became much more cautious than was necessary, and on some occasions they were even reluctant to accept medical advice that she could participate in certain activities without danger to her health. The continual contacts that the child had with middle-class professional personnel through hospitalization and clinic visits led her to accept certain middle-class American values more than did the rest of the family, and the family was continually expressing the feeling that she had different attitudes after hospitalization and contact with hospital personnel. The disliked attitudes ascribed to the child were in general those of middle-class American culture.[15] Not only abnormalities but general body type could become the symbol to call forth scapegoating. In two families, the spouses had many problems in their sexual life. Rather than face these maladjustments directly, the problems were expressed through concern about the masculinity and normality of a slender, graceful son.

While the general process of symbolization of a scapegoat is very similar to the dream symbolization, there is one problem in the family selection of a scapegoat which is not met in the selection of a dream symbol, and that is the problem of availability. While in dreams, any symbolic representation is open to the dreamer, in the family only a very small number of children are available as the potential scapegoats. Hence, when there is a serious family problem and no child is an appropriate symbol of the problem, there must be considerable cognitive distortion in order to permit the most appropriate one available to be used as a scapegoat. For example, in one family which was very concerned about the problems of achievement, the focus of the family's problems was the eldest son. Although he was receiving passing grades in school, whereas the

parents had had very poor school records, the parents were very critical of his school performance. Because of this pressure, the child worked hard and was able to get somewhat better marks on his next report card. However, the mother stoutly maintained that her son didn't deserve those grades, that he must have cheated, and she continued to criticize him for his school performance.

The other aspect of the problem of availability resulted from the fact that the parents apparently have had tensions since early in marriage. As nearly as it was possible to reconstruct the marital history, it appeared that the spouses had selected each other partly on the basis of the fact that they shared many of the same conflicts and understood each other quite well. Not long after marriage, however, they seemed to have become polarized in their conflicts, so that one parent represented one side of the conflict and the other represented the other side. This seems to have given each of the spouses a way of handling his own conflicts and allowed each to remain fairly consistent and well integrated by projecting difficulties onto the partner. However, it also led to very severe difficulties in the marital relationship and created many tensions which were quickly displaced onto the first available and appropriate object, very often the first child. Since the eldest child was the first one available for scapegoating, he often seems to have been assigned this role and, once assigned, has continued in it. Perhaps because of his prior availability and his closer involvement in the adult world, he is a more appropriate object for the scapegoating.[16] In the one case in which a child was able to escape the scapegoat role by decreasing his attachment to the home, the

---

and Prevention of Neurosis," *Journal of Abnormal and Social Psychology,* XXIII (1928), 4–11.

[15] In the well families, there were cases of comparable physical illness which did not result in the same type of anxieties in the family.

[16] No adequate large-scale studies are available to provide an estimate of the proportion of emotional disturbances found in the eldest child. Many small-scale studies have been made, but they are inconsistent and contradictory. See John P. Spiegel and Norman W. Bell. "The Family of the Psychiatric Patient," in Silvano Arieti (ed.), *American Handbook of Psychiatry* (New York: Basic Books, Inc., 1959). In the present study, slightly more than half were eldest children, a finding similar to that in another small sample of emotionally disturbed children: Sydney Croog, "The Social Backgrounds of Emotionally Disturbed Children and their Siblings" (Unpublished Ph.D. thesis, Yale University, 1954). It has also been noted that eldest sons are more likely to be involved in problems of inheritance and rivalry, and are more likely to be adult-oriented. See such diverse studies as George Peter Murdock, *Social Structure* (New York: Macmillan, 1949); Sigmund Freud, *Moses and Monotheism* (New York: Alfred A. Knopf, 1939); and Charles McArthur, "Personalities of First and Second Children," *Psychiatry,* XIX (1956), 47–54.

next most appropriate child was used in the scape-goat role.

3. INDUCTION OF THE CHILD INTO THE SCAPEGOAT ROLE

If the child is to be a "satisfactory" scapegoat, he must carry out his role as a "problem child." The problem behavior must be reinforced strongly enough so that it will continue in spite of the hostility and anxiety it produces in the child. This delicate balance is possible only because the parents have superior sanction power over the child, can define what he should or should not do, and control what he does or does not do. This balance necessarily requires a large amount of inconsistency in the ways parents handle the child.

The most common inconsistency was between the implicit (or unconscious) and the explicit role induction.[17] In all cases, certain behavior of the child violated recognized social norms. In some instances stealing, fire-setting, expressions of hostility, or unco-operativeness affected the child's relationships with people outside the family. In other instances, bed-wetting, resistance to parental orders, or expression of aggression to siblings affected relationships in the family. But in all instances, while the parents explicitly criticized the child and at times even punished him, they supported in some way, usually implicitly, the persistence of the very behavior which they criticized. This permission took various forms: failure to follow through on threats, delayed punishment, indifference to and acceptance of the symptom, unusual interest in the child's symptom, or considerable secondary gratification offered to the child because of his symptom. The secondary gratification usually took the form of special attention and exemption from certain responsibilities. While the parents had internalized social norms sufficiently to refrain from violating the norms themselves, they had not sufficiently internalized them to prevent giving encouragement to their children for acting out their own repressed wishes. The

wish to violate these norms was transferred to the child, but the defenses against this wish were never as strong in the child.[18]

Another type of inconsistency seen was that one parent would encourage one type of behavior, but the other parent would encourage an opposing type of behavior. The result again was that the child was caught in the conflict. This also permitted one spouse to express annoyance to the other indirectly without endangering the marital relationship. For example, in one case, the father objected to the son's leaving toys lying around and would violently explode at the child for such behavior, implying that the mother was wrong in permitting him to do this. The mother realized that the father exploded at such behavior and did not stop the father since she "knew he was right." Nevertheless, she often indicated that the child need not bother picking up the toys, since she felt that he was too young to have to do such things by himself and that the father was too strict. If the mother's encouragement of the behavior annoying to the father was explicit, there would be danger that the father's hostility would be directed at the mother rather than the child. By keeping the encouragement implicit the mother was able to deny that she had encouraged the child. The father was usually willing to accept this denial, even if he did not believe it, rather than risk an explosion with his wife. In some instances, however, the other spouse was angered or felt compelled to criticize the other for not handling the child properly. Then the encouragement of the child to behave in a certain way would have to become more subtle to avoid criticism of the other spouse, another delicate balance to maintain. A parent had to give sufficient encouragement to the child to perform the act, without making it so obvious that his spouse felt obliged to criticize him.

In addition to the inconsistent pressures resulting from the difference between explicit and implicit expectations and from the differences between the expectations of the two parents, the child also had to deal with changes in each parent's expectations. From the parent's conscious point of view, this inconsistency resulted from an attempt to reconcile two conflicting desires: teaching the child to behave

[17] The way the parent gives the child implicit approval to act out his own unconscious wishes has already been well described for the relationship between a single parent and a single child. Adelaide M. Johnson, "Sanctions for Superego Lacunae of Adolescents," in Kurt R. Eissler (ed.), *Searchlights on Delinquency* (New York: International Universities Press, 1949); Melitta Sperling, "The Neurotic Child and his Mother: A Psychoanalytic Study," *American Journal of Orthopsychiatry*, XXI (1951), 351–64. For a more detailed account of family role-induction methods, see Spiegel, "The Resolution of Role Conflict within the Family" (Reprinted in this volume).

[18] Here again, the analogy to the individual personality system is instructive. Just as Freud's hysteric patients expressed a *belle indifference* to their symptoms and a surprising reluctance to change them, so did these parents have a *belle indifference* to the symptoms of their children. Just as the individual's symptom represents an expression of his own unconscious wish, so does the child's symptom represent an expression of his parents' unconscious wishes.

properly and not being "too hard on the child." When a parent was consciously attempting to teach the child proper behavior, he was extremely aggressive and critical.[19] At other times, the parent felt he had been too critical of the child and permitted him to behave in the same way without punishment, and would be extremely affectionate and supportive. While the explanation given for this inconsistency was that he wanted to teach the desired behavior without being "too hard on the child," its latent function was to prevent the child from consistently living up to the ostensibly desired behavior and to preserve the disliked behavior. The period of not being "too hard on the child" served to reinforce the disapproved behavior and the period of "being firm" permitted the parents to express their anxieties and hostility. This balance was also very delicate since it was always possible that negative sanctions would become so severe that the child would refuse to behave in such a way that parents felt he could legitimately be punished.

The delicacy of this balance was perhaps best exemplified by the problem of bed-wetting. Parents complained about bed-wetting, but at the same time they could not bring themselves to do anything to alter the child's behavior. If the therapists could get both parents to be firm at the same time, the child would usually stop bed-wetting. Very soon, however, by putting a rubber sheet on the bed, or buying special night clothes "just in case he wets," the child was encouraged again to wet. One mother succeeded several times in finding methods to stop her son's wetting, but immediately stopped using them "since he's stopped now." In several cases, the parents would alternate in being concerned and trying to be firm and being unconcerned and implicitly encouraging the behavior, at all times remaining inconsistent, one with the other. It seemed clear that whether or not the child wet his bed was a relatively sensitive index of just where the balance of rewards from the parents lay. In general, however, the implicit demands carried the greater sanction power and the child continued with the behavior of which the parents unconsciously approved

[19] While the control imposed by parents in well families sometimes appeared to be extremely aggressive and punitive, this aggression was not such a massive critical attack on the child and did not carry the threat of such severe sanctions as did the aggression by the disturbed parents. In the well families, the punishment of the child was not regarded by the child as so damaging, and there was ordinarily the possibility of escaping further punishment by behaving in a different, desired way. There were few possibilities for the child to escape this hostility in the disturbed family.

and consciously disapproved. Presumably, the sanctions of the parents against bed-wetting would increase as the child grew older, and the balance would become delicate only at that later time.

Since these conflicting expectations existed over a long period of time, it is not surprising that the child internalized these conflicts. Once a child was selected as a deviant, there was a circular reaction which tended to perpetuate this role assignment. Once he had responded to his parents' implicit wishes and acted in a somewhat disturbed manner, the parents could treat him as if he really were a problem. The child would respond to these expectations and the vicious cycle was set in motion. Both the child and the parents, then, had complementary expectations. The particular role assigned to the child was appropriately rewarded. It is difficult, if not impossible, to distinguish just at what point the parents began treating the child as if he were a problem and at what point the child actually did have internalized problems. There does not seem to be any sudden development of the child's problems; rather, it is a process occurring over a period of time. By the time the family was seen in the clinic, the vicious cycle was well established, and the child had internalized his disturbed role to such an extent that it was difficult to effect change only by removing external pressures. This was, of course, particularly true for older and more disturbed children. The fact that the child becomes disturbed adds stability to the role system, so that once set in motion, scapegoating did not easily pass from one child to another. In the well families, when scapegoating did take place, it was less severe and did not become stabilized with one child as a continual scapegoat.

4. THE RATIONALIZATION OF SCAPEGOATING

When a scapegoating situation was established, a relatively stable equilibrium of the family was achieved. However, there were difficulties in maintaining the equilibrium. Parents had considerable guilt about the way they treated the child, and when the child was identified as disturbed by neighbors, teachers, doctors, or other outside agencies, pressure was brought to bear for some action to be taken. When called upon to explain, parents did not have much difficulty in explaining why they were so concerned about the child, but they did have great difficulty in rationalizing their aggressive and libidinal expressions to the children.

One way in which the parents rationalized their behavior was to define themselves, rather than the children, as victims. They stressed how much difficulty there was coping with all the problems posed by their child. For example, mothers of bed-wetters complained about the problems of keeping sheets clean and the impossibility of the child staying overnight at friends' or relatives' homes. Such rationalizations seemed to relieve some of the guilt for victimizing the children and served as a justification for continued expressions of annoyance toward the children.

Another way was to emphasize how fortunate their children really were. For most of these parents, the standard of living provided for their children was much higher than the standard of living they enjoyed when they were children. One of the central complaints of these parents, particularly the fathers, was that the children wanted too much and got much more than the parents ever got when they were children. This was seen by the parents as a legitimate excuse for depriving their children of the toys, privileges, and other things they wanted, and for refusing to recognize the children's complaints that they were not getting things. A closely related type of rationalization stems from the change of child-rearing practices over the past generation. The parents felt that their parents were much stricter than they were with their children and that children nowadays "get away with murder." Many of the parents had acute conflicts about how strict to be with children, and when the parents did express aggression to the children, they ofen defined it as beneficial strictness and "giving the child a lesson." Since their own parents were much more severe with them, their own children don't realize "how good they have it."

The parents also used various specific norms to justify their behavior. Even though the parents may be giving implicit encouragement to break these norms, the fact that these social norms are explicitly recognized gives the parents a legitimate basis for punishing the children. As long as the permission for disobeying the sanctions is implicit, it is always possible for the parents to deny that they are really giving it. In general, these parents were reluctant to admit that their child had an emotional disturbance or that he was behaving the way he was because of certain inner problems. They generally interpreted the disturbed child's behavior as willful badness. They felt that the child could behave differently if he really wanted to. Hence, what was needed, in their view, was not consideration, advice, and help, but a "lesson" in how to behave, i.e., severe reprimands and punishment; but even this they could not give. At times, the parents attempted

to deny completely that they were scapegoating this particular child. They insisted very rigidly that "we treat all the children just the same." At other times, the parents insisted that this one particular child was just different from all others, implying that this child deserved punishment and that they were good parents since their other children have turned out so well.

Frequently, the mothers expressed, although inconsistently, unusually strong affection for a son. They justified this almost invariably in the same way: the child had problems and difficulties and thus needed more help and care than the other children. However, what they considered care and protection far exceeded the usual limits. This can be seen for example in the mother who carried her twelve-year-old son from the bed to the bathroom so that he could avoid bed-wetting, in the mother who continually fondled her adolescent son and called him "lovie," and in the frequent slips of the tongues by a variety of family members which identified the mother and son as spouses. Fathers, on the other hand, often had special attachments to, and fondness for, daughters.

All these attempts of the parents to rationalize their behavior had a very defensive quality and showed the difficulty these parents had in reconciling their own behavior with general social norms about child-rearing. In the more severe disturbed families, the pressing nature of their problems required serious distortion of social norms, but in the mildly disturbed families, more attention was given to the social norms, and attempts were made to express emotions in more acceptable ways. In any event, much energy was required to keep the balance stable, a state which required co-ordination of many subtle and inconsistent feelings and behaviors. It was, in effect, an "armed truce," and the danger of an explosion was constantly present.

5. FUNCTIONS AND DYSFUNCTIONS OF SCAPEGOATING

a) Functions — Although the present paper has been concerned with the dynamics of the family as a group in relation to an emotionally disturbed child, some comments should be made on the functions that scapegoating serves for the parents individually and for external social systems. For the parents, scapegoating served as a personality-stabilizing process. While the parents of these children did have serious internal conflicts, the projection of these difficulties onto the children served to minimize and control them. Thus, in spite of their personality difficulties, the parents were able to live up to their commitments to the wider society, expressing a minimum of their difficulties in the external economic and political systems. Most of the parents were able to maintain positions as steady workers and relatively respectable community members.

While the scapegoating of the child helped the parents live up to their obligations to the community, often they did not live up to their obligations as adequately as other families, and the whole family became a scapegoat for the community. Then the same mechanisms existed between the outer community and the family as between parents and child. The families, like their children, seldom fought back effectively; instead they channeled their additional frustrations and tensions through the child. Once established, many forces may play into the scapegoating situation. Though the child suffered additional burdens through the medium of the family, he helped drain off the tension of the broader community in relation to a particular family.

From the point of view of the family, the primary function of scapegoating is that it permits the family to maintain its solidarity. In all the disturbed families, there were very severe strains which continually threatened to disrupt the family.[20] In all the disturbed families, very serious dissatisfactions between spouses came to light during the course of therapy, which were much more severe than those found in the well families. In the two families with the most severely disturbed children, when the scapegoating of the child eased up during therapy, the explosions between parents became so severe that there was serious fear that the family might break up. In the one case in which the problems between spouses remained relatively latent throughout therapy, marital problems emerged more clearly after the termination of therapy, and this led to serious anxiety attacks of the father. Yet, considering these internal strains, all of these families have shown surprising stability. Only in one family had there been a brief period of voluntary separation between the parents, and it had occurred before their first child was born. By focusing on one particular child, the families were able to encapsulate problems and anxieties which could potentially disrupt various family processes. There seemed to be an added solidarity between the parents who stood united against the problem child. The fact that it is a child who is disturbed permits the parents to continue to perform the tasks necessary for household maintenance with relative sta-

[20] In one well family, when there was considerable marital tension it was handled in a very overt fashion, and marital problems were not dealt with through the child.

bility. Since the child is in a dependent position and contributes relatively little to family task activities, his malfunctioning does not seriously interfere with family stability.

b) Dysfunctions — While the scapegoating of a child is effective in controlling major sources of tensions within the family, when a child becomes emotionally disturbed, this leads to disturbing secondary complications which are, however, generally less severe than the original tensions. One dysfunction is that certain realistic problems and extra tasks are created for the family. The child does require special care and attention. If, for example, the child is a bed-wetter, then the family must either wake him up regularly, or wash many sheets and take other precautions. This becomes particularly acute when traveling, visiting, or attending camp. Often the child cannot be left alone, and someone must continually look after him. If the child is to receive treatment, then the parents must expend time and money in providing this.

In addition, while the child is responsive to the implicit sanctions of his parents, he, too, may develop mechanisms of fighting back and punishing his parents for the way they treat him. Often the child becomes very skilled in arousing his parents' anxieties or in consciously bungling something his parents want him to do. Of course, the mother, being present during most of the day, experiences more of this counteraggression, and this in part accounts for her readiness to bring the child in for treatment. In most of these families it was the mother who took the initiative in seeking treatment. It would appear that as long as she can carefully control the amount of hostility the child expresses to her, she can tolerate this dysfunction, but when hostility rises above a certain point she is willing to seek outside help.

While the functions of the scapegoat within the nuclear family clearly outweigh his dysfunctions, this is typically not the case with the child's relationship outside the nuclear family. While the family gives the child sufficient support to maintain his role in the family, the use of him as a scapegoat is often incompatible with equipping him to maintain an adjustment outside the nuclear family. This problem becomes particularly acute when the child begins important associations outside the nuclear family in relationship with peers and his teachers at school.[21] It is at this time that many referrals to

[21] At adolescence, the time when more demands for independent existence are made, a large number of acute disturbances appear. Many who were adequately adjusted to the roles they were assigned within the family, were

psychiatric clinics are made.[22] While the child's behavior was perfectly tolerable to the parents before, his behavior suddenly becomes intolerable. While he may still be performing the role the family wants him to play in order to be a scapegoat, this comes into conflict with his role as a representative of the family. The family is thus in conflict between using the child as a scapegoat and identifying with the child because of his role as family representative to the outside. Both sides of this conflict are revealed most clearly in the one family which carried on a feud with the outside and alternated between punishing the daughter for her poor school behavior and criticizing the teachers and children in school for causing problems for their daughter. In nearly all of these disturbed families, school difficulty was a crucial factor in the decision to refer the child for psychiatric treatment. While the child's behavior was rewarded at home, it was not rewarded at school, and while the family could tolerate the child's maladaptive behavior at home, when the school took special note of the child's behavior, this proved embarrassing and troubling to the parents.

This problem in relation to the outside world is perhaps most striking in the case of the school, but it is also true, for example, in relationships with neighbors and relatives. Neighbors and relatives are likely to be very critical of the family for the child's disturbed behavior, and it is often at such times that the family makes the greatest effort to get rid of the child's maladaptive behavior. In those families which alternated between punishing and rewarding the child's behavior, difficulty with the outside was often a cue to the family to move into the stage of punishing and criticizing the child's behavior.

While, as a whole, the child's disturbance served to relieve family tensions, it often led to further family tensions. To the extent that outside norms or standards, by which the child does not abide, are considered legitimate, inevitable frustrations arise. While the parents made strenuous efforts to interpret this as a result of the child's behavior and not of their own behavior, this effort was never completely successful. In accordance with modern child rearing theory to which they are at least exposed, they consider themselves at least partly responsible for the disturbance of the child, and this seems to have been particularly true at the time of therapy. Thus, the child's disturbance feeds back into the problems which must be faced by the parents, and the marital pair often project the responsibility for the child's disturbance onto each other. The mother will say, for example, that the father doesn't spend enough time with the children, and the father will say that the mother doesn't manage the children properly. While this was thus dysfunctional to the marital relationship, it never became so prominent that the parents ceased using the child as a scapegoat. The predominant direction of aggression was still toward the badly behaved child rather than toward the other spouse.

While the disturbed behavior leads to some dysfunctions for the family, it is the personality of the child which suffers most as a result of the scapegoating. Any deviant or scapegoat within a group feels strong group pressure which creates considerable conflicts for him.[23] While other groups may also maintain their integration at the expense of the deviant, in the nuclear family this can be stabilized for a long period of time and result in far more serious personality impairment of the child assigned to the deviant role. The development of the emotional disturbance is simply part of the process of internalizing the conflicting demands placed upon him by his parents. While in the short run the child receives more rewards from the family for playing this role than for not playing this role, in the long run this leads to serious personality impairment. In short, the scapegoating mechanism is functional for the family as a group but dysfunctional for the emotional health of the child and for his adjustment outside the family of orientation.

unable to meet the new adjustment outside the family. See, for example, Nicholas J. Demerath, "Adolescent Status and the Individual" (Unpublished Ph.D. thesis, Harvard University, 1942). A large number of acute psychoses also occur as soon as the army recruit leaves home and enters military service. Under ordinary circumstances, the socialization of the child prepares him for the social demands of external society. See, for example, Talcott Parsons, "The Incest Taboo in Relation to Social Structure and the Socialization of the Child," *British Journal of Sociology*, V (1954), 101–17; and David Aberle and Kaspar Naegele, "Middle-Class Fathers' Occupational Roles and Attitudes toward Children," *American Journal of Orthopsychiatry*, XXII (1952), 566–78 (reprinted in this volume).

22 The importance of difficulties with the associations outside the nuclear family in directing the family for psychiatric treatment has long been recognized by clinicians. See, for example, Anna Freud, "Indications for Child Analysis," in *The Psychoanalytic Study of the Child*, Vol. I (New York: International Universities Press, 1945).

23 See, for example, the analysis of the case of Long John's nightmares in William F. Whyte, *Street Corner Society* (Chicago: University of Chicago Press, 1943); and a report of Asch's experiments in Solomon E. Asch, *Social Psychology* (New York: Prentice-Hall, 1952).

RENÉ A. SPITZ

The Psychogenic Diseases in Infancy*
An Attempt at Their Etiologic Classification

I. INTRODUCTION

In the following we will attempt to enumerate the psychogenic manifestations we have been able to observe in the course of the first years of life, which impressed us as deviating from the picture offered by the normal infant. We consider these manifestations as abnormal because, on the one hand, they are to be found only in a relatively small minority of children at that particular age. On the other hand, one and all seem to be the result of a damaging process taking place in the infant. In each of these manifestations we have been able to establish a psychogenic factor, without excluding that in some of them other factors, e.g., congenital ones, may be present. We will attempt to formulate these manifestations as distinct nosological pictures, and then to classify them according to certain principles to be discussed further on.

Any study of psychogenic conditions in infancy will have to begin by making a clear distinction between adult and infant psychiatry. The reason for this lies in the structural and environmental differences involved. The infant does not possess the same personality structure as the adult, while at the same time the infant's environment also is vastly dissimilar from that of the grownup.

To begin with the personality: The adult personality is a structured, well-defined organization which provides certain individual attitudes representing personal initiatives in a circular interaction with the environment. The infant at birth, on the contrary, though he has individuality, has no comparable personality organization, develops no personal initiatives, and his interaction with the environment is a physiological one. The newborn is not conscious: no organization is demonstrable in its psychic apparatus. It is only toward the second half of the first year that a central steering organization, the ego, is gradually developed. During the whole period of which we are speaking, i.e., the first year of life,

this ego remains rudimentary. It would be completely inadequate for self-preservation were it not complemented by an external helper, a substitute ego as it were, to whom the major part of the executive, defensive and perceptive functions are delegated. This delegate, who complements the infant's ego, is its mother or her substitute. We can speak of her as the infant's external ego; like the adult's internal ego the infant's external ego controls the pathways leading to motility during the first year of infancy.

The second variable, the environment, consists in the case of the adult of a multiplicity of factors, inanimate and animate, of numerous individuals and groups. These and other dynamic constellations of varying dignity provide constantly shifting patterns of force which impinge on and interact with the adult's organized personality. Environment for the infant consists, crudely speaking, of one single individual: the mother or her substitute. And even this one individual is not experienced by the infant as a separate object, but is fused with the infant's need and gratification pattern. Consequently, in contrast to the adult, the normally reared infant lives during its first year in what we may call "a closed system." A psychiatric investigation of infancy will, therefore, have to examine the structure of this "closed system." As the system is a simple one and consists only of two components, the mother and the child, it is the relationship within this "dyad" which has to be investigated. We are well aware that in reality the total situation, i.e., the interrelations of roles within the household or the institution in which the child is reared, form his universe; yet this universe is mediated to him by the one who fulfills his needs, i.e., the mother or the nurse. Therefore, the personality of the mother on the one hand, the personality of the child on the other, will have to be brought into relation with each other.

The reason for these differences between adult and infant lies in the fact that the psychic system is not yet differentiated from the somatic system in the infant. What we might call psyche at this stage is so

* Reprinted by permission from *The Psychoanalytic Study of the Child*, Vol. 6, 1951, pp. 255–275.

completely merged with the physical person that I would like to coin for it the term *somato-psyche*. Subsequently the psychic and somatic systems will be progressively delimited from each other. Step by step, in the course of the first six months a psychological steering organization will be segregated from the somato-psyche. This steering organization serves the needs of defense and of mastery. It is characterized by its organization, its structure, and by the quality of consciousness. This organized, structured and conscious steering organization is the nucleus of what we call the ego, a body ego in the beginning. It is thus delimited from the remaining unconscious part of the somato-psyche, which we will designate as the id.

The differentiation of the ego from the id takes place under the pressure of the need for survival. The physical demands on the individual made by the physical environment force it to develop the adaptive mechanism of defense and mastery which form the first ego organization. Hartmann (3) has defined this part of the ego as the conflict-free ego sphere.

This process of differentiation is followed by an integration. I have elaborated upon this alternation of differentiation and integration in the course of psychological development in a paper read at a meeting of the Vienna Society for Psychoanalysis in 1936 (10).

The differentiation of ego and id takes place progressively in the course of the second half of the first year, and is accompanied by the usual transitional hazards which characterize every phase of differentiation. In the course of the second and third year a further development of ego functions will follow. The new ego functions transcend the conflict-free sphere of the ego. A new process of differentiation begins, this time under the pressure of psychological needs, and produces a further set of mastery and defense organizations. The psychological needs in question are in the nature of demands made upon the individual by its human environment and are centered predominantly on the anal level. This psychological need pressure will gather momentum in the years to follow and eventually will lead to the formation of a further organization, that of the super-ego. This process, however, does not concern us in the present paper.

These successive processes of differentiation are the evidence of the progressive segregation of a psychic apparatus out of the somato-psyche. This segregation has to start from the inchoate beginnings of the infant, during which responses are manifested more or less indiscriminately, reminding one of over-flow phenomena; it is difficult to assign the earliest responses to either the somatic or the psychological field, as they occur mostly in such a manner as to express the characteristics of both psyche and soma. Much of what we discuss in our present article will be of this nature, for it takes place during the first year, in the course of which the boundaries between these two systems are being established progressively. It is hardly necessary to stress that we do not believe that a rigid separation between soma and psyche can ever be postulated in the course of human life; but the functions assigned to the two systems are differentiated more and more clearly in the course of development.

II. ETIOLOGICAL FACTORS AND THEIR CLASSIFICATION

We have stressed in our introductory remarks that the number of factors operative during the first year of life is limited. This has facilitated our work so that the modest amount of information we have gathered in the course of our research already enables us to make a preliminary attempt at an etiological classification of psychogenic diseases in infancy. We will eliminate the consideration of congenital disease which does not belong in our province. Like the question of congenital disease, we also will eliminate from our considerations the possible consequences of physical infirmity. With this eliminated the factors which can operate in producing a psychological influence in infancy are more or less reduced to the sole mother-child relation. Our first proposition then will be that if the mother-child relation is normal, there should not be any disturbance in the infant's psychological development, barring physical interference in the nature of lack of food, sickness, etc. As for a satisfactory mother-child relation, we will define it as being satisfactory both to mother and child.

Limiting the action of psychological influences in infancy to the mother-child relationship contains implicitly our second proposition that harmful psychological influences are the result of unsatisfactory mother-child relations. Such harmful influences fall into two possible classes:

(1) The wrong kind of mother-child relations.
(2) An insufficient amount of mother-child relations.

(1) The wrong kind of mother-child relation can develop in various ways. We have found a number of specific psychogenic conditions which can be re-

lated to specific inappropriate forms of mother-child relations. In such cases the mother's personality acts as a disease-provoking agent, a psychological toxin, as it were. We will, therefore, call this first group the *psychotoxic diseases of infancy.*

Inappropriate maternal attitudes found in psychotoxic diseases of infancy can be classified and divided into six subgroups:

1. Overt primal rejection.
2. Primary anxious overpermissiveness.
3. Hostility in the garb of anxiety.
4. Rapid oscillation between pampering and aggressive hostility.
5. Cyclical alternation of long duration in the mother's mood.
6. Hostility, consciously compensated.

The sequence in which the different etiologies are listed is mainly one of their chronological occurrence in the first year of life.

Our own detailed investigations on large numbers of infants cover the conditions of points 3, 4, 5, and 6. The first two conditions were included in view of their general familiarity to the observer of infants. They have not been investigated specifically by us, though we possess a number of individual observations on these conditions.

(2) The second main group, the restriction of the mother-child relations, can be compared in its structure to a class of diseases well known to internal medicine, namely, the deficiency diseases. We will, therefore, call our second main group *emotional deficiency* diseases. According to our present findings, this group can be divided into two subgroups, which

reflect the measure of the deficiency inflicted on the infant:

1. Partial deprivation.
2. Total deprivation.

It need hardly be stressed that total deprivation of the child of relations with its mother or her substitute refers only to emotional interchange. It is self-evident that a minimum of physical care consisting in food, hygiene, warmth, etc., has to be insured to any infant if it is to survive at all.

In the following table we present the psychogenic diseases in infancy which up to this time we have been able to segregate as distinctive nosological entities. In the left-hand column of the table we give the diseases; in the right-hand column the maternal attitudes we have found to be significantly related to the manifestations of the particular diseases.

III. THE INDIVIDUAL SYNDROMES

A. *Psychotoxic Diseases*

1. *Overt Primal Rejection* — The maternal attitude of overt primal rejection consists in the mother's global rejection of maternity and concurrently of the child. It is manifested often during pregnancy, but always beginning with the delivery. In an article published in 1937 (8), Margaret Ribble described the reactions of newborn infants to rejecting mothers. In extreme cases the babies became stuporous, fell into a comatose sleep with Cheyne-Stokes respiration, extreme pallor and diminished sensitivity. These infants had to be treated as in states of shock, by saline clysis, intravenous glucose and blood transfusion. After recovering they had to be taught to suck by

■ TABLE 1 / Etiological Classification of Psychogenic Disease in Infancy According to Maternal Attitudes

	Infant's Disease	Etiological Factor provided by maternal attitude
Psychotoxic Diseases	Coma in newborn (Ribble)	Overt primal rejection
	Three-months colic	Primary anxious overpermissiveness
	Infantile neuro-dermatitis	Hostility in the garb of anxiety
	Hypermotility (rocking)	Oscillating between pampering and hostility
	Fecal play	Cyclical moodswings
	Aggressive hyperthymic (Bowlby)	Hostility consciously compensated
Deficiency Diseases	Anaclitic depression	Partial emotional deprivation
	Marasmus	Complete emotional deprivation

stimulation of the mouth. If the situation was not dealt with immediately, it threatened the life of the neonate (8).

I have had the opportunity to observe such cases and to take a motion picture of one of them (11). The case history follows:

Case No. Mat. 55: The mother of the child is a sixteen-year-old, unusually good-looking girl, unmarried. She was employed as a servant and seduced by the son of her employer. Allegedly only one intercourse took place, resulting in impregnation. The child was undesired, the pregnancy accompanied by very severe feelings of guilt, as the girl was a devout Catholic. The delivery took place in a maternity hospital and was uneventful. The first attempt to nurse, after twenty-four hours, was unsuccessful and so were the following ones. The mother, allegedly, had no milk. We found no difficulty in producing milk by manual pressure. Neither was there any difficulty in feeding the infant from the bottle. The observation of the mother showed her to behave during nursing as if her infant was completely alien to her and not a living being at all. Her actual behavior was one of withdrawing from the baby, with a rigid and tense attitude of body, hands and face. The nipples, though not inverted, were not protruding and nursing did not appear to provoke turgor.

This state of affairs continued for five days. In the final attempts, one of which was filmed, the baby was seen to sink back into the stuporous, semi-comatose condition described by Ribble. Energetic methods had to be applied, including tube feeding and saline clysis, to bring the baby out of this condition.

In the meantime, an attempt at indoctrination of the mother was made in view of her youth and background. The method used was not interpretative, but authoritarian, starting with exact instructions and exercises in how to treat her nipples to produce turgor and making nursing possible. After this indoctrination, and from the fifth day on, the nursing went on relatively successfully and the child recovered, at least for the subsequent six days during which I could observe it.

It remains, of course, an open question what the subsequent course of an infant's development will be when the mother's rejection is as manifest from the beginning as it was in this case. We have the suspicion that even when the threat to life involved in this primal reaction is successfully overcome, other though less severe psychosomatic consequences will appear, and that certain cases of vomiting of infants during the first three months of life probably also belong in this category, as illustrated by the following case history:

Case No. WF 3: This child was breast-fed by its mother in the beginning. The mother then refused to continue and formula was introduced. Both during breast feeding and formula feeding the mother was full of complaints and recriminations. Breast feeding was, she said, unsatisfactory because the child vomited; but the formula was not right either, because the child vomited also. After three weeks the mother contracted influenza and was separated from the child. The formula was fed to the child by a substitute. The vomiting ceased immediately. Six weeks later the mother returned. The vomiting started again within forty-eight hours.

If we were to formulate the impression we have gained from such observations, our statements would have to remain extremely general and tentative. It is evident that, at present, we do not have sufficient observational material at our disposal; nor do we have an adequate hypothesis regarding the kind of maternal personality structure which results in this form of global rejection. We are, therefore, unable to formulate a theoretical assumption covering these cases.

As the child grows, maternal rejection will, of necessity, take on a different form and lead to a different result. The infantile personality will become progressively more diversified with increasing age; the maternal hostility will clash with this more developed infantile personality; individual and varied maternal hostility patterns will evolve. In contrast to this, maternal rejection of an objectless nature, so-to-speak, not directed at an individual child, but at the fact of having a child in general, will be encountered in the pure form only during the very first weeks and perhaps months of the baby's life. It is to be assumed that the attitude of these mothers — i.e., of generalized hostility toward maternity — is related to their individual history, their relations to the originator of the pregnancy, their individual way of solving their oedipal conflict and their castration anxiety. In the course of a few months the further relations with the baby will play their part, and a secondary elaboration of the generalized hostility into specific forms will take place.

We will call the original, and at that time still unstructured, rejection of maternity seen in these cases *overt primal rejection.* It impinges on an infant who has not even begun to develop any method of defense or adjustment. For at birth the infant is in the earliest narcissistic stage, in the act of developing the earliest patterns of orality, which will progressively be structured into what is known in psychoanalysis as the oral stage. In this earliest stage the contacts of the infant with the environment have just been shifted from the umbilical cord to the mouth and to intake. It is not surprising then that the symptoms manifested in the cases we have described are in the nature of a paralysis of intake during the very first days of life, in the nature of a rejection through vomiting at a somewhat later stage.

2. *Primary Anxious Overpermissiveness* — The maternal attitude of primary anxious overpermissiveness consists in a special form of overprotection during the first trimester of life. David Levy (7) introduced the term of "maternal overprotection." This term has been used rather indiscriminately by various authors to cover a wide range of behavior patterns and attitudes without too much regard for underlying motivations. In the following we will try to differentiate various forms of overprotection with the help of investigations directed at the maternal motivations underlying the individual forms, and we will attempt to correlate them with specific clinical pictures of the infant. For the first of these forms I have coined the term of "primary anxious overpermissiveness"; its consequences in the child we believe to be the so-called "three-months colic."

The "three-months colic" is a condition, well known in pediatric circles, with the following clinical picture: After the third week, and up to the third month, the infants begin to scream in the afternoon. They can be temporarily reassured by feeding. They appear to be subject to colicky pains. Changing of formula, or introducing formula instead of breast feeding, is of no avail. Various measures have been tried, all without success. The stools of these infants show nothing pathological, though at times diarrhea may be present. The pains may go on for several hours and then subside, only to start again the next day. The time of the day may vary. Around three months the condition has the tendency to disappear as inexplicably as it had appeared, to the great relief of mother and pediatrician.

I was struck by an interesting observation of Spanish and South-American pediatricians on this subject. They also were familiar with the "three-months colic" which they call "dispepsia transitoria."[1] But first Alarcon (1) and later Soto (9) observed that the "three-months colic" is unknown in institutionalized children.

This is an observation which we can fully confirm

[1] A similar condition has been described by Finkelstein under the name of "Spastische Diathese" and ascribed by Weill to lack of tolerance of mother's milk on the part of the infant.

from our own experience. In none of the institutions which we observed was "three-months colic" a problem. It was least so in the institutions where the infant had no maternal care whatsoever. It appeared most frequently in the institution we called "Nursery," in which the mother-child relations were at their best. Even there it was rather rare. In the relatively small number of infants in private families we observed, however, it was not infrequent.

Soto's explanation of the absence of "three-months colic" in institutions is that the children here are not "pampered," as he puts it; he describes institutions where the nurses look after the physical needs of the children, but the children do not get toys, and there is just "no nonsense." In contrast with this, he says, children in private families are "extremely pampered."

The observation appears to have merit. It is a pity that Soto ignores the other consequences of institutionalization which are infinitely more serious than "three-months colic." If, however, we translate his conclusions into our current conceptual framework, he appears to assume "maternal overprotection" of some kind as the causative factor in the "three-months colic."

This is a finding which lends itself to demonstrate the misleading nature of such over-all application of the term "overprotection." Indeed, Alarcon's and Soto's findings will have to be confronted with a series of observations made recently by Milton I. Levine and Anita I. Bell (6). They found in a series of twenty-eight infants observed over a period of three years, who had developed "three-months colic," that in 90 per cent of the cases the condition disappeared when the infants were given a pacifier.

However, "giving a pacifier" is certainly a measure which would be classified as "overprotective." How can we reconcile Alarcon's and Soto's findings with those of Levine and Bell? Certain aspects of the Levine-Bell patients duplicate closely the Alarcon-Soto assumptions. Thus all the twenty-eight children were raised in private families and not in institutions; but over and beyond this, with very few exceptions, the Levine-Bell babies were on a self-demand schedule. The assumption that the mothers of the babies were particularly permissive is, therefore, justified.

On the other hand, Levine and Bell state that in almost every instance the infants in question were hypertonic. Their work does not inform us whether the hypertonicity was observable already at birth and consequently represents a congenital factor. If so, we may advance a two-factor hypothesis in which the infants' congenital hypertonicity would represent a bodily compliance, to which the mothers' overpermissiveness would have to be added to result in the "three-months colic." We might even go further and presume that such overpermissive mothers are perhaps more prone to develop anxiety when confronted with unpleasure manifestations of the child; that they can only deal with such unpleasure manifestations by increasing their permissiveness still more, and that thus a vicious circle will develop in which the child's cry, which in reality expresses the need for tension release, is answered by a proffering of food which increases the tension and produces further colic. This vicious circle is then interrupted when the pacifier is introduced; for the pacifier lends itself to reduce tension without interfering with metabolic processes.

A clarification of the sequence would be desirable, for it is perfectly possible that (even without the congenital hypertonicity) the mother's anxiety in itself could produce the vicious circle, and that the hypertonicity will result from this vicious circle without necessarily being congenital. The decision which of the two assumptions is the more probable one can only be made through a detailed investigation of a significant number of children.

The assumption that the pacifier acts as a release of tension and consequently as a cure for the "three-months colic," is in accordance with David Levy's findings. He showed that sucking frustration, an oral frustration which increases tension, leads to increased finger sucking.

However, not only oral frustrations and tensions, but, as we stated, any kind of tension finds its release primarily through an activity of the oral zone in the first trimester of life. K. Jensen (5) demonstrated manometrically that newborn infants who were exposed to a series of stimuli (among which heat, cold, pinching of toe, pulling of hair, sudden dropping, etc.) reacted in a statistically significant number of cases with a sucking response. Therefore, the assumption that the pacifier acts as a release of tension and consequently as a cure for the "three-months colic," appears perfectly plausible.

3. *Hostility Garbed as Manifest Anxiety* — The maternal attitude in this clinical picture consisted in manifest anxiety, mostly in regard to the child. It became soon clear that this manifest anxiety corresponded to the presence of unusually large amounts of unconscious repressed hostility.

A study was made by the author of this paper, jointly with Katherine M. Wolf, on 220 children. We followed them in the environment called Nursery (12) and observed 28 children who developed skin affections during the first year of life. Of these, 24 were studied thoroughly, and the diagnosis of eczema was made in 22 cases by the pediatrician.

The mothers' unconscious hostility became evident in the frequency with which they barely avoided inflicting serious damage on their babies, such as feeding them an open safety pin in the cereal, dropping the baby several times on its head, consistent intolerable overheating of the baby's cubicle, knotting the baby's bib so tightly that the baby became blue in the face and barely escaped strangulation, etc. The same mothers showed a curious inhibition: they were afraid to touch their children or they refused to touch them, which is hardly surprising in view of the combination of repressed hostility and overt anxiety. This fear showed itself particularly vividly in some of these mothers who were always trying to get others to diaper, wash or feed their children. This fear was also manifest in some of the statements protocolled by us, like, e.g.: "A baby is such a delicate thing, the least false movement might harm it."

We investigated the personality of the children with the help of tests and developmental profiles (4). As described elsewhere (15), these tests provide quantifiable measures for the personality sectors of perception, body mastery, social relations, memory, manipulative ability, and intelligence as well as an over-all developmental quotient. In the group suffering from eczema, a characteristic retardation was observable in the sector of learning (memory and imitation). Less conspicuous, but mostly present also was a consistent retardation in the sector of social relations (Fig. 1).

A detailed discussion of the findings regarding this eczema group is in preparation (18). We may, however, mention some of the conclusions we have reached in this study in regard to the dynamics we have assumed to be present.

In the case of the eczema child, we have an anxiety-ridden mother who avoids touching her baby because of her more or less repressed aggression. If the mother avoids touching her baby, she makes it impossible for her child to identify with her and that at an age at which the baby is still in the stage of primary narcissism, when the child's ego is incomplete, and when the mother assumes the functions of the ego. In the process of psychological development in the course of the first year the child acquires its ego with the help of numberless identifications with its mother which are made possible through the sensory experiences offered by her. Among the most important of these, if not *the* most important are the tactile experiences which include both superficial and deep sensitivity.

When this external ego, represented by the mother, withdraws psychologically because of anxiety, the child cannot develop its own ego with the help

□ **Figure 1**

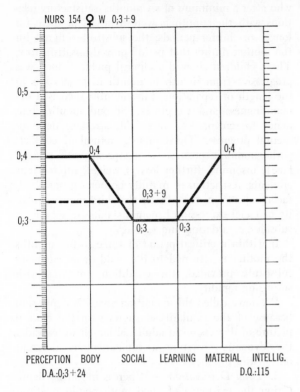

NURS 154 ♀ W 0;3+9

PERCEPTION BODY SOCIAL LEARNING MATERIAL INTELLIG.
D.A.:0;3+24   D.Q.:115

regard to normal and pathological motor patterns on the other.

Within the group of hypermotility there is one form which appears in large numbers, particularly in the institutional environment. This is the well-known rocking behavior of infants. In itself, this behavior can hardly be called a pathological pattern, for it is manifested occasionally in a transitory way by most children. In the cases observed by us, it differed, however, by becoming the principal activity of the children affected, by substituting for most of their other normal activities, by its frequent, striking violence which appears out of proportion with the physical resources of the child, and by the fact that it seems actually to involve a much larger amount of motor behavior than is seen in the average normal child of the same age. Its phenomenology consists in rocking movements, mostly in the knee-elbow position, not infrequently in the supine position at earlier ages, and not infrequently either in the standing position at later ages.

We studied this condition with the collaboration of Katherine M. Wolf in a group of 170 children and discussed our observations and our conclusions in our article "Autoerotism" (16).

Clinically the children show, apart from hypermotility, a characteristic retardation in the social and in the manipulative sectors of their personality (Fig. 2). We concluded that rapidly changing maternal attitudes, oscillating between overpampering and extreme hostility, will impair the formation of object relations of all kinds in the psychic sphere, while resulting in hypermotility, manifested as rocking, in the physical sphere.

5. *Cyclical Mood Swings of the Mother* — The maternal attitude toward the child remained stable for a number of months, after which it would change into its opposite and again persist for a number of months.

For the purpose of this study (16) we observed 153 children and their mothers. In 16 of these children we found fecal play and coprophagia in the fourth quarter of the first year. On investigation the mother-child relation turned out to be highly significant. We found that the bulk of psychosis in these 153 mothers was concentrated on those whose children manifested fecal play.

The clinical symptoms of depression with long-term mood swings were evident in the mothers of the coprophagic children. The mothers' attitude toward the children would be oversolicitous for many months and then suddenly change to extreme hostility with rejection. In our publication we offer a dynamic proposition as to the reason why such an

of identifications with her. This is specifically true in the second half of the first year when it has begun to delimit itself from the mother through the formation of secondary identifications. The anxiety-ridden mother, as part ego, offers no opportunity for secondary identification in bodily activities of a manipulative and imitative kind. Therefore, the infant's libidinal and aggressive drives which normally would be discharged in the course of the handling of the mother and converted into identifications, remain undischarged. It seems that they are discharged in the form of a skin reaction. The comparison may seem far-fetched, but one is reminded of the discharge phenomena taking place in adults in the peptic ulcer syndrome.

4. *Oscillating Between Pampering and Hostility* — We have found that a maternal attitude oscillating *rapidly* between pampering and hostility appears to lead frequently to a disturbance of motility in the child. In the following we will encounter several other such disturbances of the motor system. From the descriptive point of view these disturbances can be divided into two principal groups, namely hypermotility and hypomotility. In both groups further distinctions can be made in regard to quantitative increase or decrease of motility on the one hand, in

□ **Figure 2**

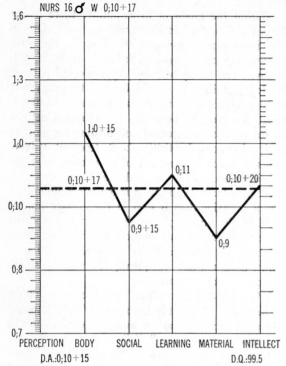

NURS 16 ♂ W 0;10+17

1;6

1;3

1;0 + 15

1;0

0;11

0;10 + 17   0;10 + 20

0;10

0;9 + 15

0;9

0;8

0;7

PERCEPTION   BODY   SOCIAL   LEARNING MATERIAL INTELLECT
D.A.:0;10+15   D.Q.:99.5

attitude should result in coprophagia, that is in the oral introjection of an "object," during the transitional period from the oral to the anal phase.

6. *Maternal Hostility, Consciously Compensated* — The term is self-explanatory. The parents of these children are more eager to use them for their own exhibitionistic and narcissistic purposes than as a love object. They realize that their behavior toward the child is not appropriate and consciously overcompensate it with sub-acid syrupy sweetness.

We have observed only a few cases of this type, of which we have described one (13). The data and follow-up studies on these cases are not sufficient to permit more than a tentative assumption. We believe that children confronted with this maternal attitude stay retarded in the social sector of their personality during the first year of life, while at the same time they are advanced in all other sectors. They present a picture in the second year in which hostility is predominant.

Our tentative assumption is that in the course of their later development they will present the picture of the aggressive hyperthymic, described by John Bowlby (2).

B. Deficiency Diseases

1. *Partial Emotional Deprivation* — In a study made with the assistance of Katherine M. Wolf (15)

on a total of 170 children, we observed 34 children who after a minimum of six months' satisfactory relations with their mothers were deprived of them for longer or shorter periods; the substitute offered for the mother during that period proved unsatisfactory. These children showed a clinical picture which was progressive from month to month in proportion to the length of separation: First month: increased demandingness and weepiness. Second month: tendency to scream, loss of weight, arrest of developmental progress. Third month: refusal of contact, pathognomonic position (lying prone with averted face), insomnia, further loss of weight, intercurrent ailments, restriction of motility becomes generalized, facial expression rigid. After the third month: rigidity of facial expression becomes stabilized, weepiness subsides, retardation and lethargy.

If within a critical period of three to five months the mother is returned to the child or an adequate substitute provided, the condition improves with surprising rapidity.

We have called this condition anaclitic depression because of the similarity it shows with the clinical picture of depression in adults, although we consider the dynamic structure a fundamentally different one in the infant.

2. *Total Deprivation* — Whereas in partial deprivation the existence of good mother-child relations prior to the deprivation is a prerequisite, this is immaterial in total deprivation. Regardless of the mother-child relations existing prior to total deprivation, its consequences will lead to the severest of the emotional deficiency diseases we have observed until now.

For the purposes of this study (12) we observed 91 children in a foundling home situated outside of the United States where the children were raised by their mothers during the first three to four months of their lives. During this period they showed the picture and developmental level of average normal children of the same country. After three to four months they were separated; they were adequately cared for in every bodily respect, but as one nurse had to care for eight children officially, and actually for up to twelve, they were emotionally starved.

After the separation from their mothers, these children went rapidly through the stages we have described for partial deprivation. Then the picture for motor retardation became fully evident. The children became completely passive, lying in their cots in a supine position. They did not even reach the stage where they could turn around sufficiently to perform a withdrawal by lying prone. The face became vacuous, eye co-ordination defective, the expression often imbecile. When motility returned after a while, spasmus nutans in some, and bizarre finger movements in all were manifested, reminiscent of decerebrate or catatonic movements (12). The developmental level (Fig. 4) regresses by the end of the second year to 45 per cent of the normal; sitting, standing, walking, talking are not achieved even by the age of four (see Fig. 3).

The progressive deterioration and the increased infection-liability lead in a distressingly high percentage of these children to marasmus and death. Of the 91 children followed by us for two years in Foundling Home, 37 per cent died (Fig. 5). In contrast, in another institution, Nursery, where the children were cared for by their mothers, not a single death occurred among 220 children observed during a four-year period. It appears that emotional starvation leads to progressive deterioration, which is in direct proportion to the duration of the deprivation which the child has undergone.

IV. CONCLUSIONS

The discussion of the single diseases tabulated in Table 1 shows that our classification at this stage is a crude attempt to orient ourselves in the field of psychogenic disorders in infancy. We have used for this purpose the criteria of etiology. At the present stage of our knowledge this approach cannot provide as diversified or detailed a picture as would a symptomatological approach. It would be possible, for instance, to divide the psychogenic affections in infancy according to the systems which they involve predominantly, like the motor, the intestinal, the circulatory, the respiratory, or other systems.

I believe, however, that such an approach would be both difficult and confusing. As discussed in the first part of the paper, in infancy the boundary lines between the different systems, both psychic and somatic, are fluid. We will always find more than one system involved in each of the conditions and, as can be seen for instance in the picture of the emotional deficiency diseases, in the progressive course of the ailment one system after another becomes involved. I believe also that it would be much more difficult to establish nosological entities with the help of symptomatic criteria than with the help of an etiological classification.

As in all research of this nature, our understanding of the fact that more than one or two nosological en-

□ **Figure 3**

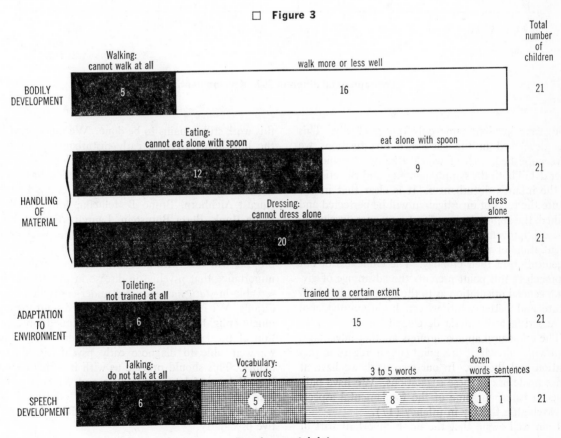

Developmental data.

□ **Figure 4**

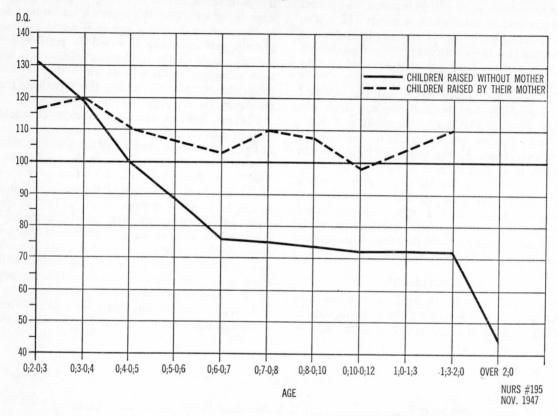

Environmental differences in development.

tities were involved came only very gradually. This was developed in the successive investigations we have published, each of which attempts to study in finer detail both the symptomatology and the etiology of the infant's disturbances. It is clear that in the future the tools of investigation will be perfected and refined, the approaches modified, new ones developed. These improvements will result in a far greater differentiation of nosological pictures and more exact specification of their etiology. The crudeness of our approach at this point presents the advantage of giving a general orientation as to the directions in which future and better solutions can be attempted, and more satisfactory criteria developed.

The etiological approach offers another advantage. It provides already at this point cues in regard to prevention and therapy. In our own work we have at times made use of these suggestions. We have published a paper on some of the fundamental aspects of psychiatric therapy in infancy (17).

I am well aware that the most important part of

this work still remains to be done. We must provide the link between these early disturbances and the psychiatric and somatic conditions which will develop in later life. As yet no clinical connection has been established with the pioneer work of Anna Freud, August Aichhorn, Bruno Bettelheim, John Bowlby, Beata Rank, Berta Bornstein, Lauretta Bender, and all the others who have investigated the psychiatric disturbances of the pre-school child. Future research projects will take into account that it is of decisive importance that psychiatric disease in infancy is observable in *statu nascendi* and under controlled conditions. We can expect, in the not too distant future, much enlightenment from the continued observation of the later development of children in whom we were able to diagnose early psychiatric abnormality. This should provide us with information on the etiology of later psychiatric and medical problems of childhood, adolescence and adulthood as well as with valuable pointers in the field of preventive psychiatry.

☐ **Figure 5**

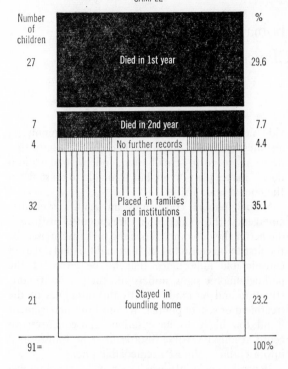

SAMPLE

Number of children		%
27	Died in 1st year	29.6
7	Died in 2nd year	7.7
4	No further records	4.4
32	Placed in families and institutions	35.1
21	Stayed in foundling home	23.2
91 =		100%

V. SUMMARY

1. The differences between the organization of the infant's personality and environment and that of the adult are discussed.

2. In view of these differences the possible etiological factors operative in psychogenic diseases in infancy are considered and reduced to the sole mother-child relation.

3. Variations of this etiological factor are reduced to the wrong kind of mother-child relation conducive to psychotoxic diseases on the one hand, to the insufficient amount of mother-child relation conducive to emotional deficiency diseases on the other.

4. A classification of nosological pictures in infancy on the basis of these criteria is presented.

BIBLIOGRAPHY

1. ALARCON, A. G. 1929, *Dyspapsie des Nourrissons*, Paris: Ballière.
2. BOWLBY, J. *Forty-four Juvenile Thieves.* Ballière, Tindall & Cox, London, 1946.
3. HARTMANN, H. "Ich-Psychologie und Anpassungsproblem," *Int. Ztsch. f. Psa.*, XXIV, 1939.
4. HETZER, H. AND WOLF, K. M. "Baby Tests," *Ztsch. f. Psychol.*, CVII, 1928.
5. JENSEN, K. "Differential Reactions to Taste and Temperature Stimuli in Newborn Infants," *Genet. Psychol. Monog.*, XII, 1932.
6. LEVINE, M. T. AND BELL, A. I. "The Treatment of 'Colic' in Infancy by Use of the Pacifier," *J. of Pediatrics*, XXXVII, 1950.
7. LEVY, D. *Maternal Overprotection*, Columbia Univ. Press, New York, 1943.
8. RIBBLE, M. A. "Clinical Studies of Instinctive Reactions in Newborn Babies," *Am. J. Psychiat.*, XCV, 1938.
9. SOTO, R. "¿Porque en la Casa de Cuna no Hay Dispepsia Transitoria?" *Revista Mexicana de Puericultura*, VIII, 1937.
10. SPITZ, R. A. "Differentiation and Integration," read at the Vienna Society for Psychoanalysis, 1936.
11. SPITZ, R. A. "LAM 44 — Film," 1944.
12. SPITZ, R. A. "Hospitalism: An Inquiry into the Genesis of Psychiatric Conditions in Early Infancy," *This Annual*, I, 1945.
13. SPITZ, R. A. With the assistance of Wolf, K. M. "The Smiling Response," *Genet. Psychol. Monog.*, XXXIV, 1946.
14. SPITZ, R. A. with the assistance of Wolf, K. M. "Anaclitic Depression," *This Annual*, II, 1946.
15. SPITZ, R. A. "La perte de la mère par le nourrisson," *Enfance* (Nov.–Dec.) 1948.
16. SPITZ, R. A. "Autoerotism," *This Annual*, III/IV, 1949.
17. SPITZ, R. A. "Psychiatric Therapy in Infancy," *Am. J. Orthopsychiat.*, XX, 1950.
18. SPITZ, R. A. "Eczema" (in preparation).

LEON EISENBERG

School Phobia
*Diagnosis, Genesis and Clinical Management**

What pediatrician has not been confronted with the child who experiences nausea, abdominal pain or non-specific malaise recurrently on school mornings, but rarely on weekends? Physical examination reveals an apparently healthy child, and recovery occurs with gratifying rapidity once the hour for school is safely past. The physician may recognize the secondary gain of the symptoms and dismiss them with an indulgent smile as he recalls his own early years. When such episodes are persistent, they become less amusing and may engender a vigorous comment that the patient is malingering and should be packed off to school forthwith. But, somehow, the parents prove unable to induce the child to return to school, and the physician is faced with a family crisis. He may perhaps conclude that the child is too "nervous" or "sensitive" and should be granted home leave for the remainder of the term. To his dismay, the physician finds that the convalescence fails to achieve its presumptive goal in tranquilizing the child and that the difficulty of inducing him to return to school is, if anything, greater with the arrival of the new school year. From the transient "Tom Sawyer" type of school-morning sickness, we have passed to a clinical variant of an important psychologic disorder: school phobia.

I have deliberately placed the problem of school phobia in the context of a symptomatic continuum to emphasize that we are not dealing with a rare psychiatric entity, but rather with a common pediatric problem. There is, let it be said, a world of psychologic difference between the occasional "normal" use of somatic complaints to avoid an unwelcome task, and the phobic child's uncontrollable psycho-physiological symptoms. But the transition from one to the other occurs at times in an insidious fashion and will be detected in time only if the pediatrician is sensitized to its occurrence and significance. The syndrome of school phobia may, of course, present itself frankly as a fear of attending school and pro-

* Reprinted by permission from *Pediatric Clinics of North America*, by Leon Eisenberg, pp. 645–666. Philadelphia: W. B. Saunders Company, 1958.

vide no diagnostic quandary. More commonly, it assumes a somatic disguise. The child protests that he wants to go to school (and, indeed, part of him does), makes plans to go, but is unable to do so when the crucial hour arrives.

School phobia constitutes an acute psychiatric emergency; the sooner proper treatment is instituted, the better the outcome. Since the pediatrician may be the first to be consulted by distraught parents, it is of considerable importance that he be aware of the pathognomonic signs, understand the psychodynamic structure and be familiar with the principles of the treatment of school phobia. Medical mismanagement is all too likely to have serious consequences; an acute, readily reversible disorder may be transformed into a chronic, almost irremediable one.

Beyond its own intrinsic importance, school phobia serves as a paradigm of neurotic disorders in children, for it illustrates with special clarity the relation between symptoms in the child and the psychologic structure of the family. The principles of its treatment highlight general considerations in the psychotherapy of emotional disorders. Only if the physician, the school authorities and participating social agencies coordinate therapeutic efforts is rehabilitation of the family unit likely to be successful.

DEFINITION

School phobia may be defined phenomenologically as partial or total inability to go to school that results from an irrational dread of some aspect of the school situation. It is accompanied by physiologic symptoms of anxiety or even panic when school attendance is imminent. Somatic manifestations may be the most prominent feature and may take the form of anorexia, nausea, vomiting or diarrhea, syncope, asthenia, headache, abdominal pain, diffuse or focal muscle aches, malaise or even unexplainable recurrent low grade fever. The overt expression of fear of school may be totally absent and may only be inferred from the correlation of symptoms with school days and their absence on holidays. At times the physiologic symptoms are not actually experienced, but only feared; i.e., the child may avoid going to school lest he vomit or faint once he is there.

If the child is able to put his fear into words, he may relate it to a particular teacher or the principal, to one or more of his classmates or to the dread of failing an examination. This frequently leads to well-meaning efforts to circumvent the difficulty by changing class, course or school — rarely, however, with any success. In itself, this leads us to suspect that the manifest reason for the symptoms is not the actual one.

It is essential at the outset that we distinguish sharply between school phobia and truancy. Both lead to irregular or failing attendance, but here the similarity ends. The truant "makes no bones" about his dislike for school, whereas the phobia child wishes he could attend and usually has ambitions that require academic training. The chronic truant starts off for school, but does not arrive, or leaves shortly after arrival; he spends his day pursuing his pleasures on the streets. He has usually been a poor or indifferent student; he is typically aggressive and not infrequently sociopathic. He acquires skill in fabricating excuses to cover up his behavior so that considerable time may elapse before the facts come to light. He stays away from both school and home, unless home is an inviting haunt because his parents are away at work.

The child with school phobia, by contrast, draws attention to his inability to leave home to get to school. Usually he spends the school hours in his home and is very much concerned lest anyone know he is not at school. Typically, he has other fears which restrict his mobility; he may be unable to go to church, club meetings, parties or movies unless his parents accompany him and remain with him. In the usual case his previous academic record has been good so that school authorities are at a loss to understand his behavior. In most cases the acute onset of the phobic state has been preceded by a history of hesitance about going to school manifested by a spotty attendance record, ostensibly because of "colds," "GI upsets," and so forth.

Apprehension about going to school is not uncommon among kindergarten or first-grade pupils. It may occur transiently in older elementary school students at the beginning of a term or upon transfer to a new school. When, however, symptoms persist for more than a few weeks, the possibility of an incipient school phobia must be considered. Unfortunately, there is a prevailing myth to the effect that the normal child, especially the "red-blooded" boy, does not — indeed, should not — like school. This sterotype

is a reflection of the anti-intellectual trends of recent years; it contributes, in itself, by shaping attitudes toward learning, to the poor levels of academic achievement now causing national concern in the race for scientific productivity. The case is quite the contrary. A normally intelligent child, offered a decent educational opportunity, will welcome and enjoy his school experience. When he does not, we should examine the quality of his schooling, the attitudes of his family, the mores of his culture and his personal adjustment. *A persistently negative attitude toward school is invariably expressive of social or personal pathology.*

The definition of school phobia offered at the outset of this discussion — partial or total inability to go to school that results from an irrational dread of some aspect of the school situation — is based upon the manifest symptoms. Johnson and her co-workers(3, 7) have suggested that the syndrome be redefined in terms of an etiologic analysis. The basic difficulty, they point out, is not that of going to school, but rather that of *leaving home*; i.e., anxiety about separating from the parents. This places school phobia within the neurotic category of *separation anxiety*, a usage followed by Kanner.(8) Johnson has defined separation anxiety as "a pathological emotional state in which child and parent (usually the mother) are involved in a relationship characterized primarily by an intense need on the part of both to be in close physical proximity." This widens the focus of our attention from the behavior of the child, so perplexing when viewed in isolation, to the patterns of interaction within the family unit. It implies the necessity for dealing with the emotional conflicts of both parent and child if a successful return to school is to be effected.

The phenomenologic definition has the virtue, however, of stressing the symptomatic manifestations by which the syndrome may be identified. It involves no commitment to an exclusive theory of causation. Although my own clinical experience is in general agreement with the dynamic etiology so lucidly expressed in Johnson's formulation, the issues are neither completely nor quantitatively set forth in this thumbnail sketch of the problem. Nor, as the literature is reviewed, are all students of the subject in complete agreement upon it. Consequently, it would seem best for the moment to adhere to a descriptive statement and to classification by manifest symptoms.

PREVALENCE

There is a dearth of reliable information upon which to base an accurate estimate of the prevalence of school phobia. The relative paucity of psychiatric literature on the subject until recent years reflects the customary mode of disposition of cases: to the truant officer or his equivalent, rather than to the child psychiatrist. Within the past decade, however, cases of school phobia have been referred to psychiatric clinics in ever increasing numbers. For example, the rate of clinic admissions to the Children's Psychiatric Service of the Johns Hopkins Hospital rose from four cases of school phobia per 1000 admissions for all causes in 1948 to 17 per 1000 in 1956. Current figures are approximately 30 per 1000.

Whether there has been any real increase in the actual incidence is a matter for conjecture. It is difficult to argue from clinic figures; most certainly, a larger part of the increase in clinic experience stems from changes in the traditional methods of management, as school authorities and family physicians have become more aware of the psychiatric implications of the disorder. That there is a large unreported reservoir of cases is demonstrated by the report of Hahn.[5] In a clinical study of school phobia in a suburban Boston area, it was found that about seven children with this problem were being referred to the clinic in the course of a year (about the same as our experience in 1956). When, however, a special study unit was established *within* the school system and the availability and purpose of the service were publicized to the teachers, 24 cases were found in less than four months, a rate some 10 times greater! This verifies our expectation that estimates of prevalence based upon psychiatric referrals will grossly underestimate the number of cases in the school population.

CLINICAL FEATURES

In contradistinction to most childhood psychiatric disorders which affect boys far more frequently than girls, school phobia is no less common in girls than in boys,[2, 13] if not more common.[12] Almost all patients have been of normal or superior intelligence. This is, at least in part, almost a matter of definition. The defective child, who is misplaced in school and is consequently reluctant to attend, can hardly be said to be suffering from an "irrational dread." With appropriate change in his classroom situation, his attitude is likely to change remarkably for the better. There is, however, no inherent reason why a defective child may not be caught in the same web of neurotic conflicts which lead to school phobia in the normally intelligent. The good intelligence of the usual phobic child only emphasizes the fact that the essential problem is not an academic one.

The somatic symptoms displayed by these children when school attendance is imminent are equally remarkable for their overwhelming quality and for their plasticity. Impressive as they may be at 8:30 a.m., they are usually not much in evidence during the rest of the day, on weekends and on holidays, except in the more seriously disturbed child. In the typical case an observer who did not know the history would be at a loss to detect any great abnormality in adjustment from the behavior of the patient in the clinic, at least after the first or second visit. Whereas symptoms may be prominent in the presence of the parents as the child arrives at the clinic, the simple act of closing the door between the patient and his mother may bring about a remarkable transformation in his overt behavior.

Asked to discuss his difficulty, the child is usually at a loss to explain it. He avers his desire to attend and may readily agree to a plan for attendance, only to be unable to carry it through. When the interviewer shifts to a discussion of family affairs, after he has established rapport with the child, significant data are readily elicited. Play methods, with the younger group of patients, are usually effective in bringing family difficulties into sharp focus.

This remarkable discrepancy between the anxiety and panic when separation is threatened, and the relative normality of behavior under other circumstances is a feature of the majority of children with school phobia who are at an elementary school level. Their symptoms are clearly situational products of a currently active family problem. The adolescents, on the other hand, evidence a much more serious *intrinsic* disturbance of general adjustment. The family stress may or may not be currently active, but its action over a period of years has resulted in psychologic malfunction with a driving force of its own that is no longer simply resolved by a reordering of family affairs. While one will occasionally find such cases in the younger group and, conversely, an easily managed problem in a junior high school student, it has been our experience that there is a great difference in severity in the two groups with a fairly sharp cutoff point at about the seventh grade.

Coolidge et al.[1] and Waldfogel,[13] on the basis of similar observations, suggest that the syndrome of school phobia be divided into (*a*) neurotic and (*b*) characterologic types. Johnson[6] feels, however, that the diagnostic differentiation is unwarranted, since the basic problem is essentially the same in the two groups. Whatever merit the terminologic dispute may have from the standpoint of psychiatric theory, it is important to be aware of the difference (that in our experience has been correlated with age) in the prognosis of the two groups. The skillful pediatrician and school social worker can usually anticipate success from their joint psychotherapeutic efforts with the nursery or elementary school child, but had best refer the older child for more intensive psychiatric care.

It should hardly be necessary to add that the study of each case should begin with a careful investigation of whatever complaints the child may bring about the school. A sadistic teacher, an organized gang of delinquents or an unreasonable academic load may precipitate fear of going to school. If the fear is justified by the external facts, then treatment must begin with an effort at their correction. However, such factors are remarkably rare as a sufficient cause for the development of a school phobia. Even when an unpleasant event has occurred at school as a *precipitating* factor, there is usually good evidence of *predisposing* neurotic elements in the patient.

Pamela R. had an acute school phobia which she related to having been slapped by the principal. He stoutly denied the incident, but admitted it with considerable remorse a week later. He had lost his temper, felt acutely ashamed of what he had done (for the first time in 30 unblemished years of teaching!) and, in a panic, had tried to cover up. This was obviously an especially upsetting experience for the child, involving not only a blow, but also a lie. When the facts had emerged and the principal had apologized personally to the child, Pamela remained unable to return. It then came to light that she had had a previous history of intermittent school attendance and was living in the midst of a decompensating family situation. Only with psychiatric help to the family was Pamela enabled to return to school. It is instructive to note that a second child had been struck by the principal under similar circumstances that week, but he had been attending school without further difficulty.

DYNAMICS OF SYMPTOM FORMATION

School phobia is usually precipitated by some factor or factors that threaten the security of the child and his mother and increase their mutual dependency needs. Thus an illness which necessitated an absence from school, a move to a neighborhood strange to the family, or a transfer to a school about which the child has heard frightening tales may be the source of increased anxiety. Changes in the family situation, hospitalization of the mother, the arrival of a new baby, or marital turbulence between the parents, alone or together with a school incident, may lead to the appearance of phobic symptoms in a predisposed child. The sequence of events from this point will be determined in large part by the manner in which the child's anxiety is handled by his parents.

With calm assurance and matter-of-fact recognition that school attendance is mandatory, he can usually be eased back into school. The further experience of confronting and overcoming his fears, in the presence of supportive parents, will then result in a diminution in his symptoms, particularly as he continues to enjoy the satisfactions of a normal school experience.

Unfortunately, the problem is usually not so resolved, for the very reason that the parents, immobilized by their own neurotic involvement, serve only to multiply the child's difficulty with separation. The mother of such a child is all too likely to seize upon his complaints of nervousness or fatigue as an adequate excuse for remaining at home. She may go through the verbal formula of reassurance, but in a strikingly unconvincing manner. She is too ready to agree that the teacher is too strict, the curriculum too demanding and the other children too rough. She thus cooperates with the child in displacing his fears from the nuclear family problem on to the school.

I have reported in greater detail elsewhere the prototypical interpersonal transactions between such parents and their children.(2) The essential psychologic mechanism is the provision to the child of *contradictory verbal and behavior cues* at one and the same time. The child may be urged to leave his mother's side, but she simultaneously tightens her grasp about him. He may be told he has nothing to fear by a father whose visible tremor indicates that some disaster lies in store. He may be "ordered" to go in a hesitant and wavering voice that lets the child know that the "order" need not — indeed, should not — be followed.

Complementary patterns of behavior may be observed by the physician in the course of his contacts with the family. The doctor will be "warned" in the child's presence that "he'll never go to your office alone with you;" as this is said, mother's tight hold on the child will guarantee the validity of the prediction. If the doctor suggests a plan for returning the child to school, it is likely to meet with the response: "Oh, but, Doctor, I can't stand to force him!" or "What do I do when the plan doesn't work?" This constant anticipation of failure is a not too subtle derivative of the mother's *need* to have the plan fail.

Observations of the behavior of mothers in a nursery school setting permitted validation of this concept of the parental role in the genesis of the symptoms:

On the first few days in the nursery the child might hover by his mother's side. As he began to display interest in the group and wander from his mother's side, she would almost invariably move in order to be closer to him. Or she would intrude herself in his activities on the guise of wiping his nose, taking him to the toilet, protecting him from a fight, and so forth. When the time for her departure was set, her anguish on leaving was often greater than the child's. Typically, she would return for several goodbyes. Her 2 hours away from school might be described as the hardest she had ever spent. On return, she would be overaffectionate, as though the absence had been one of 2 weeks rather than 2 hours. Several mothers were visibly perturbed to learn that their children had played happily in their absence.

Instances of overt sabotage of school plans by mothers were not infrequently encountered among these cases.

Stanley R., 15, was due to resume his school attendance. At the last moment his mother argued that it was raining too hard. When he persisted in his intention to follow through on his pledge, she suggested that his father be consulted. Called at his office, he insisted that Stanley go. At this point mother hung up the phone and told Stanley his father thought he should stay home.

Henry L., who had missed 6 weeks of school because of morning symptoms of nausea and vomiting, had been enabled to resume daily attendance through clinic efforts. After 2 weeks of faithful attendance his mother reported in passing at her next regular interview that he had been absent the previous 3 days because of a moderate snow. He lacked overshoes, she explained, and she had been concerned about his health. This might not have seemed too unreasonable, had we not learned from Henry that he had been permitted by his mother to be out sledding on those very 3 days!

Thus far the discussion has been focused on the modes of parental behavior which block the child's efforts to emancipate himself from pathological dependency. When the covert communication from mother is that of permission for gratifying egocentric wishes, the child exhibits behavior efficiently designed to secure his whims; the skill he displays is born of long experience; he is more able to manage his parents than they him. When the covert cue from mother betrays her own anxiety, fear or hostility, the child responds with anxiety or even panic. Not only is he threatened by the unwelcome message about mother's feelings toward him, but in addition he is afraid of his own hostile impulses which his mother has proved ineffectual to check. What he seeks, above all, is a parent stronger than he, despite his

railing against control; what he finds is an adult no more capable than he is of mastering his inner turmoil.

The child's behavior at the moment of separation is only partially understandable in terms of the immediate interpersonal transactions between his parents and himself. At a deeper level it is evident that *he cannot leave home because he is anxious about what may occur during his absence from the home.* At times this fear may be a realistic one. He may fear that his parents will separate or that his father will injure his mother.

Robert P. had a vexing school phobia over many months. Only after prolonged psychotherapeutic efforts was it discovered that he lived in constant dread that his divorced father might return home to kill his wife, as he had repeatedly threatened to and once attempted. (This important bit of history had been withheld by Mrs. P. until it was revealed by Robert.) When this came to light, Robert's therapist could discuss with him the external guarantees against this event and explore the complex inner feelings involved in it. Only then was Robert able to return to school.

With more or less justification, he may be afraid that a younger sibling, of whom he is jealous, will consolidate his favored position in the family during his own absence from the competition while at school.

Most often the fears of the phobic child are comprehensible as projections onto the outer world of socially forbidden wishes about which he has overwhelming guilt. The psychic structure of the young child is governed by a conviction of the magic omnipotence of thought. As he learns language, he gains a powerful tool in controlling the world; his verbal expressions order the events and the objects about him into a more understandable whole. His statements modify the behavior of the significant persons in his social world. Intoxicated by his new power, he passes through a stage of animistic thinking in which to name is to control, to think is to do. Gradually, too, he acquires consensually validated concepts and gives up his own egocentric world view. But this is available only for ideas that can be expressed and checked against the ideas of others. The feelings which a repressive environment may not tolerate may be denied access to correctional feedback and may continue in the shadowy world governed by magical thinking.

Thus the child whose security is threatened by a younger sibling may be unable to leave home lest something happen to that sibling. The apparent solicitude is an inverted psychic representation of angry feelings which, if not guarded against, will magically produce the feared (wished) injuries. The same dynamic mechanisms are operative in the frequently expressed concern about the welfare and safety of one or another parent. This should not be misunderstood as any real wish for harm to befall the person in question. Indeed, the child is, as his behavior shows him to be, strongly attached to this parent. What distresses him is the psychic ghost of hostile feelings toward loved ones, normal in every child, but unmanageable in the phobic child because of the inability to tolerate the merest hint of such feelings as a grave transgression of the fundamental commandment that one honor one's parents.

The strength and duration of these factors, as well as accessory ones, which may run the full gamut of psychopathology, will determine the severity of the disorder. Chronic exposure to an anxiety-laden family environment that consistently inhibits growth toward independence will ultimately result in a neurotic inner structure with its own momentum. Reactions of withdrawal, regression and flight may become the inveterate modes of response to stress. The more extensive the intrinsic neurosis, the more intensive will be the psychiatric efforts required for its extinction and the substitution of more adequate patterns of behavior. In the early case, clearly responsive to the psychic fields of force that impinge upon the child, external management and support will usually suffice; the tearful infantile behavior customarily ceases on the threshold of the classroom. In the more severe one, however, the child may no longer be able to perceive his environment clearly, so distorting are the psychic forces swirling within him; extensive reconditioning is required before he can assimilate the class experience.

THE FAMILY ENVIRONMENT

A detailed account of the psychologic characteristics of the parents of phobic children is beyond the scope of this paper. The general statements that follow are offered solely as clues to the problems which may be relevant. No inference is intended that they are universally present; careful study of the individual case is necessary to identify the pertinent issues for the particular family. Summary descriptions unavoidably oversimplify and, to some extent, distort the subtleties of actual life situations. There is, however, some justification for the schematization of key themes recurrent in these families; the remarkable similarity of the findings of different investigators (1, 2, 3, 5–9, 11–13) indicates that the patterns of interaction within the family can be meaningfully related to the genesis of symptoms in the child. The papers by Waldfogel,(13), Talbott,(12) Klein(9) and Coolidge et al.(1) summarize the family patterns in substantial series of cases. The case analysis by Estes et al.,(3) written from a psychoanalytic orientation, exemplifies the psychologic features in a fairly typical family; this paper is noteworthy for a clever and incisive set of cartoons illustrative of crucial issues.

Cases of school phobia occur among families of widely varying socio-economic class, religious affiliation and ethnic origin. In the overwhelming majority the parent principally involved in the separation anxiety of the child is the mother; this was true, for example, in 24 of the 26 cases I reported.(2) But this clearly implies a fault in the marital relationship as well, for the mother who is a partner in a mature and satisfying marriage is hardly likely to have such a symbiotic relationship with her child. If the discussion focuses on the mother, this should not be taken to exculpate the father; it merely reflects a psychiatric focus on the most effective point for the application of therapeutic leverage: the mother-child relationship.

The mother of the phobic child is closely identified with her child; i.e., there is little psychologic distance between them. Both share a common perspective, almost a *folie-a-deux* that distorts the perceptions of each. The mother can be seen to relive vicariously through her child the unresolved problems of her own childhood. She is a person who has been trapped in a dependent relationship with her own mother. This is frequently part of a current problem with mother or mother-in-law and not merely a hangover from the past. She empathizes too readily with her anxious child because of her own anxieties; in the process she overreads and overreacts to his tensions. Several of Suttenfield's cases(11) — and two of my own — were instances of school phobia in successive generations.

The relationship with the child has been an unusually close one from the very beginning of infancy. This is not entirely a matter of overcompensation for hostile feelings, though this enters into every case to some extent, but is an expression of a strong primary emotional tie. I emphasize this point lest the genuine affection of the mother for her child be dismissed by overanalyzing the compensatory mechanisms; Waldfogel(13) has raised the same caution. It is rather the hostile feelings that are likely to be secondary as the mother becomes exasperated at her own helplessness in extricating herself from a symbiosis that both she and the child ultimately find suffocating. Each cherishes the intensity of the relationship; each resents the excessive dependency; neither can find a way out of the trap.

The pathologic strength of the attachment of mother to her child is expressed in an overprotective attitude. The dependency and infantilization this fosters bring in their wake constant demands from the child who has been blocked in developing means of satisfying his needs other than through mother. While at first seizing upon this dependence upon her as a symbol of intense love, the mother finds herself increasingly frustrated. Her own initiative and freedom of movement are restricted by a child who will not tolerate her leaving him. He disappoints her by failing to measure up to achievements of more mature children of his age. She cannot accept her angry feelings toward him, since they jeopardize her exalted image of devoted motherhood. The repressed resentment periodically explodes in anger disproportionate to the provoking incident. Laden with guilt at her hostility and even more at her unjustified outbursts, she returns to her overprotective and permissive position. The cycle then recapitulates itself as the child exploits her inability to set limits.

This may be represented in the following diagrammatic fashion:

Overprotective, overpermissive
maternal attitudes
↓
Dependent, demanding,
clinging child
↓
Maternal hostility
(repressed)
↓
Periodic outbursts of
disproportionate anger
↓
Maternal guilt

The question remains: Why have the overprotective and oversolicitous attitudes that initiate the cycle developed in the first instance? Here the mechanisms may vary widely from case to case. The child may have been a late arrival after many years of sterility and frequent miscarriages; it is rare for such a child not to be surrounded by a great deal of apprehension. In another case the child may symbolize an earlier relationship of great significance to the mother.

Wendy Q. was conceived during the terminal illness of Mrs. Q's mother; she was born shortly after the grandmother died. In Mrs. Q's words: "She took my mother's place. I was never as close to my first child. She was my husband's, but Wendy was mine."

For a complex of reasons the mother may relive through a particular child her own childhood traumata.

Mrs. S. stated: "When Paul cried, I could remember how unhappy I had been as a child. I saw how lonely and frightened he looked in the classroom. I couldn't leave him there. My father never had any sympathy for my fears. When my husband punished Paul and said he was a baby, I felt so bad I was ready to leave him. Paul came to me for help. How could I, knowing how he felt, turn him away!"

Mr. R. had been victimized by a sadistic father who abandoned him early, but returned periodically with promises that were eagerly received and invariably led to further frustration. Mr. R. was determined that his son would have all those paternal attentions he had never had. By fathering Harry in the image of an all-giving parent, he was playing the roles of father and son by turns. So closely identified was he with the child that when Harry complained of nausea, Mr. R. would respond by vomiting.

When the child has been conceived as a tie for a failing marriage, he becomes a hostage who traps the parent in a relationship that may be deeply resented. He has to be the source of those satisfactions normally derived from the marriage. As the only worthwhile product of the union, he may be cherished and fondled to the point of seduction. At the same time he is resented as a further barrier to freedom.

Mrs. O. married a perennial bachelor some 15 years her senior. At the point of divorce she agreed to have a child. To her dismay, twins were born. Her inadequate husband was even less competent as a father. Now convinced that she should have left him, she was no longer capable of supporting herself and saw no escape from a frustrating existence. The twins were at once the objects of her love and her hatred. The latter sentiment was incompatible with her conception of motherhood and led to manifest behavior of complete submission of her needs to those of the children. She could only reassure herself that she loved them sufficiently when they gave proof of their "devotion" to her by becoming completely dependent upon her.

These few examples must suffice to indicate the complexity of the life patterns that may generate the symbiotic relationship with the child.

The role played by the father in the family drama is less well defined. With the exception of two cases, one of which, Mr. R., has already been cited, cases in which the fathers behaved like caricatures of anxious mothers, the complicity of the father is more frequently one of omission than commission. It is what he fails to do to sustain his wife; what he fails to provide his child; what he lacks as a mature man with whom a positive identification could occur that constitutes his share in the problem. Most commonly, he is uninvolved and has abandoned both parental roles to his wife. If he takes any part, it is likely that of a disgruntled and carping sideline critic.

Mr. S., with the skill of a prosecuting attorney, indicted his wife's failings with Richard. Intoxicated by self-satisfaction, he explained that he had warned her step by step of the inevitable consequences of her mismanagement of the child. With unpardonable pride, he reported that each of his dire predictions had come true. Richard used to obey when father did things his way — but father had stopped trying. His wife wouldn't listen, so why try? What stopped were the few constructive efforts he had made in earlier years; what remained were his acidly ironic comments on the futility of Mrs. S.'s actions. Badgered and bewildered, his immature wife, herself the sheltered baby of overindulgent parents, was reduced to a chronic state of anxious indecision.

The father may be angered, not only by his child's inability to carry on in adequate fashion at school and elsewhere, but as well by his resentment of the manifest preference displayed for the mother. The father frequently resents hearing about his wife's difficulties with the child on the grounds that he has enough to worry about at work. It is not unusual to find that he spends little time at home. The marriages, while under constant strain, are likely to be quite durable, since each partner serves certain neurotic needs of the other. A common source of stress is the father's relationship with his own family, resented bitterly by the wife for its closeness and exclusion of her as an outsider. He, on the other hand, cannot accept his wife's dependence on her family and proves insensitive to her frequent pleas to him for help in altering the basis of this relationship. These centrifugal forces weaken the marital bond; the weakness of the marital bond itself leads each to need even more the family resented by the other.

Father's mode of response to the child's phobic symptoms is likely to be one of angry and unsympathetic dismissal. This threatens the insecure child, who turns to mother for "reassurance," the price for which is submission. Mother is then apt to side with the child and further widen the cleavage between him and father, who storms out of the situation. This sequence of events is by no means uniform, however.

Father may be simply absent psychologically, hardly looking up over his morning paper. Or he may share his wife's anxieties and respond with helpless bewilderment. Rarely is he capable of taking decisive and effective action independently, although with psychiatric guidance he is more readily able to take over the situation than is his wife.

TREATMENT

Essential to the entire treatment process is *early return to school*. This may seem gratuitously self-evident; absence from school is, after all, the presenting complaint. It is nonetheless necessary to stress the point. All too frequently the physician shares, quite unwittingly, parental anxieties about the effect of pressure on the child. Moreover, valuable emphasis on etiologic understanding, techniques of uncovering, and the achievement of insight obscures at times the importance of symptom control, which may be contemptuously dismissed as "flight into health." There is no gainsaying the desirability of altering basic psychopathologic mechanisms if substantial and persisting improvement is to be achieved. But phobic symptoms are significant *in themselves*, not merely as symbolic manifestations of underlying neurotic conflicts.

The very existence of the phobic symptoms in this syndrome materially alters the patient's subsequent behavior. The phobic state denies him the experiences necessary for his growth and forces him into more intimate contact with the sources of his psychologic impasse. He fails to attend school, which he must for his own further social and intellectual development; he remains at home, a sullen captive to the mother from whom he must liberate himself. Mutual dissatisfaction with this frustrating state of affairs feeds the latent resentment of each toward the other; largely unexpressed, this chronic hostility fuels the fires that impel the overt neurotic mechanisms. The "success" of the child's anachronistic infantile behavior reinforces the probability of its recurrence, as it magically achieves its neurotic goals.

Superimposed upon the psychologic problems that have initiated the phobic state are realistic secondary factors. The child falls behind in his school work so that now he is in danger of failing. It becomes progressively more difficult for him to rationalize his prolonged absence from school to classmates and teachers. The teacher herself is likely to become involved secondarily. She is apt to regard her inability to get the child into class and to keep him there as a failure on her part. If she is a focus of his fears, particularly if the parent blames her for strictness, unfairness, and so forth, it is difficult for her not to retaliate against the child, thus further complicating the problem.

The longer he remains at home, the harder does he find the task of leaving it. It is, after all, common experience that the barrier to the performance of a feared action increases directly with the delay in undertaking it. For the phobic patient his misperception of the situation upon which his anxieties are displaced becomes the more distorted the longer he denies himself the possibility of a corrective experience, which requires re-exposure. Indeed, the very persistence of the invalidism at home means to the child that what is feared is real; the paralysis of his family signifies their participation in the unspoken conspiracy to act as though the problem lay outside the home.

If the physician accepts the impasse and provides a medical certificate legalizing the absence from school, he, in essence, becomes a co-conspirator. The situation is rendered far too comfortable for all concerned by providing a home teacher. The symbiotic union is preserved with little sacrifice; mother and child may now avoid facing their anxieties without jeopardizing his academic progress. A great impetus for movement in treatment has been removed. This may somewhat overstate the case. It is not too far from the truth, however, as indicated by a recent study of children on home teaching in Baltimore. Eight of the 108 children receiving this service were certified as in need of it because of school phobia. *All had been out of school no less than one year, and one as long as three years* (J. B. Hardy: personal communication). This, it should be noted, does not represent a terminal state, but merely the course up to the present.

Klein(9) emphasizes the importance of getting the child into the school building, if only to the principal's office, to the counsellor or to the teacher after class for his homework. The key point is the development of measures which will serve to maintain some contact between child and school while a more fundamental reintegration is sought. At the same time the firm emphasis on the reality of compulsory school attendance helps to mobilize the anxiety necessary for psychotherapeutic progress. This action orientation of a psychoanalytic therapist has its theoretical justification in a modification of orthodox technique which Freud found necessary in analyzing phobias. According to Fenichel,(4) the analyst "must induce the (phobic) patient to expose himself to the feared experiences for the purpose of bringing the full force of his neurotic conflict into the open." Lippman,(10) formerly an exponent of removing all pressure for attendance from the child, now agrees that the ap-

propriate use of firmness in properly selected cases facilitates the therapeutic task.

The plan for resuming school attendance must be made in terms of the particular child, family and school. *From the outset the treatment effort is best conceived as a joint undertaking between medical and school personnel.* Thus a conference with school authorities is a fundamental part of the first stage of therapy. This provides an opportunity to clarify for the teacher and principal the dynamic motivation of the child's behavior. The recognition that the physician sees the causes of the difficulty as arising primarily from without the school diminishes the teacher's defensiveness and reduces unrealistic expectations of what she alone can accomplish. The school will then be enabled to play a more constructive role in rehabilitation. Instead of resenting the sting of parental criticism and moving to retaliate, often to the child's detriment, the principal can now see the parental behavior as part of a neurotic disorder toward which a therapeutic rather than a punitive response is appropriate.

The plan for resumption of school attendance, to be realistic, must take into account the severity both of the child's problem and of his mother's neurotic involvement. In the majority of instances it is not necessary to work out a plan for the return to school on a special part-time basis; once the family has been helped to understand the problem, effective guidance by the parents under psychiatric supervision will ensure prompt return on a normal basis of attendance. There will be cases, however, in which the tolerance for anxiety is so low that compromise plans will be more effective: getting homework from the teacher after class as a first step; beginning school return by spending an hour in the counsellor's office; having mother remain in the classroom or a nearby office for a specified period, and so on. Gradually the child is weaned from one step to the next. Such plans require a fully cooperative school and are not without hazard. Time limits are essential if movement is to occur. These dates should be set with the child exercising limited choice. Equally important is strict compliance with the contract by parents and school. Under no circumstances should mother, if she has promised to remain, try to slip out when the child's attention is diverted. This is likely to produce a severe exacerbation of anxiety and to jeopardize the success of treatment.

Two fundamental considerations should be made explicit to the child and his parents in the course of negotiating the plan for return to school: Attendance is mandatory under law; the child is capable of resuming his place in the community of his peers. The issue is not whether he will return, but how and when. Let me caution against any misinterpretation of this therapeutic procedure. It is not a matter of relying on the threat of punishment; on the contrary, it focuses on the process of establishing controls. It is precisely the lack of inner control that gives rise to anxiety in the child who cannot master his upsurging impulses; the failure of his parents to stand fast and lend him strength results in the breakdown of function. The physician's confident expectation that the patient can accomplish the task of separation enhances the likelihood of its accomplishment, just as parental doubts had lessened it. By setting limits the therapist mobilizes the constructive elements in the patient; at the same time the limits provide a measure of the parental motivation for change.

So long as progress is perceptible toward the goal of return to school, the physician may properly intervene to lessen legal sanctions. But he must be alert lest "treatment" be converted into a sham formalism; it can be misused to perpetuate the symbiotic union by providing a technical excuse to bypass the school law requiring compulsory attendance. In several cases in which I was convinced that the child was ready to return, but the mother insufficiently motivated to follow through, I did not hesitate to inform the child and his parents that I was referring the matter back to the school for appropriate action. When the school authorities set a date for a juvenile court hearing, a prompt and complete return to school followed. It is clearly the physician's responsibility not to permit himself to be used in the service of illness if he is to meet his obligation to the patient and to the community.

It is at times difficult to persuade psychiatrists as well as pediatricians of the correctness of this stand. It is mistaken for the assumption of a judicial prerogative. This is not at all the case; compulsion resides, and properly so, in the laws of the community. The physician is merely removing himself from the untenable position in which he has been placed by the family. He is being used in order to declare the patient sick and therefore not appropriately subject to legal action, and to maintain the fiction that the patient is being treated. In the cases mentioned the child was not only not harmed by the legal process, but actually helped over a barrier to his maturation. In no instance in my experience in which I permitted the school law to be invoked has there been untoward psychologic consequence for the patient beyond transient turbulence which promptly subsided and was succeeded by more effective function. Obviously, it would not be appropriate for the severely disturbed child, whose school phobia is but one symptom of a total pattern of maladjustment. This emphasizes once again the importance of the initial diagnostic study.

When this material was presented at the 1957 Meeting of the American Psychiatric Association, the discussion offered by Dr. Norman Nixon, Director of the Child Study Center, Institute of the Pennsylvania Hospital, emphasized the importance of this therapeutic approach. With his kind permission, I quote the following excerpt from his remarks on that occasion:

In spite of this increased awareness of the problem (of school phobia), there still is much confusion about both the etiology and the treatment of school phobia. Our experience coincides with Dr. Eisenberg's and I am in complete agreement with his formulation. We also recommend that the children with school phobia who are referred to the Child Study Center be returned promptly to school following diagnostic evaluation as the first step in therapy. Unfortunately, many physicians . . . and that includes a number of psychiatrists who should know better, are still recommending the cautious handling of these children through their isolation at home on an indefinite medical excuse and a home teacher. While we see the same kinds of mother-child separation anxiety in our nursery school groups and younger school-age children, the problem is usually handled without too much difficulty. When the school-phobic child is in junior or senior high school, however, the problem is much more difficult. Yet it can be handled quite effectively in most instances, provided there is close coordination of the clinic's efforts with the school and, in some cases, the court.

It is this close coordination, however, that is difficult to attain unless the clinic, or the child's private physician, provides the leadership. Our procedure, once the diagnosis is made, is to hold a conference with the school counselor and the attendance officer. If the pediatrician or family doctor has been involved, he, too, is invited to the conference, especially if he has previously excused the child from attending school. At this time, we inform the school authorities that, in our opinion, the child is physically and psychologically able to attend school. This requires confirmation of our recommendation by the Chief of Medical Services of the Board of Education so that any previous excuses can be rescinded. The home teacher, if one had been assigned to this patient, is withdrawn.

Then follows a family conference attended by the patient and his parents and the clinic team (psychiatrist, social worker, psychologist and director of the Center). The school counselor and the attendance officer also are present to exemplify the unity of purpose of both school and clinic. Our clinical impressions are summarized and our recommendations for therapy for the child, as well as his parents, are presented. We assure the family that the child-patient is able to attend school and that we have found no reason, either physically or psychologically, why he cannot return immediately. Of course, the onus is placed on the law which says that every child of school age must be in school unless officially excused for illness. The school authorities at the conference then use the dynamic of authority. It is made clear that the child will return to school or the case will be referred to the magistrate. The clinic director emphasizes the child's (and the parent's) need for psychotherapy, but that his return to school is a prerequisite for beginning the therapeutic program.

In most cases, this procedure is successful in getting the child back in school. Here again, close cooperation is essential. During therapy, if the child does not appear in school, the counselor notifies the attendance officer immediately so that he can ascertain through direct contact with the home the day of the absence and whether it is excusable. A home visit sometimes is made and the clinic also is made aware of the situation in the event of absence, so that the family is confronted with a united front in their therapeutic sessions.

Of course, these are not easy cases to handle. Often, the pattern is of such longstanding that a long period of psychotherapy is essential. But psychotherapy alone, regardless of how intensive it is or how frequently the sessions are held, is not enough. It is the coordinated efforts of both clinic and school, together with the pediatrician or family physician, which are mandatory if the desired results are to be attained.

I have stressed the importance of a psychotherapeutic orientation toward early return to school because it is insufficiently appreciated; I do not mean thereby to imply that it is the be-all and end-all of treatment. There must be a concurrent program for the identification and correction of the neurotic components within family relations that have permitted the phobic state to crystallize and persevere. The child needs help in recognizing, expressing and accepting the conflicted feelings whose disguised derivatives cause him such anguish. His parents are just as urgently in need of insight into the sources of their neurotic interactions with each other and the child. At the outset of treatment they require a good deal of support to alleviate feelings of guilt and anger, and direct guidance in substituting construc-

tive patterns of behavior. The duration and intensity of the required therapeutic program will vary with the severity of family pathology. The acute early case in the young child can be treated effectively by the pediatrician *if* he is sensitive to psychologic issues, *if* he is willing to take the necessary time, and *if* he is able to collaborate with the school social worker in a joint therapeutic effort. The more seriously disturbed child, particularly if he is in the older age group, is best referred promptly to the psychiatric clinic for treatment.

The main therapeutic problem the physician will encounter in dealing with the mother is the task of handling her *marked ambivalence*. In the psychotherapeutic situation this takes the form of simultaneous dependence on the therapist and hostile resistance to him. He is implored to tell her what to do to get out of the impasse with the child; at the same time his suggestions are subtly sabotaged and his successes resented. Any attachment the child forms to the therapist may be jealously regarded as an intrusion on her possessive "love" affair with the child. She is apt to seek the therapist's tacit approval in displacing responsibility onto the school and to be angered by his efforts to help her to examine her own involvement. She projects onto him her dissatisfactions with her husband, her child and her own parents.

This ambivalence is best understood as a cross-sectional sample of the forces whose longitudinal development has been outlined in an earlier section of this paper. The parent is motivated by contrary emotional drives, one of which is usually denied access to her awareness so that it manifests itself covertly in her actions. Side by side with the compelling urge to retain the child as a projection of herself is resentment of the constraint his dependence imposes on her own freedom. On the one hand, she takes sustenance from his need to be with her constantly, which counterfeit of love she takes for real love; on the other, she is dismayed by his immaturity and paralysis of function. She professes to be motivated solely by tender feelings; dimly perceiving her angry impulses, she is laden with guilt. The therapist is welcomed as the agent who can help her regain health; he is feared as the person who will cost her the treasured closeness with her child.

If this amalgam of contradictory drives be understood, the therapist can avoid the error of mistaking the hostility for which he becomes the repository as directed at him personally — and of retaliating in a punitive manner. The mother's dependent needs require to be met in the initial stages of treatment without issuing any unrealistic promise of magical solutions. Only in the latter stages of therapy can they be interpreted. She must be prepared for the possibility that the child will act out his own angry feelings in a rather direct manner. The mother should be forewarned that this may be a byproduct of treatment and helped to understand that it should be no more than a transitory stage in the course of improvement. It requires to be met, with neither counterhostility nor supine acceptance, but rather with firmness tempered by understanding. If the mother is not prepared for this eventuality, she may respond to it by sudden withdrawal from treatment.

This oversimplified version of the dynamic forces at work is intended as a preliminary guide for the therapist. It should not occasion premature ex-cathedra "interpretation" to the child or parent before evidence has been secured for the relevance of these general expectancies to a particular family structure — and certainly not before the ground-work has been laid in treatment which will enable the patient to formulate these insights in native terms. It is not possible here to go further into the problems of treatment. The articles in the bibliog-raphy should be consulted for additional discussion.

It may be of interest to indicate the results that can be anticipated from this therapeutic program. I reviewed the records of 27 cases, 11 in nursery, 10 in elementary and six in junior high school and high school. Of the first group, all but one were able to adjust rapidly to a special nursery program; (2) the one child was withdrawn by her mother and lost to the study. Of the 10 elementary school children, all were able to return to school; only one

has had a serious recurrence and is again in therapy. Results were far less satisfactory in the adolescent group. Two are attending school regularly; one is a therapeutic failure; the remaining three have been in and out of school and are still in need of treat-ment (after two years of intermittent therapy).

Talbott (12) reported on the outcome in 24 pa-tients, 20 of whom were able to resume full atten-dance (two with remissions). Of the remaining four, one was able to go to school only so long as her mother remained with her in the classroom, two were not yet in school, and one moved out of the clinic area. Klein (9) indicated that seven of his 10 patients were back in school on a full-time basis; the other three were in treatment and were judged to be making progress toward the goal of return. Suttenfield (11) was able to help four or five children to resume full attendance. The papers by Waldfogel (13) and Coolidge et al. (1) do not specify the statistics of outcome, but imply largely similar results. The outcome reported in the larger series in the recent literature is summarized in the following table, which probably understates the likelihood of improvement, since lost cases as well as those in which only partial progress had been obtained are categorized together with failures.

One final word as to treatment may be in order. It is frequently stated that the initiative for con-tinuing treatment may be lost once the child has returned to school. In my own experience, only one of the 10 nursery, one of the nine elementary and neither of the two high school patients dropped out of treatment when return had been accom-plished. Of six failures, all but two have continued to seek help, albeit inconsistently.

■ TABLE 5 / Outcome of Treatment in School Phobia as Reported in the Psychiatric Literature

Investigator	Total Number in Series	Full School Attendance	Partial or Total Failure
Talbott[12] (mixed group)	24	20	4
Klein[9] (mixed group)	10	7	3
Suttenfield[11] Elementary school	3	3	0
High school	2	1	1
Eisenberg[2] Nursery school	11	10	1
Elementary school	10	9	1
High school	6	2	4
Total	66	52	14

REFERENCES

1. COOLIDGE, J. C., and others: School Phobia: Neurotic Crisis or Way of Life. *Am. J. Orthopsychiat.*, 27:296, 1957.

2. EISENBERG, L.: School Phobia: A Study in the Communication of Anxiety. *Am. J. Psychiat.*, 114:712, 1958.

3. ESTES, H. R., and others: Separation Anxiety. *Am. J. Psychotherap.*, 10:682, 1956.

4. FENICHEL, O.: *The Psychoanalytic Therapy of Neurosis.* New York, W. W. Norton & Co., 1945, p. 215.

5. HAHN, P. B.: Cooperation between Clinic and School (in the Management of School Phobia). *Am. J. Orthopsychiat.*, 27:769, 1957.

6. JOHNSON, A. M.: Discussion of paper by Coolidge et al. *Am. J. Orthopsychiat.*, 27:307, 1957.

7. JOHNSON, A. M., and others: School Phobia. *Am. J. Orthopsychiat.*, 11:702, 1941.

8. KANNER, L.: *Child Psychiatry.* 3rd ed. Springfield, Ill., Charles C Thomas, 1957.

9. KLEIN, E.: The Reluctance to Go to School; in Eissler, R. S., and others: *Psychoanalytic Study of the Child.* New York, International Universities Press, 1945, Vol. 1, p. 263.

10. LIPPMAN, H. S.: Discussion at Workshop on the Development, Meaning and Management of School Phobia. *Am. J. Orthopsychiat.*, 27:776, 1957.

11. SUTTENFIELD, V.: School Phobia: A Study of Five Cases. *Am. J. Orthopsychiat.*, 24:368, 1954.

12. TALBOTT, M.: Panic in School Phobia. *Am. J. Orthopsychiat.*, 27:286, 1957.

13. WALDFOGEL, S.: Family Relations in the Development of School Phobia. *Am. J. Orthopsychiat.*, 27:754, 1957.

MARY E. GIFFIN, ADELAIDE M. JOHNSON, AND EDWARD M. LITIN

Symposium, 1954: Antisocial Acting Out

*2. Specific Factors Determining Antisocial Acting Out**

Delinquency is unquestionably on the increase in this country. The individuals involved in such behavior, if unassociated with any gang group, can be treated, but only with the enormous expenditure of energy by highly trained people. Successful therapy of children at home can be accomplished only by intensive collaborative treatment of parents and child. Successful treatment of the average *neurotic* adolescent is a simple task, by contrast.

For treatment to be rational, etiology must be explicit. Arrival at our understanding of clinical evidence for etiology has necessitated drastic changes in our previous understanding of traditional psychoanalytic theory. Psychoanalysts' first interest was in the neuroses, and with few exceptions research has been concerned largely with this aspect of psychopathology. In understanding the neuroses one conceives of a too-punitive superego. Until recently, pathology of the superego was viewed only in terms of its being too punishing to patients. For years any antisocial acting out was explained in terms of a patient's being excessively guilty about conflicts or being driven by constitutionally unmanageable instinctual drives. The reflected preventive attitude for all patients has been "Do not repress the child so drastically or he will become neurotic or act out."

Therapists, as well as parents, have become greatly confused, thinking that prohibitions in all forms lead to too much guilt and thus, neurosis. Some therapists have unwittingly permitted and fostered acting out in, especially, the sexual sphere. Prohibitions in themselves do not lead to unhealthy guilt; rather, they are an important aspect of security. So far as the prevention of neurosis is concerned, the prohibition of antisocial activity merely requires the presence of a parent sufficiently well integrated to accept in legitimate ways the hostility expressed by the child over the limit-setting that society demands.

* Reprinted from *American Journal of Orthopsychiatry*, Vol. 24, 1954, pp. 668–684. Copyright, the American Orthopsychiatric Association, Inc. Reproduced by permission.

It has become increasingly clear that many parents, particularly those with poorly integrated impulses, have become uneasy about setting limits, even concerning matters which are specifically destructive to society, such as stealing, sexuality or even murderous intent. Yet it is evident that certain specific things, such as stealing, fire-setting, murder and sexual destructiveness, cannot be countenanced in our society — they must be prohibited completely and definitively. As most of us clearly recognize, there is, then, specific behavior, the expression of which should arouse guilt in everyone. The guilt alone is not unhealthy. Neurosis need be feared only if great rage has been repressed, along with the prohibition of such antisocial activity.

Our concern in this paper is with the development of that form of pathologic superego which permits antisocial behavior. Clinical evidence shows it to be lacunar, weak in some respects, punitive in some and normal in still other areas.

Many people have strong latent antisocial impulses, yet never act out such fantasies. We are concerned with defining the specific stimulus to the acting-out behavior. We shall first consider the problems of the direct acting out of forbidden antisocial impulses; namely, stealing, truancy, fire-setting and direct sexual acting out. Later in the paper, we shall consider the problems found in those *structurally* more complicated cases in which acting out is associated with perversions.

Since the early work of Szurek and one of us (Johnson) (7), collaborative studies on antisocial acting out have continued. From the initial studies emerged the thesis that antisocial acting out in a child is unconsciously initiated, fostered and sanctioned by the parents, who vicariously achieve gratification of their own poorly integrated forbidden impulses through a child's acting out. One or both parents in addition unconsciously experience gratification for their own hostile and destructive wishes toward the child, who is repeatedly destroyed by his behavior. It is possible in every case adequately studied to trace the specific conscience defect in the child to a mirror image of similar type and emotional charge in the parent. The focus of these observations has been not on the activities of the kind seen among deprived and other sociologically determined gang groups, but rather among individual children of poor or of privileged class, frequently from families of "good" reputation and high social standing.

The superego defects in these children are frequently in only one or two areas and are rarely widespread. A child may steal, but never be truant. Another may set fires and do nothing else that is anti-social. In another, only the sexual sphere will be implicated through the acting out. To be sure, like other people, these patients have neuroses with conflict and guilt, but they have also the superego weakness in one or more areas, permitting discharge of tension.

There is frequently confusion regarding the use of the phrase "acting out." The expression "acting in the transference" was first used recurrently by Freud to refer to the phenomenon which was seen during psychoanalytic therapy in which the neurotic patient repeated in the transference, without insight, certain salient episodes of his earlier life.

Eduardo Weiss (13) aptly described it in the following way: "By acting out is meant the behavior of a person who repeats without insight an unconscious psychic situation out of his past in terms of current reality. A man, for instance, repeats intense feelings of hostility towards his brothers and sisters by quarreling with his fellow workers."

Weiss continued, "Freud considered transference as a form of acting-out. According to Freud one acts out instead of remembering. However, psychoanalytic experience teaches us that patients in analysis often act out emotional situations which they have already remembered." Weiss stated that "Freud's formulation can be modified by saying that one acts-out instead of remembering fully with the appropriate attending emotions." He continued, "While acting-out is a substitute for recall, it does not have the therapeutic effect of the latter. The patient who acts out has still to acknowledge that *his present behavior is a reproduction of past experiences.*" Weiss concluded, "I agree fully with Anna Freud who says that the patient who acts-out *exclusively* cannot be analyzed."

In more recent years the phrase "acting out" has come to be used almost exclusively in referring to that behavior against authority which is specifically forbidden by our society. Actually, except for the moral issue, there is no sharp line of demarcation between the acting in the transference and the kind of phenomenon expressed by the unconscious acting-out problems with which we are here dealing. This is in keeping with the view commonly held today: That ego and superego are not separate entities, but merge imperceptibly on the spectrum of reality testing. At one end are observed highly moral aspects of the ego; here there can be no alternatives to conforming morally. Proceeding to the opposite end of the spectrum, increasingly complicated alternatives and choices become obviously permissible, since ethics is not involved; it is more in this latter area that acting out during analysis occurs.

The provocative contributions of Reich (10), Alexander and Healy (2), Healy and Bronner (5), Schmideberg (11), Gardner (4) and many others have been extensively reviewed in our previous communications. It was Aichhorn (1) whose contributions first unquestionably moved delinquency out of the nihilistic depths of constitutional inheritance, into the realm of dynamic understanding. Every worker in the field of childhood and adolescent acting out has been stimulated by and greatly indebted to this man who genuinely understood delinquents.

We follow the emphasis of Szurek (12), who as early as 1942 described the psychopathic personality as being only a delinquent grown older, as an individual defective in personality organization, specifically in the individual's conscience. Szurek distinguished those individuals from the sociologically stimulated gang lawbreakers, and presented one of the earliest contributions to the dynamic understanding of these problems. He wrote, "Clinical experience leaves the impression that the definition of psychopathic personality is no greater mystery than other syndromes in psychopathology. Almost literally, in no instance in which adequate psychiatric therapeutic study of both parent and child has been possible has it been difficult to obtain sufficient evidence to reconstruct the chief dynamics of the situation. Regularly, the more important parent, usually the mother, although the father is always in some way involved, has been seen unconsciously to encourage the amoral or antisocial behavior of the child."

It is impossible to understand the dynamic concepts behind the behavior of these individuals unless one has clearly in mind the development of the normal superego. One must understand the reaction of the well-integrated parent, and the subtle conscious and unconscious ways in which this behavior directs the development of the child's superego. Identification with the parent consists of more than incorporation of the manifest behavior of the parent; it necessarily involves inclusion of the subtleties of the parent's conscious and unconscious image of the child. The healthy parent fantasies his child as capable of becoming law abiding. The well-integrated, mature mother does *not* immediately check on a child following an order or request; she unconsciously assumes that the order will be carried out. The neurotic mother, who immediately checks or warns that if the job is not done dire consequences will follow, merely conveys to the child that an unstated alternative exists in the mother's mind. It is frequently with this alternative image in the mother's thoughts that the child more strongly identifies. This is true because the child senses the peculiar parental emotional need conveyed in the anxious, vacillating tone of the parent's expression.

The child internalizes, then, not only the positive, socially consistent attitudes of the parent, but also the frequently unexpressed, ambivalent antisocial feelings. We cannot agree with those who state that the child identifies only with idealized aspects of the parent. The child identifies with all facets of the parent — to be sure, repressing those parental characteristics which cause conscious confusion, anxiety and shame.

The patients with whom we are specifically concerned in this paper are those manifesting what are frequently called "superego lacunae." The apparent "punched-out" aspect of this kind of superego is misleading except from the point of view of society. From the point of view of the patient there is a positive, undeniable drive toward acting in the manner in which the parent unconsciously wishes, even though it be antisocial in direction. The conception of a deficit within the superego structure must be elaborated to include the overwhelming parentally determined dynamic push toward antisocial behavior which the child senses and with which he necessarily complies. Although we are not here concerned with sociologically delinquent gang members, there is frequently overlapping of the individuals who act out antisocially, these latter often moving into gangs.

If our thesis is correct that parents unconsciously initiate and foster antisocial behavior in order to experience gratification for themselves, accurate documentary evidence must be defined in answer to two basic questions:

1. How is sanctioning communicated to the child?
2. Why is one child implicated in a family in which all of the other children are quite conforming?

Not only is it possible by careful questioning and observation to define the process by which a specific child is chosen and the dynamic factors behind the choice of a particular form of socially disapproved behavior, but it is also possible to detect the highly personal technique by which the parent transmits the double talk, interest, permissive tone or structured situation by which the activity is fostered.

During the process of definitive treatment, it is clearly seen why one child becomes emotionally chosen to be the outlet of expression for these forbidden impulses. An adopted child, whose behavior can be blamed on heredity, becomes a natural victim through whom to express antisocial trends, with simultaneous expression of hostile feelings in the parent toward this child. Sometimes the only son of a woman who is disturbed by unresolved hostile dependent problems with her own father, and permitted by her own mother to carry on petty stealing, may become the means of expressing both her unconscious anger and her poorly integrated stealing impulses through her fostering such socially destructive activities in her child.

Proper understanding of case material is impossible unless one is aware of the many innuendoes of communication which occur without conscious awareness between parents and child. Such communications are by all conceivable means of approach sometimes errors of omission, frequently ones of frank commission. Knowing *what* to listen for, and *how*, the diagnostician gradually defines these operations from direct quotations, double talk, facial expressions, and often through histrionic portrayal by some parents who dramatize the actual interchange between themselves and the child. In the more subtle cases the casuistic, disingenuous rationalizations of these parents can reduce the whole spirit of an ethical principle to a quibbling absurdity.

The specific manner in which, for instance, the truancy from home was handled on a particular day must be obtained; frequently, when this is done, one finds that the mother met the girl with the comment, "If you don't like us and our house, find another; we can get along without you." If this mother is merely asked for adjectival descriptions of the relationship between herself and Jennie she will, without realizing it, forget to indicate this kind of response.

The entranced parental facial expression apparent to the child describing a stealing episode, a sexual misdemeanor, or a hostile attitude toward a teacher conveys to the child that the parent is achieving some pleasurable gratification. No amount of subsequent punishment will act as a deterrent against the recurrences of the acting out. A child wishes to do the thing which he senses gives the parent pleasure, even though he may be punished. We frequently see parents who describe the child's delinquent behavior with obvious pleasure. Suspicious questioning often conveys the parents' unconscious wish that the child comply by doing the thing *verbally* warned against.

Frequently, parents verbalize evasion and deceptions such as, "Here is an extra quarter, but don't tell your father"; "You can get into the movie for half-price, since you certainly don't look twelve years old"; "Fires are dangerous, but if you must get it out of your system, then we'll set some in the yard."

A mother can make such a suggestion, yet she would never recommend that her child take a trial run in front of cars on the street. The mother of a 14-year-old girl was not genuinely interested in prohibiting her child's stealing; she said to her daughter,

"Why did you take the money from your *aunt's* purse instead of from mine?"

Children hear their parents gloating about short-changing the grocer; naturally they sense the parental pleasure. Some parents do not follow through when the facts of stealing are perfectly clear. For instance, they hesitate to go with the child to the dime store to make proper restitution for a stolen trinket. A mother who has poorly integrated prohibitions concerning her own hostile sexual impulses may fantasy that her eight-year-old daughter will "get into sexual difficulties" as adolescence approaches. With her provocative warnings accompanied by anxiety she is a predictable stimulus to vacillating sexual behavior in such a child.

We frequently have patients whose parents tell the child to ask the physician for permission to do something they already well understand to be forbidden. Parents complain of *children's* breaking family rules when the parents themselves consciously or unconsciously break rule after rule and promise after promise without apology or comment.

The process of vicarious gratification now becomes clearer. The antisocial behavior of the implicated child becomes a means of parental expression by which poorly integrated antisocial impulses of the parent are expressed through the child. As Emch (3) lucidly stated it, the child is "acting-out the caricatured reproduction of past parental behavior." In addition to this use as a mode of expression for parental impulses; such a child is the recipient of a hostile destructive drive in the parent; in close relationship lie vicarious gratification through the child and the wish to destroy this same child. Such family behavior in the end is destructive to both the parent's ego organization and that of the child.

For purposes of research, particularly, but also for the proper controlled therapy of nonresidential acting-out patients, collaborative therapy is the only adequate technique. There continues to be misunderstanding about the actual procedure, and it must therefore be pointed out that the term "collaborative therapy," as we use it, refers to that particular form of dynamic psychotherapy in which the individual treatment hours of each patient are reviewed in great detail, hour by hour, among all the psychiatrists acting as therapists. It is not the task of a social work follow-up, nor is it concomitant therapy in which two individuals of the same family unit are undergoing therapy during the same period of time; it is a form of highly specialized therapy in which the individual treatment is intensive and the interchange between therapists is regular and frequent. The availability of each physician to the other must be immediate. Material pertinent to the current problem is discussed openly between therapists and with the patients, as it may be useful to them. Transference problems arising from such interchange of timely material are actively analyzed. The purpose and advantage lie in the convenient interchange of information between therapists, material which helps the understanding of each patient and hastens the treatment of all. By means of it, adequate and suitably timed limit-setting is possible, long before its need might be apparent in individual therapy.

ANTISOCIAL ACTING OUT: ILLUSTRATIVE CASES

Scientific proof of causation is not satisfied merely by demonstrating the invariable presence of the suspected cause (unwitting parental permissiveness) whenever the effect (antisocial behavior of children) is observed. In addition, it must also be shown that whenever the suspected cause is present, the effect is also seen. Our first case demonstrates the factors that must be satisfied for scientific proof of causation.

Stealing — Ten years ago one of us was asked to treat a young single woman of 22 years who was depressed. Her married sister, the only relative in that city, came to give some family history and assist with medical arrangements. At that interview, this sister, in commenting on the personalities of her *own* three children, said of her only son, 9-year-old Mark, "He runs circles around us all—he is so brilliant that schoolwork is no challenge to him. I often wish he had been born more dumb so he would be forced to work hard. I tell him that since his schoolwork requires no effort, he will never learn how hard it is to make an honest living. He has not stolen yet, that I know of, but I cannot see him working hard to make an honest living."

We were very interested at the time in recording these exact words because they indicated a hostile wish and image that the boy not be a straightforward citizen. In the course of 2½ years' treatment of Mark's 22-year-old maternal aunt, it was observed that her oldest brother, Bob, a brilliant fellow, was always permitted by his parents to cut corners to the point of frank cheating and stealing. Although his parents ostensibly favored him over the girls by this sanctioning, they were literally destroying him, and the law finally intervened. He was imprisoned for a few years, to the bitter humiliation of our patient and Mark's mother.

By the time Mark was 12 years old his parents came to see us because he had been caught with another boy stealing four jackknives from a sporting-goods store. Needless to say, when questioned closely the parents had absolute evidence of stealing from the mother's purse for at least a year; the only punishment for such transgressions had been a casual remark, which is now so familiar to us, "You are just Uncle Bob over again." In brief, when that mother became our patient, it was unmistakably clear that all Mark's life she had identified him with her hated brother and conveyed this image to the boy in countless ways.

The most alarming attitudes were those expressed quite unconsciously in the diagnostic interview with the parents as they related the episode of the stolen jacknives. When the parents were asked if they had any ideas as to why the child had stolen the knives, the mother immediately answered, *and* to the father's great discomfort, "Children don't realize it, but grownups know that stealing and cheating are on the short route to seriously injuring someone."

The husband burst out angrily, "Jean, your wild ideas run away with you. What do you mean? Mark has never hurt anyone. You've always had him so scared stiff of you that he won't even play a little baseball, let alone hurt anyone."

To this the wife responded angrily, "You don't listen to me — I've been telling you that for the past year when I slap him his eyes blaze with anger — there's terrible temper there, even if he does not *say* anything." Later in her treatment the mother's fantasies that this boy could steal and murder *"if driven to it"* had to be actively dealt with as a manifestation of her own fantasies. The normal parent neither anticipates impending disaster nor dismisses monetary or other transgressions as trivial.

When one discovers the presence of stealing in one family member, its occurrence in at least one other is predictable. Such a relationship is also true of firesetting, truancy and direct hostile or sexual acting out. A case of the last is appropriate.

Direct murderous acting out. — Very attractive, prominent parents in a large city came with their 14-year old adopted son for study. There were three older sisters, and one older brother, all unadopted. The parents' only concern was that sexually their son might not be developing normally — that his slight plumpness might be an endocrine problem. Fortunately, this boy was away in a private school from the age of 10 years, yet when he came home on vacations the mother bathed him, cleaned his penis thoroughly and felt of his testes, ostensibly to ascertain if they were firm and large enough. She laughingly spoke of her amusement when her son called her by the name of a currently enticing actress as she herself strutted about in the nude. She complained bitterly of how defiant her boy was, yet when questioned by her husband, she could not describe any real naughtiness. The boy did surreptitiously take out anger in mild ways on colleagues — yet never had he dared an open battle. When this mother was alone with us, without the father's being present, she described fantasies which aptly reflect her image of her son's future. We could hardly believe the material spontaneously given by this well-dressed, intelligent, attractive woman.

"He is very affectionate — he hugs and kisses me. The school wanted his eyes checked for blinking. I wanted his male organs checked — they seem too small. His brother's seem bigger and firmer. He says I'm prettier than he — nicer in the breasts. We like our baths together. I'm afraid to turn him loose with boys for what he might do — a bad blow — afraid for him to have a gun. I worry he might rape or butcher someone — not just sexually. There are cases of boys who carved up people's organs, heads and faces. I have the feeling that an attraction to a girl would develop in him a wish to mutilate her — stab her in the back, slice her throat, cut her from head to foot."

When the father was seen alone, he was, of course, not told of the mother's fantasies given to us, but in relating the family history he described his wife's background. Her father was brutal to her mother when he was drunk, a condition which was habitual. He was always kindly to our patient and she adored him. When she was 6 years old she saw her intoxicated father beat up the mother and throw her cruelly across the room. The 20-year-old son in the family picked up a bat and crushed his father's skull, killing him. This son, the maternal uncle of our 14-year-old patient, was imprisoned for a time. Our unfortunate parent, bewildered at what could happen and indeed did happen before her eyes as a child, had no capacity within herself to believe in her own son's control. It was not surprising that the mother, however, implicated the adopted son's heredity.

The boy himself, attractive and well built, showed the most rigid compulsive defensive attempt at inner control associated with considerable depression. His unconscious fantasy life was filled with murder, retribution, and "then everyone lived happily in the end."

In the foregoing case we see the poorly integrated seductive and hostile components of the mother's personality tragically coercing her son into mounting rage over the seduction, rage completely frightening in view of *her* concept of how anger is handled. These are truly terrifying cases, and often initially in treatment, for safety's sake, the child is treated best by removal to the medical floor of a hospital. The apparent mystery of adolescent homicides can be quickly dissipated if adequate background material is available.

TREATMENT OF ANTISOCIAL ACTING OUT

Since our concepts of etiology are relatively new, we cannot detail the therapeutic procedures employed with any finality. The broad outlines of therapy, however, may be indicated. Most of our treatment has dealt with the adolescent who comes to the clinic and lives at home — this has permitted more adequate focus on etiology, research which has necessitated close study of the parents as well as of the child. In this communication we must restrict ourselves to the mention of basic tenets. It should be remembered that the task is prodigious. One adolescent girl and her parents now in treatment under the three authors' care involve a minimum of 12 hours a week, and this for months and years.

Frequently, the child with acting-out problems is brought to treatment only after a series of pressures from neighbors, teachers and often the law. At times a younger child is brought at the insistence of one parent who is better integrated than the other. Implicit in these situations is the fact that motivation for treatment is often superficial and ambivalent. Obviously, a parent who receives gratification, albeit unconscious, is not anxious to remove his source of supply, and a child attempting to satisfy parental wishes is not driven to seek help which will separate him from a needed parent. Frequently, however, by the time an *adolescent* comes to treatment he is frightened by the increasing discrepancy between parental and social standards, and he appears as a sullen, distraught and confused child.

No area in psychoanalysis involves the possibility of greater intensity of countertransference problems than the realm of delinquency. Disruption of treatment frequently follows inadequate resolution of such problems. A few aspects of this problem can be discussed.

1. The use of collaborative therapy in the handling of any psychiatric problem involves the proper resolution of countertransference problems. All collaborative therapy is based on the premise that we are dealing with family pathology; a therapist's overidentification with his patient, and narcissistic competitive complications arising from such overidentification create chaos. It must not matter *which* patient gets well first; the goal of successful collaborative therapy is the recovery of *all* members of the family.

2. The problem of limit-setting, even though dynamically timed, is disturbing to some therapists. The resorting to the historical concept of the analyst as

utterly noninterfering may well be used as a rationalization for some vicarious gratification on the part of the therapist, achieved through the acting out. Brian Bird has elaborated extensively and with very apt illustrations on this point in his discussion of this paper.

3. It must be remembered that even healthy parents are not omnipotent; actually they do make mistakes. Therapists who cannot face these facts develop such contempt for erring parents and such over-identification with the child that they cannot casually and directly point out a lie, deception, or confusing corruption in a parent, and deal with the immediate hostility. Every good therapist grows with each patient he treats; likewise, every parent has the right to grow with his child in treatment.

4. Just as in the treatment of a neurosis in which the patient may relapse or become more disturbed, so in the treatment of acting-out problems, the mature therapist does not become discouraged or contemptuous when some complicated re-educational measure has not taken hold as yet, or when some hitherto unrecognized pressure leads to recurrence of acting out.

We shall mention a few rules relative to the treatment of the child, followed by generalizations about therapy of the parents. Treatment of the child must take into account the following:

1. As many have recognized, the patients most successfully treated on a clinic basis are those who are able to develop early some positive feelings for the therapist.

2. Any initiation of interviews by asking a child to give an account of misdemeanors only pushes him into further falsification.

3. We are aware that the normal superego develops through identification with a parent who unconsciously assumes that the child will learn to be as honest as the parent; we assume that similar identification is possible, in time, with these delinquent children if they are able to make some contact with us. We indicate that in time, as we know each other, the adolescent will find himself handling these troublesome matters more and more easily. This is a detailed meticulous re-education process, in which the therapist assumes that the child has capabilities eventually to learn a new mastery of impulses heretofore unconsciously given free rein.

4. Since for a long time the child has known consciously or unconsciously that his antisocial behavior was ambiguously condoned at home, he has developed a pattern of expectation that adults will overlook misdemeanors. The therapist's own corruptibility is immediately tested, since the child automatically responds in his usual pattern. When we are positive of the facts, we catch little things early, so that the child does not commit greater misdemeanors and then feel betrayed when we interfere with only a large issue.

5. We certainly do *not* begin by asking a child why he acted out. He does not yet know that this behavior is in keeping with the parent's wish that he comply in this fashion. We shall see how this comes about in treatment.

6. The initiation of dynamic therapy, associated with limit-setting, the core of re-education, comes about in the following way.

All therapists watch for the first current evidence showing unmistakably that parents themselves are acting out with the child. For instance, when all three therapists agree that such an act is a fact, then each takes it up with the patients involved. A short illustration will make this more clear.

The seductive father of an adolescent girl who was acting out sexually finally confessed, with considerable anxiety, that he had called his daughter an "s.o.b." and a "whore." The father's therapist helped him understand that his regret would be meaningful to his daughter, should she know from her therapist of her father's real concern and remorse about the outburst.

For some time the child's therapist had known that this girl was overwhelmed by some very disturbing comment from her father, whom at one time she had loved very much. She had been unable, however, to mention the distressing names. When the therapist told the child that her father had expressed great remorse about having used these epithets, the child reflected amazement, followed by a pathetic inquiry, "You mean he really told *that?*"

This was the first evidence of real anxiety and conflict in the girl, and it was followed by a rather dramatic deepening of attachment to the therapist.

Again, when the mother broke a very definite rule that had been established between the three patients, this was called to her attention at once. When this was discussed with the daughter, it had truly dynamic merit in making her more consciously aware of her previous *automatic* compliance with the mother's uninhibited behavior. If parents break rules continuously with evasions, the child automatically does the same. The collaborator treating the child can tactfully discuss with the child any matter about which the family has confusion and of which they had been unaware.

Treatment of the parents is probably a more formidable and prolonged procedure than that of the child. Therapists differ in their views as to the means of successful enlistment into treatment of parents of any child, neurotic or delinquent. Every therapist must handle this in the manner which works most successfully for him. We have some definite views on this matter, ideas which have been elaborated in another communication (6). Detecting the clues of unconscious permission as they operate between parents and child, and bringing this to the parent's awareness, naturally arouses anxiety and anger. This must be dealt with very actively, and the anger must be absorbed by the therapist, who maintains his stand with society on the corrupting issue. The parents unconsciously try every artifice and perfidy to engage the therapist in condoning the forbidden issue in question. After hours of accepting the anger, but with no capitulation on the moral issue, one can begin to see better integration within the parent. This, however, is achieved only by active analysis of all transference indications of mounting tension related to the parental neurotic equilibrium that is now being disturbed by the limit-setting.

Many therapists seriously question the wisdom of helping the child to recognize the manner in which the parents unwittingly operate. These skeptics maintain that such recognition detracts from the parents' esteem and mobilizes unmanageable guilt in both parents and child. However, therapy cannot be a swindle; the problems recognized unconsciously by all participants must be made conscious. Hilde Bruch, in her discussion, emphasizes that confidentiality between patient and therapist becomes a mockery when a patient unconsciously feels he is engaging his therapist in a contract of secret misrepresentation. When we call a deception to the patient's awareness with no contempt on our part, but with firmness and friendliness, absorbing the anger, the patient can then begin to deal with the real issues. It is remarkable to observe the almost revelatory experience with which the parent suddenly becomes conscious for the first time of his own deceptive heritage.

PROBLEMS OF SEXUAL ABERRATION

As with the direct activities of stealing and fire-setting, so with the perversions: One can invariably detect, with proper study, the interdigitation of parent-and-child conflicts. These are dynamically more complicated cases because of the additional regressive step which will be elaborated. Many individuals become aware, particularly during the course of psychotherapy, of strong latent homosexual, transvestite or exhibitionistic trends, yet it never occurs to them to act out such fantasies, just as many neurotics show tendencies to set fires or steal, yet never act out such desires. We are here concerned with evaluating the specific stimuli to the overt behavior.

The etiology of perverse behavior follows a similar, but more complicated, pattern to that of direct acting out. With proper means of research it is possible to define: 1) the specific details of a confused and unsatisfactory parental relationship; 2) evidences of pathologic seduction of a particular child, with condoning by the other parent; 3) a pattern of genital frustration following the initial pattern of seduction; 4) the impetus from the parent toward an abnormal pattern of sexual behavior.

As an antisocial acting out, the choice of the specific child in terms of the parents' background and neurosis is similarly definable. This is a very simplified statement of the factors entering into the acting out of aberrant sexuality. One must keep in mind that this is no simple one-to-one relationship, but rather, a relationship which depends upon all of these factors' interrelating with the total intrapsychic life of the patient.

It is necessary to understand that by the term "seduction" we are referring to a pathologic form of a parental sexual temptation which is completely inappropriate temporally for the child. Under the guise of tenderness, it confronts the child with an ambivalent, genital passion which he cannot understand or begin to integrate. Faced with what is overtly parental love, he becomes unconsciously aware of the hostile parental feelings; in incest or with genital frustration the hostile guilty, shameful feelings of the parent are absorbed by the child, who experiences in himself confusion, guilt, fear of detection and anxiety. Out of the parents' own guilt another form of personally acceptable sexual expression must be defined. Unconsciously, this has been previously emphasized by the parent during the polymorphous sexual period of the child.

How is the defining of a permitted regressed (perverse) outlet to the tension *generated* by seduction and frustration? Here we must observe the very early pregenital behavior of the child and mother, beginning with the ambivalence of the oral dependency on up to the genital struggles. In these cases of perversion we always see overstressing of at least one aspect of polymorphous sexual behavior of the young child, such as to lead to unusual selective hypertrophy. Although at such an early age there is no orgasm, and therefore this cannot be called a "perversion," still the hypertrophy can be so *profound* and *organized* that we cannot accept this as just the unorganized sexuality of the polymorphous perverse child. We shall not include here a report on a child of this age; a case in which extreme transvestitism began in a child at 2½ years is now in press (9).

We shall present only one case of adolescent perversion, that of exhibitionism.

A 17-year-old boy was apprehended by the police while exhibiting himself to three young women in a park. Investigation revealed that although the boy's transgressions never had been brought to the attention of the police before, certain neighbors had complained of his behavior to his parents for the three years preceding the incident in question. Medical help was not spontaneously sought by the moderately wealthy parents, both of whom were active in civic organizations.

Both parents were seen separately and together diagnostically. The father was humiliated and filled with rage and contempt toward the boy.

"I've been telling his mother for years that that kid would come to a bad end with her coddling and drooling over him like a spoiled pup. I despise her youngest brother, who was pampered and coddled by his mother — he isn't worth a darn. Of course, I admit his father never paid an hour's attention to him in his life, and then probably only to pull a few strings with politicians to bail him out of jams. I know my wife has been ashamed a hundred times of her brother, but she gets furious if I say one word of truth about the bum."

The mother was first interviewed by a man. The interviewer was immediately aware of her frank, rather intimate, seductive approach. No sign of anxiety was apparent in this woman.

When asked what she thought about the immediate problem, she said, "I don't understand Don — we have always been completely frank with each other about everything, but when I try to talk to him about this, he won't talk."

When the interviewer remained silent, she went on, "He is our only son and so many terrible mistakes were made with my youngest brother that I vowed to keep things friendly and frank with our boy. I've answered all his questions and he has told me everything until now. I admit he didn't tell me about these other things with women, and I didn't talk to him because I knew he would tell me in due time — my husband was so angry that I wouldn't let him talk to Don, but I can't trust my husband — he gets so angry and rigid with the child."

At this point the psychiatrist asked the mother if she could give some elaboration of how frank and confidential the boy had been with her. This opened a recital of wholly unconscious tragic seduction and unhealthy intimacy between this mother and Don. There were no restrictions on nudity, or the bathroom, and talk was endless about sexual matters. The mother went into great detail with the boy about her own sexual life, to the point of revealing frequency of intercourse, her husband's hostile demands, and her rearing concerning the duties of a wife.

The 15-year-old daughter, from 7 years on, would have none of this frankness; she demanded privacy in the bathroom and would not be lured into sexual discussions.

The father frequently rebuked the mother for carrying on her "long harangues" with the boy and shouted that he would be better off "learning stuff the hard way on the streets," as he did.

There is no need to include the boy's great detail in describing his mother's appearance, her breasts and other anatomic attributes; these attitudes of her son were given by the mother with a dreamy, pleasurable expression. She herself expanded at length about her son's fine physique, including what she called his "beautiful masculine endowment." The seduction between mother and son was obvious to any listener.

But how did this boy come to choose exhibitionism as a means of discharging his rage and sexual drive? The mother fostered and showed the keenest interest in exhibiting herself and in looking at the nude boy from his earliest years. Until Don was 13 he and the mother often showered together, especially when the father was away on trips. The mother commented, "Loneliness brings one closer to a child."

The boy hated his father; as this mutual dislike mounted, Don and the mother became even closer. Subsequent interviews with the mother revealed a most unhappy marriage, the husband being engrossed in business as well as openly flirtatious with other women; the mother was humiliated, but unable, because of her own background and conflicts, truly to enter a love relationship with her husband.

Don, a handsome, strongly built boy, was barely defending himself against murderous feelings toward both parents. His identifications with them were so confused as to suggest that no treatment was safe without his initial removal from home. Intensive therapy for Don, his mother and father was necessary.

TREATMENT OF PERVERSIONS

We shall give only the briefest summary of basic ideas concerning the collaborative therapy of a case of perversion. More detailed material is now in press.

In this group of cases it is imperative to have preliminary interviews with parents before the child is even seen, since these children are even more withdrawn, sullen and uncommunicative than many of the other delinquents. The initial contacts divulge the basic clinical data, exposing unconscious seduction and unwitting condoning of the perverse outlet. Such material is used as the steppingstone to the therapy of parents and child as well, making possible the enlistment into treatment of a child who might otherwise be lost.

During the interviews with the parent it is possible to define two sets of clues; the first, seductive; the second, permissive. The first include incidents and conversations which reveal current, unconscious, ambivalent seduction, such as sleeping with the child, nudity or excessive freedom in the bathroom. The second group of clues consists of evidences of parental permissiveness, distinguising the special form of permitted perversion or abnormal sexuality. With the interpretation of specific examples of unconscious seduction and unconscious permission, the dynamic therapy of parent and child begins.

These are in part acting-out problems between all participants. Early limits must be set with parents and child about the current ambivalent seduction, whether it be sleeping together, bathing together, mutual bathroom gratifications or nudities. From the child's point of view, when such seduction ceases he does not have so strongly the original need to act out through the perverse outlet. From the parents' point of view, as soon as a limit is set on the parents' seductive behavior toward the child, great tension will develop in the parent stemming from his own poorly integrated sexual drives and the associated hostility. This must be very actively analyzed in the transference. Usually, the first evidence of the tension in the transference is acute anger of the parent toward the therapist. As this is absorbed by the therapist in a manner quite different from the parents' experience with their own parents, the transference deepens, and analysis of the distorted genital and pregenital life of the patient is under way.

As treatment progresses, if the child continues perverse acting out, it means either that seduction has transpired at home or that the child's therapist has appeared as a seductive threat. In the first instance, information from the combined treatment hours permits more definite limit-setting. In the second, transference material must be more actively analyzed. With etiology more explicit, experimental technical modifications in the treatment of adult overt homosexuals have been presented in a paper now in press (8).

When the acting out then seems well controlled in all patients, analysis proceeds as in any complicated neurosis, with intensive therapy for the resolution of all the complex pregenital fixations inherent in these disorders.

SUMMARY

In this communication we have discussed the etiology of individual antisocial acting out, and of sexual aberrations. Latent unconscious impulses to steal, set fires and murder, as well as fantasies about such practices as homosexuality and transvestitism, are frequently seen in many patients. We have been concerned with defining the specific stimuli to their becoming overt.

Antisocial acting out is seen as a superego defect which stems from unconscious parental initiation and fostering because of poorly integrated forbidden impulses in the parents. These impulses, and their permission to be acted upon, are communicated usually unconsciously to the child. In his acting out the child affords to the parents vicarious gratification for their own forbidden impulses, and concomitantly satisfies parental destructive feelings toward the child. Such behavior is destructive toward both the child's and parent's ego organization, as well as toward society, unless adequate collaborative therapy is instituted.

Sexual aberrations are seen to develop as a result of ego adaptation to highly specific, often unconscious, family attitudes impinging on the child; these attitudes subtly coerce and distort the child's psychosexual development. The parent, because of his own problems, unconsciously seduces the child, then sets *genital* limits and unwittingly defines the direction for regressed perverse outlets.

The emphasis of this paper has been on factors in etiology. The basic tenets important in intensive collaborative therapy of parents and children stem from a more rational concept of etiology. Our thesis necessitates the early establishment of definite limits to behavior, the timing of which varies with the case. As has been seen, the concepts emerging in this paper place the emphasis in acting-out problems on a pathologic superego which is weak in certain specific areas; this is in contrast to the neurotic superego, which is too punitive.

It is the responsibility of psychiatrists to resolve the confusion in the treatment of individuals with weak superego structure. To be sure, we are cognizant of the confusion which accompanies transition from puritanic mores of a culture to greater individuation. But it is not alone this transition which has led to many improper treatment plans, and far too permissive, ill-defined, so-called preventive psychiatric suggestions to parents. With clearer definition of etiologic factors in this group of patients, we are in a better position to be definitive about when we should be permissive of anger in order to offset neurosis, and when we must be prohibitive of amoral impulses in order to prevent acting out. No one should give tacit consent to behavior which acts against the individual's best interests in our society. Parents increasingly can be helped to absorb and to channel in constructive fashion the child's hostilities when society's prohibitions are imposed emphatically. When psychiatrists achieve greater clarity, parents, educators and those executing the law will function with less confusion.

REFERENCES

1. AICHHORN, AUGUST. *Wayward Youth.* (Transl. from 2nd German ed.) Viking Press, New York, 1935.
2. ALEXANDER, FRANZ, and WILLIAM HEALY. *Roots of Crime.* Knopf, New York, 1935.
3. EMCH, MINNA. *On the "Need to Know" as Related to Identification and Acting Out.* Internat. J. Psa., 25: 13–19, 1944.
4. GARDNER, GEORGE. E. Personal communication to the authors.
5. HEALY, WILLIAM, and AUGUSTA F. BRONNER. *New Light on Delinquency and its Treatment.* Yale Univ. Press, New Haven, 1936.
6. JOHNSON, ADELAIDE M. "Collaborative Psychotherapy: Team Setting," in *Psychoanalysis and Social Work* (Marcel Heiman, Ed.), pp. 79–108. Internat. Univ. Press, New York, 1953.
7. JOHNSON, ADELAIDE M., and S. A. SZUREK. *The Genesis of Antisocial Acting Out in Children and Adults.* Psa. Quart., 21: 323–343, 1952.
8. KOLB, L. C., and ADELAIDE M. JOHNSON. *Etiology of Overt Homosexuality and the Need for Therapeutic Modification.* Psa. Quart., in press.
9. LITIN, E. M., MARY E. GIFFIN, and ADELAIDE M. JOHNSON. *Parental Influence in Unusual Sexual Behavior in Children.* Psa. Quart., in press.
10. REICH, WILHELM. *Der triebhafte Charakter.* Internat. Psa. Verlag, Vienna, 1925.
11. SCHMIDEBERG, MELITTA. *The Mode of Operation of Psychoanalytic Therapy.* Internat. J. Psa., 19: 314, 1938.
12. SZUREK, S. A. *Notes on the Genesis of Psychopathic Personality Trends.* Psychiatry, 5: 1–6, 1942.
13. WEISS, EDUARDO. *Emotional Memories and Acting Out.* Psa. Quart., 11:477–492, 1942.

MARY A. SARVIS AND BLANCHE GARCIA

Etiological Variables in Autism*

Autism is a childhood psychosis characterized by widespread ego disturbance. Impairment of reality testing, withdrawal, and unevenness of development in all areas — motor, psychological, social — are prominent. Compulsive-aggressive behavior, rituals, magical thinking, inappropriate affect, pseudoretardation, or unreliable precocity and perceptual disturbances are common. Our basic hypothesis in this paper is that autism is a reaction occurring in a particularly vulnerable developmental stage, and that an autistic reaction may be set in process, during this vulnerable period, by any or all of a series of etiological gradients or vectors in any combination. These etiological variables will be discussed, with illustrative case material.

The term *autism* is objected to by some authors; Maenchen, for instance, prefers to call the syndrome *atypical development*.[1] Maenchen feels that autism connotes too narrow a syndrome because the term, as originally coined by Kanner, described a particular kind of relationship between a child and a "schizophrenogenic mother."[2] Kanner himself more recently, however, has broadened the term to include a syndrome of multiple causes,[3] and it is beginning to be widely used in the literature with this broadened meaning. Atypical development seems to us to be too loose a term, which could include a heterogeneous group of difficulties ranging from autism to simple mental retardation. We therefore prefer the term autism, with the understanding that we believe it is a syndrome of multiple origins.

Multiple factors in the origin of autism are acknowledged by most authors, although not by all. Szurek, for instance, hypothesizes that it is a purely

* Reprinted by special permission of The William Alanson White Psychiatric Foundation, Inc., from *Psychiatry*, Vol. 24, 1961, pp. 307–317. Copyright by The William Alanson White Psychiatric Foundation, Inc.

[1] Anna Maenchen, "Notes on Early Ego Disturbances," pp. 262–270, in *Psychoanalytic Study of the Child*, Vol. 8; New York, Internat. Univ. Press, 1953.
[2] Leo Kanner, "Problems of Nosology and Psychodynamics of Early Infantile Autism," *Amer. J. Orthopsychiatry* (1949) 19:416–426.
[3] Leo Kanner, "Childhood Schizophrenia, Round Table, 1953," *Amer. J. Orthopsychiatry* (1954) 24:526–528.

psychogenic disorder, the result of a disturbed mother- or family-child relationship.[4] Bender, on the other hand, describes it as a result of organic embryological dysmaturation.[5] Psychoanalytically oriented authors in general have focused more on the deficits and distortions of development, with the consequent structural ego disturbances, than on problems of etiology.

According to our hypothesis, the vulnerable developmental period for the development of autistic reactions — as contrasted, for instance, to phobic or hysterical reactions — is the period during which the mother is the primary object to the child, usually about six months to three years. Mahler and Gosliner[6] and other psychoanalytic authors have similarly stressed the period of individuation of self from mother as the period during which the child is most vulnerable to autistic disease. Walking seems to be one critical factor in helping the child to differentiate himself from his mother and gradually to relate to her as a separate person.

Autism thus merges, on the one hand, with Spitz's marantic and anaclitic syndromes,[7] which he related to deprivation in mothering or earlier loss of the mother, and, on the other hand, with symbiotic child psychosis or childhood schizophrenia. Autism and symbiotic psychotic pictures certainly overlap, although the pathological behavior in the latter syndrome is deferred until child and mother are separated. It is possible that in symbiotic childhood psychosis, the child is able to master the primary paranoid reaction, which we consider basic to the autistic reaction, by total introjection of the mother image.

During the period of differentiation of self and gradual perception of the mother as a separate person, the mother is still the primary object. Therefore, anything that happens to the child, whether from the inside or from the outside, is apt to impress the child as persecution by the mother and cause him to adopt the *paranoid attitude* which we feel to be central in the promotion of an autistic reaction.[8] Feeling the mother to be responsible for his difficulties, the child rejects the mother. We call this paranoid rejection the *autistic reaction* (see Figure 1).

The mother is now faced with the child's paranoid rejection and withdrawal. In return, she faces a temptation to counterreject or withdraw from the

□ **Figure 1**

Any combination of etiological variables operating as gradients.

Environmental and all other influences on mother, including many of the original etiological variables.

Stage 1
Autistic reaction in child. Child rejects mother (basic paranoid position.)

Stage 2
Mother counterrejects or withdraws from child.

Stage 3
Chronic autistic disease. Consolidation of paranoid attitudes; appearance of such restitutional behavior as compulsive, magical, autonomous efforts to reconstitute world.

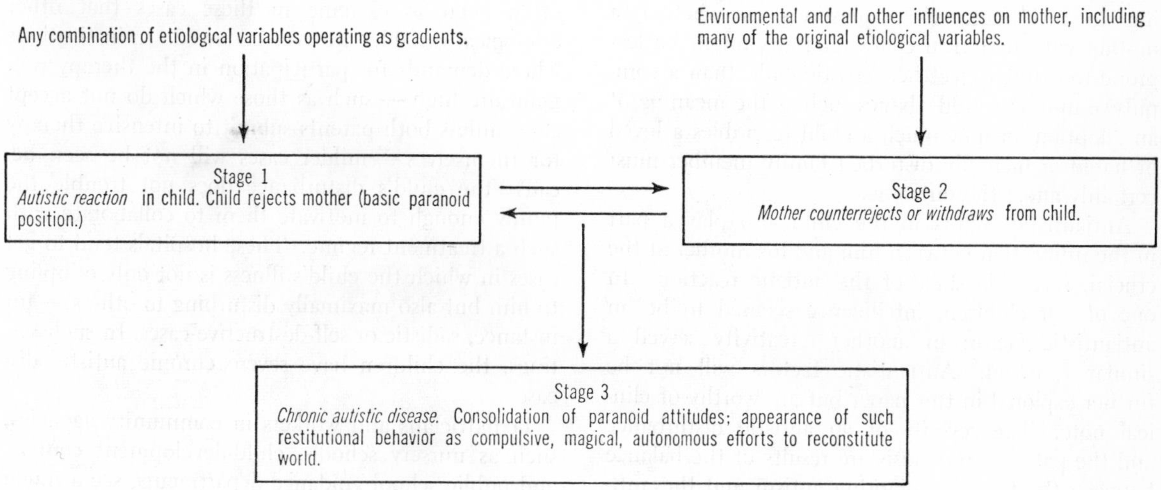

[4] S. A. Szurek and I. N. Berlin, "Elements of Psychotherapeutics with the Schizophrenic Child and His Parents," Psychiatry (1956) 19:1–9.
[5] Lauretta Bender, "Childhood Schizophrenia," Amer. J. Orthopsychiatry (1947) 17:40–56.
[6] Margaret S. Mahler and Bertram J. Gosliner, "On Symbiotic Child Psychosis," pp. 195–214, in *Psychoanalytic Study of the Child*, Vol. 10; New York, Internat. Univ. Press, 1955.
[7] René A. Spitz, "The Psychogenic Diseases in Infancy," pp. 255–275, in *Psychoanalytic Study of the Child*, Vol. 6; New York, Internat. Univ. Press, 1951.

child. The reactions of other family members are especially important at this stage (stage two, Figure 1). For instance, the attitude of a father who views his child as defective and does not support the mother in trying to relate to him sometimes promotes counterrejection or withdrawal by the mother. However, the effect of parental attitudes cannot be directly in-

[8] Paul Kramer, "On Discovering One's Identity," pp. 47–74, in *Psychoanalytic Study of the Child*, Vol. 10; New York, Internat. Univ. Press, 1955.

ferred from the *presence* of an attitude. In some of our cases, paternal rejection of the child caused intensification of maternal concern, and diminished maternal counterrejection of the child at stage two.

Refusal by the mother to counterreject the child may result in reversal of the autistic reaction. This refusal to counterreject is not a simple function of the mother's general emotional maturity or mental health; much more specific factors seem to be involved. In one case, for instance, we felt that we could detect three antiautistic features in the mother.[9] (1) Her character type was hysterical (within normal limits on psychological tests). She minimized hostility and countered the child's paranoid rejection with the attitude that this could not be basic reality: love was bound to win. (2) The child was adopted, and, to this particular mother, this seemed to mean that she was not really responsible for the illness (although consciously she took the responsibility). (3) The mother had been told that she had a probably fatal disease and felt that if she did not help the child before she died, no one else would be able to tolerate him (which, on the basis of long-term clinical evidence, was true). There is certainly no simple quantitative factor, such as degree of neurotic disturbance in the mother, which determines the severity of her counterrejection. It would be interesting to investigate such questions as whether a mother with hysterical character traits might be less prone to counterreject her autistic child than a compulsive mother would. Issues such as the meaning of an adoption, or how much a child resembles a loved or hated or mentally disturbed family member must certainly affect the outcome.

Antiautistic factors in the child also play a part in the interaction between him and his mother at the crucial, reversible stage of the autistic reaction. In one of our children, intelligence seemed to be an antiautistic factor; in another, creativity served a similar function. Antiautistic factors will not be further explored in this paper but are worthy of clinical note. The severity of an autistic disturbance and the patient's prognosis are results of the balance between the factors promoting autism and the antiautistic factors combating it. Therapy, of course, may be a powerful antiautistic factor.

In any event, at stage two, if the mother seriously counterrejects or withdraws from the child, the child tends to be confirmed and frozen in his paranoid reaction and may develop the more intransigent, less reversible state which we have called *chronic autistic*

disease (stage three, Figure 1). At this stage, restitutional behavior becomes prominent; the child, having turned his back on the world of human relations, tries to relate to himself as an object, to inanimate objects, or to part objects (such as breasts, eyeglasses). Evidences of his original negativism and paranoid attitudes remain, but the focus has shifted to compulsive, magical, autonomous efforts at mastery of the disturbance. Marked unevenness of development, impairment of reality testing, and so forth, are the inevitable result, and these, in turn, further promote consolidation of the chronic autistic disorder.

Regardless of antiautistic factors within a family, occasionally massive autistic factors — for example, overwhelming physiological assaults — may in themselves be sufficient to produce irreversible autistic disease. Much of the time, however, such a result is not inevitable.

A major impediment in the study of etiological factors in autism has been that many of the children studied have been institutionalized. Beres correctly states that one cannot make fine differentiations about these institutionalized children because the disruption in their early human relationships has been so severe and overwhelming.[10] Psychiatric hospitals also tend to receive only the most severely disturbed autistic children. Parental pathology has often been so extreme in these cases that other etiological variables are overshadowed. In institutions where demands for participation in the therapy program are high — such as those which do not accept cases unless both parents submit to intensive therapy for themselves — milder cases will not be seen because the child's disturbance does not trouble the family enough to motivate them to collaborate with such a treatment regime. These hospitals tend to get cases in which the child's illness is not only crippling to him but also maximally disturbing to others — for instance, sadistic or self-destructive cases. In such settings, the children have severe chronic autistic disease.

Pediatricians and workers in community agencies, such as nursery schools, child-development centers, and public school guidance departments, see a much broader range of children with autistic reactions. Children are seen with varying degrees of paranoid reactions, withdrawal, bizarre or eccentric behavior, and preoccupation with isolated compulsive activities such as plate-spinning, darting to investigate apertures such as cupboards or drawers, or repetitive engrossment with light switches or plugs. Arguments for-

[9] Mary A. Sarvis, "Psychiatric Implications of Temporal Lobe Damage," pp. 454–481, in *Psychoanalytic Study of the Child*, Vol. 15; New York, Internat. Univ. Press, 1960.

[10] David Beres, "Ego Deviation and the Concept of Schizophrenia," pp. 164–235, in *Psychoanalytic Study of the Child*, Vol. 11; New York, Internat. Univ. Press, 1956.

merly raged in many staff conferences about whether these less severe cases should be called autistic. In our opinion, this argument is unproductive in studying etiology since it tends to limit the diagnosis of autism to children with massive chronic autistic disease. It was similarly unproductive in studying the etiology of adult schizophrenia to limit the diagnosis to severely disturbed, hospitalized patients. In such patients, the range of etiological variables is lost and the meaning of the patient's behavior is often obscured because of the number of secondary, restitutional symptoms which have been developed to 'master' the original conflicts. We would like to emphasize that cases involving milder degrees of autistic behavior are fairly common, and are far more frequent than the cases of chronic autistic disease seen in institutions and hospitals.

Beres has raised the question of whether cases in which regression is prominent should be differentiated from those in which fixation is more marked.[11] In our opinion, all these ego disturbances in early childhood merge into each other and are arbitrarily demarcated on empirical grounds. There is no clear-cut sudden point at which the mother ceases to be the primary object and other object relations appear. The further self and objet differentiation has advanced, the more any disturbance may include regressive features as well as fixation. By analogy, Erikson's description of the way in which various libidinal modes and zones surge gradually into pre-eminence, and then gradually subside but do not disappear, is pertinent here.[12]

Regardless of how mild or how severe his disturbance, the child has experienced difficulties at a vulnerable developmental stage. He has adopted a basically paranoid position, regarding his mother as the persecutor. He may master his basically projective attitude by introjecting the persecuting mother image; in a sense he struggles with whether the world or he himself is unalterably evil. Similarly, he is caught between his own destructive aggressive impulses and fear of the world as overwhelmingly hostile and destructive to him. Love and mothering are fused into one image with hate and destruction. In treatment, a critical phase is the redifferentiation of these fused images.[13]

ETIOLOGICAL VARIABLES

We have observed the following variables, operating in all combinations and intensities, which in the

vulnerable developmental stage may cause a child to develop an autistic reaction.

(1) Family Psychodynamics Specifically Promoting Austism

(1a) Autism meets specific unconscious need in parents — This category is analogous to the group of families described by Johnson and Szurek, in which the child's delinquent behavior met and "satisfied" certain specific unconscious needs in one or both parents.[14] The parent's psychic equilibrium could not be maintained unless the child was acting in a specific way. Similarly, some of the parents we have observed unconsciously need to have their children act autistic; they specifically promote autistic reactivity in the child. Either the autistic reaction itself or the child's general development — particularly with respect to Oedipal problems — has specific unconscious meanings to the mother. She either promotes autism directly or needs to prevent the child's development because of its malignant meaning to her, so that autism results. We have seen several children, for instance, who have had to wean themselves from pacifiers, literally over their mothers' protests, at five or six years.

(1b) 'Tone-deaf' mothers — Tone-deaf mothers promote autistic reactions by virtue of their inability to empathize with the child. Category 1b conforms to Kanner's concept of the "schizophrenogenic" or "Frigidaire" mother.[15] These remote, unempathic, compulsive mothers have been widely described in the literature as major etiological agents in infantile autism. We prefer the term tone-deaf mother because it emphasizes the lack of emotional empathic ability, which seems analogous to color blindness, literal tone deafness, and other perceptual deficiencies. The mothers or fathers in this category are, as we have seen them, compulsive, meticulous people who give the impression to an observer of being either cold or very poignant. They are by no means consciously monstrous in their attitudes; often a mother has spent years trying to get help for her child, conscientiously doing everything she was told by pediatrician, nursery school teacher, or psychiatrist, and is bewildered by

[11] See footnote 10.

[12] Erik H. Erikson, Childhood and Society; New York, Norton, 1950; pp. 44–92.

[13] Blanche Garcia and Mary A. Sarvis, "Evaluation and Treatment of Autistic Children," unpublished manuscript.

[14] Adelaide M. Johnson, "Sanctions for Superego Lacunae of Adolescents," pp. 225–245, in Searchlights on Delinquency, edited by K. R. Eissler; New York, Internat. Univ. Press, 1949. Adelaide M. Johnson and S. A. Szurek, "The Genesis of Antisocial Acting Out in Children and Adults," Psychoanalytic Quart. (1952) 21:323–343.

[15] Quoted by Margaret S. Mahler in "Severe Emotional Disturbance: Psychosis," pp. 816–839, in American Handbook of Psychiatry, Vol. 1, edited by Silvano Arieti; New York, Basic Books, 1959.

the lack of beneficial results to the child and hurt by the child's rejection of her. The difficulty lies not in what she has done but in the way she has done it. She has 'serviced' the child like a machine, because of the basic deficit in empathy, which perhaps may be related either to the mother's infantile relationship to her own mother, or to constitutional factors in the mother.[16] We are not impressed by the evidence, however, that this tone deafness is always and entirely psychogenic.

(2) *Family Psychodynamics Enabling Autism to Occur*

(2a) *Family events not primarily directed at child* — Maternal depression, paternal compulsivity, marital difficulties, illness in the family, birth of a sibling, and similar events may enable an autistic reaction to develop in a child in the vulnerable developmental period even though there is no conscious or unconscious intent on the part of the parent to promote autism. The mother of one of our patients had a malignant melanoma removed during her pregnancy with him. She responded with severe depression and lethargy; the father was also depressed. Shortly after the child's birth, the father was drafted and away from home for months. The family could not accompany him, and the mother's depression continued. The child's overt autistic symptoms began at two, when a sibling was born.

(2b) *Infantilization or pushing of the child* — Infantilization or pushing of a child may occur and be a factor promoting an autistic reaction without the specificity implied in categories 1a and 1b. An intellectual and proud father overreacted to his three-year-old son's precocious — probably already autistic — absorption with intellectual material such as a history of mankind written for adults. The father's overcathexis of intellectuality showed that it had a specific unconscious meaning to him, but there was no unconscious need on his part for an *autistic* reaction per se, as there was in the case of 1a mothers, whose fear of Oedipal masculinity in their sons and need to prove men were crazy babies led them to keep the boys addicted to the pacifier.

In another case, the parents were moving toward divorce as the climax of severe marital difficulties when the patient was an infant (2a), and the mother, in a reactive way, severely infantilized him (2b).

By the time a family is seen, of course, category 2 may have been given some category 1 quality because of the prolonged presence of an autistic child in the family. Aside from direct parental counterre-

jection of the autistic child, family members react to his presence and his management in the home with depression, hysterical defenses, apathy, rivalry, overprotectiveness, and so forth. In evaluating a given family, an effort must be made to separate reactive from original etiological variables. This separation is important because it may bear on prognosis, even though it is recognized that once a vicious circle is set up, reactive attitudes become etiological agents too.

(3) *Circumstance*

This category consists of situations over which the family could exert no reasonably conceivable control, such as the father's being drafted into the service. We feel it should be narrowly defined. In one of our cases, a housing shortage necessitated living arrangements which resulted in overstimulation of the child. This was coded 3 and 4b-3.

(4) *Assaults on the Child*

This category shifts the focus to the child and often, therefore, is coded with another category which considers the same event in terms of parental psychodynamics or circumstance. The preceding example illustrates this.

(4a) *Maximum developmental insult* — This category describes an illness or injury which is specific, in mode or zone, to a given developmental stage, such as colic, diarrhea, or severe constipation in the oral and anal periods, or immobilization of the legs in the toddler period. This is called maximum developmental insult because the very function or body part with the highest libidinal cathexis at the time in question is the one selected for traumatization. Examples are seen in some of the detailed cases presented below.

(4b) *Underreactivity or overreactivity of the perceptual apparatus* — This category includes all perceptual underreactivity or overreactivity, whether inborn, produced by temporal lobe disease, or the result of handling. Interference with accurate perceptual recording of stimuli seems to bear a very special relationship to paranoid reactions, as can be seen, for example, in infantile autism and in the prominent tendency to paranoid reactivity in the deaf person. Correction of the disturbed perception helps to neutralize the paranoid reaction.

(4b-1) *Inborn* — Bergman and Escalona described a group of children who seemed to have a "thin protective barrier" against stimuli.[17] When

[16] See Maenchen, footnote 1.

[17] Paul Bergman and Sibylle K. Escalona, "Unusual Sensitivities in Very Young Children," pp. 333–352, in *Psychoanalytic Study of the Child*, Vols. 3/4; New York, Internat. Univ. Press, 1949.

seen, these children seemed to have exceptional artistic gifts, but the authors felt that their ultimate destiny was psychosis. Since family psychopathology did not seem to be sufficient to account for the children's reactivity, an inborn factor was postulated. Several of our cases support the hypothesis that such a factor exists, and other observations on young children also show a wide range in reactivity to stimuli.[18] We have also observed underreactivity of the perceptual apparatus.

(4b-2) *Temporal lobe disease* — In temporal lobe damage, emotional storms and aggressive outbursts occur. There are also various disturbances of perception: the patient may experience hyperreactivity of taste, smell, or hearing, tinnitus, and *déjà vu* phenomena or feelings of unreality; and may show complex disturbances of gait and coordination. Objects coming toward him — for example, a ball — may apparently change in size and speed of travel.[19] Among the 80 autistic children studied by one or both of us, there are 8 with temporal lobe damage shown by EEG. In six additional cases, clinical evidence points strongly in this direction, but neurological examinations are not yet complete. Since the use of temporal lobe activators in EEG examinations is a rather recent innovation in our area, and since many of the 80 children were never studied from this point of view, it seems clear that these are minimal figures. Temporal lobe disease is a powerful gradient promoting autism if it occurs when the child is in the vulnerable developmental period.

Two of the children had prolonged, severe diarrhea concomitantly with the temporal lobe pathology and perhaps produced by it, since no other cause was ever found. This thus also constituted a maximum developmental insult (4a). A boy who was intensively studied and reported elsewhere illustrates the gradients involved in autistic reactions and the way in which such reactions can abate with the diminution of one or more gradients.[20] His illness began abruptly at nine months with the presumed onset of the temporal lobe disease (4b-2) and with severe diarrhea (4a). He reacted with severe classical autistic symptoms. There were strong antiau-

tistic gradients in both boy and family, and when his diarrhea subsided, between the ages of two and one-half and three, the autistic reaction immediately began to subside, although he continued to have the aggressive outbursts and perceptual disturbances which characterized his temporal lobe disease.

(4b-3) *Overstimulation or understimulation* — Lack of shielding from stimulation may produce the same functional result in a child as an inborn thin protective barrier against stimuli.[21] Understimulation — in terms of the needs of a given child — also promotes an autistic reaction. Children isolated from human contact for long periods in cribs or play pens show such reactions. A constitutionally thin-skinned child requires more shielding from stimulation than his less reactive brother; maternal empathy is a crucial variable in adjusting the stimulus level to the needs of the child.

An even more powerful gradient in the production of autistic reactions is alternation between overstimulation and understimulation. As the culmination of a long period of family stress, the father of one of our patients was engrossed in studying for very difficult examinations and insisted on complete quiet in the house. The patient's mother was depressed, lethargic, and suffering from an as yet undiagnosed pelvic infection, and functioning almost without ability to respond emotionally. The patient was markedly understimulated most of the time. When the parents tried to "make it up to him" with bursts of tense, overstimulating play, which relieved their guilt, his autism was markedly aggravated.

In another case, an older father and a young, naïve mother moved to the Pacific Northwest, where they ran a combined bar, restaurant, bakery, and barbershop. They were panicky and overworked. The baby was left upstairs in his crib for long periods of time. At other times he would be brought into the bar, with its highly stimulating atmosphere, but firmly prevented from "being a nuisance" to anyone — that is, he received massive stimulation but was unable to discharge it by any participation in the group.

(4c) *Miscellaneous* — In this category we have included the gradients which could not be included elsewhere. For example, prematurity is a gradient coded as 4c; if there were temporal lobe damage as a result of prematurity, it would also be coded 4b-2. Also included in the 4c category are congenital defects; accident or disease which is not a maximum

---

[18] Margaret E. Fries and Paul J. Woolf, "Some Hypotheses on the Role of the Congenital Activity Type in Personality Development," pp. 48–64, in *Psychoanalytic Study of the Child*, Vol. 8; New York, Internat. Univ. Press, 1953. Augusta Alpert, Peter B. Neubauer, and Annemarie P. Weil, "Unusual Variations in Drive Endowment," pp. 125–163, in *Psychoanalytic Study of the Child*, Vol. 11; New York, Internat. Univ. Press, 1956.

[19] For a detailed description of temporal lobe damage and its relationship to an autistic reaction, see Sarvis, footnote 9.

[20] See footnote 9.

[21] L. Bryce Boyer, "On Maternal Overstimulation and Ego Defects," pp. 236–256, in *Psychoanalytic Study of the Child*, Vol. 11; New York, Internat. Univ. Press, 1956.

development insult (4a); perceptual disorders that are not the result of temporal lobe disease — for instance, deafness; brain damage which is not primarily the result of temporal lobe disease. Nonperceptual constitutional factors of nonspecific nature and Bender's embryological dysmaturation are also included here.

We would like to emphasize that we are discussing autism as a disease or reaction of a particular developmental stage and saying that when the variables discussed above assault the child during this vulnerable stage, they tend specifically to promote autistic reactions. At a later stage of development, when differentiation of self and object are more firmly established, these same assaults on the child would promote a psychological disturbance that would either not be autistic or not as typically autistic. Obviously, stages of development and symptoms are not clear-cut, either-or phenomena. Central to our concept is the idea that the variables promoting autism operate in any or all combinations as *gradients* with varying degrees of intensity. We do not have the knowledge, at present, to reduce these gradients to quantitative weights or numbers, although perhaps such rating systems could be developed. We do feel that we can usually assess any variable as severe, moderate, or minimal. In the cases which follow, we make an effort to show the interlocking impact of several variables occurring in varying degrees of severity. An effort to assess or code etiological variables should be used only to facilitate diagnostic thinking. Coding should not limit consideration of further individual factors.

Case Histories

Jon [2a, 3, 4b-2, 4b-3; minimal counterrejection by family]. Jon is the first boy and second child in a family of four children. None of the others has shown serious psychopathology. At two years of age, Jon was referred to a nursery school by the family minister because he showed a moderately severe autistic disturbance, which had chronic features. He had poor spatial orientation, was a severe headbanger, did not talk at all, and showed extremely self-destructive behavior. With rigid body, he catapulted powerfully through space without regard for objects in the way or for his destination. He had aggressive outbursts in which biting and spitting were prominent. He was withdrawn and did not relate to children or adults. He improved in nursery school, but his behavior still differed so much from that of the other children that the parents requested individual therapy. One of the authors has seen him individually for a year, and this experience has been coordinated with group experience in nursery school.

Jon's father, a second-generation Hawaiian-Japanese, is a public school teacher; his mother, a Chinese who had been raised in California, is a college-educated housewife. The patient developed normally until he was nine months old, when circumstance 3 required that the family move back to the paternal family in the Hawaiian Islands for a year. Because of the housing shortage, they had to move into the paternal household, which already consisted of 10 adults. Jon's mother was highly ambivalent about this and reacted with guilt about the overcrowded situation they were causing. She felt that she should make amends by keeping house for the workers and scholars in the home. Hence, she often isolated Jon for hours in a bedroom during the day while she cleaned house, ironed white shirts daily for all the men, and cooked. When the extended family returned home, Jon was taken up, passed around, held, cuddled, roughhoused, and otherwise stimulated. This alternation between understimulation and overstimulation (4b-3) seemed to play a major part in his autistic reaction. He did not walk until he was forced to at 18 months. He began to develop the self-destructive accident-proneness we have mentioned. His difficulties were aggravated by the birth of a sibling when he was only a year old (2a).

Certain features of Jon's reactions, especially his problems of spatial orientation, also suggested a possible temporal lobe factor (4b-2), which was subsequently verified.

The mother handled this patient's disturbance with considerable understanding of the way in which both her own desire to placate the father's family and the circumstantial factors had contributed to it. She did not counterreject Jon. The father did not react rejectingly to the autistic disturbance either, but he did handle all his children with a good many oral-sadistic mechanisms — for example, rough teasing, which included biting — that have been little modified.

At present, Jon is making satisfactory progress. He is beginning to talk and does so with phallic energy and pride, although missing teeth contribute to defective speech. The present issue is whether to enter him in kindergarten at the usual age or to retain him for a year in nursery school.

William [1b, 2a, 4a, 4b-1, 4b-3, 4c; family counterrejection marked]. William is the younger of two children. His sister has not shown gross psychopathology in any form. At four years, when he was first seen in a child development center, William showed severely autistic symptoms. He was withdrawn, would not talk, and would not eat solid foods. He had serious spatial disorientation, and went into a panic if he was lifted off the ground. He fluttered his hands constantly. He was obsessively preoccupied with light plugs and lights, with turning faucets off and on, and with flushing toilets. The family seemed so unmotivated for any kind of treatment that foster home placement was recommended. From the foster home, he was institutionalized on a children's psychiatric ward, where he remained for a year and a half. In the psychiatric hospital he improved moderately. He returned to the foster home at six and lived there until he was eleven. Firm and rather heavy-handed treatment in the foster home resulted in some further improvement but also in a 'sealing off' of pathology and the development in William of compulsive, automaton-like behavior with marked defects in spontaneity, affect, and relations to others. He was seen again in treatment when he was about nine and showed further improvement. His therapist arranged for William's return to his own family when he was eleven. The family has been worked with at the counseling level. The mother says, "We realize that we have a good many problems but we can't change our basic personalities." Nevertheless, they have been able to modify many of their attitudes toward William, and the boy is now functioning moderately well in a public school; his academic performance is one year behind his correct age-grade placement. His muscle tone and development have improved markedly, and he is more independent, has much better relations with other children, is more spontaneous, and usually is able to express feelings freely and appropriately.

In the etiology of William's autistic reaction, the following features were of note. He had a severe intestinal illness throughout the first year of life (4a). He reacted by massively rejecting his family and demonstrated the typical paranoid attitude which we feel is central in the autistic reaction. His father is a scientist who is distant in relations with people, has difficulty in expressing feelings, and is oriented toward things and concepts rather than toward relationships (2a). During William's childhood, his mother was vague, lethargic, and ineffectual, her frustration tolerance was low, and it was felt that she was diffusely depressed (2a). Both parents showed marked counterreactivity to William's autistic reaction. The father counterrejected the boy and the mother counterwithdrew. They showed little opposition to the foster home placement.

Other variables also played a part. This boy probably falls into the group of children who have thin protective barriers against stimuli (4b-1). He has a tremendously hypercathected sense of time and memory, which have been intensified by his marked compulsivity. In addition, his mathematical ability is extremely precocious, and periodically he becomes completely absorbed in mathematical problems. His preoccupation with time and time-binding suggested that a temporal lobe factor should be investigated. On an electroencephalogram done some time later, diffuse brain damage (4c) was demonstrated. William's mother showed some features of the tone-deaf mother (1b); her child seemed so odd and different that she felt unable to understand him. In response, she was unsuccessful in meeting his needs and did not shield him sufficiently from stimulation (4b-3). If we were coding this mother, we would say that she showed some aspects of 1b behavior, resulting partly from the child and partly from 2a factors in the mother.

Debby [2a, 3, 4c; family counterrejection absent]. Debby was grossly psychotic when seen for the first time at three. The mother reported that Debby's symptoms had been severe for about a year, but the exact onset is not known because the mother had been absent from the home. Debby behaved like the wolf boy of Aveyron. She spent her life anxiously, tensely flitting and flying about, as if she wanted to climb the walls. Any effort to approach her made her run; if she were touched, she fought or went rigid. She chewed things constantly in a tense, birdlike fashion. She mouthed gibberish with no attempt at communication. She was so tense and undifferentiated in her responses to events that interpretation of her behavior was impossible.

Debby was born with severe congenital disorders of heart, sight, and hearing (4c). When she was born, heart surgery had not yet been perfected and she was not expected to live beyond the age of two. Her father's personality in general would warrant a coding of 2a; he was a withdrawn, compulsive man who had been a subject in a study of children of genius-level intelligence. Debby's apparently fatal prognosis seemed to give the family permission to be indulgent with her so that 2a factors were minimal. When Debby was one, the mother developed tuberculosis (3) and was away from home for a year. Although the housekeeping help was not conspicuously bad, Debby was grossly autistic by two. At two and a half she had cardiac surgery with good results. Her defects in eyesight and hearing were diagnosed much more gradually and their severity was not fully recognized when she was first seen.

These parents, particularly the mother, did not reject their autistic child and have continued to work with her. Debby was a participant in the child development center nursery school for three years and was seen individually for two of those years. Since then, there has been some counseling with the parents and she has been followed minimally by her public school guidance department. She attended regular classes in public school for about three years, and was then put into classes for the hard of hearing, where she is doing well academically and socially, although about one year behind the usual age-grade placement. She does not show autistic features.

Eben [4a; family counterreaction absent]. This boy was first seen at three with an acute autistic reaction which was obviously in an early stage. He displayed diffuse, distracted, frantic anxiety. When separated from his mother he screamed hysterically and almost went out of contact. He also had screaming spells for no identifiable reason. His speech was pressured and infantile. He turned lights off and on obsessively and had an obsessive interest in music. He was markedly paranoid toward his mother, and this reaction seemed to keep him from passive withdrawal.

The mother reported that Eben's development had been normal in the first year of life. Sometime during that period the boy developed a hernia which was undiagnosed. When he began to walk at 13 months, walking made him cry, and the autistic symptoms gradually developed (4a). Eben cried with pain, but the pediatrician felt that he was spoiled and advised the mother to ignore his crying. As he continued to cry, the hernia tended to strangulate and the pain became more severe. Finally, when Eben was two, an emergency herniorrhaphy was done.

The parents of this boy were frustrated and irritated but not counterrejective. The father was an electronics engineer, a thoughtful, slow-moving man of Scandinavian ancestry. He and his wife were singularly nondefensive and were equally concerned that their son get help with his problems (anti-autistic in categories 1 and 2).

Eben was seen during only four months of individual psychotherapy (two months at once a week and two months at twice a week). When family finances necessitated interruption in his individual therapy, Eben had already improved remarkably and was able to enter a cooperative nursery school. Although this boy has recovered from his acute autistic reaction, continued follow-up is planned.

Ginny [2a (father), 4a, 4b-2, anti-1 and anti-2 (mother); family counterreaction minimal]. Ginny was a middle child with an older brother and a younger sister, both of whom are considered to function well although they have potential neurotic problems. Her father is a lawyer; her mother has worked as a biological technician, although she is more interested in the social sciences. Both parents entered psychotherapy because of marital and intrapsychic difficulties; by the time Ginny was entered in nursery school, divorce was imminent (2a). Ginny, when seen at three and a half, was grossly autistic. She had almost no speech, isolated herself from human contacts, lacked appropriate affect, showed massive restriction of motility, suffered from spatial disorganization, and had serious concerns with being aggressed against or about her own aggression. Temporal lobe damage (4b-2) was suspected at this time and confirmed some years later.

Ginny had also had a severe intestinal illness in the first year of life (4a), which caused her to react autistically. In addition — and this was also during a period of parental turmoil — at the age when Ginny was learning to walk, her legs were placed in casts to correct congenital anomalies (4a). Her autistic reaction increased, and she was referred for study.

In this family, the father's compulsive make-up and dissatisfactions with the mother and children must be considered a 2a variable. He regarded Ginny as defective and tended to withdraw from her and the total situation. The mother, on the other hand, did not respond to Ginny's autistic reaction by counterwithdrawal. Despite the marital difficulties, she did not react, as many parents do, by turning to the child and infantilizing her. The mother was coded anti-1 and anti-2. She concentrated on efforts to counterreact the autistic reaction and she progressively developed awareness of the psychological factors within herself which had formerly made close, spontaneous human contact difficult for her.

This child has been followed for seven years. Management has consisted of individual treatment at periods of heightened anxiety, counseling with the mother, working with personnel in nursery school and in public school, and tutoring. Ginny required two or three years to form enough relationship with teachers to enable her to learn; however, with several exceptionally fortunate teacher relationships, she is now learning academically. At 10, many of her more bizarre behavior patterns have diminished and she is able to function in a public school program. She still appears as an eccentric child and requires some special understanding. In therapy, she is beginning to cope successfully with Oedipal problems.

CONCLUSIONS

In the 80 or more autistic children we studied, the two most striking observations were: (1) the difficulties invariably involved the particular developmental stage when the mother was the primary object to the child, so that the disturbance caused the child to adopt a basic paranoid attitude toward the mother; (2) the children manifested all degrees of disturbance from very mild to very severe, from transitory autistic reactions to chronic, intransigent autistic disease. Children seen in institutions and psychiatric hospitals usually fall into the latter category.

When we try to evaluate an autistic child in terms of the etiological variables described in this paper, we see that there are practical implications in planning for treatment.[22] Parents in the 1a or 1b categories must be seen in therapy for themselves if there is to be a reasonable hope of working with their autistic child. In category 1a, the unconscious parental attitudes promoting autism must be uncovered and worked through. In category 1b, a prolonged relationship with the parent, the opportunity for her to identify with the therapist, and education to counteract the tone deafness are essential. Experi-

[22] See footnote 13.

ences in parent groups in nursery schools and opportunities to observe other young children are at least as important for 1b mothers as individual therapy. Category 2a parents may need treatment because of the disturbance within themselves, but in terms of the child, counseling may be sufficient. Reactive infantilization or pushing of the child may similarly yield to counseling or to identification with and education within a nursery school parents' group. Categories 3 and 4 suggest counseling with and education of the parents but primarily therapeutic work with the child, who has the internalized problem of how to interpret and overcome the assaults which have beset him. This individual work with the child has proved to be useful, even with preschool children. A combination of group and individual experiences, of nursery school and formal therapy, of interpretation and education, of permitting necessary regression and encouraging appropriate growth, has proven optimal in working with these children.

We feel that trying to evaluate the concrete variables involved in the autistic reaction of a given child and planning a treatment regime to meet these concrete needs enables one to proceed with moderate optimism about the prognosis of many autistic children.

DON MOSER

The Nightmare of Life with Billy*

"When his father's car pulled out of the driveway, I'd bolt the doors, lock the windows and the nightmare would begin." Thus Billy's mother, Pat, describes a terrifying existence in which she was at the mercy of a small boy so cunning and so violent that he almost propelled her into a nervous breakdown.

Pat's story is significant in two respects. First, it indicates that it is virtually impossible for an intelligent, well-intentioned parent to cope with an autistic youngster. Second, it shows why Pat and her

husband, along with the parents of the other children, so eagerly embraced Lovaas' program even though it involved shock and other forms of punishment.

The causes of autism are no clearer with Billy than with the other children. He had suffered a traumatic birth, one that places great strain on the infant. Pat was 17 hours in labor, and when doctors had finally delivered him by Caesarean section, it was 90 seconds before he breathed, another 90 before he cried. Nor was his early environment always pleasant. His parents' marriage was going through a difficult period. His father, a doctor, was serving his internship; every other night he was at the hospital, and when he came home he had no energy left to do anything but fall into bed. Later, called into the Navy, he was separated from Billy and Pat for long periods.

Whatever the causes — organic, environmental or both — it was clear by the time Billy was 2 years old that something was very wrong with him. He had not started to speak. He threw uncontrollable tantrums. He never seemed to sleep. Pat and her husband took the child from one psychiatrist or neurologist to another. All gave the same analysis: Billy was retarded.

Before long, however, Pat realized that Billy was diabolically clever and hell-bent on destroying her. Whenever her husband was home, Billy was a model youngster. He knew that his father would punish him quickly and dispassionately for misbehaving. But when his father left the house, Billy would go to the window and watch until the car pulled out. As soon as it did, he was suddenly transformed. "It was like living with the devil," Pat remembers. "He'd go into my closet and tear up my evening dresses and urinate on my clothes. He'd smash furniture and run around biting the walls until the house was destruction from one end to the other. He knew that I liked to dress him in nice clothes, so he used to rip the buttons off his shirts and used to go in his pants." When he got violent Pat punished him. But she got terribly distraught, and for Billy the pleasure of seeing her upset made any punishment worthwhile. Sometimes he attacked her with all the fury in his small body, once going for her throat with his teeth. Anything that wasn't nailed down or locked up — soap powder, breakfast food — he strewed all over the floors. Then, laughing wildly, he dragged Pat to come see it.

She had to face her problems alone. It was impossible for her to keep any household help. Once Billy tripped a maid at the head of the stairs, then lay on the floor doubled up with laughter as she tumbled down. And Billy was so cunning that his father didn't know what was going on. "Pat would tell me about the things he did while I was away, but I couldn't believe her," he says.

As time went on, even his father realized that they had a monster on their hands. Enrolled at a school for retarded children, Billy threw the whole institution into an uproar. Obsessed with a certain record, he insisted on playing it over and over for hours. He sent the children in his class into fits of screaming misbehavior. "He was just like a stallion in a herd of horses," his mother says. Billy ruled his teacher with his tantrums until, a nervous wreck herself, she could no longer stand to have

him in the class. "He became a school dropout at the age of 5," says Pat.

At home things were taking a macabre twist. Billy had a baby brother now, and at any opportunity he tried to stuff the infant into the toy box and shut the lid on him. His parents had bought him a doll which resembled the baby, and which they called by the baby's name, Patrick. Every morning Pat found the Patrick doll head down in the toilet bowl. Terrified of what might happen, she never left the two children alone together.

As he grew older Billy's machinations seemed far too clever for a retarded child, and so his parents took him to see another expert. There, given a puzzle to test his intelligence, Billy simply threw the pieces against the wall. The expert delivered the same old verdict. Billy was retarded.

At the retarded children's school, the youngsters occasionally got hamburgers for lunch from a drive-in chain. Inexplicably, Billy became hooked on them — hooked to the point that he would starve himself rather than eat anything else. Within a few weeks Pat and her husband became slaves to Billy's hamburger habit. Every morning and every night Billy's father stood in line at the drive-in and bought cheap hamburgers by the sack. Eventually he became so embarrassed — he is a small, thin man, and the waitresses had begun to look at him curiously — that he cruised the city looking for drive-ins where he wasn't known. Billy ate three cold, greasy hamburgers for breakfast, more for lunch, more for dinner. "He was like Ray Milland in *The Lost Weekend*," Pat shudders. "To make sure he wouldn't eat them all at once I'd hide them all over the house — in the oven and up on shelves. In the middle of the night he'd be up prowling around, looking for them. A month later I'd find ossified hamburgers in hiding places I'd forgotten."

When they were out driving with Billy, they had to detour around any drive-ins. Billy flew into such a frenzy at the sight of one that he frothed at the mouth and tried to jump out of the moving car.

Pat knew that the boy could not survive on a diet of cheap hamburgers. She took him to places where they served hamburgers of better quality; Billy refused to eat them. Frantic, she contrived an elaborate ruse. Buying relish and buns from the drive-in, she bought good meat and made the patties herself. She put them into sacks from the drive-in, even inserting the little menu cards that came with the drive-in's orders. When she presented this carefully recreated drive-in hamburger to Billy, he took one sniff and threw it on the floor.

Then there was Billy's Winnie-the-Pooh period.

Billy had become obsessed with a particular kind of Teddy bear, marketed under the trade name of Winnie the Pooh. Without it, he'd go berserk. The family was moving about a good deal then, and Pat was terrified that she would have no replacement when Billy lost his bear or tore it up. "Just to make sure I'd never run out, I found where to buy a Winnie wherever we might be going. I knew a place in San Diego and a place in La Jolla and a place in San Francisco. I even knew where to buy a Winnie in Las Vegas. I always kept some in reserve just so we wouldn't run short in a hotel. Our whole life became one long Winnie trip. Once, when we were moving, Winnie got put into the van by mistake, and we had to have the movers take everything out so we could find it. We were afraid to make the trip with Billy without a Winnie bear — we were starting to go nutty ourselves."

Pat became so desperate that when she found something that frightened the boy, she used it as a weapon of self-defense. The one thing that did the trick, appropriately enough, was Alfred Hitchcock. For some reason, when Hitchcock came on television Billy took off like a rocket and hid under the bed. When Pat learned that photographs of Hitchcock had the same effect, she started cutting them out of TV magazines. When Hitchcock appeared on LIFE's cover, she bought a whole stack of magazines and stuck the covers up all over the house — on the icebox to keep Billy from opening it, on the fireplace to keep him from crawling around in it. When she took a bath she put Hitchcock pictures outside the bathroom door so Billy would leave her in peace.

"It was crazy," Pat remembers. She was at bay in a house with the doors bolted and the windows locked, the baby stuffed in the toybox and the Patrick doll with its head in the toilet, hamburgers hidden on shelves and a closet full of cast-off Pooh bears and the breakfast food strewn all over the floor, and little Billy raging around like an animal, attacking pictures of Alfred Hitchcock with a long stick.

By now Billy was getting so big and strong that Pat could hardly control him physically, and she and her husband were thinking of building a fence around their house to keep him from endangering others. But before doing so, they took him to one more psychiatrist. "You can't build a fence high enough," the psychiatrist said flatly. "He'll be a Frankenstein monster. Put him away."

Miserable though they were, Pat and her husband couldn't stand the thought of abandoning the boy to an institution. "We were supposed to put him away and throw away the home movies and tear up the scrapbook pictures," she said "We just couldn't do it."

A few weeks later a psychiatrist connected with the retarded children's school told Pat and her husband that Billy might not be retarded but autistic. He suggested they take him to the Neuropsychiatric Institute at UCLA where Dr. Lovaas and his colleague, Dr. James Simmons, a psychiatrist, were choosing autistic children for a new experimental program. Pat and her husband were enthusiastic, even though they knew about the punishment that Billy would be subjected to.

Their one fear was that Billy, erratic child that he was, would flunk his audition in front of Lovaas. But they knew that one of the criteria was that the children accepted must like to eat, and must be willing to expend a lot of energy to obtain food. So Pat and her husband talked things over, and they had an idea.

When they took Billy to see Dr. Lovaas, they made a stop on the way at the drive-in. Billy, given the hamburgers during the interview, passed the entrance exam with flying colors.

Psychotherapy / 9

No book of readings on the subject of abnormal psychology would be complete without a section devoted to the varieties of techniques available for treating emotional disorders. Psychotherapy is a helping relationship, an intimate encounter between patient and therapist with the goal of bringing stability and wholeness to an uncertain and fragmented personality. All therapeutic procedures begin from certain basic givens — that the patient is experiencing pain and is engaged in hurtful, self-defeating behavior. How to go about easing this pain and ending disruptive behavior, and how to understand the process of such change, are questions all our contributors seek to answer.

For many years psychotherapy was synonymous with psychoanalysis, and innovations in psychotherapeutic techniques were essentially modifications within the context of the psychoanalytic tradition. However, the passage of time has seen an increasing number of methods of psychotherapy developing out of theoretical positions other than psychoanalysis. In the following papers, we have not attempted to examine all these innovations in psychotherapy, but have sought to present a sampling of the major theoretical approaches and techniques.

In the first paper, Frieda Fromm-Reichmann discusses the recent advances in psychoanalytic procedures. She examines the differences between the concepts of classical psychoanalysis and those arising from more recent psychodynamic theorizing, how these new ideas have affected therapeutic methods and techniques, and types of patients who can be treated by psychoanalytic therapy. Her main emphasis is on the contributions of the interpersonal theorists such as Harry Stack Sullivan and the increasing analytic concern with ego processes.

Carl Rogers is best known for his development of the client-centered approach to psychotherapy which stresses the importance of working within the client's frame of reference. The present paper is unique in that it represents an attempt by Rogers to formulate a view of psychotherapy from an external frame of reference. This is both a conception of the process of psychotherapy and a developmental theory of personality change in a more general sense. In the course of therapy, Rogers sees the total functioning of the individual as shifting from a rigid, fixed position to one of greater fluidity and flexibility.

The past decade has seen a significant increase in attempts to apply learning theory to psychotherapy and in the development of both new treatment procedures and formulations of therapeutic change. However, Bandura asserts that the implications of a learning-theory approach have not been fully appreciated and that the potential of treatment methods based upon counterconditioning, extinction, discrimination learning, reward, punishment, and social imitation have yet to be adequately explored. He argues against several prevalent attitudes which impede the acceptance of learning-theory principles.

In his provocative paper, Wolpe argues that the techniques developed for eliminating experimental neuroses in animals can be applied to the reduction of anxiety in humans. He argues that laboratory experiments suggest the general proposition that if a response inhibitory to anxiety can be made to occur in the presence of anxiety-evoking stimuli, so that the latter are accompanied by complete or partial suppression of the anxiety response, the bond between these stimuli and the anxiety response will be weakened. He then describes a specific technique known as "systematic desensitization," which is based upon the generalizing effects of a behavioral response, in this case, muscle relaxation.

The paper by Jackson and Weakland examines the advantages of involving the entire family in the therapeutic process. They begin with the assumption that emotional disorder is a function of distortions in family transactions, involving communication and affective elements. They postulate that the distorted family interaction patterns should be the focus of the therapist's concern, and that changes effected there will lead to a healthier re-organization of the family system, a new homeostasis.

Attempts to apply the scientific method to the study of psychotherapy have raised a number of critical issues, not only about the validity of psychotherapy, but also about the efficacy of psychotherapy research itself. Protagonists in these debates generally fall into one of two camps: the scientifically-oriented researcher; and the clinically-oriented and intuitive therapist. Strupp, who has tried to combine both roles, comments upon the issues central to this ongoing debate and offers the opinion that the voluminous research, for better or worse, has exerted little demonstrable influence upon the theory and practice of psychotherapy. ■

FRIEDA FROMM-REICHMANN

Recent Advances in Psychoanalysis*

Before attempting any discussion of recent advances in psychoanalysis a brief review should be given of some basic concepts of classical psychoanalysis versus its modifications in recent modern dynamic psychoanalytic conceptual thinking, so that a useful frame of reference may be established.

Advances achieved in psychoanalysis in recent years are in relation to these conceptions, to the method and technique of therapy, and to the types of patients who can be treated by psychoanalytic psychotherapy.(1)

BASIC PSYCHOANALYTIC CONCEPTS

Psychoanalysis understands the functioning of the human mind as the result of the dynamic interaction between mental operations on various levels and with different qualities of awareness. (Freud: Conscious, preconscious, unconscious.) Thoughts and feelings which are incompatible with the standards of a person himself, with those of significant people in his environment or of his culture at large may be barred from awareness and recall ('repressed,' 'dis-

sociated') because of the effect of anxiety they would produce were they to remain in awareness. Unknown to the person, these repressed experiences remain alive in his mind and influence his thoughts, feelings, and actions. At times, this is the reason for people expressing things which are seemingly not meaningful. As psychoanalysts have learned to realize that their origin is on other levels of awareness, hence qualitatively different from those in which the person communicates, they have learned to understand that all mental and emotional manifestations are meaningful and, at least potentially, understandable.

This dynamic conception of the modes of operation of the human mind is in contrast to the pre-analytic, descriptive, psychiatric approach to an understanding of the working of the mind as a static entity. Poets and philosophers, of course, have known for centuries about the functional dichotomy of the human mind. It is the scientific discovery of its application to psychiatry and to psychology, and more specifically in the context of this paper, of its medical application to psychiatry, to psychotherapy, and to medicine at large (psychosomatic medicine), that I am discussing here.

To gain an understanding of human personality as characterized by psychoanalytic dynamic psychia-

* Reprinted by permission from *Journal of the American Medical Women's Association,* Vol. 4, 1959, pp. 320–326.

try, its functioning must be explored and understood genetically, that is, from its total history. The early developmental history of infancy and childhood plays a predominant role in the formation of character and personality and especially in the formation of patterns of human interrelationships. This early history is understood in terms of three elements complementing one another. They are: constitution, or that which a person brings with him, the influences of external circumstances at large, and, most of all, the specific important interpersonal experiences of the infant and young child with the significant people of his early environment. The latter play a portentous role, due to the length of time and the extent of the biological and psychological dependence of the human.

Unknown to the person, this pattern formation and its reappearance hold true also for the early traumatic interpersonal experiences which have been subjected to the process of dissociation or repression. Because they have been dissociated there can be no participation of such experiences in the growth and maturation of the rest of the personality. It is their reflection in the interpersonal experiences of later life which is the salience of many distorted evaluations of and responses to these experiences throughout life, on the one hand, and of the mental patient's unwitting, compulsive search for their repetition, on the other. Whether the connection of these early, unclarified interpersonal experiences is with love, hatred, pain, anxiety, or other feelings and emotions, their transference to the people of one's later life plays a very important role in all relationships.

So much, in brief, about the generally accepted basic psychoanalytic concepts of the functioning of the human mind and personality. I shall endeavor now to outline briefly a few highlights of the various psychoanalytic conceptions of human developmental history because they form the frame of reference for all genetically oriented psychoanalytic psychotherapy.

DEVELOPMENTAL HISTORY

The early developmental history as conceived by Freud is psychosexual in nature.(2, 3, 4, 5) He understands the various phases of a person's development to be the outcome of a response to the lust obtainable and the interpersonal expression available by means of the bodily zones of food intake and elimination. Consequently, Freud speaks of an oral, anal, and phallic state of one's pregenital psychosexual development, all of which precede the ability

of a person to feel genital lust. The sexual energy manifesting itself in these psychosexual pregenital and genital interests and activities, Freud calls libido. He conceives the course of character development and personality in its ultimate mentally healthy outcome to be the result of this libidnal energy having run a complete and uninterrupted course, from the early oral state to the time at which the human gains the ability to feel primarily genital lust in relation to another person of the opposite sex.

According to Freud, a person matures as he learns to take care of the desexualization of his pregenital libido by means of sublimation, reaction formation, over-compensation, etc. Subsequently he develops the ability for orgastic genital experiences with a mature person of the opposite sex.

OEDIPUS COMPLEX

This is done first in terms of the Oedipus complex, the situation in which the genitalization of libido is felt in connection with a tender and sexual affection, for the parent of the opposite sex and concomitant feelings of rivalry and hatred for the parent of the same sex. The Oedipus constellation in the mentally healthy is resolved by the child's tendency to use the parent of the same sex as a model for its own further developmental patterns and ideal formations, and the parent of the opposite sex as a person through whom it learns to develop friendly interpersonal relationships.

The ability to amalgamate feelings of emotional tenderness and of sexual attraction toward one and the same person is considered another evidence of matureness. Freud views love as an outcome and a concomitant feeling of sexual attraction to another person.

In the course of neurotic character development, according to Freud's concepts, the progress of libidinal energy from oral to genital primacy is interrupted and incomplete. The libidnal charge is fixated or attached emotionally to one of the pregenital levels of the psychosexual development. Also, the neurotic person has not succeeded in overcoming the early conflicts of the original Oedipus constellation. According to Freud, these early conflicts constitute one universally valid reason for the later development of neurotic disorders.

The doctrine of the ubiquitousness and of the sexual nature of the Oedipus complex has been revised by many psychoanalytic authors and cultural anthropologists. (Boehm, (6) Fromm, (7) Malinowski, (8) Mullahy, (9) et al). They would demonstrate, first, that in matriarchal societies it may not be the father but an uncle who is the target for the little boy's hatred; second, that the boy's hatred against the father, where encountered, is much more frequently based upon his resentment of the authoritative prerogatives of the father figure and/or his envy of the interpersonal intimacy between the father and mother, than upon a sexual origin.

Sullivan viewed the various phases of developmental history in terms of the interpersonal experiences characteristic of each of these phases of development. (10) He referred to the period of infancy, the childhood period, the juvenile era, preadolescence, and, as a last developmental phase, adolescence.

The period of infancy he refers to as the time during which the human is in contact with the mothering one by empathic linkage, the state of non-verbal contact through non-sensory channels which is characteristic of the early mother-infant relationship. In varying degrees, empathy may operate in people throughout their lives. It is the quality due to which non-verbalized, meaningful communication is frequently successful and its operation becomes therapeutically important in the psychiatrist's dealings with his mental patients, especially with mute or inarticulate ones.

The childhood period, Sullivan characterizes by the development of mutual, verbalized communication, contentment in a communal life with authoritarian adults, and the more or less personalized pets, toys, and other objects.

The juvenile era is characterized by maturation of the need for compeers and of one's talents for such interpersonal phenomena as co-operation, competition, and compromise.

Preadolescence is a time during which the need for a chum to love is a predominant interpersonal factor. Love, as defined by Sullivan and Fromm, (11) is the state or relatedness in which a person is as interested in the loved one's wellbeing, satisfaction, and security, growth, and maturation, as he is in his own.

Adolescence is the period that is characterized by the process of puberty, gradually producing a maturing sense of self realization. This is the time when there is a need to break away from the authoritative people of childhood in a rather dramatic way, via the detour of exchanging them for dependence upon and admiration for one's heroes and heroines. In this way the ability to form independent evaluational judgments is finally gained and ultimately the capacity is developed for establishing durable relationships of intimacy.

PSYCHIATRY—THE SCIENCE OF INTERPERSONAL RELATIONSHIPS

This interpersonal concept of the developmental history is an illustrative part of Sullivan's total doctrine of psychiatry as being the art and science of interpersonal relationships, which means that human personality functions and can be understood only in terms of a person's actual or phantasy relationships and through the medium of a person's contacts and exchange with others.

The emotional importance of the bodily zones of intake and elimination and of their functions during early life is not denied, of course, by any of the modern psychoanalytic psychiatrists. (Fromm, (12) Horney. (13)). However, many of them do not believe that character and personality trends can be understood as the outcome of various forms of desexualization, as has been described in the review of the basic classical psychoanalytic concepts. Fromm, for instance, sees the fundamental basis of character formation in the specific kind of relatedness of a person to the world as it is molded in childhood by the family, the psychic agent of society. His concept of a receptive, exploitative, hoarding, and marketing character versus a productive character who is able "to use his powers and to realize the potentialities inherent in him," in a positive, life-furthering sense are illustrative of his approach.

We see from these concepts, then, that modern developmental psychoanalytic theory is characterized by the maintenance of the paramount significance of the total developmental history and by the negation of its classical psychosexual interpretation.

Freud's conception of the emotional significance of immediate environmental influences for the understanding of human personality and for the treatment of human psychopathology has been broadened in the direction of the inclusion of cultural influences on a general scale versus his otherwise predominantly biological approach to human psychopathology. The concepts of Fromm, (12, 14) Horney, (13, 15) Kardiner, (16) Sullivan, (10, 17) et al, on the Oedipus constellation, may serve as an example for this development.

PSYCHOANALYTIC CONCEPTS OF ANXIETY

Another expression of the changes and advances in psychoanalytic thinking and therapy is with regard to some mental symptoms, among them the most outstanding one: anxiety. The study of the concepts of anxiety as developed in the various schools of psychoanalytic thinking is of greatest importance for any student and practitioner in the field, since the understanding and adequate handling of the patient's anxiety plays a crucial role in all psychopathology, hence in all psychoanalytic psychotherapy.

Freud has defined anxiety in his early writings as the correlate of repressed libidinal strivings. Later he saw it as a person's fear at the realization of culturally inacceptable inner strivings. (18) This definition is similar to the one Sullivan gives in his interpersonal frame of reference. (10, 19) In Sullivan's definition, anxiety is the discomfort which the child learns to feel in the presence of the disapproval of the significant adult who first uses the arousal of this discomfort as a tool while training the child to abide by the basic requirements of acculturation. With great variations as to the threshold of endurance, anxiety remains effective throughout people's lives in response to disapproval from important people which interferes with a person's security and prestige. Sullivan has taught the understanding of all mental disorders as an expression of and an attempt at warding off anxiety. Horney speaks of four principal modes of defense against anxiety: affection, submissiveness, power, withdrawal. She teaches that the craving for affection, for power, and for control plays a paramount role in the development of neuroses and neurotic personalities.

Where there is anxiety there is insecurity; where there is insecurity there is lack of self-respect; where there is lack of self-respect there is lack of respect for others. Anxiety causes impairment of relatedness to others, fear of friendliness in giving and taking, loneliness and hostility, all well-known symptoms in mental patients.

This brief outline of psychoanalytic concepts may suffice as a background for the following discussion of the recent advances in the method and technique of psychoanalytic psychotherapy and the types of patients who may be treated by modern, dynamic psychoanalytic psychotherapy.

ETIOLOGY OF MENTAL DISORDER

In the light of the dynamic and genetic conceptions of the working of the mind, human psychopathology is understood by all dynamic psychiatrists as the outcome of early warp, thwarting experiences, and severe frustrations in relation to a significant person in the infant's or child's environment. In the upbringing of our present day, circumscribed as it is by family life, as a rule, it is a parent who is responsible for warping experiences, the threat of which is too great

to be offset by other benign influences. The type of emotional disturbance which a person develops will depend upon the timing of the first decisive blow of a set of such traumatic experiences and from the presence or absence of other benign or malignant interpersonal influences. Many emotional experiences of his later life will be undergone, actually or by his interpretation, as if they were really repetitions of the original traumata in the childhood setting.

In other words, whenever a person who has undergone too severe or too frequent early traumatic experiences is exposed to later life experiences engendering pain, hostility, anxiety, etc., he has to cope not only with the actual experience as such, but in addition with its repetitional validity. This repetitional aspect stems from his early dissociated, therefore never satisfactorily integrated, traumatic experiences with all their immature misevaluation and their concomitant anxiety.

In order to avoid misunderstanding, I wish to state at this point, that in discussing the psychopathological effects of keeping emotional experiences from awareness, I do not mean to say that all dissociative or repressed processes are psychopathological in nature. The contrary is true. Man depends upon successful dissociations and processes of selective inattention for the mastery of his psychobiological existence. It is the surplus of painful and anxiety-arousing emotional experience, whose barring from awareness creates psychopathological problems. If a patient's original traumatic material is brought to awareness in psychotherapy, it can be submitted to revaluation on the present level of the patient's matureness, anxiety can be relieved and recent traumatic experience can be freed from the additional weight stemming from non-integrated previous experience. Hence, the bringing to awareness and the subsequent evaluation of repressed material must be an integral part of the psychotherapeutic process just as will the investigation of those feelings, the reflection of which will be transferred to the people of one's later life.

PSYCHOANALYTIC PSYCHOTHERAPY

In the situation of psychoanalytic psychotherapy these feelings, unknown to the patient himself, will be transferred to the psychotherapist and so they can be studied *in statu nascendi* by psychiatrist and patient. Otherwise, treatment must be directed toward resolving psychopathological repression and dissociation and understanding the patient's difficulties in terms of his developmental history. This aim is attained in using the following psychotherapeutic tools: collecting data from the patient regarding biographical and historical facts which the patient is able to offer; his presenting problems, previous problems and crises situations; biographical data especially regarding his developmental history; his private mental experiences, such as dreams and daydreams, hallucinatory and delusional experiences.

The means for collecting the data are listening intelligently, as a participant observer, to all that the patient has to say; asking simply meaningful and pertinent questions; encouraging associative thinking; and picking up marginal thoughts and physical sensations, where direct information is failing. Further therapeutically valid material presents itself in the repetition and reactivation, during treatment, of the powers which originally motivated the patient's dissociative procedures. As mentioned before, this also takes place, and is of the essence for therapeutic use in the vicissitudes of the doctor-patient relationship, in its real and in its distorted, "parataxic," aspects — in classical terminology, in the patient's "transference" experiences. Once the pertinent data is carefully collected, interpretative collaboration between the patient and the psychotherapist follows, with regard to the understanding of the hidden meaning of the previously dissociated material, as to its genetics, dynamics, and content.

INTERPRETATION

Interpretation means translating into the language of awareness, and thereby bringing into the open, that which the patient communicates, without being conscious of its contents, dynamics, revealing connections with other experiences or of various implications pertaining to its factual or emotional background.

At the present state of development in psychoanalytic psychotherapy, special interpretative attention is given to the clarification of the dynamic significance of the defense mechanisms, the security operations which the anxious mental patient uses, wittingly or unwittingly, in his dealings with his fellow men, including the psychotherapist. These security operations are directed against anxiety producing, real or alleged, threats to the patient's safety and prestige which he expects from the people of his environment. This makes it advisable that great attention be paid to the actual interpersonal experiences of the patient in his everyday life, both previous to and during the treatment situation, and

that special attention be paid to the crises which may have precipitated his entering treatment, and as they recur while he is undergoing psychotherapy. (15, 10, 29).

Part of the previously hidden meaning of the patient's material reveals itself and part of his dissociations resolve themselves by the mere process of relating the data to the doctor, that is, by bringing his hitherto private covert experiences into contact with outward reality. Another part gets clarified in the course of the interpretative investigation of the patient's security operations. Only what remains unclarified by these two devices should be uncovered and revalued by direct interpretation of content. By and large, content interpretation, *per se*, is not considered as important today as it was in the early years of psychoanalysis, and it is used with ever-increasing thriftiness, caution, and discrimination.

No cure is accomplished according to present classical and modified psychoanalytic knowledge by any single, one-time understanding of any single symptom or any single previously dissociated experience. All emotional experiences which are made accessible to the patient's awareness and mature emotional judgment have to be recognized and accepted ("worked through") repeatedly in various contexts. In doing so, psychiatrist and patient should be guided by what gradually transpires as the patient's central problem. Working through should be continued until the time is reached when the intellectual understanding of this problem, its previously dissociated causes and its various interlocking mental and emotional ramifications are gradually transformed into real creative emotional insight.

FREE ASSOCIATIONS

The encouragement of the patient's "free associations" is considered to be a backbone of classical psychoanalytic therapy. It is designed to eliminate the patient's conscious control over his mental productions, thus bringing out previously repressed and dissociated material.

Since the psychoanalytic doctrine and method were first conceived, an impressive body of knowledge and experience as to the modes of operation and expression used in interpersonal processes which are outside of awareness has been collected. Therefore, many modern dynamic psychotherapists do not feel the indiscriminate use of the so-called method of "free association" to be a basic requirement in psychoanalytic therapy. This marks another change in psychoanalytic therapy.

Many psychoanalysts feel that a sufficient amount of recognizable dissociated material comes to the surface and may arise into awareness in more directed psychotherapeutic interchange and directed focused associative thinking.

DREAM INTERPRETATION

Scientific dream interpretation continues to be considered an important means of understanding many thoughts and feelings that the patient cannot express while awake, because of the fact that, during sleep, control and censorship of his mental processes are eliminated or at least greatly reduced. The extent to which dream interpretation may be used in any single psychotherapeutic process depends upon the therapeutic usefulness of both the nature of a patient's dreams and the understanding and interpretative skill of the psychotherapist.

DIDACTIC PSYCHOANALYSIS

In this connection, emphasis may be placed upon the fact that the extent and nuance of the use of the various psychotherapeutic tools in each course of treatment will, of necessity, be co-determined by the assets and liabilities of both persons concerned, the patient and the doctor as participant observer. This being so, a personal psychoanalysis is among the training requirements for any psychiatrist who wishes to do psychoanalytic psychotherapy.

SET-UP IN PSYCHOANALYTIC PSYCHOTHERAPY

The trend toward more therapeutic attention being paid to the actual realities in the patient's life is responsible for several practical changes in the set-up of the treatment situation. Among these recent trends is the relinquishment, by many psychoanalysts, of the binding rule that the patient must lie on the couch, the doctor seated invisibly behind him. As is now understood by many psychoanalytic psychotherapists, this arrangement interfered, for quite a number of patients, with an experience of reality and spontaneity in the exchange between patient and doctor. This feeling of reality and a spontaneous interchange should be encouraged, notwithstanding the maintenance of the strictly professional character of the doctor-patient relationship. Present arrangements of many psychoanalysts allow for patients to sit or to lie down, depending upon the way it appears to work best with each patient. With some patients this may be decided upon at once for the entire course of treatment,

with others changes of position once or repeatedly may be advisable during the course of the treatment.

BRIEF PSYCHOTHERAPY—GROUP PSYCHOTHERAPY

Other recent changes in psychoanalytic psychotherapy stem from research and practical endeavor directed toward shortening the psychoanalytic process with a carefully selected group of patients. Important work in that direction is under way at one of the leading psychoanalytic training centers in this country, the Chicago Psychoanalytic Institute. (20, 21) The successful introduction of psychoanalytic concepts into group psychotherapy as it has been developed in many psychotherapy centers during and after the last war should also be mentioned in this connection. (22, 23, 24)

PSYCHOSOMATIC MEDICINE

The technique of psychoanalytic psychotherapy was originally created for the special application to psychoneuroses. Treatment of physical symptoms was in terms of an interpretative approach to the "conversion symptoms" of the hysteric.(2, 3, 4, 5) Modern developments in psychosomatic medicine are mainly due to psychoanalytic research.(25, 26, 27) Two sets of results, which have become of great significance for practically all branches of modern medicine, stem from this advance in psychoanalytic development. One is the psychotherapeutic approach to the emotional roots of the etiological factors of somatic symptomatology, where previously symptoms and syndromes were approached in terms of their clinical appearance. The other is the finding of certain laws governing the correlation between certain types of psychoneurotic personalities and their choice of bodily disturbances. The psychosomatic significance of high blood pressure, gastric ulcers, and the various types of colitis, asthma, and hay fever is by now known to every physician as representative of these findings.

PSYCHOSES

There is one more important progressive step in psychoanalytic psychotherapy, which is signified by a modification in the technique of psychoanalysis for the application to the psychoses.(28–34) An early attempt at doing classical psychoanalysis with a manic depressive was made by Abraham.(35) Recently research and therapeutic endeavor focused around the manic depressive group has been done in England.(36) In this country, severely disturbed schizophrenics have been approached with modified psychoanalytic techniques. This became possible in line with the previously described recent changes in psychoanalytic technique and as a result of the two aforementioned great discoveries of psychoanalytic psychiatry: that all mental manifestations, including those of the mentally disordered, are potentially meaningful; and that there is interpersonal interaction between any two people who meet, including the mentally disturbed patient and the psychotherapist.

Out of this grew the psychopathologically significant insight: that the difference between healthy, neurotic, and psychotic people is much more one of degree than one in kind; that the mentally handicapped may have assets which may not be found in the healthy, and that the healthy may have liabilities not duplicated in the mentally disturbed.(36) In brief, that we are all "Much more simply human than otherwise."(10)

Some psychoanalytic psychiatrists hope that it is not too optimistic to harbor the dream that this psychiatric insight may in time develop into a small contribution toward improving the mutual understanding between the peoples of the disturbed world of today.

BIBLIOGRAPHY

(1) FROMM-REICHMANN, FRIEDA, Recent advances in psychoanalytic psychotherapy, Psychiatry, 4: 161–164, May '41.

(2) FREUD, SIGMUND, A general introduction to psychoanalysis, Boni & Liveright, New York, 1920.

(3) BRILL, A. A., The basic writings of Sigmund Freud, Modern Library, New York, 1938.

(4) HENDRICKS, IVES, Facts and Theories of Psychoanalysis, Alfred Knopf, New York, 1939.

(5) FENICHEL, OTTO, Outline of Clinical Psychoanalysis, W. W. Norton, New York, 1934.

(6) BOEHM, FELIX, Intern. Ztschr. Psychoanalyse, 12: 66–79, '26. Not translated.

(7) FROMM, ERICH, in The Family, Its Function and Destiny, A Synthesis; Anshen, Ruth Nanda, ed., Chapters XVII, XIX, Harper & Brothers, New York, 1949.

(8) MALINOWSKI, B., Sex and Repression in Savage Society, Harcourt, New York; K. Paul, Trenck Trubner & Co., London, 1927.

(9) MULLAHY, PATRICK, Oedipus Myth and Complex, Hermitage Press, Inc., New York, 1948 (offers orientation on the attitude of all psychoanalytic schools to the problem).

(10) SULLIVAN, H. S., Conceptions of modern psychiatry, William Alanson White Memorial Lectures, Psychiatry 3: 1–117, Feb. '40. Reprinted as monograph. The William Alanson White Psychiatric Foundation, Washington, D.C., 1947.

(11) FROMM, ERICH, Selfishness and self-love, Psychiatry, 2: 507–523, Nov. '39.

(12) FROMM, ERICH, Escape From Freedom, Farrar and Rhinehart, Inc., New York and Toronto, 1941.

(13) HORNEY, KAREN, The Neurotic Personality of Our Time, W. W. Norton & Company, New York, 1937.

(14) FROMM, ERICH, Man For Himself; an inquiry into the psychology and ethics, Rhinehart, New York, 1947.

(15) HORNEY, KAREN, New Ways in Psychoanalysis. W. W. Norton & Company, Inc., New York, 1939.

(16) KARDINER, ABRAM, The Individual and His Society, Columbia University Press, New York, 1939.

(17) SULLIVAN, H. S., A note on the implications of psychiatry, the study of interpersonal relations, for Investigations in the Social Sciences, Amer. J. Sociol., 43: 848–861, May '37.

(18) FREUD, SIGMUND, The Problem of Anxiety, W. W. Norton & Company, New York, 1936.

(19) SULLIVAN, H. S., The meaning of anxiety in psychiatry and in life, Psychiatry 1: 1–13, Feb. '48.

(20) ALEXANDER, FRANZ, FRENCH, TROMAS M., and others, Psychoanalytic Therapy, Ronald Press, New York, 1946.

(21) Proceedings of the Psychotherapy Council, Chicago Psychoanalytic Institute, 1946.

(22) ABRAHAM, JOSEPH, Group psychotherapy; remains on its basis and application, Med. Ann. District of Columbia, 16: 612–616, Nov. '47.

(23) ACKERMAN, N. W., Dynamic patterns in group psychotherapy, Psychiatry, 7: 341–348, Nov. '44.

(24) SLAVSON, S. R., An Introduction To Group Therapy, Commonwealth Fund, London, Oxford, 1943.

(25) The Journal of Psychosomatic Medicine, The Williams and Wilkins Company, Baltimore, Md.

(26) DUNBAR, H. F., Emotions and Bodily Changes, Columbia University Press, New York, 1938.

(27) WEISS, E., and ENGLISH, O. S., Psychosomatic Medicine, W. B. Saunders Co., Philadelphia and London, 1943.

(28) SULLIVAN, H. S., Environmental factors in etiology and course under treatment of schizophrenia, Med. J. and Rec., 133: 19–22, Jan. 7, '31.

(29) SULLIVAN, H. S., Therapeutic investigations in schizophrenia, Psychiatry, 10: 121–125, May '47.

(30) FEDERN, P., Psychoanalysis of psychoses, Psychiatric Quarterly, 17: 3–19, '43.

(31) FEDERN, P., Principles of psychotherapy in latent schizophrenia, Am. J. Psychotherapy, 1: 129–144, Apr. '47.

(32) FROMM-REICHMANN, FRIEDA, Transference problems in schizophrenics, The Psychoanalytic Quarterly, 8: 412–426, Oct. '39; reprinted in Contemporary Psychopathology, S. S. Tomkins, Ed., Harvard University Press, '43.

(33) FROMM-REICHMANN, FRIEDA, Psychoanalytic psychotherapy with psychotics, Psychiatry, 6: 277–279, Nov. '43.

(34) FROMM-REICHMANN, FRIEDA, Notes on the development of treatment of schizophrenics by psychoanalytic psychotherapy, Psychiatry, 11: 263–273, Aug. '48.

(35) ABRAHAM, K., Selected Papers, pp 473 ff., Internat. Psycho-analytical Library, No. 13.

(36) KLEIN, MELANIE, A contribution to the psychogenesis of manic-depressive states, Internat. Journ. Psycho-analysis, 16: 145–174, Apr. '35.

(37) FROMM-REICHMANN, FRIEDA, Remarks on the philosophy of mental disorder, Psychiatry, 9: 293–308, Nov. '46.

CARL R. ROGERS

A Process Conception of Psychotherapy*

I would like to take you with me on a journey of exploration. The object of the trip, the goal of the search, is to try to learn something of the *process* of psychotherapy, or the *process* by which personality change takes place. I would warn you that the goal has not yet been achieved and that it seems as though the expedition has advanced only a few short miles into the jungle. Yet perhaps if I can take you with me, you will be tempted to discover new and profitable avenues of further advance.

THE PUZZLE OF PROCESS

My own reason for engaging in such a search seems simple to me. Just as many psychologists have been interested in the invariant aspects of personality — the unchanging aspects of intelligence, temperament, personality structure — so I have long been interested in the invariant aspects of *change* in personality. Do personality and behavior change? What commonalities exist in such changes? What commonalities exist in the conditions which precede change? Most important of all, what is the process by which such change occurs?

Puzzling over this problem of getting at the process has led me to realize how little objective research deals with process in any field. Objective research slices through the frozen moment to provide us with an exact picture of the interrelationships which exist at that moment. But our understanding of the ongoing movement — whether it be the process of fermentation, or the circulation of the blood, or the process of atomic fission — is generally provided by a theoretical formulation, often supplemented, where feasible, with a clinical observation of the process. I have thus come to realize that perhaps I am hoping for too much to expect that research procedures can shed light directly upon the process of personality change. Perhaps only theory can do that.

A Rejected Method

When I determined, more than a year ago, to make a fresh attempt to understand the manner in which such change takes place, I first considered various ways in which the experience of therapy might be described in terms of some other theoretical framework. There was much that was appealing in the field of communication theory, with its concepts of feedback, input and output signals, and the like. There was the possibility of describing the process of therapy in terms of learning theory or in terms of general systems theory. As I studied these avenues of understanding, I became convinced that it would be possible to translate the process of psychotherapy into any one of these theoretical frameworks. It would, I believe, have certain advantages to do so. But I also became convinced that, in a field so new, this is not what is most needed.

I came to a conclusion which others have reached before: in a new field perhaps what is needed first is to steep oneself in the *events*, to approach the phenomena with as few preconceptions as possible, to take a naturalist's observational, descriptive approach to these events, and to draw forth those low-level inferences which seem most native to the material itself.

* Reprinted by permission from *American Psychologist*, Vol. 13, 1958, pp. 142–150.

The Mode of Approach

So, for the past year, I have used the method which so many of us use for generating hypotheses, a method which psychologists in this country seem so reluctant to expose or comment on. I used myself as a tool. I have spent many hours listening to recorded therapeutic interviews — trying to listen as naively as possible. I have endeavored to soak up all the clues I could capture as to the process, as to what elements are significant in change. Then I have tried to abstract from that sensing the simplest abstractions which would describe them. Here I have been much stimulated and helped by the thinking of many of my colleagues, but I would like to mention my special indebtedness to Eugene Gendlin, William Kirtner, and Fred Zimring, whose demonstrated ability to think in new ways about these matters has been particularly helpful and from whom I have borrowed heavily.

The next step has been to take these observations and low-level abstractions and formulate them in such a way that testable hypotheses can readily be drawn from them. This is the point I have reached. I make no apology for the fact that I am reporting no empirical investigations of these formulations. If past experience is any guide, then I may rest assured that, if the formulations I am about to present check in any way with the subjective experience of other therapists, then a great deal of research will be stimulated, and in a few years there will be ample evidence of the degree of truth and falsity in the statements which follow.

A Basic Condition

If we were studying the process of growth in plants, we would assume certain constant conditions of temperature, moisture, and sunlight in forming our conceptualizations of the process. Likewise in conceptualizing the process of personality change in psychotherapy, I shall assume a constant and optimal set of conditions for facilitating this change. I have recently tried to spell out these conditions in some detail (7). For our present purpose, I believe I can state this assumed condition in one word. Throughout the discussion which follows, I shall assume that the client experiences himself as being fully *received*. By this I mean that, whatever his feelings — fear, despair, insecurity, anger; whatever his mode of expression — silence, gestures, tears, or words; whatever he finds himself being in this moment, he senses that he is psychologically *received*, just as he is, by the therapist. There is implied in this term the concept of being understood, empathically, and the concept of acceptance. It is also well to point out that it is the client's experience of this condition which makes it optimal, not merely the fact of its existence in the therapist.

In all that I shall say, then, about the process of change, I shall assume as a constant an optimal and maximum condition of being received.

The Emerging Continuum

In trying to grasp and conceptualize the process of change, I was initially looking for elements which would mark or characterize change itself. I was thinking of change as an entity and searching for its specific attributes. What gradually emerged in my understanding as I exposed myself to the raw material of change was a continuum of a different sort than I had conceptualized before.

Individuals move, I began to see, not from a fixity or homeostasis through change to a new fixity, though such a process is indeed possible. But much the more significant continuum is from fixity to changingness, from rigid structure to flow, from stasis to process. I formed the tentative hypothesis that perhaps the qualities of the client's expression at any one point might indicate his position on this continuum, might indicate where he stood in the process of change.

SEVEN STAGES OF PROCESS

I gradually developed this concept of a continuum of process, discriminating seven stages in it, with examples from recorded therapeutic interviews illustrating the qualities of the process at each stage. It would be quite impossible to give all of this crude scale here, but I shall try to suggest something of its nature by describing very briefly Stages 1 and 2, to illustrate the lower end of the continuum, and describing more fully Stages 5, 6, and 7, to fill in the upper end of the scale.[1]

First Stage

The individual in this stage of fixity and remoteness of experiencing is not likely to come voluntarily for therapy. However, I can to some degree describe the characteristics of this stage:

There is an unwillingness to communicate self. Communication is only about externals.

[1] An amplification of this paper, giving the whole scale with more extended illustrations, may be obtained from the author by those who are interested in using it for research purposes.

Feelings and personal meanings are neither recognized as such nor owned.

Personal constructs (to use Kelly's helpful term, 4) are extremely rigid.

Close and communicative relationships are construed as dangerous.

No problems are recognized or perceived at this stage. There is no desire to change.

There is much blockage of internal communication.

Perhaps these brief statements will convey something of the psychological fixity of this end of the continuum. The individual has little or no recognition of the ebb and flow of the feeling life within him. He construes his experience rigidly in terms of the past. He is (to borrow the term of Gendlin and Zimring) structure-bound in his manner of experiencing, reacting to now "by finding it to be like a past experience and then reacting to that past, feeling it" (3). The individual at this stage represents stasis, fixity, the opposite of flow or change.

Second Stage of Process

When the person in the first stage can experience himself as fully received, then the second stage follows. We seem to know very little about how to provide the experience of being received for the person in the first stage, but it is occasionally achieved in play or group therapy where the person can be exposed to a receiving climate, without himself having to take any initiative, for a long enough time to experience himself *as received*. In any event where he does experience this, then a slight loosening and flowing of symbolic expression occurs, which tends to be characterized by the following:

Expression begins to flow in regard to nonself topics.

Ex. "I guess I suspect my father has often felt very insecure in his business relations."[2]

Problems are perceived as external to self.

Ex. "Disorganization keeps cropping up in my life."

There is no sense of personal responsibility in problems.

Ex. This is illustrated in the above excerpt.

Feelings are described as unowned, or sometimes as past objects.

Ex. Counselor: "If you want to tell me something of what brought you here. . . ." Client: "The symptom was

[2] The many examples used as illustrations are taken from recorded interviews, unless otherwise noted. For the most part, they are taken from interviews which have never been published, but a number of them are taken from the report of two cases in a chapter of a forthcoming book (6).

— it was — just being very depressed." This is an excellent example of the way in which internal problems can be perceived and communicated about as entirely external. She is not saying "I am depressed" or even "I was depressed." Her feeling is handled as a remote, unowned object, entirely external to self.

Feelings may be exhibited, but are not recognized as such or owned.

Experiencing is bound by the structure of the past.

Ex. "I suppose the compensation I always make is, rather than trying to communicate with people or have the right relationship with them, to compensate by, well, shall we say, being on an intellectual level." Here the client is beginning to recognize the way in which her experiencing is bound by the past. Her statement also illustrates the remoteness of experiencing at this level. It is as though she were holding her experience at arm's length.

Personal constructs are rigid, and unrecognized as being constructs, but are thought of as facts.

Ex. "I can't ever do anything right — can't ever finish it."

Differentiation of personal meanings and feelings is very limited and global.

The preceding example is a good illustration. "I can't ever" is one instance of a black and white differentiation, as is also the use of "right" in this absolute sense.

Contradictions may be expressed, but with little recognition of them as contradictions.

Ex. "I want to know things, but I look at the same page for an hour."

As a comment on this second stage of the process of change, it might be said that a number of clients who voluntarily come for help are in this stage, but we (and probably therapists in general) have a very minimal degree of success in working with them. This seems, at least, to be a reasonable conclusion from Kirtner's study (5), though his conceptual framework was somewhat different. We seem to know too little about the ways in which a person at this stage may come to experience himself as "received."

The Fifth Stage

I shall omit any description of Stages 3 and 4. Each involves a further loosening of symbolic expression in regard to feelings, constructs, and self. These stages constitute much of psychotherapy. But going beyond these stages, we can again mark a point on the continuum and call it Stage 5. If the client feels himself received in his expressions, behaviors, and experiences at the third and fourth stage, then this sets in motion still further loosenings, and the freedom of organismic flow is increased. Here I believe we can again delineate crudely the qualities of this phase of the process:

Feelings are expressed freely as in the present.

Ex. "I expected kinda to get a severe rejection — this I expect all the time . . . somehow I guess I even feel it with you. . . . It's hard to talk about because I want to be the best I can possibly be with you." Here feelings regarding the therapist and the client in relationship to the therapist, emotions often most difficult to reveal, are expressed openly.

Feelings are very close to being fully experienced. They "bubble up," "seep through," in spite of the fear and distrust which the client feels at experiencing them with fullness and immediacy.

Ex. Client is talking about an external event. Suddenly she gets a pained, stricken look. Therapist: "What — what's hitting you now?" Client: "I don't know. (She cries) . . . I must have been getting a little too close to something I didn't want to talk about." The feeling has almost seeped through into awareness, in spite of her.

There is a beginning tendency to realize that experiencing a feeling involves a direct referent.

The example just cited illustrates this in part. The client knows she has experienced something, knows she is not clear as to what she has experienced. But there is also the dawning realization that the referent of these vague cognitions lies within her, in an organismic event against which she can check her symbolization and her cognitive formulations. This is often shown by expressions that indicate the closeness or distance the individual feels from this referent. Ex. "I really don't have my finger on it. I'm just kinda describing it."

There is surprise and fright, rarely pleasure, at the feelings which "bubble through."

Ex. Client, talking about past home relationships, "That's not important any more. Hmm. [Pause] That was somehow very meaningful — but I don't have the slightest idea why. . . . Yes, that's it! I can forget about it now and — why, it *isn't* that important. Wow! All that miserableness and stuff!"

There is an increasing ownership of self feelings, and a desire to be these, to be the "real me."

Ex. "The real truth of the matter is that I'm not the sweet, forbearing guy that I try to make out that I am. I get irritated at things. I feel like snapping at people, and I feel like being selfish at times; and I don't know why I should pretend I'm *not* that way." This is a clear instance of the greater degree of acceptance of all feelings.

Experiencing is loosened, no longer remote, and frequently occurs with little postponement.

There is little delay between the organismic event and the full subjective living of it. A beautifully precise account of this is given by a client. Ex. "I'm still having a little trouble trying to figure out what this sadness — and the weepiness — means. I just know I feel it when I get close to a certain kind of feeling — and usually when I do get weepy, it helps me to kinda break through a wall I've set up because of things that have happened. I feel hurt about something and then automatically this kind of shields things up and then I feel like I can't really touch or feel *anything* very much . . . and if I'd be *able* to feel, or could *let* myself feel the instantaneous feeling when I'm hurt, I'd immediately start being weepy right then, but I can't."

Here we see him regarding his feeling as an inner referent to which he can turn for greater clarity. As he senses his weepiness, he realizes that it is a delayed and partial experiencing of being hurt. He also recognizes that his defenses are such that he can not, at this point, experience the event of hurt when it occurs.

The ways in which experience is construed are much loosened. There are many fresh discoveries of personal constructs as constructs, and a critical examination and questioning of these.

Ex. A man says: "This idea of needing to please people — of *having* to do it — that's really been kind of a basic assumption of my life (he weeps quietly). It's kind of, you know, just one of the very unquestioned axioms that I *have* to please. I have no choice. I just *have* to." Here he is clear that this assumption has been a construct, and it is evident that its unquestioned status is at an end.

There is a strong and evident tendency toward exactness in differentiation of feelings and meanings.

A client speaks of "Some tension that grows in me, or some hopelessness, or some kind of incompleteness — and my life actually is very incomplete right now. . . . I just don't know. Seems to be, the closest thing it gets to, is *hopelessness*." Obviously he is trying to capture the exact term which for him symbolizes his experience.

There is an increasingly clear facing of contradictions and incongruences in experience.

Ex. "My conscious mind tells me I'm worthy. But someplace inside I don't believe it. I think I'm a rat — a no-good. I've no faith in my ability to do anything."

There is an increasing quality of acceptance of self-responsibility for the problems being faced, and a concern as to how he has contributed.
There are increasingly freer dialogues within the self — an improvement in, and reduced blockage of, internal communication.

Sometimes these dialogues are verbalized. Ex. "Something in me is saying 'What more do I have to give up? You've taken so much from me already.' This is *me* talking to *me* — the *me* way back in there who talks to the *me* who runs the show. It's complaining now, saying, 'You're getting too close! Go away!' "

I trust that the examples I have given of this fifth phase of the process continuum will make several points clear. In the first place, this phase is several hundred psychological miles from the first stage described. Here many aspects of the client are in flow, as against the rigidity of the first stage. He is very much closer to his organic being, which is always in process. He is much closer to being in the flow of his feelings. His constructions of experience are decidedly loosened and repeatedly being tested against referents and evidence within and without. Experience is much more highly differentiated, and thus internal communication, already flowing, can be much more exact.

As a general comment on the description thus far, it would be my observation that a person is never wholly at one or another stage of the process. There is, however, a general consistency in his manner of experiencing and expressing. Thus, a client who is generally at Stage 2 or 3 seems unlikely to exhibit any behaviors characteristic of Stage 5. This is especially true if we limit observations to a single defined area of related personal meanings in the client. Then I would hypothesize that there will be considerable regularity, that Stage 3 would rarely be found before Stage 2, that Stage 4 would rarely follow Stage 2 without Stage 3 intervening. Such tentative hypotheses can, of course, be put to empirical test.

The Sixth Stage

If I have been able to communicate some feeling for the scope and quality of the increased loosening, at each stage, of feeling, experiencing, and construing, then we are ready to look at the next stage, which appears, from observation, to be a very crucial one. Let me see if I can convey what I perceive to be its characteristic qualities.

Assuming that the client continues to be fully received in the therapeutic relationship, then the characteristics of Stage 5 tend to be followed by a very distinctive and often dramatic phase. It is characterized as follows:

A *feeling which has previously been "stuck," has been inhibited in its process quality, is experienced with immediacy now.*
A *feeling flows to its full result.*
A *present feeling is directly experienced with immediacy and richness.*
This immediacy of experiencing, and the feeling which constitutes its content, are accepted. This is something which is, not something to be denied, feared, struggled against.

All the preceding sentences attempt to describe slightly different facets of what is, when it occurs, a clear and definite phenomenon. It would take recorded examples to communicate its full quality, but I shall try to give an illustration without benefit of recording. A somewhat extended excerpt from the eightieth interview with a young man may communicate the way in which a client comes into Stage 6.

Client: "I could even conceive of it as a possibility that I could have a kind of tender concern for me. . . . Still, how could I be tender, be concerned for *myself*, when they're one and the same thing? But yet I can *feel* it so clearly. . . . You know, like taking care of a child. You want to give it this and give it that. . . . I can kind of clearly see the purposes for somebody else . . . but I can never see them for . . . myself, that I could do this for me, you know. Is it possible that I can really want to take care of myself, and make that a major purpose of my life? That means I'd have to deal with the whole world as if I were guardian of the most cherished and most wanted possession, that this *I* was between this precious *me* that I wanted to take care of and the whole world. . . . It's almost as if I *loved* myself — you know — that's strange — but it's true." Therapist: "It seems such a strange concept to realize. Why, it would mean I would face the world as though a part of my primary responsibility was taking care of this precious individual who is me — whom I love." Client: "Whom I care for — whom I feel so *close* to. Woof!! That's another *strange* one." Therapist: "It just seems *weird*." Client: "Yeah. It hits rather close somehow. The idea of my loving me and the taking care of me. [His eyes grow moist] That's a very, very nice one — very nice."

The recording would help to convey the fact that here is a feeling which had never been able to flow in him, which is experienced with immediacy, in this moment. It is a feeling which flows to its full result, without inhibition. It is experienced acceptantly, with no attempt to push it to one side or to deny it.

There is a quality of living subjectively in the experience, not feeling about it.

The client, in his *words*, may withdraw enough from the experience to feel about it, as in the above example, yet the recording makes it clear that his words are peripheral to the experiencing which is going on within him and in which he is living. The best communication of this in his words is "Woof!! That's another *strange* one."

Self as an object tends to disappear.

The self, at this moment, *is* this feeling. This is a being in the moment, with little self-conscious awareness, but with primarily a reflexive awareness, as Sartre terms it. The self *is*, subjectively, in the existential moment. It is not something one perceives.

Experiencing, at this stage, takes on a real process quality.

One client, a man who is approaching this stage, says that he has a frightened feeling about the source of a lot of secret thoughts in himself. He goes on: "The butterflies are the thoughts closest to the surface. Underneath there's a deeper flow. I feel very removed from it all. The deeper flow is like a great school of fish moving under the surface. I see the ones that break through the surface of the water — sitting with my fishing line in one hand, with a bent pin on the end of it — trying to find a better tackle — or better yet, a way of diving in. That's the scary thing. The image I get is that *I* want to be one of the fish myself." Therapist: "You want to be down there flowing along, too."

Though this client is not yet fully experiencing in a process manner, and hence does not fully exemplify this sixth point on the continuum, he foresees it so clearly that his description gives a real sense of its meaning.

Another characteristic of this stage of process is the physiological loosening which accompanies it.

Moistness in the eyes, tears, sighs, muscular relaxation are frequently evident. Often there are other physiological concomitants. I would hypothesize that in these moments, had we the measures for it, we would discover improved circulation, improved conductivity of nervous impulses. An example of the "primitive" nature of some of these sensations may be indicated in the following excerpt:

The client, a young man, has expressed the wish his parents would die or disappear. "It's kind of like wanting to wish them away, and wishing they had never been. . . . And I'm so ashamed of myself because then they call me, and off I go — swish! They're somehow still so strong. I don't know. There's some umbilical — I can almost feel it inside me — swish" [and he gestures, plucking himself away by grasping at his navel]. Therapist: "They really do have a hold on your umbilical cord." Client: "It's funny how real it feels . . . like a burning sensation, kind of, and when they say something which makes me anxious I can feel it right here [pointing]. I never thought of it quite that way." Therapist: "As though, if there's a disturbance in the relationship between you, then you do just feel it as though it was a strain on your umbilicus." Client: "Yeah, kind of like in my gut here. It's so hard to define the feeling that I feel there."

Here he is living subjectively in the feeling of dependence on his parents. Yet it would be inaccurate to say that he is perceiving it. He is *in* it, experiencing it as a strain on his umbilical cord.

In this stage, internal communication is free and relatively unblocked.

I believe this is quite adequately illustrated in the examples given. Indeed the phrase "internal communication" is no longer quite correct; for, as each of these examples illustrates, the crucial moment is a moment of integration, in which communication between different internal foci is no longer necessary, because they become *one*.

The incongruence between experience and awareness is vividly experienced as it disappears into congruence.

The relevant personal construct is dissolved in this experiencing moment, and the client feels cut loose from his previously stabilized framework.

I trust these two characteristics may acquire more meaning from the following example. A young man has been having difficulty getting close to a certain unknown feeling. "That's almost exactly what the feeling is, too — it was that I was living so much of my life, and seeing so much of my life, in terms of being *scared* of something." He tells how his professional activities are just to give him a little safety and "a little world where I'll be secure, you know. And for the same reason. [Pause] I was kind of letting it seep through. But I also tied it in with you and with my relationship with you, and one thing I feel about it is fear of its going away. [His tone changes to role-play more accurately his feeling.] Won't you let me have this? I kind of *need* it. I can be so lonely and scared without it." Therapist: "M-hmm, m-hmm. 'Let me hang on to it because I'd be terribly scared if I didn't!' . . . It's a kind of pleading thing too, isn't it?" Client: "I get a sense of — it's this kind of pleading little boy. It's this gesture of begging" [putting his hands up as if in prayer]. Therapist: "You put your hands in kind of a supplication." Client: "Yeah, that's right. '*Won't* you do this for me?' kind of. Oh, that's terrible! Who, *me? Beg?* . . . That's an emotion I've never felt clearly at all — something I've never been . . . [Pause] . . . I've got such a confusing feeling. One is, it's such a wondrous feeling to have these new things come out of me. It amazes me so much each time, and there's that same feeling, being scared that I've so much of this. [Tears] . . . I just don't know myself. Here's suddenly something I never realized, hadn't any inkling of — that it was some *thing* or some *way* I wanted to be."

Here we see a complete experiencing of his pleadingness, and a vivid recognition of the discrepancy between this experiencing and his concept of himself. Yet this experiencing of discrepancy exists in the moment of its disappearance. From now on he *is* a person who feels *pleading*, as well as many other feelings. As this moment dissolves the way he has construed himself, he feels cut loose from his previous world — a sensation which is both wondrous and frightening.

The moment of full experiencing becomes a clear and definite referent.

The examples given should indicate that the client is often not too clearly aware of what has "hit him" in these moments. Yet this does not seem too important because the event is an entity, a referent, which can be returned to, again and again if necessary, to discover more about it. The pleadingness, the feeling of "loving myself" which are present in these examples, may not prove to be exactly as described. They are, however, solid points of reference to which the client can return until he has satisfied himself as to what they are. It is, perhaps, that they constitute a clear-cut physiological event, a substratum of the conscious life, which the client can return to for investigatory purposes. Gendlin has called my attention to this significant quality of experiencing as a referent. He is endeavoring to build an extension of psychological theory on this basis (2, especially Chap. 7).

Differentiation of experiencing is sharp and basic.

Because each of these moments is a referent, a specific entity, it does not become confused with anything else. The process of sharp differentiation builds on it and about it.

In this stage there are no longer "problems," external or internal. The client is living, subjectively, a phase of his problem. It is not an object.

I trust it is evident that in any of these examples it would be grossly inaccurate to say that the client perceives his problem as internal or is dealing with it as an internal problem. We need some way of indicating that he is further than this and, of course, enormously far in the process sense from perceiving his problem as external. The best description seems to be that he neither perceives his problem nor deals with it. He is simply living some portion of it knowingly and acceptingly.

I have dwelt so long on this sixth definable point on the process continuum because I see it as a highly crucial one. My observation is that these moments of immediate, full, accepted experiencing are in some sense almost irreversible. To put this in terms of the examples, it is my observation and hypothesis that with these clients, whenever a future experiencing of the same quality and characteristics occurs, it will necessarily be recognized in awareness for what it is: a tender caring for self, an umbilical bond which makes him a part of his parents, or a pleading small-boy dependence, as the case may be. And, it might be remarked in passing, once an experience is fully in awareness, fully accepted, then it can be coped with effectively, like any other clear reality.

The Seventh Stage

In those areas in which the sixth stage has been reached, it is no longer so necessary that the client be fully received by the therapist, though this still seems helpful. However, because of the tendency for the sixth stage to be irreversible, the client often seems to go on into the seventh and final stage without much need of the therapist's help. This stage occurs as much outside of the therapeutic relationship as in it and is often reported, rather than experienced, in the therapeutic hour. I shall try to describe some of its characteristics as I feel I have observed them:

New feelings are experienced with immediacy and richness of detail, both in the therapeutic relationship and outside.
The experiencing of such feelings is consciously used as a clear referent.
There is a growing and continuing sense of acceptant ownership of these changing feelings, a basic trust in his own process.

This trust is not primarily in the conscious processes which go on, but rather in the total organismic process. One client puts it: "I seem to work best when my conscious mind is only concerned with facts and letting the analysis of them go on by itself without paying any attention to it."

Experiencing has lost almost completely its structure-bound aspects and becomes process experiencing — that is, the situation is experienced and interpreted in its newness, not as the past.

An example in a very specific area is given by a client in a follow-up interview as he explains the different quality that has come about in his creative work. It used to be that he tried to be orderly. "You begin at the beginning and you progress regularly through to the end." Now he is aware that the process in himself is different. "When I'm working on an idea, the whole idea develops like the latent image coming out when you develop a photograph. It doesn't start at one edge and fill in over to the other. It comes in all over. At first all you see is the hazy outline, and you wonder what it's going to be; and then gradually something fits here and something fits there, and pretty soon it all comes clear — all at once." It is obvious that he has not only come to trust this process, but that he is experiencing it as it is, not in terms of some past.

The self becomes increasingly simply the subjective and reflexive awareness of experiencing. The self is much less frequently a perceived object and much more frequently something confidently felt in process.

An example may be taken from the same follow-up interview with the client quoted above. In this interview, because he is reporting his experience since therapy, he again becomes aware of himself as an object; but it is clear that this has not been the quality of his day-by-day experience. After reporting many changes, he says: "I hadn't really thought of any of these things in connection with therapy until tonight. . . . [Jokingly] Gee! maybe something did happen. Because my life since has been different. My productivity has gone up. My confidence has gone up. I've become brash in situations I would have avoided before. And also, I've become less brash in situations where I would have become very obnoxious before." It is clear that only afterward does he realize what his self as an object has been.

Personal constructs are tentatively reformulated, to be validated against further experience, but even then to be held loosely.

A client describes the way in which such a construct changed, between interviews, toward the end of therapy: "I don't know what [changed], but I definitely feel different about looking back at my childhood, and some of the hostility about my mother and father has evaporated. I substituted for a feeling of resentment about them a sort of acceptance of the fact that they did a number of things that were undesirable with me. But I substituted a sort of feeling of interested excitement that — gee — now that I'm finding out what was wrong, I can do something about it — correct their mistakes." Here the way in which he construes his experience with his parents has been sharply altered.

Internal communication is clear, with feelings and symbols well matched, and fresh terms for new feelings.

There is the experiencing of effective choice of new ways of being.

Because all the elements of experience are available to awareness, choice becomes real and effective. Here a client is just coming to this realization: "I'm trying to encompass a way of talking that is a way out of being scared of talking. Perhaps just kind of thinking out loud is the way to do that. But I've got so *many* thoughts I could only do it a little bit. But maybe I could let my talk be an expression of my thoughts, instead of just trying to make the proper noises in each situation." Here he is sensing the possibility of effective choice, perhaps approaching this seventh stage rather than being in it.

By no means all clients move this far on the continuum; but when this seventh stage is reached, it involves us in another dimension. For it will be evident that the client has now incorporated the quality of motion, of flow, of changingness into every aspect of his psychological life. He will therefore continue to be a continually changing person, experiencing with freshness and immediacy in each new situation, responding to its newness with real and accepted feelings, and construing its meaning in terms of what it *is*, not in terms of some past experience.

RECAPITULATION

I have tried to sketch, in a crude and preliminary manner, the flow of a process of change which occurs when a client experiences himself as being received, welcomed, understood as he is. This process involves several threads, separable at first, becoming more of a unity as the process continues.

This process involves a loosening of feelings. From feelings which are unrecognized, unowned, unexpressed, the client moves toward a flow in which ever-changing feelings are experienced in the moment, knowingly and acceptingly, and may be accurately expressed.

The process involves a change in the manner of experiencing. From experiencing which is remote in time from the organic event, which is bound by the structure of experience in the past, the client moves toward a manner of experiencing which is immediate, which interprets meaning in terms of what is, not what was.

The process involves a loosening of the cognitive maps of experience. From construing experience in rigid ways which are perceived as external facts, the client moves toward developing changing, loosely held construings of meaning in experience, constructions which are modifiable by each new experience.

The process involves a change in the self. From being a self which is not congruent with experience, the client moves through the phase of perceiving self as an object, to a self which is synonymous with experience, being the subjective awareness of that experience.

There are other elements, too, involved in the process: movement from ineffective to effective choice, from fear of relationships to freely living in relationship, from inadequate differentiation of feelings and meanings to sharp differentiation.

In general, the process moves from a point of fixity, where all these elements and threads are separately discernible and separately understandable, to the flowing peak moments of therapy in which all these threads become inseparably woven together. In the new experiencing with immediacy which occurs at such moments, feeling and cognition interpenetrate, self is subjectively present in the experience, volition is simply the subjective following of a harmonious balance of organismic direction. Thus, as the process reaches this point, the person becomes a unity of flow, of motion. He has changed; but, what seems most significant, he has become an integrated process of changingness.

REFERENCES

1. BERGMAN, D. V. Counseling method and client responses. *J. consult. Psychol.*, 1951, **15**, 216–224.

2. GENDLIN, E. The function of experiencing in symbolization. Unpublished doctoral dissertation, Univer. of Chicago, 1958.

3. GENDLIN, E., & ZIMRING, F. The qualities or dimensions of experiencing and their change. *Counseling Center Discussion Papers*, 1955, **1**, No. 3. (Univer. of Chicago Counseling Center)

4. KELLY, G. A. *The psychology of personal constructs.* Vol. I. A theory of personality. New York: Norton, 1955.

5. KIRTNER, W. L. Success and failure in client-centered therapy as a function of personality variables. Unpublished master's thesis, Univer. of Chicago, 1955.

6. LEWIS, M. K., ROGERS, C. R., & SHLIEN, J. M. Two cases of time-limited client-centered psychotherapy. In A. Burton (Ed.), *Case studies of counseling and psychotherapy.* New York: Prentice-Hall, in press.

7. ROGERS, C. R. The necessary and sufficient conditions of therapeutic personality change. *J. Consult. Psychol.*, 1957, **21**, 95–103.

Psychotherapy as a Learning Process*

While it is customary to conceptualize psychotherapy as a learning process, few therapists accept the full implications of this position. Indeed, this is best illustrated by the writings of the learning theorists themselves. Most of our current methods of psychotherapy represent an accumulation of more or less uncontrolled clinical experiences and, in many instances, those who have written about psychotherapy in terms of learning theory have merely substituted a new language; the practice remains essentially unchanged (Dollard, Auld, & White, 1954; Dollard & Miller, 1950; Shoben, 1949).

If one seriously subscribes to the view that psychotherapy is a learning process, the methods of treatment should be derived from our knowledge of learning and motivation. Such an orientation is likely to yield new techniques of treatment which, in many respects, may differ markedly from the procedures currently in use.

Psychotherapy rests on a very simple but fundamental assumption, i.e., human behavior is modifiable through psychological procedures. When skeptics raise the question, "Does psychotherapy work?" they may be responding in part to the mysticism that has come to surround the term. Perhaps the more meaningful question, and one which avoids the surplus meanings associated with the term "psychotherapy," is as follows: Can human behavior be modified through psychological means and if so, what are the learning mechanisms that mediate behavior change?

In the sections that follow, some of these learning mechanisms will be discussed, and studies in which systematic attempts have been made to apply these principles of learning to the area of psychotherapy will be reviewed. Since learning theory itself is still somewhat incomplete, the list of psychological processes by which changes in behavior can occur should not be regarded as exhaustive, nor are they necessarily without overlap.

COUNTERCONDITIONING

Of the various treatment methods derived from learning theory, those based on the principle of coun-

ter-conditioning have been elaborated in greatest detail. Wolpe (1954, 1958, 1959) gives a thorough account of this method, and additional examples of cases treated in this manner are provided by Jones (1956), Lazarus and Rachman (1957), Meyer (1957), and Rachman (1959). Briefly, the principle involved is as follows: if strong responses which are incompatible with anxiety reactions can be made to occur in the presence of anxiety evoking cues, the incompatible responses will become attached to these cues and thereby weaken or eliminate the anxiety responses.

The first systematic psychotherapeutic application of this method was reported by Jones (1924b) in the treatment of Peter, a boy who showed severe phobic reactions to animals, fur objects, cotton, hair, and mechanical toys. Counterconditioning was achieved by feeding the child in the presence of initially small but gradually increasing anxiety-arousing stimuli. A rabbit in a cage was placed in the room at some distance so as not to disturb the boy's eating. Each day the rabbit was brought nearer to the table and eventually removed from the cage. During the final stage of treatment, the rabbit was placed on the feeding table and even in Peter's lap. Tests of generalization revealed that the fear responses had been effectively eliminated, not only toward the rabbit, but toward the previously feared furry objects as well.

In this connection, it would be interesting to speculate on the diagnosis and treatment Peter would have received had he been seen by Melanie Klein (1949) rather than by Mary Cover Jones!

It is interesting to note that while both Shoben (1949) and Wolpe (1958) propose a therapy based on the principle of counterconditioning, their treatment methods are radically different. According to Shoben, the patient discusses and thinks about stimulus situations that are anxiety provoking in the context of an inter-personal situation which simultaneously elicits positive affective responses from the patient. The therapeutic process consists in connecting the anxiety provoking stimuli, which are symbolically reproduced, with the comfort reaction made to the therapeutic relationship.

Shoben's paper represents primarily a counterconditioning interpretation of the behavior changes brought about through conventional forms of psycho-

* Reprinted by permission from *Psychological Bulletin*, Vol. 58, 1961, pp. 143–159.

therapy since, apart from highlighting the role of positive emotional reactions in the treatment process, no new techniques deliberately designed to facilitate relearning through counterconditioning are proposed.

This is not the case with Wolpe, who has made a radical departure from tradition. In his treatment, which he calls reciprocal inhibition, Wolpe makes systematic use of three types of responses which are antagonistic to, and therefore inhibitory of, anxiety. These are: assertive or approach responses, sexual responses, and relaxation responses.

On the basis of historical information, interview data, and psychological test responses, the therapist constructs an anxiety hierarchy, a ranked list of stimuli to which the patient reacts with anxiety. In the case of desensitization based on relaxation, the patient is hypnotized and given relaxation suggestions. He is then asked to imagine a scene representing the weakest item on the anxiety hierarchy and, if the relaxation is unimpaired, this is followed by having the patient imagine the next item on the list, and so on. Thus, the anxiety cues are gradually increased from session to session until the last phobic stimulus can be presented without impairing the relaxed state. Through this procedure, relaxation responses eventually come to be attached to the anxiety evoking stimuli.

Wolpe reports remarkable therapeutic success with a wide range of neurotic reactions treated on this counterconditioning principle. He also contends that the favorable outcomes achieved by the more conventional psychotherapeutic methods may result from the reciprocal inhibition of anxiety by strong positive responses evoked in the patient-therapist relationship.

Although the counterconditioning method has been employed most extensively in eliminating anxiety-motivated avoidance reactions and inhibitions, it has been used with some success in reducing maladaptive approach responses as well. In the latter case, the goal object is repeatedly associated with some form of aversive stimulus.

Raymond (1956), for example, used nausea as the aversion experience in the treatment of a patient who presented a fetish for handbags and perambulators which brought him into frequent contact with the law in that he repeatedly smeared mucus on ladies' handbags and destroyed perambulators by running into them with his motorcycle. Though the patient had undergone psychoanalytic treatment, and was fully aware of the origin and the sexual significance of his behavior, nevertheless, the fetish persisted.

The treatment consisted of showing the patient a collection of handbags, perambulators, and colored illustrations just before the onset of nausea produced by injections of apomorphine. The conditioning was repeated every 2 hours day and night for 1 week plus additional sessions 8 days and 6 months later.

Raymond reports that, not only was the fetish successfully eliminated, but also the patient showed a vast improvement in his social (and legal) relationships, was promoted to a more responsible position in his work, and no longer required the fetish fantasies to enable him to have sexual intercourse.

Nauseant drugs, especially emetine, have also been utilized as the unconditioned stimulus in the aversion treatment of alcoholism (Thirmann, 1949; Thompson & Bielinski, 1953; Voegtlen, 1940; Wallace, 1949). Usually 8 to 10 treatments in which the sight, smell, and taste of alcohol is associated with the onset of nausea is sufficient to produce abstinence. Of 1,000 or more cases on whom adequate follow-up data are reported, approximately 60% of the patients have been totally abstinent following the treatment. Voegtlen (1940) suggests that a few preventive treatments given at an interval of about 6 months may further improve the results yielded by this method.

Despite these encouraging findings, most psychotherapists are unlikely to be impressed since, in their opinion, the underlying causes for the alcoholism have in no way been modified by the conditioning procedure and, if anything, the mere removal of the alcoholism would tend to produce symptom substitution or other adverse effects. A full discussion of this issue will be presented later. In this particular context, however, several aspects of the Thompson and Bielinski (1953) data are worth noting. Among the alcoholic patients whom they treated, six "suffered from mental disorders not due to alcohol or associated deficiency states." It was planned, by the authors, to follow up the aversion treatment with psychotherapy for the underlying psychosis. This, however, proved unnecessary since all but one of the patients, a case of chronic mental deterioration, showed marked improvement and were in a state of remission.

Max (1935) employed a strong electric shock as the aversive stimulus in treating a patient who tended to display homosexual behavior following exposure to a fetishistic stimulus. Both the fetish and homosexual behavior were removed through a series of avoidance conditioning sessions in which the patient was administered shock in the presence of the fetishistic object.

Wolpe (1958) has also reported favorable results with a similar procedure in the treatment of obsessions.

A further variation of the counter-conditioning procedure has been developed by Mowrer and

Mowrer (1938) for use with enuretic patients. The device consists of a wired bed pad which sets off a loud buzzer and awakens the child as soon as micturition begins. Bladder tension thus becomes a cue for waking up which, in turn, is followed by sphincter contraction. Once bladder pressure becomes a stimulus for the more remote sphincter control response, the child is able to remain dry for relatively long periods of time without wakening.

Mowrer and Mowrer (1938) report complete success with 30 children treated by this method; similarly, Davidson and Douglass (1950) achieved highly successful results with 20 chronic enuretic children (15 cured, 5 markedly improved); of 5 cases treated by Morgan and Witmer (1939), 4 of the children not only gained full sphincter control, but also made a significant improvement in their social behavior. The one child with whom the conditioning approach had failed was later found to have bladder difficulties which required medical attention.

Some additional evidence for the efficacy of this method is provided by Martin and Kubly (1955) who obtained follow-up information from 118 of 220 parents who had treated their children at home with this type of conditioning apparatus. In 74% of the cases, according to the parents' replies, the treatment was successful.

EXTINCTION

"When a learned response is repeated without reinforcement the strength of the tendency to perform that response undergoes a progressive decrease" (Dollard & Miller, 1950). Extinction involves the development of inhibitory potential which is composed of two components. The evocation of any reaction generates reactive inhibition (I_r) which presumably dissipates with time. When reactive inhibition (fatigue, etc.) reaches a high point, the cessation of activity alleviates this negative motivational state and any stimuli associated with the cessation of the response become conditioned inhibitors $(_sI_r)$.

One factor that has been shown to influence the rate of extinction of maladaptive and anxiety-motivated behavior is the interval between extinction trials. In general, there tends to be little diminution in the strength of fear-motivated behavior when extinction trials are widely distributed, whereas under massed trials, reactive inhibition builds up rapidly and consequently extinction is accelerated (Calvin, Clifford, Clifford, Bolden, & Harvey, 1956; Edmonson & Amsel, 1954).

An illustration of the application of this principle is provided by Yates (1958) in the treatment of tics. Yates demonstrated, in line with the findings from laboratory studies of extinction under massed and distributed practice, that massed sessions in which the patient performed tics voluntarily followed by prolonged rest to allow for the dissipation of reactive inhibition was the most effective procedure for extinguishing the tics.

It should be noted that the extinction procedure employed by Yates is very similar to Dunlap's method of negative practice, in which the subject reproduces the negative behaviors voluntarily without reinforcement (Dunlap, 1932; Lehner, 1954). This method has been applied most frequently, with varying degrees of success, to the treatment of speech disorders (Fishman, 1937; Meissner, 1946; Rutherford, 1940; Sheehan, 1951; Sheehan & Voas, 1957). If the effectiveness of this psychotherapeutic technique is due primarily to extinction, as suggested by Yates' study, the usual practice of terminating a treatment session before the subject becomes fatigued (Lehner, 1954), would have the effect of reducing the rate of extinction, and may in part account for the divergent results yielded by this method.

Additional examples of the therapeutic application of extinction procedures are provided by Jones (1955), and most recently by C. D. Williams (1959).

Most of the conventional forms of psychotherapy rely heavily on extinction effects although the therapist may not label these as such. For example, many therapists consider *permissiveness* to be a necessary condition of therapeutic change (Alexander, 1956; Dollard & Miller, 1950; Rogers, 1951). It is expected that when a patient expresses thoughts or feelings that provoke anxiety or guilt and the therapist does not disapprove, criticize, or withdraw interest, the fear or guilt will be gradually weakened or extinguished. The extinction effects are believed to generalize to thoughts concerning related topics that were originally inhibited, and to verbal and physical forms of behavior as well (Dollard & Miller, 1950).

Some evidence for the relationship between permissiveness and the extinction of anxiety is provided in two studies recently reported by Dittes (1957a, 1957b). In one study (1957b) involving an analysis of patient-therapist interaction sequences, Dittes found that permissive responses on the part of the therapist were followed by a corresponding decrease in the patient's anxiety (as measured by the GSR) and the occurrence of avoidance behaviors. A sequential analysis of the therapeutic sessions (Dittes, 1957a), revealed that, at the onset of treatment, sex expressions were accompanied by strong anxiety reactions; under the cumulative effects of permissiveness, the anxiety gradually extinguished.

In contrast to counterconditioning, extinction is likely to be a less effective and a more time consuming method for eliminating maladaptive behavior (Jones, 1924a; Dollard & Miller, 1950); in the case of conventional interview therapy, the relatively long intervals between interview sessions, and the ritualistic adherence to the 50-minute hour may further reduce the occurrence of extinction effects.

DISCRIMINATION LEARNING

Human functioning would be extremely difficult and inefficient if a person had to learn appropriate behavior for every specific situation he encountered. Fortunately, patterns of behavior learned in one situation will transfer or generalize to other similar situations. On the other hand, if a person overgeneralizes from one situation to another, or if the generalization is based on superficial or irrelevant cues, behavior becomes inappropriate and maladaptive.

In most theories of psychotherapy, therefore, discrimination learning, believed to be accomplished through the gaining of awareness or insight, receives emphasis (Dollard & Miller, 1950; Fenichel, 1941; Rogers, 1951; Sullivan, 1953). It is generally assumed that if a patient is aware of the cues producing his behavior, of the responses he is making, and of the reasons that he responds the way he does, his behavior will become more susceptible to verbally-mediated control. Voluntarily guided, discriminative behavior will replace the automatic, overgeneralized reactions.

While this view is widely accepted, as evidenced in the almost exclusive reliance on interview procedures and on interpretative or labeling techniques, a few therapists (Alexander & French, 1946) have questioned the importance attached to awareness in producing modifications in behavior. Whereas most psychoanalysts (Fenichel, 1941), as well as therapists representing other points of view (Fromm-Reichmann, 1950; Sullivan, 1953) consider insight a precondition of behavior change, Alexander and French consider insight or awareness a result of change rather than its cause. That is, as the patient's anxieties are gradually reduced through the permissive conditions of treatment, formerly inhibited thoughts are gradually restored to awareness.

Evidence obtained through controlled laboratory studies concerning the value of awareness in increasing the precision of discrimination has so far been largely negative or at least equivocal (Adams, 1957; Erikson, 1958; Razran, 1949). A study by Lacy and Smith (1954), in which they found aware subjects generalized anxiety reactions less extensively than did subjects who were unaware of the conditioned stimulus provides evidence that awareness may aid discrimination. However, other aspects of their findings (e.g., the magnitude of the anxiety reactions to the generalization stimuli were greater than they were to the conditioned stimulus itself) indicate the need for replication.

If future research continues to demonstrate that awareness exerts little influence on the acquisition, generalization, and modification of behavior, such negative results would cast serious doubt on the value of currently popular psychotherapeutic procedures whose primary aim is the development of insight.

METHODS OF REWARD

Most theories of psychotherapy are based on the assumption that the patient has a repertoire of previously learned positive habits available to him, but that these adaptive patterns are inhibited or blocked by competing responses motivated by anxiety or guilt. The goal of the therapy, then, is to reduce the severity of the internal inhibitory controls, thus allowing the healthy patterns of behavior to emerge. Hence, the role of the therapist is to create permissive conditions under which the patient's "normal growth potentialities" are set free (Rogers, 1951). The fact that most of our theories of personality and therapeutic procedures have been developed primarily through work with oversocialized, neurotic patients may account in part for the prevalence of this view.

There is a large class of disorders (the undersocialized, antisocial personalities whose behavior reflects a failure of the socialization process) for whom this model of personality and accompanying techniques of treatment are quite inappropriate (Bandura & Walters, 1959; Schmideberg, 1959). Such antisocial personalities are likely to present *learning deficits*, consequently the goal of therapy is the acquisition of secondary motives and the development of internal restraint habits. That anti-social patients prove unresponsive to psychotherapeutic methods developed for the treatment of oversocialized neurotics has been demonstrated in a number of studies comparing patients who remain in treatment with those who terminate treatment prematurely (Rubenstein & Lorr, 1956). It is for this class of patients that the greatest departures from traditional treatment methods is needed.

While counterconditioning, extinction, and discrimination learning may be effective ways of removing neurotic inhibitions, these methods may be of relatively little value in developing new positive habits. Primary and secondary rewards in the form of the therapist's interest and approval may play an important, if not indispensable, role in the treatment process. Once the patient has learned to want the interest and approval of the therapist, these rewards may then be used to promote the acquisition of new patterns of behavior. For certain classes of patients such as schizophrenics (Atkinson, 1957; Peters, 1953; Robinson, 1957) and delinquents (Cairns, 1959), who are either unresponsive to, or fearful of, social rewards, the therapist may have to rely initially on primary rewards in the treatment process.

An ingenious study by Peters and Jenkins (1954) illustrates the application of this principle in the treatment of schizophrenic patients. Chronic patients from closed wards were administered subshock injections of insulin designed to induce the hunger drive. The patients were then encouraged to solve a series of graded problem tasks with fudge as the reward. This program was followed 5 days a week for 3 months.

Initially the tasks involved simple mazes and obstruction problems in which the patients obtained the food reward directly upon successful completion of the problem. Tasks of gradually increasing difficulty were then administered involving multiple-choice learning and verbal-reasoning problems in which the experimenter personally mediated the primary rewards. After several weeks of such problem solving activities the insulin injections were discontinued and social rewards, which by this time had become more effective, were used in solving interpersonal problems that the patients were likely to encounter in their daily activities both inside and outside the hospital setting.

Comparison of the treated group with control groups, designed to isolate the effects of insulin and special attention, revealed that the patients in the reward group improved significantly in their social relationships in the hospital, whereas the patients in the control groups showed no such change.

King and Armitage (1958) report a somewhat similar study in which severely withdrawn schizophrenic patients were treated with operant conditioning methods; candy and cigarettes served as the primary rewards for eliciting and maintaining increasingly complex forms of behavior, i.e., psychomotor, verbal, and interpersonal responses. Unlike the Peters and Jenkins study, no attempt was made to manipulate the level of primary motivation.

An interesting feature of the experimental design was the inclusion of a group of patients who were treated with conventional interview therapy, as well as a recreational therapy and a no-therapy control group. It was found that the operant group, in relation to similar patients in the three control groups, made significantly more clinical improvement.

Skinner (1956b) and Lindsley (1956) working with adult psychotics, and Ferster (1959) working with autistic children, have been successful in developing substantial amounts of reality-oriented behavior in their patients through the use of reward. So far their work has been concerned primarily with the effect of schedules of reinforcement on the rate of evocation of simple impersonal reactions. There is every indication, however, that by varying the contingency of the reward (e.g., the patient must respond in certain specified ways to the behavior of another individual in order to produce the reward) adaptive interpersonal behaviors can be developed as well (Azran & Lindsley, 1956).

The effectiveness of social reinforcers in modifying behavior has been demonstrated repeatedly in verbal conditioning experiments (Krasner, 1958; Salzinger, 1959). Encouraged by these findings, several therapists have begun to experiment with operant conditioning as a method of treatment in its own right (Tilton, 1956; Ullman, Krasner, & Collins, in press; R. I. Williams, 1959); the operant conditioning studies cited earlier are also illustrative of this trend.

So far the study of generalization and permanence of behavior changes brought about through operant conditioning methods has received relatively little attention and the scanty data available are equivocal (Rogers, 1960; Sarason, 1957; Weide, 1959). The lack of consistency in results is hardly surprising considering that the experimental manipulations in many of the conditioning studies are barely sufficient to demonstrate conditioning effects, let alone generalization of changes to new situations. On the other hand, investigators who have conducted more intensive reinforcement sessions, in an effort to test the efficacy of operant conditioning methods as a therapeutic technique, have found significant changes in patients' interpersonal behavior in extra-experimental situations (King & Armitage, 1958; Peters & Jenkins, 1954; Ullman et al., in press). These findings are particularly noteworthy since the response classes involved are similar to those psychotherapists are primarily concerned in modifying through interview forms of treatment. If the favorable results yielded by these studies are replicated in future investigations, it is likely that the next few years will witness an increasing reliance on conditioning forms of psychotherapy, particularly in the treatment of psychotic patients.

At this point it might also be noted that, consistent with the results from verbal conditioning experiments, content analyses of psychotherapeutic interviews (Bandura, Lipsher, & Miller, 1960; Murray, 1956) suggest that many of the changes observed in psychotherapy, at least insofar as the patients' verbal behavior is concerned, can be accounted for in terms of the therapists' direct, although usually unwitting, reward and punishment of the patients' expressions.

PUNISHMENT

While positive habits can be readily developed through reward, the elimination of socially disapproved habits, which becomes very much an issue in the treatment of antisocial personalities, poses a far more complex problem.

The elimination of socially disapproved behaviors can be accomplished in several ways. They may be consistently unrewarded and thus extinguished. However, antisocial behavior, particularly of an extreme form, cannot simply be ignored in the hope that it will gradually extinguish. Furthermore, since the successful execution of antisocial acts may bring substantial material rewards as well as the approval and admiration of associates, it is extremely unlikely that such behavior would ever extinguish.

Although punishment may lead to the rapid disappearance of socially disapproved behavior, its effects are far more complex (Estes, 1944; Solomon, Kamin, & Wynne, 1953). If a person is punished for some socially disapproved habit, the impulse to perform the act becomes, through its association with punishment, a stimulus for anxiety. This anxiety then motivates competing responses which, if sufficiently strong, prevent the occurrence of, or inhibit, the disapproved behavior. Inhibited responses may not, however, thereby lose their strength, and may reappear in situations where the threat of punishment is weaker. Punishment may, in fact, prevent the extinction of a habit; if a habit is completely inhibited, it cannot occur and therefore cannot go unrewarded.

Several other factors point to the futility of punishment as a means of correcting many antisocial patterns. The threat of punishment is very likely to elicit conformity; indeed, the patient may obligingly do whatever he is told to do in order to avoid immediate difficulties. This does not mean, however, that he has acquired a set of sanctions that will be of service to him once he is outside the treatment situation. In fact, rather than leading to the development of internal controls, such methods are likely only to increase the patient's reliance on external restraints. Moreover, under these conditions, the majority of patients will develop the attitude that they will do only what they are told to do — and they will do as they please once they are free from the therapist's supervision (Bandura & Walters, 1959).

then often only half-heartedly — and that they will do as they please once they are free from the therapist's supervision (Bandura & Walters, 1959).

In addition, punishment may serve only to intensify hostility and other negative motivations and thus may further instigate the antisocial person to display the very behaviors that the punishment was intended to bring under control.

Mild aversive stimuli have been utilized, of course, in the treatment of voluntary patients who express a desire to rid themselves of specific debilitating conditions.

Liversedge and Sylvester (1955), for example, successfully treated seven cases of writer's cramp by means of a retraining procedure involving electric shock. In order to remove tremors, one component of the motor disorder, the patients were required to insert a stylus into a series of progressively smaller holes; each time the stylus made contact with the side of the hole the patient received a mild shock. The removal of the spasm component of the disorder was obtained in two ways. First, the patients traced various line patterns (similar to the movements required in writing) on a metal plate with a stylus, and any deviation from the path produced a shock. Following training on the apparatus, the subjects then wrote with an electrified pen which delivered a shock whenever excessive thumb pressure was applied.

Liversedge and Sylvester report that following the retraining the patients were able to resume work; a follow-up several months later indicated that the improvement was being maintained.

The aversive forms of the therapy, described earlier in the section on counterconditioning procedures, also make use of mild punishment.

SOCIAL IMITATION

Although a certain amount of learning takes place through direct training and reward, a good deal of a person's behavior repertoire may be acquired through imitation of what he observes in others. If this is the case, social limitation may serve as an effective vehicle for the transmission of prosocial behavior patterns in the treatment of antisocial patients.

Merely providing a model for imitation is not, however, sufficient. Even though the therapist exhibits the kinds of behaviors that he wants the patient to learn, this is likely to have little influence on him if he rejects the therapist as a model. Affectional nurturance is believed to be an important precondition for imitative learning to occur, in that affectional rewards increase the secondary reinforcing properties of the model, and thus predispose the imitator to pattern his behavior after the rewarding person (Mowrer, 1950; Sears, 1957; Whiting, 1954). Some positive evidence for the influence of social rewards on imitation is provided by Bandura and Huston (in press) in a recent study of identification as a process of incidental imitation.

In this investigation preschool children performed an orienting task but, unlike most incidental learning studies, the experimenter performed the diverting task as well, and the extent to which the subjects patterned their behavior after that of the experimenter-model was measured.

A two-choice discrimination problem similar to the one employed by Miller and Dollard (1941) in their experiments of social imitation was used as the diverting task. On each trial, one of two boxes was loaded with two rewards (small multicolor pictures of animals) and the object of the game was to guess which box contained the stickers. The experimenter-model (M) always had her turn first and in each instance chose the reward box. During M's trial, the subject remained at the starting point where he could observe the M's behavior. On each discrimination trial M exhibited certain verbal, motor, and aggressive patterns of behavior that were totally irrelevant to the task to which the subject's attention was directed. At the starting point, for example, M made a verbal response and then marched slowly toward the box containing the stickers, repeating, "March, march, march." On the lid of each box was a rubber doll which M knocked off aggressively when she reached the designated box. She then paused briefly, remarked, "Open the box," removed one sticker, and pasted it on a pastoral scene which hung on the wall immediately behind the boxes. The subject then took his turn and the number of M's behaviors performed by the subject was recorded.

A control group was included in order to, (a) provide a check on whether the subjects' performances reflected genuine imitative learning or merely the chance occurrence of behaviors high in the subjects' response hierarchies, and (b) to determine whether subjects would adopt certain aspects of M's behavior which involved considerable delay in reward. With the controls, therefore, M walked to the box, choosing a highly circuitous route along the sides of the experimental room; instead of aggressing toward the doll, she lifted it gently off the container.

The results of this study indicate that, insofar as preschool children are concerned, a good deal of incidental imitation of the behaviors displayed by an adult model does occur. Of the subjects in the experimental group, 88% adopted the M's aggressive behavior, 44% imitated the marching, and 28% reproduced M's verbalizations. In contrast, none of the control subjects behaved aggressively, marched, or verbalized, while 75% of the controls imitated the circuitous route to the containers.

In order to test the hypothesis that children who experience a rewarding relationship with an adult model adopt more of the model's behavior than do children who experience a relatively distant and cold relationship, half the subjects in the experiment were assigned to a nurturant condition; the other half of the subjects to a nonnurturant condition. During the nurturant sessions, which preceded the incidental learning, M played with subject, she responded readily to the subject's bids for attention, and in other ways fostered a consistently warm and rewarding interaction with the child. In contrast, during the nonnurturant sessions, the subject played alone while M busied herself with paperwork at a desk in the far corner of the room.

Consistent with the hypothesis, it was found that subjects who experienced the rewarding interaction with M adopted significantly more of M's behavior than did subjects who were in the nonnurturance condition.

A more crucial test of the transmission of behavior patterns through the process of social imitation involves the delayed generalization of imitative responses to new situations in which the model is absent. A study of this type just completed, provides strong evidence that observation of the cues produced by the behavior of others is an effective means of eliciting responses for which the original probability is very low (Bandura, Ross, & Ross, in press).

Empirical studies of the correlates of strong and weak identification with parents, lend additional support to the theory that rewards promote imitative learning. Boys whose fathers are highly rewarding and affectionate have been found to adopt the father-role in doll-play activities (Sears, 1953), to show father-son similarity in response to items on a personality questionnaire (Payne & Mussen, 1956), and to display masculine behaviors (Mussen & Distler, 1956, 1960) to a greater extent than boys whose fathers are relatively cold and nonrewarding.

The treatment of older unsocialized delinquents is a difficult task, since they are relatively self-sufficient and do not readily seek involvement with a therapist. In many cases, socialization can be accomplished only through residential care and treatment. In the treatment home, the therapist can personally administer many of the primary rewards and mediate between the boys' needs and gratifications. Through the repeated association with rewarding experiences for the boy, many of the therapist's attitudes and actions will acquire secondary reward value, and thus the patient will be motivated to reproduce these attitudes and actions in himself. Once these attitudes and values have been thus accepted, the boy's inhibition of antisocial tendencies will function independently of the therapist.

While treatment through social imitation has been suggested as a method for modifying antisocial patterns, it can be an effective procedure for the treatment of other forms of disorders as well. Jones (1924a), for example, found that the social example of children reacting normally to stimuli feared by another child was effective, in some instances, in eliminating such phobic reactions. In fact, next to counterconditioning, the method of social imitation proved to be most effective in eliminating inappropriate fears.

There is some suggestive evidence that by providing high prestige models and thus increasing the reinforcement value of the imitatee's behavior, the effectiveness of this method in promoting favorable adjustive patterns of behavior may be further increased (Jones, 1924a; Mausner, 1953, 1954; Miller & Dollard, 1941).

During the course of conventional psychotherapy, the patient is exposed to many incidental cues involving the therapist's values, attitudes, and patterns of behavior. They are incidental only because they are usually considered secondary or irrelevant to the task of resolving the patient's problems. Nevertheless, some of the changes observed in the patient's behavior may result, not so much from the intentional interaction between the patient and the therapist, but rather from active learning by the patient of the therapist's attitudes and 'values which the therapist never directly attempted to transmit. This is partially corroborated by Rosenthal (1955) who found that, in spite of the usual precautions taken by therapists to avoid imposing their values on their clients, the patients who were judged as showing the greatest improvement changed their moral values (in the areas of sex, aggression, and authority) in the direction of the values of their therapists, whereas patients who were unimproved became less like the therapist in values.

FACTORS IMPEDING INTEGRATION

In reviewing the literature on psychotherapy, it becomes clearly evident that learning theory and general psychology have exerted a remarkably minor influence on the practice of psychotherapy and, apart from the recent interest in Skinner's operant conditioning methods (Krasner, 1955; Skinner, 1953), most of the recent serious attempts to apply learning principles to clinical practice have been made by European psychotherapists (Jones, 1956; Lazarus & Rachman, 1957; Liversedge & Sylvester, 1955; Meyer, 1957; Rachman, 1959; Raymond, 1956; Wolpe, 1958; Yates, 1958). This isolation of the methods of treatment from our knowledge of learning and motivation will continue to exist for some time since there are several prevalent attitudes that impede adequate integration.

In the first place, the deliberate use of the principles of learning in the modification of human behavior implies, for most psychotherapists, manipulation and control of the patient, and control is seen by them as antihumanistic and, therefore, bad. Thus, advocates of a learning approach to psychotherapy are often charged with treating human beings as though they were rats or pigeons and of leading on the road to Orwell's 1984.

This does not mean that psychotherapists do not influence and control their patients' behavior. On the contrary. In any interpersonal interaction, and psychotherapy is no exception, people influence and control one another (Frank, 1959; Skinner, 1956a). Although the patient's control of the therapist has not as yet been studied (such control is evident when patients subtly reward the therapist with interesting historical material and thereby avoid the discussion of their current interpersonal problems), there is considerable evidence that the therapist exercises personal control over his patients. A brief examination of interview protocols of patients treated by therapists representing differing theoretical orientations, clearly reveals that the patients have been thoroughly conditioned in their therapists' idosyncratic languages. Client-centered patients, for example, tend to produce the client-centered terminology, theory, and goals, and their interview content shows little or no overlap with that of patients seen in psychoanalysis who, in turn, tend to speak the language of psychoanalytic theory (Heine, 1950). Even more direct evidence of the therapists' controlling influence is provided in studies of patient-therapist interactions (Bandura et al., 1960; Murray, 1956; Rogers, 1960). The results of these studies show that the therapist not only controls the patient by rewarding him with interest and approval when the patient behaves in a fashion the therapist desires, but that he also controls through punishment, in the form of mild disapproval and withdrawal of interest, when the patient behaves in ways that are threatening to the therapist or run counter to his goals.

One difficulty in understanding the changes that occur in the course of psychotherapy is that the independent variable, i.e., the therapist's behavior, is often vaguely or only partially defined. In an effort to minimize or to deny the therapist's directive influence on the patient, the therapist is typically depicted as a "catalyst" who, in some mysterious way, sets free positive adjustive patterns of behavior or similar outcomes usually described in very general and highly socially desirable terms.

It has been suggested, in the material presented in the preceding sections, that many of the changes that occur in psychotherapy derive from the unwitting application of well-known principles of learning. However, the occurrence of the necessary conditions for learning is more by accident than by intent and, perhaps, a more deliberate application of our knowledge of the learning process to psychotherapy would yield far more effective results.

The predominant approach in the development of psychotherapeutic procedures has been the "school" approach. A similar trend is noted in the treatment methods being derived from learning theory. Wolpe, for example, has selected the principle of counter-conditioning and built a "school" of psychotherapy around it; Dollard and Miller have focused on extinction and discrimination learning; and the followers of Skinner rely almost entirely on methods of reward. This stress on a few learning principles at the expense of neglecting other relevant ones will serve only to limit the effectiveness of psychotherapy.

A second factor that may account for the discontinuity between general psychology and psychotherapeutic practice is that the model of personality to which most therapists subscribe is somewhat dissonant with the currently developing principles of behavior.

In their formulations of personality functioning, psychotherapists are inclined to appeal to a variety of inner explanatory processes. In contrast, learning theorists view the organism as a far more mechanistic and simpler system, and consequently their formulations tend to be expressed for the most part in terms of antecedent-consequent relationships without reference to inner states.

Symptoms are learned S-R connections; once they are extinguished or deconditioned treatment is complete. Such treatment is based exclusively on present factors; like Lewin's theory, this one is a-historical. Non-verbal methods are favored over verbal ones, although a minor place is reserved for verbal methods of extinction and reconditioning. Concern is with *function*, not with *content*. The main difference between the two theories arises over the question of "symptomatic" treatment. According to orthodox theory, this is useless unless the underlying complexes are attacked. According to the present theory, there is no evidence for these putative complexes, and symptomatic treatment is all that is required (Eysenck, 1957, pp. 267–268). Quoted by permission of Frederick A. Praeger, Inc.)

Changes in behavior brought about through such methods as counter-conditioning are apt to be viewed by the "dynamically-oriented" therapist, as being not only superficial, "symptomatic" treatment, in that the basic underlying instigators of the behavior remain unchanged, but also potentially dangerous, since the direct elimination of a symptom may precipitate more seriously disturbed behavior.

This expectation receives little support from the generally favorable outcomes reported in the studies reviewed in this paper. In most cases where follow-up data were available to assess the long-term effects of the therapy, the patients, many of whom had been treated by conventional methods with little benefit, had evidently become considerably more effective in their social, vocational, and psychosexual adjustment. On the whole the evidence, while open to error, suggests that no matter what the origin of the maladaptive behavior may be, a change in behavior brought about through learning procedures may be all that is necessary for the alleviation of most forms of emotional disorders.

As Mowrer (1950) very aptly points out, the "symptom-underlying cause" formulation may represent inappropriate medical analogizing. Whether or not a given behavior will be considered normal or a symptom of an underlying disturbance will depend on whether or not somebody objects to the behavior. For example, aggressiveness on the part of children may be encouraged and considered a sign of healthy development by the parents, while the same behavior is viewed by school authorities and society as a symptom of a personality disorder (Bandura & Walters, 1959). Furthermore, behavior considered to be normal at one stage in development may be regarded as a "symptom of a personality disturbance" at a later period. In this connection it is very appropriate to repeat Mowrer's (1950) query: "And when does persisting behavior of this kind suddenly cease to be normal and become a symptom" (p. 474).

Thus, while a high fever is generally considered a sign of an underlying disease process regardless of when or where it occurs, whether a specific behavior will be viewed as normal or as a symptom of an underlying pathology is not independent of who makes the judgment, the social context in which the behavior occurs, the age of the person, as well as many other factors.

Another important difference between physical pathology and behavior pathology usually overlooked is that, in the case of most behavior disorders, it is not the underlying motivations that need to be altered or removed, but rather the ways in which the patient has learned to gratify his needs (Rotter, 1954). Thus, for example, if a patient displays deviant sexual behavior, the goal is not the removal of the underlying causes, i.e., sexual motivation, but rather the substitution of more socially approved instrumental and goal responses.

It might also be mentioned in passing, that, in the currently popular forms of psychotherapy, the role assumed by the therapist may bring him a good many direct or fantasied personal gratifications. In the course of treatment the patient may express considerable affection and admiration for the therapist, he may assign the therapist an omniscient status, and the reconstruction of the patient's history may be an intellectually stimulating activity. On the other hand, the methods derived from learning theory place the therapist in a less glamorous role, and this in itself may create some reluctance on the part of psychotherapists to part with the procedures currently in use.

Which of the two conceptual theories of personality — the psychodynamic or the social learning theory — is the more useful in generating effective procedures for the modification of human behavior remains to be demonstrated. While it is possible to present logical arguments and impressive clinical evidence for the efficiency of either approach, the best proving ground is the laboratory.

In evaluating psychotherapeutic methods, the common practice is to compare changes in a treated group with those of a nontreated control group. One drawback of this approach is that, while it answers the question as to whether or not a particular treatment is more effective than no intervention in producing changes along specific dimensions for certain classes of patients, it does not provide evidence concerning the relative effectiveness of alternative forms of psychotherapy.

It would be far more informative if, in future psychotherapy research, radically different forms of treatment were compared (King & Armitage, 1958; Rogers, 1959), since this approach would lead to a more rapid discarding of those of our cherished psychotherapeutic rituals that prove to be ineffective in, or even a handicap to, the successful treatment of emotional disorders.

REFERENCES

ADAMS, J. K. Laboratory studies of behavior without awareness. *Psychol. Bull.*, 1957, **54**, 393–405.

ALEXANDER, F. *Psychoanalysis and psychotherapy.* New York: Norton, 1956.

ALEXANDER, F., & FRENCH, M. T. *Psychoanalytic therapy.* New York: Ronald, 1946.

ATKINSON, RITA L. Paired-associate learning by schizophrenic and normal subjects under conditions of verbal reward and verbal punishment. Unpublished doctoral dissertation, Indiana University, 1957.

AZRAN, N. H., & LINDSLEY, O. R. The reinforcement of cooperation between children. *J. abnorm. soc. Psychol.*, 1956, **52**, 100–102.

BANDURA A., & HUSTON, ALETHA, C. Identification as a process of incidental learning. *J. abnorm. soc. Psychol.*, in press.

BANDURA, A., LIPSHER, D. H., & MILLER, PAULA, E. Psychotherapists' approach-avoidance reactions to patients' expressions of hostility. *J. consult. Psychol.*, 1960, **24**, 1–8.

BANDURA, A., ROSS, DOROTHEA, & ROSS, SHEILA, A. Transmission of aggression through imitation of aggressive models. *J. abnorm. soc. Psychol.*, in press.

BANDURA, A., & WALTERS, R. H. *Adolescent aggression.* New York: Ronald, 1959.

CAIRNS, R. B. The influence of dependency-anxiety on the effectiveness of social reinforcers. Unpublished doctoral dissertation, Stanford University, 1959.

CALVIN, A. D., CLIFFORD, L. T., CLIFFORD, B., BOLDEN, L., & HARVEY, J. Experimental validation of conditioned inhibition. *Psychol. Rep.*, 1956, **2**, 51–56.

DAVIDSON, J. R., & DOUGLASS, E. Nocturnal enuresis: A special approach to treatment. *British med. J.*, 1950, **1**, 1345–1347.

DITTES, J. E. Extinction during psychotherapy of GSR accompanying "embarrassing" statements. *J. abnorm. soc. Psychol.*, 1957, **54**, 187–191. (a)

DITTES, J. E. Galvanic skin responses as a measure of patient's reaction to therapist's permissiveness. *J. abnorm. soc. Phychol.*, 1957, **55**, 295–303. (b)

DOLLARD, J., AULD, F., & WHITE, A. M. *Steps in psychotherapy.* New York: Macmillan, 1954.

DOLLARD, J., & MILLER, N. E. *Personality and psychotherapy.* New York: McGraw-Hill, 1950.

DUNLAP, K. *Habits, their making and unmaking.* New York: Liveright, 1932.

EDMONSON, B. W., & AMSEL, A. The effects of massing and distribution of extinction trials on the persistence of a fear-motivated instrumental response. *J. comp. physiol. Psychol.*, 1954, **47**, 117–123.

ERIKSON, C. W. Unconscious processes. In M. R. Jones (Ed.), *Nebraska symposium on motivation.* Lincoln: Univer. Nebraska Press, 1958.

ESTES, W. K. An experimental study of punishment. *Psychol. Monogr.*, 1944, **57** (3, Whole No. 363).

EYSENCK, H. J. *The dynamics of anxiety and hysteria.* New York: Praeger, 1957.

FENICHEL, O. *Problems of psychoanalytic technique.* (Trans. by D. Brunswick) New York: Psychoanalytic Quarterly, 1941.

FERSTER, C. B. Development of normal behavioral processes in autistic children. *Res. relat. Child.,* 1959, No. 9, 30. (Abstract)

FISHMAN, H. C. A study of the efficiency of negative practice as a corrective for stammering. *J. Speech Dis.,* 1937, **2**, 67–72.

FRANK, J. D. The dynamics of the psycho-therapeutic relationship. *Psychiatry,* 1959, **22**, 17–39.

FROMM-REICHMANN, FRIEDA. *Principle of intensive psychotherapy.* Chicago: Univer. Chicago Press, 1950.

HEINE, R. W. An investigation of the relationship between change in personality from psychotherapy as reported by patients and the factors seen by patients as producing change. Unpublished doctoral dissertation, University of Chicago, 1950.

JONES, E. L. Exploration of experimental extinction and spontaneous recovery in stuttering. In W. Johnson (Ed.), *Stuttering in children and adults.* Minneapolis: Univer. Minnesota Press, 1955.

JONES, H. G. The application of conditioning and learning techniques to the treatment of a psychiatric patient. *J. abnorm. soc. Psychol.,* 1956, **52**, 414–419.

JONES, MARY C. The elimination of childrens' fears. *J. exp. Psychol.,* 1924, **7**, 382–390. (a)

JONES, MARY C. A laboratory study of fear: The case of Peter. *J. genet. Psychol.,* 1924, **31**, 308–315. (b)

KING, G. F., & ARMITAGE, S. G. An operant-interpersonal therapeutic approach to schizophrenics of extreme pathology. *Amer. Psychologist,* 1958, **13**, 358. (Abstract)

KLEIN, MELANIE. *The psycho-analysis of children.* London: Hogarth, 1949.

KRASNER, L. The use of generalized reinforcers in psychotherapy research. *Psychol. Rep.,* 1955, **1**, 19–25.

KRASNER, L. Studies of the conditioning of verbal behavior. *Psychol. Bull.,* 1958, **55**, 148–170.

LACEY, J. I., & SMITH, R. I. Conditioning and generalization of unconscious anxiety. *Science,* 1954, **120**, 1–8.

LAZARUS, A. A., & RACHMAN, S. The use of systematic desensitization in psychotherapy. *S. Afr. med. J.,* 1957, **32**, 934–937.

LEHNER, G. F. J. Negative practice as a phychotherapeutic technique. *J. gen. Psychol.,* 1954, **51**, 69–82.

LINDSLEY, O. R. Operant conditioning methods applied to research in chronic schizophrenia. *Psychiat. res. Rep.,* 1956, **5**, 118–138.

LIVERSEDGE, L. A., & SYLVESTER, J. D. Conditioning techniques in the treatment of writer's cramp. *Lancet,* 1955, **1**, 1147–1149.

MARTIN, B., & KUBLY, DELORES. Results of treatment of enuresis by a conditioned response method. *J. consult. Psychol.,* 1955, **19**, 71–73.

MAUSNER, B. Studies in social interaction: III. The effect of variation in one partner's prestige on the interaction of observer pairs. *J. appl. Psychol.,* 1953, **37**, 391–393.

MAUSNER, B. The effect of one partner's success in a relevant task on the interaction of observer pairs. *J. abnorm. soc. Psychol.,* 1954, **49**, 557–560.

MAX, L. W. Breaking up a homosexual fixation by the conditioned reaction technique: A case study. *Psychol. Bull.,* 1935, **32**, 734.

MEISSNER, J. H. The relationship between voluntary nonfluency and stuttering. *J. speech Dis.,* 1946, **11**, 13–33.

MEYER, V. The treatment of two phobic patients on the basis of learning principles: Case report. *J. abnorm. soc. Psychol.,* 1957, **55**, 261–266.

MILLER, N. E., & DOLLARD, J. *Social learning and imitation.* New Haven: Yale Univer. Press, 1941.

MORGAN, J. J. B., & WITMER, F. J. The treatment of enuresis by the conditioned reaction technique. *J. genet. Psychol.,* 1939, **55**, 59–65.

MOWRER, O. H. *Learning theory and personality dynamics.* New York: Ronald, 1950.

MOWRER, O. H., & MOWRER, W. M. Enuresis — a method for its study and treatment. *Amer. J. Orthopsychiat.,* 1938, **8**, 436–459.

MURRAY, E. J. The content-analysis method of studying psychotherapy. *Psychol. Monogr.,* 1956, **70** (13, Whole No. 420).

MUSSEN, P., & DISTLER, L. M. Masculinity, identification, and father-son relationships. *J. aborm. soc. Psychol.,* 1959, **59**, 350–356.

MUSSEN, P., & DISTLER, L. M. Child-rearing antecedents of masculine identification in kindergarten boys. *Child Develpm.,* 1960, **31**, 89–100.

PAYNE, D. E., & MUSSEN, P. H. Parent-child relationships and father identification among adolescent boys. *J. abnorm. soc. Psychol.,* 1956, **52**, 358–362.

PETERS, H. N. Multiple choice learning in the chronic schizophrenic. *J. clin. Psychol.,* 1953, **9**, 328–333.

PETERS, H. N., & JENKINS, R. L. Improvement of chronic schizophrenic patients with guided problem-solving motivated by hunger. *Psychiat. Quart. Suppl.,* 1954, **28**, 84–101.

RACHMAN, S. The treatment of anxiety and phobic reactions by systematic desensitization psychotherapy. *J. abnorm. soc. Psychol.,* 1959, **58**, 259–263.

RAYMOND, M. S. Case of fetishism treated by aversion therapy. *Brit. med. J.,* 1956, **2**, 854–857.

RAZRAN, G. Stimulus generalization of conditioned responses. *Psychol. Bull.,* 1949, **46**, 337–365.

ROBINSON, NANCY M. Paired-associate learning by schizophrenic subjects under conditions of personal and impersonal reward and punishment. Unpublished doctoral dissertation, Stanford University, 1957.

ROGERS, C. R. *Client-centered therapy.* Boston: Houghton Mifflin, 1951.

ROGERS, C. R. Group discussion: Problems of controls. In E. H. Rubinstein & M. B. Parloff (Eds.), *Research in psychotherapy.* Washington, D.C.: American Psychological Association, 1959.

ROGERS, J. M. Operant conditioning in a quasi-therapy setting. *J. abnorm. soc. Psychol.,* 1960, **60**, 247–252.

ROSENTHAL, D. Changes in some moral values following psychotherapy. *J. consult. Psychol.*, 1955, **19**, 431–436.

ROTTER, J. B. *Social learning and clinical psychology.* Englewood Cliffs, N.J.: Prentice-Hall, 1954.

RUBENSTEIN, E. A., & LORR, M. A comparison of terminators and remainers in out-patient psychotherapy. *J. clin, Psychol.*, 1956, **12**, 345–349.

RUTHERFORD, B. R. The use of negative practice in speech therapy with children handicapped by cerebral palsy, athetoid type. *J. speech Dis.*, 1940, **5**, 259–264.

SALZINGER, K. Experimental manipulation of verbal behavior: A review. *J. gen. Psychol.*, 1959, **61**, 65–94.

SARASON, BARBARA R. The effects of verbally conditioned response classes on post-conditioning tasks. *Dissertation Abstr.*, 1957, **12**, 679.

SCHMIDBERG, MELITTA. Psychotherapy of juvenile delinquents. *Int. ment. hlth. res. Newsltr.*, 1959, **1**, 1–2.

SEARS, PAULINE S. Child-rearing factors related to playing of sex-typed roles. *Amer. Psychologist*, 1953, **8**, 431. (Abstract)

SEARS, R. R. Identification as a form of behavioral development. In D. B. Harris (Ed.), *The concept of development: An issue in the study of human behavior.* Minneapolis: Univer. Minnesota Press, 1957.

SHEEHAN, J. G. The modification of stuttering through non-reinforcement. *J. abnorm. soc. Psychol.*, 1951, **46**, 51–63.

SHEEHAN, J. G., & VOAS, R. B. Stuttering as conflict: I. Comparison of therapy techniques involving approach and avoidance. *J. speech Dis.*, 1957, **22**, 714–723.

SHOBEN, E. J. Psychotherapy as a problem in learning theory. *Psychol. Bull.*, 1949, **46**, 366–392.

SKINNER, B. F. *Science and human behavior.* New York: Macmillan, 1953.

SKINNER, B. F. Some issues concerning the control of human behavior. *Science*, 1956, **124**, 1057–1066. (a)

SKINNER, B. F. What is psychotic behavior? In, *Theory and treatment of psychosis: Some newer aspects.* St. Louis: Washington Univer. Stud., 1956. (b)

SOLOMON, R. L., KAMIN, L. J., & WYNNE, L. C. Traumatic avoidance learning: The outcomes of several extinction procedures with dogs. *J. abnorm. soc. Psychol.*, 1953, **48**, 291–302.

SULLIVAN, H. S. *The interpersonal theory of psychiatry.* New York: Norton, 1953.

THIRMANN, J. Conditioned-reflex treatment of alcoholism. *New Engl. J. Med.*, 1949, **241**, 368–370, 406–410.

THOMPSON, G. N., & BIELINSKI, B. Improvement in psychosis following conditioned reflex treatment in alcoholism. *J. nerv. ment. Dis.*, 1953, **117**, 537–543.

TILTON, J. R. The use of instrument motor and verbal learning techniques in the treatment of chronic schizophrenics. Unpublished doctoral dissertation, Michigan State University, 1956.

ULLMAN, L. P., KRASNER, L., & COLLINS, Beverly J. Modification of behavior in group therapy associated with verbal conditioning. *J. abnorm. soc. Psychol.*, in press.

VOEGTLEN, W. L. The treatment of alcoholism by establishing a conditioned reflex. *Amer. J. med. Sci.*, 1940, **119**, 802–810.

WALLACE, J. A. The treatment of alcoholics by the conditioned reflex method. *J. Tenn. Med. Ass.*, 1949, **42**, 125–128.

WEIDE, T. N. Conditioning and generalization of the use of affect-relevant words. Unpublished doctoral dissertation, Stanford University, 1959.

WHITING, J. W. M. The research program of the Laboratory of Human Development: The development of self-control. Cambridge: Harvard University, 1954. (Mimeo)

WILLIAMS, C. D. The elimination of tantrum behaviors by extinction procedures. *J. abnorm. soc. Psychol.*, 1959, **59**, 269.

WILLIAMS, R. I. Verbal conditioning in psychotherapy. *Amer. Psychologist*, 1959, **14**, 388. (Abstract)

WOLPE, J. Reciprocal inhibition as the main basis of psychotherapeutic effects. *AMA Arch. Neurol. Psychiat.*, 1954, **72**, 205–226.

WOLPE, J. *Psychotherapy by reciprocal inhibition.* Stanford: Stanford Univer. Press, 1958.

WOLPE, J. Psychotherapy based on the principle of reciprocal inhibition. In A. Burton (Ed.), *Case studies in counseling and psychotherapy.* Englewood Cliffs, N. J.: Prentice-Hall, 1959.

YATES, A. J. The application of learning theory to the treatment of tics. *J. abnorm. soc. Psychol.*, 1958, **56**, 175–182.

The Systematic Desensitization Treatment of Neuroses*

Some years ago, studies on the induction and elimination of experimental neuroses in animals (23) showed that these conditions were persistent habits of unadaptive behavior acquired by learning (conditioning); and that their therapy was a matter of unlearning. The central constituent of the neurotic behavior was anxiety, and the most effective way of procuring unlearning was repeatedly to feed the animal while it was responding with a weak degree of anxiety to a "weak" conditioned stimulus. The effect of this was to diminish progressively the strength of the anxiety response to the particular stimulus so that it eventually declined to zero. Increasingly "strong" stimulus situations were successively dealt with in the same way; and finally, the animal showed no anxiety to any of the situations to which anxiety had been conditioned. The basis of the gradual elimination of the anxiety response habit appeared to be an example, at a more complex level, of the phenomenon of *reciprocal inhibition* described originally by Sherrington (17). Each time the animal fed, the anxiety response was to some extent inhibited; and each occasion of inhibition weakened somewhat the strength of the anxiety habit. The experiments suggested the general proposition that *if a response inhibitory to anxiety can be made to occur in the presence of anxiety-evoking stimuli so that it is accompanied by a complete or partial suppression of the anxiety response, the bond between these stimuli and the anxiety response will be weakened.*

I have argued elsewhere (24, 27, 28) that human neuroses are quite parallel to experimental neuroses. On this premise and during the past twelve years, the writer has applied the reciprocal inhibition principle to the treatment of a large number of clinical cases of neurosis, employing a variety of other responses to inhibit anxiety or other neurotic responses. In a recent book (27) an analysis has been given of the results in 210 patients, of whom 89 per cent either recovered or were much improved, apparently lastingly, after a mean of about 30 interviews.

* Reprinted by permission from *The Journal of Nervous and Mental Disease*, Volume 132, 1963, pages 189–203. Copyright ©, 1963, The Williams & Wilkins Co., Baltimore, Md. 21202, U.S.A.

In the case of neurotic responses conditioned to situations involving direct interpersonal relations, the essence of reciprocal inhibition therapy has been to instigate in the situations concerned new patterns of behavior of an anxiety-inhibiting kind whose repeated exercise gradually weakens the anxiety response habit (16, 19, 20, 25, 27, 28). Neurotic responses conditioned to stimuli other than those arising from direct interpersonal relations do not lend themselves, as a rule, to behavioral treatment in the life situation of the patient; and consulting-room applications of the reciprocal inhibition principle have been necessary. The most straightforward examples of neurotic responses requiring such measures have been the phobias. Relatively "simple" though they are, they have hitherto constituted a difficult therapeutic problem. For example, Curran and Partridge (2) state, "Phobic symptoms are notoriously resistant to treatment and their complete removal is rarely achieved." A very different picture is in prospect with the use of conditioning methods (1, 4, 10–12, 14, 15), which are no less effective when used for much more subtle neurotic constellations. Examples will be found below.

In the office treatment of neuroses by reciprocal inhibition, any response inhibitory of anxiety may in theory be used. The almost forgotten earliest example of therapy of this kind (7) involved inhibiting the anxiety of phobic children by feeding (just as in the animal experiments mentioned above). Conditioned motor responses have occasionally served the same end (27, p. 173); and Meyer (14) and Freeman and Kendrick (4) have made use of ordinary "pleasant" emotions of daily life (see also 27, p. 198). But the behavioral response that has had the widest application is deep muscle relaxation, whose anxiety-inhibiting effects were first pointed out by Jacobson (5, 6). It has been the basis of the technique known as *systematic desensitization* which, because of its convenience, has been most widely adopted (1, 9, 11, 12).

Though several descriptions of the technique of systematic desensitization have been published (*e.g.*, 26, 27) it is now clear that more details are needed to enable practitioners to apply it without assistance. It is the aim of this paper to present a more adequate account, and also for the first time to give a separate statistical analysis of results obtained with this treatment.

A TECHNIQUE OF SYSTEMATIC DESENSITIZATION

It is necessary to emphasize that the desensitization technique is carried out *only after a careful assessment of the therapeutic requirements of the patient.* A detailed history is taken of every symptom and of every aspect of life in which the patient experiences undue difficulty. A systematic account is then obtained of his life history with special attention to intrafamilial relationships. His attitudes to people in educational institutions and to learning and play are investigated. A history of his work life is taken, noting both his experiences with people and those related to work itself. He is questioned about his sexual experiences from first awareness of sexual feelings up to the present. Careful scrutiny is made of his current major personal relationships. Finally, he is asked to describe all kinds of "nervousness" that may have afflicted him at any time and to narrate any distressing experiences he can remember.

The problems posed by the case are now carefully considered; and if there are neurotic reactions in connection with direct interpersonal relations, appropriate new behavior based on the reciprocal inhibition principle is instigated in the patient's life situation (19, 20, 25, 27, 28). Most commonly, it is assertive behavior that is instigated. When systematic desensitization is also indicated, it is conducted as soon as possible, and may be in parallel with measures aimed at other sources of neurotic anxiety.

Systematic desensitization is used not only for the treatment of classical phobias involving anxiety responses to nonpersonal stimulus constellations (like enclosed spaces or harmless animals), but also for numerous less obvious and often complex sources of neurotic disturbance. These may involve ideas, bodily sensations, or extrinsic situations. Examples of each are to be found in Table 1. The most common extrinsic sources of anxiety relate to people in contexts that make irrelevant the use of direct action, such as assertion, on the part of the patient. As examples, one patient reacts with anxiety to the mere presence of particular persons, another to definable categories of people, a third to being the center of attention, a fourth to people in groups, a fifth to inferred criticism or rejection, and so forth. In all instances, *anxiety has been conditioned to situations in which, objectively, there is no danger.*

In brief, the desensitization method consists of presenting to the imagination of the deeply relaxed patient the feeblest item in a list of anxiety-evoking stimuli — repeatedly, until no more anxiety is evoked. The next item of the list is then presented, and so on, until eventually even the strongest of the anxiety-evoking stimuli fails to evoke any stir of anxiety in the patient. It has consistently been found that at every stage a stimulus that evokes no anxiety when imagined in a state of relaxation will also evoke no anxiety when encountered in reality.

The method involves three separate sets of operations: 1) training in deep muscle relaxation; 2) the construction of anxiety hierarchies; and 3) counterposing relaxation and anxiety-evoking stimuli from the hierarchies.

TRAINING IN RELAXATION

The method of relaxation taught is essentially that of Jacobson (5) but the training takes up only about half of each of about six interviews — far less time than Jacobson devotes. The patient is also asked to practice at home for a half-hour each day.

The first lesson begins with the therapist telling the patient that he is to learn relaxation because of its beneficial emotional effects. He is then directed to grip the arm of his chair with one hand to see whether he can distinguish any qualitative difference between the sensations produced in his forearm and those in his hand. Usually he can, and he is asked to take note of the forearm sensation as being characteristic of muscle tension. He is also enjoined to remember the location of the flexors and extensors of the forearm. Next, the therapist grips the patient's wrist and asks him to pull, making him aware of the tension in his biceps; and then, instructing him to push in the opposite direction, draws his attention to the extensor muscles of the arm.

The therapist now again grips the patient's wrist and makes him tense the biceps and then relax it as much as possible, letting go gradually as the patient's hand comes down. The patient is then told to "keep trying to go further and further in the negative direction" and to "try to go beyond what seems to you to be the furthest point." He may report sensations like tingling and numbness which often accompany relaxation. When it appears that the patient has understood how to go about relaxing he is made to relax simultaneously all the muscles of both arms and forearms.

At the second lesson in relaxation, the patient is told that from the emotional point of view the most important muscles in the body are situated in and around the head, and that we shall therefore go on to these next. The muscles of the face are the first to be dealt with, beginning with the forehead. This location lends itself to demonstrating to the patient the step-like manner in which tension is decreased; and I do this by contracting the eyebrow-raising and the frowning groups of muscles in my own forehead very intensely simultaneously, and then relaxing by degrees. The patient is then made aware of his own forehead muscles and given about ten minutes to relax them as far as possible. Patients frequently report spontaneously the occurrence of unusual sensations in their foreheads, such as numbness, tingling, or "a feeling of thickness, as though my skin were made of leather." These sensations are characteristic of the attainment of a degree of relaxation beyond the normal level of muscle tone. At this session attention is drawn also to the muscles in the region of the nose (by asking the patient to wrinkle his nose) and to the muscles around the mouth (by making him purse his lips and then smile). After a few minutes he is asked to bite on his teeth, thus tensing his masseters and temporales. The position of the lips is an important indicator of successful relaxation of the muscles of mastication. When these are relaxed, the lips are parted by a few millimeters. The masseters cannot be relaxed if the mouth is kept resolutely closed.

At the third lesson, attention is drawn to the muscles of the tongue, which may be felt contracting in the floor of the mouth when the patient presses the tip of his tongue firmly against the back of his bottom incisor teeth. Thereafter, with active jaw-opening, infra-hyoid tensions are pointed out. All these muscles are then relaxed. At the same session, the tensions produced in the eye muscles and those of the neck are noted and time given for their relaxation.

The fourth lesson deals with the muscles of the shoulder girdle, the fifth with those of the back, thorax and abdomen, and the sixth with those of the thighs and legs. A procedure that many patients find helpful is to coordinate relaxation of various other muscles with the automatic relaxation of the respiratory muscles that takes place with normal exhalation.

CONSTRUCTION OF ANXIETY HIERARCHIES

This is the most difficult and taxing procedure in the desensitization technique. Investigation of any case of anxiety neurosis reveals that the stimuli to anxiety fall into definable groups or *themes*. The themes may be obvious ones, like fear of heights, or less apparent ones, like fear of rejection.

Hierarchy construction usually begins at about the same time as relaxation training, but alterations or additions can be made at any time. It is important to note that the gathering of data and its subsequent organizing are done in an ordinary conversational way and *not under relaxation*, since the patient's *ordinary* responses to stimuli are under scrutiny.

The raw data from which the hierarchies are constructed have three main sources: 1) the patient's history; 2) responses to the Willoughby Questionnaire (22); and 3) special probings about situations in which the patient feels anxiety though there is no objective threat. Abundant material is often obtained by setting the patient the homework task of listing all situations that he finds disturbing, fearful, embarrassing, or in any way distressing.

When all identified sources of neurotic disturbance have been listed, the therapist classifies them into groups if there is more than one theme. The items of each thematic group are then rewritten to make separate lists and the patient is asked to rank the items of each list, placing the item he imagines would be most disturbing at the top and the least disturbing at the bottom of the list.

In many instances, the construction of a hierarchy is a very straightforward matter. This is true of most cases of such fears, as of heights (where the greater the height the greater the fear), or enclosed spaces, or, to take a somewhat more complex instance, fears aroused by the sight of illness in others. In such instances as the last, exemplified in Case 1 below, although the items have only a general thematic linkage and do not belong to a stimulus continuum (as do, for example, the items of a height hierarchy), all that has to be done is to obtain a list of situations embodying illnesses in others and then to ask the patient to rank the items according to the amount of anxiety each one arouses.

In other cases, hierarchy construction is more difficult because the sources of anxiety are not immediately revealed by the patient's listing of what he avoids. For example, it may become clear that he reacts to social occasions with anxiety, and that different kinds of social occasions (*e.g.* weddings, parties, and the musical evenings) are associated with decreasing degrees of anxiety. There may then be a temptation to arrange a hierarchy based on these types of social occasions, with weddings at the top of the list and musical evenings at the bottom. Usually, little effective therapy would follow an attempt at desensitization based on such a hierarchy, and more careful probing would almost certainly reveal some facet of social occasions that is the real source of anxiety. Frequently, fear and avoidance of social occasions turns out to be based on fear of criticism or of rejection; or the fear may be a function of the mere physical presence of people, varying with the number of them to whom the patient is exposed. The writer once had a patient whose fear of social situations was really a conditioned anxiety response to the smell of food in public places. A good example of the importance of correct identification of relevant sources of anxiety is to be found in a previously reported case (27, p. 152) where a man's impotence was found to be due to anxiety related not to aspects of the sexual situation as such, but to the idea of trauma, which in certain contexts, especially defloration, enters into the sexual act.

It is not necessary for the patient actually to have experienced each situation that is to be included in a hierarchy. The question before him is of the order that, "If you were today confronted by such and such a situation, *would you expect* to be anxious?" To answer this question he must *imagine* the situation concerned, and it is usually not much more difficult to imagine a merely possible event than one that has at some time occurred. The temporal setting of an imagined stimulus configuration scarcely affects the responses to it. A man with a phobia for dogs has about as much anxiety to the idea of meeting a bulldog on the way home this evening as to recalling an encounter with this breed of dog a year previously.

A small minority of patients do not experience anxiety when they imagine situations that in reality are disturbing. In some of these, anxiety is evoked when they *describe* (verbalize) the scene they have been asked to imagine. As in other patients, the various scenes can then be ranked according to the degree of anxiety they evoke.

To a therapist inexperienced in the construction of anxiety hierarchies, the most common difficulty to be encountered is to find that even the weakest item in a hierarchy produces more anxiety than can be counteracted by the patient's relaxation. In many cases, it is obvious where weaker items may be sought. For example, in a patient who had an anxiety hierarchy on the theme of loneliness, the weakest item in the original hierarchy — being at home accompanied only by her daughter — was found to evoke more anxiety than was manageable. To obtain a weaker starting point all that was needed was to add items in which she had two or more companions. But it is not always so easy, and the therapist may be hard put to find manipulable dimensions. For example, following an accident three years previously, a patient had developed serious anxiety reactions to the sight of approaching automobiles. At first it seemed that anxiety was just noticeable when an automobile was two blocks away, gradually increasing

until a distance of half a block and then much more steeply increasing as the distance grew less. This, of course, promised plain sailing, but at the first desensitization session even at two blocks the imaginary car aroused anxiety much too great to be mastered: and it was revealed that the patient experienced anxiety at the very prospect of even the shortest journey by car, since the whole range of possibilities was already present the moment a journey became imminent. To obtain manageable levels of anxiety, an imaginary enclosed field two blocks square was postulated. The patient's car was "placed" in one corner of the field and the early items of the hierarchy involved a trusted person driving his car up to a stated point towards the patient's car, and of bringing this point ever closer as the patient progressed. Another case in whom weak anxiety stimuli were not easily found was a patient with a death phobia, whose items ranged in descending order from human corpses through such scenes as funeral processions to dead dogs. But even the last produced marked anxiety, when they were imagined even at distances of two or three hundred yards. A solution was found in retreating along a temporal instead of a spatial dimension, beginning with the (historically inaccurate) sentence, "William the Conqueror was killed at the Battle of Hastings in 1066."

DESENSITIZATION PROCEDURE

When the hierarchies have been constructed and relaxation training has proceeded to a degree judged sufficient, desensitization can then begin. First "weak" and later progressively "strong" anxiety-arousing stimulus situations will be presented to the imagination of the deeply relaxed patient, as described below.

When relaxation is poor, it may be enhanced by the use of meprobamate, chlorpromazine, or codeine given an hour before the interview. Which drug to use is decided by trial. When pervasive ("free-floating") anxiety impedes relaxation, the use of carbon dioxide-oxygen mixtures by La Verne's (8) single inhalation technique has been found to be of the greatest value (27, p. 166) and with some patients this method comes to be used before every desensitization session. In a few patients who cannot relax but who are not anxious either, attempts at desensitization sometimes succeed, presumably because interview-induced emotional responses inhibit the anxiety aroused by the imagined stimuli (27).

It is the usual practice for sessions to be conducted under hypnosis with the patient sitting on a comfortable armchair. He may or may not have been hypnotized in an exploratory way on one or more occasions during earlier interviews. With patients who cannot be hypnotized, and in those who for any reason object to it, hypnosis is omitted and instructions are given merely to close the eyes and relax according to instructions. (There is a general impression that these patients make slower progress.)

The patient having been hypnotized, the therapist proceeds to bring about as deep as possible a state of calm by verbal suggestions to the patient to give individual attention to relaxing each group of muscles in the way he has learned.

The presentation of scenes at the first session is to some extent exploratory. The first scene presented is always a neutral one — to which a patient is not expected to have any anxiety reaction whatsoever. This is followed by a small number of presentations of the mildest items from one or two of the patient's hierarchies. To illustrate this, we shall make use of a verbatim account of the first session of Case 2, whose hierarchies are given below. After hypnotizing and relaxing the patient, the therapist went on as follows.

"You will now imagine a number of scenes very clearly and calmly. The scenes may not at all disturb your state of relaxation. If by any chance, however, you feel disturbed, you will be able to indicate this to me by raising your left index finger an inch or so. (*Pause of about 10 seconds*) First, I want you to imagine that you are standing at a busy street corner. You notice the traffic passing — cars, trucks, bicycles, and people. You see them all very clearly and you notice the sounds that accompany them. (*Pause of about 15 seconds*). Now, stop imagining that scene and again turn your attention to your muscles. (*Pause of about 20 seconds*). Now, imagine that it is a work day. It is 11 A.M. and you are lying in bed with an attack of influenza and a temperature of 103°. (*Pause of about 10 seconds*). Stop imagining the scene and again relax. (*Pause of 15 seconds*) Now, imagine exactly the same situation again. (*Pause of 10 seconds*) Stop imagining the scene and relax. (*Pause of about 20 seconds*) Now, I want you to imagine that you are at the post office and you have just sent off a manuscript to a journal. (*Pause of 15 seconds*) Stop imagining the scene and only relax. (*Pause of about five seconds*) In a few moments, I will be counting up to five and you will wake up feeling very calm and refreshed. (*Pause of about five seconds*) One, two, three, four, five. (*The patient opened his eyes looking somewhat dazed*).

On being brought out of the trance, the patient is asked how he feels and how he felt during the trance, since it is important to know if a calm basal emotional state was achieved by the relaxation. He is then asked to indicate whether the scenes were clear or not. (It is essential for visualizing to be at least moderately clear.) Finally, the therapist inquires whether or not any of the scenes produced any disturbance in the patient, and if they did, how much. It is not common for a patient to report a reaction to the neutral control scene. It is worth remarking that even though the patient has a signal at his disposal with which to indicate disturbance, the fact that he has not done so during a scene by no means proves that it has not disturbed him at all, for it is a rare patient who makes use of the signal if only mildly disturbed. But the provision of a signal must never be omitted, for the patient will use it if he has a strong emotional reaction, which may not be otherwise manifest. *Exposure, and prolonged exposure in particular, to a very disturbing scene can greatly increase sensitivity.* With less marked disturbance there may be perseveration of anxiety, which makes continuance of the session futile.

At subsequent sessions, the same basic procedure is followed. If at the previous session there was a scene whose repeated presentations evoked anxiety that diminished but was not entirely extinguished, that scene is usually the first to be presented. If at the previous session the final scenes from a hierarchy ceased to arouse any anxiety, the scene next higher is now presented, except in a few patients who, despite having had no anxiety at all to a final scene at a previous session, again show a small measure of anxiety to this scene at a subsequent session. It must again be presented several times until all anxiety is eliminated before going on to the next scene.

In order to gauge progress, the following procedure is adopted after two to four presentations of a particular scene. The therapist says, "If you had even the slightest disturbance to the last presentation of this scene, raise your left index finger now. If you had no disturbance, do nothing." If the finger is not raised, the therapist goes on to the next higher scene in the hierarchy. If the finger is raised, the therapist says, "If the amount of anxiety has been decreasing from one presentation to the next, do nothing. If it has not been decreasing, raise your finger again." If the finger is now not raised, this is an indication for further presentations of the scene, since further decrements in anxiety evocation may be confidently expected; but if it is raised, it is clear that the scene is producing more anxiety than the patient's relaxation can overcome, and it is therefore necessary to devise and interpose a scene midway in "strength" between this scene and the last one successfully mastered.

There is great variation in how many themes, how many scenes from each, and how many presentations are given at a session. Generally, up to four hierarchies are drawn upon in an individual session, and not many patients have more than four. Three or four presentations of a scene are usual, but ten or more may be needed. The total number of scenes presented is limited mainly by availability of time and by the endurance of the patient. On the whole, both of these quantities increase as therapy goes on, and eventually almost the whole interview may be devoted to desensitization, so that whereas at an early stage eight or ten presentations are the total given at a session, at an advanced stage the number may rise to 30 or even 50.

The *duration* of a scene is usually of the order of five seconds, but it may be varied according to several circumstances. It is quickly terminated if the patient signals anxiety by spontaneously raising his finger or if he shows any sharp reaction. Whenever the therapist has a special reason to suspect that a scene may evoke a strong reaction he presents it with cautious brevity — for one or two seconds. By and large, early presentations of scenes are briefer, later ones longer. A certain number of patients require fifteen or more seconds to arrive at a clear image of a scene.

The *interval* between scenes is usually between ten and twenty seconds, but if the patient has been more than slightly disturbed by the preceding scene, it may be extended to a minute or more, and during that time the patient may be given repeated suggestions to be calm.

The *number* of desensitizing sessions required varies according to the number and the intensity of the anxiety areas, and the degree of generalization (involvement of related stimuli) in the case of each area. One patient may recover in as few as a half-dozen sessions; another may require a hundred or more. The patient with a death phobia, mentioned above, on whom a temporal dimension had to be used, also had two other phobias and required a total of about a hundred sessions. To remove the death phobia alone, a total of about 2,000 scene presentations were needed.

The *spacing* of sessions does not seem to be of great importance. Two or three sessions a week are characteristic, but the meetings may be separated by many weeks or take place daily. Occasional patients, visiting from afar, have had two sessions in a single day. Whether sessions are massed or widely dispersed, there is almost always a close relation between the extent to which desensitization has been accomplished and the degree of diminution of anxiety responses to real stimuli. Except when therapy is nearly finished, and only a few loose ends of neurotic reactions are left (that may be overcome through emotions arising spontaneously in the ordinary course of living (27)), very little change occurs, as a rule, between sessions. This was strikingly demonstrated by Case 1 (below) in whom the marked improvement of a severe claustrophobia achieved by a first series of sessions remained almost stationary during a three and one-half year interval, after which further sessions overcame the phobia apparently completely.

EXAMPLES OF HIERARCHIES FROM ACTUAL CASES

Single or multiple anxiety hierarchies occur with about equal frequency. Each of the following two cases had multiple hierarchies. (*The most disturbing item, as always, is at the top of each list with the others ranked below it.*)

CASE 1

Mrs. A. was a 50-year-old housewife, whose main complaint was of very disabling fears on the general theme of claustrophobia. The fears had begun about 25 years previously, following a terrifying experience with general anesthesia, and had subsequently spread in a series of steps, each associated with a particular experience, to a wide range of situations. The patient also had other phobias, the most important of which, concerning illness and death, had its origin during childhood. In 46 desensitization sessions between March and July, 1956, all phobias were overcome except the most severe of the claustrophobic possibilities indicated in the first three items of the hierarchy given below, and with item 4 still incompletely conquered therapy was terminated when the writer went overseas for a year. The patient returned to treatment in October, 1959, having maintained her recovery in all areas, but having made very little additional progress. During the next two months, 16 additional sessions were devoted to desensitizing to numerous scenes relevant to the "top" of the claustrophobia hierarchy. She was eventually able to accept, in the session, being confined for two hours in an imagined room four feet square, and reported complete freedom from fear in tunnels and only slight anxiety in "extreme" elevator situations.

Hierarchies

A. Claustrophobic Series

1) Being stuck in an elevator. (The longer the time, the more disturbing.)
2) Being locked in a room. (The smaller the room and the longer the time, the more disturbing.)
3) Passing through a tunnel in a railway train. (The longer the tunnel, the more disturbing.)
4) Traveling in an elevator alone. (The greater the distance, the more disturbing.)
5) Traveling in an elevator with an operator. (The longer the distance, the more disturbing.)
6) On a journey by train. (The longer the journey, the more disturbing.)
7) Stuck in a dress with a stuck zipper.
8) Having a tight ring on her finger.
9) Visiting and unable to leave at will (for example, if engaged in a card game).
10) Being told of somebody in jail.
11) Having polish on her fingernails and no access to remover.
12) Reading of miners trapped underground.

B. Death Series

1) Being at a burial.
2) Being at a house of mourning.
3) The word *death*.
4) Seeing a funeral procession. (The nearer, the more disturbing.)
5) The sight of a dead animal, *e.g.*, cat.
6) Driving past a cemetery. (The nearer, the more disturbing.)

C. Illness Series

1) Hearing that an acquaintance has cancer.
2) The word *cancer*.
3) Witnessing a convulsive seizure.
4) Discussions of operations. (The more prolonged the discussion, the more disturbing.)
5) Seeing a person receive an injection.
6) Seeing someone faint.
7) The word *operation*.
8) Considerable bleeding from another person.
9) A friend points to a stranger, saying, "This man has tuberculosis."
10) The sight of a blood-stained bandage.
11) The smell of ether.
12) The sight of a friend sick in bed. (The more sick looking, the more disturbing.)
13) The smell of methylated spirits.
14) Driving past a hospital.

CASE 2

Dr. B. was a 41-year-old gynecological resident who had felt anxious and insecure for as long as he could remember. Five years earlier, when anxieties were intensified by divorce proceedings, he had consulted a follower of Harry Stack Sullivan, who had tided him over the immediate situation but left him with attitudes of "acceptance" which had resulted in his becoming more anxious than before. After a few weeks' assertive training, he felt considerably better, but was left with the anxious sensitivities ranked in the hierarchies below. After six desensitization sessions he was completely free from anxiety responses to any actual situations similar to those contained in the hierarchies.

Hierarchies

A. Guilt Series

1) "Jackson (Dean of the Medical School) wants to see you."
2) Thinks "I only did ten minutes work today."
3) Thinks "I only did an hour's work today."
4) Thinks "I only did six hours' work today."
5) Sitting at the movies.
6) Reading an enjoyable novel.
7) Going on a casual stroll.
8) Staying in bed during the day (even though ill).

B. Devaluation Series

1) A woman doesn't respond to his advances.
2) An acquaintance says, "I saw you in Jefferson Street with a woman." (This kind of activity had locally acquired a disreputable flavor.)
3) Having a piece of writing rejected.
4) Awareness that his skill at a particular surgical operation left something to be desired. (Anxiety in terms of "Will I ever be able to do it?")
5) Overhearing adverse remarks about a lecture he delivered that he knows was not good.
6) Overhearing, "Dr. B. fancies himself as a surgeon."
7) Hearing anyone praised, *e.g.*, "Dr. K. is a fine surgeon."
8) Having submitted a piece of writing for publication.

■ TABLE I/Basic Case Data

Patient, Sex, Age	No. of Sessions	Hierarchy Theme	Outcome	Comments
1. F, 50	62	a) Claustrophobia	++++	See case data above.
		b) Illness and hospitals	++++	
		c) Death and its trappings	++++	
		d) Storms	+++	
		e) Quarrels	++++	
2. M, 40	6	a) Guilt	++++	See case data above.
		b) Devaluation	++++	
3. F, 24	17	a) Examinations	++++	
		b) Being scrutinized	++++	
		c) Devaluation	++++	
		d) Discord between others	++++	
4. M, 24	5	a) Snakelike shapes	++++	
5. M, 21	24	a) Being watched	++++	
		b) Suffering of others	++++	
		c) "Jealousy" reaction	++++	
		d) Disapproval	++++	
6. M, 28	5	Crowds	+++	
7. F, 21	5	Criticism	++++	
8. F, 52	21	a) Being center of attention	0	No disturbance during scenes. Was in fact not imagining self in situation.
		b) Superstitions	0	
9. F, 25	9	Suffering and death of others	+++	
10. M, 22	17	Tissue damage in others	++++	
11. M, 37	13	Actual or implied criticism	++++	
12. F, 31	15	Being watched working	+++	
13. F, 40	16	a) "Suffering" and eeriness	++++	This case has been reported in detail (26).
		b) Being devalued	++++	
		c) Failing to come up to expectations	++++	
14. M, 36	10	a) Bright light	++++	
		b) Palpitations	++++	
15. M, 43	9	Wounds and corpses	+++	
16. M, 27	51	a) Being watched, especially at work	+++	No anxiety while being watched at work. Anxious at times while watched playing cards.
		b) Being criticized	++++	
17. M, 33	8	Being watched at golf	+++	
18. M, 13	8	Talking before audience (Stutterer)	0	No imagined scene was ever disturbing.
19. M, 40	7	Authority figures	++++	
20. M, 23	4	Claustrophobia	++++	
21. F, 23	6	a) Agoraphobia	0	Later successfully treated by conditioned motor response method (27).
		b) Fear of falling	0	
22. M, 46	19	a) Being in limelight	+++	
		b) Blood and death	++++	
23. F, 40	20	Social embarrassment	++++	
24. F, 28	9	Agoraphobia	0	
25. F, 48	7	Rejection	+++	
26. M, 28	13	a) Disapproval	+++	
		b) Rejection	++++	
27. M, 11	6	Authority figures	++++	
28. M, 26	217	a) Claustrophobia	++++	
		b) Criticism (numerous aspects)	+++	Finally overcome completely by use of Malleson's method (13).
		c) Trappings of death	+++	
29. F, 20	5	Agoraphobia	++++	
30. M, 68	23	a) Agoraphobia	++++	
		b) Masturbation	++++	
31. F, 36	5	Being in limelight	++++	
32. M, 26	17	a) Illness and death	+++	
		b) Own symptoms	+++	

TABLE 1—*Concluded*

Patient, Sex, Age	No. of Sessions	Hierarchy Theme	Outcome	Comments
33. F, 44	9	a) Being watched	++++	
		b) Elevators	++++	
34. F, 47	17	Intromission into vagina	+++	After 15th session gradual in vivo operation with objects became possible, and subsequently, coitus with husband.
35. M, 37	5	a) Disapproval	++++	
		b) Rejection	++++	
36. F, 32	25	Sexual stimuli	++++	
37. M, 36	21	a) Agoraphobia	++++	
		b) Disapproval	++++	
		c) Being watched	++++	
28. M, 18	6	a) Disapproval	+++	Instrumental in overcoming impotence
		b) Sexual stimuli	++++	
39. F, 48	20	a) Rejection	++++	Stutter markedly improved as anxiety diminished, partly as result of desensitization, and partly due to assertive behavior in relevant situations.
		b) Crudeness of others	++++	

RESULTS

Table 1 presents basic details of 39 cases treated by desensitization. These patients, comprising about one-third of the total number so treated up to December, 1959, were randomly selected (by a casual visitor) from the alphabetical files of all patients treated. They are considered to be a representative sample of the total treated patient population. Rather than to summarize results from nearly 150 cases, it was felt desirable to present some details about a more limited series.

Many of the patients had other neurotic response habits as well, that were treated by methods appropriate to them. Interspersed among the 39 cases reported were six others eligible for desensitization who had between two and six sessions, but who are excluded from the series because they terminated treatment for various reasons (even though usually showing some evidence of progress). It is felt proper to exclude these, as in evaluating the therapeutic efficacy of an antibiotic it would be proper to omit cases that had received only one or two doses. Also excluded are two cases that turned out to be schizophrenic. Psychotic patients do not respond to this treatment and of course receive it only if misdiagnosed as neurotic. On the other hand, every presenting neurotic case is accepted for treatment.

Outcome of treatment is judged on the basis of several sources of information. In addition to the patient's report of his reactions to stimuli from the hierarchies during sessions, there frequently is observable evidence of diminished anxious responding, inasmuch as many patients display, when disturbed, characteristic muscle tensions (such as grimaces or finger movements). The greatest importance is attached to the patient's reports of changed responses, in real life, to previously fearful situations. I have not regularly checked these reports by direct observation, but in several cases in whom I have made such checks the patient's account of his improved reaction has invariably been confirmed. In general, there is reason to accept the credibility of patients who report *gradual* improvement. A patient who wished to use an allegation of recovery in order to get out of an unsuccessful course of treatment, would be likely to report recovery rather suddenly, rather than to continue in treatment to substantiate a claim of gradual recovery.

Degree of change is rated on a 5-point scale ranging from 4-plus to zero. A 4-plus rating indicates complete, or almost complete, freedom from phobic reactions to all situations on the theme of the phobia; 3-plus means an improvement of response such that the phobia is judged by the patient to retain not more than 20 per cent of its original strength, 2-plus means 30–70 per cent, and 1-plus indicates that more than 70 per cent of the original strength of the phobia is judged retained. A zero rating indicates that there is no discernible change. (It will be noted that only 4-plus, 3-plus and zero ratings have been applicable to the patients in this series.)

Table 2 summarizes the data given in Table 1. There were 68 phobias and neurotic anxiety response habits related to more complex situations among the 39 patients, of whom 19 had multiple hierarchies. The treatment was judged effective in 35 of the patients. Forty-five of the phobic and other anxiety habits were apparently eliminated (4-plus rating) and 17 more were markedly ameliorated (3-plus rating). (It is entirely possible that most of the latter would have reached a 4-plus level if additional sessions could have been given; in cases 16 and 29, progress had become very slow when sessions were discontinued, but this was not so in the other cases.)

■ **TABLE 2 / Summary of Data of Table 1**

Patients	39
Number of patients responding to de-sensitization treatment	35
Number of hierarchies	68
Hierarchies overcome	45 ⎱ 91%
Hierarchies markedly improved	17 ⎰
Hierarchies unimproved	6 9%
Total number of desensitization sessions	762
Mean session expenditure per hierarchy	11.2
Mean session expenditure per successfully treated hierarchy	12.3
Median number of sessions per patient	10.0

Among the failures, cases 8 and 18 were unable to imagine themselves within situations; case 22 could not confine her imagining to the stated scene and therefore had excessive anxiety, but was later treated with complete success by means of another conditioning method (27, p. 174); case 25 had interpersonal anxiety reactions that led to erratic responses and, having experienced no benefit, sought therapy elsewhere.

The 39 patients had a total of 762 desensitization sessions, including in each case the first exploratory session although in many instances scenes from the hierarchies were not presented at that session. The mean number of sessions per hierarchy was 11.2; the median number of sessions given to patients 10.0. It should be noted that a desensitization session usually takes up only part of a three-quarter hour interview period, and in cases that also have neurotic problems requiring direct action in the life situation there may be many interviews in which a session is not included.

At times varying between six months and four years after the end of treatment, follow-up reports were obtained from 20 of the 35 patients who responded to desensitization. There was no reported instance of relapse or the appearance of new phobias or other neurotic symptoms. I have never observed resurgence of neurotic anxiety when desensitization has been complete or virtually so.

DISCUSSION

The general idea of overcoming phobias or other neurotic habits by means of systematic "gradual approaches" is not new. It has long been known that increasing measures of exposure to a feared object may lead to a gradual disappearance of the fear. This knowledge has sometimes (21), but unfortunately not very often, contributed to the armamentarium of psychiatrists in dealing with phobias. What is new in the present contribution is 1) the provision of a theoretical explanation for the success of such gradual approaches and 2) the description of a method in which the therapist has complete control of the degree of approach that the patient makes to the feared object at any particular time. The situations, being imaginary, are constructed and varied at will in the consulting room.

The excellent results obtained by this method of treatment are naturally viewed with skepticism by those who in the psychoanalytic tradition regard phobias and other neurotic anxiety response habits as merely the superficial manifestations of deeper unconscious conflicts. Some attempt to clarify the issue must be made. In the majority of cases a phobia is found to have begun at a particular time and in relation to a particular traumatic event. Before that time, presumably the patient already had his assumed unconscious conflicts, but did not feel any need for treatment. At the very least, then, it must surely be admitted that if through desensitization the patient is restored to the state in which he was before the traumatic event, something important has been gained from the point of view of his suffering. The reply could, of course, be made that unless the unconscious conflicts are brought to light and resolved, the patient will relapse or develop other symptoms; but in keeping with follow-up studies on the results of non-analytic psychotherapy in neurotic cases in general my experience has been that relapse or the appearance of new reactions is rare, unless a major group of stimuli in a desensitized area has been neglected.

At the same time, it is indisputable that only a minority of individuals exposed to a given traumatic event develop a phobia; some predisposing condition or conditions must determine which individuals do. The psychoanalysts are undoubtedly right in insisting on this point. But we are not therefore compelled to accept their version of the nature of the predisposing conditions, especially as the factual foundations of that version are far from satisfactory (30). Objective behavior theory can also point to factors that may predispose an individual to particularly severe conditioning of anxiety. First, some people are apparently endowed with much more active autonomic nervous systems than others (e.g., 18). Second, previous experience with similar stimulus constellations may have induced low degrees of anxiety conditioning which would sensitize a person to the traumatic experience. Third, there may be circumstances in the moment of trauma that may bring about an unusually high degree of focusing upon certain stimulus constellations. The second of these suggested factors is probably the most important, for patients do frequently tell of minor sensitivity having pre-existed the precipitating event. In the course of desensitization, these original sensitivities also come to be removed, along with whatever has been more recently conditioned.

Critics of the conditioned response approach to therapy of the neuroses frequently assert that when the desensitization method leads to recovery, it is not the method as such that is responsible, but the "transference" established between patient and therapist. If these critics were right — if desensitization were incidental to rather than causal of recovery — it would be expected that improvement would affect all areas more or less uniformly, and not be confined to those to which desensitization had been applied. The facts are directly contrary to this expectation, for practically invariably it is found that *unless different hierarchies have unmistakable common features desensitization to one hierarchy does not in the least diminish the reactivity to another (untreated) hierarchy.* For example, a recent patient had both a widespread agoraphobic constellation, and a fear of airplanes, extending to the sight and sound of them. Having constructed hierarchies to both series, the writer proceeded to desensitize the patient to the agoraphobia, but ignored the airplane phobia until the agoraphobia had been almost completely overcome. At this stage, re-assessment of the airplane phobia revealed not the slightest evidence of diminution. This is in accord with observations made in connection with experimental neuroses, in which eliminating anxiety conditioned to visual stimuli does not affect the anxiety-evoking potential of auditory stimuli that were conditioned at the same time as the visual stimuli(23, 27).

From the point of view of the scientific investigator the desensitization method has a number of advantages that are unusual in the field of psycho-

therapy: 1) the aim of therapy can be clearly stated in every case; 2) sources of neurotic anxiety can be defined and delimited; 3) change of reaction to a scene is determined during sessions (and accordingly could be measured by psychophysiological means); 4) there is no objection to conducting therapy before an unconcealed audience (for this has been done without apparent effect on the course of therapy); and 5) therapists can be interchanged if desired.

SUMMARY

The desensitization method of therapy is a particular application of the reciprocal inhibition principle to the elimination of neurotic habits. The experimental background and some theoretical implications of this principle are discussed.

A detailed account is given of the technique of desensitization and an analysis of its effects when applied to 68 phobias and allied neurotic anxiety response habits in 39 patients. In a mean of 11.2 sessions, 45 of the neurotic habits were overcome and 17 more very markedly improved. Six month to four year follow-up reports from 20 of the 35 successfully treated patients did not reveal an instance of relapse or the emergence of new symptoms.

REFERENCES

1. BOND, I. K. AND HUTCHISON, H. C. Application of reciprocal inhibition therapy to exhibitionism. Canad. Med. Ass. J., 83: 23–25, 1960.
2. CURRAN, D. AND PARTRIDGE, M. *Psychological Medicine.* Livingstone, Edinburgh, 1955.
3. EYSENCK, H. J. *Behavior Therapy and the Neuroses.* Pergamon Press, New York, 1960.
4. FREEMAN, H. L. AND KENDRICK, D. C. A case of cat phobia. Brit. Med. J., 2: 497–502, 1960.
5. JACOBSON, E. *Progressive Relaxation.* Univ. of Chicago Press, Chicago, 1938.
6. JACOBSON, E. Variation of blood pressure with skeletal muscle tension and relaxation. Ann. Int. Med., 13: 1619–1625, 1940.
7. JONES, M. C. The elimination of children's fears. J. Exp. Psychol., 7: 382–390, 1924.
8. LAVERNE, A. A. Rapid coma technique of carbon dioxide inhalation therapy. Dis. Nerv. Syst., 14: 141–144, 1953.
9. LAZARUS, A. A. The elimination of children's phobias by deconditioning. Med. Proc., 5: 261, 1959.
10. LAZARUS, A. A. *New group techniques in the treatment of phobic conditions.* Ph.D. dissertation. Univ. of the Witwatersrand, 1959.
11. LAZARUS, A. A. AND RACHMAN, S. The use of systematic desensitization in psychotherapy. S. Afr. Med. J., 31: 934–937, 1957.

12. LAZOVIK, A. D. AND LANG, P. J. A laboratory demonstration of systematic desensitization psychotherapy. J. Psychol. Stud., 11: 238, 1960.

13. MALLESON, N. Panic and phobia. Lancet., 1: 225–227, 1959.

14. MEYER, V. The treatment of two phobic patients on the basis of learning principles. J. Abnorm. Soc. Psychol., 55: 261–266, 1957.

15. RACHMAN, S. The treatment of anxiety and phobic reactions by systematic desensitization psychotherapy. J. Abnorm. Soc. Psychol., 58: 259–263, 1959.

16. SALTER, A. Conditioned Reflex Therapy. Creative Age Press, New York, 1950.

17. SHERRINGTON, C. S. Integrative Action of the Nervous System. Yale Univ. Press, New Haven, 1906.

18. SHIRLEY, M. The First Two Years. Univ. of Minnesota Press, Minneapolis, 1933.

19. STEVENSON, I. Direct instigation of behavioral changes in psychotherapy. A. M. A. Arch. Gen. Psychiat., 1: 99–107, 1959.

20. STEVENSON, I. AND WOLPE, J. Recovery from sexual deviations through overcoming nonsexual neurotic responses. Amer. J. Psychiat., 116: 737–742, 1960.

21. TERHUNE, W. S. The phobic syndrome. Arch. Neurol. Psychiat., 62: 162–172, 1949.

22. WILLOUGHBY, R. R. Some properties of the Thurstone Personality Schedule and a suggested revision. J. Soc. Psychol., 3: 401–424, 1932.

23. WOLPE, J. Experimental neuroses as learned behavior. Brit. J. Psychol., 43: 243–268, 1952.

24. WOLPE, J. Learning versus lesions as the basis of neurotic behavior. Amer. J. Psychiat., 112: 923–927, 1956.

25. WOLPE, J. Objective psychotherapy of the neuroses. S. Afr. Med. J., 26: 825–829, 1952.

26. WOLPE, J. Psychotherapy based on the principles of reciprocal inhibition. In Burton, A., ed. Case Studies in Counseling and Psychotherapy, pp. 353–381. Prentice-Hall, Englewood Cliffs, N. J., 1959.

27. WOLPE, J. Psychotherapy by Reciprocal Inhibition. Stanford Univ. Press, Stanford, 1958.

28. WOLPE, J. Reciprocal inhibition as the main basis of psychotherapeutic effects. A. M. A. Arch. Neurol. Psychiat., 72: 205–226, 1954.

29. WOLPE, J. Recoveries from neuroses without psychoanalysis: Their prognosis and its implications. Amer. J. Psychiat. In press.

30. WOLPE, J. AND RACHMAN, S. Psychoanalytic "evidence": A critique based on Freud's case of Little Hans. J. Nerv. Ment. Dis., 131: 135–148, 1960.

DON D. JACKSON AND JOHN H. WEAKLAND

Conjoint Family Therapy
Some Considerations on Theory, Technique, and Results*

The paper presented here is a product of the Family Therapy in Schizophrenia Project of the Palo Alto Medical Research Foundation, and thus reflects the ideas and experience of the entire project staff and associated therapists.[1] In it we should like primarily to report some observations based on this particular experiment in conjoint family therapy with schizo-

* Reprinted by special permission of The William Alanson White Psychiatric Foundation, Inc., from Psychiatry, Vol. 24, Suppl. to No. 2, 1961, pp. 30–45. Copyright by The William Alanson White Psychiatric Foundation, Inc.
[1] This investigation, directed by Gregory Bateson, was supported by Mental Health Project Grant OM-324 from the National Institute of Mental Health, U.S. Public Health Service, by the Veterans Administration Hospital, Palo Alto, and The Mental Research Institute, Palo Alto Medical Research Foundation.

phrenics — that is, in treating the identified patient and other members of his family together as a functioning natural group. We shall have little to say about the work of others, except by way of acknowledging and illustrating a growing trend toward this form of treatment. There is still only a limited amount of such work being done, and less published, so perhaps the best way to introduce something that is bound to be somewhat new and strange is to have the reader accompany us on our own voyage of exploration and discovery, in part. As we go, we shall also attempt to formulate more systematically what we ourselves have been learning along the way.

Our research group stumbled onto conjoint family therapy by accident, or at least tangentially. In 1954 we wished to view the schizophrenic patient communicating and behaving in his natural habitat, which was not the hospital, and we inevitably turned to the family as the proper milieu in which to view his interactions. Our thinking in this direction was spurred by experiences with relatives in our private practice; by chance home visits made in connection with schizophrenics we had in individual therapy; and by stories we heard from various staff members at the Veterans Administration Hospital about their encounters with families.

In order to study the patient directly in relation to his parents and siblings, it was necessary to bring them together and, more important, to observe them together over a period of time. An answer to this practical problem seemed to lie in interviewing the schizophrenic patients and their family members as family groups, a procedure which would provide data for us (especially since all our interviews are recorded) and some therapeutic help for them. In setting up this work, we had no clear plans for family treatment, nor did we know at the time that family therapy was going on elsewhere. However, our experience soon demonstrated that, once one begins to talk directly with these families with a schizophrenic member, there is rapid development of pressures to treat them. Situations arise in which it is important to consider them from a therapeutic point of view, both to keep some control of the family's tendencies to involve the interviewer in their problem and to help them with their increasingly evident difficulties. So our own work in family therapy began.

Against this background, however, it is interesting to note that, as has happened repeatedly in the history of science, similar developments were occurring about simultaneously elsewhere; and in retrospect a rationale for this broad development, and a pertinent need to which it is a response, can be outlined rather clearly.

As we have been increasingly involved in studying and working with families over the past five years, we have been struck to come upon various other people who have independently gotten into similar work. Some of these — for instance, Lyman Wynne and his co-workers, Murray Bowen and his group (both originally at NIMH), and Ivan Boszormenyi-Nagy and his associates in Philadelphia — have like ourselves been most interested in schizophrenia. Others have been interested in a range of psychiatric problems, like Nathan Ackerman in New York, Kalman Gyarfas and Virginia Satir in Chicago, John Bell of the U. S. Public Health Service, and Eugene MacDonald in Galveston; while still others have been primarily interested in another particular problem, as in Charles Fulweiler's work with the families

of delinquents in Alameda County, California. But all share a basic orientation toward understanding and treating the family as a unitary system.

Some of the background of this development is clear enough. Ever since Freud's early work, the fact that the patient's family is important has been recognized at least conceptually. But, practically, this fact has been dealt with mainly by segregating the patient and therapist and excluding all relatives from contact with the patient's treatment. An important and increasing exception to this practice, however, has been in the treatment of child patients; here at least the mother has become more and more an object of therapy also. Yet this leaves some problems hanging — for example, what to do about the father? — and raises new ones about the need for time and for adequate communication between therapists if parents and child are not seen by the same therapist. Similar problems arise in the treatment of marital partners. Meanwhile, there are serious practical problems attending individual treatment that are made especially evident in the case of hospitalized schizophrenics. On the one hand, hospital personnel frequently experience difficulties in necessary dealings with relatives, sometimes in being unable to get together with the relatives effectively when necessary and sometimes in being unable to get the relatives off their backs. On the other hand, when patients are successfully helped in relative isolation in the hospital, their return to the family too often is marked by upsets — of the parents, or of the patient, who then relapses, or of both.

The essential point to be gleaned from all these matters of common knowledge is that treatment of a psychiatric patient *necessarily* involves dealing with members of his family, and with family relationships, either directly or indirectly. Clearly, even setting up a rule of excluding the family from the therapy involves handling these matters, and drastically, though perhaps simply. The question at issue, then, is not *whether* the members of a patient's family are to be dealt with, but *how* they are to be dealt with. This paper is concerned with describing our work with conjoint family treatment as a means of dealing with this problem in the case of schizophrenic patients particularly.

THEORETICAL BACKGROUND

To understand our attempts at treating these families and formulating our treatment approach, it is necessary to understand the theory under which we labor, since our present practices and present conceptions have both developed out of the interplay of some very broad original orientations and our groping attempts at treatment of actual families.

At the outset of our program of work with families of schizophrenics our two main concepts were (1) the double bind[2] and (2) family homeostasis.[3] The concept of family homeostasis arose from observations that psychotherapeutic efforts with one member of a family might be hindered by the behavior of other members, or that another member might become disturbed as the member in treatment improved. These observations, in connection with existing ideas about homeostatic systems generally, suggested that a family forms such a dynamic steady-state system; the characters of the members and the nature of their interaction — including any identified patient and his sick behavior — are such as to maintain a status quo typical of the family, and to react toward the restoration of this status quo in the event of any change, such as is proposed by the treatment of any member.

The double bind concept is grounded in our most basic conception about communication as the chief means of human interaction and influence: that in actual human communication a single and simple message never occurs, but that communication always and necessarily involves a multiplicity of messages, of different levels, at once. These may be conveyed via various channels such as words, tone, and facial expressions, or by the variety of meanings and references of any verbal message in relation to its possible contexts. The relationships among these related messages may be very complex. No two messages, at different levels of communication, can be just the same; however, they may be similar or different, congruent or incongruent. Difference and incongruity appear fundamental to the richness of human communication, as when certain combinations of words and tone define styles of expression, such as irony or humor; however, they also appear fundamental to the origin and character of much psychopathology, as in the symptom "inappropriate affect," considered as an evident incongruence between words and tone or expression. Further, the use of double-level messages seems increasingly central to therapy in ways we shall mention later.

The double bind concept refers to a pattern of pairs or sets of messages, at different levels, which are closely related but sharply incongruent, occurring together with other messages which by concealment, denial, or other means seriously hinder the recipient from clearly noticing the incongruence and handling it effectively, as by commenting on it. Instead, he is influenced toward incompatible behavioral responses while enjoined not even to notice either influence or incompatibility. We believe that, within an important relationship, where messages cannot merely be ignored or avoided, the combination of extensive experience of such communication being uttered and the recipient's learning to participate by accepting incongruence without question can be productive of schizophrenic behavior.

It is not hard to note that these two main concepts are both concerned with the description and specification of interaction among actual persons, by various means of communication, at a level of directly observable behavior. This focus implies further an emphasis on what is real and on what is current and continuing to occur. Taken together, these emphases define a broad 'communicational' and transactional orientation to the study, understanding, and treatment of human behavior — including that special class most interesting to psychiatrists, symptomatic behavior. This orientation, while related to earlier work, especially Sullivan's, and currently increasing in acceptance, still is considerably different from the strong traditional orientation of psychiatry emphasizing the individual patient and constructs about the unreal or unobservable: fantasies or misperceptions of reality; past, mainly childhood, experience; and intrapsychic organization and content.

In brief, we are much more concerned with influence, interaction, and interrelation between people, immediately observable in the present, than with individual, internal, imaginary, and infantile matters. It is worth making this difference in basic orientation explicit, since to do so helps clarify the nature of our main specific concepts, indicates some important connections between them, and provides a background essential for understanding our whole therapeutic approach — what we do and what we do not do, especially some of our differences from other therapeutic concepts and practices.

The family homeostasis and double bind concepts, with some expansion and modification,[4] continue to be of major significance in our family work. Since these ideas have not always been clearly understood by others, particularly the importance of difference in levels of messages, some more concrete

[2] Gregory Bateson, Don D. Jackson, Jay Haley, and John Weakland, "Toward a Theory of Schizophrenia," *Behavioral Science* (1956) 1:251–264.

[3] Don D. Jackson, "The Question of Family Homeostasis," *Psychiatric Quart.*, Suppl. (1959) 31:79–90.

[4] For instance, John H. Weakland, "The 'Double Bind' Hypothesis of Schizophrenia and Three-Party Interaction," pp. 373–388, in *The Etiology of Schizophrenia*, edited by Don D. Jackson; New York, Basic Books, 1960.

discussion of them seems to be in order here. Some of our critics have felt that the double bind situation is essentially an either-or situation, a damned-if-you-do and damned-if-you-don't predicament or merely a complicated way of describing ambivalence.[5] The double bind situation is all of these things. But it is more. As an illustration, take the predicament of an innocent person who undergoes a lie detector test. It is common practice in such tests to invoke a standard situation for the establishment of a base line. One such situation is to have the subject draw a card from a deck, look at it, and replace it. He is then told not to reveal which card he drew even should the examiner guess it. When the card drawn is guessed and the subject answers, "No," the squiggles on the tape reveal how much he reacts to a lie. However, a theory merely invoking guilt over the telling of a lie fails to account for some of the complexities in the situation. Most subjects in his situation cannot be confident of innocence because a person cannot know *a priori* what his body will do and thus the subject's literal innocence is no protection against the context being one in which the power rests in the hands of the examiner. Since the examiner has asked him to lie, is this really a "lie" or is it not the truth — that is, a correct perception of what it takes to make the machine work? The double level situation renders the subject especially vulnerable because if he denies what he totally perceives, he has put into play a self-deception that does not come equipped with clear boundaries. Suppose at the completion of the test, the examiner stated to the subject, "You have been lying." Could the subject be sure that the examiner was referring only to his deliberate 'cooperative' lie? Could he be sure that he is not a person who is in a chronic state of not processing all the data available to him and thus subject to self-deception?

THE THERAPEUTIC PROCESS—
ARRANGEMENTS AND TECHNIQUES

"The family" we are talking about in practice usually consists of father, mother, and patient. They are seen together once a week for sixty to ninety minutes in a room equipped with a microphone for tape recording and a one-way window for occasional observation and supervision. The meetings may be

[5] Despite our previous discussion of the "illusion of alternatives" in John H. Weakland and Don D. Jackson, "Patient and Therapist Observations on the Circumstances of a Schizophrenic Episode," *AMA Arch. Neurol. and Psychiat.* (1958) 79:554–574.

conducted more frequently than once a week when indicated, but time limitations have not made this possible on a regular basis, and it does not seem essential. Any combination of the basic group's members may be seen as outside necessity — such as trips or illnesses — dictates, or if the therapist feels it is technically wise. We used to be fairly rigid about meeting only if all members could be present. Now, although the general emphasis remains on the whole group, there is variation on this among our several therapists.

The status of the patient's siblings remained obscure for some time and is still only partially settled. We have found them reluctant to be drawn into a potentially unpleasant situation. In retrospect, it appears that we attributed more health to them than they had in fact, and unconsciously went along with their characteristic defense: "This is a situation I am not involved in." For example:

The younger brother of a chronic schizophrenic was visiting this country on vacation from his European job. The therapist had anticipated his arrival by getting him to agree to three family sessions during his visit, since it appeared likely that he would not be available again during the course of therapy. At the first session, the brother appeared to be everything his parents claimed he was and everything the patient was not. During this session, he maintained a pleasant aloofness and claimed amnesia for any events that the therapist felt had been important in the patient's life. At the end of this session, his mother stated that she knew he would be happy to return, but the therapist, discouraged, made it clear that he realized this was a great imposition on the brother's limited time and, without realizing it, left an excellent opportunity for the brother to back out. However, he did return for the next session, and the several days he had spent with his parents brought to the fore more data than could have been hoped for. He expressed genuine regret at the end of the third session that he could not continue to participate in the family meetings and stated that his life abroad probably protected him from a crack-up.

Currently, we have no hesitation about trying to include one or more siblings in the family sessions if they are living with the parents. If they have established other residences, we generally limit the contact to occasional meetings, usually for our own data needs.

Given this basic group of at least three persons, what is the therapist's orientation toward them and his goal? In other words, how does he envisage the therapeutic process, and how does he structure the situation for the group?

When we started to try family therapy in treating schizophrenia, we assumed from our previous work that the identified patient was on the receiving end of double binds from a parent or parents; and we knew that we needed the parents' cooperation, about which we were uncertain, at least to the extent that they keep coming for a period of time. Accordingly, our initial efforts were crude attempts to protect the patient from his parents and to impress the parents with how much help we might derive from the data that they might furnish about the patient. It rather quickly dawned on us, however, that: First, the patient was not a delicate violet and was quite capable of upsetting his parents and blocking the therapist's ambitions; and, second, the parents were unhappy people who potentially could benefit from psychotherapy.

By now, the ten or so therapists involved in the schizophrenia project appear to be reasonably uniform in their impressions as to why they and the family are in the room. All of the therapists while still inexperienced were patient-oriented, but they quickly achieved the realization that the three persons confronting them are bound together in a mutually destructive way and that the primary symptom presented by all three is a crippling entanglement that from the surface is apparent only in the patient. The parents initially try to preserve this surface view, and hence every initial session is replete with remarks about poor X and his unfortunate illness. Once, however, they respond to the lure of the therapist's curiosity about them, the brittle surface cracks and the utter desolation that can only be experienced by two people living together in apartness begins to ooze from below. It is at this point that the therapist's humane interest can still save the day. It is at this point no longer enough that the parents come for the patient's sake. An abbreviated but typical sequence in early family sessions is as follows:

The patient is a 30-year-old man with some five years of hospital experience who is currently living at home. The parents are disturbed with his inactivity, sloppiness, and delusions. Their attempts to push him into activity or to get him out of the house boomerang and result in unpleasantness not only between them and the patient but sometimes between the parents themselves. In the initial interview, the patient is hugely sloppy, quiet, and makes a point of not appearing involved. The parents are careful to point out their own attainments in con-

trast to the patient's many faults, which of course are labeled sickness, and there is a sticky back-and-forth exchange between them and the therapist over the details of therapy time — the frequency of sessions and so on.

During the second session, the parents have been thinking about the patient's illness and recall anecdotes from the past having to do with outside events or acts of God that they suggest may have caused it. Typically the schools and school teachers are mentioned as culprits. In this session, the patient demonstrates some of his symptoms with obvious encouragement from the parents.

During the third session, the therapist expresses curiosity about the parents, their background, how they met, and their early marriage. He introduces these topics deliberately, at the suggestion of his supervisor. Although the parents start out initially to report factually, there appears to be more tension in the air. Finally, well along in the session, the mother says to the father, "Why don't you tell the doctor about New York?" Her reference is to a not completely estimable escapade on the father's part, and he responds with an unhappy but gallant attempt to face the music. But the focus does not stay on the parents and off the patient for long. In the course of recounting this episode, it is stated that the patient was living with the father temporarily. This is quite correct, but largely irrelevant. The son was only about ten at the time and his staying in one city with the father temporarily, while the mother remained in another, was the parents' arrangement and indeed one related to their problem being discussed. But once the son is mentioned, the parents are soon off again on his difficulties and the father is off the hook.

During the fourth session, the therapist attempts to clarify the experience alluded to in the previous session and to discuss further some aspects of the parents' marriage. During this session, the patient appears interested and laughs heartily on several occasions when the father is willing to make himself the butt of a particular story. There is more of a feeling that, however unhappy they are, these people do share something together.

In the next session, the father appears alone. The mother is said to be down with some vague illness, and the patient is waiting in the car. The father has come in only to tell the therapist that they won't be arriving that evening. However, he stays to chat and, to the therapist's surprise, writes on a matchbook cover (presumably so it won't be overheard by the tape recorder) that he and his wife are having terrible fights. He then retrieves and destroys the matchbook cover. The father is almost totally unable to break down and to allow the therapist to sympathize with him over his marital discord; nevertheless, a breach has been made, and subsequent sessions reveal that the mother was not ill but that there had been a family quarrel before the session and she had refused to come. This leads to further consideration of their difficulties as well as those of the patient.

This example illustrates some of the typical characteristics of our families and typical responses they show to the situation posed by initially entering into therapy together. We may explicitly summarize some of these before going on to list and illustrate certain standard initial moves we have developed to deal with the problems these features pose, and then to consider the further course of therapy similarly.

In most of the families we have seen, perhaps especially in middle-class ones, the mother appears as the prime mover about therapy, with the emphasis on her concern for her child; many mothers also appear as 'lay experts' on schizophrenia and its treatment on the basis of long experience with their child's illness, often plus reading up on the subject. In some cases the father is more in the foreground, but on closer inspection he seems usually to be so largely as a spokesman or front man for the mother. Often it is found that the father is physically absent from the family a lot, as by being very much occupied with his business. In fact, in many of the families it seems that the members hardly ever get together except in the therapy room, although they have little independent life as individuals either.

The father and mother both center their initial discussion on the subject of their child, especially on his illness; this might seem natural in the circumstances, except that this focus is extreme while at the same time it often centers on minor aspects of the illness, such as details of the patient's dress and manners. The parents are able to get together and agree fairly well when the patient's illness is thus the topic of discussion, although they may both speak of this in a disjointed or incongruent way — that is, at one moment they may insist that the patient is too sick to be held responsible for anything, and the next complain in extreme ways about his irresponsible misbehavior, making this abrupt transition without giving the cues or structuring that ordinarily accompany such a shift. Yet this area of agreement stands out, especially as it soon becomes evident that these two people can agree very little on any other matter. The patient, meanwhile, is appearing helpless and hopeless, yet by

withdrawal or acting-up is influencing everyone and upsetting the therapy situation in part. It is thus very easy to see from these early sessions why observers without further experience would naturally tend to draw big distinctions between the "sick" patient and the "well" parents and siblings. Yet, on closer and more extended contact with these families, we have been struck by the observation not only that the parents also have considerable personal difficulties, but that their difficulties are apt to be fundamentally like those the patient exhibits via his symptomatology.[6]

A number of problems connected with these characteristics tend to arise very quickly in the therapy. The parents keep their discussion centered on the patient and by this avoid talking of themselves and their relationship. The patient often helps them in this by some kind of overt "goofing up" or going too far which aids in keeping him labeled as *the* patient; this may occur especially at points when the parents do happen to approach some topic that is hot for them, and so strongly that even the therapist is likely to turn on the patient, away from the parents, without quite noticing what he is doing.

If the therapist does attempt to put the focus on the family, or to define the parents as equally patients with their child, certain other difficulties are expectable. Either the mother or the father may move to involve the therapist in individual and private communication, by phone calls or before or after the family session. Fathers tend to avoid involvement in the family therapy by distancing devices; sometimes actual absences from meetings, sometimes withdrawal by silence, or intellectualization under the label of "objectivity." Mothers seem to feel more guilty about their possible relationship to the child's illness, and they tend to be correspondingly active in one way or another. In some cases, there is danger that the mother will be so concerned as to terminate therapy very rapidly once the "family therapy" idea really is clear. In others, sessions may continue but be dominated by the mother, who may take over the therapist's position by endorsing everything he says, by being more expert and scientific than he, usually with biological and chemical theories of schizophrenia which deny her guilt, or even in a few cases by taking blame on herself so strongly and indiscriminately that examining actual family interactions again is badly hampered. Indeed, such examination is difficult at best, since it is a real project to get clarity about anything with these

6 Don D. Jackson and John H. Weakland, "Schizophrenic Symptoms and Family Interaction," AMA *Arch. Gen. Psychiatry.* (1959) 1:618–621.

families; the statements of the various members do not agree, and each tends to be vague and shifting, or to bury everything in details, or both. Of particular importance is the fact that the family members present their behavior in terms of responses to outside situations, so that it is difficult even for the therapist to keep in mind and in view how much they are responding to each other, and to begin to clarify this with them.

FRAMING OF THE THERAPY

If such typical initial problems are not dealt with adequately, they are likely to become acute or chronic, ending the therapy quickly or leading into a repetitive stalemate similar to the family's usual circle of interactions, only with the therapist drawn in as one more player in this game with no winners. On the other hand, effective dealing with these initial problems is correspondingly valuable. As we see it, 'patient management' in family therapy, which includes management of all the family members involved in the therapeutic situation, is a central part of therapy, and by no means only superficial in its effects. Thus, the standard procedures we have evolved to utilize in the initial family sessions represent much more than merely a means of avoiding limited particular difficulties. They involve a framing of the therapy as a whole, a setting-up of continuing broad standards and expectations. Also, the means by which the therapist does this framing are illustrative of much about our over-all technical orientation and practice.

In the initial session, the therapist customarily expresses a philosophy of "We are here to work together on better understanding one another so that you all can get more out of your family life." Such a statement implies that the parents are as much involved in the family unhappiness, specified or unspecified, as the patient, and also that they equally have something to gain from therapy. This replaces our former tendency to open the initial interview by asking what they would like to get out of the sessions, an approach that resulted in the standard answer, "Nothing is wrong except poor Bill," or whoever the identified patient happened to be. Such mention of "working on understanding" also implicitly focuses on communication as deeply involved in their difficult relationships and as a means of therapy. There are similar implications in our usual handling of the problem of private communication. Formerly, it was customary for the therapist to receive a phone call from one or both parents during the early weeks of therapy asking if the patient shouldn't be put on tranquilizers or shouldn't be getting more exercise, and so on. Then the therapist would feel awkward about bringing this up at the next family meeting and awkward if he did not bring it up because it implied a conspiracy with one or the other of the parents. Now, in the initial session, the therapist casually announces that all parties are privileged to all information about contacts with the therapist; and, like most rules that are brought up matter-of-factly, this is accepted.

Alternatively, the therapist may sometimes handle similar matters less by implication and more by making fairly explicit statements, while attaching to these a prefabricated framing interpretation. For example, he may state that all families develop habitual patterns of communication, including some avoidances by which the family members protect each other, and therefore part of the therapist's job is to clarify these patterns and avoidances when they stand in the way of resolving important blocks between the family members; it is the therapist's responsibility to them all — while treating them impartially, although naturally each of them will feel at times he is not doing so — not to let the solution of such problems be missed even by such protective tendencies. Thus the family is given credit for their good intentions, while the therapist's position of stirring things up at times is defined as a positive duty for their benefit. Also the therapist will point out that they must have some important relationship with each other, regardless of their difficulties, since they have stayed together for a long time; in addition, they really know each other better than anyone else, including the therapist, can, and thus they are the best possible therapists for each other. This framing places responsibility for helpful participation on all the family members equally, which both calls on the more withdrawn ones to take more part and undercuts the usual tendency of some one family member to take over the situation from the therapist.

The members of our group also tend to be active in similar ways in connection with many of the more specific issues that arise initially. For example, we commonly avoid some dreary time-wasting by politely interrupting the parents' attempts to focus exclusively on the patient's illness. In addition, we tend to discipline the patient if he attempts to utilize the "I am the sick one so I am not responsible" ploy, as the following example shows.

The therapist was questioning the parents in the initial session about their living. The mother was uneasy, apparently about her alcoholism which had not yet been disclosed. At this point, the schizophrenic son broke in to announce how much he had benefited from shock therapy in the hospital. Immediately both parents discussed this with him, and the father asked if he wished more. The mother stated that maybe he needed tranquilizers and then thought to ask him if he was currently taking them, to which the patient replied, "No." At this juncture, the therapist broke in to ask the patient in a rather commanding tone, "Bob, you're not on shock therapy now? Right?" The patient replied that he was not. The therapist added, "And you said you were not on drugs." Again the patient acknowledged that this was true. The therapist continued, "So it's fortunate then that you are *you* this morning here with us. In other words, you and mom and dad and I are all responsible for what we say and that makes it easier to understand each other."

The patient's rescue operations which dig his own hole deeper are usually an issue in the first few minutes of the initial session. The therapist's criticism or irritation at these attempts implies not only that this kind of thing is not acceptable, but also that the patient can do better. This attitude is in contrast to that of the parents, who usually will drop whatever they are engaged in and follow up the patient's intervention like a hound dog in pursuit. (However, an alternative approach that is sometimes feasible is to accept this line of joint interest in the patient's symptoms but to press the inquiry in such a way as to include more of the family circumstances surrounding symptomatic behavior and their relevance to it.) Another matter that comes up in the first session is the question of what to do if someone in the family is absent from one of the sessions. It may seem to be borrowing trouble to anticipate such a happening, but experience has taught us that the multitudinous excuses proffered for someone's not appearing would delight a sage truant officer. It seems more efficacious to announce to the family that there will be times when they do not wish to come and that such absence is a rather powerful lever to use against the therapist and against family members; or to announce that they are likely to feel reluctant to come just when important progress is occurring. Such announcements also emphasize our philosophy that family members do have a great effect on each other and that there is no such thing as not commenting even if the "No comment" is attempted through silence or through a nonappearance.

In summary, a few principal means that the therapist may use — separately, jointly, or alternatively, according to taste and circumstances — in handling the typical problems arising at the start of family therapy might be listed as follows. First, there is a certain place for being very clear, direct, and explicit. This is comparatively limited, applying mostly to practical details such as the schedule of meetings; unless the therapist is quite clear and definite, even such a simple matter can set off a long, inconclusive discussion. Second comes the making of certain matter-of-fact statements whereby the important messages are conveyed implicitly. Third comes the making of statements about some aspect of the therapy which are accompanied by some comment that serves to anticipate and disarm resistance — for example, "I intend to be impartial, though each of you will surely doubt that I am at times." This may be carried all the way to an "inversion of meaning" statement such as "There will be times, just as real progress is being made, when you will feel like not coming to the meetings."

From the discussion so far it must now be evident that active intervention in and management of family interaction has an important place in our initial work; and, indeed, this holds true of the further course of family therapy also. This active orientation, however, grew out of our experience and was not a predisposition except that experience in treating individual schizophrenics presses one toward an active and varied style of therapy. Nevertheless, in beginning our work with families, we were concerned lest activity on the part of the therapist would obscure family operations and dim the light of our research. Actually, it has been so difficult to keep the sicker families involved, to produce shifts and not mere repetitions of the standard patterns characteristic of any one family, that we are no longer so concerned about the therapist remaining a flyspeck by his own design and efforts, and more concerned with avoiding being put into such a useless position by the family.

If it is kept in mind that families have horizontal as well as vertical layers, then the pattern of response to the therapist's intervention can simply be viewed as a further unfolding of the range of this particular family's transactions. By vertical, we mean going back in time; by horizontal, we mean layers of complexity of communications or, as they might be called, layers of defense in concentric circles. One of the things that the tyro therapist must experience is that he will have to deal with the same problem over and over again in different forms and guises, as the following example suggests.

Initially, the father of a paranoid patient complained to the therapist of his son's obesity and requested a diet for him. He and his wife expressed futility about "doing anything with him." They occasionally took action of an interesting sort, considering their son's suspicious nature; for example, the father sneaked out early one morning to tell the milkman that he was to ignore any requests for ice cream. The therapist held fast to his recommendation that the patient would change himself when he was ready, and several sessions later the patient announced that he had lost some weight. As the therapist tried to congratulate him, the mother cut in to discuss her own weight problem, and the father topped her by recounting a rather bizarre episode in which he was found unconscious and taken to a hospital in peril of his life.

This sequence was characteristic for this family. The patient's statements tended to be ignored or rationalized away, the mother usually sounded a serious note about something, and the father topped it by telling something on himself which, while dramatic, inevitably made him out to be slightly foolish. A kind of closure was usually attained at the end of these sequences by the father, mother, and son all chuckling slightly at the father's expense. This sort of closed sequence, however, constitutes the sort of pathological family homeostasis that it is the therapist's business and duty to alter.

FURTHER TECHNICAL MEANS

As family therapy proceeds, we are ordinarily not much concerned with the topics and content of the family discussions, except perhaps when there is evident talking of one matter to avoid something else. Indeed, it may be valuable at times to shift the discussion from a hot topic to a less important one involving the same sort of family alignment and interaction, in the hope that the nature of the interaction can better be seen and some revision inaugurated while dealing with a more minor matter.

Such alteration of self-reinforcing and mutually destructive networks of interaction is the most general goal of our work with families, and our emphasis correspondingly is on means of influencing these patterns rather than on examining their content, or even on describing the pattern as such.

Our experience with this kind of repetitive pattern is that pointing it out to the family does little good. However, its meaning, intent, or focus can be shifted by the therapist's intervention; and after a series of such interventions, the pattern loses some of its highly stereotyped repetitiousness. Various means may be essayed in relation to this formidable task, several of which have already been mentioned. Implication is a powerful tool in the therapist's

hands; but making explicit what the family members communicate only implicitly can be equally important. Framing or interpretation of messages — in a communicational, not psychoanalytic, sense of interpretation — is most important, and occurs in many varieties: the therapist may frame his own message, and, equally important, he may reframe and reinterpret the messages of family members. By this means, the positive side of difficult or provocative behavior in the family can be shown, sense made out of craziness, and congruence out of incongruence. Such inverting is a powerful lever for change. Certain sorts of dualistic positive-and-negative messages also are important, such as criticism administered with personal attention for easier swallowing or a strong comment given in a mild tone; in this sort of "quiet bombshell" there is an evident similarity between our communicational orientation and more orthodox psychiatric thought and practice.

We may also give advice. However, our aim in advising is not to tell family members the proper thing to do; rather it is to enable them to accept interest, advice, and help, for they ordinarily are so defensive as to disqualify and reject whatever is offered, even if they have been demanding it. If we can present a little advice in an acceptable way, in accepting it from us as experts, they take a first step toward accepting from each other.

The giving of some rather specific instructions as a technique in therapy illuminates this area still further. We do not expect to achieve change directly by giving instructions on how to behave, and we ordinarily avoid doing so, especially on matters of obvious practical importance — although this is where our advice and instructions are most likely to be solicited. Instead, we are apt to choose an apparently minor matter — which still will be involved in some significant pattern of interaction — and give an instruction to do A, expecting that the person, from our knowledge of his reactions, will in fact do B, which will cause change C in a family relationship. An example may clarify this complicated but significant situation:

The mother of a 15-year-old schizophrenic boy was a very managing woman, taking over everything from her nearly mute son, her rather quiet husband, and also from the struggling therapist. Yet she was very unhappy and anxious. Finally she was able to say one day that she was upset because she felt that her husband was distant; she couldn't get in close touch with him. Yet she felt wrong if she reacted to this, even if only by becoming silently upset. The main emphasis was on the problem of feeling wrong uncontrollably, even when she thought she had some just cause for distress. The therapist then suggested that she could act to resolve this problem of feeling wrong, if she seriously wanted to, by following a simple instruction. After a pause, she agreed. The therapist's instruction was that, during the following week, she should deliberately do something that she considered wrong. The only conditions imposed were that the wrong was not to be a really serious one and was to involve some other family member in some way; other than that she should choose the action. During the next session, she revealed that the daring deed she had committed was subscribing to a book club.

The members of the research group laughed as they heard this section on the tape, thinking how constricted she was to commit such a minor sort of sin. However, they had failed to appreciate the limitations placed on the range of action in this family, because the father, who in the session heard for the first time what she had done, angrily disapproved. Although his reasons were a bit obscure, they appeared to concern the expense involved. In fact, since this was not great, and money was used by the father as a means of control, the mother's independence seems more important. From this episode, the therapist and the group as a whole learned a little more about why this woman had to breathe her sick son's every breath. The fact that she was severely controlling did not mean that she was not similarly controlled by herself and her husband. And if control is this severe, then even the small change of behavior, change of evaluation, and change in relationship with her husband that this act represented, though initiated by the therapist's instruction, may be correspondingly significant.

FAMILY PATHOLOGY AND THERAPY; A THEORETICAL SUMMARY

Perhaps we can now utilize the preceding material to attempt a more condensed and general statement of our ideas on the pathology of these families and its treatment. Even though such a theoretical statement is bound to be oversimplified and incomplete at this stage of our knowledge, it will provide a basis for some comparison between our theoretical and therapeutic slants and those of other workers.

Summing up very broadly then, it appears that these families of schizophrenics are enmeshed in a pathological but very strong homeostatic system of family interaction. That is, regardless of their past history — although that might be enlightening — they are *at present* interacting in ways that are un-

satisfying and painful to all, provocative of gross symptomatology in at least one, and yet powerfully self-reinforcing. Their overt behavior may appear varied or even chaotic, but beneath this a pervasive and persistent pattern can be discerned, and one that is quite resistant even to outside therapeutic efforts at change.

How and why is this so? On what basis may such homeostasis be clarified and understood? We may at least begin to do so by using further our basic concepts of the double bind and the still broader concept of the necessary multiplicity of messages, of different levels, in all communication. These ideas, which were helpful in understanding the occurrence of schizophrenic behavior, are also helpful in attacking the more fundamental problem level: Why does pathological behavior or organization persist, even under pressure to change? We have not solved this problem, but we can state a few leading ideas. First, the double bind pattern itself tends to be circular and interactive in a self-perpetuating way, even though we may speak of it carelessly as if it were a one-way matter, with a "binder" acting on a "victim." Actually, if A sends incongruent messages to B, B is very likely to respond with a correspondingly incongruent set of messages in reply. The one main difference likely to exist between their communications only serves to intensify the vicious circularity: If the incongruence between A's messages is concealed and B falls in with this, then the incongruence in B's reply is apt to be correspondingly *exaggerated* the typical case for schizophrenic utterance. This in turn influences A toward further incongruence, even more concealed or denied, and so on. In three-party situations,[7] essentially the same process may occur. If A and B are parents giving incongruent messages to C, their child, C is likely to respond in a disturbed way with markedly incongruent messages and ones likely to have some reference to the family relationships; at this A and B are very likely to insist more strongly that there are no differences in what they think and say, rather than admitting differences, as we have described earlier.

Second, the existence of a multiplicity of messages obviously offers great possibilities for interaction among family members in which nothing is ever clarified because *both* agreement and disagreement can be avoided. It is possible, with incongruent messages, to agree with another person, yet not agree, by agreeing at one level of message yet disagreeing at another or indicating that it is not really the speaker who is agreeing. And similarly with

---

[7] Discussed in Weakland, footnote 4.

disagreement; this also can be no-yet-yes. We find that members of families in which there is a schizophrenic are likely to communicate largely by remarks we may call "disqualifying" — that is, they effectively negate what someone else has said, only in an indirect way, so that statements are not really met. This sort of communication and its paralyzing effects have been particularly striking in some standard interviews that we have given experimentally, since these interviews focused on family organization, leadership, and planning, first by asking the family members to plan something they would like to do together, and then by inquiring who was in charge of the family.

This sort of problem may be seen from a somewhat different angle by considering the two sorts of families of schizophrenics discriminated by Lidz:[8] One ("skew" families) in which harmony is conveyed overtly, but with covert persistent disagreement; the other ("schism" families), in which there is constant overt scrapping yet the family members somehow remain together for many years. Both may be seen as types of pathological organization whose stability is related to the existence of such incongruent double messages about family relationships plus the avoidance of recognition and acknowledgment of such incongruence by family members.

Any move toward change or therapy, finally, immediately encounters difficulties similar to those just mentioned. The members of these families have long been adept at using incongruent messages. Thus, if some change in behavior or family organization is proposed, what is more likely than that it will be met with agreement that is not agreement; with disagreement that is not disagreement; with agreement from one member and disagreement from another, while they insist they are together on the matter, and so on? If a specific change can be brought about in the behavior of some member, it is likely to be negated by a shifting of the general context, by the same person or another: "Yes, my husband is behaving better to me now; but of course that's just because you told him to, not that he cares any more about me." Or a more general shift may be negated by a specific change; or the two parents may both change at once so that they remain on opposite sides of whatever fence divided them, even if reversed from their original stands. All this also throws light on why description or labeling of family behavior is usually ineffective, even where

[8] Theodore Lidz and Stephen Fleck, "Schizophrenia, Human Integration and the Role of Family," pp. 323–345, in *The Etiology of Schizophrenia* (see footnote 4). For other references and more extensive discussion, see Weakland, footnote 4; pp. 380–382.

the members themselves appear to grasp it; thus we are more concerned with altering interaction than with "insight."

In other words, these families have a tremendous aptitude for "plus ça change, plus c'est la même chose." It appears increasingly clear to us as we work with them that to be effective we must meet them on their own ground, though with different orientation — toward positive change instead of defensive maintenance of a sick system. That is, the therapist must himself employ dual or multiple messages involving such incongruences as will serve to come to grips with the whole complexity of the messages of the family members he must deal with. A reconsideration of the techniques we have mentioned earlier shows readily enough that for many this is already explicitly so, and it is implicit for most of the others. That is, we have been concerned with using explicit statements that convey concealed and unexpected implicit meanings as well; with using content messages joined with framing statements; with giving instructions whose carrying-out will constitute a further message. We have spoken of this elsewhere, perhaps too narrowly, as the "therapeutic double bind"; the broad principle described here, of using multiple — and often incongruent — messages therapeutically, is what needs recognition, and then further investigation.

OURSELVES AND OTHERS: FAMILY THERAPY AS A COMMUNICABLE DISEASE

Except for political rallies, baseball games, and burlesque shows, it is difficult to imagine a situation more capable of arousing enthusiasm among therapists than conjoint family therapy. It is not completely clear to us why this should be, but it does make us cautious about accepting new adherents and we do attempt to review our work with the limited objectivity available to us.

There is little question that exposure to conjoint family therapy alters the psychotherapeutic approach of the exposed, both in his private and research work. Most of those engaged in our family therapy research project have private practices on a part-time basis. It is fascinating and predictable to note that their psychotherapeutic approach undergoes at least the following changes:

(1) The therapist will become more 'active' in individual therapy, especially in suggesting the meaning of other people's behavior vis-à-vis the patient.

(2) The therapist will be less interested in diagnosis or the accepted dynamic formulations; he will tend, rather, to describe his patients in terms of an

interlocking milieu, consisting mainly of the immediate family situation, but drawing also upon the wider family context and sometimes including ethnic or subcultural factors.

(3) The therapist will greatly increase the number of couples he treats, mostly in the conjoint situation. We believe it is rare for our therapists not to have met the spouses of all their patients.

These tendencies, in other words, parallel several distinctive emphases in the orientation of our family therapy: activity of the therapist rather than passive listening; more concern for alteration of behavior than for 'insight'; more intense focus on the present than on the past; and more attention to interaction than to intrapersonal experience.

Perhaps two brief examples will illustrate how the family therapy bug affects its victim:

Example A — A catatonic young woman was discharged from a Midwestern state hospital because her parents were moving to California. She was referred to one of us for recommendations as to local hospital care. Although the patient was mute and stiff, she appeared evanescently pleased by the suggestion that if she and her parents were willing to start family therapy, we could see how it would work out to have her live at home, with a practical nurse assisting the mother during the daytime. She has remained out of the hospital now for two years and appears to be functioning fairly adequately. Previous to our family work, it would have been unthinkable that such a catatonic patient who did not appear to be in good contact would not be hospitalized.

Example B — On an emergency home visit, one of us met a 60-year-old woman who had made a mild suicidal gesture. She appeared to be in a typical agitated depression, and the question seemed to be where to hospitalize her and whether it should be in an institution where she would receive electroshock therapy. After speaking to her for a few minutes, the psychiatrist asked her daughter with whom she was living to join them; and he noted that, despite a smiling cooperative kindliness, not all was well between daughter and mother. When this was touched on, the daughter mentioned that she had her husband and her own 17-year-old daughter to worry about and perhaps her mother's attitude was a little bit too much. The mother sparked noticeably at this and implied that the daughter didn't have a complete romance with her husband and had in fact invited the mother to live with her partially on this

account. The patient was not sent to a hospital but was seen in conjoint therapy with her daughter, son-in-law, and granddaughter. After a very brief time, the blocked communication in the family had noticeably improved and the mother decided she would like to live by herself. In retrospect, it seemed fairly certain that getting the patient's daughter involved after a few minutes of the initial visit, and the orientation of the therapist, altered what would have been fairly standard psychiatric disposition.

TRANSFERENCE, COUNTERTRANSFERENCE, AND INTERACTION

Many analysts have had strong doubts about the idea of family therapy, which are often put on transference and countertransference grounds. Thus the terms "transference and countertransference" are troublesome unless it is kept in mind that they refer strictly to aspects of a very special situation — psychoanalysis. We have no doubt that our therapists have feelings about the family members and vice versa; on the other hand, no clarity is achieved if we label such states of mind transference and countertransference. There are several reasons for this:

Transference is a manifestation related to the inactivity prescribed for standard psychoanalytic treatment. The patient, on the basis of minimal cues, creates a framework and embroiders it with past personal references. In conjoint psychotherapy, there is a good deal of activity, even if the therapist is only acting as a traffic cop. If skillfully managed, the interaction is largely among family members and not with the therapist. Thus we would consider the proper intervention when a wife is chopping her husband to ribbons, not to be "Look what you're doing to the poor man," but to ask *him* if she always shows her attachment to him in this way. The wife will be fascinated awaiting his reply and will be busy with her rebuttal.

That is, with so much interaction among the family members, and active therapeutic focus on this, there is no emergence of standard transference phenomena. What we do see can better be labeled parataxic distortions since the data consist of discrete examples of expectations on the part of a family member that the therapist does or does not fulfill. Some of these instances even seem to be a combination of ignorance and misinformation as to what one can legitimately expect of a therapist, while others appear to result from explanatory concepts that the person brought with him into therapy, such as, "All men are . . . ."

It is difficult to explain the difference between these phenomena in individual and family therapy unless one has observed or participated in both forms of psychotherapy. A statement by a family member, which if it occurred in an individual psychotherapeutic session may be labeled evidence of transference, can have a very different meaning in family therapy. Thus, a comment by the wife that the therapist is the only one who has ever understood her is apt to be an expression of dissatisfaction with her husband, a pointing out of a direction he should take; and before the therapist can label this himself as father transference, the husband's reaction will have to be dealt with, plus one of the children, plus the wife's reaction to her husband's reaction, and so on.

The same difficulties apply to countertransference. If the therapist is active, he becomes aware of his feelings partially through the kind of action he takes, and often not until a supervisory session. An experienced, fairly secure therapist may change the direction of a beginning feeling in himself by taking an action opposite to the feeling. For example, if he finds himself irritated by the mother's quietly nagging, martyred tone, he may turn to the father and ask what he experienced in himself during the time when the wife was speaking. On the surface, it would appear that the therapist simply passes the buck to the father and that this technique might be a fairly destructive one. On the other hand, if it is kept in mind that the father has been having thoughts for years about his wife's attitude, and that now is his chance to express them with the support of another male present, a different face is put on the situation. By the time the husband has made his comments, the therapist may then be in a mood to reaccept the wife and to help find out what she has to complain about. Such interlocking transactions are part of the ordinary family life and have been referred to in papers on everything from pecking order to role playing.

RESULTS

We are not yet in a position to support any claim that family therapy is better or worse than the more usual methods of treating schizophrenics. Insufficient time has elapsed, and unusual and difficult problems of evaluation are posed by our interest not only in the identified patient, but in the parents and siblings and especially in the functioning of the family as a whole, while means for evaluation at this level are largely lacking in psychiatry at present. Thus it is appropriate that the emphasis in this

paper has been on our ideas and methods; we have pointed out that family therapy differs from individual therapy, in ways we have tried to outline, and that this difference helps to shape a new orientation in the therapist. We may, however, end by discussing briefly the inconclusive yet promising results of our therapeutic efforts so far.

Various studies have shown that prognosis for recovery from schizophrenia is importantly related to the history of the illness — that is, its duration, amount of hospitalization and other treatment without success, and so on. Therefore, our evaluative scheme for family therapy, with reference to the identified patients, is based on comparing the level of their social adaptation before family therapy and currently, against the background of information on the prior history of their illness. On this basis, our cases can hardly be considered other than difficult ones. We have worked with eighteen families so far. Of the identified schizophrenic patients in these families, eleven were males ranging in age from 13 to 41, and seven were females ranging in age from 14 to 34. Of these eighteen, six had been originally diagnosed as schizophrenic between 10 and 16 years ago, four between 5 and 10 years ago, and eight less than 5 years ago. Perhaps four of these eight were first seen by us as fairly new or acute cases, but fourteen of our eighteen patients could be labeled as already chronic cases when we first saw them. Some had been diagnosed in early childhood, as young as 3 years; the maximum age at first diagnosis was 25. Eleven of these patients had been hospitalized at some time, from a minimum of 2 months up to 6 years maximum, the average being 3 to 4 years. Of the seven patients never hospitalized, probably three or four were clinically sick enough to justify hospitalization and had avoided it only because they were so young or had such passive-withdrawing symptomatology that their behavior could still be tolerated or handled within the home.

Information on prior treatment other than hospitalization, although it is certainly not complete, shows that at least seven patients had received EST, one insulin shock, eight had had tranquilizing drugs, and twelve had received individual psychotherapy ranging from a minimum of 3 sessions to a maximum of 9 years of intermittent examination and treatment. In several cases family members — usually the mother — had also had some individual psychotherapy. In only four instances, all young persons and fresh cases, had there been no therapy before family treatment was started.

At the time of writing, our families had been seen, usually on a once-weekly basis for an hour or an hour and a half, from a minimum of 3 months up to 41 months in one case, the average being about 12 months. Most of our families are still in treatment, although four terminated therapy against our advice.

There were seven patients hospitalized at the outset of family therapy. Of these, one is still in the hospital, three are living at home and able to go out unaccompanied, one is living at home but working, one is living alone and caring for her child though still financially dependent on the parents, and one is living alone, working part-time but financially dependent on her parents. Thus, six of these seven have shown a noticeable improvement in terms of social adaptation and independence. Of the remaining patients, nine were young persons, mostly never hospitalized, who were living with parents and restricted to the home or, if going out, not productive — that is, not working or doing badly in school. All but two of these improved in such degree as starting

to school again, changing from failure to passing, starting to work, or at least starting to go out unaccompanied, as did the two remaining patients who had previously been confined to their homes after release from hospitalization.

It is still more difficult to characterize results with the parents and siblings, and with the family as a whole. But, very broadly, it can be said that the other family members generally have improved, though less noticeably than the identified patients. More than half of the fathers were judged improved by their therapists, with the rest showing no distinct change. The picture for the mothers was similar except for two cases where it was judged that the mother was worse. And limited data on siblings showed about evenly divided improvement and no change, excepting again one sibling judged worse.

Finally, though it often appeared a severe course of treatment, all of our therapists seem to have been helped, without exception.

HANS H. STRUPP

Some Comments on the Future of Research in Psychotherapy[*][1]

As you know, we have never prided ourselves on the completeness and finality of our knowledge and capacity. We are just as ready now as we were earlier to admit the imperfections of our understanding, to learn new things and to alter our methods in any way that can improve them.

SIGMUND FREUD (1919)
(1955, Volume XVII, p. 159)

There is a growing consensus today which says that the future of psychotherapy is that of a scientific discipline. In recent years this point of view has been advanced by numerous writers, who add that any other course would tend to relegate psycho-

* Reprinted by permission from *Behavioral Science*, Vol. 5, 1960, pp. 60–71.
[1] The writing of this paper was supported, in part, by Research Grant M-2171 of the National Institute of Mental Health, U.S. Public Health Service. I am deeply grateful to the National Institute of Mental Health for its continued and generous support.

therapy to a doctrine, a faith, or a gospel (Kardiner, 1958; Kubie, 1956). While Freud often spoke of psychoanalysis as a "movement" and "cause," he never conceived of it as anything but a science. Moreover, he feared greatly that institutionalization would lead to stagnation and the emergence of a cult rather than to scientific development. This apprehension, it must be conceded, has not been altogether groundless, but fortunately there is a countertrend; and it is this countertrend with which many of the foremost thinkers in the area ally themselves. I am referring to the increasing emphasis on controlled research and experimentation, that is, the application of the scientific method to furthering our understanding of the psychotherapeutic process. During the past fifteen years the quantity as well as the quality of research contributions has grown, and there is every reason to believe that the coming decades will see an intensification of this effort. Has research exerted a demonstrable influence on the theory and practice of psychotherapy? In my opinion, the influence has been slight, and I propose to examine, in this paper, some of the reasons for this seemingly pessimistic conclusion. I am also prompted by the belief that, somehow, we should be able to do better.

First it will be necessary to clarify what 'research contribution' is intended to mean in this context. The term "research" is broad indeed and connotes very different things to different people. To American psychologists and social scientists schooled in the tradition of empiricism, positivism, and operationism, the meaning is fairly clear: basically it means the formulation and testing of a hypothesis to aid in building a theory. The ground rules for this process are often intricate and complicated, but the insistence is always on empirical evidence for any assertion and an explicit statement of the means by which knowledge is derived. Such knowledge is public rather than private; it is demonstrable, reproducible, and communicable. These stipulations are those of any science, and they must be adhered to insofar as psychotherapy aspires to the status of a scientific discipline.

To Freud and those working in the psychoanalytic tradition, "research" had a similar but not identical meaning. To be sure, he diligently searched for empirical evidence; he was concerned with making explicit the procedures by which knowledge was acquired; he recognized the need to replicate findings; and he strove for a distinction between clinical findings and the theoretical formulations he devised to explain them. Nevertheless, he was far less rigorous in his investigations than contemporary researchers, if — let it be noted — infinitely more productive. Certainly, one of Freud's greatest and probably most lasting achievements is that of having devised a novel and unique method of investigation (the psychoanalytic situation) and having incisively explored its essential ingredients. Psychoanalytic research was and largely continues to be done in the clinical setting; this setting led to the emergence of the cardinal principles upon which psychoanalysis as a therapeutic technique is built; this setting, too, by its very nature imposes serious restrictions on the rigor which is part and parcel of the scientific method.

True, it has its built-in "controls": it defines the therapeutic situation as well as the role of the analyst (within rather broad limits); it seeks to maximize the patient's contribution to the situation while holding the analyst's constant; it imposes relatively strict rules upon the role behavior of the analyst; but it fails to insure that the analyst's observations (and the inferences he draws therefrom) are *reliable*, that is, more than purely subjective experience.[2]

Limiting the discussion to the American scene, it may be noted that knowledge about the psychotherapeutic process is enriched from two major sources: (a) analysts working in the tradition of Freud, and (b) research workers whose approach is more eclectic. The former group, largely on account of the restrictions imposed on psychoanalytic training, consists principally of analysts whose background training has been in medicine; the second group, primarily of psychologists whose training and experience has been in clinical psychology. With the rise of clinical psychology as a science and profession during the last decade, and as a result of increased contact of psychologists with psychoanalytic principles and techniques, research workers bring to bear upon their investigations a vastly greater understanding and appreciation of the subject matter, problems, and concerns of psychoanalysis than was true before 1940.[3] Psychoanalysts, on the other hand, have begun in some instances to seek the collaboration of psychologists whose training has stressed research design and methodology as well as clinical experience in psychotherapy. In short, there seems to be a tendency for psychoanalysts to know more about research (in a rigorous sense) and for research workers to know more about the dynamics of psychotherapy as an interpersonal process. Consequently, there is an expanding meeting ground, hence greater possibility for communication and collaboration.

[2] Not long ago a British follower of Melanie Klein reported that she was "shocked" to learn from a conversation with an American analyst that he and most practicing analysts in this country do very little research. As she saw it, *every* case at her institute is a "research" case. A similar comment was made to the writer by a British child analyst trained by Anna Freud. There are indications that the younger generation of American analysts, perhaps as a result of more extensive training in the natural and social sciences, tend to use the term "research" in a stricter sense.

[3] A comprehensive survey prepared in 1943 (Sears) revealed a widespread preoccupation to "validate" psychoanalytic concepts and principles through methods then current in academic psychology. Significantly, Sears dispensed with reviewing "A few studies . . . of the psychoanalytic process itself, . . . since none of these was designed to test any theoretical point" (Preface, p. x).

This statement is not intended to suggest that the millenium has arrived. The cleavage between the two kinds of research contributions — with a few notable exceptions — continues to be a rather sharp one. On the one hand, there is a plethora of papers which, while usually starting with clinical observations, pile inference upon inference and arrive at conclusions which typically are not capable of verification. On the other hand, there are numerous investigations whose attention to matters of methodology, sampling, quantitative assessment, and statistical control is reasonably adequate, but which fall short of illuminating the phenomena they purport to clarify. It is noteworthy that by and large the first kind of contribution tends to appear in "psychoanalytic" journals, the second kind in "psychological" ones. It is a hopeful sign that in papers of the first kind there is increasing emphasis on scientific rigor; with respect to researches of the second kind there is greater stress on meaningfulness and relevance. Very probably, the future will bring even greater rapprochement, and perhaps an eventual amalgamation of the two approaches. At present, however, it remains true that the former studies focus on the individual case, stressing longitudinal development, idiosyncratic richness, and depth; the latter place greater confidence in the cross-sectional approach, in which one or a few variables are systematically investigated in a sample of patients, therapists, etc. Here the individuality of the single case is subordinated to considerations of experimental design and statistical inference.

This problem is familiar to all who have witnessed the battle over psychometric *vs.* projective tests, and it seems hardly necessary to belabor the issue. Although new statistical techniques (which are still not very widely employed) have opened new vistas for the study of the individual case, the problem remains with us. Let it be conceded without further discussion that both sides have a contribution to make, and that a scientific discipline of psychotherapy can and does profit both from exhaustive studies of individual cases and from cross-sectional researches. The one may suggest hypotheses which can be more conclusively investigated by the other, and in general there is little danger that either approach will soon have to be abandoned for lack of problems.

At the same time, it is clear that the development of psychotherapy tends in the direction of greater specificity, explicitness, precision. This movement is inescapable if psychotherapy is to be taught, described, and explicated. It is becoming an axiom that concepts must be defined more stringently, and that the vagueness inherent in the subject matter must be diminished. The demands for operational definitions — or at least demonstrable empirical referents — can hardly be sidestepped. These desiderata are expounded with considerable vigor at scientific meetings, but, with the exception of a small minority of researchers, most practicing clinicians and psychotherapists are none too mindful of these injunctions. And, in a sense, rightly so; they cannot suspend their clinical work until such time as research sharpens their tools; they must go ahead, meet the vast clinical demands, and do the best under existing conditions.

The increasing split between the clinical function and the research function is undoubtedly due to many complex reasons, of which the technical difficulty of combining scientific rigor with therapeutic objectives is merely one. By contrast, it is interesting to note Freud's assertion that, in psychoanalysis, therapy and research always go hand in hand. Indeed, he considered this one of the distinctive features of the method. To him, each individual patient was the proving ground for his previous theories and the *fons et origo* of new clinical discoveries, which were then woven into subsequent formulations. He found it impossible to divorce research from the process of therapy, and conceived of himself more as a scientist than as a "healer." In fact, he came to the final conclusion that the possibilities of psychoanalysis as a research tool far overshadowed those of a treatment technique. To Freud, "research" meant *clinical* research, i.e., the painstaking study of individual patients. However, he applied the scientific method and, through the study of new cases, tested his hypotheses in an approximate way, without however achieving strict experimental control. In some instances, his observations led Freud astray, but it is a tribute to his genius that he succeeded in making valid generalizations on the basis of exceedingly small samples. At any rate, he found the roles of scientist and therapist quite congenial, and the thought of applying a therapeutic technique routinely was utterly alien to him. Nevertheless, as he envisaged the future of psychoanalysis, he foresaw a growing group of analysts who were primarily practitioners rather than researchers and who would rely on others to forge and refine the tools needed for clinical work.[4]

Furthermore, Freud held the view that research on psychoanalysis (as a therapeutic instrument) could *only* be conducted in the psychotherapeutic situation — at least he did not foresee other possibili-

---

[4] Rogers (1955), on the other hand, feels that he cannot simultaneously function in both roles: if, in the clinical situation he attempts to be a scientific observer, he feels his empathic ability suffers. He considers the two roles diametrically opposed and essentially irreconcilable.

ties. Even today a strong belief is held in many quarters that in order to do research on the psychotherapeutic process, particularly long-term, analytically-oriented psychotherapy, it is mandatory to leave the therapeutic situation undisturbed, even though various research techniques may be used as long as they do not interfere with the therapeutic situation proper. Another group of researchers seems to feel that relevant and meaningful research can be conducted experimentally or quasi-experimentally. The first group, harking back to Freud, asserts that the analytic situation represents a specific method of investigation, and that *psychoanalytic* research cannot be performed without this method; the latter group, without questioning the value of the method for therapeutic and other purposes, believes that other approaches, too, may yield fruitful and provocative data, which eventually, may find their way back into the treatment situation.

So far, I have tried to indicate that essentially there are two kinds of research approaches to the psychotherapeutic process: the clinical, used preponderantly by practicing analysts and therapists; and the experimental, exemplified chiefly by clinical research psychologists. While changes are gradually taking place, it appears that clinical penetration and scientific rigor have varied inversely. Furthermore, the two approaches undoubtedly reflect the temperaments of the proponents. If the advances of psychoanalysis as a therapeutic technique are compared with the experimental research contributions, there can be little argument as to which has more profoundly enriched theory and practice of psychotherapy. To make the point more boldly, I believe that, up to the present, research contributions have had exceedingly little influence on the practical procedures of psychotherapy. This, in view of the advocacy of more and more research, the expansion of facilities and the greater availability of federal and private financial support, is a deeply disquieting state of affairs requiring closer scrutiny. Why is this so? Why have research contributions had so little impact? Is it that they have nothing to teach the practicing therapist? Are therapists so impervious to scientific findings that they are unable to profit from them? Is our knowledge of the subject matter so rudimentary that at this stage research cannot possibly be expected to have left its mark on clinical practices? I raise these questions, not as a therapeutic nihilist but as a researcher who feels that important answers should come from research. But, I must confess that I am not fully convinced that they will. A closer look at the contemporary scene may not enable one to discern trends to forecast the future, but it may help to clarify the schism that

divides practicing therapists and investigators doing research on the therapeutic process.

The therapist-clinician might speak as follows: Psychotherapy, first and foremost, is a clinical art, not a science. My task is to aid and promote personality growth, or, more accurately, to help a troubled human being in his struggle with his emotional difficulties. I assume that the patient is fully capable of steering his own life course once the obstacles which stand in his way are removed. My task is to aid him in this process. I don't "handle" a case, I don't "manipulate" a person, I don't apply a "technique." My whole effort is concentrated upon *understanding* this person and his difficulties in living. If I am a psychoanalyst or an analytically-oriented therapist, I follow certain technical rules (based on such concepts as transference, resistance, defense, etc.) which usually accelerate the therapeutic process. From this vantage point, I don't see how it would help me to know that persons having certain psychological characteristics are better candidates for intensive psychotherapy than persons having some other characteristics; that interpretations of a certain kind tend to produce resistance in certain kinds of patients at a certain stage in therapy; that under certain conditions the therapist's personal problems tend to interfere with the therapeutic process; that certain patterns of personality characteristics in a therapist are more conducive to progress in therapy than certain others; that interpretive techniques are more effective in the hands of certain therapists with certain kinds of patients under certain circumstances, etc. How do such findings help me to understand my patient, Joe Smith, whom I am seeing three times a week, who relates to me, a particular therapist, in a particular way, who tells me about his anxieties in highly specific situations and whose style of life, defensive patterns, life goals, fantasies, wishes are a unique constellation? True, there are important clinical papers which have influenced me deeply: they are the papers of a host of sensitive therapists — not the kinds of investigations which are based on a sample of patients often treated by student therapists, which report results at the .05 or .01 level of statistical confidence. I am in sympathy with the point of view which says that we must achieve greater clarity about our concepts and our operations, but I doubt whether an experimenter standing *outside* the therapeutic situation can deepen my understanding of patient qua living human beings.

The researcher-scientist might speak thus: I fully recognize that the major contributions to the theory and practice of psychotherapy are based on careful observations of perceptive clinicians. Freud and those who followed in his footsteps have revolutionized our thinking about psychic conflicts and developed a unique method for effecting fundamental and lasting personality change. Certainly, clinical observation and painstaking efforts by individual therapists have taught us most of what we know about the principles of psychotherapy and psychotherapeutic technique. It is possible that these insights will not be equaled or even approached in another century. However, we must not lose sight of the fact that Freud considered psychoanalysis a *science*, and he strove until his dying day to preserve the scientific attitude which formed the basis of his most notable discoveries. Unlike some of his followers, he did not consider his formulations as final pronouncements or immutable truths. To be sure, his methods were relatively uncontrolled, nor was he able to marshal the scientific rigor that is demanded of investigations today; but he applied the scientific method as clearly and unmistakably as an experimental psychologist who runs rats through a maze or a physiologist who measures the contractions of a muscle. The differences are quantitative rather than qualitative.

Furthermore, it must be rocognized that our knowledge of psychotherapy is at a very rudimentary stage. As Kubie (1956, p. 102) points out, we stand at the threshold of a new era; discoverers like Freud have pointed the way, but it remains for others to systematize his insights, to document the wealth of his observations, to sift, discard, build, and revamp. Reluctant as the clinician may be to bring the searchlight of dispassionate and objective research to bear upon his clinical operations, no other course is open. It may be a long time before our knowledge is reorganized in revolutionary ways, and, compared to the sweeping discoveries of Freud, the patient and laborious investigations of the researcher may appear pedestrian, obsessive, and even picayune. Nevertheless, they are needed and may surely be counted upon to advance the frontiers of knowledge. Possibly none or very few of the current research investigations provide principles which *radically* change therapeutic technique or even have a marked influence on clinical practice. But neither have clinical insights during the last decades led to momentous changes in therapeutic technique. Progress in this area has been slow, but by no means negligible. Besides, the clinician's attitude of respect, empathy, and understanding has nothing to do with what research has to contribute; on the contrary, greater specificity which will come from research will strengthen and illuminate the clinical framework of his practical operations and gradually enable him to be of better help to his patients.

These arguments, based as they often are on emotional commitments, have a familiar ring. They underlie the nomothetic-ideographic controversy; they are mirrored in the fundamental differences between the *geisteswissenschaftliche* approach of German psychology and the naturalistic-positivistic approach of American psychology; they have recently been revived in existentialist thinking and *Daseinsanalyse* (May, Angel, & Ellenberger, 1958); and they are rooted in the subject-object schism of Western philosophy. These basic philosophic convictions determine one's view of psychology as a science, the methods by which knowledge is acquired about psychological processes, as well as one's conception of psychotherapy and of the role and function of the psychotherapist.

It is instructive to note that after having lived with Freud's discoveries for half a century, and viewed the individual patient as the battleground of impersonal forces shaping his destiny, we are still largely ignorant of the nature of the therapeutic action, and renewed attention is being focused on the psychotherapist as a *person*, who — some suspect — plays a larger part in the therapeutic endeavor than has hitherto been acknowledged or made explicit.[5]

[5] In one of his last papers Freud makes this highly significant point: "Amongst the factors which influence the prospects of an analysis and add to its difficulties in the same manner as the resistances, we must reckon not only the structure of the *patient's* ego but the personal characteristics of the *analyst*. . . . The analyst . . . , because of the peculiar conditions of his work, is really impeded by his own defects in his task of discerning it in a manner conducive to cure. So there is some reason in the demand for a comparatively high degree of psychical normality and correct adjustment in the analyst as one of his qualifications for his work. And there is another point: he must be in a superior position in some sense if he is to serve as a model for his patient in certain analytic situations and, in others, to act as his teacher. Finally, we must not forget that the relationship between analyst and patient is based on a love of truth, that is, on the acknowledgment of reality, and that it precludes any kind of sham or deception." (Freud, 1952, pp. 351–352). As in earlier papers, the emphasis rests on those aspects of the therapist's personality which might create an impediment to therapy; however, Freud also recognizes that the therapist must be "in a superior position in some sense if he is to serve as model for his patient. . . ." Unfortunately, one is left to guess what is meant by "superior position," but I wonder whether Freud meant that the therapist had to be somewhat of a *Persönlichkeit*. If in the passage immediately following he expressed doubts that the candidates would acquire the "ideal qualification" for his work *solely* in his personal analysis, he clearly had the removal of "blind spots" in mind; but perhaps he also questioned whether the candidate could ever become a *Persönlichkeit* solely through his personal analysis unless his analyst in turn embodied the "model qualities" which Freud alluded to.

Working with widely different methods of investigation, theoretical orientations, and therapeutic objectives, numerous investigators appear to converge on this point. Alexander, after a lifetime of experience in psychoanalysis, refers to "the most opaque area of psychoanalysis, the question of the therapist's influence on the treatment process by the virtue of being what he is: an individual personality, distinct from all other therapists." (1958, p. 311). Frank, speaking as a researcher concerned with experimental controls, sees as a chief problem "to distinguish the effects of the therapist's personality or attitude, from the effects of his technique." (1959). And further: "The most important, and unfortunately the least understood, situational variable in psychotherapy is the therapist himself. His personality pervades any technique he may use, and because of the patient's dependence on him for help, he may influence the patient through subtle cues of which he may not be aware." (Frank, 1959). Elsewhere Frank considers the possibility that the patient's faith and trust in the therapist may be the single most important variable in therapeutic change (1958). Rogers speaks of the therapist's "genuineness in the relationship," his "unconditional positive regard," and "empathy." He views the therapeutic relationship "as a heightening of the constructive qualities which often exist in part in other relationships, and an extension through time of qualities which in other relationships tend at best to be momentary" (1957, p. 101). In the same paper, Rogers comes to the conclusion that "the techniques of the various therapies are relatively unimportant" (1957, p. 102) and, stressing the overriding importance of the therapist's attitudes:

"Any of the techniques may communicate the fact that the therapist is expressing one attitude at a surface level, and another contradictory attitude which is denied to his own awareness. Thus one value of such a theoretical formulation as we have offered is that it may assist therapists to think more critically about those elements of their experience, attitudes, and behaviors which are essential to psychotherapy, and those which are nonessential or even deleterious to psychotherapy" (1957, p. 103).

The present writer, basing his conclusion on a study of psychotherapists in an experimental situation regards the therapist's contribution to the treatment process as both personal and technical:

"His personal attributes (maturity, warmth, acceptance, etc.) enable him to create the kind of interpersonal relationship in which constructive personality change can take place; his knowledge of psychodynamic principles permits him, in and

through this relationship, to initiate the kinds of emotional unlearning and learning experiences that are considered necessary to the alleviation or resolution of neurotic conflicts. The latter would be impossible without the former; the former, by itself, would never be sufficient." (Strupp, 1958, p. 66).

There appears to be, then, a growing disenchantment with psychotherapy as a "technique," American preoccupations with technology notwithstanding. The keynote of this development was perhaps sounded by Freud himself. His attention to the technical aspects of psychoanalytic therapy declined toward the middle and end of his career, and contrary to his theoretical revisions in other areas he had relatively little to add to his earlier papers on technique. While he considered the therapist's personal attributes important, he stressed their potentially noxious influences, leaving the positive aspects largely unformulated (Freud, 1952). True, at one time he conceived of psychoanalysis as a kind of "after-education" but later on expressed a distaste for the conception of the therapist as an "educator" or "mentor." (See, in this connection, Burchard, 1958.) He feared that the therapist might make similar mistakes as the patient's parents in "indoctrinating" him with a set of values and rules which would impede his free development and self-direction. In the 1920s and '30s much emphasis was given to interpretations, their timing, correctness, and adequacy. Concomitantly, the person making the interpretations tended to be lost sight of, and under Freud's impetus the essence of psychoanalytic therapy was seen as the resolution of the transference neurosis through appropriate interpretations — a process, one surmised, which would reel off, regularly, automatically, and inexorably, if but the "correct" technical procedures were followed. This is not the place to trace subsequent developments except to draw attention to a trend culminating in the "rediscovery" of the therapist as a person, whose attitudes, personality, and values presumably play an exceedingly important, if not crucial, part in the therapeutic process. Concomitantly, it is being realized that increasing effort must be expended to elucidate his personal influence, which may far transcend his technical contribution.[6]

Could it be that we have come full circle? Starting from the age-old view of the potentially beneficial effects of love, friendship, and acceptance of one's emotional well-being, we seem to have traversed an era in which a highly technical procedure

[6] For a more extended discussion of this point, see Strupp, in press.

(psychoanalysis) came to the ascendency. Here the therapeutic task was conceived as an effort to bring about a reconciliation of impersonal forces — to help the ego come to terms with an irrational id and an unreasonable, overly severe superego. Moving along a spiral, the developments of ego psychology have stressed a conception in which the ego's autonomy and integrative functions again came to the fore. Contemporaneously, the psychotherapeutic situation is again seen as an encounter between two *persons*. The patient is regarded as an individual with problems in living, but also as a human being striving to realize his potentialities. The therapist is viewed, not as an analytic manipulator or technician, but as a human being who, aided by technical training *and* experience in living, attempts to *understand* the patient as a person. This understanding is to be accomplished through emotional participation in living with the other person over an extended period of time, to the end that the therapist's influence conduces to constructive personality growth. The focus is upon the experiential components of the situation, to which everything else becomes subordinate, including the technical operations by which the experience is facilitated. Consequently, the operations of psychotherapy are not simply to be explained by rules which tell the novice when to interpret and what; rather they presuppose a deep understanding of the principles governing the whole gamut of human collaboration. Aware of this complexity, though speaking in a different context, Freud said:

> Anyone who hopes to learn the noble game of chess from books will soon discover that only the openings and end-games admit of an exhaustive systematic presentation and that the infinite variety of moves which develop after the opening defy any such description. This gap in instruction can only be filled by a diligent study of games fought out by masters (1955, Vol. XII, p. 123).

This analogy illustrates a point, but like all analogies it has its limitations. It asserts that (a) there are rules governing the conduct of psychotherapy; (b) these rules are explicit and communicable, hence teachable; (c) there is an over-all strategy in psychotherapy as there is in chess, i.e., there is a specific objective; (d) while knowledge of the basic rules is a prerequisite, it does not, in and of itself, enable one to play the game with any degree of skill; in other words, the general rules must be applied in highly specific and concrete situations, and once a measure of skill is acquired, the basic rules seem to recede to the background, so that the player is

largely unaware that he is employing them; (e) one learns the skill by watching and studying closely the operations of experts; in doing so, one learns to avoid pitfalls and refines his technique which ultimately becomes interwoven with one's personality. One of the important shortcomings of this analogy is that the rules of psychotherapy are established empirically, not, as in chess, a priori. Furthermore, they are modifiable in the light of empirical findings, that is, their validity is to be established by reference to an external criterion. As the analogy suggests, the expert is more "successful" in playing the game than a novice, as evidenced by the fact that he wins more games. Is the expert psychotherapist more "successful" than the novice? This is a purely empirical question, which so far as I know has not been answered to anyone's satisfaction. One of the important reasons that it has not been done is the difficulty of *comparing* the performance of an expert with that of a novice, under rigidly specified conditions, and to note differences in outcome. Such a comparison presupposes the definition and measurement of dimensions which are hypothesized to make a difference (maturity, technical skill, for example). In all probability, the expert does differ in his therapeutic performance from the novice, but this must be demonstrated unequivocally, beyond a reasonable doubt. One approach might be to study the therapeutic behavior of a group of experts to see what they have in common. One might then search for the same common characteristics (therapeutic ingredients) in a group of beginners and determine whether differences exist. If so, they should lead to predictably different outcomes. If not, the results may be due to other factors yet to be defined. Freud attributes the results of psychoanalysis primarily to certain technical operations on the therapist's part; Rogers is inclined to search for them in the area of the therapist's "unconditional regard"; Frank hypothesizes a series of nonspecific factors, such as faith and trust. I suspect that technical skill and salient characteristics of the therapist's personality interact to make possible a new emotional experience, cognitive learning, and the gradual acquisition of new attitude patterns.

Preoccupations with psychotherapeutic technique have increasingly come under criticism in recent years. In this country, Rogers has been an eloquent spokesman for the view that *understanding* the patient is the therapist's first and foremost task. In Europe, the rise of existential psychotherapy has brought with it a further deemphasis of technique. In explicating this point of view to American readers, May states: "Existential analysis is a way of understanding human existence, and its representatives believe that one of the chief (if not *the* chief) blocks to the understanding of human beings in Western culture is precisely the overemphasis on technique, an overemphasis which goes along with the tendency to see the human being as an object to be calculated, managed, 'analyzed' " (May et al., 1958, p. 76). The central issue is "whether the human being is an object to be analyzed or a being to be understood." (May et al., 1958, p. 81). However, the emphasis on the here-and-now relationship neither obviates technical training nor should it discourage research on problems of technique. In May's words, this relationship

> . . . is in no way an over-simplification or short cut; it is not a substitute for discipline or thoroughness of training. It rather puts these things in their context — namely, discipline and thoroughness of training directed to understanding human beings as human. The therapist is assumedly an expert; but, if he is not first of all a human being, his expertness will be irrelevant and quite possibly harmful. The distinctive character of the existential approach is that understanding *being human* is no longer just a 'gift,' an intuition, or something left to chance; it is the 'proper study of man,' in Alexander Pope's phrase, and becomes the center of a thorough and scientific concern in the broad sense. The existential analysts do the same thing with the structure of human existence that Freud did with the structure of the unconscious — namely, take it out of the realm of the hit-and-miss gift of special intuitive individuals, accept it as the area of exploration and understanding, and make it some extent teachable (1958, pp. 82–83).

Thus, it is of little avail to investigate whether psychotherapy "works," or even whether one technique is more "effective" than another. Rather one must ask: Is this particular therapist, by virtue of being a particular person, capable of creating the kinds of conditions in which a given technique or techniques can attain their maximum usefulness? The question of the relative effectiveness of techniques still has to be answered, but the primary focus is on the *person* of the therapist by whom a particular technique is used. Can he understand the patient as a human being struggling with life's problems? Can he communicate this understanding, to the end that the patient feels deeply understood? For methodological reasons, research may emphasize one aspect or the other, but the totality of the therapist and technique in interaction with a particular patient cannot be ignored.

There appears to be a serious danger in overemphasizing either relationship or technique at the expense of the other. To avoid these pitfalls it would appear that ways and means must be found to conduct investigations which do justice both to the demands of scientific rigor and the depth and breadth of the therapeutic undertaking. To this end, researchers must become better and more insightful clinicians, and clinicians must develop a greater awareness of the ideals which the scientist espouses. Among other things, such a rapprochement may result in a larger number of research contributions which are meaningful and relevant to the therapist. Similarly, it may inspire that tentativeness, caution, and respect for error in human observation which is still seen lacking in many clinicians.

The subject-object split which still pervades the science of psychology seems a particularly grave obstacle to the interpenetration of clinical practice and research in psychotherapy. Russell (1948), quoted by Szasz (1957), has eloquently dealt with this issue and defined psychology as a science dealing with essentially private experience. Among psychologists, Allport (1955) has taken issue with the prevailing behaviorist tendency to regard the human person as "empty." In the area of psychotherapy, the investigations of Rogers and his students are perhaps the best illustration that fruitful research on the process of psychotherapy can be done, while retaining something of the uniqueness of the persons participating in the process (Rogers & Dymond, 1954). These are but beginnings, but they seem important beginnings in studying objectively the subjective experiences of patient and therapist in interaction.

Erwin Straus's dictum that "Whatever is related to my particular existence lessens and obscures knowledge" (May et al., 1958, p. 145) seems to strike at the core of an important dilemma in research on psychotherapy. In order to expand scientific knowledge of the therapeutic process, it is necessary to objectify essentially subjective experiences, but as one succeeds in doing so, one runs the danger of sacrificing the essence of what one is studying. Therefore, the obverse of the quotation likewise appears to be true: Knowledge lessens and obscures whatever is related to my particular existence. This, of course, is precisely what science attempts to do in all areas of investigation. Is psychotherapy an exception? If so, it can hardly become a science. If not, the search for invariance amidst change must go forward; common elements must be abstracted; and the unique aspects of the therapeutic encounter may have to go by the board. In one sense, I seem to have suggested that the future *may* bring the development of techniques for *simultaneously* achieving both objectives. This is a hope which may never materialize. We may find that we can't have our cake and eat it. In that event, the therapist and the researcher in psychotherapy may move further apart, unless the clinician abandons his commitments, which seems to be as doubtful as that the researcher will forsake the ideals of science.

Among other things, it will be fruitful to learn how a particular patient is perceived, experienced, and reacted to by a particular therapist and *vice versa*. But if "objective" knowledge in psychotherapy is possible we must also learn more about what patient and therapist are "really" like, as seen by *external* observers. There is reason to suspect that preconceptions on the therapist's part (e.g., notions about the treatability or nontreatability of certain "conditions") may blind him to the patient's potentialities and assets (Strupp, 1958). Of course, the therapist should develop maximal self-awareness of all factors which might adversely affect his therapeutic attitudes. But, important as the study of subjective elements and biasing factors may be, it must not overshadow the thorough scrutiny of interpersonal processes (e.g., transference manifestations) qua objective facts which, as every analyst knows, usually emerge in the treatment process irrespective of the therapist's unique personality characteristics even though they may be colored by the latter. And — to continue on this side of the fence — it seems that the latter-day emphasis on "encounter," "here-and-now experience," "understanding," etc. does scant justice to the painstaking and prolonged process of "working through" — a highly *technical* operation — which is considered an integral part of all fundamental personality change achieved through intensive psychotherapy. Difficult as controlled research on these problems will be, I am sure the limits have not been tested. However, I am not fully convinced that it will be possible to reconcile successfully scientific rigor with the richness and subtle complexity of interpersonal dynamics.

CONCLUSION

The questions raised at the beginning of this paper still loom large. It is disquieting to contemplate the large discrepancy between clinical and philosophical insights on the one hand, and research accomplishments, on the other. As researchers we seem to lack methods for making greater inroads on the phenomena with which psychotherapy deals — the broad spectrum of human experience. For instance: How do we assess and measure such qualities in the therapist as: respect for the patient's struggle toward self-realization and self-direction; capacity for empathy; warmth; acceptance of the human-ness of another person; depth of one's *Weltanschauung* and life experience; emotional maturity; ability to serve as a model of reality; and so forth[7] — all of which undoubtedly play an important role in determining the extent to which the therapist can participate in and collaborate with the patient's striving for realizing his human potentialities? By contrast, the quantitative and comparative analyses of technique, formidable as they are, appear like child's play.

The fact that techniques for measuring significant personality attributes are in their infancy does not mean that they are doomed to remain there. The fact that so far the contributions from researchers to psychotherapeutic theory and practice have been relatively slight need not remain an immutable truth and omen for the future. The task poses a challenge to our imagination as researchers. We must show greater penetration in forging our research tools and refuse to purchase precision in measurement at the expense of shallowness of concepts. If we agree to the proposition that psychotherapy's future is that of a scientific discipline, we have no choice but to undertake the laborious and painful drudgery of checking the empirical value of brilliant clinical insights glimpsed by intrepid pioneers and to sharpen our research instruments that they may become adequate to deal with the phenomena in our domain. It is just barely possible that a few crumbs of insight left over by the giants may be the reward of the patient researcher, not to mention the gratification of demolishing along the way some hypotheses which contemporaneously enjoy the status of a creed.

[7] We need to specify those qualities of character which give the therapist stature as a mature personality and model of reality. Compare reference footnote 5 for a statement of Freud's position.

REFERENCES

ALEXANDER, F. Unexplored areas in psychoanalytic theory and treatment. *Behav. Sci.*, 1958, 3, 293–316.

ALLPORT, G. W. *Becoming: Basic considerations for a psychology of personality.* New Haven: Yale University Press, 1955.

BURCHARD, E. M. L. The evolution of psychoanalytic tasks and goals. *Psychiatry*, 1958, 21, 341–357.

FRANK, J. D. Problems of controls in psychotherapy as exemplified by the psychotherapy research project of the Phipps Psychiatric Clinic. In E. A. Rubinstein & M. B. Parloff (Eds.), *Research in psychotherapy.* Washington, D.C.: Amer. Psychol. Assn., 1959. Pp. 10–26.

FRANK, J. D. Some effects of expectancy and influence in psychotherapy. In J. H. Masserman & J. L. Moreno

(Eds.), *Progress in psychotherapy, Vol. III.* New York: Grune & Stratton, 1958. Pp. 27–43.

FREUD, S. Analysis terminable and interminable. In *Collected Papers, Vol. V.* London: Hogarth Press, 1952. Pp. 313–357.

FREUD, S. Further recommendations in the technique of psychoanalysis. In *Complete Psychological Works of Sigmund Freud, Standard Edition.* London: Hogarth Press, 1955.

KARDINER, A. New Horizons and responsibilities of psychoanalysis. *Amer. J. Psychoanalysis,* 1958, 18, 115–126.

KUBIE, L. S. Some unsolved problems of psychoanalytic psychotherapy. In Frieda Fromm-Reichmann & J. L. Moreno (Eds.), *Progress in psychotherapy 1956.* New York: Grune & Stratton, 1956. Pp. 87–102.

MAY, R., ANGEL, E., & ELLENBERGER, H. F., (Eds.). *Existence: A new dimension in psychiatry and psychology.* New York: Basic Books, 1958.

ROGERS, C. R. Persons or science: A philosophical question. *Amer. Psychologist,* 1955, 10, 267–278.

ROGERS, C. R. The necessary and sufficient conditions of therapeutic personality change. *J. consult. Psychol.,* 1957, 21, 95–103.

ROGERS, C. R. & DYMOND, ROSALIND F. (Eds.), *Psychotherapy and personality change.* Chicago: University of Chicago Press, 1954.

RUSSELL, B. *Human knowledge: Its scope and limits.* New York: Simon & Schuster, 1948. Ch. 6.

SEARS, R. R. *Survey of objective studies of psychoanalytic concepts.* New York: Social Science Research Council, 1943.

STRUPP, H. H. The psychotherapist's contribution to the treatment process. *Behav. Sci.,* 1958, 3, 34–67.

STRUPP, H. H. Toward an analysis of the therapist's contribution to the treatment process. *Psychiatry,* in press.

SZASZ, T. S. *Pain and pleasure: A study of bodily feelings.* New York: Basic Books, 1957. Ch. 2.